Adobe®
GoLive™ 5 Bible

Adobe®
GoLive™ 5 Bible

Deborah Shadovitz

IDG Books Worldwide, Inc.
An International Data Group Company

Foster City, CA ✦ Chicago, IL ✦ Indianapolis, IN ✦ New York, NY

Adobe® GoLive™ 5 Bible

Published by
IDG Books Worldwide, Inc.
An International Data Group Company
919 E. Hillsdale Blvd., Suite 300
Foster City, CA 94404
www.idgbooks.com (IDG Books Worldwide Web site)

ISBN: 0-7645-3347-9

Printed in the United States of America

10 9 8 7 6 5 4 3 2 1

1B/RU/RS/QQ/FC

Distributed in the United States by IDG Books Worldwide, Inc.

Distributed by CDG Books Canada Inc. for Canada; by Transworld Publishers Limited in the United Kingdom; by IDG Norge Books for Norway; by IDG Sweden Books for Sweden; by IDG Books Australia Publishing Corporation Pty. Ltd. for Australia and New Zealand; by TransQuest Publishers Pte Ltd. for Singapore, Malaysia, Thailand, Indonesia, and Hong Kong; by Gotop Information Inc. for Taiwan; by ICG Muse, Inc. for Japan; by Intersoft for South Africa; by Eyrolles for France; by International Thomson Publishing for Germany, Austria, and Switzerland; by Distribuidora Cuspide for Argentina; by LR International for Brazil; by Galileo Libros for Chile; by Ediciones ZETA S.C.R. Ltda. for Peru; by WS Computer Publishing Corporation, Inc., for the Philippines; by Contemporanea de Ediciones for Venezuela; by Express Computer Distributors for the Caribbean and West Indies; by Micronesia Media Distributor, Inc. for Micronesia; by Chips Computadoras S.A. de C.V. for Mexico; by Editorial Norma de Panama S.A. for Panama; by American Bookshops for Finland.

For general information on IDG Books Worldwide's books in the U.S., please call our Consumer Customer Service department at 800-762-2974. For reseller information, including discounts and premium sales, please call our Reseller Customer Service department at 800-434-3422.

For information on where to purchase IDG Books Worldwide's books outside the U.S., please contact our International Sales department at 317-572-3993 or fax 317-572-4002.

For consumer information on foreign language translations, please contact our Customer Service department at 800-434-3422, fax 317-572-4002, or e-mail rights@idgbooks.com.

For information on licensing foreign or domestic rights, please phone +1-650-653-7098.

For sales inquiries and special prices for bulk quantities, please contact our Order Services department at 800-434-3422 or write to the address above.

For information on using IDG Books Worldwide's books in the classroom or for ordering examination copies, please contact our Educational Sales department at 800-434-2086 or fax 317-572-4005.

For press review copies, author interviews, or other publicity information, please contact our Public Relations department at 650-653-7000 or fax 650-653-7500.

For authorization to photocopy items for corporate, personal, or educational use, please contact Copyright Clearance Center, 222 Rosewood Drive, Danvers, MA 01923, or fax 978-750-4470.

Library of Congress Cataloging-in-Publication Data

Shadovitz, Deborah.
  Adobe GoLive 5 bible / Deborah Shadovitz.
    p.   cm.
  ISBN 0-7645-3347-9 (alk. paper)
  1. Adobe GoLive. 2. Web site--Design.   I. Tapley, Rebecca.   II. Title.
TK5105.8885.A34 S48   2000
005.7'2--dc21   99-058463

ABOUT IDG BOOKS WORLDWIDE

Welcome to the world of IDG Books Worldwide.

IDG Books Worldwide, Inc., is a subsidiary of International Data Group, the world's largest publisher of computer-related information and the leading global provider of information services on information technology. IDG was founded more than 30 years ago by Patrick J. McGovern and now employs more than 9,000 people worldwide. IDG publishes more than 290 computer publications in over 75 countries. More than 90 million people read one or more IDG publications each month.

Launched in 1990, IDG Books Worldwide is today the #1 publisher of best-selling computer books in the United States. We are proud to have received eight awards from the Computer Press Association in recognition of editorial excellence and three from Computer Currents' First Annual Readers' Choice Awards. Our best-selling ...*For Dummies*® series has more than 50 million copies in print with translations in 31 languages. IDG Books Worldwide, through a joint venture with IDG's Hi-Tech Beijing, became the first U.S. publisher to publish a computer book in the People's Republic of China. In record time, IDG Books Worldwide has become the first choice for millions of readers around the world who want to learn how to better manage their businesses.

Our mission is simple: Every one of our books is designed to bring extra value and skill-building instructions to the reader. Our books are written by experts who understand and care about our readers. The knowledge base of our editorial staff comes from years of experience in publishing, education, and journalism — experience we use to produce books to carry us into the new millennium. In short, we care about books, so we attract the best people. We devote special attention to details such as audience, interior design, use of icons, and illustrations. And because we use an efficient process of authoring, editing, and desktop publishing our books electronically, we can spend more time ensuring superior content and less time on the technicalities of making books.

You can count on our commitment to deliver high-quality books at competitive prices on topics you want to read about. At IDG Books Worldwide, we continue in the IDG tradition of delivering quality for more than 30 years. You'll find no better book on a subject than one from IDG Books Worldwide.

John Kilcullen
Chairman and CEO
IDG Books Worldwide, Inc.

*Eighth Annual
Computer Press
Awards* ➣*1992*

*Ninth Annual
Computer Press
Awards* ➣*1993*

*Tenth Annual
Computer Press
Awards* ➣*1994*

*Eleventh Annual
Computer Press
Awards* ➣*1995*

IDG is the world's leading IT media, research and exposition company. Founded in 1964, IDG had 1997 revenues of $2.05 billion and has more than 9,000 employees worldwide. IDG offers the widest range of media options that reach IT buyers in 75 countries representing 95% of worldwide IT spending. IDG's diverse product and services portfolio spans six key areas including print publishing, online publishing, expositions and conferences, market research, education and training, and global marketing services. More than 90 million people read one or more of IDG's 290 magazines and newspapers, including IDG's leading global brands — Computerworld, PC World, Network World, Macworld and the Channel World family of publications. IDG Books Worldwide is one of the fastest-growing computer book publishers in the world, with more than 700 titles in 36 languages. The "...For Dummies®" series alone has more than 50 million copies in print. IDG offers online users the largest network of technology-specific Web sites around the world through IDG.net (http://www.idg.net), which comprises more than 225 targeted Web sites in 55 countries worldwide. International Data Corporation (IDC) is the world's largest provider of information technology data, analysis and consulting, with research centers in over 41 countries and more than 400 research analysts worldwide. IDG World Expo is a leading producer of more than 168 globally branded conferences and expositions in 35 countries including E3 (Electronic Entertainment Expo), Macworld Expo, ComNet, Windows World Expo, ICE (Internet Commerce Expo), Agenda, DEMO, and Spotlight. IDG's training subsidiary, ExecuTrain, is the world's largest computer training company, with more than 230 locations worldwide and 785 training courses. IDG Marketing Services helps industry-leading IT companies build international brand recognition by developing global integrated marketing programs via IDG's print, online and exposition products worldwide. Further information about the company can be found at www.idg.com. 1/26/00

Credits

Acquisitions Editor
Michael Roney

Project Editors
Chris Johnson
Linda Turnowski

Technical Editor
Richard Gaskin

Copy Editors
Michael D. Welch
Dennis Weaver
Laura Stone
Cindy Lai
Lane Barnholtz
Julie Campbell Moss

Proof Editor
Patsy Owens

Project Coordinator
Louigene A. Santos

Graphics and Production Specialists
Bob Bihlmayer
Rolly Delrosario
Jude Levinson
Michael Lewis
Victor Pérez-Varela
Ramses Ramirez

Quality Control Technician
Dina F Quan

Permissions Editor
Laura Moss

Media Development Specialist
Jamie Hastings-Smith

Media Development Coordinator
Marisa Pearman

Book Designer
Drew R. Moore

Illustrators
Gabriele McCann
Mary Jo Weis
Karl Brandt

Proofreading and Indexing
York Production Services

Cover Illustration
Lawrence Huck

About the Author

Deborah Shadovitz's first career was in television, video, and audio-visual production and editing. (She also dabbled in radio and theater production.) Her affinity toward GoLive is a result of her design and communications background. Like many of us, she's enamoured by the Web for its unique communication capability. Because of this, she appreciates GoLive's vision of making this communication easier for all, and loves showing off GoLive's easy designer-oriented methodology and power. She enjoys helping others use GoLive effectively and wanted to write this book since using GoLive 2 (then called GoLive CyberStudio).

Deborah is well known in the Mac community as an author, instructor, and speaker. She started out on computers using DOS and followed the path to Windows, so she's also familiar with the Windows environment. She's done stints on several Los Angeles–area Internet group advisory boards and is an active participant in the user group community. Deborah is also on the GoLive Advisory Committee (as you can see if you watch the GoLive splash screen long enough).

Deb is known internationally for her well-received column, "Mac Efficiency 101," at www.maccentral.com. She is coauthor of the award-winning *Macworld Office 98 Bible*, *ClarisWorks Office For Dummies*, and *AppleWorks 5 For Dummies*, as well as a contributor to other books including *My iMac* (all from IDG Books Worldwide). She's a regular speaker/instructor at Macworld Expo, other trade shows and events, and at computer user groups. And of course, she teaches GoLive—you can catch her at various user-group meetings, trade shows, or private seminars.

About the Tech Editor

Richard Gaskin is founder and president of Fourth World Media Corporation, a Los Angeles–based software and Web development firm. While Richard has been developing interactive media since before the Web was invented, today much of his company's work relies on Adobe GoLive.

Having contributed software engineering, testing, and documentation services to a variety of both commercial software products and internal process enhancement tools, Richard has a deep appreciation for the contributions GoLive makes for his company and those of his clients.

Passionate about usability, Richard is acting chair of the Los Angeles chapter of the ACM Special Interest Group for Computer–Human Interaction, and has given presentations on user-interface design and prototyping at Macworld Expos in San Francisco and Boston.

When he's not developing software or editing books, Richard keeps himself sane by hiking in the Santa Monica mountains, camping in the Mojave desert, and taking his employees to Disneyland.

To Cathy Scrivnor, official Book Mom and fabulous friend, for all of your long nights testing theories and methods, and discussing topics with me until the right words came through. (Good thing it's a local phone call! Tom can have his wife back now.) Her name is not in many places in this book, but her words, wisdom, and spirit sure are.

To Richard McLean, Oliver Zahorka, Rob Keniger, and to all the other people who have added to my knowledge of GoLive, some of whom I know in person and many I have yet to meet, but am proud to know nonetheless. In other words, to all the people who have participated on the GoLive e-mail lists over the years — those who asked great questions and those who patiently answered them.

And to my family, for all of your support during this very long process. Mom, thanks for the temporary laundry service. Dad, thanks for the grocery delivery. David and Orly, thanks for the meal delivery. (I'm back to doing my own laundry, shopping, and cooking now.) Donna, thanks for the grammar checks. Kiddies, thanks for the play breaks.

Foreword

On behalf of everyone at Adobe Systems, Inc. and speaking for all those who are responsible for driving the success of Adobe GoLive 5 in the professional Web design community, I wish to express my gratitude for the Herculean effort put forth by Deborah Shadovitz, including the supportive crew at IDG Books Worldwide, to make this impressive book a reality for all to enjoy and learn from.

I can assure you that Deborah's writing efforts required more than simply mastering all the features included in Adobe GoLive 5 — itself a daunting task. Due to the nature of the Web itself, writing about GoLive requires a thorough understanding of the challenges that Web designers confront on a daily basis, along with browser-compliance considerations, and contemplating how GoLive 5's many new and advanced features might be used to create engaging, dynamic Web sites.

My thanks go to the many members of the GoLiveTalk mail list as well as our GoLive Advisory Council members and valued beta testers who shared their insights in helping us deliver this product. I encourage everyone to subscribe to the TalkList (see Chapter 4 for how to do this) and join the Adobe online Web community at www.adobe.com, where you will find interesting Web design discussion, including many new tips and techniques in mastering the product. Here, you will also find GoLive Extensions and Actions to extend the power of the application.

At Adobe Systems, we are committed to developing a comprehensive set of integrated professional Web design tools. Our goal is to provide individuals and teams the greatest creative freedom and control in mastering the Web design process. Adobe GoLive 5.0, among its 100+ new features, includes numerous innovations, including an onboard interactive editor for editing multimedia, "360Code," that provides complete control over any Web design source code, superior site planning and management, workgroup collaboration (including "asset" synchronization and check-in and check-out through WebDAV support), and "smart links" that provide drag-and-drop object-sharing with other Adobe products. What's more, an integrated development environment that extends the GoLive feature set, plus advanced functionality such as Dynamic Link, together simplifies the incorporation of dynamic database and e-commerce capabilities.

GoLive is best viewed as many-apps-in-one. Cases in point are seven areas of the product that I consider standalone products because of their feature set and level of product integration: Photoshop's Save For Web image-optimization engine, QuickTime Editor, JavaScript Editor, JavaScript Debugger included with the GoLive SDK, Site Design, Site Reporting, and GoLive Dynamic Link for ASP. These are all extremely powerful applications built into the product. Together, they help the serious Web designer reach new levels of productivity.

Moving forward as the Web evolves, and thanks to the constant feedback we receive from our customers to enhance our products, Adobe Systems will continue to address emerging technologies and challenges that Web designers face, and translate these advances and challenges into compelling new product features. I encourage you to submit your feature wish-list requests to golivewishlist@ adobe.com; one of my primary roles in the organization is to make sure your wishes are acted upon in future product releases.

Without the continuing support provided by our valued customers, Adobe Systems would be hard-pressed to deliver a comprehensive set of integrated Web design tools that best meet your needs. Thanks to feedback received for GoLive and Adobe's industry-standard Web design toolset, which includes Photoshop, Illustrator, and LiveMotion, we are excited about the future.

Thanks for purchasing this book. With this book's expert guidance, I'm confident your work using Adobe GoLive 5 will help pave the road to success for your professional Web design efforts.

John Kranz
Senior Product Manager
Adobe Systems, Inc.

Preface

Whether you're considering building or taking over management of your first presence on World Wide Web, or whether you're an old-timer who has been hand-coding Web pages since the rickety dawn of the Internet, GoLive is written for you — and so is the *Adobe GoLive 5 Bible*.

Like its namesake and topic — Adobe GoLive — this book is designed to be the ultimate tool for creating a Web site and going live with it on the Web. Both could also easily (if not for copyright) go by the subtitle *Staying Alive* because the key to success on the Web is not just getting your site up there, but keeping it fresh. GoLive makes that easy, too. GoLive is as easy to use after you publish your site as it is to publish it in the first place. Built-in file transfer, complete with incremental upload, enables you to enjoy the same easy-to-use visual design interface to update or add to your site. You can upload any new or changed pages with just two clicks (or three by your own preference).

GoLive was written with designers in mind so the interface is easy to use and is consistent with Adobe's other excellent design applications. At the same time, it accommodates users who want to do serious programming within their page code. It was written for today's Web; with GoLive, adding all of the popular multimedia types is a cinch, and it's easy to make your sites interesting and fun. There's a lot to GoLive, so there's a lot to this book.

This book goes beyond just telling you how to use GoLive. It not only explains what the various tools and capabilities of GoLive are, but shows you what each thing is *for*, and gives you an idea of how you might use it. It even provides the materials you need to try various features of GoLive and capabilities of the Web, so you don't have to scrounge around for sample files or wonder how something works. Many of these materials are waiting for you right on the CD-ROM included with this book. Other materials are more appropriately available on the Web so their addresses are noted within the book or at www.golivebible.com, this book's companion site — it is a constantly growing resource for you as you work with GoLive and this book.

Welcome to the world of GoLive, and to the Web if you're new to that neighborhood, too.

Is This Book for You?

In short, if you're interested in creating a Web site and like working as efficiently as possible, this book is for you.

Are you a designer who's been asked by clients to create Web sites? GoLive was created with designers in mind. I, and many of the contributors to this book, share this background with you. You'll find both GoLive and this book are easy to identify with and use.

Have you been hand-coding sites for years? If so, you deserve a break. GoLive's site management puts an end to broken links and difficulty moving files. (If you use this book and GoLive just for that one feature, you'll free up hours in your life. Then, while you're at it, look at the FTP features and win back some more hours of your life.) You don't have to alter your existing sites or pages to begin managing them in GoLive. Chapter 4 shows you how. In fact, you can continue to hand-code your pages all the time, or any time.

Are you fairly new to the Web and wondering if a Web site is beyond you? It's not. GoLive is powerful and does a lot, but its palettes and windows are friendly and consistent. I've been teaching computers to beginners for years and still remember my first years very well. I love passing on the power of computers and great software, not showing off my own knowledge. My directions are simple and straightforward. I even tested them on beginners. As long as you comfortably know your way around your computer (Windows or Macintosh), you'll have no problem. The beauty of a book is that you can read it and reread as you experiment. In addition, this book's companion Web site at www.golivebible.com has some real-life pages you can explore and even look at within GoLive to see how they are done.

GoLive's System Requirements

Written to be platform-independent, this book covers both Macintosh and Windows 95/98/NT versions of GoLive 5. Adobe Systems has the following system requirements for the software:

Macintosh

✦ PowerPC-based Macintosh computer processor with CD-ROM drive

✦ OS Version 8.6 or 9.0

✦ 48MB of available RAM (to enable all modules)

✦ 35MB of available hard-disk space

Windows

+ Intel Pentium 200 MHz (or faster) or compatible processor with CD-ROM drive

+ Microsoft Windows 98, 2000, or Windows NT 4.0 (or later) with Service Pack 4

+ 48MB of available RAM for Windows 98, or 64MB of available RAM for Windows NT 4.0 (to enable all modules)

+ 60MB of available hard-disk space

How This Book Is Organized

More than 900 pages of important information can be rather daunting to contemplate, let alone digest, so I've divided the book up into logical parts. Consider this book a Chinese restaurant menu from days of old, where you can choose an item or two from column A and another from column B. Take what you need and pass on the rest; it'll still be there for you when you're hungry for more later. Here's what's on the menu.

Part I: Introducing GoLive 5

This part introduces you to the GoLive basics. Here's where I show you the fundamental tools you use to build your presence on the Web. Wondering what GoLive can do for you? Wondering if it can handle your site? Here's the answer. (Well, the answer is yes, but here are the details of GoLive's powerful site management and creative design capabilities.)

Part II: Starting to Build Your Site

Ready to get started? This is the place to learn how. Whether you're starting a new site from scratch, converting a site from another application, or bringing a hand-coded site into GoLive, this part covers the details of actually starting your site.

Part III: Adding Text, Graphics, and Links

Whether you've got pictures to speak for you or you've got your thousands of words on hand, this is the part that shows you how to deploy them. As you create your message, the linking techniques you learn here enable you to build your site in earnest.

Part IV: Using GoLive's Advanced Tools

After you've got the basics down, you can add a navigation bar, logo, or other more advanced feature to your site using GoLive's Components, and jazz up your interface with fancy buttons. You can also format your pages with style sheets—a very good idea. Want to lay things out in tables or use frames to present your site? That's here too. This is the place to learn how to really take control of your pages and get the formatting just right.

Part V: Adding Multimedia, Movement, and Interactivity

Here's where the Web becomes fun. This part shows you how to add video, animation, or sound files to your site. It's also where you learn about using Dynamic HTML (DHTML) to add movement to your site without video files. Want to make one of those cool effects where text or images magically appear when the mouse rolls over a screen element? That's DHTML—and this is the place for learning how to do it. The basics in Part III are a prerequisite to this part.

Part VI: Going Live — The Final Touches

After your pages are complete, come here to learn how to add some professional touches that'll help your site be found—and help visitors find what they seek at your site. Then learn about optimizing your site for delivery on the Web. This part shows you how to polish your site in a variety of ways. It's also where you'll learn how to get your site onto a server—to *go live* with it.

Part VII: Using GoLive's Advanced Site-Planning Tools

A site's not very lively if you can't easily make changes to it after it's live. GoLive makes updating a cinch. I show you how to do it right here. After you get all the basics of site design down, and know the power of GoLive, you may want to become part of a design team—perhaps a team that presents design ideas to clients, or an international design team with codesigners all over the world. Those powerful high-end professional design features are the subject of this part, too.

Appendixes

At the back of this book you'll find Appendix A, which tells you about everything that is on the CD-ROM. In addition, you'll find four additional appendixes on the CD-ROM, all containing valuable bonus material that I couldn't squeeze into the book. In those appendixes you can introduce yourself to the JavaScript language, read about how forms communicate, learn how to set up an e-commerce site, and discover great information about extend scripts and the GoLive SDK.

Conventions This Book Uses

I use the following conventions throughout this book.

Windows and Macintosh conventions

The *Adobe GoLive 5 Bible* is a cross-platform book. As a result, I give you instructions for both platforms whenever there's a platform difference. In the case of the keyboard, where the difference is a constant, I've merged the commands to make reading easier. Here's what you can expect:

♦ On your keyboard, if you're using Windows, or perhaps a third-party Mac keyboard, you'll have the word "Enter" on the key that sends the cursor to the next line. However, on the Mac keyboard, you'll have "Return." Wherever this key is mentioned, it appears as "Enter/Return."

♦ The key that deletes text that comes before the cursor is called Backspace in Windows, but Delete on the Mac. This key is shown as Backspace/Delete.

Keyboard shortcuts can be great time savers so I want you to be able to identify the shortcut you need quickly. Following the Mac and Windows interfaces you're familiar with, I use a hyphen between Mac keys and a plus sign to show Windows keys. For example, this is what the shortcut to create a link looks like: ⌘-L (Mac) and Alt+L (Windows).

Menu commands

To show you where you can select a command from a menu, I put the menu name first, followed by an arrow pointing to the specific command. For example, to tell you to open GoLive's Inspector window from the Window menu, I say to choose Window ⇨ Inspector.

Where the command to be chosen is a submenu of a main menu command, you'll see each command separated by an arrow. For example, to tell you to open a new site by choosing Blank from the New Site submenu under the File menu, I say to choose File ⇨ New Site ⇨ Blank.

Mouse instructions

On both Windows and Mac, clicking an item is a main way of selecting an object. To click an item, move the mouse until the tip of the arrow pointer touches the object, and then click the mouse button one time. With the Windows mouse, you click the left mouse button. When an object is selected, its color inverts, or it becomes the color you've selected in your operating system's Control Panel. To select more than one item, select the first, press the Shift key, and then click the next object while you hold down the Shift key. To move selected items, keep the mouse down after the item (or last item) is selected, and then drag the mouse until the item is in the desired location. Then release the mouse. Click in a blank area of your page or window to deselect the selected items so you don't inadvertently issue another command to them.

GoLive is replete with a full set of contextual menu commands. A contextual menu is one that consists only of commands that are appropriate for the item you're pointing at as you call up the menu. For example, when pointing to a cell in a table, one available command is Select Cell. But if you point to a file in the Site Window, there is no cell to select so the Select Cell command is not available. To call up a contextual menu in Windows, click the right mouse button. Macs use a one-button mouse, so you press the Control key as you click the mouse button to produce a contextual menu. In this book you'll see the words "Control-click (Mac) or right-click (Windows)" to describe this process. (But just so it doesn't get too boring, sometimes I'll simply tell you to call up the contextual menu.)

Typographical conventions

I use *italic* type for new terms and for emphasis, and **boldface** type for text that you need to type directly from the computer keyboard.

Code

A special typeface indicates HTML or other code, as demonstrated by the following example:

```
<html>
  <head>
    <title>Welcome to Adobe GoLive 5</title>
  </head>
  <body bgcolor="#ffffff">
    <p>GoLive 5!</p>
  </body>
</html>
```

This book also uses the same code font within paragraphs to designate HTML tags (such as <body>), attributes, and values. All HTML tags are presented in lowercase, which is the current standard for HTML coding and the way GoLive generates HTML.

Tools of the Trade

I wrote this book on an Apple Macintosh 7600, running as a 450 MHz G3, thanks to an XLR8 upgrade card, with an Inside Out Networks USB card and hub and a Swann FireWire card. It was backed up to a VST FireWire hard drive using Dantz Retrospect software. I ran GoLive on a variety of machines, predominately a Windows PC running Windows 98, a G3 Mac running OS 8.6, my own 7600 (as a G3), and even using Virtual PC running Windows 98 on the beige G3. EarthLink's DSL service kept those many beta versions coming in and book files flying across the Internet. All machines had DSL Internet connectivity thanks to an Xsense XRouter Pro. Backup dial-up access was via a Swann Mac2k USB v.90 modem. Typing was done with the help of TypeIt4Me and SpellCatcher. The Mac and VPC screen shots were taken using Snapz Pro while the Windows shots were done with Snag-It. For more hardware and software details, see www.golivebible.com.

Navigating Through This Book

This book is presented to you in short paragraphs so they're easy to follow. In many cases, numbered steps are outlined to help you proceed. In addition, the following icons guide you to some extra special facts:

 Tips provide the secrets of true power. This icon helps point these powers out to you.

 In the spirit of the Internet, several experts share their tips with you. Look for this icon to learn from a variety of Web professionals.

 Notes point out something extra of interest that you should, well, take note of.

 This icon is the hyperlink of the *Adobe GoLive 5 Bible*; it lets you know where you can find more information about a topic (although clicking it won't do more than produce a pretty sound).

 If you're already a GoLive user and you're wondering where a menu or capability went, watch for these icons to save your sanity.

 The CD-ROM icon lets you know about something on the CD-ROM that comes with this book.

 Once in a while there's something you need to be careful about.

Where Should I Start?

If you are new to GoLive, I recommend you start at the very beginning with Chapters 1 and 2. These chapters provide the foundation for understanding GoLive's interface. From there, you can move to Chapter 4 so you can start your site. Then consider following the order of the chapters in Part III, as they build the basic knowledge you'll need to create your site. From there, jump to the chapter in Part IV or V that provides what you need. Finally, use Part VI to take your site live.

If you're upgrading from a previous version of GoLive, Chapter 2 points out the Site Window, menu, and window changes, saving you a bit of hunting. (And Chapter 1 may prove useful; you may discover another strength you didn't even know GoLive had.) After those introductory chapters, you can skip directly to the chapter that covers the task at hand.

Acknowledgments

First, thanks to the folks at IDG Books Worldwide. This book would simply not exist if not for Michael Roney. It was Mike who recognized the need for this book in the Internet community, proposed it to his IDG Books teammates, and then oversaw the entire process of getting it into your hands. I've had the honor of working with Mike before (on the *Macworld Office 98 Bible*) and am honored that he remembered my love of GoLive and picked me as the person to complete his vision of this book. Mike is always there to run an idea by, which enabled me to do something very different in this book: bring in various GoLive, visual, and Internet experts to provide you with what we've dubbed "Expert Tips." Thanks Mike, for seeing GoLive's power and believing in me to create this book.

Thanks to Chris Johnson for his patience, creative approaches to problem-solving, and project coordination. My appreciation goes to Michael Welch, Dennis Weaver, Laura Stone, Cindy Lai, Lane Barnholtz, and Julie Moss for their excellent copyediting work. And thanks, too, to the entire production staff at IDG Books for expert layout and design. Thanks also to Linda Turnowski and Michael Christopher for their help along the way. Thanks to Debbie Gates for her file transfer support and to Stephanie Rodriguez and Sandy Rodrigues.

Thanks to the entire really cool Adobe GoLive team. They not only created this amazing application, but also did their best to be available to answer questions, listen to (and implement!) feature requests, and work through work-flow thoughts. Special thanks to Jens Neffe, Lance Lewis, Lars Peters, Veronika Schlick, Sebastian Dimpker, Jan Stoeckmann, Robert McDaniels, and Sam Hui. A standing ovation for Irv Kanode and Matt Ridley. Boy, did Irv and Matt ever answer the call — no matter what I asked for. Also thanks to Kim Platt and Daniel Brown. And most of all, thanks to John (jfk) Kranz, GoLive product manager, for, well, *sooo* much.

Thanks also to my agent Christian Crumlish for making this project possible for me and for keeping me going when covering all of GoLive's power seemed endless.

Thanks to LA Bridge, an excellent Los Angeles ISP, for hosting www.golivebible.com during the book's creation process.

Thanks to Mordechai Kamornick and Jeff Klein, to Sheri and Mario Salinas, Mark Treitel, and to Cathy Scrivnor for coming to my rescue around the clock whenever I needed equipment or someone to kick a thought around with. To Moe Wodnicki for the house call to keep my HP 4M printing. Thanks to the helpful guys of the Web405 list: Kynn Bartlett, Joe Crawford, and Mark Jaress.

Thanks to the generous contributions of the talented people who have provided materials for you to work with on the CD-ROM. (You can learn more about these materials in Appendix A.)

This book has one name on the cover, but many great names inside, so a great big thanks to people who went all out reviewing my chapters, trying out services such as WebDAV with me, and writing up some of their Expert Tips or verifying my own tips:

- Sheri and Mario Salinas and Cathy Scrivnor for the outline and flow of the book, and for help testing WebDAV and learning its intricacies.

- Richard McLean for writing half of Chapter 2, and doing the entire update of Chapter 16 and the forms appendix. You won't see his name there often but his words are sure there.

- Oliver Zahorka for his many contributions to Chapters 15 and 22 and the JavaScript appendix. Also for the WebDAV server. And for the bonus OUTactions!

- Rob Keniger, first for writing all the SDK appendix. Next, for adding the new forms variables information to Chapter 16. And also for his additions and verifications in Chapters 11, 17, 18, 22, and 30.

- Steven Shmerler for fully updating Chapter 10 and adding his graphic expertise and for his many contributions to Chapter 13.

- Pete Zimowski for doing so much in Chapters 11, 25, and 26.

- Ken Martin, GREP guru, for his contributions to Chapters 3, 14, and 25.

- Doug Fairchild for making Appendix D shine. And to Mark Tiextera for his e-commerce help.

- Lynne LaMaster for her contributions to Chapters 6 and 10. And to her son, Doug LaMaster, for his Flash and LiveMotion images.

- Jeep Hauser for the WebDAV server and testing.

- Bob Stein for his color-on-the-Web sidebars.

- Also to Beate de Nijs, Nini Tjäder, and Frederico Russo, for miscellaneous GoLive details. And to David Shadovitz, my middleware guru.

- More thanks to Cathy Scrivnor for writing all of Chapter 24, and her counseling and testing on every other chapter as well, particularly on Chapter 19.

Cathy adds: Thanks to Brian Sooy, Scott Myers, Frederico Russo, and Paul Ferguson for helping her out with the intricacies of Dynamic Link, especially during those crazy beta days when one never knew which part of the puzzle was missing from beta to beta. And to Bernard Questel for teaching the finer details of Access.

And thanks to Richard Gaskin, for his role as official technical reviewer.

Contents at a Glance

Contents

• •

Part II: Starting to Build Your Site   101

Part III: Adding Text, Graphics, and Links   189

Part IV: Using GoLive's Advanced Tools   343

Chapter 12: Making Image Maps and Using Advanced Links 345

Part V: Adding Multimedia, Movement, and Interactivity   567

Chapter 18: Applying GoLive's JavaScripts: Actions and Smart Objects 569

Part VII: Using GoLive's Advanced Site-Planning Tools   913

Chapter 28: Updating Your Site 915

Bonus Appendixes   On the CD-ROM

Appendix B: Introducing the JavaScript Language

Appendix C: How Forms Communicate

Appendix D: Understanding the E-commerce Puzzle

Appendix E: Extend Script and the GoLive SDK

Introducing GoLive 5

This part introduces you to the GoLive basics. Here's where I show you the fundamental tools you use to build your presence on the Web. Wondering what GoLive can do for you? Wondering if it can handle your site? This chapter has the answer. (Well, the answer is yes, but here are the details of GoLive's powerful site-management and creative design capabilities.)

Introducing GoLive's Features

Do you remember the days (oh so long ago) when normal presence on the Web was a single page? Nowadays, full-fledged Web sites — multiple pages — are more common. The Web has matured significantly in its brief lifetime. Once upon a time a picture on a site was special. An animated GIF was jaw-dropping. Nowadays you can add still graphics, animated graphics, streaming sound, videos, and animations. Web sites have certainly become more intricate to create and manage. Thankfully, there's Adobe GoLive 5.

This book can actually have a few different introductions. I can introduce it as a great tool for beginners because it enables you to easily create great pages and get them on to the Web quickly. I can introduce it as a great tool for designers because it integrates well with Adobe's other amazing design tools. I can introduce it as a great tool for old-fashioned coders because it not only provides all the tools you need for coding, but also allows you to simultaneously view your results. I can introduce it as a tool for QuickTime content creators because it contains an entire QuickTime Editor that takes full advantage of the QuickTime API (application program interface). I can introduce it as a tool for small-site designers because it is easy to use for designing a small site, getting it documented and up and going, and perhaps more important, it can remain your tool of choice as your site grows. I can introduce it as a tool for large-site designers because GoLive handles large productions with its site architecture document generation capability. GoLive also efficiently handles site management and Web Distributed Authoring Versioning (WebDAV) features for team development , and makes it easy to add, adapt, edit, and project manage your site through all phases. The following are some further points to keep in mind:

✦ GoLive is not just a tool for designing a page; it's a tool for designing an entire site from site architecture to creation.

✦ GoLive is not only a tool for designing an entire site, it's a tool for updating, expanding, and maintaining your site.

✦ GoLive is a state-of-the-art Web site creation program that supports all widely accepted advanced Web capabilities.

✦ GoLive is a project management tool for an entire Web development team.

✦ GoLive is a complete FTP tool for uploading your site or for incremental uploads with full file tracking to ensure that all your updates make it to the server.

✦ GoLive 5 is now completely cross platform.

✦ GoLive 5 is now a part of the Adobe family of creative tools in every way; it , includes the popular Adobe interface and has the capability to work between other Adobe applications such as Photoshop, Illustrator, and LiveMotion. (GoLive 4 users can easily upgrade to Version 5.)

Introducing the GoLive Web Site Creation Tool

Using GoLive is simple. You collect your site's asset files such as graphics, videos, and sounds in a window. You open a page, enter some type, drag some file icons or the Objects palette icons onto the page's unique Point and Shoot feature to connect the files, make sure everything is positioned right . . . and that's about all you need to do.

Just so your Web life isn't a total *drag*, GoLive throws in an intuitive Inspector with a few easy-to-use pop-up menus or a places to enter information. As you work, GoLive manages your site and tells you when an error occurs. And to fix an error? Just click a button or drag to reconnect the file.

So what exactly does GoLive do? In a nutshell, it provides ease of use, ease of site conceptualization, management, flexibility, error checking, browser compatibility, HTML formatting, page interactivity, forms creation, JavaScripting, Cascading Style Sheets formatting, DHTML coding, QuickTime editing, site building and streamlining, database, e-commerce and XML support. How does it do this? Mostly through the magic of its Site Window where files are recorded and tracked, with the help of a palette full of objects for your pages, and with the aid of its multifunctional Inspector.

Whether you're new to Web page creation and only plan on building a small site for you and your family, whether you're a professional graphic designer expanding your design skills to the Web, or whether you're a Web-wise old-timer and want a break from hand-coding to take you to the next level of design and management, GoLive is packed with useful and commanding features that can handle sites ranging from a few pages to hundreds of pages.

Taking a Quick Tour of the GoLive Interface

What sets GoLive apart from other Web site tools on the market? Its powerful and technologically advanced features. Here are the main ones:

✦ **Site Window.** This is your main site management interface, similar to your computer's desktop list view (details) interface. You place all of the files that comprise your site here so GoLive can manage them. Instead of having to keep track of all of your site's *assets* (pieces), you just drag each graphic, sound, movie, PDF (Portable Document Format file), downloadable file, and so on into the Site Window. From there, GoLive provides file management and when you FTP, it ensures all of your files are correctly uploaded to the Web server. When you link to pages from within the Site Window, GoLive tracks your links — providing full link error checking. When you collect external URLs from the Site Window, GoLive verifies those URLs. GoLive even tracks the colors and fonts you designate on the pages of your site. There's more, but in short, GoLive tracks all the elements that comprise your site from within the easy-to-use but powerful Site Window.

✦ **Point and Shoot.** This is GoLive's incredibly simple and intuitive linking technique. Ask experienced GoLive users how to sum up GoLive in very few words and the chances are that they will say *Point and Shoot* pretty quickly. Point and Shoot is literally that. You place the text or graphic that you want to turn into a link. You then press Option (Mac) or Alt (Windows) as you click this would-be link and you drag it over to the page or to the marker that's your link's destination.

✦ **Objects palette.** This palette provides the page element icons for you to drag and drop into place on your page. Each icon has an *Inspector* that shows you what you can do to set up that object once it's on the page. *Contextual menus* compliment the Inspector when you're pointing to an item, but also provide many of the menu and toolbar commands.

✦ **In & Out Links palette.** This feature lets you see all of your links for pages and individual files at a glance. When you select a page in the Site Window, the In & Out Links palette shows you every file that links to the page and every file that is linked from that same page.

When you select a file, such as a graphic or video, you see all pages it is used on, and any links that graphic may contain as well. This palette does more than report links; it also enables linking. You can use the Point and Shoot button to swap any graphic, link, or other destination.

GoLive provides the preceding easy-to-understand tools, in addition to others. They include the Frames editor and the Frames tab of the Objects palette that work together to make building a frameset as easy as drag and drop—and getting it set up right as easy as Point and Shoot, drag, and click. You can drag the Table icon to your page to build a table. The Color palette enables you to choose a color from any number of color options—and even pick up any color on your monitor! Additionally, customizable keyboard shortcuts make it easier for you to perform any function that's available within GoLive's menus. Figure 1-1 shows GoLive's interface, including the Site Window and the Inspector.

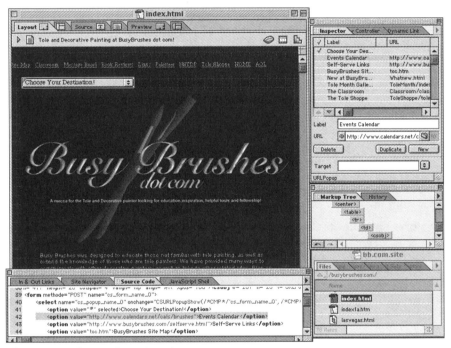

Figure 1-1: The GoLive 5 interface

Using GoLive

GoLive maintains a level of ease that beginners are comfortable with, yet is packed with power that even the highest end designers and coders find appealing. It truly has a full range of features for anyone who designs for the Web.

GoLive is a great tool for any of the following types of users:

✦ **Beginners** will find it easy to create great pages and get them onto the Web fast.

✦ **Designers** will appreciate its integration with Adobe's other innovative design tools.

✦ **Old-fashioned coders** will like it because it not only provides all the tools needed for coding, but also offers a parallel view of the results.

✦ **Scriptors and developers** are provided the Software Development Kit (SDK) that enables the extension and customization of GoLive's already comprehensive capabilities.

✦ **QuickTime content creators** will benefit from using the QuickTime Editor that takes full advantage of the QuickTime API.

✦ **Small-site designers** will find it is easy to use for architecting, documenting, and setting up a small site. Perhaps more importantly, it can remain a tool of choice as the site grows.

✦ **Large-site designers** and project managers will like the way GoLive competently handles large productions with its site architecture document generation for clients. Its site management and WebDAV features for team development make it easy to add, adapt, edit, and project manage your site through all phases.

GoLive is for beginners

Well, actually, it's for everyone who understands that you don't have to work hard to work smart. GoLive's entire interface is geared toward simplicity and ease. It's Site Window tracks all the actions you do and lets you know when you're doing well or when you have an error — and it lets you know what and where that error is.

You don't have to know HTML or any other code, to create simple or intricate Web sites. With GoLive 5, you don't even need to have a design in mind. GoLive's templates enable you to get a site up quickly even if you're not a designer. Simply choose File ➪ New Site ➪ Copy From Template and build your site based upon one of Adobe's starter sites.

GoLive's Window menu is rich with palettes and windows that provide the tools you need to build an amazing site. Keep the Objects palette open to add elements to your site. Keep the Inspector open as you work and it enables you to configure and adjust your pages or the elements on your pages. Open extra palettes as you work on a specific element or task that has a palette name associated with it.

GoLive is for designers

In addition to being great for beginners, Adobe GoLive is a true designer's tool. It is visual (WYSIWYG), enabling you to concentrate on the look and feel of your site, not the hypertext markup language (HTML) code behind it. However, anytime you wish, it's a cinch to look at, and work in, the HTML. In fact, using GoLive can even help you learn and perfect your understanding and use of HTML and emerging code technologies.

GoLive streamlines the entire Web design process from start to finish. When I say *start* I mean from *concept*. GoLive provides tools to conceive and *storyboard* (graphically layout) the architecture of a new site. This process is so easy that you can create several site layouts and document them in print or Adobe Acrobat PDF files for professional graphical client presentations.

As a designer, you can create your page *mockups* (comps) in Photoshop and add them to your Web site as full-page tracing guides and cut individual optimized sections from them with amazing ease. Some of GoLive's designer-oriented features include the following:

✦ **Smart Objects** (new to GoLive 5) makes it easy to import original layered files you create with Photoshop, Illustrator, or LiveMotion — and edit the originals *live* as needed. A Smart Object from your page links to both your original layered artwork (the source file) and an optimized Web-ready version (GIF, JPEG) that is created from within GoLive during the Smart Object linking process using the *Save For Web* feature first introduced in Photoshop. You store the optimized version in your Site Window so it uploads to your Web server when you publish your site. Any time you want to resize or edit your artwork, double-click the Smart Object on your page in the document window to open the source file in its original application (such as Photoshop). You edit the original and when you save the original, GoLive automatically saves a new optimized version and overwrites the previous one onto your page.

✦ **Image tracing** (new to GoLive 5) enables you to import Photoshop graphics for use as an underlying design and layout guide. Many designers and art directors create the layout and look of a Web page in Photoshop, and then give this image to the Web developer to cut up and lay out on the page as close to the Photoshop image as possible. With Tracing Images this process is much easier. You import the entire Photoshop image into your page, which basically functions as would any page background image, enabling you to place text and images on top of it. Unlike a background image however, you can reduce the opacity to make it a guide so you can place corresponding images and text over it.

In addition, you can cut out sections of the Tracing image itself, from within your GoLive page and, using the Save for Web dialog window, optimize and save the section. Each cutout appears as a floating box in your Web page in the exact location of the underlying Tracing image layout. From here, you can change the position or apply animation to these floating boxes or drag the image out of the floating box. When you are finished with your page and all elements line up to your liking, you can then remove the underlying Tracing Image.

✦ **Import Photoshop as HTML** (new to GoLive 5) enables you to import a layered Photoshop file and have each layer import as a separate image in its own GoLive floating box on a Web page. Each imported Photoshop layer is presented to you with its own Save for Web dialog box so you can optimize each layer independently. You can use the floating boxes for your Dynamic HTML needs or drag the graphics out of the floating boxes, delete the boxes, and use the images as standard HTML images on your page.

✦ **The Layout grid** enables you to design a page by moving its elements around anywhere you want them — just like you would within a page-layout program such as InDesign, PageMaker, or Quark. The grid is GoLive's own invention — really a jazzed up table. As you work on the grid, GoLive is writing the code for a plain old (albeit intricate) standard HTML table. You can convert your grid to a regular table or turn a plain table into a grid anytime.

GoLive is for hand-coders

Hand-coding HTML takes time — lot of time. As the Web and Web design become more complicated, sites with hundreds of pages, and advances such as JavaScript, Cascading Style Sheets, Dynamic HTML (DHTML), Active Server Pages (ASP), and others take too much time to hand-code. Furthermore, consider all those seconds toggling between source code and browser views. Would it surprise you to learn that they add up to hours that a WYSIWYG authoring environment like GoLive eliminates? Not to mention all the site development and management tools at your disposal. If you are building large sites for fun or for a living, simply too many pages, too many links, too much code, and too few hours exist not to take advantage of GoLive's capabilities.

For example, using GoLive to create a navbar with let's say half a dozen rollovers may take five to ten minutes, while hand-coding all the JavaScript and defining all the image links can take hours! But GoLive is not just about WYSIWYG display. GoLive is a full-featured professional authoring environment with intuitive tools to conceive, create, maintain, and manage any level site.

Using GoLive doesn't mean saying good-bye to hand-coding. On the contrary, GoLive realizes that certain advanced and proprietary sites require "getting under the hood." GoLive supports this with its Simultaneous Views feature, which introduces a new visual dimension to your work. With GoLive, you can work in code — and *see* the results of your work *as* you work. You can also see a view of your layout in outline view by using the Markup Tree palette (discussed in the following list).

Serious coders (and others) can take advantage of the following features:

✦ **Source Code palette** shows you the HTML of a page as you work in Layout mode in the page window. Open your page in Layout mode to see it in a visual state, and then open the Source Code palette to code within. You can position each window wherever it's most comfortable for you on the screen. Type your code into the source code, and then click anywhere in the page layout to see the results.

✦ **Markup Tree palette** provides you with an outline of the HTML tags that lead to any item within your page. Click a tag in the Markup tree and it becomes selected in Layout mode and in the Source Code palette if it is open. In an intricate layout this capability can help you select any element quickly. (Elements such as invisible borders on nested tables and invisible GIFs can be difficult to select with the cursor in layout but an HTML tag in the markup outline is a full-sized target to click.) You can also move back and forth between your selections to get back to any item.

✦ **Layout Preview** simulates how your pages will display on various platforms and browsers, which is an incredible timesaving development tool. For example, you can view a simulated display of Internet Explorer 4.0 for Windows or Macintosh, or Navigator 3, 4.5, or 5 for Mac or Windows, all in the time it takes to click a pull-down menu in GoLive.

✦ **360 Code** ensures that what you code is what you get. GoLive 4 parsed your HTML each time you switched from the Source mode back to Layout mode, which created some problems for nonstandard HTML code. By popular demand, GoLive 5 does not touch code it doesn't understand. This means you can use nonstandard HTML code or scripting in Source mode and it remains intact.

✦ **Rewrite Source Code** complements 360 code, enabling you to have GoLive rewrite your source code (based on GoLive's Web settings, which you can customize).

✦ **Find by Element** is a unique find and replace tool created specifically for working within HTML. With it you can easily edit your code.

GoLive is for scriptors and developers

GoLive may be drag-and-drop simple, but that doesn't mean it doesn't have powerful capabilities. Some other enhanced GoLive features include the following:

✦ **JavaScript Editor** enables you to write your own internal or external JavaScripts by typing it yourself, by dragging prewritten snippets of JavaScript code into place, or by using a combination of both methods. You can use prescripted *GoLive Actions* or write your own.

✦ **AppleScript** enables Mac users to automate just about any task using standard AppleScript procedures.

✦ **The GoLive SDK (Software Development Kit)** is included with GoLive 5. You can use it to customize the GoLive interface. For example, you can add your own menus or commands to GoLive's existing menus. You can add tabs to the Objects palette. You can add Dialog boxes. You can create your own Inspectors, and more. You do all these by using JavaScript (and the built-in JavaScript Debugger) and XML; you don't need to be a C or C++ programmer, or to use outside programming tools. GoLive is all you need, but you can call external C libraries on Mac and Windows as well.

✦ **XML.** Once upon a time there was standard generalized markup language (SGML). It worked well but it was considered complicated. So programmers created hypertext markup language (HTML), a subset of SGML that was easier for people to understand and use. So much so, that HTML literally changed the world as the Web's growth exploded. As with any expansion, the limitations of a language created in 1989 demanded some new thinking. Enter XML (extensible markup language), another subset of SGML that defines custom tags called Document Type Definitions (DTD). GoLive's XML support enables you to read and edit XML documents as objects in the Outline Editor or as text in the Source Editor. GoLive recognizes XML code and reads and writes it without any problems, leaving the code intact.

GoLive is for project managers

GoLive supports WebDAV to help you manage a collaborative development environment. Using a WebDAV server, your site is built in a *staged* area with permissions and page check-out and check-in tracking so that a page cannot be updated by more than one person at a time. Your team can edit, add, delete, duplicate, rename, move, upload, or download no differently than they would locally using the WebDAV browser tab in the Site Window. When your site is completed, you move it from staging to live for publication to the online world. (See the next section, "GoLive is for large projects," for details.)

GoLive is for large projects

No job's too big for GoLive 5. It's designed to handle *sites of any size*. A 10,000-page site should respond as fast as one that's 100 pages. It won't cost you 10,000 pages' worth of memory because GoLive handles that for you by keeping only the pages you're working on active instead of keeping all pages in memory at the same time. After all, even the best Web designers can only do a certain number of tasks at once (not 10, 000).

A large site is much easier to build if you begin with a good structural design that enables you to place information within easy reach of your visitors. GoLive has an entire menu, appropriately called the Design menu, to provide *site diagramming* and *structural review*. (You can learn all about it in Chapter 29.) It'll even build you a table of contents based on your page titles. GoLive provides superior site development with the following tools:

✦ **Site Designer** (new to GoLive 5) enables you to create multiple plans for a site, run them by your clients or mull them over in your own head, and then submit a design to GoLive. When you submit the design, GoLive instantly creates the pages for you; you just add content. Changing your mind is not a problem; you can recall any page later (except content-containing pages) and choose another layout.

✦ **Navigation View** lets you view your site in an organizational chart manner. You can use it to rearrange your site's structure, to create new pages, and record your intentions to link pages (by shooting to them, of course). The Spotlight feature lets you easily see which pages are related to any specific page. You can use Navigation View in many ways to help you clearly see the big picture.

✦ **Links View** shows you all the links in your site, and I do mean *all*, in a hierarchical view of your site.

✦ **WebDAV** enables collaborative authoring and GoLive takes that several steps further by being one of the first applications to support it. In the spirit of the Web, which accelerates communication and accessibility, GoLive enables you to use WebDAV (Web Distributed Authoring and Versioning), a protocol for uploading and downloading your site's files to a common area accessible by an entire worldwide design team. With WebDAV, you can be designing a page, someone else is adding text to another page, and yet another person is designing a different page or adding graphics to the site, all at the same time. You have a choice of two file protection methods: simple locking and unlocking of files or GoLive's advanced check-out and check-in feature. With WebDAV the world just got smaller again — and hopefully your communication costs will decrease too.

Note   You need access to a WebDAV server to use this feature. Servers include Microsoft IIS 5 (included with Windows 2000), Apache (with the mod_dav module), Novell NetWare 5.1, and Mac OS *x*.

Recycling with GoLive

Like the saying goes, why reinvent the wheel? After you create an element, you don't need to re-create it. Instead, you can use it over and over again. The following GoLive features enable you to use elements repeatedly:

✦ **Stationery** enables you to create the basics of a page once, and then use that page as a starting point for countless other pages. All you do is create the page in the same way you create any other page, and then save or move it into a special folder aptly called "Stationery." After that it's available from the Objects palette any time you want it.

✦ **Components** provide a unique level of flexibility in your pages. Components enable you to create an element once, and then incorporate it into multiple pages. You design a Component in the same way that you create a page. The only difference is the folder in which you save it. After you create the Component it appears in your Objects palette. You then simply drag the Component from the Objects palette into place on any page. (That's any place on any page. Each page can be totally different, except for the Component, of course.) Later, when you need to change an item within the Component, you get to see the true glory of it. Just change the Component and GoLive updates every page of which it is a part. Components are useful for navigation bars and mastheads.

✦ **Custom tabs in the Objects palette and Site Window** enable you to store HTML snippets and objects. After you create an object, you can store it for future use. To use it in any site you create using your copy of GoLive, place it in the Objects palette's custom tab. To use it only within the site on which you're working, drag it into the Custom tab of the Site Window. Later, you can place that object on any page by just dragging it into place.

✦ **Cascading Style Sheets** add a new level of page control to the Web while enabling you, as the designer, flexibility to change the look of your pages easily.

You don't have to know style sheet syntax to create a style sheet. In GoLive you select your styling options from a dedicated Style Sheet Inspector. Need color? Click the color swatch and chose it from the GoLive-standard Color palette. Need a font or entire font set? Choose it from the pop-up menu. Want margins? Enter the number into the margin fields and choose your measurement unit.

With an external style sheet, you can make a change across the entire site by making one small change in the style sheet instead of having to change every page. Or you can link an external style sheet to just some of your pages and effect just those pages. You can have multiple style sheets, and even use more than one on any page. Prefer internal style sheets? Not a problem; the same easy-to-use interface is there for you. In fact, GoLive can even convert an internal style sheet to external and vice versa. There's a lot more to this style sheet ease. I cover Cascading Style Sheets fully in Chapter 17.

Creating Multimedia and Interactive Pages

Embed, create, animate—you can do it all in GoLive. Multimedia makes the Web fun and provides you with interesting ways to say more in less space. Some of GoLive's multimedia capabilities are as follows:

✦ **Customized plug-in icons** (and a Generic plug-in) enable you to *embed* a piece of multimedia within your page. With GoLive you can add multimedia files such as QuickTime or QuickTime VR (movies), Flash, Shockwave, LiveMotion (SWF files), or Scalable Vector Graphics (SWG files).

These types of animations need a plug-in in the user's browser in order to work on the user's end. That same browser plug-in works within GoLive when you place it in GoLive's plug-ins folder. You can also easily add Java applications.

Just drag the multimedia file into the Files tab of the Site Window, drag the prewritten Plug-in icon from the Objects palette to your page, and then Point and Shoot from the icon to the file. The Inspector is also there to help you, as always. Of course, you can create a regular link too, instead of embedding your multimedia file into your page. Chapter 20 gives you the lowdown on importing audio and video.

✦ **QuickTime** support abounds in GoLive. QuickTime is the most flexible and mature application for implementing video and sound on the Web, and GoLive has it big time. The GoLive QuickTime Editor, with the help of a dedicated QuickTime tab in the Objects palette, enables you to edit an existing movie or begin an entirely new one by starting fresh with a blank new movie container, and then adding your pieces. You can add multiple tracks of video and sound, and then use filters or transitions to combine them in a smooth flow. You can also do much more: Do you have an *SWF* file to add to your site? You can build upon that animation by placing it into a QuickTime container, either alone or with other elements. Do you want to add a *text* track, live *links*? You can. How about *animated sprites*? You can create those in Photoshop or elsewhere and bring them in to add animation and interactivity to your site. If your movie becomes too long you can divide it into *chapters* too. Want to stream just a par of your movie, for reliability or for copyright reasons, perhaps? That's as easy as dragging in a track and linking to it, just like you would add any other effect to your movie. The bottom line is that the GoLive QuickTime Editor enables you to perform the same functions as in QuickTime.

✦ **DHTML** animation is easy to create using GoLive's *floating boxes* and animation *TimeLine Editor*. Floating boxes give you the same effect as layers do in a drawing or graphics program, but can do far more than just stack images on one another. They can be used to do some great animations. You can put any text or image within a floating box, and then animate it by recording your actions or by using the TimeLine Editor. Another effect is to have mouseover actions show and hide a floating box when the user runs his or her mouse over the trigger item. You can add several floating boxes to a page to aid in the effect. To learn about floating boxes see Chapter 19.

✦ **JavaScript** is perhaps the most popular way to add interactivity or action to your site. GoLive richly supports JavaScript and comes with many preprogrammed JavaScripts, called GoLive Actions, ready for you to customize via the Inspector. Drag a JavaScript icon to your page and set it up in the Inspector or Actions palette.

✦ **ActiveX** controls can be set up by using the Object icon from the Basic tab of the Objects palette along with the Inspector. ActiveX is primarily a Windows-only tool for interactive features and can only be set up (and function from) a Windows machine.

GoLive's Web Database

The secret behind GoLive's knowledge of HTML is its Web database. All of HTML's code is stored here, enabling GoLive to create and manage your pages. Just in case HTML changes in some way before GoLive comes out with an update, you can edit within the Web database to accommodate these codes. However, if you are a novice page designer and don't possess a deep understanding of HTML, do not mess around with this database.

Creating Forms

Forms enable you to collect data from and send it to your visitors, and gather information for support functions such as customer service. Some forms, with the addition of a database on the server, enable you to have your user search for, add or update information, do e-commerce, host bulletin boards, and much more. GoLive provides an entire tab in the Objects palette just for forms creation. (Chapter 16 discusses forms thoroughly.)

It's easy to create forms, thanks to the Forms tab of the Objects palette. This tab enables you to build entire forms with drag and drop ease. Forms communicate by calling upon an intermediary called a Common Gateway Interface (CGI), which is a mini application that contains instructions. You can store your CGI script directly within your site's folder or you can store it at a more common level on the Web server. (Your Web server administrator may have rules about this.) Either way, you can easily link it to GoLive within the Form tags and Form Inspector.

Dynamic Link enables you to write the code needed to have your page communicate with middleware applications, such as ASP (the first Dynamic Link interface), without knowing programming. With Dynamic Link, you can design your page visually. When the layout is approved, you connect to the server that hosts the database, and use a dedicated Inspector to *associate* (bind) your sample data or empty form fields to the fields within the database. Somewhere along the line, someone has to design the database and put it up on a server, but that someone doesn't have to be you and you don't have to become a database programmer.

Tracking Your Work in GoLive

You need to keep track of a lot of items as you create a site. GoLive's tracking and reporting aides allow you to concentrate on creating a site and not worry about where everything is. These features include the following:

✦ **Multiple undos** enable you to change your mind about an action and undo it, going back up to 20 changes.

✦ **History palette** tracks the additions you make to your page and what you do to set the object up, writing a history of them in the History palette. (Specifically, each history is a page history; that is, changes to any page are tracked, not application-wide actions such as Preference settings.) You can move back in this history, to any state of the page, up to 20 steps backwards. Each time you save your page or close it, the history begins anew. It also clears and begins anew when you switch layout views, such as moving from Layout to Source, or to Outline or Preview (but not when you switch between Layout view and the Source Code window).

✦ **Site Reports** give you the details of your site's health. You can view and even print a report telling you which pages need a page title, which take more than any number of clicks for users to reach from the index page, whether a page is missing attributes, and much more. In Figure 1-2, you can see a Site Report set up to report all pages more than three clicks away from the site's home page.

✦ **Find & Replace** lets you locate anything in your site, on a page, or in your code. After you set up even the most intricate search, you can save it for reuse. You can also Find and Replace in Layout view, in the source code on one page or one folder, or on every page on the site.

✦ **File naming restrictions** alert you to any documents that don't adhere to the name restraints you set up for it to help you avoid uploading those files to a server that won't be able to handle them. (Predefined constraints may be all you need, but this option is here for you just in case.) This feedback is in the usual places: the Status column in the Files tab, the Errors tab, and the File Inspector. (If you have a file set to Never Publish, GoLive won't waste time checking on that file.)

✦ **Network Status window** captures a log of communications that occur between GoLive and the FTP or WebDAV server with which you're working. Errors are always tracked and are there for you to view anytime (File ⇨ Network Status). You can choose whether you also want to view warnings and status messages (which can be very helpful).

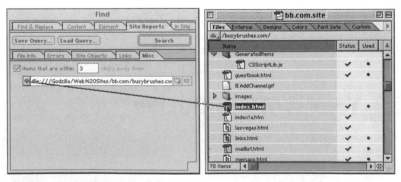

Figure 1-2: Setting up a site report

Taking Your Site Live with Ease

When it's all said and done, Web site creation is about going live on the Web. GoLive makes it easy to . . . well, go live. In fact, GoLive gives you three options for getting your site onto the Web. One of those lets you set your site up to well, go anywhere. GoLive even enables you to edit your site live on the Web.

The following are GoLive's three site-publishing interfaces:

✦ **Site Window FTP** enables you to upload your files with a click or a drag and see your files on the server in a side-by-side listing, next to your files tab. The Incremental Upload and Upload Modified Files Only features make it easy to keep your site up-to-date as it evolves.

✦ **FTP Browser** is a generic FTP client that you can use at any time to get to any server. This adds convenience when you're working on one site and need to access a site on another server. It's handy for uploading one-off items, such as files that go to a Streaming Server.

✦ **Export** enables you to create a Web-ready folder that you can pass on to clients, archive, or FTP to a Web server using the FTP Browser or a third-party FTP program.

GoLive has Web site design features and capabilities for beginners, designers, coders, scriptors, developers, and project managers — and you can take advantage of it now. Don't worry about learning all of its features. In fact, many people who have successfully created well-designed, popular sites have done so without knowing much of what is covered in this book. You can start using GoLive with only a fraction of what's in this book — although, of course, I hope this book offers a lot more information that you're not likely to know intuitively. You can build your site and take it live — and then start experimenting with other features of GoLive or other interesting effects you can add to your site. GoLive is great as an updating tool so your site can continue to evolve.

If you're new to GoLive, I recommend that you read Chapter 2, which introduces the way GoLive works. You're welcome to read Chapters 3 and 4 of course, but to follow the progression of learning, read Chapters 5–14 and 17, which provide the best foundation.

If you're an old hat at Web design but new to GoLive, you definitely want to read Chapters 2 and 5 so you can import a site to work on and then get started. From there, go on to whatever strikes your fancy.

✦   ✦   ✦

Getting to Know GoLive's Interface

As you use GoLive with the help of this book, you'll become more familiar and comfortable with GoLive's interface. Throughout this book, as you call upon any part of its interface I give you the steps clearly and concisely. However, it's always best to have a good foundation to build upon. This chapter is your GoLive foundation.

As you add pages, graphics, and other elements to your Web site, you accumulate many individual files that must be stored where they're accessible, and then uploaded to the Web server when it's time for your site to go live. You need to remember to upload all files in your site, and your pages need to be able to find these files — or you'll end up with broken images and broken links. GoLive solves this problem, tracking and managing your files for you in one easy-to-use place. You don't have to keep remembering where you stored all the files you use, and continually switch from GoLive back to the Windows desktop or the Macintosh Finder to move them around. You don't have to worry about remembering to get them to the server. And you don't have to worry about broken links.

Meeting the GoLive Visual Team

When you create a new site, GoLive creates a file called the site document, along with two folders where it stores all of the site's files. Each time you want to work on a site, you just open its site document. This file keeps track of everything you do; as you build and design the site, it notes what you're doing. The site document isn't like a typical document, though; you don't see it as a page, but as something called the Site Window instead. In Figure 2-1, you can see a site document and its corresponding Site Window. Notice that everything within the Site Window is also within the site's actual folder, along with the site document.

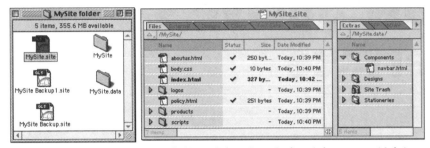

Figure 2-1: A site document (left) and the Site Window it becomes (right). Everything created or organized in the Site Window happens in the site's actual folder.

The *Site Window* is your main site management interface. It contains all the elements belonging to your site. The Site Window is also home to external URLs (for easy access), custom clippings you create for reuse, error checking, and more. On top of that, it enables FTP access so you can get your site onto the Web server, and WebDAV access for collaboration with other Web site designers. Using the Site Window, you can even connect to your server and edit a page on the spot, even though you've already posted it. (The Site Window is discussed in more detail later in this chapter.)

Your next main interface is the *Inspector* — GoLive's Swiss Army knife. Rather than sending you on a menu hunt, GoLive focuses its main controls within this single palette. This could certainly be a very busy, cluttered window, but it's not. It's actually very clean, simple, and elegant. Why? Because the Inspector is *context sensitive* — it only displays the controls relevant to the selected page element. For example, Figure 2-2 shows the Inspector palette transformed into the Table Inspector because a table is selected. GoLive simplifies the process of setting and changing object attributes by bringing them together in this single palette.

Of course, at the heart of a Web site is its pages. GoLive's page-creation window is also clean and efficient. In one simple-looking tabbed window GoLive gives you a page on which to design visually, a full HTML programmer's view, and a unique outline view of HTML that provides the power of working directly in HTML without reading through a maze of tags, attributes, text, and comments. Also in the page window is a Preview mode that, along with some choices in the Inspector, enables you to get an accurate idea of how your page will look in a browser. Topping the page window is the context-sensitive toolbar, which only displays controls that fit the view you're working in. (You can see a page and toolbar above, in Figure 2-2; toolbars are discussed later in this chapter.)

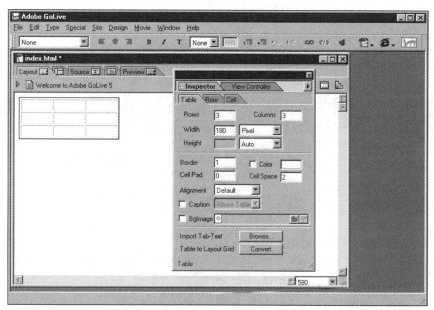

Figure 2-2: The Inspector changes to show the controls for the attributes of a selected table. (Also shown is the page and the full toolbar in Windows.)

Aiding you further in your quest for the perfect Web page is the Objects palette, from which you can drag the necessary items onto the page. Its window-mate, the Color palette, enables you to place virtually any color on your page, and even pick up colors from anywhere on your screen.

For linking and site planning, you have the In & Out Links palette (see Figure 2-3), which shows you all pages that link to a selected page as well as all files used on that page—and enables you to change any of those linked items or pages. It can also show you every page on which a URL, color, font set, or particular graphic/media file is used—and let you change that item across all of those pages at once.

The In & Out Links palette is so called because it shows all links in and out of the selected element. When you select a page, it shows you the elements on that page as well as any pages in your site to which the selected page is linked to. When you select another object (such as a graphic or external link) the In & Out Links palette displays the pages that include or link to that object.

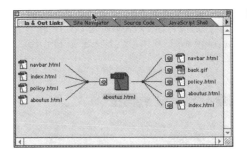

Figure 2-3: The In & Out Links palette

As you build your site, the Design menu provides you with various interactive maps of your site. In the Navigation window, you can see all existing pages and their relationships to one another (both actual and pending). In its partner, the Links view, you can see all pages within your site, and the way every page links to one another. Then there's the Site Designer, which provides you with endless blank design canvases on which you can plan your entire site, or new sections for it. Designs you make on the design canvas can be submitted to your site and used as real pages, or they can remain as visualizations.

The Window menu contains several more palettes, as well. Each is dedicated to one GoLive ability and presents just what you need in a clear, uncluttered way. Palettes are grouped into six windows, logically grouped so you only need to be using one palette within a group at any time. To make life even easier, you can *tear off* any palette and let it stand alone or move it to another window. (More on that later under "Exploring the Palettes.")

Although you won't need to travel to them often, GoLive's menus provide some helpful features. For example, you can view document statistics to get an idea of the time it will take for visitors to download (and therefore see) your page. You can also view document statistics for an individual file. This can help you decide whether a particular graphic is worth using. The menus are also the home to a spell checker that can check a single page or your entire site. And then there's the amazing, full-featured site report. Among other things, it can tell you how many pages are more than, say, three links always from your home page! Or, it can tell you if you've forgotten to give your page a title—which you also definitely want to know if you want an effective, impressive site.

Note There's more stuff, too; things that let you dig into HTML, JavaScript code, Cascading Style Sheets, GREPs, and more. But I'll get to that all later in the book. For now, I'll concentrate on the basic page/site design interfaces.

Discovering the Site Window

The Site Window is where it all starts. It's the hearth of the GoLive home. Each time you create a new blank site, or import a site, GoLive creates a site document and opens it, which in turn opens up a new Site Window for you. This Site Window is your main interface to your Web site. It's where you store the files that are part of your site, collect and see external links (links to other Web addresses, e-mails, and so on), and find colors and font sets you use or want to use. It's where you can see and plan the layout of your site.

Before you place any element on your page, you add it to the Site Window by dragging the item from the hard drive (or CD-ROM or other mounted drive) into the Files tab of the Site Window. If dragging is not your style, you can use the Add Files window. Should you decide you don't want to use something you added to the Site Window, just select its icon in the Site Window and delete it. Your pages live here, too — easily added whether pre-existing or new. To open a page for editing and development, you double-click that page's icon here in the Files tab.

If errors occur in your site, they are reported here. A bad link within a page is depicted by a green bug in the Files tab, as is a bad external URL in the External tab. All referenced or potential colors and font sets can also be stored within the Site Window for easy access and sharing between sites. There's also a Custom tab here, waiting to collect your own creations so you don't have to reinvent the wheel. When you are ready to send your site to your Web server, you can also do it from here.

Figure 2-4 shows the Site Window for a new site, called MySite. No extra pages, graphics, media files, and so on have been added to the site yet. Therefore, only the first, automatically created page, called index.html by default, is in the Site Window. (It could also have been created as default or with .htm instead of .html; there's a preference to control that.)

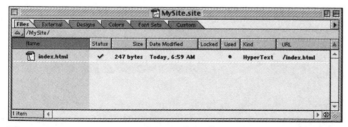

Figure 2-4: A new Mac Site Window for a site named MySite

The Site Window works in conjunction with your computer's operating system. Whenever you add a file to this window, it is automatically copied into a parallel folder on your computer, so the original file is not moved from its place on your hard disk. Instead of dragging things in and out of the folders on your hard drive, you move them around in the Site Window. When you add a new folder to the Site Window and name it, GoLive makes and names a new folder on your hard drive.

By placing things in the Site Window, you are storing them in one central place, enabling yourself to use that element over and over again. But more than that, you enable GoLive to keep track of that item's usage, and in the case of linked page elements, to swap one for another.

Note   Because the Site Window is the key to your Web site, it should be open whenever you're working on the site. Should you close it while you are working, reopen it to continue. You can double-click the site document again, or choose it from File ⇨ Open Recent Files. Recent site documents appear at the top. Individual pages appear at the bottom of this list. You want to be sure to open a site document when you wish to work on a site.

The Site Window contains the same controls you'd expect for any window you open on your computer:

✦ In Windows, the upper-right corner contains the usual buttons to minimize, maximize, and close your window, respectively from left to right.

✦ On the Mac, the title bar has a Close box at the top left and Resize and Collapse boxes at the right. in addition, it becomes a tabbed pop-up window when dragged to the bottom of your screen.

Tip   While you are concentrating on your page's design, you may find the Site Window intrusive, but as I said, you don't want to close it. On each platform there's a platform-ish solution. In Windows, you can minimize the Site Window. On the Mac, you have something similar to tabbed folders: drag it to the bottom of your screen until it tabs. Click its tab to restore it. Yet another feature to help you is the Select Window button. See the "Organizing Your Screen" section later in this chapter.

Focus on Your Site

By Lynne LaMaster, Specialized Publishing (www.specialpublish.com)
Certified Expert in Photoshop

As you design your site, remember that it's important that your site be focused. In other words, you need to know why you are going to have an Internet site in the first place. When I meet with clients, I have a questionnaire that we fill out together. Here are some of the things we consider:

1. What is the purpose of the site?

• To sell

• To educate & inform

- To communicate
- Combination of some or all of the above? Which is primary?

2. Who do I want to reach?

- Potential clients?
- Other professionals in my field
- Friends and family

3. What do I need to present in order to achieve my purpose?

- Graphics & images: logos, illustrations, textual graphics, color
- Photographs: examples, visual rest, people
- Factual information: statistics, straight information, graphs and charts
- Opinionated Information: regular articles, pull quotes
- Nonchanging elements: logo, header, navigation elements, background

4. How do I reach my potential audience?

- Find them
- Attract them
- Give them what they desire
- Sell them my stuff

5. How do I present my information in order to attract and keep my audience interested?

- Fast download
- Well-planned pages
- Strong use of color
- Optimized visual graphics
- A site with "focus"
- Well-presented, relevant information
- Something for them to "keep"
- Easy to navigate
- A welcome feeling
- Easy-to-find contact information

Continued

Continued

If you can't answer questions 1 and 2, you're not ready to create a site. Here's the trick: make sure that *everything* on the page relates to the first point above: What is the purpose of my site?

For example:

✦ Perhaps for a fabric or clothing site, you have a background that looks like a wonderfully textured piece of fabric (keep it subtle, though.)

✦ A music clip would not be appropriate at a pharmaceutical site. It would probably need a plug-in for the browser and take a long time to download. This will be irritating and people will leave.

✦ If it's a realty site, make sure it has pictures of property — nice, clear pictures.

Step out of the role of the designer and think about potential visitors. Then go ahead and design your site — with *them* in mind.

The main part of the Site Window

The Site Window has six tabs:

✦ Files tab

✦ External tab

✦ Designs tab

✦ Colors tab

✦ Font Sets tab

✦ Custom tab

Together, these tabs contain and manage all of the different kinds of elements in your site.

The Files tab

The *Files tab* holds all of the files that are physically part of your site. Your pages, the .html documents, are the main pieces stored there. All of the graphics you place on your pages are also stored there. So are sounds, QuickTime movies, or other animations, such as LiveMotion or Flash. If you provide files for your visitors to download, those are placed here too. External Cascading Style Sheets and JavaScripts share the space, as do CGIs. If you include other types of pages, such as Acrobat PDFs or Web pages made in other programs, they are also stored here. To place an item into the Files tab, you simply drag it from your hard drive, disk, CD-ROM, and so on. (Or choose Add Files to collect them.) No matter where you drag a file from, GoLive copies the file, leaving the original intact. If you drag an entire folder into the Files tab, the entire folder and all of its contents are copied.

When you create a page and put a graphic on that page, the locations of each — because they're in this tab — are tracked. If you move either the page or graphic later on, and it contains links of any sort, GoLive notices and asks you for permission to update the links (a.k.a. *paths*) to the moved file. This enables you to organize and reorganize your site as you work.

The Files tab also reports the integrity of the pages in your site. If any page contains an incomplete or inaccurate link, a green bug alerts you. Widen the column and you see a more detailed text message, stating the nature of the errors and number of errors. Missing pages or pages not yet worked on are also reported. If your pages are within a folder, you'll see a smaller version of the Error icon beside a folder-type arrow. When a page's links are all intact, a checkmark informs you. This tab also displays file types and shows the URL for each file in relation to your site. As this tab is used to hold so much, its use is covered in several chapters throughout this book. In Figure 2-5, you can see a Site Window and some errors reported.

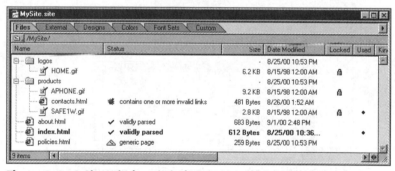

Figure 2-5: A Site Window (Windows) as a site is in progress

Within the Files tab, folders can be stored in subfolders, just like files always can be. To reveal the contents of a folder on the Mac, the arrow beside the folder reveals the folder's contents. In Windows, you click the plus sign (same function, different system-like icons). You can also double-click a folder to make it the main focus of the Site Window's view. Then, to get back to the main folder, click the blue arrow (Mac) or upward-pointing folder (Windows) above the Files list and below the Files tab. Beside that Folder Navigation icon is the path to the folder you're currently within. You'll read plenty about using the Files tab throughout this book as its use comes up often.

The External tab

The *External tab* can (and should) be used to hold all of the references to elements that you call for within your site but really reside outside of your site. Unlike the Files tab, which holds actual files, this tab holds markers that note the addresses of the pages, files, or e-mail addresses to which your page links. By creating an address element in this tab, you enable yourself to call upon that address multiple times without having to enter the address over and over. More importantly, if you take advantage of this tab, you can change an address here just once (via the Inspector) and GoLive will update the address throughout your site. (GoLive asks first, of course. You can tell it not to change specific links, or any links, if you want.) You have many ways to place addresses in this tab, as you can learn in Chapter 11.

This tab also displays each address and notes whether you've used it yet by placing a bullet in the Used column, as you can see in Figure 2-6. When you're connected to the Internet, a Green Bug icon in the Status column can even alert you when a particular URL is not valid by selecting Site ➪ Check External Links.

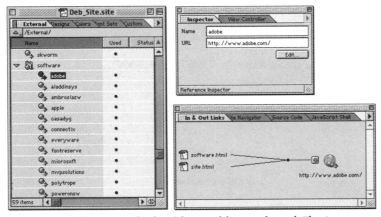

Figure 2-6: The External tab with an address selected. The Inspector, also shown, enables its editing of the selected address while the In & Out Links palette, also shown, informs you of pages that use this address.

While in the External tab, the Inspector enables you to enter or edit the external addresses while its companion, the View Controller, lets you determine which columns are visible.

The In & Out Links palette plays its usual two roles here: you can view all pages that use an address, and you can substitute any address with another address within your External tab. You can learn more about the External tab and all of these features in Chapter 11, which covers links in detail.

The Designs tab

The *Designs tab* is home to any site designs you experiment with as you design your site. The Design tab shown in Figure 2-7 only provides a list of each design you create using the Design menu. However, double-clicking any design listed here opens a window dedicated to that particular design. (You can have several design windows open at once to compare designs.)

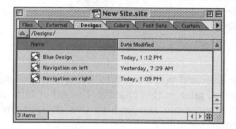

Figure 2-7: The Designs tab reports all site designs you've experimented with.

The Site Design window is explained fully in Chapter 29, which is all about using the GoLive Site Designer to plan your site.

The Colors tab

Colors can pop up all over your pages. Text, table or grid backgrounds, page backgrounds. . . , The Colors tab enables you to record of all colors you may use or do use in your site. Colors saved here also appear in a dedicated tab of the Color palette, providing easy access. You can place a color in the Site Window before you use it—making it handy when you're ready for it. In fact, it awaits you in your own special tab (called the Site tab) in the Color palette. Or, you can use it first, and then have GoLive gather it for you. Either way, storing a color in the Site Window offers several benefits.

When a color's in this tab, you have feedback that it's one of the 216 Web-safe colors or not. Here, you can also see whether you've used the color yet. Another benefit of storing a color in the Site Window is that you can easily copy that color into any other site's Site Window for use in that other site. To use a color in another site, just open that site's Site Window and drag the color from your current Color tab to the other site's Color tab.

By clicking a color within the Colors tab and checking the In & Out Links palette, you can see exactly which pages you've used the color in so far, as shown in Figure 2-8. (All pages that use this color appear to its left, leading into it.) However, unlike files and external addresses, colors can't be swapped within pages by using any of these windows. (That's because the color information isn't linked, but is embedded within the page's HTML code. Notice that no Point and Shoot button exists there.) Changing a collected color within the color's Inspector changes the color listed in the Color tab for future use, but doesn't change instances where the prior color was already used.

Figure 2-8: The Colors tab of the Site Window and the In & Out Links palette, which reports use of colors

Note   Because colors are used all over your site, and you'll need to know how to use them right away, color is covered in detail later in this chapter. The other tabs of the Site Window are more targeted to one specific purpose, so they're each covered later in the book, where they're more pertinent.

Collecting colors in the Site Window

To automatically collect colors into the Colors tab after it's used in your page, follow these steps:

1. Close all open pages, because colors cannot be collected from an open page.

2. Bring the Site Window forward and click the Colors tab to make it active.

3. Then choose Site ⇨ Get Colors Used. (You can also click the Update button on the toolbar, but it will only get colors when you're in the Colors tab.) The colors automatically appear in a folder named New Colors.

   • You can rename this folder by selecting the name and typing a new one in either the Colors tab or in the Inspector.

   • You can move the colors out of it by dragging the color's icon.

   • Each color is named "untitled color," "untitled color 1," and so on. To rename a color, select its name in the list and type the new name. (Or select the color and then rename it in the Inspector.)

Even if you move or rename a color, GoLive still knows you collected that color already and won't gather it again.

Tip   The Update button always performs whichever update or scan option is appropriate for the tab that's active in the Site Window. Therefore, in the case of colors, because the Colors tab of the Site Window is active, the Update button does the same thing as Site ⇨ Get Colors Used.

You can also manually add a color to your Site Window. I'll show you the Color palette a little later in this chapter. From the Color palette, you can drag a color into the Site Window's Colors tab. (By the way, if you do, the Colors tab may not be active when you get to the Site Window, but rest over the Colors tab and it jumps forward for you.) The color comes in with its name, "untitled color," automatically selected so you can type a descriptive name for it. That name assigned here also appears in your Color palette's site tab, but is only for your own benefit.

Removing colors from the Site Window

To remove a single color from the list, select that color and click the Trash button on the toolbar.

To remove all unused colors from the Site Window's Color list, select the Color tab again and choose Site ➪ Remove Unused Colors.

The Font Sets tab

A *font set* is a list of fonts that you can assign to text blocks. The font set lists, in order, the fonts you prefer for the display of your text. When a user's browser reads the set, it chooses the first font it recognizes as active on the user's computer to render that text. Font sets can be applied to any occurrence of text on your page, or they can be used in a style sheet, which is far more flexible and generates far less code in your page.

The Font Sets tab is much like the Colors tab. You can collect your font sets here, see whether you've used a set, and select it to have the In & Out Links palette show you exactly where you've used it, but you can't substitute one font set for another within pages where a font set is already used. Chapter 8 fully covers font sets and this tab.

The Custom tab

The Custom tab enables you to collect snippets of text and HTML code so you can use them again and again at any time within Layout mode or Source mode as you create your site. To take advantage of it, just drag selected text into this tab, and then drag the snippet over to any page later on. You can also reuse graphics and even compilations of items, such as entire tables or a page footer with your copyright information. You can also drag entire objects into this tab. You see the same Untitled Snippet icon and the content lists the code, but when you drag this snippet back onto a page, its code describes the object and you have a copy of you dragged-over object to enjoy.

Unlike the other tabs of the Site Window, items in this tab are not displayed within the In & Out Links palette. You can learn more about the Custom tab and its use in Chapter 14, which covers all reusable items.

Note   Items that you place in the Custom tab of the Site Window are available only when you have the Site Window open. If you would like a custom item to be available to you in all your sites, place it in the Custom tab of the Objects palette.

Color Designing Your Web Site

By Bob Stein, VisiBone (www.visibone.com), maker of several printed and online color resources for Web designers

How do you find great color? How do you implement it on a Web site? Color on the Web is a collision of intuition and logic. The artiste in you knows great color when you see it. The curious cat in you tinkers the technology into delivering it.

Color can decorate and make mood, like the blush of morning on a bedroom wall, the lurid growth after a spring rain or the dream-catching distance of a clear horizon. Color can inform and empower when it resonates with the structure of a site. Use color schemes for recognition, like the sections of Amazon.com, or use it to mark off complexity like the headings on IMDB.com. This power is lost without superhuman stability and consistency.

Finding great color is an essential art. I distrust formulas for compatible colors about as much as I distrust computer matchmaking. They're blind to the enormous talent you have to bring to the task. Besides millions of generations of chromatic sight entwining emotions with colors, you've had a lifetime of observation. It all counts toward a set of colors appealing or not, impressing or not, annoying or not. I suggest the best machine we have for predicting these effects is reading these words right now. You're designed to recognize in less than one breath: friend, foe, beauty, nourishment, danger, opportunity. When you color a lip or a car or a Web site, you're exploiting this legacy to attract attention, to compel, to seduce.

So I made a free online tool with which to feed your intuition hundreds of color combinations in a few minutes: the Webmaster's Color Lab. All the colors are symmetrically arrayed. Every click chooses or removes one, changing the scheme. It's your 21st-century version of an artist's paint box. Use the force, Luke, and you will take our breath away. You can find the Webmaster's Color Lab at `www.visibone.com/colorlab` or on the CD-ROM at the back of this book.

As technology matures, that second part of the colorsmith's challenge will diminish. It now looms large. Because of the limitations of monitors, networks, and the coding of content and presentation, the Web artist is forced to become a Web technician. This is why there's a profession for the fusion of these talents: Web designer. Web designers must master the numbing intricacy of Web machinery, and they must divine and express vision. When combined seamlessly, when a site works and looks great, when form makes love with function, it is true brilliance.

For more on color limitations, see the sidebar, "Web-Safe Color at the Century's Dawn," later in this chapter.

Viewing the "hidden" part of the Site Window

The Site Window also contains a second section, hidden by default. To reveal and access this section, click the double-headed arrow at the bottom right of the Site

Window. Doing so opens a new section at the right. This section contains four more tabs:

✦ Errors tab

✦ Extras tab

✦ FTP tab

✦ WebDAV tab

File access within this "hidden" part of the Site Window works just like access within the main part.

You can resize the proportion of the left and right sections by moving the mouse over the section dividing line in the center and dragging when the pointer becomes a hand.

The Errors tab

The Errors tab shows you any missing or orphaned files. Orphans are files that need to be copied into your Site Window. To fix them, you just drag the orphan over to the desired folder in the Files tab. Missing files are those GoLive can't locate on your hard drive. They need to be found and then dragged to the Files tab.

 Cross-Reference   Chapter 25 provides the complete story of the Errors tab.

The Extras tab

The Extras tab, shown in Figure 2-9, contains the following four folders:

✦ The **Components** folder holds any components you create to use within your site. Components are an easy-to-use way of enabling you to create something once and use it multiple times, and update it across all pages at once. After you create a Component, you add it to your pages via the Site Extras tab of the Objects palette, not directly from this folder. For more information about Components, see Chapter 14.

✦ The **Designs** folder contains all of the pages-to-be that you create within each site design you experiment with to plan your site. The Site Designer is explained fully in Chapter 29.

✦ The **Site Trash** folder holds all files you delete unless you change the preferences to send your deletions to your computer's actual trash. Dragging a page or file into this folder keeps your files safe and maintains its links in case you decide you want to use it after all. Clicking the Trash Can icon to send a page or file here keeps the file safe within your site's files but does not track the file's link. To use a file, drag it back into the Files tab. To permanently delete it, select it in the Site Trash folder and use the Delete/Backspace key.

✦ The **Stationeries** folder holds pages you create as starting points for more pages later on. As with Components, you add your Stationery to your site via the Site Extras tab of the Objects palette, not from within this folder. For more information on Stationery, see Chapter 5.

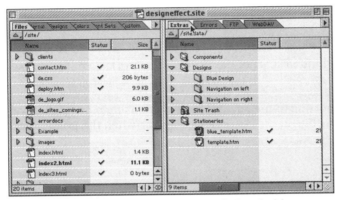

Figure 2-9: The Extras tab of the Site Window holds your Components, designs, files you send to the site trash, and finally, it holds Stationery.

The FTP tab

The FTP tab enables you to upload your site to the Web with the click of the Upload to Server button, the choice of the Upload Modified Items command, or by dragging the files from the Files tab over to the FTP tab. FTP is discussed fully in Chapter 27.

The WebDAV tab

GoLive 5 ushers in a new era of collaborative design as one of the very first applications to support and build upon WebDAV. WebDAV, which is short for Web Distributed Authoring and Versioning, enables multiple users to access a server (the WebDAV server) simultaneously or separately in order to build the pages of a site. Users can preview and edit pages without the fear that someone else is also working on changes to the same page and causing work to be lost, because it enables you to lock a page while you need to make changes to that page. GoLive builds upon WebDAV by adding its own Workgroup Support features, such as file check-out. Adobe GoLive lets you manage files and folders on a WebDAV server in the same way that you manage them on your desktop, including copying, deleting, renaming, and moving Web pages. Available WebDAV servers include Microsoft IIS 5 (included with Windows 2000), Apache (with the mod_dav module), Novell NetWare 5.1, and Mac OS X Server.

Adobe GoLive provides a function that lets you synchronize both the site on your local platform and the site on the WebDAV server, and it does so in either direction. Files that are missing on one site but exist on the other are dimmed in the

Synchronize dialog box. If a synchronization conflict occurs, such as the same file having been changed on the local site and on the remote site, you can decide which synchronization action you want to take to resolve the conflict. The system has built-in synchronization actions for each file: upload, download, skip, and delete. Icons are displayed with each action in the dialog box. You can synchronize the entire site or just selected files.

Customizing the Site Window

You can customize the look of the Site Window to make it easier to see its contents. You can determine which columns you see, and therefore what information the tab presents. While you are in any tab within the Site Window, the View Controller, which sits beside the Inspector by default, enables you to control the columns of information you view. Simply click the Show Columns pop-up in the View Controller, and then select a listed column to turn it off or on. (All columns are on by default, except the Name column in the Files tab, which lists the file's name.) A checkmark beside each column heading tells you the column is already on.

You can make any column wider so you can read longer names or more information, or you can shorten a column so you can fit more columns on your screen. To resize the columns, move your mouse over the border of the column and drag when the mouse becomes a two-headed arrow. This works for any columns that have a common border.

You can also change the order of the columns. To do so, press ⌘ (Mac) or Ctrl (Windows) and drag the column's heading right or left to the new heading position. You can sort by any of the column headings by clicking a heading. You can also reverse the sort order of the column you are sorting by clicking the column heading. On the Mac, the triangle to the right of the column headings reflects the sort order; clicking this triangle also reverses the sort. In Windows, just look at the result.

You can also tear off any tab from the Site Window (except the Files tab) to view it within its own window. To tear off any tab, click that tab's dotted area at the left, and then drag away from the Site Window until the new window's outline appears in addition to just the tab's outline. (More information about this can be found in the section "Exploring the Palettes," next.)

To put a tab back into the Site Window, click that tab's dotted area at the left and then drag it back into the desired position, or choose Site ⇨ View ⇨ Default Configuration.

At any time as you work, you can return the Site Window to its initial state again by selecting Site ⇨ View ⇨ Default Configuration. This resets all Site Window tabs and columns. (This does not affect any of the palettes — just the Site Window.)

Exploring the Palettes

GoLive 5 includes tools for working with all of the elements of your pages. Most of these tools are grouped into palettes that work with a particular area of GoLive. For instance, the Objects palette contains all of the different types of elements you can add to your pages, the Color palette for working with color, and the Table palette for working with tables. table rows, and cells. All of GoLive's palettes can be grouped in different combinations to save valuable screen real estate and can be dragged and dropped onto each other to easily combine or separate different palettes (shown in Figure 2-10).

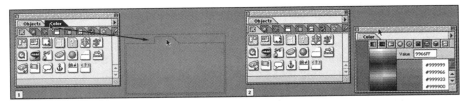

Figure 2-10: Palettes can be separated and combined into customized groupings to suit your workflow: (1) shows the Objects and Color palettes combined, and (2) shows the separated palettes after dragging the Color palette to a position outside the palette group.

Tip   If you are looking for a way to reclaim that little bit of precise screen space, try this. Tear off the Color palette and close it. The Color palette opens automatically when you click any of the color swatches in GoLive. Next, add the Objects palette to the Inspector. You might be thinking "they are the two most used palettes!" and you'd be right, but you never use them both at the *same time.* After placing an object, double-click it or use the keyboard shortcut to bring up the Inspector. (This tip probably isn't applicable to power users with lots of screen space to work with, as it does need the extra click to bring up the Inspector, but if you are on a small screen or a PowerBook, you may find it extremely handy.)

The Inspector

While the Site Window is your organizational interface, the Inspector is the master control for every file and element within your Site Window, whether used or unused. No matter what you're doing, the Inspector provides the controls you need to fine-tune your work. You've already seen that there's an Inspector to go along with every tab of the Site Window. For example:

✦ When you select a page in the Files tab of the Site Window (or in the Navigation view or Links view), the Inspector turns into the File Inspector, and then provides five tabs in which it tells you all about the file. (Its Contents tab even provides a preview.)

✦ If you select a graphic in the Files tab of the Site Window, as in Figure 2-11, the Inspector, as the File Inspector, enables you to preview the image — even showing you animations, videos, or QuickTime VR — as well as name your graphic and set publishing controls.

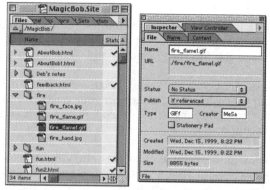

Figure 2-11: The three tabs of the File Inspector for a graphic file within the Files tab

✦ After you place a graphic on your page and select it, the Inspector, becomes an Image Inspector (see Figure 2-12) enabling you to select or enter specific attributes for that particular instance of that graphic. You can add an alternate text label, size the graphic, turn the graphic into a button or image map, set actions that can happen when your visitor uses point or click with the mouse, and more.

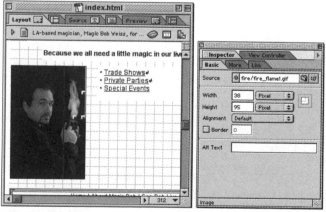

Figure 2-12: Three of the tabs of the File Inspector for the same graphic as in Figure 2-11 after placement on a page

✦ After you place any text on a page and then select it, the Inspector turns into the Text Inspector and enables you to assign a URL and actions to the text. (It doesn't do the text formatting — the toolbar provides for that.)

✦ When you select other objects such as Button Image or URL Pop-up on a page, the Inspector changes to offer whatever specifics are needed for that object. For example, each Smart Object has its own Inspector.

✦ When you're previewing a page, the Inspector enables you to see the page approximately the way it will look in different operating systems (Windows and the Mac OS) and browsers (Internet Explorer and Netscape Navigator).

There's actually more the Inspector does. It'll always be there to provide the appropriate options for any element that you select, either on your page or in the Site Window. In each chapter, as I show you how to set up an element, I show you the Inspector and how to work within it.

To open the Inspector choose Window ➪ Inspector (Mac) or View ➪ Inspector (Windows). On the Mac, the exact name that appears in this menu depends on what object or file is currently selected, but you'll still recognize it as the Inspector.

The Objects palette

Like an artist's palette supplies the pigments for a painting, GoLive's Objects palette provides the elements for your creation. When you want to add text to your page, you drag a Text icon to your page from the Objects palette, which is shown in Figure 2-13. To add form fields where users enter information, you drag form items to your page. To add a JavaScript, you drag a JavaScript icon. Throughout this book, I introduce each item in the palette as it comes into play in your site's design.

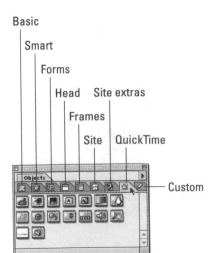

Basic
Smart
Forms
Head   Site extras
Frames
Site   QuickTime
Custom

Figure 2-13: The Objects palette, with the QuickTime tab active

The default installation of GoLive installs nine tabs within the Objects palette, shown below. Each provides a category of tools for you to build your page with. A tenth tab becomes active when you turn on the WebObjects Module in the Preferences section.

Here's a list of all the tabs:

✦ The **Basic** tab contains elements that are available for use on the body of your page (or any element you design visually — but not the head, for example). Basic tags come up in several chapters.

✦ The **Smart** tab includes a collection of prewritten elements that provide action or interaction on your page. New to GoLive 5 are the Smart Objects for Photoshop, Illustrator, and LiveMotion. These objects allow for close integration with GoLive by enabling you to create images directly from the source files, without having to export them to GIF or JPEG first (for more information, see Chapter 10. The Modified Date icon adds a report of the last time you saved the page. For easy-to-build fancy links, there's the a prebuilt three-stage button rollover and the URL pop-up. The Component icon is here, too, to help you place across-the-board content on multiple pages. Two JavaScript Action sets are also here: one for the head and one for the body of your page and a browser switch JavaScript that enables you to note your visitor's browser/platform and switch to an alternative page.

✦ The **Forms** tab is dedicated to the things you need to build a form on your page. It provides the HTML tag to tell the page it'll act as a form, and provides all the building blocks for the data-containing elements such as text fields, buttons and checkboxes, and pop-up menus. Chapter 15 covers forms in detail.

✦ The **Head** tab provides the HTML tags that go into the head of a page. These tags affect the way the page behaves. For example, the Refresh tag enables you to have visitors automatically taken to another page after a specified amount of time. Head tags are mentioned as they come into play.

✦ When you design a site based on frames, you begin with the **Frames** tab. This tab provides several different frame layouts for you to choose from. To put one into action, all you do is drag the icon for the look you want onto your page. (In the page window is a tab you switch to in order to use frames.) After you choose a frame layout, you can customize the look any way you want (within the rules of HTML, of course). Chapter 15 goes into frames in detail.

✦ The **Site** tab provides objects for adding a new generic page to the Files tab or the Site Window, address markers to the External tab of your Site Window, colors to the Site Window's Colors tab, and font sets to the Font Sets tab. It also provides folders for organizing your site. You can drag into the Site Window's tab in order to categorize your files, media, colors, and so on. Each item within this tab is noted again in its respective chapter.

✦ The **Site Extras** tab includes Stationery pages and Components that you create. When you use the Inspector to turn a page into Stationery or a Component, it appears in the Stationery or Components folder in the second part of the Site Window and also in this tab of the palette. A pop-up menu in the bottom right switches between Stationery pads, Components, and items from the Site Window's Custom tab. (For more on Stationery, see Chapter 4; Components and the Custom tab are covered in Chapter 14.)

✦ On the **QuickTime** tab, you'll find everything you need to build a fully featured QuickTime masterpiece. (See Chapter 21 for more.)

✦ The **Custom** tab is your very own storage area. Anything you create on your page can be selected and dragged here. Once it's here, you can drag your creation to any page. This'll save you tons of redundant formatting, such as setting up tables or grids to your liking. (For instructions, see Chapter 14.)

✦ The **WebObjects** tab does not appear with the standard GoLive installation. If you've added WebObjects capability by turning on the WebObjects Module under your preferences, it appears in the Objects palette. The WebObjects tab contains everything you need to use WebObjects on your page. WebObjects is a programming tool beyond the scope of this book, but if you're familiar with WebObjects, the Objects palette items will be familiar to you.

Note   You can collapse the Objects palette to the side of your monitor by Control-clicking the title bar. To reopen it, just click the header of the collapsed palette.

The Color palette

The alter ego of the Objects palette is the Color palette, which is shown in Figure 2-14. You have many ways to add a color to your page. You can add a color to the entire background, or to the background of a table, grid, or floating box, or to the cells of a table, or to text. Whenever you can add color, I show you how. GoLive enables you to use virtually any color, not just Web-safe colors, so in this section I show you all the possible colors you can create or choose.

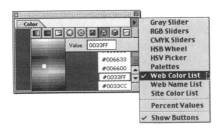

Figure 2-14: The Color palette. You can use the color space buttons, or you can choose the color space from the fly-out menu at the top-right corner of the Color palette. You can also choose to show or hide the buttons from within the menu.

Whenever you're working with text, the toolbar provides a Color button for you. Just about any other time you have the option to add color, the Inspector provides a small square color swatch area beside the word *color*. You have two ways to select a color, as follows:

✦ If it's one of the 216 Web-safe colors you want for sure, Control-click (Mac) or right-click (Windows) on any color button. Then move to, and click, the desired color.

✦ To choose from any color, click once within any of these color swatches to open the Color palette to the color and Color tab you last used. Unlike the other palettes, which just become active when a button for them is clicked, the Color palette literally jumps open. You can also open the Color palette through the menus using Window ⇨ Color, explore the various color tabs as desired, and then click, or mix, the desired color. As you click any color, it becomes the chosen color and appears in the color swatch. You can keep clicking/mixing colors until you hit the one you want.

After you mix or choose the desired color in the Color palette, you can also drag the color from the preview area into place in your Inspector, toolbar, Outline mode, or source code.

Tip   Each of the Color tabs is connected to the other. When you select a color in one palette, the same (or closest) color is reported in the other palettes. This means that, for example, someone can give you the CMYK color they want and when you enter it, you can see the nearest color within the other Color tabs.

The Color palette's tabs

Nine color subtabs exist in the Color palette (see Figure 2-15), each providing a different grouping of colors, known in the designer's world as a "color space," enabling you to view or choose any color you can think of.

When you select a color in any of the other slider-based tabs, you see the equivalent color in each of the other tabs (except the Palettes tab). If you select a color that's within either the Web Color list or the Web Name list, it will be selected when you switch to that tab. If it's a Web List color, it'll be selected within that tab. If not, the Color list jumps to the nearest color match. This can help you match colors. For example, you can match a CMYK color to a Web list color for use on your page.

✦ The **Grayscale** tab is for working in grayscale. It enables you to choose a shade of gray or, working in reverse, choose a color in another color space and discover its gray value.

✦ The **RGB** tab works with the red, green, and blue colors that comprise a color in terms of a TV or computer monitor. In this tab, you can use the red, green, and blue sliders to "mix" a color and see the result in the preview area.

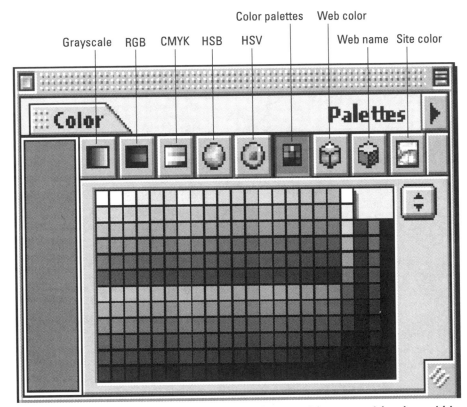

Figure 2-15: The nine subtabs of the Color palette enable you to pick colors within almost any color space you choose.

✦ The **CMYK** tab works with the cyan, magenta, yellow, and black colors that comprise a color in terms of printed ink. In this tab you can use the respective sliders to "mix" a color, or enter those values, to see the end result.

✦ The **HSB** and **HSV** tabs enable you to choose any color available in your particular computer. This is dependent on your video card, and therefore varies from computer to computer. In the HSB tab, you can choose a brightness. In the HSV tab, you can select a hue from the circle and see the available colors within the square inside it. Then you can slide around within the square to pick up the desired color, moving horizontally to increase or decrease saturation, or vertically to locate a color value.

✦ The **Palettes** tab enables you to pick a color using your system's color space. Use the pop-up menu to choose the number of colors you can view. This limits your choice of colors. You can also set up a palette comprised of you own desktop colors. Additionally, you can create your own Color palette here by copying colors.

✦ The **Web Color List** tab displays only the 216 browser-safe options. (See the "Web-Safe Color at the Century's Dawn" sidebar, coming up shortly, for more information.) This is the only color space that's 100 percent safe to use on the Web.

Click in the color patch to jump to a color. This selects the color in the scrolling list to its right. Use the scrolling list of all available colors, which are grouped with other similar shades, to locate a specific color, or just explore your options. Each color is displayed in the list with both a "chip" and its corresponding six-digit hex value. (The hex value, is how HTML identifies your color choices, so this combination of letters and numbers is what appears in your page's source code.) To select any color in this list, click it. You can tell a color is selected by a black rectangle around it. The selected color appears in the larger preview area of the tab.

The Value field, above the scrolling list, can be used to seek out a specific color by hex value. Enter a value in this field and the corresponding color appears in the scrolling list. This can be useful when you're collaborating with another person. You can tell each other the values of the color you're discussing and each of you can see it to consider it. You can also copy a value from the Value field in order to paste it elsewhere.

✦ The **Web Named List** tab displays the extended set of colors current browsers are capable of calling up. Many computers today use thousands or millions of colors and can display these colors, but they are not guaranteed to look the same across all platforms or various versions of any platform. This tab works the same as the Web Color List tab but doesn't provide the color tool.

✦ The **Site Color** tab is where your own colors appear after you collect them into the Color tab of the Site Window. (See "Collecting colors in the Site Window," earlier in this chapter.)

You can collapse the Color palette to the side of your monitor by Control-clicking (Mac) or right-clicking (Windows) on the title bar. To reopen it, just click it.

Note

Not all colors work on the Web, because different browsers and platforms have different color limitations. On the Web, the only *fully* safe color space is the 216 colors within the Web Color List tab, with the Web name colors coming in safe for most modern computers. The other tabs may be handy, however, in helping you recognize colors from other venues. See the "Web-Safe Color at the Century's Dawn" sidebar below for more information.

Web-Safe Color at the Century's Dawn

By Bob Stein (stein@visibone.com), VisiBone (www.visibone.com), maker of several printed and online color resources for Web designers

In 1994, Netscape initiated a brilliant solution to a perennial problem with graphics operating systems that Web browsers had just made much worse. Most computers at that time could only display 256 colors at a time. The choice of those colors was at the whim of application developers, and then, Web site designers. When more than one program or Web page was visible at a time, and the colors they clamored to display totaled more than 256, there was pandemonium. Users would see ridiculously distorted color. Netscape defined a set of 216 colors that would have priority; six levels each of red, green, and blue, evenly spaced throughout the RGB color space. Web pages that used those colors exclusively would have a much better chance of looking right.

Some consequences of using colors outside the Web-safe palette on 256-color computers are: no effect at all, a speckled compromise called "dithering," radical color replacement (for example, gray); or color thrash when switching applications.

In 2000, the advantages to Web designers, and those they serve, of avoiding non-Web-safe colors are not nearly as strong as they once were. The avoidance only benefits users limited to 256 colors, and most computers can now theoretically display millions of colors at a time. There have always been distinct disadvantages. Pastels and earth tones are especially sparse in this set. Many designers have cast off the Web-safe yoke for convenience or to more precisely realize the colors they envision. In a statistical sampling of Web pages in November 1999, I found that 27 percent of the colors for text and background, other than black and white, were not Web-safe.

The number of users limited to 256 colors for whatever reason is in gradual steady decline, from 20 percent in May 1998, to 8 percent at the turn of the century, according to the voluminous data at www.thecounter.com (thanks to Morten Wang for pointing this out). The figures are unclear on a full 20 percent of the users, perhaps due to older browsers or disabled JavaScript, but even 8 percent is probably a larger portion of your users than you want to vex unnecessarily.

Antique computers that only display 256 colors at a time remain in service. But not all 256-color users are on old computers. A Web designer ran into 256-color mode on a client's laptop while trying to show off his work. Some game programs insist on reconfiguring to *256-color mode* to animate faster. A developer switches to 256-color mode to trade off for higher resolution and faster operation.

Thanks to a discussion on the webdesign-L mailing list, I've come up with a simple way to measure the color depth of users for any Web site through the statistics logs, www.visibone.com/palettesurvey.html. Figures (as of this writing) indicate 5 to 14 percent of the people who visit the VisiBone home page have computers limited to 256-color mode.

The large rectangle at the left of the Color palette is the preview area. In this area, you can see the selected color separate from the group so you can see its true appearance.

You can resize the Color palette by dragging the lower-right corner. As the palette grows, so do the colors in the color patch and in the scrolling list. And, of course, the longer you make the palette, the more colors you can see in the scrolling list.

Tip

The color patch of the Web Color List tab contains a secret power—a color picker that enables you to pick up any color that's anywhere on your screen (even outside of GoLive). To pick up a color, click in the color patch, and then keep the mouse button down as you move across the screen. As you drag the mouse, you'll see the color in the preview area and see its hex value appear in the Value field. Of course, not all colors on your screen are Web-safe. Here's the trick to seeing whether the color you're considering is Web-safe: if the color you're resting over happens to be Web-safe, it appears and is selected in the scrolling list. Due to the way colors are rendered onscreen, if your screen is set to thousands of colors, the color picker may not pick up a color as one of the 216 color-safe colors even if the color really is Web-safe. You'll do better to set your monitor to millions of colors, or back to 256 if you don't have millions.

As you're perusing colors, feel free to drag any color into the Colors tab of the Site Window for future use. It then becomes available in the final Color tab—your site's Color list.

Markup Tree palette

In addition to the HTML Outline Editor tab in the document window, GoLive offers the Markup Tree palette, an HTML navigational tool that shows the hierarchical position of a selected object within the HTML element tree structure. For example, the Markup Tree palette might show that a selected image is contained inside a paragraph element, the body element, and the HTML element, as in Figure 2-16. Clicking any of these elements in the palette shows a new hierarchy based on the element you click and selects every object (including text) on the page within that element. To return to the original hierarchy for the image, click the Select Previous Item button in the palette. Use the Markup Tree palette as you work in Layout view, along with the new Source Code palette, to quickly and precisely select the elements you want.

Expert Tip

If you are having trouble selecting a small object on your page, using the Markup Tree palette makes it very easy. For instance, if you have a small image inside a floating box and, when trying to select the image, you always end up selecting the floating box, open the Markup Tree palette. Select the <DIV> tag that represents the floating box, and then select the <IMG> tag to select the image on your page.—*Richard McLean, Web developer,* www.designeffect.com

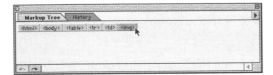

Figure 2-16: The Markup Tree palette gives you an easy way to select nested or small elements on your page.

Table palette

Tables are easier than ever to design and edit. You can work directly in the table in your document, use the Table Inspector, and use the new Table palette, shown in Figure 2-17. The Table palette contains two tabs — With the Select tab, you can Shift-click to select multiple table cells, and cut, copy, and paste entire blocks of contiguous cells. It also enables you to more easily select individual table cells, rows, and columns, and sort your table's content. Your table content can be easily sorted numerically or alphabetically, in descending or ascending order, and by rows or columns. The Style tab, which contains a set of predefined table styles, enables you to change the appearance of your table instantly by applying a preset table design. You can even create your own table styles and add them to the Table palette's Style tab for multiple use.

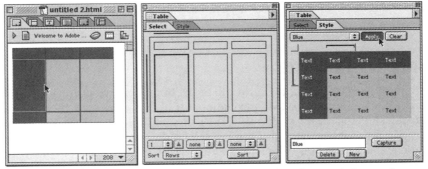

Figure 2-17: The Table palette enables you to easily select and change formatting for sections of your table and sort columns and rows (middle), and apply preset or custom table styles (right).

History palette

As you add objects to your page, GoLive tracks your additions and actions, writing a "history" of them in the History palette. (Specifically, each history is a page history; that is, changes to any page are tracked, not application-wide actions such as preference settings.) You can move back in this history to any state of the page by clicking that state, as in Figure 2-18, up to 20 steps backwards. When you go backward, the later steps gray out and the page reverts to that point in history. You can then click a gray step to go forward again. Each time you save your page or close it, the history begins anew. Unfortunately, though, it also clears and begins anew when you switch layout views, such as moving from Layout to Source, or to Outline or Preview, so bear this in mind before you switch views if you're experimenting with something.

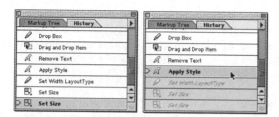

Figure 2-18: Go back in time with the History palette if you make a mistake or want to do something differently.

When you switch between the various pages you're working on, the history for each page is retained; you simply see the history for the page in which you are currently working, while the other page's histories remain in GoLive's memory.

> The History palette tracks actions on pages, not in the Site Window. For example, it doesn't track the addition of files to your site, creation of folders, moving files within the Files tab, or deletion of items in the Site Window. The palette also clears when you change from one mode in the page window to another (For instance, from Layout to Source mode, or vice versa.)

Source Code palette

Use the Source palette to view changes in your layout and code simultaneously. You can code in HTML and see how it looks in layout, or watch how changing your layout changes your source code. The Source Code palette only "fires up" its changes when it loses the *focus*. In other words, when you work in the Source palette, its code takes effect in your page when you click the page to make the layout view active again.

Transform palette

The Transform palette provides options for positioning an object or a group of objects, resizing objects proportionally, grouping and ungrouping objects, and changing their layering. Multiple selected objects are moved as a group without changing their position relative to each other. When you use the Size option to set width and height values, you can then resize an object or a group of objects proportionally. Often, if not always, whenever this palette is an option, the toolbar provides the same input so you have a choice of places to work.

When you work with objects that have a stacking order (Z-Order) or overlap each other, you want to be able to control how they overlap and in what order they appear. The Z-Order option now lets you put objects in front of or behind other objects. This is especially useful for map shapes (hotspots) in image maps.

Align palette

In addition to the alignment features on the toolbar, GoLive provides the Align palette. The Align palette aligns objects on a layout grid, regions on images (image maps), floating boxes, tracks in the Layout view of the QuickTime Movie Viewer, and page objects in the site design window.

When you select one or more of these items, you can use the alignment options provided by the Align palette, which include aligning an object or group of objects relative to a parent object or relative to each other. You can align objects left or right, top or bottom, or center. Other options exist that equally space or distribute objects relative to their vertical or horizontal axes.

The Toolbar

Just below the menu bar when you start GoLive, you will see a toolbar, as shown in Figure 2-19.

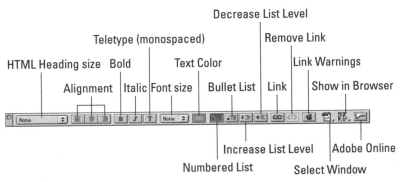

Figure 2-19: GoLive's default toolbar

The options and buttons in the toolbar will change depending on the objects you have currently selected in the work area (whether it be an image on a page, or a folder in the Site Window, or a style sheet). Figure 2-20 shows you the various toolbars. This makes the toolbar a very powerful part of the GoLive interface, which you can use to perform a lot of the tasks involved in creating and maintaining your Web site. Whatever task you take on, whenever you select a new object, take a look at the toolbar and see what it can do for you.

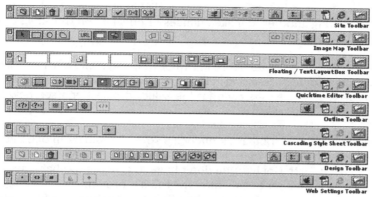

Figure 2-20: The context-sensitive toolbar changes to reflect the options of the current object selected, or the current mode you are in.

The Page Window

Of course, you can't design a Web site until you have a page to start with. When you create a new blank site, GoLive automatically creates your home page for you. All you have to do to begin working on it is double-click its icon in the Files tab of the Site Window. In Chapter 4, I show you the various ways to create more pages for your site.

The GoLive page window has tabs for every occasion. The first tab to the left is called Layout and is for designing your page visually, in what is known as WYSIWYG (What You See Is What You Get) mode. Layout mode is where you get to drag and drop the elements of your design and work as if in any page layout program.

Then comes the Frames tab, in which you set up your frameset (if you are using frames on a page) and choose the page that will appear in each section of the frame.

Next come two tabs for working in HTML code. In the Source tab, you can view and work within raw HTML as well as gain very valuable feedback about browser compatibility. In the Outline tab, you can view HTML in an unique outline, whereby each of the page's elements appears like a heading and all relative attributes for it appear below its heading. (It's cool because you don't have to know HTML to work here.)

The last tab (or two if on a Mac) enables you to preview your page without launching a browser. (If you're using a Mac, you'll find one Preview tab for regular pages and a separate one for previewing a page that uses frames. Windows users will see all previews within their one Preview tab.) The next sections describe each page view in more detail.

As you work, you can switch between any view by clicking the view's tab. You can work in any view, visiting another to make changes or check in on the affect of your addition.

Tip   When you select an object or text while in Layout view and then switch views, the code for that object or text is selected in the other view. This is a great way to learn HTML because you can see the code for the selected object and see how the object fits in to the code around it.

Above the page window is the toolbar. Actually it's several toolbars in one because each time you change the mode you're working in, the toolbar changes to provide the tools you may need. With GoLive, you don't have to give the toolbar a second thought other than to remember to call upon the tools it provides when you need them. You have no extra toolbars to turn on or off and no customizing to do. It's all done for you automatically, and in very little space.

Layout view

Layout view is where you'll spend your most time if you're a designer or like working visually, seeing your results as you create. If you are used to working in Illustrator, FreeHand, Photoshop, or even AppleWorks, you'll be comfortable here. Here you can work "inline" like within a word processing program and as is common in Web design, or with a layout grid as is common in page layout programs. Here, you can display rulers at the borders of your page for easy alignment, or align objects relative to one another.

Two layout views actually exist. The first is the Layout Editor tab where you create your page, as shown in Figure 2-21. The next is the Frame Editor where you place and arrange frames, if you choose to use them. (You don't actually create pages in this tab. Instead, you link the frame section to a page you design using the first tab. But the Frame tab is where you set the size of your frames, therefore determining what size to make the design area of each of your pages. More about frames in Chapter 15.)

This book focuses on designing a site with Layout view because that's part of what sets GoLive apart for the other Web design programs.

The toolbar has two incarnations that accompany the Layout view. One is the Layout toolbar, available whenever you are working on a text line. The other is the Grid toolbar. The Layout toolbar turns into the Grid toolbar whenever you place a layout grid on a page and then work within the grid.

The Inspector also has several incarnations that you work with in Layout view. There's a general Page Inspector for setting up the basics of the page. Then there's an Inspector for each item you place on the page. As you select any item on your page, you'll see the Inspector do its morphing thing.

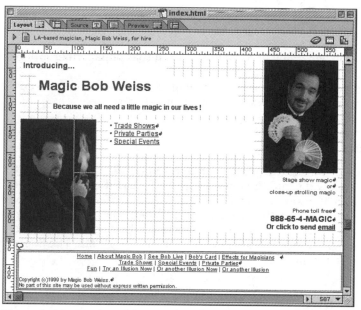

Figure 2-21: Magic Bob's completed page as it appears in Layout view

In addition to the view tabs within the page window, a few buttons hang out there — all at the top right. The functions of each of these buttons are discussed later in their respective chapters.

Along the top you'll find:

✦ The Java Bean icon opens the JavaScript Editor. In this editor, you can write your own JavaScripts. As you do, the code you enter is entered directly into your page. Whenever you're in the JavaScript Editor, the Inspector becomes the JavaScript Inspector and provides a wide assortment of JavaScript functions and constructs that you can drag into place within the JavaScript Editor. It doesn't make your JavaScript creation fully drag and drop, but it takes you as far as possible.

✦ The Filmstrip icon opens the TimeLine Editor. Using the TimeLine Editor in conjunction with floating boxes, you can create your own custom animations. As with any standard TimeLine Editor, you place *keyframes* along the timeline at any desired interval, and then set the position of the floating box that corresponds to that keyframe. And, of course, you can create multiple *tracks*. You can learn all about this feature in Chapter 19.

✦ The Stair-step icon symbolizes cascading and opens the Style Sheet Editor for creating a Cascading Style Sheet (CSS).

Cross-Reference To learn about Cascading Style Sheets, see Chapter 17.

Above the right scroll bar, you'll find the Rule button that pops a ruler into place.

At the bottom right of the page window is the Page Size pop-up menu, discussed in the sidebar, "Sizing Your Page Windows," coming up shortly.

Source view

Source view is where you see the pure, unadulterated HTML that describes your page—where you really dig into the nitty-gritty of HTML and can tweak code like a programmer. To make it easier to identify the code that creates an object, select the object in Page Layout view and then switch views. When you switch to Source view, the code that corresponds to your selected objects will be selected. This can be a helpful trick if you want to become somewhat familiar with HTML. The Source view is covered in detail in Chapter 3.

The Outline Editor

The Outline view is GoLive's very own invention. This unique view enables you to see each of your code choices under collapsible/expandable headers, enabling you to see what you have code-wise, without training yourself to read through HTML tags.

Cross-Reference The Outline view is covered in detail in Chapter 3.

In this view, you see all of the page's elements clearly displayed in bold text within collapsible lines. By clicking the arrow to the left of the tag, you can see the details of the object, as in Figure 2-22. When you're designing in Layout view most of this time, this option is an excellent way to see the HTML code behind your page without having to read between all the HTML code.

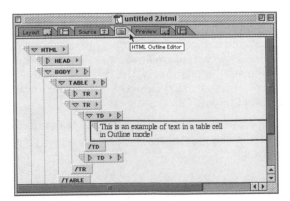

Figure 2-22: A page shown in Outline view with a few elements expanded

Preview view

Switch to the Preview tab any time to get an idea of how your page will look in a browser on the Web. In Preview mode, you are able to see how your movies and animations will play: animated GIFs play, and, if you have the correct plug-in, so do QuickTime movies and other multimedia. (In some cases you may see the first frame rather than the full animation.) As the Preview tab depends on the Preview module, you can turn it on or off using the Modules Manager in GoLive's Preferences window.

In Preview mode, you can test your links. Links to pages on your site are served from your hard drive. Links to pages on the Web will actually connect you to the Web and call up the page, providing your computer is set to dial up or otherwise connect automatically. However, instead of having the linked pages replace the first page you are previewing, each page opens in a new window.

Note
If you are working on a Mac and previewing pages that contain frames, use the Frame Preview tab. When you are not using frames, the frames preview just says No Frames.

On the Mac, Preview tab gives you can approximation of how your page will look in Netscape Navigator and Internet Explorer 3, 4 and 5 on both Mac and Windows. To use this ability, you choose the Preview tab in the page window and then open the View Controller palette. When you choose any browser, the page redraws. Unfortunately, in the Windows version the Preview tab uses Internet Explorer only due to the integration of Internet Explorer into Windows.

Layout mode, which is shown in Figure 2-23, also presents an opportunity to see how your page will look in IE or Netscape on Mac or Windows — and this preview ability is available on both Windows and Mac. At any time as you work within Layout mode, you can open the View Controller and choose from the available browsers and platforms. View a page that uses a style sheet and you'll see how Version 3 browsers will render it. View a page as a Version 3 or 4 Mac browser and then the corresponding Windows browser and you'll see the platform font size issue. This preview is new to Windows — and very handy.

You can also preview your pages in any Web browser that you have available on your computer. See "Previewing Your Page," later in this chapter.

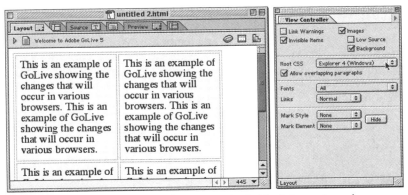

Figure 2-23: A page as viewed on a Mac in GoLive's Layout mode; simulating IE4 in Windows.

Sizing Your Page Windows

With so many monitor sizes in the world, the question of what size window to design for is an often-discussed issue. While GoLive can't solve the problem, it does make it easier to see how much fits on your page at various widths. The page size, noted in the lower-right corner of the page window, is actually a pop-up menu like the one you see here, which provides several preset page widths — the two most helpful are presets for a 14" and 17" monitor:

The Window Settings pop-up enables you to quickly resize your window.

When you choose a size from this pop-up menu, the page window snaps to that size. This does not lock the page width — you can still resize it. As you add elements to your page, the window will not grow, but the elements may extend past the desired window size. You'll need to widen the window to work with these objects. You can do this by dragging the bottom corner of the page, just like with most programs. After you do, the ability to return quickly to one of these preset sizes comes in very handy.

After you set a window to your desired size, you can make that size your default. All of your new and newly imported HTML pages will open at that size. (After you open an HTML document in GoLive and resize it, it will open to the last-used size, not the default.)

To set a default page size, follow these steps:

1. First set the desired size.

You can size the length by dragging the bottom-right corner, as is common with any document in any program. You can also set the width by dragging. Or, to accurately set the width to a preset size, click the Page Size pop-up and choose a width.

2. Click the page size pop-up menu again and choose Window Settings.

3. In the Window Settings dialog box, shown below, make sure there's a check next to HTML Windows. Then click OK.

The Window Settings pop-up enables you to quickly resize your window.

Remember that this page size does not actually affect the size of your page. It simply acts as a guide so you can see what will fit within your page area. And, of course, it provides your working area.

When you consider page width, consider more than the number of pixels on the user's monitor. Don't forget to take into consideration the width of the browser's scroll bars, and any other space-takers such as Internet Explorer's side panel.

Organizing Files

As you collect files or referenced items in the Files, External, Colors, and Font Sets tabs of the Site Window, it may become hard to locate what you need when you need it. By adding folders to these tabs, you can keep things neatly filed and labeled. To add a folder, you simply drag it from the Site tab of the Objects palette into the appropriate tab in the Site Window. There's a specific folder icon for each type of folder:

✦ The plain folder is for organizing files in the Files tab.

✦ The folders with the World icon and the icon with the faces are for external URLs and e-mail addresses, respectively. They are both for use in the External tab.

✦ The folder with the Color icon is for organizing colors within the Colors tab.

✦ The folder with the Font icon is for organizing your font sets in the Font Sets tab.

You can't drag an incorrect folder to a tab; it is rejected. But try it just for fun — it's fun to watch the Folder icon jump back into the Objects palette. Folders always come in called untitled. You name a folder (or change it anytime) by clicking its name, selected the desired text, and then typing a new name.

Tip   You can turn a URL folder into an Addresses folder and vice versa. When you select the folder within the External tab, the Inspector provides the appropriate choices.

When you export a site for posting to the Web, GoLive gives you the option of keeping the files organized exactly how you have them in the Site Window or of putting all pages (except the home page) in a Pages folder and all other physical files into a Media folder. (Actually, you have more choices and you can change those folder names in the Preferences window, but that's another story.) As a throwback to those days when export was necessary, before GoLive's innovative Site Window FTP, GoLive users got into the habit of creating those folders in the Files tab and working with that organization. Now you can have any folders for your pages and/or files. At any time you can drag a plain folder from the Objects palette into the Files tab, name it, and then drag files into it within the Site Window.

You can add folder and reorganize your files at any time. As you move files, URLs, or e-mail addresses around, GoLive keeps track and reorganizes the folders in your hard drive for you accordingly. If you move a file that is in use on any of your pages, GoLive asks permission to update pages that use the moved item. In most cases, you should click OK and permit the update your site. (Files within the Files and Site tabs are the ones that need to be tracked. The items in the other tabs are not actually files, but more like information holders. When you reorganize the items in the Color, External, or Font Sets tab, or change the information in these other tabs, the contents of your pages are not updated.)

Note   When a file is directly in the list of the Files tab, it is in the root-level folder of the site. When a file is inside a folder, its path becomes the name of the folder it is in, and then a slash, and then the file's exact name.

In the next sections, I'll go through the details of moving files around the Site Window, both for the Macintosh and for Windows.

Moving files within the Site Window

Opening folders and moving files from folder to folder is very similar to working on your desktop or within any folders. You have two ways to see what is in a folder, as follows:

✦ As in the Mac Finder and Windows Explorer, you can reveal a folder's contents without opening the folder by clicking the Expand button to the folder's left (blue triangle on Mac, plus box (+) on Windows). When you do this, the arrow points downward (Mac) or the plus changes to a minus sign (Windows), and the files inside that folder appear indented beneath the folder. You can have many folders open like this at the same time, although it may greatly increase your need to scroll. Clicking the Expand button again hides the folder's contents.

✦ The other way to see what's in a folder is to open that folder so its contents are the only things in view. To open the folder like this, double-click the folder. When a folder is open, its name appears in the Navigation pop-up menu above the column header. (This mimics standard Open and Save dialog boxes.) Whenever a folder is open like this, the blue arrow to the right of the pop-up menu activates. You can click that arrow to quickly return to the main (root) level of your site's folder, or you can use the pop-up menu to navigate any-where between the current folder and the root folder.

To move a file from the main (root) level into a folder, just drag it into the desired folder. To drag the file from one folder to another, click the arrow by the folder to reveal its contents and then drag any file from within that folder to any other visible folder, as in Figure 2-24. If you've placed a file within a folder and want to move it out of that folder so it resides in the main level of the Site Window's file list (the root level), drag the file onto the heading (which says Name) at the top of the Files list. Alternately, you can drag a file onto the name of another file that's already in the root level.

Figure 2-24: Moving a file from the NewFiles folder into the Pages folder

Note   You can move several at once by first Shift-clicking or marqueeing them to select them.

Folders are "spring loaded." As you drag a file into a folder, resting over the destination folder causes the folder to spring open. If a folder springs open and it's not the folder you seek, just move your mouse to the column's heading (Mac) or Folder icon above the column heading (Windows) and the folder springs closed. (Later, when you start using Point and Shoot you'll find this feature handy. I explain Point and Shoot later in this chapter).

When you're in a folder, only that folder's files appear. To return to the main folder, (called the root folder) click the arrow (Mac) or Next Folder Up button (Windows) to the left of the site's name beneath the Files tab. You can also drag the file to the left of any other file that is already at the root level and drop it there to put it into the root.

Introducing Point and Shoot

Point and Shoot provides a simple way to a create link with GoLive, whether linking from one page to another, from a page to an external URL, or from a page to a graphic or media file you wish to include on the page. Whenever Point and Shoot is an option, GoLive provides a Point and Shoot button, which looks like a curled-up rope, in the Inspector.

Throughout this book, wherever Point and Shoot is an option, I let you know and show you how to use it (particularly in Chapter 11, which focuses on link creation). But, just to familiarize you with it, keep the following points in mind:

✦ To create a link from text or a graphic, you simply press Command (Mac) or Alt (Windows) as you click the text or graphic and drag from it. Continue dragging until you reach the desired page target. (See Figure 2-25.)

✦ To create any link or to link a placeholder to a file, select the item that will be the link's origin, and then drag the Point and Shoot button from within the Inspector to the destination.

Point and Shoot makes you feel a bit like a cowboy as the rope extends to your destination. For real fun, start to Point and Shoot but release the mouse before you reach a destination and watch the rope snap back.

GoLive's file management and Point and Shoot work together to make it incredibly easy to change the destination of any link—even when it is used within many pages. Because graphics are merely linked to a page, too, you can actually change a graphic in one place and have it change on tons of pages.

Files, Folders, and Their Effects

As you add pages to your site, and then graphics, movies, sounds, and other media files, the Files tab in your Site Window can become a busy place. Like on your computer, you can organize and group your files into logical folders and arrangements to make it easier to manage them and remember where you've stored everything.

When I started Magic Bob Weiss's site, I had a folder for each category of entertainment he did. I figured it was neatest to keep the page for each, along with the graphics and other media files, all organized by category. However, looking at the URL of each page, Bob decided he'd like a person to easily bookmark `magicbobweiss.com/tradeshows.html` instead of `magicbobweiss.com/trade/ tradeshows.html`. So, the easy fix was to pull the pages out to the main folder of the Site Window.

In retrospect, had I known he was concerned about users bookmarking the individual pages as separate units, I would have made a folder called "tradeshows" and put the page about trade shows into that folder, naming that page `index.html`. That way, the URL would have been `magicbobweiss.com/ tradeshows`. No specific page name would be needed, as the index page within that folder would be called automatically. I would have done this for every page in his site that was about another topic. Truth is, it's not too late to do that. GoLive makes page naming easy. As you rename a page, all references to it are updated. And as you move pages around within folder, all paths to and from that page are updated. Perhaps by the time you visit his site, you'll see the new paths in effect.

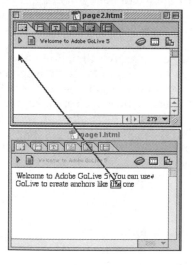

Figure 2-25: Pointing and Shooting directly from text to a destination page

When you select any file within your site and open the In & Out Links palette, you see all of the links in and out of the page, as explained earlier in this chapter. But there's more. You also have a Point and Shoot button beside every page and graphic/media file. At any time, you can drag any of these Point and Shoot buttons from its file to another file. This replaces that file with the new one. One such use of this feature might be to change a background image. If you use a background image throughout your site, and then change your mind, you can substitute another background graphic—just by Pointing and Shooting once.

In addition to being able to easily swap one file for another within your site, you can change the links within Acrobat files that you place in your site. And for Flash files. In Chapter 11, you can read all about links and how easy it is to change them.

Organizing Your Screen

As you work in GoLive, you need to see not only the page you're creating, but a few other things as well. You're bound to fiddle around with your workspace until you find a setup that works well for you. The most common configuration seems to be placing the page to the left, as is standard computer practice, and then placing the Objects palette and Inspector to the right of the page. The Objects palette can be resized to fit just about any space. The Inspector can be resized, but its size depends on its contents. The Site Window must always be open as you work.

As with other page layout programs, a large monitor (or two large monitors) is a true blessing. But in case you don't have the luxury of a large screen, or a second monitor, GoLive gives you some space-saving features.

Many functions and key commands are built into GoLive to help you manage your screen real estate. In addition to some common aids, each platform (Windows and Mac) also has its own unique space-saving mechanisms.

There will be many times when you need to view you page, but then Point and Shoot to a file in the Site Window. In case you don't have room for both onscreen, you can keep the Site Window directly on top of your page, and then use the Select Window button on the toolbar to bring either forward as needed. You have two ways to use the Select Window button. If you have just one page open on screen, just click the button to switch between it and the Site Window. But if you have more than one page open, click the Select Window button and hold on a moment until it reveals a pop-up menu, as in Figure 2-26. This menu shows each of the open pages as well as the Site Window, so you can choose between any open page in addition to choosing the Site Window.

Figure 2-26: You can toggle between your page or pages and the Site Window by using the Select Window button.

In addition to covering up your Site Window, you can also place it out of the way on your screen. In Windows, you can minimize the Site Window, and then maximize it. On the Mac, you can Control-click the Site Window's title bar or drag it to the bottom of the screen until it tabs (much like pop-up folder windows), and then click it once to bring it back to its original position. Pages work exactly the same way in their respective operating systems, by the way.

One of the easiest space savers is the ability to collapse your palettes, including the Inspector, against the right edge of your monitor by pressing the Control key as you click the top of the palette. When collapsed, only the name tabs of each tab are visible. The palette lands level to where it is onscreen, so you know where to look for it. (If you're using multiple monitors, your palette collapses onto the main monitor, so if you have two palettes at the same level on different screens, one may overlap the other. Remember where to look for it.) To restore your palette to its pretabbed position ready for use, just click the tab.

As you work with the various palettes, your screen can become a busy place and you may find a palette or two inconveniently covering parts of your page-in-progress. You can quickly get a clear view of your page by hiding all palettes and even the toolbar with a simple keystroke. On the Mac, just press Control-Tab. In Windows, press Ctrl-J. Only your open pages and the Site Window will remain in view. The same keys restore your palettes and toolbar to view.

On the Mac, you can also click the "windowshade" box at the right end of the title bar or double-click the title bar of any window or palette to reduce it to its title bar, or "windowshade" it. Palettes don't have Minimize buttons in Windows, though. And, of course, both platforms have their respective Close window controls to close any palette. In Windows, the GoLive application fills the whole screen when you launch it and you cannot move your palettes out of the application window. You can obtain maximum flexibility on your screen by clicking the Restore button, and then maximizing the window again. After you do this, you should be able to move your palettes anywhere on your screen (and onto your secondary monitor if you have one). If you cannot move a palette or the Inspector outside of the application window, press Control as you drag it into place. And, you can always choose Window ➪ Cascade to stagger your windows so the title bars shows, by using Tile Horizontally or Tile Vertically — which reduces the size of all the windows so that they can all be seen next to each other.

Previewing Your Page

The real test of a Web page is how it looks in the various browsers on the various platforms. GoLive makes this testing simple as can be: from within GoLive, you can preview your page in any browser that is installed on your computer — which takes care of checking for browser compatibility, at least for the platform on which you are working.

All it takes to have GoLive show you how a page will look in any installed browser is to have the page open and choose the browser with the Show in Browser button on the toolbar. You need to do a small bit of setup first, though: you have to tell GoLive to add the browser to the button's list. The first time you click the Show in Browser button, GoLive even jumps to the setup automatically.

To set up for browser preview, choose Edit ➪ Preferences, click the Browsers icon on the left side to display the Browser preferences, and then click Add to add one specific browser at a time, or click Add All to have GoLive search all mounted volumes and add every browser it finds. The location of each browser is clearly noted so you can determine if you wish to keep on the list. You can remove a browser from the list by clicking it in the list within the Preferences dialog box, and then clicking the Remove button. After a browser is in the list, it becomes available in the pop-up menu on the toolbar. Choose the browser to see how it displays the active page.

Note   Due to limitations within Internet Explorer, you cannot open Versions 2 or 3 after you've installed Version 4. You can install these older versions, but double-clicking them or otherwise trying to open them is fruitless — they just call up Version 4. In order to preview in Internet Explorer 2 or 3, you'll need to install each on another startup disk. With Internet Explorer 5, Microsoft became more flexible, so you can have and use Version 5 and 4 on the same startup disk. This is true on both Windows and Mac.

Cross-Reference   Remember that several differences differentiate computer platforms. See Chapter 26 for more on making sure your pages look good on other platforms.

And, of course, you'll want to test your site once it's posted to the Web as well, just to make sure you've uploaded all the necessary files, and that your file names are appropriate for the type of server you're using.

File Transfer

GoLive gives you not one, but three ways to go live with your site. Two are built-in FTP features, while the third exports your site for you to pass along for uploading. Why two FTP programs? Because one (the File menu) lets you FTP to anyplace anywhere on the Web, while the other (the Site menu) provides a direct path directly to the specific site you're working on.

The simplest, and dare I say coolest, of the options is the Site Window's FTP. After you set up your server info once for your site, it's remembered with the site (stored within the site document). Then, whenever you want to move your site files to the server, or delete or download a file, you're only a click or two away. Of course, you always have control over what gets uploaded. You have several ways to do so.

Under the File menu, you'll find another full-function FTP program. This one enables you to quickly use GoLive to check up on a site, add or delete folders, move things around, or make changes to the site—all that without opening that site's site document, which can be very helpful when you don't have that site's site document stored on the hard drive you're currently working from.

Note   GoLive even enables you edit your site live on the Web. After you connect to your server (using either FTP) just double-click any page within the FTP tab or browser and the page opens on your screen. Change it, save it, and close it. That's it. It's cool—and it can come in very handy when you're away from your home machine and need to make a change immediately.

If you prefer not to use the FTP tab, you can use GoLive's Export command to create a Web-ready folder. Then you can use GoLive's own built-in FTP program or a third-party FTP program to put your site up. Or you can send the exported site, replete in its folder, off to a customer via e-mail or on a removable disk.

Cross-Reference   You can learn all about GoLive's FTP abilities and uploading or updating your site in Chapters 27 and 28.

✦   ✦   ✦

Viewing and Editing HTML

GoLive's visual interface gives you a beautiful way to create Web pages. But . . . (there's always a *but,* isn't there?) . . . no matter how terrific it is, the bare fact is that behind any Web page, lies plain, hard code. And, sometimes, or someday, you'll need to look into that code. Maybe you'll want to learn a tag in order to use it in a style sheet. Or maybe you'll want to try applying a nonstandard attribute to an object on your page. When that day comes, you can either bite the bullet and check the HTML reference guides and books to learn that tag, or you can see if the attribute you seek even exists. . . . Or you can discover the answer in just a few easy clicks within your own page layout or in either of the HTML interfaces right within GoLive. Seriously, just a few clicks.

GoLive gives you two ways to peer into — and work with — this code behind your pages. One way is Source mode, which shows the raw HTML; the other way is Outline mode, which provides an easy-to-view and unique look at the HTML tags on your page. This chapter examines all of these interfaces, and how you can use them.

Viewing and Working in Source Code

HTML is the nitty-gritty of what makes a Web page. It's the code behind all the cool things you do when you drag objects from the Objects palette to the page. It's full of tags that tell the browser what to do, how to render an element, where to find an image, and where to take the user when a link is clicked.

GoLive actually provides two interfaces for you to view straight HTML and to work with it (and other code within your page). The first is the Source Code window (a.k.a. *Source Code palette*), which enables you to see your code as you build your page in Layout mode, and it is also for entering code into. And the second is the HTM Source Editor, built with features especially for HTML programming (coding).

Using the Source Code window

As you work in Layout mode, you can view the source of your page within the Source Code window. To do so, simply choose Window ➪ Source Code. You can learn much about HTML programming just by having this window open while you are creating pages.

With this simultaneous view of your page, you can watch the HTML in your page change moment by moment as you work. While you are dragging an object from the Objects palette onto your page, you can see the code that renders the object. And because any new object on your page is automatically selected on your page, the new code for this object is even highlighted, making it easy for you to notice the code. By watching this window, you can learn much about HTML programming. In fact, I use it throughout this book to show you what the code for an object looks like.

The Source Code window isn't just for watching HTML. It's for programming, too. Any time it's open, you can click inside it and edit your code. The edit takes effect as soon as you click back in your layout.

Note   The Source Code window shows you the HTML of your page when you're working in any view within your page, except the Source tab.

The Source Code window has a few settings that are worthwhile to know about. You choose the settings by selecting them from the fly-out menu at the top-right corner of the Source Code window, as shown in Figure 3-1. Each item is a toggle. Select an item when it's off to turn it on, and vice versa to turn it off.

Local mode

By default, the Source Code window shows you all of the HTML for your page. Local mode (see Figure 3-2) narrows the focus of the Source Code window, showing you only the code for whatever object(s) and/or text that is currently selected. Normally, when you drag, say, a table, from the Objects palette, the code for that table becomes selected in the Source Code window, but the rest of the page's code also appears. Should you click within the Source Code window, you lose that selection, leaving it up to you to figure out where the table's code begins and ends. In Local mode, when you drag that table onto the page, only the code for the table appears. Even when you click within the Source Code window, only that table's code is in view. This enables you to roam around in source code, typing away, knowing where you are. Then, as soon as you click back in the page, you'll see your results.

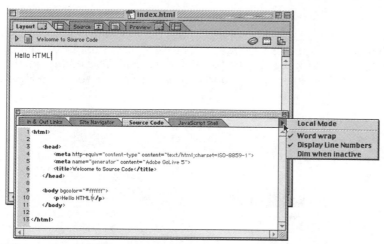

Figure 3-1: The fly-out menu of the Source Code window enables you to customize your view of your page's HTML.

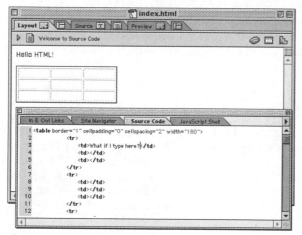

Figure 3-2: Local mode shows you only what is currently selected on your page—. in this case, just a table. Here, text entered in the table cell in source code hasn't appeared in the table yet because the user has not returned to the page.

Tip

Local mode is an excellent way to learn HTML. Switch to local mode any time you want to see a specific bit of code. It's great for learning and great for quick, specific source code edits, too!

You can switch in and out of Local mode any time by returning to the fly-out menu.

Word wrap

In HTML, the contents of a table cell, for example, count as one line of code, regardless of how that content appears to wrap on your page. This can make it difficult to read the code, as the closing tag may be far off screen. With Word Wrap on, the HTML wraps between the edges of the Source Code window, as shown in Figure 3-3.

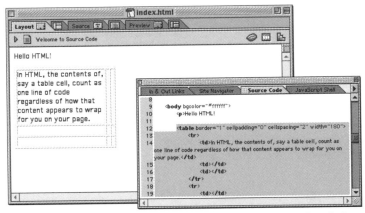

Figure 3-3: By wrapping the text within the Source Code window, you can perhaps more easily see your opening and closing tags.

Display line numbers

Line numbering can enable you to more easily identify bits of code within your page. With this feature on, numbers appear in a gray margin at the left side of the Source Code window. Of course, if the line numbering changed every time you resized the width of the Source Code window, the numbers wouldn't be much help. You would never be able to make notes to yourself concerning a particular issue on a certain line number. Instead, line numbering counts lines of code. When text that would normally appear on one line is wrapped, it is not assigned a numbered line. (You can see this in Figure 3-3.)

Dim when inactive

By default, when you are working on your page in Layout mode, the contents of the Source Code window are slightly dimmed. When you click the Source Code window to make it active, the text becomes brighter so that you can more easily focus on it. On the other hand, turning off this feature causes the code to always appear brighter. It may be handy for you.

Note You can change some of the behaviors of the Source Code window within GoLive's Preferences under the Source section. To learn about these settings, see Source Editor Preferences later in this appendix.

Using the HTML Source Editor

While the Source Code window provides a simultaneous view of your page in code, the Source Code tab of the your page's window provides a full-featured HTML editor. This is the place where programmers can be at home. But even if you're an HTML novice, or you don't really want to know that much about HTML, you can learn something here.

As with the Source Code window, you can learn the code that's generated when an object is built on your page or as it is tweaked. Simply select an object in Layout view and then switch views to see the corresponding code selected in source, too.

Drag and drop

You might think that GoLive's drag-and-drop page building is only a WYSIWYG feature, but it's not! You can drag tables, links, Smart Objects, form elements, and some other items from the Objects palette into place in the HTML source. Colors can also be dragged and dropped. As you drag an item, you'll see a vertical bar representing the placement of the object in the source code. Drop the item, and the code appears!

Word wrap and line numbering

As in the Source Code window, the word-wrap feature wraps your code so that it fits into your page window, while the line-numbering feature counts lines of code. You can turn each of these features on independently of each other by clicking their respective buttons on the toolbar.

Tip GoLive's Source preferences enable you to turn either of these features on so that they're on each time you return to this tab. To do so, choose Edit ⇨ Preferences, click the Source topic, and then check Line Numbers and/or Word Wrap, as desired.

Syntax highlighting and checking

As is common with other HTML editors, GoLive provides color coding, called *Syntax Highlighting,* so you can differentiate between all code and content, media and links, server side code, or just URLs, at a glance. Convenient buttons on the window's button bar make it simple to switch between color coding with a single click. This can be extremely useful when troubleshooting a problem file.

The default Syntax Highlighting is *Detailed syntax highlighting*, which identifies tags, attributes, values (as well as other items), by coloring them "intelligently." If GoLive sees that a required character is missing, the coloring after the error is different. For example, if you have a file that contains the following, you will see everything colored properly because this code is correct:

```
</html>
<<html>
  <head>
  </head>
  <body bgcolor="#ffffff">
    <img src="kiwi.gif" width="132" height="136">
    Some text
  <body>
</html>
```

But . . . delete some code, such as the closing quotation mark from the end of an image name, and you can see the rest of your code change color as your code is reinterpreted. Put in the right code, and it's all fixed and back to the correct coloring.

You don't even have to follow the color coding or figure out what's missing or wrong. GoLive tells you! The Source Editor's button bar contains Syntax Checking. With it, GoLive can give you error alerts and warnings about your HTML. Because different browsers interpret HTML differently, a pop-up menu on the toolbar enables you to check your code for compatibility with different groups or sets of browsers.

Getting back to the example, click the Check Syntax button, and it opens an error display above your code and lists any errors in your page, line by line. At any time as you work on your site, you can switch to the Source tab and see if GoLive has any errors or warnings to report. If you're working exclusively in Layout mode, you shouldn't have errors. But when you get into experiments with global regular expression prints (GREPs—see the "Find and Replace in Multiple Files" section in Chapter 25 for more information about GREPs) or start hand-coding or pulling out tags with source code, you might find this checking to come in quite handy.

Check Syntax compares the code in your page to GoLive's Web Database, which keeps track of HTML tags and how they should be used. Check Syntax then alerts you to any differences between the code in your page and the code in the GoLive Web Database. You can view, and even edit, this Web Database. It's at Edit ➪ Web Settings.

Caution   All of GoLive's code generation comes from the Web Database. Do not mess around in it unless you are sure you know what you are doing—and don't mess around in it while you are working on a site that you care about. Test it first and be prepared to reinstall GoLive before working on any more pages.

Click once to select the Display Errors button. This button displays a list of serious errors in the HTML code, as shown in Figure 3-4. The errors are listed with a red bullet preceding each one. Clicking the error automatically selects the text that triggered the error.

Errors are displayed here

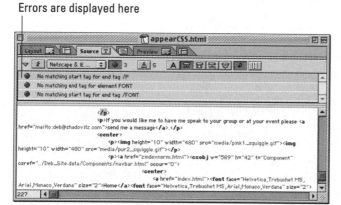

Figure 3-4: The Display Errors feature of the Source Editor's Syntax Checking. When I pulled out font tags from a four-year-old site by hand (because I was being silly), I ended up with quite a mess. The Display Errors feature came in handy.

Click once to select the Display Warnings button, which similarly displays less critical warnings, mostly minor browser incompatibilities. These warnings are displayed with a yellow yield-sign bullet, as shown in Figure 3-5.

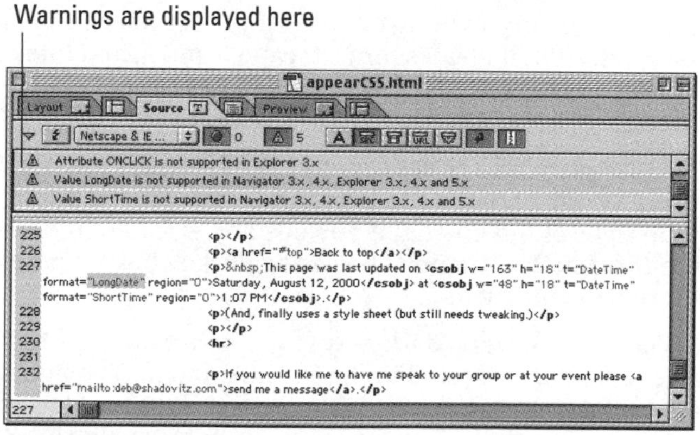

Warnings are displayed here

Figure 3-5: The Display Warnings feature of the Source Editor's Syntax in action

Overview of the Source Editor toolbar and features

When you work in Source view, an extra in-page toolbar provides buttons that show errors and help identify code. Figure 3-6 shows these buttons.

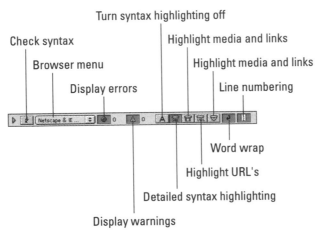

Figure 3-6: The HTML Source Editor's toolbar

Following is a description of each of the main buttons:

✦ **Check syntax.** As already discussed in the preceding section, "Syntax highlighting and checking," clicking the Check Syntax button opens the error reporting area. The errors reported here are determined by the next three items in the toolbar. After an error or a warning is reported, the browser version concerned is noted.

✦ **Browser menu.** This menu enables you to choose which browser the error checking checks for. By default, it checks for Netscape 3 and 4, and Internet Explorer 3, 4, and 5. You can choose just Netscape or just Internet Explorer browsers, if you prefer.

✦ **Display errors.** This button, when dark gray, counts the errors in your page for the browsers currently selected in the browser menu. The number of errors is noted to the right of the button. If you see any errors noted, click Check Syntax to see the details. The button is a toggle, so clicking it when it is on (dark) turns it off, and vice versa.

✦ **Display warnings.** This button, when dark gray, counts the warnings in your page for the browsers currently selected in the browser menu. The number of warnings is noted to the right of the button. If you see any warnings noted, click Check Syntax to see the details. The button is a toggle, so clicking it when it is on (dark) turns it off, and vice versa.

✦ **Turn syntax highlighting off.** By default, Syntax Highlighting is turned on. When on, the HTML on a page is displayed in color. Coloring, that is items highlighted, depends on which of the next buttons on the toolbar are selected. If you prefer not to see highlighting at all, click here to turn this button off. All code then appears as black. Although this button is a toggle and clicking it when it is deactivated turns it back on, the highlighting that was on prior to deactivating it does not reappear. You'll need to choose a highlighting from the next buttons.

✦ **Detailed syntax highlighting.** As noted by its name, this highlighting provides the most detailed highlighting. With this button selected, tags are blue, values you choose are brown, and body text is black. This makes it easy to read your page as you code.

✦ **Highlight media and links.** This option turns all code black, except for the media on your page (that is, images and sounds), which turns turquoise, and your external and e-mail links, which turn a red.

✦ **Highlight URLs.** This option turns all code black, except the actual addresses on your page, such as e-mail, external links, and image file names, which turn a red.

✦ **Highlight server side code.** This option turns all code black, except the server side code in your page.

✦ **Word wrap.** Off by default, unless otherwise set in Preferences, this wraps the code on your page so that you can see it all instead of seeing long, long lines that scroll on and on and on. It's a toggle, so if it is on (even by default), you can click to turn it off, and vice versa.

✦ **Line numbering.** When on, this button numbers your lines of code so that you can easily refer to them. If the button is off, click it in order to turn it on. If the button is on, click it in order to turn it off. Line Numbering is off by default, but you can turn it on by default within your GoLive Preferences under Source.

Source editor preferences

GoLive enables you to set several preferences so that your code can appear in a way that's most comfortable or familiar to you. To set preferences, choose Edit ⇨ Preferences and then click Source. Preferences come in five categories. Each category and its options are self-explanatory. Actually, the best way to see what each does, is to try them for yourself.

General source preferences

This section, shown in Figure 3-7, determines what your source code looks like. It also enables you to use drag and drop within both source code views. It provides a live demo of the effect of each option as you select or deselect it.

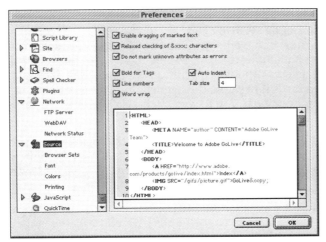

Figure 3-7: The HTML Source Editor's main preferences

Browser sets

This section determines the browser checking sets that appear in the pop-up menu of the toolbar. You can create your own sets, as shown in Figure 3-8. To create a new set, click New, name your set, and then check the desired browsers. You can also choose a new default set. To do so, select the set and check Default Browser Set. The dot to the left of the current default set moves to the newly chosen set.

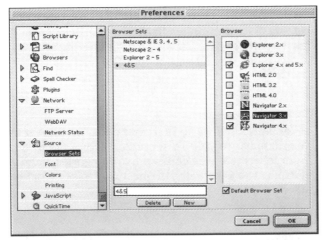

Figure 3-8: Creating a new browser set to check only Netscape 4 and Internet Explorer 4 and 5. The new browser set is also set as the default.

Font

This section enables you to choose the font used to display your code. It also enables you to choose font size and whether the font appears as bold, italic, or with other formatting.

Colors

Here, you can determine the colors used for the Syntax Checking. Choose the highlighting set for which you want to change a color and then click any color swatch to change the color of the highlighting set. Color preferences is also a great place to learn exactly which items are highlighted for each set.

Printing

In case you print your code, this area enables you to determine how your code prints. Choose to show Syntax Highlighting, show tags as bold, or use line numbering. You can also choose a font, other than the one displayed onscreen.

Introducing Outline View

As you may gather from its name, Outline view displays your page in outline form. That is, it displays the code behind your page in outline form. Instead of presenting a page full of tags inserted all over the place, Outline view displays your page's elements clearly, in bold text within collapsible lines.

For example, by looking at the page depicted in Figure 3-9 within Outline view, you'll see the contents of Figure 3-10. This way, at a glance you can see the HTML tags that make up your page. Each tag appears not between brackets that you normally have to ignore or seek out in source code, but in its own outline heading (which GoLive's Help refers to as a "box").

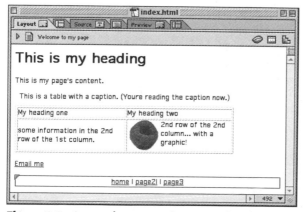

Figure 3-9: A sample page as it appears in Layout view

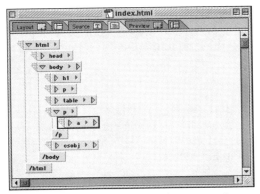

Figure 3-10: The same sample page as it appears in Outline view

By clicking the arrow to the left of the tag you can see the details of the object, as shown in Figure 3-10. When you're designing in Layout view you can see the HTML code behind your page without having to read between all the HTML code.

But this is still a bunch of HTML tags. So, how does it *really* help if you don't already know the tags? Say, for example, you want to understand the code that renders a table. You've looked into source code but all those ⟨td⟩ and ⟨tr⟩ tags are confusing. While in Layout mode, because you want to know the exact tag for the actual table, select the entire table. *Then*, with the table selected, switch to Outline. As demonstrated in Figure 3-11, the actual table tag stands out. For one thing, it's selected by a black box around it, and for another, the *attributes* of the table are visible. You know they're a part of the table tag because they appear indented, like any subsection of a heading does in any outline.

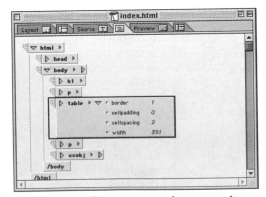

Figure 3-11: The same sample page as it appears in Outline view after the table has been selected in Layout mode

If, instead, you want to know exactly what the tag is for in a table cell, you can select any table cell within Layout mode and then switch to Outline mode to see that tag revealed and highlighted. Because the table cell shares a row with another cell, the entire row unfolds and both cells appear — but only your selected cell is selected, and only it displays its attributes. So, again, you have the opportunity to clearly know the exact code that defines a cell. (It's <td>, by the way.)

While viewing any tag, you can also easily learn what other attributes HTML provides for your page-creation pleasure. That's coming up. But first, a close look into how the outline headings and other tag displays work.

Expanding and collapsing tags

By default, when you switch to Outline view, all items on your page are collapsed, except for the object that is selected within Layout mode at the time. If your cursor is in a line of text, the tag that contains that line of text appears expanded.

You can expand any object's tag while in Outline view without having to go back to Layout mode and selecting that object. To expand any object's tag, just click the blue arrow to the tag's left. (This is the arrow that points *to* the tag.) The arrow turns downward as the tag's contents are revealed. Of course, you can click the same arrow again to turn the arrow sideways again and, therefore, collapse the tag's contents.

As you view the page's outline, you'll notice gray lines (or black, if the item is selected) along the left side of the outline. These lines connect the opening and closing tags of an element. In other words, they show you where an item begins and ends. Everything alongside a line is within that object. For example, the entire page is within the html tag set. When you place a table and expand it, you'll be able to tell what's within that table.

Note

What *are* a tag's contents? That depends on the tag. The contents of the entire HTML tag are the code for the entire document. The contents of the head or body tag are the head section or body of your page, respectively. The contents of a table tag are the caption and rows. The contents of a table row's tag are the cells in that row (one per column). The contents of a column's tag are the text and/or graphics, and so on with what is within that cell. Each tag's or item's contents are indented to the right at the same level to show that they're within that tag or item.

Normally, when you expand an object's tag, each tag directly under that tag appears. This means that if you, for example, expand the body tag, you'll see the names of the tags that fall within the body of your page, as shown in Figure 3-12. Should you want to see the body's contents in fuller detail without having to expand each tab, you can press Option (Mac) or Shift (Windows) as you click the expansion arrow. This action automatically expands every tag within the tag you're expanding, as shown in Figure 3-13.

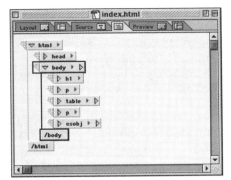

Figure 3-12: Click the arrow to the left of a tag to reveal the tags within it. Here, using the same page as in Figures 3-10 and 3-11, the body's tags are revealed.

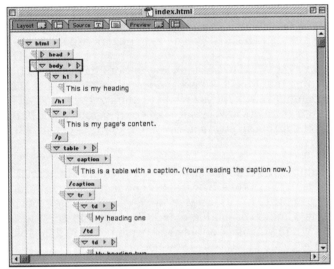

Figure 3-13: By pressing Option (Mac) or Shift (Windows) while clicking the arrow to the left of a tag, you also expand all tags within the tag you've clicked. Here, using the same page as previously, the body's tags are revealed and expanded.

Likewise, when you close a tag and open it again, normally the state it was in when it was last closed or opened remains in effect. But you may have had enough of those expanded tags and want them all to close again. To do so, click the same tag again, once more pressing the same modifier key, Option (Mac) or Shift (Windows).

Tip   Once any tag is visible, you can use any of these techniques to open or close that tag.

Another way to expand everything below an item is to press Option (Mac) or Shift (Windows) and the right arrow key. This only works if the item is closed. If the tag is already expanded, use the left arrow key to close it first and then the right arrow key to open it again.

You can also have all tags beneath a tag open automatically when you first make the switch from Layout view to Outline view. Simply select the object to be viewed while still in Layout mode and then press Option (Mac) or Shift (Windows) when you click the Outline tab.Finally, you can easily close or open any paired (binary) tag from the keyboard—after it's selected. Just press the Enter/return key in the alphabetic section of your keyboard.

New Feature

In GoLive 4, the full outline was expanded by default. In GoLive 5, the entire page is collapsed by default, instead. This should make it easier for you to locate what ever you seek. Now, GoLive reveals just the selected element—if you select something in Layout mode before switching.

Selecting tags

To select any tag within the outline, point to any edge of that tag's rectangular area as you click. (Clicking inside the area is more difficult because you may accidentally select many items within the area.)

After any one tag is selected, you can move up or down through the outline to select any other tag by using the up and down arrows on your keyboard. This moves you through every tag that's visible.

The View Controller enables you to quickly see all occurrences of each element on your page. When you choose to see any of these elements, the outline expands as necessary to show you each occurrence and then marks each occurrence with a yellow highlight. This highlight doesn't affect your ability to work with an element; it just makes it easier to notice the element. You can mark as many elements as you want at a time, but if you have multiple types of elements open, you can not unmark a type of element without unmarking the others.

To bring up the View Controller, either click the View Controller tab of the window that it shares with the Inspector or choose Window ➪ View Controller. You can choose elements from two menus. Simply click the arrow and make your choice from the desired menu, as follows:

✦ The Set Mark pop-up menu enables you to view and mark all text, all comments, or all Generic Elements.

Text, in this case, includes all internal JavaScript code and internal style sheet code.

✦ The Mark Element pop-up menu (see Figure 3-14) reveals and marks any tag in use on your page. This menu is dynamic; every tag you place on your page appears here, and if you delete a tag it is removed from the list.

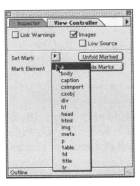

Figure 3-14: Choose any tag from the Mark Element menu of the View Controller in order to have GoLive automatically reveal all occurrences to that tag.

Choosing to mark, for example, your heading-1 elements, doesn't reveal the actual text within the h1 tags or expand the tags to reveal the closing tags. It simply highlights the h1 tag. To reveal the material between the marked tag, click Unfold Marked.

Tip   One of the most frustrating experiences in Web design is losing an invisible GIF on your page. Because the GIF is invisible, it's difficult to see it in Layout mode. (It's even harder if the GIF is only 1 pixel × 1 pixel.) The Mark Element menu, though, enables you to easily notice even a tiny invisible graphic because it shows you the tag that links the graphic into your page. (I'm assuming you know the GIF's name.) Just choose img from the Mark Element menu. You can now edit the size of this spacer as desired, add a border to it so that you can see it as you work, or delete or move it if it's in the wrong place. See these respective topics within this chapter to learn how.

To remove all currently highlighted highlights, click Hide Marks. (This doesn't collapse the expanded areas.)

Viewing images

In addition to seeing the tags and text that comprise your page, you can also see the images that comprise it. Not just the links *to* the images, but the images themselves. To see your actual images within the outline, open the View Controller (Window ➪ View Controller) and check the Images option at the top-right corner.

The counterpart to the image-viewing option, Low Source, tells GoLive to show you the low-resolution version of your image instead of the full version. With this option on, anywhere you have a low-resolution image, that image appears on your page. Images on your page that don't have a high-resolution version appear as generic placeholders in the same generic size as when you first drag a placeholder onto your page.

Tip

This feature can also help you find a lost, invisible GIF on your page. Turn on the Images viewing and then check Low Source so that the generic image placeholder appears. This is not helpful, though, unless you happen to expose the tag that the image is placed within. The mark images trick can be faster. Or mark the image tags and then turn on images, but leave Low Source off. This way you just have to look for the expanded tags that don't have a graphic showing.

GoLive remembers the two image viewing choices so that in the next site you work on the same checkmarks are in effect.

Viewing link warnings

As in page Layout mode, you can tell GoLive to point out your broken links. Here, they also appear marked in red (by default), but it's the tag that's marked.

You can turn Link Warnings on by checking the option in the View Controller or within the toolbar. (The Outline view toolbar contains the same green bug Link Warnings button you're used to from Layout mode, and it even keeps the button in the same place.) When you turn on Link Warnings, GoLive automatically expands any necessary tags to reveal the bad links, as shown in Figure 3-15.

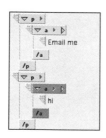

Figure 3-15: A healthy link (top link) and bad link (lower link) as they appears in Outline view

Editing your page

In addition to just seeing the parts of your page in Outline view, you can, of course, edit you page here. You can add elements by dragging them from the Objects palette, just like in Layout mode (except that you don't get visual layout feedback). You can delete elements by selecting them and then pressing Backspace/Delete, as you'd expect. And you can edit elements here.

Tip The reason Outline view is so great for learning HTML is that when you click the arrow at any object's right, the only attributes you see are the one's that apply to that particular object. Any time you're wondering if you can do something to an object, you can select the object in Layout view, switch to Outline view, and then check the object's pop-up attribute list. In most cases, if an attribute is available, you can use it in the Inspector. However, if something is not widely supported (by browsers), it may only appear in outline view.

Adding an element

One way to add an item to your page is to drag it into place from the Objects palette, as follows:

✦ Before dragging the object, be sure to expand your outline so that the object is visible that you want to place the new item after.

✦ As you drag, a thick gray line shows you where the new item will land when you release the mouse to drop it into place.

Your new item appears as a heading, marked by whatever the HTML tag for that item happens to be. In the case of Figure 3-16, a new bold element tag that says br, appears just below the text and above the closing table cell tag (/td).

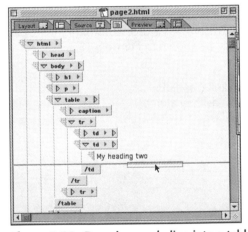

Figure 3-16: Dragging a rule line into a table cell, just after the phrase "My heading two"

Note You cannot add links here by dragging a page icon or external address from the Site Window. These items come in as text, instead. To add a link, you need to use the toolbar to add a tag, and then you need to code the tag.

The other way to add an item to your page is by placing generic tags via the Outline toolbar, shown in Figure 3-17.

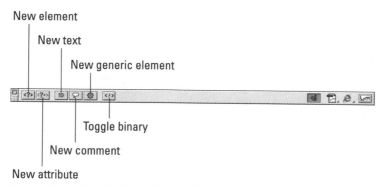

Figure 3-17: The Outline view toolbar

To place generic tags via the Outline toolbar, though, you need to know the HTML tag for the element that you wish to add. Here are the steps:

1. Select the tag immediately above where you want the new element to appear.

2. Click the appropriate button on the Outline toolbar. This places a new, blank tag below the previously selected element.

3. Type the HTML code for your new element, without typing the brackets, and then press Enter/return or click elsewhere in the page to set the change. You don't need to enter the code for the closing tag; GoLive does that for you.

4. If your new element's tag doesn't have a closing tag, the Toggle Binary button becomes active. Click the Toggle Binary button to remove the closing tag that GoLive automatically generates.

Comments here are gray to differentiate them from text.

In addition to using the toolbar, you can choose each element from your contextual menu within Outline view, or choose elements by selecting them from the Special menu.

To check for tag or attribute syntax errors, switch to Source Code view. See Appendix B for more information.

The Outline toolbar contains the following buttons:

✦ **New Element** places a new HTML tag.

✦ **New Attribute** places a new HTML attribute.

✦ **New Text** places a field into which you can type new text.

✦ **New Comment** places a new HTML comment box.

✦ **New Generic Element** places an empty tag for adding code other than HTML to your page.

✦ **Toggle Binary** removes unnecessary closing tags when the tag entered is not paired. This button activates when appropriate.

Moving elements around

You can also move items around on your page while you work. To drag any element into a new position, click the dotted handle at the element's far left and then drag the element. After you click the handle, the entire element becomes selected, as depicted by the thick black border around it. As you drag, a horizontal gray line shows you where the element will land if the item is dropped at that moment.

Adding an attribute to an existing element

After you have an object in place on your page, whether placed within Layout mode or in Outline (or Source) mode, you can easily add any attribute to the object. In fact, you can even add some attributes that aren't available in the Inspector.

Discovering an Element's Attributes

From time to time, you will probably wonder if there's a way to perform a particular task on a page. "Does HTML provide a tag to do this task?" you may ask yourself. Or you might ask the question to the GoLive lists or to an HTML writers list. But with the Outline view in GoLive, like Dorothy from *The Wizard of OZ*, you have the answers already. Outline view is just waiting to show you — if you know how to ask the questions.

Outline view is your magic pair of ruby-red slippers, and the directions under "Adding an Attribute to an existing element" are your good witch.

Just remember that the attributes you're most likely to turn to Outline mode for are the nonstandard attributes. And those attributes don't appear in Layout mode or Preview mode, so you'll need to preview your addition in a browser. In fact, in several browsers.

To add any attribute, follow these steps:

1. Expand the outline so that the element's tag is visible.

2. Click the small gray arrow to the item's right. This reveals all of the item's possible attributes or formatting possibilities.

3. Choose an attribute from the list. The codes here are HTML coding, but they're fairly descriptive, so you should be able to figure out what you're looking for. The selected attribute appears below the currently active attributes. It's code is selected, but don't change it.

4. Press Tab to move to the field to the right of the attribute. This is where you set up the parameters. What you enter here depends on the attribute. The best way to learn available parameters is by using GoLive's Layout mode and then seeing the choices in the Inspector.

Although color attributes provide a color swatch, adding a color here is a bit different from the rest of GoLive. It's a throwback to the GoLive 4 method of adding a color swatch. Double-click the color swatch to open the Color palette (as with Layout mode). Then, locate the desired color and then *drag* the color into the empty color swatch to the right of the word color. (Clicking the color in the Color palette doesn't work in Outline view.)

To link to an image, as for a background image, click the gray arrow that appears to the right of the attribute's code (see Figure 3-18). This opens the Open dialog box. Navigate to the desired graphic and select it.

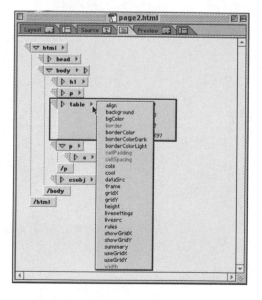

Figure 3-18: Click the small gray arrow beside an element to see and choose from all possible HTML attributes

Note People frequently want to add a border color to a table on a page. Because adding a border color to a table is not well-supported in HTML, it is not available to do in the Inspector. Figure 3-18 happens to show you the attribute for doing this.

Deleting an element

To delete an element or attribute, follow these steps:

1. Select the tag or attribute you wish to delete, as follows:

   • Select the outside border of an element (tag).

   • Click the small blue dot to the left of the attribute.

2. Press the Backspace/Delete key.

✦   ✦   ✦

Getting Help

Learning any new software can be a daunting task, but when that software involves designing for the Web, you also need to know many things beyond the actual page creation, such as changing browser and platform compatibility, evolving standards — and such things are ever-changing. GoLive's revolutionary interface is brilliant, convenient, and easy to use. But it's such a powerful program, and a complex site has so many details to keep track of, that you'll probably need help at some point.

In this chapter I not only show you how to use GoLive's Help and tell you about other sources of help using GoLive; I also offer sources of help with Web-specific issues. You can never have too many sources for help when you're learning something new.

Using Onscreen Labels

You've got enough to think about in life without memorizing the names of every button, tab, and icon. Fortunately, GoLive doesn't expect you to.

To learn the name — and function — of a toolbar button, all you have to do is rest over the button until the Tooltip, a small yellow rectangle, pops up by the tab. In Windows, the button or tab's name also appears in the lower-left corner of the GoLive window.

The Objects palette is the other place where it can be difficult to recall tab or icon names, so again labels are available. To learn what any tab of the Objects palette holds in store for you, just rest over the tab until the Tooltip appears. Then, to learn the name of any icon *within* the Objects palette, look in the lower-left corner of the palette as you pass over the icon.

On the Mac, the Tooltips are optional and can be turned off by choosing Help ➪ Hide Tooltips. After it has been turned off, the Help menu command changes to read Show Tooltips. To turn it back on, select Help ➪ Show Tooltips.

Finding Onscreen Help

GoLive's onscreen Help provides you with a handy version of the information provided in the GoLive user manual. It's well organized by topic, easy to use, and rich with images that help you understand what is being explained.

To launch GoLive's Help, choose Help ➪ GoLive Help (or, in Windows, press F1). This launches your browser and opens the main Help page. The tab at the top-left corner of the Help page presents three ways to access the help you seek. You can use the Table of Contents, which lists all help topics by subject. You can use the alphabetic Index to locate help by keyword. Or, you can use the Search page to look into the topical Help pages for mention of the specific word you seek. Each provides a different way of arriving at the Help page for the topic you're interested in, but all get you to the same place eventually. By clicking the tabs at the top-left corner, you can switch between the different search interfaces.

Tip   Because Help is HTML, you can launch and use it from directly within any browser. It's a frameset (as in Chapter 14), so you need to open the main frameset page to get the full benefit of its Table of Contents. To launch Help when not in GoLive, locate Help.html within the Help folder in the GoLive application folder, and then drag it onto your browser's icon, alias, or shortcut.

Because GoLive Help is displayed within your browser, you can navigate, print, and copy text just like you do within any Web page. Because the Help system uses frames, the same issues that pertain to all frames also come into play here.

Seeking help by content listing

Each time you launch GoLive Help, you're presented with the main Contents listing, which contains about 30 basic topics listed in a logical progression. This is the best way to begin a search for general GoLive knowledge. You can see this listing and some of the topics in Figure 4-1. Each topic is, of course, a link as you can see when you move your cursor over the topic. Clicking any of these topics takes you to the first Help page pertaining to that topic. As you explore the Help, the Contents list remains in place while the actual help is presented to the right.

When you first click a topic link, the right panel usually presents another list; the list of sections (subheadings) that relate to the topic (see Figure 4-2).

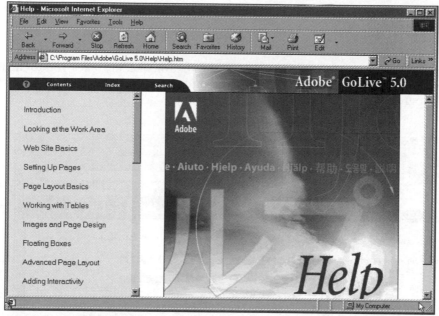

Figure 4-1: The Contents tab provides help by category. Clicking any category takes you to an introduction to the topic.

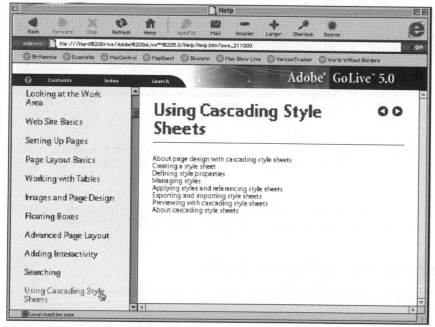

Figure 4-2: The first page of any topic contains a list of subtopics covered. Click any subtopic or click the forward arrow to move to the first topic.

Tip   You can click any of these subheadings to jump directly to the specific information you seek.

Clicking the forward arrow to the right of the section heading takes you to the first subheading. Each Help page contains a forward arrow to move you forward through the progression of subheadings (see Figure 4-3).

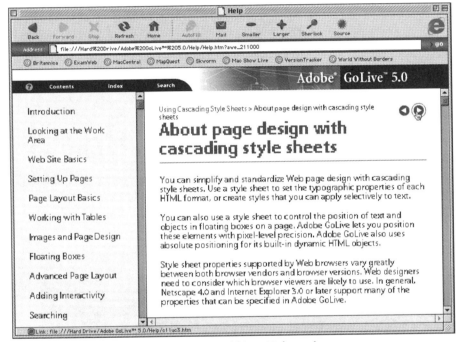

Figure 4-3: The first information page within a Help topic

Each page of information is as long as it needs to be in order to cover the topic. Some contain images or steps. Blue text within any page indicates a link to related information.

Tip   Because Help is presented within your chosen browser, you can use the same browser controls you're used to using to control the look of the Help.

Seeking help using the Index

If you have a pretty good idea of what you're looking for, it may be faster to find it using the Index instead of the Contents listing. To use the Help Index, click the

Index button at the top-left corner of the Help page. An alphabetical listing appears at the top of the left frame. Click any letter for a listing of all words beginning with that letter.

Scroll through the list until you see the information you seek. If there, it is followed by a red number "1" to tell you it's listed once. If there's second occurrence of your topic, there's a number "2" and so on. Click any of these red numbers to see that particular occurrence of your topic, as shown in Figure 4-4.

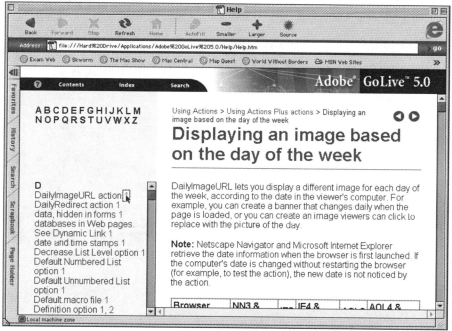

Figure 4-4: The Index feature of GoLive's Help shows you occurrences of a bit of information by topic.

Seeking help using Search

The Search tab provides you the most powerful way to search for help. When you have a specific keyword or phrase to search for help on, the Search tab can get you to the information you seek most quickly. When you choose Search, you're presented with a simple Search field at the top-left corner of the left frame. As with a typical search field on the Web, you enter the work you seek and then press Enter or Return, or click the Search button.

As with the Index search, all pages that contain mentions of your word appear to you, listed in a scrolling field below the Search field. Each listing is a link that, when clicked, presents the topic instruction, as shown in Figure 4-5.

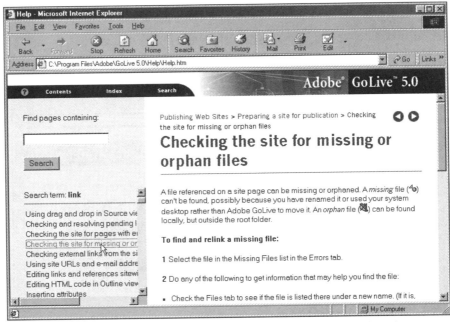

Figure 4-5: Using Search to see all mentions of the word link, and learning something about links

Printing a Help page

Frames are tricky to print. The secret to printing the Help information contained in GoLive Help is to click within the actual Help content area, and then click Print.

Bookmarking a Help page

Help pages are displayed within the right frame of a frameset, so if you try to book-mark the page, you'll simply arrive back at the main Help page. The trick to book-marking just the desired page is to use the contextual menu *from within the desired frame*. Control-click (Mac) or right-click (Windows) in the Help area of the Help page and choose Add Page to Favorites. This will bookmark that particular page so you can return to it later. However, it bookmarks only that page. From there, you can use the path headings at the top or bottom of the page in order to move through that particular topic, but you'll be viewing those pages out of the context of the frameset, so you won't have the Contents listing, Index, or Search.

Copying Help text

As usual within a browser, you can copy any page's text by selecting the text and choosing File ➪ Copy. From there, paste the text into any document.

Tip   If you're displaying the Help within Internet Explorer 5 for the Mac, you can select the desired text and then drag it to the Desktop or anywhere within the Finder. As always within IE5 for Mac, this creates a SimpleText document for you.

Quitting Help

Because the Help system runs within your browser, quitting the browser quits Help. However, because you're likely to be previewing your pages within your browser, you may prefer not to quit it. Instead, just close the Help page.

Looking for Other Adobe Help

In addition to the program Help files, several other helpful items are accessible via the Help menu.

Note   Each of these options, located beneath GoLive Help in the Help menu, requires the Adobe Online Software. If the Adobe Online Software is not installed on your computer, you'll receive a dialog box informing you and asking if you'd like to install it now.

Support

The Support option under the Help menu is your fastest path to GoLive's online support. Choosing Help ➪ Support takes you directly to the GoLive Support options page of the Adobe Web site. Here you can follow links to Top Issues, Updates, Plugins, Patches, the Support Database, Adobe's User to User Forums, and to Tech Support. You'll also find a field for searching the Support database.

Downloadables

With the new Downloadables feature, you'll never have to scour www.adobe.com for new modules, Actions, or other items that are, or can be, part of GoLive.

Instead, just choose Help ➪ Downloadables and the top part of the window will present you with a list of available files. The options on the bottom of the window are self-explanatory, enabling you to choose which files you see and how they are downloaded and installed.

Registration

If, upon installing GoLive, you missed the opportunity to submit your registration to Adobe, you can do so at any time. Just choose Help ➪ Registration, and then select the option to register online or to print the form, and proceed from there as directed.

Adobe Links

The submenu under Help ➪ Adobe Links leads you directly to a wealth of information to help you use GoLive. Each is clearly marked. Of course, you can still visit www.adobe.com within your browser without the help of this menu, but this menu makes it much easier to find what you seek.

Adobe Online

This menu option leads you directly to the Adobe Online Software setup. Click Preferences to begin your setup. You can make your choices directly within the Preference area, or use the Setup Wizard to guide you through the steps to tell the software how you connect to the Web and what your settings are.

Searching for Helpful Resources on the Web

Adobe GoLive enables you to develop a presence on the Web, so it's perfectly logical to expect the Internet to also be a source of help for using it. Many Web sites can help you, as can newsgroups and e-mail lists. Some are dedicated specifically to GoLive, while others cover other aspects of Web site creation.

Independent GoLive resources

The resources I list here are active as I write this, but remember that in the ever-evolving world of the Internet, things can change rapidly and easily.

GoLiveTalk

GoLive Talk is an e-mail discussion list. You can receive messages as they are posted or you can subscribe to the digest. A searchable archive also exists, so before you post a question, be sure to check to see whether your questions have already been answered; the answers may be waiting for you there. At the Web site `www.blueworld.com/blueworld/lists/golive.html`, you can learn about this list, search it, and subscribe to it.

GoLive Heaven

GoLive Heaven (`www.goliveheaven.com`) is a general news and information site dedicated to GoLive. You'll find news about anything that might be important to you as a Web designer, some GoLive-specific tutorials, some HTML information, JavaScript tutorials, and more.

GoLive Headquarters

GoLive Headquarters (`www.golivehq.com`) is another news and information site focusing mainly on GoLive. You'll find forums, tips, and news, among other things, which can be of great use as you design your Web site in GoLive.

CYB — A French-language site

If you are more comfortable thinking in French, you'll appreciate the independent GoLive list and the news at `http://go-cyb.com`.

HTML help resources

This is by far not a complete list of places to learn the HTML standard and how to use it. But it's a very good start.

The HTML Writers Guild

The HTML Writers Guild (`www.hwg.org`), founded in 1994, is a nonprofit educational group of members helping members. According to its membership reports, the guild is "the world's largest international organization of Web authors with over 98,000 members in more than 130 nations worldwide." Its purpose is to assist members with their authoring capabilities. It has several topical mail lists, online classes, town hall meetings, and more. This is a membership organization, but they offer a free trial so you can see what it's all about. Be sure to check out their newsletter tips section at `www.hwg.org/opcenter/newsletters/tips`.

W3C (World Wide Web Consortium)

This is the place to go for the bottom line on HTML — past, present, and proposed future. A good place to start is the Help area: `www.w3.org/Help`. You can also learn the history of the Web here.

Web Standards Project

This group (www.webstandards.org) formed because Web designers "were (and are) mad as hell and aren't gonna take it anymore." It's a coalition of Web developers and users whose mission is "to stop the fragmentation of the Web, by persuading browser makers that standards are in everyone's best interest. Together we can make the Web accessible to everyone."

The NCSA (at UIUC) Beginner's Guide to HTML

This page (www.ncsa.uiuc.edu/General/Internet/WWW/HTMLPrimer.html) is a small part of the National Center for Supercomputing Applications' site. The center is a research institution of the University of Illinois — the group that created Mosaic (the first Web browser). The entire site is filled with helpful information about the Web and other aspects of computers, but the Primer is the most relevant to understanding the Web.

Liszt

The mailing list directory Liszt (www.liszt.com) says it has over 90,000 lists to be found in its searchable list directory. There's a presorted Internet category and one under that just for the Web. DejaNews, at www.dejanews.com, is an excellent complement to Liszt.

The Web Developer's Virtual Library

There's a lot here at http://wdvl.com, including lists, to help you on your way and keep you learning and sharing.

HTML books

Some additional good books to start with, all from IDG Books Worldwide, include the following:

✦ *Creating Cool HTML 4 Web Pages, 2nd Edition* by Dave Taylor

✦ *HTML 4 Bible, 2nd Edition* by Bryan Pfaffenberger and Bill Karow

✦ *HTML For Dummies, 3rd Edition* by Ed Tittel, Natanya Pitts, Mike Wooldridge, and Chelsea Valentine

✦ *HTML 4 For Dummies Quick Reference* by Deborah S. Ray and Eric J. Ray

General Web site development help

Design is a big part of your site. GoLive provides the tools, but it's up to you to provide the design skill. A good Web page is *not* just a good printed page online, so if you come from a print standard these sites may help you become familiar with Web design considerations. Again, this is not a full list by any means.

Internet.com

There's a lot here at `http://internet.com`. Among those things offered are a plethora of free e-mail newsletters and discussion lists about the Net. Follow the Resources list. Many good leads for other resources lead back here.

Webreview.com

This site, found at `webreview.com/wr/pub/guides/style/unsafegrid.html`, provides lessons and lists covering varied Web design issues from a technical perspective.

Internet 201

The focus of this site (`www.powerdesign.com/201/index.html`) is graphic design for the Web.

Web-Page Design for Designers

If you already know print design, then come to this site (`www.wpdfd.com/wpdhome.htm`) to learn design for the Web.

A List Apart—For People Who Make Websites

A List Apart, by Jeffrey Zeldman and Brian Platz (`www.alistapart.com`), describes itself as "a weekly online magazine for people who make Web sites, and a moderated discussion list of over 6,000 professional designers, writers, and programmers." It covers "Everything connected with making the Web—from pixels to prose, coding to content."

Interface considerations

It doesn't matter how great your site looks if visitors can't figure out how to use it. If you can't get there from here, as they say, your site will do you little good. Human Factors International (`www.humanfactors.com`) is a company specializing in creating user interfaces. While they design sights (and software and other things) themselves, they also hold training seminars you may be interested in, and share some of their knowledge within the site.

An AOL Guide for Webmasters

AOL is well aware that there are, shall I say, "special" issues to consider if you want your site to be AOL-browser friendly. This site is put up by AOL to address those issues. You'll find it at `http://webmaster.info.aol.com`.

Developer.WebTV.net

Like all platforms, WebTV interprets your site in its own way. (WebTV *really* has its own way.) This site (`http://developer.webtv.net`), created by the WebTV people, introduces you to those considerations and guides you in development. At this site you can also download the WebTV Viewer, an application that enables you to simulate how your site will look on WebTV, so you don't have to go out and buy one or bug your friends to test your site.

Browser Watch

If you have a question about a browser or plug-in, turn to Dave Garaffa and his Browser Watch at `www.browserwatch.com`. Here you'll find "breaking news in the browser and plug-ins industry, as well as one of the most complete lists on development of different plug-ins and browsers."

Accessibility

The Web is still a new medium with the potential to be accessible to everyone. Those who cannot see can have your pages read to them. Those who also cannot hear can have their Braille readers print out the words on your pages in Braille (if you design with accessibility in mind). The following resources can help you design your pages to be as accessible as possible for Net surfers with disabilities.

Web Accessibility Initiative (WAI)

This is the W3C (`www.w3.org/WAI`) again, but I list it separately to make sure you know about this initiative. The resources here will help you learn what you need to do — or not do — to enable everyone to benefit from your site.

The Center for Applied Special Technology (CAST)

Part of CAST's goal is "to expand opportunities for people with disabilities through the innovative uses of computer technology." That's where their Bobby (`www.cast.org/bobby`) comes in. Enter the URL of your site and Bobby analyzes your pages to let you know how accessible your site is to people with disabilities. It pinpoints your problem areas to help you improve their accessibility. After you're approved, you may post the Bobby Approved icon on your site. Bobby is offered free, as a public service. I encourage you to take advantage of it.

The AWARE (Accessible Web Authoring Resources and Education) Center

The AWARE Center (`www.awarecenter.org`) is a part of the HTML Writers Guild, and a pet project of the ever-caring Kynn Bartlett. It's a wealth of information.

The Royal National Institute for the Blind (RNBI)

This RNBI's page (www.rnib.org.uk/wedo/research/hints.htm) starts out by pointing out something we all need to think about: Between perfect vision and blindness, a wide range of people see, but need certain levels of contrast or font size flexibility in order to be able to see your site. This site wisely informs designers that, "Accessible Websites are not dull Websites. Attractive, dynamic designs, which are fully accessible, can be achieved. Websites that are designed intelligently benefit all Net users, not just those with disabilities." Don't miss this group's excellent page full of tips for designing sites that can be used by all.

VisiBone's Color-Deficient Vision page (colorblindness)

Bob Stein, the man behind VisiBone, and master of color charts, provides the most helpful tool I've ever found to enable color-sighted people to comprehend color-deficient vision and design with it in mind. Be sure to visit VisiBone's Color Deficiency page (www.visibone.com/colorblind) to see for yourself. His color card and color chart have been eye-opening experiences for me. (No bad pun intended. I highly recommend this chart to all.) This page also contains some very helpful links that further explain and even test (online) for color-blindness.

Note Web and database programmer Andrew Oakley is a color-blind man who did an excellent job of explaining color-blindness and describing the experience. "One in twenty white men are color blind," he says. That means one in twenty men may not be able use your site because your words and pictures disappear into the background. Unfortunately, his site has moved and I cannot locate it. However, as I write this, one key color-blindness page remains (www.cimmerii.demon.co.uk/colourblind/design.html) and provides clear and easy guidelines to help you be aware of color issues.

Legal

The Internet makes the exchange of ideas easier than ever before in recorded history. That ease is terrific, but it also makes it easy for people to lift your words, graphics, photographs, and so on. How can you protect yourself? Conversely, legal issues exist regarding the use of other people's materials.

Ivan Hoffman's legal articles

Ivan Hoffman is an attorney and an expert when it comes to knowing what you should know as the creator of content. Amazingly, he's put up an entire four-time award-winning site (www.ivanhoffman.com) to share some of his knowledge. While it doesn't take the place of having an attorney to guide you (such as Ivan in person), it is very helpful in introducing you to issues. Check out the links under the headings "Articles for Web Site Designers and Site Owners" and "Articles about e-thics."

World Intellectual Property Organization

The World Intellectual Property Organization (WIPO) is an intergovernmental organization with headquarters in Geneva, Switzerland. It is one of the 16 specialized agencies of the United Nations system of organizations. WIPO is responsible for the promotion of the protection of intellectual property throughout the world through cooperation among States, and for the administration of various multilateral treaties dealing with the legal and administrative aspects of intellectual property. You can learn about it, its activities, and membership at `www.wipo.int`.

Marketing

Having a site is one thing. Marketing it (that is, getting people to come visit) is another. These are a few sites to help you with marketing.

eMarketer

This site (`www.emarketer.com/estats/welcome.html`) provides news and statistics covering the growth of the Internet and e-commerce. The site offers a free newsletter covering eMarketer news highlights, statistics, and other hot tidbits.

Search Engine Watch

If you're vying for notice and position with the various search engines that may lead the public to your site, this service (`www.searchenginewatch.com`) is a very helpful resource. It provides the complete lowdown on how search engines work and explains how to design with them in mind. It also offers a free monthly newsletter.

Nielsen//NetRatings

This site (`www.nielsen-netratings.com`) is packed with lots of good stats, such as Web user data and daily statistics, such as the average time people spend on the Web. They also have a good newsletter. And, of course, they offer their commercial service.

CyberAtlas

The CyberAtlas (`www.cyberatlas.com`) byline is "the Web marketer's guide to online facts." It has been a popular, award-winning site since it started in 1996 and is now owned by internet.com. The site continues to "provide readers with valuable statistics and Web marketing information, enabling them to understand their business environment and make more informed business decisions. CyberAtlas gathers online research from the best data resources to provide a complete review of the latest surveys and technologies available."

✦　　✦　　✦

Starting to Build Your Site

Ready to get started? This is the place to learn how. Whether you're starting a new site from scratch, converting a site from another application, or bringing a hand-coded site into GoLive, this part covers the details of actually starting your site.

Starting Your Web Site

Are you totally new to Web page creation, or do you just happen to be starting a new site from scratch? If so, you'll be starting a blank site—or perhaps using a template to give your site a substantial head start. Have you begun the site, or just a single page, using another Web page program or text editor—and do you have this page or site on your hard drive or another volume you can mount on your desktop? If so, you'll appreciate the Import from Folder command.

Have you already created a site and posted it to the Web? Or are you taking over a project that is already on the Web? In these cases, you can import it into Adobe GoLive for further development by using the Import from FTP command.

You're welcome to read through all the options and instructions in this chapter, but it's not necessary. Just jump to the section that applies to you.

Starting a New Site

GoLive provides two ways to begin a new Web site. You can create a new blank site and design it from the ground up or you can begin with a predesigned site template.

Beginning a blank site

It's easy to create a new blank site. Just choose one command from the File menu, and then save one document. GoLive does the rest, creating a new blank Site Window and a set of site management folders.

Each time you launch GoLive, by default it presents you with a new blank page. While you *could* begin designing on this page, this default does not start a new Site Window, which you need for storing and managing your site's elements. Therefore, I recommend you not use this default page. Instead, immediately close that page without adding anything to it or saving it. Then use the following steps to begin your site:

1. From the File menu, select New Site ➪ Blank. This opens the Create New Site dialog box. It looks different depending upon your computer platform and operating system, but the function is always the same.

2. The Site Name field contains the generic name "New Site," which is preselected for you. Any text you type replaces those words, so without clicking, type your new site's name, shown in Figure 5-1 as "MyNewSite."

Name	Date Modified	Size	Kind
▽ 🗋 MyNewSite	Today	—	folder
📄 index.html	Today	4 K	Adobe GoLive HTML p
📄 MyNewSite Backup.site	Today	1 MB	Adobe GoLive Site
▽ 🗋 MyNewSite.data	Today	—	folder
▷ 🗋 Components	Today	—	folder
▷ 🗋 Designs	Today	—	folder
▷ 🗋 Site Trash	Today	—	folder
▷ 🗋 Stationeries	Today	—	folder
📄 MyNewSite.site	Today	1 MB	Adobe GoLive Site

🗋 MyNewSite folder
9 items, 5.8 GB available

Figure 5-1: The Create New Site dialog box (Windows), where you name your site, create its folder, and choose its destination. Here, the site is named "MyNewSite" and placed in a folder called Websites.

If you click or type within the field, you'll be editing the name, not replacing it, so you may have to select all of the text within the Name field to rename the new site.

Note

You may have already heard that strict rules govern the naming of files and directories (folders) used on the Internet. This is true. However, the name you give your site and its folder here is of little consequence. The name you choose here becomes your site document's name, but this document is merely the file (Site Window) that manages your site. It never goes to the Web server. The site's name also becomes the name of the site's folder, but that's mainly for your own identification while you're creating the site. Consider it a working name.

3. Use your computer's standard navigation to select the location (partition, disk, drive, or folder) where you want to save your site. (In Windows, click Browse to locate your destination; on the Mac, use the controls in the dialog box to navigate directly to the desired location.)

By default, GoLive automatically creates a folder with the same name as your site name, and places it in the location you choose as your site's destination. Everything you add to your site is housed in this automatically created folder.

If you uncheck the Create Folder option, GoLive does not create a folder. Instead, it places all your site folders/documents in the location you chose. Should anything else already be in that location, things will become confusing. I strongly recommend you leave this option checked so your site's folder's names will all match. However, you could uncheck the Create Folder option if you are certain you're saving the new site to an empty folder already (or if, on the Mac, you use the New Folder button to create and name a new folder specifically to house your site).

4. Click Save. Behind the scenes, GoLive automatically creates the folder it needs to manage your site (if you left the Create Folder option checked). You won't see this folder unless the folder you saved it into happens to be open. (See the "Watching GoLive Create a New Site" sidebar later in this chapter.)

You're presented with the Site Window that bears the name of your site. In it you'll find your home page, index.html, waiting. (By default, this page is called index.html, but you can change its name, or choose another home page, later.)

That's it. You don't have to save at this point because the site was saved when it was created. You can close the Site Window now and come back later, or you can continue working right now.

Once the Site Window appears, you are ready to design your index page, create more pages, or add content (such as the graphics you want to use on your pages) to your Site Window. If you have a master plan in mind, you can transfer that plan into your site's layout by using the Navigation view under the Design menu. (The "Envisioning Your Site Structure" sidebar later in this chapter introduces this planning feature.) If you're more the type to look squarely at a blank piece of paper (or blank computer document) and start by playing around on it, you can skip to the section called "Adding pages to the Files tab" later in this chapter, or to Chapter 6, to begin designing your index page.

Watching GoLive Create a New Site

When you type the name for a new site, such as **MyNewSite**, in the Site Name field and keep the Create Folder box checked, GoLive creates a group folder entitled MyNewSite. This group folder will contain a document folder, data folder, and site document file. (Later, GoLive also creates a backup of the site document file.)

The document folder, called MyNewSite, stores the files that comprise the Web site — all the pages, graphics, and any other elements that are part of the site's features (such as sound files and downloadable files). MyNewSite.data stores the behind-the-scenes elements of your site, such as any components and Stationeries you may create later, your site trash, and any site designs.

The site document is named MyNewSite.site. This site document, when opened, becomes the Site Window. It's the file that records and manages the structure of the site and all pertinent information. This is the file you double-click to open your site in order to work on it.

GoLive also creates the first page for your new site, named index.html by default. This file name identifies the page as the home page of the site. Because it is a page within your site, it is stored within the folder that contains the site's documents, as shown in the following figure. You will see it in the Files tab of the Site Window when you launch the site document.

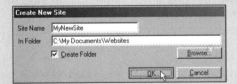

A site's actual storage folder (not the Site Window). You don't need to access it directly, but it's nice to know what's in it.

You don't directly work within these folders or add or remove items from them. Instead, with GoLive's unique interface, all site file management should be done via the Site Window. Directly accessing files within the physical folder will confuse GoLive. The only thing you access in this site's folder is the site document — which you double-click to open the Site Window in order to work on your site.

When you open the site folder to launch the site document, you will also see a backup file. (In this case, it would be called "MyNewSite backup.site.") A new backup is created every time you open your site document. (You can disable the automatic backup in Preferences if you don't want the security it provides. Some people choose to do this because of the few seconds it takes for GoLive to write the file each time you relaunch the site.)

Tip

Because the new blank page that GoLive automatically opens upon its launch is not particularly helpful in Web site creation, you might as well tell GoLive not to bother. To do so, select Edit ⇨ Preferences. If it's not already selected, click the General icon. In the At Launch menu, choose Do Nothing. Alternatively, you can choose Show Open Dialog, which tells GoLive to show you a standard Open dialog box from which you can navigate to, and open, any Web site. (But I think it's easier to just double-click the site document for the site you wish to open.)

Beginning a new site based on a template

If you have just launched GoLive and a new blank page automatically opened, close that page without saving. Then follow the directions listed here to begin your new site based on a template:

1. Select File ⇨ New Site ⇨ Copy from Template. This opens the Copy Site from Template dialog box. Each available site template is listed by name, along with a description if one has been provided.

2. Click the name of an available template once to select it. You can see a miniature image of a page and mini Navigation view map too, if these images have been provided by the template's creator.

3. Replace the default name of the site with your own name. This name has no bearing on the domain name where the site will ultimately reside; it's a working name only and should be descriptive. Avoid spaces, though, to make path names simpler during development.

4. Click Browse to determine where your site will be stored as you develop it.

5. Click OK to create the site. A new Site Window appears, complete with pre-designed pages ready for you to customize.

Note

If you have installed extensions to GoLive, you may see an alert that the site cannot be created, telling you to open the site once directly. Click OK to cancel the creation. Then open the GoLive application folder, and then the Site Templates folder, and open the folder of the template you wish to use. Double-click the site document (ending with .site) for the site. When its Site Window opens, close the Site Window without saving. Then return to the File menu and begin again.

You can customize your new site any way you like. To learn about any element on a page, select the element and check the Inspector. To learn where it is used, open the In & Out Links Inspector (under the Window menu).

Envisioning Your Site Structure

After you create a GoLive Site Window, you're ready to begin building your site. Your new Site Window comes complete with your first page, the home page. Of course, you'll want to add more pages — and GoLive gives you plenty of ways to do that. Adding a page is covered in the following section. Then, after you add more pages, you can get down to adding content to your pages and getting your site going — live on the Web!

In the Navigation window, you can select your home page and then add pages that will branch out from it. Then you can select any of those new pages, and add pages that branch out in any direction. The pages you add this way can be blank, generic pages, or pages created from any Stationery you create. (See "Adding Pages to Your Site" later in this chapter to learn how.)

In Navigation view, you can set up a master plan. GoLive keeps track of where you add each page. If you move any page around within this view (as you can by dragging it), GoLive recognizes your new plan.

Why a master plan? Because it helps you plan your user's experience at your site. It lets you see how many clicks it will take for a user to get to specific information.

What do you do with this plan? For one thing, you can return to it at any time and easily see which pages still await links. Just click the fly-out menu at the upper right of the Navigation View window and choose Spotlight Pending. This turns on red arrows that point out pending links. The arrow points from the page that will contain the link, to the page that the link is to. While here, you can double-click any page to open it, and then create the links you see are needed. Another thing you can do is reorganize the flow of your pages. Just drag any page into place by another page. When you reposition a page, all pages below it move along with it. (You can clearly see that the pages below it move by choosing Spotlight Family from the fly-out menu before making the move.)

Cross-Reference

Whether you use them now or not, you can always switch to the Navigation and Link views, review what your site looks like so far, and add or delete pages. This is helpful because, no matter how much you plan, Web sites grow and it's common to want to add pages or groups of pages. To learn more about the Navigation and Link views, see the "Envisioning Your Site Structure" sidebar above or check out Chapter 29.

Importing an Existing Site

Perhaps you already have a Web site, maybe started in another Web page creation program or written directly in HTML. This work isn't wasted. It's easy to import your existing site into GoLive to continue working on it. That is, GoLive will look at your file structure and create a site document/Site Window to reflect it, creating a GoLive folder structure.

Importing a site from a local drive

You can import a site from any volume you can mount. However, GoLive does not automatically copy your original files from the original drive or volume to the home of your new site. Instead, you have to do that yourself.

Note   If the site you're importing is already on the volume you'll be importing to, you may want to back up your site before you begin the import.

To import a site from your own computer, follow these steps:

1. On the hard drive or volume where you want your new GoLive site to reside as you work, create a new folder to house your new site.

   This folder can have any name. It doesn't have to comply to Web naming standards because it won't be transferred to the Web as part of your site in the end — short and descriptive is always good, though.

2. Place your existing site's folder into the folder you created in Step 1, as shown in Figure 5-2. If the site you are importing is on another hard drive or volume, this copies the existing site's files into your new GoLive site so they become a part of your new site.

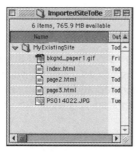

Figure 5-2: Moving an existing site into a new folder called ImportedSiteToBe

3. If GoLive is not already running, launch it. If a new page automatically opens, close that window.

4. Choose File ➪ New Site ➪ Import from Folder. This opens the Import Site Folder dialog box, as shown in Figure 5-3.

5. Click the Browse button in the top half of the of the Import Site Folder dialog box, and then navigate to and select the folder that you just moved or copied into the folder you created in Step 1, as is being done in Figure 5-4. If the folder is in view, instead of browsing, you can drag that folder into the top half of the of the Import Site Folder dialog box.

Figure 5-3: The Import Site Folder is where you tell GoLive which site you're converting into a GoLive site.

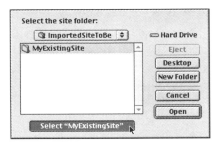

Figure 5-4: Selecting the existing site to import: in this case, importing a site named MyExistingSite

The path to the folder appears in the top half of the dialog box, as in Figure 5-5.

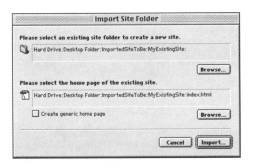

Figure 5-5: The Import Site Folder dialog box as the site's original folder is selected and the home page is designated. It is ready for import.

If a page exists called index.html or default.html, GoLive assumes it to be the site's home page and identifies its path in the lower part of the dialog box. If no home page is defined, or if you want to indicate another home page, go ahead to Step 7, clicking Import. Otherwise, go to Step 6.

6. If GoLive did not automatically identify your home page, or if it chose the wrong page, do one of the following:

- To handpick an existing page from within the folder you're importing, click the Browse button in the lower half of the dialog box and then navigate to and select the desired home page from within the folder you're importing. (Or, if the site's folder is in view, instead of browsing, you can drag that home page into the lower half of the dialog box.)

- To have GoLive create a new blank home page for you, check the Create Generic Home Page option.

The path to the home page appears in the dialog box.

7. Click Import. GoLive creates your new site document and presents you with a Save dialog box. The new site document is automatically named based on the name of the folder that you moved into the encompassing folder in Step 2. Be sure to save your new site document into the encompassing folder that you created in Step 1. Click Save, as in Figure 5-6.

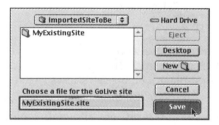

Figure 5-6: The new site document is created, named, and ready to save.

After you save the site document, GoLive opens it for you so you can get to work. (The site document you saved in Step 7 opens up to become the Site Window you see in Figure 5-8, which is shown in the following section.) GoLive also automatically creates a data folder in the same location as your original folder. A backup site document is also generated. Those folders and files are within the folder to which you saved them and not actually visible. The new Site Window is shown in Figure 5-7.

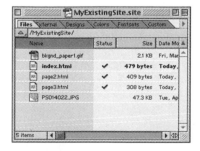

Figure 5-7: The new Site Window, in which you work. Notice that the original files are all reflected in the Site Window.

You are ready to begin working on the site. GoLive will manage the files on your hard drive via the Site Window, as it always does.

Downloading a Web site from a remote server

Do you already have a Web site, but it's on the Web server somewhere and you don't have a copy on a disk? (Maybe it's your own site, or maybe you've been hired to work on a site that's already live?) Not a problem. Just get the FTP info (address, username, and password) from the server's administrator and you can easily bring it down to your computer and into GoLive for further development. GoLive downloads the site's pages and media from the Web server, reads the site's structure, and builds a site document.

If you are just launching GoLive and a new page is automatically open, close that window as discussed earlier in this chapter. If any other Site Windows are open, close them to avoid confusion. Have the server access information handy. Then follow these directions to import an already active site via FTP download:

1. Choose File ➪ New Site ➪ Import from FTP Server.

   This opens the Import Site from FTP Server dialog box.

2. Enter the information needed to access the site you are importing. The person who hosts the site must supply this information (the same information needed to put the site on the Web in the first place). Figure 5-8 shows the settings you'll need for most FTP transfers.

   The following is more information about the settings shown in Figure 5-8 that you'll need for most FTP transfers:

   • *Server.* The server is the part of the URL that comes after `http://` and ends with .com, .net, .gov. .edu, or some other designation. If the domain for the site being imported begins with `http://www.golivebible.com`, the Import dialog box would have `www.golivebible.com` in the Server field.

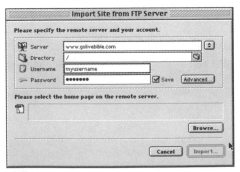

Figure 5-8: Sample information for importing a site from FTP

- *Directory.* The directory is the path to the site, including the final folder the home page resides in. If the URL to the Web site is simply the domain name, then no directory exists within the server folder and you must type a / here. For example, if the URL to the site being imported is http://www.golivebible.com, the Import dialog box would have / in the Directory field. If, however, the URL to the site being imported is http://www.golivebible.com/myexistingsite, the Import dialog box would have /myexistingsite/ in the Directory field.

Tip

If you're not clear on the path to directory of the desired site, click the Browse button (the Folder icon) in the Directory field. This connects you to the server, if you're not already connected, and shows you a list of what's in that domain's folder. Then select the site's folder and click OK.

- *Username.* This is the name necessary to log onto the Web server. Often, it's the name chosen by the owner of the site.

- *Password.* This is the password that goes along with the username. It's the password of the site owner or administrator. To enter it, click in the Password field and type your password. (For security, bullets replace the actual characters you enter.) If you forget to enter the password, upon connection attempt you'll be prompted for it before you are connected. Another option is to select Remember Password, which means you won't need to enter the password again when GoLive attempts to connect to the server.

- *Port.* If the host of the site tells you the port number is other than the standard, click the Advanced button, select the current number, and enter the port number.

- *Use passive mode.* The host of the site will tell you whether or not to check this box. Click the Advanced button to access this option and check it.

Tip

If you plan to access this server again, click the pop-up arrow next to the Server field and choose Add Current Server. The next time you want to access this server, choose the server from the same pop-up menu. You may have to reenter the password (unless you've checked Remember Password), but the server, directory, and username information will automatically fill in.

Now it's time to import the site. In the next step you will connect to the server. If you're not already connected to the Internet, make your connection now. (This is not a GoLive feature; connect to the Internet the way you usually do. Your computer may be set to connect as needed.)

3. Click the Browse button in the section that says, "Please select the home page on the remote server."

This makes the connection to the server and presents you with the Select Home Page dialog box.

4. In the Select Home Page dialog box, select the home page. (You may need to open a folder within the list in order to see the home page.) Then click OK, as shown in Figure 5-9. (Or just double-click the home page.)

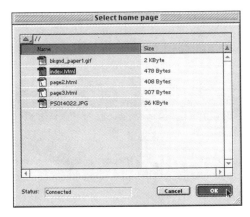

Figure 5-9: Selecting the home page file as the imported site's home page

The path to the folder appears in the dialog box.

5. Click Import.

6. In the Save dialog box, name the new site's folder. This folder's name doesn't have to comply with Web naming standards because it won't be transferred to the Web as part of your site in the end. Name it as you'd name any project folder on your computer.

7. Navigate to where you want GoLive to put the imported site's files, and then click Save.

Note   Be sure to keep Create Folder checked so your new site's files will land in one neat folder.

There will be a pause and you will see the Download Progress dialog box as GoLive downloads your files and creates the new site document. When your new Site Window appears, you can begin working on your site. There's no need to save at this point; that's been done for you.

GoLive imports files well; links do not break during import. However, if the imported site had broken links to begin with, your import will also have broken links. A quick glance at the Site Window alerts you to any errors; if errors are present, a green bug will appear. If a file becomes orphaned or is missing, you can see this from a quick glance at the right pane of the Site Window, under the Errors tab.

Cross-Reference   You can learn about fixing broken links in Chapter 11. To learn about fixing errors, see Chapter 25.

Your Site's Map

If you are working on a site that you just imported, you probably already have more than one page. It can be helpful to see the reality of that site's structure. Navigation view (Design ⇨ Navigation View) enables you to get a feeling for the flow of your existing pages, and then add more pages if you desire. Because you've imported the site, you should see all of the pages as they relate to one another. If you see only one icon, but you know your imported site is comprised of two or more linked pages, choose Design ⇨ Rebuild Hierarchy.

Links view (Design ⇨ Links View) shows you the flow of the links from each page. This is not just a cursory view, but a very detailed view found in the highest caliber of planning applications. Every single page shows every link to every page that it, in turn, links to. (You can see links to absolutely everything on each page, not just the page-to-page links; but for now, just focus on the page links.)

While in the Navigation or Links window, you can hide or show any branch of your site map to make viewing easier on large, complex sites. If the page has pages below it, above it, or to its side, a plus sign is visible. Click the plus sign to reveal those pages. When pages are hidden, or collapsed, they appear as icons behind the page to which they link.

To see if you have any other pages in the site that are not linked into it, choose Scratch Pane from the fly-out menu at the upper-right side of the window while in Navigation view.

To see if any of the site's pages are awaiting planned links, choose Pending Pane from the fly-out menu while in Navigation view. This opens the Pending pane in the right side of the window. Then click once on the page you are wondering about. All pages awaiting links from that particular page appear in the Pending pane. (Note that the Pending pane shows links that are due to link from the selected page, not into it.)

To see which pages directly link to a specific page, click that page to select it and then choose Spotlight Family from the fly-out menu.

Remember, you can always switch to the Navigation and Link views, review what your site looks like, and add or delete pages from Navigation view. This is helpful because, no matter how much you plan, Web sites grow and it's often necessary to add pages or groups of pages to it. For more on the Navigation and Links views, and other site planning, see Chapter 29.

You are ready to begin working on the site. GoLive will manage the files on your hard drive via the Site Window, as it always does.

Note

When you import a site that was created in GoLive, you may see an area on a page that has light gray or dotted oddly placed lines through it. This area is one that, upon the original page's creation, was a layout grid. The layout grid, or grid, is one of GoLive's unique strengths. You can easily turn this area back into a proper GoLive layout grid. Just select the table, so the Inspector shows you the Table Inspector, and then, in the Table tab, click the Table to Layout Grid Convert button.

GoLive 4 users will recognize the Navigation and Links views as a separation of what used to be the Site tab of the Site Window. The old Site tab's functions have been split up to provide a clearer picture. In the Site tab, linked pages were connected by solid lines and unlinked pages were connected by light dotted lines. Now, navigational lines are green and appear only in the Navigation view, and actual link paths are blue and appear only in the Links view.

Adding Pages to Your Site

You may think I'm getting ahead of things by talking about adding pages to a site when you haven't even had a chance to work on your first page. But you may not want to work on your home page first, and may prefer to begin with a secondary page instead. Or, you may have imported your site and only want to work on new pages now.

You can add pages to a blank site or to an imported site that has existing links. You have several ways to add pages to your site. You can add your pages loosely into the Files tab, or you can add them into the Navigation view so you can see where they fit within your master plan and track the progress of getting them integrated. You can add blank pages, or add preformatted pages — after you format them, of course. You can even add pages from other GoLive sites if you can view that site's Site Window on your monitor.

Of course, you can add pages at any time. You can also add any combination of pages: a few generic blank ones, some pages from one or more Stationeries, pages from another site, and so on.

Adding pages in Navigation view

Using the Navigation window to add pages to your site produces several benefits. Its site overview helps you envision your site in full, enabling you to determine how each page will relate to other pages. By adding pages here, you see how the page will fit into the flow of your site, using *navigational links* to define the page's relationship to another page. A navigational link quickly marks your *intent* to create a real, physical link between the pages. At any time you can open the Links window and see whether you've actually created the physical link. In fact, you can tear the Links tab away from the Navigation tab so you can see the two side by side.

You can also see the state of any page's intended links and completed links by opening the page, selecting the Page icon at the top-left corner, and then looking in that page's Inspector's Pending tab. This is a list, rather than a graphical view. It's covered in Chapter 29.

You can add as many pages as you like while working in the Navigator window. Of course, you can also leave this view, work on any aspect of your site, and return here any time in the future to continue adding pages. But even easier than that, you can double-click any page here to open it and work on it.

Follow these steps to add blank pages using Navigation view:

1. Open the Navigation view by choosing Design ⇨ Navigation View.

If the site is new, there will only be one page, the default page. Otherwise, click the plus sign to reveal all pages below the home page.

2. Click once on the page to which you want to add the new page.

3. Click one of the four new page buttons in the toolbar:

- *New Next* creates a page to the right of the selected page, designating a *sibling* page that will follow.

- *New Child* creates a page below the selected page, designating a child page that branches from the selected page.

- *New Previous* creates a page to the left of the selected page, designating a sibling page that comes before the selected page.

- *New Parent* creates a page on top of the selected page, designating a page that will lead down to the selected page.

If the site is new, the only page is the default home page, so you can only add children to it.

Figure 5-10 shows a blank site to which three child pages have been added. The yellow Caution Sign icon tells you the pages haven't been worked on yet. Notice that as the pages are created, they appear in the Site Window's Files tab, in a folder called NewFiles.

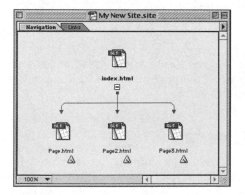

Figure 5-10: Three new blank pages added to a new site by clicking the New Child Page button within the Navigation view. The Site Window (behind) shows the new pages, too.

Alternately, you can add a new page by dragging a Generic Page icon from the Objects palette's Site tab or add a page based on a Stationery by dragging the Stationery from the Site Extras tab (if any Stationery has been created for your site). A dark line shows you where the new page will fall if you release the mouse. You can even give your page a head start by adding a Stationery page this way. Just drag the desired Stationery (after you create it, of course) from the Site Extras tab of the Objects palette, as shown in Figure 5-11.

4. Because the default "page" names are not very descriptive, you should name your page to help you visualize your site. Click the default name to select it, and then type a new name. It's important to keep the .html extension, so GoLive does not select that part of the name.

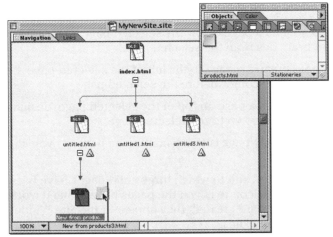

Figure 5-11: A new page being created by dragging Stationery from the Objects palette into place to the right of another page created the same way

Note   Don't be afraid to experiment. You can easily delete added pages if you're not happy with the results. Simply select the page you don't want by clicking it, and then click the Trash icon in the toolbar.

Adding pages to the Files tab

If you're not into visualization, you can add pages directly into the Site Window instead of using the Navigation view. One reason to do so is if you know you want to create a page but have no idea how it will fit into the scheme of things until after your site evolves. Because a page added via the Files tab doesn't have any intended links recorded, it won't appear in the Navigation view. However, it will appear in the

Scratch pane within Navigation view. Later, when you know where the page fits in, you can drag it from the Scratch pane into any position in the Navigation view.

You have a few ways to add pages to your site via the Files tab. You can create a blank new document using the File ⇨ New command, making sure you save it to the correct location on your hard drive. You can drag a page into the Site Window from anywhere on your hard drive; this copies a page into your site. Or, you can turn a page into Stationery and then drag the Stationery from the Objects palette.

Pages from the File menu

As with just about any application, you can create a new blank document — in this case, a page — by choosing File ⇨ New. When you use File ⇨ New, you begin your page and then save it using File ⇨ Save. However, when you save this page, you have to be careful to save it into the correct folder on your hard drive in order for it to be recognized within the site. If you're not comfortable with your computer's Save dialog box and filing system, this should not be your new-page method of choice.

Cross-Reference You'll find detailed instructions on saving a page started with File ⇨ New in Chapter 6.

Pages from Stationery

After you've created a basic Stationery template, you can easily drag a copy into the Files tab to begin a new page that contains the Stationery's elements. In fact, you can even add Stationery from another GoLive site — if you can open that site's Site Window on your monitor. To work on a page created from Stationery, all you need to do is double-click to open it, work as usual, and then choose File ⇨ Save to save your work.

To add Stationery to the Site Window, follow these steps:

1. If it's not already open, open the Objects palette by choosing Window ⇨ Objects.

2. Click the Site Extras tab, and then select Stationery from the pop-up at the bottom-right corner of the palette.

3. If you have more than one Stationery document, and cannot determine which one you want by the custom icon alone, move your mouse over the icons to see each Stationery's name.

4. After identifying the desired Stationery, drag it into the Files tab of the Site Window.

   If you begin to drag to the Site Window but the Files tab is not front-most, rest the mouse over the Files tab until it moves to the front and then continue to drag into the window files area. You can place the page directly within the Files tab, or place it inside any folder within the tab. You can also move the page anywhere else within the Files tab later on.

5. To customize the page's name, click its existing name and then type a new name, befitting of your current site. (Only the part of the name before the .html is selected, so you don't have to worry about typing over this important extension.)

Tip

To use Stationery from another GoLive site, open that site's Site Window, but make sure you can still clearly see your current site's Site View window. Then, follow the same steps for adding Stationery from your current site, except in Step 3 have the other site's Site Window active as you go to the Objects palette. That way, you'll see the other site's Stationery. Then drag that Stationery into place within your current site's Site View window. If you plan to use this page of Stationery often, you can turn it into Stationery within this current site, or you can drag the Stationery from the first site directly into your current site as Stationery.

Copying a page from another site

It is also possible to copy a regular page from another GoLive Site Window into your current Site Window. To copy a regular page from another GoLive Site Window, follow these steps:

1. Open the Site Window of the site that contains the desired page. Position it so you can still clearly see your current site's Site View window.

2. Locate the desired page, and then drag it out of its Site Window into your target Site Window.

   The original page within the first site remains in place, while an exact copy is added to the destination site.

Duplicating a page that's within your site

Yet another method of adding a new page to your site is to duplicate one already in your Site Window. To do so, you select a page within the Files tab of the Site Window and then choose Edit ➪ Duplicate. However, if the page you're duplicating contains linked graphics or files, or links to other pages, this can get sticky. It's far better to turn a page into Stationery first, and then use the Stationery. Saving a page as Stationery is covered in Chapter 6; it makes little sense to save a page as Stationery until after you've begun designing it.

Moving a page from your hard drive into your site

You can bring any page from another source into your site. The page doesn't have to be created in GoLive. To add a page into your site, you simply drag it into the Files tab of the Site Window. This automatically copies the page into your site instead of physically moving the existing page, so the original page remains intact. You can bring in a page regardless of whether it contains links.

Follow these steps to copy a page that has no links to other pages or graphics into your site:

1. Open the folder that contains the file so you can see it and drag it.

2. Have your Site Window in view.

3. Drag the file into the Files tab of the Site Window.

   The page is copied safely into your site and you're finished adding the page.

Follow these steps to copy a page that does contain links to images or other pages:

1. Open the folder that contains the file so you can see it and drag it.

2. Have your Site Window in view.

3. Drag the file, and all images or other media that belong to the page, into the Files tab of the Site Window. If the images and media are within a folder, you can drag the entire folder. GoLive will create a folder within the Files tab. If you don't locate and drag all of the associated files, the missing files are reported as orphans.

4. Because the file contains graphics, other media, or links to other pages, the Copy Files dialog box opens. In the Copy Files dialog box, approve the update.

5. Click the double-headed arrow at the bottom-right corner of the Site Window to open the right side of the Site Window, and then click the Errors tab to make it active. If any orphan files exist in your site, an Orphan Files folder will also exist. If any missing files exist, a corresponding Missing Files folder will also exist.

   If an Orphan Files folder exists, open it by clicking the arrow (Mac) or plus sign (Windows) beside the folder, and then drag the orphan files into the Files tab in the main section of the Site Window. This copies those files into the current site.

   If a Missing Files folder exists, open it by clicking the arrow (Mac) or plus sign (Windows) beside the folder. Then you need to locate the missing files and copy them to the Files tab.

Cross-Reference You can learn more about missing and orphan files in Chapter 25.

Note As you view your files in the Files tab in the Site Window or in Navigation view, you may notice a green bug on some. The green bug is GoLive's way of letting you know that somewhere on that page a link is broken or incomplete. (GoLive is very good at watching your site's integrity at all times.) Green bugs, and how to correct them, are discussed in Chapter 11.

Saving Your Site

As you add files to your site, GoLive records the changes. Changes are also recorded when you create folders and move files. Actually, everything you do within the Site Window is automatically saved. However, it's not a bad idea to manually save once in a while, just in case.

Just have the Site Window active and choose File ⇨ Save.

Deleting Pages

You have three ways you can delete pages from your site. You can delete files from your site but still maintain their links — just in case you change your mind. You can delete them without having GoLive continue to track the file's links, but still have them on hand in case you want reinstate them. Or, if you're certain you want to delete them, you can delete them fully by moving them out of GoLive altogether and directly into your computer's Trash/Recycling Bin.

The safest way to delete a file is to have GoLive continue to maintain its links. To do this, you drag the files into the site trash. GoLive always tracks links of files that are dragged.

To delete a file but maintain its links, follow these steps:

1. Click the double-headed arrow at the lower-left corner of the Site Window to open the right Site Window panel. Then click the Extras tab.

2. Drag the file(s) to be trashed from the Files tab, or Navigation or Links view, into the Site Trash folder, which is shown in Figure 5-12.

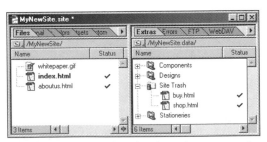

Figure 5-12: Two files that have been moved into the Site Trash folder

3. Click OK when GoLive asks to update all affected files.

Organizing Pages in the Files Tab

As you add pages and graphics to your site, it can become hard to find things within the Files tab. One common way to organize your files is to create one folder for all of your pages and another folder for all media. An alternate method is to make one folder for each logical section of your site. You can make those folders now or add them at any time. Either way, as you move files into a folder or between other folders you create, GoLive updates the links for you. To add a folder in which to keep your pages, drag the plain Folder icon from the Site tab of the Objects palette and drop it into the Files tab. Or, while the Files tab is active, click the New Folder button on the toolbar. Click the name of the folder (untitled folder) and type your own name for it.

You know that the links are being maintained because the files are updated en route to the trash. If you select a file that is deleted this way, and then choose Window ⇨ In & Out Links, you can see that all links remain intact. When a file is dragged to the site trash this way, dragging it back to the Files tab or Navigation view updates the links again, restoring them. Therefore, you can restore the file(s) just by reversing the process and dragging the file(s) from the Site Trash folder back into the site's files. You don't have to return the files to the same place from which they are deleted because GoLive updates the links as you return them to the site's structure.

The next method of deleting files either moves files to the site trash or directly to your computer's trash, depending on the preference settings you choose. Unless you've changed GoLive's default, a deleted page is moved to your site's Site Trash folder, rather than to your hard drive's Trash/Recycle Bin. This enables you to move it back into your site if you change your mind. Files in your hard drive's Trash/Recycle Bin remain available for restoration only until you empty the Trash/Recycle Bin. Files in the site trash are not counted among the site's files, and are not exported.

To delete a page without maintaining links, follow these steps:

1. Click the page in the Files tab, or Navigation or Links view, to select it.

   To delete multiple items at once, select all of the items using your system's usual methods: Shift-click (Mac) or Ctrl-click (Windows) as you select pages, or drag a marquee around the pages. (In Windows, you can also easily select contiguous pages by Shift-clicking.)

   If you are in the Files tab of the Site Window and are in Dual-pane mode, the file is in the left pane.

Caution

When you delete a page in Navigation view, all pages below it and next to it are removed as well.

2. Click the Trash button on the toolbar or choose Edit ➪ Clear (Mac) or Edit ➪ Delete (Windows). When in Navigation view or Links view, you can also press your keyboard's Delete/Backspace key.

3. A dialog box asks if you are sure you wish to move this file to the site trash. Click Move (Mac) or Yes (Windows). The page will move to the Site Trash folder. If you've changed GoLive's default to have files go directly to your hard drive's trash, the dialog box will ask if you are sure you want to move this file to the Finder Trash (Mac) or the Recycle Bin (Windows). If you've unchecked the Show Warning option, you will not see the Warning dialog box.

Tip

To delete the file without bothering with the warning, press Option (Mac) or Alt (Windows) as you issue any of the delete commands in Step 2. The file still moves to the site trash or hard drive's Trash/Recycle Bin, as set in your preferences. I recommend that you do not change the default deletion options. Instead, if you are ever absolutely certain you want a page fully deleted, you can remove the file from the site trash later on.

If you use the Trash button to delete a page, deleting a page that is linked to from other pages will create a bad link on each of those other pages. In this case, you'll see a green bug appear on the affected pages to inform you. You then need to open these pages and break the link or remove the object (text or graphic) that acts as the link.

When you are certain you no longer need a file in your site, or no longer wish to keep it just in case, you can move it from the site trash to your computer's trash. This breaks all links for good. Next time you empty your computer's trash, the file will be gone for good (unless you have a backup of it somewhere).

Here's how to remove a file from the site trash:

1. Click the double-headed arrow at the lower-left corner of the Site Window to open the right Site Window panel. Then click the Extras tab.

2. Open the Site Trash folder by clicking the arrow (Mac) or plus sign (Windows) next to the site trash.

3. Select the file or files to be deleted.

4. Click the Trash button in the toolbar or choose Edit ➪ Clear (Mac) or Edit ➪ Delete (Windows). (You won't be asked to confirm this deletion.)

In case you're curious about GoLive's Trash options, Figure 5-13 shows you the preferences for this.

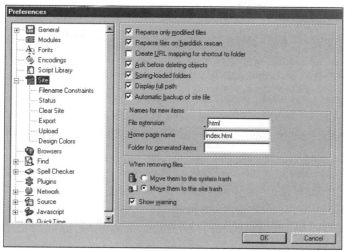

Figure 5-13: GoLive's Trash preferences — options for handling files you no longer want in your site

No Undo command exists for undeleting pages or files, and the History palette does not track deletions. However, depending on where the files have been moved, you may be able to restore a deleted page or file as described in the next section, "Restoring Deleted Files."

Actually, all file deletion works the same way. You can remember this method to delete any unused graphics from your site, too. However, you have a better way to clear your site of unnecessary items. It's aptly called the Clear Site command.

Note   If you have a file in your site that links to files that were not copied into your site, that file causes you to have orphan files (listed in the Errors tab of the right side of the Site Window). When you delete a page from your site, whether by moving it to the site trash or to the hard drive's trash, the orphan files disappear.

Restoring Deleted Files

Depending on how you deleted a file, you can either restore it fully, partially, or not at all. If you dragged your file to the site trash, dragging it back into the site's structure restores the file and its links fully. If you used the Trash button, dragging the file back into the site structure restores it partially but loses track of some files. If, prior to using the Trash button to delete a file, you set the file removal preference to move your files directly to the computer's trash, your files are definitely no longer tracked and may no longer be on your hard drive.

To restore a file from the site trash, follow these steps:

1. Open the Site Window's right pane by clicking the double-headed arrow at the window's bottom-right corner.

2. Click the Extras tab in the right Site Window pane to bring that tab forward.

3. Reveals the Site Trash folder's contents by clicking the arrow (Mac) or plus sign (Windows) to the folder's left.

4. Drag the file from the site trash back into the desired location within the Files tab.

   To restore multiple files at once, Shift-click (Mac) or Ctrl-click (Windows) and then drag them all to the left pane.

5. A dialog box informs you that the links to the restored pages need to be updated. Click OK. The updating success depends on the deletion process, as follows:

   • If you originally dragged the file to the site trash, all links between pages and files for the restored page are accurately corrected to reflect the page's location — even if you move the file to a folder it wasn't in prior to its deletion. The file's place in the site's hierarchy may be lost, though. You can discover this by checking the Scratch pane of the Navigation view (as explained in Chapter 29).

   • If you used the Trash button, links from other pages to this restored page should be restored, leaving those pages bug-free. However, links from this restored page may become inaccurate. If you see any green bug warnings, you'll need to repair those links. You can learn more about this in Chapter 11.

   • If you have moved the file to your hard drive's trash and not emptied it, you can restore it to your site by dragging it back into the Files tab, although all links are lost. However, if you've already emptied the Trash/Recycle Bin, your only option is to try hard drive file restoration using a third-party utility. That's beyond the scope of this book. If you can successfully restore the file to your hard drive, you can add the file to your site again by dragging it back into the Site Window. Because dragging a file into the Site Window actually copies the file, rather than moving it, you will still have the original copy of the file in the Trash/Recycle bin. This works the same for deleted graphic files and such.

✦   ✦   ✦

Setting Up Your First Page

As you begin to design your Web page, you'll need to set some global page settings, such as page name, background color and image, text and link colors, and page margins.

In GoLive, you'll find the overall settings in the Page Inspector. To get to the Page Inspector, enter Layout mode and click the Page icon at the top left of the page, directly under the Layout tab icon. In the lower-left corner of the Inspector, which must be open, you'll see the word Page to let you know you're in the Page Inspector. The Page Inspector has four tabs. The physical page settings are under the Page tab. As with a word processor or design program's page, these settings are only for the current page. Each page can have its own page settings.

After the common basics of the page are set, you can continue to develop the page in any way you wish, or you can save the page and use it as a model for future pages. Actually, no matter what you choose to do with your page after you've begun to set it up, you'll still need to save it. GoLive automatically saves the changes you make in the Site Window, but it's up to you to save your pages after you do anything you wish to keep.

Are you wondering about using the page as a model for the future? There's the option of saving your page as Stationery. Stationery works like a template, so you can easily create multiple pages that all start with the same common look. (It's never too early to save a page as Stationery because you can always save another version of it later on in the page's development.) There is also one other way to save a page, so it becomes your default page whenever you choose the File ⇨ New command. Because this is an option, this chapter tells you how to use it, although this method isn't all it's cracked up to be. If you're not the designer type, but still want an impressive Web site, you can use one of GoLive's premade sites. Just choose a template and then edit the text and swap the pictures.

Opening a Page

In order to work with any page, you must first open it. You have several ways to do this, as follows:

✦ **From the Site Window.** Under the Files tab (the first tab) of the Site Window are all the pages you have created so far. To work on your home page (the default page that visitors first see) double-click index.html. Otherwise, double-click the page you wish to develop. You can also open the page by pointing to the document as you right-click (Windows) or Control-click (Mac) and choose Open in Adobe GoLive from the document's contextual menu.

✦ **From Navigation or Links View.** While inspecting your site's navigation flow in Navigation or Links View, double-click the page.

✦ **From anywhere.** No matter where you are, you can open a page by choosing File ➪ Open and then navigating to your site's folder, down into the folder named for your site.

Note   If the page you wish to work on does not exist yet, you can add a new page. To learn about adding a page to your site, see "Adding Pages to Your Site" in Chapter 5.

Opening the Page Inspector

As you work in GoLive, either initially setting up the page (as covered in this chapter) or setting the page up later on, you'll find yourself returning to the Page Inspector. Because of this, many roads lead to the Page Inspector. You'll know you're in the Page Inspector when the word Page appears in the lower-left corner. (The name of the Inspector is always reported there.) Three tabs are present (plus one ColorSync tab on the Mac), but all count as the Page Inspector.

You have two ways to activate the Page Inspector after the page is open and in Layout mode. You can click the Page icon at the top-left corner of the page's window (under the Layout tab), or you can press Tab. (If the Inspector window is not open, choose Window ➪ Inspector to open it.) Whichever way you activate the Page Inspector, press Tab again to return to your prior Inspector mode. (The Inspector reverts back to inspecting for the object currently selected on your page.)

If the Inspector is not open, you can open it as you switch Inspector modes. While your cursor is anywhere in the page, right-click (Windows) or Control-click (Mac) to bring up the contextual menu and choose Document ➪ Page Properties, as shown in Figure 6-1. (If you point to the Page icon when you call up the contextual menu, the Page Properties command appears directly in the menu instead of under a Document submenu.)

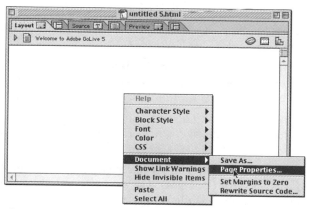

Figure 6-1 Opening the Page Inspector with a contextual menu

Note The Inspector is only functional in Layout mode. In Source and Outline modes, you have no page icon to click and the Tab key has different functions.

Naming your page

Just like any document, Web pages have names. But Web pages actually have two names. The name of your document is not the name that appears in the top of the window, as you'd expect from your normal day-to-day document creation. Instead, the name of your document becomes part of the URL (or address) that people enter in order to arrive at the page. The name that appears at the top of the browser window is, instead, the *title* you give it from within the page itself. If you haven't noticed page titles before, go to any page on the Web and look at the top of the document window.

The title doesn't just make the page look pretty. It is also the name used when the page is bookmarked or set as a favorite. It is also recognized by search engines, helping others to find your site. Therefore, a good page title should clearly and concisely describe the page's contents.

Here are some ideas for choosing a title:

✦ Keep it concise. This way, your page is easily identifiable when it's bookmarked. (The title becomes the bookmark name.)

✦ Spaces in a title are okay. They remain viewed as spaces when part of the title. (It's the spaces in a file name that are converted to symbols, such as %20.)

✦ If you forget to give the page a title, it will bear the default title "Welcome to Adobe GoLive 5." (GoLive's Site Report, covered in Chapter 25, helps ensure this won't happen to you.)

✦ In Internet Explorer, the title appears in a user's browser history for a number of days. Therefore, a descriptive title can help users return to your site days later, even if it wasn't bookmarked the first time the site was visited.

✦ The title is often displayed at search engine sites, and it is almost always a key factor when your site is indexed by these engines. Therefore, a descriptive name may help bring people to your site.

✦ Title lengths have limits. After a certain number of characters, a title may be cut off within the window's name or bookmark. For example, with Internet Explorer 4.5 (Mac) the title cuts off at 47 characters.

To give your page a title, follow these steps:

1. Click anywhere on the phrase "Welcome to Adobe GoLive 5" at the top-left corner of your page, just to the right of the Page icon. Select the existing text and type in the name of the page, as shown in Figure 6-2. To edit the text, instead of replacing it all, place your cursor over the text and double-click the I-beam within the title area. You can then add additional text or select and replace specific parts of the text.

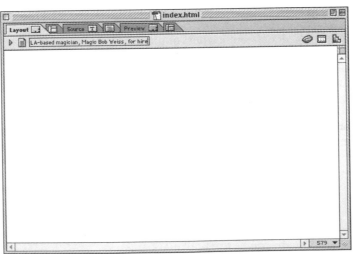

Figure 6-2: Click the title area to replace the default page title.

2. When you are finished typing your new page title, press Return, Enter, or Tab. This sets the title and also moves the cursor onto the body of the page, in case you wish to begin entering text onto your page. Alternately, you can use the mouse and click anywhere on the page to deselect the title and go on with your page creation.

You can also title your page in the Inspector. To do this, have the Inspector open and then click the page icon in the page window's header. This turns the focus of the Inspector to the Page Inspector, as noted by the word Page at the bottom-left corner. Switch to the Page tab if you haven't already done so. Now type the new title into the Page Title field at the top.

A Look into the HTML

At this early stage of page design, while the HTML is sparse, taking a look at some of your page elements can help you understand the interaction between GoLive's visual interface and its generated HTML code. You have several ways to check in on the HTML code, as follows:

✦ If the palette containing the Source Code tab (shown in the following figure) is open onscreen, click this tab to see the HTML. (If it's not open, choose Window ➪ Source Code to open it.) You can even edit the title right in this tab. Simply click in the tab to activate the HTML, and then select and edit the current title. Just be sure to leave the `<title>` and `</title>` tags intact.

✦ Another way to see the HTML is to click the Source tab of your page window. You will see your title between the `<title>` and `</title>` tags at the top of the page within the `<head>` and `</head>` tags. You can also edit the title by selecting any of the current title text and then typing over it.

✦ You might also try switching to the Outline tab to see where the title falls into place. To see the title, click the large blue arrow of the `head` tag's block so that you can see the title tag, and then click the `title` tag's blue arrow. Again, you can edit the title here. Just click the current title, select it, and then type as desired.

A new page title as it appears in the Source Code tab

Adding Background and Text Colors

After giving your page a title, the next logical step is either to set your background or to set your text and link colors. For me, having a background in place helps me make decisions about text and link colors. I always want my background to feel right for my site's focus and the images on the pages.

Perhaps you have a specific image to use as a background. Or maybe your priority is the color of your text. Some people feel the text color is more important and then prefer to choose a background that works well with the text.

Even if you're using Cascading Style Sheets (CSS) to set the look of your site, set text and background colors using the procedures explained in this section, too.. That covers you for the browsers that don't recognize style sheets. If you don't set these colors, the default colors in the Page Inspector are used. When you set the overall text colors for your page using the Page Inspector, the colors are noted only once on each page and the dreaded font tag is not added. (The font tag causes problems for style sheets and clutters your code, as explained in Chapter 8.)

Setting a background color

The background of your page plays a large part of setting the page's mood. Background can be a solid color, a texture, or a graphic. Colors are provided in GoLive's Color palette, which shares the Objects palette window by default.

Note   You might think that using an image as a background precludes you from needing a color. Indeed, they do seem redundant, but there are good reasons to use both. For example, say you're using a light text on a dark background image. If your reader's browser doesn't have image viewing on or if the image fails to load, your light text won't have the same contrast and may not be visible.

Setting a color as a background

Using a color as a background is incredibly easy. To set a page's background color, follow these steps:

1. Open the Page Inspector.

2. In the Page tab, double-click the color swatch next to the word Color in the Background section. (Don't bother to check the Color option because GoLive does this automatically.) This selects the color swatch, as noted by the dark border inside it, and opens the Color palette.

3. In the Color palette, click the tab that contains the set of colors from which you want to select a color.

4. Click the desired color, as shown in Figure 6-3. In the six far-right color tabs, click directly on the desired color. Alternately, in any color tabs where there's a slider, you can click the slider or drag it to set the color. If you drag the slider, the color sets when you release the mouse. (Clicking in the preview area at the left doesn't set the color.) If you are not happy with a color you chose, simply click another color.

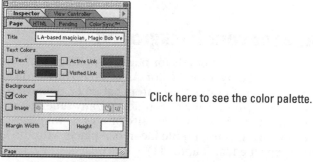

Click here to see the color palette.

Figure 6-3: To set a background color, after selecting the Inspector's color swatch, click the desired color.

Note When you switch color tabs after clicking the background color swatch in the Inspector, the color you select doesn't always take hold. If the Inspector's color swatch does not remain selected, you can either select it again and then click the desired color, or you can drag the desired color from the large preview area of the Color palette into the Inspector's color swatch, or you can drag it directly onto the Page icon in the page window.

5. Save the page (File ➪ Save).

Tip You can also set the color by dragging the color from the Color palette onto the Page icon at the top-left corner of your page.

As an added flair, you can use a GoLive Action (or your own JavaScript) in order to have your page's background color to change upon a mouse action or as part of an animation. To learn how to use Actions see Chapter 18. Background color can also be defined as part of a style sheet. See Chapter 17 to learn about Cascading Style Sheets.

Removing a background color

At any time, you can change a page's background color the same way you add a color.

To revert back to GoLive's default white background, open up the Inspector and uncheck the Color option in the Background section. Your last selected color may remain in the color box by the option, but the page reverts to white. Checking the Color option again reapplies the color last tried.

The History palette can also help you remove a background color, if you also want to remove all other actions you've done since adding that background color. To learn about the History palette, see Chapter 2.

Using an image for your background

Images are commonly used as backgrounds for pages—perhaps more than you realize. Using a color provides only a solid color. Any rich textures you see on a Web page are actually graphics. Besides the customization or richness a graphic achieves, there's another benefit to using a graphic. If at any time you want to change your background across the entire Web site or on several pages, you can easily do so simply by changing your graphic file in one place, with the help of the In & Out Links palette (explained in Chapter 11).

You have several ways to place an image as your background. But regardless of which method you use, you can try one image after another to see each image's effect. The newly placed image simply replaces the last one used.

No matter which way you choose to set your background image, I cannot stress enough that it is always safest to place your images in the Site Window before using them. The background image, like all other page elements, should be placed in the Site Window prior to placement on the page. Placing the image in the Site Window tells GoLive to manage that file. (See Chapter 2 for more about Site Window management and getting files into the Site Window.) If the image you wish to use is not yet in the Site Window, open the folder that contains the image and drag the image into the Files tab of the Site Window.

 Backgrounds are important to the overall feeling of any site, so, with the help of some terrific people, I've included a variety of backgrounds on this book's CD-ROM. They're all ready for you to use. Each has a Read-Me file that spells out the copyright arrangement for the use of these graphics.

Adding a background image by dragging

If the image you wish to use is not in the Site Window yet, open the folder that contains the image and drag the image into the Files tab of the Site Window (or choose Add Files from the Site Window's contextual menu). The background image, like all other page elements, should be placed in the Site Window prior to placement on the page. Placing the image in the Site Window tells GoLive to manage that file.

What Makes a Good Background Image?

By Lynne LaMaster, Specialized Publishing (www.specialpublish.com)
Certified Expert in Photoshop

Background images can make or break a Web site. Remember, when you design your site, it needs to be focused, and that means that the background needs to add to the general purpose of the design and not just be tossed in.

File size and format

The background image needs to be as small as possible in file (K) size, hopefully no more than 15K, but 7K or 8K is much better. Background images are usually in either GIF or JPEG format. Theoretically, a PNG format could also be used, but so far PNG is not widely used because only the newest (5.0) browsers recognize it (and older browsers never will, unless the appropriate plug-ins are developed).

Tiled backgrounds

Background images *tile*, which means they repeat over and over, like a tiled pattern on a wall or a floor. The trick is to make the background appear as one image without "seams" showing. In other words, you don't want visitors to notice where the edges meet.

You can use this tiling to your advantage if you design a small image to repeat over and over in a pattern. I have seen a background image as small as 1 pixel by 1 pixel that was even an animated GIF that changed colors so gracefully and gradually that you hardly even noticed until the purple had become blue, and then green, and so on. A good example of a seamless tiled background is the foxtrot border at www.foxtrot.com/comics/index.html.

The right graphic can also look like a texture and be so realistic that users want to touch the screen to see if it really is burlap or velvet. As a matter of fact, background images are often called *textures*. An elegant, rich texture can lend to the intangible message of a site and even promote reading of the information there.

Poorly done graphics send an amateurish message and look bad. They reduce the visitor's ability to get the message of the site. Two frequent problems are the repeat being too visible and the graphic too busy. Poorly tiled images can be distracting and even offensive to viewers' eyes, rendering a site unreadable. So, use caution when adding a tiled background, and preview its tiling effect before you add content to your page and as you add content. A good image for tiling has soft edges that blend

Cross-Reference See Chapter 2 for more about Site Window management and for more about getting files into the Site Window.

The fastest way to set your image as the background is to drag the image from the Files tab of the Site Window onto the Page icon in the header section, which is just below the tabs of the Page window. When a black outline appears around the Page icon, release the mouse. The effect of the image is immediately visible. If you don't like that image, drag another onto the Page icon.

Tip

If you're experimenting with various images, it is understandable if you don't want to copy all of them into the Site Window. This is a rare case where I suggest breaking the rules. Perhaps the fastest way to try an image is to open its folder beside your page and drag each image onto the page icon in turn to quickly see how each will look. But . . . when you've selected your final image, or narrowed down the possibilities, don't forget to put those final images into the Files tab of the Site Window and then to drag the selected image onto the page icon to set it.

Placing a background image using Point and Shoot

In many cases, GoLive's unique Point and Shoot is the greatest time-saver. However, in this case, it actually involves extra steps.

To set the background using Point and Shoot, follow these steps:

1. Position the Site Window and Inspector so that you can see both of them at the same time. Have at least the top part of your page window in sight, as well.

2. Open the Page Inspector as explained in the section "Opening the Page Inspector," earlier in this chapter.

3. Check the box next to the Image option in order to activate the Point and Shoot button (the curly button) and add the phrase "(Empty Reference!)" to the image's path field.

4. Click the Point and Shoot button and drag toward your image file within the Site Window. When the tip of your arrow touches your destination file and the file darkens to let you know it's selected, as shown in Figure 6-4, release the mouse.

Browsing from the Inspector to place a background image

With the Browse button, you can use your computer's Open dialog box to locate and place a background image.

Tip

Some users prefer the browse method because with it you don't have to open the file's folder and drag the file into the Site Window. Also, this is another way to check out the results of using many images without copying all of them into the Site Window.

To place a background image using the browse method, follow these steps:

1. Open the Page Inspector as explained in "Opening the Page Inspector," earlier in this chapter.

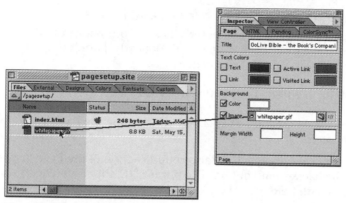

Figure 6-4: Point and Shoot is one way to select a background image.

2. Check the Image option in the Background section of the Page Inspector to activate the background image area and its Browse button.

3. Click the Browse button, which is the small folder icon to the left of the image's field.

4. Navigate to the desired image, click the image file name, and then click Open. The background immediately appears on your page.

Caution

As always, if you browse to a file that has not yet been placed within your Site Window, that file is not copied into the site. Therefore, GoLive cannot manage or upload it. If the file you selected was within your Site Window, be sure to copy it into the Site Window now, as directed in Step 5, or remember to use the Clean Up Site command before you upload your site. (See Chapter 25 to learn about the Clean Up Site command.)

5. *(Optional)* If you have any doubt that the file you selected was within your Site Window, click the double-headed arrow at the bottom-right corner of the Site Window to open the right side of the window.

If no Orphan Files folder exists, you're all set.

If an Orphan Files folder does exist, open the folder. If the file you just selected as your background is listed, it was not within your Site Window. Drag the file from the Orphans folder over to the Files tab. GoLive will ask if you'd like to update the page to which you just added the background image. Agree to the update. GoLive will copy the file into your Site Window.

Manually entering the path to a background image

Entering the path through your computer's files to your background image by hand is definitely more of a programmer's method. Honestly, I don't think the GoLive team expects you to do this. But you can.

Follow these steps to enter a path to the image file:

1. Open the Page Inspector as explained in "Opening the Page Inspector," earlier in this chapter.

2. Check the Image option in the Background section of the Page Inspector to activate the background option. The phrase "(Empty Reference!)" appears in the image's path field.

3. Select the phrase "(Empty Reference!)" and type in the path to the desired image. Press Enter or Return when you've finished typing.

Removing a background image

If after trying out an image or two you opt not to use any image and prefer to use a plain color instead, you must break the link to the last image you tried. To do so, follow these steps:

1. Open the Page Inspector as explained in "Opening the Page Inspector," earlier in this chapter.

2. Uncheck the box next to the Image option.

Note   If you have an image already assigned to your page, it will override any color. To have the color take effect, click the Page icon, open the Inspector (now the Page Inspector), and then uncheck the option for Image in the Background section of the Inspector.

Choosing your text and link colors

You can make any text, down to the individual character, any color. However, for design consistency, it is advisable to set one overall text color. Traditionally, links are a different color to help distinguish them. Actually, links can appear in three possible colors. One color sets them apart from the regular text as a link. A link may become another color when the user is actively clicking the link. Then a link may change to another color after it has been clicked, to show your visitors they've already followed that link.

Creating Nontiling Backgrounds

By Lynne LaMaster, Specialized Publishing (www.specialpublish.com)
Certified Expert in Photoshop

Sometimes tiling will undo the effect you seek. What if you want a background image, but you don't want it to tile? One way is to use a Cascading Style Sheet (CSS). But pre-4*x* browsers don't support style sheets. However, not all browsers will support a nontiling background. Here's the trick to achieve this effect without CSS: Start a new document in Photoshop or other image editing program and set up a page that has a large image size for your total background. It should be about 1,200 pixels × 1,000 pixels or a length to match the content that will be on the page. (A pixel is a unit of measurement; each inch has 72 pixels.) Design within the upper-left corner of the background area, in an area about 600 pixels wide by 300 pixels high or smaller, as shown later. Leave the rest of the background area empty. You can fill it with a solid color, or make it transparent if it's a GIF. As the user widens the browser, chances are that only more of this solid area will come into view. Although this background will actually still tile when the browser window becomes wider than the graphic's full width, it's unlikely anyone will see the repeat because this requires an *extremely* large screen.

When designing a page, you should understand that your visitors might not actually see your chosen text colors. By default, browser settings usually allow each Web page to specify the text colors displayed, which means your choices as the designer of the page are honored. However, each user may elect to view your page with the browser's own default text color settings. Users may even override the browser text color defaults by choosing their own color preferences. For example, a person who is color blind may choose a text color that he or she is more certain to see against any background color.

Although you have no guarantee that your design will be honored fully, it is still nice to set your own text and link colors, providing the best potential look for your page. Just remember, as you design to take browser defaults into account. Try to be consistent with standard protocols, not to contradict them. For example, because royal blue is the color that both Netscape browsers and Internet Explorer use for links not yet visited, if you use royal blue for your visited links, your viewers may wrongly believe they have not been to your pages. Likewise, Netscape browsers and Internet Explorer use a purplish-eggplant color to represent visited links, so you want to bear this in mind. Because these defaults may change with any update, as a rule it is best to notice the default colors of the common browsers and either honor those colors or use entirely different colors. WebTV, by the way, does not use colors to represent links, so you needn't worry about that browser.

To set the overall text color for your page, follow these steps:

1. Open the Page Inspector as explained in "Opening the Page Inspector," earlier in this chapter.

2. In the Page tab, double-click the color swatch next to the word Text.

   This selects the Text color swatch, as noted by the dark border inside it. It also opens the Color palette.

3. In the Color palette, click the tab that contains the set of colors from which you want to select a color.

4. Click the desired color. In the six far-right color tabs, click directly on the desired color. Alternately, in any color tab where there's a slider, you can click the slider or drag it to set the color. If you drag the slider, the color sets when you release your mouse. (Clicking in the preview area at the left doesn't set the color.) If you are not happy with a color you chose, simply click another color. As soon as you click a color, GoLive automatically checks the Text option in the Page Inspector and places the selected color in the Text color swatch, as shown in Figure 6-5.

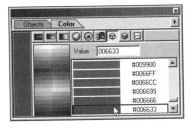

Figure 6-5: Setting the default color of a page's text to a Web safe color from the Web Color List (Windows)

5. Save the page (File ➪ Save).

Note   If the color doesn't take hold, either click the Color swatch in the Inspector again and reselect the color again, or drag the desired color from the large preview area of the Color palette into the Text color swatch within the Page Inspector.

To set the color of any of your links, repeat the preceding procedure, clicking the appropriate color swatch. GoLive lets you set the colors for three types of links:

✦ **Link.** One not yet visited.

✦ **Active Link.** A color that flashes for a moment to indicate that you've actually clicked that link. In case you're wondering, the active link doesn't have a user-defined default in Internet Explorer or Netscape.

✦ **Visited Link.** One that has already been followed by this particular visitor or has already been followed by a user of this computer and browser who is viewing your site.

You can come back and repeat the procedure at any time to change the text or link colors in any particular page.

Making Side Strips

By Lynne LaMaster, Specialized Publishing (www.specialpublish.com) Certified Expert in Photoshop

Side strips are often used as a way to simulate a framed site, adding a nice designer touch to the left or top of the page. These top and side strips are usually a color, or texture, often with a drop shadow.

For a strip that has a side stripe, create a graphic that is about 1,200 pixels wide by about 72 pixels high. Make sure your stripe is as wide as you want. For example, you may want it to accommodate your buttons. Be sure to leave room for another color to serve as the background.

Follow this guideline to create a top stripe with a drop shadow.

For a top stripe, do the opposite: Create a graphic that's about 72 pixels wide by about 1,200 pixels long.

Setting Page Margins

By default, any text you type, or any object you place on a page, is placed about 6–8 pixels from the left side of the page and about the same distance from the top of the page. This is intentional because without the space, your page contents can come so close to the user's browser controls that your message becomes too hard to read. (In good page layout a bit of well-placed space can go a long way.)

However, there may be times when you don't want this default space because you will be adding your own margins. For example, on the layout grid you have the ability to place your page's elements exactly where you want them. Therefore, the preset margin is not needed, and adds an inexact margin to your page. Tables are another example. By using a table border, alignment, cell padding, and the like, you can control your contents' positioning. And, of course, using Cascading Style Sheets (including floating boxes), you have absolute control of positioning.

So, how do you remove the default margins? In GoLive 5 it is easy, as both margin settings are entered within the Page Inspector.

The fastest way to remove the default top and left margins, setting them to 0, is to point your cursor anywhere in the page window as you Control-click (Mac) or right-click (Windows) and choose Document ⇨ Set Margins to Zero.

Alternately, you can remove the margins in the Inspector. The Inspector provides the added opportunity to set a page margin of any size. To manually remove or alter the default top and left margins of the browser window, follow these steps:

1. Open the Page Inspector as explained in "Opening the Page Inspector," earlier in this chapter.

2. To set the distance from your contents to the left side of the browser, enter the desired number in the Margin Width field. To remove all distance, enter **0**.

3. To set the distance from your contents to the top of the browser window, enter the desired number in the Height field. To remove all distance, enter **0**.

 In Layout mode, you'll see your page contents move flush against the left edge. This provides you with a good idea of your layout, but you won't see any difference in the space at the top. You'll see that in the browser.

If you decide you're not happy with the spacing you've selected and you want to revert the page back to the browser offset defaults, open the Page Inspector again and delete the zeros (or other numbers) from the margin fields.

Saving Your Page

Anytime after you begin working on a page, it's a good idea to save it. GoLive automatically records the changes you make to the Site Window, but saving the page is up to you. (Which is good, because it gives you the control.)

Saving your page can be as easy as File ➪ Save, or it can take a few extra steps, depending upon how you chose to start your page.

Saving a page opened from the Site Window

If the page you are working on was opened from the Site Window, it is already written to your hard drive and recognized as part of the site. Therefore, to save any changes you make to it, simply use the File ➪ Save command (⌘-S for Mac or Ctrl+S for Windows) before closing the page's window. If you close the window without saving, GoLive asks you if you'd like to save your changes.

 This simplicity is the reason I strongly recommend always creating your pages from within the Site Window and opening them from there. To learn more, see Chapter 5.

Saving a new page opened from the file menu

If you started your new page by using the File ➪ New command, your page is not yet recognized as part of your site. In order for GoLive to manage that page as part of your site, you must save the page into the Site Window.

Here are the steps to save a new page:

1. To save the work you have done on your new page, choose File ➪ Save or press ⌘-S (Mac) or Ctrl+S (Windows). This opens a Save dialog box.

2. In the Save dialog box's naming field, "untitled" is preselected, while the .html (or .htm) extension is not preselected, so just type your page name and the .html extension intact, unless your site requires the alternative .htm extension. (Your site host can tell you whether to use .hmtl or .htm as your extension.)

Note

You can actually save your page without changing the default name. Just like any other page in GoLive, you can always change its name later. To do so, you click the page's name within the Files tab or Site tab, and then select the unwanted text and type your new name over it. When GoLive asks for permission to update the changed page and all pages that link to it, allow this update.

3. Click the GoLive icon (button) and then choose Root from the pop-up menu, as shown in Figures 6-6 and 6-7. This brings you directly to the root (main) level of the site folder for the site you're currently working on.

Figure 6-6: Use the GoLive pop-up button (the GoLive icon) in the Save dialog box to ensure a page is saved to the folder that houses your site. (This is the Mac Save dialog box with Navigation Services off.)

The GoLive icon that provides the pop-up menu is only available when you have a Site Window open. If you have GoLive running, but no Site Window open, you will only have the computer's regular save options. The GoLive icon is in a different place depending on whether you're using Windows, or whether you're using a Mac with or without Navigation services.

Figure 6-7: Save to the Site Window's Files tab (also known as the Root folder) via the GoLive pop-up button in the Save dialog box. (This is the Windows 98 dialog box.)

4. Click Save. This saves the page to your site's folder on your hard drive and enables GoLive to recognize and manage your new page. You can continue to work on your page after you save it, or you can close it and move on.

Caution

Saving your page into the site's folder works only when the Site Window is open. If you don't have a Site Window open, you can still save a file to the site's folder. You'll have to manually navigate to the correct folder — the folder on the same level as the ".data" folder. However, if you do this, GoLive will not recognize the page properly as part of the site. Likewise, if you save the page to the hard drive and then move it to the site's folder, it will not be recognized. In these cases, you must tell GoLive you've added the page to the Root folder. To do so, if there are no graphics or other media on the page, when you later open the Site Window, click in the Files tab and then click the Update (checkmark) button on the toolbar. (This is the same as choosing Site ➪ Rescan "Yoursitename.") The pages should immediately appear in the Files tab. If there are images or other media on the page, you create orphan files and will need to move the orphans from their listing in the left side of the Site Window over to the Files tab. This procedure copies them in. This is much messier than simply starting with a Site Window, saving the orphan files directly into the Site Window, and properly collecting objects into the Files tab prior to use.

Setting the Publish status

Now that you have begun work on your page, consider setting or updating the Publish status. You can change the Publish status while the page is open or when it is closed.

To set the Publish status of a page, follow these steps:

1. Click the page once within the Files tab to select the page. You can also click it to select it while viewing your site structure in the Navigation View or in the Links View.

2. In the Inspector, acting as the File Inspector, choose one of the following options from the Publish pop-up menu:

   - *Never* tells GoLive never to upload this page to the Web server when doing any type of automatic upload. You can still manually upload it, though. You might use this status while your page is in development and then change the Publish status to Always or "If referenced" upon completion of the page. You can also use this status when a page is not intended for use on the server (for example, on a page you'll never actually use in your site, such as a graphic source file or a media file that will be hosted on a streaming server, or a page you are using as a model).

   - *Always* tells GoLive to upload this page to the server when appropriate, as you do any type of automatic uploading. This is the default. Keep it at Always if you want the page uploaded to the Web server, no matter what stage it is in and whether it is linked into your other pages or not.

   - *If referenced* tells GoLive to upload this page (or file) during an automatic upload when appropriate, only if the page is actually connected to some other page in your site. This prevents pages that are not yet an active part of your site from wasting upload time and server space.

As you're editing a page, you might want to set the status to Never so that the page does not accidentally replace a viewable version that is already live. Publishing a page in progress can be embarrassing. When the edit is complete, you can change the status to If referenced so that GoLive can upload it intelligently.

The Publish status is not a part of the page, but of the Site Window, so you don't have to resave the page if you change the state while the page is open.

Cross-Reference   You can learn more about how the Publish status comes into play in Chapters 27 and 28.

Reusing Your Page

Because you'll probably use the same text and background colors throughout a site, it pays to set up a blank page with these settings once, and then use it as a common starting point for future pages. GoLive provides two options for this. One is to set your page as the default New Page setting. The other is to turn it into Stationery. The default new page is an application-wide preference, so it affects every new page you create in GoLive. Stationery offers more flexibility.

A blank page with just background, text, and link colors set can be a great starting point for other pages. However, you may wish to include other elements covered in later chapters, such as a grid or a navigation bar, on your default page or Stationery. That's fine; saving a page as Stationery or setting it as the default new page now doesn't mean you can't change your mind later. You can always reset the New Page option or resave a page as another Stationery when you add more elements that you want to appear throughout the site.

Making your page the default new page

You can choose one page as the new page starting point by making it the page that opens via the File ➪ New command. The only limitation is that this page shouldn't contain any links or graphics because links break if you save your newly made pages to a folder other than the folder that the original page is in. To reuse pages with links, Stationery is the correct option, as links are automatically updated on Stationery pages.

When you set a default page, you set the look of every new page you create by choosing File ➪ New in GoLive for the current site and for every other site you work in. That is, as long as GoLive can find the default page. If you move the default page or delete it, GoLive reverts back to its own default.

Any changes you make to this page, even after setting it as the default, will be part of each new page.

New pages created from within the Site tab of the Site Window do not contain these default page settings.

Follow these steps to set your page as the New Page default:

1. Create your page, set it up as desired, and then save it.

   Name the page in a way that tips you off to its being a template. For example, call it newpage1.html, whitebkg.html, or such.

If you save this page to the root level of your site folder, as with your other pages, it can be stored and backed up along with your site. Don't store this page in the Stationery folder, as Stationery is available only within the for which it was created, not for all other sites. However, if you store the page within a site, remember that if you remove that site from your hard drive, the page will no longer be available, and GoLive reverts back to its own new default new page. Another option is to save the default page in another folder that you don't move.

2. Choose Edit ➪ Preferences and click General.

3. Check the box next to New Document.

4. Click the Select button.

5. Navigate to the page you just saved and click Open to choose it.

6. In the Preferences dialog box, click OK.

After you set this page as your New Document, a copy of it opens whenever you choose File ➪ New to begin a new page.

If you edit the original that you selected as the default, your changes are reflected on all new pages from that point on. If you decide you're not happy with this default page, you can always come back and choose another default new page.

Saving a page as Stationery

Pages saved as Stationery can be called upon time and time again as a starting point for your new pages. This enables you to have multiple pages start off with the same basic elements. You can have many different Stationery pages and then pick any page as your starter. (See "Adding Pages to Your Site" in Chapter 5.)

Unlike the default new page, Stationery is stored within a specific site and is available only within that site. However, you can always copy a Stationery from one site to another. (See "Sharing Stationery Between Sites" later in this chapter to learn how.)

You can save a page as Stationery when you do the initial save, or you can turn an existing page into Stationery at any point.

You can save a page as Stationery during the initial save early in the page's development and then continue to save copies as the page progresses, or alter the saved Stationery page.

To save your new, unsaved page as Stationery, follow these steps:

1. Open the Save dialog box as usual, by choosing File ➪ Save.

2. In the Save dialog box, select the "untitled" and type a descriptive page name over it, leaving the .html extension intact. (If your Web server requires .htm instead of .html, change it here.)

Tip

If your Web server uses .htm instead of the preset default (.html), set GoLive's preference to write that for you each time you create a new page. Choose Edit ➪ Preferences and then choose Site. Just edit the entry for File Extension. (While you're at it, if your Web server prefers "default" instead of "index" for the server's default page, change this too.)

3. Click the GoLive icon and then choose Stationeries from its pop-up menu. This brings you directly to the Stationeries folder (that's in the data folder) for the site you're currently working on.

The GoLive icon that provides the pop-up menu is in a different place depending on whether you're using Windows, or whether you're using a Mac with or without Navigation services. The GoLive icon is available in your Save dialog box only while you're using GoLive and have a Site Window open. (It's the same one as shown back in Figure 6-6.)

4. Click Save.

Note   When you save a page as Stationery, it is saved into your site's folder, into the .data folder. In the Site Window, the page is reflected in the right side of the window, in the Stationeries folder, as you're about to see in the next section, "Editing Stationary." But, unless you're editing the page, you'll be using it from within the Objects palette.

You have several ways to turn an existing page into Stationery. You can simply convert your existing page, or you can turn a copy of the page into Stationery, leaving the original intact. Either way, the Stationery functions the same.

To turn an existing page into Stationery, follow these steps:

1. Close the existing page.

2. Click the double-headed arrow at the bottom-right corner of the Site Window to open the right section of your Site Window, and then click the Extras tab to make it active.

3. Drag the page from the Files tab of the Site Window into the Stationeries folder within the Extras tab, as shown in Figure 6-8. (If the Extras tab is not the active tab, rest over the tab as you drag. It will come forward, enabling you to continue the move.)

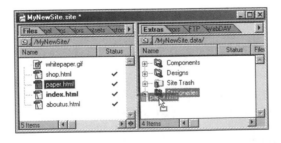

Figure 6-8: Move a page into the Stationeries folder to turn it into a reusable Stationery template.

Upon placement in the Stationeries folder, the icon of the page changes from that of a regular document to that of a pad. (If it doesn't change immediately, don't worry, as the icon will update in time.)

This page no longer exists as a regular page in the Files tab. To create a page based on this page, you'll create a new copy of it via the Object palette. Another alternative is to keep the page you currently are working on but also to create a copy as Stationery. You have two ways to do this: Do a Save As or copy as you drag the page to the Stationeries folder.

Note   You'll have the same result if you create the Stationery without making a copy and then create a new page from that Stationery.

Follow these steps to create a copy of an existing page as Stationery using Save As:

1. When your page is at the stage you desire, choose File ➪ Save As.

2. In the Save dialog box, select the "untitled" and type a descriptive page name over it, leaving the .html or .htm extension intact.

3. Click the GoLive icon and then choose Stationeries from its pop-up menu. This brings you directly to the Stationeries folder for the site you're currently working on.

4. Click Save.

Because you use Save As instead of Save, your original page is still a normal page within the Files tab, while a copy is saved to the Stationeries folder for future page generation.

To create a copy of an existing page by dragging, follow these steps:

1. Close the existing page.

2. Click the double-headed arrow at the bottom-right corner of the Site Window to open the right section of your Site Window and then click the Extras tab to activate it.

3. You will actually make a copy of the page you just worked on. If you are working in Windows, press Ctrl as you drag the file into the right pane. If you are on a Mac, press Option as you drag the page into the right pane. If the Extras tab is active, drag directly into the Stationeries folder. If another tab is active instead, drag the file onto the Extras tab, rest for a moment until the Extras tab moves forward, and then drop your page into the Stationeries folder.

As you drop the page icon into the Stationeries folder, a small plus sign (+) at the back end of your cursor informs you that your page is being copied. Your original page remains in the Files tab of the Site Window as a page on your site. The copy lands in the Stationeries folder, and its icon changes to symbolize a reusable Stationery pad. (If the icon doesn't change immediately, don't worry, as the icon will update in time.)

When you want another new page based on this Stationery, add a new page from this Stationery into your site. (See Chapter 5 to learn all about adding pages.)

As you work on the original page, only that original page is affected. (It was not turned into Stationery; the copy you made when you dragged became the Stationery.)

Note On a Mac, you actually have one more way to create Stationery, but I don't recommend it. You do it by selecting the page in the Files tab, and then checking the Stationery option in the File Inspector. However, that doesn't move the page to the Stationeries tab and make it accessible in the Objects palette, which can cause confusion. (Additionally, pages in the Files tab may be uploaded, depending on your upload settings, and this page would just unnecessarily take up space on your server.)

Each Stationery icon in the Site Extras tab of the Objects palette should appear with a custom icon depicting that page. If, instead, you see a generic GoLive page icon, GoLive simply hasn't generated the custom icon yet. Give GoLive a chance. Eventually, you'll see a full-color thumbnail of the page there. Otherwise, you can "edit" the Stationery to instantly cause the icon to be drawn. You don't really have to edit it — just open it, add a space somewhere, delete that space, and then save the "change."

Editing Stationery

After you create a Stationery, you can still edit it. After an edit, all new pages started from that Stationery will reflect the changes. For example, you can add several more items, such as a logo, other graphics, a navigation or button bar, a copyright, and so on. Pages you've already created from that Stationery will not be affected.

To edit a Stationery, follow these steps:

1. Click the double-headed arrow at the bottom-right corner of the Site Window to open the right section of your Site Window and then click the Extras tab to activate it.

2. Open the Stationeries folder so that you can see its contents. To do this on a Mac, click the blue arrow next to the folder. In Windows, click the plus sign (+) next to the folder.

3. Double-click the Stationery that you want to edit. A dialog box asks you whether you'd like to modify the existing Stationery or create a new one. Figures 6-9 and 6-10 show you this dialog box for Windows and for a Mac, respectively. Click Yes (Windows) or Modify (Mac). This action opens the existing Stationery page.

4. Make any changes to the page, as desired.

5. Save the changes the same way you save any page — by using File ➪ Save.

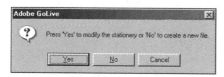

Figure 6-9: The Modify Stationery dialog box (Windows)

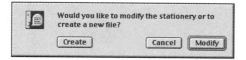

Figure 6-10: The Modify Stationery dialog box (Mac)

The next time you drag a copy of this Stationery from the Objects palette, the new page will begin with the new look.

Note   Editing a Stationery does not change any pages you have already created using that Stationery. Stationery is a master starting point, not a master template.

Sharing Stationery between sites

If you develop a Stationery page in one site and want to use it in another site, you can easily do so. The process is similar to that of copying any page from one site to another.

To share stationary between sites, follow these steps:

1. Open both sites — the site that contains the Stationery and the site you want to copy to.

2. Click the double-headed arrow at the bottom-right corner of the Site Window to open the right section of your Site Window and then click the Extras tab in order to activate it.

3. Open the Stationeries folder so that you can see its contents. To do this, click the blue arrow (Mac) or plus sign (Windows) next to the folder.

4. Drag the Stationery from its Stationeries folder in the original Site Window to the Stationeries folder of the destination Site Window.

As usual, when you drag a file into a Site Window, it is copied. Therefore, this procedure copies the Stationery page, rather than actually moving it out of the original folder.

✦   ✦   ✦

Using a Grid as a Layout Tool

The GoLive layout grid is a designer's dream, enabling you to arrange the elements of a page pixel by pixel, or move page elements around independently of one another. Until the GoLive layout grid came along, arranging elements on a page in such a way was just not possible when designing Web pages.

A regular Web page works somewhat like a word-processing document, enabling only line-by-line object placement. Tables let you line up objects a bit more precisely, but only by deal-ing with table cell sizes and relative alignment — not fun for a designer, and certainly not conducive to creative flow. The layout grid truly broke new ground in Web-design flexibility. It's often greeted by rounds of loud *oohs* and *aahs* when demonstrated.

Welcome to the grid, a unique page element on which you can place or align objects independently of one another. On the lay-out grid, you can drag elements into place or use arrow keys to nudge them into precise position. Welcome to the rare world of true creative design on the Web.

This chapter tells you all you need to know about the GoLive layout grid: the how-tos, pros, cons, caveats, and tips.

Introducing the Layout Grid

HTML-wise, and therefore browser-wise, a layout grid is actu-ally just a normal table that GoLive builds on the fly as you place elements upon it and move them around. To build this table on the fly, GoLive simply adds a parameter it calls `cool` inside the opening table tag. In GoLive the `cool` parameter is used and recognized, giving you the benefit of a layout grid, but when a browser sees the `cool` parameter it simply ignores it. No harm is done; no extra work takes place.

When you look at the HTML code on a page that contains a grid, you see the standard table tags. As you add content to your grid, GoLive generates some spacer tags. Although in an intricate layout, this may look busy or complicated, the spacer tag is actually just a simple tag that helps provide the most accurate element placement possible. GoLive uses spacer tags because of a glitch in Netscape browsers that causes the browsers to have problems drawing tables. Internet Explorer simply ignores these spacer tags.

Some HTML purists frown upon the grid, advocating the use of tables instead. The grid *is* a table. It's simply a much easier type of table to work in because GoLive creates the table's cells for you. However, because you may not want to keep the grid code in your page, when you export your page you can easily tell GoLive to strip its proprietary tags and/or the spacers.

I must share one piece of information with you up front before you begin using a grid. Because the layout grid is actually a table, it is not recognized by browsers that don't recognize tables. This eliminates viewing by users of Version 2.0 or older browsers. Some people advocate designing for the lowest common denominator, or browser, but doing so eliminates most of the cool stuff you can do on the Web. These days designing for old browser versions is like producing television shows in black and white in case some viewers don't have color television sets yet. The reality is that fewer than 10 percent of all Web users are on browsers that do not recognize tables (and therefore, the grid).

Why use a layout grid?

When designing for print, you can plan a page by using placeholders when you don't have the actual graphics or text yet. You can also place a block of text on a page, and then place another elsewhere, and add a graphic anywhere else — all independently of each other. Then you can select page elements and drag them around or use relative alignment to set them into place. The layout grid enables you to use placeholders and rearrange blocks on Web pages, too.

Without a layout grid, a Web page works somewhat like a word-processing document, where content must be placed line by line. Your cursor even looks and acts like a text tool's I-beam. However, Web pages are also very different from regular word-processing documents. In a word-processing document, the text wraps to the next line when it hits the right margin of the printed page. But in a plain Web page, the line expands to fit the width of the browser window. In other words, the *user* determines the right margin by sizing the browser window. You *can* add custom line breaks by using a soft return or a paragraph marker, but even that's cumbersome and time-consuming. Besides, those tags have formatting limitations.

 Cross-Reference   To learn more about formatting text in GoLive 5, take a look at Chapter 8.

Want to position a few separate text phrases? A grid makes precise text and object placement easy. Just place a text boxtype next to your sentence inside the text box and then place another. You can resize the boxes and drag them into place anywhere on the grid. Want to place a graphic beside some text? You can put the text in one table cell and the graphic in another cell, and then figure out the alignment. Or you can use a grid, which lets you set a right margin simply by dragging the size of a text box, and then drag your graphic into place right next to the text. The number of words that fit within a line inside a text box and the length of the text block varies depending upon other factors, but you can control the sides and know your graphic will stay put.

The bottom line is that the grid provides much of the same design control you are used to if you've done page layout.

> **Tip**   You might want to add a grid to your page prior to saving it as stationery. That way, you are able to easily replicate page after page with the same look without having to place and resize the grid each time.

Tips for placing a grid

Grids are really cool and very easy to use but, to make your page most efficient, don't use them where you really don't need to. Don't begin every page by placing a full-page grid. Instead, think about what you are putting on the page. If the top of your page is just text spanning your page, there may be no reason to put it in a grid. Instead, you could simply type and format your text. Then you could add a grid for the part of the page where you want to do some creative object positioning. When you again have need for only a simple stretch of text, you can again type that text on the regular part of the page, below the grid. You can then add a second grid after that text. Or you may prefer the text to be placed within a simple table in order to confine the text between specific margins. In that case, you can use a table before, after, or between grids.

When you place a grid, you might as well begin by having it span the entire width of your page. If it turns out that you don't use the right side of the page, you can always reduce the grid later. (See "Optimizing a Layout Grid" later in this chapter.) If you won't need the grid across the entire page, you can have it span just part of your page, and then use alignment to move the grid and its contents. (See the "Aligning a Layout Grid" section later in this chapter.) Or, you can place a table on your page, and then place a grid in any of the table cells.

You cannot place other elements next to a grid. HTML dictates that a table, and therefore a grid, must have its own line. Therefore, the following rules are true:

✦ You cannot place a grid next to another grid. (It would make more sense to have a single wider grid anyway.)

✦ You cannot place a grid next to a table. That is, you can't do so directly on a page. But you can achieve a similar effect by placing a grid within any cell in a table.

✦ You cannot start a line with text, and then add a grid to that line, or type text after a grid on the same line. However, no reason really exists for wanting to do this because you can put your text on the grid instead, and gain full control over its placement.

However, you *can* do one of the following with grids:

✦ **Place one grid beneath another.** You might do this if some of your material spans the entire width of a page (or much of it) and other material above or below only spans a narrow area. You might also do this if some material needs to be on one side while other stuff should be on the other. In that case, one grid can be left-aligned and the other right-aligned.

✦ **Place a grid within a table cell.** The common scenario for this is when certain graphics (such as buttons) need to remain tightly grouped. Those graphics are placed in one table cell, while the grid is placed in another cell, enabling items to be freely placed within the gridded cell's area. For example, you might create a two-column table with no visible borders and then place a navigation bar in the left column and a grid in the right. Figure 7-1 shows an example of this. (You can also find the live version of Figure 7-1 at www.golivebible.com.)

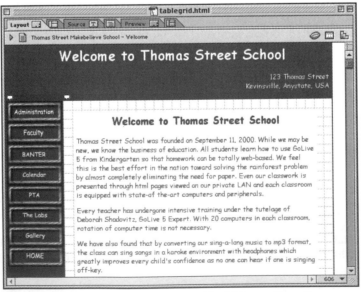

Figure 7-1: You can place a layout grid within a table cell.

✦ **Place a grid on top of another grid.** However the only time it makes sense to do this is when you have a reusable object — a Component or Custom Object — that is created on a grid, and you want to place it on a page in an already gridded area. (To learn about reusable objects, see Chapter 14).

Caution

Don't get carried away placing grids in tables or tables on grids. In most cases it is not necessary and creates unnecessarily complex and redundant code.

No set rule exists as to whether it is faster or better to use one large grid or several smaller grids. Part of the issue is how many objects are on the grid. Apparently Internet Explorer can have problems with more complex tables, and the grid reaches this complexity at about 20 objects. That said, if some objects are exactly aligned to the same grid line, they create less complex code than the same number of objects that are not aligned. If your grid contains many elements, you can check Special ⇨ Document Statistics to see the file size of the page. If your page grows to over 75K or so, and the design is on a grid, experiment with breaking your grid into smaller grids, which may generate less code. Of course, the grid may very likely not be responsible for a large page size. Some other ways also exist to keep your page-size down. I mention several throughout this book, as they come up.

Cross-Reference

Other factors go into the decision of whether to use a grid as well. Chapter 13, which covers tables, helps provide a greater understanding of the differences between the grid and a table.

Adding a layout grid to your page

You can place a grid anywhere on a page. It can cover your entire page, or just a small area. For example, you can use the regular line-by-line page structure for the first few lines, add a grid as the foundation for the next part of your page, add some more lines, and then end with another grid.

To add a layout grid to your page, you simply drag the Layout Grid icon from the Objects palette, which is shown in Figure 7-2. If the page is blank, the grid snaps to the top-left corner. If other elements exist on the page, including empty lines, you choose where to place the grid.

Figure 7-2: The Layout Grid icon on the Objects palette

To add a layout grid to your page, follow these steps:

1. If the Objects palette is not already open choose Window ➪ Objects palette to open it.

2. If the Basic tab is not the front-most tab, click it to bring it forward. (The Basic tab is the first tab.)

3. Drag the Layout Grid icon on to your page, as shown in Figure 7-3.

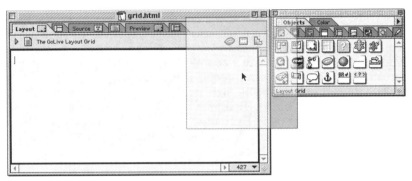

Figure 7-3: Dragging a layout grid onto a page (notice the cursor flashing at the top-left corner of the page; this is where the grid begins)

4. Save the page.

If you're placing the grid on a totally blank new page, you don't actually get to drag it into place because the only place it can land is at the cursor, which is flashing at the top-left corner on the first (and only) line. The grid snaps into place inline with this cursor. After you have more lines, a table, or another grid on your page you have more options for placing a grid.

When placing the first grid on a page, you can position it lower by adding more lines by pressing Shift as you press Enter/Return, and then dragging the grid to one of those lines. This action inserts <br> tags before the table to move it down. However, because you're probably moving the grid down to add lines of text above it, you might as well enter that text first. You can enter that text by simply typing. After you place a layout grid you can resize it and set its alignment.

Removing the default page margins

When you place a grid on your page, you should notice that it doesn't quite touch the top or left side of your page layout window. That's due to a default browser off-set, or margin. When text or images are placed directly on a page, they look awkward touching so close to the browser controls. The default offset of seven to eight pixels helps to balance the page. But when you're working on a grid, you have the ability to place your page's elements exactly where you want them. Therefore, the margin is unnecessary — and it can also upset the balance of your page.

To place your grid flush against the top and left margins of the browser window, choose one of the following easy methods:

✦ Control-click (Mac) or right-click (Windows) and choose Set Margins to Zero from the Document submenu.

✦ Control-click (Mac) or right-click (Windows) and choose Document ⇨ Page Properties. This opens the Page Inspector. Then enter **0** in each of the margin fields (or just in the one you want to have no margin for).

✦ With the Inspector open, click the Page icon at the top-left corner of the page, and then enter **0** in each of the margin fields, as desired.

If you change your mind for some reason, open the Page Inspector again and delete the zeros from the margin fields. This reverts the page back to the browser offset defaults.

Resizing a Grid

When you drag a new layout grid from the Objects palette to your page, it comes in as a 200 by 200 pixel square. You can make it any width or length you need it to be. One common size accommodation is to widen the grid immediately so it spans your full page. Another is to size it to fully fill a table cell. Yet another may be a wide, but short grid on which you can stagger design elements.

You cannot lock a grid size. It sometimes grows to accommodate elements you add to it. If the layout grid grows, you can use the History palette to remove the item that caused it to grow and return the grid to its original size.

You can either resize the grid visually, by dragging it, or more precisely by entering measurements into a dialog box. Both methods are explained in this section.

Resizing the layout grid visually

Follow these steps to resize the layout grid by dragging:

1. Select the layout grid by moving your mouse over any edge of the grid, and then clicking when the cursor icon gains a box-like symbol (the object selection icon) at its tail, as shown in Figure 7-4. (If you just placed the grid, it is already selected so you can skip this step.)

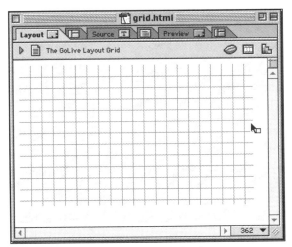

Figure 7-4: To select a grid, click when your cursor turns into the object selection icon.

When the grid is selected, handles appear on the right, bottom, and lower right corner.

2. Move your mouse over the appropriate handle until the mouse becomes an arrowhead, and then drag the handle until you achieve the desired size. You have the following options:

   • To widen the layout grid, move your mouse over the right handle.

   • To lengthen the layout grid, move your mouse over the bottom handle.

   • To widen and lengthen at the same time, move your mouse over the handle in the bottom-right corner.

As you drag, a dotted line shows you the new size, while the original outline and handles remain in place (see Figure 7-5). After you release the mouse button, the grid takes on its new size.

3. Save the page.

Tip

Once you know where the resizing handles are located and what the light blue arrowhead looks like, you can resize the grid in one step. Without selecting the grid, simply move your mouse over one of the three handle areas. Even though the handles are not visible, the resizing arrow appears when you move over it. When it does, click and then drag the handle.

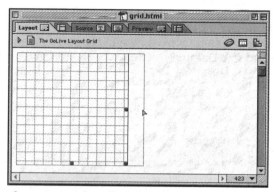

Figure 7-5: A handle being dragged to widen a grid

As you resize your grid visually, it may help to have feedback about its size. You can get a feel for the size of the grid by sizing the page, by using the ruler, or by viewing the page's size in the Inspector, as follows:

✦ A pop-up window at the bottom-right corner of your page window reports the width (in pixels) of your window (see Figure 7-6). You can set the size of the window to the size you want your page to be; then, as you drag the grid, you can see how it fits.

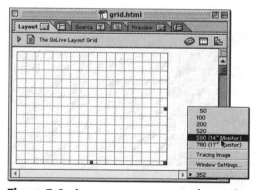

Figure 7-6: A pop-up menu on each page's window helps you know the size of your page.

Note

The pop-up menu on each window offers suggested sizes for the most common monitors. Using these sizes helps ensure that your pages fit well within most users' viewing areas. The 14-inch monitor size is the most common. Therefore, it is suggested you keep your pages between 560 and 600 pixels in width. GoLive's recommendation is 580 pixels. Wider pages cause many viewers to have to scroll sideways.

✦ A ruler in the document window also enables you to track the size of your grid, page, and other elements. To show the rulers, click the ruler icon in the top-right corner of the page's window, as shown in Figure 7-7. When you drag to resize the grid, the grid size is noted by the white section of the ruler, as shown in Figure 7-8.

The ruler button

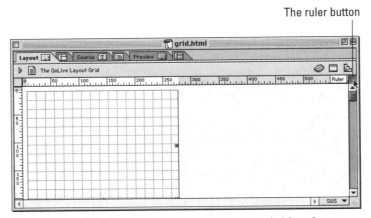

Figure 7-7: Click the ruler button to see top and side rulers.

White area

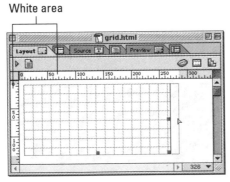

Figure 7-8: The white area in the ruler shows the size of a grid when it is resized.

✦ You can use the Inspector to measure the size of your grid. As you drag the grid, its size is reflected in pixels in the Inspector, as shown in Figure 7-9.

Figure 7-9: The Layout Grid Inspector dynamically reports the current grid size.

Resizing the layout grid numerically

If you know the size you want your layout grid to be, the fastest way to size it is to enter the size in the Inspector. If your grid is to be the full width of the page, then you definitely know the width to set for your grid.

Follow these steps to resize the grid using the Inspector:

1. Click anywhere on the grid to turn the Inspector into the Layout Grid Inspector. (If the Inspector is not open, open it now.)

2. Select the number in the Width field of the Layout Grid Inspector to widen the grid or the Height field to lengthen the grid. Then type a new number.

   The new grid size is entered. When you tab or click anywhere in GoLive to do whatever you do next, or press Enter or Return, the grid jumps to its new size.

3. To size the grid in the other direction simply type in the other proportion.

   Again, the new grid size is entered and is reflected as soon as you move on.

4. Save the page.

Aligning a Layout Grid

The layout grid, like any element on a page, can be aligned left, centered, or right. This may seem like an innocuous property, but it can greatly affect the look of your page. Why? A layout grid is a container for all the elements you place on top of it. Therefore, when the Grid moves, it carries along all elements that are on it. If you inadvertently choose an alignment option from the toolbar while the grid is selected, you might find yourself wondering why stuff on your page moves every time the browser window is resized. That's when the knowledge in this section comes in handy. It may also come in handy if you place a grid inside a table. The movement of a grid and its elements may be even more noticeable when the grid is inside of a table because the table can move in addition to the grid being able to move within the table's cell.

When you place a grid directly on a page, it aligns to the left side of the window by default. But you can change the alignment of a grid in several ways. Changing a grid's alignment doesn't affect the items that are on the grid. They just go along for the ride when the grid moves.

The method you use to align your grid depends upon where your grid is placed: The first point to understand about aligning a grid is that a grid's alignment is somewhat relative to the container it is placed within. For example, consider the following possibilities:

✦ If the grid is directly on a page, the size of the page (which in reality is the user's browser) can affect its placement. This doesn't matter as long as the grid remains aligned left, but affects your page when the alignment is changed.

✦ When a grid is within a table's cell, the grid always travels with the table. Additionally, the grid travels with the cell it is in. Finally, the grid may move according to the alignment of the cell that holds it.

✦ If a grid is placed within another grid, it moves along with the underlying grid.

Setting a grid's alignment

By choosing an alignment option in the Layout Grid Inspector, you can set a grid's alignment. However, this alignment remains relative.

The Align pop-up menu provides the master control for a layout grid. Three options for alignment exist:

✦ **Default** enables the grid to be aligned based upon the alignment settings of whatever container the grid is placed within. For example, if the grid is on a line by itself the toolbar's alignment buttons can control its alignment. If you place the grid within a table cell, the cell's alignment controls the grid.

✦ **Right** tells the grid to always keep its right edge up against the right edge of the container. For example, if the grid is directly on the page, as the user widens the browser the grid and its contents move right; if it's in a table, as the table cell widens, the grid moves right.

✦ **Left** makes sure the grid is kept against the left edge of whatever container it is within. This option may seem redundant because the grid starts out aligned against the left edge, but it isn't. Because resizing the browser window doesn't change the left side of the browser, this is the safest option for keeping your grid's elements where you want them.

The effect of left and right alignment is demonstrated in the following two figures. The same page is shown twice using Preview—first in a window that is 580 pixels wide (see Figure 7-10) and then as the window becomes narrower (see Figure 7-11). Notice how the images move closer together. The left image is attached to the left of the browser, being set to left alignment in the Layout Grid Inspector. Likewise, the right image is aligned right. The text above the images is not on a grid, but directly on the page. It wraps with the browser edges. All in all, none of the elements on this page is permanently placed. If all the elements were on one layout grid they would all remain in place in relation to one another.

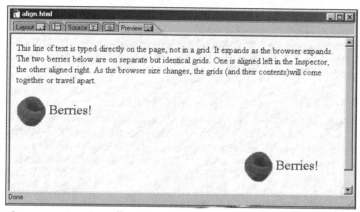

Figure 7-10: A left-aligned grid and one that's right-aligned, as displayed in an average window

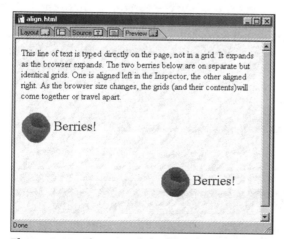

Figure 7-11: The same left-aligned and right-aligned grids, when the browser window narrows

Aligning a grid on a line

If a grid is part of a line, its position is relative to the user's browser window. Browser windows grow toward the right while the left edge remains in place. Therefore, if you align a grid to the left, the grid remains where it is put. However, if you align a grid to the right, that binds the right edge of the grid to the right edge of the browser window. When the user expands his browser window, the grid moves toward the right, carrying it further away from the left edge and any elements that are at the left of the page. The objects that are on the grid remain in place relative to one another, but are carried along with the grid. If you choose center alignment for a grid directly on a page, the grid remains centered but the center changes depending upon the right edge of the browser window.

You have two ways to choose a grid's alignment when it is directly within the page. You can use the Align pop-up of the Layout Grid Inspector or you can use the toolbar.

If you choose right or left alignment in the Layout Grid Inspector, this setting takes control and the toolbar buttons have no effect. Otherwise, you can leave the Layout Grid Inspector's option at Default alignment (which happens to be its default). Then you can use the alignment buttons on the ruler in much the same way as you align text in a word processor.

Tip   As an alternative to the alignment options in the toolbar you can choose Type ➪ Alignment ➪ Left/Right/Center.

To align a grid using the toolbar, first select the grid as an object by moving your cursor over the edge of the grid and clicking when the cursor becomes the object selection icon. Then click the desired toolbar button. The three buttons are shown in Figure 7-12. To align the grid at the left edge of the browser window click the left-alignment button. To center it between the edges of the user's browser, click the center alignment button. To place the grid's right edge against the browser's right edge, click the right-align button. Figure 7-13 shows you the effect of each alignment.

Alignment buttons

Figure 7-12: The three alignment buttons on the toolbar affect a grid's alignment when the grid is part of a line.

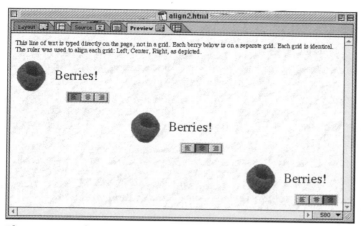

Figure 7-13: The effect of changing a grid's alignment, as seen in Preview mode

Tip

If you use a layout grid over your entire page and choose left alignment, you avoid alignment issues. All of your page's elements are stable within the grid. A grid does not expand when a user expands a browser. The background simply appears and remains blank.

Aligning a grid within a table

The important concept to understand about aligning a grid within a table cell is that the table itself can move around depending upon its settings. Tables are subject to the same alignment controls and issues that layout grids are when the grid is placed directly on the page.

The control you have for a grid within a table is the control over how the grid aligns within the cell that houses it. If you leave the Layout Grid Inspector's option at Default alignment, the grid aligns according to the left, right, or center settings of that cell. If the cell grows and its alignment is right or center, the grid moves within that cell. You can override the cell's alignment by choosing left or right alignment from the Layout Grid Inspector's Alignment pop-up menu or by clicking an alignment button on the toolbar when the grid is selected. (See Chapter 13 to learn more about alignment within tables.)

Aligning a grid on another grid

If a grid is placed on top of another grid, it moves left or right, or centers, whenever the underlying grid moves. However, it is treated like any other object on a grid and is aligned in relation to the other objects. See the object placement sections later in this chapter for more information about aligning objects on a grid.

Setting Up a Layout Grid's Lines

Do you like seeing grid lines to help you place objects? Or do you find grid lines a distraction? Do you like having objects snap into place along a grid, or not? Do you like a loose grid, or a tight grid? Perhaps you want one set of behaviors for one grid, but elsewhere on your page you feel differently. You can choose how each of your layout grids looks and behaves by making a few simple selections or changes in the Layout Grid Inspector (see Figure 7-14). Each grid is independent of any others and has its own set of properties.

Figure 7-14: The Layout Grid Inspector window. Here's where you set up your grid.

Grid lines are the light gray lines that appear within a grid by default. They don't print, but can be helpful as a visual aid while you're setting up your page. You can adjust the spacing between the horizontal lines in your grid, as well as between the vertical lines.

Grid spacing can be a visual cue or can play an active role in your design. When the Snap option is on, as it is by default, the grid is magnetic—the top-left corner of objects placed on that grid snap into place along the nearest grid line. You can set the horizontal and vertical grid independently of one another, as demonstrated in Figures 7-15 and 7-16. The top row of options in the grid area affects the Horizontal grid, while the lower row of options sets the vertical lines of the grid. The grid spacing in no way affects the amount of HTML code generated by GoLive, so don't worry about smaller grid increments making your page size larger and therefore slower to load.

Note   If you choose to use the Snap feature, when you move elements around with the arrow keys, the objects jump the distance between grid lines. You can over-ride this and move the object one pixel at a time by pressing Option (Mac) or Ctrl+Alt (Windows) as you use the arrow keys.

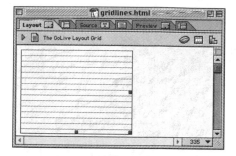

Figure 7-15: A grid with no horizontal grid lines and vertical lines set at 10 pixels so objects snap to 10-pixel increments

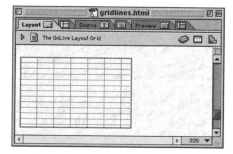

Figure 7-16: A grid with magnetic lines every 30 pixels horizontally and closer at 10 pixels vertically

Adding a Background Color to a Layout Grid

By default a layout grid is transparent, enabling the page's background to show through. However, you can set a gridded area apart as a design element by adding a color to the grid's background. Each layout grid can have its own background color. A layout grid cannot have an image.

Background color is set within the Inspector. To set the color, follow these steps:

1. Click anywhere on the grid to turn the Inspector into the Layout Grid Inspector. (If the Inspector is not open, open it now.)

2. Click the color swatch next to the word Color in the Background section. (Don't bother to check the Color option as GoLive does this automatically.) This selects the color swatch, as noted by the dark border inside it, and opens the Color palette, as seen in Figure 7-17. If the Color palette isn't already open, it opens automatically. (If, the palette window doesn't open to the Color palette, click the color swatch one more time.)

Select colors here

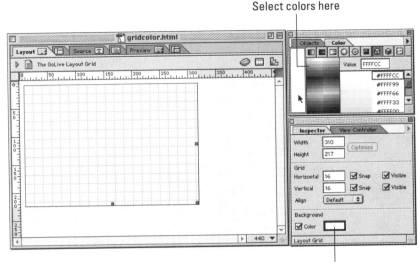

Click here to open color palette

Figure 7-17: The grid, after a background color is set. The color swatch is selected in the Inspector, and the Color palette, where the color was chosen, is open.

3. In the Color palette, click the tab that contains the set of colors from which you want to select a color.

Tip

If you have saved the desired color into the Site Window, just pick that color from the Site Color List tab. No searching necessary.

4. Click the desired color.

Cross-Reference

If you're not familiar with the issues of color on the Web, see Chapter 2 before you settle on a color for your site.

In the six right-most color tabs, click directly on the desired color, as is being done in Figure 7-17 where a color is being selected from the Web Color List. (One or two have a slider also; you can use either this method or the next for those tabs.)

In any color tabs where there's a slider, the key is to click the slider or drag it to set the color. If you drag the slider, the color sets when you release mouse. (Clicking in the preview area at the left doesn't set the color.)

In any case, if you are not happy with a color you chose, simply click another color.

5. Save the changes you just made to this page (File ➪ Save).

Note

When you switch color tabs after clicking the background color swatch in the Inspector, the color you select doesn't always take hold. If the Inspector's color swatch is not still selected, you can either select it again, and then click the desired color, or you can drag the desired color from the large preview area of the Color palette into the Inspector's color swatch or directly onto the Page icon in the page window.

If, at any time later, you wish to change the background color, repeat the same steps. If you decide you don't want the color, uncheck the box next to the word Color.

Placing Text on a Grid

You can add text to a layout grid by typing it, by pasting it in from another document, or by dragging it from another document. First you place a text box on the layout grid. After you place the text box, you can position, resize, and add text to it — in any order.

After text is placed on the grid it is pretty much edited and formatted the same as text on a plain page or text in a table. To learn about text editing and formatting, see Chapter 8.

Adding a text box

As with page layout programs, on a GoLive layout grid you must place a text area on the grid before you can add text — regardless of how you add the text. Text boxes always land on the page as 32 pixel by 32 pixel squares (regardless of grid size). After you place a text box, you can size it by enlarging it in any direction.

Follow these steps to add a text area:

1. Open the Objects palette (Window ➪ Objects) and click to bring the Basic tab forward if it's not already front-most.

2. Drag the Layout Text Box icon from the Basic tab of the Objects palette into place on your grid.

If the grid is set to snap horizontally or vertically, a dark box shows the grid line(s) the block snaps to when placed. Figure 7-18 illustrates this.

Text layout box

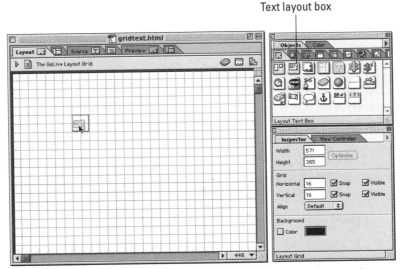

Figure 7-18: Dragging a Layout Text Box into place. The shadow lines show where it will snap horizontally and vertically.

You can also add a text box by double-clicking on the Layout Text Box icon in the Objects palette. This pops the text box into the first available space starting at the top-left corner of the page.

After you place a text box you can move it around and resize it to your heart's content.

Cross-Reference

Text is fully discussed in Chapter 8. Refer to that chapter for more about adding and handling text on a grid.

Resizing a text box

After you place a text box, you drag its handles to adjust its size. You can size it to give yourself a feeling of how the text will look and fit, even if you don't have the copy yet. If you are ready to add the text right away you can begin entering text without changing the default size. However, as you add text, the box expands downward. This pushes any elements below it further down on the page. Therefore, it is most efficient to size the box to the desired width before you add text, so the rest of your layout is more likely to remain intact.

Here's how to resize a text box:

1. If the box is already selected, move your mouse over the handle you plan to drag, so your cursor becomes a light blue arrowhead.

   If it is not already selected, move the mouse to the corner you want to drag. When you're over a handle area, a light blue arrow appears.

   To expand (or later decrease) a text box to the right, click the right, top-right, or bottom-right handle. To change sizing on the left, choose a left handle. You can also affect sizing upward or downward by choosing a top or bottom handle.

2. While you mouse is an arrowhead, drag the handle until you reach the desired size. Figure 7-19 shows a text box being dragged wider.

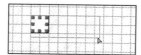

Figure 7-19: Resizing a text box: making this one wider and longer

Repositioning a text box

To move a text box, move your cursor over the box until the object selection icon appears, and then drag the box into position. You can move it anywhere on the grid.

If Snap is turned on, the outline snaps into place as you drag. Figure 7-20 shows a text grid dragged with snapping, and Figure 7-21 shows text grid dragged without snapping to the grid.

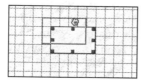

Figure 7-20: Dragging a text box with the snapping option on

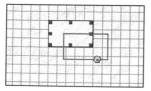

Figure 7-21: Dragging a text box without the snapping option

To override the snapping feature and move the box pixel by pixel, press Option (Mac) or Ctrl+Alt (Windows) as you use the arrow keys.

Adding text to a text box

You can add text to a text box at any time after you've placed it on the grid. You can type or paste your text. You can also drag text from another page, or even from another program.

You can add text to a text box in several different ways, as follows:

✦ **To type your text,** click in the text box to activate the cursor, and then start typing.

✦ **To paste text,** first copy it from your other document. Then click in the text box to activate the cursor. If you are adding text to existing text, place the cursor where you want the next text to come in. With the cursor flashing in the desired spot, use the Edit ⇨ Paste command. (You cannot paste text without adding a text box first.)

✦ **To drag text from another document,** position both windows so you can see both of them. Then select the text in the other document and drag it to the text box. A wide line similar to a cursor lets you know where the text will come in. Mac and Windows users also have the following drag options:

  • *Mac users* can also drag text clippings into GoLive. However, text clippings from Word 98 are not standard text clippings so they don't work as editable text. Instead they come into GoLive as a graphic.

  • *Windows users* can also drag a Word 97 Text Scrap into GoLive. (You can create a Text Scrap by dragging text out of Word 97 onto the Desktop.)

Text wraps within the sides of the text box, regardless of the box's width. The sides won't expand, except perhaps a bit to fit a large word that almost fits anyway (see Figure 7-22). However, the length is flexible. As you type or paste text, the bottom edge grows to accommodate the text. If another text box or an image is below the text box, the box continues to expand, pushing down the object below it.

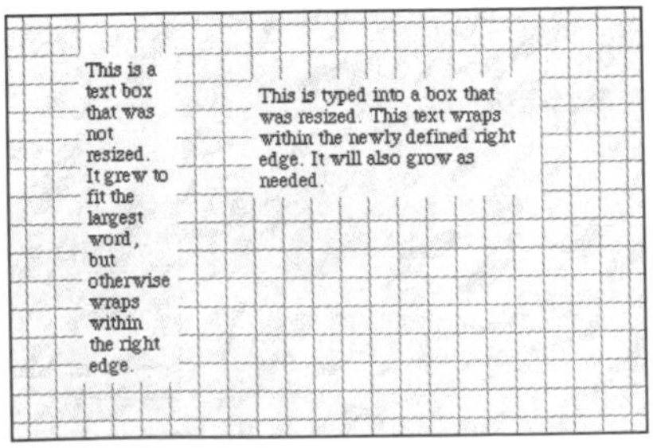

Figure 7-22: The effects of text in the default box (left) and a resized box (right)

If you leave the grid lines visible it is easier to see where your text boxes are.

You can constrain the side of a text box so it won't expand, even if more text exists than can fit in the box.

Here's how to constrain the side of a text box:

1. Select the text box.

2. Open the Inspector, if it is not already open.

3. In the Layout Textbox Inspector, click Allow Content Overflow (see Figure 7-23).

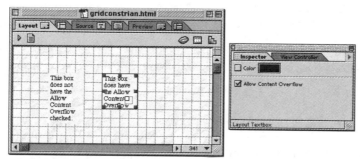

Figure 7-23: A text box that doesn't have Allow Content Overflow turned on (left) and one that does (right)

Note In case you're confused about the Inspector: Two Inspectors actually exist for text placed on a grid. When a text box is selected as an object (with handles) the Inspector becomes the Layout Textbox Inspector. When the cursor is active inside the text box, the Inspector becomes the Text Inspector.

Adding a background color to a text box

By default a text box is transparent, enabling the page or grid's background to show through. However, you can add a color to the text box, helping set the text apart from the rest of the grid's contents.

To set the color, follow these steps:

1. Select the text box, and then open the Inspector if it is not already open. The Inspector becomes the Layout Textbox Inspector.

2. In the Layout Textbox Inspector, double-click the color swatch next to the word Color. (Don't bother to check the Color option as GoLive does this automatically.)

This selects the color swatch, so a dark border appears inside it, and opens the Color palette.

3. In the Color palette, click the tab that contains the set of colors from which you want to select a color.

4. Click the desired color. (In the six right-most color tabs, click directly on the desired color. (One or two have a slider also; you can use either this method or the next for those tabs.)

   In any color tabs where there's a slider, the key is to click the slider or drag it to set the color. If you drag the slider, the color sets when you release the mouse. (Clicking in the preview area at the left doesn't set the color.)

To use a different color, just click the next color. (You may have to click the Inspector's color swatch again before clicking the new color.) If you decide you don't want the color, uncheck the box next to the word Color.

Caution   Not all browsers support the table tag attribute for color. This exists in Version 4.0 and later browsers, but users of earlier versions may not see the background color.

Using Objects on the Grid

If you're familiar with the basics of layout and design in any page layout or design program, you should find most of the concepts here familiar.

The first step to placing an object, such as a graphic, a video, or a JavaScript, is to place an object holder on the page. After an object holder is placed in the layout grid it needs to be filled it with the appropriate content. You can do that right away if the content is available. That's the easiest way to design your page because it helps form the complete look of your page. However, if you don't have the specific content yet you can move, resize, and arrange the container without the content, and then fill it later.

Cross-Reference   This section does not go into full detail about the objects discussed here. Rather, it focuses on how you get an object onto a grid and how you handle it as an object once it is on the grid, whether empty or full. Details about how each object performs are addressed as each object is covered throughout the book.

You can include many objects on your Web page, and you can place several of these on a layout grid. Most of these objects reside on the Basic tab of the Objects palette. They are Floating Box, Image, Plug-in, SWF (Shockwave file), QuickTime, Real (Real Audio file), SVG image, Java Applet, Object, Line (Horizontal Rule), JavaScript, and Marquee (for IE only). In addition to those, you can also add Smart Photoshop,

Smart LiveMotion, Smart Illustrator, Components, Rollovers, Modified Dates, and URL Pop-ups from the Smart tab. You may also be able to place your own Custom items, depending upon the item.

Other objects from the Basic tab and other tabs of the Objects palette can also be dragged onto the grid. However, it is not practical to use these other objects on a grid. For example, as you place items on a grid, GoLive generates the correct spacing, so adding a spacer to a grid would not serve any purpose. Form elements are another set of objects that are best not used on a grid.

Note You can place a table on a grid, but it is most likely redundant and unnecessary as the grid already gives you pixel-level alignment control. If you want the specific look of a table, consider placing it above or below a grid, or even between two grids. Placing a table on a grid creates unnecessarily complex code.

Because text is contained in Text blocks, text also counts as an object here on the grid. A text box is selected, moved, and aligned just like any object on the grid.

One particular action exists that you may be interested in that you won't find here. As wonderful as grids are, due to the limitations of HTML a grid still can't let you place objects in front of, or behind, other objects. To achieve this effect you can use a floating box, which is supported by Version 4 and 5 browsers, but not older ones.

Note You can add comments to your grid, and perhaps should, if the comment is best noted when placed near a specific page element. Remember, though, that whatever you add to the grid increases the complexity of the grid. So place the comment very close to the object being commented on to keep the grid's resulting table simpler. Better yet, consider placing your comments at the top or bottom of the grid for simplicity.

Placing objects on the grid

You have two ways to place an object on a grid. You can drag it, or you can double-click. To place an object exactly where you want it to go, drag it from the Objects palette directly into place.

Here are some guidelines for placing objects on a grid:

✦ If not enough space exists where you attempt to place an object, GoLive rejects the placement, popping the icon back in the palette. Rearrange whatever is blocking your new object's space or enlarge the grid, and then try placing the object again.

✦ Sometimes when not enough room exists on the grid GoLive may place the object in the closest available space. In this case, an outline designates where it suggests that the object fits so you can position the icon accordingly before you release the mouse to place the object.

✦ Floating boxes are an exception to normal object placement. Although you can have a floating box appear over a grid, when you place the floating box on the page, you should drag its icon to the top-left corner of the page. Then you can move the floating box itself into place. See Chapter 19 to learn about floating boxes before you try to use them.

Alternatively, you can double-click the object in the Objects palette. It pops into the next available space from the top-left corner. You need to move it from there.

After an object is on a grid, you can move it around at any time. You can move an object in three different ways:

✦ **You can drag an object.** To do so, move your mouse over it until your pointer becomes an object selection icon, and then drag the object to the desired location. If not enough room exists for it in the new location it lands in the nearest space that's large enough. As you drag the object around, a wide gray line appears on the grid to show you where the object will land if you release the mouse at that time.

✦ **You can use the alignment functions.** See the "Aligning Objects on the Grid" section later in this chapter.

✦ **You can position it to a specific pixel coordinates within the grid.** To do so, move your mouse over the object until your pointer becomes the object selection icon, and then click to select the object. The toolbar changes, providing horizontal and vertical position fields, respectively. Enter the desired number in either of these fields, and then confirm the change by pressing Enter or Return or by clicking anywhere at all as you continue to work. (See Figure 7-24.) Bear in mind that these numbers are the object's position on the grid, not on the page. The grid itself can be moved to another line on the page or have its alignment within the page change.

If you'd like to get started filling your first containers, you can select the object and investigate its Inspector. The Inspector is the key to setting up any object's functionality. Many object holders require links to the file they hold the place for. You'll most likely use Point and Shoot to link from the object holder to the file. The file must be available within the Site Window in order to Point and Shoot to it. Otherwise, you're likely to use the Browse button, also located in the object's Inspector. Again, the file should be in the Site Window before you use it. Smart Objects are the exception to the rule about items being in the Site Window before use. It's a good idea to store the original files you use with Smart Objects in a safe, stable place, but it is not necessary or wise to place them in the Site Window as they can be rather large. See Chapter 10 to learn more about Smart Objects.

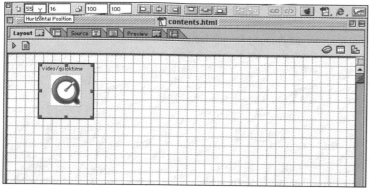

Figure 7-24: An object (QuickTime placeholder) being repositioned horizontally with the aid of the Horizontal Position field in the toolbar

Cross-Reference

For more information about inserting different types of objects, turn to the chapter that discusses the object you're interested in, and then return to this point to learn more about how the object is handled on the grid.

Resizing objects on the grid

In many cases it is not necessary to resize the object holders. Most resize automatically to accommodate the size of the object they contain as soon as you link the object holder to a file. However, as stated earlier in this chapter, you may want to plan the look of your page or site before you have all the graphics or elements available. In this case, you may want to resize the object holders. (If the actual item turns out to be smaller than you make the placeholder, GoLive can easily make the size correction.) All the object boxes can be resized except for Comments and JavaScript holders, which aren't seen by users anyway. If you want to know whether you can resize an object, just click it to select it — if you see handles you can adjust the size; if not, sizing is not applicable.

Tip

GoLive makes it easy to resize an image. However, it is far better to set your image size in a graphics program such as ImageReady or Photoshop, before you bring it into GoLive. If you use GoLive to reduce the size, you have not actually reduced the image. Therefore, your user downloads the full sized image and the sizing takes time each time your page is visited. Or, if you use GoLive to enlarge your image, the image is stretched and becomes jagged looking. For more about resizing graphics, and about using Smart Objects, which are alternatives, see Chapter 10.

When a graphic is on the layout grid you have three ways to resize it. Two are by entering exact dimensions in pixels. The other is by dragging.

You have several ways to resize objects on a grid, as follows:

✦ **Use the Width and Height fields on the toolbar.** Select the object by moving your mouse over the object until your pointer becomes an object selection icon, and then click. This changes the toolbar to provide horizontal position and vertical position fields (as in Figure 7-25). Toolbar resizing is only available for objects when they are on the layout grid.

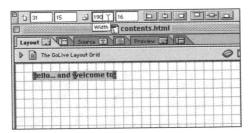

Figure 7-25: Changing the dimensions of a selected object (Marquee) using the Width and Height fields in the toolbar

✦ **Use the Width and Height fields in the Transform palette,** shown in Figure 7-26. Move the mouse over the object until the pointer becomes an object selection icon, and then click to select the object. Choose Window ➪ Transform to open the Transform palette. Enter the new width and/or height in the Width and/or Height fields. This palette offers one feature not on the toolbar: you can constrain the dimensions of your object so sizing it in one direction identically resizes it in the other. To do this, just check Constrain Proportions. This resizing is only available for objects when they are on the layout grid.

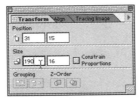

Figure 7-26: Resizing a selected graphic using the Width and Height fields in the Transform palette

✦ **Select the object, and then drag its handles in the desired direction.** Corner handles enable you to resize both width and height. Side handles move only in the direction of the side they are on. To constrain dimensions click the corner handle, and then press Shift as you drag.

Tip

If you want to know whether you can resize an object, just click it to select it. If you see handles you can adjust the size. If not, sizing is not applicable.

Aligning objects on the grid

You can align objects with respect to the edges of the layout grid or to one another.

To align objects to the edges of the layout grid you use the six alignment buttons that become available on the toolbar as soon as an object is selected, or use the Align palette. You can align as many objects as you want with a single click. To align objects relative to other objects, you use the Align window.

Aligning objects with respect to the grid

Follow these steps to align objects with respect to the grid:

1. Select the object or objects you wish to align using one of the following methods:

   • Click the first object to select it, and then press the Shift key as you click each subsequent object you wish to select.

   • To select contiguous objects, drag over each object you're selecting. If any objects can't be reached this way, press Shift as you click the additional objects. If any object is inadvertently selected, press Shift and click it to deselect it.

2. Click the desired alignment button in the toolbar, or open the Align palette (Window ⇨ Align), and then click the desired alignment button under the Align to Parent section. Either way, the alignment options and the buttons that depict them are identical (see Figure 7-27). You have the following options:

   • *Align Left* moves the object to the left edge of the layout grid.

   • *Align Center Horizontally* moves the object to the horizontal middle of the layout grid.

   • *Align Right* moves the object to the right edge of the layout grid.

   • *Align Top* moves the object to the top edge of the layout grid.

   • *Align Center Vertically* moves the object to the vertical middle of the layout grid.

   • *Align Bottom* moves the object to the bottom edge of the layout grid.

Not all options are available at all times. For example, if you have a text box to the left of a graphic, the graphic — by itself — can't be aligned at the left side of the layout grid. Therefore, the Align Left button is grayed out on the toolbar. However, if you select both the graphic and the text box, then you can align both of them. (See the following Note.)

After an object is aligned with respect to the grid it always aligns with the grid, moving if you resize the grid.

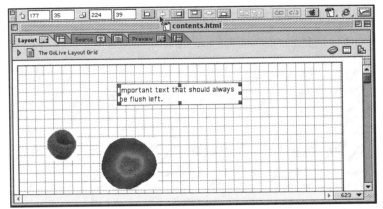

Figure 7-27: A block of text that has just been set to align in the center of the grid at all times. The Align Center button is gray because it is the alignment in effect. Five other alignment choices surround this button.

Note   If you select multiple items to align, they remain proportionately spaced in relation to one another and all move as a block, as if grouped together. If you want each item to align separately from one another, select and align each individually.

To undo alignment, simply drag the object to any new location.

Aligning objects with respect to one another

In addition to aligning objects with respect to the grid, you can align objects with respect to each other. You can align the objects along their top or bottom edges, or their horizontal or vertical centers. You can also automatically distribute the space between objects evenly.

To align objects with respect to one another, follow these steps:

1. Select the object or objects you wish to align, using one of the following methods:

   • Click the first object to select it, and then press the Shift key as you click each subsequent object you wish to select.

   • To select contiguous objects, drag over each object you're selecting. If any objects can't be reached this way, press Shift as you click the additional objects. If any object is inadvertently selected, press Shift and click each to deselect it.

2. Open the Align palette (Window ⇨ Align) and click the desired alignment. The options available vary depending on the initial placement of the items to be aligned. The buttons each depict their alignment effect. In Figure 7-28 two objects are selected and, because their sides overlap, their vertical lines cannot be aligned. However, they can be aligned side by side. The left-most button aligns the tops of both objects, the middle button aligns their horizontal centers, and the last button aligns the bottoms of the selected images.

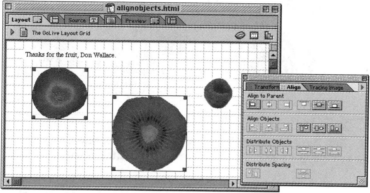

Figure 7-28: Performing a simple alignment of objects on a grid; aligning the centers of two objects

Distributing object spacing

In addition to merely aligning objects horizontally or vertically, you can also align them by evenly distributing the space between them. Using the center two buttons of the Align palette, you can distribute the spacing between multiple objects as well as align them along their horizontal or vertical lines. Figure 7-29 shows three objects before and after spacing is distributed.

You can also simply distribute the spacing between objects without moving them along their horizontal or vertical lines. The bottom two buttons take care of that for you. When you select multiple items, and use one of the Distribute Spacing buttons, each outer-most item remains in place, while any objects in between them are distributed evenly with the space between. Figure 7-30 demonstrates this feature.

Another way to align objects is to note their position on the ruler. To display the ruler, click in the small ruler button above the top-right scroll bar. When you select an object the area it occupies is shown in white along the ruler. As you move the object, its new position is noted.

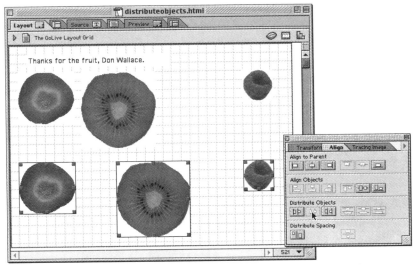

Figure 7-29: *Top:* Three objects before their spacing is distributed. *Bottom:* The same objects after the distribute centers button is used.

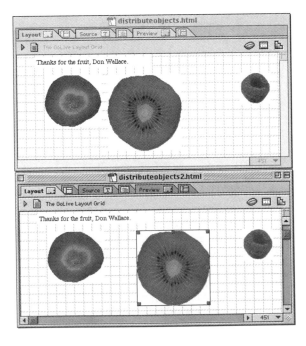

Figure 7-30: *Top:* Three objects aligned at the top, before they are distributed evenly. *Bottom:* The same objects after the left Distribute Space button is used.

Grouping objects

As your grid fills with objects you may find it easier to work if you join several objects together in a group. You can group any object you use as a design element on the grid.

To group objects, simply select them, and then click the Group button on the Layout Grid toolbar or in the Transform palette (Window ➪ Transform), or choose Edit ➪ Group. (Both Group buttons are shown in Figure 7-31.)

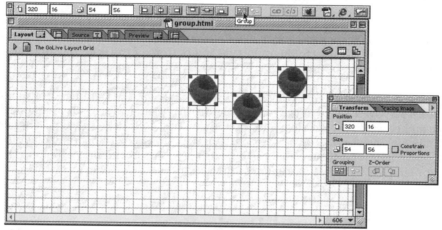

Figure 7-31: Selected objects being grouped with the Group button on the toolbar

After you group objects they act as one. This way you only have to select one object instead of several when you want to move those elements, as in Figure 7-32. Grouping also saves you from inadvertently selecting objects when you're trying to select and work with other objects.

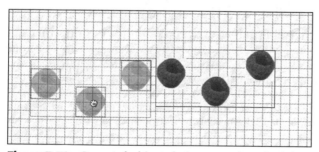

Figure 7-32: Grouped objects being moved to the left as one unit

To ungroup, select the group and click Ungroup on the toolbar or in the Transform palette (Window ⇨ Transform), or choose Edit ⇨ Ungroup. The Ungroup button (and menu item) becomes active whenever a group is selected.

Optimizing a Layout Grid

After your page (or at least the section that contains the grid) is complete, you can choose to optimize it. Optimizing reduces the size of the grid to accommodate the elements on it, which eliminates any unnecessary code.

To optimize a grid, select the grid, and then open the Inspector (now the Layout Grid Inspector). Then, just click the Optimize button if it is active. If the grid's elements extend all the way to the right side and bottom of the grid, this button is inactive because no optimization is available.

Optimization works by removing the extra grid space at the right and bottom of the grid. If it removed space at the top, it would move your grid's position up on the page and carry its design elements with it, affecting your page's design. Therefore, optimization leaves the top and left parts of the grid alone. Depending on your layout, you might want to select all the objects on your grid and move them to the top and/or left of the grid for maximum optimization.

Tables to Grids and Back Again

Your decision to use a grid — or not to use one — is never final. Neither is your decision to use a table instead of a grid. You can turn a table into a grid or a grid into a table at any time — even if that table or grid has contents!

It's not a good idea to abuse this ability though. Switching between a table and grid sometimes mixes up the code and causes the grid to draw a bit oddly.

Converting a table into a grid

If you've been working with a table and wish to convert it into a grid, you can easily do so. This ability might come in handy in a few other instances. Some examples of this include if you inherit a site that was created using another application, or convert your own site from another application, or if the site was created with GoLive but the GoLive tags were stripped during export. Additionally, if under some rare circumstance, your grid suddenly just appears as a sort of table but with dotted outlines, you can simply turn the table back into a functioning grid.

Follow these steps to turn any table (or a broken grid) into a layout grid:

1. Move your mouse over the top or left side of the table until the cursor turns into the object selection icon, and then click to select the table.

2. Click the Table to Layout Grid Convert button at the bottom of the Table Inspector. (You need to open the Inspector if it's not open already.) The table appears as a layout grid.

3. If the grid's full contents don't appear, locate the bottom handle and drag downward to reveal the rest of the grid. You may have to select the grid so you can see the handles. To do so, move your mouse over any grid edge until your cursor becomes the object selection icon, and then click to select the grid.

   If the grid's lines are not showing and you'd like to see them, select the grid and click one or both Visible boxes in the Inspector (which is now the Layout Grid Inspector).

Note You can turn a table into a grid at any time by using the Table Inspector. But once it's a grid, the Layout Grid Inspector doesn't present you with an option to turn it back into a table. To turn a layout grid into a plain table, you need to use the HTML, as described next.

Converting a grid into a table

If, while you're creating a page, you decide you'd rather work with a table instead of a grid, you can easily do so.

Here's how to convert a grid into a table in Source view:

1. Select the grid if it's not already selected.

2. If the Source code window isn't already open, choose Window ➪ Source Code to open it.

   Because the grid is selected, its code is selected too. It looks a little like this:

   ```
   <table cool width="201" height="201" usegridx="yes"
   usegridy="yes" showgridx="yes" showgridy="yes"></table>
   ```

3. Double-click the word "cool" and delete it by pressing the Delete/Backspace key.

4. Click anywhere on your page, outside of the grid/table.

   Gray lines now appear denoting the table cells that were created as you worked on the grid.

Note   You can also do this by switching to the Source View tab of the page and deleting the word "cool." Of course, the reverse works to turn a table into a grid. Just type **cool** after the word "table." (Remember that you can also click the Convert button in the Table Inspector, as shown in the previous section.)

To convert a grid into a table using Outline mode, follow these steps:

1. Select the table if it's not already selected.

2. Click the HTML Outline Editor tab — the tab with the outline icon — to switch to the HTML Outline Editor view.

   The code for the table is highlighted by a dark rectangle around it.

   The table's attributes appear by the table's heading. The attribute that turns the table into a grid is a unique-to-GoLive attribute called "cool." Figure 7-33 demonstrates how the table heading and the cool attribute appear in Outline mode.

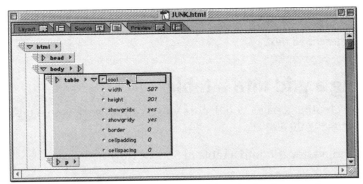

Figure 7-33: The Cool tag ready to delete in Outline mode

3. Click the word Cool and press Backspace/Delete.

   Although the line that contains the cool tag remains for now, it disappears when you switch to Layout mode.

✦   ✦   ✦

Adding Text, Graphics, and Links

Whether you've got pictures to speak for you or you've got your thousands of words on hand, this is the part that shows you how to deploy them. As you create your message, the linking techniques you learn here enable you to build your site in earnest.

Entering and Formatting Text

Although the success of the Web is due in part to its multimedia abilities, the written word remains a key to our communication. Just as important as what you say, though, is how you present the words on your page: especially on the Web, words are not just words. The actual characters you choose, their font face, size, color, and positioning all add to the impact and interpretation of your message.

If you're a print designer, or even if you work in video, you're used to strict control of every aspect of your text. Aside from a few lingering color issues, the way you set up a file is the way it will look — whether you are creating a printed page, a film, or a television screen. Because of the interpretive nature of the browser, though, Web pages are different creatures.

What happens with Web pages is similar to what happens with a word processing or page layout document when you send someone the electronic file instead of printing it. If the recipient doesn't have the fonts you used, the page won't look anything like your design. Most likely, your carefully chosen typeface will be substituted with a basic system font. Unless you've used returns, either soft or hard, the lines will wrap at different places depending on the size of the font face that's substituted. Words may no longer fall near the graphics, fall on their intended lines, or fall correctly in relation to each other. Well, the Web is even worse. On the Web, even the page width and font size can change. Designing for the Web is about planning for all contingencies.

GoLive's job as a Web site creation tool is to offer you all of the tools you need to do anything that's possible — and GoLive makes everything very easy. However, just because you *can* do something doesn't mean it's the best thing to do. This chapter provides all of the basics of text input and formatting. However, some of the formatting abilities covered here are things you *can* do — but aren't necessarily the best way to do things. For some formatting, Cascading Style Sheets provide a cleaner, leaner, more flexible alternative. As I show you each formatting possibility, I let you know when a style sheet is a good alternative to consider.

Adding Text

Before you can set the look of your text, you need to get the text into your document. You have a few ways you can do this, depending upon where you place the text. Getting text on your page is the simple part — after you choose the words, at least.

Four types of containers exist into which you can add your text: a blank Web page, a table, a text box on a layout grid, and a floating box. Each container plays a specific role in helping to organize your page and create its look, as follows:

✦ A **blank Web page** starts off the same as a regular word-processor page — with a cursor flashing. You can add text at this cursor in all the standard ways. Text directly on the page wraps automatically at the right edge of the browser window. The tricky thing is that you don't control the browser's size; the user resizes it at will, which changes the point at which text moves to the next line.

✦ As with a word processor, you can add a **table** to your page. Within a table you can click in any cell and add text at that cell's flashing text cursor. Because you can control the width of the table, you can set the width of the text area.

✦ GoLive's unique **layout grid**, which functions like a page-layout program, enables you to place text boxes anywhere on the gridded area and move them around pixel by pixel. You control the width of the text area by resizing the text box. (Text wraps within the text box.)

✦ **Floating boxes** are sort of like the grid's text boxes, except they literally float above the rest of your page. When you click inside a floating box, you'll also find the familiar flashing text cursor. And, of course, you can add text at this text cursor just like you add text anywhere else. (Text wraps within the text box.)

This chapter tells you how to add text to each of these containers. You can find the details of the layout grid, tables, and floating boxes, each in Chapters 7, 13, and 19 respectively.

No matter which text area you're adding text to, the methods are the same. Here's how you add text:

✦ You can type just like in a word processor. As with a word-processor or page-layout program, you don't need to press Enter/Return at the end of each line. The text wraps automatically when it hits the right edge of the browser window, the text box, the cell, or the floating box's right edge. Use Enter/Return only to start a new paragraph. To type text into the grid's text box, a table cell, or a floating box, click inside the box to place the I-beam text cursor (if it's not already flashing). Once the I-beam is flashing, type away. Figure 8-1 shows you the various text areas, each with some text and the cursor flashing.

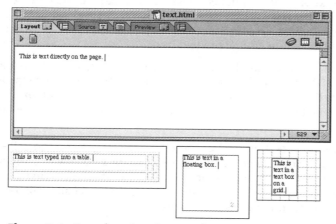

Figure 8-1: Samples of each type of text area and its I-beam

✦ You can copy text from another document and then paste it into place. Go to the original source, select the desired text, and copy it using Edit ⇨ Copy. Then return to your Web page, move your cursor to the place you want the text to appear, click to place the text I-beam cursor, and then use Edit ⇨ Paste.

✦ You can also drag text from most drag-aware programs directly onto the page. Select the text within the other program, and then drag it on the GoLive page. As you drag, a dark line indicates the exact place your text will land when you release the mouse. You can drop it into any text container: a page, text box, table cell, or floating box.

✦ Mac users can also drag in text clippings made from most programs. Just drag the text clipping into place on the page. This works just like dragging text from a drag-aware program.

✦ Windows users can also drag document scrap text (created by dragging selected text from Word to your desktop or a folder). Simply drag the document scrap text file onto the page wherever text can normally be typed.

Note When you copy or drag text from another source, such as a word processor, character and paragraph formatting will be lost. When you copy or drag text from within GoLive, character formatting remains intact.

When adding text in GoLive, consider the following:

✦ As you add text to the grid's text box, it wraps automatically between the left and right edges of the text box. As you type, the box grows downward if more space is needed. However, the nature of the grid is that any item directly below the text box will be pushed down on the grid. Because this can affect the layout of your page, if you have anything on the grid below the text box, it's best if you adjust the size of the text box yourself in anticipation of the size you'll need before adding the text itself.

✦ Within a floating box, text also wraps between the left and right edges, and the box expands downward if more space is needed. However, because a floating box actually floats over the rest of your page, it doesn't affect anything else on the page when it grows. Therefore, it's not necessary to resize the box prior to adding text.

✦ Within a table cell, text wraps between the cell's edges and the cell expands downward as space is needed. As this cell expands downward, any other cells in the same row also expand to the same height. Therefore, anything in the rows below will also move down, but their contents will stay aligned with the other things in the other cells in those rows.

Editing Text

Any good writer knows that his or her words need to be edited — to be refined. If you're writing your site's copy as you create the site, you can expect GoLive's word-processing-like abilities to come in very handy. Even if your words are already composed, you may come to need an edit here and there.

Introducing the Text toolbar

When you work with text, the Text toolbar becomes active. Figure 8-2 introduces the Text toolbar.

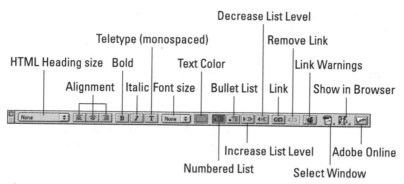

Figure 8-2: The Text toolbar

Selecting text

Before you can move text, cut it, copy it, or apply a style to it, you have to select it. All of the selection techniques common to word processors work here, too.

As in a word processor, you have several ways to select text:

✦ You can select any block of text by inserting the cursor where you want the selection to begin, and then keeping the mouse button down as you drag over the text to be selected.

✦ To quickly select a word, double-click it.

✦ To quickly select a line, triple-click in the line. This actually is different from word processors. In GoLive, a line is exactly one line of text rather than a sentence. This is true whether you're in a layout grid's text box or a floating box, or you're working directly on the page. If you select one line and then resize the page or element, the original selection holds.

✦ You can select words letter by letter by pressing Shift as you press the arrow keys. Pressing Shift and Ctrl selects word by word. Use the right-, left-, upward-, or downward-pointing arrow key to extend the selection in the corresponding direction. Using an opposing key undoes the selection. The left and right arrows select character by character. The up and down arrows select line by line.

✦ Press ⌘-Shift (Mac) in conjunction with the left or right arrow key to select a line from the point of the cursor to the end of the line. The up or down arrow selects the text upward or downward line by line.

✦ You can select a block of text, no matter how large, by placing the cursor in front of the first word you want selected and then pressing Shift as you click where you want the selection to end. You can also do this in reverse, placing the cursor at the end first, and then the beginning. You can adjust the selection as long as the text remains selected. To do so, press Shift again and click in the new start or end location.

When you select text in GoLive, the selection is relative to the location of your cursor at the time of selection. This goes for both dragging over text and for using Edit ⇨ Select All. If your cursor is directly on the plain page, and you drag across all or any of the text on the page, or you use Select All, layout grids and floating boxes appear to become selected. However, if you apply any text attribute, the text within the layout grids and floating boxes will not be affected.

To select text that's in a layout grid's text box or within a floating box, you must click within that individual text box or floating box. Within either box, you can either drag over the text or use Select All. Select All only selects all of the text within that box.

Cross-Reference

To learn about layout grids and how to use them, see Chapter 7. For information on floating boxes, see Chapter 19.

Cutting and copying text

In GoLive, you edit text the same way as in a word-processor or page-layout program — using Cut/Copy and then Paste or by dragging. Text can be moved between the main part of the page, grids, and floating boxes by using either method. You can move text freely between the page, grids, and floating boxes; from one text area to another; or between like areas. Of course, you can also move text between pages.

To move text, you can do either of the following:

✦ Select and cut it, and then click where you want the text to be inserted and paste it into the new location.

✦ Select it, and then drag it from its existing location on any GoLive page to a new location — even between pages. As you drag, a heavy black line indicates where the text will land when you release the mouse.

To keep your existing text, but place a copy of it in another location, do either of the following:

✦ Select and copy it, and then click where you want the text to be inserted and paste it into the new location.

✦ Select it, and then press Option (Mac) or Control (Windows) as you drag it from its existing location to a new one. As you drag, a plus sign on the pointer tells you that you're making a copy, and a heavy black line indicates where the text will land when you release the mouse.

If you're dragging or copying text to a grid, keep these points in mind:

✦ If you drag onto the blank area of a grid, a text box is automatically created around the dragged text.

✦ If you drag into an empty text box, the text lands at the cursor.

✦ If you drag into a text box that already has text, you can place the text anywhere within the existing text or immediately after it. A heavy cursor indicates where the text will land when you release the mouse.

If you're dragging or copying text to a floating box, keep the following points in mind:

✦ You must create a floating box before you can add text to it.

✦ If you drag into an empty floating box, the text lands at the cursor.

✦ If you drag into a floating box that already has text, you can place the text anywhere within the existing text or immediately after it. A heavy cursor indicates where the text will land when you release the mouse. In Figure 8-3, the word *can* is being moved from the regular page area into a floating box.

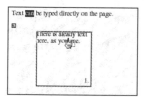

Figure 8-3: Moving a word from a line of text into text within a floating box

Using different editing methods

Each method of editing has its benefits: copy and paste or dragging — that is, besides choosing the one that's most comfortable for you. Here are some points you might want to consider:

✦ To move text large distances, it is usually easier to copy and paste than drag. That way, you avoid holding the mouse as you wait for the page to scroll long distances.

✦ When you cut or copy text, it is temporarily stored on your computer's clipboard. Therefore, you can paste this text not just once, but over and over again. It remains in place on the clipboard until something else is cut or copied, replacing it. When you drag, text isn't put on the clipboard. Therefore, if you want to use some cut or copied text in more than one location, use Cut or Copy.

✦ If you want to reuse some text that is on the clipboard (having been cut or copied), but also want to move or copy other text, use the drag method to handle the second text, leaving text on the clipboard intact.

Clearing text

You can also clear text using Edit ⇨ Clear (Mac), or Edit ⇨ Delete (Windows). This removes text completely. Cleared/deleted text cannot be pasted back in as with the Cut command. You may choose to use Clear/Delete when you need to remove text and don't want to disrupt the contents of the clipboard.

Duplicating text boxes

When you're working on a layout grid you can use the Duplicate command (Edit ⇨ Duplicate) to create identical copies of already-placed text and its layout box, and use these copies as a starting point for your new text areas. When you choose the Duplicate command, a dialog box asks you how many copies you'd like and how far from the original you want the new box to land horizontally and vertically. Enter the height and width of the text box as the preset offset. If the grid does not have enough room for you to place the requested number of duplicates, no new text boxes are created when you click OK. In such a case, you must cancel, expand the grid, and then try again. The Duplicate Command only works on the grid, so text that is directly inline on the page or in floating boxes can't be duplicated with this command.

You can achieve the same effect as the Duplicate command by copying and pasting an entire text box. This also works with a floating box. A pasted text box lands in the next available space. A pasted floating box lands directly on the original. After you paste a copy, you can edit the text as desired. (To learn about floating boxes, see Chapter 19.)

Setting Up Headers

Headings, called headers in HTML, guide the reader, break up your page, and help call attention to the topics. They also provide structure to the page, which enables a voice-synthesizing browser to make sense of, and better read, your page to the blind as well as to print it in Braille for the blind.

A heading is applied to an entire paragraph; it cannot be applied to single words or characters within a line or paragraph. (This is just like in word processing or page layout for print.)

To create a heading, place your I-beam in the paragraph to which you're assigning the header and then choose from the Header choices under the Type menu (see Figure 8-4) or the Paragraph Format pop-up menu that's on the toolbar whenever you're working with text. They're exactly the same headings — the ruler just adds another closer location. (The ruler also provides feedback as to what style is applied, after it is applied.) This defines your text as a heading in HTML terms.

Best of Both Worlds?

Are you planning on using a Cascading Style Sheet and wondering what you can do to enable non CSS-savvy browser users to also see your page as you want them to see it? The wisest way to go about this is to use the HTML tags that apply *structure* to your page, and then, in the style sheet, use those same tags to provide further formatting, or *presentation*.

These tags, such as the headings, block quote, and list tags create a structured page for non CSS-savvy browsers, but only use the browser's defaults for their look. When you create a style sheet, you tell the style sheet to look at specific tags and apply formatting to them based on your instructions. The formatting you add within the style sheets can get as fancy as you'd like. It in no way imposes upon the structure of your document. This is the best of both worlds.

The only downside to working this way is that your page may look rather bland to those using the pre-CCS browsers.

If, instead, you fill your page with HTML tags that provide presentation, rather than structure, you can tell a non CSS-savvy browser what to do, but . . .

✦ You add a lot of unnecessary code to the page and that code needs to be downloaded

✦ You make it harder for voice-synthesizing browsers to read your page

✦ You can confuse the CSS-savvy browser

You'll need to consider your audience and design for them.

If you choose to go ahead and add presentation-only HTML tags into your page, be sure to test the page in the various browsers and platforms and see what happens. Results will vary based on the specific tags involved. I also try to note which formatting may cause a conflict in CSS-savvy browsers.

When you choose an HTML header, the browser determines exactly how the heading will look. The actual font size, typeface, spacing before or after the heading, and other heading attributes such as bolding the text are selected by the browser — not by you, the designer. (It typically places a line or so of space to set it apart from the body text and renders the heading in bold.) You are choosing a relative heading level: a Header 2 is a subheading under Header 1. But the browser settings determine the actual styles applied to Header 1 and Header 2.

If you don't want to stick with the browser defaults, you *could* adjust the size, color, and typeface used in the headers by using some of those formatting tools on the toolbar. However, these attributes add the <font> tag to your page and that tag is known to cause problems for browsers trying to interpret a style sheet. (More about these attributes later in this chapter.) The more elegant and flexible alternative is to use a Cascading Style Sheet.

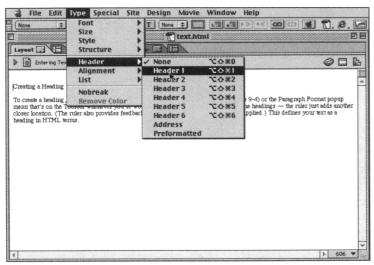

Figure 8-4: Using the Type menu to apply a Header 1 to the line where the cursor flashes. The pop-up menu at the left of the ruler contains the same heading formats and can also be used.

Cross-Reference   I recommend you read Chapter 17 to learn about style sheets before adding any more formatting to your headings.

You *could* also create the *visual effect* of a heading just by selecting the text and choosing a font size (as described in the next section, "Adjusting Font Sizes"). However, by specifically assigning the text as a header, you ensure uniformity and bring a level of organization to your page that is needed by voice-synthesizing browsers and perhaps by hand-held devices. Also, a style sheet will have an easier time discerning and applying the specific look you want for the header and not confuse this text with other text that happens to be the same font size. The W3C accessibility standard is to use headings for the overall organization of your page's sections rather than assign a font size.

Adjusting Font Sizes

Controlling font size on the Web is one of those never-ending debates. The user's browser preferences determine the basic size of a font; then, with HTML, your control is limited to setting it to be equal to, larger, or smaller than that default.

Note   Style sheets enable you to have more precise control and are discussed later in the book. Here and now, the focus is on HTML-set font size.

Changing a font size requires just two steps:

1. Select the text to be changed.

2. Choose a size from the Size submenu of the Type menu, or from the font size pop-up on the Text toolbar. Figure 8-5 shows the toolbar's pop-up menu.

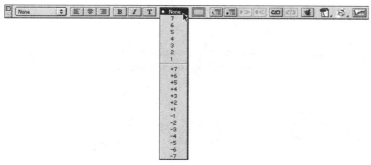

Figure 8-5: The font size pop-up menu on the toolbar

Seven sizes exist, each relative to the user's browser preference. Size 1 is the smallest, and 7 is the largest. (Figure 8-6 illustrates the relative sizes.) Size 3 is the Web-standard default when no size is specified. GoLive does not write any size in when you add text, so your pages are viewed using the standard default. This way, the user's browser determines the size at which the font will render. If you specify a font size, the user's browser will show your text in that font size when first viewing your page. The user can then choose to make your fonts larger or smaller by using the option in the browser. This method of relative sizes enables you to determine that sections of your text will be larger or smaller than other parts.

When you apply a font size to text, that text is surrounded by the font tag. For example, here are the words, "This is size 2" formatted with size 2:

```
<font size="2">This is size 2</font>
```

You can see the font tag in the Source Code view (Window ⇨ Source Code) as shown in Figure 8-7, or the Source tab of the page. Although in other places I warn against using the <font> tag, accessibility-wise, sizing your fonts this way is all right to do. Just remember not to use it in lieu of adding true structural instructions to your page.

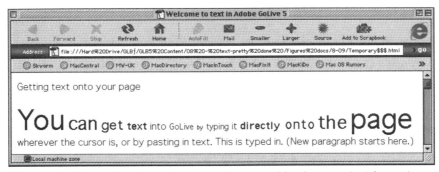

Figure 8-6: The various font sizes, from 7 to 1 and back up again (shown in Internet Explorer 5, Mac)

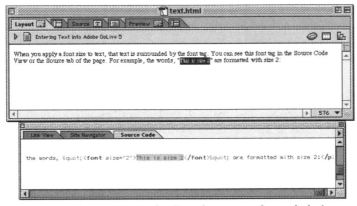

Figure 8-7: The Source Code view shows you the code being generated when you set the font size.

Caution

If you specify a font size on top of a header, you're telling the browser to display the text both at the specified header size *and* at the specified font size. Each browser works with its own priorities, so your results may be unpredictable.

Without using style sheets, the only way to mandate a specific point size is to create a GIF image of the text, and then place it as an image. However, three problems can occur with this practice. If users turn off images to browse faster, they'll never see your words, and users of items like a Palm hand-held won't see the images either. Additionally, speech and Braille readers will miss your message. You can combat these problems by using an alternate text tag (see Chapter 10) to reflect the message contained in the GIF. Another problem is speed. An image takes time to download. If your page is image heavy or has other things that need time to load, you risk losing the visitor.

It's important to remember that different computer platforms and monitor resolutions will display the same text differently. For example, because the same exact font and font size draws larger on Unix and Windows than on a Mac, a font that is readable on Windows can be miniscule on a Mac. Monitor size and screen resolution can also make a difference in how a font is displayed.

Font size isn't the only thing affected by these differences. For instance, resolution also affects the size of images onscreen, as discussed in Chapter 10.

Formatting Paragraphs

Text, of course, can become very unreadable if it's not broken up into readable sections. Headings and subheadings help quite a bit, but when it comes down to it, paragraphs are the most common separating devices.

Creating paragraphs

Like with a word processor, you can end one paragraph and begin another in GoLive by pressing Enter/Return. However, unlike a word processor, this does not just begin another line. Instead, it acts more like a work processor paragraph that is using a "space after" command. This is an HTML standard, not just GoLive's. As you add text to your page, GoLive writes the paragraph tags. Each page starts out with a set of paragraph tags, `<p>` and `</p>`; you can see them in the Source Code window (Window ⇨ Source Code) if it's open. When you press Enter/Return, GoLive places the correct HTML code to close the current paragraph and starts a new one. Because the paragraph tag adds one full line of space between paragraphs, you don't have to press Enter/Return an extra time. Figure 8-8 shows the spacing between paragraphs, as viewed in Internet Explorer 5 for Macintosh. (In Windows, it looks very much the same.)

If you use a style sheet, you can easily adjust the amount of space between paragraphs, as discussed in Chapter 17.

You can avoid the extra space between the paragraphs by using the HTML equivalent of word processing's "soft return," which is the "line break." You can create a line break by pressing the Shift key as you press Enter/Return instead of just pressing Enter/Return. However, the line break has a different behavior than a paragraph tag. With a line break, you carry the formatting of the previous paragraph to the postline-break paragraph because you are not actually creating a new paragraph. In many cases, such as when creating a list, this won't do. See "Inserting Line Breaks," later in this chapter, to learn more about the line-break feature.

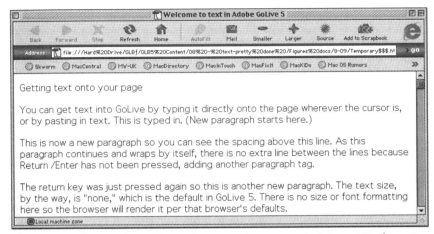

Figure 8-8: The spacing effects of paragraphs as seen in Internet Explorer 5 on a Mac

Note   You may be used to showing the invisible formatting when you work in a word-processor or page-layout program. You can do the same in GoLive. However, GoLive doesn't display a symbol for new paragraphs in Layout mode—it only shows line breaks. To toggle the invisible formatting on and off, use Edit ⇨ Show Invisible Items or Hide Invisible Items.

Creating block quotes

As in the print world, when quoting a paragraph, you use a *block quote*. A block quote is a paragraph that is indented on both the left and right margins to set it apart, as shown in Figure 8-9.

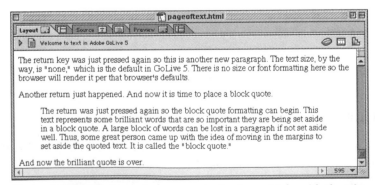

Figure 8-9: A block quote, as seen in the Layout tab, with the View Controller emulating Internet Explorer 4 for Windows

To set a block quote, follow these steps:

1. Place your cursor anywhere in the paragraph you want to indent. Because the format affects the entire paragraph, you don't have to select all the text in the paragraph. However, if you want to indent several paragraphs, you need to select at least part of each paragraph.

2. Choose Type ⇨ Alignment ⇨ Increase Block Indent.

   To indent the paragraph(s) further, repeat Step 2.

To decrease a block quote, choose Type ⇨ Alignment ⇨ Decrease Block Indent. A button appears on the toolbar that appears at first glance to do the same thing. However, this button is for increasing list indents, which indents the left side only, leaving the right side unaffected.

Note   You can use a block quote whether you're adding a style sheet or not. The style sheet simply enhances its look.

Indenting paragraphs (or other lines)

Another difference between the Web page and a word processor is that HTML doesn't recognize a tab to create an indent. Nor does it recognize multiple spaces for indenting text. Instead, you have a few options.

The most sophisticated way to indent a paragraph is to use a Cascading Style Sheet. But whether you use a style sheet or not, if you really want your indents to be seen in older browsers, you have to turn to one of the other methods. In the print world, many people gave up indenting paragraphs a few years ago, so your viewers don't necessarily expect indents. Perhaps your best decision is to designate indents in the style sheet, but let the rest of your users see the text without any indents. With this consideration in mind, here are a few ways you can physically create an indented first line for a paragraph — the nonbreaking space, a horizontal spacer, an invisible image, and the Preformatted text style.

Caution   If you use a physical method to create an indent, and then configure an indent using a style sheet, viewers using CSS-savvy browsers may end up with huge indents. You'll need to add specific style code (a class) to counteract this. You can learn about that in Chapter 17.

Indenting paragraphs with nonbreaking spaces

Using nonbreaking spaces is the best solution for indenting without using a style sheet. Because a nonbreaking space is a text element, it resizes along with the text, making it the most flexible method. To insert a nonbreaking space press Option-spacebar (Mac) or Shift+spacebar (Windows). It just looks like a regular space; it has no special marker to differentiate it. However, in Source view you'll see   in the code, as shown in Figure 8-10.

Figure 8-10: The effect of a nonbreaking space as it appears on the page, shown along with the HTML that creates the space

Caution   If you use nonbreaking spaces to create an indent, and then configure an indent using a style sheet, viewers using CSS-savvy browsers end up with huge indents. You will need to accommodate for this within the style sheet, as discussed in Chapter 17.

Indenting paragraphs using the horizontal spacer

The horizontal spacer is another indent method. It's a great little idea. It can be stretched to any size, creating an indent for you. The only, not-so-slight problem is that the spacer is only a Netscape protocol; users of Internet Explorer will not see an indent. To insert a spacer, drag its icon from the Basic tag of the Objects palette into place within your text. Then drag its handle to size it or enter the desired width into the Spacer Inspector.

Inserting Nonbreaking Spaces the Old-Fashioned Way

As a bit of insight into HTML, here's how you'd insert nonbreaking spaces without GoLive's convenient shortcut:

1. Open the Source Code window (Window ➪ Source Code).

2. In the Layout mode of your page, select part of the text that comes right before where you want to add the space. This highlights that text in the Source Code window.

3. Place your cursor into the HTML in Source Code window at the point where you want the space and then type ** ** once for each space you'd like to add, pressing the spacebar once between each space code sequence.

4. Use Layout mode to check out the results. If you want to add or delete indent spaces, repeat Steps 2 and 3, adding or removing the   — but be sure to use the entire six characters.

Because the effect of this space is lost in Internet Explorer, I definitely don't recommend using it. The same caution about the space effect being added on top of a style sheet still holds. However, I don't provide style sheet code for dealing with this effect.

Indenting paragraphs with an invisible image

The invisible image — a one-pixel GIF — is a solution that works in all browsers. Place the GIF the same way you place any image, and then use its Inspector to stretch the GIF several points.

For your convenience, a one-pixel GIF is provided in the graphics folder on the CD-ROM.

If you use an invisible GIF and then use a style sheet to create an indent, the GIF's effect will be added to the style sheet's effect, increasing your indent. Chapter 17 discusses a style code that tells the browser to ignore the GIF.

Indenting paragraphs using the Preformatted style

Another way to add space is to use the Preformatted style (Type ➪ Header ➪ Preformatted). The idea behind using it in this case is that because this style interprets your typing exactly, you can add spaces to indent the text and they won't be ignored. This has limitations, though. Because it works on an entire paragraph at once, you can't type the spaces, set them as Preformatted, and then have the line's text appear in another font. Instead, you're stuck with the Courier or monospaced font that the user's browser uses for this tag. This is not a commonly used style any longer.

Inserting space between paragraphs

In a word processor, you press Enter/Return an extra time to add space between paragraphs. This isn't necessary on a Web page. Instead, when you press Enter/Return to end a paragraph, HTML automatically adds a line. Again, a Cascading Style Sheet provides full control over spacing between paragraphs, but a plain HTML page doesn't. If you will not be using a style sheet, you can use several tricks to achieve certain desired effects. (Bear in mind, though, that mixing any of these techniques with the use of a style sheet can cause unpredictable outcomes. Consider skipping these methods and letting those with older browsers simply see the default spacing, which is quite sufficient.)

Note The options in this section are all visual effects only. In other words, they are for presentation, not structure. They can make your page look better, but they don't help a voice-synthesizing browser, or someone using a text-only browser, to read your page more effectively the way headings do.

Using a horizontal spacer to set paragraphs apart

One option is to use a horizontal spacer. However, as noted earlier in this chapter, this spacer is only recognized by Netscape browsers and has no effect in Internet Explorer.

Using an invisible GIF to set paragraphs apart

Another option is to use an invisible one-pixel GIF, and then resize its height to the number of points that you want for the line space. Take a look at Chapter 10 to learn how to insert and size graphics. You'll find a ready-to-use invisible GIF in the graphics folder on the CD-ROM.

Using a table to contain text

Yet another option is to use a table. To do so, you create a table that has several rows and one column, and then place each paragraph in a separate row. By adjusting the cell padding, you can add space between each line. See Chapter 13 to learn more about tables.

Cross-Reference Cascading Style Sheets are the most sophisticated way of controlling paragraph spacing. For more information on style sheets, see Chapter 17.

Using a horizontal rule (line) to set paragraphs apart

The last option doesn't actually add space, but it adds a dividing line that can break up paragraphs nicely, as shown in Figure 8-11. This dividing line is called a *horizontal rule*, or *rule*, in HTML terms. Its code is `<hr>` with no closing tag to go with it. While a horizontal rule can share a line with text, it would either wrap to a new line or remain on the same line as your text depending on how the user sizes his or her browser. Don't count on a user to have the same width browser you have. Instead, create a new line just for your rule line.

To insert a horizontal rule, follow these steps:

1. Create a new empty line into which you will place the line.

2. Drag the Line icon from the Basic tag of the Objects palette up to the blank line.

3. Use the Inspector to set the line's width. (It doesn't have handles to drag.) You have the following options:

   • Choose between a shadowed line (the default) and a plain line style. You can see the look of each within your page in Layout mode.

- Set the line's width. **Full** sets it to automatically cover the entire width of the user's browser. **Pixel** lets you set a specific length; enter the number of pixels into the blank field there. **Percentage** renders the line in relation to the size of the user's browser window; you enter the desired percentage.

- **Height** sets the height of the line, in pixels. Depending on the style you choose, your rule can either be solid or appear as more of an outline.

- **Alignment** tells the line to butt up against the left or right side of the browser, or to remain centered regardless of the user's browser width.

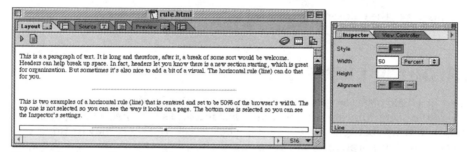

Figure 8-11: Two lines breaking up paragraphs: one not selected and one selected to demonstrate the Inspector settings

People often ask about adding color to a horizontal rule line. No color option exists within the Inspector because color is not commonly supported for this rule. You can add color to your line, but don't count on viewers seeing it.

To add color to your line, follow these steps:

1. Select the line in Layout mode.

2. Switch to Outline mode. The section that contains the ⟨hr⟩ code is selected.

3. Click the small gray arrow directly to the right of the ⟨hr⟩ and choose Color from the menu that pops up.

4. Click in the color swatch that appears next to the word "color." This opens the Color palette.

5. Locate the desired color and drag it to the color chip in the Outline view so the color appears in the color swatch.

The color will not appear in Layout view. Preview the page in Internet Explorer — or another colored-rule-supporting browser — to see the result. (Perhaps by the time you read this Netscape will support colored rules, too.)

You can also add color to your line in Source mode, as follows:

1. Open the Source Code window (Window ➪ Source Code).

2. In Layout mode, click the rule line to select it.

3. Open the Color palette and locate the color you'd like to add.

4. Drag the desired color from the Color palette into the Source Code window and place it just after the "r" in `<hr>`, so that the color code lands inside the bracket. The resulting code looks like this: `<hr color="#ff6633">`.

   The code for adding the color is automatically added to the HTML.

Again, to see the colored rule, preview your page in a browser.

Controlling Lines

Text in a plain page (outside of a grid's text box, table, or floating box) wraps according to the user's browser window width. Inside a grid's text box, a table, or floating box, text wraps between the edges of the box or cell. But there may be times you want to end a line on purpose for phrasing or esthetics, or perhaps you want to ensure a line doesn't break midphrase. Either way, your wish is HTML and GoLive's command.

Inserting line breaks

When you are certain you want a line of text to end and another to begin, you want a line break. A line-break command is somewhat similar to word processing's soft return — it begins a new line without starting a new paragraph.

Because you're still within the same paragraph, any paragraph-level formatting remains in effect. This includes its heading, if you've applied one, and the paragraph's alignment. However, you cannot have a line of text align flush left and then use a break and center the next line. (There's more on aligning later in the chapter.)

Character-level formatting can differ from one word to another within a paragraph broken by a line break. This includes physical formatting, such as bold, and structural formatting, such as emphasis. (More on all this later in the chapter.)

You have two ways to enter a line break:

✦ Drag a line break from the Basic tab of the Objects palette (see Figure 8-12), placing the break between the words you wish to break — in front of the word you want to have start the new line.

✦ Place your cursor in front of the first character you want on the new line, and then press Shift along with Enter/Return.

Figure 8-12: Dragging a line break from the palette to break up a line

The symbol for the line-break icon is the HTML code for break —
 along with the in-text symbol for it. Each time you place a line break on your page, GoLive writes the <br> tag into the page's HTML. In Figure 8-13, you can see both the Layout view's symbol and the HTML code.

Figure 8-13: The look and effect of line breaks in Layout mode

Line breaks can also help you wrap text around a graphic. See "Aligning Text" later in this chapter.

To remove a line break and rejoin your lines, delete the line-break character the same way you delete a text character. (If you do not see the line-break character, choose Edit ➪ Show Invisible Items.) Another way to delete a line break is to click it, select it as an object, and then press Backspace/Delete.

Preventing line breaks

Sometime you want to be sure two words or a phrase remains together on the same line for effect. For example, you might want a name — Ms Jane Doe — to remain on one line, even if the browser window is resized. You can do this easily using the Nobreak command under the Type menu.

Here's how to keep words together:

1. Select the words you wish to keep together.

2. Choose Type ➪ Nobreak

Aligning Text

As with a word processor, you can align each paragraph of text. Alignment is a paragraph-level format. When you place the cursor anywhere in a paragraph and choose an alignment option, the entire paragraph takes on that alignment. This is just like in word processing or page layout, except that HTML doesn't provide for text justification. By default, text is aligned flush left, so there's often no need to adjust alignment at all.

Style sheets provide more alignment control, also enabling you to justify text. If you'll be using a style sheet, you don't need to use the alignment discussed here to code the alignment into the HTML. You *can* use the alignment buttons for older browsers and also use a style sheet, as long as the alignment matches. (Otherwise, the instructions may clash.)

When you use the toolbar to align your text, you are not adding the `<font>` tag to your text. Alignment uses the `<div>` tag. This means it in no way conflicts with accessibility standards.

Alignment works the same whether the text you're aligning is on the plain page, in a text box on a grid, or in a floating box. To align your text, follow these steps:

1. Place your cursor anywhere within the paragraph you want to align. If you want to align more than one paragraph, select at least a part of each paragraph.

2. Click one of the three alignment buttons on the Text toolbar:

   • **Align Left** aligns the text along the left edge of the browser window. As the user resizes the browser window, the left edge remains constant. However, the words that fall at the left edge change as the text reflows to fit the window. Left alignment is the default.

   • **Align Center** aligns the center of each line at the exact center of the browser window. As usual, text reflows to fit the window, so the words contained on each line change.

   • **Align Right** places the text along the right edge of the browser window, leaving the left edge ragged (uneven). (Sentences still read left to right.) This alignment is the most affected by the resizing of the browser window as the text (and graphics within the paragraph) attaches to the right side. That means the effect of the reflowing lines is more noticeable.

Figures 8-14 shows text aligned three ways.

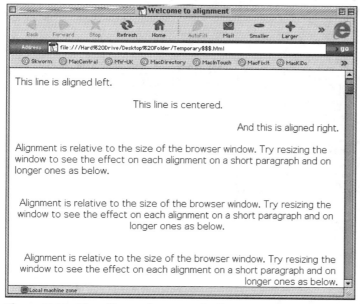

Figure 8-14: The effects of paragraph alignment

Alignment also affects any graphics or other objects that are within the text line. If you have a graphic within your body of text, it will move along with the text alignment. Grids and tables are also affected, as they are attached to a line via the cursor. If you select a grid or table as an object and choose a paragraph alignment, it will move accordingly. Items on the grid or within the table are not affected; they remain in place. However, the actual grid or table moves and therefore carries its contents along with it.

You can also set line breaks to have text align or flow around a graphic, as shown in Figure 18-15.

It takes a bit of playing around with, but here are the basics for positioning text with graphics:

1. Put your graphic in the line of text and align it left or right.

2. Place the line breaks where desired. (See the section "Inserting Line Breaks," earlier in this chapter.)

3. Select the line-break character that is immediately above the line you wish to align.

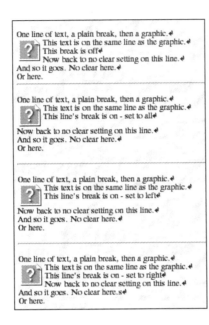

Figure 8-15: The effects of each line-break setting

4. Check the Clear checkbox in the Inspector, now called the Line Break Inspector.

5. Choose All, Left, or Right from the pop-up menu, as follows:

- **All** moves the next line of text to below the graphic.

- **Left** moves the next line of text to below a left-aligned object.

- **Right**, in conjunction with a left-aligned object, has the same effect as not using the Clear checkbox : the text remains up closer to the line-break-containing line.

- **Right** moves the next line of text to below a right-aligned object. Using Clear and Left beside a right-aligned object has the same effect as not checking Clear at all. Rather than move the next line down below the object, the text remains immediately below the line that has the break.

Note If you're wrapping text around a floating box, you must first align the floating box to the left or right.

Adding Pizzazz to Words with Font Styles

As with a word processor, you can assign attributes to specific words or phrases to help them stand out or get your point across. In addition to the attributes you are familiar with in a word processor, two other attributes exist for the Web — Teletype and Blink. These styles are assigned to individual characters, as opposed to entire paragraphs, so you can affect a single character or word.

When creating Web pages, you have two ways to format text using standard HTML tags. (CSS is a third method.) You can use the original Internet standard of selecting *relative*, or *structural*, styles and letting each browser render the style according to the user's preference — or you can take more control by assigning *physical* attributes such as specific font faces, sizes, and other styling. Designers tend to prefer physical styles because bold definitely renders as bold, and so on. However, the intent of the HTML standard is to continue with the idea that formatting tags should carry semantic connotations and enable style sheets to build upon those structural tags. The Style menu is the source of all of these styles — both relative and physical. Either is perfectly safe for you to use.

The attributes in this section work well with style sheets. You can use any of these to help get your message across to viewers, and then, if you'd like, use a style sheet to further jazz up the text. In fact, you can use these tags to build styles upon.

Note The items under the GoLive Type Style menu are actually not styles but text attributes. Technically, a style is a collection of attributes — not just in GoLive, but in all programs. Somewhere along the line, someone started calling bold, italic, underline, outline, and so on text styles and the term stuck. I don't call these choices attributes here just because of HTML geek stuff. I do it because I'd rather keep terms straight for computer-using humanity.

The attributes under the Type ⇨ Style menu are physically assigned to the characters to which you apply them. When you make a word bold, it will definitely be drawn bold by any user's browser. This provides absolute control over your text. Bear in mind, though, that although you know the font will be rendered in bold, unless you're using a style sheet, you still cannot be certain what size your viewers will see. Figure 8-16 shows the physical styles.

The physical styles shown in Figure 8-16 are as follows:

✦ **Plain Text** is text, plain and simple, with no formatting. After you've changed your text, you can remove formatting from your text by first selecting the text and then choosing Type ⇨ Style ⇨ Plain Text or pressing Shift-Option-P (Mac) or Shift+Control+P (Windows).

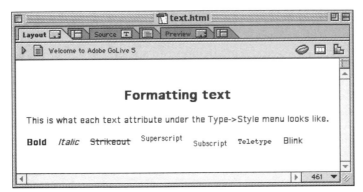

Figure 8-16: The effects of the Style menu, as seen in Netscape Navigator

✦ **Bold** is the same bolding effect you know from word processing. Use it to bring attention to your words. To make your text bold, select the text and then click the Bold button on the toolbar, or choose Type ➪ Style ➪ Bold or press Command-Shift-B (Mac) or Control+Shift+B (Windows). The bold tag — <b> — is commonly used in style sheets to further add to the look of text.

✦ **Italic** text adds emphasis to words. Be careful, though, because italics are hard to read at small sizes onscreen. Your visitors may be viewing your text several sizes smaller than you wish they would. To make your text italic, select the text and then click the Italic button on the toolbar, or choose Type ➪ Style ➪ Italic, or press Command-Shift-I (Mac) or Control+Shift+I (Windows). This tag — <i> — is commonly used in style sheets to further add to the look of text.

✦ **Underline** places an underline beneath your words. However, because links are known by underlines, using this underline can be confusing. In fact, it is now obsoleted by the HTML standards and its use is absolutely discouraged. But because it's a choice in GoLive, we'll tell you that to use it, select it and then choose Type ➪ Style ➪ Underline, or press Command-Shift-U (Mac) or Control+Shift+U (Windows).

✦ **Strikeout** places a line through your text. To strikeout your text, select it and then choose Type ➪ Style ➪ Strikeout, or press Command-Shift-A (Mac) or Control+Shift+A (Windows).

✦ **Superscript** raises your text above its baseline. Be careful with this because it adds extra space above the line, throwing off the look of a paragraph. To use it, select the text and then choose Type ➪ Style ➪ Subscript or Command-Shift-+ (Mac). (No shortcut exists in Windows.)

✦ **Subscript** moves your text below its baseline. Be careful with this because it adds extra space below the line, unbalancing the look of a paragraph. To use it, select the text and then choose Type ➪ Style ➪ Subscript or press Option-Shift- - (hyphen) (Mac). (No shortcut exists in Windows.)

✦ **Teletype** is not actually a definite effect. It is meant to provide an old-fashioned typewritten look and does — Courier is set as your viewer's monospace font. Otherwise, it draws in whatever the monospace font is set to in the user's browser. With a style sheet, you can be more exact in requesting Courier. To use teletype, select the text and then click the Teletype button on the toolbar, or choose Type ➪ Style ➪ Teletype, or press Command-Shift-T (Mac) or Control+Shift+T (Windows).

✦ **Blink** causes your text to blink constantly. To have your text blink, select it and then choose Type ➪ Style ➪ Blink. The Blink effect isn't visible in the GoLive Preview mode. To see it, you must preview your page in a browser. To do so, click the Show in Browser button on the toolbar. Think twice and thrice about choosing Blink; it's a distracting effect that is not well received by viewers, and is ignored by Internet Explorer.

You can also select the preceding formatting options by choosing each respective style's name from the Style heading in the contextual menu.

The Type menu also provides a submenu called Structure. The choices in this submenu assign relative, or structural, styles as opposed to a physical look. After you choose a structural look for your words, the browser implements its own rendition based on the browser's behavior. If you are using a style sheet, you can also use these tags inline to define the look of text based on what you want the text to represent. These styles were created in the first days of the Web when the Web was used for exchange of scientific knowledge, as the names and functions reflect. Figure 8-17 shows the structural styles.

Figure 8-17: The effects of the Structure submenu

The structural styles shown in Figure 8-17 are as follows:

✦ **Plain Structure** returns the text to its unstyled state. If you apply formatting and wish to remove it, you can choose this style to do so.

✦ **Emphasis** is intended to add emphasis to your words. It does so by italicizing them.

✦ **Strong** calls attention to your words by making them bold.

✦ **Quotation** lets readers know you are quoting another person's words. By convention and default, this italicizes the font. Although GoLive calls this Quotation, the HTML tag applied is `<cite>`. This tag is going to continue to grow in power and use in upcoming HTML specifications — a good reason to use it rather than to just make your text italic when your intention is to quote someone.

✦ **Sample** is similar to Quotation, but is used when text is a sample from another source. This is usually displayed in the viewer's designated monospaced font.

✦ **Definition** tells the reader you are noting a definition. This is usually done with plain text.

✦ **Variable** is part of noting program code. It's usually shown in italic.

✦ **Code** is used to show program code and is usually drawn in a monospaced font.

✦ **Keyboard** tells the reader this text is to be typed. It is typically depicted by the monospaced font designated by the user's preferences. Courier, the font of typewriters, is the typical browser default for monospaced text.

Each of the preceding formatting options is also available in the contextual menu. However, instead of being under a menu heading called Structure, they are in the lower part of the Style menu heading.

Changing Font Colors

As explained in Chapter 6, you can assign a master color for all of the text on your entire page and easily change that color at any time, even after there's plenty of text on your page. But at times you are bound to want certain bits of text to be a color other than the main text color. Doing so is easy. But you have more to consider than just the ease of adding a color. You should consider what it takes to change the color and how much code the added color places in your page. This is discussed later in this section.

To change the color of a single character, a word, or any contiguous text, follow these steps:

1. Select the text you want to color.

2. Click the Text Color color swatch in the toolbar to open the Color palette.

3. Click the desired color in the Color palette.

If you seek one of the 216 Web-safe colors for your text, instead of choosing a color from the Color palette, you can select the text to be colored and then point to the Text Color color swatch in the toolbar and Control-click (Mac) or right-click (Windows), and then choose your color from this pop-up color chart.

The HTML surrounding text colored in this manner looks like this:

```
<font color="#663399">This text is purple.</font>
```

If you color text that is midsentence or in the middle of other text, the text on each side still uses the current body text color. However, if you apply the new color to the end of your existing text, and then keep typing, the new text comes in with the new color and that new color continues until you begin a new paragraph. To remove that second color and get your new text back to the body color, or to remove a secondary color anytime, select the text and choose Type ⇨ Remove Color. This completely removes the font color tags that surrounded it.

After you've changed the color of specific text, when you change the whole page's color within the Page Inspector, this text color remains intact, unaffected.

Tip

You can remove all secondary colors from the main part of a page at once by selecting all of the text on the page and choosing Type ⇨ Remove Color. However, this doesn't remove the color from a gridded area, from within a table, or from within floating boxes. To remove color from those areas, you must select all the text in those areas and then use the Remove Color command.

Color and the Font Tag

When you assign a color to an entire page using the Page Inspector, you are setting a one-time-per-page tag called `<body text>`. However, adding color to a specific block of text inserts the font tag (`<font>`) in the HTML code. This tag was originally a somewhat good idea in that it gave you control of text characters, but a bad idea in its implementation. To use it, you must apply its attributes, such as font face and color, to every single block of text individually. This can add a lot of extra HTML code to your page. It also requires you to resort to changing font colors by hand in the HTML source or using Find and Replace if you want to change them later. Style sheets do the job much more easily. Therefore, the `<font>` tag has been deprecated (phased out) and is not planned for the next HTML standard. If you use this tag now, you may just have to remove it later. Another very good reason not to use this tag is that it causes problems for screen readers, speech browsers, and other access tools used by people with visual impairments. The `<font>` tag says nothing about the structure of your document, just the visual appearance—which is contrary to accessibility standards.

Tip

To help you weigh the need to add color this way, consider these facts. If you're planning on using style sheets for your page, you don't want font tags in the body of your document because there's a good chance they'll conflict with the style sheet. Version 4 browsers and Internet Explorer 3 can see color when you use a style sheet. Therefore, the only users this color addition benefits are those using Version 2 browsers or the Netscape 3 browsers. (Font color specification was not part of Version 1 browsers.)

Using Font Sets

Font sets, introduced by Internet Explorer 3, were the Web's first way to give designers some control over what font their pages were rendered with. Prior to font sets, fonts were displayed in the font dictated by the browser or by the user's preferences. Designers, hungry for control over the look of their pages, happily embraced the font face attribute and it was soon widely used.

The idea behind the font set is rather brilliant. A browser can only display text using the fonts that are installed on the user's computer — and you have no control over which fonts a user has. Therefore, if you assign a particular font to any of your text and the user doesn't have that font installed, the user won't see your text in the desired font. So instead of assigning a single font to the text, you can assign a list of fonts. As the page builds, the browser refers to the list. If the first font is installed, the text is rendered with it. If it's not, the browser checks for the next font on the list, and so on. By choosing fonts of a similar design (size and shape), and listing at least one that's common on each platform, you gain control over the look of your page. (If the user has none of your set's fonts installed, it uses the default font.)

Unfortunately, the way a font set was integrated into a page was by the addition of a new tag called `<font face>`. And this font tag turned out to be more trouble than it was worth. It adds a lot of code to your page, slowing the download when a user calls for your page. And worse, it doesn't play nicely with its predecessor, style sheets.

As the Web progressed, Version 4 browsers brought the ability to use Cascading Style Sheets, lessening the need for the font face tag. However, as style sheets aren't backward compatible (and were not totally reliable), the font face tag remained in wide use. These days, some designers still don't trust style sheets and prefer the font face tag. Using it is your call.

The Font Face Tag: Should You or Not?

When you use the Type ⇨ Font menu to apply a font set to your text, you add the `<font face>` tag into your page's HTML. Should you do it? What can it do for you? Here's what it boils down to:

✦ No Version 1 or 2 browser sees the font tag. (Not a big deal these days.)

✦ Netscape 3 doesn't see the font tag.

✦ Version 4 and 5 browsers can take advantage of the cleaner style sheet method of assigning a font set.

✦ The only benefit of using HTML to apply a font set is for those viewing your site with Internet Explorer 3. That's a pretty small viewership for such a hassle. (Unless, for some reason beyond me, you don't choose to use a style sheet.)

Fortunately, you have another way to implement a font set without adding tons of HTML code to your page. You can assign a font set within a style sheet. That way, the entire list of fonts as well as the nine-character HTML tag are listed only once instead of for every occurrence of the set's use. Additionally, a style sheet provides more control over the font set. See Chapter 17 to learn about this use of a style sheet. But keep reading here to learn how to create your own reusable font set.

Note

Are you wondering why one single place doesn't exist where you can enter a font preference for the entire page the way you enter a font color for the whole page? There is a tag that does that. It is called `<basefont>`. It goes in the `<head>` section of the HTML and looks something like this: `<basefont face="Arial, Helvetica" size=3 color="#999999">`. However, GoLive doesn't provide an interface for it because it is a "deprecated" tag. In other words, it is being officially phased out (in favor of Cascading Style Sheets).

Creating font sets

It's easy to create a font set. After you do, you can store it and reuse it any time. You can also share it between pages and sites.

Before you create a new set, consider making the set a default set so it will be globally available to all new pages and sites you create in GoLive. There's no harm in having it in case you want it again. If you are creating a default set, you don't have to have any site open when you create it. To create a set for a specific page, you have to have that page open. However, you can also share page-related sets easily, as discussed later in this chapter.

Follow these steps to create a font set:

1. Choose Type ⇨ Font ⇨ Edit Font Sets to open the Font Set Editor.

2. Determine whether the set will be globally available in GoLive or just available for that page, or when that page is open. Here are some guidelines:

   • If no page or Site window is open, the set will automatically be available globally.

   • *In Windows*, you make a font set global by choosing Default Font Sets from the Font Sets pop-up menu at the top left of the window. Otherwise, the default choice is Page Font Sets.

   • *On the Mac*, you make a font set global by choosing the Default icon in the far left of the window. Otherwise, if a page is open, the set will be available to the current page only; the Page icon is selected at the far left.

3. Under the Font Sets list on the left side, click New, as shown in Figures 8-18 and 8-19. This starts a new empty font set, which appears in the Font Sets list.

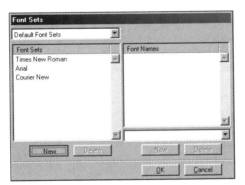

Figure 8-18: Creating a new default (global) font set in Windows

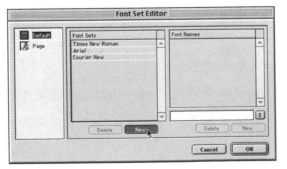

Figure 8-19: Creating a new default (global) font set in Mac

4. Add the first font to the set as follows:

- If the font you want to add is installed in your system, click the arrow pop-up list and choose a font from the list.
- If you don't have the font you want to add, type the name of the font in the Name field. This is the field that says "New Font by default."

The new font's name appears in the list at the right in the Font Names column.

To add another font, and as many fonts as you'd like, click the New button on the right side (the Font Names side) of the window and repeat Step 4.

5. Click OK to save the set.

New sets take on the name of the first font selected. You have no way to change the name of the font set within the Font Set Editor.

If your new font set doesn't show up in the Type ⇨ Font menu, close the page that's currently open and open it again. If no page is open when you create the font set, simply open a page or start a new page and the font sets will be available.

When creating a font set, consider the following:

✦ In order to have your pages render as closely as possible to the look you want, use similar fonts within a set. This means using only serif fonts together or sans serif fonts. It also means matching strokes and shapes as closely as possible. Otherwise, a rounder font will take up more room than a narrower font, and your text will wrap at different places depending on which font actually gets used on the viewer's browser.

✦ Don't choose fonts that it's extremely unlikely your viewers will have. If a set contains fonts that are typically installed by the user's operating system, you have the most chance of success. This isn't as much of a problem if you are designing for an intranet, because you can control or be aware of the fonts that users have installed.

GoLive starts you off with a few font sets containing the commonly installed fonts available on both Mac and Windows. For example, a sans serif set exists consisting of Arial, Helvetica, Geneva, Swiss, and SunSans-Regular.

After you create a set and apply it to any text on your page, you can easily add that set to the Site window. To learn how and why, read on.

Storing font sets in the Site Window

The Site window manages your entire site, so of course it enables you to store font sets too. In the Site window, a font set is easy to use share with other sites — and even to use when creating a style sheet. Perhaps the best reason to store your font sets in the Site window is that you can then see where your set is used by selecting the set and viewing the In & Out Links Inspector. You have three ways to add a font set to the Site window: by dragging text that uses the font set into the Font Sets tab of the Site window, using the Get Font Sets Used command, or using the Clean Up Site command.

Regardless of the method you use to get your font sets listed in the Font Sets tab of the Site window, you'll see the following feedback in this tab:

✦ A bullet in the Used column tells you the set is in use within the site.

✦ The Font Set column lists the fonts in each set. You can expand the column to see the list fully. To do so, move your mouse over the column's divider, and then drag when the mouse icon becomes a double-headed arrow.

Manually adding a font set to the Site Window

One way to add a set to your Site window is to add it manually after you use it. This only works if you apply a font set to text within the page, adding the font face attribute. It doesn't work if you use a style sheet to apply a font set.

Here's how to add a set manually after using it:

1. In Layout mode, apply the font set to selected text.

2. Select any of the text that uses the font set and drag it from the page into the Font Sets tab of the Site window. If the Font Sets tab isn't active, as you drag, rest the mouse over that tab then continue to drag after the tab moves forward, and drop the text into the window area.

The set automatically takes the name of the first font listed in the font set. To change the name, click the existing name to select it and then type the new name.

Automatically collecting font sets

When using style sheets to format your text, this is the method for collecting your used font sets into the Font Sets tab. This command gathers all sets defined for the entire site, including sets in internal and external style sheets and font sets you have not used yet. However, the sets are not named, which is confusing. Additionally confusing is that if you've edited a set, all of the versions you experimented with become listed even though they are not actually used.

To collect all of a site's font sets at once, follow these steps:

1. Click the Font Sets tab in the Site window to make it active.

2. Close all open pages.

GoLive cannot gather font sets from open pages. The command will work, but the open page's sets will not be collected.

3. Choose Site ⇨ Get Font Sets Used (available only when the Font Sets tab is active) or click the Update (checkmark) button on the toolbar (which performs the Get Font Sets Used command too, but, like the menu command, only when the Font Sets tab is active).

After GoLive scans and notes all font sets used in your site, a new folder appears in the tab. (The folder opens automatically, but should you need to open it yourself later.) Click the arrow (Mac) or plus sign (Windows) beside the folder. Inside the folder you'll find each set used, as shown in Figure 8-20.

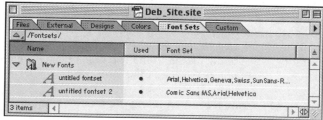

Figure 8-20: Font sets newly added to the Font Sets tab of the Site Window

The sets appear in the Site window without names. You can name a set at any time by clicking the words "untitled font set" to select that text and typing a new name. The new name appears in the bottom part of the Type ⇨ Font menu as well. However, it doesn't change the name as it appears in the top part of the menu or in the Edit Font Sets dialog box. (Nothing you do in the Font Sets tab affects the font sets stored in the menu and Edit Font Sets dialog box.)

Collecting font sets with the Clean Up Site command

Finally, you can let your font sets be collected as part of the package when you use the Clean Up Site command (Site ⇨ Clean Up Site). However, it makes more sense to use the other methods so the sets are more easily available to you.

To collect fonts sets with the Clean Up Site command, follow these steps:

1. Close all pages.

2. With the Site window active, choose Site ⇨ Clean Up Site.

3. Uncheck all options except for font sets under the Add Used (top) section.

4. Click OK.

Caution Clean Up Site can also delete your files, so be careful not to leave anything checked unless you are sure of what will happen. Clean Up Site is covered in Chapter 25.

Using a font set

You have two ways to assign a font set to your text (other than using a style sheet). You can use the Type ➪ Font command or you can drag and drop from the Site window. In order to use drag and drop, the set has to be stored in the Font Sets tab of the Site window first. The method you use doesn't affect the font set's behavior within the page where it is used.

Caution After you apply a font set to text, you can still edit the font set. (See the section entitled "Editing font sets" later in this chapter.) However, editing the set will not necessarily update the text to which that set is already applied. You can only change a set on a page-by-page basis, which can become tedious, or by using Find/Replace, which takes practice. Therefore, I strongly recommend that you choose a font set carefully and test it before applying the set to many blocks of text—unless you are using style sheets and can therefore easily edit the fonts used.

Follow these steps to assign a font set to text using the menu command:

1. Select the text you want to use with the font set.

2. Choose Type ➪ Font and then choose a set from the submenu, as shown in Figure 8-21.

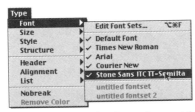

Figure 8-21: Selecting a font set from the Font menu

Font sets in the first section of the menu are sets available to the current page—both global, which are available all the time, and page sets for that page only. Sets below the separator are the ones that are in the Site Window.

Here are the steps for assigning a font set to text using drag and drop:

1. Select the text you want to use with the font set.

2. Drag the font set from the Font Sets tab of the Site window onto the selected text.

Sharing or transferring a font set

What if you create a font set for one page only and want to use it on another page? You have two ways to do this. You can copy a font set between Site windows, or you can do this without collecting your sets in the Site window.

Transferring a font set between Site Windows

To use a page-specific font set within another site, follow these steps:

1. Open the Site window of the source set and click the Font Sets tab.

2. Open the Site window of the destination set and click the Font Sets tab.

3. Drag the desired set from the source Site window into the destination Site window.

   If you did not click the Font Sets tab in Step 2, linger over the tab as you drag. The tab will move forward so you can continue dragging.

4. Rename the set, if desired, by clicking the set's name and typing a new one.

When you move the set into the new Site window, GoLive copies the set so it exists independently in each site.

Transferring a font set by pasting text

When you copy text from one page within GoLive to another, all of that text's attributes — font tag, bold, italic, and so on — are copied along with it. When the text has a font set assigned, even the font set comes along with it.

To copy and paste a font set, follow these steps:

1. Open the page that contains the font set.

2. Copy some of the text that uses the font set.

3. Switch to the page on which you want to use the font set, and then paste.

That's it. The font set is transferred. If you delete all the pasted text, the font set is removed from the source code. But if you edit the text, leaving part of it in place, the set remains in the page. When you use the Get Font Sets Used command, the set will collect into the Font Sets tab just as if you created the set within the Font Set Editor. You can then use it over and over by selecting the text and dragging the font set name from the Font Sets tab onto the text.

The HTML Behind a Font Set

It's important to understand that the `<font face>` tag is placed around every block of text that you apply the set to. For example, even if you select every cell within a table and apply the same font set to that table, the tag set is applied to each cell's text. The code shown in the following figure is for a one-row, three-column table. Notice the redundant code — and notice that the code is, ironically, longer than the actual text that's displayed.

```
<table border="4" cellpadding="0" cellspacing="2" width="400">
  <tr>
    <td><font face="Arial,Helvetica,Geneva,Swiss,SunSans-Regular">Left cell&#146;s text.</font></td>
    <td><font face="Arial,Helvetica,Geneva,Swiss,SunSans-Regular">Center cell&#146;s text.</font></td>
    <td><font face="Arial,Helvetica,Geneva,Swiss,SunSans-Regular">Right cell&#146;s text.</font></td>
  </tr>
</table>
```

The HTML behind a one-row, three-column table when a default font set is applied to the text in all three cells

Actually, pasted text is something to caution you about, too. If you copy and paste text, you have no choice but to inherit the font set. If you don't want a font set within your new page, you'll have to delete the font face code from the pasted text's page. You can do this by selecting the text and choosing Type ⇨ Style ⇨ Plain Text. If you have many individual blocks of text to do this to, consider using GoLive's Search and Replace in the Find window. See Chapter 25 to learn how to do this.

Editing font sets

The most important thing to understand about editing a font set is that when you edit a set, the set is not necessarily updated within all of the pages where you've used it already. When a page is open, you can edit a set that is used within that page and the HTML will update within that page. But under no conditions can you edit a set and have the entire site change to reflect that edited set.

You have two ways to edit a font set:

✦ You can edit it the same way you added the fonts in the first place. In this case, you can edit a default set or you can edit a set for the open page only.

✦ You can edit a set by using the Inspector that becomes available to sets stored within the Site window.

However, editing the set via the Site window and Inspector does not update the text to which that set is already applied. Therefore, I strongly recommend that you edit your font sets from the Edit menu only.

Caution

When you edit a font set, even just to remove a font from the set, GoLive will update the default-listed set, but may also create another set and list both the old and new set as belonging to the page. This can be confusing, as both sets will have the same name. When assigning or editing a set, you have to be sure to select the correct set.

To change, add, or delete a font from an existing set via the Edit Font Sets menu (which I recommend as your main method), follow these steps:

1. Choose Type ➪ Font ➪ Edit Font Sets to open the Font Set Editor.

2. Decide whether you'll edit a default (globally available) set or a set within the currently open page only.

   By default, the Page icon is selected. This will change the set for that page only — even if the font set used initially was a global set. By choosing the Page version, you create a "this-page-only" version of the font set.

3. Click the name of the font set you want to edit, as in Figure 8-22. A list of its fonts appears in the Font Names list at the right.

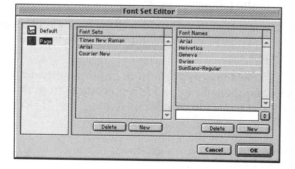

Figure 8-22: Editing a font set

4. To replace a font, click the name of the font you want to replace, and then do one of the following:

   • If the font you want to add is installed in your system, click the arrow pop-up list and choose a font from the list. The new font's name appears in the list at the right in the Font Names column.

   • If you don't have the font you want to add — and you may not if it's a font from another platform — type the name of the font in the Name field. This is the field that says "New Font by default."

To add a new font, click New under the Font Name list on the right side, and then add fonts as you do when creating a new set and click OK when you're finished.

To delete a font from the set, click the font's name in the Font List at the right side of the window and then click Delete. (The Delete button becomes active only when a font is selected.)

5. To add and/or delete more fonts, repeat Steps 3 and 4.

6. Click OK to save your changes.

Edits from within the Site window are not reflected in the Edit Font Sets dialog box, and therefore are not reflected in the font sets that appear in the top part of the Type ⇨ Fonts menu.

Follow these steps to replace, add, or delete a font from an existing set in the Site window:

1. In the Font Sets tab of the Site window, click the set you want to edit.

2. If the Inspector isn't already open, open it. It will be the Font Set Inspector. In the Inspector, take one of the following steps:

   • To replace a font, select that font and then either pick a replacement from the pop-up menu or type the font name into the Name field. (It's the only field you can type in.)

   • To add a new font, select an existing font in order to activate the New button. Click New and then either pick a replacement from the pop-up menu or type the font name into the Name field.

   • To delete a font, select that font and then click Delete.

Repeat Step 2 as desired. No save button exists for changes made in the Font Set Inspector. These saves are automatic.

Tip You can also change the set's name in the Font Set Inspector by editing it in the top field. As with other font set edits made within the Site window, this only changes the name within the Site window's list of sets.

After you edit a font set, if you use the Site ⇨ Get Font Sets Used command to gather your used sets in the Site window, an edited set will be collected as a new set.

Tip If you want to see whether a font set has changed within your page, open the Source Code window, and then select some of the text and see what follows in the `<font face>` tag in source code.

Quickly Updating Fonts with Search and Replace

Editing a set does not update text that already has the set applied. To be sure your text is all updated, you have to reassign the font set to each group of text in order to have the changes go into effect. This is easier if you use the Search and Replace features.

1. Open the Source Code window (Window ⇨ Source Code).

2. In your page, select one occurrence of the old font set's text and change the font set.

3. In Source View, copy an occurrence of the old set's text, such as `<font face="Arial,Helvetica"` — including the opening bracket to help avoid inadvertently replacing places where the text is used in another capacity.

4. Choose Edit ⇨ Find, select the Find & Replace tab, and then paste the set into the Find field.

5. Open the Replace section of the Find dialog box.

6. Back in the page, select the new set's text (again up until the end quote of the fonts) and copy it.

7. Paste it into the Replace section of the Find dialog box.

8. Click Replace All — if you know that no places exist where you've used the entire Font Face command, including the opening bracket elsewhere such as in links. Otherwise, use Replace & Find to review each replacement. If you have multiple pages, you'll need to accommodate them too.

Removing unused font sets

At any point, you can clean up the Font Sets tab of the Site window, removing all sets that are not in use on your site's pages. This doesn't delete an unused set from the Type menu. It simply removes it from the Site window. If you have several font sets created under the Type menu, but haven't used them all on your site, those sets remain intact under that menu.

Removing unused font sets is straightforward:

1. Click the Font Sets tab in the Site window to make it active.

2. Choose Site ⇨ Remove Unused Font Sets. (This command is only available when the Font Sets tab is active.)

At any time you can manually remove a font set from the list in the Font Sets tab of the Site window. Simply click the set's name to select it, and then click the Trash icon in the toolbar.

Another way to remove unused sets is the Clean Up Site command. This also removes sets listed in the Site window, not sets in the Type menu. Choose Site ➪ Clean Up Site, and then uncheck everything but font sets under the Remove section. Then click OK.

Using Special Text Characters

Special characters are for the most part the characters that aren't directly on your keyboard but are typed by using key combinations. This includes currency and legal symbols (such as ¢, €, ®, and ©) as well as foreign language character marks (such as ë, è, and ç), and punctuation such as the em (—) and en (–) dashes. Most of these are hidden key combinations, although a few, such as $ and %, are right out there in view on of the top line of the number keys.

All you really need to know is that when you type these symbols, GoLive puts them on your Web page. GoLive shields you from the code-techie stuff. What's really going on is that because HTML only knows a very basic character set, GoLive substitutes the HTML special codes to provide you with any symbol your heart or employer desires. For example, to type quote marks before and after a sentence, all you have to do is press Shift and the quote key as with a word processor. But a quick glance at the HTML behind the scenes reveals that GoLive really inserted the tag <&quot> before and after your words.

One thing you might miss in GoLive if you are used to word processing is having automatic smart (also known as curly) quotes. When you type Shift and the quote key you get a straight, typewriter-style quote. To make life a bit easier for you, Table 8-1 shows you the keys for smart quotes and some of the other most common special characters. These are the keys you type on your keyboard, not the HTML characters that GoLive substitutes for you.

If you're using a Mac, you can also use Key Caps to help you insert special characters, or you can use the very popular and incredibly handy Pop Char Pro.

On the CD-ROM

On the off chance that you don't already have Pop Char Pro, it's included on the CD-ROM.

If you're using Windows, you can use its built-in character map to copy the special characters, and then paste them into GoLive. To see the character map, click Start ➪ Programs ➪ Accessories ➪ System Tools ➪ Character Map.

	Table 8-1	
	Special Characters in GoLive	
Symbol	**Mac Keys**	**Windows Keys**
"	Option-[	Alt+0147
"	Shift-Option-[	Alt+0148
¢	Option-$	Alt+0162
€	Shift-Option-2	Alt+0164
¥	Option-Y	Alt+0165
•	Option-8	Alt+0149
©	Option-G	Alt+0169
®	Option-R	Alt+0174
™	Option-2	Alt+0153
--	Shift-Command-- (hyphen)	Alt+0151

Note The code that gets written into the HTML is different than the keyboard shortcuts. Because GoLive shields you from the HTML codes, I won't make this book heavier by listing the many pages of special character (or entity) codes. If you're interested in them, we recommend the *Hip Pocket Guide to HTML* by Ed Tittel, *HTML 4 For Dummies* by Ed Tittel and Stephen Nelson James, and the *HTML 4 Bible* by Bryan Pfaffenberger and Alexis D. Gutzman (all from IDG Books Worldwide).

Checking Your Spelling

Misspellings can be pretty embarrassing, and the folks on the GoLive team want you to look your best. So, of course, there's a full-featured spell checker built in. It's easy to check any page — or to check your entire site in one fell swoop. It even checks any pages you have in the Site Trash when you check the whole site — just in case you change your mind about using them.

To check a single page, open that page before choosing Edit ➪ Check Spelling. To check the entire site, begin with all pages closed. As GoLive finds a questionable word, it opens the page that contains that word.

Here's how to do a spelling check:

1. Choose Edit ➪ Check Spelling to open the Check Spelling dialog box. Alternately, you can press ⌘-Option-U (Mac) or Ctrl+Alt+U (Windows).

2. Choose a language from the Language menu.

3. You can tell GoLive what types of words to look for or ignore. To do so, click the triangle by More Options. This reveals seven options you can check or uncheck, as shown in Figure 8-23.

Figure 8-23: The spelling checker's More Options choices revealed (Mac version)

4. Click Start (or on a Mac, you can also press Enter or Return) to start.

GoLive starts checking the first page in the Site window and then automatically moves on to the next page, moving down the list in alphabetical order by page name. As it checks each page, the name of the dialog box states the page name in the window title bar. When GoLive stops at a questionable word, or questionable punctuation, it opens the page that contains the word and highlights the word in question. At the top of the Spell Checker window, the problem is stated. Below that, GoLive shows you what it guesses to be the best option. Below that, GoLive displays all of the suggestions it comes up with, such as the following:

- If the word is spelled correctly you can add it to your own custom dictionary by clicking Learn, as in Figure 8-24.

- If the word is spelled correctly but you prefer not to add it to your own custom dictionary, click Ignore. You can also choose Ignore All if you want GoLive to not stop each time it comes across this word during the current search.

- If the word is misspelled and the suggestion below the misspelling is correct, click Change.

- If the word is misspelled but one of the other suggestions in the Suggestions area is correct, double-click the word you prefer in order to insert that word. (Or take the long way, clicking the word and then clicking Change.)

- If the word is misspelled and you aren't happy with any of the suggestions, click in the top field, select the listing, and type over it, or edit the suggested word. For example, if you've forgotten a space between words, you can click in between the words and insert a space. Then click Change.

- If you prefer not to check a page, click Next File at any time to move on to the next page.

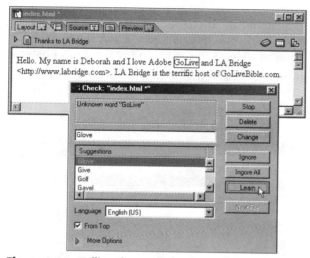

Figure 8-24: Telling the spell checker to learn the word "GoLive" (Windows version)

When the spelling dialog box completes the last page within your Files tab, the dialog box reverts back to saying "Check Spelling."

Editing your personal spelling dictionary

As you check spelling and click Learn, you add the questionable word on your page to your personal dictionary (the file with UDC extension that lives in the Modules folder, within the Dictionaries folder). You can edit this dictionary any time in case you want to remove or repair a word you've added. You can also add words directly into the dictionary instead of waiting until GoLive comes across it while spell checking.

To edit your custom dictionary, follow these steps:

1. Choose Edit ⇨ Preferences to open the Preferences dialog box.

2. In the Preferences dialog box, click Spell Checker from the preference list on the left.

The dictionary doesn't contain any words until after you've added some yourself, either in this Preferences window or in the Check Spelling dialog box. You can click New to start your custom dictionary.

3. Perform any of the following functions:

- To delete a word, select the word and then click Delete.

- To edit a word, select the word so it appears in the field below. Then make any changes within the field, as shown in Figure 8-25. (you won't see an OK button to confirm the change. If you want to be sure the entry is updated, click elsewhere in the list to see the entry change.)

- To add a new word, click New and then replace the words "new word" in the white editing field with your new word. Click the arrow to the field's right or press Enter or Return to confirm.

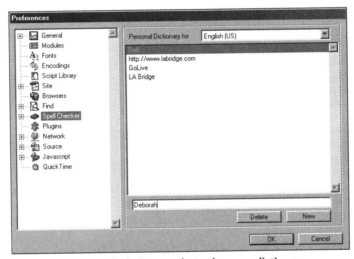

Figure 8-25: An edit being made to the user dictionary

✦　　✦　　✦

Creating and Formatting Lists

Lists can be an excellent way of displaying information in an easy-to-read, well-organized manner. They also add an element of interest to what can otherwise be monotonous text. And, of course, you can turn any word, words, or line of a list into a link, which creates a nice index, directory, or table of contents. Lists can consist of a few simple words or they can be particularly intricate.

Creating a list in GoLive is much like creating one in a word processor. It's really just a matter of selecting text and clicking a button. From there, it's the organization that makes your list — and button clicks here and there to indent its levels for you.

Lists are excellent organizational tools. The HTML code that creates lists is fully recognized by voice synthesizing browsers, so a list's contents and hierarchy can be known to the blind and deaf. Additionally, these tags play well with Cascading Style Sheets so you can add pizzazz to your lists without reducing their accessibility.

Introducing Ordered and Unordered Lists

Lists are typically seen in the form of numbered lists or bulleted lists. In the Web world numbers require or denote a specific order, so a numbered list is known as an *ordered list*. Bulleted lists are classified as *unordered*. Both types are demonstrated in Figure 9-1.

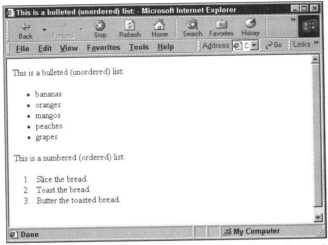

Figure 9-1: The two main types of lists: ordered and unordered

Numbered lists and bulleted lists can be used in conjunction with one another, so you can have a numbered list that has a bulleted list under one of its list items — and vice versa.

There's also a third list on the Web — called a *definition list*. Definition lists are used for noting terms and their definitions. Definition lists aren't as frequently used, but they'll come in handy when you've got some explaining to do.

Creating Lists

You have two ways to turn text into a list. You can select existing text and apply a list style. Or you can type up to where you want your list to begin, and then apply the list style so that when you type the text it is automatically formatted in the list style. This is exactly how formatting works in word processing.

Each method has its benefits. If you first do all the typing, and then select the list text, only the list items are formatted. If you apply the list style as you type, then you need to remove the list style when you no longer want it for the next text.

You can create a list by clicking the bullet or numbered list buttons, which can be found on the toolbar, or by choosing a list type from the List submenu of the Format menu. The two buttons on the toolbar (pictured in Figure 9-2) apply the HTML default unordered or ordered list styles. The Format menu (shown in Figure 9-3) provides more options in addition to the two default list styles. However, as you'll soon learn, I recommend that you stick to the defaults.

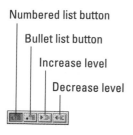

Numbered list button

Bullet list button

Increase level

Decrease level

Figure 9-2: The List buttons on the Text toolbar: two for creating the lists and two for adjusting a list item's levels

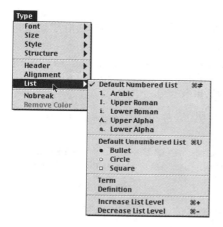

Figure 9-3: The List options in the Type menu: the same as the four buttons plus a few more (this image is from a Mac; it looks a bit different in Windows)

The key to understanding lists is that *list formatting is applied by the paragraph.* As with word processing, GoLive and HTML don't care whether the text you apply a list format to is a few words or several lines. Any text that falls between one occurrence of pressing the Enter/Return key and another simply counts as one paragraph and therefore gets moved as one element in your list. If you use a soft return, called a Line Break (`<br>`) in HTML, the text before and after that break counts on the same list level, as shown in Figure 9-4. (That's because a soft return does not count as a paragraph break.)

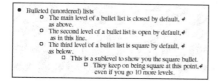

Figure 9-4: Line breaks don't create new list items; they just move the text to the next line.

Creating a list as you type

Follow these steps to create a list by formatting it as you go:

1. Type the introduction to your list, and then press Enter/Return to begin the new line on which your list will start.

2. Choose a list format. As you do, you'll see the first list number or marker appear on your line. This can help guide you in your choice. You have the following options:

   - To create a *default numbered list*, click the Number List button on the toolbar or choose Type ➪ List ➪ Default Numbered List. On the Mac, you can also press Option-#.

   - To create a *default bulleted list*, click the Bullet List button on the toolbar or choose Type ➪ List ➪ Default Unnumbered List. Alternatively, you can press Option-U (Mac) or Ctrl+U (Windows).

   - To use a bullet or number format, other than the default order, choose Type ➪ List and choose a style.

Tip For a bullet (unordered) list, the recommendation of the W3C is to use the default bullet, and then use a style sheet if you wish to have your bullets rendered in a shape other than the default.

3. Begin typing your first list item.

4. At the end of your first list item press Enter/Return to start a new line. This creates another line on the same level of the first line. You can then do any of the following:

   - To add another item at this list level, just type.

   - To make this new line a sublevel of the last line, click the Increase List Level button on the toolbar.

   - To change the bullet or number style, click the toolbar button for the type of list you want to apply, or choose Type ➪ List, and then choose a style. You can mix bullets and numbers without a problem. (However, you're better off using a style sheet to alter the default rendering. If you choose a nondefault list style, check for clashing results in various browsers.)

5. Repeat Steps 3 and 4 for every line of your list. If you've created some lines and want to take a step back to a higher level, click the Decrease List Level button on the toolbar.

6. When you've completed your list and want to return to unlisted text format, press Enter/Return to start a fresh line. Then click the Decrease List Level button on the toolbar as many times as it takes to return to the main level, plus one more to switch the line from being a list to being regular text.

If you find any line of text is getting too long, consider adding a line break (soft return) to move the next text to a new line without creating a new list item. To add a new break to a line, place the cursor where you want the break, and then press Shift as you press Enter/Return.

Creating a list from existing text

What if you've already typed all, or even part of the text that you want to format as a list? You don't have to retype it. Instead, you can turn this text into a list. The same goes for text you paste from another source.

The following steps are intended to help you understand list formatting, although this is actually the long way to operate. Read on to find out the easier way to actually format your lists, once you have this understanding.

To turn already typed text into a list by entering it first, and then formatting it, follow these steps:

1. Type or paste in all the information you want your list to contain — or type any information you have so far. (You can always add the rest later, as you get it.)

   One element to pay attention to: A tab in a word processor translates to a space in HTML. You can see the spaces in Figure 9-5, which shows you both the original Word document as well as the result of copying the list into GoLive. (It also shows you the HTML created in GoLive.)

Figure 9-5: *Left to Right:* The text within Word, the same text pasted into GoLive, and the Source Code written behind the scenes by GoLive

2. Place your cursor in the first line you wish to format as a list. Typically, this would be the first element in your list, and you'd want it at the main level.

   You don't have to bother selecting all of the text in the line because the formatting applies to the entire paragraph — all text that comes between the last Enter/Return and the next one.

3. Choose a list format, as follows:

- To create a *default bulleted list*, click the Bullet List button on the toolbar or choose Type ➪ List ➪ Default Unnumbered List. You can also press Option-U (Mac) or Ctrl+U (Windows).

- To create a *default numbered list*, click the Number List button on the toolbar or choose Type ➪ List ➪ Default Numbered List. On the Mac you can also use Option- #.

- To use a bullet or number format other than the default order, choose Type ➪ List and choose a style from the submenu. (Bear in mind though, that the W3C recommends using a style sheet to alter the look of bullets. You can learn about this in Chapter 17.)

When you format a line (or paragraph), only that line is formatted. Lines (paragraphs) above and below are unaffected, as you can see in Figure 9-6.

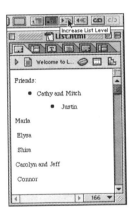

Figure 9-6: The same text again, after a subline is formatted as a bullet, and Increase List Level is clicked one time

4. Place your cursor in the next line you wish to format as a list and do one of the following:

- If this line is another element to be at the top level of your list, choose the same list format you selected in Step 3.

- If this line is to become a sublist under the first element in your list, choose the desired list format, and then click the Increase List Level button on the toolbar.

Note   The Increase List Level button does not become active until you specify the list type.

5. Repeat Step 4 until your entire list is complete. For any lines that need to be moved several levels inward, click the Increase List Level button on the toolbar enough times to move it where you want it. If you go too far, or change your mind later, you can use the Decrease List Level button to move the text back toward the left margin.

I've just told you the longest way to go about formatting a list, so you can gain the best understanding of what's happening. Now, here are the shortcuts you can take.

When formatting a pretyped list, you don't have to format the list line by line. Instead you can do the following:

1. Begin by selecting the entire list and applying your first-level formatting choice. In a numbered list this gives every line a number. In a bulleted list it gives every line the same bullet.

2. Return to the top of your list text and select any lines under the first line that you wish to turn into a sublevel of the first line. If you have several, select them all. It doesn't matter if this includes text that is to be even more indented. With all this text selected, click the Increase List Level button on the toolbar. Now you have your first level-two indent. Repeat this step as needed within the level one formatted text that you want to move to level two.

3. If the text formatted as level two in Step 2 includes text you want at level three, select that text and click the Increase List Level button on the toolbar. (This step works exactly as Step 2.) Repeat this step as needed within the level two formatted text that should become level three.

Working with pasted lists

When the text you paste is already formatted as a list in the application you copy it from, the numbers or bullets from that list paste into GoLive as hard-typed characters. In other words, they count as text, not a fluid numbering system like they were in the other application. You can see this for yourself two ways:

✦ You cannot select bullets or numbers that are HTML-rendered by GoLive.

✦ In the Source Code you can see that in each pasted line the number was pasted as if it were text.

Because of this, when you apply numbering or bullets you have the old numbers or bullets in addition to the list format you apply in GoLive. This is illustrated in Figure 9-7, where a bullet was applied to the first line of the pasted-in list.

At some point, either after formatting your list in GoLive or before, you need to delete the imported letters, numbers, or bullets.

Figure 9-7: *Left to Right:* The list as numbered within Word; the list pasted into GoLive, with the first line formatted as a bullet in GoLive; and the Source Code

Turning a list back into plain text

At any time after you create a list, you can turn the entire list, or any individual line of the list, back into regular text. To do so, you pretty much reverse the creation steps, except that you don't have to remove style.

To turn a single line back into regular text, place the cursor anywhere in that line, and then click the Decrease List Level button until the line returns to the margin. When it does, the bullet or number disappears.

To turn multiple lines (or even the entire list) back into regular text, select the lines, and then click the Decrease List Level button until the lines return to the margin and the bullets or numbers disappear. The lines don't necessarily have to be at the same list level in order to do this. Each line simply hits the margin at its own rate and hangs out while the others continue their trek to the margin.

You might expect that you could place the cursor in a list's line and, if a list button is highlighted on the toolbar, click the highlighted button again. However, in GoLive clicking a selected button has no effect. Likewise, you might expect that you could select the lines, and then return to the Type ➪ List submenu and choose the list option to deselect it. However, this action doesn't toggle the menu option to off.

Applying list styles

So when do you use a bulleted list and when do you use a numbered one? Well, numbers, as I've said, are used for ordered lists. Numbers imply a ranking — the first item is more important than the second, or should be done before the second, and so on. Numbers are a natural choice for lists of steps, for example. Bullets, on the other hand, imply equal thoughts or ideas. Use bullets when the items in your list can be switched around without sacrificing any meaning.

Bullets and numbers can be mixed and matched in a single multilevel list. For example, you can have a numbered list, and then under one of the numbers you can have several bullets to enforce your point. Placing a list within a list is called "nesting" in HTML.

> As with other text formatting, you can use the ruler and Type menu to create bullets embedded directly in your page or you can use Cascading Style Sheets. Whichever way you choose to fancify your bullets, GoLive gives you the power to do so easily. However, per the W3C, I recommend sticking with style sheets to alter the look of your lists.

Bulleted list styles

Three bullet styles exist, as follows:

✦ **Bullet.** The solid bullet, just like you get using Option-8 (Mac) or Alt+0183 (Windows). This is the same bullet you get when you choose Default Unnumbered List.

✦ **Circle.** The same size and placed bullet as the regular, solid one, but hollow. This is also the default second level bullet that you get when you choose Default Unnumbered List and do no extra formatting.

✦ **Square.** A hollow square. This is also the default third level bullet that you get when you choose Default Unnumbered List with no extra formatting.

When you apply the Default style, each of these styles is called into place according to the level of your list item. Alternately, you can apply any of these styles by choosing Type ➪ List, and then selecting the desired style. However, it is best to use a style sheet to customize your lists. Users of non-CSS-savvy browsers still see the order; however, they just see the browser's default bullet rendering instead of your custom bullets.

Numbered list styles

Five numbered, or ordered, list styles exist, as shown in Figure 9-8. They are as follows:

✦ **Arabic.** The standard numbering system (1, 2, 3, 4, and so on) such as in the numbered instruction lists in this book. This is the type of number you get when you choose Default Numbered List.

✦ **Upper Roman.** Uppercase roman numbering, as in I, II, III, IV, V, and so on.

✦ **Lower Roman.** Lowercase roman numbering, as in i, ii, iii, iv, v, and so on.

✦ **Upper Alpha.** The uppercase alphabet, as in A, B, C, and so on.

✦ **Lower Alpha.** The lowercase alphabet, as in a, b, c, and so on.

```
I. Arabic
II. Upper Roman
iii. Lower Roman
D. Upper Alpha
e. Lower Alpha
```

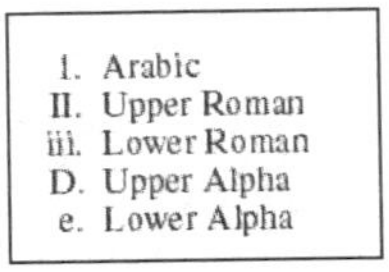

Figure 9-8: The various styles for ordered (numbered) lists

Unlike bullets, which change as you get into sublevels of an outline, number formatting remains the same for each of the secondary levels. You *could* apply a specific format from the Type ⇨ List submenu to create a sublevel numbering system, but that is best done with a style sheet, per the recommendation of the W3C.

Each time you start a numbered (ordered) list, the numbering (order) begins anew. You cannot start an order, break it up with nonlist text, and then have the number list continue automatically. However, you can *tell* the second list what number to begin with, so you can create the *look* of a list numbering continuation.

Follow these steps to continue a number sequence after breaking up a numbered list:

1. Enter your list contents as normal.

2. Use the list choices to assign the desired numbered (ordered) list style to the first part of the list, and then the second part of your list. At this point, you have two separate lists, each starting with "1" or "A" or such.

3. Open the Source Code window (Window ⇨ Source Code) if it's not already open.

4. In Layout mode, click the first line of the second list. This pops the corresponding HTML into view within the Source Code window.

5. In the Source Code window (see Figure 9-9), click inside the `<li>` tag, just in front of the closing bracket.

6. Type a space, and then type **value="X"** where *X* is the number you want your line to have as its number. This value attribute tells the browser to show that list item as the number you specify.

That's it. Each line that follows, and has been formatted as part of the numbered list, automatically takes on the value of *X* + 1. The new numbering does not appear in either Layout or Preview mode, but it does appear within a browser. To see your results, use the Preview in Browser button.

Using Images as BulletsSmall images can be an interesting and attractive alternative to HTML's generic bullets. You can create an entire list using one custom graphic repeatedly, or you can use a different bullet for each element, adding a visual clue as to what a point may be about. Additionally, you can link an image bullet, providing further navigation to your page.

```
Link View    Source Code
    <p>This is the first part of the list:</p>
    <ol>
        <li>Line one of the list</li>
        <li>Line two of the list</li>
        <li>Line three of the list</li>
        <li>Line four of the list</li>
    </ol>
    <p>Now, something that does not get a number. Then back to the list.</p>
    <ol>
        <li value=5>Line five of the list. (But it begins as the first line by default.)</li>
        <li>Line six of the list. (This automatically takes on the value of line five + one.)</li>
    </ol>
```

Figure 9-9: Manually entering a line number value for a numbered list to provide the appearance of continuous line numbering

You have two ways to use graphics as bullets in your list. You can create a single style in a style sheet or you can use a table. To learn how to use a style sheet see Chapter 17. To learn how to create a list in a table, read on. Technically speaking, when you use graphics to create a list, you aren't really creating a list. Instead, you're creating several lines of text that each happen to begin with a bullet-like graphic in order to create the overall effect of what is known, in "everyday language," as a list. If the text for each list item is short, you can place your graphic-bulleted list directly on your page or perhaps on a layout grid. However, if the words that follow any of your custom bullets take up several lines, or are in any way possibly going to wrap to a second line, you're better off putting your list's elements into a table. The reason a table becomes the clear choice for wrapping text has to do with ensuring your bullets and text remain together in all browser circumstances.

Note   Actually, I'm jumping the gun a bit by going into graphics or tables before fully covering them in dedicated chapters. You might want to read about graphics in Chapter 10 and tables in Chapter 13 before actually attempting the following procedure. But for now, you can just look over this material to get basic idea.

To create a list of short phrases using graphics as bullets, follow these steps:

1. Begin by placing a graphic at the start of the first line of your list.

2. Type the text for that line beside the graphic. Keep this line very short to ensure that it does not wrap.

3. Press Enter/Return after the end of the first line.

4. Repeat Steps 1 through 3 until your list is complete.

This type of list looks similar to Figure 9-10, although your own graphic can be any size or shape.

Tip   To add a space between each graphic and text, add a nonbreaking space tag (< >) by pressing Option-spacebar (Mac) or Shift+spacebar (Windows).

Figure 9-10: An unordered list using a graphic as a bullet, without a space, and then again with a nonbreaking space

Here are the steps to create list of long phrases using graphics as bullets:

1. Create a table that is two columns wide and has as many rows as you have list elements. (You can always add or delete rows, so don't worry about being exact for now.)

2. Place a graphic in the left cell of the first line of your list.

3. Click in the right cell of the first line of your list, and then type the text for that line. Text wraps within the cell so the text can be any length.

4. Repeat Steps 2 and 3 until your list is complete.

Want to add some coolness to your lists, and potentially save your viewers from a lot of extra scrolling? Just as Mac users click an arrow and Windows users click a plus or minus sign to reveal or hide lists, you can make your lists collapsible using JavaScript.

Setting up Definition Lists

Definition lists are used for glossaries, product descriptions, and similar lists. When you create a definition list, you need to specify two parts for each list item: the *definition term,* which is on one line, flush against the left margin; and the *definition description,* which appears indented on the next line, as shown in Figure 9-11. Of course, after you create your definition list you can always jazz it up by creating styles for the term and description in a style sheet.

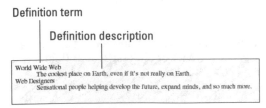

Figure 9-11: A definition list

To create a definition list, follow these steps:

1. Begin your definition list with a fresh new line. Type your first term. Leave the cursor flashing after your text.

2. Choose Type ⇨ List ⇨ Term to format the term.

   You can have two terms in a row without placing a definition between them. To do so, just press Enter/Return after you enter and format the first term, and then type the next term.

3. Press Enter/Return to create a new line for the definition, and then type that definition and leave the cursor flashing at the end of the definition.

4. Choose Type ⇨ List ⇨ Definition to format the first description.

   If you want to add another definition for the same term, press Enter/Return, and then type away. You don't have to format this next definition because it inherits the formatting from the previous line.

   If you have another term to add, press Enter/Return and repeat from Step 2.

5. To complete your definition list and return to regular formatting, press Enter/Return to start a new line, and then click the Decrease List Level button on the toolbar. The cursor returns to the left margin, showing you that you're out of the list formatting.

In case you find a description getting too long, you can add a line break as with all other text. A line break moves the next text to a new line indenting at the same place as the first line of the description. To add a new break to a line, press Shift as you press Enter/Return.

Tip

One Web site element that lends itself perfectly to a list is a Table of Contents. As a matter of fact, GoLive thought of that—and included an automatic table of contents generator. It would be rather silly to generate a Table of Contents until your contents are at least somewhat set, so this is too early in the game to show you how to do it. To learn how to have GoLive create your Table of Contents for you, see Chapter 26.

✦　　✦　　✦

Putting Images on Your Pages

The Internet was conceived as a text-only network by the United States Army in the early 1960s. The ability to display graphic content only occurred in 1989 with the invention of hypertext markup language (HTML) protocol by Tim Berners-Lee at CERN. Although CompuServe invented the capability to animate an image with its GIF89a format that same year, it wasn't until the mid-90s that the animated GIFs became widely know and used among developers.

Today, displaying full-color images is taken for granted. However, as recently as 1995, discovering a GIF could be animated was *the* hot topic of the day. When you consider the speed in which graphics capabilities have evolved from the animated GIF to PNG and SVG formats, interactive graphics using rollovers, full-screen animations with SWF, *live* Webcasts and streaming video with audio . . . it's miraculous.

And as these technologies have evolved, so has the way the developer community creates Web sites and arranges content on the page. Using a WYSIWYG interface, GoLive 5.0 provides several ways to place graphics on your Web pages with ease, options, and control.

Understanding Images on the Web

Unlike text content, images are not physically placed or stored directly in a Web page. Instead, images are separate files typically stored in an "images" directory or folder. When you place an image on your page, you actually create a link in the page's HTML source code, so it looks something like this:

```
<img src="images/image.gif" height="50"
width="50" alt="My Image">
```

This source code tells the browser to display an image called "image.gif" that resides in a directory called "images." The image is 50 pixels square and is called "My Image" in the alternative text. (See the sidebar, "The Importance of ALT Tags," later in this chapter.) When a browser is pointed to a Web-page URL, it downloads the page source code, which is made up of page and text formatting, interactive scripts, text, all links, and so on. If the page contains image links, each image is downloaded as well. (Next time you are waiting for a page to download look at the bottom-left status bar of your browser to see the page components as they are requested and downloaded one by one.)

Once an image downloads to a user's computer, it is stored in the browser cache and you can use it again without causing another download from the Web server.

Tip   To set your browser's cache, go to its Preferences and enter a new number, in megabytes. Depending upon how much free hard disc space you have, 1 to 5MB of browser cache is a good start. Once this cache fills up, the oldest files will be deleted first as new cached files are downloaded into the cache.

From a Web design point of view, you can take advantage of the cache by using the same image multiple times. For example, if you're using a graphic as a bullet, by using the same exact one rather than, say, different colored bullets, you save page download time because the browser will display the image that is already on the local computer instead of downloading it again each time it is referenced (linked). GoLive provides several ways to do so and makes it easy. But remember, GoLive is a layout and site-management program, not a graphics-creation application. While GoLive does provide some image translation and the capability to scale the size of a graphic onscreen on-the-fly, these tools are only offered for convenience. It is best to prepare graphics in a graphics program such as the Photoshop/ImageReady bundle to accomplish the best image and compression optimization. By optimizing your images you'll provide a smooth-looking, fast-loading Web experience for your visitors.

Tip   A good rule of thumb is that it takes 1 second to download 1 kilobyte on an average 28.8 Kbps modem. If you have a page that's 15K of code and calls for four images that are 20K each, the total amount of information for download is 95K [(20 × 4) + 15], which may take about 95 seconds (1:35 minutes). If the server and/or Web connection is slow, the download time can be much longer even with a fast modem. Even if you drive a Porsche, in bumper-to-bumper traffic, it can still be slower than a bicycle.

Graphic formats — A quick overview

Web graphics are currently displayed using four main image formats. GIF and JPEG (also JPG) are the two most commonly supported. PNG and SVG, being newer, are not widely used (yet) and therefore require browser plug-ins. Each of these formats use different methods of file size compression to optimize graphics at screen resolution.

Doing the Math

By Steven Shmerler, Web site designer

If you have a page with four images, you create five download requests from the Web server (one page, four images).

Question: Which is quicker to download? A 48K GIF or four 10K GIFs?

Answer: Probably the one larger GIF, because it takes only one request and one open connection. The other requires four requests. That's four open connections, four downloads, and four closed connections. This is why one graphic may be quicker than the same image sliced into separate image files — and one image map may be faster than multiple separate buttons. This is not an absolute, though, so you'll have to experiment.

GIF — Graphics Interchange Format

GIF is an 8-bit color graphics file compression format developed by CompuServe used for transmitting raster images over the Internet. GIF is a *lossless* compression format, meaning that it retains the integrity of the original file bit for bit. File size depends on the physical size (height and width) of the image plus the number of colors actually used in the image (up to a maximum of 256). Any color from the original image that is not in the GIF palette is assigned to the next closest color in the palette (this process is known as *dithering*), which can be set during compression. The GIF format enables one color to be transparent in addition to enabling animation. GIFs are best used with text, line drawings, computer-generated images, and images with large areas of single colors.

To learn about the GIF specification, visit www.lintilla.demon.co.uk/gif89a.htm.

JPEG — Joint Photographic Experts Group

JPEG is a 24-bit *lossy* compression method that supports millions of colors. Lossy compression involves taking advantage of how the eye sees color versus brightness. JPG removes selective image information to achieve significant file compression. Therefore it is best to always work from an original image and not a compressed JPG file. A *Progressive JPG* is similar to an *Interlaced GIF*, whereby the browser first displays a low and then full resolution version of the image. JPEG does not support transparency or animation, but is supported by all browsers and is best used with continuous-tone images such as photographs and those with gradients.

For more information about JPEG you can check out the JPEG Committee site at www.jpeg.org or JPEG FAQ at www.faqs.org/faqs/jpeg-faq.

PNG — Portable Network Graphics

PNG is an extensible and streamable lossless file format that was originally created as a patent-free alternative to GIF. Two PNG formats exist: PNG-8 and PNG-24. PNG-8 uses 256 colors like GIF, but supports transparency and compression more effectively while allowing for smaller file sizes. PNG-24 supports millions of colors like JPEG, background transparency, and, unlike JPEG, is lossless.

At present, older browsers don't support either PNG format without a plug-in. Version 4.0 browsers support PNG partially. Also, PNG-8 doesn't support animation and PNG-24 is not as effective as JPEG for file-size compression.

You can learn a lot about PNG at the PNG Home Site, maintained by Greg Roelofs, at `www.libpng.org/pub/png`. The PNG specification is outlined at `www.w3.org/TR/REC-png.html`.

SVG — Scalable Vector Graphics

SVG is an extensible graphics language in XML, which enables vector graphic shapes, images, and text objects. You can use Cascading Style Sheets to define font, text, and color, and — unlike GIF, JPEG, and PNG — text remains as text and can be modified at any time in addition to being searchable online. SVG images can be dynamic and interactive, allowing for complex vector graphics animation and event handlers such as mouseovers, onclick, and other events.

SVG images are scalable, enabling users to zoom in and out without image degradation. Unlike GIF, SVG enables any line within a vector graphic to be transparent, translucent, or even opaque. SVG files are smaller than GIF and JPG, but can only be viewed with a SVG viewer or browser plug-in. Because of this different nature of SVG, and its multimedia capability, its placement and set up are covered in Chapter 20.

Adobe Illustrator 9.0 supports SVG and can save to this format. For more information on SVG, consult the following sources:

✦ SVG specification: `www.w3.org/Graphics/SVG`

✦ Adobe SVG viewer: `www.adobe.com/svg/viewer/install`

✦ SVG overview/tutorial: `www.adobe.com/svg`

Note   In addition to recognizing the preceding Internet graphic formats, GoLive can also handle the standard bitmapped image formats — PICT on the Mac and BMP in Windows — by translating them into GIF, JPEG, or PNG. This capability is provided as a convenience to help you for preview and layout purposes only. GoLive's translation is not high quality and not intended for online publication.

Scanning Meets Photography

If you're working with images for the Web, you probably use, or will use, a scanner or digital camera at some point. Recently, I saw a demo of Lightshow 3D made by 3D SCAN (www.3dscanner.com) of its scanner add-on hardware. It is unique, amazing, and worth noting if you're doing any kind of image capture by scanner *or* camera.

Lightshow 3D sits on top of your scanner and turns it into a desktop photo studio. It quickly creates photorealistic images that you can import into any graphics or desktop publishing applications without a camera or any of the usual production set-up or photography costs. Now that's cool! It creates amazingly realistic images that are perfect for object capture, artwork, desktop publishing, Web sites, engineering, prototyping, modeling, and more.

The Lightshow 3D unit is self-contained and conforms with most scanner footprints and works for both Windows and Mac. You can export files in most 2D software formats. You can create 3D models for the Internet and desktop by capturing several 2D scans and importing the files into its 3D modeling software. The company's site explains the details nicely.

Collecting Images in the Site Window

To best use GoLive's powerful site-management system, all pages and all items you place on your pages are best stored within the Files tab of the Site Window — with the exception of native source image files for Smart Objects and Tracing Images. Graphics files are typically stored in an "images" directory within the Site Window's File tab. You can place a graphic or group of graphics into the Files tab at any time.

Collecting images

To place a graphic in the Site Window, open the folder, CD-ROM, disk, or volume that contains the graphic. Then, drag the file into the window of the Files tab where your image files are listed. As you collect images, keep the following points in mind:

✦ Before you begin to drag the image into the Site Window, if the Site Window is not the top active window, bring it to the front by clicking any visible underlying part, choose it from the Window menu, or click the Select Window icon in the toolbar.

✦ If you begin to drag the image only to discover that the Site Window is hidden, you can bring it forward as you drag the file and then continue to drag the file into place. To bring the Site Window forward, rest over any part of it that's exposed or rest over the Select Window button on the toolbar. (If, on a Mac, you have the Site Window tabbed, you can rest over the tab to have the Site Window pop up. After you drop your image in, it pops back down.)

✦ If you reach the Site Window but the Files tab is not active, bring your cursor to rest over the Files tab until this tab becomes active, and then continue.

The files you place here are not physically moved from the original location. Instead, GoLive makes a copy of the original file(s). After you add the copy of the image to the Site Window you can change its name without affecting the original. To help make identification of your files easier, use short, descriptive file names with no spaces.

Caution If you use the Clean up Site command, note that it has an option to delete any unreferenced files. If you've placed graphics in the Site Window in order to use them later, but have not yet used them, be sure to uncheck this option or those files will be removed. Make sure you understand this command (covered in Chapter 25) thoroughly, so you don't inadvertently trash needed files.

Organizing your images

As with any project, it helps to plan and get organized. Whether you're developing a large enterprise site that is fully preplanned and flowcharted down to the last page and image, or a small hobby site and growing it as you go, GoLive's powerful Site Window, Site Navigator, and In & Out Links window let you see, develop, and manage your site's structure at a glance. And regardless of your site's size, structure, or complexity, if you ever need to reorganize, you can restructure with ease by simply dragging your files into place and letting GoLive update the links automatically and flawlessly. This is an amazing feature.

To create a folder, drag a folder icon from the Site tab of the Objects palette, as shown in Figure 10-1, into the body of the Files tab of the Site Window, or click the folder icon on the toolbar in the upper-left while you're in the Files tab.

Site tab

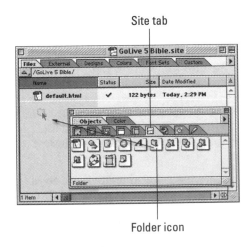

Folder icon

Figure 10-1: Drag a folder from the Site tab of the Objects palette into the Files tab of the Site Window to organize your site's images and other files.

By default, your new folder is named "folder," but is selected so all you have to do is type to rename it, as shown in Figure 10-2. You can keep all of your images within this folder or place other folders within this one. For example, you might have a folder in the images folder called "rollovers."

Figure 10-2: Creating a folder named "images" in which to store your images makes it easier to manage your site files and to update it later.

Tip   If you have a folder full of images on your hard drive that you want to use in your GoLive site, you can add the entire folder at once by dragging it into the Files tab or into the "images" folder within the Files tab.

Previewing Images

You can preview images in two ways: File Preview and Page Preview. You can preview file content using the Content tab in the File Inspector and page content using the Layout Preview tab in the Document Window.

File Preview

File Preview enables you to view a file before you use it, in order to help determine whether it's the file you'd like to use. After you add a file to the Site Window, you can preview it in the Content tab of the File Inspector.

The Content tab displays all image types covered in this chapter: GIFs, JPEGs, Progressive JPEGs, PNGs, and Animated GIFs.

Page Preview

Page Preview enables you to see the result of adding a graphic to your page. After you have linked a graphic to a page in your site you can preview the page and its content in the Layout Preview tab of the Document Window. Simply click the Preview tab of the Document Window. Some images require a plug-in to work in page preview.

Previewing an image file

To preview an image file, follow these steps:

1. Click the image file to select it within the Files tab of the Site Window.

2. In the File Inspector, click the Content tab (see Figure 10-3).

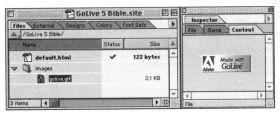

Figure 10-3: From the Site Window, you can preview a selected image by switching to the Content tab of the File Inspector. The hand cursor enables you to move large images for viewing.

3. *(Optional)* Resize the Inspector so you can see your image fully. Or, if the image is larger than the Inspector, use the scroll bars that appear or use the hand cursor to drag the image around within the Inspector.

Note

After you finish previewing graphics in the Contents tab, switch the File Inspector back to the main tab. Otherwise, each time you select a file in the Files tab while the Inspector is open, GoLive will draw the image. This task can slow things down for you considerably because, in addition to loading QuickTime movies, it even draws previews of an entire page.

To preview an image in the context of your Web page, follow these steps:

1. If the page is not open, open the page that contains the image(s) you want to preview.

Note

You can set the display view you want to see when GoLive launches a page. The default is "Layout Editor," which I recommend. To change to another view, choose Edit ➪ Preferences. Beside the General icon select the view you want from the Default Mode pop-up menu.

2. In the Page window, click the Preview tab, which toggles to the Layout Preview.

That's it. You should see your image in place on the page, closely approximating how it will look on the Web.

If your image is a PNG and you don't see it on your page or in preview, check to see that the PNG Image Format module is turned on in your Preferences.

Tip   To become familiar with your files quickly, you can place the Inspector to the side of the Site Window with the Content tab selected, click the first file you want to inspect, and then use the arrow keys on your keyboard to move up and down the list of images in the Files tab.

Placing an Image by Dragging

Adding an image to a Web page is easy with GoLive. No matter where you want to place your image, inline with text, into a table, onto a grid, or into a floating box, you can place it there simply by dragging it. You can drag an image from the Site Window or from its preview in the Content tab of the Inspector.

When you drag an image into place, any text or object(s) to its right and below it are moved further right and/or down to accommodate the graphic. Once on the page, you can change the image's alignment attributes in the Basic tab of the Inspector and also change the space surrounding the image (HSpace and VSpace) in the More tab of the Inspector. Each of these attributes affects how text and other objects appear in relation to this image. When you drag an image into a table cell, floating box, or grid, each of these structures grows to accommodate the size of the graphic.

Dragging an image from the Files tab

To add an image file to a page as shown in Figure 10-4, simply drag it from the Files tab of the Site Window over to your page and drop it wherever you want it. You can always move it later.

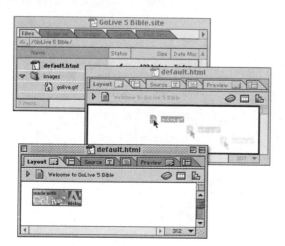

Figure 10-4: To add an image to your page, just drag it from the Files tab of the Site Window.

Dragging a previewed image

When you don't recall an image's name or you're not sure which one you want, use GoLive's Preview feature. You can preview your images and drag the desired one directly from the preview.

Follow these steps to drag an image from the preview:

1. Select the image within the Files tab of the Site Window.

2. In the Inspector, click the Content tab.

3. If the image you want is displayed, go to Step 4. If not, you can click another image to preview it, or use the arrow keys on your keyboard to move up or down to the next file.

4. With your cursor, grab the image in the Content tab and drag it into place on your page. Figure 10-5 shows an image in mid-drag.

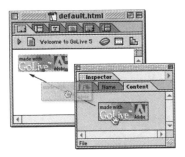

Figure 10-5: You can add an image to the page by dragging it from the Content tab's preview.

5. In the Inspector, switch to the Basic tab and enter a short description of your graphic into the Alt Text field shown in Figure 10-6. (See the following sidebar, "The Importance of ALT Tags" for details.)

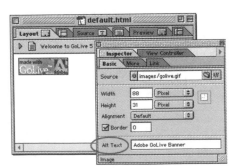

Figure 10-6: To add Alternative Text to your image, type in the text in the Image Inspector Alt Text field.

The Importance of ALT Tags

Whenever you use a graphic on any Web page you should make it a habit to add what is known as *alternative text* that briefly describes the graphic or its function. If your graphic contains text information such as a company name or a button's directions (for example, "Home," "Products," "Contact Us," and so on), the graphic's message will be lost to a user who cannot see your images. Instead of seeing an empty image space, alternative text provides users with information in text form that you put into the artwork. Graphics may not display because of slow connections or if image display is turned off in the browser preferences.

You can supply alternative text simply by typing in some text. When you do, GoLive generates an <alt> tag within the HTML tag that calls the graphic. This description, called ALT text or an ALT tag, serves several purposes — all good and all helpful.

Keep the following points in mind when working with ALT tags:

✦ ALT text is read by voice-synthesizing browsers so your visitors can experience your site, even if they are hearing your page instead of seeing it.

✦ ALT text is translated into Braille so visitors who can't see or hear your page can still get a lot out of it.

✦ ALT text is displayed by text-only browsers so those using nongraphical browsers, whether on an ancient PC or a newfangled hand-held device, can still get your message.

✦ ALT text can help keep users at your site by getting them around faster. This text displays in the browser before the graphic loads. Therefore the user has an idea of what's to come, giving them an opportunity to make choices without waiting for the graphics to fully load.

Here's how to add a text message as an alternative to a graphic:

1. Click the image to select it.

2. In the Image Inspector's Basic tab, click in the Alt Text field and type your text exactly as you want it to appear. Spaces are acceptable, but be brief. This is not the place to be wordy.

A good example of alternative text is the explanation of a graphical navigation bar, and alternative direction, shown in Figure 10-6. The HTML for an alt tag is <alt>. It is placed within the image tag. For example:

```
<img height="155" width="144" src="Images/mygif.gif" alt="This is
the alt text.">
```

Adding an Image by Using a Placeholder

Whether you're designing your site commercially for a client, or creating it for yourself, at times you may want to plan and lay out your page but don't have all the page's elements. In such a case, an image placeholder can hold the area open and give you a feel for the layout, as shown in Figure 10-7.

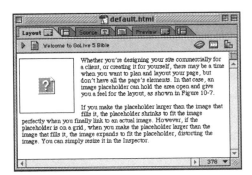

Figure 10-7: An image placeholder can help you lay out your page before you have all the final elements.

Note   If you make the placeholder larger than the image that fills it, the placeholder shrinks to fit the image perfectly when you finally link to an actual image. However, if the placeholder is on a grid, when you make the placeholder larger than the image that fills it, the image expands to fit the placeholder, distorting the image. You can simply resize it in the Inspector.

You have a few different ways to add an image with a placeholder. I'll cover all of them in the next sections.

Pointing and Shooting an image from a placeholder

With this method you can follow Steps 1 and 2 first, and then come back to complete Step 3 any time in the future. It's as easy to use as any point-and-shoot camera. This is a win-win page design option.

To Point and Shoot an image from a placeholder, follow these steps:

1. Add a placeholder to your page in one of these two ways:

    • *Dragging.* For the most control, drag the graphic placeholder from the Basic tab of the Objects palette into place on your page. In Figure 10-8 an image placeholder is being dragged to a grid.

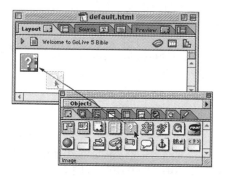

Figure 10-8: Place an image placeholder by dragging it from the Basic tab of the Objects palette into the Files tab of the Site Window.

- *Clicking.* Tell GoLive where you want the placeholder to appear by placing your cursor on the page or by selecting an area of the page. Then double-click the graphic placeholder in the Basic tab of the Objects palette, which places the placeholder at the cursor on your page. If you selected a floating box or clicked in an empty table cell, the placeholder lands in that box or cell. If you selected a grid, it lands in the first available space on the grid.

2. Prepare for the image that will fill the placeholder:

- Fine-tune the position of the placeholder.

- Arrange your page to accommodate the graphic.

- Resize the placeholder to approximately the size of the graphic you expect to fill it with. To resize the placeholder, drag the bottom-right or bottom-left handles (as with any object). To resize any placeholder, drag a handle. The bottom-right corner is always available and draggable. A table cell or floating box expands as you drag the image placeholder (a grid won't expand).

3. To tell GoLive which graphic you want to place in the placeholder spot, press ⌘ (Mac) or Alt (Windows) as you click the placeholder, and then drag to the graphic file in the Files tab of the Site Window, as shown in Figure 10-9.

Figure 10-9: You can Point and Shoot directly from a placeholder to the desired graphic as long as the graphic is in the Site Window.

Using the placeholder and Image Inspector

If you tend to keep the Inspector open, then it's as convenient to place an image placeholder and then Point and Shoot from the Image Inspector as it is to Point and Shoot directly from the placeholder.

Here's how to Point and Shoot an image from the Image Inspector:

1. Add a placeholder to your page in one of these two ways:

    • *Dragging.* For the most control, drag the graphic placeholder from the Basic tab of the Objects palette into place on your page.

    • *Clicking.* Tell GoLive where you want the placeholder to appear by placing your cursor on the page or by selecting an area of the page. Then double-click the graphic placeholder in the Basic tab of the Objects palette. This pops the placeholder into place. If you clicked in any line of text, the placeholder lands at the cursor. If you selected a floating box or click in an empty table cell, the placeholder lands in that box or cell. If you selected a grid, it lands in the first available space on the grid.

2. Resize the placeholder to the approximate size of the graphic, and then rearrange the objects on your page. This can give you an idea of the page's look when you don't yet have the graphic handy. To resize the placeholder, drag the bottom, right, or bottom-right handles. Be aware that GoLive will report this placeholder as an error as long as the link source still says "(Empty Reference!)."

3. Open the Inspector, now called the Image Inspector. If the Basic tab is not already active, click this tab to bring it forward. From the Source field at the top of the Basic tab, do one of the following:

    • Drag the Point and Shoot button to the desired graphic in the Files tab of the Site Window, as shown in Figure 10-10.

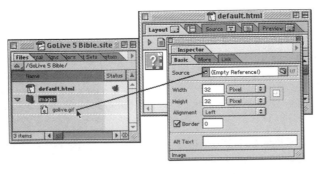

Figure 10-10: You can Point and Shoot from the Point and Shoot button in the Image Inspector to link a placeholder to a graphic.

- Rest your cursor over the toolbar's Select Window button to bring it forward. (You can also rest over any part of the underlying Site Window that's visible and click.) When you get to the Site Window, if the File tab isn't front-most, click it with your cursor.

- If the Inspector is in your way, release the mouse to abandon the shoot. Then move the Inspector to a better position and Point and Shoot again. The Site Window only moves in front of the page you are linking, not in front of the Inspector.

4. You have two ways to link your images to the placeholder:

- *Browsing.* Click the Folder icon to the right of the Source field in the Basic tab of the Image Inspector to browse to your image. Then use the Open dialog box to locate and select the file you want to link. Browse can only link files on your hard drive, which means links within your site. If you have many images in your Site Window and it becomes tedious to have to scroll through them all to Point and Shoot, you may prefer to Browse to your graphic(s).

  You can also use Browse if the destination page isn't already in the Site Window. However, once again, it is much better and safer to place all your images in the Site Window first and then link to them.

- *Typing the file path.* Type the name of the file in the text field in place of the default text "(Empty Reference!)" by pasting or by typing it in the field. To paste, select the file's name in the Files tab of the Site Window, copy the name, and then paste it into the Source field, replacing the words "(Empty Reference!)." To type, select the words "(Empty Reference!)" and type the name.

  If the graphic is inside a folder in your Site Window, you have to add the name of that folder and a forward slash in front of the graphic's name. For example, if you have an image called logo.gif and it is located in the Files tab of the Site Window, you type or paste **logo.gif**. However, if you made a folder called Images, you need to type **Images/logo.gif**. Some servers are case-sensitive, so it is a good idea to only use lowercase in all your coding (for your own consistency). But either way, pay attention to the capitalization of your folder and file names because "logo.gif" and "logo.GIF" would be regarded as different files on a case-sensitive server. Unnoticed spaces are another error that can break the link.

  When you successfully enter the correct file name and path, the graphic appears on your page. If you later move the file in or out of a folder, the file's path will be updated as with all moved files.

Caution

Using Browse to link to files that are *outside* the GoLive Site Window root folder does not collect the referenced files into the site folder that GoLive is managing. If you use this method, you *will* have orphan files that *must* be reconciled before you upload your site to the Web server or the graphics will not appear on your page. See Chapter 25 to learn about orphan files. It's not only easier, but better structurally and managerially to put all graphics in the Site Window because they are then integrated in to GoLive's file management. *After* a file is in the Files tab, you can Point and Shoot or Browse to it; these methods are the safest ways to maintain the integrity of your site.

Dragging a file directly onto a page

You have one last way to add a graphic to your page. It's mentioned last because it's not the wisest way to go. However, there's a good chance you'll discover this capability, especially because it looks so easy, so I owe it to you to explain what happens when you do this.

You can place a graphic on your page simply by dragging it onto the page directly from any folder that's on your hard drive or any volume you can access with your computer (floppy, external drive, Zip, Jaz, CD-ROM, and so on). When you do this, the image immediately appears on your page and all seems well. Indeed, you've got the image in place and it's nice because with one very simple step you can see exactly how it looks there. However, as when placing a graphic from outside the Site Window, such images are only linked externally; they are not copied into the site and are not handled by GoLive's file management.

You have two ways to get a file into the Site Window after it's been added to a page in the way mentioned previously. The file will appear as an *orphan* in the Errors tab of the Site Window. You can drag it from there into the Files tab. Alternately, you can use the Site ➪ Clean up Site command. However, this command can produce complications depending on the Clear options you select.

Cross-Reference

For a discussion on the reasons for using the Site Window to collect all your files, see Chapter 2. For more information about the Errors tab, see Chapter 11. And to learn about the Clean up Site command, see Chapter 25.

So how can you use this capability to drag graphics directly to the page wisely? You can use it to see how an image will look without actually making an extra copy of it by placing it in the Site Window. Drag the graphic onto the page and look at it. If you don't like it just delete it using the Backspace/Delete key. If you do like it, drag the orphaned graphic from the Errors tab to the Files tab of the Site Window. If the graphic was not final or optimized, when you have a final version, you can replace it. In addition, with the advent of GoLive's powerful Smart Objects feature, you can initiate an update of the original image at any time by double-clicking the image from within GoLive. Very cool. See the "Using Smart Objects" section later in this chapter for more information.

A Look into the HTML

Whether you place an image by dragging it directly to the page or via the image place-holder, the HTML (hypertext markup language) code is identical:

```
<img height="86" width="72" src="myimage.jpg">
```

If the image is in another folder, such as "images," the path to that folder is quoted after the `src`, as follows:

```
<img height="86" width="72" src="images/myimage.jpg">
```

When you place a graphic, the HTML that GoLive adds is the `<img>` tag to the source code, which is the standard tag for GIFs and JPEGs. From time to time in the world of HTML, you will hear about the `<embed>` tag. The `<embed>` tag is typically called for when a plug-in or helper application is needed by the Web browser to handle a media type. If, for some reason, you want to have GoLive place an `<embed>` tag, use the Plug-in icon found in the Site tab of the Objects palette.

Placing Sliced Images

All Web graphic files are actually square or rectangular. The only way to get round or curved shapes is by creating them inside the box. For example, if you want a one-inch-diameter circle, you could create a one-inch-square graphic file in your favorite graphics editor and then draw a circle inside it. If the background of the image is the same color as the background of your Web page, or if you make the image background transparent using GIF, when you place the image on your page, the eye will see only the circle.

Take a look at Figure 10-11. Circle 1 shows the relationship of the round art to the rectangular file space. To create the illusion of a circle on a Web page, the white corners (negative space) could be made a transparent color (GIF) or match the background color of the page the circle will be placed on. Circle 2 shows an imaginary dotted border for the file's edges. Circle 3 is what the eye would actually see.

Figure 10-11: All image files are square or rectangular, but the art inside a file doesn't have to be.

As Web-access speeds and Web usage increased, Web design and layout became more sophisticated, demanding more artwork on the page. But HTML has layout limitations regarding text and image alignment. To work around the limitations, Web designers began slicing up the emerging larger graphics and placing them into tables as a way of placing HTML text and images side by side in a way that standard HTML does not accommodate. Figures 10-12 and 10-13 illustrate how a typical Web page might be sliced and laid out.

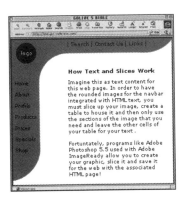

Figure 10-12: A typical Web page layout that requires slicing to make the best and most efficient use of the page space

Note   With DHTML and floating boxes you can place text and images where you like, but be aware that not all browsers support this capability.

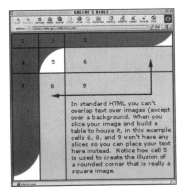

Figure 10-13: By slicing larger graphics into sections and placing them in a table, you can eliminate large portions of image space. This has been done in sections 6, 8, and 9 where you can place HTML formatted text.

Another reason to slice an image is to more easily create a *mouseover* effect (also called a *rollover*) on one or more parts of an image. For example, you might embed an animated GIF inside a large image so you can control the best optimization file size for different parts of the image. The animation might need a larger palette while the other parts of the image might be optimized with fewer colors. In addition, standard navigation bar (also called the *navbar*) rollovers are a snap using Photoshop, ImageReady, and GoLive's Tracing Image feature.

If you use a Web graphic creation program such as Photoshop, ImageReady, or Fireworks, these programs provide the added benefit of optionally exporting an accompanying HTML page that pieces together the slices into the perfectly formatted table.

You have two ways to place a sliced image: manually or by using a preformatted sliced image. The first works for any sliced image, while the other is for images you've prepared in a program such as ImageReady, which can export an HTML page that describes how the slices fit together by using a table.

Placing sliced images manually

This method works no matter what program you use to slice up your image. Even if you are using ImageReady or Fireworks, reading through these steps can provide a good foundation for understanding other methods of Web design.

Manual image placement involves making a graphic, slicing it, and creating a table to house the slices. Tables are commonly recommended for containing sliced images because of the tight control a table provides to keep image slices properly aligned. Even if you're working in a grid, place a table on the grid to contain the image.

If you do not use a table and place your sliced images directly on a grid or page, expanding text or browser differences pull the graphics apart.

The process begins in your image-preparation program. When you save the image slices, save them into their own empty folder. This way you are clear on which image pieces belong to the image. If an artist is providing the image segments to you, ask for them in a folder that contains nothing besides these image files. You'll thank me later. . . .

Creating Rollover Navbars Using Photoshop 5.5

By Steven Shmerler, Web site designer

You can easily create *rollover* (also called *mouseover*) navbars using Photoshop 5.5 and ImageReady. In Photoshop, first create your navbar buttons that are in the *off* state. This is the nonmouseover state. Duplicate the layer and modify these buttons to their *on* mouseover state, such as a glow or different color. Separate the buttons by dragging guides as cut lines. Jump to ImageReady (Edit ⇨ Jump To) and, in ImageReady's Slice menu, select "Create slices from guides." Then, using ImageReady's Rollover window, configure each button with the images for the *off* and *on* (also called *over*) states. From the Edit menu select Save As Optimized. Set your image names and HTML file preferences, if any, and you're ready to import your new rollover navbar into your GoLive Site Window.

Follow these steps to add a sliced image to your page:

1. Add the individual images to the Files tab of your Site Window. For organization's sake I suggest keeping them within their own folder. You can do either of the following:

   • Drag the images folder directly from your hard drive or volume that contains your image files into the Files tab. This places the images neatly in a folder within the Files tab.

   • Create the folder in the Files tab of the Site Window, and then drag the images into this folder. To create the folder, drag a folder icon from the Site tab of the Objects palette into the Files tab or click the New Folder button on the toolbar while the Files tab is active. Then, return to the slice-containing folder and drag all the image slice files into the new folder in the Files tab.

2. Open your page and drag a table icon from the Basic tab of the Objects palette into place on the page. The table is the key to keeping the pieces of the image held tightly together and aligned properly. Don't format the table.

3. Drag the top-left piece of the image into the top-left corner cell within the table. The cell expands to fit the slice.

   Both ImageReady and Fireworks name the slices intelligently by default (in Fireworks leave "auto-name slices" enabled). Each segment is named with the original file name, then the row number, and then the column number. The first image in the first row is 01-01, the first image in the second row is 02-01, and so on.

4. Continue dragging each image piece into place until all are in the table. In Figure 10-14 you can see another section of an image being added to a table manually. If you place any parts out of place, simply drag them to the appropriate cell to fix it.

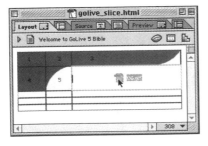

Figure 10-14: You can build your own table and manually place the image slices.

5. Select the edge of the table, and then select the Table tab of the Table Inspector to set the table's border, cell padding, and cell spacing all to zero. This will eliminate any space in the cells so the slices connect seamlessly as one large image. The width and height attributes should be set to Auto.

For the full lowdown on creating and formatting tables, see Chapter 13.

Adding a preformatted sliced image

Photoshop/ImageReady and Fireworks not only slice an image; each can also generate an HTML page with table and image links to fit the entire sliced image seamlessly back together for you. You can use this auto-generated HTML file as the basis for your GoLive page, and then continue building on that page.

ImageReady provides a preference setting for your HTML to be consistent with GoLive or other editors.

Using Photoshop/ImageReady or Fireworks, slice the image. Then save the image as sliced, saving the slices into an empty folder to avoid file inventory confusion. Save the HTML file along with the image slices. Do not change the names of any of these files as doing so would break the links to the images in the corresponding HTML file.

Next, follow these steps to add the sliced images and table into GoLive:

1. Add the folder that contains the ImageReady or Fireworks-generated images, and HTML page, to your Site Window. For organization's sake I suggest keeping the images within their own folder. The page can go wherever you're storing pages.

   Regardless of where you place the items in the Site Window, GoLive updates the paths between the HTML page and the files, so let GoLive perform the update it requests.

Always add *all* the slices and the HTML page at the same time. If you drag the page first, the links will point to the original graphics outside the Site folder. (The graphics then appear as orphans in the Errors tab.)

2. Navigate to open (double-click) the ImageReady- or Fireworks-generated HTML.

3. The entire image should appear on the page. Black lines mark the divisions between table cells and, therefore, image segments. The lines denote table cell divisions while you are in Layout mode, but won't display in Preview mode or in any browser.

4. Do a quick check to see that all of the slices made it into the Site Window; to do this, check the Errors tab on the right side of the Site Window. You can quickly repair an orphan simply by dragging it from the Orphans folder into place where you want it in the Files tab.

   If you choose to use this page and further develop it for use in your site, you're finished with these steps. You can then develop this page the same way you develop any page.

If you prefer to place this sliced image compilation into a preexisting page within your site, continue with the following steps.

5. After dragging the sliced images and auto-generated HTML page into the Files tab of the Site Window, open the auto-generated HTML page and the page where you want to place your sliced image. Make sure you can see both pages.

6. On the auto-generated HTML page, select the entire table by dragging across it.

7. Drag the entire table from the HTML page into place on your destination page, as shown in Figure 10-15. As you drag, a wide black line shows you where the image table will land when you release the mouse. Use this guide to position the table, and then release the mouse to place the table.

8. Close the HTML page. This page isn't needed any longer. You can move it to the Site Trash or wait until you clean out your site during the final site check.

Cross-Reference   To learn about final site checking, see Chapter 25.

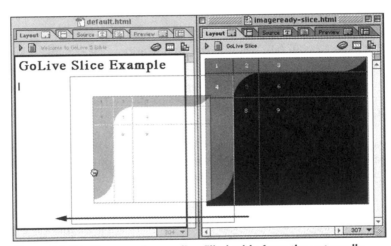

Figure 10-15: You can drag a slice-filled table from the externally generated page into place on an existing page.

One more way to add a preformatted sliced image

You can add a preformatted sliced image to your page in yet another way. You could open the ImageReady or Fireworks HTML file in GoLive, and then drag the image-filled table into place on an existing page from there. However, with this method, the images you see on the page in GoLive are actually still back at the other page; they're orphans that are not in the Site Window and won't make it to the Web server. So, to get those images into GoLive, you need to do some orphan repair or gather the images in one of two ways:

✦ Open the Errors tab on the right side of the Site Window and drag all of the slices from the Orphans folder into place where you want them in the Files tab.

✦ Close all windows, choose Site ➪ Clean up Site, and then check *only* the Add Used Files option. The pieces that comprise the image automatically appear in the Files tab of the Site Window inside a folder called NewFiles, and the process is complete. Then you can rename the NewFiles folder to better reflect the image on the page or move the image's pieces out of the NewFiles folder to wherever you want them. Either way, let GoLive perform the requested update so the links to the images remain valid.

To better understand about orphans and the Clean up Site command, see Chapter 25.

Using Thumbnails

When you have a lot of images to display on a page, it isn't practical to present users with a page of large high-quality images because of the lengthy download time required. For example, consider an online store, or an artist's portfolio. In each case, a search or summary page could feature a number of small, quick downloading thumbnail images of the larger ones, along with some descriptive overview text. Typically, the thumbnail image and some corresponding text will link to another page with full details about the item along with the larger, higher-quality image. The small thumbnails are made from the original, larger image in a graphic creation program such as Photoshop.

Adobe Photoshop 5.5 offers a very cool feature called Web Photo Gallery that creates thumbnails of an entire folder of images in addition to all the associated HTML pages, one for each image, on the fly, automatically! The first page displays all the thumbnails that are linked to the corresponding large images page. In Photoshop, go to File ➪ Automate ➪ Web Photo Gallery. First create your Web Photo Gallery in Photoshop and them import and customize the pages in GoLive.

GoLive 5 has an Update Thumbnails feature in the Design menu that should not be confused with image thumbnails discussed here. Update Thumbnails is for updating the thumbnail images that GoLive generates for each page.

Creating a Low-Resolution Image

When you're using a large image on your page, you may not want to risk losing your visitors while the image downloads to the user's computer. To make the wait tolerable and even possibly interesting, a style known as *progressive rendering* was adopted into the GIF and JPEG image standards.

The built-in progressive effect

The progressive effect is that a low-resolution version of the image downloads first, followed by more and more of the graphic's information. As more of the graphic arrives at the browser, the image fills in, becoming clearer and clearer. Both GIF and JPEG images have progressive rendering formats. In a GIF the effect is called *interlaced* and for a JPEG it is called *progressive*. In each of these cases, the display effect is built into the structure of the image itself.

The <lowsrc> progressive effect

In addition to the built-in progressive effects, you can use the <lowsrc> HTML tag created by Netscape. <lowsrc> tells the browser to load two versions of one image: first a low-resolution, quick-download version (called the *low-source* version) while the rest of the page is loading, and then the low-source version is replaced by a quality one. (This was an important idea in the days of the 14.4 Kbps modem, but the use of this tag has decreased as transmission speeds have increased. On faster modems, viewers do not even see the first image and the process just adds an extra trip to and from the server.)

Creating a low-resolution image automatically

To take advantage of this option, you need a low-resolution version of your image, which GoLive can create for you.

To create and link to a low-resolution image, follow these steps:

1. After you place the image on the page, click the image to make sure it is selected. Then go to the More tab of the Image Inspector.

2. In the Source field at the top of the More tab, click the Generate button.

3. GoLive generates a new image and sets it up to load automatically. The name of this newly created image appears in the source field. The box by the Low option is automatically checked. Figure 10-16 demonstrates these effects.

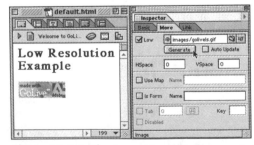

Figure 10-16: The Image Inspector generates a low-resolution image with just a click of the Generate button.

4. *(Optional)* Check Auto Update to have GoLive automatically update the low-resolution image every time you make a change to its parent image.

The new image appears in the same location as the original within the Files tab. Its name is that of your original image except that "ls" (for "low-source") is added to it.

By default the low-resolution image is created in black and white. You can choose to have a color image generated instead. Choose Edit ➩ Preferences, then General, and then Images. In the Low Source area choose Color from the pop-up menu, as shown in Figure 10-17.

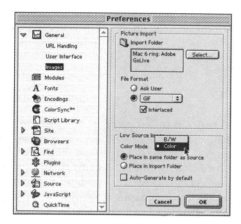

Figure 10-17: In the Image Preferences you can set GoLive to generate low-resolution images in color instead of the default black and white.

Another option in Preferences is to place the low-source image in an Import Folder. If you choose this option, instead of having your image go into the Site Window, it will go into a folder you designate to store all images that GoLive generates for you. You can designate a folder in the same Image Preferences panel. As usual, I recommend you keep all images in the Site Window instead so you can be sure your images are always with your site.

If the image you are generating a low-resolution version of is composed of slices, you *could* use the low-resolution loading method but I definitely don't recommend it. You'd need to generate a low-resolution image for each piece. This would greatly increase the number of calls between the browser and server, so having a low-resolution image version in addition to using a sliced image may actually defeat the purpose of both features.

Note   As mentioned previously, in the More tab of the Image Inspector, the Auto Update checkbox option generates a low-resolution image automatically.

Using your own low-resolution image

If you prefer to create your own image and have it load first, place that image in the Site Window along with all other images. Then use the Point and Shoot button just above the Generate button in the More tab of the Image Inspector to link to your low-resolution image. (Or click the image as you press Shift-⌘ (Mac) or Shift+Alt (Windows) and point from the image to the low-resolution image.)

Arranging Images on Your Page

Once you've placed an image on your page, you'll want to make sure that it fits well with the other page elements, such as text and other graphics. You have several ways to manipulate your image or tweak your page to make the page look good. This section tells you how.

Resizing an image

After you place an image on a page you can resize it by dragging or by entering dimensions in the Basic tab of the Image Inspector. When an image is resized in this way, the dimensions are sent to the browser, which resizes the image on the fly. The actual image is not affected. Therefore, it is possible to have the same image appear in different sizes on the same page or between pages. However, having the browser resize your images on the fly adds to the server workload and may affect your page's download time. Therefore, I don't recommend browser image resizing, except to experiment with layout or quickly see how a resized image fits on the page.

When you resize an image with the browser, the browser loads the original file anyway so if your goal is to improve download time, the best method is to create the images in the actual physical size you want.

However, if you want to see how a resized image will fit on a page, follow these steps:

1. Move the mouse over the bottom-right corner until the cursor becomes a blue arrow, and then click and drag to the desired size. (If the image is already selected when you begin, you can click any handle. However, you don't need to see handles in order to drag the corner, provided the cursor is blue.)

2. To maintain the image's proportions, press Shift as you drag.

   If you have the page's rulers showing, you can measure the image's size. The image area is the white section in the ruler while the image is selected. To show the rules, click the ruler button on the right side of the page's window, above the vertical scroll bar. (The ruler button is square and looks like rulers meeting in a corner.)

If you want more precise control than by dragging, you can adjust the size of an image numerically by selecting the image, and then entering the dimensions into the Image Inspector. Just choose Pixel or Percentage in the Width and Height pop-up menus, and then enter the desired numbers in the Width and Height fields. If you enter a number or numbers, and then change the size option between pixel and percentage or vice versa, GoLive maintains your chosen image sizing.

When an image has been resized in GoLive's Layout view, a resize warning icon appears in the lower-right corner of the image to alert you, as in both images in Figure 10-18. In addition, a matching resize warning button in the Basic tab of the Image Inspector is active. Should you wish to return to having the browser display the image in its actual size, select the image, open the Basic tab of the Image Inspector and click the Resize button, as shown in Figure 10-19.

Figure 10-18: A resize warning icon appears to alert you whenever an image has been resized. The image on the left was made smaller, and the image on the right was enlarged.

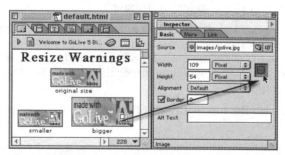

Figure 10-19: To return a resized image back to its original dimensions click the Resize button in the Image Inspector. This button is only active for a placed image when the image is not on the page at its true size.

Tip
For the most flexibility with the sizing of images, use GoLive 5's new Smart Objects feature. See the "Using Smart Objects" section later in this chapter.

Aligning an image

An image's alignment is defined in relation to the text it is "in line" with. Hence the name, "inline image." With the exception of Left and Right alignment, all other alignment options affect only one line of text as defined by the width of the page. When the line of text that is aligned with an inline image reaches the end of the page, the text wraps underneath the image. The point to understand is that, unlike page layout, with HTML inline images affect and are affected by text and other images they are inline with.

By default, images sit on the same line as the baseline of the text, with descenders falling below the bottom of the image line. You can choose from several other alignment possibilities to best fit your image in with the flow of your text, as follows:

✦ **Default** aligns the image with the baseline of the text or image that it is next to. Text descenders fall below the bottom of the image line.

✦ **Top** aligns the image's top with the top of the text or image it is next to.

✦ **Middle** aligns the vertical center of the image with the baseline of the text halfway between the top and bottom of the image.

✦ **Bottom** aligns the image with the baseline of the text or image that it is next to. Descenders fall below the bottom of the image line (same as *Default*).

✦ **Left** aligns the image to the left of the text. Unlike the other alignment options, Left (and Right) affects all text to the right (and left, respectively) of itself for the height of that image. All text moves to the right of the image and will text-wrap. If more text exists than the image's height, the text will flow under the image. (See the next section for more on text wrapping.)

✦ **Right** aligns the image to the right of the text. The image moves to the right edge of the browser window and all text moves to the left of the image. Similar to Left, all text moves to the left of the image and will text-wrap. If more text exists than the image's height, the text will flow under the image. (See the next section for more on text wrapping.)

✦ **Text Top** aligns the image with the top of any text that is on the same line as the image.

✦ **Abs Middle** (absolute) aligns the vertical center of the image with the actual absolute center of the text halfway between the top and bottom of the image.

✦ **Baseline** aligns the image with the baseline of text that is on the same line as the image. Descenders fall below the bottom of the image line.

✦ **Abs Bottom** (absolute) aligns the image so its bottom is in line with the absolute bottom of the text—not the baseline, but the bottom of the descenders.

Follow these steps to change the alignment of an inline image that is in a line of text:

1. Click the image to select it.

2. In the Image Inspector's Basic tab, choose an alignment option from the Alignment pop-up menu, as shown in Figure 10-20.

Figure 10-20: The Image Inspector enables you to select from a variety of alignment options.

Image alignment on a grid is a different situation. The only time the preceding alignment would be valid on a grid is when the graphic is placed inside a text field. To learn about aligning objects on a grid, see Chapter 7.

Use a table if you have an image with text that you want *middle* aligned, but the text is long and wraps underneath the image. To keep all the text to the right and middle of the image, create a two-column, one-row table and place your image in the first column and your text in the second column. Align your text as you would normally using Table Cell alignment in the Table Inspector. — *Steven Shmerler, Web site designer*

Wrapping text around an image

In the print world, it's easy to wrap text around a graphic. People have become used to seeing the effect and designers are used to doing it. Text wrapping is not as easy on the Web, but tools such as image alignment help.

To have text wrap around an image, follow these steps:

1. Place the image at the beginning or within a line of text.

2. Select the graphic and align it right or left (as in Figure 10-21).

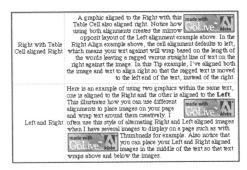

Figure 10-21: You can achieve the look of text wrapped around a graphic by aligning an image to the right, as shown here, or left.

3. Move the image up and down in the lines of text to find the best balance of text wrap. To move a graphic, click it and drag it. A dark line shows you where the graphic will land when you release the mouse. Placing the graphic is not an exact science when alignment is involved so experiment.

Remember, inline images align in relation to the text and images surrounding them. Therefore, you have no guarantee that the layout on your computer will display the same way from user to user. Each user can set his or her browser to display the text font and size of their choice, plus different browsers and platforms display text size differently. In general, Windows browsers display text one-third larger than Mac browsers. You should view your pages on various browsers and platforms. GoLive's View Controller in both the Layout and Preview mode is an excellent quick view to get a sense of the differences. The rule of thumb for good design is: *Test, Test, Test!*

Tip When layout is critical, designers often use tables to isolate text, or if a minimal amount of text exists, consider making the text an image in your graphics program so that it cannot be changed by browser or user preference (with the exception of "images off"). Keep in mind that image text takes longer to download than HTML text and if your user has images turned off he or she won't see this text image. Therefore, always use Alternative Text on your graphics. (See the sidebar, "The Importance of ALT Tags," earlier in this chapter.)

Wrapping looks better when enough text exists to fit around the graphic. To control the width of a text area, place a text box on a layout grid. When text is on a grid, you can alter the height and width of the text box, therefore changing the wrap of the text.

Note Because text appears at different sizes on different browsers and platforms, the exact wrapping can differ so be sure to check the results in different browsers and platforms. Watch for the difference in proportion between the text size and the graphic.

Setting Your Images Apart from Your Page

Sometimes it's a good idea to set your image apart from your page. This is a good idea, for example, when your background clashes with the image. To do so you can add a border and/or space around your image.

Creating a border

Sometimes placing a border around a graphic sets it apart and enhances it. You can easily add a border around any graphic you select on your page in GoLive.

Here's how to add a border:

1. Click the image to select it.
2. In the Basic tab of the Image Inspector, check the Border option.
3. Enter a number (in pixels) in the Border field.

The border immediately appears around your graphic. To change the border, enter a new number. To remove the border, uncheck the Border option or enter zero. If your image will be a link, and if you've set the border option in the Inspector, the border displays with the color of your Link and VLink page settings, which may not be the color or effect you want. To correct this, set the border to zero.

If you need a border on a linked image and don't want the color associated with the links for that page, then create the image with a border in the original artwork.

Note
    I use the border option only when I have a lot of images that need a border and are already compressed as JPEGs or GIFs. If an image needs a border, I prefer to add one in a graphics program to put the border into the art. This way you can reliably control border size and color. Also, if anyone else ever updates your page, the border cannot be mistakenly removed from the HTML.

Adding space around an image

It is often visually pleasing to separate your graphic from surrounding elements (whether text or graphics) by placing a space around the image, especially with Left and Right alignment. You can do this in GoLive by using HSpace and VSpace located in the More tab of the Image Inspector.

To add space between a graphic and text, follow these steps:

1. Click the image to select it.
2. Open the Image Inspector to the More tab.

3. HSpace adds space to the left and right of the image. Enter a number (in pixels) in the HSpace field. This space is immediately added to the image's area. To change the spacing, enter a new number in the HSpace field.

4. VSpace adds space above and below the image. Enter a number (in pixels) in the VSpace field. This space is immediately added to the image's area. To change the spacing, enter a new number in the VSpace field.

Note   If you have objects next to an image and you add VSpace, depending upon the objects' alignments they may move up or down along with the new boundaries of the image.

Because a grid enables exact text and image placement, this method doesn't work on a grid; just move the image where you want it instead.

If you've sliced an image, the HSpace and VSpace attributes cause alignment problems because they add space between sliced pieces of the image that need to be adjacent, thus breaking up the image. To add space around a sliced image, place it on a grid or put the image-containing table into another table. The grid provides more control in this case.

All three examples you see in Figure 10-22 show left-aligned images. Example 1 has no margin of space in the actual image and does not have any HSpace applied. Example 2 has a 5-pixel HSpace applied. Notice how a margin appears on both the left and right of the image? A nice space exists between the text on the right, but the image is pushed out of alignment with the text below on the left. Example 3 does not use HSpace as in Example 2. Unlike Example 2, Example 3 has a 5-pixel white space added on the right using Photoshop.

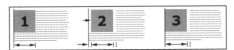

Figure 10-22: Managing left-aligned images

Managing Margins

Space is often needed to create a margin between an image and text such as with Left or Right align. Keep in mind that HSpace adds space to the both the left and right sides of an image, which may not be what you want in your layout. An example is if you have a left-aligned image and you want to add a margin of space between the image and text on the right. When you use HSpace, you get the same amount of margin on both sides of the image. This pushes the text to the right away from the image, but also pushes the image to the right away from the left page or cell margin and therefore out of alignment with whatever is below it. In cases such as this it is better to add the margin you want to the artwork in a graphics program such as Photoshop.

Editing or Deleting an Image

After you see an image on your page, you may decide it needs editing. You can do this very efficiently. It can be as easy as double-clicking a graphic wherever it is on your page.

Tip Smart Objects provide the cleanest editing options by returning you to the original nonoptimized image and actually generating a new optimized image that replaces the image already on your page. See the "Using Smart Objects" section later in this chapter to learn about this feature.

Editing existing optimized Images

When you double-click a Web-ready graphic on your Web page or the image file directly in the Files tab of the Site Window, GoLive calls for the graphic to open in an appropriate application: either its native application or a type-compatible program. Photoshop is the default setting to open GIFs and JPEGs, but in case you don't have Photoshop, you can tell GoLive that you want all GIF or JPEGs to open in the editing program of your choice.

Try double-clicking any of your graphics in an existing GoLive-authored site and see what happens. In addition, you can check out the file-mapping preferences to see the default file formats and their associated programs. (File mapping is discussed in the following section.) To take a look, choose Edit ➪ Web Settings, click the File Mappings tab, and then scroll through the list of file types.

If you use the default application setting to open a GIF file (Photoshop) when you double-click a GIF image anywhere on your page or in your site, the image opens in Photoshop. Any editing you do to that image is immediately reflected on your page when you save those changes from within Photoshop. If the same graphic is used in several places on your site, the change is universal. This is because when you place an image in more than one place, you are linking the same exact image each time.

If you created a new alternative file and you wish to swap it for the originally used file, you need to change the links from the old file to the new one wherever you want the change.

Cross-Reference See Chapter 11 to learn about the In & Out Links palette's ability to help you with updating links.

If you edit the image directly from a page where the image is used and you change the size of the image, the new size won't automatically be reflected on the page. Instead, the new image resizes to fit the old space it was allotted earlier. Be sure to click the Resize button in the Image Inspector to update the image's size on the page.

Caution

If you haven't read the information about Web file types and compression at the beginning of this chapter, please go back and read about GIFs and JPEGs. It is okay to edit GIFs because they use a *lossless* compression, but it is not a good idea and is not recommended to edit JPEGs because they use a *lossy* compression and can become distorted when you recompress them. For JPEGs it is best to go back to the original file and edit that or a production file. You can read about GoLive's new Smart Objects features later in this chapter.

Changing file mapping

If needed, you can change the default file mapping settings in the File Mapping tab. When a file type is mapped to an application, that application opens whenever the mapped file type is double-clicked.

To map a file to a specific application, follow these steps:

1. Choose Edit ➪ Web Settings, and then click the File Mappings tab, which is shown in Figure 10-23.

MIME type sets

Figure 10-23: To tell GoLive to open all files of a certain type, begin by selecting the file MIME type such as image/.

2. Open the MIME type set you want to edit, such as image/.

3. Select the file type for which you want to change the associated application, such as a GIF file(see Figure 10-24).

4. Note the default application in the File Info Extension Inspector (for GIF it is Photoshop).

5. To change to another application, click the Browse icon at the right of the Application field and navigate via the Open dialog box to your desired application and click it (Mac) or select Open (Windows). This new application will be listed in the Application field of the tab and will open the edited file (see Figure 10-25).

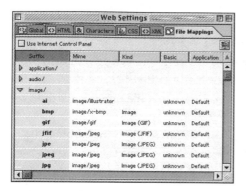

Figure 10-24: To change the application that opens GIF files, select the image/ MIME type set and then GIF. Changes are then made in the File Info Extension Inspector.

Figure 10-25: The File Info Extension Inspector is where you make file mapping changes. To complete the preference setting, choose an application for GoLive to call whenever you double-click files of the type you've selected.

To create a new extension, do the following:

1. Choose Edit ➪ Web Settings, and then click the File Mappings tab (see Figure 10-26).

Figure 10-26: The File Mappings tab of the Web Settings window toolbar

2. Open the MIME type set to which you want to add, such as image/.

3. Click the New Extension button on the toolbar.

4. Using the File Info Extension Inspector, fill in the missing file information or use the Browse icon to the right of the Application field.

5. When the Open dialog box appears, navigate to a file on your hard drive that is the same file type that you want to add.

6. Double-click (Mac) or Open (Windows) the file to fill in the missing file type information needed in the File Info Extension Inspector. This completes the process of adding a new extension type.

Alternatively, you can create a new extension file type by duplicating an existing file type. To do so, follow these steps:

1. Select Edit ➪ Web Settings, and then click the File Mappings tab.

2. Open the MIME type set you want to add to such as image/.

3. Click the Duplicate button on the toolbar.

4. Using the File Info Extension Inspector, change the missing file information or use the Browse icon to the right of the Application field.

5. When the Open dialog box appears, navigate to a file on your hard drive that is the same file type that you want to add.

6. Double-click (Mac) or Open (Windows) the file to fill in the missing file type information needed in the File Info Extension Inspector. This completes the process of adding a new extension type.

Double-clicking any GIF file opens that file in Photoshop by default, or in any application that you change the file map to. (The application needs to be on your system, of course.) If you wish to change the application for another file type such as JPEG so that it opens in a different application rather than Photoshop, scroll to that file type (JPEG), click it and repeat the preceding steps. Then, click OK to activate the change.

Note Mac users who are using the pre OS 8.5 Internet Config control panel or the OS 8.5+ Internet control panel can check the Use Internet Config box. This tells GoLive to use the file mapping you've previously set up on your computer so you don't have to set things twice.

Removing an image couldn't be easier than if you could do it by crossing your arms and blinking your eyes. All you have to do it click the image and press the Backspace/Delete key. To delete a sliced image, select and delete the entire table. Or, if you just want to delete a segment of the image, select and delete that one part.

Other Tricks You Can Do with Images

Images add a lot to a page and you can do plenty of cool things with them. You can turn an image into a button by linking it to a URL or e-mail address. To learn how, see Chapter 11.

You can turn specific parts of a graphic into links so each part links to another destination. For more on creating these image maps, see Chapter 12.

For an animated effect, you can place an image in a floating box and define a path on which the box travels. This is different from using an animated GIF. However, you can also place an animated GIF in a floating box. You can do several tricks with floating boxes. I show you how to use and animate floating boxes in Chapter 19.

You can use an image as a Submit button in a form page. To learn about forms, see Chapter 16.

You can use image text in place of HTML text when you want your text to be unaffected by variations in platforms, Web browser display, or user-defined type size preferences. With imaged text, you have total control and you can apply various graphic filters such as anti-aliasing or drop shadows, and not have to worry whether the user has the font that you want to display. However, a word of caution. Imaged text takes more time to download than HTML text so if your page is already large, you need to weigh the pros and cons of your design needs versus added download time. Also, if a user has image display turned off in his or her browser, or he or she is visually challenged, or your graphics are not loading because of server load (if too much of your information is in graphic form), your messages may not be conveyed.

Knowing how and when to compromise is a large part of the challenge and expertise required for building Web sites. The key to good Web design is knowing the goals, the target audience, and what level of features your site should have to satisfy all these objectives.

Using Smart Objects

Linking with Smart Objects is a major advance in Web authoring. Graphical content can now be generated, implemented, and managed from GoLive through the integration with and linking to Adobe Photoshop, Illustrator, and LiveMotion files. By using a two-way link, called a *Smart Link*, to the original source file, Smart Objects eliminates the need to track, manage, and store unnecessary intermediary production files that are typically created during Web-site production. With Smart Objects, you have one master source file and one optimized Web-ready version of the source file, which streamlines the entire graphics creation and updating process! (You have to have Photoshop, Illustrator 9, or LiveMotion installed for the Smart Linking to work with that program, of course. GoLive doesn't display a Smart Object icon for a program you don't have installed on your computer.)

Before Adobe created Smart Objects, Web graphics were created in a graphics program and then a smaller optimized Web-ready copy was created from the original. The original file was (hopefully) saved and the Web-ready file was used in the Web site and linked to the Web page. Smart Objects are similar to the traditional method of simply linking to an optimized graphic in some way, but have two simultaneous links instead of one, as follows:

✦ **Source files.** Smart Objects link to an original source file made in Photoshop, Illustrator, or LiveMotion (called *native* or *source* applications).

✦ **Web-ready files.** Web-ready files are optimized versions of their original source file using compression technology such as GIF, JPEG, PNG, and so on. In addition to linking to the source file, Smart Objects also link to the optimized Web-ready version that is created during the linking process.

Caution Source files are not directly used or placed on your Web pages, but once linked, GoLive maintains a Smart Link to them for updates. Once linked, if you move either the Web-ready or source files, your Smart Links will break.

Web-ready files are no different in file format from any other Web-optimized file such as GIF, JPEG, PNG, and so on. The only difference is that instead of being created from their native application such as Photoshop or an optimization program such as Debabilizer or Fireworks, Smart Object Web-ready files are created within GoLive using the Save For Web window during the Smart Linking process.

Web-ready images display normally as with any Web graphic in your GoLive pages and browser. So what's the difference? The big difference comes when you want to make a change to a Web-ready image on your page. To do this, you simply double-click the Web-ready image on your page, which is a Smart Linked Smart Object. GoLive opens the original source file in its native application (such as Photoshop). You make your changes and when you Save them and return to your page or the Site Window, GoLive updates the Web-ready version on your Web page automatically with the same optimization as you set before. Now *that's* pretty smart!

To use Smart Objects, you drag a Smart Object icon from the Smart tab of the Objects palette to your page. Using the Smart Objects Inspector, you link to the original source file and tell the Smart Image Inspector where you want the Web-ready version stored (for example, the images folder). GoLive launches its Save For Web window where you set the desired optimization settings. GoLive then creates an optimized Web-ready version of the source file and places it in the folder you specified. GoLive maintains a link to both the source and Web-ready files using a Smart Link. Figure 10-27 illustrates how the different files interact.

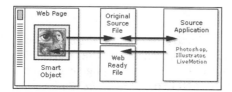

Figure 10-27: Smart Objects link to both the source file and an optimized Web-ready version. Double-clicking the Smart Object opens the source file in its native application. Any changes in the source file are automatically made to the Web-ready file.

If you've spent any time making or working with graphics for Web pages, you have no doubt experienced the duplicative efforts required. First you make a source image, and then you save it in an optimized Web format for your site. If you need to update the image on your page, you open the original source file, make your changes, and then optimize a new version, bring it into your site, delete the old version on your page, and link to the new one. How many times have you seen files named something like myimage6.gif? Presumably, there were five previous versions that each had to be updated, optimized, and linked into the page. This duplicative work is thankfully eliminated using Smart Objects.

Working with Smart Objects

As you can see from the preceding overview, working with Smart Objects is similar to placing regular graphics on your page in that you use the familiar "icon" place-holder from the Objects palette and link to your images using an Inspector. The difference is that Smart Objects have two links: one to the source file and one to the optimized Web-ready version of the source file that is created within GoLive instead of your graphics program. Not surprisingly, the GoLive Save For Web window uses the same basic Save For Web interface used in other Adobe graphic applications. If you're not familiar with Save For Web optimization, it is simple and easy to learn and use.

Smart Objects link to Photoshop, Illustrator, and LiveMotion files (source files) and launch the corresponding native application when the Smart Object is double-clicked. To work properly, the native application of the source file must be installed on your computer. GoLive only offers Smart Object icons in the Objects palette for corresponding applications on your computer.

GoLive accepts Photoshop, Illustrator, and LiveMotion source files in any of the following formats: PSD, BMP (Windows only), PICT (Mac only), PCX, Pixar, Amiga IFF, TIFF, and TARGA.

Note

If you don't have a copy of the native application of your source file, you can't use the Smart Objects feature, but you can still use regular image links. Create an optimized Web-ready version and then place your graphics on your Web pages using the regular Image icon from the Basic tab of Objects palette, as discussed earlier in this chapter.

Using Smart Links

At present, Smart Objects link to Photoshop, Illustrator, and LiveMotion files called *original* or *source* files. This link is called a Smart Link. It opens the source file through its native application when the Smart Object on your page is double-clicked (and you have the source application installed). For the examples in this section, I use a Photoshop Smart Object on a page called smartlink.html.

Note   I assume some user familiarity with the native application of the source file you wish to Smart Link (Photoshop, Illustrator, or LiveMotion). For more information regarding these applications, please refer to their respective user manuals.

Follow these steps to place a Smart Object on your page:

1. Drag a Smart Object placeholder from the Smart tab of the Objects palette into place on your page, as shown in Figure 10-28.

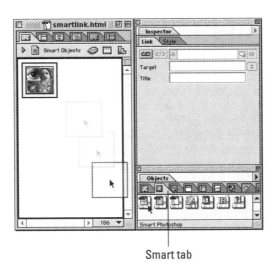

Smart tab

Figure 10-28: The three windows you will be using: your page, the Inspector, and the Objects palette. Here, a Smart Photoshop icon is dragged to the Web page.

2. Using the Smart Image Inspector, browse to the source file, as shown in Figure 10-29. The source file must be of the type that matches the Smart Object.

Tip   You can skip Steps 1 and 2 by dragging the graphic directly onto your page. This places the Smart Object placeholder on your page and opens the Save For Web window, bringing you directly to Step 3.

3. After navigating to and selecting your source file, GoLive presents you with a Save For Web window, as shown in Figure 10-30, where you set the optimization for the Web-ready version of the source file for your page. Choose the settings you want (GIF, JPEG, and so on) and click OK.

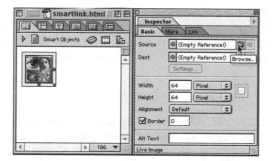

Figure 10-29: Click the Source Browse button to link to the source file, and then use the Dest Browse button (*Dest* is short for "destination") to tell GoLive where to store the Web-ready version of the source file.

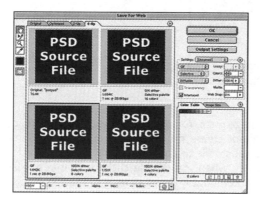

Figure 10-30: In the Save For Web window you set the optimization. You can compare two or four different Web settings and choose the best one.

For more information about file optimization, I recommend you read the *Photoshop 6 for Windows Bible* or *Macworld Photoshop 6 Bible*. Both books are by Deke McClelland, and are available from IDG Books Worldwide.

4. When the Specify Target File window appears, click the GoLive pop-up button and choose Root, bringing you directly to your site's folder. Once there, save the Web-ready file to the desired folder within your site's root folder (such as the customary images folder), and click OK.

5. GoLive returns you to your page.

After you use a Smart Object to create a Web-ready graphic, this graphic exists in your Files tab just like any other graphic. You can use this graphic multiple times in your site using the traditional linking method. However, you *must* bear in mind that if you edit the Smart Object, this graphic is automatically altered and will update any instances where this graphic is used — and may effect the layout of those pages.

In the Smart Objects linking process you link to a source file as listed in the Source field, create a Web-ready version of the source file, and place it within your site as listed in the Dest field of the Live Image Inspector. Notice in Figure 10-31 that the Smart Object on the page has an identifying icon in the lower-right corner to signify that it is a Smart Object.

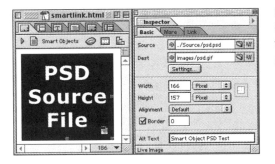

Figure 10-31: A properly linked Smart Object. (Notice that the designer filled the Alt Text field, which is always a good practice.)

Caution   You can only use a source image once. You can use its resulting Web-ready graphic multiple times, but you cannot create multiple renderings of the same source image. If you use the same source file to create multiple different versions of the same source graphic, inevitably, when you double-click the Web-ready file to alter one usage of the graphic, it automatically alters all uses of this file.

To make changes to Web-ready images on your page, follow these steps:

1. Double-click the Smart Object on your page to open the original source file in its native application. This example uses Photoshop.

2. Make your changes in the native application and save.

3. When you return to GoLive, you see the Updating from Source File alert telling you that GoLive is making the changes you made in the source file to the Web-ready Smart Object on your page, as shown in Figure 10-32.

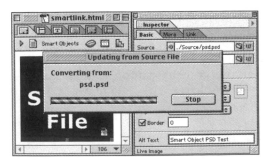

Figure 10-32: GoLive automatically updates the Web-ready file from the source file.

4. After the conversion is complete, GoLive displays the updated Web-ready image on your page. You can see the changes instantly on your page, as illustrated in Figure 10-33.

Figure 10-33: The source file's background and font color were changed. The changes are updated to the Web-ready file. You no longer need to create a separate Web file for each change.

5. To update this file, simply double-click the Web-ready Smart Object again and go through the preceding steps.

Changing settings of a Web-ready image

If you change your source file in a way that effects how you would optimize the Web-ready image, you will need to reset the optimization settings after the conversion update because GoLive automatically uses the existing settings.

For example, in the first black-and-white image in Figure 10-33, this image was saved as an eight-color GIF. When I updated it, I added a white background, and a drop shadow to the text, which I changed to dark gray. These changes added a number of grays to the image's palette, which increased the palette to 185 colors. For the updated file to display on the screen to my liking, I wanted to use a higher GIF setting of 128 colors instead of the previous eight colors.

Here are the steps to change the optimize settings:

1. Select the Smart Object Web-ready image on your Web page.

Note   Select the file, don't double-click it, as double-clicking opens the file's native application.

2. In the Live Image Inspector, click the Settings button under the Dest location field to launch the Save For Web window.

3. Change the settings to your liking and save.

Your changes are instantly reflected in the Smart Object Web-ready image on your page.

Storing your Smart Object files

A Web-ready file, which is linked to your page, should be stored along with the other graphics in your site, as you're reminded by the presence of the GoLive button in the Save window.

Source files, however, are production files that need to remain linked to your page, but never inhabit your page. Therefore, source files do not need to be inside the Site Window or uploaded to your server. In fact, they shouldn't be stored in your Site Window, because when there, they will be uploaded to you server, which is not necessary. These nonoptimized files will be fairly large so you want to avoid that. For this reason, I recommend that you create a new folder and call it Source Files, placing the new folder within the enclosing site project folder that GoLive creates for you when you create a new site. This way the source files are in their own folder beside the folders in which GoLive stores your site files and site data files, as shown in Figure 10-34.

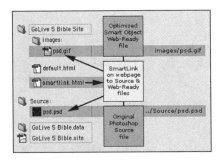

Figure 10-34: In this example, the site project folder is called "GoLive 5 Bible Site" and you can see a new source files folder, called Source, beside the files (root) folder and the .data folder.

Tracing Images

GoLive 5's new Tracing Image feature enables you to use your Photoshop (or other) graphics as the basis of your GoLive Web pages. You can use it to prototype your Web page, and then import the prototype layout from Photoshop, and use it as a layout guide by turning down its opacity and adding your page elements *over* it. Or, you can turn the prototype into your actual page elements by cutting out sections from the tracing image, and then using GoLive's Save For Web window to turn the sections into final Web-ready GIFs, JPEGs, PNGs, or other formats.

In addition to importing Photoshop files, you can import the following file formats for your tracing image: GIF, JPEG, PNG, TIFF, PICT (Mac only), BMP (Windows only), TARGA, PCX, Pixar, and Amiga IFF.

To add a Tracing Image to your page, follow these steps:

1. Open the Tracing Image palette (Window ⇨ Tracing Image), and then check the Source checkbox at the top of the palette to activate the import.

The Source field's URL defaults to "(Empty Reference!)."

2. Browse to the tracing image you wish to import. (Although Point and Shoot is available as an option, you need to have the image document within the Files tab of the Site Window in order to Point and Shoot, and storing this document there is unnecessary.) The image appears in the upper-left corner of your page.

3. Set up your page and the image to be traced by doing one of the following:

   • If you'd like your page size to match the size of the image you're about to trace, click the Change Window Size pop-up menu at the bottom-right corner of the document window and choose Tracing Image as the window size. This setting resizes the page automatically.

   • If the image is not intended to fill your entire page, or the image to be traced is only to comprise a portion of the page, position the tracing image on your page, click the Move Image Tool button (hand) on the Tracing Image palette, as shown in Figure 10-35, so your cursor becomes a hand. Then drag the image into the desired position on your page. (Alternately, you can enter the desired distance, in pixels, from the left and top edges of the page into the Position fields.)

Figure 10-35: Use the Tracing Image palette to link to your tracing image, set the position, opacity, and cut sections.

4. *(Optional)* Slide the Opacity slider to set the tracing image's opacity so it can act as a layout guide for the elements on your page, as shown in Figure 10-36, which features a prototype page layout.

Note
You can stop here and use the grayed-out version of your graphic as a background template guide, or you can continue to turn any square or rectangular sections of your graphic into individual graphics that will comprise your final page.

5. Click the Cut Out button on the Tracing Image palette to activate the tool.

6. Click and drag within your graphic to select the section you wish to turn into an individual graphic. This action defines the section.

7. Once defined, click the Cut Out button or double-click the section to launch the Save For Web window.

Figure 10-36: Tracing images can work as a positioning guide for your grid, tables, or floating boxes.

8. Set the optimization values you want for GIF, JPG, PNG, or other format, and click OK.

9. In the Specify Target File window, use the GoLive button to save the file into the root folder (your Files tab) and then choose any folder within the Files tab. Change the default name of the new graphic if you wish, and then click Save.

   GoLive places your optimized image section into a floating box and positions it on top of the tracing image, as shown in Figure 10-37.

Figure 10-37: The floating box is placed over the tracing image in the proper location.

Note

If you leave GoLive to work in another application, the tracing image disappears from your page, although it is still noted as linked in within the Source field. To get your tracing image back so you can continue working with it, uncheck the Source checkbox, and then immediately check it again. (Future revisions of GoLive may fix this disappearing tracing image issue so you may not need to do this.)

10. *(Optional)* Continue to cut out sections of your tracing image until you've cut out all desired sections.

11. When you are finished using the tracing image, uncheck the Source checkbox in the Tracing Image palette so the traced image will go away. (You may want to keep the traced image in view for a long time, though.)

Tip

If you do not want to use floating boxes but do want to use the Tracing Image cut-out feature, after your Web-ready image is saved to a floating box, simply drag the image out of the floating box onto your page. Then select the floating box container by clicking an edge of the rectangle and then press Delete. The floating box is deleted, leaving you with the optimized Web-ready image.

Importing Photoshop Layers as HTML

Import Layers as HTML enables you to import layered Photoshop files directly into your GoLive pages. Each layer can be individually optimized and imported into its own floating box layer. Web-ready images have never been easier to create or faster to place into an HTML or DHTML authoring environment.

Expert Tip

In Photoshop, name each layer of your image descriptively before importing it into GoLive. (You can name layers in Photoshop even after you've created the image.) The names of each layer are recognized in GoLive, automatically becoming the names of each respective floating box. This can save you a lot of time because you don't have to select each newly made floating box to name it in order to work with it later on. — *Cathy Scrivnor, Web site designer*

Here's how to Import a Photoshop layered graphic:

1. With your page open, choose File ➪ Import ➪ Photoshop as HTML.

2. Locate the Photoshop file to be imported, and then choose Open.

3. Select the folder in which you want to store the imported image files. This should definitely be a folder within your Files tab, such as a new folder you call "images" to keep things organized. GoLive launches the Save For Web window in which you will set optimization for each layer being imported from the Photoshop file.

4. Set the optimization preferences for the first layer and click OK. Then set the optimization preferences for the remaining layers, as a new Save For Web window opens for each layer in turn.

Honoring Copyright

I want to make quick mention about copyright. Copyright protects creators of text as well as graphical and audio content. In the United States, the instant you create something original, it's automatically copyrighted. Going live with a Web page on the Internet is an act of electronic "publication," which is protected by United States copyright law. If you haven't generated the content yourself, make sure you have permission from the creator to publish it. A copyright violation can carry a stiff penalty.

Likewise, you don't want others publishing your content without your permission. You have no foolproof way to restrict others from downloading your copyrighted material, but Walter Blady's CopyrightNotice.action is a nice reminder to users. Walter Blady has created more than 30 excellent Actions, which are prewritten JavaScript procedures that you just plug in and use right off the bat. Check them out at www.wblady.com/actions.html. Copyright-Notice.action will display a © copyright notice alert when a user clicks a graphic (Version 4 browsers only). You also have the option of opening a second window and loading an HTML page that displays more detailed copyright, purchase, and contact information.

Tip   If the optimization settings will be the same for all layers, when you set the first layer press Control when you click OK to do the first export. GoLive then applies these settings to the remaining images without showing you the Save For Web window again. You can use this trick at any point from which all layers are to use the same settings.

Once the import is complete, you can keep the images in the floating boxes and arrange them to design your page, or you can take them out of the floating boxes to place them in a table, on a grid, or as you please on the page. You can also animate the floating boxes using the Floating Box Inspector's animation option or the DHTML Time Line Editor.

Cross-Reference   See Chapter 19 to learn what you can do with floating boxes.

✦   ✦   ✦

Adding Navigational Links to Your Page

To borrow a concept from science, if you could distill the World Wide Web down to its most basic element, that element would be the link. There could be no Web pages without links. In many ways the HTML that makes up a Web page is merely a shell to support links. You've already seen in Chapter 10 how an image on a page is actually placed there by a link that tells the browser the image's location, border, size, and so on.

This chapter explores how to turn your text and images into links that can take your readers anywhere around the Web. Your navigational links can transport people within a page, to another page in your site, or to a page on any other site on the Web — the itinerary is practically endless. You'll see how you can use links to add more advanced elements to your pages, such as Adobe Acrobat files, Adobe LiveMotion files, Macromedia Flash files, or Macromedia Director files. You'll learn how to make a link that can send an e-mail and that can even address it first, and you'll learn how to link a file so that someone can download it right from your site. Finally, you'll also see how to use GoLive's powerful link tools to create, modify, manage, and maintain your links, and how to even correct them when they lose their "sense of direction."

The Four Basic Links

Navigational links generally fall into the four following categories, listed in the order of most common use to the least common:

✦ Linking from one page to another page within your site

✦ Linking to a page outside of your site

✦ Linking to another point within your page

✦ Linking to a specific point on a separate page

Any of these links can be in the form of text, as in body text, a line of links across the bottom of a page (commonly called the *nav bar*), or a table of contents. They may also be in the form of an image or images, as in a single linked image (called a *button*), or an image divided into hotspots that each link to their own destination (which is called an *image map*). Any type of link can jump to any type of destination.

Linking from one page to another page within your site

The most common link found in Web sites is a link on one page that opens another page within the same site. This kind of link is known as an *Internal link* because it stays within your site. The home page shown in Figure 11-1 contains five links, each to a different section of the site. Every site needs internal links so that viewers can get around and see all the great content within the site. Efficient and effective use of this kind of link is crucial to a good site.

Linking to a page outside of your site

One great power of the Web is its capability to instantaneously link to any other page within any other site anywhere in the world. These days advertising and business cards commonly provide URLs, but most sites are still discovered via links from other pages. When you link from your own page to another person or company's page, you are helping spin the World Wide Web, increasing traffic to their site, as well as yours. You are also creating what is known as an *External link*.

As part of GoLive's complete site management, External links are managed within the Site Window along with all other parts of your site—in this case, within the External tab of the Site Window (see Figure 11-2). Therefore, as with all other files you use in GoLive, you can collect them in the Site Window in order to manage them. You can collect them before linking to them, or after. Because these are not destinations that are physically part of your site, you don't physically drag (copy) them into the Site Window as you do with files. Instead, you collect or enter the addresses of these destinations and then link to the address icons.

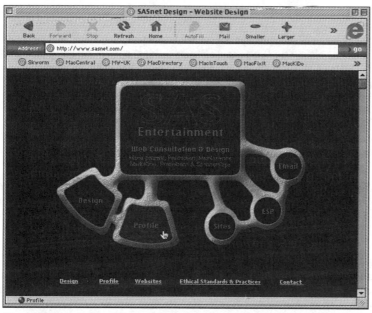

Figure 11-1: Steven Shmerler's home page basically consists of links to the parts of his site. His metallic control panel makes entering his site fun.

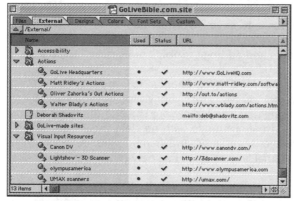

Figure 11-2: External addresses managed within the Site Window

You have many ways to collect URLs of other Web sites and also to collect e-mail addresses. In this chapter, I show you how to create the link first. Later on, in "Collecting URLs and E-mail Addresses," I show you many ways to gather or enter the destinations into the Site Window. This way, you can see the potential benefits of collecting the destinations before taking the time to do so.

While you're linking to other sites, bear in mind a few of the implications of doing so:

✦ Linking to someone else's page is an inexact science because you don't have control over that site. The Web master may delete, move, or redesign that site at any time. Rather than linking to a specific page, product, or topic, it is often safer to link to a home page.

✦ When you link to a page outside of your own site, you cannot link to a specific point within that page, unless it's a page you built or if there's already an anchor on the page for you to link to. Sometimes you can get the designer to place an anchor into the page for you. (See "Linking to Specific Parts of a Page Using Anchors" later in this chapter.)

✦ For the most part, linking to another site provides a common benefit to you and the other site. You lead people to the other site, which makes their site more valuable or useful. Then, perhaps you can arrange for them to link to you, if that makes sense. But some sites may not want the traffic increase because it may tax the site's server, or your link may bypass their advertising or home page, which might not coincide with the Webmaster's or company's plans or needs. If you're referring your visitors to an online publication or a software company, you can be fairly sure your link will be welcome. If you're uncertain as to the reception of a referring link, check with the Webmaster before you link.

When you create an External link (or any link, for that matter), GoLive's default setting is to deliver that page within the browser window that's currently open, taking the place of the current page. When you link to pages within your site this is fine. However, if this external page takes your visitor away from your site, you risk losing this visitor. One way to avoid this is to have External links open pages in a new browser window. I'll show you how to do this when I show you how to create a link. The sections on adding text links and adding graphics links provide full instruction.

Caution   If you set your page up using frames (see Chapter 15), the external site's page opens within your site's frame. You won't lose your visitor, but you stand the good chance of creating a confusing hodgepodge of your site and the other site, possibly a frames-within-frames visual nightmare with no clear means of escape. You can solve the dilemma for both unframed and framed sites (as appropriate or needed) by setting your external links to open in a new browser window.

The other method is to use a GoLive Action, which is JavaScript. Without going into too great detail, with Actions you can present pages in their own windows that open over or around your main window, enabling you to provide additional information while still having your main page visible.

Cross-Reference   Chapter 18 covers Actions in greater detail.

Linking to another point within your page

It's common to organize a site by topic, creating a separate page for each topic. However, sometimes a topic has subtopics that don't belong on pages of their own — either because there's not enough text to warrant a separate page or the time that it takes to download it, or because the content reads better in one place on one page. If you've spent time on the Web, you've probably seen this type of page. These pages can be long, requiring the user to scroll the page. Therefore, the efficient way to set this type of page up is by listing the subtopics at the top of the page, like a table of contents, providing a sense of what's contained. In addition to acting as a content guide, each subtopic is an active navigational link. However, instead of linking to another page, the links take the reader to the respective text on the same page, as is done on the www.wiredlaw.com Legal Pad shown in Figure 11-3. This type of navigational link is often referred to as an anchor link. This is one situation where you'd want a link to another point on the same page. You may find others. You can create an anchor link or links within any HTML page on your site.

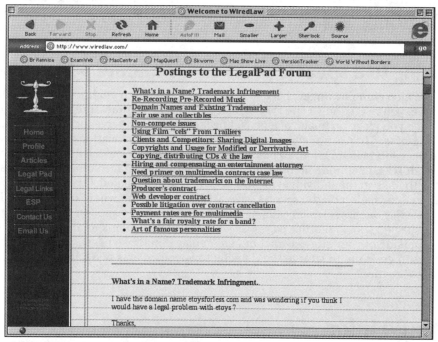

Figure 11-3: The top of the Wired Law page contains a list of questions. Each question in the list links to the full question and its answer — which is lower down on the same page. Clicking any question jumps users to the exact location on the answer.

Links within the same page are created by linking to an *anchor* within the page. This is an HTML standard, not just a GoLive method. GoLive makes it incredibly easy to do. After you create the anchor link within your page, you can move its destination anytime just by dragging the anchor. You can also break the link and delete the anchor if you wish. All you need to create an anchor link within a page is the text or image you're linking from and the text you are linking it to. If linking from a graphic, you need the Inspector open.

When you create a link within your page, you tell the browser which line to display when the link is clicked. Another way to think of an anchor link is as an instant automatic scroll to a place elsewhere on the same page. Be aware, though, that each browser may handle this request a bit differently. Each browser will scroll your page to display your destination line within the window but may have the line land in a different spot — so the line you link to may land at the top of the browser's window or somewhere in the center. If the part of the page that the anchor link links to is already viewable in the browser, it's possible that the page won't scroll at all. If there's more than one linked section as you get to the end of a page, often those links can only take you to the bottom of that page because not enough vertical space exists to bring the remaining linked sections to the top of the browser's window.

Linking to a specific point on a separate page

You can also combine linking between pages with linking to anchors. Let's say, for example, you're creating a site for a business that has several store locations. On one page you place an image of a map showing their twenty-five locations across the United States. There's not enough information about each location to warrant a separate page for each location, so on one separate page you make a list of each location's address, telephone number, and so on. On the first page you create an image map with links to the individual locations, which, when clicked, takes readers to the location information on the second page, which may be anywhere on the page. This is done using anchors, which can link not only to a specific spot on the same page, but to specific spots on other pages, as well. You can even link to anchor points on pages outside of your site — if anchors are in place on those pages. Again, I cover anchors in great depth later in the "Linking to Specific Parts of a Page Using Anchors" section.

Creating Links

Any text on your page can become a link — whether a single character, an entire line, or a full paragraph. Likewise, any graphic on your page can also be turned into a link. When a graphic acts as a link it is commonly called a *button*.

Whether your link is from text or from a graphic, it performs the same way. That is, it can trigger a jump to another part of the same page, to another page within your site, to a page elsewhere on the Web, to a Portable Document Format (PDF) page, a page that contains an .swf animation, or to an e-mail address. You can even link to a downloadable file.

The initial creation of text and graphic links varies slightly because a graphic already is a link of sorts. That is, the graphic is not really on your page (as explained in Chapter 10) but linked into it. This section shows you how to begin each link. Then, the following sections show how to actually complete the link by choosing the link's destination.

Traditionally, when text is linked, it appears with an underline. As underlines are distracting to the reader, it's often better not to turn an entire paragraph into a link but to instead have several words act as a link. Figure 11-4 shows an example of text links with descriptive sentences that help guide the reader. After you create a link, you can still edit it to change the words that describe it.

Text links

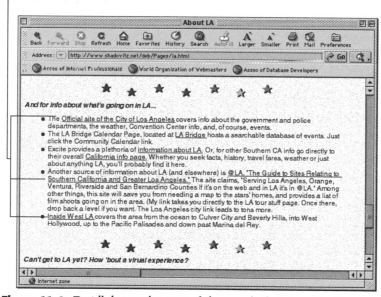

Figure 11-4: Text links can be part of the words that describe them.

When creating a new page, make sure you save it into your site before linking from or to it. GoLive *will* let you create a link on an unsaved page to a saved page, but that link will be to a directory location on your hard drive — not to the location within your site. GoLive will *not* let you make a link *to* an unsaved page.

To create a link, follow these steps:

1. Select the text or graphic you want to turn into the link, as follows:

   • If linking from text, select the exact words or characters that you want underlined and appearing in the color of linked text. Typically, the text is descriptive of the link. (You can always change the words, so don't fret too much over the choice of words. You can also remove part of the text from the link later, if you decide to shorten the link.) When you select the text, the arrow-pointer cursor acquires a box icon (because selected text can also be moved).

   • If linking from a graphic, simply click the graphic to select it.

Tip

If your linked text is at the end of an existing line, type a space after the text. Then, select the link text but leave the space unselected. As a result, the link only includes the exact text, and when you go on to type more, the new text will not be part of the link. Likewise, if linking from a graphic that's inline with the I-beam, type a space after the graphic so that anything that follows the graphic will not become part of the link.

2. Tell GoLive you want to create a link and activate the URL field. Choose one of the following five ways to do this:

   • Choose Special ➪ New Link.

   • Control-click (Mac) or right-click (Windows), and then choose New Link from the contextual menu.

   • Press ⌘-L(Mac) or Ctrl+L (Windows).

   • Click the New Link button on the toolbar.

   • Click the New Link button on the Link tab of the Inspector, as shown in Figure 11-5.

Note

The Inspector doesn't have to be open in order to use the menus or shortcuts.

Each of these methods has the same effect, activating the URL area of the Inspector and placing the phrase "(Empty Reference!)" in the URL field beside the Link buttons. At this point a Bug icon also appears by the page in the Files tab of the Site Window because the link is not yet complete.

3. In the Inspector, tell GoLive where the link should lead. You have three ways to do this, as shown in Figure 11-6.

New link

Selected text to be linked

Remove link

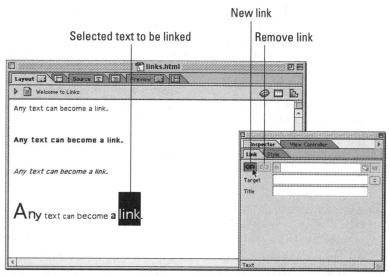

Figure 11-5: The New Link button is one way to turn a selection into a link.

Point and Shoot to destination link

Type or paste destination link

Browse to destination link

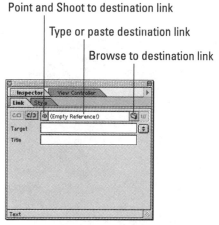

Figure 11-6: The URL Getter area of the Inspector provides three ways to designate a link's destination after text has been selected and the New Link button is clicked.

Point and Shoot. You can Point and Shoot by dragging the Fetch URL button of the Inspector to a destination within the Site Window. As you drag, a rope-like line depicts the connection. Your goal is to reach and select the page or item that is your link's destination. Here are some details to keep in mind:

- If your link is an HTML page, a .swf or .pdf document, an anchor link listed beneath any HTML page, or even a compressed file for users to download, it's in the Files tab. (See the "Creating a Downloadable File" section later in this chapter for details.)

- If your link is to another location within your current page, drag to that exact location. When you release the mouse, an anchor is created. That anchor is the link's destination. (See the "Linking to Specific Parts of a Page Using Anchors" section later in this chapter.)

- If your link is to an external URL or an e-mail address, it's in the External tab. That is, if you've already collected the address there. (See the "Collecting URLs and E-mail Addresses" section later in this chapter.)

If the Site Window isn't visible as you begin to drag, rest the cursor over the Select Window button in the toolbar to bring the Site Window forward (see Figure 11-7) while dragging the Fetch URL button and then continue on to your link's destination. If any part of the Site Window is peeking out from behind the page, you can instead drag over that part to bring the Site Window forward.

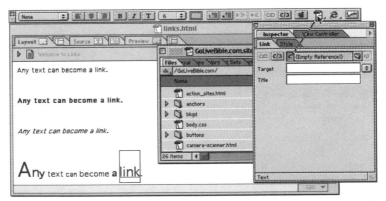

Figure 11-7: The Point and Shoot rope, resting over the Select Window button, brings the Site Window forward so that you can drag the rope toward the link's destination.

If the tab that contains your destination is not active, rest the cursor over the desired tab until the tab moves forward and then continue downward into the body of the window.

If you arrive at the Site Window's tab only to find that a subfolder is open and that you need to move up to the main level of the tab's contents, hover the cursor over the blue arrow (Mac) or Folder Navigation button (Windows) located above the file list (directly below the Files tab). When your destination or your destination's folder appears, you can continue. When you reach and point to the destination page, URL, or address and it becomes selected, release the mouse to make the connection, as shown in Figure 11-8.

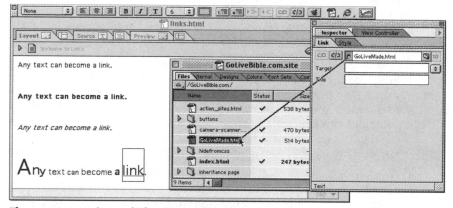

Figure 11-8: Point and Shoot provides an easy way to connect words to a page. In this case, the page being linked to is GoLiveMade.html.

Browse. Click the Browse button, which is the small folder icon to the right of the URL field. Then use the Open dialog box to navigate to and select the file you want to link to.

Browse only works for linking to pages and downloadable files; you can't use it to link to external addresses or to anchors (specific points within a page). Some people prefer using browse when their screens are too crowded to see the Site Window easily.

If you browse to a file that isn't already in the Site Window, it's important to understand that browse does not actually collect the referenced file into your project folder. After using browse you'll see the added page and its elements, but their URLs are still in their original locations, not within your Site Window. You will also notice that the URLs are not in your Files tab, but they appear in the right side of the Site Window in the Orphan or Missing folder.

Cross-Reference

See Chapter 25 to learn how to deal with these errors.

As you type or paste within the URL in the Inspector's URL field, you might find the area too small to see your entire URL. While the URL is selected, press Command-E (Mac) or Ctrl+E (Windows) to open a larger edit field. (Or press Option [Mac] or Alt [Windows] so that the Browse icon — the folder — turns into a pencil and then click the pencil.)

Manually. Select the phrase "(Empty Reference!)" and type or paste in the destination.

For an e-mail link, you can simply enter the actual address. GoLive adds the mailto: code for you. This automatic addition of the mailto: code can be turned off in the URL Handling section of the Preferences dialog, should you want this naming feature off for some reason.

(Mac only) While the Inspector is open you can instantly select the URL field in the Inspector by pressing ⌘- , (comma). This automatically selects the words "(Empty Reference!)" so that you're ready to type or paste your URL. (Need more room to see what you're typing or pasting? Press ⌘-E to open the URL field into a larger edit window.) Use this tip together with the ⌘-L shortcut mentioned in Step 2 of the how to create a link discussion for maximum speed. That is, ⌘-L, ⌘- , (comma), type the address, and then you're done.

4. *(Optional)* By default, all links created in the Inspector are *relative*. If you specifically want your link to be *absolute*, press Return or Enter (or click anywhere in the Inspector) to confirm the address you just entered. This activates the Absolute Link button (//:) at the far right of the URL Getter area. Click this button to turn your link absolute. (See the next section, "Absolute and relative paths," for more about this topic and to learn how to set up URL mapping.)

5. *(Optional)* If you're linking to an external page (that is, a page outside of your own site) you can have the target page open in its own new browser window instead of replacing your page. To do this, choose "_blank" from the pop-up menu next to the Target field at the bottom of the Inspector, as shown in Figure 11-9. (The rest of those choices pertain only to frames.)

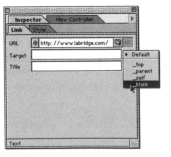

Figure 11-9: To have a destination page open in its own window choose "_blank" from the Target menu.

6. *(Optional)* You can also give your link a title by entering title text in the Title field. This title is different from the Title you give your own pages. Instead, this is a bit like the alternate text you add for graphics. The text can be read by a voice synthesizing browser to help users learn about the destination page. Giving the link a name is supposed to improve accessibility and contain the title of the page to which you are linking so that the title can be read or converted into Braille. However, this feature not really defined or supported, and in some browsers it creates a pop-up in a small note pane similar to conventional Tooltips.

While the Title attribute for a link is not yet a well supported standard and its actual usage is in question, it provides an excellent opportunity for you to save much time and effort if you're using middleware to connect to a database.

After you complete the link, return to your page by clicking the page. Mac users can also press ⌘- ; (Command-semicolon) in order to return to the text that you selected to make into the link.

Tip

When you're linking from text, you can bypass going to the Inspector and Point and Shoot directly from the text. Just select the text (as mentioned in Step 1 of the how to create a link discussion), and then press Option (Mac) or Alt (Windows). The arrow pointer gains a curly point-and-shoot symbol by its tail. Keeping this key down, click the selected text and drag to the target page within the Site Window.

When your text is successfully linked, it appears underlined in your page layout (unless the page already uses a style sheet that defines an alternative style for your links). Because buttons are links, in previous versions of GoLive they were automatically marked by a border the same color as a text link's underline. However, in response to popular demand, Adobe removed this default border. If you'd like any button to have a border color that matches the color of its corresponding hyperlink text, select the graphic button and in the Basic tab of the Image Inspector replace the 0 border width with a larger number. (The larger the number, the wider the border.) The color of the border is the same color as the one you designate for all links. Blue is the default.

Cross-
Reference

How to change the color of all of your links within the Inspector is explained in Chapter 5. Another method that uses a Cascading Style Sheet is explained in Chapter 17.

Absolute and relative paths

After you create any link to a page with your own site, the URL area in the Inspector offers you a checkbox to make the URL absolute. But before you make the URL absolute, make sure that you understand the differences among physical, absolute, and relative URL paths.

✦ A **physical path** is a fully qualified URL beginning with a protocol and a domain (the physical name of the server, `http://www.domain.com/`) and including the full path to the page (for example, `http://www.domain.com/yourpage.html` or `http://www.domain.com/subdirectory/subdirectory/yourpage.html`). To create fully qualified physical paths in GoLive, use the URL Mappings feature described later in this section. If you decide to use physical paths and to set up a URL mapping for your site, GoLive will track the file and update its path from the Web root while you're working on the site. However, if after you export or upload the site you move the site to another domain, browsers will be unable to find the page or file.

✦ **Absolute paths** (also called *root-relative* paths) are specified from the root of the Web server (`/`) to the page (for example, `/subdirectory/yourpage.html`). This is the type of path that GoLive creates when you click the absolute link button in the URL inspector. These types of links will work regardless of which page they are called from, as long as the directory structure of the site remains unchanged. Unlike physical paths, absolute paths remain valid if you switch domains. Absolute paths will *not* work, however, if your site is served from a directory other than the root of the Web server (for example, if your Web site address is `www.domain.com/~mywebsite`). You can tell GoLive to automatically make new links absolute in Edit ➪ Preferences ➪ General ➪ URL Handling.

✦ **Relative paths** (the GoLive default) are specified relative to the current page. So, if you have a page in a subdirectory of the Web server root called "pages" and you want to access a page in another subdirectory of the server root, your link would be written as follows: `../subdirectory/yourpage.html`. The "`../`" means "go back one level in the directory structure." In order to go back two directory levels, you would use "`../../`", and so on. By keeping a path relative, the link remains valid wherever you move the site, as long as you maintain the file directory (folders for Mac) structure.

To set up a URL mapping in order to create fully qualified physical links, with the Site Window active, choose Site ➪ Settings ➪ URL Mappings and click New. In the first field, enter the full URL of your side (for example, `http://www.yourdomain name.com`). Then select "root of this site" from the pop-up menu to the right of the second field at the bottom. Any new links that you create will now be fully qualified physical links.

Note The Head tab of the GoLive palette contains an icon for a Link tag. You may have noticed that I haven't discussed using this Link tag as a way to create a link. That's because it isn't necessary to use it when you manage your pages in the Site Window. To learn about this tag, you can refer to the GoLive manual.

Now that you know the basics of creating a link, you're ready to learn the details of the various link destinations.

Other ways to create links between pages

GoLive actually provides the following two lesser-known ways to create text links between the pages of your site:

✦ Dragging the link destination into place

✦ Dragging the page icon to the source page (Mac only)

Dragging the link destination into place

You can drag the destination page or external address directly into place on the desired page. The link takes on the exact name of the HTML file, URL, or address you've dragged. If you've named your external URL or e-mail links well, this is a great method to use for those links. (It's not as logical for links to pages because page names are things such as "products.html," and that's not exactly the text you want on your page. However, you can always edit the link's text.)

To create a link by dragging the link's destination, follow these steps:

1. Enter the link's introductory text on your page. (Don't include the text to be linked. Don't type a space after the last word. It will be added automatically, so you'll end up with an extra space if you add your own.)

2. Locate the URL or e-mail address in the External tab of the Site Window and drag it into place on the page, as shown in Figure 11-10. You can drag the file into any line of text, including a text box on a grid, text in a floating box, or a table cell. The name of the address appears as a completed link.

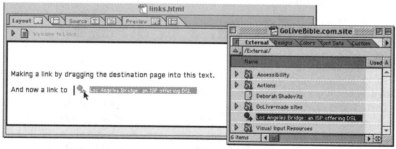

Figure 11-10: Drag an address from the Site Window onto the page to create an instant link. Here, the link is still selected, as the External URL icon (still selected in the Site Window) was just dropped into place.

Note   You can also drag between existing text. In fact, GoLive wisely places a space before and after your new link. (If you already have spaces in your text, as you most likely do, watch for extra spaces that you may need to delete later.)

3. Click the page to deselect the link and place the cursor to continue working. A space is automatically added after the link, so the next text you type the new characters will not be part of the link.

This step is not necessary if you've dragged the link in between existing text.

You can, of course, edit the name of the link at any time. If you will be linking to this destination again and realize you prefer to call it something different on the page, you can choose the address in the Site Window and rename the address with the more convenient name.

Dragging the page icon to the source page (*Mac only*)

If you happen to have both the page you want to link from and the page you want to link to open, you can drag a link between those pages. The result of this is the same as dragging an address from the Files tab of the Site Window — the link takes on the name of the page. It's not very likely you'll find yourself in a position to use this method. But just in case, here are the steps you should follow:

1. Position the pages so that you can see the Page icon at the top of the target page and the place you want the link to fall in the page from which you are linking.

2. Drag the Page icon from the top of the target page into where you want the link.

3. Click anywhere in the page to deselect the link and then place the cursor to continue working.

Edit the link's name as desired. You can edit this text as you edit any text.

Linking to Specific Parts of a Page Using Anchors

Normally, when you link from one page to another, the link automatically takes you to the top of the destination page. As an alternative, you can have a link take the user to a specific point within the destination page. You can also have a link take the user from one part of a page to another part of the same page. To link to any spot within a page, place an anchor within the page and then link to the anchor by using one of two methods: create the link and anchor at the same time on the fly as you Point and Shoot, or place the anchor first and then link to the anchor.

You have basically the two following ways to link to anchors within your own site:

✦ Create the anchor on the fly by Pointing and Shooting directly to the desired anchor point within a page. If linking to a page other than the one the linked text or graphic is in, the destination page must be open. It must be an HTML page, and the page must be within your site.

✦ Link to pre-existing anchors by Pointing and Shooting to the anchor where it is listed in the Files tab. To link within another page format, the page must already have the anchors defined prior to their placement in the Site Window.

Following is a method to link to an external page:

✦ To link to an external anchor, first create an external link complete with the anchor information as part of the destination and then link to this address in the External tab.

See Figure 11-3 (shown previously in this chapter) for a real-life example of linking within a page.

Creating an anchor on the fly

You can create the anchor and link to that anchor all at once simply by Pointing and Shooting to the destination. (What could be easier?) This works whether the link and destination are on the same page or on different pages within your site.

If linking to another part of the same page, all you need open is that one page. If you're linking to a specific location within another page of your site, you need that other page open in order to do this.

Tip   Linking from one part of a page to another part of the same page? When the destination of a link is fairly close to the originating point, the quickest way to create a link within a page is to Point and Shoot. As your destinations are farther down the page, scrolling becomes necessary with this method, so it becomes time to switch to the next method — placing an anchor and then using the Site Window to make the connection.

Follow these steps to create an anchor on the fly as you create the link:

1. On the originating page, select the text or graphic that you want to turn into the link.

2. In the Link tab of the Inspector, click the New Link button to begin the link.

3. Drag the Point and Shoot button over to your target text, as in Figure 11-11, and then release the mouse to place the anchor and to complete the link.

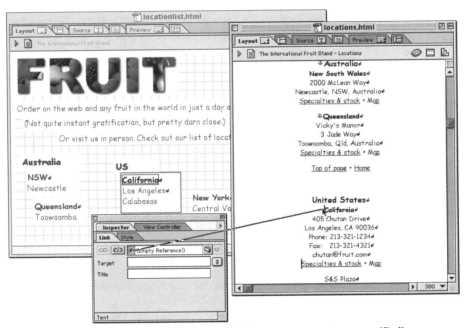

Figure 11-11: Pointing and Shooting to link from one page to a specific line on another page

If at all possible, place your anchor inline with the main cursor on your page, rather than in a table or on a grid. Some browsers do not recognize an anchor in a table cell (or the text area of a grid) as a link destination. Therefore they jump to the top of the table (or grid). If the bulk of your page consists of a single table or grid, consider breaking it up into smaller tables or grids. Then place the anchor in front of or after the relevant table or grid. If your link destination is a graphic, place the anchor just before or after the graphic.

You have no need to stop and name the anchor during this process because the anchor is automatically named, using the word directly after the link's destination. The name will be something like `Anchor-yourtext-49575`. You can rename it by selecting the anchor on the page and by using the Anchor Inspector. The anchor name actually becomes part of the link's URL, so keep the name short, avoid spaces, and follow Web naming protocol. Make the name descriptive so that you can identify the anchor later, in case you wish to create other links to it. Don't use a name twice in the same page because then the link won't know which anchor to jump to.

Tip

If you're linking from text, you can cut this down to one step. Simply Point and Shoot from the text to be linked directly to the destination text. That is, select the text to be linked and then press ⌘ (Mac) or Alt (Windows) as you point to the text and drag it to the desired destination.

Linking to an anchor

Creating an anchor on the fly can get out of hand when the pages involved are long and, therefore, require much dragging. In these cases, it's easier to place your anchors within the destination page first and then to link to those anchors. You may also find it easier to preplace the anchors when a page has several anchor destinations. This method involves two steps: First, create the anchor. Second, link to the anchor.

Here are explanations of the steps for creating a link with this method:

1. Open the destination page and have the Objects palette in view. Drag the anchor icon from the Basic tab of the Objects palette into place on the page, as shown in Figure 11-12.

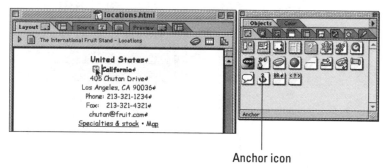

Anchor icon

Figure 11-12: Dragging an anchor from the Objects palette to the page

Place the anchor inline with the main cursor on your page. If your destination is within a table or on a grid, place it in front of or after the table or grid, rather than in a cell or in a text area on a grid. This is advisable because some browsers don't recognize link destinations, and they jump to the top of the table (or grid) instead. If the bulk of your page consists of a single grid or table, consider breaking it up into smaller grids or tables so that the anchor can be before or after the grid or table but still be close to your intended destination. If your destination is a graphic, place the anchor just before or after the graphic. If your anchor doesn't land where you want it to land, drag it into place. (You can also move it later, in case you want to tweak its position.)

If you want to have multiple jumping points within the page, place an anchor to each point. (You can add more anchors later, but you might as well place them all at the same time.)

Anchors are reported in the Files tab of the Site Window as a sublisting of the page on which they reside. Your new anchor should be visible automatically. (In case it's not, clicking the light gray arrow to the left of the page's icon reveals the page's anchors.)

2. With the anchor still selected on the page, open the Inspector and replace the generic name, "Anchor," with a short descriptive name, unique within the page, as shown in Figure 11-13. (It is okay to have one anchor named "Anchor" on a page, but if two exist, only the first one will be recognized.) The name becomes part of the URL and needs to be matched by the browser, so keep the name short. As with other URLs, use only lowercase letters and avoid spaces.

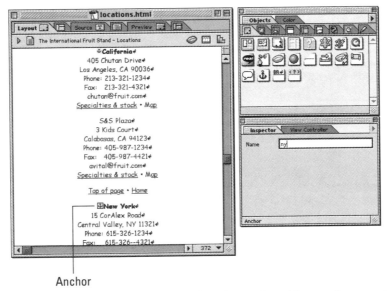

Anchor

Figure 11-13: A page of anchors placed from the Objects palette, and naming them using the Anchor Inspector

Unlike most items in the Site Window, an anchor cannot be renamed by clicking its name there, nor can you call up the Anchor Inspector by selecting an anchor in the Site Window. To alter any anchor, open the page it is on, and then locate and select the actual anchor.

3. On the originating page, select the text or graphic you want to turn into the link.

4. In the Link tab of the Inspector, click the New Link button to begin the link.

5. Point and Shoot to the anchor in the Files tab (as shown in Figure 11-14).

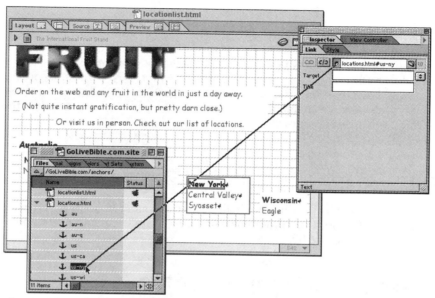

Figure 11-14: Point and Shoot to an anchor marker in the Files tab in order to link directly to a specific point within the destination page.

If the Site Window, or the part of it you need, isn't showing, rest the cursor over the Select Window button in order to bring the Site Window forward. Or if any part of the Site Window is visible, rest the cursor on that part in order to bring the entire window forward. Then continue dragging.

In each case, the target anchors appear beneath their respective pages. If the anchor isn't already showing, rest the cursor over the page's name or gray arrow as you Point and Shoot to reveal the anchor(s). Release the mouse when the anchor's name becomes highlighted.

Links to anchors are composed of the page's name followed by the number sign/hash mark (#) and then the anchor's name. This is the URL that appears when the link to the anchor is inspected in the Inspector, when a cursor rests over the anchor, or when you click the anchor in a browser.

To link to a specific part of a page that's outside of your site, don't place the anchor. Instead, use an existing anchor — if the destination has one. On the Web, visit the exact location you're targeting and copy the entire URL, including the pound sign and the rest of the anchor name. Then link to it the same way you link to any External link: either by creating the link and pasting the copied destination into the URL field in the Inspector or by adding this URL to the External tab in the Site Window.

Testing anchor links

You can test the link by switching to Preview mode. However, Netscape and Internet Explorer each jump to the anchor a little bit differently. It's best to preview the page in each browser. (Platforms aren't an issue here, just browsers.) After testing, you may wish to move an anchor up or down in the page in order to affect the point to which the browser jumps.

Using Externally Created Pages

The pages in your Web site don't all have to be made in GoLive. You can create your pages in other software programs and incorporate them into a site you created using Adobe GoLive 5.

Using LiveMotion or ImageStyler

If you've created an entire page within LiveMotion (or ImageStyler) and saved the document as an HTML page, you can bring that page into GoLive and link to it just like you link to any other HTML page. Within LiveMotion (or ImageStyler) use the Export As command, which exports the page and its graphic elements, creating one HTML file and a folder called Images. To incorporate the LiveMotion- or ImageStyler-made page into you site, drag the HTML file and the Images folder into the Files tab of the Site Window, letting GoLive perform the requested update. In GoLive, link to the HTML page as you link to any other page in your site. After you move the HTML page into the Site Window, treat the HTML page as you do any GoLive-made HTML pages. You can also use the In & Out Links Inspector to see all links into and out of the page (as with other HTML files), relink the URLs and addresses, and even relink the buttons and other graphics used on the page.

Using PDF files

Besides HTML files, you might want to include an Adobe Portable Document File (PDF) page as part of your site. This is a popular solution for distributing forms, product guides, or brochures. Create the PDF file outside of GoLive, drag it into the Files tab of the Site Window, and then link to it as you link to any other page on your site.

Expanding the Functionality of PDFs

PDFs have more functionality, such as annotation and markup, when opened independently of a browser (in the actual Acrobat Reader program). Additionally, when a PDF opens within a Netscape 4.x browser, the PDF can hang up and need reloading. Also, if a PDF opens within a frame, it can freeze if the user tries to resize the frame. For these reasons and more, most people prefer to have users download PDFs instead of viewing them in a browser. Most browsers preconfigure Acrobat as a helper application by default, so Acrobat or Acrobat Reader launches if the user has one or the other installed. But for full control as the site designer, one surefire way to ensure your PDF will download (not open in the browser) is to place the PDF file on an FTP server and then to create an External link to the file using the URL to the FTP location. Another method is to compress the PDF and then link to the compressed file.

If the user does not have the Adobe plug-in placed within the browser's plug-ins folder, the PDF file downloads to the user's hard drive when the link to it is clicked. If the Adobe Acrobat plug-in is installed, clicking a PDF file link opens the file within the browser window. Users who have the PDF plug-in can optionally download the file for viewing independently of the browser by choosing "Download to disk" from the links choices.

After you move a PDF into the Site Window, you can view and update its embedded links (if it has any). View its links the same way you view any other file's links, by clicking the file in the Site Window and opening the In & Out Links Inspector. Change its links in the same way, by Pointing and Shooting to any other destination file. (See "Reviewing and Changing Links" in the In & Out Links palette.) Just be aware that readers are likely to view your PDF outside of the browser and not within the context of your site, so links within the PDF should be absolute, not relative. In other words, include the entire URL to the destination.

You can perform many tricks by combining various file formats into a PDF before bringing it into GoLive. For example, you can put a Flash file in a QuickTime 4 movie (the Flash file will still keep its interactivity), put the QuickTime or QuickTime VR movie into a PDF, and then link the PDF into your Web site.

The Adobe Acrobat read-me document contains helpful information and considerations for using a PDF on your site. I recommend you take the time to read this document.

Using SWF or Director pages

There may be times when you want your entire page to be a Macromedia Flash (.swf), Shockwave Director movie (.dcr), or LiveMotion (.swf) page. For example, this is a popular way to have an interesting splash screen on your site. Linking to these pages is really no different than linking to any other page in your site. The only difference is that any of these pages have two parts. The HTML page enables it be viewed on the Web, and the .swf file (for Flash or LiveMotion) or .dcr file (for Director) actually contain the animation. To show a Flash or LiveMotion movie, place both files in your Site Window and upload both to the Web at a later time. To call upon a page of animation, link to the HTML file just like you link to any other Web page. That HTML file, in turn, calls upon the animation content file. The HTML page is just a simple page with the standard header and body code.

Tip   When you hire a designer, depending upon your agreement, you may be given just the Flash, LiveMotion, or Director movie, or only the movie along with an HTML page. If using Flash or LiveMotion and the designer only supplies the .swf, you can embed it into your own HTML page yourself. (See Chapter 20 for details.) If your animation is in Director, it's much easier to request that the designer provide the encompassing HTML file. (The designer should also give you the entire authoring file, so you own the design and have full control over it.)

To link to Flash, LiveMotion, or Director movies, follow these steps:

1. Drag the pair of files into the Files tab of the Site Window, as follows:
   - If using Flash, you'll have the HTML file and its accompanying Flash (.swf) document.
   - If using LiveMotion, you'll have the HTML file and its accompanying LiveMotion (.swf) document.
   - If using Director, you'll have the HTML file and its accompanying Director (.dcr) file.

   If a .swf file contains links, GoLive notices the links and asks to update them. Click OK.

2. Use your favorite linking method to link from your page to the HTML file.

To properly preview the page with the full effect, open the page and preview it in a browser. But remember that your browser will only render one of these formats if the Flash plug-in is in the browser plug-ins folder.

In addition to linking to a Flash file, you can also view and change the Flash file's embedded links (if it has any). Because the links are embedded within the original animation file, the .swf file, select the .swf file in the Files tab to change the link destinations. After selecting this file, open the In & Out Links palette and proceed as with any other file. See the "Reviewing and Changing Links in the In & Out Links Palette" and "Verifying and Repairing Links" sections later in this chapter. (In case you're wondering why GoLive doesn't allow you to work on Director's embedded links, it's because the programming code, also known as API, has to be public for things like this. The Director API needed for this is not in public release.)

Tip If hiring a Flash or LiveMotion designer, it's a good idea to have the designer build a forward link (called a *Get URL*) into the movie. This is the link to which the user is taken when the movie play has completed or when a user clicks the optionally placed Skip Intro button. Remember, you can change the destination of that link at any time, as described previously in this section.

QuickTime movies

Of course, you can also include QuickTime movies in your site. Most commonly, you will place a QuickTime movie or sound file within a page and then link to the page just like you would link to any other page. If you link directly to the QuickTime file and the user has MoviePlayer or another program that plays QuickTime movies, the movie opens independently of the Web page within the application that it plays in.

You can also link to, see link errors in, and edit the links within QuickTime movies. If a QuickTime file contains links and has a bad link, a Bug icon appears by it in the Files tab of the Site Window, just like with any other file. To view or edit a QuickTime file's links, select it and look at the In & Out Links palette, also like with any other file.

Cross-Reference Details on putting together QuickTime movies in GoLive can be found in Chapter 20.

Collecting URLs and E-mail Addresses

By recording link destinations into the Site Window, you enable GoLive to manage and keep track of those link destinations, as well as enabling GoLive to verify the external URLs. By placing a URL or destination in the External tab of the Site Window, you can easily add that destination over and over again, as well as copy it to another Site Window to use on another site. You can either place the URLs and addresses in the Site Window before you create links, or you can create a link (entering the URL or address manually) and then have GoLive gather and add the link to the Site Window later.

You have many ways to get your URLs and e-mail addresses into the Site Window. You can add them individually or add entire collections. And, of course, you can enter any URL or e-mail address manually. Each browser and platform is different, so not every way will work for every browser. However, browsers evolve, so what doesn't work in one browser at this writing may work by the time you read this.

Gathering URLs and e-mail addresses from your pages

If you create any links, whether external URLs or e-mail addresses, by pasting or typing the address into the URL field in the Inspector, it's handy to collect the links into the Site Window at some point. It's easy to do, and you can do it any time.

In fact, you can do it as often as you like because addresses that are already in the Site Window are acknowledged; you don't have to worry about duplication. You don't need any pages open. All pages are automatically checked, and all addresses that are not yet in the External tab are gathered.

Here's how to gather link addresses from your pages:

1. Bring the Site Window forward and click the External tab to make it active.

2. Choose Site ➪ Get References Used in order to click the Update button on the toolbar.

   Because the External tab of the Site Window is active, the Update button does the same thing as Site ➪ Get Referenced Used. (The Update button always performs whichever Update or Scan option is appropriate for the tab that is active in the Site Window.)

   The URLs and addresses automatically appear, complete with descriptive names. URLs are put in a folder called New URLs, while addresses land into a folder called New Addresses. You can rename these folders or move the addresses out of these folders.

   That's it. You can now easily link to these addresses over and over.

By linking to a gathered address, you make it easy to change the address as a link destination. Editing the address in the External tab changes that destination for all links that call upon it. If, instead, you link to the same destination twice, but manually type the destination both times, GoLive sees two different destinations, and you'll have to edit that address in both links.

Manually adding a URL or e-mail address

If you know the URL or e-mail address you wish to have your site link to, you can add it's address to the External tab at any time by typing it. The good part is that you don't have to be connected to the Web to do this. The bad part is that you have to type.

To manually add a URL or e-mail address to the Site Window, follow these steps:

1. Drag a URL icon (or Address icon for e-mail) from the Site tab of the Objects palette into the External tab of the Site Window, as shown in Figure 11-15.

   You now have an untitled URL (or untitled address). Because it comes in selected, you can name it immediately by typing a name for it. However, it's also easy to name it in the Inspector in the next step.

   You can save some extra work later by giving your link an appropriate name here. How? Drag a link from the External tab of the Site Window directly onto your page. The name appears as the text for the link.

URL icon

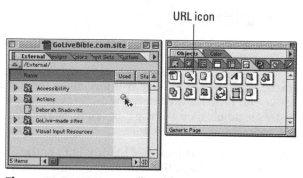

Figure 11-15: To manually add a URL to the External tab, drag the URL icon into the tab.

2. Open or bring forward the Inspector, now the Reference Inspector, because a URL or e-mail address is selected. If you have named the URL or address in the Site Window, that name appears in the Name field. If you didn't name it, now is the time to select the default text and enter a name. (If you don't see the URL or address information in the Inspector, click anywhere in the Site Window's tab and then select the new URL or address icon again.)

3. Tab to the lower field and enter the link's destination.

If you are adding a URL, the second field is the URL field. Keep any appropriate part of the untitled URL (see Figure 11-16) and replace the rest so that the desired URL is now listed. Move on to your next task or press Enter/Return to confirm the change.

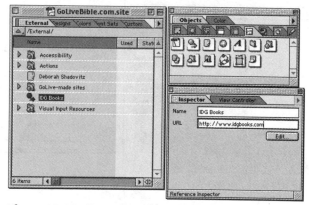

Figure 11-16: Enter the address information of an external link into the Reference Inspector.

That's it. This external address is now ready for you to link to it.

Other ways to add addresses

Here are several other ways to add addresses to your Site Window (not all methods work in all cases, but they're always worth a try):

1. To add any URL or e-mail address to the Site Window, make the External tab of the Site Window active and position the Site Window so you can see it. Make sure that you can also see at least a bit of the Site Window while you can also see the window that contains the URL or address.

2. Drag the URL or address into the main area of External tab of the Site Window or into any folder within the tab. Keep the following details in mind:

    • While visiting a site, you can easily add its address to the Site Window. This automatically provides you with a properly named address icon, making it easy to link to later. Drag the bookmark icon at the left of browser's location bar (Netscape) or the @ icon in the location bar (Internet Explorer) into the External tab, as shown in Figure 11-17.

Note This works with Netscape 4 browsers, with Internet Explorer 4 (Mac), with Internet Explorer 5 (Mac), and with Internet Explorer 5.5 (Windows).

    • You don't actually have to be at the page or the site in order to collect its link or to place its link on your page. Whenever you see a link on any page, you can collect it. This works in Netscape browsers and in Internet Explorer, both online and offline. However, this does not work in Internet Explorer for Windows.

Figure 11-17: Drag the Favorite/Bookmark icon for a current page into the Site Window to collect the URL.

    • Collect a URL or address from any text document. Select the link within the page and drag it into the External tab. (This does not work in every browser or text document, but it is always worth a try.)

- Collect individual Netscape bookmarks or Internet Explorer favorites. In Netscape Navigator choose Bookmarks ➪ Edit Bookmarks or in Internet Explorer choose Favorites ➪ Organize Favorites. Locate the desired bookmark or favorite and then drag it into the External tab, as shown in Figure 11-18.

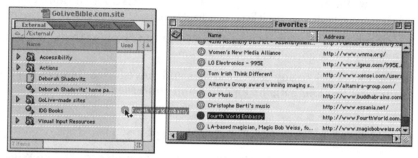

Figure 11-18: You can add a URL to your Site Window by dragging it from a bookmark.

- Collect an entire Favorites/Bookmark file at one time. In GoLive, choose Site ➪ Import Favorites as Site Externals. In the Open dialog box, locate the file you wish to import and then click Open or double-click the file to open and import it. Upon import, GoLive places your new URLs in a new folder named for the import (such as Bookmarks for Yourname or Favorites).

  (Mac only) Netscape's Bookmarks.html is in the System Folder ➪ Preferences ➪ Netscape Users ➪ Yourname. Internet Explorer's Favorites.html is in the System Folder ➪ Preferences ➪ Explorer. You can also import the Internet Explorer History file this way.

  (Windows only) Netscape bookmarks.htm is in C drive ➪ Program Files ➪ Netscape ➪ Users ➪ Yourname ➪ bookmark.htm. In order to import favorites from Internet Explorer, you first need to export them using the Import/Export Wizard opened via the File ➪ Import and Export command. Export to the desktop and then perform the import.

- Collect a specific folder of favorites from Internet Explorer. (It is helpful if you keep your Favorites folder well organized.) On a Mac, while in Internet Explorer, choose Favorites ➪ Organize Favorites, open the folder you want to export, and then choose File ➪ Export Favorites. Choose a location to save the file to and then click export. In Windows, choose File ➪ Import and Export and then use the Wizard to export the desired folder. In GoLive, choose Site ➪ Import Favorites as Site Externals. In the Open dialog box, locate the exported file and then double-click it to open and import it. GoLive places your new URLs in a folder named for the Favorites folder.

- *(Mac only)* Import any day's history. In Internet Explorer choose Go ⇨ Open History. Double-click that day's History folder to open it in its own window. Choose File ⇨ Export. In the Save dialog box, tell Internet Explorer to save to the desktop or someplace else where you can easily find the particular History folder and then click Save. In GoLive, choose Site ⇨ Import Favorites as Site Externals, locate the exported History file within the Open dialog box, and then click Open or double-click the file. GoLive places the URLs in a folder named for the date of the history.

3. *(Optional)* After you add an address, you can change the name by clicking the existing name and entering a new name.

4. *(Optional)* Delete any unwanted files and move files around as desired. (See the next section, "Organizing URLs and addresses.")

Organizing URLs and addresses

As you add more and more URLs and/or e-mail addresses to the Site Window, the Site Window may get out of hand, making it hard to find what you need when you need it. If so, sanity is at hand by way of folders. At any point in your site's development, you can drag a folder from Objects palette into the External tab of the Site Window. GoLive provides a folder specifically for grouping URLs and another folder specifically for e-mail addresses. These folders are called URL group and Address group, respectively. It's completely possible to put URLs in an address folder and vice versa; it may confuse you due to the visual icons on the folders, but you can do it if you choose.

Each folder comes into the External tab of the Site Window called "untitled group." The folder name is selected so that you can immediately type a descriptive name for the folder. (The folders won't be much help if you can't tell what's in them.)

To place a URL or an address into a folder, simply drag it into the folder. You can also move a file between folders, or move it out of a folder so that it is loose again. Organizing files and folders in the Site Window is much like organizing files and folders on a computer's hard drive.

Cross-
Reference

To learn more about opening folders and moving files around, see Chapter 2.

Extending E-mail Links

A typical e-mail link calls up the user's e-mail program and automatically addresses the e-mail. However, you can also have your e-mail link enter a subject line so that you can easily identify e-mail that comes from that link. You can even have the e-mail start body text, too. You have two ways to accomplish this: with a standard HTML link or with a JavaScript via GoLive's Action interface.

Why preaddress e-mail? You'll find plenty of reasons, but I'll start you off with one great one. Let's say you maintain and update several sites. By preaddressing this link with a specific Subject field, you can ensure (for the most part) what the subject will be. So, if you have a link for more information from Site #1, your subject might be, "Site #1: Request for Information." Then from your second site, your subject can be "Site #2, Request for Information." This is far more effective than leaving the subject up to the discretion of the user. You can have a link on each site for reporting bad links, one for making suggestions, and one for saying "great site." (Okay, maybe I'm joking about that last one.) You can then filter and read your mail efficiently. Of course, a user can change the subject line and mess up your brilliant system, but not everything can be perfect.

Adding to your e-mail link using standard HTML

You can create a link that automatically enters a subject, one or more carbon copies, one or more blind carbon copies, and even any amount of message body text. All it takes is a question mark (?) after the address to denote that the address has ended, and then the simple code for what you're adding. Use an ampersand (&) to connect each additional address element. Additional addresses can be placed in any order. You can add as many recipients as you'd like, but just one subject and one body.

To extend the functionality of your e-mail link, follow these steps:

1. Begin your e-mail link as normal by typing the recipient's address.

   You don't have to type `mailto:` when you enter the address. GoLive recognizes an e-mail address and adds that part of the address for you when you press Enter/Return or move out of the URL field.

2. Extend the e-mail link to include more information by adding a question mark (?) after the address.

3. Add one of the following strings of text, as shown here (but with your own words after the equal sign):

   ```
   subject=your subject text
   body=your body text
   cc=recipent@domain.com
   bcc=recipent@domain.com
   ```

   Figure 11-19 demonstrates the addition of the subject line.

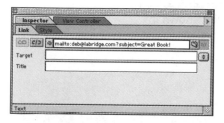

Figure 11-19: The URL in this figure creates an e-mail with a predesignated subject. In this example, the recipient is deb@labridge.com and the subject is "Great book."

4. *(Optional)* To add another addressee, a subject, or body, add an ampersand (&) and then another of the four options listed previously in Step 3.

Repeat Step 4 to add more recipients, to add a subject, or to start the body text. Figure 11-20 shows an e-mail link that's all tricked out.

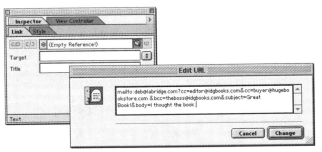

Figure 11-20: The URL in this figure creates an e-mail with multiple addressees, a subject, and the beginning of the body text.

To test your e-mail link, preview the page in a browser and click the link, as shown in Figure 11-21. E-mail links cannot be tested within the GoLive Preview. If you have your browser set up to communicate with your e-mail program, a new e-mail message opens and is addressed as you wish.

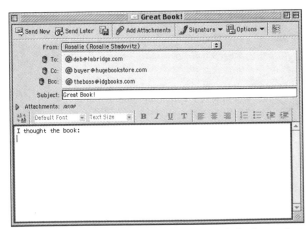

Figure 11-21: The result of clicking the link shown in the previous figure

A link that contains any of this extra information is considered separately from a regular link just to the person's e-mail address. Therefore, the link with this extra information appears as a separate link within the External tab in the Site Window. Bear this in mind when updating addresses. (See "Updating e-mail addresses" later in this chapter.)

Adding to an e-mail link using a GoLive Action

Another alternative to the extended link is to use a GoLive Action. Although GoLive doesn't come with an e-mail Action, the brilliant and Action-prolific Matt Ridley (www.matt-ridley.com) created a great one, called Emailer Action. It's easy to use — and free. It works with both Internet Explorer 3 and higher and with the Netscape browsers from Version 3 and higher, so it's pretty safe to use.

By using this Action, you avoid having to know the syntax (exact code to type) of the HTML needed to create an extended link. (I showed you the code in the preceding section, but you may not care to refer to it each time you create a link.)

You can download Emailer Action from www.matt-ridley.com. To install it, open the GoLive application folder, the Modules folder, the JScripts folder, and then the Actions folder. Place the new Action directly with this folder or within any sub-folder. The folders are organized by function, so use your own judgment as to where to store the Action. (I think the Link folder is a logical place for it.)

Cross-Reference

You can learn all about the GoLive-installed Actions in Chapter 18, but here in Chapter 11 I only discuss Ridley's Action.

You begin the link the same way as any other text or graphic link. Then, after you enter the e-mail address in the URL field, you move to the Actions tab of the Inspector and set up the Action as a Mouse Click event.

To create an e-mail link using Matt Ridley's Emailer Action, follow these steps:

1. Select the text or graphic that is to become the mailto: link and create a link.

   One easy way to create the link is to click the link icon on the toolbar or to press ⌘-L (Mac) or Ctrl+L (Windows).

2. To create a link from text in the Text Inspector, click the Link tab. Type, paste, or Point and Shoot to the e-mail address in the URL field, and then click the Enter arrow or press Enter/Return. (I've found that you don't have to enter the e-mail destination. You can simply place a "#" in the URL field and the Action will still work. However, by entering the address, your link should still work in non-JavaScript compliant browsers. At any rate, Matt Ridley says to enter the real e-mail address in this URL field.)

To create the link from a graphic, click the Link Tab and then type, paste, or Point and Shoot to the e-mail address in the URL field. Next, click the Enter arrow or press Enter/Return. (See the preceding comment about this topic.)

3. Click the Actions tab.

4. Select Mouse Click from the Events list so that the e-mail will be created when the user clicks the link.

5. Click the Add Action button to enable an Action.

6. Click the Action pop-up button and select the Emailer Action from wherever you placed it. (If you are in the Links folder, move down to Links and then over to Email Action.)

   In the lower part of the Inspector, three fields appear: Email Address, Email Subject, and Email Message.

7. Enter the e-mail's destination, subject, and body message in the three fields, respectively. (The subject and body are actually optional.)

Unlike the regular HTML link, when a user's mouse cursor rests over this link, only the e-mail's destination appears in the browser's status area, not the subject and the other predetermined information.

You should take a couple of matters into consideration before using this or any Action for creating an e-mail, though. Most important, an Action requires a JavaScript-capable browser. However, all this means is that, most likely, users of older browsers will end up with a regular e-mail, without the subject and body. Also, the e-mail may behave oddly in older e-mail clients (the program a user uses to read and write e-mail). For example, Ridley reports one quirk: In the old Claris Emailer, a Mac e-mail program, the body text ends up in the subject field.

Updating e-mail addresses

At any time you can change an address (or other link destinations) within your entire site in one fell swoop. To do this, click the External tab of the Site Window. If the address is not already in this tab, click the Update button on the toolbar to collect the e-mail addresses referenced in your site. Select an address, open the Inspector, change the address, and then click the now-active Enter button (the arrow) or press Enter/Return. When GoLive asks to update the links that refer to this address, click OK.

If you have an extended link that includes a *cc*, a *bcc*, a subject, or a body, this link is considered separately from a link to the same person that doesn't have all this extra stuff. Therefore, if you have your plain e-mail address in the External tab (without the extra stuff), changing this regular address doesn't update the extended links. You must locate all extended links within the External tab and update them, too.

Reviewing and Changing Links in the In & Out Links Palette

As your site grows, it can be difficult to recall all the pages that link into or out of any particular page. Not knowing your site's links can make it difficult to manage and plan changes to your site. The In & Out Links palette provides an interactive visual diagram of all of the links in your site on a page-by-page or item-by-item level. When you click a page in the Site Window, the In & Out Links window shows you all pages that link into the page and all links out of it.

But wait, there's more. . . . the In & Out Links palette doesn't only show you links — it enables you to change those links by simply Pointing and Shooting from a reported file to the one with which you want to replace it. Actually, it also shows you all files that comprise the page — the graphics (including a background image if one exists), QuickTime videos, sounds, external URLs, e-mail links, and so on. Any part of the page that's in, or belongs in, the Files tab or External tab is tracked and identified in the In & Out Links window. But that's another story. For now, the focus is on links that act as transport to other pages or files.

To open the In & Out Links palette, click the Open In & Out Links palette button on the toolbar or choose Window ➪ In & Out Links. If no file is selected, the In & Out Links window is blank. You can resize it or collapse it as with any other window.

To view an item's links, click the item within the Site Window. This selected item becomes the focus of attention, as is "about_me.html" in Figure 11-22. All pages that link *to* it appear on the left. Files that link *from* it are at the right.

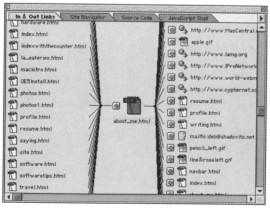

Figure 11-22: The In & Out Links window reveals all links into and out of any page (or file) selected in the Site Window.

Note   On the right in Figure 11-22 are links to the graphics, sounds, and so on that are part of the page (whose files can also be relinked here via Point and Shoot). You can ignore them for now. In fact, you can turn them off, if you like, by choosing Palette Options from the fly-out menu. See Chapter 24 for details.

You can easily replace one page with another by dragging the Point and Shoot button located next to any page to any other page within the Files tab of the Site Window. You can also swap e-mail addresses or external URLs in the same way. (See "Changing a Link," coming up soon.)

To change one instance of a link's destination, inspect the page it is on and then Point and Shoot from where the link is listed as a destination. The link is listed as a destination on the right side of the page. To inspect and change all occurrences of the address where it is a destination, inspect the address. That address appears in the center of the palette as the center of attention. That's where you Point and Shoot from.

When you view an External URL or address stored within the External tab, all pages that use that address appear at the left, leading into the address's icon. Figure 11-23 demonstrates the use of an e-mail address.

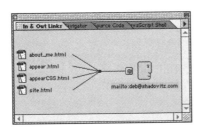

Figure 11-23: External addresses called for in a site are reflected in the In & Out Link palette.

Tip   One great benefit of the In & Out Links palette is that it provides the capability to view — and edit — the links contained within a PDF file and even in a Flash or LiveMotion file. By clicking the .swf file in the Files tab of the Site Window and viewing the file's links in the In & Out Links palette, you can see all of the file's *embedded links*. That is, the links out of the document. As with the other link destinations you inspect in this palette, you can swap any existing destination for another. The only thing you can't do is edit the look of the page to change what the user sees as the link.

Verifying and Repairing Links

You have several ways to learn that your link is complete — and when your link has an error. As you work in Layout mode, GoLive can show you incomplete and invalid links by marking them in red. You can also see these errors in Outline mode. At any time while you are working, you can also preview your page and try the links. The In & Out Links palette is always available to lend a hand. The Errors tab of the Site Window can help, too. Once identified, to repair a broken link, use any of the same methods you used to create the link in the first place.

The same interface that enables you to check for broken links and to repair them also enables you to check for any items, such as graphics, movies, and sounds, that may be missing from a page. Because this error checking is all encompassing, link verification and repair are covered later, in Chapter 25. That is not to say you should not, or cannot, check links as you work. GoLive's visual feedback and ease of link repair are among its best strengths. For now, here's the short version.

Whenever GoLive detects a bad link on your page, it displays a green error Bug icon in the Status column of the Files tab. (Normally, there's a checkmark there.) To discover the cause of the bug, you can do the following:

✦ Open the page and click the Link Warnings button on the toolbar or choose Edit ➪ Show Link Warnings. With Link Warnings turned on, any bad links are marked by a wide, red border, as in Figure 11-24. This same red also identifies the bad link within the Inspector.

Highlighted broken link

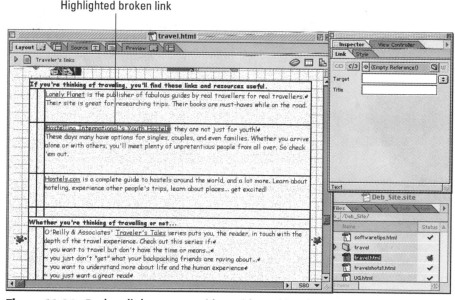

Figure 11-24: Broken links appear with a wide, red border in Layout mode and highlighted red in the Inspector when the Link Warnings (green Bug icon) button in the toolbar is on.

In the case of a graphic, the bad link can either be to the graphic on the page or to the link that is its destination.

✦ Open the In & Out Links palette and select the error-containing page for inspection. Look for any links going in or out that are blank and have the words "(Empty Reference!)" or that have a question mark instead of a page or file name (see Figure 11-25).

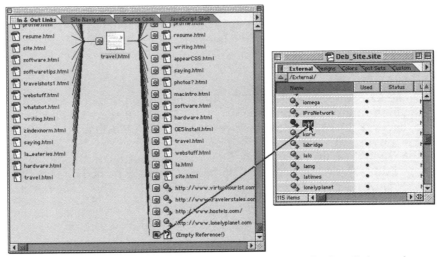

Figure 11-25: The In & Out Links palette reveals that of the four links on the selected page, one is incomplete.

The "(Empty Reference!)" is caused when a link has been started, but no file is linked to it. The question mark denotes a file that GoLive can't identify.

✦ Open the Errors tab to view orphan and missing files.

✦ Another way to become aware of bad links is to switch to HTML Outline Editor mode while Link Warnings is on.

Cross-Reference   Chapter 3 explains the Outline Editor.

You can also discover broken links by switching to Preview and trying the links. (Some pages don't fully render in Preview, so some links may not work in Preview.) Or preview by using the "Show in Browser" button and trying the links. These previews enable you to try the links, but GoLive doesn't mark them in any way. After you're previewed the page, return to the page's Layout mode to fix the problem.

You can also have GoLive check your external links. To do this, while connected to the Internet, go to the External tab of the Site Window and then choose Site ➭ Check External Links. GoLive will begin verifying your links. During this process a green connection icon will appear in the Status column of the Site Window. When a link is verified, a black checkmark appears. If an external link cannot be found, a Green Bug icon appears in the Status column, and you should investigate this problem.

Changing a Link

One of the easiest things to do in GoLive is to change a link—even if the link's destination is used in a hundred places. Once again, all you do is Point and Shoot.

Using the In & Out Links palette

The In & Out Links palette is an incredibly handy visual representation of all of the files within your site. Any time you click a file within the Files tab or External tab and then open the In & Out Links palette, you can see every place that file is used.

Follow these steps to change a link, either in one place or everywhere it's used on your site:

1. In the Site Window, click the icon that represents the file you want to change.

   If the link you're changing is a target URL, click that URL in the External tab. If the link is a page within your site, click it in the Files tab, and so on.

2. Open the In & Out Links palette.

   The palette not only enables you to change the link; it enables you to first see where the link is used. This prevents unwanted repercussions. In Figure 11-26 an external URL is selected and is identified as being used on two pages.

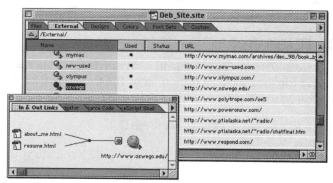

Figure 11-26: Inspecting the links to SUNY Oswego shows it is used on two pages.

3. To change the link, drag the Point and Shoot button by the file in question and to the new desired link location within the Site Window. Release the mouse when the new file is selected.

   Figure 11-27 shows how a purple bullet used on multiple pages can be replaced by another bullet with one point–and-shoot action.

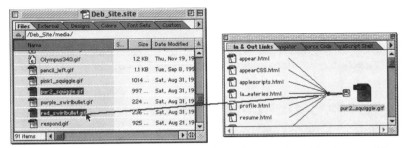

Figure 11-27: A purple squiggle is replaced by a red swirl wherever it's used on various pages by dragging the Point and Shoot button from the In & Out Links Inspector to the new link destination.

The In & Out Links palette shows that all links from the former destination are now linked to the newly selected destination. If you click the icon of the former destination the In & Out Links palette will show it no longer has any links.

The In & Out Links Inspector can be fun, but it can also be a bit tricky. When you click any file depicted in the In & Out Links palette, that file becomes the focus of the Link Inspector. This Inspector not only shows links between pages; it also shows links to all files used within a page. Click any connecting item and the entire focus jumps to reflect that item. If a graphic is used only once in the site, suddenly it appears alone. If you click a page, suddenly all the links change. This can throw you off if your reflex is to double-click a page to view it.

Changing all references

Another way to change all references to a file in your site is by using the "Change all References" button on the toolbar. This option lacks the feedback that the In & Out Links palette provides, so use it with care. No Undo command exists for it.

To change all references to a link, follow these steps:

1. In the Files tab or External tab of the Site Window, click the file you wish to replace.

2. Click the "Change all References" button on the toolbar to open the Change References dialog box. The file to be changed appears in the top section of this dialog box.

3. Assign the new destination that you want to have replace the current destination in all files within your site, as follows:

   • Use the Point and Shoot button in the dialog box to link the new destination within the Site Window, as in Figure 11-28. This method ensures that the destination is in your Site Window.

   • Type or paste a new destination in the URL field.

- Use the Browse button to locate and to choose a new location. Remember that selecting a file for use is not the same as placing it in the Site Window. You'll need to use the Clean Up Site or Update command to actually include the file.

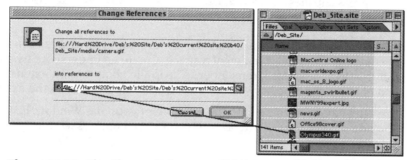

Figure 11-28: The Change References dialog box enables you to fully substitute one file or destination for another across your entire site.

Creating a Downloadable File

From time to time you may want to enable your guests to download a file that you provide. When you create a link to a downloadable file, it's a good idea to tell users what they will receive. Provide an explanation of what the file is and its file size to let readers decide whether they want to spend the time downloading it. Also provide the platform and system requirements required to use the file. It's also a good idea to explain that the file is compressed and to provide expansion instructions.

Here's how to link to a file that will download:

1. Encode and compress the file so it can travel over the Internet. If you have several files to download at once, place them in a folder first and then encode and compress them. Encoding is necessary so that the data within a file isn't lost as the file travels between various computers (gateways) of the Internet. Keep the following platform differences in mind:

   - (*For Windows visitors*) Windows users are often familiar with .zip files. If you're on a Mac, you can use ZipIt, a shareware program by Tom Brown, or you can use StuffIt Deluxe by Aladdin Systems to create a zipped archive to accommodate your Windows guests. Windows users can also decompress .sit and .sea files by using the free StuffIt Expander 5 for Windows. But because this is a new option for Windows, it helps to tell users about this and to link to the Aladdin Systems download site. If you're in Windows, you can use a Zip program such as WinZip or use DropStuff Windows to create zipped files for your Windows visitors.

- *(For Mac visitors)* Mac users are often familiar with .hqx (BinHex), .bin (Binary), .sit (StuffIt archive), or .sea (StuffIt Self-extracting) files. If you're in Windows, use DropStuff by Aladdin Systems to create a StuffIt archive to accommodate your Mac visitors. Mac users can use StuffIt Deluxe or DropStuff to compress files for their Mac users. Mac users can also decompress .zip files with StuffIt Expander, a freeware program common to Mac users, or with ZipIt.

When you name the compressed file, be sure not to have spaces in the name. Use an underscore (_) in lieu of a space. Create an underscore by pressing (Shift- - [hyphen]). Also, remember to keep the compression extension at the end of the name. The browser acts upon your file by reading the extension.

2. Drag the compressed file into the Files tab of your Site Window, just like how you add any file to your site. If you rename the compressed file, be sure to keep the extension intact.

3. Link to the compressed file the same way you link to any other file within your site.

When you upload your site to the Web server, the compressed file(s) upload along with your pages and images. Then when users click the link, the file automatically downloads.

On the CD-ROM You can find the various StuffIt programs and ZipIt on our CD-ROM or at www.aladdinsys.com and www.maczipit.com, respectively.

Editing and Removing Links

GoLive 5 provides you with the ability to fully edit a text link. You can change the text within a link, remove text from the link, and even break a link into two. Editing text within a link is no different from editing unlinked text. Just place your cursor, and then add or delete text as normal.

Editing a Link

Depending upon where you place the cursor to begin editing, GoLive acts differently. Let's say you select a word embedded in a sentence on your page and make it a link. If you place the cursor right in front of the linked text and begin typing, the letters are not considered part of the link. If you place the cursor after the last letter of the linked word, each letter you type will be considered part of the linked word. When you begin a new line by using Enter/Return, GoLive will not carry the link over into the next text you type. However, if you press Shift as you press Enter/return to start a new single-spaced line, but continue on with the existing paragraph, GoLive continues the previous link, until you tell it to do otherwise by breaking the link. GoLive 5.0 differs from previous versions when removing links, either from text or images. Now, you can remove the "linkage" from text (or images) in the beginning, middle, or end of a linked area, without destroying the linkage in the entire area.

The Look of Links

The look of your links can be set up in two ways: in the Page Inspector, as covered in Chapter 5; and by using a style sheet, as covered in Chapter 17. But before you make any changes, be sure to consider the implications of doing so. Is it wise to change the look of your hyperlinks? If so, how will you point out your links?

If you are designing a site for internal company use, you can create any type of look for a site because you can let your users know what to look for as a link. However, if your site is out on the Web for public consumption, you never know who your audience will be or how Web-savvy it will or will not be.

If you expect or want a wide variety of visitors to come to your site, it is wise to do what you can to make sure that the visitors will recognize links. The standard look of a link is the now-familiar underline denoting the actual clickable link. The underlined linked word is as a rule royal blue, and it turns a purplish-eggplant color after it has been clicked. Changing the colors of links should not present a problem, as this has become fairly common. (See Chapter 5 to learn how to set a page-wide link color.) However, remove an underline with caution. Underlines and colors have been the convention used to designate links from the inception of the Web. If you remove an underline, users may miss your links—even if you make the link bold or do something else to set it apart. (Removing the underline can only be done by using a style sheet. See Chapter 17 to learn about style sheets and how to change a link's *decoration*.)

Even the standard underline might not be enough, depending on your audience. To make your site more understandable to newcomers, you might even want to somehow tell your readers to "click here."

Removing part of a text link

Say, for example, you happen create a link at the end of a line of text, and then go on to add more text to the line, or even place a graphic — and the new material became part of your link, although that's not what you intended. This can even carry down to new lines or new paragraphs. Or, say you have one very long link, and then decide it is too distracting. Instead, you'd like fewer works linked. But you'd actually like a few words at the start of the long link to remain linked, and also want another word toward the end to link to that same destination. Neither of these things is a problem.

To remove part of a link, do one of the following:

✦ While that text or item is selected, choose Remove Link from the contextual menu.

✦ Select the text or objects that are not supposed to be part of the link, and then click the Remove Link button on the toolbar. (Or press ⌘-Option-L on Mac or Ctrl+Alt+L in Windows.)

Everything that was not selected remains intact as a link. Only the selected text or objects cease to be part of the link.

Removing a link completely

Sometimes you simply change your mind about having a link. It's easy to remove a link any time after you create it. To keep the text intact, but unlink it, select the entire link's text and then click the Remove Link button on the toolbar or in the Text Inspector.

New Feature

In previous versions of GoLive, a link was all or nothing. The ability to break only part of a link, while keeping the rest intact, is new to Version 5. Because a link was all or nothing before, all you had to do was click anywhere in the link to break it. Now only the selected text is unlinked, so you must select all linked text to fully remove a link

Removing a graphic link

To keep a graphic on your page but unlink it so that it's not a button any longer, click the graphic to select it and then click the Remove Link button on the toolbar or in the Link tab of the Inspector.

To remove the link and the graphic as well, select the graphic and press Backspace/Delete to delete the graphic.

Removing anchor links

Anchor links are no different from other links as far as breaking the link goes. However, breaking these links does not delete the anchor itself. To delete an anchor, return to the page that the anchor is on. Click the anchor to select it and then press Backspace/Delete, or choose Edit ⇨ Cut. (Mac users can also choose Edit ⇨ Clear. Windows users can also choose Edit ⇨ Delete.)

✦   ✦   ✦

Using GoLive's Advanced Tools

After you've got the basics down, you can add a navigation bar, logo, or other more advanced feature to your site using GoLive's Components, and jazz up your interface with fancy buttons. You can also format your pages with style sheets — a very good idea. Want to lay things out in tables or use frames to present your site? That's here too. This is the place to learn how to really take control of your pages and get the formatting just right.

Making Image Maps and Using Advanced Links

In addition to the basic links of text or a single image covered in Chapter 11, you can add zest and functionally to your page by creating fancier links.

You can define hotspots within a single image to create an image map, providing separate link areas within a single image. You can add alternative images to a button so it presents the user with an alternative image when the mouse is over it and yet another image when the button is clicked. Or, you can concentrate multiple links into the space of one — a pop-up menu that, with the help of JavaScript, automatically transports users to whichever URL is selected.

Introducing Image Maps

A picture is not only worth a thousand words; a picture can also be more fun than a thousand words. For example, consider a list of worldwide locations. You can present a list of every country, region, city, or state — many lines of words or a pop-up menu longer than your monitor — or you can show a map of the world. Clearly, the map is more concise and appealing in a case such as this.

This handy type of image is called an *image map*, or more specifically a *clickable image map*. An image map enables you to define any part or parts of a solid image as a hotspot that can act as a button when clicked, or trigger an event the way a link does. Each region can do something different from its fellow regions; one can be a simple button while another is a rollover, and another region isn't a button at all, but triggers an Action.

Image maps are also a great way to create a navigation bar. Instead of having several buttons that have to come down from the server, just one image has to load. Because it's one image, its look can be clean and unified. The image can have a nice background, effects, or a theme.

An image map is a somewhat complicated object. Creating one involves laying a coordinate map on top of an image and then noting the coordinates of each specified area within the map, and assigning URLs or other instructions to each set of coordinates. Luckily, GoLive handles the complicated coding stuff itself, behind the scenes. All you see is the easy, creative stuff. To make an image map, all you have to do is place the desired image, use some simple drawing tools to mark each hotspot on top of the image, and then Point and Shoot to the hotspot's destination.

Two types of image maps exist. The original type held the instructions at the Web server so whenever a user clicked an image map area, the browser had to send a request back to the server so the server could tell the browser what to do with the request. GoLive uses the newer, easier, more popular type of image map, called a *client-side map*. With this type of map, the client (which is the browser) has all the map's instructions to begin with and knows exactly what to do as soon as the user clicks an area. If you look at the HTML source code after you create a map, you can see the instructions directly within the HTML that defines your page.

This chapter introduces you to everything you need to know about creating an image map in GoLive. After you become familiar with these basics, you can learn how to use buttons to create fascinating pages or interfaces.

Although I hate to put a damper on the fun and benefit of image maps, I do have to remind you that not everyone can see the graphics you use on your site. Bear in mind the people who rely on having your pages read aloud by a speech-synthesizing browser, and those on the Web via older computers or hand-held devices. In addition to the image map, include some sort of text navigation within your page. The text version can be at the bottom, and does not have to be as intricate as the detailed list of worldwide locations in our opening example.

Starting an Image Map

These are the first steps for creating an image map—the boring stuff. The exciting creative steps come next. After you place the image, the key players in image map setup are the image on the page and the Image Inspector.

To set up an image as an image map, follow these steps:

1. Place the image on your page, just as you'd place any other image.

   In case you're wondering, you can move an image map around just like you move any other image. You simply move the image. The mapping on top of it will follow.

2. Select the image.

3. As with any image, you should provide text to guide visitors who don't get to see the image. To do so, simply type your message in the Alt Text field of the Basic tab of the Image Inspector.

The Alt Text field is also covered in Chapter 10.

   The alternate text should be concise but tell users what type of navigation this image provides and direct them to some alternate text links, possibly at the bottom of your page. For example, if your image map is providing navigation for your site, as it most likely is, you might write something like, "Navigation menu. See text links below."

4. *(Optional)* Set the image border to zero (no border), or give your image any border width you'd like. To do so, check the Border box. Zero is pre-entered and goes into effect when you check the border option. To set a specific width, enter a border width just like you'd do with any image.

5. Switch to the More tab in the Image Inspector and then check Use Map, as shown in Figure 12-1.

Figure 12-1: The magic that turns an image into an image map starts when you check the Use Map option in the More tab of the Image Inspector.

This tells GoLive the image is to be a client-side image map. It also turns the Image Inspector into the Clickable Image Map Inspector and activates the Image Map toolbar. However, you don't actually have an image map until after you define and link the regions.

6. *(Optional)* When the Use Map option is checked, GoLive automatically names the image map, but you can change it to be more descriptive. To do so, select the name and enter a new one.

Now that GoLive knows this is an image map, you can begin to define the regions and set up their links, as described in the "Defining Regions" and "Linking a Region" sections below.

Defining Regions

The next step in creating an image map is to divide the image into regions of any shape. Each region you define is a potentially active area — a button-to-be. The Image Map toolbar provides three basic tools for defining regions (the Circle, Rectangle, and Polygon tools) and an arrow tool for manipulating areas (the Selection tool). Three tools also exist to help you see the regions as you define them (URLs, Frame Regions, and Color regions, plus a color swatch to choose a color with which to view them), and two arrangement tools (Move to front and Move to back). Hot Help identifies each of these tools as you rest the pointer over it. Figure 12-2 identifies them as well.

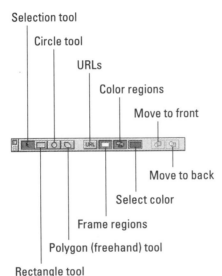

Figure 12-2: The nine tools in the Image Map toolbar enable you to create regions of any shape, and even overlapping regions.

Selection tool
Circle tool
URLs
Color regions
Move to front
Move to back
Select color
Frame regions
Polygon (freehand) tool
Rectangle tool

To define a region, you click a drawing tool to select it, drag the tool over the image, and release the mouse when you've got the shape you want. Don't worry about being completely precise, though; you can edit the shape of the region by selecting it and dragging the handles that appear. (There's more on that in the "Editing Regions" section later in this chapter.)

Because regions can overlap, you don't have to make region borders match perfectly side by side. You'll be able to send any shape to the back of other shapes or in front of other shapes. When regions overlap, the one in front will be the effective button, while the one in back is dormant. (For more about overlapping, see the "Arranging Overlapping Objects" section later in this chapter.)

Note   As soon as you add a map region to your page, the Image Inspector morphs into the Map Area Inspector. You can define that region's link immediately, or you can define all your regions first and then go back and link each one.

The three map-drawing tools are the Rectangle tool, the Circle tool, and the Freehand Drawing tool. You can use a different tool to define each region.

Using the Rectangle tool

The Rectangle tool enables you to make rectangles in any proportion. To place a rectangle, click the Rectangle tool to select it. Then move the cursor to the page and drag over the shape you want to mark. Release the mouse to place the shape. You can drag any of the sides in or out later on.

Using the Circle tool

The Circle tool makes perfect circles. Click the Circle tool to select it, and then move to the page and drag over the shape you want to cover. The circle grows or shrinks proportionately as you drag. Release the mouse to place the circle. Figure 12-3 shows a circle being created. Figure 12-4 shows the look of the image map after the circle is complete.

Figure 12-3: As you define a region, you see its outline as a guide.

Figure 12-4: After you complete a region, colored shading helps you see the defined hotspot.

Using the Polygon (Freehand) tool

The Polygon tool is the toughest tool to master, but it's the one that enables you to create irregularly shaped regions using a freehand method.

To begin defining your region, first click the Polygon tool to select it. Then click the image to place the first handle. Then click again to plant a handle at the second desired spot. Each time you click, you can see a line being laid to continue the form.

After the first three handles, you'll have a triangle. Don't let that throw you. Just keep clicking along the outline of your image in a logical order and the polygon will reshape.

Each time you click, you place a handle. The more handles, the better for editing later. Figure 12-5 shows the beginnings of an irregular region being defined.

Note   You might not want your hotspot to exactly fit the image beneath it. Instead, consider where the user is most likely to click, or can click easily.

At some point your region's shape may be bigger than the desired area you want to cover. That's okay. As you place more handles, the handles pull the region back in, as is happening in Figure 12-6.

Figure 12-5: The beginning of an irregular hotspot region

Figure 12-6: As an irregular hotspot region takes shape, you can pull in the region's shape to fit the image beneath it.

If you accidentally click a handle that isn't the last one placed, you'll create the effect of dragging the wrong handle and disrupt the shape of the region. If this happens, undo the last point by choosing Edit ➪ Undo or by removing the last Action in the History palette (Window ➪ History). You can undo many Actions this way, until you get back to the shape you desire. Don't forget, though, that as soon as the basic region is laid, you'll be able to drag any point to refine your image map area.

When you complete your shape, click the Arrow Tool button in the toolbar to tell GoLive you don't want to work on that region any more. The region remains selected; in Figure 12-7, you can see the handles around the perimeter of the overall shape's area.

Figure 12-7: The banana is now complete as a hotspot region and ready for fine-tuning or linking.

Editing Regions

Chances are, when you initially drag the Rectangle or Circle tool to define a region, you won't get the region's shape perfectly into place. After you place the region, you can always move the entire object or drag its handles to define the area more clearly.

Tip   As you work, you can turn the region's color overlay on or off or make the color lighter. This color is a visual guide for you. Turning it off won't remove the map region. See the "Seeing Your Work Clearly" section later in this chapter.

Editing a circle or rectangle

After you place a circle or rectangle, you can drag its handles to reshape it so it more accurately defines the image beneath it. Along with moving the handles, consider moving the entire shape. To edit a circle or a rectangle, follow these steps:

1. Click the Arrow Tool button in the toolbar.

2. Make sure all regions are deselected so you don't inadvertently move the wrong area. To do so, click somewhere on your page outside of the image map area and away from any other element you might select.

3. Click the defined area to select it, and then drag any of its handles, as in Figure 12-8.

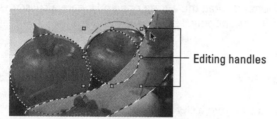

Editing handles

Figure 12-8: Drag a handle to resize a shape.

Note that circles remain perfect circles regardless of which handle you drag.

The side handles on a rectangle enable you to make a rectangle wider; the top and bottom handles make the rectangle longer. Corner handles can be dragged both wider and longer at the same time.

Editing a polygon

When you create your irregular shape, the more points you place within it, the more control you have when editing it. In this step, you can move any point to best fit the image beneath it.

Follow these steps to fine-tune a polygonal shape:

1. Double-click inside the area.

   This causes the individual handles to appear.

2. Drag any handle into a better position, as in Figure 12-9. As you drag a handle, a dotted outline shows you where the new path will lie. Don't forget to click somewhere off the image to deselect the image after you've completed your edits.

This dotted line defines the new shape

Figure 12-9: When you drag a handle to refine an irregular shape, a dotted line helps guide you by showing the results of the adjustment.

Note

You cannot delete individual handles. Instead, if you find that a handle is making your shape less refined, cheat by dragging the unwanted handle very close to one that is wanted. If you decide to move either of these close-by handles later, you'll be in for fun if you inadvertently drag the wrong one and create a crisscross shape. That's a situation that calls for undoing.

Moving a Region

Two reasons may compel you to move a defined hotspot region. One is to more accurately have it represent the image it represents. The other reason is to place one region safely out of the way in order to edit an overlapping region.

To move a defined region, follow these steps:

1. Click the Arrow Tool button in the toolbar.
2. Make sure all regions are deselected so you don't inadvertently move the wrong region. To do so, click somewhere on your page outside of the image map area and away from any other element you might select.
3. Click within any defined area to select it, and then drag the region as desired.

Linking a Region

The basics of links from an image map are the same as other navigational links. The big difference is that instead of clicking a button to define a link, any region is automatically expected to be a link, so all you have to do is drag the Point and Shoot button.

As with any link, you can link to another location on the same page, another page in your site, a page outside of your site, or an e-mail address. If you're using frames, the link can also link to another frame target.

See Chapter 15 to learn about frames.

Here's how to link a hotspot to a page or file:

1. Select the image area if it's not already selected.

2. To create the link, do one of the following:

   • Click once on the region you wish to turn into the link. Then press Ô (Mac) or Alt (Windows) as you click the image to be linked, and then drag the Point and Shoot line to the destination. (Rest over the Select Window button on the toolbar if your Site Window is not accessible.)

   • Click once on the region you wish to turn into the link. This turns the Inspector into the Map Area Inspector, which comes complete with a preactivated URL Getter area. Drag its Point and Shoot button to the link's destination, as shown in Figure 12-10. (Rest over the Select Window button on the toolbar if your Site Window is not accessible, which was the case in this example.) As with other links, you also have the option of hand typing or pasting the URL or of using the Browse button.

Figure 12-10: Using the Inspector to Point and Shoot to a target page within the Site Window

Refer back to Chapter 11 to learn about links in detail.

3. *(Optional)* If you want the destination page to open in its own window instead of replacing the page that contains your image map, select _blank from the Target menu in the Map Area Inspector.

4. *(Optional)* Enter the title of the page you're linking to by entering it in the Title field. (This title is not the same as the title for your page. Its usage is somewhat undefined and most site designers are confused by how to use it. In Internet Explorer, the title sometimes appears as a Tooltip, but that is not the intended use.)

5. Type your short description of the mapped region's image into the Alt field. (Technically, this is optional as the image map works without it. However, alternative text is an accessibility guideline, so I highly recommend you add it.)

Tip   Upon creation of a link, the file name and path appear in the URL field. You can look there to see that the link has been created. However, perhaps the easier way to see which map areas have completed links is to turn on Display URLs. When on, the link's destination appears directly over the region on the page. (See "Displaying URLs" later in this chapter.)

To test your link, switch to the Preview tab, and click the hotspot. You can also test it by previewing in a browser.

Seeing Your Work Clearly

Image maps can become confusing when you can't see which areas are hotspots. A few tools exist to help you see your work clearly, as follows:

✦ The **Frame Regions** button enables you to see the outline of each region. This button is a toggle switch. If the outlines are on, this button turns them off. If they are off, it turns them on. Figure 12-11 shows you what an image looks like with Frame Regions off.

✦ The **Color Region** button enables you to turn the color on or off in the defined regions. This button is a toggle switch, so clicking it turns color on if it's off and off if it's on.

As the example image was worked on, it became hard to see the shape of the grapes through the other fruit that was already mapped. Turning off Color Regions helped the grapes become visible again, as shown in Figure 12-12. (The other option would have been to change the region coloring, as explained next.)

✦ With **Select Color**, you can choose the color that fills the hotspots by performing the steps in the following procedure. Lighter colors make it easier to see the image beneath the color.

Figure 12-11: When Frame Regions are turned off, the outlines of the regions aren't visible.

Figure 12-12: Turning color off can help you see the shape you're trying to create a map region for.

To choose a color, follow these steps:

1. Click the color swatch on the toolbar to open the Color palette.

   Because this isn't a color that will appear on the Web, you can use any color from any color tab.

2. Choose any color tab in the Color palette and then click the desired color.

   The new color appears immediately in the image map, unless you've turned off the Color Regions. If you're not happy with the first color you pick, just click away in the Color palette until you like what you see on your image map.

Displaying URLs

As you work, it can become confusing trying to figure out which defined hotspots have links and which don't. GoLive provides instant feedback on this by enabling you to see the URLs directly on top of the defined region. Undefined hotspots say "(Empty Reference!)." Linked regions show the name of the destination. In Figure 12-13, some links are complete, while others remain to be done.

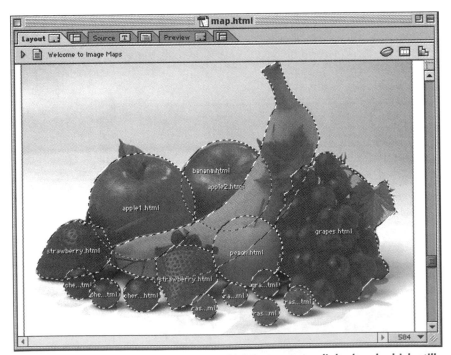

Figure 12-13: It's much easier to see which hotspots are linked and which still need links by turning on the Display URLs button.

Arranging overlapping objects

When hotspot regions overlap, the front-most region becomes the active region, responding with its URL when clicked. Regions behind this active region are ignored. Use the Bring Region to Front and Send Region to Back buttons to move regions forward or backward, as follows:

✦ **Bring Region to Front.** To bring a hotspot forward, click the region to select it and then click this button.

✦ **Send Region to Back.** To send a hotspot to the back of the other hotspots, click the region to select it and then click this button.

You can place a region in front of one object but behind another by using the commands on several regions.

In the example I've been using throughout this chapter—food stylist Don Wallace's fruit image—several fruits overlap, so the Send Region to Back and Bring Region to Front buttons become very important. The banana is behind most of the elements, but in front of the apples. To accomplish the correct order, I sent the banana to the back first. Because the front-most fruits were defined after the banana, they are already in front of it. However, to be safe, I send the large apple to the back. After that, I send the small (right) apple to the back so it lands behind both the banana and the larger apple. This gives the banana precedence over the apples, and the larger apple priority over the smaller apple. As you move items forward and backward, the change is very subtle, but you can see the outline of a shape become less noticeable when a region is sent behind another.

When overlapping image maps become busy, you can use the various visual area definition aides to see more clearly.

Adding Button Rollover Effects

A regular button shows the user one image and jumps to the link's destination when clicked. But add JavaScript to the mix and a button can present the user with an alternative image when the mouse is over it and yet another image when the button is clicked. This fancier button is called a Rollover button in GoLive and is easy to set up using the Rollover Smart Object.

Button *rollovers* are one of the most popular JavaScript items on the entire Web—and with good reason. They look great, they're easy to do, and they add visual feedback for the user by making it apparent which button is selected. And besides . . . they're fun to use. With a rollover effect, buttons come to life.

A button rollover combines the three most common events: mouseover, mouseout and onclick. Up to three different images can be assigned to a single button. The *primary image* displays when the page loads and whenever the user's mouse is not over the button (or perhaps clicking the button). The *secondary image* appears when the user moves the mouse over the button image. (This is a mouseover or, in the Actions palette, Mouse Enter trigger.) When the mouse pointer moves off the button image, the first image swaps back, restoring the original look. (That's a mouseout or Mouse Exit trigger.) The third image displays when the button is clicked. (That is the onclick or Mouse Click trigger.) The third image, the click image, is optional.

A good example of a button rollover is the effect of having a button glow, change color, or use an alternate word when the user moves the mouse over it. To do this, you use two images that are identical in shape but use a different color, effect, or wording for the second (and third if you want) button states. Or, you can have some more fun with your images, as Cathy Scrivnor did with her buttons. On rollover, each button not only "glows," but also displays a funny alternative label, as you can see in Figure 12-14.

Figure 12-14: This whimsical navigation bar by Cathy Scrivnor is an example of a GoLive rollover. In order, they are normal state, during rollover, and during the mouse click.

Note   GoLive users often wonder whether a button image can be used in a Component. The answer is yes, as long as you're certain to export the JavaScript code using GoLive's external code feature as described later in this chapter.

Ideally, all three images should be the same size before you create the button. This ensures that each image will look its best. It's physically possible to use different-sized images, but the button effect will vary. If your image sizes vary, the size of your button is determined by the size of the button you place first. The second and third buttons will grow or shrink to the size of the first-placed button. However, if you select any button set for any stage, and use the Resize button, the other images will resize to fit that space.

To add a rollover button image to your page, follow these steps:

1. Drag a Rollover icon from the Smart tab of the Objects palette into the desired position on your page.

This turns the Inspector into the Rollover Inspector, as shown in Figure 12-15.

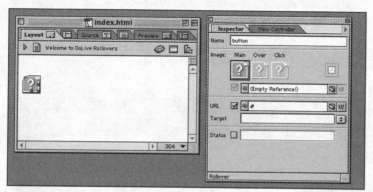

Figure 12-15: The Rollover Inspector just after a Rollover Smart Object is placed on a page

You may notice that the URL area of the Inspector contains a # mark. That's because as a JavaScript, the button needs to be a link at heart. Once a link is created, if the URL for the link is blank, the words "(Empty Reference!)" appear and the link is reported as a green bug error. This marker prevents the error, so you don't have to keep investigating the source of that page's bug. As you view any page that contains a rollover, you'll see a link to the "#." That's your tip that a rollover is on the page. (Or, if you use that same mark as an error-presenter for all of your Actions, you'll see it and know a JavaScript of some sort exists on the page.)

2. In the first tab of the Rollover Inspector, select the default name (which says "button" by default) and then enter a short descriptive name for your rollover button. (Don't use spaces.) A rollover must have a name in order for it to be called by an Action later.

If you don't name the Rollover button, the next Rollover you add will be called "button2" by default so that each button has a unique identity.

3. The three button states are labeled "Main," "Over," and "Click," and each has its own icon underneath the label. The main button state is preselected for your convenience.

To set the image for the Main (initial) state of the button, link it to an image as you link any other button: by using the Point and Shoot icon in the Inspector, or by using browse (with the usual caution that if the image is not in your Site Window already, you will have an orphan to deal with later). You can also select the words "(Empty Reference!)" and hand-enter the path and button name if you're secure in doing so. (The image's path is relative by default. If you prefer it to be absolute path as explained in Chapter 11 instead, check the Absolute checkbox.)

A thumbnail of your new button image replaces the Main image so you can easily keep track of your button. The full size view of the image appears on your page in place of the rollover placeholder.

4. Click the Over icon to select the mouseover image placeholder.

5. To activate the button's second stage, click the checkbox to the left of the Link Reference field, as shown in Figure 12-16.

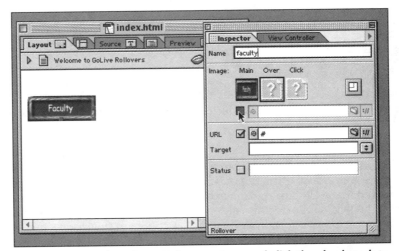

Figure 12-16: Select the next button stage and click the checkmark to activate the URL Getter so you can assign the image.

This enables the Point and Shoot button and Browse button, and adds "(Empty Reference!)" to the field.

Note You did not need to click this checkbox for the Main image, because it's already selected by default and cannot be deselected.

6. Again, Point and Shoot (or otherwise link to) the image that will appear when the user rolls the mouse over this button. The second button appears in the Inspector. However, it is not reflected on your page.

Note If you're only creating a two-stage button effect, you are finished at this point. To add a third image that appears when the user actually clicks the button, continue. However, this button stage only shows for the moment the user is clicking the button, so bear that in mind and weigh the time it will take users to download the extra image.

7. To add a third image, click the Click icon to select the onclick image place-holder.

8. To activate the button's third stage, click the checkbox to the left of the file reference.

9. Point and Shoot, or otherwise link to the image you wish to display while the user clicks the mouse.

10. *(Optional)* If you want your button to connect to another page or location when clicked, check the URL checkbox, and then link to the location and set up the link, as shown in Figure 12-17. (As with any link, if you want the URL's path to be absolute, click the Absolute Link button. To have the destination page open in its own new browser window, choose _blank from the Target pop-up menu. If using frames, select the target frame as the target.

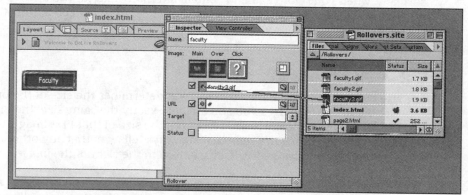

Figure 12-17: Linking the third image

 Note   The URL is for the Rollover button as a whole; you cannot set a separate URL for each image in the rollover.

11. Check the Status checkbox and then enter a message in the Status text box.

 Note   Adding a message to this Status field causes that message to appear in the Status area in the lower-left corner of the user's browser window when the mouse is over your button. Normally, a status message would be optional. However, due to the way GoLive is programmed, this particular status area doubles as the image's alternate text (alt) tag. So, in order to aid Web accessibility, you need to add your descriptive alternative text to this Status field.

Making Buttons Sticky

Normally, with a button, the image defaults back to the initial image once the user's mouse rolls off of the image. However, it's very helpful to have the rollover image remain active after the user is transported to the linked page within your site. This provides feedback to show the users which page they're in — and which button they last clicked to get there. Buttons that, in effect, remain clicked until the next button is clicked are commonly called "sticky" buttons. OUTactions (www.out.to/actions) provides a ready-made Action, called Lock Rollover, which is part of the Rollover Control Action Suite, that enables you to easily add sticky buttons to your site — even when your buttons are in a Component, or in a different frame. I highly recommend this solution.

Normally, when you set up a link to contain alternate images, you have to set those alternate images to preload. However, the Rollover Smart Object, automatically sets up the preloads.

Resizing an image

The size of the first image added to a rollover determines the size of the button. If either of the next two images you add are not exactly the same size, the different-sized image is automatically resized to match the size of that first image. GoLive alerts you to this resizing the same way it always tells you that any other image has been resized — by activating the Resize button to the right of the images.

To return any image to its original size, select that image in the Inspector and click the Resize button. Returning any image to its original size automatically resizes the other two images to match that image's size. No matter what you do, all images will be matched in size.

Converting buttons

What if you already have a plain button (an image turned into a link) or simply a plain, unlinked image on your page and want to create a rollover button? You can turn a plain button or plain image into a rollover button image by simply dragging a Rollover icon from the Smart tab on top of the existing button on the page. Click someplace on the page, and then click back on the button to reselect it and you'll see the Inspector reflect the change.

Other Actions

If you prefer to have the button do something other than take the user to a link, open the Actions palette and make the appropriate selections as with the setup of any Action. Although the images remain intact in the Rollover Inspector, the second and third button images no longer function. In addition, the link you set up by placing a link in the URL field of the Rollover Inspector may clash with anything you set up in the Actions palette, so just be aware of that possibility.

Minimizing code

Depending on your GoLive preferences, GoLive may be writing the JavaScript code for your rollover and other JavaScripts directly into your page or into an external document. If you have a folder called GeneratedItems and a document called CSScriptLib.js inside it, your code is already being written to that external document. However, you can do one more thing to ensure that minimal code exists in your page. While the page is open, select the Page icon at the top-left corner so the Inspector becomes the Page Inspector. Then click the HTML tab and, if it's not already chosen, choose Import GoLive Script Library. When you do this, only the minimal code needed for your buttons remains in the page. Finally, just before you upload your site to the Web server, you should use the Flatten Script Library command to have GoLive weed out all unused JavaScript code from the external (.js) file.

Cross-Reference See Chapter 25 to learn about stripping used code from your JavaScript files.

Adding URL Pop-up Menus

How do you put many links on your page without taking up large areas of your page to list those links? With a pop-up menu, which, in effect, provides multiple links in the space of only one. When the user selects a destination from the pop-up menu, he or she is automatically taken there. A pop-up menu is not fancy, but it lets a reader see an entire selection of choices while taking up very little space on the page.

When the user first sees this pop-up, only the first label, "Choose" is visible. You can change the word or words that appear here. When the user clicks the menu, all links you add here become visible. When the user moves to one of the choices and releases the mouse, he or she is automatically transported to the link's destination.

To put a URL pop-up menu on your page, follow these steps:

1. Drag the URL Popup icon from the Smart tab of the Objects palette into place on your page. (Or, double-click the icon to automatically place it at the end of all the other elements on the current page.)

2. In the Inspector, now the URL Popup Inspector (see Figure 12-18), click the label Choose, which is the default word that appears in the pop-up on the page. Press your Tab key to move to the Label field (or click in the field and select the text there), and then type the words you want as a guide for your visitors.

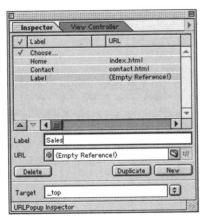

Figure 12-18: The URL Popup Inspector

This first label is a guide for visitors only. You cannot set a URL for it.

3. Click the default first link, to "Adobe Systems Inc.," and then click Delete to remove it and start fresh.

4. To create a new link, click the New button.

This adds a new line to the list at the top, with the default label, "label." It also preselects this default label in the Label field so you can immediately enter your own label.

5. Type the label you'd like as a guide for the user. This is what the user sees when the menu is clicked. Press Enter/Return to set the entry.

Note   Do not use an apostrophe in the label. Apostrophes break JavaScript, so the menu will not work. In fact, avoid most punctuation. Hyphens are safe, though.

6. Select the destination for this link just as you would set any link: you can Point and Shoot, browse, paste, or hand-enter the destination.

7. If you're working with frames, select the desired frame target (as explained in Chapter 14) from the Target pop-up at the bottom of the Inspector. If the link is to a page outside your site and you want the target destination to open in its own new window, choose _blank as your target.

8. Repeat Steps 4 through 7 for each link you want to include in the menu.

Instead of clicking New each time, you can duplicate a link by selecting it and clicking the Duplicate button. This can be useful if you're referencing several different pages at the same site because you can leave the bulk of the URL intact and change only the end of the URL (the destination page within that site).

To edit any link's label at any time, just click that label in the list of links, and then tab to the Label field and edit the existing label.

To edit any link's destination at any time, just click that label in the list of links, and then set the new link the same way you set up any link.

To change the order in which links appear in the list, select the link you want to move. This activates blue up and down arrows at the bottom-left corner of the links list. Use the arrow to move the selected label/link up or down.

✦　　✦　　✦

Creating and Laying Out Tables

In This Chapter

Adding tables to
your Web page

Converting and
deleting a table

Selecting tables
and cells

Adding content to
your tables

Adding and
removing rows
and columns

Formatting your table

Applying GoLive's
table styles

Performing table
tricks for page
formatting

You don't get very far into the Web page design world before you hear the word *table*. What exactly is a table? A table is a bunch of rows and columns, like a spreadsheet. When you want numbers and data to line up perfectly, you put them into a table. Those rows and columns of perfectly aligned cells don't exactly seem conducive to creative page design, though, do they?

So, why a table? Remember that Web pages do not have precise dimensions — a viewer can make the browser window wider or narrower than you designed for and even set the type on the page to be two or three times the size that you specified. Your text will wrap to fit the browser window, so you never know where a line break might fall. You may want a certain sentence to fall side by side with a certain image, but you can't ensure that will happen — at least not on a plain Web page.

An answer to that problem is the table. You can't always control where a table will fall on a page when the page reflows due to browser size — but you know that the first and second cells in the second row will always be side by side. No matter how a user views a page, a row of cells remains side by side on the same exact level and a column is always perfectly straight. Therefore, whatever you put inside table cells remains aligned.

Besides using a table in its obvious way — to stack related information — you can use a table to keep images such as navigation buttons together and aligned. You can use tables in many creative ways. This chapter shows you how to use GoLive to add and format tables for the best effect.

Adding Tables to Your Web Page

Confining your design elements to table cells and having to adjust each cell isn't part of the print world's creative process, but on the Web you've gotta do what you've gotta do. Thankfully, GoLive makes tables fairly easy to deal with. And, if you happen to begin a table and decide you prefer to work with a grid, you can always convert your table into a grid.

Placing a table on your page

As with every structural element you add to a page, you can add a table to your page by simply dragging it from the Objects palette. You can place a table directly on the page, on a grid, or in another table.

To place a table, drag the Table icon from the Basic tab of the Objects palette into place on the page, as shown in Figure 13-1. As you drag the table onto the page, a dark cursor-type of line shows you where your table will land. If it is being placed on a grid, the icon can land anywhere. If it is being placed anywhere else, it will attach to a line.

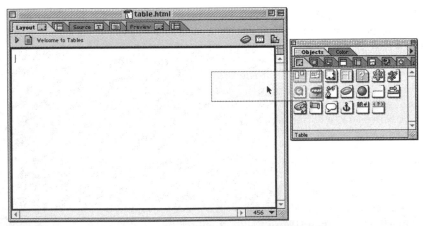

Figure 13-1: Adding a table to a blank page by dragging from the Basic tab of the Objects palette

If the table is the first element on a new page, it will land in line with the cursor at the top of the page. If you already have contents on the page and want the table placed between what you have, watch the cursor to see where it will land. Tables need to live alone on their own line, but you don't have to worry about creating that line ahead of time because GoLive writes the new line (<p>) for you.

Tip If you are placing a table inside another table (a.k.a. nesting), first drag a Comment icon from the Objects palette into the cell where you will add the next table. This provides a separation of the two tables, making it much easier to select these tables later. The comment appears as a visual element in Layout mode, but not in any browser. If it throws off your perception of your page as you design, choose Edit ➪ Hide Invisible Items.

By default, the new table size is three columns and three rows, 180 pixels wide, as shown in Figure 13-2.

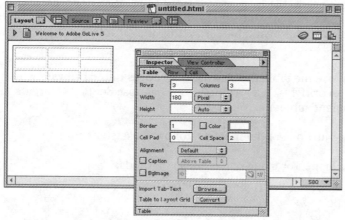

Figure 13-2: A new table on a blank page. Tables always come in with three columns and three rows, as reported in the Table Inspector.

Tip You are not limited to always starting with the defaults of a new table from the Objects palette's Basic tab. You can set up an empty table any way you like, and then store it in the Custom tab of the Objects palette. After your custom table is in the Custom tab, you can drag it to your pages over and over. Actually, you could even store a table that's not empty there too.

Cross-Reference To learn more about reusing elements, see Chapter 14.

After you place the table, you can add your content and adjust its look. What to do next depends on what you're doing with the table, what elements you have ready to work with, and what your design is. Tables resize to accommodate content, so you may want to hold off on all other table formatting until you have the content in place. The only thing you may need to right away is add more columns or rows in which to place some of your content. If you're importing data from a spreadsheet or database, the resulting table will be automatically configured to contain the number of rows and columns of your imported content.

Tip Sometimes a browser will not render a table until all of its elements are down-loaded. This is not usually an issue unless you overload a table. If, when you test your page, the table takes too long to appear, consider dividing the table into two or more smaller tables.

Removing or changing the page margins

When you place a table on your page, you'll notice it isn't flush against the top or left side of your page. That's because browsers have a default offset of about 6–8 pixels. This default margin prevents text from starting so close to the edge that it is hard to read or notice due to the browser controls. Depending how you're using your table, you may prefer to override either the top margin or side margin default, or both, in favor of using your own table formatting to control the distance of your page's visual elements.

The fastest way to place the table flush against the edges of the browser window is to Control-click (Mac) or right-click (Windows) and choose Set Page Margins to Zero from the Document submenu.

If you want to change just one of the margins, follow these steps:

1. Open the Page Inspector using one of these methods:
   - Control-click (Mac) or right-click (Windows) and choose Document ⇨ Page Properties.
   - Click the Page icon at the top left of the page. This changes the Inspector to the Page Inspector. (If the Inspector isn't open, open it.)
   - Option-click anywhere on your page. This changes the Inspector to the Page Inspector. If the Inspector isn't open, open it.
2. Define the size of each margin by entering the desired number of pixels in each of the margin fields. If you want the margins to revert back to the default setting, leave the fields blank.

Converting or Deleting a Table

At any time in you design process, you can convert your table into a grid — no matter what content your table holds. Simply select the table and then click the Convert button in the Table Inspector. Or, point to the table's border as you ⌘-click (Mac) or right-click (Windows) and then choose Convert to Grid from the resulting contextual menu.

To delete a table, select it by clicking its top or left border when the Mouse icon turns into the Object Selection icon and then press the Backspace/Delete key. Be careful, though, because the caption and all of the cell's contents are deleted along with the cell. If you want to keep any of the table's contents, be sure to drag that content out of the table before deleting the table.

You can also select a table for deletion by dragging the cursor over the table when the cursor is a text I-beam. This selection method selects the table as if it's just one more bit of text, so it works for deleting but not for activating the Table Inspector.

Selecting Tables and Cells

You're probably eager to begin adding text and graphics to your table, but before you can add elements to the table, the table or cells must be selected. This section introduces you to all the ways you can select the table, cells, rows, and columns.

With GoLive 5, the folks at Adobe introduce the Table palette (Window ⇨ Table), a miniature version of your table's structure that enables you to select cells, rows, or columns within a compact area of your table. This minimizes your mousing around time. If your table is particularly large, you'll definitely appreciate this new tool. The Table palette is resizable, just like most windows. Simply drag the bottom-right corner and drag it to any size you'd like (within the size of your monitor, of course).

Selecting a table

The fastest and most common way to select your entire table is to move to the top or left edge of the table. At these edges, your mouse icon becomes an Object Selection icon, as in Figure 13-3. When it does, click once. A thin dark line tells you it's selected. When selected this way, the Inspector becomes the Table Inspector and jumps to the Table tab. Because that's the tab in which you set your table-level controls, this is the best way to select a table.

1	2	3
21	22	23
31	32	33

Figure 13-3: When the Mouse icon becomes an Object Selection icon, click to select a table.

Cross-Reference

If your table happens to be on a grid, you select it as an object on the grid instead. See Chapter 7 to learn more about using the layout grid.

If you already have any cell or cells selected and want to select the entire table entity, you can press Ctrl along with the Enter/Return key on the letter pad. If you have one table inside another, this is handy because pressing Control-Return or Ctrl+Enter again selects the next outside table. Another way to select a table is by selecting all of its cells using the contextual menu. Control-click (Mac) or right-click (Windows) on the bottom table border and then choose Select All. This calls the Table Inspector up, jumping to the Cell tab. To do overall table formatting, you need to switch to the Table tab.

Selecting a cell or cells

You have several ways to select cells. Regardless of how you select a cell, the results are the same. A line appears around the cell to indicate it is selected and the Table Inspector jumps to the Cell tab.

To select the cell directly on the page, do one of the following:

✦ Click its right or bottom inside edge. (Specifically, aim for the inside border of the cell.)

✦ Point inside the cell and then Control-click (Mac) or right-click (Windows) and choose Select Cell.

✦ Click inside the cell and press Control along with the Return (Mac) or Enter (Windows) key on the letter pad.

Either way, to select additional cells, press Shift as you click anywhere within the next cells. To deselect any cell, press Shift as you click anywhere within that cell.

To select the cell in the Table palette, do either of the following:

✦ Click the cell. To add more cells to your selection, press Shift as you click the next cells.

✦ Drag over the cell, as shown in Figure 13-4. To select more cells, just keep dragging. If you go too far, drag backwards to deselect cells. To add noncontiguous cells, you'll need to press Shift as you click those cells, because you can't reach them by dragging.

Selecting a row or column

You can select an entire row or column of cells at a time. After selecting the rows or columns, you can add individual cells to your selection.

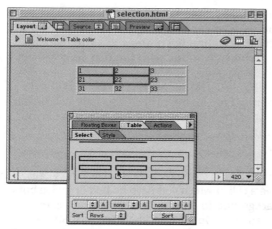

Figure 13-4: Selecting cells by dragging within the Table palette

To select a row or column directly on the page, choose from these options:

✦ Move your cursor to the left edge of the table. (Your cursor becomes a hand.) Then press the Shift key. This turns the hand cursor into a blue arrow that points inward to the row. Click to make the selection. To select a column do the same, but from the top edge.

✦ To add more rows to your selection, drag upward or downward. To add more columns, drag sideward. (You can release the Shift key once you have the arrow cursor.) To add individual cells to your selection, press Shift again and click in the individual cells.

To select the row or column in the Table palette, choose from these options:

✦ Move the mouse to the left side of the row (or top of the column) until your cursor turns bluish and points toward the row. Then click.

✦ To add more rows to your selection, drag upward or downward. To add individual cells to your selection, press Shift and click in the individual cells.

Filling Your Table with Content

A table is made up of cells. You add content to an individual cell within the table. Just about anything you can put on a Web page can go into a cell. You can add text to a cell or add graphics. You can even put another table into a table's cell or put a grid in a cell.

When you click inside a cell, you can see a standard text cursor flashing. A table's cell is very much like a word-processing page: text starts at the left, flows within the cell, and wraps when it reaches the right edge of the cell. When you place a graphic or movie into a cell, it is technically inline with the text so it will act just like it does on the main part of the Web page.

You can add content to any cell at any time in any order. Cells can also be left empty. In fact, that's commonly done when the table is used as a page layout tool. If you decide you don't want something in a cell, you can delete the content or drag it to another cell.

Note   Table cells require an object within them to trigger their display. Empty cells do not appear in browsers. If you have a cell in which you have no text or image but want formatting such as a color background to appear, the workaround is to place an ASCII space in the cell. To do so, type Option-spacebar (Mac) or Shift+spacebar (Windows).

One thing to avoid placing in a table cell is the SB control for a floating box. This is because Internet Explorer tends to read the box's position as being inside the table cell while Netscape Navigator reads it as being at the start of the table, outside of the table. You'll have a more consistent floating box effect if you keep the SB outside of any tables.

Later in this chapter I tell you about cell padding and spacing, borders, and alignment. You can use these techniques to create spacing between columns or align items to your liking. But you can also skip an entire row or column, leaving it empty—setting it at a set width or height in pixels to provide a definite space between the rows or columns.

Adding text to your table

Inside a cell, life is much like that on a regular Web page or a word processing page. Adding text is the same too.

Follow these steps to add text to a cell by typing or pasting:

1. Click inside the cell into which you want to enter the text. If the cell is empty, the cursor flashes inside the cell at its left edge by default—or elsewhere, depending upon the alignment set for the cell. If text already exists in the cell, the cursor flashes wherever you click. You can move it by clicking again or using the arrow keys. If an image of any type exists in the cell, the cursor appears beside the graphic, depending upon the alignment in that cell.

Note

Sometimes it's difficult to place the cursor within a narrow cell or in a cell having only an existing image object with no cell padding. In this case, if you can successfully click inside another cell, do so, and then press Tab until you're at the desired cell, or press Shift+Tab to move backward through the cells. Alternately, you can temporarily increase the cell padding to place your cursor, and then press Enter/Return to insert some lines to hold extra space. Then reset your padding. When you're all finished, remove the extra lines.

2. You can type or paste text into a cell, much like you would in a word-processing program. Or, you can drag the text from another cell, another part of the page, another page within the site, or even a document created in another application. Just select the text and drag it into place within the cell. As you drag over the cell, a black flashing line shows you where the text will be entered when you release the mouse.

Note

Mac users can also drag a text clipping into the cell. (Windows users can drag scrap text, such as is created by dragging text out of Word.) You have no need to preselect the cell or place the cursor first. Just drag the clipping file into place. As you drag over the cell, a black flashing line shows you where the clipping's text will land when you release the mouse. You can place the text between any other text, or by a graphic in the cell. (A Word 98 text clipping doesn't work, though, due to Microsoft's clipping creation. It comes in as a graphic instead, so GoLive's Save for Web feature kicks into action.)

As you add text to a cell, the cell may grow in an odd manner while its adjacent cells shrink. Don't let it throw you. When you add text or other content to those cells, they'll even out. After you see the content in place and have an idea of your layout and sizing, you can set the cells to have specific sizes (if you want to). If the neighboring cell becomes so small that you feel you can't click inside it to place the cursor, use the Tab key to move into it. Once the cursor is flashing in any cell, tabbing moves the cursor to the next cell, and then the next, and so on. Shift+Tab to move backward through the cells.

Importing a text file into your table

If you are using the table to hold rows and columns of organized data, and you already have the data in another spreadsheet or database, you can import that data directly into a table. This avoids typing, typos, and manual table formatting because all the necessary rows and columns are created during the import. This can be a big timesaver.

The first step is to export the data from the spreadsheet or database. There's no reason to import data you won't be using, so in the spreadsheet select the cells (or in the database, the records) that contain the data you want to export before you do the export. Then export the data, choosing a Save As Text export format. The most common and reliable export/import type is "tab-delimited." Exact export instructions will vary according to your spreadsheet program, but as a guideline I can tell you that in Excel 98 you do the export by choosing File ➪ Save As, and then choosing Text, tab-delimited from the list of formats you can save as. After you save the exported file, return to GoLive.

Here's how to import the exported spreadsheet or database into GoLive:

1. Select the table.

2. Open the Table Inspector if it's not already open. If it didn't automatically go to the Table tab, make the Table tab active.

3. At the bottom of the Table tab, click the Browse button next to Import Tab-Text.

4. Navigate to the exported file and click it to select it.

5. Make sure the column selector matches the export type for your file, as follows:

   • The default is tab, which matches the tab-delimited export type.

   • If you used another export type, choose the matching format from the pop-up menu. (You cannot do so after you select the file.) The choices are tab, comma, space, and semicolon.

   The data imports, creating all the necessary cells and filling the table with the data.

Note   If you import a large file, you may run out of memory. Either check to be sure that you didn't export too much, or quit GoLive and bump up the memory you've allotted to it.

Working with table text

After the text is in your table, it's time to work with it. As with all text, you can change the font, color, and style of text inside a table. You can also wrap text.

Text wrap

By default, text wraps within a cell. However, you can turn off the text wrapping on a cell-by-cell basis. To do so, select the cell and check the box by the No Text Wrap option in the Cell tab or the Table Inspector.

Moving text

After you place text, you can move it at any time. You don't have to move all of the text; only the text you select is moved, exactly like within a word-processor or page-layout program.

To move text, follow these steps:

1. Select the text you want to move. (You work directly in the table to do this, not within the Table palette.)

2. Drag the selected text to the new cell within the table or out of the table to anyplace there's a cursor, as follows:

   • If the location is within the same page, the text is removed from its original spot and placed in the new location.

   • If the location is on another page in your site, the text remains intact in its original spot while a copy is placed in the new location.

To place a copy of your text in a new location while keeping the original text in place, select the text (as in Step 1) but press Option (Mac) or Ctrl (Windows) while you drag to the new location. Of course, you can also cut or copy text and then paste it elsewhere.

 Tip   You can easily turn any contiguous cells within a table into their own standalone table. Simply select the desired cells (as I show you later in this chapter), copy them, and then paste them wherever you want the new table to appear. The original table and all of its contents remain intact.

Applying a header style

A table header style is one way to quickly set a row, column, or even an individual cell apart from the rest of the table.

When you apply GoLive's Header Style option to a cell, all text within the cell becomes formatted; however, the browser interprets the table header `<th>` tag, which is commonly displayed as bold and centered.

To apply this style, select the desired cell or cells and then check the Header Style option in the Table Inspector's Cell tab, as shown in Figure 13-5. (The Inspector jumps to the Cell tab whenever you select an individual cell or cells.)

The HTML tag for a cell with a header style is `<th>yourtext</th>` instead of the standard `<td>yourtext</th>` for a regular table cell.

The Header Style option works independently of the styles that GoLive's Table palette provides. You can add a header to cells and still use a style. Or, you can make your own style that includes the header style.

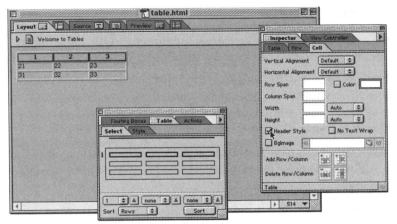

Figure 13-5: Applying a header style to the top row of cells

Coloring or assigning a font set to text

Text can be colored or assigned a font set as with any other text in your site. However, in a table there's an easier way to do this than by selecting the text. Instead, you can select one cell or all the cells to which you want to add the color or font set — but rather than selecting the cells in the table itself, which may require scrolling, you get to do it in a minitable in the Table palette. (The Table palette is new to GoLive 5.)

Follow these steps to change the color of a cell's text or assign a font set:

1. Open the Table palette (Window ➪ Table).

   This palette will be blank until you select table.

2. Select the entire table. (The easiest way is to click the top or left border when your Mouse icon becomes a hand.)

   A miniature version of your table is displayed in the palette. (If your table is large and the table appears too small, drag the bottom-right corner to enlarge the palette and image.)

3. In the Table palette, select the cells in which you want to add the color or font set.

   The border of each selected cell becomes bold so you can tell it's selected.

4. Add the color or font set, as follows:

   • To add a color to the text within the selected cells, click the Color button/swatch in the toolbar. This opens the Color palette. In the Color palette, locate the desired color and then click that color. (This is the same as adding color to any other text. See Chapter 8 for more information.)

• To assign a font set to the text in the selected cells, choose the desired font set from the Font Sets submenu under Type ⇨ Font or drag a font set from the Font Sets tab of the Site Window onto any part of the selected border.

You can also change the color of, or add a color or font set to, individual characters within a cell. To do this, select the text directly within the table cell and then use the same procedure you would for any other text — click the Color button in the toolbar and choose a color; or choose a font set from the Type ⇨ Font menu.

Caution

Before you add colors and font sets to your table, consider that adding these attributes adds more code to your page. When you add a color to a cell, the font color tag is added to that cell. Adding the same color to an entire row, column, or table adds the same color tag code to every cell; it is not just added once. Consider using style sheets instead.

Cross-Reference

Take a look at Chapter 17 to learn more about style sheets.

Sorting text

What happens if, after you get all of your data entered into a table, you learn that you've got more to add? Is all that hard work for nothing? Do you manually pick through the information in your table, figuring out where each line of new information should be added? Thankfully, not. Using the Table palette, you can sort tables easily and quickly. Just add the extra rows or columns to the end of your table and then re-sort the contents. Of course, sorting comes in handy in other ways besides this example. You'll be able to sort lists of names or merchandise you'd like presented in order, and all sorts of other stuff. (No pun intended.)

The Sort feature enables you to sort by one primary field, and then do two subsorts.

Here's how to sort the contents of your table:

1. Select the table you wish to sort.

2. Open the Table palette (Window ⇨ Table) to the Select tab.

3. Choose the column or row you wish to sort by picking a number from the first pop-up menu. (If you have four rows, the numbers 1–4 appear in the pop-up menu. When you have six rows, you see numbers 1–6, and so on.)

4. Choose a sort order. By default, the sort order is A to Z or 1, 2, 3, and so on, as depicted by the triangle that goes from smaller to larger. To reverse the sort, click the triangle so it is wider on top.

5. In the Sort menu, determine whether you'll sort columns or rows.

6. (*Optional*) Choose a secondary sort order using the next pop-up menu and Triangle Sort Order button.

7. (*Optional*) Choose a third subsort order using the next pop-up menu and Triangle Sort Order button.

8. Click Sort to perform the sort.

If you're not happy with the results, you can undo the sort by choosing Edit ⇨ Undo, or by removing the sort from the History palette.

Adding graphics or other media to your table

You add a graphic to a table using the same methods as for adding a graphic to a page, as follows:

✦ Drag the image or media file into the cell from the Site Window.

✦ Drag the appropriate placeholder from the Basic tab of the Objects palette into the cell, and then Point and Shoot from the placeholder to the file in the Files tab of the Site Window.

A cell grows to accommodate an image even if its height and width, and even the total height and width of the table, are set to a smaller size.

After you place a graphic or media file, you can move it to another cell in the table or elsewhere on the page by dragging it to the new location, as follows:

✦ To move an item to a new cell or location on the page, click it and drag it to the new location.

✦ To place a copy of the item in a new location while keeping the original in place, press Option (Mac) or Ctrl (Windows) while you drag the item.

✦ You can move an item from one page to another by dragging it into the other page. When you drag between pages, the original remains intact in its location. A copy is made on the destination page.

Adding and Deleting Rows and Columns

You have two different ways to add rows or columns. One method adds new columns at the right side of the table and new rows at the bottom. It also enables you to add many rows or columns at the same time. The other method enables you to specify where the new row or column is added.

Empty cells appear as one large seemingly undefined area. In reality, individual cells exist, so don't let this throw you.

Adding rows or columns to the end of a table

To add columns to the end or rows to the bottom of a table, follow these steps:

1. Select the table by moving your mouse to the top or left border of the table and clicking when the cursor turns into a hand. A line appears around the table to indicate it's selected.

   The Table Inspector, if open, jumps to the Table tab because anything you do while the entire table is selected affects the entire table. (If the Inspector is not open, open it now.)

2. Add new rows and/or columns, as follows:

   • To add new rows, select the existing number in the Rows field at the top of the Inspector and then replace that number with the new one.

   • To add new columns, select the existing number in the Columns field at the top of the Inspector and then replace that number with the new one.

   With either method, the new columns are added at the right side of the table, as shown in Figure 13-6.

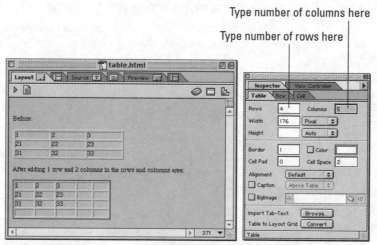

Figure 13-6: You can add any number of new rows and columns to the edges of a table by using the Table Inspector.

Now that you understand how the Table Inspector handles the number of rows and columns, try this trick. To add any number of new rows at the end of your table, press Command (Mac) or Ctrl+Shift (Windows) as you point to the bottom border of the table (the cursor gains a plus sign), and then click and drag downward. As you drag, dotted lines show you the number of rows you'll have if you release the mouse at that moment. In Figure 13-7, two new rows are about to be added. You can drag back upward to reduce the number. Release the mouse when you have the desired number of rows. The same works for adding columns, but with the right edge of the table and dragging to the right.

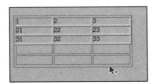 **Figure 13-7:** You can also add any number of new rows and columns to the edges of a table by holding down the ⌘ button (Mac) or Ctrl+Shift (Windows) and dragging the bottom or right edge.

Inserting a new row between existing rows

You have two ways to add rows within your table. In both cases, the new row comes in on top of the row you select.

Follow these steps to insert a new row between existing rows:

1. Select the cell below where you want the new row to appear.

   The Table Inspector, if open, jumps to the Cell tab so you can do work related to that cell. (If the Inspector is not open, open it now.)

2. Click the Add Row button in the Table Inspector, as shown in Figure 13-8.

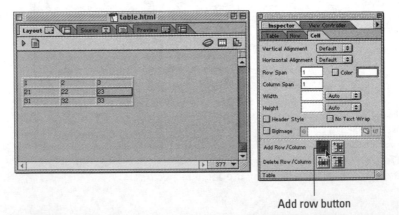

Add row button

Figure 13-8: To add a new row above a specific existing row, use the Add Row button in the Cell tab of the Table Inspector.

The new row appears above the cell you selected, as shown in Figure 13-9.

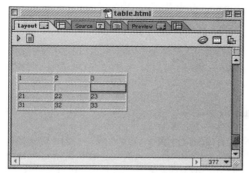

Figure 13-9: A new row added above a specific existing row

3. (*Optional*) To add more rows, click the Add Row button once for each row.

Tip   Another way to add a row between any rows within your table is to select the cell below where you want the new row to appear, and then Command-click (Mac) or right-click (Windows) and choose Insert Row.

Sometimes you need to insert a row *below* an existing row instead of above it. You can do this, too, but not in the Inspector. Instead, select any cell within the row you want to add a new row above. Then point anywhere within the selected cell and Command-click (Mac) or right-click (Windows) to call up the contextual menu and choose Insert Row Below.

Inserting a new column between existing columns

You have two ways to add columns within your table. In each case, the new column comes in to the left of the column you select.

To insert a new column between existing columns, follow these steps:

1. Select the cell to the right of where you want the new column to appear. To select the cell, click its right or bottom inside edge (or use the Table palette or contextual menu). A line appears around the cell to indicate it is selected.

   The Table Inspector, if open, jumps to the Cell tab so you can do work related to that cell. (If the Inspector is not open, open it now.)

2. Click the Add Column button in the Table Inspector. The new column appears to the left of the cell you selected.

3. (*Optional*) To add more columns, click the Add Column button once for each column.

Tip   You can also add a column by selecting the cell to the left of where you want the new column and then Command-clicking (Mac) or right-clicking (Windows) and choosing Insert Column.

Sometimes you need to insert a column to the *right* of an existing row instead of to its left. The command to do this is not yet in the Inspector, but it is available in the contextual menu. Select any cell within the column you want to add columns to the right of. Then point anywhere within the selected cell and Command-click (Mac) or right-click (Windows) to call up the contextual menu and choose Insert Column Right.

Removing rows and columns

Because a new table always has three rows and three columns, you may need to delete a row or column or two from time to time. Of course, the possibility also exists that you'll need to delete a row or column simply because you were overzealous in your additions earlier. Delete with care, though; any content in deleted cells is deleted along with the cell.

Here's how to delete a row or column:

1. Select any cell in the row or column you wish to delete. To select the cell, click its right or bottom inside edge.

   Alternately, to select the cell you can click the corresponding cell in the Table palette, or Control-click (Mac) or right-click (Windows) as you point inside the desired cell, and then choose Select Cell.

   The Table Inspector, if open, jumps to the Cell tab so you can do work related to that cell. (If the Inspector is not open, open it now.)

2. Click the Delete Row or Delete Column button in the Table Inspector. The entire row or column is removed.

Tip   Another way to delete a row or column quickly is to select any cell in the row or column to be deleted and then Command-click (Mac) or right-click (Windows) and choose Delete Column or Delete Row. (You can even use the contextual menu to first select the cell, by pointing within the cell as you call up the contextual menu.)

Adjusting the Size of Your Table

By default, table cells grow to perfectly fit whatever you place in them. You can take advantage of this by placing your content first and fine-tuning the table dimensions later, or you can preset the size of your table or its individual cells prior to placing content.

If you don't make any changes, the default settings for the table (as shown in the Table tab) and each cell (in the Cell tab) are all Auto — that is, if the contents of the table or cell grow beyond the default table size of 180 pixels, the table and cells adjust to fit the contents. When you change the size of either the table or a cell, you must choose between pixels and percent. Be careful with this, because if you mix pixels and percents within the same table, conflicts may arise. (More about pixels, percent, and other table measurement details in the paragraphs that follow.)

Understanding table measurements

You can make a table wider or narrower simply by dragging or by entering the desired dimensions in the Table Inspector.

Before I show you how to set the size of a table, a discussion of the measurement options is worthwhile. You can set a table's dimensions as an exact size by entering them in pixels, or you can set a table to size as a percentage of the width of the browser.

If you set a size in pixels, the table stays that size (for the most part). For example, if you make a table 580 pixels wide it will occupy most of the browser when a user's window is open all the way on a screen that's 640×480 (pixels). But if a person on a larger monitor expands the width of his or her browser to anything wider, the table will not expand to fit the new browser width. If a user makes the browser narrower than 580 pixels, then your entire table, which remains 580 pixels wide, no longer fits in the window — so scrollbars appear at the bottom of the screen and the user must scroll to see your entire width. The strength of a set width is that the objects in your table stay put.

If you set the size of your table as a percentage, the table grows when the user expands the width of the browser and shrinks when the user narrows the browser window. As the table resizes, though, the cells all resize, which can affect the cell's content. By default, text wraps within a cell. So if you have a medium-size cell, the text may look perfect. However, as you shrink the width, the text wraps oddly, and if you expand the cell, the text may look lost within a mostly empty cell. If you also have an image in that cell attached to the text line, the image will move around and end up falling anywhere within the cell. For the most part, this is a layout designer's nightmare. However, occasionally it's great to have the table resize. For example, if you want an image to be perfectly centered at all times, you can build a one-cell table into which you put that image. Then, by setting the image to center in the cell and setting the cell to be 100 percent of the browser window, the image will realign to remain centered no matter what size the browser becomes.

The last sizing option is Auto, for automatic. With this sizing option, the cell shrinks or grows to fit content while working in GoLive. Once your layout is complete and the page is viewed in the browser, the size is fixed, as with pixel sizing. When you use pixel or percentage sizing, the cells grow to fit content, but don't shrink.

Adjusting a table by dragging

The advantage of adjusting the width by dragging is that you can work visually instead of guessing at the size by numbers. If you're going for a visual effect with the table, you may prefer this method.

Making a table wider or narrower by dragging is so easy that it only takes one step. You don't even have to select the table! The Table Inspector doesn't have to be open either, but if it is you can watch as the width is reported pixel by pixel as you drag. Dragging to resize always sets the dimensions in pixels.

To adjust the width and/or height of a table by dragging, keep the following choices in mind:

✦ To adjust the width, move your cursor over the outside of the right edge of the table until your mouse becomes a dark blue double-sided arrow, and then drag left or right, as shown in Figure 13-10.

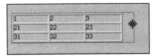

Figure 13-10: The dark blue double-sided arrow enables you to drag a table to a new size.

If the cursor fails to turn into the arrow, press Option (Mac) or Alt (Windows) as you move the mouse over the right edge of the table.

When the cursor is on the inside edge of the outside of the table, the right-most cell will be resized instead. To help you differentiate between the table and cell sizing, the arrow that adjusts table width is always dark blue while the arrow for adjusting cell width is light blue.

✦ To adjust the height, move your cursor over the bottom inside edge of the table and press Option (Mac) or Alt (Windows) until your mouse becomes a dark blue double-sided arrow and then drag upward or downward.

As you change the width, the cells grow wider or narrower. As you change the height, the cells grow taller or shorter. Because the size is measured in pixels, the size you set for the table will remain intact even when the cells are empty.

Adjusting a table in the Table Inspector

The other way to size a table is by entering specific dimensions into the Table Inspector.

To set the size of a table in the Table Inspector, follow these steps:

1. Select the table by moving your mouse to its top or left border and clicking when the cursor becomes an Object Selection icon.

   The Table Inspector jumps to the Table tab because anything you do while the entire table is selected affects the entire table. (If the Inspector isn't open, open it now.)

2. To adjust the table's width, choose the method of sizing from the pop-up menu after the Width field and enter a number in the Width field. Table width is set at 180 pixels by default. If you want your new measurement to be an exact amount, just replace the 180 and enter the new number. If you prefer to size your table in proportion to the browser window, choose Percent from the pop-up menu next to the Width field.

3. Table height is automatic by default, with each cell being one line. This is because as you add content to a cell, the cell grows to accommodate your lines of text or your graphic. If you provide a set height for a table, the total height is distributed among the rows, adjusting the height of each row evenly. To adjust the height of the table, first select Pixel or Percent from the pop-up menu beside the Height field to activate the Height field. Then enter the desired height in pixels or percentage. If you choose Pixel and enter a number, then change to Percent, the percentage will be chosen automatically from the proportion of the table's size (while in pixels) to the width your page window is set at.

Tip

If a table is wider than the browser, the user will see a horizontal scrollbar across the bottom of the page, and your page will have to be scrolled sideways to be read. Because factors such as the table's border can come into play with the width, to ensure a browser won't have horizontal scrollbars you can set your table to be 98 percent instead of 100 percent as a size.

If a table's width is set to a specific number of pixels or percentage, the table will — for the most part — remain constant at that size regardless of the sizing within the cells. While the first columns will take on the size you assign them, the last cell will make up the difference between the sum of the cells to its left and the size of the table instead of becoming the size you request. The table sort of steals space as is available. However, at some point if insufficient space exists, the table will actually grow past your set width or percentage. Therefore, if you are assigning specific sizes to the cells in your table, change the table's size to Auto. The same happens when you set a table's height. However, because the table's height is automatic by default, you are less likely to come across this problem.

Adjusting the size of cells

You can't actually change just the size of a *single* cell (unless you have a one-column or one-row table). When you change the width of a cell you actually change the width of the *entire column* that cell is in. Likewise, changing the height of a cell changes the height of the *entire row*.

When you set the size of cells in a table, don't mix pixels and percentages or you'll confuse the table. Also, make sure the sum of all the cells in a row equals the width of the table, or set the table to Auto. Make sure the sum of the cells in a column equals the height or set the height to Auto.

Resizing a cell by dragging

By dragging a cell's border to size it, you can see the way the cell looks onscreen in relation to the other items on your screen. However, the text within it doesn't reflow until after you stop dragging. As you drag, you can also see the size in pixels or percent if you have the Table Inspector open to the Cell tab.

Remember, to resize a cell, you move its column border, or row border, or both.

Follow these steps to adjust the width of a column by dragging its border:

1. Move your cursor over the right side of the cell so it points to the dividing line.
2. Press Option (Mac) or Alt (Windows) to turn the mouse into a double-sided light blue arrow.
3. Drag right or left until you achieve the desired size.
4. Release the modifier (Option or Alt) key and mouse.

Follow these steps to adjust the height of a row by dragging its border:

1. Move your cursor over the bottom of the cell so it points to the dividing line.
2. Press Option (Mac) or Alt (Windows) to turn the mouse into a double-sided light blue arrow.
3. Drag the arrow down or up until you achieve the desired size.
4. Release the modifier (Option or Alt) key and mouse.

Resizing a cell with the Table Inspector

Instead of dragging to set the size of a cell, you can enter the size in pixels or as a percentage directly. Here's how to do it:

1. Select the cell by clicking its right or bottom inner edge, or via the contextual menu or the Table palette. A line appears around the cell to indicate it is selected. The Table Inspector jumps to the Cell tab so you can do work related to that cell. (If the Inspector is not open, open it now.)

2. Choose Pixel or Percent from the pop-up menu by the Width and/or Height field.

3. Enter a number in the Width and/or Height field.

Merging Rows and Columns

After you set up your table, you can set up a cell to span horizontally across multiple columns or up and down over multiple rows. (In HTML this appears as `<colspan>` and `<rowspan>`, respectively.)

When you extend a cell's span across other cells in its row, it extends to the right. The selected cell becomes one (merges) with the cells that currently occupy the columns to the right that are included in the span. For example, in a table that consists of three columns and three rows, if you want only one long cell in a particular row instead of three cells in that row, you change the cell span to span three columns and the two cells to its right disappear. Anything within those other two cells is deleted. One cell can span an entire row, but it can't span more columns than exist in the table. Likewise with columns, when you extend a cell to span down several rows, it encompasses the cells below it and can span the entire number of rows within the table.

Merging cells in a row

When you merge a cell across a row, you widen the cell by having it cover multiple columns. You have two ways to merge a cell across a row. You can use the Inspector to make the change numerically, or you can work visually. You can merge cells to the right, but not to the left.

To visually merge a cell with others in its row, follow these steps:

1. Select the left-most cell that you want included in the merge.

2. Press the Shift key as you press the right arrow to expand your cell across columns to the right. If you go too far, use the left arrow to undo the merge.

While you're merging cells, you can also use the down arrow to lengthen the cell. If you go too far, use the up arrow to undo the merge.

Follow these steps to merge a cell with others in its row by using the Inspector:

1. Select the left-most cell that you want included in the merge.

2. Open the Table Inspector if it's not already open, and switch to the Cell tab if it doesn't go there automatically.

3. Enter the number of columns you want this cell to cover in the Column Span field. The cell expands as in Figure 13-11, removing anything in the cells it now encompasses.

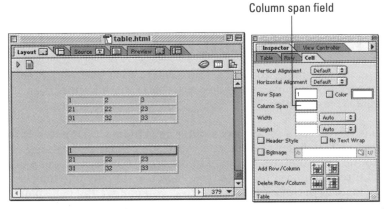

Figure 13-11: To extend a cell across several columns, enter the number of columns in the Column Span field.

Merging cells down a column

When you merge a cell in a column, you expand the cell downward, lengthening it so it covers multiple rows. You can merge a cell downward, but not upward. You can merge the column visually or do it numerically within the Inspector.

The following steps demonstrate how to visually merge a cell down a column:

1. Select the top-most cell that you want included in the merge.

2. Press the Shift key as you press the down arrow key. Each time you press the down arrow you move the cell down to cover one more row.

   If you find you've covered too many rows, use the up arrow key to return a cell to its independence.

While you're merging cells, you can also use the right arrow to merge the cell across columns, widening the cell. And, of course, use the left arrow to undo a merge.

To merge a cell with others in its column using the Inspector, follow these steps:

1. Select the top-most cell that you want included in the merge.

2. Open the Table Inspector if it's not already open and switch to the Cell tab if it doesn't go there automatically.

3. Enter the number of rows you want this cell to cover in the Row Span field. The cell expands, removing anything in the cells it now encompasses, as in Figure 13-12.

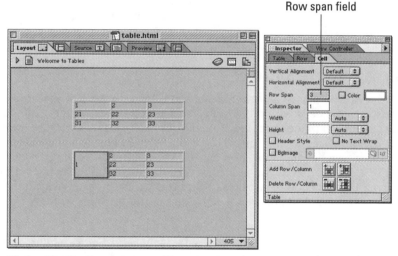

Figure 13-12: To merge a cell across several rows, enter the number of rows in the Row Span field.

Note

At times you may find that in, say, a three-column table, you have every row of the table spanning across the third column. In effect, then, you really only need a two column table. In this case, in order to help browsers display your table consistently, it is better to delete the unused columns, and then resize the table accordingly. By having one row that contains the set number of columns, you provide a control for the browser. The same holds true for rows—if you have a four-row table, at least one column should actually have four cells. By the way, GoLive does this for you automatically within the layout grid.

Tweaking Your Table's Basic Appearance

Every part of a table is adjustable, so you can make it look just how you want it — or give it no look at all. The border, cell padding, and cell spacing of your table can do a lot to make your material presentable. A bit of space here and there can help readers see and absorb the table content. This section shows you how to give your content space — how to set your text apart from the structural part of the table, how to use the table's structure to add to the presentation, or even how to make the table totally invisible so it can do its job behind the scenes. You can make these changes at any time. However, it makes the most sense to do this after you've added the content. That way, you can see the effects of the formatting.

After you set up a table's look, you may want to be able to use that look again in another table or in another site. GoLive 5 introduces table styles, which enable you to do this with ease. In a later section, "Table Styles," I show you how to save your table's look as a style and then easily apply it elsewhere — even to an existing table full of content.

Adding a table border

The border option places a border around the entire outside of your table and adds lines between any cells within the table. A table without a border is effective for holding a layout in place. A table with a border can become a picture frame. Make a one-cell table, place the picture in the cell, and then create a wide border. A wide border takes on a beveled look. You can see the results of a few table widths in Figure 13-14. Remember, if you add a border to a cell it counts as part of the cell's width, even though each browser may not reflect this the same way. Keep this in mind to avoid unwanted horizontal scrollbars in the browser window.

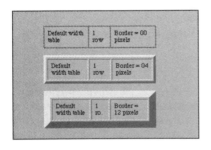

Figure 13-13: Various border widths, as they appear in Layout mode. When no border exists, the lines appear as dotted by default.

For a greater understanding of how borders affect table size, see the "Cell Sizing Experimentation" sidebar later in this chapter.

Follow these steps to set a border or remove the default 1-pixel border:

1. Select the table by clicking the top or left border of the table.

2. Open the Table Inspector to the Table tab if it's not already open and at that tab.

3. Enter the desired border in the Border field.

   By default, each table has a border 1 pixel wide. To remove the border, replace the number 1 with 0.

When the border is 0, GoLive shows the table's cell divisions as dotted lines to let you know you're viewing a table, aid you in the design of your table, and give you the ability to select cells. If you prefer not to see the cell divisions at all, select Edit ➪ Hide Invisible Items. (Or choose Hide Invisible Items from the contextual menu.) When you switch to the Preview tab the divisions disappear, as they will in the browser.

Tables can be interpreted differently in each browser. Figure 13-14 demonstrates the effect of various border widths in Internet Explorer and Netscape browsers.

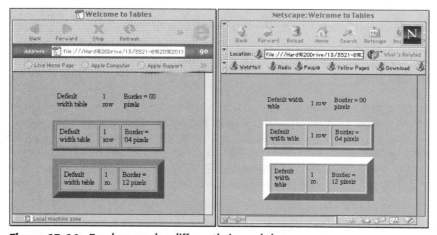

Figure 13-14: Borders render differently in each browser.

Adjusting cell padding

Cell padding adds a space between the cell's contents and the inside edges of the cell, as depicted in Figure 13-15. Padding is set on a table-wide basis, so the padding for one cell is the same as for the rest.

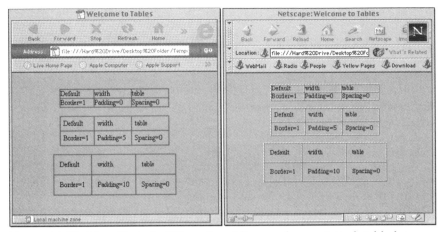

Figure 13-15: The effect of a little cell padding can be great. Each table here has six points of padding.

To set cell padding, follow these steps:

1. Select the table by clicking the top or left border of the table.

2. In the Table tab of the Table Inspector, enter the desired number of pixel spaces in the Cell Pad field. Press Enter/Return or click anywhere to confirm the entry.

Note

You can create the effect of having text over a colored square by using a one-column by one-row table. Drag in a table icon from the palette and set it to column = 1, row = 1, border = 0, spacing = 0. Add the color to the cell. Next, add your text into the table cell. (You can color the text, too.) At this point the text butts up to the cell edges, looking cramped, so increase the cell padding to extend the background color beyond the text, creating an esthetically pleasing margin of color.

Adjusting cell spacing

Cell spacing enables you to put some space between the cells and the table's border as shown in Figure 13-16. It's set table-wide. The amount of spacing you enter is the space between the outside cells and the table's border as well as the amount of space between the cells themselves. The difference between cell padding and cell spacing can be confusing at first. Although both add space to a table, padding adds space inside a cell and spacing adds space between each cell. The best way to see the subtle difference is to experiment. (For a greater understanding of how spacing affects table size, see the "Cell Sizing Experimentation" sidebar later in this chapter.)

Cell Sizing Experimentation

When you're setting up tables with exact sizing, it helps to understand exactly what affects the total size of a table.

To understand how cell sizing, padding, spacing, and borders all add up, try this experiment. Create a table with three columns and three rows. Make the height and width Auto. Set the border, padding, and spacing to 0. Make each cell 40 pixels × 40 pixels (because it's an easy number). Then select the table as a whole and change the height and width pop-ups to pixels. Note that GoLive calculates the height and width to 120 pixels because $40 \times 3 = 120$.

Change the height and width pop-ups back to Auto and change the padding to 5. Then change the pop-ups back to pixels. Now the height and width are reported to be 150, an addition of 30 pixels. That's because each of the three cells has 5 pixels on each side of your content so each cell grew by 10 pixels, enlarging your table.

Again, change the height and width pop-ups back to Auto and this time change the spacing to 5. Change the pop-ups back to pixels. Height and width are now 170, an addition of 20 pixels. This time the addition is the 5-pixel width of the walls. Each cell divider is 5 pixels wide and four dividers exist (because the outside walls count too), totaling 20 pixels (5 pixels × 4 dividers = 20 more pixels).

For the last part of the experiment, change the height and width to Auto one more time and add a table border of 2 pixels, and then change the height and width back to pixels. This one's an odd one: If 2 pixels exist on each side of the table, the increase should be 4, bringing the table size up to 174. However, the table size is reported by GoLive as 182. Perhaps by the time you read this GoLive will address this table border issue, but as of the 5.0 release it holds true. You'll know by the final total you see at the end of this experiment. If you try this and get a total of 172, when you're setting the size of your table to an exact size, remember that you have to manually enter the table's width or height, adding once more the size of the border if you have a border. (This is critical to avoid horizontal scrollbars on your page and if you're creating an exact page width.)

Now that you understand how GoLive calculates table sizes, there's one more consideration. In the wild world of the Web, there seems to be no law when it comes to table rendering. As various figures in this chapter show you, each browser can interpret a table differently. Netscape browsers and Internet Explorer sure do. Which is right and which is wrong depends on how you look at it. Internet Explorer counts padding and border width as extra widths, widening the table, while Netscape counts them as part of the cell and table's width.

Here's how to set cell spacing:

1. Select the table by clicking the top or left border of the table.

2. In the Table tab of the Table Inspector, enter the desired pixel space in the Cell Space field. Press Enter/Return or click the Return button to confirm the entry.

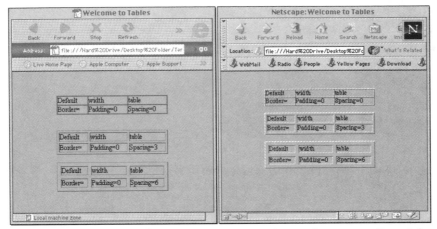

Figure 13-16: Cell spacing provides separation of space between cells and the border as well as between cells within the table.

Aligning tables and their contents

Tables have two levels of alignment: alignment of the entire table and the alignment of items within each table cell. Each alignment is independent of the other.

Table-level alignment

The table's alignment tells the browser where to place the table in relation to the browser's borders and the text in the line that follows the table. A table's alignment has no effect on the alignment of items within the cells.

Cross-Reference   If your table is directly on a grid, table alignment has no effect. See Chapter 7 to learn how to align a table as an object on a grid.

Remember that you place a table inline with the page's cursor. Therefore, you align a table in relation to the page just like you align text. The three standard options apply for a table's alignment: left, center, and right. However, because you're dealing with HTML, you have two different ways to perform table alignment, and the HTML tags for each method are different, as are the results. You can align a table within the page (browser window) using the ruler — which affects only the table — or you can align the table using the table tag of the Inspector — which affects not only the table but the text that follows the table.

To set the alignment of a table on your page but not affect the text or elements that follow the table, you use the text controls on the toolbar. This is not necessary to do, because the table, like all other elements on a page, is rendered flush left in a browser by default.

To set a table's alignment *only*, do one of the following:

✦ Select the table, and then click one of the three alignment buttons (left, center, or right) on the toolbar.

✦ Place the cursor directly before or after the table, and then click one of the three alignment buttons (Left, Center, or Right) on the toolbar.

The HTML tag generated by GoLive when you use the toolbar alignment is the `<div>` tag.

By using the alignment options in the Table Inspector, you can align your table and cause the text that follows the table to wrap around it on the left or right side of the table. This method of alignment writes the align attribute into the `<table>` tag.

To set a table's alignment and also effect text wrap, follow these steps:

1. Select the table.

2. In the Table Inspector's Table tab, choose one of the following alignments from the alignment pop-up menu:

   • *Left* alignment forces the table against the left edge of the browser window. The causes text to be rendered after the end of the table, to its right. The text then continues along its right edge until it reaches the bottom of the table, and then, after the table ends, it flows against the left border and falls across the entire page. Text must remain left-aligned to create this effect.

   • *Right* alignment forces the table against the right edge of the browser window. When the browser is made wider or narrower, the table moves along with the right edge of the browser, repositioning the table in relation to the items around it. Text then flows up to the left edge of the table, wrapping to the next line when it gets to the table. It continues to flow up to the table's left edge until it reaches the bottom of the table, and then falls across the entire page. Text must remain left-aligned to create this effect.

   • By default when you place a table, the option selected is *Default* and no alignment attribute is written. The default alignment has no text wrapping effect. It provides no specific instruction for the table, so the table takes on the alignment of the line that contains it. When you want to remove the alignment attribute from the table tag, select Default.

Figure 13-17 demonstrates the default alignment of a table and the effect of aligning the same table to the left.

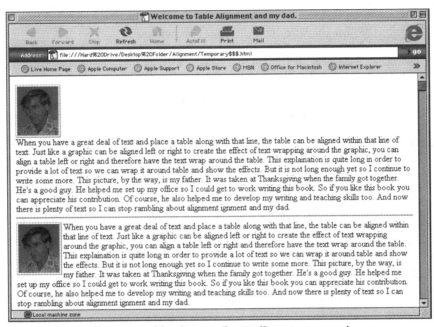

Figure 13-17: Aligning a table align attribute affects text wrapping on a page. In this figure, the image is in a one-cell table and the text is loose on the page. *Top:* Default alignment. *Bottom:* Left alignment.

Tip   To center a table, you can also place it within another table that is set to span 100 percent of the browser window and set it to be centered within the encompassing cell. See the "Table Tricks" section later in this chapter.

Cell-level alignment

A cell's alignment tells the browser where to place the contents of a cell. You can choose a vertical alignment, a horizontal alignment, or one of each. Each cell's alignment is recorded in the HTML independently of the others. You can align a single cell at a time, or align multiple cells, an entire row or rows, or an entire column or columns at once.

To set a cell's alignment, follow these steps:

1. Select the cells, rows, or columns you want to align.

2. If the Table Inspector isn't already open, open it.

3. (*Optional*) Choose a vertical alignment from the pop-up menu in the Cell tab of the Table Inspector, as follows

- *Default* alignment places the text in the middle of the cell between the top and bottom. If you have set a specific alignment for a cell's row, default takes on that alignment.

- *Top* alignment places the text against the top of the cell.

- *Bottom* alignment places the text against the bottom of the cell.

- *Middle* alignment places the text in the middle of the cell.

4. (*Optional*) Choose a horizontal alignment from the pop-up menu in the Cell tab of the Table Inspector, as follows:

- *Default* alignment is flush left against the left edge of the cell.

- *Left* alignment places the text against the left edge of the cell. Text comes in and moves to the right as you add it.

- *Right* alignment places the text against the right edge of the cell. As the cell grows wider or narrower, the text moves along with the right edge of the cell. Text extends to the left as it's added.

- *Center* alignment places the text smack in the center of the cell. As the cell grows wider or narrower, the text remains centered in the cell. Text extends outward in both directions as it's added.

In Figure 13-18, you can see how the Table Inspector looks after a cell has been aligned both vertically and horizontally. GoLive's layout view accurately depicts the way this alignment appears in browsers.

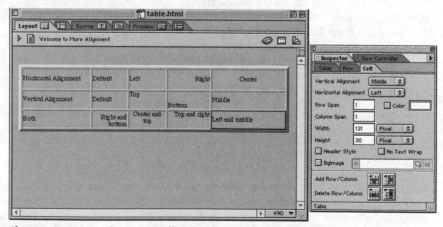

Figure 13-18: To change a cell's alignment, choose a horizontal and/or vertical alignment from the Cell tab of the Table Inspector.

Row-level alignment

Although GoLive provides a dedicated Row tab, you'll notice that GoLive doesn't switch you to this tab when you select a row. That's because using it can lead to confusion. The issue is that the Row tab writes your alignment in to the table row <tr> tag, while the Cell tab writes code for the cell into the table cell <td> tag. While it may be convenient to apply alignment to an entire row using the Row tab, those alignment attributes will not show up in the Cell tab when you select one or more cells of that row. Therefore, you have no feedback about your chosen alignment while in the Cell tab. Also, any attributes you give individual cells will override whatever attributes you may have given the row. Because the Cell tab (and cell tag) enables you to choose more formatting options, it is wisest to use that tab (and therefore tag) only. Lastly, if you want to design using style sheets, you will have to base table alignment styles on the table cell <td> tag as styles based on <tr> will be ignored completely.

You can align the contents of cells within an entire row at one time by using the Row tab of the Table Inspector.

Follow these steps to align a row:

1. Select the entire row using one of the following ways:

   • In the Table palette, point to the row from the left edge of the row so the cursor turns bluish and then click.

   • In Layout, if any cell is already selected, click anywhere outside of the table to deselect all cells, press the Shift key as you point to the row from the left edge, and click.

2. In the Cell tab — not the Row tab — of the Inspector choose a vertical and/or horizontal alignment for the selected row. If, upon taking the issues into account, you want to use the Row tab to align the entire row, you can select the row as in Step 1 and then switch to the Row tab of the Table Inspector and choose a vertical and/or horizontal alignment for the selected row.

Adding color

You can add a background color to an entire table, to a row, or to one or more individual cells. Each row or each cell can have its own color. Whether you set a background color for the entire table, a row, or individual cells, the color fills the cells but doesn't affect the border.

Note

If your table or any of the cells are empty when you add the color, the color will not be visible in a browser. This is because empty cells collapse If a cell is to remain empty and you wish the color to appear, place a nonbreaking space in the cell. You can do this by typing Option-spacebar (Mac) or Shift+spacebar (Windows), or by using the contextual menu to select the cell and then again to choose the Insert   command. Don't forget to delete that space if you add content later or you'll be wondering why your alignment is off.

Applying a background color to a table

Table color is supported starting with Internet Explorer 3 and Netscape 4 browsers.

Here are the steps for setting a background color for the table:

1. Select the table by clicking the top-left corner of it.

2. In the Table Inspector, double-click the color swatch to the right of the word "Color." This selects the Color field and opens the Color palette.

3. In the Color palette, choose a color. (Remember, the Web Color List contains the 216 designated Web-safe colors.) As you click a color, the Color option's checkbox becomes checked automatically in the Inspector and the color immediately takes effect in the table. If you're not happy with that color, simply click another one.

 If you have collected your colors in the Color tab of the Site Window, you can select those colors from the site Color List tab.

Applying a background color to a row

Because it is common to identify information within a spreadsheet or table, HTML tables support adding color to a table on a row-by-row basis.

To set a background color for the row, follow these steps:

1. Select the row by doing one of the following:

   • In the Table palette, place your cursor at the left edge of the row pointing to the row so the cursor turns bluish, and then click.

   • In Layout, place your cursor at the left edge of the row and press the Shift key as you point to the row, and then click.

2. In the Table Inspector, switch to the Row tab. (If the Inspector isn't already open, open it.)

3. Click in the color swatch to the right of the word "Color" to select the swatch and open the Color palette.

4. In the Color palette, choose a color. (Remember, the Web Color List contains the 216 designated Web-safe colors.)

 If you have collected your colors in the Color tab of the Site Window, you can select those colors from the site Color List tab.

As you click a color, the Color option's checkbox becomes checked automatically in the Inspector and the color immediately takes effect in the table. If you're not happy with that color, simply click another one.

Applying a background color to a cell or cells

Because it is common to identify information within a spreadsheet or table by color, HTML tables support adding color to a table on a cell-by-cell basis. You can add color to one cell at a time or to many at once.

If you are placing a graphic or some type of media within a cell, a color within that cell can set it off nicely, blend it into the page, or add a nice effect. By placing a table within another one-cell table that has cell padding and a background color, you can create a more complex border for your table.

Note   Cell color is supported starting with the Version 4 browsers, but not in any Version 3 browser.

To set a background color for a cell or cells, follow these steps:

1. Select the cell either by clicking its bottom or right edge, by clicking it in the Table palette, or via the contextual menu.

2. (*Optional*) To select additional cells, press the Shift key as you click the next cell or cells, one at a time, either within the actual table or within the Table Inspector. If you inadvertently select a cell, you can deselect it by repeating the action.

3. In the Table Inspector, switch to the Row tab. (If the Inspector isn't already open, open it.)

4. Click in the color swatch to the right of the word "Color" to select the swatch and open the Color palette.

5. In the Color palette, choose a color. (Remember, the Web Color List contains the 216 designated Web-safe colors.) As you click a color, the Color option's checkbox becomes checked automatically in the Inspector and the color appears in the cell or cells that are selected. If you're not happy with that color, simply click another one.

Note   After a cell has a colored background, you can select that cell by clicking any empty area within the cell. (Clicking a graphic selects the graphic and clicking text positions the text cursor at that location.)

Adding a color border to a table and cell divisions

Border color is only recognized in the newer browsers — and even then it displays differently in each browser, so don't depend on it. But, because people often ask how to apply color to a cell's border, I show you how to do it in GoLive.

An Inspector interface doesn't exist for adding color to a border because it is not HTML 4–standard. However, GoLive recognizes it as a possible attribute, so you can add it in Outline mode.

Tip Because border colors render differently in each browser, they can't be counted on. You have a better way to add a color around a table, and even to control the addition of color between the cell divisions. See the section "Table Tricks" at the end of this chapter to learn about it.

Follow these steps to add color to your table's border:

1. Select the table by clicking its top-left corner when the cursor becomes an Object Selection icon.

2. Switch to Outline mode by clicking the Outline tab at the top of the page window.

   Because the table was selected in Step 1, it is delineated by a black rectangle and should be visible without scrolling.

3. Click the small gray triangle to the right of the word "table," and then choose borderColor from the pop-up menu that appears, as shown in Figure 13-19.

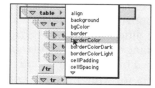

Figure 13-19: To add color to a table's background, choose the borderColor attribute from the table tag's pop-up menu in Outline mode.

The table's attribute list is now open. Because this is a color attribute, a color box appears next to the attribute.

4. Click the box in the Outline mode to open the Color palette.

5. Bring the appropriate color tab forward.

   Remember, only the 216 colors in the Web Color List colors are designated Web-safe. If you have collected your colors in the Color tab of the Site Window, you can select those colors from the site Color List tab.

6. Drag the desired color into the color box, as shown in Figure 13-20.

This color doesn't appear in Layout view. To see the result in Windows, you can switch to Preview mode or preview the page in a browser. Either works because Windows' preview uses the Internet Explorer engine. On the Mac the color will not appear in Layout or Preview mode, so to see the results, preview the page in a browser. The effect of adding a color to a border can be significantly different in each browser.

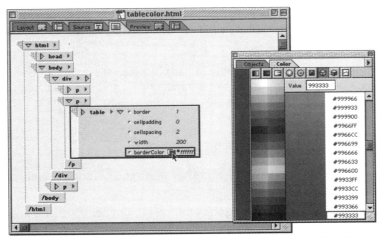

Figure 13-20: Drag a color from the Color palette into the borderColor attribute's Color field to apply that color to a table's border.

Placing an image as a table or cell background

Although not part of the HTML 4.0 specification, it is possible to use an image as a background for a table or cell — if you are willing to take the risk. Netscape 4 and Internet Explorer 4 were the first browsers to support use of an image as a background of a table or cell. But they each support it differently. Internet Explorer 4 will not display a table or table cell background image if the page the table is on also uses a background image. However Netscape 4 browsers do. If you use this effect, be sure to preview it in each of the browsers for which you are concerned about compatibility.

Note | Take care that your table looks right in browsers where the background image does not appear. For example, if you use a text color designed to show up on the image, give the table or cell a background color that somewhat matches the image to ensure that your text will be visible if the image isn't. That way, older browsers and those not loading your image will see the color while the others see the image, and all users can see and read the text.

Another reason to preview this effect is to make sure the image looks good inside the table. Several considerations exist. As with an image used as a page background, an image used as a background for a table or cell will tile if it is smaller than the table or cell. Additionally, if the image is larger than the table or cell, it will be cut off. You also want to make sure the image doesn't clash with the information presented — and that the text will be clearly visible.

Note The ability to set up a table or cell background image in the Inspector is new to GoLive 5. As it is not HTML 4–standard, it was not encouraged visually in earlier versions. Instead, you added it using Outline mode. Although still not HTML-standard, it gained a home in the Inspector by popular request.

Like the table background, an individual cell can also have a background, but you cannot count on the background appearing to all viewers. Again, be sure to preview the results in various browsers.

To add a background image to a table, follow these steps:

1. It is always best to have an image safely placed within the Site Window prior to using it, so begin by dragging the image into the Site Window. If the image file is already there, skip this step. If you're using a Smart Object graphic, the original shouldn't be in the Site Window.

2. Select the table by clicking its top or left edge.

3. In the Table tab of the Table Inspector, check the BgImage option.

4. Select the desired image by using Point and Shoot or browse, or by manually enter the path to the file. (This is a link to an image, just like any other.)

Here's how to add a background image to a cell:

1. Select the cell.

2. In the Cell tab of the Table Inspector, check the BgImage option.

3. Select the desired image by using Point and Shoot or browse, or by manually enter the path to the image file. (This is a regular image link.)

If nothing exists in any the cell that contains the background, the background won't appear in Layout mode. This is a good reminder that the cell will collapse so its background won't appear in a browser. Add your content in order to see the background. If the cells will remain empty, add a nonbreaking space. To type this invisible character, press Option (Mac) or Shift (Windows) as you type a space in the cell. (Or, you can point to the cell as you call up the contextual menu and choose Select Cell, and then call the contextual menu again and choose Insert   from the menu.)

Creating a caption for your table

It is often helpful to have an explanation of what your table represents or presents. While you can add introductory text on any line above or below the table, including a caption is more elegant. The caption becomes part of your table, so it will move along with your table if you move the table and will not become separated by text size differences.

Although attached to the table, in every other way a caption is just like other text. You can do anything to a caption that you can do to other text. Actually, you can even add graphics to a caption area.

To add a caption to your table, follow these steps:

1. Select the table.

2. In the Table tab of the Table Inspector, check the Caption option. (Open the Inspector if it's not already open.) A black outline appears around your table. This outline includes extra space at the top of your table, running across the entire table width, as shown in Figure 13-21.

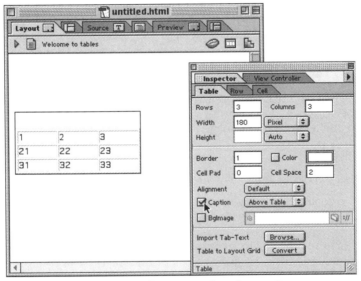

Figure 13-21: When you choose Caption, the caption area appears at the top of your table; you can choose to place the table's caption below the table instead.

3. *(Optional)* If you prefer your caption to appear below the table instead of above it, choose Below Table from the pop-up menu now available beside the Caption option.

4. Click within the caption area and type your caption, as in Figure 13-22.

When you enter the caption area, the Inspector turns into the Text Inspector. Any time you select the table again, it becomes the Table Inspector again so you can switch the caption's position or make other adjustments to the table.

You can align your caption using the Text toolbar, and format it there too. (Or, you can use a style sheet to add formatting. The tag for a caption is simply `<caption>...</caption>`, as you can see in the Source Code window.)

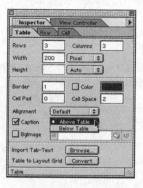

Figure 13-22: Captions are just like any text. Simply type as you please.

Adding a caption doesn't affect the way you select a table—you still move your cursor to the top-left corner of the cells, wait until your cursor becomes a hand, and then click. However, the dark line around the table no longer appears to show you the table is selected. Use the Inspector as your cue by seeing that it turns into the Table Inspector.

Applying Table Styles

With GoLive 5's new Table Styles feature, you can format the look of your table in three easy clicks. You can choose from the styles that come with GoLive, or you can create your own style to use again later.

Applying a style

To apply an existing style to a table, follow these steps:

1. Select the table by clicking the left or top border of the table.
2. Open the Table palette (Window ➪ Table) and then bring the Style tab forward.
3. Select a style by name from the pop-up style list at the top of the palette.

   A sample of the style appears in the palette. If you're not happy with that look, choose another until you see something you'd like to try.
4. Click Apply.

If you decide not to use a style after seeing how it looks on your table, you can apply a new style, revert back to what you have prior to adding the style, or clear your table of all styles, as follows:

✦ To choose another style, first remove the previously applied style by choosing Edit ➪ Undo or using the History palette. This ensures that none of the former style's code is left in your page. Then choose the new style from the from the pop-up style list at the top of the Table palette.

✦ To safely remove the newly applied style, reverting back to your former table formatting, choose Edit ➪ Undo or use the History palette.

✦ To remove *all* styling from the table click the Clear button in the Table palette. However, if you had your own styling prior to trying the Style palette's style, your own formatting will be gone.

Creating a style

After you create a table and get the style just right, you can save the style for use again and again in any site. Table styles are stored in a file called styles.xml. It is located in the GoLive application folder. GoLive ➪ Modules ➪ Table Styles. You can share your styles between computers by sharing this file. And, if you want to back up your styles, this is the document to back up.

Here's how to create a new style:

1. Select the table whose styling you wish to capture and reuse.

2. Open the Table palette (Window ➪ Table) to the Style tab.

3. In the Table palette, enter a name for your new style in the field at the bottom of the palette.

4. Click the Capture button.

Your new style becomes an option in the style pop-up menu.

Doing Page Formatting Tricks

Here are a few creative ways to use tables on your page.

Togetherness

To ensure that an image will always be aligned side by side with text, create a one-row, two-column table. Then place the image in one cell and the text in the other. By default, a row of cells will always grow tall enough to accommodate the contents of the cell that contains the tallest content.

Tip

Practice good table manners: life is nicer when your tables can get along with all the nice browsers out there. In theory, you can place a second table within every single cell of a table or place a table within a table's cell, within another table's cell, and so on down the line. However, the more complicated your tables become, the harder the browser has to work to display the table and the more the chances for errors.

Two tables cannot be placed side by side; tables each get their own line due to the way HTML works. But one trick lets you place two tables side by side. Make the two tables, but also make a third that is one row by two columns. Then place each of the two tables in one of the third table's cells. Set the border on the third table to 0 so it isn't visible. Again, that third table is simply an alignment container.

Be a cut-up

Cut an image up and use table cells to hold the pieces. Does that sound crazy? Why slice an image if you're just going to put it back together? Because it enables you to use different image or media types within an otherwise single image. Because it helps you mix text and graphics. Because it enables you to have various rollover buttons. As you get familiar with the Web, you may discover many tricks you can perform this way.

Keep a close eye on graphics as they load and you'll see what I mean. You'll notice that some images load in small sections as if the overall image were sliced up. And if you look at the source code, you'll probably find the slices are being held together in a table. For example, at www.magicbobweiss.com, the photo of Magic Bob Weiss doing a fire trick is actually part JPG (because it's a photo and I wanted Bob to look good) and part animated GIF. I sliced it and used ImageReady to animate the flame.

Cross-Reference

To learn about placing a sliced image, see Chapter 10.

Framing

Rather than rely on the table color attribute, which looks very different in each browser, try this simple and reliable trick. Create your table, add all the contents, and size it as you want it to appear—but don't use a border. Create a second table above or below the first table and make it one row by one column. Keep its size set to Auto and, for starters, keep its border at 1 and its padding at 0, but change the cell spacing to 0. Fill this table's single cell with the color you want for the border and division color of the first table. Optionally, drag a Comment icon from the Objects palette to this single-cell table so it can act as a divider between tables while you're working in GoLive's Layout mode. Then, drag the first table into the second table. The cell spacing in the inner table becomes filled with the color of the outer table's cell color.

Now both tables can be fine-tuned. Add padding to the inner table to set your text and graphics off. Add or decrease cell spacing to adjust the amount of color between the cells.

Adjust the outer table's cell padding as desired — the padding adds the background color all around the inner table. When all else is complete, fine-tune the outer table border as desired. It's best to leave this for last because if you set the outer table border to 0, it becomes harder to select the inside table (unless you use the optional Comment icon tip). For a 3D look, widen it. You can set the outside table's border color to match the inside color, but remember that the color table border can't be counted upon to render as you want it.

Centering

If you absolutely always want everything on your page to be 100 percent centered in the user's browser no matter how large or small that browser window might become, take advantage of centering and percentages.

Make a one-cell table (1×1) with no border and set it to 100 percent high and 100 percent wide. You can add cell padding to keep the page's elements from going too close to the edge. Then, either create your entire page layout within the cell or create your page in another page, and then drag it in. Use Edit ➪ Select All to select everything within the cell, and then click the Center Align button on the toolbar. This aligns the entire cell's contents in the center of the cell — and the cell is always 100 percent of the browser's width. You don't have to align top to bottom because everything inside a cell is aligned in the middle by default.

✦   ✦   ✦

Creating Reusable Components, Items, and Text

Part of good design in a multipage print publication is consistency, and the same is true on the Web. In order to have your guests recognize a page as part of your site, a consistent logo, masthead, or navigation system is important. Actually, on the Web the logo, masthead, and navigation system may well be one and the same. You already know that you can create a graphic once, reuse it in many places across many pages, and still be able to replace it with one simple Point and Shoot to a replacement graphic. But what about an area of your page, such as a masthead or navigation bar, that comprises several elements (of any sort)? That's where *components* come in. Components are GoLive's unique way of enabling you to compose an entire area of elements and then place it on several pages. Plus, you can update any part of this area across all pages just by changing it in one place. That's power!

Whether you're designing a rough prototype for a client or a polished final version of your own site, components add ease and flexibility. The one thing constant (so far) about the Web is that nothing remains constant. You're bound to want to add or remove pages from your site, update your logo, or reword something. In print you simply skip the desire to do so because it's so time-consuming or costly. With GoLive and the Web, you just double-click your component on any page in which it's contained, make the change once, save, and the change is in effect on every page that contains the same component. When you add a new page, it's a cinch to add the new link within the component. Need to change your masthead? You can add or remove an element, change the text, move things around . . . and save—just once, and the whole site is changed.

Components are always an excellent choice for navigation bars, whether at the top, bottom, or side of the page. If you have a header or footer you place on all or many pages, making it a component will also be a great time-saver. If your logo consists of more than one graphic, consider using a component for that, too. After you experiment with components a bit, you're bound to find creative uses for them. The more you incorporate your page design into components, the more flexible the design may become. (Did I tell you yet that you can have several separate components on one page?)

In addition to components (the most powerful, dynamic way to share your efforts across pages), you have many other ways to reuse you work after you create something. The Custom Items tab of the Objects palette enables you to store any object or collection of objects, such as a populated table or a grid, and then place the object or objects on any other page simply by dragging. The Custom tab of the Site Window lets you drag text off your page after you enter it and then drag it back onto any other page within your site. (You can also share it between sites.) Last but not least, GoLive are Text Macros — entire strings of code you create and then call into your page's code just by typing the shortcut you assign. In this chapter, I show you how to create and use all of these features. First, components, and then custom items and custom text, and finally text macros.

Creating a Component

You create, and later edit, a component just like you create any other page using GoLive. Almost anything you do to a page or add to a page anywhere else can be added to a component. A few things should not go into a component. I address these shortly. You can begin a component with a new blank page, or you can turn an existing page into a component.

It may seem confusing to start an entire page for a component when you are only creating a part of a page. However, that's how it's done. You'll need to use your imagination a bit to visualize how the component will look within the context of a page. After you create the component page, it remains a separate page (with some tags removed) listed in the Files tab of the Site Window. To incorporate the component page into a page, add a component placeholder and then link to the component. However, the contents of a component are not really linked to the page in the same way another page or a graphic is. Pages and graphics remain separate entities that must be copied to a Web server in order to be used, whereas components are physically written into the HTML code of a page. When you make a change to a component, GoLive rewrites the part of each page that contains the component. You'll notice this when you use the upload feature to have GoLive automatically upload all files that have changed; all pages that contain the component will be re uploaded even though you didn't open each of those pages to alter them.

Note In case you're wondering how a component works, GoLive adds a custom tag—`<csobj>` and `</csobj>`—to the HTML of the page in which the component is inserted. When a browser comes across a tag it doesn't recognize, it simply ignores the tag. Only GoLive knows that this tag means to be on the lookout for something that may change and need GoLive's diligent updating. Anything you put in the body of your component's page is placed within those tags. If you've placed a background color or background image into the component, GoLive ignores it, using only the background color or background image of the encompassing page. Actions and styles that you put in the component's page are put into the head section of the encompassing document. A special ID mechanism enables a component with dynamic elements to appear multiple times on a page.

Component considerations

When considering the items you place in the component, remember that although the component becomes incorporated into another page, it is a separate document within the Site Window. Therefore, you might think of adding some elements that might not be appropriate for your component; they can be added and will function—just maybe not the way you want them to.

The Modified Date Smart Object is a good example of this. It's nice to let readers know the last date and time your page was modified so that GoLive provides a Smart Object to make that easy. When you add the Modified Date Smart Object to your page, each time you save the page GoLive writes in the date and/or time it was saved. If you place this Smart Object in a component, the date and/or time is written each time you change the component. Therefore, if you don't want to count changes to the component's contents as a change to every page the component is in, place your date and time Smart Object on each page instead of in the component. (No other Smart Objects need this consideration, although the Head Action and Browser Switch fall under the don't-use-head-items-in-a-component rule, which follows in the next section, "Head Actions in Components.")

Head Actions in components

Because you create a component the same way you create any other page in GoLive, you can *physically* put any Head Action item into a component. However, this is not always appropriate and should sometimes be avoided. When a component is incorporated into a page, the Head Action items are moved from the component's page into the encompassing page. This means that if the main page already contains the same action in its head, your action may occur twice.

If you want an action to control a page, put it in the main page. If you're creating a component from scratch, don't add page-level Head Actions. If you're converting a page you've already created, simply remove the page-level Head Actions you may have placed. Two Smart Objects, the Head Action and Browser Switch, are page-level Actions.

A Head Action that preloads an image is a different story. That's a Head Action that makes sense to use in a component because it controls an item specifically within the component and is only added to the containing page after the component is inserted. That action would not already be within the encompassing page, so it is not going to be repeated. In addition, because it refers to one item specifically within the component-added page, no chance exists of it adding conflicting instructions.

Rollovers in components

The question of using rollovers in components often comes up, so it deserves addressing and understanding. You can definitely use rollovers in a component, whether you create them using the Rollover icon from the Smart tab in the Objects palette or whether you create them using the Actions tab of the Inspector. (In fact, you can use any JavaScript that is provided by the Objects palette or Actions tab.) GoLive handles this by putting the JavaScript for the rollovers into an external document. That way, the JavaScript is not lost when the component is incorporated into another page.

Here's how it works: When you create a component, GoLive automatically creates an extra document called CCScriptLib.js and places the extra document in a folder in your Files tab. GoLive calls the folder GeneratedItems. You can see the preference for this set itself when you click the Components button in the Page Inspector. When you upload your site to the Web server, you also upload this folder and document. (For the complete lowdown on Actions, see Chapter 18.)

It is also possible (and easy) to create rollovers in ImageReady and then to use those rollovers in a GoLive component. With ImageReady 2.x the preferences can be set to write its rollovers as GoLive code when you use the option File ➪ Save Optimized As and click the HTML Options button. In the bottom-right corner is a pop-up menu labeled "Code:ImageReady." You can change that to "Code:GoLive." Click OK and make sure that you select the Save HTML File option, as well as the Save Images option. Keep that preference setting and then save your file directly into your GoLive site folder. After doing so, open the Site Window, click the Files tab, and then click the Update button (checkmark) on the toolbar. (If you've created your rollovers in ImageReady 1.0, I recommend that you bring the rollovers into Version 2 and redo them.)

Creating a component from scratch

To create a component by beginning with a blank page, follow these steps:

1. Choose File ➪ New to start a new page.

   Because the component page is just used as part of a "real" page and, therefore, doesn't link to other pages on a unique one-to-one basis, beginning the page within the Site tab of the Site Window doesn't have any benefit. In the last step the page will safely be saved to the Site Window.

2. Open the Page Inspector.

- With the Inspector open, click the Page icon at the top-left corner of the page.

- With the Inspector open, press Tab.

- Point anywhere in the content area of the page, Control-click (Mac) or right-click (Windows), and choose Document ⇨ Page Properties.

- Point to the Page icon on the page, Control-click (Mac) or right-click (Windows), and choose Page Properties.

3. In the Page Inspector, go to the HTML tab and then click the Component button at the bottom of the Inspector, as shown in Figure 14-1. In the tab you may see the JavaScript Functions radio button change from "Write Code into page" to Import GoLive Script Library. The rest of the work is done invisibly.

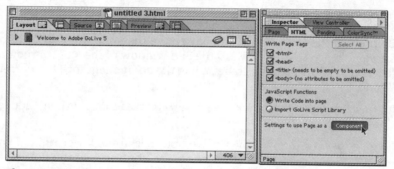

Figure 14-1: The Components button is the first step to turning a page into a component.

4. Design your page, adding the grid, text, graphics, or such, as desired.

As mentioned before, a component can contain almost anything a regular page permits. However, because the component becomes a section of a page, only items in the body of the page will be seen or used when the component is incorporated into the encompassing page. Anything in the head of the page won't be recognized, as that page will already have its own head section. The other things that won't be recognized when the component is put on a page are the text and link colors if you set those colors in the Page Inspector. All text without in-line style attributes takes on the coloring of the incorporating page. Notice the example navigation page shown in Figure 14-2.

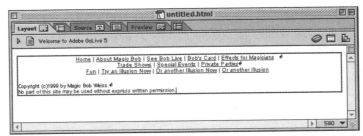

Figure 14-2: A page created to become a component. No page title or background color is necessary.

Tip

To see for yourself whether something is part of the head tag, open the Source Code window (Window ➪ Source Code).

5. Select File ➪ Save to open the Save dialog box.

Before you start the save, if you have more than one site (Site Window) open for some reason, bring forward the Site Window of the site this component is for. That way, you're sure to be saving the component into the correct Site Window.

6. In the Save dialog box, click the pop-up GoLive icon and then choose Components.

If you're using Windows, the GoLive button is at the lower right. If you are on a Mac and have Navigation Services on, the button is at the bottom-right corner; but if you have Navigation Services turned off, the GoLive button is at the top-right corner. In either case, the pop-up menu looks like the one shown in Figure 14-3. You are taken directly to the Components folder for the site you are currently working on.

GoLive icon button

Figure 14-3: The GoLive icon is a pop-up button; click it to save your creation directly to the Components folder for use in your site. (Mac with Navigation Services off.)

7. Give the component a descriptive name to help you identify it for use later. (The Save dialog box looks something like Figure 14-4.) Then click Save.

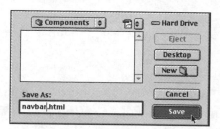

Figure 14-4: Give the component a descriptive name and save it to the Components folder that belongs to your site.

The component appears in the Components folder in the right pane of the Site Window. It may take a moment for it to appear. Figure 14-5 shows a component in the Components folder.

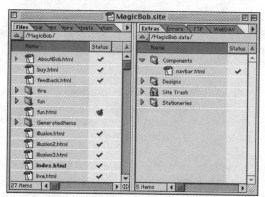

Figure 14-5: The component's file is stored in the Components folder in the Site Window.

That's all there is to creating a dynamic component. After you create it the next step is to add it to your pages, as covered in "Placing a Component on Your Page," later in this chapter.

Creating a component from an existing page

As I said, you can also turn an existing page into a component. The process is similar to the process of creating a component from scratch, except you have to drag the page into the Components folder within the Site Window.

To turn an existing page into a component, follow these steps:

1. Open the page that you wish to turn into a component.

2. Open the Page Inspector:

   • With the Inspector open, click the Page icon at the top-left corner of the page.

   • With the Inspector open, press Tab.

   • Choose Document ⇨ Page Properties from the contextual menu.

3. In the Page Inspector, click the HTML tab and then click the Component button at the bottom of the Inspector.

4. Save the page.

5. Drag the page from the Files tab of the Site Window into the Components folder (in the right Site Window pane).

   GoLive automatically saves this change to the site.

Note Another alternative is to do a Save As, which makes a new copy of your page as a component while leaving the original in place. However, this alternative leaves the original page you designed it on sitting in your Files tab, which is probably unnecessary and may be confusing.

After you create a component it not only appears in the Components folder in the Site Window but also in the Site Extras tab of the Palette when you select Components from the pop-up menu at the bottom-right corner of the Palette. GoLive should render a custom icon to represent your component with the Palette.

Tip If you see a generic GoLive page icon instead of the custom component icon, you can convince GoLive to create the custom icon by making any small change to the component and saving the change. See the "Editing a Component" section later in this chapter. Of course you don't have to keep the change you make. You can simply nudge a graphic one pixel and then nudge it back, or type a space and then delete the space. The trick is getting GoLive to rewrite the file.

You can also turn an existing page into a component by doing a Save As and following the same steps outlined previously under the section, "Creating a component from scratch." This leaves your original working component page within the Files tab as a regular page, though, so don't let that confuse you.

Placing a Component on Your Page

With GoLive you can place a component using Point and Shoot or using drag and drop. Each method is described in this section.

To place a component you must have already created it, of course. The component can be open or closed, but the page into which you add the component must be open.

Using Point and Shoot

To place a component on a page using GoLive's Point and Shoot feature, follow these steps:

1. Open the page into which you want to place the component (if it's not already open).

2. Open the Inspector and click the Smart Objects tab. From there, drag the Components icon (see Figure 14-6) into place on your page.

Smart Objects tab

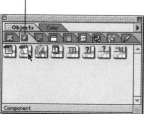

Figure 14-6: The Component placeholder in the Smart Objects tab of the Objects palette

The component icon appears on your page as a rectangle with a green triangle at the top-left corner, as shown in Figure 14-7. It is selected and ready to be work with. Don't resize it; it automatically accommodates the component. (If placing the component on a grid, you *may* have to resize it manually later to reveal the entire component, but not now.) Meanwhile, the Inspector becomes the Component Inspector.

3. If the right pane of the Site Window isn't open, click the double-headed arrow at the bottom-right corner of the screen in order to open the Site Window; then click the Extras tab to bring the Site Window forward.

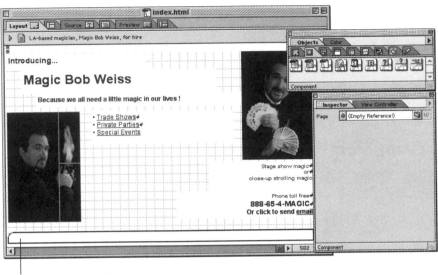

Component placeholder

Figure 14-7: The Component placeholder awaits linking to a component within the Components folder of the Site Window.

4. In the Component Inspector, drag the Point and Shoot icon over to the Component in the right pane of the Site Window. (This is just like Pointing and Shooting to any other file, except that the destination is in the right Site Window pane instead of in the Files tab.)

   • If the Site Window is hidden behind the page, pause the cursor a moment while dragging over the Select Window button to bring it in front of the page.

   • *(Mac)* If the Site Window is tabbed at the bottom of your screen, click the tab to open it back up.

   • *(Windows)* If the Site Window is minimized, click it to open it back up before Pointing and Shooting.

   • If the Components folder is not already open, pause the pointer over the folder until it opens and then continue to Point and Shoot.

If you prefer not to use Point and Shoot, you can click the Browse button, navigate to the Component file within your site's folder, and then select it. (Be sure you're selecting a component from the current site's folder.) When your Site Window is loaded with stuff or your screen is cluttered, you may prefer this method.

After you select the component file, its name and path appear in the Component Inspector's URL area. On the page, the component holder resizes to perfectly accommodate the component. After the component is placed on your page, you can reposition it as with any object.

Using drag and drop

To drag and drop a component onto your page follow these steps:

1. In the Objects palette, choose the Site Extras tab, click the pop-up menu at the bottom-right corner of the Objects palette, and then select Components.

   Any components you've already created for this site appear in this palette. You can identify the components by name by moving your mouse over each component. The component's name appears at the bottom-left corner of the palette. Additionally, each component should have a custom icon so that you can easily identify it. If the component doesn't have a custom icon, you can cajole GoLive into creating the icon by modifying and saving the component. See the "Editing a Component" section later in this chapter.

2. Drag the desired component from the Objects palette into place on your page, as shown in Figure 14-8. In Windows, it appears in place surrounded by a solid border. On a Mac, it appears in place surrounded by a wide dotted border, as shown in Figure 14-9. You can reposition a component at any time, the same way you move any other object around on a page.

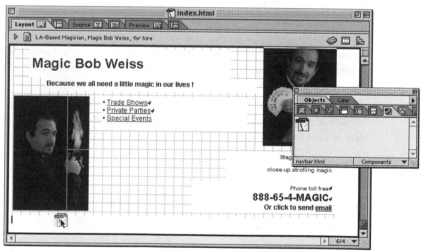

Figure 14-8: You can add a component to your page simply by dragging it from the Site Extras tab of the Palette into place on the page.

Note

If your component is on a layout grid, you may have to resize it manually in order to reveal the entire component.

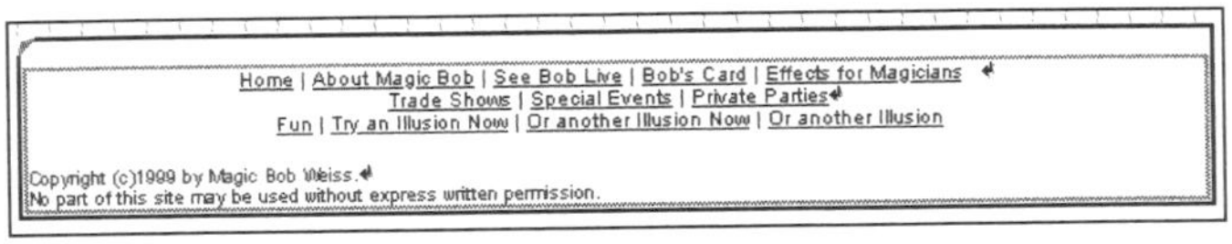

Figure 14-9: A component in place on a page. A dotted gray line around it and a green triangle at the top-left corner identify the area as a component on the page.

Editing a Component

The whole reason for using dynamic components is because you can change them easily. You can change a component either by opening it from the Site Window or by calling it up from any page on which it appears. When you save a change to any embedded component, all pages that contain it are automatically updated to reflect the change.

To make a change to any element within a component, follow these steps:

1. Do one of the following:

   • If you are working on a page that contains the component and notice something you'd like to change, double-click any place within the component area. You can even double-click a graphic. The graphic won't open in its native or other application as normal because it is not really on that page — it's on the component page.

   • If you realize you'd like to change the component but aren't in a page on which it appears, you can open the Components folder and double-click the actual component file.

   Either way, the component page opens just like any other page.

2. Edit the component page the same way you'd edit any page in your site.

3. Save the page using File ⇨ Save or an equivalent keyboard shortcut.

   If you forget to save and try to close the page it will ask you to save just like any normal page.

4. The Updating Component dialog box appears with a list of all pages that contain the component, as shown in Figure 14-10. Click OK. Next, you'll see the Update Progress dialog box, so you know what's going on.

   If GoLive does not ask you to let it perform the update and you know the component is used within your site, you can manually tell it to do the job by pressing Option (Mac) or Ctrl (Windows) and then choosing Site ⇨ Reparse All. After a moment, the Parse dialog box appears to show you the progress.

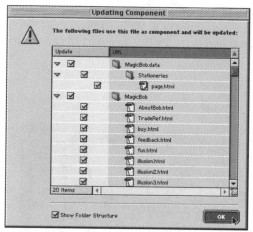

Figure 14-10: The Update dialog box shows you which pages will be updated to reflect your change. (This image shows Mac OS 8.6 with Navigation Services turned on.)

GoLive provides the capability to actually open a page after it is on your server and to edit that page. However, you can *only* update components and their files while they are on your hard drive. After you make a change to a component and let GoLive perform the update, you need to re-upload all of the updated pages to the server. (See Chapter 27 to learn about uploading your pages to a server.)

Switching a Component

You can substitute one component for another exactly the same way you substitute any page or graphic. You can also change the component out for a noncomponent file, but, of course, noncomponent file won't have the flexibility that the component had.

The only thing to be careful about when switching components is the size of the new component or replacement item. Substituting a new file of a different dimension may shift several items around on any given page.

And, of course, you have to have the replacement file in existence before you can substitute it. Note that you don't have to have any component-containing page open to do this.

To switch a component on all of its pages at once, follow these steps:

1. Open the Components folder of the Site Window and click once the component you want to replace in order to select it.

2. Open the In & Out Links window (Window ⇨ In & Out Links), which is shown in Figure 14-11. The component file appears in the middle of the Link Inspector between the pages that use it and the files that are part of the component.

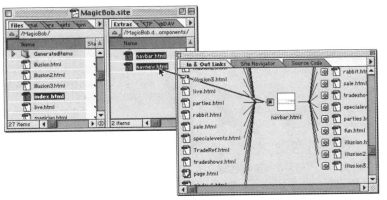

Figure 14-11: Using Point and Shoot from the In & Out Links view to switch one component with another

3. Drag the old component's Point and Shoot button to the file you wish to use as a replacement.

4. After you select the new component, the Updating Component dialog box asks for permission to update all pages that contain the component. Chances are, you want this, so click OK.

To switch a component in a single page, follow these steps:

1. Open the page on which you want to replace the component (if it's not already open).

2. Move your mouse over any edge of the component to select it.

3. Open the Inspector, now the Component Inspector, and Point and Shoot to the new component within the Components folder of the Extras tab in the Site Window.

   Alternatively, use the Browse button and then navigate to the component file and choose it. (Be sure you're selecting a component from the current site's folder.)

Note

You cannot replace an existing component by dragging a second component from the Objects palette onto the first component. That just places the second component on the page along with the original.

Deleting a Component

All in all, a component is simply another object on a page. To delete it, select it and press Backspace/Delete. Deleting a component from a page doesn't delete it from any other page or from the Site Window. It is still there for the other pages and for use again anywhere.

If you decide you are never going to use a component, you can remove it from the Site Window the same way you delete any file. To do so, open the Components folder in the Site Window and click the component file once to select it. Then click the Trash button on the toolbar. This moves the component to the Site Trash, unless you've changed the default preference. You might want to let it hang out in the Site Trash in case you change your mind. Otherwise, to remove it completely, open the Site Trash, select the file, and click the Trash icon on the toolbar again. (If you've changed the Trash settings in the Site panel in Preferences, the file is moved to the computer's real trash the first time you click the Trash button.)

Using Custom Objects and Snippets

Besides components, GoLive provides another way to reuse items after you've created them—just store them on the Customs tab. Two Custom tabs exist, one in the Palette and one in the Site Window (new to GoLive 5). These Custom tabs are simply an easy way to store your items for convenient reuse without having to locate and open the page on which you created the item. This works for any element, such as a table or a table full of content, a grid or a grid full of information, or a block of text. (A button comprised of rollovers can also be stored, but links to graphics become buggy and require some extra attention.) You can make these items available in every site on your computer by storing them in the Objects palette, or you can make them available only within a specific site by storing them in the Site Window. Items stored in the Objects palette are called "Custom Objects." Items stored in the Site Window are called "Custom Snippets."

The Custom tabs are particularly useful when you have an intricate item that you'll want to use in basic form again and again, but you need each instance to be just a bit different. Unlike components, each time you place an item from one of the Custom tabs, it becomes an independent element. Changing the item on one page does not affect the other pages it is on.

Actually, the Custom tabs—particularly the tab in the Objects palette—are even very helpful in the creation of blank objects. For example, say you tend to like tables that are 580 pixels wide, with 2 columns, 3 points of cell spacing, 2 points of cell padding, and a first row column span of 2. You can set up a blank table like this once and drag it to the Custom tab for safekeeping. Then whenever you want a new empty table that is just this configuration (or even close to it), instead of starting with a generic table and changing all the settings over and over again, simply drag your preformatted table from the Custom tab to your page. The same works for presizing a grid. Take advantage of this to store anything you think you may have to repeat.

Tip   The contents of your Objects palette's Custom tab are stored in a file called AGLPalette.dat, which is located in the Modules folder of the application folder. You can back up this tiny file so that you can restore it in case you need to reinstall GoLive. The contents of your Site Window's Custom tab are stored along with your site, so you have nothing extra to back up in order to save them.

Creating Custom Objects

To store an item in the Custom tab of the Site Window, follow these steps:

1. After you have finished designing the element, select it and drag it into the Custom tab of the Objects palette, as shown in Figure 14-12. This tab tends to disappear when you narrow down the palette, so if you don't see the tab, drag the palette's bottom-right corner to the right in order to widen the palette. After the item lands in the Objects palette, GoLive gives it a custom icon to help you identify it.

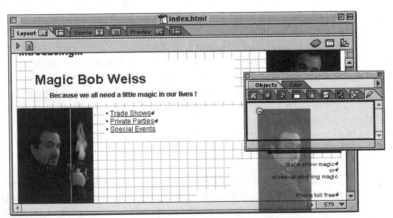

Figure 14-12: Drag an item into the Custom tab for easy reuse later on. This item is a three-cell table containing a sliced image.

2. Name the item to make it easier to identify later. Double-click the object in the palette to open the Object's Palette Item Editor (see Figure 14-13), enter a descriptive name, and click OK. Names can be very long. (I stopped counting at 101 characters.) After you name the item, the width of your Objects palette determines how much of the name you'll see. Whenever you want to use the stored item again, drag it from the Objects palette onto your page.

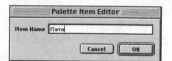

Figure 14-13: To name a Custom Object, double-click the item and then enter a name in the Palette Item Editor.

Caution

When an item stored in the Custom tab contains graphics or other media files, the item is reliant on those original files. If you delete the original graphics and/or media files or remove the site from your hard drive (therefore removing the original graphic), the item remains listed in the Custom tab. However, when you place the item, the graphics or other files that comprise it will be missing.

Using Custom Objects in other sites

Custom Objects stored within the Custom tab of the Objects palette are not only available for the site from which you dragged them. These items are available to you for any site you create with the installed copy of GoLive with which they were created. They will appear in the Objects palette whenever you open any other site or create a new blank site.

On the CD-ROM

You'll find tables and other useful Custom Items on the CD-ROM. They're on a GoLive page waiting for you to drag into your own Objects palette to use in your own sites.

When an item is purely a GoLive-generated object, such as a custom-sized table or grid, it can be used in any other site. However, if the item you store in the Custom tab relies upon a graphic or other media file, you need to know a few details.

When an item is stored in the Custom tab, it is not copied to any special files folder. The original remains in the site from which you created the Custom Object. This is not a problem, but requires an extra step or two. However, if any of the images within the Custom Object are no longer within the originating site, whether you have a problem with the object or not depends upon whether you kept a copy of the original graphic or media file.

To use a custom object in a site other than the one it was created on, follow these steps:

1. Place the Custom Object on your page, as usual, by dragging it from the Custom tab of the Objects palette into place on your page. The item should look exactly as it did when it was first created. If graphic images or other media files are involved, they should be there and functioning normally.

2. Open the right pane of the Site Window by clicking the double-headed arrow in the lower-right corner.

When you place the Custom Object on your page, if it has a placeholder icon instead of the correct image, then files are missing. If your object is something like a Rollover Smart Object, the image on the page may look fine, but the second or third image may be missing. You can tell by looking at the object's Inspector. Or you can check the Errors tab of your Site Window, looking for one of the following conditions:

✦ If no Orphan folder exists, you're finished and all is well.

✦ If you see an Orphan folder, open it and drag the items from this folder into the Files tab. You can put these items in any appropriate folder, such as adding a graphic into the folder that contains your other graphics. This dragging copies the Custom-item-containing files into your current site. That's it. You never have to open the originating site, and because the files are only copied, the originals remain intact in your originating site.

✦ If you see a Missing folder, it may mean that one of the images within your Custom item is missing. Open the folder to see if the missing file is part of this Custom item.) The good news is that this tab tells you the image is missing from the originating site. However, because that file was once copied into that site, not moved to it, you may still have a copy of the original file (from before you ever copied it into the originating site).

If you still have the original file, locate it and drag it into the Files tab (which copies it into the current site). Then select the missing file in the Orphan folder, switch to the Inspector, now called the Error Inspector, and Point and Shoot to the file you just placed in the Files tab. This removes the Missing file from the Missing Files folder and tells GoLive where to find the file it needs.

You can see for yourself the source of a file you've placed on the page by selecting the file and checking the Inspector. For example, a simple graphic or Rollover created from a Smart Object lists the path to the graphic file in the Basic tab.

Tip

Because items stored in the Custom tab are reliant on the original files from which the items were created, it might be best to create a special site just for storage, and you use it to create all of your custom items. That way, you don't have to worry about inadvertently deleting parts of your custom items; you just have to keep this master site on your hard drive. (And be sure to back it up, too.)

Items stored within the Custom tab of the Site Window are only available for the site from which you dragged them. (Anything in the Site Window is stored within that site's folder, not within GoLive's application folders.) However, you can drag any item from one open Site Window to another in order to copy it to another site for use there.

Creating Custom Snippets

Follow these steps to create Custom Snippets:

1. After you have finished designing the element, select it and drag it into the Custom tab of the Site Window. (Remember that you can rest your mouse over

the Site Window or Select Window button to bring the Site Window forward and rest over the Custom tab, if that tab's not already the furthest-forward tab.

The Custom Snippet, called No Name by default, appears in the Site Window, as shown in Figure 14-14. The Content column displays the text content to help you reuse it later.

Figure 14-14: The Custom Snippets as they appear in the Site Window. The top snippet contains new paragraph tags, while the next is simply text, and the third contains text coloring tags.

2. Give the snippet a custom name for easier recognition in the future. Just select the phrase No Name and type your new name.

To reuse a Custom Snippet, just drag it from the Custom tab of the Site Window into place on the page.

You can also view the HTML code behind and a Custom Snippet and even edit it. Select the snippet in the Site Window and then view or edit its code in the Inspector.

Deleting Custom Objects and Custom Snippets

When you place a custom item on your page, it becomes part of the page just like anything else, so a custom item can be deleted the same way you'd delete it if it wasn't added as a custom item.

To remove an item from either the Custom tab of the Objects palette or the Site Window, click the item in the tab and then press Backspace/Delete, click the Trash button on the toolbar, or choose Edit ⇨ Clear (Mac) or Edit ⇨ Delete (Windows).

Using Text Macros

Text macros are a programming feature, designed to make your HTML, JavaScript, or WebObjects programming easier. They eliminate the need to keep retyping intricate strings of code that you'd type repeatedly over any period of time. The only trick is to remember the shortcut you need to type to call the macro into action.

A text macro works in your page's HTML Source Code (both the Source tab and the Source Code window), the JavaScript Editor, and the WebObjects Editor. There's a macro document dedicated to each of these three editors. Unlike anything else in GoLive, though, you don't work within the GoLive visual interface, or any other GoLive interface, to create macros. Instead, you add macros as you would within any text-editing program.

To create a text macro, you actually open and edit a document, stored within the GoLive application folder. Four documents exist there, one for each of the language editors in which they work (HTML, JavaScript, and WebObjects), plus a default macro document for macros that are to be loaded before any language-specific macro.

Introducing text macros

The best way to begin to understand what a text macro is and how it works is to try one, and then see where it comes from. So, before I get to the actual instructions for using or creating a macro, you may want to try this minitutorial.

Because your page's source code may be somewhat familiar to you, try the following HTML macro first. Rather than mess up your hard work, try this in a new page. You won't save this page. It's just a test page. Here are the steps:

1. Open a new blank page using File ⇨ New.

2. Open the Source Code window by choosing Window ⇨ Source Code.

   Alternately, you can click the Source tab for the page, but if you work in that tab when you use text macros for real, you won't see the result in Layout as you work.

3. In the Source Code window, click after the following body tag:

   ```
   <body bgcolor="#ffffff">
   ```

   Then press the Return/Enter key to start a new line.

4. Type **img** and then press ⌘-M (Mac) or Ctrl+M (Windows).

   Notice that this expanded the shortcut, img, into an entire section of code. That code happens to be one of the default macros that GoLive provides for HTML macros. Now, take a look at how this macro looks in the Text Macro document.

5. In your hard drive, open the GoLive application folder, and then the Modules folder, and finally the Macros folder.

6. In the Macros folder, double-click to open the document called, "HTML Source.macro."

Take a look at the last line of the document. Notice that it first contains the same shortcut you typed to trigger the macro. That's the macro's name. Then, after a space, and inside an apostrophe mark, is the same code that the macro shortcut expanded to.

Therein lies the secret of a text macro. You can close both pages now, without saving. And then, if you're game, go on to the next section to learn how to create your own text macros.

Creating text macros

Macro documents are not places to write code, but to store it. First, within the appropriate editor, write the code you wish to reuse. The following steps take it from there for creating a text macro:

1. In GoLive, open the editor that contains the code you wish to reuse. Then select and copy that code.

If you are copying code from elsewhere, instead, locate that code and copy it.

2. Open the Text Macros folder, located within the Modules folder within the GoLive application folder on your hard drive (GoLive folder ⇨ Modules folder ⇨ Macros folder).

3. Double-click to open the document that reflects the macro you're creating.

- For an HTML-creating macro that works in the Source tab and the Source Code window, open the HTML Source.macro document.

- For a macro to use when writing JavaScript, open the JavaScript Source.macro.

- For a macro to use when writing WebObjects, open the WebObject Source.macro.

- Open the Default.macro for macros you will want to use in any language editor.

4. Press Enter/Return after the last macro to start a new line.

5. Enter a name for your macro.

This name is the text you'll type inside the editor as the first part of the macro trigger. (The second part is Ctrl+M [Windows] or ⌘-M [Mac].)

The name can consist of any combination of letters and numbers. Other characters are sometimes used in the programming code and can cause confusion within the editor.

6. Type a space after the name.

7. Type a single quotation mark to mark the beginning of the macro contents.

The quotation mark is the *delimiter* character that tells the macro to begin. Actually, the delimiter could also be something like double angled brackets (<<) or a quotation mark ("). But because the default macros in the document use the single quotation mark, I also suggested it.

8. Paste the code you copied from the editor (in Step 1).

9. Type another single quotation mark to mark the end of the macro contents.

This quotation mark is the closing *delimiter* character that tells the macro to finish typing. The closing delimiter must match the opening delimiter, so if you used double angled brackets (<<), you need to use the other part of that pair (>>) now. The same goes for the quotation mark ("), which needs a closing quotation mark (") here.

10. Save and close the macro document.

Your text macro is ready to test and use.

Using a text macro

You place a text macro's code into the desired editor, just like in the minitutorial.

To place your text macro's code into HTML source code, follow these steps:

1. Open the editor you want to place the code within.

The editor you use can be either of the Source Code views GoLive gives your for hand-entering HTML, or it can be the JavaScript Editor or the WebObjects Editor.

2. Type the shortcut assigned to the desired macro — the macro name.

The shortcut appears in the editor.

3. Press ⌘-M (Mac) or Ctrl+M (Windows).

The shortcut disappears and is replaced by the macro's text.

Remember, the macro's name is case sensitive. If the macro is called AS, then typing "as" or "As" won't trigger its insertion.

Real Life Uses of Text Macros

By Ken Martin, digitalcyclone.com

It's hard to talk yourself into spending those extra few minutes setting up a macro—it often seems easier to just type—but macros have helpful uses. If you use PHP, JSP, Cold Fusion, Lasso, or some other language in your pages, you'll find that things need to be written in a very specific way (just ask anyone who's had to chase down a missing single quotation mark). Using macros can give you a perfect framework with which to build your code.

For example, as I've been learning to code JSP, I've saved my "HTML Source.macro" file to look something like the following:

```
; HTML macros

Selection = @

DEC          '<%! @String s = ""@; %>'
EXP          '<%= @x@ %>'
SCR          '<% @SCRIPTLET@; %>'
TERT         '<% @TEST@ ? TRUE : FALSE; %>'
FULLIF    '<% if (@TEST@) { %>
RESULT_TRUE
<% } else { %>
RESULT_FALSE
<% } %>'
```

Now, by going into source (or the Source Code palette), typing **FULLIF** (or **fullif** in the Source Code palette), and then pressing ⌘-M, I get a complete and properly structured JSP if-else scriptlet. (Notice that the macro can span multiple lines.) TEST, RESULT_TRUE, and RESULT_FALSE describe what needs to be entered by me, and TEST is highlighted so that I can quickly enter this conditional's test. This is really nice when you're just learning.

Using Lasso? Have code that you're tired of typing over and over? How about trying this:

```
CURDATE   ~[Date_Format:(Date_GetCurrentDate),
DateFormat='@%m/%d/%Y@']~
EN        ~EncodeNone~
FP        ~Form_Param:'NAME',$EN$~
INLINE    ~[Inline: search,
database='@THE_DB@',
layout='THE_LAYOUT',
FIELD='($FP$)']~
```

How do you keep track of all these little macros? First, try to name them something you consider useful or logical (perhaps something you'd type anyway, such as "inline"). Second, and terribly low-tech, just print the "HTML Source.macro" file and pin it up somewhere nearby. Having this printout hanging conveniently nearby is not just a simple reference, it's also a great tool to help learn both the macros and the actual code!

Nesting text macros

There's a peculiar quirk in GoLive's handling of nested text macros that you need to be aware of. If, instead of the results you expected, you're ending up with the name of a macro inserted rather than its contents, you've probably created a *circular reference*. A circular reference results when an attempt to call a macro from within another macro would lead the program process to go back to an earlier part, thus, creating an endless loop. GoLive handles circular references by halting macro processing and inserting the name of the macro that contains the circular reference.

✦   ✦   ✦

Designing Your Page with Frames

Normally, when a user clicks a link within your site, he or she is taken to an entirely new page. That new page loads into the browser, drawing the new page in its entirety. This means that elements, such as buttons, that appear on every page of your site, are redrawn on each page. (If they are graphics and are cached to the user's hard drive, they don't have to download again, but they still reload into the new page.) The alternative to this behavior is to present the user with multiple pages so that one page remains loaded and only the changing content has to load. This set-up is based on frames, which are the focus of this chapter.

Frames enable you to display a group of completely independent, separate Web pages, all within one browser window at the same time. Each frame can have its own colors, backgrounds, images, links, and more. Frames can either be separated from other frames by thin borders, or be "frameless," which means the border lines are hidden. Each frame can have a scrollbar to enable users to scroll through the frame's contents, or it can appear without a scrollbar, giving a more frameless look to the page.

While frames provide some excellent convenience, they also present some downsides that must be considered. One downside is that the content page can't reliably be bookmarked; the menu command correctly bookmarks only the URL to the main (frameset) page. If the user creates a bookmark using a contextual menu, the bookmark captures the page within the frame, not the frameset it should be presented within. Actually, that's not a downside for everyone; some consider this good because it forces visitors to always come to the home page.

Scrollbars represent another downside. If they are not handled well, they can break up the continuity of the page. For example, because users can easily enlarge the size of their text on your page, critical content can be cut off without scrollbars. But if you enable scrollbars to appear as needed, the unified look of your page is cut by them.

Note Frames were first supported in Netscape 2, but not with all attributes, and then became fully supported in Version 3. Internet Explorer began its support with Version 3. Consequently, no frame support exists in Netscape Navigator 1, Internet Explorer 2, and some of the more exotic browsers and text-only browsers such as Lynx.

Some site creators avoid frames because they're hard to code correctly in HTML. Of course, that's not an issue when you're designing with GoLive. GoLive takes a lot of the pain and potential problems out of creating pages using frames. You simply drag one of several framesets from the Objects palette, and then just Point and Shoot from each frame section to the page you wish to display within each frame. In one easy-to-use visual layout, you can link a page into a frame, see how it looks, and then set up borders, scrolling and resizing, and resize the frame as desired. No guesswork. With GoLive, you can focus on whether frames serve a purpose for you, and weigh the pros and cons of using frames. The coding difficulty that turns some people away from frames is not an issue.

Introducing Frames

When you hear the word *frame* do you think of a picture frame creating a container for a picture (or one that holds multiple pictures), the framework that holds up a house and divides it into rooms, or a window frame that contains individual panes? Each makes a good analogy to explain frames in Web pages. In each case a framework has been created to hold contents. The same is true with a Web page. A page that uses frames begins with a *frameset,* a simple HTML page, that defines each of the sections. The frameset then calls for, and displays, the page that you assign to it. That's where any of the analogies end though, because in the Web situation, the contents of any frame can be changed independently of the other sections in the frameset.

The frameset is the page that actually contains the frames. This is the page that you tell users to call up in their browsers (in other words, it's the URL you hand out to have visitors initially arrive at your site). When you set up this page, you determine how many sections the frameset will have, and set the size of each section. The pages the frameset calls into each frame are the framed pages. A frame-based page begins with the selection of a frameset — the organizational layout of the page. The frameset determines where each page is displayed, whether a border appears between frames, and whether the user sees a scrollbar to resize that section of the "page." But it's the actual framed page that provides the content that the user sees. The Objects palette contains an entire tab full of different frameset arrangements. If you were hand-coding the HTML for a frameset you'd be facing a fairly complicated challenge and would have to try a few times (at least) to produce the desired results. Using GoLive, all you need to do is drag one of the many premade framesets onto your page, and then drag any frame's inner edges to tweak its size. To add another frame to a frameset you just drag a single frame into place from the Objects palette, or, add another entire frameset into the first. To tell the browser which page to display within each frame you just Point and Shoot as usual.

 Note   Unlike regular Web pages, for which you can provide a background color and preferred text colors, you do not set these options up for a frameset. Because the frameset is merely a placeholder or page organizer, each frame's actual content comes from the pages placed (linked) within the frame. Therefore, each frame area gets its background and its text color, along with the rest of its content, from each actual page within the frame. If you add a background to the frameset itself, or set text and link colors for it, these effects won't be seen in frames-savvy browsers. However, they will be seen in older browsers that don't recognize frames. See the "Creating a <noframes> Alternative" section later in this chapter for more about accommodating older browsers.

Using Frames

Why use frames? In a nutshell, it's worth using frames to enable at least part of the page to remain in place while the rest of the "page" presented to the user changes. Typically, you want to do this to minimize redraw time and to present the user a consistent navigation panel. This section looks at a few examples that speak for themselves.

 Expert Tip   Don't use frames just because you can or because you think they make you look like a better, fancier designer. Most of the time, a well-designed site will not need frames. Remember that a site design should be planned with focus, and just because something is cool is no reason to use it. Use frames only when they add to your purpose and you have a real reason to use them. — *Lynne LaMaster, Designer, Specialized Publishing*

Loading special effects

One reason to use frames is to enable effects, such as audio, to load into the user's browser only once and stay there. For example, you could have music play all the time while visitors remain at a site, as with Lynne LaMaster's Cornerstone Church site (www.cornerstone-efc.com). The main page of this site that you see in Figure 15-1 doesn't begin with frames, but the next page enters a frameset. The top frame, which remains constant, contains the music (which autostarts and loops). This way, no matter what visitors do at the site, the music continues without needing to reload and therefore breaking up.

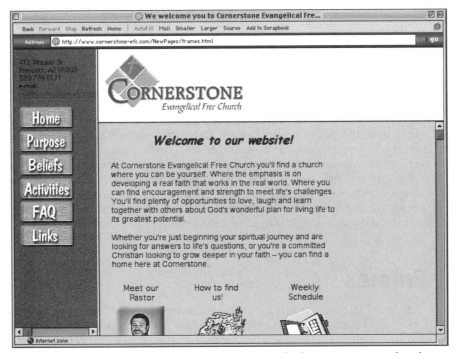

Figure 15-1: Lynne LaMaster used frames to provide the Cornerstone Church site with music.

Hiding code within frames

Just as you can place music within a frame so it remains constant, you can place code within a frame so it's always available. The frame that contains the code may be visible or it may even be totally unseen and unknown.

In Bob Stein's Webmaster's Color Laboratory, a free online service at www.visibone.com, one frame contains the code that generates its companion frame. Bob's left frame remains constant, providing his excellent Web-safe color chart. Then, as you click a color in the chart, the right frame displays another page that redraws to show you that color, as shown in Figure 15-2.

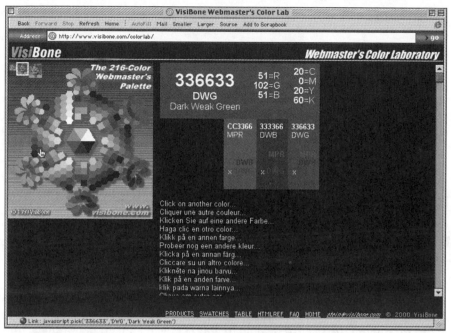

Figure 15-2: The Webmaster's Color Laboratory (www.visibone.com), where JavaScript in the left frame custom-writes the HTML for the right frame's page on the fly

As Bob explains:

It's been a curse and a blessing, using frames but this site absolutely *must* use frames, or be a very different thing. (I would not need them for Internet Explorer with its richly evolved object model, but for the other browsers . . .)

The Color Lab displays a collection of colors with text/background combinations. To do this without the Java Virtual Machine, and without the Web server being involved, one must compose new HTML. The only portable (that is, to Netscape, WebTV) way to do this was with frames: The HTML of the entire right frame is regenerated from scratch by JavaScript in index.html. Clicking a color to add it to the collection causes no server access, it all happens locally on the user's computer. (How fast it happens is some indication of the speed of the JavaScript in the user's browser and his or her computer.)

The page that contains your code doesn't always have to show as it does with the Webmaster's Color Laboratory. You can create a page that contains all sorts of intricate code, and then hide the page from view within a frame that has a width or height of zero, so users never see it. GoLive guru Frederico Russo does this often for his intricately programmed sites. He explains:

> You can use frames to reliably execute dynamic functions and interactions with databases and other objects. For example, calls from Flash or QuickTime to hidden frames can pull up both client-side JavaScript and server-side CGI, Perl, Lasso, WebSiphon, and so on. Time JavaScript functions, such as BodyOnLoad, OnFocus, or OnBlur would otherwise choke on a buggy Flash or QuickTime plug-in. Frames are also an excellent way to reduce the bandwidth required to transmit a bunch of code you might not otherwise need, preload predicted resources undistracted, and so on.

Using frames to frame dynamic media

Frames can be especially useful if you have a page composition in which you want only a part of it to change, with the rest remaining static and not redrawn. Richard Gaskin, Web Developer, Fourth World Media Corporation, explains:

> We took this approach to present a series of linked QuickTime VR panoramas with a graphic frame around them. The panoramas contain clickable hotspots that link to other pages containing panoramas from different locations on the site. We wanted the user to be able to jump between linked panoramas, but we didn't want the surrounding graphic to redraw each time.
>
> The solution was to create a frameset containing five frames: the center frame contains the panorama, while the top, left, right, and bottom frames contain sliced graphics that comprise the border. When the user clicks a hotspot in the panorama, only the middle frame changes to show the new panorama. (See Figure 15-3.)
>
> Another benefit to this approach is a greater sense of "physicality" to the interface. By having the graphic elements remain in place while only the panorama frame changes, the design looks and behaves more like a physical object, a sort of viewing port into this virtual world. If we had placed the border images on each panorama page rather than in a frameset, they would erase and redraw every time the user clicks a hotspot in the panorama, which would take more time, be less visually appealing, and destroy the visual consistency we wanted for the border graphics to appear more like a physical object.

Using a frame to contain a navigation bar

You can also use one frame within a page to contain the site's menu or navigational bar, as Oliver Zahorka, of OUT Media Design GmbH, does at www.holzforum.ch and www.moon-music.ch. This use of frames enables the navigation bar to remain constant and it does not have to reload each time the user switches pages. The site also contains a larger frame in which the main content is displayed. The menu's page contains links that call up the desired page into that main viewing frame.

Figure 15-3: QuickTime VR panorama in the middle frame of a composition that uses four other frames to hold the surrounding slices of a GIF image.

Frame Caveats and Issues

A page that uses frames is actually composed of not one page, but several. This creates a unique set of issues. It's important to consider these issues before deciding to use frames. Many experts recommend that beginners stay away from frames, that they are the realm of only those with some serious Web design experience under their belts. This section is designed to shorten the frame learning curve, so maybe you'll feel comfortable taking the plunge.

Note   For more on the downside view of frames, see Jakob Nielsen's famous article, "Why Frames Suck (Most of the Time)," at www.useit.com. (You'll find it under the article heading, "Top ten mistakes of Web design.")

Frames and search engines

As just mentioned, a page that uses frames is actually composed of not one page, but several. Search engines have unique challenges when dealing with frames. When the search engine finds your main frame page, the frameset, all is well and visitors are taken to the frameset with all initial frames correctly displayed. But what happens when the search engine locates one of your content pages, designed to be displayed within a frame? In such a case, the content page appears to the user, but without your navigation frame, site identification information, banner adds, or any other information you may have placed within your other frames.

Here are some ways to help people find your page:

✦ Do all you can to lead search engines to your frameset page by using a good title and all appropriate keywords for the site in the frameset (see Chapter 26).

✦ Place a title and keywords on all pages within the site, even though they are technically a subsection of the site. But be sure to provide help to get users to the main frameset from there. See "Solving Frame Navigation Issues" later in this chapter.

✦ Give search engines and directory staff good, concise, friendly information about your site wherever you can. The <noframes> page is a perfect place to do this (see the "Creating a <noframes> Alternative" section later in this chapter). You can also find more information at http://searchenginewatch.com/webmasters/frames.html.

✦ Place a link on each main content page to lead your visitors to the frameset page. All you need is a regular clickable link that has the target set as _top (so the visitor doesn't end up in a mis-nested set).

✦ Use JavaScript that automatically takes the user to the frameset page when he or she first arrives at the content page. GoLive provides the ForceFrame Action to do this for you. See "Solving Frame Navigation Issues" later in this chapter.

Frames and bookmarking

The tricky part of setting up frames is dealing with bookmarks so users can find your site again — or the part of your site they need to get to quickly. When a user is within your framed page and uses the menu at the top of the screen to bookmark your site, that frameset page is properly marked (at least in some cases). But what happens when a Windows user right-clicks or a Mac user Control-clicks to set the bookmark? Or when a Mac user holds the mouse down and bookmarks the page from the pop-up contextual menu? No matter where this user is reading, the mouse has got to be within a frame — consequently, what gets bookmarked is the URL to the page that happens to be displayed within that frame at the time. Thus, only that frame is called up when the user attempts to return to your site — not the frameset. As a result, the presentation of your site is incomplete, and information such as navigation within your site is missing from the user's screen. The next section provides a possible solution to this problem.

Sometimes a user spends precious time combing your site trying to find specific information, and then bookmarks your site in order to return to the information. What if, upon returning, the user is back at the main frameset, the site's intro, only to find it necessary to search through your site yet again to locate the information thought to be safely bookmarked? You want people to return to your site, but certainly not to be frustrated.

Finding the Way Home

How can you direct a user who lands in one of your meant-to-be-in-a-frame pages when the navigation frame is missing — and this user doesn't have JavaScript functioning? (It's not too common these days but it can happen.) How does the user find the way home?

Savvy users will edit the URL address at the top of the browser, but not all users know to do that. To account for this, you can take the precaution of always including a link to the main frameset (URL) on each page that sits within each frame.

Cross-Reference This issue of enabling a user to quickly get to the desired information is greatly lessened by good site planning and navigation. Have your site clearly labeled and have all information available within just a few clicks. To learn how GoLive can help you plan your site, check out Chapter 29.

By placing GoLive's ForceFrame Action (or another such JavaScript) in each individual page, you can enable the user's browser to automatically transport the user to the full frameset. Specifically, the page from which the bookmark was made remains within the frameset while the rest of the frameset loads. However, that's only a partial solution. It's great if the user bookmarks from within the page, but not if the user bookmarks from the browser's main menu. (Are you beginning to see that no single or all-encompassing solution exists for reliably bookmarking framed pages?)

Frames and printing

Frames can be tricky to print. It's hard, if not impossible, to ensure that your entire frameset will print when the user chooses the print command. If a user clicks within a frame, that may well be the frame that prints. Users may end up with a printout of your navigation bar, rather than the information desired, or else your information may print, but without your site's identification. There's no way to force the entire frameset to print.

If you intend for your site's content to be printed, you will have to either create print-ready pages that open outside of the frameset, or create a PDF (Adobe Acrobat) file and then link to that for viewing or download.

On the other hand, if your site doesn't really provide material that lends itself to being printed, you may not share this concern. Just in case, though, check that the files are print-presentable.

Accessibility

Framed pages often rely highly on visibility, presenting an obstacle for those who cannot see. However, you can take a couple of steps to keep your frames-based site accessible:

✦ Be sure to make good use of the `<noframes>` page and enable it to provide navigation through your site's pages.

✦ Name your frames descriptively and use the title attribute to describe the page your link leads to within any frame.

I'll address these issues as they arise in this book.

Designing a Frames Site

It's easy for a designer to get carried away with frames, and therefore easy for frames to become confusing to the user. Think of the user as you design your frames. Keep the sections of your site clear in form and function. Consider the following factors and questions as you design your frames site:

✦ Think carefully about your intended audience. If you're designing to reach the general public, do you want those on browsers without frame support (Netscape Navigator 1; IE 2, and text-only browsers such as Lynx) to be able to see your site? If so, consider that they cannot see frames at all. You'll need to create an alternative frameless site for them. See the "Creating a <noframes> Alternative" section later in this chapter. You may find that using frames merely causes you to create your site in duplicate, so frames may not be right for you at all. You could tell users to upgrade their browsers before using your site, but you need to be willing to risk losing that user forever.

✦ Can the user easily notice your navigation tools? Providing one frame that clearly displays your navigation does the trick.

✦ When the user clicks a link will he or she know where to look to see the result? Provide one area of the window that clearly presents the main content. Because content is king, as they say, this main content area should be large enough to easily display yours. Your content area may be one large frame, or it may be some intelligent combination of frames.

✦ If a user likes your site and bookmarks it, will returning be successful? (For more on bookmarking, see "Frame Caveats and Issues" earlier in this chapter, and "Solving Frame Navigation Issues" later in this chapter.)

✦ Make sure the content of each of the frame's pages is consistent in its layout and the type of content it presents (navigation, contact info, main content, and so on).

✦ Don't let frame borders and colors cut up your site. Design so that frame divisions add to the look of your site, or so the page appears to be frameless.

✦ Make sure the size of each frame fits the contents nicely — or scrolls elegantly to present it. If you've got a banner that's 500 pixels wide, you'll need a frame that's 500 pixels wide to properly display it. If the frame will scroll, place it so the scrollbar doesn't break up the unified look of the site.

✦ Design your content pages with the frameset in mind, remembering that their content needs to fit inside the frames — and design your frameset with your site's content in mind.

The frameset you choose must be able to accommodate your content. The frameset icons you choose from the Objects palette provide excellent depictions of the frameset structures. Take a look at them in Figure 15-4 or in the Objects palette itself to help you envision your page.

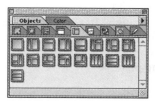

Figure 15-4: GoLive's predesigned framesets

Frames can wreak havoc on a site's continuity — if done badly. Don't design pages too full for the frame in which they'll be displayed. Doing so causes the need for scrollbars, which can easily break up your overall page. (See "Turning Scrollbars On or Off" later in this chapter.)

Expert Tip   Make clever use of framesets. Try to create a single frameset for the whole site. A frameset is meant to be your site's interface, not to be replaced every second click. If you start calling on duplicates of the main frameset for each section and subsection of your site, rethink the site design. — *Oliver Zahorka, OUT Media Design GmbH, Switzerland*

If a page will fill a vertical space, place the content on the left side of the page. Then fill the rest of that page with a background that won't conflict with the overall look of the full frameset. This way, if the frame size expands, it won't conflict with what's next to it. Likewise, for a page that will be viewed within a horizontal frame, place that page's content at the top of the page. Whether its frame will be at the top or bottom of the frameset page, its contents are viewed from the top down.

Note   Even if your page will live at the right side of the screen, you should still place that page's content on the left side of the page. When the page is viewed within the frame, the left side of the page begins at the left side of the frame. How much of the page the user will see is determined by the width of that frame.

Creating Frames and Framesets

Normally, the "page" a user downloads is mostly a framework that includes directions for downloading various elements to fill that framework. The only page content it really contains is the text. When you design your page using frames, the "page" a browser collects is even more of a framework. It doesn't even contain text. The URL for a framed page simply calls up a frameset that contains the instructions to call for the pages you link into that set.

To build a page using frames, you begin with a master frame document — the frameset — and then add or adjust the rows and/or columns of frames that fit within the frameset. To add the content to your page, you actually create several "regular" Web pages. Then you link each page to the frame you want it to appear within.

You can set up your home page using frames, or your home page can be a "regular" page that later calls upon the frame-using page when frames are beneficial.

If you have existing pages and wish to turn them into a frames-based page, create a new page and lay out the frameset on that page. Size one frame to fit your existing page. Then link that frame to your existing page. You cannot apply frames to existing pages by dragging a frameset on top of the existing page.

To help you practice using frames, the *Adobe GoLive 5 Bible* CD-ROM includes practice framesets and pages by me and by Oliver Zahorka, of OUT Media Design GmbH. You can find them inside the Exercises folder.

Placing a frameset on a page

The first step in creating a page with frames is to place the frameset on the page. In GoLive, you'll find a page layout view just for working with the layout of a frameset. Actually, it's the only layout in which you can add work on a frameset. To build a frameset page, follow these steps:

1. Open the page in which you'd like the frames to appear.

   This is a regular new blank HTML page that should be in the Files tab or your Site Window before you begin. This is also the page whose URL users will call upon if the frameset is the home page, or that will link from the home page if a regular page is the home page.

2. Click the Frame Editor tab of the document window.

   The Frame Editor is the where you create and tweak a frames-based page. Before you add frames the page will simply say "No Frames." After you add your frameset, it is where the frames structure is displayed and edited.

   The Frame Editor is the where you create and tweak a frames-based page. Before you add frames the page will simply say "No Frames." After you add your frameset, it is where the frames structure is displayed and edited.

Understanding Frameset Construction

Normally, when a user changes the size of a browser window, the entire page expands or contracts. However, frames are a different story. If every frame within the page changed size when the browser resized, you'd have nothing but an uncontrollable mess, with no control over how much of any frame's content would appear. Instead, with a frames page, you set at least one section to a definite (or proportionate) size, letting another change size to accommodate the browser resizing.

When a frameset has at least two frames side by side (even if only part of the frames touch), one of those frames is always set to a fixed width, while the other scales. The fixed-width frame can be exactly wide enough to display your navigation buttons, a graphic, or a table of set size that contains certain content. Then the other frame beside it can grow or shrink as the user resizes the window, but the information in the set-size frame is not compromised. If both of those side-by-side frames were scaled, the browser would give each frame half of the window, and there would either be too much or too little room in each. If both were set with fixed widths in pixels, and the user made the window wider or narrower than the sum of the two frame widths, the browser wouldn't be able to draw either frame properly. The same goes for frames that share the height of a window.

When it comes to setting a size for your frames, you have the choice between pixels, a set size, and percentages, which tell a frame to render a specific proportion of the entire window.

To gain a fuller understanding, experiment by dragging the various framesets onto your page, and then looking at the sizes of each frame. Or, simply examine the frameset icons on the Objects palette, noticing the colors.

3. Drag the desired frameset from the Frames tab in the Objects palette onto the document window.

Seventeen icons exist on the Objects palette, shown previously in Figure 15-4, but you actually have 16 frameset choices because the first single frame is for adding frames to your set later. (If you don't see them all you can scroll or expand the Objects palette.)

If none of the frame layouts in the Objects palette meets your needs exactly, pick the one that is closest to your design in order to begin. You can easily customize the frameset later by adding or deleting frames.

Each frameset icon contains at least one blue frame. There's more to that than just looking pretty. In each frameset, there should always be at least one frame that can be scaled. The blue frame represents a frame that is, by default, set to scale. (However, you can change the frame scaling at any time, choosing another frame to scale instead.)

The frameset looks something like the one shown in Figure 15-5, except that yours will reflect your selected set. Notice that within each frame is an icon with a question mark and the words "Empty Reference" beneath it, letting you know that no page is assigned to that frame yet. When you add a frameset the Inspector becomes the Frameset Inspector.

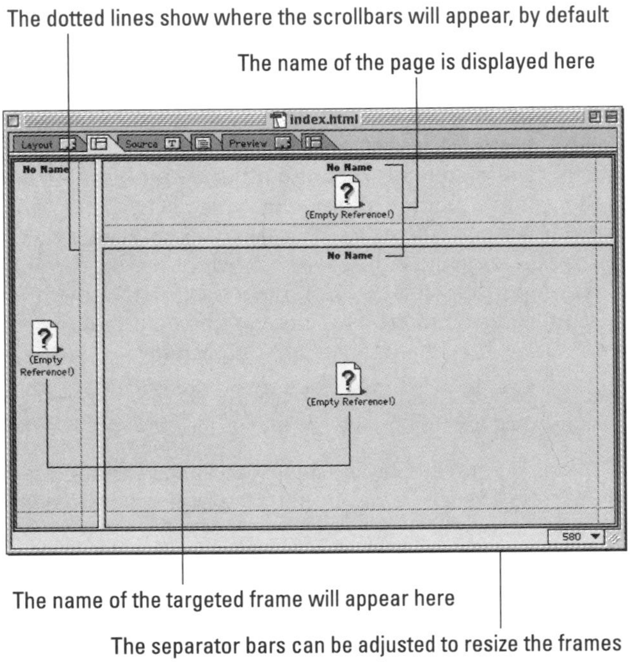

The dotted lines show where the scrollbars will appear, by default

The name of the page is displayed here

The name of the targeted frame will appear here

The separator bars can be adjusted to resize the frames

Figure 15-5: A new frameset in the Frames Editor view, with the frames choices displayed on the Objects palette (the lower-right frame is selected)

After you add the frameset you can adjust it as needed. You can move the frame borders, or add more frames or delete unwanted frames. Or you can link your pages first, and then adjust the frames after. Whatever you do, as always, remember to save the page by choosing File ⇨ Save.

If you're not happy with the frameset you choose, undo the addition (Edit ⇨ Undo) or select the set and delete it. Then drag another set onto the Frames layout tab. (Dragging another frameset icon over an existing frameset doesn't replace the existing frameset. Instead, it places the second frameset inside the first.)

Tip

When you add a frameset to any page within GoLive, the Page icon, visible in the top-left corner of the Layout view, changes to represent frames. This will tip you off to the fact that the page contains frames and that you should switch to the Frames Editor view in order to work on them. The Page icon isn't visible in Frames Editor view so you won't notice this icon change as you're working on your frames.

Adding another frame or frameset to your set

You can have almost any kind of arrangement of frames on a page. If the framesets available in the Objects palette don't exactly meet your layout needs, you can easily add extra frames to your page after placing the initial frameset. You can also add a new frame after you've linked pages to the frames, and even while you have Preview Frame turned on (see the next section). However, you may have to reassign pages after adding a new frame.

Tip   The single-frame icon in the Frames palette is for adding a frame to an existing set, not for creating a single-frame page. A single frame on a page doesn't offer any advantages over the standard nonframes page. What's more, Netscape browsers (at least through Version 4) do not interpret single-frame Web pages properly.

To add a frame to an existing frameset, you drag the single-frame icon from the Frames tab of the Objects palette and release the mouse where you wish the new frame to be placed. You can also add another frameset to the frameset on your page by dragging another frameset icon into place. Inserting frames or framesets within an existing frameset can be tricky, so here are a few clues to guide you:

✦ If you have two vertical frames and want to add a third vertical frame between them, drag the new frame icon onto the line that divides them.

✦ If you have two horizontal frames and want to add a third horizontal frame between them, drag the new frame icon onto the line that divides them.

✦ To divide a vertical frame into two, drop the new frame within the page area of the existing frame. Regardless of whether you drop the new frame to the top or bottom of the existing frame, the new section appears at the bottom. The frame into which the new frame lands becomes outlined by a dark line within the frame.

✦ To divide a horizontal frame into two, drop the new frame within the page area of the existing frame. Regardless of whether you drop the new frame to the left or right side of the existing frame, the new section appears at the right. The frame into which the new frame lands becomes outlined by a dark line within the frame.

✦ Dropping an entire frameset works the same way; you either drop it onto the border between frames or into a frame's area. Dropping a frameset onto a border adds the new frames between the existing frames. Dropping a new set into a frame subdivides that frame's space.

✦ Remember, you always have the Undo command (Edit ➪ Undo); you'll need it while getting the hang of inserting frames.

Tip   You can, and should, add one frameset inside another to create vertical and horizontal frames, but don't divide the page into so many frames that users don't know where to look first, or where to expect the results of an action to appear. Simpler is always better in Web-page design, especially when it comes to using frames.

Deleting a frame or frameset from your set

You can delete an entire frameset, or any single frame within your page, at any time. In short, all you do is select, and then press the Delete/Backspace key. When a frame or set is selected, a dark line appears around it.

To delete the entire frameset, and begin anew with a blank frameset page, click any of that set's borders. If you've nested one set inside another, clicking a border within that set selects that set, not the outer set.

To delete a nested frameset, click one of the borders within that set. You'll see that set's border become surrounded within the enveloping set.

To delete any single frame, click inside that frame (not on its border). You can delete any individual cell, whether you added it as a single cell or as part of a set. If, by accident, you select the entire frameset, call upon your trusty Undo command (Edit ⇨ Undo). No need to start all over again.

You can also use the Undo command to remove a frame or frameset if it was the last thing you did.

The History palette records all frame additions and deletions, so it can help you revert to a prior arrangement, unless you've added content in the meantime and want to keep that content. (You cannot selectively remove individual steps within the History.)

Moving frames around

At any time after you place a frameset on your page, you can move any of the frames around—with some limitations. To move a frame to another part of the page click anywhere within the frame and drag it to its new location. Moving a frame or frameset doesn't change its size.

Within an original frameset from the Objects palette, you can move a vertical frame from the left side of the page to the right, or move a frame from the top of the page to the bottom. However, you cannot move a horizontal frame into a vertical space. When you try to drag it, it just won't go. When you add another frame and it subdivides an original frame space, you can move the added frame within that space.

After you've inserted a second frameset into a frame, you can move that frameset in its entirety too. To do so, press ⌘-click (Mac) or right-click (Windows) on any border within that frameset and you can reposition it within the frame to which you added it.

Whatever you do, if you don't like the result, you can undo it. Or, if you've done something else in the meantime, simply drag the frame back to its original location, or even to another location at any time.

Changing a frame's orientation

After you've started your initial frame layout, you might find that your page would work better with two frames beside one another rather than on top of one another or vice versa. GoLive makes it very easy to make this type of change. To do this, you actually change the orientation of the divider between the two frames you want to change. You can do this before you assign a page to the frame, or after. You can also do this while the Preview Frame is displayed in the Inspector.

To change the orientation of the divider between the two frames, do the following:

1. Click directly on the border you wish to change.

   This selects the border and turns the Inspector into the Frameset Inspector. By the subject of Orientation, either the Horizontal or Vertical radio button is already selected.

2. Click the radio button that reflects the orientation you wish for the selected frame border.

Because the frame's size and shape in no way affects the contents of the page or pages that are viewed within the frame, you can make this type of change — and change it back if you don't like the result — at any time.

Naming a frame

When pages are displayed within a frameset, each page must be told which frame to appear within. This is called *targeting* a frame. Setting the target frame is simply a matter of choosing the frame by name, when you create the link (see "Setting Up Links Across Frames" and "Using Generic Targets" later in this chapter). However, you can't choose a frame by name until you give that frame a name. You can name your frames at any time.

Here's how to name a frame:

1. If the frame is not already selected (it'll have a dark line around it), click within the frame to select it.

   This turns the Frameset Inspector into the Frame Inspector for that page.

2. Select the default words, "No Name," in the Name field (as shown in Figure 15-6), and then type a short descriptive name into the field.

   It's best to keep the name simple and logical. For example, use "menu" for a frame that is acting as your site's menu, or "main" or "content" for a page that displays the site's main content.

After you name a frame, GoLive lists it within the Target menu (for the current site).

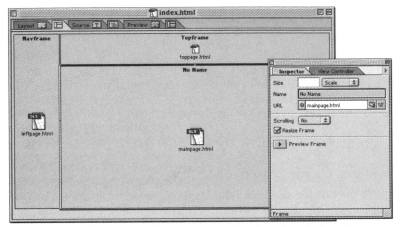

Figure 15-6: The page and Inspector, as they look just before the lower-right frame is named. The left and top frames are already named.

Placing Content into Frames

While the frameset provides the structure for your page, the content of each frame is supplied by the individual page you link to that frame. To tell a frameset to display a page within a specific frame, you link the frame to its respective page. The page then displays within that frame. By setting the size of the frame, you determine how much of the page is visible to the user.

As a rule, don't link pages from other people's Web pages into your own frames. Those pages are designed for viewing within the context of their owner's site and taking their content out of this context opens you to all sorts of copyright conflicts. Perhaps this is okay in certain circumstances, but obtain permission first. Instead, open links to a foreign site in a new window (Target = _blank). — *Oliver Zahorka, OUT Media Design GmbH, Switzerland*

Link a page to a frame using one of the following methods:

✦ Drag the desired page from the Files tab or the Site Window into the particular frame in which you wish that page to display, as shown in Figure 15-7.

✦ Drag the desired URL from the External tab or the Site Window into the particular frame in which you wish that page to display. This method is the easiest way to link to a page that's not a part of your site.

✦ Press Option (Mac) or Alt (Windows) as you click inside a frame and then drag to Point and Shoot directly from the frame to the desired page in the Site Window's Files tab or the external page's address in the External tab.

Name That Frame

By Oliver Zahorka, OUT Media Design GmbH, Switzerland

Name all of your Frames. Use a unique name for each, using clear names that contain "_frame" as part of the name—for example, `content_frame`. If you tend to use these names for several clients, it may even be clever to attach the site or client's name—for example, `acme_content_frame`. This may sound like silly overkill at first, but will be highly appreciated if the site gets more complex and you start using JavaScript to manipulate the content of frames and pop-up windows.

Do not use punctuation marks or spaces in the name. Don't use reserved words such as `_top`, `_blank`, or JavaScript object names for a frame name. Unexpected things can happen then; for example, a frame named "top" will confuse JavaScript that tries to access it because "top" is used as a synonym for the top-most window in a frame window hierarchy.

If you have a `navigation_frame` frame that contains lots of links to pages to appear in a `content_frame` frame, instead of using `target=" content_frame "` for each link, you can place a base URL metatag with `target=" content_frame "` in the navigation page.

✦ Select the frame in which you wish that page to display by clicking in it. Then use the URL area of the resulting Frame Inspector to Point and Shoot to the page, browse your way to it, or type in the page's address.

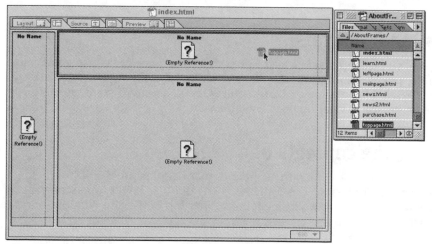

Figure 15-7: Drag a page into a frame to have that page display within that frame. The lower frame already has a page assigned, while the left frame is still unassigned.

Once a page is linked to a frame, the Frameset Inspector becomes the Frame Inspector.

An icon representing the page appears in place of the question-mark icon. A generic page icon represents a page from within your site. The external URL icon represents a link to a page that is elsewhere on the Web. The address of the linked page replaces the words "Empty Reference." At the top of each frame you will see the words "No Name" at first. You have the opportunity to name each frame within the Frame Inspector.

> **Note**
>
> If you happen to have the Inspector open and handy, and you have not yet named the frame you're working in, this is a good time to do so. Frames will need to be named in order to set up the navigation between the pages of your site. If the frame is not already selected (it'll have a dark line around it), click within the frame to select it, turning the Frameset Inspector into the Frame Inspector for that page. Then type a short descriptive name into the Name field. Choose a logical name such as `top_frame`, `main_frame`, or `nav_frame`. (As already mentioned, don't just use "top" as that's a standard target name and can cause confusion.)

After you place content into your frames, you may want to see the overall effect. Then you're likely to need to tweak the look of the various frames. As you do, be sure to preview the page in both Internet Explorer and Netscape, and remember to account for platform differences.

If you're working on a Mac, there's a convenient sort of semipreview you can easily do. After you've placed a page in a frame, while you're still working in the frame, click the Preview Frame button. For details see "Previewing Your Frames," coming up shortly.

Nesting framesets

The page you call up inside a frame doesn't always have to be a "regular" page. It's possible to have another frameset appear within one of your frames. This is called *nesting*. While it's possible to do, it requires careful content planning. It's easy to create confusing navigation problems this way.

Editing the contents of a page

The frameset page is merely the container that handles the display of the pages you place within it. To change the contents of any of those pages, open the page as you usually would (by double-clicking it in the Files tab of the Site Window) and then edit as you edit any page.

Previewing Your Frames

Normally, as you work on a page, you get to see its overall look. Framesets are different because the frameset is just a container in which various pages are displayed. Therefore, you'll want to check the overall look of your frameset as you tweak it. GoLive provides several ways to preview individual frames or the entire frameset. On the Mac you can even preview the contents of your frames as you work, making the process easier.

Browser preview

To most accurately preview your page, use the Preview in Browser feature. The page you need to preview is the one that contains the frameset. With that page active, simply click the Preview in Browser button, as with any other page you create in GoLive. The browser finds the pages within your Site Window and previews each page in the designated frame.

During this preview all of the links within your frameset will work just as they would on the Web. If any of your frames display an external link, you'll need to be connected to the Internet to access that page.

GoLive preview

As with all pages, you can easily do a quick preview of your page simply by switching from the Frames Layout tab to the Preview tab (if on a Mac, use the Frames Preview tab). Preview mode lets you somewhat check the overall look of your page. However, as with any other preview, you cannot make any changes to your frameset or any of its content pages while previewing a frameset.

In this preview mode, you can test all links within your frameset. On the Mac, as you click any link from one page to another, the destination page appears in the frame you've targeted. However, in Windows, although each link successfully opens the destination page, the new page doesn't open within the targeted frame. Thus, for a proper preview and link check, you'll need to preview your frameset in a browser.

Normally, on the Mac, the View Controller helps you get a feel for how the page will look in Netscape and Internet Explorer (both Mac and Windows), and even in Opera (a Windows browser). However, View Controller is not available in the Frames Preview.

Semi-editable preview (Mac only)

If you're working on a Mac, you can see what the page looks like within the frame — as you work. This enables you to tweak the size and look of your frame without switching page tabs — somewhat. Bear in mind, though, that although this preview shows you the frame's page contents, it isn't compensating for browser differences, font sizes, margins, and so on. To most accurately see those details, you'll want to preview within a browser, regardless of which platform you're working on.

To preview a frame's contents in Frame Layout mode, click within the frame to turn the Frameset Inspector into the Frame Inspector for that page, and then click

Preview Frame, as shown in Figure 15-8. You can preview multiple frames at the same time by selecting each frame and clicking Preview Frame, one at a time. You can also preview the entire page by clicking any frame border to select the entire frameset, and clicking Preview Set in the Frameset Inspector.

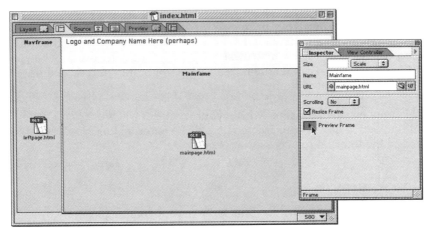

Figure 15-8: The Frame Editor (Mac) after the initial pages have been linked to pages within your site. The bottom-right frame is being set for preview. The top-right frame is being previewed.

If the pages linked to these frames are within the Files tab of your Site Window or otherwise accessible on your hard drive or network, they will become visible. However, if any linked page is elsewhere, out on the Web, that page cannot be seen and the URL icon and address will remain within the frame. You'll need to preview those pages in a browser while connected to the Internet.

While in this preview mode, you can drag the divider between the frames, or use the other settings within the Frameset Inspector to tweak the look of your page. Click Stop Preview to return to a view of the generic icon and see the frame's destination.

Note   While you are previewing your entire frameset (page), if you change one of the initially placed pages, that frame reverts back to the nonpreview state, identifying the icon and URL of the newly placed page. To preview the contents of this frame along with the rest of the page, with this frame selected simply click the Preview Frame button in the Frame Inspector.

Now that you know all about previewing your work, you're ready to finish setting up your frameset.

In case you're wondering why this feature doesn't exist in the Windows version, due to the way Internet Explorer is bound to the Windows operating system, it's just not possible.

Web Design Frame by Frame

By Oliver Zahorka, OUT Media Design GmbH, Switzerland

Here are some tips to help you get along with frameset-specific oddities:

1. Netscape is genuinely inaccurate when calculating the sizes of frames. This is due to the frame size calculation algorithm, which does all calculations in percent instead of pixels. Therefore, a fixed pixel size frame happens to be off by as many as five pixels (that's what I've seen so far; this inaccuracy can be even greater if the real estate of the screen is larger).

2. Do not try to have *all* frames set to a fixed pixel size. The browser will fail to calculate proper dimensions, and yield unpredictable results for window sizes that are not the exact sum of the frame sizes.

3. To turn off all kinds of frame borders in Netscape and Internet Explorer, in the Frameset Inspector set BorderSize to 0 (`border="0" framespacing="0"`) and Border Frame to No (`frameborder="no"`).

4. If you have a complicated frameset that seems to misalign some of the content, check that all measurements are as desired and add up to the full window size. For example, if you have a frameset of three rows containing three columns, and you experience some shift of the left border across the three rows, check to make sure each frame within the first column is the same size, and then check each frame within the second column, and so on.

Tweaking the Look of Your Framed Page

After the pages are assigned to their frames you can clearly see your page and complete its setup. As with the previous frames setup, this is also done in the Frames layout tab of your page window. And of course, the Frameset Inspector and Frame Inspector are there to help.

It's easiest to tweak your page while you can see what the page looks like. As explained in the previous section, you can see a frame's contents within the Frame Layout view by selecting a frame, and then clicking the Preview Frame button in the Frame Inspector.

Adjusting a frame's size

In each frameset, some frames are set to fixed pixel widths and at least one is designated scalable. (Remember, in the Objects palette, blue identifies a scalable frame.) You can change the size of any fixed frame, either by entering a new size in the Inspector or by dragging the frame's border. The scaling frame never has a size assigned; its size is determined by the fixed frames that border it, and by the total size of the user's browser window.

Note   You can change any scalable frame to fixed, or any fixed frame to be scalable. In fact, when you nest one set into another, you should do this so all the frames will work together correctly. Just be sure to always leave one frame across the width and height of the window scalable so the page can draw properly.

If you're happy with the predetermined frameset and just wish to change a frame's width or height a bit to fit your content, following these two steps:

1. Click the border of the frame you want to adjust, and then drag the frame, as shown in Figure 15-9, until your image, table, text, and so on show to your liking. (This may be more helpful to Mac users, as they can turn the cell preview on and see the frame's content as they drag.)

2. Click inside the cell to select it, and then change the number in the Size field of the frame's Inspector. When you have a graphic, because you're certain of the size of the graphic (in pixels), it is easy to match that size by typing in that size within the Inspector. If the cell is horizontal, the size specifies the height of the frame. If the cell is vertical, the number determines the width.

 Note   When two sections of a row or column share a row or column, enlarging one reduces the other.

If you'd like to customize the frameset, you can change the size of a preset frame from pixels to a percentage. Or you can change a scalable frame to fixed, and then change its complementary frame to scalable.

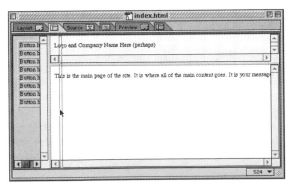

Figure 15-9: Dragging the left frame's border to resize it to fit the buttons in the navigation frame

Here are the steps for changing the sizing method for a frame:

1. Click within the frame you want to resize.

2. In the Frame Inspector, choose Pixel or Percent from the menu next to the Size field. Or, choose Scale to let the rest of the frames determine the frame's size.

Here's what each of the three options do, and some recommendations on their use:

- *Pixel* enables you to specify the exact size of a frame in pixels. This is the default for all but one frame in each GoLive-provided frameset.

  Pixel is the best choice when the frame will contain a graphic that has a set size. The frame can then match the size of the graphic exactly. Because the frame and graphic match exactly, the user will always see the entire image perfectly, never needing to scroll or resize the frame, and never missing any part of the image. Pixel is also a good choice when a frame contains text. However, because text can be resized by the user, there's a good chance that some users will not see all of your text within the designated frame area. To account for this possibility, set the frame size to accommodate the most common font size. Then, enable scrollbars and/or user resizing.

- *Percent* enables you to determine the size of the frame in relation to the rest of the browser window. When the user resizes the window, percent-sized frames resize in the mandated proportion.

  When the width of a window is composed of two (or more) side-by-side frames, you need to make sure the sum of the two (in percentages) equals 100 percent — the total width of the browser at any given time. GoLive doesn't tally this total automatically, so when you change one, you must remember to adjust the bordering frame too.

  Percentage is tricky because you have no real control over how much of your page the user will see within the frame. You'll need to experiment to get the page looking right. Netscape is particularly odd about rendering frames using percentages.

- *Scale* is the absence of a specific size. It enables the frame to resize on the fly, when the user changes the size of the browser window, taking up all available space after the neighboring frames claim their predetermined pixels or percentages.

  Scale is the default for one frame (sometimes two) per GoLive-provided frameset. One frame should always scale so the other frame's proportions aren't distorted as the user widens or lengthens the browser window.

3. If your selection for sizing is Pixel or Percent, do the following:

- Enter the desired size in the Size field. If the cell is horizontal, the set percentage or number of pixels specifies the height of the frame. If the cell is vertical, the number determines the width.

- Click the border you want to move, and then drag it. You can drag a vertical border sideways and drag a horizontal border up or down.

Note

You can drag to move the border between any frames within a set. When you drag the border between two frames, you're not actually setting the size property of both of those frames. You're actually affecting the size (in pixels or a percentage) of the fixed frame. The other frame simply continues to scale in order to let the user's window draw properly.

As you set up the frame's size to fit your content, don't forget about the browser off-set built into each page by default. Those few pixels that act as a left and top margin affect the contents of each page your frames will display. Remember that you can set those margins to zero if you'd like. You do this directly within each page that's linked into the frame, not within the frame's settings. Fortunately, the preview you see within the Frame Editor accurately reflects the page's margins, so you can decide on a page-by-page basis whether to change the default margins or not. (Be sure to preview within each browser, though, as the offsets are not identical in each.)

Turning scrollbars on or off

As with most windows that you and your users are used to seeing on a computer, frames can have their own scrollbars. The upside of a scrollbar is that it enables a user to scroll when all of a page's information isn't visible. This capability comes at a cost. The downside is that the scrollbar may disrupt the page's complete, unified look.

You can set the scrollbar for each frame of your page individually. Here's how to set a scrollbar:

1. Select the frame you want to affect by clicking in that frame.

2. Choose the desired scrolling option from the pop-up menu. You have three options, described as follows:

   • *Auto* (the default) tells the browser to turn the scrollbar on when all of your content is not visible within the frame.

     When the scrollbar is set to Auto, a dotted outline represents the scroll-bar area. (That way you can remember to design your page to accommo-date the scrollbars.)

     During frame preview (Mac only), the scrollbar area is always displayed, showing the scroll items if content exists to scroll to, and showing just the blank area if not.

   • *Yes* turns the scrollbar on all the time. If all of the frame's information is already visible, the scrollbar area will appear as you demand, although it will not contain the arrows or draggable "elevator" box.

   • *No* turns the scrollbar off whether the frame's full contents are visible or not. When the scrollbar is off, the page has a better look of solidarity. Depending on your frame's *size* setting, that frame may become larger when (if) the user enlarges the browser window. But if the user has no more room onscreen to enlarge the page, or if you've set a definite frame size, if impor-tant information can't be seen by the user, the user can do nothing about it.

     When you set the scrollbar to No, the outline representing it disappears in the Frame Editor.

Making frames user-resizable

One alternative to having scrollbars show is to enable users to drag any frame border as they view your page. The upside of enabling this is that all of the information in your frame will always be viewable. Unfortunately, the user is likely not to know this can be done.

In addition, if you resize one frame it changes the size of the neighboring frames, therefore affecting their visible content and possibly upsetting the balance of your page. All in all, though, given the flexibility this option adds, I prefer to turn on resizing.

To make your frames user-resizable, simply select the frame you want the user to be able to resize, and then check Resize in the Frame Inspector. You can control this setting on a frame-by-frame basis.

Changing the width of borders between frames

This setting is made within the Frameset Inspector, rather than the Frame Inspector, because it changes the appearance of the frame, not the presentation of the frame's contents. You can set each border independently of the others within a frameset.

Note   BorderSize and BorderFrame place `<frame>` tag attributes (border, framespacing; frameborder) that are not reliably supported by all versions of either Netscape Navigator or Microsoft Internet Explorer for either Macintosh or Windows. Therefore, it is possible the results will not be seen by some of your viewers.

To reduce or enlarge the width of a border between frames, follow these steps:

1. Click directly on the border you wish to change.

   This selects the border and turns the Inspector into the Frameset Inspector.

2. Check the box labeled BorderSize.

   GoLive's default border size, 6 pixels, appears.

3. Select the default number in the field by the BorderSize option, and then enter your desired number.

   For a wider border enter a larger number. For a thinner border enter a smaller number, and zero for no border. However, a border of 0 may still result in a thin line appearing in some browsers so if you don't want any border, be sure to set the BorderFrame option to No. (See "Turning Borders Between Frames On or Off" later in this chapter.)

Changing the color of borders between frames

As with changing the width of frame borders, this setting is made within the Frameset Inspector, rather than the Frame Inspector, because it changes the appearance of the frame, not the presentation of the frame's contents. You can set each border independently of the others within a frameset.

Note BorderColor is a ⟨frame⟩ tag attribute not reliably supported by all versions of either Netscape Navigator or Microsoft Internet Explorer for either Macintosh or Windows. Therefore, it is possible the results will not be seen by some of your viewers.

To set the color of a border between any two frames, follow these steps:

1. Click directly on the border you wish to colorize.

   This selects the border and turns the Inspector into the Frameset Inspector.

2. Check the box labeled borderColor.

   This activates the color swatch area.

3. Double-click within the color swatch.

   This opens the Color palette if it's not already open on your screen.

4. Click the desired color within the Color palette.

   The border color appears in the color swatch and in the Frame layout (if you have borders turned on for the frameset).

Note Setting the BorderFrame option to No overrides the borderColor setting (and BorderWidth), as a border no longer exists to which to apply weight or color.

Turning borders between frames on or off

If you prefer not to have any border appear between any two frames, you can turn it off totally. You can turn each border on or off independently of the others within a frameset.

This setting is done within the Frameset Inspector, rather than the Frame Inspector, because it changes the appearance of the frame, not the presentation of the frame's contents.

Note BorderFrame is a ⟨frame⟩ tag attribute not reliably supported by all versions of either Netscape Navigator or Microsoft Internet Explorer for either Macintosh or Windows. Therefore, it is possible the results will not be seen by some of your viewers.

To disable (or enable) a border between frames, follow these steps:

1. Click directly on the border you wish to change.

   This selects the border and turns the Inspector into the Frameset Inspector.

2. Check the box for the BorderFrame option.

3. Choose Yes or No from the menu.

   Yes sets a border to display and No turns off the border.

Note   If you also have a borderColor set up, it will appear in the Frames Layout and (on Mac) Frames Preview. However, it won't appear in the browser.

Setting Up Links Across Frames

When you link pages to one another when using frames, you not only tell the link what page to jump to, but also which frame to display the page within. If links are not targeted properly, you'll have pages opening in the wrong frame, or opening within their own windows on top of your page. Fortunately, GoLive makes it simple to set up your links correctly.

Creating links that change the contents of one frame

For the most part, links within frames are just normal links that link from one of your pages to another page, whether the destination page is your own or an external page. However, each link must contain a *target*—that's the secret to designating which frame the page is to appear within.

Note   If each frame is not already named, name them now, as described previously in the "Naming a Frame" section. By naming each frame you make it easier to specify the correct frame for each newly called-upon page to land in.

Follow these steps to set up the links between your frames:

1. Set up your frameset and link the pages that will display in each frame initially.

2. Double-click anywhere inside the frame that contains that page on which you're placing your links. (Even if you already have the links created, you may need to tweak the links to properly target your frames.)

   This opens the page as if you'd double-clicked the page within the Files tab of the Site Window.

3. Create your first link the same way you create any other link. Leave your I-beam within the text if it's a text link or keep the graphic selected if the link is a graphic.

   If the link was created prior to this, select that link now. (If it's a text link, select the text or just place the cursor anywhere within that text. If the link is a graphic, select the graphic.)

Cross-Reference   Chapter 11 covers the topic of linking more fully. You can also link to a specific line within the destination page. To learn about anchors, see Chapter 11.

4. In the Inspector used to set your link's destination, click the Target menu (the arrow to the right of the field) and select the name of the frame into which you want this linked page to display.

Your frames appear at the top of the target list, above the more cryptic generic names. If you have not named a frame, it will say "No Name." If, for some reason, you don't want to pick a specific frame by name, you can select a generic frame destination. These generic targets are explained after the linking process.

5. In the Title field, enter a descriptive title for the page to which you are linking.

This may seem redundant, as the page you link to already has a title. But a speech synthesizing browser may read it, helping improve Web accessibility to those who cannot see your page. What should you put here? You might enter something like "menu and navigation frame" or "main content page." When you test for accessibility later on, you can learn how your titles work out.

Note   This Title field is different from the page's title tag. This one is an attribute sometimes available for elements on the page. This title is an attribute of a link. It's not standardized and may have different results in different browsers, For example, in some cases it may create a yellow Tooltip, but because it offers an accessibility benefit, I recommend using it.

The most important thing when setting up links for a frames site is to accurately specify the link's target. If your page already contains the links, run through all the links and set their targets. If you are first making the links, be sure not to forget the target as you create each link. If you forget to specify a target for any link, clicking that link causes the linked page to load into the frame from which the link is clicked.

Using generic targets

Instead of choosing a specifically named frame in which to present your site's pages, you can choose a generic target: *top*, *parent*, or *blank*.

Given the differences between browser implementations, you'll want to test your frames in as many different browsers as possible. For example, in some versions of Netscape the top and parent targets behave the same.

Here's a description of each of the generic frame targets:

✦ **_top** opens the destination page within the current browser window, replacing your frames page with a full window display of only the newly called page. This means you are now without navigation around your site, unless the newly called page is meant to be a complete unit for your site, or unless the user thinks to hit the browser's Back button.

✦ **_parent** opens the destination page into the already-open browser window so the linked page replaces the frameset. Or, if another frameset first led the user to the current page, it opens the new page back in that original frameset.

✦ **_self** tells the new page to load in the same frame in which the link is clicked. If the link is clicked within your navigation area, your navigation aid will be replaced by the new page, potentially leaving the user unable to get around within your site. (The browser's Back button may return the frame's original contents, but the user may not figure that out.) If the link is clicked from within your main content area, and is meant to replace the current main content, the target can do the job.

✦ **_blank** opens the destination page in a new browser window on top of the framed page from which it was called. If the user closes the newly opened browser window, your page will still be open and intact.

After you create the links within your frame content pages, it's a good idea to test them.

Tip The top target is the best way to break out of frames when you want to return to a regular page.

Testing your links

Mac users can test local links within the Preview in Browser feature shown in Figure 15-10. On the Mac, pages load correctly into the designated frame in this preview. Unfortunately, in the Windows preview tab, links open within new pages instead of loading into the target frame. Because of this, Windows users must test all links by using the Preview in Browser button.

To test external links, you definitely have to preview the frameset page in a browser by clicking the Preview in Browser button. (Connect to the Internet to fully test your page.)

Changing two frames at once

You can also have a single link change the pages in two frames at once. For this, you use a GoLive Action, called Target2Frames. Bear in mind, though, that any Action relies on JavaScript so you cannot fully depend on it to be available for all users. By creating a "real" link to your primary page, you're ensured that your most important information is displayed.

Note An alternative to this GoLive-provided Action is Goto URL by OUT Media Design GmbH. Goto URL is an alternative to the standard Goto Link Action and a much better and more flexible choice than Target2Frames of the Actions Plus Package. It handles nested framesets, does link checking, and allows for suppression of history entries!

Cross-Reference See Chapter 18 to learn about Actions.

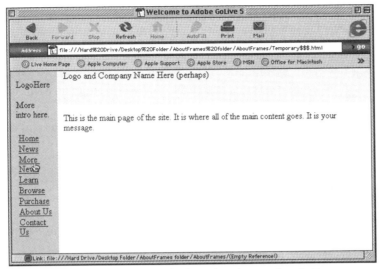

Figure 15-10: You can test links by using the Preview in Browser feature. When one of these links is clicked, a new page opens within the main viewing area (main frame).

To set up the Target2Frames, follow these steps:

1. Begin your link as normal, linking it to the more important of the target pages.

2. Open the Actions window (Window ⇨ Actions) and follow the common procedure for starting Actions:

   • Click the plus sign at the top-right corner to start the Action.

   • Click the user action once that will trigger the frame change. Commonly, this is Mouse Click.

3. Click the Actions pop-up menu, and then choose Target2Frames from the Actions Plus submenu.

4. In the text field next to Frame 1, type the name of one frame into which you want a new page to load.

Note   This link will be redundant, as it links to the same page as the original link. That's just part of covering for non-JavaScript browsers.

5. Use your preferred linking method to link to the page you want to have load into this frame.

6. In the text field next to Frame 2, type the name of the other frame into which you want the other new page to load.

7. Use your preferred linking method to link to the page you want to have load into this frame.

In Figure 15-11 you can see a completed setup for the Target2Frames Action.

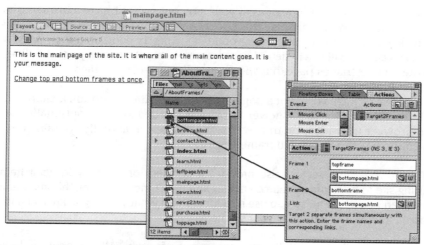

Figure 15-11: Setting up the Target2Frames Action to have one link change the contents of two frames at once

To test these links, use the Preview in Browser button. (Actions are JavaScript and therefore require a browser to function.)

Cross-Reference   A few other alternative Actions do the same or similar things. You can find them at the sites listed in Chapter 18.

Linking to a page outside of your frameset

What happens when you want to break out of your framed page and take users back to regular pages displayed one per page within a browser window? As with all pages within a framed page, the secret is the target attribute.

Why might you want to do this? When you link to an outside resource, it's not fair to stuff that outside page into your own frame. Doing so has two downsides. For one, it crams a page designed for a full browser window into a much smaller space, making it harder for the user to read the page. For another, you are not doing justice to the person or company providing that other information.

To have one of your links open in its own window, rather than within one of your frames, set up the link the same as any other link but set the target for that link as _blank, using the generic target at the bottom of the list. That's all.

Creating a <noframes> Alternative

What happens when a visitor arrives at your site, but doesn't have a browser that recognizes frames? What will this visitor see? By default, they'll see nothing — just a plain blank window with a white background. It's a pretty good idea to provide something these visitors will see in lieu of your frames — an alternative page that lives within the regular frames page, but within specific <noframes> tags.

The <noframes> page is sort of a page within a page. It can contain a simple message alerting the visitor that a newer browser is needed and can optionally contain links to browser upgrades. Or, the <noframes> page can actually contain your page's content — in a simplified frameless format.

Tip The <noframes> section also provides a priceless opportunity for your frame-using site to be found by search engines and directories. They see this information and can use it — so be sure to use it to show them what you've got. Present a thorough, friendly description of your site here.

GoLive automatically sets up this alternative page for you. All you need to do is add content. By adding this content, you can safely provide something for everyone, whether visitors are using a frames-compatible browser or not. Of course GoLive is about visual page creation — so of course you can design your <noframes> page in Layout mode. To add your <noframes> page content simply switch to Layout mode and design away. Don't forget to save when you're finished.

To see what the <noframes> code looks like, open the Source Code view (Window ⇨ Source Code) or switch to the Source tab.

You will see code like the following (although what you see between your own <Frame Set> tags will differ depending upon the frame pattern you select):

```
<html>

  <head>
    <meta http-equiv="content-type"
content="text/html;charset=iso-8859-1">
    <meta name="generator" content="Adobe GoLive 4">
    <title>This page contains only the Frame Set</title>
  </head>

  <Frame Set cols="80,*">
    <frame src="(Empty Reference!)" name="No Name" noresize>
    <frame src="(Empty Reference!)" name="No Name" noresize>
  </Frame Set>
  <noframes>

    <body>
    </body>

  </noframes>
</html>
```

The code that contains the `<noframes>` setup is that last part:

```
<noframes>

  <body>
  </body>

</noframes>
```

This message appears only to nonframe browsers, so you will not see it in the frame preview. Instead, check out the regular Preview tab to see your results. Of course, for a more accurate preview you should use Preview in Browser. You need a Version 1 or 2 browser for this preview. (Otherwise your preview will be of the frames.)

Expert Tip

To preview your page in a later-version browser, design it in a separate normal page, check it in your normal browser, and revise until satisfied. When you finish, copy all the content into the frame page. Or, if you are using Internet Explorer to preview you pages, you can also switch the frame display off by choosing Preferences ⇨ Web Content ⇨ Page Content ⇨ Show Frames. — *Oliver Zahorka, OUT Media Design GmbH, Switzerland*

Solving Frame Navigation Issues

Recall that a page that uses frames is actually composed of not one page, but several pages working together to present your information. Consequently, you need to account for the times when a user somehow ends up at one of the pages that are intended only to be viewed within a frame as a single part of your entire presentation. You can use JavaScript to automatically transport the user to your frameset page, but you also need to add a regular link a user can click manually in case the user does not have JavaScript functionality. Using the JavaScript automatic correction is optional, although recommended. Adding a manual link is absolutely necessary.

Adding a manual link

Place a link on each main content page to lead your visitors to the frameset page. To do so, follow these steps:

1. Enter the text to explain the situation, as desired.

2. Within this explanation, select the text that will become the link.

3. Click the Make Link icon on the toolbar.

4. Using your favorite linking method, link to the frameset page.

5. From the Target menu, choose _top.

Now, whenever a user lands at this page instead of your frameset page, he or she will see the link, understand that this page is not meant to be viewed alone, and (hopefully) click the link to arrive at your fully presented frameset.

Adding an automatic correction

The ForceFrame Action compensates for when a user bookmarks your site from within a specific frame. When the user returns to the bookmarked page, the Action redirects the browser to your actual frameset page, and then inserts the book-marked page into place within the proper frame. This way the user gets to the information desired, but it is presented properly within your page, so your logo, navigation, and other details are all there too.

GoLive's ForceFrame Action is JavaScript that, when on your page, is automatically called into action whenever a Web browser begins to load the page as a standalone page instead of as part of the main frameset. When you use it, as long as the user has JavaScript working, your page will be viewed in its proper context within your full frames page, no matter how the page was bookmarked. It's a great help, and a must if you're using frames. To use it, you place it in each page that you want to always have displayed within the frame page. (This means the navigation page, the banner ad page, the hidden frame page . . . every page.)

Cross-Reference   To learn more about Actions, see Chapter 18.

Caution   A couple of bugs have been found in the ForceFrame Action by users of GoLive 4. Perhaps they won't pop up in the rewritten GoLive 5 code, but in case they do, I want you to be aware of them so you don't think you're going crazy. One is that, under certain circumstances that users were not able to track down, it called the proper page, but disallowed any link to progress from any of the pages of the frameset. Instead, it reloaded the first called page over and over again. The other bug happens when two of your frames contain pages with links. Links from one frame work fine, but links from the second frame work intermittently, sometimes needing another click, or sometimes only calling up the page originally designated for that frame. (Thank you to Nini Tjäder for documenting this.)

As handy as it is, GoLive's ForceFrame Action doesn't handle nested framesets. If you use it to load a page into a single frame, or another frameset, that was nested within a default frameset, the page and frame will not appear when the frameset page loads. Fortunately, OUT Media Design, at its OUTactions site (`http://out.to/actions`), sells an excellent and stable alternative that does handle nested framesets. (It's a very reasonable $10, and I definitely recommend it.)

On the CD-ROM   For your convenience, a copy of the OUTactions, complete with descriptions of their Actions and the Actions files, is included on this book's CD-ROM. (But check the live site on the Web for the most current updates and additions.)

To set up the ForceFrame Action, follow these steps:

1. Drag a Head Action icon from the Smart tab of the Objects palette into the head section of the page. (If the head section isn't open, hover over the arrow next to the Page icon until the section opens, and then continue to drag the icon in place.)

2. From the Exec menu, choose OnParse.

   OnParse happens while the page is fetched from the server; OnLoad happens after all the elements of the page have been loaded into the browser's memory.

3. Click the Action pop-up menu and choose Actions Plus ⇨ ForceFrame.

4. From the Frameset URL area, link to the frameset page using your preferred linking method. (That's the page in which you've created the frameset.)

5. In the Frame field shown in Figure 15-12, type the name of the frame into which you want the new page to load. (This is another great reason to name your frames, and why it's good to name them clearly and concisely.)

Figure 15-12: Setting up a page called mainpage.html to open in the frame called Main within the index.html page

Because this solution is an Action (which is JavaScript), it requires a browser to function. So, to test your results, use the Preview in Browser button. Preview the page that you've just placed the Action in and, when it opens in the browser, it should open, not as a standalone page, but within the frameset in the correct target frame.

✦   ✦   ✦

Adding a Form to Your Site

Chances are good that you've filled out a few forms in your day. When the form is on paper, you complete the relevant information and then someone most likely transfers the information to a database or some sort of list — doing so by reading your information and typing (or retyping) what you've already entered.

The Web introduces a new era for forms, enabling the data you enter to land directly in the database or list without being touched by human hands. (Or, at the very least the data goes into an e-mail and is sent to you to be copied and pasted.)

So what might you do with a form on the Web? You can collect information, as you'd expect. For example, you can ask users for their names, e-mail addresses, shipping addresses, music preferences, favorite Thomas the Tank Engine railroad car, and so on.

GoLive provides an excellent, easy-to-use interface for creating forms on your pages. There's an entire tab in the Objects palette replete with all of the field-building elements you need to create a beautiful form — fields, radio buttons, checkboxes, list boxes, buttons, and form tags.

Understanding How Forms Work

Did you ever imagine using a secret decoder ring? Well, Web page forms aren't exactly rings (unless you count the data's trip to the server and back a circle), but when you use a CGI you're definitely working with a decoder. In fact, you're also working with the encoder.

Gathering data with the form document

What the user sees on a page when he or she submits information is just a part of the form story. Behind the scenes an encoded message is being constructed from commands called *form actions,* from any *hidden fields* you have placed within the form, and from the form's *controls* (which are the various types of fields that collect the user-entered information). It's not being encoded for secrecy, though. It's encoded so it can make the trip across the Internet in one piece. When you choose a ready-made CGI or other agent, the person who created it will tell you what command you need to provide in the form.

Telling the form what to do with the data

The parts of the form that the user fills out are called the *controls.* They contain, for the most part, all the information you desire from the user. In order to tell that information where to land within a database or how to look in an e-mail or elsewhere, you provide a set of *matching information,* such as the name of the field that matches the user's input.

In addition to the information the user provides, you may need to know things like what browser or platform a user is sending from so you can send back a page nicely formatted for each user, or because you're counting how many people from each platform use your site. (You can't collect private information from a user's hard drive — just the browser-information-type stuff. For example, the server's name, path, realm, or IP number. The capability to collect this must be programmed into the CGI [or other agent].)

If a user provided a username and password, you don't want to ask for them each time, so you can hide the information within the page, too — just while dealing with that one user. If you're creating an online order system, the form needs to carry product codes along with the user-entered quantity.

The form needs to know where to send the data, so the form has to be assigned some sort of Action; this is called the Form Action, and you supply that too. The form also needs to know how to carry the information to the Web server, so you have to tell it which Method to use.

As you create your form, the page takes on the look the user will see while the Inspector shows you the behind-the-scenes stuff that you need to provide but not bother the user with. Be sure to keep the Inspector open and handy.

Now you're armed with possibly more than you ever wanted to know about forms, like the one shown in Figure 16-1. In this chapter, I'll show you each of a form's building blocks and how GoLive enables you to add them easily to a page.

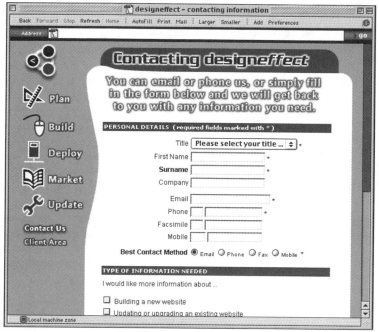

Figure 16-1: Forms are a good way to collect information about your customers.

Starting a Form

A form can exist anywhere on your page, as long as you place it inside the Form container. The form doesn't care where you place it on the page. However, due to the way browsers may render form elements differently (and display them in different sizes), in order to have your form look its best and keep the fields, directions, and labels lined up, place your form items within a table inside the Form Container. You can also place them directly inside the Form container (using the cursor), or you can use a combination of both. Grids are not recommended.

> **Note**
>
> Previous users of GoLive will notice that the way forms are constructed in GoLive 5 is different than in previous versions. Whereas you used the Form Start and End tags before, GoLive now uses a container that writes the end tag for you (the reason for this is so your forms always meet the W3C HTML specifications). This may result in a misaligned tag becoming visible in Layout mode. This is dealt with later in this chapter in the "Form Troubleshooting Issues" section.

Later I mention that another option for setting up your form is to use the new HTML 4 fieldset. See "Placing fieldsets in a form" later in this chapter.

To create a form using a table to contain your form elements, follow these steps:

1. Place the Form container on your page, as shown in Figure 16-2.

Form icon

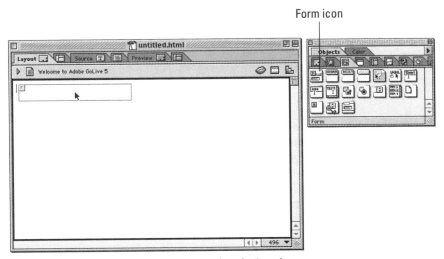

Figure 16-2: Add a form to your page by placing the Form icon from the Objects palette's Form tab.

2. Place the table into your Form container and format it.

Typically a form has one column at the left for labels — text that serves as a visual clue to tell your viewers what you seek. The fields are usually placed in a column to the right. You may also want to put a narrow column between the label and field columns to provide a bit of space between the two, or you may be able to use cell padding or spacing to separate the columns.

Cross-Reference   To learn about tables, see Chapter 13.

To create a form directly on your page, drag the Form icon into place, and then add the form elements inside the Form container as needed.

The Form Inspector, which becomes active whenever the form tag is selected, is where you provide the basic necessary directions for your form (see Figure 16-3). The rest of this section explains each of the Form Inspector's form information areas.

Figure 16-3: The Form Inspector

Naming your form

Naming your form simply helps you keep your sanity by helping you easily identify the form when you need to work with it — if you give your form a descriptive name. Putting more than one form per page makes a name even more important. Your form name should be unique to your site.

For example a form that enables a person to add his name to a list or sign a guest book can be called "AddGuest" or "GuestAdd."

Specifying an Action

Every form must have an Action. The Action tells the user's browser where to go with the information sent when the user presses the Submit button.

The Actions are specific to the CGI or server-side technology you're using. Commonly, the Action is the URL of the CGI document or the name of the page that contains the code for whatever server-side technology you're using.

To enter an Action, follow these steps:

1. Make sure the Form icon on your page is selected so the Inspector window says Form Inspector.

2. Specify the Action in the Actions field.

   If you're using a server-side technology other than a CGI, check with its documentation or with your site host.

   If you're using a CGI, the Action is the address of your CGI script, which is a file that either resides within your site or in a specified directory on the Web server. Check with your site host about this.

   • If the site host is providing the CGI, it probably provides a list of specific CGIs in a common folder and the address of each of them.

- If you are permitted to use your own, you'll be told where on the server to store the CGI so you'll know the path to it; then add the name of the CGI along with any other specific instructions the CGI provides. CGIs are commonly stored either in a common folder on the server, or within a specifically labeled folder set up for you within your own folder on the server.

The Action sometimes contains more than just the name of the CGI or server-side program. Sometimes it includes a command the program will recognize. The program's documentation will guide you.

If your CGI script is on the Web server and your site host tells you to use a full URL (beginning with http://) you can store the address in the External tab of the Site Window, and then use Point and Shoot to designate it. The reverse is also true. If you type the full URL into the Inspector, it will automatically be added to the External tab of the Site Window if you are working with a site open.

If your site host lets you store your CGI script in your own folder on the server, you can store the CGI script in your Site Window. In that case, if the script is already in your Site Window, you can Point and Shoot to it or use the Browse button.

 To learn about storing URLs, take a look at Chapter 11.

Targeting form results when using frames

After your form calls upon the CGI, the CGI returns results — presented with another page. You might assume the Target option in the Inspector is where you tell the CGI which page to return, but it's not. The page to be returned is more commonly designated in a hidden tag unless it is permanently embedded in the CGI or uses another scheme.

The target GoLive provides for in the Form Inspector is only applicable when you are using a frameset. When your CGI returns a page, the target determines which frame the page will land in. If you are using frames, choose a frame target from the pop-up menu. If you are not using frames, leave this field blank. To learn about frames see Chapter 15.

Encrypting form results

If your site is on a secure server, choose the server's encryption method from the pop-up menu. Check with your site host if you're not sure whether this is the case, or, if it is, what encryption method to select. Encryption is not commonly used and requires that the server be running specialized encryption software.

Of course, it is preferable to encrypt sensitive information. Another, simpler way to encrypt information, such as a credit card field, is to use a simple Perl script or JavaScript that can work on a field-by-field level. Many such scripts are floating around on the Web. I point you to a few script archives at the end of this chapter. This does not require use of the Inspector's Encryption field.

Choosing a method

The method your form uses determines the way that information is carried from the user's browser to the server. Two methods are available, as follows:

✦ **Get** adds the user's information to the URL that is sent back to the server. This is a very limited method, as URLs can only contain a specific number of characters and then cut off the rest of what you may need sent. It also limits you to using only ASCII characters. Additionally, the sent information appears in the URL — not cool if your form contains hidden data. One reason you might want to use the GET method is if you would like visitors to your site to be able to bookmark specific queries (because the values sent are stored in the URL).

✦ **Post** is the preferred method. It can carry as much data as desired, and the information carried isn't visible in the URL.

 Note Some hosts only permit the use of GET, although this limitation is rare these days. Check with your host before creating your form.

After you have entered this basic form information, you are ready to begin building your form. Information or search requests are submitted via the various fields on you form.

Using hidden tags

Hidden tags are sort of secret codes you place in your form to communicate with your CGI. No one set of such codes exists. Instead, each CGI requires its own specific tags and may call them commands, variables, or perhaps something else.

For example, say you're using a database that has many layouts. A hidden tag would tell the database which layout to access. Another tag can tell your CGI script which page to return to the user upon completion of a specific exchange of data. A hidden tag can also pass information from one page to another.

 Note Passing information within hidden tags makes it easier for you, the page creator, to update the information without having to learn how to open the CGI and hard-code these values into the CGI. Support for the hidden tags must be built into the CGI in the first place, though.

Hidden tags can be placed anywhere within your form tags. It is common, and recommended, that you place your hidden tags at the beginning of the Form container. That gets the work out of the way so you can go on to focus on the fields and the aesthetics of your page. No limit exists to the number of hidden tags you can place in a form. In fact it's common to call upon several.

To use a hidden tag, follow these steps:

1. Drag a Hidden tag from the Forms tab of the Objects palette, placing it inside the Form container (outside of the table) or within a cell. Placement of the hidden tag is not actually critical, but it's most logical to provide all such information up front or in logical groups.

   A hidden tag appears as a small square with a capitol H on it (as shown in Figure 16-4).

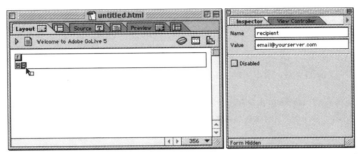

Figure 16-4: A selected hidden tag and the information it contains

2. Open the Inspector, now called the Form Hidden Inspector.

3. In the Name field, enter the name of the variable (command) you are passing.

   Your CGI script or middleware may call for several hidden tags. You can place them one after another. Their order is of little consequence unless you're instructed otherwise. Choose the variable you need to use and enter it here. For example, a variable that tells a database which layout to receive information into may be called "layout," so you would enter the word "layout." A variable can also be a customer ID number or the quantity of an item ordered. In Figure 16-4 the Hidden field carries the e-mail address where the information will be sent after the form has been processed.

4. In the Value field, enter the value that you wish to pass along with the chosen command.

   This value must be one that is appropriate for the variable you enter in Step 3. In Figure 16-4, because the Name is "recipient," the corresponding information is the e-mail address.

Note To learn about the Disabled option, see "Setting User Navigation Within a Form" later in this chapter.

All hidden tags look the same on a form. To see what each contains, select the tag while in Layout Mode and look at the Inspector, which will be the Form Hidden Inspector. You can also learn a tag's contents by keeping the Source code window open as you work, or by using Outline mode or Source mode. The code for a hidden tag, by the way, is as follows:

```
<input type="hidden" value="hiddenValue" name="hiddenName">
```

Adding Form Fields

Form fields, or *controls* as they are generically called, are the areas where the user enters data. If your form collects names and addresses, the fields are where that information is placed. If the form requests a search, the fields are where the search criteria are entered.

GoLive fully supports all standard field types (available form fields are determined by the HTML specification, not by GoLive). You can choose a type of field for each piece of information you want collected on your form. Two field types (text field and text area) enable freely typed text; an additional field (password) enables text but hides it for passwords. The rest of the field types enable you to provide predetermined responses (radio buttons, for example). Your choice of which to use determines whether the user must pick only one response, or may pick several.

The only set rule about placing fields is that you have to place them inside the Form container. Any values that are set in fields placed outside of the Form container are ignored and do not get sent to the Form processor. Other than that you can place your fields anywhere you want, using the same formatting and alignment controls for working directly on the page or working within a table. As mentioned previously, placing fields in a table helps keep them well aligned. After you create the form you can set up the *tab order,* the order in which users will jump from field to field when they press the Tab key.

For users to know what is expected of them in each field, you can provide directions by adding text labels as you do on any page or in any table. For example, to let users know you want their first names entered in a field, you would use a Label from the Form tab of the Objects palette to label that field "First Name."

All form fields are placed on the page the same way as just about everything in GoLive: Drag them from the Objects palette into place on your page, or double-click the icon in the Objects palette to have it land by the cursor. All settings for the fields are then entered in the Inspector. The settings vary depending upon the function of the field.

Note

Remember that you need to tell your user what is expected for any form field or data input element. You have two ways to do this. You can simply type instructions and field labels for the user or you can use the label tag. The Label tag adds excellent functionally to all fields, especially radio button and checkbox fields. To find out all about Labels, see the "Adding labels to form fields" section.

Because the most efficient way to organize a form is within a table, you can put field labels (whether hand-typed or placed using the label icon) into the left column of a table, and then put the actual form fields in the right. To place a space between the label and field you can have a third column between the label and field columns. Set the middle column to a few pixels set width. (See Chapter 13.)

One field setting to pay close attention to is the name. Your CGI may require certain naming conventions. For example, if your form is feeding information into a database or requesting a search within a database, the form fields probably have to *exactly match* the names in the database. Be careful not to add extra spaces to the name as that can throw off the CGI and the data will not arrive at the database. The same may hold true for other destinations as well. (If you're using a prewritten CGI, see its instructions. If you've asked someone to write a script for you, ask your provider for specific directions when you receive the script. If you've written the script yourself, you should know what to do.)

In the next sections, I'll go over all available form fields and provide instructions for using each one.

Note   You can use JavaScript to validate a form when it loads into the user's browser, or to validate that a user has completed all form fields properly prior to submitting the form. (Some simple examples of this appear later in this chapter using both GoLive Actions and custom JavaScript.) You can also use it to create a cookie to help keep track of returning visitors, and to give people the convenience of not having to fill out the same forms over and over.

Text field and password field

A *text field* is a one-line area in which a user can type or paste text. A *password field* is exactly like a regular text field except that all characters typed into it immediately appear as bullets or asterisks so the information can't be viewed by someone looking over the user's shoulder. Figure 16-5 shows the results of using each field.

Figure 16-5: A few text fields and a password field as they might look in a browser (the labels to the left of each field were added into the left column of the table)

The setup for each field is identical. In fact, although an icon exists for each on the Objects palette, you can change one to the other and even back again by clicking a checkbox in the Inspector. The only thing that changes with each field type is the Inspector's name.

Follow these steps to add a text or password field to your form:

1. Drag the text or password field icon from the Objects palette into place on your form. The Inspector palette will now look similar to Figure 16-6.

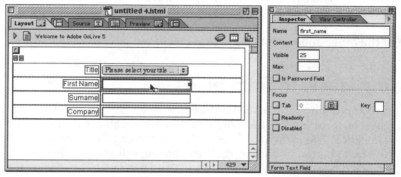

Figure 16-6: A text field being set up in the Form Text Field Inspector

2. By default, the field Name area of the Form Text Field (or Password) Inspector says textfieldName. Select this temporary name and enter your own unique field name. (Each field name must be unique within its form.)

   Remember to check about naming your fields. Often they have to match names in a database or CGI. Capitalization can often also count, as can extra spaces before or after the name.

3. *(Optional)* If you want the field to contain content by default, enter that content in the Inspector field called Content. Some people like to have a field say things like "Please enter your first name" or just "First Name." Most of the time this is left empty so users can see that they have not entered anything there yet.

4. In the Visible field of the Form Text Field Inspector, enter the width — in characters — that you wish the text field to be.

   This sets the width of the field and therefore determines the number of characters that can be seen at any one time in the field. This does not affect the total number of characters that may be entered; it is possible for text to be in the field but not appear, or for users to use their arrow keys to scroll through their entry.

   As with any other part of your page, if you make the field width longer than a browser window, the browser will show horizontal scrollbars.

   A text field's size can also be set visually on the page by dragging its right (and only) handle. As you drag, the number of visible characters automatically adjusts.

5. *(Optional)* If you wish to limit the number of characters a user may enter in this text field, enter that number, again in characters, in the Max field of the Form Text Field Inspector.

Note When you're collecting information that contains a set number of characters, such as an area code, phone number, zip code, or social security number, limiting the number of characters permitted for a field can help prevent user mistakes.

If you want to change a text field into a password field, check the Is Password Field box. To turn a password field into a text field, uncheck the same option.

Each of the other options for this field is discussed later in the chapter.

Adding labels to form fields

Labels are another new-to-HTML-4 feature that make forms easier for the user. When you create the form you link each radio button or checkbox's option to the actual button or checkbox. Then when the user clicks the label it has the same effect as clicking inside the radio button or checkbox. Aptly enough, this tag is called <label>. In source mode it begins with <label for . . .> and ends with the closing tag </label>.

Because of a label's close association with a field's choice, text readers for people with disabilities have an easier time with forms when labels are used.

Labels work staring with Internet Explorer 4 (Mac and Windows) and in iCab (Mac). They don't exhibit the added functionality in the Netscape 4.x browsers on the Mac or in Windows. In any browser that doesn't enable clicking the label, labels just appear like normal text, so you can use them in your forms without worrying about compatibility problems with older browsers.

To add a label to your form, follow these steps:

1. Drag the label icon from the Objects palette into place by the choice or option it will identify.

2. Edit the label by clicking the default label (which says Label), select that text, and then type your own words.

   The label is a text area so you can press Enter/Return to move text to a new line or press Shift along with Enter/Return to create a line break that doesn't add space between the lines of the label. Format as desired.

3. Set the label to activate the form's choice in one of these two ways:

   • Point and Shoot from the Inspector to the label's form element as shown in Figure 16-7.

- Press ⌘ (Mac) or Alt (Windows) as you click the Label's border and drag to the element you are labeling. GoLive will assign a cryptic-looking reference to the label. The reason for this is to guarantee the uniqueness of the reference when two labels might be linked to different form fields of the same name (radio buttons, for example).

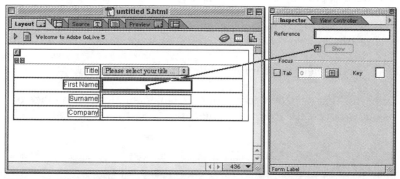

Figure 16-7: You can associate a Label and choice by Pointing and Shooting from the Label's border to the choice.

4. To verify your link between label and option, click the Show button in the Inspector. While this button is pressed, the link appears as shown in Figure 16-8.

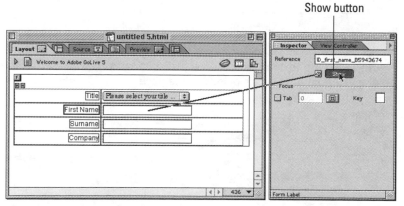

Figure 16-8: Press Show to verify an association between a label and the option it will activate.

Adding a text area field to your form

A *text area* is similar to a text field except that it provides extra lines to hold more text. A Text area also has a vertical scrollbar in order to accommodate plenty of text. Users type within a text area, as they type anywhere else on their computers. The Return or Enter key (on the letter part of the keyboard) adds a normal return, creating a new paragraph. However, the Enter key on the number pad may not have the same effect. This can differ depending on the browser (Internet Explorer may type a character, whereas Netscape usually ignores it). If this is important to the functioning of your form then you may need to tell viewers of the site that this can occur.

To add a text area field to your form, follow these steps:

1. Drag the Text Area field icon from the Objects palette into place on your form, as shown in Figure 16-9. It will then appear as shown in Figure 16-10.

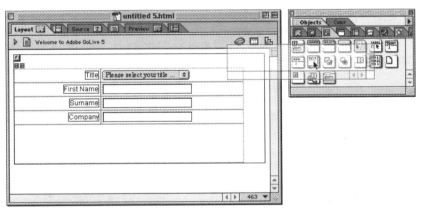

Figure 16-9: The Text Area icon as it is just starting to be dragged from the Objects palette to the page

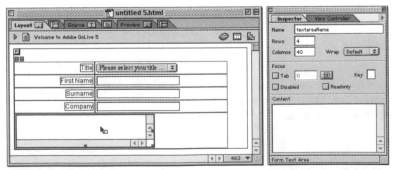

Figure 16-10: A new Text Area as it appears in a borderless cell, and its corresponding Inspector

2. By default the field name area of the Form Text Area Inspector says textareaName. Select this temporary name and enter your own field name unique to the current form.

Remember, field names often have to exactly match names in a database or CGI.

If you have two field names (regardless of kind), they'll both feed their contents or data into the same field within the database or CGI.

3. *(Optional)* If you want the field to contain content by default, enter that content in the Content field in the Inspector. This text will appear in the browser but can be deleted and typed over by the user. When the user tabs into the field the pre-entered text will be selected, and if the user clicks into this field, the cursor appears where he or she clicks. (See Figure 16-11.)

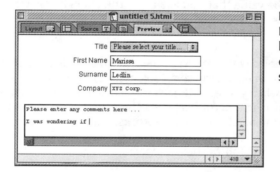

Figure 16-11: A Text Area in Preview mode demonstrates text being entered. (The user kept the original content, but it can also be selected and typed over.)

4. The text area is four rows high by default, providing four rows of visible text for the user to see without scrolling. To add or delete visible rows enter a new number in the Rows field. This has no effect on the amount of text the user may enter.

5. The text area is 40 columns wide by default, which is actually 40 characters. You can make this area wider or narrower by entering a new number in the Columns field. This width has no effect on the amount of text the user may enter.

6. In the Wrap (Mac) pop-up menu, choose an option for how (or if) text will wrap when a user enters text:

- *Default* adopts the browser's behavior.

- *Off* turns text wrap off, which means as the user types the text just keeps going and going and going. The user needs to scroll horizontally to see what he or she wrote. The user has to press Return to see the text appear at the visible part of the text area and may press Return often to read what he or she is writing. However, that actually creates a new paragraph.

- *Virtual* provides the user with the effect of text wrap, so the words are visible between the left and right edges of the Text Area field. When the field's content is sent to the server, though, it is sent as one continuous line. That way the database, e-mail, or other document that receives the text can treat it as appropriate for that application or document.

• *Physical* not only shows the user the effect of text wrap, but also adds a line break to physically cut each line at the end of the column. The words entered are sent to the server wrapping exactly the way they appear in the form. (Depending on the platform the user is on, the text you receive may have end of line characters such as "=" that you would have to clean up.)

Note   Regardless of which wrapping behavior you choose, the user must also press Return to create a new paragraph.

Adding checkboxes to your form

A checkbox enables you to have the user choose from preselected information. When the user leaves the checkbox empty, no information is sent upon submission. When the box is checked, the value that you assign to the checkbox is transferred via the browser. Checkboxes are toggles; each time the user clicks the checkbox it toggles between on and off.

Checkboxes are your best choice when you want the user to be able to choose more than one option (for example, when a form says, "select as many as desired"). Another reason to use a checkbox is when you want the user to feel in control of a choice, such as when electing to have you send him (or her) something. In this case, a yes or no set of radio buttons, or a pop-up menu of choices also works, but the checkbox is clearer.

To add checkboxes to your form, follow these steps:

1. Drag the Checkbox icon from the Objects palette into your form.

   You'll drag one checkbox for each option you want to offer.

2. Enter a name for the checkbox.

   As usual with a form, this is not an arbitrary name; it commonly must match the name of its corresponding field in the database or CGI from which it feeds or receives data.

   The name of the checkbox must be unique from other fields in the same form but not unique from the other checkboxes in its set that provide the other options. If several checkboxes provide value options for the same field within a database, you will create several checkboxes all with the same Name.

3. Enter a value. If the checkbox is selected, the value will be sent when the user submits the form.

   If the form is working in conjunction with a database, the corresponding field within the database already has values assigned to it. The values on your form need to match the database. Checkbox data can go into a corresponding set of checkboxes in the database or into text fields, not into other types of fields. For instance, if your database field only accepts entries eight characters in length, make sure that the corresponding field on your form only accepts eight characters too.

4. *(Optional)* If you want this checkbox to be checked by default when the form first appears to the user, check the Selected option. See the example of a completed checkbox in Figure 16-12.

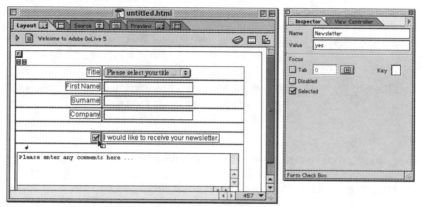

Figure 16-12: A checkbox for which *yes* will be sent to a field called Newsletter. It is preselected when the page loads.

If several checkboxes will provide value options for the same field within a Form, repeat the preceding steps to create the other checkboxes, all with the same Name. You can save time by copying the button instead of starting with a new button. Select the first button, which is already set up, copy it, and then paste as many new buttons as are needed. This way you ensure that the group name remains identical. (On the Mac you can Option-drag the original button to copy it.)

As with all form elements, you need to add a label by each option to let users know what they're selecting. For example, back in Figure 16-12, text tells the user that by checking this checkbox they're requesting to receive a newsletter. You have two ways to add labels to your form. You can simply type descriptive text, or you can use a feature new to HTML—the label tag. See the "Adding labels to form fields" section.

Adding radio buttons to your form

Radio buttons present the user with multiple choices for a specific field but force the user to *choose just one*. For example, you might ask "Do you have a credit card?" and have two radio buttons—Yes and No—that both apply to the same question field. The user can select either yes or no; when one is selected the other is automatically deselected. When radio buttons report to the same field, they are in a "group."

An empty radio button sends nothing to the server. A selected radio button sends the value that you assign to it.

Checkboxes versus Radio Buttons

Checkboxes differ from radio buttons in that more than one can be selected simultaneously by the user, meaning that the data sent from the form for this field can have more than one value. This is dealt with by sending the values as a comma-delimited list. For example, if you have a form field called "Hobbies" and someone selects the checkboxes for Bushwalking, Cycling, and Reading, the values would be sent as something similar to this:

```
Hobbies=Bushwalking,Cycling,Reading
```

You don't have to worry about the code that sends this information; the browser does it for you. The values are set using the value associated with the checkbox.

Follow these steps to add a radio button to a form:

1. Drag the Radio Button icon from the Objects palette into your form.

2. Enter a name for the radio button group; in the Form Radio Button Inspector the name goes into the Group field. If the user is asked to choose between two radio buttons, then both belong to the same field within the database so both have the same group name (as shown in Figure 16-13).

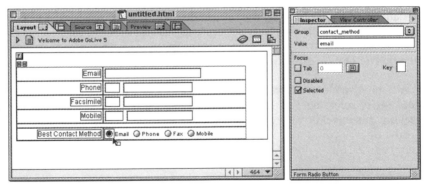

Figure 16-13: Four radio buttons, all with the same name, determine that the users will have to choose one response from four possibilities.

As usual with a form, this is not an arbitrary name; it commonly must match the name of its corresponding field in the database or CGI that it feeds or received data from.

3. Enter a value. The value is the actual data that is sent when the user submits the form. This is the same as with a checkbox.

If the form is working in conjunction with a database, the corresponding field within the database may require a particular type of value (such as an integer, a ten-letter word, a Boolean, or a date) assigned to it, so these values must match the database. The field into which the radio button value goes can take the form of a corresponding radio button or a text field, but not other types of fields.

4. *(Optional)* To have this radio button selected by default when the form first appears to the user, check the Selected option. (Only one button in the set can be selected, so only one can be preselected.)

5. Repeat these steps to add other radio buttons to the group. Each one will have the same group name but different values. You must have at least two radio buttons to offer any option. Otherwise, you have no way to deselect a radio button.

You can save time by copying the button instead of starting with a new button. Select the first button, which is already set up, copy it, and then paste as many new buttons as are needed. This way you ensure that the group name remains identical. (On the Mac you can Option-drag the original button to copy it.)

You need to add a label by each option so users know what they're selecting. For example, you need to tell users that one button is for choosing Yes and one is for No. You have two ways to add labels to your form. You can simply type descriptive text, or you can use a feature new to HTML—the label tag. See "Adding labels to forms" earlier in this chapter for details.

Creating a pop-up menu

A pop-up menu is an alternative to radio buttons. The user must choose only one of the choices you present. However, depending on how many choices exist, a pop-up menu may be a great space-saver. A large group of radio buttons can not only take up a lot of room, but also look confusing. A pop-up presents a simple, small, clean look as shown in Figure 16-14. Beware of creating too long a list, though.

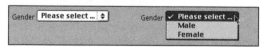

Figure 16-14: A pop-up menu as it looks normally and the same pop-up being clicked

With the other field types you have to type a label such as the Yes or No for each option offered by a radio button and place it beside the option. With a pop-up list, that option label is built into the pop-up. The choice that pops up in the list is the label that guides the user's choice. As with checkboxes and radio buttons, the actual value passed from the form does not have to be the same exact text as the label. The actual data the form sends can be something totally different. This enables you to have a friendly looking list. For example, the label can say Monday, Tuesday, and so on, while the values can be Mon, Tue, and so on—because in a database it's best to keep values short.

To create a Pop-up menu, follow these steps:

1. Drag the Pop-up icon from the Objects palette into place on your form.

2. In the Form Pop-up Inspector's Name field, enter the name for the field as defined by your CGI.

3. Click the first row under Label so the first label and value appear in the entry fields below the choice list.

   This is the first step to entering the label and value for the first choice in your menu.

4. In the choice entry area type a new label for your first choice. If the default label is preselected, just begin typing. If it's not, then select and type over this default text. This label is the first item that will appear in the pop-up. Click the Return button or press Enter/Return to confirm the change or press Tab to confirm the change automatically and also move to the Value field.

5. In the field next to the label entry area, replace the default value with your own value, as in Figure 16-15. As with the other form fields, this value must match those that exist in the corresponding field in the database. Click the Return button or press Enter/Return to confirm the change.

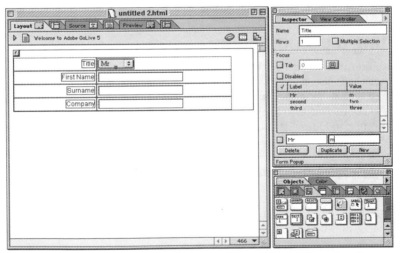

Figure 16-15: A choice's value being set after the Label is entered

When you click another item on the choice list or add a new item, the change in the value field is automatically confirmed.

6. Do the same for the next two default choices.

   If you have fewer than three choices, chances are you wouldn't use a menu, but in case you want to remove one of the defaults, click it in the list and then click Delete.

7. To add another choice click New, and then replace the default text that comes into the Label and Value fields. (The defaults are the words *label* and *value*.)

To remove any choice, select the choice in the list and then click the Delete button.

By default the first choice in the list appears in the Pop-up. However, you can set any other choice as the preselection. For example, if you have an alphabetical list of many countries, you may want one particular country to appear as the default. To preselect a choice, double-click the box to the left of the label. A checkmark then appears under the checkmark column in the choice list. (Alternately, you can check the box to the left of the entry boxes when you enter the label and value for any choice.)

Note

It's often helpful to the user to make the selected choice a helpful hint that they need to select something from the pop-up list. Using a label like "Please select . . ." or "Which size would you like?" helps give the user a visual reminder that they need to do something with the field. This becomes especially important now that browsers are letting users auto-fill forms using preselected values. It makes it very easy for a visitor to your site to miss a field that they are supposed to enter a value into.

In providing these directions I left out the Rows and Multiple Selection options. That's because adding more rows to a pop-up turns it into a *list*. Enabling Multiple Selections for a one-row pop-up prevents the pop-up from functioning at all. When working directly in HTML, adding the Rows attribute creates the change, and so it does here. By using the same Inspector interface for both a pop-up and a list, GoLive enables you to switch your field from one to another without having to re-enter the values.

Adding a list box to your form

The list is actually a variant of the pop-up menu. Unlike the pop-up menu, though, users can choose multiple responses from a list. You might say it's a cross between a pop-up menu and a group of checkboxes.

To create a list, follow the same directions as for creating a pop-up menu, with these two additions that can be performed at any point.

✦ In the Rows field, enter the number of rows that you want the user to see on the field. The more that are in view, the longer your list is. If you have six objects and three rows, scrollbars appear. Figure 16-16 demonstrates.

Figure 16-16: Both lists here contain five choices. The top list has fewer rows than choices, however, so scrollbars enable the user to see the extra choices.

✦ If you want the user to be able to select more than one choice, check the box by the Multiple Selection option.

If you enable Multiple Selection, be sure to include written instructions telling users that they can select as many as they want — and tell them how. To select more than one noncontiguous choice they need to press ⌘ (Mac) or Ctrl (Windows) as they click each choice. Or, they can press Shift as they click to select multiple items that appear one after another on the list. Shift-clicking one option and then another selects all options in between the two.

If you enable multiple selections you can have more than one choice selected by default.

On the CD-ROM

HTML doesn't provide the capability to limit the number of items that can be selected in the list, or "multiple-select," select box. However, you can use a JavaScript to provide that control. An example of code, written by David Shadovitz for you to adapt for yourself, is located in the JavaScript folder on the book's CD-ROM. Additionally, OUTactions has developed a GoLive Action just for this book that provides this function for you. You can find this Action in the GoLive Stuff folder on the CD-ROM.

If you decide you prefer a list to be a pop-up menu instead, just change the number in the Rows field to 1 and turn off Multiple Selection.

Setting User Navigation Within a Form

HTML 4 introduced some new ways to enable users to navigate through forms. One of the key additions was the concept of focus. When a visitor to your form clicks or tabs to a particular field, that field is said to have the focus. This information can be used in a number of ways, including setting the tab order of your form (which field should have focus next), setting key commands for particular fields, and other useful behaviors.

The focus area of the Inspector enables you to determine how your users will navigate through your form. Simple things like setting a logical tab order can help make it easier for your visitor to provide you with information or make requests.

The functions described in this section are new to HTML 4, so they won't work with pre-4.0 browsers, though they can be used without causing problems for the older browsers.

Setting the tab order of your fields

All browsers that read forms enable the user to tab through the forms, but they don't control the order of the tabbing and only provide for tabbing into text fields. HTML 4 enhances tab control, letting the designer set the tab order and providing for tabbing to select nontext fields. The Tab control in the Form Inspector is for set-ting the tabs as recognized by HTML 4 browsers that incorporate this capability. According GoLive's Web database, this feature, called `tabindex`, is Internet Explorer only.

When the standard is fully recognized and implemented by browsers, users will be able to tab into fields such as radio buttons and then press Enter/Return to select that choice. Tabbing in the order you specify will also be possible. For now, even though many browsers can't see your tab order (and the older browsers never will, of course), no harm or conflict is caused by setting a custom tab order.

In case you're wondering how tabs work in noncompliant browsers: In Netscape 4.6 browsers for the Macintosh, you can tab between text fields, but once you land in a text area you end up tabbing through the text area, jumping about five spaces per tab as if you are in a text document. In many browsers, the Tab key also takes you to the URL entry bar. After it cycles through the URL entry it doesn't always find its way to all of your other text fields again.

To set a custom tab order for your form, follow these steps:

1. Select the field that you want to be first in the tab order.

2. In this field's Inspector, press the # button next to the Tab field. Alternatively you can choose Special ⇨ Start Tabulator Indexing.

   Little numbered yellow boxes appear on each field that can be tabbed into. The cursor also gains a #.

3. Click each field in the order you wish the tabbing to proceed.

   As you click each field, the tab box shows its tab number. The same number is also recorded in the tab field in the item's Inspector. This number is the `tabindex`.

4. After you've assigned a tab order to all of the fields you want included, press the # button in the Inspector again or choose Special ⇨ Stop Tabulator Indexing.

Note   If you have multiple forms on your page, the other forms are also included in the tab numbering. Each form is not numbered separately. However, once a user clicks in a cell, the tabs proceed in order, so the user can still tab through each form. The focus will travel to the next form after the last cell of the current form.

After you've assigned a tab order, when the # button is selected, new tab numbers are assigned in sequence. If you click the same field multiple times, its number increments.

To edit the tab order, deselect the # button to turn off numbering, and then select the cell you want to pick up the numbering from. Turn tabulator indexing on again and start clicking. The numbering starts incrementing from the number of the cur-rently selected field.

To redo the entire tab order, select the field you want as number one and enter 1 into the Inspector. After that you can press the # button and click each field to assign new numbers.

Tip You can also click each field and enter the tab order number for each one in the tab field in the Inspector. This method has more steps, so you probably won't choose it initially. However, it may come in handy for editing the tab order.

Assigning keyboard keys

The key capability is designed by HTML 4.0 to enable you, the designer, to assign a keyboard key to a field so the user can jump directly to a specific field. This is a new idea and not widely implemented yet, though. Currently only newer versions of Internet Explorer support this function. The key command uses the Alt modifier in Windows browsers and the Control modifier in Mac browsers, meaning that if you set the Key to G, then users would press Control-G (on a Mac) or Alt+G (on Windows) to reach that field.

Caution Be careful when using this feature. So many keys are already assigned to computers that the key you choose may already do something else on the user's computer, and therefore may perform an unexpected procedure when the user follows your instructions.

To assign a keyboard key to a field, select the field that will have the key action. Then, in the Key field, type the key combination.

Disabling form elements

When you disable a form element it appears in the browser, but it is grayed out and unusable. The power of this capability, new to HTML 4, is to use it along with a script that runs a quick verification of your form and only enables the field when certain criteria are met. For example, you can have a button that only becomes available after all the fields are properly filled in, or you can have certain questions come alive depending on the way another question is answered.

To disable a form element you simply select the element and check the Disabled option. That option then appears grayed out on the form. To enable the field again, you need to write a script to do the verification and set the field as enabled. (This would perhaps be a JavaScript that is placed in the Header or Body of the page, not any special script that attaches to the actual element.)

This feature only works in Internet Explorer, though, not Netscape browsers (at least as of the time I write this). However, JavaScript provides a function that is even more useful and elegant; with JavaScript you can actually hide a field until certain criteria are met, revealing only fields (or buttons) that are pertinent to the responses a user provides or to the user's browser. (See Chapter 22 for more on JavaScript.)

Setting a field to read-only

You can set a field to read-only so the user can see the information but not change it. This can be handy when reporting information back to a user. To make a field read-only, simply select the field and check the option in the field's Inspector. A password or username is a good candidate for reading only; that way it serves as a reminder but can't be changed.

Placing fieldsets in a form

Fieldsets, literally sets of fields, are one of HTML 4's new accessibility features. The fieldset groups a number of fields within its boundary. It doesn't do anything special to contain or align the fields. It just makes it easier for speech synthesizers and text readers.

The legend that goes along with the fieldset helps make the group of fields understandable.

In the browser, a user sees a light gray line border around the cells that you place within the set's area.

However, fieldsets don't work in current Netscape browsers (they do work in Netscape 6 and Mozilla) or in Opera. They work in Internet Explorer 4 (except on a grid) and in iCab (an alternative Mac browser).

Follow these steps to place a fieldset on your form:

1. Drag the Fieldset icon to the form.

   It comes into the page as wide as your window and resizes as you resize the page.

2. By default a fieldset displays a legend — a textual description within the set's box.

   - To customize your legend with your own words, click the word Legend on the page and then type as you please.

   - If you decide you don't want a legend, uncheck Use Legend.

3. Choose a location for the Legend from the Alignment pop-up. The default alignment, called Default, is at the top left unless the browser happens to specify something different.

   Left, Right, and Center refer to the top as well as their respective horizontal alignment. An option also exists to set the alignment to the Bottom of the fieldset (you cannot set the horizontal alignment of a Bottom-aligned legend).

4. Move your fields into the set's boundary area and arrange as desired.

Adding Buttons to a Form

A form isn't much of a form until users can submit it to someone someplace. HTML provides for three types of buttons.

A Submit button submits your form, a Reset button removes all user input and returns the form to the way it looked when first sent to the browser, and a Push button attaches to a script. Each of these button types can be dragged from the Objects palette. If you place the wrong button type, you can change the type within the Inspector.

A button can optionally have an image associated with it. Each of the following button types is discussed further in the following sections:

✦ Submit buttons

✦ Normal buttons

✦ Reset buttons

✦ Universal buttons

Submit buttons

This button enables your visitors to send the entered information or request to the server. Here's how to use it:

1. Drag the button into place on your form, as in Figure 16-17.

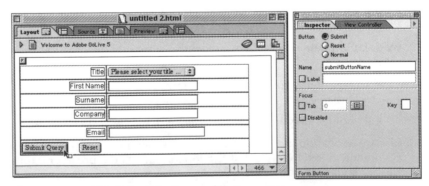

Figure 16-17: The Submit button and its Inspector

Typically a button is placed at the end of the form so users won't push it until after the form's contents are complete.

2. In the Name field enter a unique name so you can identify the button later.

A name is not required unless your CGI specifically uses a set of names as part of its instructions. However, if you have more than one Submit button on a form it will help you tell which is which. The name is included in the information passed to the server, so keep the name short.

3. *(Optional)* The Submit button says Submit Query by default. This label is merely cosmetic; it's a guide for users so they know what the button does. You can have your button say anything you want. For example, "Submit Application" or "Send your idea now." To change the words on the button, check the Label option in the Inspector and enter a new label. The button will grow to the label you give it.

It will help if you understand the HTML behind Submit buttons and know how GoLive's Inspector relates to the HTML.

The HTML for a Submit button looks like this by default:

```
<input type="submit" name="submitButtonName">
```

When you customize the label within the Inspector, you add another attribute, the *value*, as shown here:

```
<input type="submit" name="submitButtonName" value="Submit
Application">
```

The elements in this line of HTML are as follows:

✦ The *input type* is determined by the type of button it is. As long as the Submit option is active in the Inspector, the input type is submit. If you are instructed to change this type, choose the Normal button.

✦ The *name* part of the HTML is obtained directly from the Name field in the Inspector.

✦ The *value* in the HTML is entered and changed through the Label field of the Inspector. Note that unlike other form objects where the value is the data that gets passed to the server, with a button the value is merely the name that appears on the button to guide users. The value is optional.

Normal buttons

If instead of a button of input type Submit you need a button that is of input type Button, add a regular Submit button to your page and then change it to normal in the Inspector (by choosing the radio button for Normal).

This is what the HTML looks like with the normal option selected for a button:

```
<input type="button" name="submitButtonName">
```

Notice that the input type is button instead of submit. The button also says "Button." If you add a label to change the face of the button, you see something like the following code, which creates a button that says "I'm normal" on it.

```
<input type="button" name="submitButtonName" value="I'm normal">
```

Reset buttons

A reset button isn't necessary, but it can be a nice convenience for the user. When the user presses it, all of the information the user may have entered on your form is cleared. It can be helpful if a user is entering information for more than one person. It also clears a form quickly in case the user is entering a contest when his or her boss passes by. Reset doesn't send anything to the server; it does its thing completely within the browser.

Follow these steps to add a Reset button to your form:

1. Drag the Reset button into place on your form from the Forms tab of the Objects palette. Typically this button is placed at the end of the form along with the Submit button.

2. *(Optional)* By default the Reset button says Reset, but you can make it say anything you'd like. To change the words on the button, check the Label option in the Inspector and enter a new Label. The button grows to accommodate whatever you type.

You don't have anything to adjust name-wise. The Inspector is the same, but the Name field is inactive. The HTML for a Reset button is `<input type="reset">`.

Universal buttons

As this button is new to HTML 4, it is only recognized by HTML-4-compatible browsers. (GoLive's Web Settings lists it as Internet Explorer only.) It works just like any other button but is more customizable and the Inspector makes it easy to attach a script to it.

To add a universal button to your form, follow these steps:

1. Drag the Button icon from the Forms tab of the Objects palette.

2. The button says Button by default. Click the word Button on the face of the button and replace this text by typing the words you would like to have appear on the face of the button, as shown in Figure 16-18. You can adjust the text attributes too (such as font, size, color, and so on). This button face also accepts images and HTML, so you can go to town customizing its look.

3. Name the button for your own reference. The names Submit and Reset cannot be used as they are already assigned.

4. In the value field, enter the Action or value to be passed to the agent (CGI) via the server.

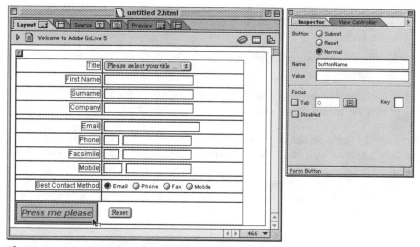

Figure 16-18: A Custom button that now says "Press me please." The name and value are unedited.

Image placeholders

Images can be used as buttons. Sometimes it's a nice touch to have the user click an icon instead of reading words.

To use an image as a button, follow these steps:

1. Drag the Input Image icon from the Forms tab of the Objects palette.

   When an image is used as a button, the Form Input Image Inspector is similar to the Inspector for other images.

2. Assign the desired image to the button.

   • Point and Shoot from the Basic tab of the Inspector to the image in the Files tab of the Site Window.

   • Browse to the image.

   • Drag an image directly from the hard drive, but remember that if the image is not a GIF or JPEG, GoLive will bring up the Save for Web window. You will then be able to set all of the attributes for the imported image and select where you would like to save the image. (See Chapter 10 for more on GoLive's Save for Web feature.)

The location of this image, as in the Source field of the Basic tab, is included in the HTML as the input source, written as follows:

```
<INPUT type="image" src="path/to/image">
```

3. Switch to the Special tab of the Inspector and enter a name to identify the image. As with the name of a plain button, this is not required unless your CGI specifically uses the name attribute as part of its communication. However, it will help you identity the button later, in case you have several buttons on your page.

   Keep the IsForm box checked, as it is by default. This tells the image it is part of a form.

4. As with all images on the Web, entering Alt text to briefly describe the image helps people whose browser reads for them or prints out your page in Braille.

You have no need to set the border image to zero (the way you might for other graphics used as buttons), as no border exists around a button image.

The HTML for a button image is `<input type="image" src="images/yourgif.gif">`. After you add a name it looks like this: `<input type="image" src="media/yourgif.gif" name="buttonname">`.

Parameters will be sent using the name to contain the coordinates of the point clicked in the image: buttonname.x and buttonname.y.

Advanced Form Fields

The form fields covered in this section are not standard elements. Consider their use carefully, as they will not be supported in every browser.

Placing a key generator on a form

If your site supports encryption, your user can choose from any encryption algorithm you list on your page. This is not a standard of HTML; it is a Netscape-only feature. Ask your site host about it before you try to set it up.

To place a key generator on your form, follow these steps:

1. Drag the Key icon to the form.

2. In the Name field, enter what your site host tells you to enter.

3. In the Challenge field enter the security level, as shown in Figure 16-19.

To facilitate discussion between you and your site host, this is the HTML that your host will be instructing you about. The items in the quotes are the words you change within the Inspector. The words before the equals sign are the codes the site host will recognize.

```
<keygen name="keygenName" challenge="publickey">
```

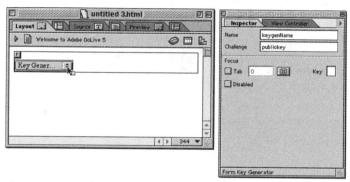

Figure 16-19: The encryption key selection field as it is being set up

Placing a file browser on a form

The File Browser is a visual interface that, along with a CGI, enables a user to browse his or her hard drive and locate a file to upload. This requires a CGI located on your server and an upload destination.

Follow these steps to place a File Browser on your form:

1. Drag the File Browser icon into place on the form.

2. In the Name field, select the default fileGetterName and place it with the path to the CGI that will do the uploading. If the CGI is within your site, you know its path. If the CGI is on the Web server, you may have to check with your site host to learn this.

3. In the Visible field enter the desired number of characters you'd like the enter field to contain.

   This field is where the name of the file to be uploaded appears after the user browses to the file and selects it. The longer this field is, the more of the file's name the user will be able to see and verify.

Validating Your Form Data

Now that you have a form set up to gather the information that you need to collect, you need to make sure that people are actually entering the right things into the right fields. It isn't going to be very useful to receive an e-mail where necessary fields are missing or wrong (as shown in Figure 16-20). This may seem like an over-the-top example, but believe me, it's not!

You have a number of different ways to validate the entries that people make in your forms before the information gets to you or gets put into a database for storage. You can check things such as if a user has entered a value in a field, whether e-mail addresses or credit card numbers are in the correct format, or if a user has entered something of a specific length or type (like a four-digit number or six-letter word).

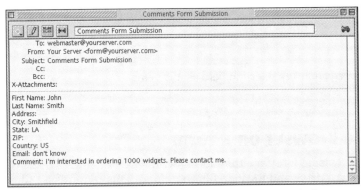

Figure 16-20: The information from this form doesn't help you because the entries weren't validated before the form was sent.

The two main different methods are client-side validation and server-side validation. Client-side validation occurs in the user's browser, either when they are entering the information (field-level validation) or when they press the Submit button (form-level validation). You can use GoLive Actions or custom JavaScript to achieve this within GoLive. Server-side validation occurs after the form has been sent to the server for processing. This is done by using a server-side language (such as ASP, ColdFusion, or PHP) to analyze the form entries and then take action from there. For instance, if the fields are correct, an e-mail should be sent or the values should be put in a database, and an error message should be returned to the user if a problem exists.

Field-level validation using the FieldValidator Action

An Action is now available for GoLive 5 called the FieldValidator Action, which enables you to do field-level validation on a form. (See Figure 16-21.) It doesn't ship with GoLive itself, but it is available through Adobe Online in the Help menu (choose Help ➪ Adobe Online and then click the Extras button — you need to be connected to the Internet to do this).

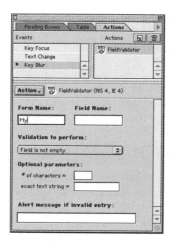

Figure 16-21: The FieldValidator Action as shown in the Actions palette

To set a field to use this Action, follow these steps:

1. Select the field you wish to validate.

2. Open the Actions palette, select Key Blur in the Events listing, and click the New Action button.

3. Choose Action ➪ ActionsPlus ➪ FieldValidator as your Action.

4. Set the Form Name to the name of the form that this field is in and the Field Name to the name of the selected field.

5. In the Validation to Perform pop-up menu, choose the type of validation you need to perform.

6. Set any optional parameters for the type you have chosen. For instance, if you have chosen "Field has this many characters," type in the number of characters the entry has to be, and if you chose "Field = exact text string," enter the text that the field must contain.

7. For cases when an error occurs, you can optionally enter the message you would like the user to see in the "Alert message if invalid entry" field.

Caution   Because this Action uses the Key Blur event to trigger the validation, you cannot use this Action on adjacent fields in your form. (This means there must be a field to tab into between fields using FieldValidator.) The problem has to do with the way that the Action is executed. It checks the form whenever you tab out of a field (which immediately puts the cursor in the next field), and then automatically pops you back to the same field if the entry is wrong. Unfortunately, if the next field has a similar Action applied, when it pops back to the first field, the Action executes on the second field also and you fall into a deadly loop. You can apply the Action as a "Text Change" event, which will solve this problem, but then it doesn't prevent the user from leaving the field blank.

Form-level validation using the VerifyForm Action

This Action by Walter Blady can be used to verify that there has been an entry in up to five text fields and one e-mail field on a standard HTML form. Each field can be set up to check for an exact match or any entered string. The E-mail field is used to check an e-mail address for proper formatting. If a mismatch exists, the form is not submitted and a dialog box warns the users to check their entries. It is available for purchase from Walter Blady's Web site at www.wblady.com/actions.html.

To add Walter Blady's field verification to your form, follow these steps:

1. Select the Actions tab and then the Mouse Click Event. Click the New Action button and select the VerifyForm.Action from the Action selection menu. The Actions palette will now look like Figure 16-22.

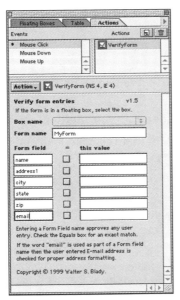

Figure 16-22: The VerifyForm Action as shown in the Actions palette

2. If your form is in a floating box, select the box name from the Box name pull-down menu.

3. Enter the name of your form in the Form name field.

4. Enter the field names that you want to verify in the Form field boxes. These names must be exactly the same as the ones you used in your form. All names are case sensitive.

5. The corresponding fields on your form will be checked for an entry, and any entry will be considered valid. If you want the user to enter an exact value, check the Equals (=) box opposite the Form field and then enter the value that the user must match in the "this value" box.

Confirming a Submission

One of the silliest things you can do is have the user submit a form and then leave the user hanging. Don't forget to confirm the submission and thank your user. While you're at it, don't miss the opportunity to send the user someplace useful.

Any good CGI will have a command that enables you to have a confirmation page returned to the user after successful submission (and also enable you to return a page noting an error). You typically send this instruction within a hidden tag. The name would be the command and the variable would be the name of the page to be returned.

If your form is simply sending an e-mail and no CGI is used, you can still send a confirmation page. To do this, you add a "redirect" JavaScript Action to the form. However, this is one case where you cannot use one of GoLive's prewritten Actions. You will have to do this manually in Source mode.

In Layout mode, select the Form tag and then switch to the Source tab. Because the form tag was selected in Layout mode, the form Action is selected so you can easily locate it. The form Action will look something like this, with the real e-mail address, of course:

```
<form name="mailform" action="mailto:mail@server.com"
method="post">
```

Place your cursor at the end of this code, immediately inside the closing bracket. Then type this:

```
onSubmit="window.location='yourcofirmationpage.html'"
```

Your entire tag will look like this (with the real name of the confirmation page, of course):

```
<form name="mailform" action="mailto:mail@server.com"
method="post"
onSubmit="window.location='yourcofirmationpage.html'">
```

If you enter a field name that includes the word "e-mail" as part of the field name, VerifyForm will perform a basic format check of the e-mail address entered by the user. If the format doesn't conform to the format necessary for a correct e-mail address, the "Form entry error" dialog box will appear.

Server-side validation

Sometimes doing validation in the client's browser doesn't provide the necessary failsafes that you need for either data integrity or security reasons. One situation that could cause this is if a user of your site has JavaScript turned off — none of your validation scripts would be triggered, and whatever they entered, or didn't enter, would be sent to the form processor to be put into a database or sent to you.

In cases where this is critical, it may be best to use server-side validation using something like ASP, PHP, or ColdFusion to check the results of the form after it has been submitted, but before the data is processed. You could then either process the data if it is correct, or represent the form (or an error page) to the user if problems occur. This approach is also very important where security or the origin of the data is critical, because you can check information like the visitor's IP address, whether the data came from your form, or whether someone had already filled out the form (important in the case of applications like polls).

Form Troubleshooting Issues

If you find a green bug symbol next to a page in the Site Window that contains a form, it may be the address of the CGI—the Form Action. This isn't a problematic bug, as you know the Action is valid. (You know a form Action is valid when the form behaves properly.) The bug appears because GoLive simply can't find this file. When you export the site, the server will be able to locate the CGI file and that's all that counts. However, having this cause a bug prevents you from being alerted to other bugs that may occur.

You can put an end to this bug by telling GoLive not to report this file (whenever it is used). All you need to do is enter a part of the Form Action's name in the URL filter. Then, any time GoLive sees a URL that contains those characters, it will know not to flag that URL as an error. For example, if you're storing your CGIs in a folder called cgi-bin, as is common, you can enter the part of the URL that contains that part of the path so all your CGIs are covered at once.

Follow these steps to set GoLive to ignore the unknown URL it is flagging:

1. Choose Preferences ⇨ Edit, or use the shortcut ⌘-Y (on Mac) or Ctrl+Y (on Windows).

2. Open the General Preferences by clicking the triangle by General.

3. Select URL Handling.

4. Under URL Filter, click the New button.

   The words New Filter appear preselected in the field above the button.

5. Type the name of the file/database your CGI accesses (the Action address) that is causing the bug, as follows:

   • If you are storing all of your CGIs in a folder called cgi-bin, as is common, you can enter **cgi-bin** as the filter. That way all files stored within that folder will not be marked as creating a bug.

   • You may not need to enter the entire address. In the case of Figure 16-23, all I typed is the common part that ends with the dollar sign. That way other pages in the site that also access this CGI won't cause bugs, even though they use an ending such as $update or $delete.

6. Click OK.

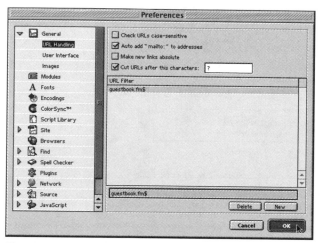

Figure 16-23: Entering a new URL filter

7. GoLive asks you if you want to update all open sites based on this new rule. Click OK unless you have multiple sites open and you have some reason not to change one of them. In that case, close the excluded site, and then repeat this procedure, accepting the change next time.

Note

You may find that other parts of your form cause GoLive to report errors. For example, if you're using PHP, you'll find that GoLive thinks that any link containing "<? . . . ?>" is bad. This type of error report can also be avoided with a URL filter. However, if you add a filter for "<?" or "?>" you also won't see errors in XML that contains that same sequence. Instead, set the filter to include more of the code that is common to the problematic PHP code. In this case, filter out <?php and your XML will not be included in the filter. (You will need to be using PHP's long style tags for this to work, as PHP can also use <?, <%, and <script type="PHP"> tags.)

Migration to GoLive 5's Form Container

In GoLive 5, Adobe has changed the form to a "container" paradigm in an effort to always write the form tags correctly according to the HTML specifications. Whereas in GoLive 4 you placed a start <form> tag and an end </form> tag, GoLive 5 takes care of this process for you. This can cause an inconvenience when first opening a form created in GoLive 4 or another HTML editor. Usually this takes the form of mis-aligned HTML tags showing up in Layout mode (as shown in Figure 16-24). This problem, while a nuisance, can be easily fixed.

If you are not familiar with HTML, by far the easiest thing to do is to simply follow these steps:

1. Make a backup of your page.

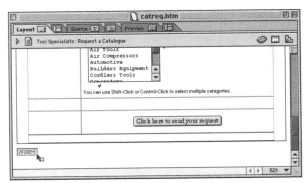

Figure 16-24: A misaligned </form> tag showing up in Layout mode after opening a form created in GoLive 4

2. Drag a new Form container from the Forms tab of the Objects palette to the beginning of your page.

3. Copy the settings from your old Form (such as Name, Action, and other attributes in the Form Inspector) to your new form.

4. Move the contents of the old form into the new one (either by copying and pasting or drag and drop). Be careful that you move any Hidden fields too.

5. Once you are sure that nothing exists in the old form container, delete it. If a misaligned </form> tag shows up on your page, delete that too.

If you do know HTML, another way to correct this problem with pages that use a single form (see the note on pages with multiple forms later in this chapter) is to move the misaligned end tag into the correct position in the HTML source (either in source mode or in the Source Code palette. You need to change to Source mode or use the Source Code palette to locate the misaligned tag pair and correct it (usually by moving the end tag that is showing in Layout mode after the </form> end tag in the source).

The layout of pages that contain multiple forms may need to be rethought slightly to accommodate the new Form container. For instance, try splitting the page into multiple tables, each one containing a form (which will usually help with page-rendering times anyway).

Using GoLive Actions with Forms

As well as validating your form data, GoLive Actions can be used to do other things with forms and form data. Sometimes you need to store or retrieve information that someone has input in a form separately from other information they have input. For instance, customers place orders on your Web site, and when they return they are welcomed with a personalized greeting or brought back to the section they were last viewing. You don't need all of the information they filled in, just the relevant fields. This is where you can use GoLive Actions such as Get Form Value and Set Cookie.

The Get Form Value Action is used to read the user's input from the text fields in a form. Typically, you'll need to do several form field value reads in order to gather all the entries (such as first name, last name, address, and so on). Each field you want to read requires a separate Get Form Value Action. Normally you would use this Action with an OnCall event triggered by a Set Variable Action attached to the form's Submit button, but unfortunately the version of Set Variable that ships with GoLive 5 doesn't work properly with the Get Form Value Action. A replacement for the Set Variable Action that does work has been developed by Robert McDaniels and is available at www.golivebible.com, and should also be available from the Adobe Web site by the time you read this.

On the CD-ROM

To demonstrate the replacement Set Variable Action written by Robert McDaniels and to give you an idea of how you could use form fields, variables, and cookies in your sites, Rob Keniger of Big Bang Solutions has prepared a simple, three-page example site showcasing the Action. Make sure you install the replacement Set Variable Action before opening the site and remember that cookies don't work on files opened from your hard disk, so you'll have to upload the pages to a server to test them.

To set an Action to get the value of a form's text field and store it in a variable, follow these steps:

1. Install the Replacement Variable Action into your GoLive ⇨ Modules ⇨ Jscripts ⇨ Actions folder.

2. Drag a Head Action from the Smart tab of the Objects palette into the header of the page, select OnLoad from the Exec menu, and then choose Actions ⇨ Variables ⇨ Declare Variable. Enter a name for the variable in the Inspector and give it a type of String.

3. Drag another Head Action into the header of the page, select OnLoad from the Exec menu, and then choose Actions ⇨ Variables ⇨ Init Variable. Choose the variable you just created in the previous step from the pop-up and give it a value of zero.

4. Drag another Head Action into the header of the page, select OnCall from the Exec menu, and then choose Actions ⇨ Getters ⇨ Get Form Value. Name the Action in the Inspector so you can use it later and enter the name of the form and the field you want to check in the appropriate inspector fields.

5. Set up a trigger. You can attach the trigger for the Action to a form, a link, or a form button. Do one of the following to attach the trigger:

   • To attach it to a form, select the form placeholder, open the Actions palette, choose "Form Submit" from the Events list, click the New Action button to add an event, and then choose Actions ⇨ SetVariable (Form).

   • To attach it to a button, select the button, open the Actions palette, choose "Mouse Click" from the Events list, click the New Action button to add an event, and then choose Actions ⇨ SetVariable (Form).

- To attach it to a link, select the link and change its URL to #, open the Actions palette, choose "Mouse Click" from the Events list, click the New Action button to add an event, and then choose Actions ⇨ SetVariable (Form).

The Action now appears in the lower half of the Inspector along with a pair of text fields into which you enter your data (see Figure 16-25).

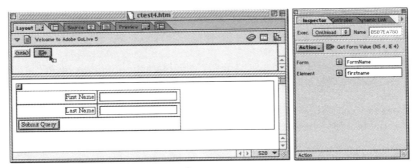

Figure 16-25: Getting a Form Value

6. Enter the name of the form in the first text box.

7. Enter the name of the text field in the second text box.

Tip

To avoid possible typographical errors which would introduce bugs into your Actions, copy and paste the object names from the appropriate Inspectors into these fields.

Now that the field is stored in a variable, you could use a Write Cookie Action to store the value so that it can be displayed on other pages. This is discussed in Chapter 18.

Dealing with Nonstandard Tags

In addition to all the HTML tags, the CGI or other server-side processing program you use is bound to have its own commands. One of the new features of GoLive 5 is 360 Code. GoLive should leave all of your custom code alone, and shouldn't break it, change it, or alter its formatting in the HTML source. If you find GoLive is having trouble with your code or making changes to it that aren't correct, you can use these tips.

The Noedit tag

You can tell GoLive not to touch any part of your code by surrounding that code with the noedit tag. Anything surrounded by this tag doesn't appear in Layout, so you don't want to surround any of your page's visual elements.

Because the code you're protecting is not standard HTML and therefore has no visual GoLive interface, you'll be entering the code in Source mode. While you're at it you might as well add the <noedit> tag set. While in Source mode, simply add <noedit> in front of the text you're protecting and then add </noedit> at the end of the code you're protecting.

Expert Tip The 360 Code feature of GoLive 5 may seem to make the <noedit> tag unnecessary, and in the sense of it protecting the code from GoLive, it is (in *almost* all situations). It is still useful though — for protecting code from yourself or other people working with your page in GoLive. It separates the code visually within your page and stops you from changing things within that specific block of code in Layout mode that may affect how it is displayed in the browser. Think of it as insurance against human error rather than insurance against GoLive. — *Richard McLean, Web developer, designeffect.com*

When you switch back to Layout mode you'll see a pinkish rectangle that says "<noedit>...</>." The protected code is between those tags, but not visible in Layout. The result of this is something like: <noedit><?php code ...; ?></noedit>

Tip If you're going to reuse this code frequently, consider storing it in the Objects palette's Custom tab. To do this, switch back to Layout mode and drag the <noedit> ... </> icon to the Custom tab. In the future, whenever you drag that saved tag back from the Custom tab to a page, you'll be adding the pair of tags, complete with the protected content.

I don't recommend adding the <noedit> tag in Layout view because it's often hard to tell where the tags belong. However, in case you really, really want to try it, to add the <noedit> tag from Layout mode, drag the Tag icon from the Basic tab of the Objects palette into place in front of the code you wish to protect. This tag doesn't have any attributes, so leave Attribute and Value blank. Finally, switch to the Content tab and type (or paste) your code.

For the rare occasions when you've created your page for a server-side application or CGI, and GoLive is having problems with it, you can use Find & Replace to add the <noedit> tag.

For example, if you are using PHP and are using the long form of PHP tags, you could search for <?php and replace it with <noedit><?php and then find all occurrences of ?> and change them to ?></noedit>.

Working in Source view

If you work *only* in Source view you can avoid the problem. You can switch to Layout (or Outline) to look at your page, but you can't make any changes to the page in these views. The act of *changing* your code in Layout or Outline causes the rewrite that is problematic.

Locking pages into Source only

If you find that when you try to work solely in Source mode, you forget and make changes while in Layout (or Outline) mode, you can set GoLive to open your page only in plain HTML source. The good news is that this trick eliminates the temptation to make changes in Layout, but the bad news is that you lose all of the great GoLive interface. This trick puts you in a plain text mode, like being in SimpleText (Mac) or Notepad (Windows).

If the pages in your site are typically using the .html extension, you will take advantage of the also-available .htm extension.

The trick is to set up GoLive's File Mapping so that pages with a specific extension only open as plain text. Here's how:

1. Choose Edit ➪ Web Settings.

2. Switch to the File Mappings tab.

3. Click the arrow next to the text/group to reveal the individual file types.

4. Scroll down to htm (listed in the Suffix column) and click that row to select it.

   The htm suffix's preferences appear in the Inspector (now the File Info Extension Inspector).

5. In the Mime Type area, change the word "text/html" to "text/plain" and then click OK.

This causes any pages that end in .htm to open as a plain text document showing pure HTML code. Then change the extension on any pages that you want to force into source mode to .htm instead of .html and work on that page in source mode. When you open this page you won't see the usual GoLive interface. You'll just see text. If you change your mind about working this way, you can change the extension of the page back to .html. File Mapping only sets the way GoLive treats your page. It doesn't change the code in the pages or the way the pages will be handled on the Web server.

> **Note** If you are using .htm as your normal page extension, reverse these instructions and set .html as the plain preference. However, if your server absolutely doesn't recognize .html, then you will have to set this extension back to .htm prior to uploading the site (or page).

Alternatively, you can set any other pages of a specific file type to open as plain text. For example, you can set all of your ColdFusion pages to open this way by adding the extension .cfm in the File Mapping preferences and then setting its Mime Type as "text/plain."

✦   ✦   ✦

Refining Your Web Pages with Style Sheets

Once upon a time, Web pages and HTML were designed for a very simple purpose: to put scientific research online. They were about sharing information, not about fancy presentation. Then the Web became accessible by a public accustomed to television and computer games, glossy magazine ads, and other visual media. Web site designers found HTML frustrating as a tool for bringing Web pages up to par with what the public expected because HTML was never intended to handle customized fonts, intricate graphics, multimedia, or precise page design. Yet due to the explosive growth of the Web, it was too late to "start over" with a more fully functional markup language. Instead, Web designers started using tricks to get the looks they wanted. HTML was used in convoluted, radical ways. That's why you might be using the `<table>` tag and/or invisible GIFs to position graphics and margins, or inserting GIFs in lieu of straight text to ensure that your design includes the exact fonts you want viewers to see. This makes HTML long, complex, and messy.

Introducing Style Sheets

You probably already know what style sheets are from your word-processing or page layout program. With a style sheet, you can decide that every chapter title in an outline should be 14-point bold Helvetica by creating a style called "chapter title." Then, instead of having to apply the font size, bolding, and font face each time you want the same look for a heading, you just select the text and choose "chapter title" from the styles menu. The basic idea behind style sheets for Web page design is exactly the same: you can exactly specify colors, fonts, and many other similar possibilities, all with one command, and then you can apply that single command specifically to the text it should affect. But this is even more special on the Web because some the attributes you can apply to your text are not even normally possible to designate in HTML.

With style sheets you can control and oversee every aspect of Web page appearance, from margins to colors to layering to text effects — even the *exact* placement of any item on a page. If you use style sheets, you don't have to use HTML to try and get exact layout. You don't have to use graphics in lieu of text to get the exact color, font size, or font type you want. You don't have to use HTML to *design* your page at all. You can use HTML just for what it was intended — to simply structure your page, provide the text, and pull in graphics and other elements — and nothing more. Because computer platforms and browsers are so different, even with style sheets, your page won't look identical across all platforms and browsers, but it'll look similar enough to make your site look good all around.

The only downside to style sheets is that they were introduced into the HTML specification late in the game and adoption by the two main browsers has been spotty. Version 1 and 2 browsers are totally prestyled sheets so they have no support at all. Netscape 3 has no support. Internet Explorer 3 has little support. Version 4 browsers have support for the most commonly used selectors, (which is why there're the most commonly used). Internet Explorer 5 has the best support, but not to full specification. To compensate for this, I'll show you how to use HTML tags that you'd be using anyway to define your styles, so your pages can provide for non style-sheet browsers too. This way, you can cover all of your visitors.

The advantages of using style sheets

To put it briefly, style sheets affect fonts, font sizes, and font colors; line spacing and horizontal alignment; margins, borders and indents; background images and colors; and image or text placement. Here are some specific advantages to using style sheets:

✦ **Style sheets give you precise control of the content of your pages.** You can have print-like layout control over the exact appearance of your Web page without complicated HTML workarounds. You can even overlap elements with layering (easily accomplished in GoLive's floating boxes) instead of resorting to images (which hinder accessibility).

✦ **Style sheets greatly reduce the size of your HTML documents (therefore speeding download time).** When you define a style sheet, the instructions for a whole document occupy only a few lines at the top of the document and, maybe, a handful of tags scattered throughout.

✦ **Style sheets let you edit and update pages very quickly.** Want to change the font you've used across your entire site? If you use the `<font>` tag, you have to change every single `<font face>` value, maybe dozens of times just in one page — not to mention in each page in your Web site. But if you use an external style sheet, you only have to change the font once. *Once.* Imagine that. (If your style sheets are internal, life is easier still, enabling you to make only one change per page.)

✦ **Style sheets are, in fact, browser-friendly.** When styles sheets are supported by your browser and they work correctly, they work very well.

✦ **Style sheets enhance accessibility.** Without the tag clutter, voice-synthesizing browsers can do their jobs better.

To put it briefly, style sheets enable you to separate the *structure* of what's on your Web page from its *form*. The structure is needed to organize and present your information. This structure enables your page to be accessible to everyone, including readers who are blind and/or deaf. You set up the structure using the standard HTML tags. For example, you start an important section with the main heading tag <h1>, use an <h2> tag as a subheading, and use the list formatting tags to create a list. This provides the structure so anyone, on any browser, can make sense of your page.

But, using these tags in their raw format, without adding font sizes, colors, and so on, doesn't make for a nice presentation. When you set text as <h1>, you're letting the browser decide how to display the font, size, color, and style of that text. If Internet Explorer displays <h1> text in 12-point bold but the Netscape browsers display <h1> text in 14-point italics, you have no choice—and that's not what you want. You want your page to look nicer. You want to *know* how your page will look. You want to *control* its look. That control is the *form* of the page. Add a style sheet and you've got form—without cluttering up the structural tags with size, color, and font face tags.

Using a style sheet you can still code a header as <h1> so the page still has structure, but now you can also specify exactly how you want that text to appear, on every browser and platform. If you want all <h1> text to be burgundy, it will be burgundy no matter what. If you want it all to be displayed in small caps, it can be. If you want it to be oblique, it can be, regardless of each browser's default style of bolding a heading. That's what style sheets enable you to do—to override a browser's HTML defaults with your own set of design specifications. HTML still defines the structure of your Web pages, but style sheets control the form each Web page element will take. And, you have a good deal of flexibility. You can create your style sheet specifications in a number of ways: based on HTML tags or your own criteria, writing the style code within a single Web page for that page only, as a standalone document for any number of pages within your entire site, or both.

Style sheets do more than just size and color your text. They can also easily add any size margin to your page or to any block of text, add padding between text and any container it's in, add borders, and more. (Tables can provide this structure, but they interfere with readers, take time to build on a page, and can lead to other complications.) Style sheets can add backgrounds and color to your page or objects on the page. They can even place objects in any precise location on the page and enable objects to overlap. (If you've ever placed a floating box on a page, you've used an internal style sheet, although you may not have realized it because GoLive does all the hard stuff for you.)

Style sheets in action

To see the effective use of style sheets in action, and understand how they affect Web pages, take a look at an excellent real-world use of style sheets — the World Wide Web Consortium's demo page (at `www.w3.org/Style`). Without a style sheet, this page's text is the default font, size and color, as you can see by viewing it in an ancient, pre-style sheet browser, as shown in Figure 17-1. This is the structure of the page.

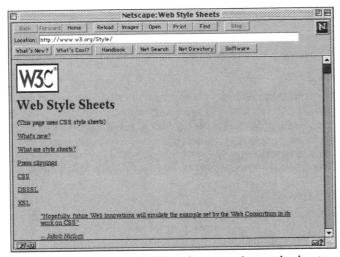

Figure 17-1: The World Wide Web Consortium style sheets page on an older, non-CSS browser (Netscape 2)

Now, enter the form defined by a simple style sheet. The same page, displayed in a modern browser, as shown in Figure 17-2, is a beautiful design full of different fonts, sizes, and colors, with varied alignment and overlapping text. (Visit this page yourself and experiment with it. Resize the browser window, and watch how the text moves to fit the window.)

Without a style sheet, the only way you'd be able to create such an effect would be by using an image. Rather than a few simple lines of text, your viewers would have to download a large GIF or JPG. And voice synthesizers, Palm Pilots, and other similar devices would know only what you wrote in the image's `<alt>` tag.

GoLive makes creating a style sheet very easy because it provides a clear, simple, visual interface. All you do is start the style sheet, click one of three buttons to assign one of the three possible style selectors, name the selector, and then choose the look of your style from the Inspector. Or, even easier, a contextual menu provides some of the common selectors, all ready to use.

Figure 17-2: The World Wide Web Consortium style sheets page on a CSS-savvy browser (IE5 on the Mac)

Note To learn about each type of selector, see "Creating an internal style sheet" and "Understanding Selectors and Style Types," later in this chapter.

Identifying Types of Style Sheets

Style sheets come in four types:

- ✦ Embedded
- ✦ Inline
- ✦ External
- ✦ Imported

Embedded and inline style sheets are internal to your page, and external and imported style sheets are called from within your page. However, of the four types, only embedded and external style sheets are widely supported enough to be counted on. GoLive provides a visual interface for them. I will discuss external and imported style sheets in this chapter, but I don't recommend you use them.

Understanding Style Sheet Syntax

All programming has a syntax, a set of rules defining how instructions are constructed. Style sheets, too, follow a syntax. Of course, GoLive provides a friendly Inspector interface, shielding you from having to know a style sheet syntax. But it helps to have an understanding of what's going on in the style sheet and see what GoLive is doing for your behind the scenes.

A style is actually no more than a specially constructed sentence of sorts, called a *rule* or *instruction*, that tells the browser what to apply a style to, and then tells it the details of the style. For example, a style that affects text first tells the browser what text to affect and what to make the text look like. The key parts to a rule are the *selector* and the *declaration*:

✦ The *selector* selects (names or states) the parts of the page that will be affected. (In this example, all text between any `<h1>` and `</h1>` tags on the page will be affected.)

✦ The *declaration*, which follows the selector, declares to the browser what the effect will be. It is set apart by curly brackets and is comprised of a *property* and a value for that *property*. In this case, that the font's weight is bold.

A single rule, also called a statement or instruction, looks like this:

```
h1{font-weight:bolder}
```

All in all, this rule has three parts, from left to right:

✦ The selector: `h1` in this case

✦ The property: `font-weight` in this case

✦ And the value: `bold` in this case

That's all there is to a style. In this case, a standard HTML tag, normally found within your Web page anyway, is used as the selector to determine which text will be formatted by the style. You have other ways to define which text on a page will be affected. I'll tell you about them a bit later in this chapter, but the important thing is that the parts of the rule are the same. There is simply a different selector. Of course, a style can have more than one declaration. Multiple declarations reside together within the same set of curly brackets but are separated with a semicolon (;) within the brackets.

Here's what that same header style would look like with two declarations:

```
h1{color:purple;font-weight:bolder}
```

With this style defined, when a browser is style sheet-savvy, all text that has the standard `<h1>` tag would appear as bold and purple.

The *embedded* style sheet is called *internal* in GoLive terminology because it is embedded internally in the top of your page. Because it is internal, it can apply only to that page. The *external* style sheet is a freestanding document and is therefore available to any page within your site. In both cases, the code for the styles and their effect is the same. And either way, you create the style sheet using the CSS Selector Inspector.

The *inline* internal style sheet and the *imported* external style sheet are the less common ones. The syntax (code) used to define these styles is also the same as the embedded and external style sheets, but the interface for creating these style sheets is not supported in the GoLive visual interface. In order to create them, you need to hand-code the style. Later, I show you how to add them to your page — just in case you want to use them.

To have any page take on the formatting defined by any external style sheet, you simply link the page to that external style sheet. By using an external style sheet, you can change the look of the text for your entire site with one simple change to the style sheet (.css) document. Or, because you choose to link each page to an external style sheet individually, you can choose not to link any page or pages to the style sheet.

You can also have a page link to several external style sheets so each external style sheet can define specific parts of your page. What if two external style sheets both use the same tag to define a style? No problem. That's the *cascading* part of Cascading Style Sheets, though I'll refer to them simply as style sheets. Only the last listing of the style takes effect. An external style sheet document, by the way, lives in your Files tab along with your pages, is uploaded to your server along with the rest of your site, and downloads to the user once (automatically) — the first time a user requests a page that uses it.

Note   As style sheets were new at the time of Version 3 browsers, Internet Explorer 3's support in these browsers is inconsistent. (In fact, the differences between the Windows versions of IE 3.0 and IE 3.02 are even greater.) Because of this varied support, designers don't count on style sheets to work in any Version 3 browser. At the end of this chapter, under "Using a different style sheet for each platform," I discuss Matt Ridley's CSS Write Action, a browser-sniffing Action that tells 3.0 browsers to ignore any external style sheets and display the page by reading only the HTML. It would be silly for me to keep telling you each of the things that don't work in various 3.0 browsers, so I don't try to.

Understanding internal and external style sheets

GoLive provides an easy interface to the two main ways to add style sheets to your page or site:

✦ You may embed an internal style sheet in each page.

✦ You may use an external style sheet that governs all, or multiple, pages in your entire site.

Both types of style sheets are easy to set up and they use the same syntax, or style sheet "grammar," so you don't have to learn new rules or procedures if you create an external style sheet and decide to embed it later on. (See the "Understanding Style Sheet Syntax" sidebar earlier in this chapter.) In fact, you can turn internal styles into an external style sheet, and vice versa, as you'll see in respective sections later in this chapter.

Why use one over the other? It's really just a matter of what you prefer. An external style sheet causes your visitor to wait for two pages to download instead of one. But . . . that only happens once for the site (unless you use multiple external style sheets). An internal style sheet downloads as part of the page, rather than separately, but this adds more data to each page. All in all, differences between download times are negligable either way.

Whether you use internal or external style sheets, you won't have a problem with browsers that don't understand CSS. An external style sheet document is referenced in the source code using the HREF attribute of the `<link>` tag. This `<link>` information tells the browser to refer to the external style sheet for instructions on how to display the page. Browsers that don't recognize style sheets simply ignore the `<link>` tag and its contents. An internal style sheet is denoted by placement of the `<style>` tag with the `<head>` tags. The actual style code is placed within comment tags within the style tag. CSS-savvy browsers know to read that code, even though it's within comment tags. But non-CSS-savvy browsers just see the comment tags and ignore them, because comments have always been known to be excluded from page structure and content.

Caution   The only browser that is a problem for style sheets is Internet Explorer 3, which understands what a style sheet is so it doesn't ignore the code, but doesn't understand enough styles to display them accurately. As for browsers that do read CSS, the style sheets always take precedence over the HTML attributes, so there won't be any misunderstandings.

An internal style sheet formats only the page it's in, so it is perhaps best used for specific needs. If you want a consistent look throughout your site, you'd have to place this same information in every page. An external style sheet can affect as many pages within a site as you'd like it to. So later, if you have corrections or changes to make, you only have to correct or change the style sheet itself rather than every single page. When using an external style sheet, you can still have certain styles apply to just specific pages rather than all of your pages. To do this, you just add another style sheet that contains that specific style (or styles) and link that secondary style sheet only to the pages you want affected.

Creating an internal style sheet

You can create your styles before adding content to the page so you can see the desired look immediately upon adding the content to your page. Or, you can get the content in and at least some of the structure down first, so you can see the effect of a style as you create it. Either way, the style sheet works the same. It's just a matter of your own preference.

To create an internal style sheet, you open the page to which you're applying the styles, and then open the Style Sheet window, which works in tandem with the Inspector. As you work in the Style Sheet window and CSS Selector Inspector, GoLive writes your choices directly into the page, placing the style sheet code between the style tags in the head section of the HTML. The effects of your styles are seen immediately on the page because the style is written directly into the page.

What Comes First: Content or Style Sheet?

What's the best work flow when you're using style sheets? Should you set up the style sheet first and then create the page content, or create the basic page, laying down its content, and then create the style sheet to fancy up the page? I asked several Web designers how they tend to work. Here's what they said:

✦ Being a long time style sheet maven (long before the Web came about, with such tools as Quark, and so on), my workflow has always been from a design side—for example, define the style sheets based on the design, knowing that you will always have to add children later. I try to implement as many styles as I can determine from the beginning, but know there will be special instances or modifications as time goes on.—*Mark Jaress,* http://jaress.net

✦ We mock up the page in Photoshop, and then build the page and the style sheet simultaneously based on the specs in the mock-up. To me, it's an integrated process. However, if I had to choose, I think the second option is probably more appropriate, because you can't plan out your types of styles until you know what content they're going to be associated with.—*George Olsen,* www.how2.com

✦ The second option sounds the most like what I do. I try to write clean HTML, and then add a link to style sheets. The idea of course is to separate style from content—and to me, pages come before style.—*Joe Crawford,* www.artlung.com

✦ I only use basic CSS (links and so on), but I usually put it in near the finalization of the site along with my metatags and other common code.—*Stace F. Graham,* www.daddyg.com

✦ I do it much more organically than either of these approaches. Each part is integrated with the other, so I build enough of the style to build more of the structure, and enough of the structure to build more of the style. It's like knitting together steel bars and silk ribbons. Once you start with relatively structured content—which is pretty easy to do—then you can grow the two side by side, interwoven. I can't imagine either producing a style sheet, first, and then the page, or the page first and then the style sheet. They're two sides of the same coin, to me.—*Kynn Bartlett,* www.hwg.org, www.kynn.com

✦ Style sheets to me are kind of an afterthought. They can be used to make an interface more intuitive, but I'm a basic Web widgets kind of guy. :) Most of the functionality in CSS is kind of superfluous, IMHO.—*Jeremy Tidwell,* http://idt.net/~tidwellj

New Feature

GoLive 5 gives you direct access to the style sheet code. As soon as you add your first selector via the toolbar, GoLive inserts the style tag in the header of HTML code: `<style type="text/css" media="screen"><!--body { }--> </style>`. All of your internal styles will be written into this area.

To create an internal style sheet, follow these steps:

1. If you're adding your style sheet to an existing page, open that page to work within it. If you prefer to create your internal style sheet before you add your page content, open your blank new page now.

2. Click the Open CSS Interface button (the stair-steps) at the top-right corner of your page to open the Style Sheet window.

   This opens a Style Sheet window specifically for that page, named yourpage. html:Style Sheet, as shown in Figure 17-3. It also changes the standard toolbar to the Style Sheet toolbar and activates the first four buttons on that toolbar: New Element Selector, New Class Selector, New ID Selector, and New Style Sheet File.

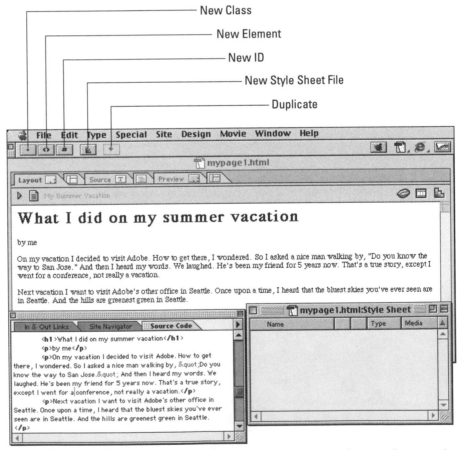

Figure 17-3: A page with existing text and the Style Sheet window newly opened. (The Source Code window shows the existing formatting, just for reference.) The Style Sheet toolbar is ready for action.

3. To create a style, click either of the first three buttons on the Style Sheet toolbar, as follows:

- *New Class Selector* to create a custom selector you can use on any individual characters, or apply by paragraphs, sections, or to the entire body. You create a class once, and then use it over and over on your page.

- *New Element Selector* to create a style based on an HTML tag that will already be in your document.

- *New ID Selector* to create a custom selector you can use *just once* on any individual characters, or apply by paragraph or section of your page.

(As an alternative to using the toolbar buttons, you can choose to add any of these from the contextual menu that appears from within the Style Sheet window.)

New Feature

The new contextual menu options also enable you to add a body, paragraph, or table tag selector in one easy step, and then skip Step 4 as they are prenamed. This contextual menu also auto-creates tag selectors for the popular link tags. (See "Defining link styles," later in this chapter.)

This creates a new style and turns the Inspector into the CSS Selector Inspector.

4. Name the selector by selecting and replacing the default name in the Style Sheet window or the Name field of the first (Pencil) tab of the CSS Selector Inspector, as shown in Figure 17-4. This identifies the text to which the style will be applied, as follows:

- When adding a new *class* style, the new selector comes in as .class. The name may contain any letters of the alphabet and/or number characters. Don't include spaces in the name. Keep it short, but name it something that will help you identify its purpose in the future. Classes begin with a dot (.), but don't type the dot yourself as GoLive adds it for you.

Figure 17-4: The Style Sheet window and CSS Selector Inspector after a tag selector is named within the Inspector

- When adding a new *element* selector, it comes in named `element`. The name must match one of the HTML tags that are, or will be, within your page. For example, to apply a style to all Heading 1 text, name the element `h1`.

- When adding a new ID style, it comes in named `#id`. Give it a unique name that describes the item it will be applied to. Again, the name can be any alphanumeric character, with no spaces.

Tip   Not sure what the HTML tag is? Open the Source Code window (Window ➪ Source Code).In Layout, select some of the text to which you want to apply the style. The Source Code window jumps to that text so you can see the tag that surrounds it. Another way to see your tag is within the Markup Tree palette (Window ➪ Markup Tree). Just place your cursor in between any characters you wish to format and the tag that applies to that text appears as the last tag in the palette.

5. Use the CSS Selector Inspector to choose your desired options from the appropriate tabs of the Inspector, as shown in Figure 17-5. As you work, remember to save the page. Your styles are saved within the page.

Figure 17-5: A style being defined within the CSS Selector Inspector. Because text already exists on the page that uses this style's tag, the effects of the style are seen immediately within the page.

Note   After you save and close the page, the next time you open it, you'll also see a Style Sheet icon, representing that code, in the head section within Layout mode. Double-clicking that icon opens the Style Sheet window again.

Creating an external style sheet

An external style sheet is identical to an internal style sheet, except that the style code resides within a standalone document and is applied to a page by a simple one-line link. You create and edit both through the same visual interface and can also view and edit the actual code of both.

Because an external style sheet is created outside of any of your pages, you don't automatically have a page on which to see the effect of your styles as you create them. Once you link the style sheet to a page, though, you can work on the page and see the effect of your styles. If you've planned your page on paper or in an application such as Photoshop, you may already know how you want your styles to look and not feel the need to see how a style actually affects your page as you set up the style. But if you are creating the look on the fly, or just like to see what you're accomplishing as you set up the style, you can link the style sheet to a page before you begin to set up the styles. There's no right or wrong for this.

The actual defining of an external style sheet is the same as the defining of an internal style sheet. Only the first and last steps are different. Here are the steps:

1. Choose File ⇨ New Special ⇨ New Style Sheet Document. Rather than opening a regular document, this opens the Style Sheet window.

   If you want to link your style sheet to a page before setting up any styles, just click a New Selector button (as in Step 2) now and proceed to saving the style sheet. Then link it to any desired page. After it's linked, you can create your styles. Open the page to which the style sheet is linked, double-click the style sheet, and then come back here.

2. Click the desired selector — New Tag, New Class, or New ID — in the Style Sheet toolbar to begin your first style rule and turn the Inspector into the CSS Selector Inspector. Or, choose a selector from the contextual menu. (The contextual menu even contains some prenamed tag selectors that are commonly of good use.) The three selector-type choices are as follows:

   • *New Class Selector* to create a custom selector you can use on any individual characters, or apply by paragraphs, sections, or to the entire body. You create a class once, and then use it over and over on your page.

   • *New Element Selector* to create a style based on an HTML tag that will already be in your document.

   • *New ID Selector* to create a custom selector you can use *just once* on any individual characters, or apply by paragraph or section of your page.

   Note   The most common use of an ID selector is with a floating box. Each time you add a floating box to your page, GoLive creates an ID selector for it and adds it as a style inside your page. The name you give the floating box in the Floating Box Inspector becomes the ID name, with a # mark in front. When using GoLive, chances are slim that you'll create and add an ID selector yourself.

3. Name the selector by selecting and replacing the default name in the Style Sheet window or by entering the name within the Basics tab or the CSS Selector Inspector, as follows:

   • A new *class selector* is named .class by default. Give it a short, descriptive name so you'll remember, later on, why you created it and where you want to use it. Use any alphabetic or numeric characters, without spaces. Classes begin with a dot (.), but don't type the dot yourself as GoLive adds it for you.

   • A new *element selector* comes in called `element`. Name it to match one of the HTML tags that are, or will be, within your page, but without the brackets.

   • An *ID selector* comes in named #id. Choose a unique alphanumeric name, without spaces, that describes the item it will be applied to.

4. In the CSS Selector Inspector, choose your desired formatting from the appropriate tabs.

Tip If you are creating another style that is similar to the one you've already created, you can duplicate it by clicking the Duplicate button in the toolbar while the style is selected. Then, rename and customize away!

5. Choose File ⇨ Save to save the external style sheet. This opens the Save dialog box and gives the document the default name, "untitled.css."

6. Name your style sheet, as follows:

    • In *Windows*, the default name, is in the "File name" field, preselected and ready for you to type the name. The "Save as type" field is preconfigured with the .css extension. Just type a name for your style sheet.

    • On the *Mac*, the default name, "untitled.css" appears in the Save As name field, with the word "untitled" preselected. The .css extension is not selected. Just type a name for your style sheet. (If you click within the name field, be sure to change only the name, leaving the .css extension intact.

7. Save the document to the root level of your site. To do so, click the GoLive pop-up button in the Save dialog box and slide over to Root folder.

8. Click Save. The style sheet document appears as a page directly under the Files tab of your Site Window. It has the same icon as a regular GoLive page, but the ending remains .css so it can act as a style sheet.

Now that your style sheet is safely begun and saved, continue adding styles to it. You can save and close it at any time, and then double-click it in the Files tab of the Site Window to return to work on it.

Note You can change the name of your style sheet within the Site Window the same way you change any page or file name. Just be sure it ends with .css when you're finished. As with any other file, GoLive updates all related pages when you change the name.

After you create the external style sheet, you can link any existing page of your site to this .css document. (See the next section, "Linking a page to an external style sheet.") You don't have to close anything in order to link a page to this external style sheet. You can proceed directly to the next section to open and link a page.

Tip Wondering which pages are using your external style sheet? Select the style sheet's icon in the Files tab of your Site Window, and then choose Window ⇨ In & Out Links. If you've set up a background image in this style sheet, the image is noted as an outgoing link.

Linking a page to an external style sheet

Recall that an external style sheet is a separate document that contains all of your style sheet instructions. To have it apply to any page in your site, you link the external style sheet to the page. (In HTML, this is one simple line of code.) When the first page that calls upon the style sheet is called for by a user, the external style sheet document downloads along with it automatically.

You can link an external style sheet to a page at any time. In fact, you have three ways to do so:

✦ File Inspector

✦ Style Sheet window

✦ Drag and drop

The style sheet can be open or not. The page can be open or not. And you can even link your style sheet to multiple pages at once.

New Feature

The ability to link an external style sheet via the File Inspector is new to GoLive 5. The other method, linking from the page's Style Sheet window, is still available as well, although changed slightly.

After you add an external style sheet to any page, an icon representing it appears in the head section of your page while in Layout mode. The icon looks like the style sheet stair-step, but has an additional link on it. (It may not appear until you close and then reopen the page.)

The code that connects a page to a style sheet is a link that looks something like this:

```
<link href="mainstyle.css" rel="stylesheet">
```

Linking via the File Inspector

To use the File Inspector to link an external style sheet to a page, follow these steps:

1. In the Files tab of the Inspector, click the page once to which you want to link the style sheet. (Or Shift-click to select multiple pages to link the style sheet to many pages at once.) This selects the page so the Inspector becomes the File Inspector for that page.

2. In the File Inspector, click the Styles tab.

3. Using the Point and Shoot button at the bottom of the File Inspector, link to the style sheet document in the Files tab, as shown in Figure 17-6. (You can also use the Browse button to navigate to the site's root folder and choose the style sheet document.) The name of the style sheet document and the path to it appear at the bottom of the URL area and the Add button becomes active.

4. Click the Add button to add this style sheet to the page(s). The style sheet document appears in the Styles list in the top section of the File Inspector, as shown in Figure 17-7.

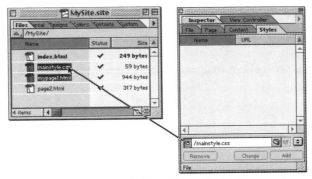

Figure 17-6: Point and Shoot from the URL area of a page's File Inspector to the style sheet being linked to the page.

Figure 17-7: The style sheet appears in the Styles list in the File Inspector of the page to which it's linked. Or shall I say, the page's File Inspector lists any style sheets that are linked to it.

Tip   After you have added an external style sheet to any one page, you can easily add it to any other page without bothering to link to it.In the Site Window, select the next page to be linked. Then turn to the Styles tab once more, but this time use the pop-up menu at the bottom-right corner to choose the desired style sheet. Then click Add to add it to the list.

At any time, you can add more external style sheets to your page. (Of course, you have to create it first. To do so, select the page again in the Site Window, and then, again, link to the other style sheet document as you did for the first one. Again, click add. The new style sheet will be added to the Styles list.

Note   You cannot change the order, or priority of the style sheets in this Inspector. To do that, you need to open the Style Sheet window for the document you want to affect. The next method enables you to do this.

Linking via the Style Sheet window

Another way to link an external style sheet to a page is via the page's Style Sheet window. This is the method more familiar to you if you used style sheets with previous versions of GoLive. Here are the steps:

1. Open the page to which you wish to apply the style sheet.

2. Click the Style Sheet button to open the Style Sheet window.

3. Click the New Style Sheet File button on the Style Sheet toolbar.

   This creates a blank new item in the External folder of the Style Sheet window. It also turns the Inspector into the External Style Sheet Inspector.

4. With the new style sheet reference still selected, Point and Shoot from the Reference area of the External Style Sheet Inspector to the desired style sheet document in the Files tab, as shown in Figure 17-8. (Alternately, you can browse to the style sheet.)

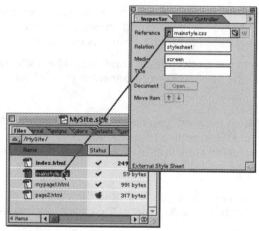

Figure 17-8: Adding an external style sheet by linking from the External Style Sheet Inspector

To add another external style sheet any time, return to the Style Sheet window, click the New Style Sheet File button on the toolbar again, and then link the new item to your next style sheet.

Linking via drag and drop

Finally, there's one more very simple way to add an external style sheet to a page. With the page open, simply drag the style sheet document (the .css file) from the Files tab of the Site Window onto the Page icon at the top-left corner of the page window.

Converting a internal style sheet to an external style sheet

If you've created a page using an internal style sheet, but later decide you'd like to use that style sheet elsewhere, you can easily export your internal styles to an external style sheet. Exporting your internal styles doesn't remove them from the current page. You can continue to use that page with internal styles, or remove them afterward.

To convert an internal style sheet to an external style sheet, follow these steps:

1. Open the page that contains the internal style sheet.

2. Click the Open CSS Interface button at the top-right corner of the page. This opens the Style Sheet window for this page.

3. Choose File ➪ Export ➪ Internal Style Sheet. The Save As dialog box appears and your new external style sheet awaits a name.

4. Type a name for your new style sheet. An external style sheet requires the .css extension. The generic name is preselected so you can simply type the new name without worrying about protecting the .css extension.

5. Save the new style sheet to the desired location. If you'll be using the style sheet within the current site, choose Root folder from the GoLive icon pop-up menu.

After your new external style sheet is saved, you can use it anywhere you'd like. If you'd like to remove the internal styles, return to the page's Style Sheet window (opened in Step 2), use your preferred selection technique to select the selectors you'd like to remove, and then choose Edit ➪ Clear.

Tip   To select all internal styles at once, place your cursor in the gray area of the window and drag across all of the selectors. As soon as the cursor touches any selector, it becomes selected.

Converting an external style sheet to an internal style sheet

In case the time comes when you'd like to take the styles from an external style sheet and import them into a page as an internal style sheet, GoLive's got you covered. Follow these steps:

1. Open the external style sheet.

2. Click the Open CSS Interface button at the top-right corner of the page to which you want to add the internal style sheet. This opens the Style Sheet window for this page.

3. Choose File ➪ Import ➪ External Style Sheet. The Open dialog box appears, awaiting you to select the external style sheet you want to import.

4. Navigate to, and choose, the external style sheet. To make it easier to get to the file, you can select Adobe GoLive HTML page from the Show menu so you only see GoLive pages. (It says HTML, but still shows style sheets.)

The selector tags immediately appear within the Style Sheet window for the open page and the styles take effect.

Understanding Selectors and Style Types

Recall that a *selector* names the parts of the page that will be affected by the specific style sheet instructions you spell out. You can use an HTML tag as a selector or piggyback two or more tags to create a more customized contextual selector. When you need formatting unique to specific text, you can invent your own selector, called a *class*, and apply it several times within your page. When you want a style for one-time use on your page, you can create an ID selector. This section shows you how to define and apply selectors.

Using element selectors

Element selectors are the easiest and most popular way to define styles. They make use of HTML tags such as <h1>, <p>, and <td>, which are necessary anyway for your page to have some formatting even in non CSS-savvy browsers. For example, using the <td> element selector to apply the color green, italic, and bolding to text in tables, a browser that supports style sheets displays that text as bold, italic, and green. But in a browser that does not support style sheets, the text will simply appear in the browser's default text style.

Another example of using a tag as a selector is using any of the style or structure tags from under the Type menu. For example, there's the <i> tag, which applies italics to text. If you use the <i> tag selector to apply the color green to text, anyone using a browser that supports style sheets sees that text displayed in green because the browser follows the style sheets instructions in addition to the browser defaults. But on a browser that doesn't support style sheets, the text will simply appear italicized as if you used the <i> tag alone. (Although styles such as italic and bold are commonly used, it is more historically or technically correct to use the choices under the Structure menu. The results are often the same in pre-CSS browsers, but the structure tags are better for browsers that read or create Braille.)

Element selectors can also be used in context with one another to, in effect, create a hybrid selector that has its own unique style attributes. For example, if you create a style called ul b, it will only be applied when the browser finds the <ul> followed by the <b> tag. The second tag does not have to follow the first immediately. The list created by the <ul> tag will inevitably contain <li> tags for each list item, but they don't disrupt the sequence. Or, you could create a style based on li b. Technically, you *could* use any number of individual element selectors to create a contextual selector. However, it's not a good idea to use more than two selectors to create a contextual selector, as Netscape has problems with longer combinations. Instead, create a class and apply your style to that class.

Adding an element selector

To add an element selector to your style sheet, follow these steps:

1. While in the Style Sheet window (for internal) or style sheet document (for external), click the New Element Selector button on the Style Sheet toolbar or choose Add Element Selector from the contextual menu. This creates an Element icon in the Style Sheet window/CSS document.

2. Select the default name, "selector," and rename the new element selector using the name of the HTML tag you wish to associate the style with. (You can also rename the selector in the Inspector's Basics tab.) For example, if you want to add a style to the <h1> tag, type **h1**. (Don't type the brackets) In Figure 17-9 you can see a selector that will affect all body text (unless another element selector closer to the text takes precedence, of course.)

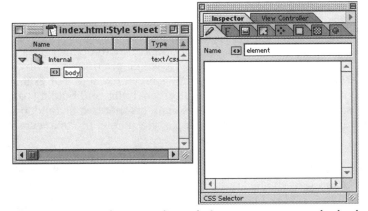

Figure 17-9: An element selector being set up to act on the body tag: Upon clicking out of the field, the word "element" in the Inspector changes to reflect the new selector.

If you're creating a contextual selector, enter the tag combination as the name. For example, for a style that's applied only where the bold tag follows the paragraph tag, enter **b p**. That's the first tag, a space, and then the second tag. In Figure 17-10, you can see the selector entry that affects the bold text within a list by using list item, and then bold as the tags to apply.

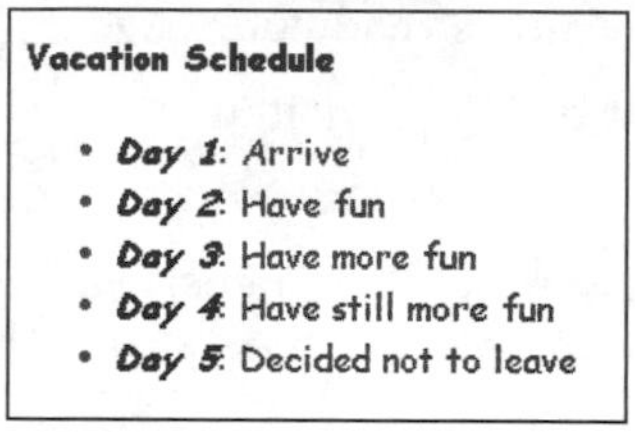

Vacation Schedule

- **Day 1**: Arrive
- **Day 2**: Have fun
- **Day 3**: Have more fun
- **Day 4**: Have still more fun
- **Day 5**: Decided not to leave

Figure 17-10: A contextual selector — li b — that turns bolded text navy and oblique when it's within a list item tag. However, the effect does not show in Layout mode.

3. Assign as many attributes — declarations — to that tag as you'd like by clicking the various tags in the CSS Selector Inspector and making your choices. For example, to assign a color to the `<h1>` tag's text, click the Font tab and choose a color. Use the pop-up menu to choose from one of the 17 browser-safe border colors that can be specified by name. Or, for greater choice, double-click in the border's color square to open the Color palette, and then locate and click the desired color. The selected color appears in the color swatch.

As you create your styles, they appear immediately on the page. However, the effect of contextual selectors don't show within GoLive's Layout or Preview mode. You'll need to preview your page in a browser to see how a contextual selector draws your document.

Defining link styles

GoLive 5 introduces a nearly automatic way to add the oft-requested link effects. Now it's easy to remove the underline from a link, have an underline appear when the user hovers over a link, and so on.

All link tags are anchor tags. Because most people use the anchor tag to format links, GoLive also provides precoded selectors with the complete selector information for each link state. These selectors are technically called pseudo-classes.

To add a predefined link element selector to your style sheet, follow these steps:

1. While in the Style Sheet window (for internal) or style sheet document (for external), Control-click (Mac) or right-click (Windows), move down to Add Selector in the contextual menu, and then choose the specific link state that you'd like to format, as shown in Figure 17-11. The link selectors, in order within the menu, are as follows:

   - *a* is the basic element of the anchor tag, providing a starting point for you to customize the look of any tag that uses an anchor. However, you may find you use the predefined pseudo-classes for most of your work.

   - *a:active* defines the look of a link at the moment the user clicks it. As the effect of this is barely visible, many people don't bother to use it.

   - *a:hover* determines how a link looks while the user's mouse hovers over it.

- *a:link* affects the link as seen while visitors read your page.

- *a:vlink* defines the look of a link that has been visited.

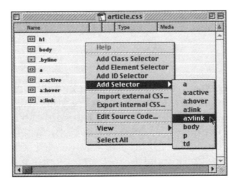

Figure 17-11: Choosing a link selector from the style sheet's contextual menu

 Note

For convenience, GoLive also provides prenamed selectors for the body, paragraph, and table cell tags.

2. With the new selector still selected, make your style choices within the CSS Selector Inspector's Font tab, shown in Figure 17-12. (That's the tab that contains all you'll need to decorate your link.) The options under Decoration are specifically designed for links. A Decoration of None removes the standard underline from your links. You can also use any other font properties to create interesting or sophisticated link effects. For example, you might remove the decoration and then have your links turn italic when the user hovers over them.

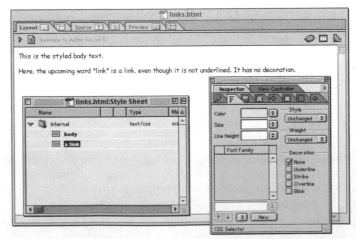

Figure 17-12: Choosing a Decoration of None removes the default underline from your links.

There's a trick to getting these styles to work properly; IE5 Mac (at least) doesn't recognize all of them unless they are in a particular order. Perhaps the order for adding element selectors isn't crucial, but the following order works well. (Thanks to designer Frédéric Berti for sharing this.) I recommend you add these selectors to your style sheet in this order so you don't have to copy and paste source code to move them around afterward. Add your element selectors for links in the following order:

1. *a:visited* (if you are using it)

2. *a:link*

3. *a:hover*

4. *a:active* (if you are using it)

5. *a:link* must be before *a:hover*, visited and active are optional.

Inheritance

Perhaps the most important thing to watch out for when using style sheets is the issue of inheritance. In short, the issue is: if you have two separate style sheet rules that seem to contradict each other, which tag wins? Inheritance is a bit like the algebra problems you did in high school. Remember the stuff in parentheses that got worked on first and then interacted with the rest of the equation?

Say you create a style sheet rule that acts on all text within the <p> tag. But within your paragraph you have some bold text and you make a rule that acts on the <b> tag. What happens to the text between the <b> tags? Because the <b> tag is within the <p> tag, do the <p> tag rules apply to them? The answer is that both can apply, but when both give the same command, such as both stating a different color, the closest tag wins.

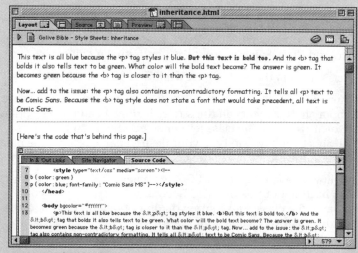

An example of inheritance

If you have already applied any of these element selectors to your style sheet and need to edit them, see the "Editing Style Sheets" section at the end of this chapter.

Defining and working with classes

Classes are custom tags that you invent yourself to use when a regular HTML tag won't do. For example, say your page calls for three different colors for the plain text: one color for the body of your content, another color for credits, and a third for sidebars. If you simply used the <p> tag to assign colors, all text with that tag would become the same color. Instead, you can create your own tag of sorts, called a *class*. Then you can apply that class multiple times on a page, applying it to a word or words here and there, to an entire paragraph at a time, or more.

 Tip If you want to create several classes, you can save time by creating them all at one time, while in the Style Sheet window and its Inspector. Then, you can switch to the page and apply the various class styles as desired.

When using classes, normal rules still apply to HTML tags. For example, if you assign a class to text that's within a <b> selector tag and don't instruct the style to do anything contrary to the bolding, (in this case, assigning a font weight), that <b> tagged text will still be bold.

Classes will work in external (linked) and internal (embedded) style sheets, but not imported ones.

Creating classes

As with any style selector, there are two parts to using a class. First you create the class, and then you apply it.

To create a class in your style sheet, follow these steps:

1. While in the Style Sheet window, click the New Class button on the Style Sheet toolbar. Or, choose Add Class Selector from the contextual menu.

   This creates a .class . icon in the Style Sheet window/CSS document.

2. Define (name), your class, giving it a short but descriptive name. A class name can contain just about anything you can think to type. It just can't begin with a dash or a numeric digit. To name the class, either select the default name, ".class" in the Style Sheet window and type your desired name or type the name in the Name field within the Basics tab in the CSS Selector Inspector window.

   Classes always begin with a leading dot (.) GoLive places the dot when you click the New Class button, but this dot also becomes selected when you select the filed to name the class. Make sure you do not delete the dot, or be sure to type it back in when you name your class.

3. Use the CSS Selector Inspector to assign declarations (style instructions). For example, to affect the font, use the Font tab. (See Figure 17-13.)

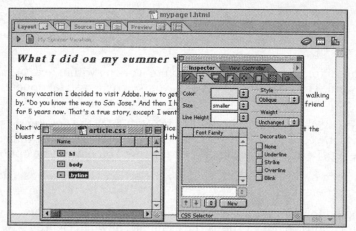

Figure 17-13: A class selector in an external style sheet. This one, called byline, will be applied to all bylines in the site.

Note
Remember that if this selector will fall between another style sheet-formatted selector, you don't have to apply redundant formatting. For example, say you've used the paragraph <p> or body <body> tag to make all your text blue. You don't have to make blue font color a part of this class because the already surrounding tag is in effect. You only have to apply a font color if you want to use a color other than the blue that is defined in the already surrounding tag.

Creating a class is one part of the equation. The other part is to tell your page where to use the class. Tag selectors act upon the HTML tags you are already using in your page. Class selectors act upon the text you specify. As with styles in word processors, you can apply a style paragraph by paragraph or you can apply one to individual characters. In HTML, the former is called a paragraph style, while the latter is called an inline style.

Assigning a class selector

After you create a class, you need to apply it wherever you want it to affect your page's look.

To assign a class style, follow these steps:

1. In the Style Sheet window, click once on the class you wish to apply. This selects the class.

2. On the page, select the text to which you want the style applied, as follows:

   • To style *specific words*, select those words using any normal text selection method.

   • To apply the style to *an entire paragraph*, click anywhere within the paragraph. Because the style is applied to that entire paragraph, you don't have to select any text.

- To apply the style to *the entire page*, click anywhere in the page.

- To apply the style to *a specific area*, such as blocks of text, select the area or object.

3. In the Text Inspector, now active because you're working within text, bring the Style tab forward. The class style (or styles) you've created so far appear listed in this Style tab with each class style on its own line.

4. Apply the style by clicking in the desired style row, under the column for the method by which you want the style to take effect. If you have more than one class style set up, be sure to click in the correct row. You have these options:

  - If you selected words in Step 2, to apply the style to those words, click in the Inline column.

  - If you opted to apply the style to entire paragraph in Step 2, click in the Par (paragraph) column. (This is the example shown in Figure 17-14.)

  - If you are applying the style to the entire page, click in the Area column.

  - If you are applying the style to an object, click in the Div column. This creates a division, which is disconnected from the normal HTML flow.

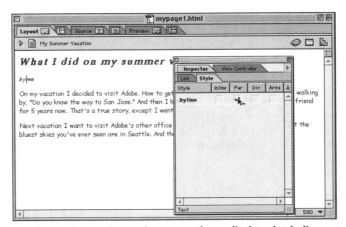

Figure 17-14: A class selector newly applied to the byline words

As extra feedback, your arrow pointer gains a green plus sign if you're adding a class style, and then gains a red minus sign if it is about to be deleted. On the page, you can see the class automatically applied to the selected text.

If you apply a class style incorrectly, with the text still selected or the cursor within the paragraph or page, simply click the checkmark that applied the style. (The cursor will have a red minus sign). This removes the checkmark and fully removes the tags from the source code.

As you work, if you keep the Source Code window open, you'll notice the words `<span class="yourclassname">` at the start of your class-applied area and

`</span class="yourclassname">` at the end. That's the extent of the code that an inline-applied class adds to your page as opposed to regular HTML, which would fully list every single attribute applied to the text.

A type of pseudo-class exists that uses a descriptive word at the start of the class, so the class becomes something like `body.main` or `body.sbar`. However, GoLive doesn't support this as a selector. In GoLive, always make sure you begin your class selector with the dot/period (.).

Creating and working with IDs

Whereas, the benefit of tag selectors is that they enable you to apply a style to all occurrences of a tag at once, and a class enables you to assign the same style to a wide variety of text or areas, ID selectors are meant for you to apply a style to one, and only one, item on your page.

GoLive doesn't provide a visual interface for adding an ID style to your page because it's not common for you to have to add one. That's not to say GoLive doesn't expect you to use the ID style in your pages, though. In fact, you are likely to use it a lot. It's just that GoLive takes care of this style for you. When you add a floating box to your page, GoLive automatically adds an ID selector to the page's internal style sheet (even if you have not started one and don't have the Style Sheet window open). It is called #layer by default (with subsequent floating boxes called #layer2, and so on). The name you give the Floating Box Inspector becomes the ID name.

Truth is, it is far easier to use a class selector than an ID, and it makes much more sense to do so. And, if you only have one table on a page, it's much easier to use the table's tags as selectors. But, in case you really want to add an ID, here's how.

Note As always, remember that font tags and other nonstructural tags may cause conflict. If you already have some and want to remove them, select the text, and then choose Type ➪ Style ➪ Plain, or Type ➪ Structure ➪ Plain to remove font tags (depending on which tags you have.

Creating the ID

Before you can use an ID selector to set the look of your page, you need to create the selector. Then you can apply it.

Here's how to create an ID:

1. While in the Style Sheet window, click the New ID button on the Style Sheet toolbar. Or, choose Add ID Selector from the contextual menu. This creates an `#id` icon in the Style Sheet window/CSS document.

2. Select the default name and type your own short, unique, descriptive name. (Alternately, you can rename the ID selector in the Name field of the Inspector's Basics tab.)

You can use any combination of letters or numbers to create an ID, but for your own sanity down the road, consider using a descriptive combination. For example, if you are creating an online magazine and want to style the classified ad section kind of uniquely, you might create IDs called #personal, #forsale, and #helpwanted. GoLive automatically adds the pound (#) sign, but it becomes selected when you edit the name so don't delete it and be sure to type it back into the name if it is deleted.

3. Use the CSS Selector Inspector to assign declarations (styles).

Tip

At this point you won't be able to see the effects of your choices, so you might want to assign just one part of the look now, and then continue with this after the style is applied within your page.

Applying the ID to an object

A visual interface doesn't exist where you can apply an ID selector, so you work in the HTML to do these next steps. Here's how to apply the ID to an object in your page:

1. Open the Source Code window (Window ➪ Source Code).

2. Open the page in which you're applying the style and select the object to which you're applying it.

   The corresponding HTML code is selected in the Source Code window.

3. Place your I-beam cursor just after the first text in the tag that creates the object to which you're applying the style.

   For example, if formatting a table, the source will look something like this, so you place the I-beam after the word table and before the word border.

   ```
   <table border="0" cellpadding="0" cellspacing="2" width="580">
   ```

4. Type a space, and then the following:

   ```
   id="youridname"
   ```

   (Don't type the "#." Just type the ID name.) The final code looks like this:

   ```
   <table id="youridname" border="0" cellpadding="0"
   cellspacing="2" width="580">
   ```

The effect of your style will not fully show up in GoLive, even with its simulated browser preview. Use the Preview in Browser feature to get an idea of the effect, but also be sure to check it on the various platforms and browsers.

Applying the ID to text

In order for an ID selector to have any effect, you have to apply it to an element on your page.

To apply the ID to text in your page, follow these steps:

1. Open the Source Code window (Window ⇨ Source Code).

2. Open the page in which you're applying the style and select the object to which you're applying it. The corresponding HTML code is selected in the Source Code window. For example, you will have something like this on your page:

```
<P>Hello world </P>
```

3. Place the I-beam after the closing bracket of the <p> tag and type the following:

```
<span id="youridname">Hello world</span>
```

The final code looks like this:

```
<P><span id="youridname">Hello world</span></P>
```

As you work on text, you can view the effect in Layout view. If you are not satisfied with the result, select the ID style in the Style Sheet window and edit its properties as desired.

Now that you're familiar with selectors, it's time to discover all the styles you can apply to your pages. Remember, in techie terms, the styles are called *declarations*.

Describing Declaration Properties

This section describes all the declarations that GoLive provides a visual interface for, along with their properties. They are grouped according to the tabs of the CSS Selector Inspector, as follows:

✦ **Font Properties.** Font and font style settings, including color, size, and line height.

✦ **Text Properties.** Spacing, case, and alignment

✦ **Block Properties.** Margins, padding, and relative location

✦ **Position Properties.** Positioning, clipping, stacking, overflow, and visibility

✦ **Border Properties.** Border styles, line width, color, and line style

✦ **Background Properties.** Background style and positioning

✦ **List & Other Properties.** Miscellaneous style sheet declarations

Caution

Just because a property is present in the GoLive CSS Selector Inspector does not mean it is supported completely by both main browsers (Netscape Navigator and Microsoft Internet Explorer) or by all versions of these browsers.

Introducing properties

Remember that a style contains a selector that indicates which element will be affected by the style sheets instructions, and then a declaration stating the style's instructions. The declaration itself has two parts, too. The first half of the declaration is the *property*, which specifies which elements on your page will be affected. The second half of the declaration is the *value,* which indicates how the element will be affected. This section covers all of the style sheet properties GoLive's CSS Inspector enables you to design your styles with. Up until now, the focus has been on text formatting, but style sheets provide excellent object formatting and positioning too, as you'll discover here.

Tip   For further understanding of what each property does, how well it is supported, and for a visual demonstration, refer to Steve Mulder's Style Sheets Tutorial at www.webmonkey.com.

Adding font properties

To add a font property to a style sheet, first select the selector selected in the Style Sheet window. Then, click the Font tab in the CSS Selector Inspector, shown in Figure 17-15.

Figure 17-15: The Font Properties tab in the CSS Selector Inspector (with a few options selected)

You can apply any of the following font properties available in the Font tab, as follows:

✦ **Color** applies the selected color to text. A always, to set a color, click in the color square to open the Color palette, and then locate and click the desired color. The selected color appears in the color square to show you it has been applied. Or, if you're just looking for one of the 16 browser-safe colors that can be specified by name, you can apply it by using the pop-up menu beside the Color field.

About Setting Sizes

Whenever you need to set a size, height, width, or other parameter, you usually have several options to choose from as your unit of measure. Options vary depending on the setting, of course.

Points, picas, and pixels are absolute measurements. So are millimeters (mm), centimeters (cm), and inches. Em and ex are relative to the font size being displayed. Percentage is also relative to the font size, browser size, and so on. Keywords also exist, which work as guidelines for the browser. With these, the browser determines what the size will be. Some keywords, such as `smaller` and `larger`, are relative to the current size.

To use a specific unit of measure, choose the unit from the menu. Then enter the desired number into the Size field. When you click elsewhere to move on, GoLive adds the unit measure to your number for you. The default unit of measure is points, so if your desired unit of measure is points, just type the number of points into the Size field. There's no need to choose the unit.

If you have a particular unit of measure you typically choose, and it's not the preset default (points), you can set up GoLive to default to that unit. Choose Edit ⇨ Web Settings ⇨ Default Unit. Then set the default unit—for example, the popular px, to make pixels the default. Then you never have to choose that unit of measure from any menu again before entering the desired size.

✦ **Size** applies a specific size to your text. Choose a unit of measure, and then enter the desired number. Or, choose a browser-determined size such as Small or Smaller. The most popular measurements seem to be pixels and ems. The size you set is the size visitors see when your page loads, so you want everyone to be comfortable with it. Each user can still use the font sizing buttons or menu choices, but he or she would have to do that for each page.

✦ **Line Height** is better known as leading in the print world. It adds space above your line of text. Specifically, it is the amount of space from one text baseline to the next.

Tip

The em is popular because it holds up well during user resizing. One em is equal to the height of the font being used, so if you choose 1.5 ems, you know the spacing will be one and a half times the space of the text height, regardless of what height the user makes the text.

✦ **Font Family** gives you some control over the font a user sees for your text. In order for a user to see text rendered in any font, the font must be installed on that viewer's computer. When you set up a list of fonts, the viewer's browser goes down your list and, upon finding one of your listed fonts, uses that font.

You can choose one font, an existing font set, or create your own font set by adding several fonts here.

Click New to add a new font or font set to the list. To choose an individual font, click the arrow button to the right of the Font field. To choose a font set, use the pop-up button to the left of the New button. To move any font or set up or down in the list order, select it in the list and then click the up or down arrows below the list.

✦ **Style** italicizes your text. If a font has an official version called italic or oblique, it uses that version. If not, it slants the text. This is much like other font use.

✦ **Weight** is the line thickness of the font. 100 is lightest, while 900 is boldest. 400 is normal. The decision of how much bolder any choice is up to the browser. The relative choices — normal, lighter, and bolder — are relative to the other thickness you've selected elsewhere. If you have not added bold style to any text, they have no effect. (The relative weights are for Internet Explorer 4 and 5 only.)

✦ **Decoration** adds a (surprise) decoration to your text. Underline, Strike, and Overline draw a line under, through, or over the text, respectively. (Netscape browsers substitute underlining instead, which is confusing as underline designates a hyperlink.) Blink, supported by Netscape browsers only, causes your text to blink (and your viewers to hate you). None, ensures that no line appears along with your text. Remembering that, by default, all links are underlined, you can catch onto the secret of None.

Adding text properties

To add a text property to a style sheet, first select the selector in the Style Sheet window. Then, click the Text tab in the CSS Selector Inspector, shown in Figure 17-16.

Figure 17-16: The Text Properties tab in the CSS Selector Inspector

You can apply any of the text properties shown in the Text tab, as follows:

✦ **Text Indent** enables you to indent the first line of text in any paragraph. The indent is measured from where the text normally begins, such as the default margin of the page or the edge of the element it's in. This is well supported.

Hiding an Invisible GIF, Nonbreaking Space, or Spacer

By Kynn Bartlett, President, HTML Writers Guild

If you use an invisible GIF and then use a style sheet to create an indent, the GIF's effect will be added to the style sheet's effect, increasing your indent. The same goes for when you use nonbreaking spaces or a spacer (which is good in Netscape only).

First create the class that will hide the spacing object (or nonbreaking spacers). No visual interface exists to create this style, so you'll be hand-coding it. (See "Creating Classes" earlier in this chapter for details.)

To create the class, follow these steps:

1. Create a class and name it something like **.hidefromcss**.

2. Select the newly created class and open the Source Code window. In the source code, the code for this new class is selected. It says: `.class {}`.

3. Place your I-beam between the brackets, and then type **display: none;**

4. Click back on the Class Selector icon. Your code reads:

   `.hidefromcss {display: none;}`

   Reselecting the class selector is not actually a part of the creation, but you need it selected to apply the class, and have to click somewhere to change the focus away from the Source Code window. Unlike most places in GoLive where pressing Return or Enter sets an entry, here it adds a line in the code.

After the class is created, you can apply it anytime, just like any other class. To apply the class, follow these steps:

1. In the page, select the invisible GIF, the nonbreaking spaces, or the spacer. Because these things are invisible, it may be tricky, but drag your I-beam over the area this covers. If you want to see the invisible GIF, open the View Controller and uncheck the Images checkbox. Depending on the size you stretched the GIF to, it may still be difficult to see it, but look closely.

2. In the Text Inspector, apply this class inline by checking the Inline column in the hidefromcss class row.

The effect of the hidden space cannot be seen within GoLive, so preview your page in a browser.

In case you're curious, the resulting code looks something like this:

```
<P> <span class="hidefromcss"> <img src="transgif.gif" width="10"
height="1" border="0" alt=" "> </span>
```

(In this case, the spacer was a GIF, called `transgif`, stretched to 10 pixels and a space was typed into the Alt text field of the image to keep with the accessibility standard.)

To create a hanging indent, specify a negative value — just like in print layout! Be careful, though. Steve Mulder states that Internet Explorer 4 and 5 can cut the first few characters, and another report is that Netscape browsers may ignore words that hang so far over the element edge that they run off the browser window.

✦ **Word Spacing** adds space between each of the words it is applied to. (Only Internet Explorer 4 for Mac supports this.)

✦ **Letter Spacing** adds space between each of the letters this style is applied to. Again, you choose a unit of measure and then enter any number to accompany it, as with font sizing. (Internet Explorer 4 and 5 only. Not recognized by Netscape Navigator 4.)

✦ **Vertical Align**, in theory, determines how your text aligns with regard to images or objects positioned beside it on a line. (Most of the options are not at all supported through Internet Explorer 5 and Netscape 4. Internet Explorer 4 and 5 support subscript and superscript, though.)

✦ **Font Variant** enables you to display your text in small caps. (However, not even Internet Explorer 5 gets it right yet. Instead, the text is all the same size, which defeats the purpose.)

✦ **Transformation** affects the case display of your text. Capitalize is what some page layout and word processor programs call Title case: the first character in every word is capitalized. Uppercase capitalizes every character. Lowercase, of course, make every character lowercase. To prevent the selected text from being capitalized by other style sheet instructions it might inherit, choose None.

✦ **Alignment** enables you to align your text relative to the edge of the element (not the edge(s) of the browser window). It works on any elements that make their own paragraph, such as paragraph, list, and header tags.

Adding block properties

To add a block property to a style sheet, first select the selector selected in the Style Sheet window. Then, click the Block tab in the CSS Selector Inspector, shown in Figure 17-17.

You can apply any of the block properties shown in the Block tab, as follows:

✦ **Margin** establishes a buffer zone of space around an element, just like with text on a printed page. A margin can also be around the outside of a box, such as a table, or around a graphic. Think *gutter* if you're coming from a print layout background. As the choices clearly depict, you can set any size margin at the top, right, bottom, and/or left, individually. You can also set an equal margin all around.

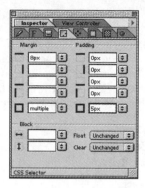

Figure 17-17: The Block Properties tab in the CSS Selector Inspector

Unlike the print world, margins are commonly applied to a whole page on the Web, so consider using the body tag as your selector to apply a margin.

You can overlap elements by using negative margin values here, so the edge of one element can cross over another. This can create some great effects. However, each browser overlaps differently, so you'll need to view the effect in each browser to see if it works for you.

Overlapping is not layering. With floating boxes, you have control over the stacking order. With overlap, stacking is up to the browser.

✦ **Padding** places space between the inside border of an element and its contents, as in a table. Again, if you're coming from print, this is familiar. You can set any amount of padding at the top, right, bottom, and/or left, individually, or set an equal border all around.

✦ **Block** represents the exact height and width of the selected element you are working with. It helps a browser to know these measurements while it is loading your page, especially if you've specified margins or padding. This is mostly useful if you have applied a style to an image.

✦ **Float** is for working with an element that is not part of the normal flow of text. It tells text to wrap around the element. To have text wrap around the right side of the floating element, you tell the object to float to the left of the text by choosing Left from the choice menu. Choose Right to place the object to the right, enabling text to wrap at its left. Choosing None causes the floating element to appear just where it occurs.

✦ **Clear** prevents floating elements from appearing on a certain side of the element you're working with. With Clear set to Left, an element will be moved below any floating element on the left side. With Clear set to None, floating elements are allowed on all sides.

Position properties

Position properties can be applied to just about anything, but their most famous implementation is probably the floating box. In fact, you may recognize some of these properties from the abilities you set up within the Floating Box Inspector. To add a position property to a style sheet, first select the desired selector selected in the Style Sheet window. Then, click the Position tab in the CSS Selector Inspector, shown in Figure 17-18.

Figure 17-18: The Position Properties tab in the CSS Selector Inspector

You can apply any of the position properties covered in the Position tab, as follows:

✦ **Kind** determines the type of positioning control a style has over the element(s) the style is applied to.

✦ **Absolute** positions a floating element in relation to the upper-left corner of the browser window. This is the positioning all floating boxes have by default. The element and everything in it have no relationship to anything on the page — just to the top and left corners of the browser. (This is positioning used by floating boxes automatically.)

✦ **Static** tells the element to flow with the surrounding text or elements, inline with the cursor it is attached to.

✦ **Relative** tells the element to flow as surrounding text allows, but positions the object with relation to whatever it is flowing with. This is a bit like a baseline shift in text layout in the print world.

✦ **Left** and **Top** set the position of the floating element in relation to the left and top sides of the browser, respectively. To determine how far from the left edge the object will appear, choose a unit of measure and enter the desired distance. This is the default positioning you set for a floating box in the Floating Box Inspector or by dragging it into position on your page.

✦ **Width** (double-headed horizontal arrow icon) and **Height** (double-headed vertical arrow icon) establishes the size of the floating element when the element is positioned absolutely. This is the setting you set for a floating box in the Floating Box Inspector or by dragging it to size on your page.

(Steve Mulder warns that height is buggy in Internet Explorer 4 and 5, as well as unsupported by Netscape 4.)

✦ **Clipping** lets you crop an element if and when it overlaps another on the page. (The Floating Box Inspector doesn't have an interface for setting clipping.) Here are the clipping options:

- *Auto* sets the clipping region to the same size as the element's rendering box. In other words, no cropping will occur. This is the default.

- *Inherit* does not specify a clipping method of its own, but instead lets the style simply adopt the clipping method of its parent. By default, this is not an inherited property.

- *Rect* lets you specify clipping by measurement on any or each of the element's four sides.

✦ **Z-Index** assigns a stacking order to the object. In the Floating Box Inspector, this control is called Depth. A box with the number 1 is at the bottom, while each subsequently z-index-numbered floating box stacks on top.

✦ **Overflow** helps you decide what to do if the contents of an element don't fit within (overflow) the height and width boundaries. (However, Steve Mulder says it is not supported in Internet Explorer 4 or 5 for Windows.) Here are the overflow options:

- *Visible* displays the entire element no matter what.

- *Hidden* shears off whatever part(s) of the element go over the browser's edge.

- *Scroll* provides a scrollbar when unseen (overflow) content exists. (Scroll works similarly in any page on your computer.)

Caution

Regardless of your choice here, a browser will still clip an element that overflows the edge of the browser window.

✦ **Visibility** controls whether the object is visible or not when the page loads. After loading, various Actions, the animation timeline, or other JavaScripts, can further control this visibility. (It's the secret to many great effects.) Here are the visibility options:

- *Inherited* is for when the object is within another object whose visibility can be set. It causes the visibility to be determined by the visibility of the surrounding object.

- *Visible*, of course, sets it to appear when the page loads.

- *Hidden* renders the object invisible on load. (It's still here. Users just don't see it.)

Note

The stuff in this tab is totally not supported by any 3.*x* browser, because it is newer than they are.

Adding border properties

The border properties enable you to set up a variety of borders around your tables, images, floating boxes, and even text blocks. These effects don't all appear in Layout mode, so be sure to preview these effects in a browser.

To add a border property to a style sheet, first select the selector selected in the Style Sheet window. Then, click the Border tab in the CSS Selector Inspector, shown in Figure 17-19.

Figure 17-19: The Border Properties tab in the CSS Selector Inspector

You can apply any of the border properties shown in the Border tab, as follows:

✦ **Border placement** is specified in the first Border column. You can choose to have a border of any width drawn at the top, right, bottom, and/or left of your object. Or, create an equal border all around. If you don't assign a border on each side, set the nonborder sides to zero. This tells the browser exactly what you want so the browser won't take its own guess. To make Internet Explorer cooperate, you have to apply a pattern style to your border. Otherwise, it doesn't create your border as ordered.

✦ **Border color** is set in the middle Border column. Use the pop-up menu to choose from one of the 16 browser-safe border colors that can be specified by name. Or, for greater choice, click in the border's color square to open the Color palette and then locate and click the desired color. The selected color appears in the color swatch.

✦ **Border pattern** is set in the third Border column. If you prefer that no border is rendered, choose None. This overrides any measurement set in the Border Width column. (According to Steve Mulder, Netscape doesn't support dotted or dashed, and neither does Internet Explorer for Windows.)

Note   Although you can choose a different color for each border, it is reported that Netscape Navigator 4 (Windows) only recognizes the first color in a list.

Adding background properties

To add a background property to a style sheet, first select the selector selected in the Style Sheet window. Then, click the Background tab in the CSS Selector Inspector, as shown in Figure 17-20.

Figure 17-20: The Background Properties tab in the CSS Selector Inspector

You can apply any of the background properties shown in the Background tab, as follows:

✦ **Image** adds a background image. Point and Shoot to the desired image file, or click Browse to select the background file.

✦ **Color** enables you to add a color background. Use the pop-up menu to choose from one of the 16 browser-safe border colors that can be specified by name. Or, for greater choice, click in the border's color square to open the Color palette and then locate and click the desired color. The selected color appears in the color swatch.

✦ **Repeat** enables you to determine whether your background image (if you're using a background image) will tile, and if so, how it tiles. When a background doesn't repeat, the background color fills in any extra browser window area. Here are the repeat options:

• *Repeat* tiles the background image both vertically and horizontally.

• *Repeat x* repeats the image horizontally only so the image tiles sideways.

• *Repeat y* tiles the background vertically only.

• *Once* sets it up to appear just once, disabling tiling altogether.

✦ **Attach** attaches the background to the text in front of it, as is normal with HTML. When the user scrolls, the background moves up the page. Text and background are fixed together. To ensure your background behaves this way, choose Fixed. However, to enable your text to scroll independently of the background, choose Scroll. It's not commonly used yet, so it makes an interesting effect (Only your Internet Explorer users will see it, though, as it is not supported by Netscape as of Version 4.)

✦ **Top** and **Left** determine where a background pattern is positioned in the browser. The various choices provide for a variety of relative placement. The numeric placements are relative to the top of the browser and its left side, respectively. Under Left, you can choose horizontal alignment. All in all, this feature enables you to have a background begin exactly in relation to another object on the page. However, this is most likely an Internet Explorer–only benefit for the time being.

Tip   When using a background, be sure to choose a background color too. This color is needed (or appreciated) by those who don't see the background. It is also seen to the right or bottom of the user's screen when a background doesn't repeat and the user's window is larger than the background image.

Adding a list and other properties

To add a list and other properties to a style sheet, first select the selector selected in the Style Sheet window. Then, click the List & Others tab in the CSS Selector Inspector, as shown in Figure 17-21.

Figure 17-21: The List & Other Properties tab in the CSS Selector Inspector

You can apply any of the List & Other properties shown in the List & Others tab, as follows:

✦ **Image** substitutes any image you select in lieu of the default bullets or numbers in a list. To add an image Point and Shoot to it in the Files tab as usual, or browse to the image and select it.

✦ **Style** determines the type of bullet that will be displayed by each list item. An image overrides bullet style, though.

✦ **Position** provides list alignment. Inside aligns the list items and the marker while Outside renders the content indented from the marker.

✦ The **Other Property** area enables you write in properties not presented within the CSS Selector Inspector—for example, the cursor property, which enables you to designate which type of cursor a user sees (in IE, at least, but not in Netscape 4.*x*). To add a property, click New. Enter the name of the property into the Property Name field at the bottom-left corner. For example, enter **cursor** to set a cursor. Then enter the name of any value available to the property into the Property Values field. For example with the cursor property, the value can be hand, crosshair, help, wait, pointer, or move.

Previewing Style Sheets

The most accurate way to preview the results of your style sheets is to preview the page(s) in a browser. To be specific, every browser on every platform you're concerned with. However, GoLive provides a built-in preview that can more easily give you a fair idea of how your page(s) will look on Mac and Windows in the most common browsers—Internet Explorer and Netscape, 3, 4, and 5.

The secret to GoLive's preview is the View Controller, that tab that sits beside your Inspector. You can preview the pages from the Layout mode, or switch to the Preview tab of your page.

To preview your pages in GoLive, follow these steps:

1. If the Inspector window is open, click the View Controller to make it active. Otherwise, choose Window ➪ View Controller to open the View Controller.

2. Choose one of the view simulators from the root CSS menu to see how your page should look in that browser, as follows:

   • Navigator 3 (Mac OS) does not support style sheets, so that option shows you how your page will look without the style sheet applied in older browsers.

   • Internet Explorer 5, Mac, shows the traditional Mac font size settings. However, Internet Explorer 5 for the Mac really comes preconfigured with the larger, PC-standard font sizing, so this preview isn't entirely accurate. No preview can be with the user controls IE introduces with that browser.

3. *(Optional)* If any of your styles have a negative margin to create an overlap, select Allow Overlapping Paragraphs to preview the effect.

4. Choose one of these options for further feedback:

   • *(Optional)* To have GoLive show you all uses of a particular style, choose that style from the Mark Style menu.

   • *(Optional)* To have GoLive show you all uses of a particular selector on your page, choose that selector from the Mark Element menu. It appears surrounded by a transparent yellow box.

Editing Style Sheets

It's a pretty sure bet that you'll want to edit your style sheets at one point or another. After all, that's part of their appeal. You can make changes to your style sheets the same way you create them. Or, if you're into code, you can work directly in the style sheet code.

Editing an internal style sheet

You can make changes to an internal style sheet anytime the page is open. You can enter your changes within the Style Sheet window or directly within the HTML. Of course, working in GoLive's Style Sheet window and Inspector is often easier and friendlier.

Follow these steps to use the Style Sheet window:

1. Click the Style Sheet icon at the top-right corner of the page window, or open the head section and double-click the Style Sheet icon that appears there.

   Either way, the Style Sheet window opens.

2. In the Style Sheet window, click the selector you wish to make changes to.

3. Make the changes within the Inspector, just like when you created the style.

If you're comfortable working in the style sheet code, you can edit it without using the GoLive Inspector interface. You edit the code within the Source Code palette, the Source tab, or the Outline tab of the page window. In the latter two, you won't see the Layout mode, though, so you won't see the effect of your changes right away.

To work directly in the HTML source code, follow these steps:

1. Double-click the page that contains the style sheet to open it.

2. View your page's source code in one of the following ways:

   • Open the Source Code palette (Window ⇨ Source Code).

   • Switch to the Source tab of the page.

   • Switch to the Outline tab of the page, and then click the arrow to the left of the Style tab. (It is somewhere between the head tags.)

3. Locate the style code. It's within the `<style>` tag. Then edit the style code that's within the comment tags (`<!--` and `-->`). (See Figure 17-22.) Then edit the text just like you work within any text editor.

4. Save your page as you work and when finished editing.

After you perform the edit, the new order of your statements appears in the Style Sheet window.

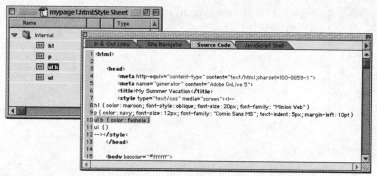

Figure 17-22: For reading or hand-editing: the Style Sheet window, with a selector selected and the corresponding style sheet code selected in the Source Code window

You could also edit the code within the Source tab or Outline tab of the page window, but because you won't see the Layout mode as you do, you won't see the effect of your changes.

To fully delete an internal style sheet, open the head section of the page, select the CSS icon (the one with the stair-step design) and press the Delete/Backspace key. After you save the page and reopen it, the styles will be gone and you'll be back to having only formatting that was done using HTML tags.

Editing an external style sheet

You have several ways to get back to your external style sheet to work on it:

✦ Double-click it in the Files tab of the Site Window. This opens the style sheet. If you want to see the effects of your choices as you work, you'll also need to open a page that uses the style sheet.

✦ If you're already working on a page when you decide you want edit the style sheet, choose one of the following options:

• Double-click the Style Sheet icon in the head section of your page. This opens the Style Sheet window for that page, which lists all style sheets (both internal and external) for a page. Then, double-click the style sheet you wish to edit.

• Click the Style Sheet icon at the top-right corner of your page or the Style Sheet icon in the head section of your page. This opens the style sheet and the Style Sheet Inspector. Here, you can check the name to be sure you've selected the correct style sheet. Then, click the Document Open button in the Style Sheet Inspector, as shown in Figure 17-23.

Figure 17-23: Opening an external style sheet from the Style Sheet Inspector

To work directly in the HTML source code, follow these steps:

1. Open the style sheet document by double-clicking it in the Files tab of the Site Window.

2. View the style sheet's code in one of the following ways:

   • Open the Source Code window (Window ➪ Source Code).

   • Control-click (Mac) or right-click (Windows) in the external Style Sheet window then choose Edit Source Code from the contextual menu.

3. Edit the text just like you work within any text editor. Enter your code, delete the style code you don't want, or replace the code you wish to change.

4. Click OK when you're done.

5. Save your style sheet by choosing File ➪ Save while in the style sheet document.

To change the order of external style sheets, follow these steps:

1. Open the page in which you wish to change the style sheet order.

2. Open the head section of that page by clicking the arrow to the left of the Page icon.

3. Click once on the icon of the external style sheet you wish to move up or down in the reading order.

4. In that style sheet's Inspector, use the Move Item arrows, as shown in Figure 17-24, to move the style sheet up or down in the pecking order.

Note   Moving a style sheet up in the GoLive Inspector increases its *weight*, which means it gives it priority over all style sheets not as high in the order. However, in the reality of HTML, it is actually moving a style sheet down that gives it priority. As the browser reads the code, from the top of the body downward, it builds the page. Therefore, the last style sheet read is the one that overrides all other style sheets with identical, conflicting, or redundant styles.

As you move style sheet's up or down in the order, you should see the changes take effect in your page.

Figure 17-24: Moving up an external style sheet (bu.css) in weight so its styles take priority over the other external style sheet

Removing an external style sheet

If you no longer wish to have a style sheet associated with any particular page, you can unlink it, yet keep the style sheet intact and safely on hand in your Site Window for other uses. Here's how to do so:

1. Open the page you wish to remove the style sheet from.

2. Open the head section of that page by clicking the arrow to the left of the Page icon.

3. Click once on the icon of the external style sheet you wish to unlink.

4. Press the Delete or Backspace key. Or, choose Edit ➪ Clear (Mac) or Edit ➪ Delete (Windows).

5. Close and save the page, and then reopen it to see the effect of removing your style sheet.

Another way to remove an external style sheet from use on a page is to select it within the page's Style Sheet window and then press Delete/backspace. You can also choose Clear from the contextual menu or choose Edit ➪ Clear (Mac) or Edit ➪ Delete (Windows).

Fixing the Netscape Cascading Style Sheet glitch

The Netscape 4 browsers have an odd glitch that drops CSS information when the user resizes the browser window, because the browser does not read in the style sheet upon redraw. This has nothing to do with GoLive — it's a universal problem. Fortunately, there's a JavaScript fix for this, and GoLive provides it as an Action. Add this Action to every page that uses a Cascading Style Sheet (or has or a floating box, which uses CSS too).

This Action doesn't require any special set up. To add it just drag a Head Action icon from the Smart tab of the Objects palette into the head section of your page. Set the Action to execute OnLoad. Then choose it from the Actions pop-up. You'll find it under Others.

To add the Netscape CSS fix, follow these steps:

1. Drag a Head Action icon from the Smart tab of the Objects palette into the head section of your page. If the head section of the page isn't open when you begin to drag the item, rest over the triangle that's next to the Page icon at the top-left corner of the page. This opens the section so you can continue placement.

2. In the Action Inspector, select OnLoad from the Exec pop-up menu.

3. From the Actions pop-up, choose Others ➪ Netscape CSS Fix.

That's it. There's no special setup to do for this Action. For more details on Actions, including screen shots, see Chapter 18.

Using a different style sheet for each platform

Due to the differences in how each computer platform renders font sizes, and how each browser handles the various style properties, you may want to set up multiple style sheets. But how would you get these custom style sheets to be seen? The answer is Matt Ridley's CSS Write Action.

With the CSS Write Action, you can assign up to six external style sheets, accommodating Internet Explorer and Netscape for both Mac and Windows. As the browser loads your Web page, it makes the call for the style sheet that matches the user's browser and platform. But if the browser is older than Version 4, and thus doesn't support style sheets well, it renders the page without any style sheet.

On the CD-ROM   You can find this Action in a folder called GoLive Stuff on the CD-ROM in the back of this book, or at Matt Ridley's Web site, www.matt-ridley.com, by following the software link.

Setting Cascading Style Sheet Preferences

Most of what takes place in the Web Settings CSS area is behind-the-scenes stuff that provides the previews we control in the Layout Controller. However, you can change a couple of simple preferences that can have a great timesaving impact on your work.

Changing the default unit of measure

The default unit of measure wherever you enter a number in any size-setting entry field is points. However, because point size is different between computer platforms, some designers recommend using pixels instead. If you find yourself choosing pixels often, you can change the default setting. That way, you don't have to bother to choose a unit of measure every time you set up a size. All you have to do is enter the number. When you leave the number entry field, the default size takes effect. (You see it appear in the size entry field.)

To change the default unit of measure, follow these steps:

1. Choose Edit ➪ Web Settings to open the Web Settings database, and then choose the CSS tab.

2. At the left side of the Web Settings window, choose your preferred unit of measure from the Default Unit menu. (You can see this setting in Figure 17-25.)

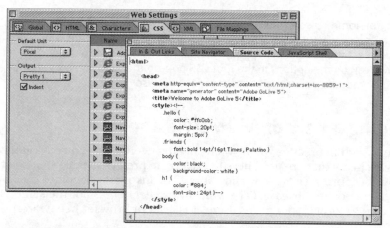

Figure 17-25: The Web Settings dialog box and sample style sheet code as it looks when Pretty 1 is the selected Output format

When you close the Web Settings window, the new unit takes effect. Next time you need to enter a size as you're setting up a style declaration, just type the number, click elsewhere, and move on. The measurement should be noted as having your selected unit.

Changing style sheet code appearance

Code can be very personal. You might want it all compressed in as few lines as possible, or you might prefer it spread out, with each rule on its own distinct line. Believe it or not, GoLive provides six code formats for you to choose from, so you can be the most comfortable reading the style sheet code you create as you work in the Inspector.

To change the way GoLive formats style sheet code, follow these steps:

1. Choose Edit ➪ Web Settings to open the Web Settings database, and then choose the CSS tab.

2. Open the Source Code window by choosing Window ➪ Source Code.

3. At the left side of the Web Settings window, choose one of the options from the Default Unit menu.

As you peruse through the options within the menu, sample style sheet code changes to show you how code is rendered and written for that style. Uncheck Indent if you prefer your style sheet code to be fully to the left.

This code format isn't just for your viewing as you work. As the name implies, the format you select becomes the final format for the style sheet code that moves to your Web server. You might just end up with the nicest formatted code on your cyberblock.

Tip

If, for some reason, you decide you don't want to use style sheets in GoLive, you can preview your page without your style sheet active. To turn your style sheets off, deselect the Allow Overlapping Paragraphs checkbox in the View Controller. Then you can try the options in the root CSS pop-up menu to see how your page would look with the default settings for various browser versions.

Creating a new preview style sheet

In theory (and in practice when you're an advanced user), you can duplicate any of the style sheets that are used here to create the preview simulation, and then create your own browser preview simulation. The Inspector becomes the Root Style Sheet Inspector, in this case. (The word *style sheet* here is not the same as the ones you create to format your pages. Here, it is a set of browser behaviors.)

Finding More Cascading Style Sheet Resources

Life on the Web is ever-changing. With browsers evolving, and with them support for Cascading Style Sheets, you'll want a few good references to run to while you're checking out the cool things you can do with style sheets. Here are a few great starting points. They'll not only help you out, but will also point you to some more good help.

✦ One of the best places to learn about CSS is from the HTM Writer's Guild. Check out their CSS Frequently Asked Questions section at `www.hwg.org/ resources/faqs/cssFAQ.html#alternate`.

✦ The oft-referred-to style sheet tutorial by Steve Mulder is a definite read. It's clear, fun, and full of examples. The full address is `hotwired.lycos.com/ webmonkey/authoring/stylesheets/tutorials/tutorial1.html`. However, you can simply type in `www.webmonkey.com`, and then choose Tutorials: Webmonkey from the navigation menu.

✦ The CSS Pointers Group (`http://css.nu/pointers/bugs.html`) is entirely dedicated to Cascading Style Sheets (CSS). There's a whole bunch of stuff to explore there.

✦ Blooberry.com's Index DOT Css — `www.blooberry.com/indexdot/css/index.html` by Brian Wilson, is another much referred-to resource for understanding CSS and learning about browser compatibility and style sheet selector usage.

✦ Eric Meyer's Browser Compatibility Charts: `http://webreview.com/pub/guides/style/style.html`.

✦ The Web Developer's Virtual Library at `http://wdvl.com/Authoring/Style/Sheets`.

✦ For a page full of CSS links, visit `www.westciv.com/style_master/academy/links.html`.

✦ For the World Wide Web Consortium CSS Validation Service, visit `http://jigsaw.w3.org/css-validator/validator-uri.html`.

✦ ✦ ✦

Adding Multimedia, Movement, and Interactivity

Here's where the Web becomes fun. This part shows you how to add video, animation, or sound files to your site. It's also where you learn about using Dynamic HTML (DHTML) to add movement to your site without video files. Want to make one of those cool effects where text or images magically appear when the mouse rolls over a screen element? That's DHTML — and this is the place for learning how to do it. The basics in Part III are a prerequisite to this part.

Applying GoLive's JavaScripts: Actions and Smart Objects

JavaScript is one of the hottest things ever to hit the Web. It's one of the easiest ways to add fun and function to your page, and it doesn't cause a huge speed hit. What can it do for you? It can create alert windows with OK buttons. It can open new windows, automatically size them, and even position them on the screen. It can verify that the contents of a form are properly completed, so improperly completed forms are not submitted to your database or e-mail. It can move layers, exchange images, force framesets and set their content, and write content of pages according to circumstances.

With GoLive, you don't have to become a JavaScript programmer to add JavaScript functions to your site because GoLive comes complete with many commonly requested JavaScripts. Some of these prewritten JavaScripts come to you in the form of Smart Objects while others come to you as Actions. Both are easy to use. Smart Objects are items you drag from the Objects palette and then set up using the object's Inspector. GoLive's Actions — the focus of this chapter — are all set up within the Actions Inspector or Actions palette.

To augment GoLive's Actions, some great Actions developers within the GoLive community offer excellent Actions for sale at amazingly great prices (or sometimes for free). Of course, if you're familiar with JavaScript you can create your own Actions or modify Adobe's.

Plenty of regular JavaScripts are also floating around the Web and available for you to use (if permission has been granted). They're easily added to your page, too, and I show you how in Chapter 22. In Chapter 22, you can also learn how to use GoLive's JavaScript Editor to write your own JavaScripts.

Are you wondering if you can use Actions in a component? This is a popular question on the GoLive e-mail lists. And the answer is, "definitely!" Actions will work perfectly well in a component. I even discuss how and why later in this chapter.

Understanding Actions

GoLive *Actions* are prewritten JavaScript procedures that you just plug in and use right off the bat. They don't require you to have any knowledge of JavaScript — you can just use them as is. Of course, GoLive is a very flexible Web development program, so if you're familiar with JavaScript, you can modify the Actions or even create your own.

Actions include such key dynamic functions as creating a pop-up alert window, moving an object from one place to another on a page, adding text or HTML code to a page, or sending the user to another Web page entirely. And of course, the famous, fancy buttons that change when a user moves the mouse over them and can even change again when the user clicks.

Triggering events

Actions take place in response to *events*. An event is something such as the page loading in a browser or something a visitor to your page does to interact with it, such as clicking a link, pressing a key, or moving the mouse over an object. One event can have multiple Actions, so Actions can become rather intricate. For example, one thing can happen on Mouse Enter for a link and another thing happens on Mouse Exit. Or, several things can happen upon mouse enter and another bunch at mouse exit. For instance, on mouse enter, one floating box can disappear while two appear.

Tip

You can create an Action group that is any two or more Actions set up as normal, but within a group so they can all be called at once. This is very helpful if you use the same group of Actions more than once. When you anticipate being in this situation, check out the "Grouping and Calling Actions Together" section later in this chapter.

Adding and Installing New Actions

Actions are like baseball cards among GoLive developers. It's common for other GoLive users to create specific Actions and share them with their fellow GoLive users. Often when a new Action is invented, the creator announces its availability and download location on the GoLive discussion lists. Some really helpful and supercool Actions are available for extremely reasonable fees. I encourage you to check out the available Actions after you've used some of the ones covered in this chapter that come with GoLive.

Some of the places you can find and download Actions are listed here:

✦ OUT Media Design's Action site — http://out.to/actions

✦ Walter Blady's site — www.wblady.com

✦ Matt Ridley's site — www.matt-ridley.com

✦ GoLive HQ — www.golivehq.com

✦ GoLive Heaven — www.goliveheaven.com

✦ *Adobe GoLive 5 Bible* companion site — www.golivebible.com

It's easy to install new Actions. For the most part, you just drop any Action into the Actions folder by following the path GoLive ➪ Modules ➪ Jscripts ➪ Actions. Inside the Actions folder, you'll find several subfolders. You can add an Action to one of those folders or create your own new subfolder by simply making a new folder in the Actions folder. Those folders create the submenus you see when you choose an Action from the Actions tab of the Inspector. Filing your Actions under descriptive categories greatly enables you to locate and choose an Action.

Some Actions rely on scripts located in their own or other folders in the JScript folder and may not work if placed improperly! Please read the installation instructions of the respective Action provider.

Three basic categories of events exist — user-triggered, browser-triggered, and timeline-triggered, as follows:

✦ User-triggered events are either caused by mouse or keyboard input.

✦ Browser-triggered events can be placed, and called from, either the header or body of the page.

✦ Timeline-triggered events happen in relation to a time frame, whether the time frame begins when the page loads or when a timeline scene is played.

User-triggered events are events that happen as the result of a user interacting with the page. A user has two means of interaction: the mouse and the keyboard. Therefore, there are mouse events, such as a click or double-click or having the mouse enter a defined area, and key-press events, which are events such as a key being pressed or released *or* pressed and released.

Browser-triggered events

Browser-triggered events reside in the head or body or the Web page and are called automatically from the page header or body to trigger the assigned Action. When in the head of a page, the trigger event can be the loading or parsing of the page, or the unloading of a page, or the event can be triggered when called for by another Action. When in the body of a page, the Action takes place as soon as that line of code is read while the browser is loading the page.

Time-triggered events

Timed events are Actions that are called automatically based on the passage of time as set within the TimeLine Editor. To trigger a timeline event, you add the Action to the TimeLine Editor.

Creating User-Triggered Actions

User-triggered Actions can occur as a result of the user interacting with some element of your page, such as text or an image. For this to happen, you first have to designate the element, and then, when the user clicks this element, moves the mouse over it, or moves the mouse off of it, the event takes place. JavaScript programmers will recognize the equivalent JavaScript events — onClick is called Mouse Click in GoLive, onMouseOver is Mouse Enter, and so on.

Setting up a mouse-invoked Action

In order to have text or a graphic act as an Action trigger for a mouse-invoked Action, the item must first become a link. (You'll notice that Actions are not available in the Action tab of the Text or Image Inspector when you first place text or an image on a page. After you create a link, the tab becomes active.)

To turn text or a graphic on your page into an Action trigger, follow these steps:

1. Select text or graphic that will become the trigger.

2. Click the Link button, or ⌘-L (Mac) or Ctrl+L (Windows), to turn this text or graphic into a link as you normally would. (You're just not really going to link it to a real destination.)

3. In the URL field of the Inspector, select "(Empty Reference!)" and replace those words with a number (or pound) sign (#).

   The number sign is not actually a link destination. It's just a sort of placeholder. If you leave the words (Empty Reference!) GoLive reports an error (green bug) for the page. By putting the # there, you avoid having to check out the reason for a bug. Also, as you check out the page in the In & Out Links palette, the standardization of the # symbol shows you there's an Action on the page.

4. Open the Actions palette (Window ➪ Actions).

New Feature

In previous versions of GoLive, the Actions interface was a tab in the Inspector. With GoLive 5, the interface is the same but moves to its own window.

5. Scroll through the list of possible user events in the Events list at the left, and then click the event once that will trigger the Action, as shown in Figure 18-1. (The link must be selected on your page in order for the Events list to appear.)

Figure 18-1: Choosing a user event (in this case, a Mouse Enter, a.k.a. mouseover) to trigger an Action

Rather than scroll through the events list, you can resize the length of the list. Move your mouse over the double divider line below the event list until the arrow becomes a double-header pointer, and then drag.

Note

You can have several event triggers attached to the same text or graphic. For example, you can have something happen when the user moves the mouse over the text/graphic, and then something else happen when the user moves the mouse away, and even another when the user clicks the text/graphic. It doesn't matter which event you choose first.

6. To add the Action for the currently selected event, click the Add Action button to the right of the Actions section heading at the top right.

As soon as you click the Add Action button, a question mark and the word "None" appear in the Actions list at the right. A bullet also appears to the right of the event name in the Event list to let you know there's an Action attached to that event.

You can have more than one Action happen for any event trigger, and can start to set the extra Actions now or later. To start the Action now, click the Add Action (which looks like a piece of stationery) button once for each additional desired Action. You can then return to the Actions list, select the next unassigned Action, and proceed to set up an Action for it.

Tip

If you have more than two Actions, you won't be able to see them all at once, so resize the length of the list. Move your mouse over the double divider line below the Event list until the arrow becomes a double-header pointer, and then drag.

7. Click the Action pop-up button and then choose the desired Action from the list of available Actions, as in Figure 18-2.

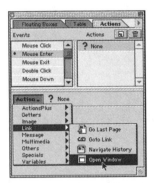

Figure 18-2: Choose an Action from the Action pop-up menu after clicking the Add Action button while an event is selected.

After you select an Action, next to the Action pop-up menu, the Action's name and icon replace the question mark and word "None" and in the Actions list. Additionally, noted to the right of the Action pop-up is feedback about the earliest browsers that support the chosen Action.

Expert Tip

The notation of the browser support may help you determine whether the Action is appropriate for your target audience. However, bear in mind that it is not derived from the JavaScript code; the developer decides what to tell you here. Testing may still be necessary. Also, if any other Actions exist on the page that need more recent browser versions, the whole page will break. And, if you use the external script library feature that supports browsers beginning with Version 4, the Action will not work in Version 3 browsers, either. — *Oliver Zahorka, OUT Media Design GmbH, Switzerland*

8. Set up the Action per the choices in the bottom part of the Inspector.

Upon completion of the details in the Inspector, you complete the setup of that Action.

9. *(Optional)* To set up another Action for the event trigger, keep the event selected, click the plus sign again, and then choose the next Action from the Action pop-up menu and proceed to set up the newly chosen Action. You can repeat this many times, adding more Actions to the user event.

10. *(Optional)* To set up another event trigger for the same text or graphic, click the next event once in the Events list at the left. Then click the plus sign to begin setting up the Action, and then choose and set up the new Action.

If you've started to set up an Action for an event and then decide you don't want the Action, select that Action from the Actions list and click the Remove Action button (the trash can) to delete it.

Setting up a key-related Action

A key-related Action is invoked when a user does something specific to a keyboard key. Rather than work on links, it is more common for a key-triggered event to act upon a part of a form. For example, at www.becauseyouforget.com, Jeremy Brown's card-entry text area counts and displays the number of characters typed, so users can more easily compose their messages.

Adding key-related Actions to your page doesn't have an adverse effect on older browsers, so you have no need to create an alternate page or use the Browser Switch Smart Object.

When you select a text or graphic link, three key events become available to you, as follows:

✦ **Key Down,** when a user pushes a key down

✦ **Key Up,** when a user releases a key (that was just down)

✦ **Key Press,** when both key down and key up have occurred

Although Key Press and Key Down seem the same, they aren't. A Key Press doesn't take place until after both a Key Down and a Key Up have occurred. It follows immediately after the Key Up, signifying that both other events have already taken place. This gives you three potential Action triggers.

Although other key-related Action events exist, in fact, little chance exists that you'll ever use them. (Prior to GoLive 5, I was unable to find anyone who ever used one of these events with a GoLive Action.) The other key-based events become available to you in the Actions palette only while their use is possible — in specific elements within Forms. Three events that you will have available while a Form field is submitted are as follows:

✦ **Key Focus,** when a form field gets the "keyboard focus" by being clicked with the mouse or by pressing the Tab key to select it, it becomes the active field where text is inserted.

✦ **Text Change,** when the contents of a text field are added, deleted or modified. This event is also triggered when a selection is made from a pop-up or list box.

✦ **Key Blur,** when the "keyboard focus" leaves the current field. This happens when you select another form field or link, either by clicking the mouse or by pressing the Tab key.

Setting up an Action for a key-triggered event is very much like with a regular link-connected user Action, so see "Setting up a mouse-invoked Action," earlier in this chapter for full details. To set up an Action to work with a form field, follow these steps:

1. Select the form field on your page.

2. Open the Actions palette (Window ⇨ Actions).

3. Choose an event from the Events list at the left. Only applicable events appear in the list and each is understandable by its description.

4. Click the Add Action button at the top right of the Actions palette.

5. Click the Action pop-up button then choose the desired Action from the list of available Actions.

Repeat Steps 3, 4, or 5, as appropriate or desired.

Sharing Actions Between Pages or Sites

You can actually create an Action on one page and then copy that Action into another page—even if that page is part of another site. You have at least three or four ways to accomplish this sharing, as follows:

✦ You can copy the trigger from one page and then paste it into the other.

✦ You can drag the trigger from one page to the other.

✦ You can drag the trigger to the Custom tab of your Objects palette so it's available for all sites you create on your computer using GoLive.

✦ You can even e-mail or FTP your Action-containing page to someone else so that person can use your Action.

All events and Actions attached to the trigger remain part of the Action. However, if the Action refers to an object specific to your page and the object isn't also transferred, it will no longer be listed in the options part of the Action setup. Because its Action remains set up, though, you can choose new objects or choices in the setup area.

When might this be useful to you? One time that immediately comes to mind (for me) is when you have an Action that hides one floating box and causes another floating box, or two or three, to appear at the same time. You get to keep the Action or Action group, and just select the floating boxes that are on your new page.

GoLive doesn't ship with any key-invoked Actions, but because I want you to be able to try one, OUTactions has kindly created Field Count Action just for owners of this book. You'll find Field Count in the OUTactions folder within the GoLive Stuff folder. It is meant for use within a form, so to see how it works, drag a form from the Forms tab of the Objects palette to any part of a page, and then drag a Text Area icon into it. Then select the text area on the page and in the Actions palette, select Key Press as the Event, click the Add Action button, and choose Field Count from wherever you placed it in the Actions menu. For Form Name, enter the default form name, FormName, and for Field Name use the default, textareaName. Use the Show in Browser button to type into the field. In the status area of the browser, you'll notice that your characters are counted each time you release the key. Now experiment with the Action's settings.

Setting Up a Page-Triggered Action

Sometimes you want an Action to take place automatically without any user interaction — for example, when you want an image to load, the browser window to resize, or a cookie to be set. You can set these Actions to happen automatically during the page loading process. You can have the Action happen as the page loads, when the page is finished loading, or when the browser gets to a specific part of the page as it is loading.

Adding head Actions

By placing a head Action in the header of your page, you enable an Action to happen automatically as the page loads into the browser or unloads.

To use a head Action, follow these steps:

1. Open the header section of your page by clicking the triangle by the Page icon in the top part of your page window.

2. Drag the Head Action icon from the Smart tab of the Objects palette into the header section. (When the header section is open, you can also double-click the icon to automatically put it at the end of any other elements within the header.)

   If the header section isn't open when you begin to drag the Head Action icon, you can rest the mouse pointer over the triangle by the Page icon until the section opens, and then continue dragging. When the head Action is selected, the Inspector becomes the Action Inspector, as shown in Figure 18-3. (This is not the Actions palette, but the actual Inspector.)

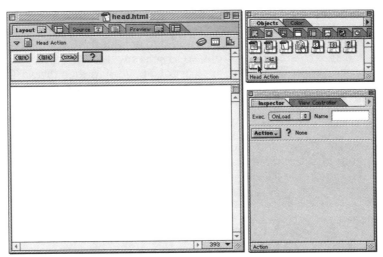

Figure 18-3: The Action Inspector, used to set up a head Action

3. In the Action Inspector, select the event you want to have trigger the Action you're setting up. You have four events to choose from, as follows:

- *OnLoad* executes the code as soon as the page is finished loading.

- *OnUnload* executes the code as the page unloads. In other words, when the user closes the page or clicks a link that will take him/her away from your page. (Have you ever landed at a porn site and tried to leave, only to find a new page for that site keeps opening as fast as you can close pages? This is the JavaScript that does it, although that's not an example your visitors will welcome.)

- *OnParse* executes the code as soon as it's read by the browser; it doesn't wait for the page to load. When choosing OnParse as the trigger, bear in mind that the part of the page you want to affect has to load before it can do anything. Until any part of the page loads, it doesn't actually "exist" in the browser.

- *OnCall* executes when another Action calls for it. Usually you would use this when you want to call an Action when an event occurs in the DHTML timeline, or when you have created an Action group to run multiple Actions from one event.

4. Select the desired Action from the Action pop-up menu. If you choose OnCall, the Name field to the right of the Exec pop-up becomes active. Enter a name for your Action into this field so you'll be able to call upon it later.

5. Select the desired settings as you would for any Action.

If you place a head Action item on a page and choose execution (or not), but don't choose an Action, and then save the page, when you reopen the page you'll find your head Action has been automatically deleted. That's a cleaning up feature—

not your imagination. This only happens when you haven't chosen an Action. The head Action item stays in place once you choose an Action, even if you haven't added any settings.

After you set up a head Action, you can copy it by copying its icon in the head, and then pasting it into the same head (to customize for a similar Action) or using it in another page. (See the "Sharing Actions Between Pages or Sites" sidebar earlier in the chapter.) Just remember that if you copy an OnCall head Action you need to give it a new name because the name is not carried to the new location. GoLive automatically gives it a code name because all OnCall Actions need names. But this code name won't be much help when you go to choose the Action from a setup menu; it really is a code.

Adding inline (body) Action items

When you place an inline Action within the body of a page, the Action happens automatically when the browser hits its code. Because an inline Action performs as it loads into the browser, there's no trigger to specify or set up. The loading *is* the trigger.

To place an Action in your page, follow these steps:

1. Drag a Body Action icon from the Smart tab of the Objects palette to wherever you want to place it on your page (or just double-click the icon to automatically put it at the end of all the other elements on the current page).

   There are no trigger options to set up. You just move directly on to setting up the item itself.

2. In the Body Action Inspector (see Figure 18-4), select the desired Action from the Action pop-up menu, and then set the Action up as with all Actions.

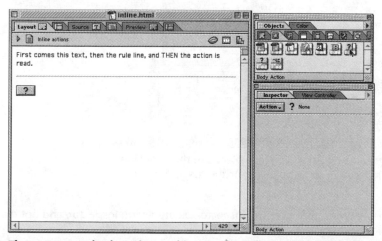

Figure 18-4: A body Action and its corresponding Action Inspector

Adding timeline-triggered Actions

It's very easy to have an Action occur automatically during the playback of an animation. All it takes is placing the Action at the desired point in the TimeLine Editor. The timeline then triggers the Action. (Of course, it's up to you what will trigger the animation that contains the Action or Actions.)

To place an Action into a timeline, follow these steps:

1. Click the Open DHTML TimeLine Editor button in the top-right corner of the page window to open the TimeLine Editor.

   Notice the gray strip below the timeline numbers. That's the Action track.

2. Move your arrow cursor to the point in the timeline where you'd like the Action to take place. Then ⌘-click (Mac) or Ctrl+click (Windows) on the Action track at this point.

   This places an Action icon — a plain black question mark in a hollow box — into place along the timeline, as shown in Figure 18-5.

   There are no trigger options to set up as the point in time is the trigger. You just move directly on to setting up the item itself.

3. In the Action Inspector, select the desired Action from the Action pop-up menu, and then set it up as you do with all Actions.

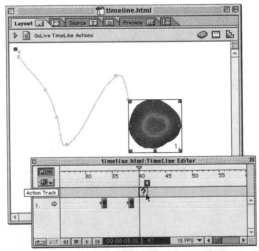

Figure 18-5: An Action icon placed in the TimeLine Editor and its accompanying Action Inspector

Note   This Action feature uses the Inspector, as the Action Inspector, and not the Actions palette.

Minimizing Code and Enabling JavaScript in Components

The JavaScript code that defines the Actions you use on your page can be placed internally (within your page) or be exported into a separate document. Putting the JavaScript into an external document enables you to have the code written just once for your entire site. Instead of having the code load each time a page loads, the pages then refer to the script page.

The external script document, CSScriptLib.js, lives in a folder called GeneratedItems within your Files tab — if you've created it and unless you've used GoLive's Preferences to change this document's name.

It's easy to export your JavaScript code. In fact, you can set this as an overall GoLive preference.

To set GoLive to write an external JavaScripts page, follow these steps:

1. Choose Edit ➪ Preferences, and then click the Script Library icon.

2. Click the Import GoLive Script Library option.

3. *(Optional)* If you prefer to change the name of the external script page (the script library), enter the new document name or folder name in the corresponding fields.

Sometimes two parts exist in the code for a script: common code and code that is specific to your script. The specific code remains in its page in order to work. All common code, however, is moved to the external document.

Components are the exception to this code separation. When you create a component, one of the steps is to turn to the HTML tab of the page's Inspector and click the Component button. You'll notice that this sets the page to write the JavaScript code into the external JavaScript library. And therein lies the secret. Normally, when you create an Action (or use a JavaScript Smart Object like the Rollover button or URL pop-up) some of the code, unique to that page, is written into the head section of that page. But when a component is integrated into a page, the code in the head section is not included because the parent page already has its own head section. By clicking the Component button and writing the code to the external library, you ensure that none of your Action's code is left behind. Instead, it's all placed in the external library and remains accessible. (Just be sure to always upload that external library.)

Upon creation of the GoLive external script library, the document appears in your Files tab, inside its own folder. Both the folder and the document are uploaded to your server when you use the Site Window FTP feature to go live with your site. (If you use the Export feature, it is exported to your Files folder, too.) That document downloads once, the first time it's called for from within a page. Because that page is cached by the user's browser, your pages load faster and the scripts become available sooner.

After you've set the GoLive application-wide preference to write to the external document, all pages you create will use that document. However, any pages you've already created prior to changing that setting need to be told to write the code externally. You do this the same way as when you are exporting code by the page, as shown next.

Instead of exporting the JavaScript code as a default, you can choose to export code from a specific page, one page at a time.

Follow these steps to export the JavaScript code from one page:

1. Click the Page icon at the top left of your page.

2. Bring the HTML tab of the Inspector forward.

3. Check the Import GoLive Script Library option.

Expert Tip   JavaScript, as a rule, is supported beginning with Version 3 browsers. However, several versions of JavaScript exist, so JavaScript programmers had to make language/support choices. GoLive's external script library feature starts its support with Version 4 browsers (JavaScript 1.2), due to its *initializing script*. Bear this in mind as you refer to the version support notice in each Action; even if it says Netscape 3 or Internet Explorer 3, support for that Action begins with Version 4.
— *Oliver Zahorka, OUT Media Design GmbH, Switzerland*

Common code stored in the external script library actually includes more than just the code created when you use Actions. It also includes the code from some Smart Objects such as the URL pop-up menu and rollovers. In addition, it stores the code you generate when you animate a floating box and when you use a component on a page.

Ensuring the integrity of the JavaScript

If you add and remove Actions as you work, you can ensure that GoLive has all necessary JavaScript code written. To do this, return to the Preference settings (Edit ⇨ Preferences, and then the Script Library icon) and click Rebuild Library.

Flatten script library

The GoLive JavaScript library is a page of JavaScript code that contains code for every part of every Action that is stored in the GoLive application's JavaScripts folder (inside the Modules folder). It's great to have tons of Actions in that folder because that makes the Actions available for use within your site. It wouldn't make too much sense to have a bunch of Actions if you can't easily use them when you want. On the other hand, you don't want to have a huge JavaScript document that the user is forced to download to use your site. The solution is a feature new to

GoLive 5 — the Flatten Script Library command in the contextual menu. (The virtual cheers were very loud on the GoLive beta list when this command made its debut there and was put to the test.)

The idea behind flattening the script library is simple. When you're about to upload the site to the server for use, you tell GoLive to go through your site. Note which Actions (or parts of Actions) are actually used in the site, and then remove all code that isn't needed to support those Actions. Later, when you work on an existing Action on any of your pages, or put another Action into use, GoLive looks at the JavaScript folder again and puts all code for all available Actions back into the external document. Thus, you have the ability to work on any Action in any way. Then, when you are again ready to upload your changes and additions, you flatten the script library again and let GoLive determine which files need to be uploaded this time around to accommodate your changes.

Implementing GoLive Actions

After you add the Action trigger to your page, you define the Action by completing the details in the lower part of the Inspector. This section shows you what each Action does, so you can determine which Action is appropriate for you; it then shows you how to set it up. GoLive organizes the Actions by what they do, so you can more easily find your desired Action. I follow this organization and suggest you at least try it for yourself.

As you peruse the list of Actions under the Action pop-up menu, you may notice that some Actions are grayed out. This is because they work in conjunction with another Action and do not detect the required Action.

Some of the Actions have an orange/red C to the left of a text/menu choice field. This is actually a button that, when clicked, provides more options from which you can choose the source of your information or target for an Action. Click once to cycle from one of the following button states to the next:

✦ The orange/red C is for either hand-entering info or for choosing from a pop-up list of the relevant items on your page. It's the most commonly used.

✦ The blue dot acquires the value of a variable defined earlier using a Set Variable or Initialize Variable Action.

✦ The green question mark enables you to call any Action on your page that is set to OnCall. (The OnCall trigger is only available in head Actions.)

Although these buttons may be there beside a choice, there may be nothing available for each of the button states.

Note   While every Action available in the GoLive installation is discussed in this chapter, the details of some specific Actions are actually within the more appropriate chapter. In this case, you'll find a cross-reference to that chapter.

Getting a floating box position

The Get Floating Box Position Action tells the browser to learn where a specific floating box is located within the page. With that information, you can have another floating box move to the position of the one whose position you're getting or you can trigger an Action based on the current position of the floating box, using an Idle Condition Action.

Before you can use this Action, the floating box you're getting the position of needs to be in place on your page. However, it doesn't actually have to have its content yet. You can record its movement if it is to move, but you don't have to at this point. (See Chapter 19 to learn more about that.)

The Get Floating Box Position Action requires the following triggers, Actions, and Action setup:

✦ **Trigger:** Head Action is set (in the Inspector) to OnCall. OnCall is the trigger of choice because the position can be called for over and over again — each time another Action *calls* for it.

✦ **Action:** Action ⇨ Getters ⇨ Get Floating Box Pos.

✦ **Action Setup:** In the Name field next to the Exec OnCall choice, name your Action with a short descriptive name that has no spaces. You'll need to recall this name in order to call for the object's position later. Then, in the Floating Box pop-up menu at the bottom of the Inspector, choose the floating box you want to get the position of, as shown in Figure 18-6.

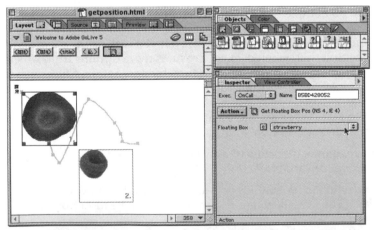

Figure 18-6: The full setup to retrieve the position of a floating box at any time this information is called for

Now that there's an Action set up to get this position whenever it's called for, you need an Action that calls for the position and does something with it.

Getting a value used in a form — Form Value

The Get Form Value Action tells the browser to *get* the data that's within one specific field within a form. (To get a user's first name and last name from a form, you need two Form Value Actions.) After it gets that data, in theory, you can use the Get Form Value Action in conjunction with other Actions such as the Write Cookie Action and the Set Variable Action. However, these capabilities were broken in GoLive 4, and they still do not work properly in GoLive 5. A replacement for the standard GoLive Set Variable Action is available at www.golivebible.com, which does work correctly with the Get Form Value Action.

Prepare to use the Get Form Value Action by setting up the form and naming the form's fields. The Get Form Value Action requires the following trigger, Action, and Action setup:

✦ **Trigger:**

- Head Action, set (in the Inspector) to OnUnload.

- Head Action, set (in the Inspector) to OnCall (typically attached to a form's Submit button).

✦ **Action:** Actions ➪ Getters ➪ Get Form Value.

✦ **Action Setup:** Enter the name of the form in the Form Name text box and the name of the field whose value you're getting in the Element field.

If the form or field name is to be obtained as the result of another Action, use the button to the field's left to toggle to the blue dot or the question mark. The green question mark lets you call up another Action. The blue dot acquires the value that must be defined earlier by another Action.

Preloading images used on your page

As you know from previous chapters, the images your viewers see are not actually a part of your Web page. Instead, images are linked into the page and the browser sends a call back to the server when an image is called for. The fancy button effects you place on your page are actually calls for extra images. The first image, the default state of the button, is called for as the page first builds. But the next image — the mouseover, or the one after that, the onClick image — is not actually called for until the user rolls the mouse over the button or clicks it. If those alternate images are not already downloaded to the user's computer, the user will most likely roll over the button and be off it already by the time the alternate button is downloaded and ready for viewing. This means the user never sees your button effect.

The way to ensure that the user will see your effects is to preload all the alternate images. By default, all images used in buttons made with the Rollover Smart Object are programmed to preload, so you don't have to worry about them. But if you're creating your own effect using the Actions window, it's a good idea to set up the

Preload Image Action to call for the extra images as the page loads. Another time to preload images is when you're using random images. Preloading an image doesn't do away with the download time. It just gets the image downloaded before the event takes place.

Prepare for the preload images function by having the image that you wish to preload in the Files tab so you can choose it. The image doesn't have to be used yet, but it is less confusing if you actually set up the Action first. That way, you're certain you are actually using the image the user is taking the time to load.

The Preload Image Action requires the following trigger, Action, and Action setup:

✦ **Trigger:** Head Action icon in the header, set (in the Inspector) to execute OnParse or OnLoad (use one head Action icon for each image).

✦ **Action:** Action ➪ Image ➪ Preload Image.

✦ **Action Setup:** Link to the image, which should be within your Files tab. In Figure 18-7, the image to be loaded is designated via Point and Shoot.

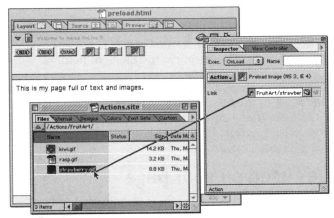

Figure 18-7: Setting up a third image, `strawberry.gif`, to preload (notice the first two Preload Image icons that are already in the head)

Displaying images at random from an image pool

Random images can provide a bit of variety for your pages. This Action enables you to designate a position into which an image will appear and then have the user see a different image at random each time the page loads. The Action enables you to designate three images to appear randomly.

The random image loads as the page loads. When the page loads initially, the base image is the one that appears. However, as soon as the page finishes loading or parsing, that base image is replaced by one of the random images.

Prepare to use random images by creating the three random images, making them the same size and adding them to your Files tab. Also place a transparent GIF in the Files tab. Place the transparent GIF on your page as the base image, a placeholder for the image that will be displayed when the page loads, sizing the GIF to the size of your three images. (The base image determines the size of the images that load randomly, so any image that's not the same size distorts to fit the size of the base image.) Name the transparent GIF, so it can be found by the Action later. To name it, select it, switch to the More tab of the Image Inspector, and type a name in the Name field (next to the IsForm checkbox).

The Random Image Action requires the following triggers, Actions, and Action setup:

✦ **Trigger:** Head Action icon in the header, set (in the Inspector) to execute OnParse or OnLoad.

✦ **Action:** Action ⇨ Image ⇨ RandomImage.

✦ **Action Setup:** Choose the base image by name from the pop-up list. Link to each of the three images, which should be within your Files tab. In Figure 18-8, the second of three images is being linked.

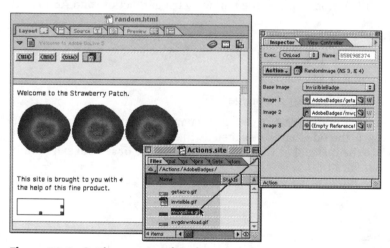

Figure 18-8: Setting up a random image

To take it further, you can make groups of random images and use the Action group Action. Or, get 6 Random Images Action — Charityware by Paul Vachier, available at www.matt-ridley.com.

Note   Steve Kitch takes advantage of the initial image of the Random Image Action in a nice way at www.artgallerystella.com. The initial image is a tiny GIF that lets visitors know an image is coming. It's small, but gives people with dial-up access something to see as the page builds.

Swapping images with the Set Image URL Action

The Set Image URL Action doesn't actually choose an image from a pool the way the Random Image Action does. It actually just lets you choose one image. However, it can be used creatively to provide the user with a variety of images in one spot on your page. When the page loads initially, the base image is the one that appears. It is then replaced by another image, depending on how you use this Action.

Prepare to use the Set Image URL Action by creating the images to be used, making them the same size you want, and adding them to your Files tab. Place the first image—to be the base image—on your page. This is the image that will be displayed when the page loads. (The base image determines the size of the images that load randomly, so any image that's not the same size distorts to fit the size of the base image.) Name the base image so it can be found by the Action later. To name it, select it, switch to the More tab of the Image Inspector, and type a name in the Name field (next to the IsForm checkbox).

Tip   Depending on your use of this Action, your base image may show for a while or not. If it doesn't show, consider using a transparent GIF the same size as your images—as the base, or initial, image. That way, no image is wasted, unseen.

The Set Image URL Action requires the following trigger, Action, and Action setup:

> ✦ **Trigger:**
>> • A link on the page, called for by any event.
>> • An Action in a timeline.
>
> ✦ **Action:** Action ⇨ Image ⇨ Set Image URL.
>
> ✦ **Action Setup:** Choose the base image by name from the Image menu. (The base image is the one that is replaced as the Action takes place.) As in Figure 18-9, link to the image that will take the place of the base image; it should be within your Files tab.

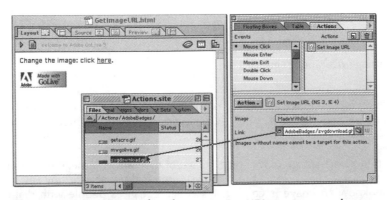

Figure 18-9: Setting up the Change Image URL to swap one image with another

Using link Actions

Four link Actions provide navigation between pages or enable users to opens new pages: Go Last Page, Goto Link, Navigate History, and Open Window.

Go Last Page — Returning to the previous page

The Go Last Page Action is the equivalent of the browser's Back button. It is often used on form result pages to take the user back to the data entry page if all fields are not properly completed. That way, the user can correct the entries and click the Submit button again to resubmit the page.

It can also be attached to a button such as a backwards-pointing arrow so the user moves back to, say, the last photograph viewed when looking through an image gallery. If this is to happen when a user clicks or rests over an image, place the image on the page, turn it into a link, and enter the number (#) sign as the link's URL.

The Go Last Page Action requires the following trigger, Action, and Action setup:

✦ **Trigger:** A link on the page, called for by an event such as a mouse click or mouseover.

✦ **Action:** Action ⇨ Links ⇨ Go Last Page. Bear in mind that you don't have a lot of control with this Action. It won't work for taking users through a predefined sequence, as the user could have jumped around the Web in any order to arrive at your page. The user's last page is relative to the user's travels.

✦ **Action Setup:** This Action has no setup.

Goto Link — Taking the user to a new URL

This Action can take your visitors to any URL you desire. You can hard-wire the URL in by linking to it just like you create any other link, or the destination can be the result of another Action or event, such as a variable Action.

If this event is to happen when a user clicks or rests over an image, place the image on the page, turn it into a link, and enter the number (#) sign as the link's URL. Or, perhaps you are using this to bring the user to an error message, or a special page of some sort, and the user is to arrive as the result of the outcome of a Condition Action.

The Goto Link Action requires the following trigger, Action, and Action setup:

✦ **Trigger:**
  • A link on the page, called for by an event such as a mouse click or mouseover.
  • A form button, called for by the Mouse Click event.

✦ **Action:** Action ⇨ Links ⇨ Goto Link.

✦ **Action Setup:** Choose the link destination the same way you normally set up a link, as in Figure 18-10. If you're linking to an external page, you can have the new page open in a new browser window by entering Blank from the Target menu. If you're working with a frameset, enter the target frame in the Target menu.

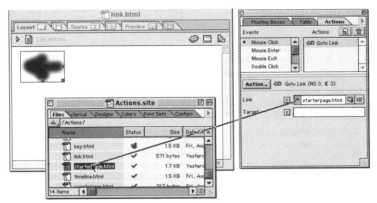

Figure 18-10: Using the Goto Link Action to link to another page in the same site

If the destination link is the result of another Action's variable, determined earlier, click the C button to switch to the blue dot, and then choose the variable from the pop-up menu. Or, you can switch to the question mark to call upon another Action.

Moving through the navigation history

The Navigate History Action is pretty much like the Go Last Page Action, but you choose how far back to send the user. Additionally, you can also go forward, as if the user clicked the browser's Forward button.

If this is to happen when a user clicks or rests over an image, place the image on the page, turn it into a link, and enter the number (#) sign as the link's URL. You'll also need to know how many links backward or forward you want the user to travel.

The Navigate History Action requires the following trigger, Action, and Action setup:

✦ **Trigger:** A link on the page, called for by any event.

✦ **Action:** Action ➪ Links ➪ Navigate History (in the Actions palette).

✦ **Action Setup:** In the Go Where text box, shown in Figure 18-11, tell the browser how many pages back or forth you want the user to be transported. Use a negative number to move the user backward through the browser history as the Back button does, and a positive number to move forward like the Forward button.

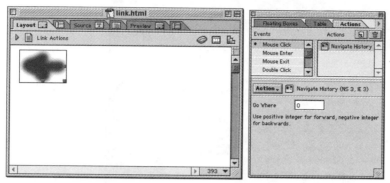

Figure 18-11: Setting up a button to take the user back or forth a certain number of pages

Open Window — Opening a new window

The New Window Action is very popular for enabling supplemental information to a page without taking the user away from the current page. In can be used to open a new window on top of the current window, just like any link when the target is set to _blank, but the special catch is that the new window can be set to a specific size and appear without the typical browser controls.

For example, on a technical page, you can provide definitions or explanations for words a user may not know. In that case, the word in question becomes a visible link the user can click to bring up the definition window. Figure 18-12 demonstrates a page's link and the extra opened window. This Action can also be called from a head Action. In that case, the supplemental window opens automatically as the page loads or parses rather than when a user moves over or clicks a link. Such an auto-open page might contain an ad banner, a special notice, or a Links palette intended to remain open as the user visits your site.

Prepare to use the New Window Action by creating the new page just like you create any other page. Glossary or supplemental pages used in this Action are typically smaller pages, just big enough to contain the definition, ad banner, Links palette, and so on. Size the page to the exact size you want it to be when it opens up.

The New Window Action requires the following trigger, Action, and Action setup:

> ✦ **Trigger:**
>
> > • A link on the page, called for by any event.
> >
> > • Head Action in the header section.
>
> ✦ **Action:** Action ⇨ Links ⇨ Open Window (in the Actions palette).

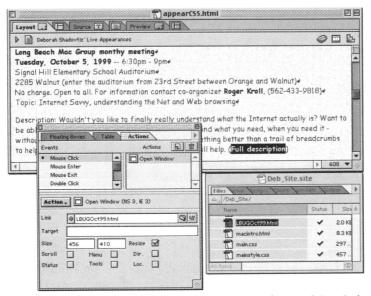

Figure 18-12: A New Window Action set up to open a plain window that can be resized to accommodate text size and closed via the standard OS Close/Minimize box

✦ **Action Setup:** Link to the destination page the same way you'd normally link to a page in the Files tab of your Site Window. To specify the new window's dimensions, enter the desired size in pixels into the size fields (width by height). It is not necessary to enter "_blank" in the Target field in order to have the new window open in its own window. That's an automatic feature of this Action.

Tip To determine the size you want your new window to be, set it to that size in GoLive's Layout mode and note the width of the window (in the lower right) or turn on the rulers to see the width and height.

All typical browser window controls are on by default, so the resulting window looks normal. Clear the checkboxes for browser features you want to disable in the new window. Regardless of which features you turn off, there will always be a title bar and Close/Minimize box to ensure that the user can close the new window. Typically, for effect, all options are turned off except Resize, as is the case in Figure 18-13.

The browser window controls are as follows:

✦ **Resize** enables the window to be resized by dragging the lower-right corner. Unchecking Resize removes the diagonal drag area. If you disable resizing, be sure to enable scrollbars so the user will be sure to see all of the window's contents regardless of text size or screen resolution.

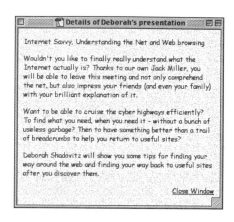

Figure 18-13: A resulting window

✦ **Scroll** provides scrollbars in the window. If you turn this off, be sure to enable resizing so the user will be sure to see all of the window's contents regardless of text size or screen resolution.

✦ **Menu** provides the menu bar in the window.

✦ **Dir.** displays the directory bar in the window.

✦ **Status** causes the status bar to be displayed in the lower left.

✦ **Tools** lets the user have the toolbar in the window.

✦ **Loc.** displays the location bar (URL area) in the window.

Tip   Although your window always has the OS's Close/Minimize box, it's a nice touch to offer a Close Window link. Close Window Action, an Action new to GoLive 5, makes this simple. It's triggered by any link and has no setup.

Employing Message Actions

The following three message Actions enable you to further communicate with your users:

✦ Document Write

✦ Open Alert Window

✦ Set Status

You've seen pop-up alert boxes and messages in status bars on zillions of pages, and whether you realize it or not, you've probably run across just about as many uses of text/HTML insertion as well.

Document Write — Inserting text or HTML code

The Document Write Action actually helps build your page content. It is a body Action, which means it is called into play the moment the browser gets to it while building the page. This means that if you are using it to add text to your page, that text is added in lieu of the Action. Wherever you place the Action in Layout mode is where the text is inserted by the browser. But you're not just limited to adding text. You can add HTML code instead. That means you can add text and format that text at the same time. Or, you can format existing page text on the fly if you use two Document Write Actions to surround the text.

Prepare to use the Document Write Action by creating your page at least up to, or around, the point where you want the message or formatting to be written into your page by this Action.

The Document Write Action requires the following trigger, Action, and Action setup:

✦ **Trigger:** A body Action anywhere in the body of your page.

✦ **Action:** Action ⇨ Message ⇨ Document Write (in the Inspector).

✦ **Action Setup:** In the HTML field, enter or choose the text or code that will be displayed in lieu of the Action when the page is read by a browser. To simply enter text or HTML, enter it while the orange/red C is active, as shown in Figure 18-14. (The results of this entry are shown in Figure 18-15.)

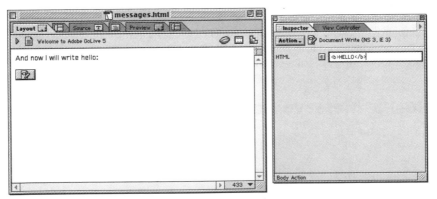

Figure 18-14: Setting up a Document Write Action

The true power of this Action comes from using it to insert information gained from another Action. For example, you can capture a user's guess in a contest or puzzle and then repeat it on the next page. To do this, you use the other options in the HTML area.

Click the C button to the left of the HTML field to switch to the blue dot to choose a value obtained from a previous Action. Click twice to arrive at the question mark and call up another Action.

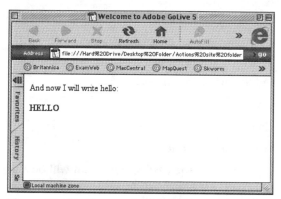

Figure 18-15: The result of the Document Write Action displayed in Figure 18-14

Note   You don't have to use HTML in the text box, even though it's labeled "HTML." If you do enter HTML code in it, make sure that it is free of errors, because no built-in error checking exists for this feature. If you do end up with a malfunctioning page, this is one of the first places to look for the source of the bug.

Opening an alert window

An alert window can provide a short bit of information that your visitor can't miss or ignore. Alerts contain two things: text and an OK button (see Figure 18-16). The user cannot proceed without clicking the OK button. Presumably that ensures the text will be read. There can be many reasons to put up an alert. One great one is Walter Blady's Copyright Action, which puts up a notice when users click an image. (That way, the user cannot click it to copy it.) Another great use is to let users know a form is not properly filled out. Rather than having the user wait while the form is sent across the Internet and into a database, where it is then rejected and sent back, one Action (or custom JavaScript) can verify the formatting and complete-ness of a form or field and the alert can request the information be corrected.

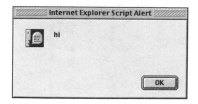

Figure 18-16: An alert window

All you need to set up for this Action is the basic page from which the alert will be called and the item that will trigger the alert. And, of course, there must be a need to display an alert.

The Open Alert Window Action requires the following trigger, Action, and Action setup:

✦ **Trigger:**

- A link on the page, called for by any event.

- An Action in a timeline.

- Head Action set to OnCall.

✦ **Action:** Action ➪ Message ➪ Open Alert Window.

✦ **Action Setup:** In the Message field, enter the text or code that will be displayed in the alert window. The alert message can be straight text that you enter here, or it can be the result of another event.

Caution Some punctuation in the Alert dialog box can break your script. If your Action doesn't work in the browser, return to the message you've entered here and remove things like apostrophes (a.k.a. single quotes). A regular quote mark is fine though.

Click the C button to the left of the Message field to switch to the blue dot in order to use a value defined earlier by another Action. Click twice to arrive at the question mark to call up another Action.

Note The title on the alert window says "Internet Explorer Script Alert," or, in Netscape, "JavaScript Application." That part is not customizable within the Action.

Putting messages in the status bar

The Set Status Action places your own custom message in the status bar at the bottom-left corner of the user's browser, as in Figure 18-17.

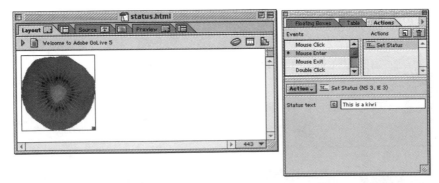

Figure 18-17: A status bar message

Prepare to use the Set Status Action by creating the basic page for which you want to change the status and the item that will trigger the status line.

The Set Status Action requires the following trigger, Action, and Action setup:

✦ **Trigger:**

- A link on the page, called for by any event.
- An Action in a timeline.
- Head Actions set to OnCall.

✦ **Action:** Action ➪ Message ➪ Set Status.

✦ **Action Setup:** In the Status Text field, enter the text that will be displayed in the status area when the user performs the specified Action. The message can be straight text that you enter here, or it can be the result of another event.

Click the C button to the left of the Status Text field to switch to the blue dot in order to use a value defined earlier by another Action. Click twice to arrive at the question mark to call up another Action.

Caution   While this can be great fun to use, the status bar's purpose is really to provide users with important browser messages. If you use it for your own messages, you're interfering with the availability of this information, so you might want to think twice about using it.

Using multimedia Actions

Most of the multimedia Actions are dedicated to the visibility, location, and movement of floating boxes. They let you specify how floating boxes will move, in response to which events, and whether or not they are even visible (you can even fade them in and out in a variety of pretty neat ways). In addition, you can also use the multimedia Actions to give users the ability to control the playing of animations (which are also floating boxes) and sounds.

Note   Chapter 19 focuses on floating boxes. Use this information to learn the technical aspects of controlling your floating boxes and Chapter 19 to learn how to place and use floating boxes to create interesting effects and dynamic HTML.

The following sections discuss these multimedia Actions:

✦ Dragging a floating box
✦ Flip Move
✦ Move By

✦ Move To

✦ Play and Stop Scene

✦ Play Sound and Stop Sound

✦ Show Hide

✦ Wipe Transition

Making a floating box draggable (Drag Floating Box)

Normally, you set the position of a floating box and perhaps have it move along a defined path using a timeline. However, you can also add some true interaction by making the floating box draggable. This way, visitors to your page can move it themselves. This can be exciting when used along with the Intersection Action.

Prepare to make a floating box user-draggable in the browser by placing the floating box on your page in the location where you want it as the page loads. Set the box up as normal, and be sure to give it a descriptive name. (Remember, without a name, a floating box cannot be called for by any Action.)

The Drag Floating Box Action requires the following trigger, Action, and Action setup:

✦ **Trigger:** Head Action icon in the header, set (in the Inspector) to execute OnLoad.

✦ **Action:** Action ➪ Multimedia ➪ Drag Floating Box.

✦ **Action Setup:** Select the floating box you want from the Floating Box pop-up menu, as is being done in Figure 18-18. (If the box is not available for selection, select the floating box and name it within its Inspector.)

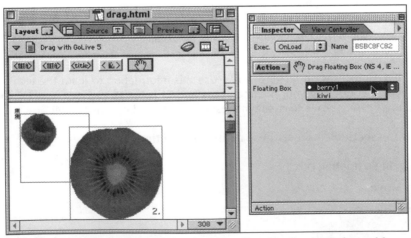

Figure 18-18: The setup to make the berry (in a floating box) draggable

Flip Move — Flipping an object between points

The Flip Move Action moves a floating box between its original location and another location that you specify. It's a toggle Action, so the second time it's triggered, the floating box returns to its original location.

 Note "Flipping" in this case is not rotation. When you flip the object, it does not turn over.

Prepare to use the Flip Move Action by placing the floating box on your page *exactly* in the location where you want it when the effect begins. (Unless attached to another fancy move, place it where it will be when the page loads.) Set the box up as normal and be sure to give it a descriptive name. If the box will flip to the location of another floating box, have that other floating box in place, too. Wherever the floating box will be moving, know the coordinates of that location.

The Flip Move Action requires the following trigger, Action, and Action setup:

✦ **Trigger:**

- Head Action, set (in the Inspector) to Load.

- Head Action, set (in the Inspector) to OnCall.

- A link on the page, called for by any event. The link can be visible text or a graphic on your page, or even be part of the contents of the floating box, as is the case with the example in Figure 18-19.

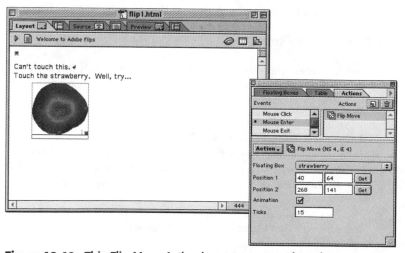

Figure 18-19: This Flip Move Action is set up to act when the user moves the mouse over the strawberry graphic (which is the link trigger) within the floating box. On mouseover, the box moves away.

✦ **Action:** Action ➪ Multimedia ➪ Flip Move.

✦ **Action Setup:**

• In the Floating Box pop-up menu, select the floating box you want moved. Use the Pos1 fields to designate where the floating box will appear at first and Pos2 to tell the box where to land. The first field determines the position on the page, in points, from the left edges of the browser window. The second field sets the position from the top of the browser. You can manually enter the locations, or use the Get button to have GoLive grab a floating box's current coordinates for you.

If your floating box is at its starting point, you can simply click Get and GoLive enters the location for you. To use Get to enter the endpoint, you can drag your floating box to the desired ending location and then click Get for Pos2. However, if you leave the floating box at position 2, it remains there when the page loads and begins the flip move from there. You'll probably want to move the box back to the starting point.

• If you'd like the movement to appear as an animation, check the Animation option and then set the number of ticks the animation should use to cover the distance of the move. The more ticks, the smoother the animation — and the longer the move may take. If you prefer the floating box's contents to just mysteriously appear in the new location, uncheck Animation and you can ignore the ticks as they're not a concern to the Action.

You can set up two flip moves so one moves one box from point A to point B and at the same time have a second floating box move from point B to point A. Then, by turning off the animation, it can appear that the two magically changed places. At www.golivebible.com, you can see this effect has green diamonds "turn" red and red diamonds turn green.

Tip   Because reentering the starting point is difficult, and the contents of the floating box will appear to jump if you don't get it exact, I recommend getting position 2 first, and then position 1.

Move By — Moving an object to a point

The Move By Action moves a floating box a set number of pixels from its current location, either vertically, horizontally, or both. Each time it is called upon, it moves the item by the same increment, continuing the item's travel over your page.

Caution   You can actually move the floating box right out of the user's browser window because you don't specify a particular endpoint, so bear this in mind.

Preparing to use the Move By Action involves placing the floating box on your page in the location where you want it as the page loads. Set the box up as normal and be sure to give it a descriptive name.

The Move By Action requires the following trigger, Action, and Action setup:

✦ **Trigger:**

- Head Action, set (in the Inspector) to Load.

- Head Action, set (in the Inspector) to OnCall.

- A link on the page, called for by any event. The link can be visible text or a graphic on your page, or even part of the contents of the floating box.

✦ **Action:** Action ⇨ Multimedia ⇨ Move By.

✦ **Action Setup:**

- In the Floating Box pop-up menu, select the floating box you want moved.

- In the DeltaX field, enter the number of pixels, if any, that you want the floating box to move horizontally, as in Figure 18-20. A positive number moves the floating box away from the left edge of the user's browser, while a negative number moves it closer to the edge. Use the DeltaY field to specify vertical movement. A positive number moves the floating box down, and a negative number moves it upward.

- If the movement is to be determined by the results of another Action, click the C button until it becomes a blue dot or question mark, and then choose the value or Action, respectively.

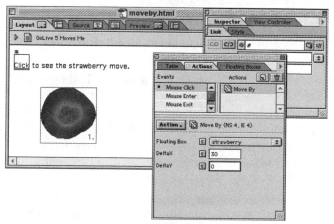

Figure 18-20: This Action is attached to the word "click" with a # as the link destination. It moves the strawberry 30 pixels to the right each time "click" is clicked.

Tip

If the trigger is a text link and you don't want the effect to be obvious, you can use a style sheet to remove the underline below the link.

Move To — Moving an object to another location

The Move To Action is virtually identical to the Flip Move Action, except it doesn't toggle the floating box between two points — it just moves the floating box from point A to point B and leaves it there. Once the object is in the new position, repeating the Action has no effect.

Prepare to use the Move To Action by placing the floating box on your page in the location where you want it as the page loads. Set the box up as normal and be sure to give it a descriptive name.

The Move To Action requires the following trigger, Action, and Action setup:

✦ **Trigger:**

- Head Action, set (in the Inspector) to Load.

- Head Action, set (in the Inspector) to OnCall.

- An Action in a timeline.

- A link on the page, called for by any event. The link can be visible text or a graphic on your page, or even be part of the contents of the floating box.

> **Tip**   If the trigger is a text link and you don't want the effect to be obvious, you can use a style sheet to remove the underline below the link.

✦ **Action:** Action ➪ Multimedia ➪ Move To.

✦ **Action Setup:**

- In the Floating Box pop-up menu, select the floating box you want moved.

- Enter the location to which you want the floating box to move. You can do this by entering the desired location or by moving the floating box in question to the desired destination and using the Get button. (If using Get, be sure to move the box back to the desired starting point.)

  The first Pos field is for the distance from the left side of the user's browser, measured in pixels. The second Pos field is for the distance, in pixels, from the top of the browser window.

- The Animated checkbox, checked by default, enables the user to see the floating box's movement. With this box unchecked, the contents of the floating box appear to jump to the new position, rather than travel there. If using animation, enter a number, in ticks, to set the number of steps for the animation, which affects the animation's speed and smoothness. Experiment to find a good number of ticks, as is being done in Figure 18-21.

- If any of these settings are to be obtained as the result of another event, click the C next to that field and choose the blue ball or the question mark, and then choose that event from the list that becomes available.

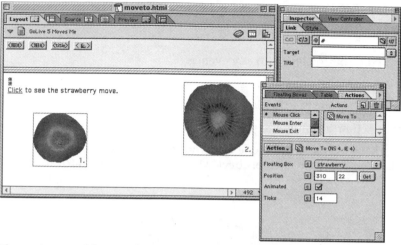

Figure 18-21: This Move To Action moves the strawberry on top of the kiwi when the triggering link is clicked. (The strawberry lands on top because it's on layer 2.)

Tip   If you're moving this floating box to the location of another floating box on the page, temporarily choose that floating box from the Floating Box menu and use Get. Then reselect the floating box that's doing the moving and continue with its setup.

Playing or stopping a scene or animation

Using floating boxes, you can create your own animated *scenes*. The Play Scene Action enables you to have the scene, well, play. You might want to have the scene play as soon as the page is finished loading, or you may want to give the user control. Or, the scene might play as the result of another event. Depending on the length of the animation, you may want to give your viewers the power to stop the scene as well, so there's a stop scene counterpart you can set up as a separate Action.

Prepare to use the Play Scene Action by creating and naming the scene. The scene doesn't have to be complete, but it does have to exist and be named so it can be found in order to call for it in the setup. If you are using multiple scenes on a page and the scene is not set to loop, place a Stop Scene Action in its timeline at the end of the scene. That way, it will not continue to play and interfere with the next scene that may be played. (Otherwise, you will need a Stop Scene Action prior to each Play Scene Action.)

Note   To play multiple scenes, you use a separate Action for each scene. (Remember that multiple Actions can be connected to the same trigger.) However, to stop multiple scenes that are playing at once, you can use one Action, Stop Complete, rather than using multiple Actions.

Play Scene requires the following trigger, Action, and Action setup:

✦ **Trigger:**

- Text or button link with any event.

- An Action in a timeline.

- Head Action set to OnCall.

✦ **Action:** Action ⇨ Multimedia ⇨ Play Scene.

✦ **Action Setup:** Choose the scene from the Scene pop-up menu, as in Figure 18-22. If no scene is available, check within the TimeLine Editor to see that you named your scene.

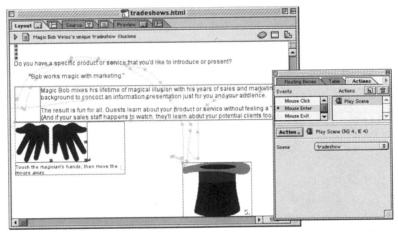

Figure 18-22: This Play Scene Action is triggered by a mouseover. You can see the paths of the scene in gray on the page while in Layout mode.

If running from one scene into another, the currently playing scene must stop before the next starts or confusion may result. If your scenes do not loop, place a Stop Scene Action at the end of each scene to avoid this problem. If your scenes do loop, use two Actions for your event: one to stop the previous scene and another to start the desired scene.

To set up a Stop Scene Action, create another Action, but choose Stop Scene as the Action. Setup is the same — just choose the scene to be stopped. To stop all scenes at the same time, choose Stop Complete as your Action. No setup exists for the Stop Complete Action after you choose it as your Action.

Play Sound and Stop Sound

The Play Sound Action is designed to enable sound to play when called for by an Action from within a timeline, by a user-triggered event, or as the result of another event set up within the head of your page. The Stop Sound Action is its counterpart, enabling the sound to cease playing. However, design is one thing, and having the tools to carry out the JavaScript commands of these Actions is another. And, unfortunately, that has not happened yet. The capability to control sound via JavaScript is not yet a reality, at least as I write this book. (Should that change, I promise I'll let you know at www.golivebible.com.)

If you can find a sound format that works on all (or most) browsers and platforms — and that can be controlled by JavaScript — you can enable your visitors to play and stop sounds on your site.

Note

> You have to have an audio plug-in placeholder in place before you can perform this task. See Chapter 19 for more information.

Prepare to use the Play Sound and Stop Sound Actions by selecting a plug-in from the Objects palette, placing the sound on your page, and then setting it up. Be sure to name the sound in the Inspector so it can be called for in the Action's setup, and therefore controlled.

The Play Sound and Stop Sound Actions require the following trigger, Action, and Action setup:

✦ **Trigger:**

- A link on the page, called for by any event.

- An Action in a timeline.

Note

> Technically, OnLoad or OnParse can also trigger a Play Sound Action, but setting a sound to autoplay within the Inspector has the same effect, and is more reliable.

✦ **Action:**

- Action ⇨ Multimedia ⇨ Play Sound.

- Action ⇨ Multimedia ⇨ Stop Sound.

✦ **Action Setup:** Choose the sound from the Name pop-up menu.

> OUTactions provides a free Action called Soundtools that provides enhanced functionality, working better in Internet Explorer. You can find this Action by opening the OUTactions site located in the GoLive Stuff folder on the CD-ROM.

Show Hide

One of the coolest things about floating boxes is that you can control their visibility. The Show Hide Action enables your floating box's contents to appear or disappear on command. Or, you can have it toggle, so if it's showing when the Action is called upon, the box goes invisible, and vice versa.

Prepare to show or hide floating box using this Action, and then setting up your floating box in place on your page. (Remember to name the floating box.) You don't have to be finished adding or tweaking the box's contents. The box doesn't even have to be in position. It doesn't even matter what visibility you have the box set to as you set up this Action. (But remember to set the starting visibility before you upload your page.)

The Show Hide Action requires the following trigger, Action, and Action setup:

✦ **Trigger:**
- A link on the page, called for by any event.
- An Action in a timeline.
- Head Action, set to OnCall (in the Inspector).

✦ **Action:** Action ➪ Multimedia ➪ ShowHide.

✦ **Action Setup:** Choose the floating box from the Floating Box pop-up menu, and then choose whether you want this event to make the box appear (show), be hidden (hide), or toggle from whatever its state happens to be at the time the Action is triggered (toggle). In Figure 18-23, a floating box named "amazing" is set to be hidden when the user's mouse moves off of the triggering text.

Figure 18-23: This text link trigger has two events: When the mouse enters the link area the floating box, named "amazing," appears; when the mouse moves off the link, the same floating box hides, or disappears.

If you set up a box to show on mouseover (Mouse Enter) and don't want it to remain visible from that point on, select the Mouse Exit event and add an Action to hide that box.

> **Note** Technically, you can also control visibility by using OnLoad or OnParse, but, because the Inspector enables you to determine whether the box appears at startup or not, that would be silly.

Wipe Transition

Not only can you make the contents of a floating box disappear or appear; you can do it with a gradual wipe — and you can control the speed of the wipe and choose from several directions.

Prepare to use the Wipe Transition Action by placing your floating box on the page, naming it, and beginning to set up its content. You don't have to have the content fully set to set up this Action, but you will get the best view of the result if the contents are complete or close to complete.

The Wipe Transition Action requires the following trigger, Action, and Action setup:

✦ **Trigger:**

- A link on the page, called for by any event.
- An Action in a timeline.
- Head Action, set to OnCall (in the Inspector).

✦ **Action:** Action ⇨ Multimedia ⇨ Wipe Transition.

✦ **Action Setup:**

- Choose the floating box from the Floating Box pop-up menu.
- Select the desired effect from the Transition menu. The choices are self-explanatory. Some make the floating box appear, as in Figure 18-24, while others wipe it out.
- Enter the number of steps for the transition in the Steps text box. The more steps, the smoother the transition.

Figure 18-24: Setting a Wipe Transition Action that smoothly causes the image in the floating box to appear, starting with the right side of the image

Exercising other Actions

The Others category is a catchall for some miscellaneous Actions. It includes the following items:

✦ Netscape CSS Fix

✦ Resize Window

✦ Scrolling the browser window automatically

✦ Set Back(ground) Color

The Netscape CSS Fix

The Netscape 4 browsers have an odd glitch that drops CSS information when the user resizes the browser window. For example, a floating box can become improperly positioned. (Remember, floating boxes are part of CSS.) This has nothing to do with GoLive; it's a universal problem. Fortunately, there's a JavaScript fix for this and GoLive provides it as an Action. Add this Action to every page that uses a Cascading Style Sheet (which includes pages that contain floating boxes). It simply tells Netscape to reread and properly parse the style sheet when it reloads the page due to user resizing.

Using this Action doesn't require preparation. Just use it if you've got a floating box on your page, or to be safe, whenever you use a style sheet.

Netscape CSS Fix requires the following trigger, Action, and Action setup:

✦ **Trigger:** Head Action icon in the header, set (in the Inspector) to execute OnLoad.

✦ **Action:** Action ➪ Others ➪ Netscape CSS Fix.

✦ **Action Setup:** None

Resize Window

The Resize Window Action enables you to set the size of the user's browser automatically. However, that gets tricky. First, because you don't know what size the user prefers or what size works best for your users (and each user is different due to font size and browser controls). But, more importantly, it is tricky because the size you set is the outside dimension of the browser, not the page area in which you design. The user may have icons showing in the toolbar or just text, toolbar buttons showing or not, and so on. All of those controls affect the page area available within the window. To see this in action (no pun intended), check out the live example of Figure 18-25 at www.golivebible.com. You don't need to prepare to use the Resize Window Action; simply have a page available.

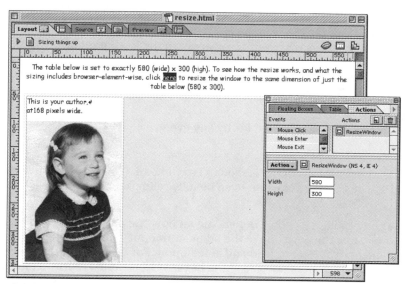

Figure 18-25: The Resize (Browser) Window Action sets the outside dimensions of the user's browser window to approximately 580×300.

The Resize Window Action requires the following trigger, Action, and Action setup:

✦ **Trigger:**
- Head Action, set (in the Inspector) to OnLoad or OnParse.
- Head Action, set (in the Inspector) to OnCall.
- A link on the page, called for by any event.
- An Action in a timeline.

✦ **Action:** Action ➪ Others ➪ Resize Window.

✦ **Action Setup:** Enter, in pixels the desired width and height for the window in their respective fields.

Scrolling the browser window automatically

The four scroll window effects — Scroll Down, Scroll Up, Scroll Left, and Scroll Right — enable you to make the user's browser window scroll, each Action affecting its respective direction, of course. The only trick to using these Actions is when to call upon them, because if you trigger them before the page builds, there's no page to scroll through.

Prepare to use a scroll window effect by having your page somewhat set up. To help give you an idea of how far you want a scroll to go, turn on the page's rulers. (That's the little button above the downward scroll arrow in the Layout mode of your page.)

Scroll window effects require the following trigger, Action, and Action setup:

✦ **Trigger:**

- A link on the page, called for by any event.

- An Action in a timeline.

- Head Action, set (in the Inspector) to OnLoad. (OnParse won't work because the page may not even be fully rendered in the browser when the Action's code is parsed.)

- A body (inline) Action. (Depending on how the page is built and therefore loads, the page above the inline Action may not be visible when an inline body Action is read and acted upon. For example, some elements need to know the final size of the page, or Netscape 4 redraws tables after they fully load.)

✦ **Action:** Action ⇨ Others ⇨ Scroll Down, Scroll Left, Scroll Right, or Scroll Up.

✦ **Action Setup:** In the Scroll Pixels field, enter the number of pixels you want the page to scroll, as shown in Figure 18-26. In the Scroll Speed field, enter the desired speed (higher numbers create faster scrolling).

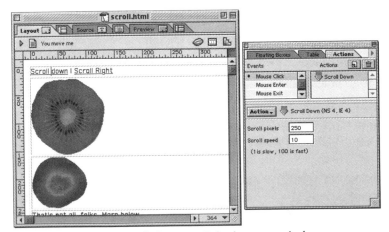

Figure 18-26: Setting a link to scroll the browser window

Setting the background color

The Set Back(ground) Color Action enables you to change the color of your page's background. If you're using an image to give your page a background texture, this effect would be lost on those who see your texture. But, otherwise, it can be a lot of fun.

There really isn't anything you must do before using this Action, except for having the page (and placing the trigger), because the Action works on the page itself.

The Set Back(ground) Color Action requires the following trigger, Action, and Action setup:

✦ **Trigger:**

  • A link on the page, called for by any event.

  • An Action in a timeline.

  • Head Action, set to OnCall.

✦ **Action:** Action ⇨ Others ⇨ Set BackColor.

✦ **Action Setup:** Click the color swatch and choose the color as in Figure 18-27, just like you choose one anywhere else.

Note   Technically, you can also use this in the head when the page loads, parses, or unloads, but the effect of the change would be lost.

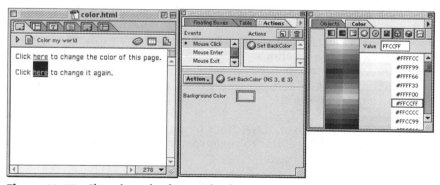

Figure 18-27: Choosing a background color

Calling upon a custom JavaScript with Call Function

The Call Function Action enables you to attach your own JavaScript to your page (providing you've written your own JavaScript or have one on hand). Any custom JavaScript that is within the head section of your page, or is in your Site Window as an external JavaScript file, can be called upon.

If calling upon an external JavaScript, have that JavaScript document in place within the Files tab of your Site Window. If calling on a JavaScript from your page, have it in place within your head section. (This is not to say you can't move either file later. It just needs to be available for the setup to take place.)

The Call Function Action requires the following trigger, Action, and Action setup:

✦ **Trigger:**

- A link on the page, called for by any event.

- An Action in a timeline.

- Head Action, set to OnCall, OnParse, or OnUnload.

- A body (inline) Action.

✦ **Action:** Action ➪ Specials ➪ Call Function.

✦ **Action Setup:** Choose the desired function from the pop-up menu. Use the Arguments field to enter any arguments needed for the function. (To understand the use of arguments, you must be familiar with JavaScript or have someone guide you regarding your particular JavaScript.)

Cross-Reference   Chapter 22 and Appendix B can help you become more familiar with JavaScript and how to get a custom JavaScript into your site.

Monitoring and acting upon conditions

Using the Idle Action, you can tell your visitor's browser to watch for a condition, or event, and then respond with one of two Actions, depending upon whether the condition is true or false. The Idle Action must be placed in the head of your page because it needs to begin monitoring for your condition as soon as the page loads. The Condition Action works in a similar way, but it must be specifically called by another event on the page, such as a mouse click or timeline event. Because they are somewhat similar, I cover them together.

Prepare to use the Condition or Idle Actions by setting up your page to include the necessary elements and directions to guide your visitors. For example, if they are expected to press a key, tell them.

The Condition and Idle Actions require the following trigger, Action, and Action setup:

✦ **Trigger:**

- Head Action set to OnLoad (for Idle Action or Condition Action).

- A link on the page, called for by any event (Condition Action only).

- An Action in a timeline (Condition Action only).
- An inline Action (Condition Action only).

✦ **Action:**

- Action ➪ Specials ➪ Condition.
- Action ➪ Specials ➪ Idle.

✦ **Action Setup:** The lower half of the Action Inspector for this Action contains three tabs in which you set up the condition and tell the browser how to act upon that condition.

In the *Condition tab*, use the lower Action menu to choose the condition to monitor. You have several to choose from, as follows:

- *Specials ➪ Intersection* enables you to have the user's browser monitor the locations of two floating boxes and act, depending on whether the two intersect or not. Simply choose the two floating boxes from those available on your page. (But, to be honest, this does not work in either GoLive 4 or 5. Perhaps it will be updated by the time you read this. Watch for news at www.golivebible.com and other GoLive sites.)

- *Specials ➪ Key Compare* enables you to have the user's browser watch for the user to press a specific key that you designate by entering that key in the CharCode field. To enter a key, enter the desired key's ASCII character code in the CharCode field. You can find the ASCII codes at www.asciitable.com or learn the most common ones on Bob Stein's HTML card available at www.visibone.com.

- *Specials ➪ Timeout* enables you to have the user's browser wait a predesignated period of time before acting in whatever way you go on to set up. For this condition, you enter the amount of time (in seconds) the browser should wait.

- *Variables ➪ Test Variable* tells the user's browser to check the value of a variable that you have previously set up using variable Actions and perform an Action depending on the value of that variable. It is discussed further in the "Working with Variables in Actions" section that follows.

In the *True tab*, if you want something to happen when the condition is met and/or tests true, choose any available Action from the lower Actions menu and set up that Action. (Not all Actions will be available; only ones that may be applicable.)

Note

The Idle Action provides an exit point so an event can happen just once and the user doesn't enter an unending loop. The out is the option to Exit Idle if Condition returns True. This enables the script to end the first time the condition is met.

In the *False tab*, set up the Action that is to happen when the condition is not met and/or tests False. That is, if you want an Action to take place. If you don't, leave this tab blank (don't choose an Action).

Note The setup for any resulting Action in the True and False tabs are the same as when that Action is used independently. Refer to the directions for each respective Action earlier in this chapter.

Working with Variables in Actions

Variables, which are expressions that represent possible values, can be very handy for use in forms, as input for the parameters of some Actions, or to create cookies. You add a Declare Variable Action to define the variable, so the browser can capture its value in any specific instance and then use that value elsewhere. Then you add an Initialize Variable Action (or the Set Variable Action) to give the variable an initial value. Then, you add the Write Cookie Action and Read Cookie Action so the browser can actually create the cookie and store it in the user's browser, and then read its content as needed later.

Note The Initialize Variable Action is used to set the initial value of the variable. You should always use this just after you have declared a variable. The Set Variable Action is used to change the value of a variable at any time, but it can also be used to initialize a variable. If you don't initialize the variable, it will have a value of "undefined" and any Actions that rely on the variable will not work correctly.

You can use variables in your pages to store values in cookies, to modify the URLs of links depending on the user's Actions on the page, and more.

Cookies are small files that are stored on the user's hard drive by the browser. Cookies enable you to store information specific to that user for later reuse on other pages — for instance, you might ask the users to enter their name on one page and then greet them by name on another, or perhaps you could create a quiz on your site and use cookies to store the current user's answers.

Declaring variables

Before you use a variable, you need to tell the browser what the variable will be called and what type of variable it is. In other words, you need to declare it.

Variables must be of a particular *data type* — that is, GoLive must know in advance if it's dealing with a word, a number, a Boolean variable (true or false), and so forth. Certain variable types are dependent on the existence of other elements on the page in which the Declare Variable Action resides.

The following trigger, Action, and setup are required to declare variables:

✦ **Trigger:** Head Action icon in the header, set (in the Inspector) to execute OnCall.

✦ **Action:** Action ➪ Variables ➪ Declare Variable.

✦ **Action Setup:**

• In the Name field, name your variable so it can be called for later on. (Use alphabetic characters only or the underscore character.)

• Select the variable's data type. For example, in Figure 18-28, the data is a text string.

• *(Optional)* Use the Cookie field to enter the name of the cookie that will hold this variable once it is acquired. (You only need to do this if you intend to use the Write Cookie Action.)

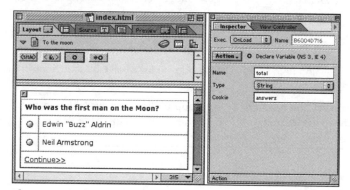

Figure 18-28: Setting up an Action in the head of a page to declare a variable

Table 18-1 lists the variable options and what they do.

Table 18-1
Types of Variables and What You Select/Enter

Data Type	What It Is	What You Assign When Initializing
Boolean	True/False	Checkbox that is True when checked
Integer	A whole number	A value text field for whole numbers
Float	Floating-point number	A value text field for numbers with decimal points
String	Alphabetical value (words)	A value text field
Layer	Floating box	A pop-up list of all available floating boxes on the page
Layer Position	Location of a floating box	Position fields and a Get button (see the Get Position Action)
Image	Image file	A pop-up list of all available images on the page
URL	Web address	A URL field and getter
Color	Color value	A color swatch for selecting a color as usual
Scene	GoLive scene	A pop-up list of all available scenes on the page
OnCall Action	Head Action item set to OnCall	A pop-up list of all OnCall Actions in the page
Function	Any JavaScript function defined in a custom head script	A pop-up list of all available function declarations on the page

Initializing variables

Declaring a variable is the creation of a placeholder that expects a value. Once a variable is declared, it needs to be given a value. This is called initializing a variable.

Prepare to initialize variables by setting up the OnCall head Action that declared the variable you now want to initialize. (See the preceding section.)

The following trigger, Action, and Action setup are required to initialize variables:

✦ **Trigger:** Head Action set to OnLoad.

✦ **Action:** Action ⇨ Variables ⇨ Init Variable.

✦ **Action Setup:** Select the variable you want to initialize, and then enter the value of the variable. Your options here depend on the type of variable you're dealing with. For instance, if you have declared the variable to be a string, you will enter some text as the value. If you had instead declared the variable as a Boolean, you would be able to assign a value of True or False to the variable.

Setting variables

The Set Variable Action is similar to initializing a variable, except that it sets the value during runtime instead of before. This enables you to change the value of a variable at any time after the page has loaded, in response to triggers such as mouse clicks, form submissions and Action calls.

Prepare to use the Set Variable Action by setting up an OnCall head Action to declare the variable you now want to initialize (see the preceding section). The Set Variable Action requires the following trigger, Action, and Action setup:

✦ **Trigger:**

- Head Action set (in the Inspector) to OnCall.

- Head Action, set (in the Inspector) to OnLoad or OnParse.

- A link on the page, called for by any event.

- An Action in a timeline.

- An inline Action.

✦ **Action:** Action ⇨ Variables ⇨ Set Variable.

✦ **Action Setup:** Choose the variable from the list of variables that are on your page. (And don't forget to name the OnCall Action if you've used that as the trigger, so it can be called upon later.) Then set up its value in whatever option areas you have. The value entry type depends upon the type of variable.

Testing variables

The Test Variable Action enables the user's browser to check the current value of a variable. This Action is meant to be used with the Condition or Idle Actions, so that you can test the variable to see if it matches a specific value and then act according to the instructions you supply for the True and False conditions.

The Test Variable Action requires the following trigger, Action, and Action setup:

✦ **Trigger:**

- Head Action set to OnLoad (for Idle Action or Condition Action).

- A link on the page, called for by any event (Condition Action only).

- An Action in a timeline (Condition Action only).
- An inline Action (Condition Action only).

✦ **Action:**

- Action ➪ Specials ➪ Idle.
- Action ➪ Specials ➪ Condition.

✦ **Action Setup:** Select Variables ➪ Test Variable in the lower Actions menu. Then choose the variable, from the Variable menu, whose value you want to test. Enter the value to test against the variable and select the comparison operation you want to apply to the test.

In the True tab, set the Action you wish to take place if the condition is true. In the False tab, set the Action you wish to take place if the condition is false.

Creating and Using Cookies

Cookies are tiny files that are created on the user's hard drive, stored and tracked by the user's browser in order to give Web designers a way to identify the user without collecting "real" information about the user. Users can set their browsers to refuse cookies. If your page or site relies on cookies, you won't be able to personalize these user's visits. It's a good idea to let them know this. Perhaps explain the cookie so users feel comfortable.

Cookies are not usually written to your hard drive unless your pages are accessed from a Web server, so GoLive's browser preview will not work. You need to upload the related pages to test your cookies.

By setting a cookie, you can perform such feats as greeting your users by name or changing the background color to suit an earlier expressed preference.

Writing cookies

The first step is to write the cookie to the user's hard drive.

Prepare to write cookies by using the Declare Variable head item. Because cookies are stored as strings, you must use the string data type for your variable. You also need to name the cookie that you are going to store the variable in at this time. This is necessary because you can store multiple cookies at once, and each cookie can hold multiple values. You then need to set the variable using the Init Variable Action in an Action head item.

The following trigger, Action, and Action setup are required to write cookies:

✦ **Trigger:** Head Action set to OnCall or OnLoad.

✦ **Action:** Action ⇨ Variables ⇨ Write Cookie.

✦ **Action Setup:**

- Enter a short descriptive name for the cookie. This must be the same name as the one you specified in the Cookie field of the Declare Variable Action Inspector.

- Set the duration of the cookie, in hours, in the Expires After field. This is the number of hours to maintain the cookie on the user's computer. If you only want to use the cookie to store very temporary values, such as answers to quiz questions, this can be set to a low value. If you want to use cookies to remember users' names, you should set it to a higher value. If you don't specify a duration, the cookie will never expire unless the user deletes it.

- *(Optional)* To protect the use of the cookie (just in case), enter the domain name and path to the Web site you're using the cookie at. This way, the cookie can only be read by your page and not misused by any other site.

- *(Optional)* If your site will reside on a secure server, you can restrict the cookie's usage to secure Web pages only by checking Secure.

Reading cookies

The Read Cookie Action enables you to read the information stored in a cookie that you have written using the Write Cookie Action and store it in a variable. You can then use that variable in an inline Action to write the value of the cookie to the page, or to use with the Test Variable Action.

Prepare to use the Read Cookie Action by setting up the page in a very similar manner to the way in which you set up the Write Cookie page. You need a Declare Variable Action head item, which must have the same name as the variable you used on the Write Cookie page, and you must have a data type of string. You must also enter the exact name of the cookie in the Cookie field.

The Declare Variable Action must be set to trigger OnParse if you want to be able to write the value of the cookie to the page. This is because JavaScript can only affect the layout of static HTML pages before the page loads, so setting it to trigger OnLoad would run the JavaScript code too late.

The Read Cookie Action requires the following trigger, Action, and Action setup:

✦ **Trigger:** Head Action set to OnParse.

✦ **Action:** Action ⇨ Variables ⇨ Read Cookie.

✦ **Action Setup:** Simply enter the name of the cookie you want read. This is the name you gave the cookie when you created the Write Cookie Action. The value of the cookie will be read into any variables that reference the cookie.

To write the cookie variable to the page, create an inline Action on the page in the position where you want the cookie text to appear and attach the Action ⇨ Message ⇨ Document Write Action to it. Next, click the little C button in the inspector until it turns into the blue dot, and then choose the variable name from the pop-up. You don't have to write the variable to the page in this way, but it is useful in many cases. You can use the Test Variable Action to test the value of the cookie instead, which opens up all sorts of interactive possibilities. You could, for example, have several quiz pages that store the total number of correct answers in a cookie, and when the user reaches the Results page, you could read the cookie and display their score.

Grouping and Calling Actions Together

Two Actions, rather than being Actions that do one particular thing, serve to make your work more efficient:

✦ Action group

✦ Call Action

I highly recommend you try these Actions and remember to consider them as you build your site.

Grouping together Actions

For any event called by a trigger, you can have multiple Actions by clicking the Add Action button once per Action, and then choosing each Action via the Action menu (see Figure 18-29). Using this technique, you can create some interesting effects. But, if you need to call upon that same group of Actions many times, it can become tedious to set each Action up over and over again. Instead, GoLive gives you the Action group. By grouping several (two or more) Actions together, you can cut your development time down.

The bad news is that if you've already created events with multiple Actions, you can't apply them to a group. You have to start a group and set up each Action within the Action group creation interface.

Tip   Because Actions can be copied from one page to another (via dragging or copy/paste) — even between sites — a group can be extra helpful.

Nothing is needed to prepare for the grouping per se, but the preparation for each of the Actions you're putting in the group must be done so you can set each up.

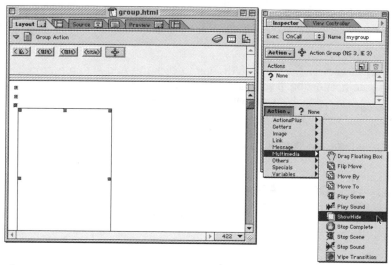

Figure 18-29: Creating an Action Group that will, OnCall, show and hide a floating box, among other tasks yet to be set up

The following trigger, Action, and Action setup are required to group together Actions:

✦ **Trigger:**

- A link on the page, called for by any event.

- An Action in a timeline.

- Head Action, set to OnCall (in the Inspector).

Tip By creating a group ready to use whenever called for, it's easy to have it handy.

✦ **Action:** Action ➪ Specials ➪ Action Group.

✦ **Action Setup:** Calling upon the Action group brings up a mini Action interface as a sort of sublevel to the main (Group) Action. You use this subinterface to add and set up each of the Actions to be grouped. To add an Action, click the Add Action button. This starts the new Action (as usual) and activates another Action pop-up menu lower down. Use the lower Action menu to choose the Action you wish to add to the group.

Be careful to make your Action selection from the lower Action menu. Choosing one from the upper menu changes the Action from an Action group to the new choice. Fortunately, though, all is not necessarily lost if you do this and notice your mistake. You can use the Undo command to get back to your Action group settings.

Add any Action you wish to the Action Group window, setting its parameters (if necessary) just as you normally would. Continue to add more Actions until you have added all the Actions you wish.

Caution

As you add more new Actions, don't forget to click the Add Action button before choosing your next Action. If you happen to select an existing one in the list, you'll change that Action to whatever new choices you make, inadvertently losing the one that was selected.

To learn how to call up the Action, read on.

Calling a previously set Action

The Call Action Action enables you to call upon an Action or Action group you've previously set up with an OnCall trigger.

Prepare to use Call Action by setting up the Action or Action group to be called.

Call Action requires the following trigger, Action, and Action setup:

+ **Trigger:** Any, except OnCall.

+ **Action:** Action ⇨ Specials ⇨ Call Action.

+ **Action Setup:** Choose the Action or Action group from the pop-up menu. This Action enables you to directly choose an Action from the C menu, or choose other Actions or results via the blue dot or the question mark.

Note

The other way to call an existing Action is by choosing the green question mark whenever you see the orange/red C button next to your setup options.

Adding a Browser Switch Item

Anytime you use advanced features such as JavaScript, floating boxes, the TimeLine Editor, or CSS on your page, you might want to create alternative pages for visitors who have older browsers. In this case, you'll need to use the Browser Switch Smart Object (a preprogrammed fairly complicated JavaScript) that takes care of all the hard stuff for you.

If, while creating your site, you wish to plan for all contingencies, you might want to create dual versions of each of your pages, or maybe of just a few critical pages. For example, you might want Windows users to see one version of a page while Mac users see another. Or, you may want people using older browsers to see a simpler, less gimmicky page.

Wondering About Writing Your Own Actions?

Are you wondering how to write your own Action? Actions are JavaScript, so it's entirely possible to write your own using GoLive's JavaScript Editor. To learn about how to write your own JavaScript in GoLive, check out Chapter 22. To learn what goes into an Action, open up the Actions folder and double-click any Action in there. It'll open up as a GoLive page. (The stuff you see on that page will make more sense after you read Chapter 22.)

After you create the alternate pages, you add the Browser Switch item to the header of the default page. Then you set this script up to check to see what brand and version of browser a visitor to your site is using. If the browser (via the script) learns that the user's browser is one of the versions checked off in the script's setup, it loads the page. But if the browser sees that the user has a version not listed, it calls upon the alternative page to load instead. The Browser Switch looks at your page, sees the floating box or such, and knows which browsers support the technology and which don't. If the browser calling for the page doesn't support the technology, the script does the switch.

The Browser Switch Smart Object requires the following trigger, Action, and Action setup:

✦ **Trigger:** Browser Switch icon from the Smart tab of the Objects palette, placed in the header. (No execution choice exists.)

✦ **Action:** The Action is preprogrammed into this Smart object.

✦ **Action Setup:** The setup for this is in the Inspector (see Figure 18-30), rather than the Actions window. The default setting is to let automatic browser checking take place, meaning that the browser switch will take care of determining if the page elements are compatible with the user's browser. All you need to do is link to the alternate page the user is to see if he/she doesn't have one of the selected browsers.

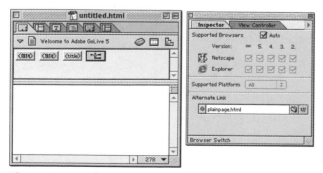

Figure 18-30: The Browser Switch Inspector

If, instead of the Auto setting, you want to manually select compatibility, deselect the Auto checkbox and then select the browsers for which you want the switch to be performed. Making the selection has two parts: choosing the browser versions and choosing the platforms. If you want the switch to happen for the same browsers on both Mac and Windows, choose All from the Supported Platforms pop-up list and check the box for each version of either Netscape or Internet Explorer that the page supports. (All means both Mac and Windows.)

To distinguish between Mac and Windows versions of browsers, first choose Mac from the pop-up and check the desired browsers, and then choose Windows from the pop-up menu and check the desired browsers for Windows. Even though you can't see both platforms in the pop-up menu, the browser choices for both are in effect.

✦   ✦   ✦

Adding Special Effects and Animation

Floating boxes are somewhat to Web pages what layers are to drawing programs. Using standard HTML, objects on a Web page cannot overlap. Basic physics: two bodies cannot occupy the same space at the same time. But a floating box *floats* above your page in a layer of its own, independently of the cursor or any table cell. That enables the contents of your floating box to float above, or overlap, anything that's on your page, whether it's inline with your cursor, on a grid, or within a table. Floating boxes can also float *above each other*. You can have multiple floating boxes on your page and place any box above or below another.

But there's more. Floating boxes (and their content, of course) *move*. You can create some cool animation by having your floating boxes move around on your page. You can create the movement by clicking a record button, and then simply dragging the box around, or you can use the full-featured TimeLine Editor. Or, you can first record the movement, and then perfect the animation using the TimeLine Editor. You can even enable your visitors to move floating boxes around in the browser window — and have events happen as a result.

And now for something completely different: a floating box can disappear, taking with it the full contents of the box. That means text and images can be invisible one moment and visible another.

In this chapter you get the full lowdown on floating boxes, from placement on the page to simple movement to some neat animation techniques. The first part shows you how to add a floating box to your page and how to add content to it. The second part focuses on the animation and effects that really make floating boxes shine. You can even see the example animations at work at the book's companion site, www. golivebible.com.

Introducing Floating Boxes

How do floating boxes perform these amazing feats? Floating boxes are *Dynamic HTML* (DHTML) in action — absolute positioning thanks to Cascading Style Sheets. (Yes, CSS does more than just format your text. It performs magic for the entire look of your page.) Thanks to CSS, you can (and always do) set an absolute position for each floating box — in three dimensions! You position the box and that's where it appears, time after time, regardless of what is on your page. It won't be pushed down by other objects or moved when text is viewed larger or smaller.

While the power of the floating box comes from CSS, the power to move it around or change its visibility, as shown in Figure 19-1, comes from JavaScript. Of course, GoLive provides easy interfaces to all of this control.

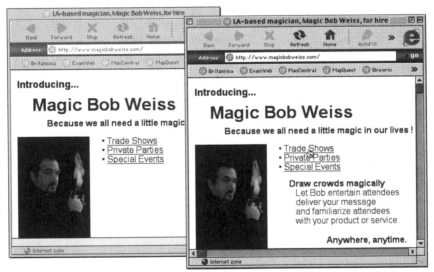

Figure 19-1: A bit of floating box magic. *Left:* the box is invisible. *Right:* as the user's mouse is over the trigger area the floating box becomes visible.

Floating boxes don't work on any browser prior to Version 4 browsers. This isn't a GoLive issue, but one of Cascading Style Sheets; the <div> tag is not known to pre-4.x browsers.

The older browsers simply ignore that tag. Unfortunately, they don't also ignore the content within the tags. Consequently, everything you place in a floating box is fully visible on your page, appearing where the SB box is located. Because the box is not recognized it cannot be invisible and you cannot control its position. This causes your pages to look very odd in pre-4.x browsers. The only solution to this is to build two versions of these pages (one being boxless) and add a browser detect (redirect) to the header of the box page to send older browsers to the boxless page (or vice versa).

If you don't place crucial content in a floating box, you can simply duplicate the page when it's complete. You then delete the boxes from one copy of the pages and have a Browser Switch Smart Object send older browsers to the boxless page. If you do put crucial content in a floating box you need to design a special boxless version of the page to which to send older browsers.

Expert Tip   You can provide users of older browsers with a bit of the effect of some of your floating boxes by converting the contents of any floating box(es) into text layout boxes on a grid using the Convert to Layout Grid command as noted later in this chapter. You then place the grid and its floating box content into the alternate page in lieu of the actual floating boxes. For example, if you are using floating boxes to create an animation, and they do not pass over any other page content, you can use this feature to capture the animation at any point and place that *freeze-frame* into the page. — *Cathy Scrivnor, Web designer*

Placing a Floating Box on Your Page

In GoLive, floating boxes are as simple to place as any other object you add to your page; just drag the floating box icon from the Objects palette. To place a floating box on your page, follow these steps:

1. Drag the floating box icon from the Basic tab of the Objects palette into place on your page. The top-left corner is the best place.

   The floating box works differently from other page objects. Although you are placing the floating box, the object actually dragged and placed is a very small SB marker that comes along with the actual floating box. Rather than place it exactly where you want the box to be on your page, place the SB box inline (in a line of text) at the top of your page. Although the SB box displaces your line of text by one line while in layout mode, it's invisible within a browser. The position of the SB doesn't affect the box's position in any way.

Caution   Although you can place the actual box anywhere on your page because it lives on top of the standard HTML, the SB needs to live within the HTML in a line of text. For stability and reliability, don't place this control within a table or on a grid. In theory the SB can be anywhere on the page but sometimes Netscape has problems when it is not placed before all other page content.

   The actual floating box appears at the top-left corner of your page, as in Figure 19-2.

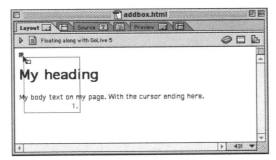

Figure 19-2: A floating box newly dropped onto the page. The cursor is still at the SB, which is selected. "My heading" is automatically pushed down a line, but only in Layout mode.

A number, 1, in the bottom-right corner may help you identify the box in case you're adding more floating boxes to your page. GoLive numbers boxes in the order they are added and uses it internally.

2. Drag the floating box into the desired position on your page (or if you're going to animate it, drag it into the starting position). To do so, move your mouse to any edge of the box until the cursor appears as a sideways hand (fingers to the left, facing into the box from the side.) When the cursor turns into the sideways hand, click and then drag the box into position, as shown in Figure 19-3. (See "Repositioning a Floating Box" later in this chapter.)

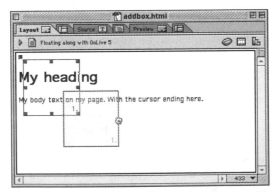

Figure 19-3: Dragging a floating box into position

Note   You can always reposition the box in the future by selecting and dragging it again.

3. Name the floating box by selecting the default name, layer1, in the Name field of the Inspector and typing in a descriptive name.

The name is important for identification in the future — especially if you are going to animate it or use an Action on it. For example, if you use an Action to change the box's visibility or to move the box, a descriptive name enables you to choose the correct box within the pop-up list. A descriptive name is much easier to identify than the default layer, layer1, layer2, and so on. Naming the box doesn't affect the white box number in the bottom-right corner.

Tip

Although I tell you here to name your floating box, in reality you may want to name it after you've added content to it. The name should reflect the content.

4. Because a floating box is actually on a layer above your page, you can assign it to a specific *depth*, from 1 on upward. The lower the number, the closer it is to the page. In other words, a depth of 3 floats above 2, which floats above 1. To assign a depth, type a number into the Depth field in the Inspector. You can change the layer number at any time.

Be sure to assign each floating box a number. Netscape doesn't like 0, so enter a 1 or above for each box. Multiple boxes can have the same number, but if you want them to stack, use a different number for each.

Resizing the box at this point is optional. It grows to accommodate any graphic you place within it so you needn't resize the box if it only contains a graphic. Text wraps within the box as it reaches the right border, so if you know you'd like the line of text to be wider than the default, you may want to widen it before adding the text. The length grows automatically to accommodate your text. Of course as you resize the box at any time, text reflows to fit the new dimensions. To resize the box, simply drag any of its handles. (Press Shift as you drag the handles to constrain the box's proportions.)

Expert Tip

If your entire page consists only of floating boxes — and no text or images directly on the page — an oddity in Netscape causes the page to render without scrollbars, regardless of page length and need. Oliver Zahorka of OUT Media Design GmbH, has a tip to prevent this bug: When first beginning the page, drag an anchor from the Objects palette to the top of your page and, in the Inspector, give that anchor a name such as **pagetop**. (This places the code: `<p><a NAME="pagetop"> </a></p>` on your page, making Netscape happier. If you have already begun the page, dragging the anchor doesn't add the `<p>` tags that are important, so place your cursor at the very top of the page (above the SB markers), press Enter/Return, and then drag the anchor icon into that newly created line. — *Oliver Zahorka, OUT Media Design GmbH*

The Code Behind the Box

Floating boxes are part of Cascading Style Sheets. Two places in HTML exist where code for a floating box is written. When you place an SB marker in the layout, GoLive creates an ID style, called #layer1, #layer2, and so forth, into an internal style sheet within the head of the page.

The HTML code for a floating box is the *div tag* (`<div>` and `</div>`). When you place an SB marker in the layout, GoLive writes `<div id="layer1"></div>` into the body of your page at that point of the HTML (see the accompanying figure). As you insert content, GoLive writes the content in between those tags. As you rename each floating box, the name between the `<div>` tags and the ID name reflect the change. (Again, a descriptive name helps you to identify it.)

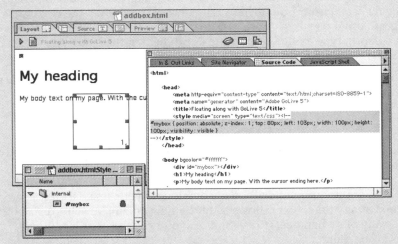

A floating box and its corresponding style sheet code

For the sake of simplicity, GoLive users get to use the floating box Inspector to set up all the basic attributes of a floating box and GoLive writes the ID tag information. It is possible, however, to also use the style sheet interface to further change the look of your floating box. For example, you can use it to set a text indent, padding, or margins. To learn more about this, see Chapter 17, which covers style sheets.

Repositioning a floating box

As you build your page, you may need to reposition your floating box in relation to the other elements on your page. By moving them into their approximate position before you add content, you may find it easier to determine which box should contain which elements.

If you are animating your floating box, place it in the position at which you want it when the page loads. If your box is invisible when the page first appears, and then appears on mouseover or such, place it where you want it to be when it appears. I discuss the various methods of creating an animation later.

You can place your floating box in any desired position by dragging it, using the arrow keys, or by entering its position into the Inspector.

GoLive uses an invisible layout-only grid to track the position of your floating boxes. This is not the same as the Layout Grid that builds a table within source code to place your items. This grid is just so that GoLive knows how to record your box's position. To view and change the default grid settings, choose Window ⇨ Floating Boxes palette, and then choose Floating Box Grid Settings from the fly-out menu arrow at the upper-right corner. In that settings dialog box, shown in Figure 19-4, choose Snap to have your floating box's move along the grid increment and enter a grid increment as well. If you choose Visible While Dragging, you can see this invisible grid as you drag your floating boxes into position.

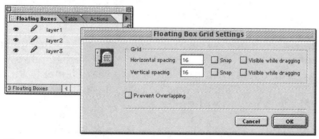

Figure 19-4: The Floating Box Grid Settings

To move your floating box into the desired starting position, do one of the following:

✦ Move your mouse to any edge of the box until the cursor appears as a sideways hand (fingers to the left, facing into the box from the side.) When the cursor turns into the sideways hand, click, and then drag the box into position.

✦ Select the box by moving the mouse to any edge of the box, and then clicking when the cursor becomes a sideways hand. After the box is selected, use the arrow keys on your keyboard, as if it is on a grid or in a page-layout program. By default, the Snap option is off in the Floating Box Grid Settings dialog box, so each arrow-key press moves the box one pixel. If that option is turned on, each arrow-key press moves the box by whatever increment is set in the page's grid. On the Mac, you can press the Option key to override the current arrow-key increment, so when the Snap option is off, each arrow-key press moves the box by the specified grid setting while the Option key is also held down. If the Snap option is on, pressing Option while using the arrow-keys moves the box in one-pixel increments.

Other methods of selecting the floating box don't work for this purpose.

✦ Select the box by moving the mouse to any edge of the box, and then clicking when the cursor becomes a sideways hand. In the resulting floating box Inspector, enter the desired coordinates into the Left and Top fields. The left field sets the distance, in pixels, of the left edge of the box from the left side of the user's browser. The top field sets the top of the floating box with respect to the top of the user's browser.

Depending on what you're doing, you may not want floating boxes to overlap. In this case, you can set GoLive to Prevent Overlapping on a page. See the "Preventing Overlapping" section that follows shortly.

Adding additional floating boxes

Add each additional floating box to your page in the same way. Although the floating box icon can be put anywhere on a page, it's best to line them up at the top of your page, above all other content. This placement makes it easier for you to locate the icons when you need them. GoLive automatically places each SB one below the other, rather than placing them side by side so that you can select any one easily.

If, instead, you were to place the SB markers within your page's content, the SB would throw off the look of your page. While the SB icon is invisible in a browser, it appears in Layout and therefore affects the spacing of the other elements in your layout. You can choose Edit ➪ Hide Invisible Items so they don't show, but other elements such as line breaks won't show either.

As you add more floating boxes to the same top corner, the cursor line appears as if it is putting the next box marker to the right of the previous one. However, when you release the mouse, the SB marker for each additional floating box is placed beneath the others, as shown in Figure 19-5.

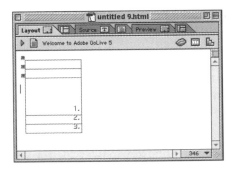

Figure 19-5: Three floating boxes added to a page before any of them are moved

Each box you add is numbered in the order it is added. Thus, the second box you add has a number 2 in the bottom-right corner and the third has a number 3. This number is not a reflection of the order in which the SB markers appear in the page.

Tip

To animate two floating boxes that need to remain together exactly as they travel, place the SB marker for one box inside the other. This *nesting* enables you to move two floating boxes at the same time, while only selecting the parent box and only creating one timeline track. However, certain limits exist as to how you can position nested floating boxes. If your nested box extends past the left, top, or bottom margin of the parent box, the contents of the extended part render improperly, creating a trail as the boxes move. Additionally, Netscape may resize your nested box automatically. In most other cases, though, it is not necessary to nest floating boxes as you can always place one floating box over another regardless of where their SB markers are.

Selecting a floating box

To align floating boxes, add a background to a floating box, or animate it, you need to select the box first. As with any object on a page, you can select that object by clicking it. Because a floating box is a container, you select it by clicking its edges — that is, the container itself, not the contents within it. Move your mouse over any edge of the box until your cursor becomes a sideways hand, and then click once. When you select the floating box this way, the handles become active as feedback.

Note

If, as your mouse is within the floating box, it appears as an arrow with a rectangle at the back end, you will not select the box if you click, but the content to which you are pointing.

To select multiple floating boxes at once, hold the Shift key down while, or after, you select the first one and click the edges of each additional box you'd like to select. (When more than one is selected at the same time, you can move both boxes together but you cannot do any formatting via the Inspector as the Inspector becomes blank.)

If you need to work in a floating box's Inspector, but not move the box or edit its contents, you can also select it by clicking its box's SB marker.

Preventing overlapping

At any time as you create your page, you can tell GoLive to not permit floating boxes to overlap one another. Once you do, you will not be able to layer floating boxes on top of each other. Whenever you move a floating box towards another, it stops when it butts up to the next floating box. If you drag one floating box over another, it snaps into place immediately next to the box you attempted to overlap.

However, any boxes that you may already have overlapping on your page remain overlapped.

To constrain overlapping of floating boxes, follow these steps:

1. In the Floating Boxes palette, click the fly-out menu (the triangle at the upper-right corner) and choose Floating Box Grid Settings.

2. Check the box labeled Prevent Overlapping.

This choice has no bearing on Prevent Overlapping Paragraphs available in the View Controller tab of the Layout Inspector.

Aligning floating boxes

You can align floating boxes in relation to one another or in relation to the page they're on, just like you can align other objects on your page. The difference with a floating box though, is that once you align it, the position on the page is absolute with regard to the top-left corner of the browser window. A floating box doesn't move in relation to the page's borders.

To quickly align selected floating boxes, do the following:

1. Choose Window ➪ Align to open the Align palette.

2. Select each box you wish to align by moving the mouse to any edge of the box, and then clicking when the cursor becomes a sideways hand.

   Other selection techniques don't work when aligning multiple boxes, but to align only one you can also select it by clicking its name in the Floating Boxes palette.

3. Click the desired alignment option in the Align palette, as shown in Figure 19-6.

   • *Align to Parent* aligns the box(es) to the browser window, from the top-left corner. This is the same as choosing an alignment option from the options that become available in the toolbar when a floating box is selected. Normally when you use this alignment option with an object on the page and you align to the bottom, left, or center of the browser, the object moves when the user resizes the window. Floating boxes are positioned absolutely though, so when you choose any alignment, GoLive reads the exact position of where the box lands and writes that exact coordinate into the ID selector tag in the internal style sheet for the page. This number does not change and the box does not move when the user resizes the browser window.

   • *Align Objects* only becomes available when more than one floating box is selected. It enables you to ensure that two or more boxes align at any edge or along their centers. The positions of these new placements are absolute on the page, not with regard to one another.

- *Distribute Objects* works like Align Objects, but evenly aligns all selected objects between the two on the ends.

- *Distribute Spacing* also becomes an option only after three or more floating boxes are selected. This option evenly distributes the space between floating boxes. The boxes on the ends remain in places while the ones in between move.

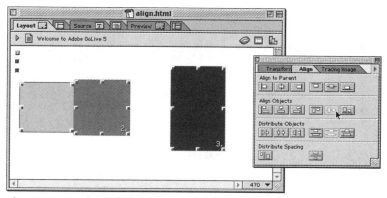

Figure 19-6: Three different-sized floating boxes (still selected) after they are aligned by their horizontal center

Absolute positioning or aligning doesn't mean you cannot move a floating box after it is aligned. You can use alignment to set up boxes in relationship to one another, and then move them anywhere you'd like.

Another way to ensure floating boxes are aligned is to use the Snap feature of the Floating Box Grid Settings.

Deleting a floating box

Follow these steps to delete a floating box:

✦ Select the actual box on your page, and then press Backspace/Delete.

Only one floating box can be deleted at a time, regardless of the number of boxes you have selected on your page when you press Delete or Backspace.

✦ Point to the box's SB marker to select it, and then press Backspace/Delete.

Only one SB marker can be selected at a time so only one box can be deleted at a time this way.

✦ Place your I-beam immediately after the box's SB marker and press Delete or Backspace or in front of that SB and use your forward delete key.

✦ Use your I-beam cursor to drag across the SB marker(s) for the box(es) you want to delete, and then press Backspace/Delete.

This is the only way to delete multiple floating boxes at once.

When you delete a floating box, all subsequently placed boxes are renumbered.

Adding a Background to a Floating Box

By default, a floating box has no background and is therefore transparent. To create an opaque background, add a background color or background image. Each floating box can have its own background color or image.

Adding a background color

Adding a background color to a floating box is very much like adding a background color to your entire page, or to any part of a table. The Inspector and Color palette make it easy for you.

Perform these steps to add a background color to a floating box:

1. In the floating box's Inspector, double-click the Background color swatch to open the Color palette.

   The Color palette opens, whether it is closed or collapsed at the side of your monitor.

2. Locate and click your desired color in the Color palette. The selected color automatically fills the swatch and the Color option as it is automatically checked. If you prefer another color, simply click the new color.

   If you've collected the desired color into the Site Window, the color is available for you in the Site Color List tab.

Tip

If the color doesn't appear in the swatch when you choose one in the Color palette, it's due to a glitch that sometimes happens. The trick is that the color swatch must be fully selected; a black box must appear around it. If you don't see the dark black box, click the swatch in the Inspector again and select your color once more. Or, if the desired color appears in the swatch but not the floating box, click the Color option to check it. (Sometimes it doesn't automatically become checked as it should.)

If you no longer want any color, uncheck the Color option box to remove all color.

Netscape browsers (4.*x*, at least) simply don't recognize color backgrounds until content is in the box and the color only appears behind the parts of the floating box that contain content. For example, if you type one word on the first line, and then press Enter /Return twice and then type more words, the color only appears behind the first word on the first line and the other words lower down. To compensate for this, enter nonbreaking spaces wherever you need to force the background to appear. To type a nonbreaking space press Option-space (Mac) or drag the nbsp symbol from the Characters tab in the Web Settings window (Windows).

Adding a background image

To add a background image to a floating box, check BGImage in the floating box's Inspector. Then Point and Shoot to the desired image in the Files tab of the Site Window.

As usual, if you prefer, you can use the Browse button and its resulting Open dialog box to locate and choose the image, but remember that if the image is not located within the Root level of your site's folder, you create an orphan file and need to remember to add that file into your site before you upload. (See Chapter 25 to learn about repairing orphans.)

If you plan to only put the background image in a floating box, type a nonbreaking space in each line of the box for the desired length of the box so the background renders in Netscape 4.*x* browsers. All you need is one space per line to make the background graphic visible. (Option-space on the Mac; in Windows, press Shift+space.)

Adding Content to a Floating Box

Throughout this book, as I discuss each element you can add to your page, I mention whether it can be added to a floating box, so you may already have a good idea about what you can do inside a floating box and how to do it. Here is some information you should know about designing within a floating box.

Although technically anything you can place on a page can be added to a floating box, using a table or grid may create problems for the user viewing your page. Therefore, it is safest not to place a table or grid in one.

Expert Tip   Netscape (at least 4.x versions) are very picky about floating boxes and tend to do better if you follow a general order of content placement. Starting with the box numbered 1 in the bottom-right corner, it tends to be happiest when you use the first layers for your text-only content. Use the next boxes for other content. Use the boxes with the highest numbers for the content that will be manipulated with DHTML. If you create your content in that order, you can move the order of the boxes' content (`<div>` tag). To effectively change the order, switch to Outline mode, click the arrow to the far right of each `<div>` tag so you can see its name, and then drag the tags into the desired order. You can also change the order by dragging the SB icon up or down among the other markers, and then switching from Layout to the Source tab and back to Layout again. However, this may prove unreliable. — *Oliver Zahorka, OUT Media Design GmbH*

Adding text within a floating box

If you prefer, you can resize the floating box before you add text to it, but it's not necessary. Text within the floating box text wraps between the side boundaries of the floating box and the box grows to accommodate the text. However, because the box floats above the rest of your page, unlike a grid's text box that can push other objects as it grows, a floating box's size doesn't affect anything else on the page when it grows. Therefore, you can add the text any time you like after adding the floating box to your page, and then resize the box any time. As you resize the box, the text reflows.

To enter text in a floating box, click inside the box. The I-beam text cursor appears so you can begin typing. It may be hard to notice the I-beam when it's up against the edge of the box but if you look closely you'll notice it. Additionally, the background of the box temporarily appears as white so you can view on your text entry. As mentioned in Chapter 8, which discusses text, you can use all the traditional text entry methods, such as pasting text or using clippings.

Text within a floating box counts as text that's on your page, so it is affected by any style sheet directions you may have. For example, if you use the body tag as a selector and define your page's text as 14-point pink Arial with a 10-pixel indent, the text within your floating boxes will also have this styling. If you have a `<p>` selector and tell text between `<p>` tags to be green, any text between `<p>` tags in your floating box will be green. (Which means any text in the box after the first time you press Return or Enter and type within the floating box.) You can define a text formatting that is unique to any floating box by using the box's ID tag as a selector. You can also do more to a floating box using a style sheet. See "Adding Additional Formatting to a Floating Box" later in this chapter.

Adding an image to a floating box

When adding an image to a floating box, it's best to first place an image place-holder icon rather than dragging an image directly from the File tab of the Site Window into place in the box. Directly dragging an image causes Netscape browsers to interpret the image as a background instead.

Note

If you're placing a Rollover Smart Object button in the box, first add a nonbreaking space, and then place the Rollover button after the space. This prevents an oddity in Netscape browsers that may cause the button to disappear. To create a non-breaking space, press Option-space (Mac) or press Alt as you press 0 1 6 0 in sequence on your number pad (Windows). Although this nonrendering Netscape oddity doesn't commonly affect other objects, you may also use this trick with other objects to help ensure all objects do appear in your floating boxes.

To add an image to a floating box, follow these steps:

1. Drag the image icon from the Basic tab of the Objects palette into place in the floating box.

2. With the image icon selected, Point and Shoot from the Basic tab of the Inspector to the desired image in the File tab of the Site Window. Or, drag your image from the Files tab and drop it *onto* the image placeholder as shown in Figure 19-7. (If you end up with an image and a placeholder, you missed.)

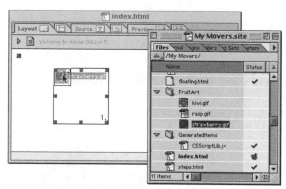

Figure 19-7: Dragging a graphic directly onto an image placeholder to place an image into a floating box

Cross-Reference

For more information about adding a graphic see Chapter 10.

Tip

When you're using graphics inside floating boxes to create an animation, it's a good idea to have the images preload so they're in place and appear when their curtain goes up. To tell the browser to preload an image, drag a Head Action icon from the Smart tab into the page's header and set it to execute `OnParse` or `OnLoad`. **Choose Image** ⇨ Preload Image as the Action and link to the image. Do this once for each image.

Adding Additional Formatting to a Floating Box

The Floating Box Inspector provides the basic setup for a floating box but when you're ready to get fancy, turn to the style sheet behind the floating box to create a more sophisticated look. Chapter 17, which is dedicated to style sheets, fully covers each of the properties you can use within a floating box. However, I feel the floating box-specific ones merit coverage here.

When you place a floating box on your page, GoLive automatically creates a style sheet ID selector for that box. (That's because floating boxes are a Cascading Style Sheet element, based on the `<div>` tag and each floating box has its unique ID so it can have unique placement and activity on the page.) All you have to do to add to the styles for that element is open the style sheet and choose your options in the Style Sheet Inspector.

Note   Some properties, such as font and text properties, are inherited from other selectors on the page.

To add to a floating box's style sheet formatting, do the following:

1. Click the Open CSS Interface button (the stair-step) in the upper-right corner of the Layout page. (The floating box does not have to be selected when you do this.)

   This opens the Style Sheet window. If you have already assigned any external style sheets to the page in progress, they are listed in this window. Any internal styles you've created for the page are there, too. But whether you've done anything with styles or not, a style exists in the Internal folder for each floating box on your page. The style for each floating box begins with a number sign (#) because it is an ID selector. The rest of the selector's name is the name you gave the floating box in the Inspector. If you have not named your floating boxes they are named #layer1, #layer2, and so forth.

2. In the Style Sheet window, click the name of the floating box for which you want to set up styles. The Inspector (which needs to be open now) becomes the CSS Selector Inspector and contains your style sheet options.

3. Proceed to the tab that contains the commands for what you want to do, and then make your choices, as shown in Figure 19-8. Most settings, such as text formatting, are visible immediately in page layout. However, others such as overflow need to be previewed in a browser. (If you set up an effect and it doesn't seem to work in layout, use the browser preview.) The following sections help you make specific adjustments to the style sheet.

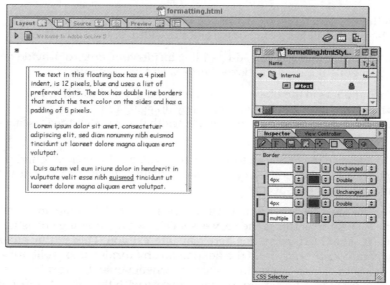

Figure 19-8: A floating box with the text set up and borders being added

Defining the look of your text

You can use the following methods to adjust the look of your font and its alignment and spacing:

✦ Use the Font tab of the CSS Selector Inspector to set color, size, and line height of your characters, as well as choose fonts. You can italicize your text by using Style, choose a thickness using Weight, and add an Underline, Strike, and Overline using Decoration. Additionally, you can set the case of your text within the Text properties tab. There, you can use Font Variant to create small caps (in theory but not in real life browser results) or Transformation to create uppercase, lowercase, or title case.

✦ To set up a list, use the List & Others tab of the CSS Selector Inspector.

✦ To align text relative to the edge of the floating box, indent the first line of your paragraphs, or add space between words or letters using the Text properties tab. In theory (but not in real life browser results), you can also align your text with regard to images or objects positioned beside it on a line, as in subscript and superscript.

Setting the look of your floating box

To adjust the look of your floating box, you can do any of the following:

✦ In the Borders tab you can create borders around your floating box, choosing which side will have one, if any, and the width, color, and pattern.

✦ In the Block tab, you can add padding inside your box, to provide an empty buffer zone between the boxes borders and its contents.

✦ The numbers in the block section are the height and width of your floating box, which you have already determined by dragging to resize the floating box or by entering numbers into the height and width fields within the Floating Box Inspector.

✦ You can use the CSS Selector Inspector to also set up background properties but the ones that concern you — background color or image — are already available in the Inspector.

✦ For the most part, everything within the Position tab is already available in the Inspector as this is the very essence of what a floating box is and why you use it. The Overflow setting here may interest you. This setting enables you to accommodate text within the floating box by turning on scrollbars within the box. Auto causes a scrollbar to appear whenever all the text in the floating box cannot fit. The scrollbars may interfere with the look of your page though.

Cross-Reference   To get the full story on style sheets and their properties see Chapter 17.

Resizing a Floating Box

Adjusting the size of a floating box is not different from resizing any other object on your pages. The floating box doesn't need to be selected to resize it; you don't need to see the handles in order to grab one. Just move your mouse to either corner or midpoint along any size, and then drag when the light blue arrowhead appears. (Of course, you can select the floating box first, and then perform the same step when you see the handles.)You can drag any handle in any direction.

Another way to adjust the size of a floating box is to press Shift as you press the arrow keys. Shift-Option (Mac) or Shift +Ctrl (Windows) resizes the floating box by the increments set in the invisible, underlying guideline-only grid. (You set the increments of this guideline grid by choosing it from via fly-out menu of the Floating Boxes palette.)

Note

Text wraps within a floating box that expands if it needs to. Users can set the font size at any size they desire. Don't forget that in Windows and for some Internet Explorer Mac users, text is far larger than for other Mac users and this causes text to wrap differently on each platform. If you don't want the floating box's text to grow downward, allow one third more room width-wise.

When you have multiple floating boxes on your page it can become difficult to adjust the size of one by dragging if another is on top of it or has handles nearby. Use the Floating Boxes palette, discussed later in this chapter, to temporarily bring the box you're working on forward.

Editing Inside the Box

Editing within a floating box is the same as editing directly on the page. To edit text within a floating box, type, select, copy, paste, or delete it just as you do with any other text. To move text, drag over it to select it, and then point to it and drag. Selected text counts as an object so when you point to it, your cursor shows the object selection cursor with the rectangle at its tail. To move a graphic, place your cursor over the graphic so the arrow becomes the object selection cursor, and then drag the graphic into its new position. Remember that items in a floating box are inline with the I-beam. The only exception is when a grid is in the box and the items are on the grid. But then, the grid is inline with the I-beam.

Converting a Floating Box to a Layout Text Box

In case you decide that floating boxes are not right for your page, you can translate them to text boxes on a Layout grid, and then work from there. This is a unique conversion; it doesn't affect your floating box-containing page and only converts the floating box(es), ignoring the rest of the page's contents in that area. The conversion doesn't actually convert your page — it makes a new page that contains only the converted floating boxes and a grid large enough to encompass them. The original page remains intact. You can do what you'd like with the newly created grid, saving its new page if you'd like or copying the grid for use in the original page or elsewhere.

The newly created page consists of a grid that extends from the top-left corner of the page to the bottom-right corner of the right-most floating box selected for conversion. On this new grid, the position of each converted floating box in relation to the page is maintained. The size of each floating box remains the same. Within each floating box, the contents remain intact.

The only limitation to this conversion is that it cannot include any overlapping floating boxes. If any of the boxes that are between the selected floating box and the top-left corner of the page happen to overlap, the option to do the conversion is not available.

To turn a floating box to a layout text box, follow these steps:

1. Open the Floating Boxes palette (Window ➪ Floating Boxes). You can do this either with or without selecting any floating box on your page.

2. *(Optional)* In the Floating Boxes palette, click the fly-out menu arrow and choose Floating Boxes Grid Settings, and then select Visible While Dragging.

   When this option is selected, the grid is visible in the resulting conversion. If it is not selected, the resulting table is identical, except that its grid lines don't appear. To turn the grid lines on or off after conversion, you can select the grid, and then check or uncheck the Visible options in the Layout Grid Inspector for that grid.

3. Return to the fly-out menu and choose Convert To Layout Grid.

   If Convert To Layout Grid is not an available option (grayed out), one or more of the floating boxes in the area to become gridded overlaps another so GoLive cannot flatten it.

The new page opens, presenting you a grid containing text boxes identical to your floating boxes, as shown in Figure 19-9.

Controlling Visibility

One of the powers of a floating box is the possibility to make it visible or invisible at any time. You can do this in two ways: based on a user event, such as when a user rolls the mouse over an item on your page, or within a timeline. It can be invisible when the page loads, and then become visible later and invisible yet again, or it can start as visible and turn invisible later.

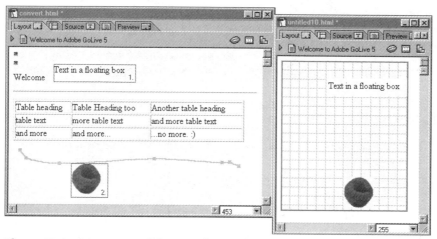

Figure 19-9: A page containing two floating boxes along with other elements and the result of converting the floating boxes to a grid

Setting the initial visibility

When you first place a box on the page it's visible. At any time, you can set its visibility simply by checking or unchecking the Visible option in the Floating Box Inspector.

> It probably makes sense to at least put the box into the desired position, or rough position, and perhaps get some of its content set up before you turn a box invisible.

When you set a box as not visible, the box and its contents literally become invisible in Layout mode. This can be very unsettling. The Floating Boxes palette, explained in the "The Floating Boxes Palette" section, enables you to view the box and its contents for design purposes, while keeping the box invisible.

In order to have a floating box's visibility change within the browser, you call upon JavaScript, either in the form of GoLive Actions (prewritten JavaScript's) or by writing your own custom JavaScript.

Visibility on call

One popular use of floating boxes is to have information appear or disappear on demand. You can easily set this effect up in GoLive, using the aptly named Show/Hide Action. Details of how to set up this Action are in Chapter 18.

For example, you can use a floating box to provide users with supplemental information about a link on your page by having more words, or even images, appear when the user rolls over that link. This not only creates an interesting effect, but also enables you to reduce screen clutter. You saw this effect earlier in Figure 19-1, where three links on a page all cause descriptive text to appear in the same location on mouseover.

Here's how it works:

✦ When a user rolls the mouse over a button or word, one or more floating boxes appear.

✦ When the mouse rolls off, the words go away.

Follow these steps to set this effect up on your page:

1. Set up your page to accommodate the effect by performing these steps:

   • Design your page with a blank area where the box will appear.

   • Place the text or graphic that, when rolled over or clicked, causes the contents of the floating box to appear.

   • Add the floating box that will appear and disappear, and then set it up how and where you want it to appear. Typically, a box for this effect doesn't have a background so the page's color or background shows through and the contents in this box appear as part of your page. If one box covers another, number the layers accordingly, with the top box having the bigger number.

   • In the floating box Inspector, give the box a depth of 1 or greater, name the floating box so you can refer to it later, and then uncheck Visible to turn the box invisible.

   • If you want more than one floating box to appear at the same time, add it too, and get it set up in place where you want it to appear. Name it and turn it invisible, too.

2. Set up the Action as follows and as explained in Chapter 18:

   • Turn the trigger text or graphic into a link, placing # in the URL field if its not really going to link anywhere, or the real link address if it does. Open the Actions palette, choose Mouser Enter as the Event, click the Add Action button, and then choose Action ⇨ Multimedia ⇨ Show/Hide.

   • In the lower part of the Actions palette, choose the name of the box you want to have appear. Choose Show from the pop-up menu.

   • If you have another box that will appear, click Add Action again and repeat the steps to choose the next box.

3. Now do this to set up the disappearing part or the floating box will remain visible.

- Still in the Actions palette, choose Mouser Exit as the Event, and then click the Add Action button, and choose Action ⇨ Multimedia ⇨ Show/Hide.

- In the lower part of the Actions palette, choose the name of the box you want to have disappear. Choose Hide from the pop-up menu, as seen in Figure 19-10.

- If you have another box that will disappear, click Add Action again and repeat the steps to choose the next box.

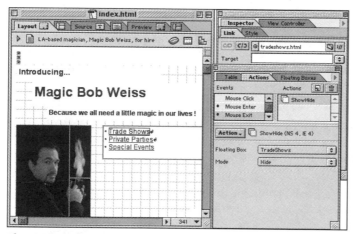

Figure 19-10: Setting up a box (named TradeShows) to disappear when the mouse moves off the selected link (Trade Shows). In this case, the link jumps users to a page called tradeshows.html.

That's all there is to it. Save your page, and then click the Show in Browser button to test the results. When the page fist loads, the floating box's content is invisible. When you roll over the link, your floating box(es) should appear. When you roll off the link, the box(es) should disappear.

You don't have to stop at having one text or button trigger on the page. Typically, an entire button bar triggers boxes to appear, or rolling over the name of each section within a site reveals information about that section. The floating boxes that appear can always appear in the common area, or they can each appear elsewhere. Floating boxes can appear all over your page. Just remember that many users only have a 15-inch monitor so having a box appear where the 16th inch would be means the user won't see the rollover effect onscreen.

Tip For a fancier twist, instead of having a blank area in which the floating box appears, have a graphic or text in that area and give the floating box a background so it covers up that page content. Or, better, don't have an empty space! Instead, use a floating box that appears when the page loads, but disappears when the other floating box appears! Both the hide action and the show action are then attached to the same rollover or click so both happen at once.

One more option in the Show/Hide Action is the Toggle command. With this, the trigger simply turns a visible box invisible and vice versa. It's a state-based toggle rather than a definite control.

A floating box can also turn visible or invisible at any point within an animation timeline. This is covered in full after I explain the timeline, but while I'm talking visibility, here it is in short.

To change visibility in a timeline, follow these steps:

1. Click the Open DHTML TimeLine Editor button at the top-right corner of the page to open the page's timeline.

2. Select the box's keyframe in the timeline.

3. Open the Inspector if it's not already open, and then uncheck the Visible option for that keyframe. When a floating box is invisible at any point, the corresponding keyframe is hollow.

   Be sure to select each keyframe for which you want the new visibility and check or uncheck Visible for that timeframe. Unfortunately you cannot Shift-click to select all desired keyframes and change the setting just once.

Working with Invisible Floating Boxes

Working with a floating box that's currently invisible on your page isn't different from working with one that's visible — except that it's, well, invisible . . . and you cannot select or edit what you cannot see.

Of course you can open the floating box's Inspector and turn a floating box visible in order to edit it, but then you have to remember to make it invisible again. (A step people *do* forget to do.) An easier way is available.

You can use the Floating Boxes palette to temporarily make the floating box visible without really altering its visibility in any way. In this state, you can use the Inspector to make changes — and actually see those changes (unlike just selecting the SB to work in the Inspector when the box is invisible. In this state you can also alter its contents in any way. You don't have to remember to change anything back because you never really change its visibility. As soon as you click anywhere else on your page, outside of the floating box, it disappears again.

Follow these steps to edit an invisible floating box:

1. Choose Window ➪ Floating Boxes to open the Floating Boxes palette.

2. Click the *name* of the floating box you want to see.

   The box temporarily appears on your page in its full glory so you can work within it. Yet, the visibility status is not altered in any way. If the box doesn't have a background of its own, the box appears white when selected for editing.

3. Click in the box to edit your text, or do whatever edit you need.

When you've finished your edits, click anywhere else on your page and the box disappears. To edit in it again, select it in the Floating Boxes palette again.

Caution

The eye or pencil icons in the Floating Boxes palette have different functions so leave them alone until you're clear on what they do. The following "The Floating Box Palette" section discusses the functions of these icons.

Your other options are the following:

✦ To make a floating box visible again in order to work with it, select the box's SB marker, and then turn on the visibility in the Inspector. Remember to turn it back off when you're finished. (One day you'll forget, see your page in a browser, and wonder bewilderedly at why images and text are showing when they're not supposed to. It happens to everyone sooner or later.)

✦ To work in the Inspector, but not with or within the floating box click the box's SB marker.

   This does not actually select the floating box for moving or drag resizing, but it does make the box's Inspector active so you can tweak the box within that Inspector. One benefit of doing this is that you can do tasks such as change the box's background or visibility, even when the box is invisible on your page.

The Floating Boxes Palette

The Floating Boxes palette (Window ➪ Floating Boxes) lists all of the floating boxes on your page and enables you to select boxes when they are visible, and to see boxes when they're not visible.

The name of each box is the key to editing. These editing abilities work even if a box is locked (via the pencil icon) or if you've used the eye icon to make a box invisible. Keep the following in mind:

✦ If a box is invisible, click its name to have it appear within your Layout enabling you to move or resize the box, or edit within the box.

✦ If a box is hidden or partly hidden behind another floating box, click its name to have it pop forward so you can work. When you're done, it pops back into its own layer. For example, if a box is at a depth of 1 and its handle is hidden by a box at a depth of 2, clicking the box's name moves it forward so you can see the edges. Move to the corner until you have a blue selection/drag arrow, and then drag to resize the box. When you complete the drag and release the mouse, the box returns to depth 1, behind the box on layer 2.

The eye icon you see in Figure 19-11 shows you the state of a box's visibility and enables you to temporarily alter that state. This helps you set up the look of your page. The following eye icon settings do not affect the actual page:

✦ When the eye is black its box is visible. Click it to have the box become temporarily invisible. The eye then becomes red to show you it is being viewed in an altered state.

✦ When the eye is gray its box is invisible. Click it to have the box temporarily appear. The eye becomes red to show you it is being viewed in an altered state.

✦ When the eye is red its box is appearing on your page as visible when it really is invisible or vice versa.

Control-click any eye icon to hide or show all floating boxes at once. If some are visible while others are not, control-clicking an invisible box makes them all visible, while control-clicking a visible box makes them all invisible.

Note   When the eye is red and you can see it on your page, you cannot move the box or edit its contents. Turning a box visible by clicking the eye icon is only to position items on your page. To see a floating box and edit it, click its name, not the eye.

The pencil icon temporarily locks or unlocks a floating box. Click a pencil icon to lock it. This dulls it out, locking it so you cannot reposition the box or edit within it. Click again to unlock it. When a box is made invisible in the floating box Inspector, it is locked within the Floating Boxes palette.

If you have several overlapping boxes it can be hard to select a given box. By locking the ones around it, you can more easily work on the one you want to reach.

Caution   At some point while you are locking a floating box you may lose the ability to change the box's depth or visibility. (These options gray out.) If this happens to you, save the page and close it. When you reopen the page, the options in the Inspector should be back to normal.

Control-click any pencil icon to lock or unlock all floating boxes at once. If some are locked while others are unlocked, control-clicking a locked box unlocks them all, while control-clicking an unlocked box locks them all.

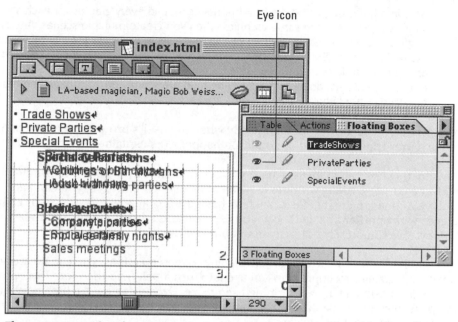

Figure 19-11: Using the eye icon in the Floating Boxes palette to temporarily show two of three hidden boxes in order to check their positioning (the bottom two eyes are red as the natural state of these boxes is invisible)

Normally, when you preview an animation using the Play button or return to the page to edit it, the Floating Boxes palette's settings revert to reflect the actual view and lock state of the page. The lock icon at the upper-right corner of the Floating Boxes palette enables you to keep that palette's temporary settings intact while the animation plays, and even when you switch between Layout and one of the other views in the page's window.

Animating Floating Boxes with a Timeline

You can use floating boxes to add animation to your page. In fact, you can add several animations to any one page. While all animations live in your page all the time, they don't all have to play at the same time. When you create an animation, you are actually creating a *scene*. To create a second, independent animation you create a second scene. You can create several scenes in one page. Each scene can use the same floating boxes, some of the same floating box, or you can introduce new floating boxes. Any floating boxes that you don't use in any given scene, you simply turn invisible.

Caution Bear in mind though, that the browser needs to load every graphic for each scene so it's best to reuse the same graphics when you create multiple scenes. Any animation you create becomes a part of your page; its instructions are a combination of JavaScript and CSS. So, also bear in mind that the code needed to describe your animation is unique to your page and therefore lives within your page's HTML. It is not in any external document, so having multiple scenes on your page can make the page rather large.

You can have a scene play automatically when the user's browser page loads, or when a user-triggered event or condition happens (as explained in Chapter 18).

Any floating box can follow any path you set, or even travel somewhat randomly within your page. Along with the movement of any box or boxes, you can add GoLive Actions to create effects such as having a box appear, disappear, or change places with another box. In theory you can also add music, but music can be rather finicky. (See Chapter 20 to learn about audio on the Web.)

By combining movement with other timeline-triggered actions, you can create some terrific effects. For example, you can use it to turn a box (and therefore its contents) visible or invisible in a predetermined sequence. Or you can have a box move across the page, become invisible, and then appear again at the other edge of the browser window again, creating a cycle.

You can add this movement by dragging the box around as the movement is recorded, or you can add it using traditional timeline tools. And, of course, you can combine the methods, which is perhaps most efficient. I recommend that you use the recording method to record the path of your floating box, and then use the timeline to properly place each box's path in time. I show you this technique here and then I show you how to set up an animation without recording.

Note When you animate floating boxes you are creating JavaScript code, so GoLive creates a document called CSScriptLib.js if it hasn't done so already for your site. This file resides by default in a folder called GeneratedItems. Both the file and its folder upload to your site during any automatic upload in the Site Window. Be sure to remember that this folder and file are important to the site (or, in the Page Inspector, tell GoLive to write all of the code into the document).

The fastest and easiest way to create an animation is to let GoLive record your movement as you drag your floating boxes around on your page. You record the movement of each floating box individually, and then view the results in the TimeLine Editor.

If you select one floating box and record a path, and then select another and record its path, the movement of each box is not concurrent, but sequential. The first recorded path plays out, and then the next recording plays. If you want the movement of your boxes to run at the same time, or to overlap, you need to adjust their starting points in the TimeLine Editor.

Recording a floating box's movement

You can add movement to a floating box simply by dragging it around on your page. As you drag, GoLive records the box's path by recording keyframes.

To record a box's movement, do this:

1. To set a specific or unique color for this animation's keyframes, click the KeyColor color swatch, and then choose a color from the Color palette. The KeyColor that's active when you record your floating box's movement becomes the color for each of the keyframes, or markers, along the animation timeline.

Tip

If you're adding several animations, using a special keyframe color can help you identify a timeline track at a glance. For example, if the item animated is red, you might use a red keyframe color.

2. Choose a type of path for your box's movement by selecting one of the following from the Type pop-up menu:

   • *None* creates a perfectly straight line with no keyframes between the start and end position. It's a direct jump.

   • *Linear* doesn't limit your path to straight lines, but it tends to draw straighter lines as you change direction.

   • *Curve* gives you a rounder path.

   • *Random* creates a scratchy line. When you have finished recording your movements, select a keyframe in the timeline and choose Random to create a nervous, jumpy movement.

   If you select and drag a floating box without choosing any path type, Linear automatically appears. If you drag on a curve, it changes to Curve.

3. Click Record. The button appears darkened while in record mode to remind you that your actions are being recorded.

4. Move your mouse to any edge of the box; when the cursor becomes a sideways pointing hand, drag the box along the desired path, as shown in Figure 19-12. As you drag the box, a gray line punctuated with many dots define the course of your path. When you finish dragging, the path polishes and the strategic points appear as keyframes in the TimeLine Editor, making it easier for you to adjust the path or add other functionality later.

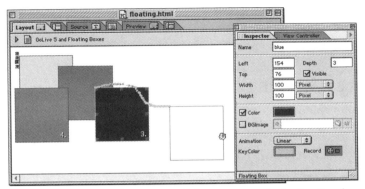

Figure 19-12: Dragging to record the movement of a floating box. The path is busy until recording is over.

As you drag to define a path, it is easy to move the box in a path that is a bit different from the one you really want. That's not a problem because you can edit the path later. For example, if you pull the box off the desired path for a moment, you can later delete the out-of-line point and the box no longer travels there. If you drag too high or low, you can reposition the box for that point in the timeline.

After you define your initial path, click the Open DHTML TimeLine Editor button at the top-right corner of the page to see and tweak the path you've just defined, as well as to name it. You can open this timeline and edit the path any time after you've recorded it.

Viewing your animation

As you create your animation, you can play it to see how it's coming together. You can play it by watching it in a browser. You can play it from the timeline and watch it within page layout—in which case you can see it in its entirety or play just a section. Or, you can use the timeline cursor to play any bit of the scene. This last option isn't close to real-time playback; it just helps you pinpoint behavior and changes.

Toward the top of the TimeLine Editor window is a set of orange arrows with a strip of paler orange between them. This denotes the actual duration of your sequence. The forward-pointing orange arrow marks the beginning of your animation while the orange backward-pointing arrow shows you the end of the animation. The last keyframe determines the end of the sequence.

Manually Creating a Scene

If, for some reason, you prefer not to record the initial movement of your floating box, you can construct its animation sequence fully in the TimeLine Editor.

Every time you add a floating box to your page, GoLive adds its first keyframe to the beginning of the timeline, as shown in this figure.

Each line of the timeline represents one floating box so if you have four floating boxes on your page, you have four timeline tracks. The left-most frame, where the first keyframe is automatically placed, represents the moment the page is opened.

To manually animate a scene, do the following:

1. Click the Open DHTML TimeLine Editor button at the top-right corner of the page.

   You see the first keyframe of each floating box on your page.

2. To place a new keyframe press ⌘ (Mac) or Control (Windows) as you click in the desired point of the timeline. (Be sure to click the track for the box with which you want to work.)

   You can also add a new keyframe by duplicating an existing one. Press Option (Mac) or Alt (Windows) as you click the keyframe closest to where you want the new one, and then drag that keyframe to where you want the new keyframe.

3. In the page, drag the floating box to the place you want it to be at this point in the animation. (Or, use the Inspector to enter its coordinates as measured from the left and top sides of the browser window to the top-left corner of the floating box.)

4. Choose the pattern for the path between the previous keyframe and the new one by selecting one from the Animation pop-up menu in the Floating Box Inspector. None causes a direct move from one to the other. Curve adds a smooth curve. Linear creates an effect that is a cross between the two — not quite a line and not a curve.

5. Continue repeating Steps 2 through 4 until you've completed your sequence.

The bottom of the TimeLine Editor window contains standard playback buttons (see Figure 19-13) you can use to see the result of your animation. The following describe what these buttons do:

✦ The single forward-pointing arrow is the Play button. When you click Play the animation plays from whatever point it is in the timeline and continues to the end of your scene. Double-click the Play button to have it play from the very beginning of the scene to its end. The Play button respects the end of your actual animation, stopping at the end of the orange area, where your last keyframe is placed.

✦ The forward-pointing arrow with the extra line is the Forward button. Each time you click this button it moves you forward on the timeline one frame at a time. Keep the button pressed and it keeps moving forward. It doesn't end at your last keyframe though. If you keep clicking, it keeps stepping forward.

✦ The backward-pointing arrow with the extra line is the Backward button. Each time you click this button it moves you backward on the timeline one frame at a time. Keep the button pressed and it keeps moving backward.

✦ The stop button stops your playback while you're previewing it.

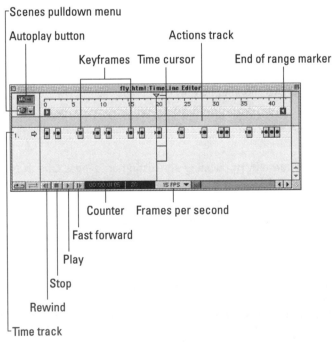

Figure 19-13: The playback controls

Next to the playback buttons is a clock and your playback speed setting that provide feedback on how long into the animation an event happens or how fast the sequence plays in a browser.

✦ The Time clock counts the length of your animation in hours, minutes, seconds, and parts of a second. It lets you know how far into a scene you are, time-wise, by multiplying the frame number by the speed you have set (which is measured in frames per second). It also shows you how long your scene runs if you take the Time cursor to the end of the scene.

✦ The Frame counter reports the frame of which you are currently viewing the state. The position of the Time cursor or selected keyframe determines the active frame.

✦ The Frames per Second drop-down menu enables you to choose a playback speed for your scene.

As your sequence plays or as you click any keyframe, the Time cursor moves across the timeline to show you exactly where you are in the timeline. You can also move the Time cursor to watch any part of your animation play out in the Layout. Point your arrow pointer to any part of the Time cursor — either the arrow at the top or the line that points out its position down through all tracks — then drag it to cause the animation to happen. You can drag it forward or back, fast or slow.

See "Setting up playback" later in this chapter for more about some of these controls.

Naming your animation

While you're viewing your animation or editing it, don't forget to name your animation scene. Your initial animation is prenamed Scene 1 so it's up to you to rename it more descriptively. If you only have one scene in your page and it places automatically, naming it isn't a big deal. But as soon as you get into multiple scenes or playing a scene from an Action, you'll be glad you can easily identify your scenes by name.

Do this to give a custom name to your first animation scene:

1. Click the Options pop-up button at the top-left corner of the TimeLine Editor window and choose Rename Scene to open the mini dialog box, aptly called Rename Scene.

2. Enter a short descriptive name in the Rename Scene dialog box shown in Figure 19-14, and then click OK.

Figure 19-14: Renaming your first scene from the default name, Scene 1

Unfortunately, the scene name does not appear in view within the TimeLine Editor.

Editing your recorded path

After you've recorded your floating box's path using the Inspector's record button, you can continue to work on that box's path and timing by opening the TimeLine Editor and working there. When you record your path, GoLive creates keyframes. In the TimeLine Editor you work with those keyframes.

When you open the DHTML TimeLine Editor, you see that page's timeline. Within that timeline, one time track exists for each floating box on the page. Within each box's track, one keyframe exists for each gray dot displayed in the box's path on the page. (That is, the position of the top-left corner of the floating box in relation to the top-left corner of the browser, or page, window.)At the top of the tracks is a timeline in which each tick represents a frame.

As you click any keyframe within a track, the box that path represents moves to that point of its travels. You can see this happen on the page so you can work with that box's animation. As you move the Time cursor over time, all boxes on the page move to their respective positions over time.

When you record the movement of multiple floating boxes, the movement appears in the timeline in sequential order so the movement of the second floating box begins when that of the first box ends. If you want them to begin together, you need to move all of the keyframes of the second floating box up to where the first one begins. Normally, when you drag a keyframe, only that one keyframe moves. To move all keyframes in an animation together at the same time, press the Shift key as you drag the first floating box that you want to move. All floating boxes that are after it on the timeline move along with it, maintaining their time intervals.

Note   After you record your initial sequence and get the timing down, you can also jazz it up by changing the depth of some boxes so they appear to move in front of or behind another box or by turning visibility on or off. See "Jazzing up your animation sequence" later in this chapter for details.

The secret to editing a box's travel, or to cause anything to happen to a box, is to use the keyframe or timeline cursor to place the box at the particular point you want to change, and then to move the box or add the Action.

Follow these steps to reposition a box at any point of its travels:

1. *(Optional)* In the page, select the box you want to edit by clicking its name in the Floating Boxes palette or by clicking the box's edge in the page.

   While not necessary, using the box's name can help you identify the track for that box. In the TimeLine Editor, you see an arrow in that track. If you've used colored keyframes you can identify each box by the colors of the keyframes.

2. If it's not already open, click the Open DHTML TimeLine Editor button at the top-right corner of the page to open the page's timeline.

3. To identify the point where you want the edit to take place, do one of the following:

   • Slowly drag the timeline cursor and stop at the edit point.

   • Click the keyframes in the track until you locate the desired edit point.

4. Click the keyframe that corresponds to the moment in time for the box to be edited.

   If no keyframe exists that corresponds to that moment, add one by pressing ⌘ (Mac) or Control (Windows) as you click the desired point of the timeline. (Be sure to click the track for the box you want to work with.) The new keyframe is automatically selected so you can move directly to Step 5.

   You can also add a new keyframe by duplicating an existing one. Press Option (Mac) or Alt (Windows) as you click the keyframe closest to where you want the new one, and then drag that keyframe to where you want the new keyframe.

5. On the page, move the box to the position in which you now prefer it to be, as seen in Figure 19-15.

   The gray line reflects the path change.

To see the result of your edit, either drag the timeline cursor across the altered part of the timeline, or click the Play button in the lower-left corner of the TimeLine Editor window.

If an animation is too choppy, try these ways of fixing it:

✦ Smooth it out by deleting keyframes. When you remove a keyframe, the path redraws between the points immediately before or after the deleted keyframe. For example, when you record an object moving from one point to another, GoLive may record several keyframes, but you may only need the first and last. Try deleting the rest in between. You can always undo the deletion. To delete a keyframe, select it in the timeline, and then press your Backspace/ Delete key.

✦ Move the keyframes backward or forward in the sequence to adjust the timing. Just drag it back or forth.

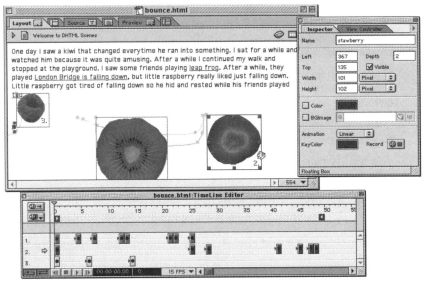

Figure 19-15: A keyframe for the Kiwi floating box selected, and the grabber hand about to drag the floating box into a new position

✦ Select a path shape for a box's travel between any two keyframes. To do this, select the arrival-point keyframe, and then choose a path from the Animation pop-up menu in the Floating Box Inspector. To change several keyframes at once, press Shift as you click each desired frame to select them all, and then choose the path shape.

When your paths are set you can jazz up your animation.

On the CD-ROM

The file depicted in Figure 19-15 (and coming up in Figure 19-17) is available in the Exercises folder on this book's CD-ROM in a site called MyMovers. In it, you can see how the various scenes are constructed, and experiment with them yourself. Other experiments in floating boxes are in this site as well. (Thanks to Cathy Scrivnor for creating the site and to Don Wallace for the use of his fruit.)

Creating additional scenes within your page

After you're created your first scene you may want to create another.

Perform these steps to create a new scene:

1. Click the Options pop-up button at the top-left corner of the TimeLine Editor window and choose New Scene, as shown in Figure 19-16.

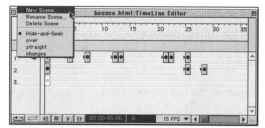

Figure 19-16: Beginning a new scene (the scene currently showing in the timeline is Hide-and-Seek, per the bullet by its name)

This opens the New Scene dialog box.

2. Enter a short descriptive name for your scene, and then click OK.

The timeline containing your first scene is put away and you have a new empty timeline within which to work.

3. Return to your page and create your new scene again, either by recording it or by manually placing keyframes on the timeline and setting up the floating boxes to correspond to each keyframe.

If a floating box exists on your page that you will not use in this new scene, select its starting keyframe (only one is available at this point) within the timeline and uncheck the Visible option in its Floating Box Inspector.

If you need new floating boxes for your new scene, add them just as you originally added floating boxes to your page.

Note Unfortunately, the scene name does not appear in view within the TimeLine Editor. To know what scene you're working in later, click the Options pop-up and note which scene is designated as active by the bullet to the left.

Jazzing up your animation sequence

You can set visibility or stacking order on a frame by frame basis by choosing the desired setting in the Floating Box Inspector at any keyframe. With these effects, items seem to morph together, or items can jump in front of each other.

When you identify a point within the timeline where a significant event will happen, you can turn the corresponding keyframe a special color to mark it. This may make it easier for you to return to that point later, or to work with that event in mind. Simply select the significant keyframe, and then click the KeyColor color swatch in the Inspector and chose a color.

Changing stacking order

You can set the stacking order (a.k.a. *depth* or *Z-index*) of a floating box on a frame by frame basis by selecting a keyframe and entering a new number in the Depth field of the Floating Box Inspector.

To change stacking order by keyframe, follow these steps:

1. If it's not already open, click the Open DHTML TimeLine Editor button at the top-right corner of the page to open the page's timeline.

2. Select the box's keyframe in the timeline.

3. Open the Inspector, and then enter a new depth for that keyframe.

4. If you have any more keyframes that follow and you want them to also reflect the new stacking order, be sure to select each one of them and change the Depth field entry for those keyframes as well. Unfortunately you cannot Shift-click to select all desired keyframes and change the depth all at once.

Changing visibility

You can set visibility on a frame by frame basis by turning a floating box invisible at any keyframe. Visibility returns with the next keyframe though, if the next is set as visible. If the keyframes are all in place, you need to select each one and set it separately.

Do the following to change visibility by keyframe:

1. Click the Open DHTML TimeLine Editor button at the top-right corner of the page to open the page's timeline.

2. Select the box's keyframe in the timeline.

3. Open the Inspector, and then uncheck the Visible option for that keyframe.

   When a floating box is invisible at any point, the corresponding keyframe is hollow.

   Be sure to select each keyframe for which you want the new visibility and check or uncheck Visible for that timeframe. Unfortunately you cannot Shift-click to select all desired keyframes and change the setting just once.

Another way to change visibility is to place the Show/Hide Action into the timeline.

Adding Actions

You can incorporate GoLive Actions (prewritten JavaScripts) into your animation. To do this, you add an Action into the Action track—the gray strip below the time-line numbers and above the animation track(s). You then set up the action just like you set up any other Action in GoLive. (See Chapter 18 to learn all about Actions.)

What Action you incorporate into your animation and how you use it depends on you and your creativity. Some that may interest you are noted at the end of this chapter under "Creating Movement in Other Ways."

Note Many Actions in GoLive are set up within the Actions palette. However, page- and timeline-triggered Actions are set up using the usual Inspector window. The interfaces are the same in both places.

To add an Action to your animation, perform these steps:

1. Use the Time cursor to determine where you'd like the Action to take place.

2. Command-click (Mac) or Alt+click (Windows) in the gray area just above track one (the Action track) at that point in the timeline.

   This places an Action icon—a plain black question mark in a hollow box— into place along the timeline.

3. Open the Inspector, and then select the desired Action from the Action pop-up menu.

4. Set up the Action in accordance with its capabilities and parameters. (In other words, choose from the options presented in the Action Inspector.)

Note You do not actually have to have floating boxes or an animation on your page to use the timeline. You can use it just to trigger an Action after the browser has been open for a certain amount of time. In that case, you just need to click anywhere in the actual timeline numbers and notice the Time clock as you do, to determine where to place the Action.

Setting up playback

After you've created your animation, changes are good that you'll want your site's visitors to see it. You can determine what causes the animation to play, as well as whether it plays just once or continuously.

Playback options

You can set up your animation to play automatically, to play once, or to repeat endlessly when a user's browser loads the page. You can also set the speed at which it plays, in frames per second.

Your animation plays automatically by default, meaning that as soon its elements are downloaded, the sequence plays. However, you may not want that, depending on the purpose of the animation. To prevent it from playing automatically, simply click the Autoplay button in the top-left corner of the TimeLine Editor window.

Because it is on by default it is darkened. When you click it to turn it off, it is no longer dark gray. If you turn off Autoplay, it's up to you to place a trigger somewhere in your page that enables the animation to start playing.

To have your animation repeat in an endless loop, click the Loop button in the lower-left corner of the TimeLine Editor. During playback, the sequence plays from the first keyframe to the last, and then jumps back to the first and repeats again. To have the sequence play front to back, and then from the last keyframe backward to the first, click the Palindrome button to add it to the mix. (It only works when the Loop button is active; the two are partners.)

Tip Whether you have your animation Autoplay or not, if you set it to loop continuously, you may want to include a trigger that enables the user to stop the playback. See the following "Controlling playback" section.

By default, an animation plays back in the user's browser at 15 frames per second, as noted in the FPS (frames per second) pop-up menu at the bottom of the TimeLine Editor to the left of the window's scrollbar. This is a safe speed for most users, considering Internet connection and browser handling. You can make your movie play slower or faster by choosing another frame rate from the FPS pop-up menu. Whatever speed you choose, test the results in various browsers at various connection speeds.

Controlling playback

By default an animation plays automatically when a user's browser loads. You can set up an animation to play when the user clicks a link or moves the mouse over a designated word or image.

Cross-Reference To learn how to set this up, see "Creating User-triggered Actions" in Chapter 18. Chapter 18 also discusses how to set up an animation to play when a certain condition is met.

If you have multiple scenes in your page, you can have one begin to play when another ends by placing the start and stop triggers in the timeline. In that case, you place the Action trigger in the timeline just as you would place other Actions in it.

In addition to providing a mechanism to begin playback, you may also want to give the user a way to stop the playback. These options are similar to the start play options so again, I refer you to Chapter 18.

The actual Action that you use to start your animation is the Play Scene Action. You can read about this in Chapter 18 under "Playing or stopping a scene or animation." Nothing fancy is involved in setting up this action. You just set up the trigger like you would for any other Action, and then choose Action ⇨ Multimedia ⇨ Play Scene and choose the scene's name from the menu that becomes available, as shown in Figure 19-17.

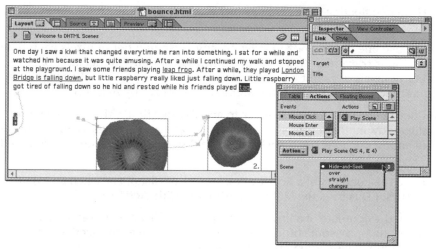

Figure 19-17: Setting up a false link to invoke an Action that plays one of four scenes in a page

Note

If you have multiple scenes on one page and are using Play Scene Actions to start each individual scene, each time you use the Action you need to add a Stop Scene Action to end the playback of the previous scene. If you don't, the prior scene continues to play in a separate layer.

Creating Movement in Other Ways

GoLive comes installed with a few Actions that enable you to manipulate your floating boxes in some interesting ways. Adobe extras and third-party Actions that are fun to use are also available if you want to experiment further. An Action here and your imagination there — and the possibilities are endless.

In addition to other tasks, GoLive's preinstalled Actions enable you to perform the following:

✦ Locate the exact location of a specific floating box on the page at any moment and use those coordinates to send another floating box to the same place. (This uses the Getters ➪ Get Floating Box Pos Action.)

✦ Enable a user to drag the contents of a floating box within the browser window. When the user drags this content, it may trigger another event. For example, you may have the draggable floating box contain an image of say, an arrow, and then have a target on the page too. The target can be a trigger set to mouse enter. When the user drags the arrow over to the bull's eye the event triggers. If the target is an image map, even more possibilities exist. (This uses the Multimedia ➪ Drag Floating Box Action.)

✦ Have two floating boxes change places. (This uses the Multimedia ➪ Flip Move Action.)

✦ Choose one floating box to move by any given number of pixels each time the Action is triggered. Or, if used along with a variable and declaration, the number of pixels does not have to be hard-set but can be ever changing based on another event. (This uses the Multimedia ➪ Move By Action.)

✦ Choose one floating box to move to another location, either hard-set or determined by another event. For example, a floating box can move to the location of another floating box, which is also on the move. (This uses the Multimedia ➪ Move To Action.)

✦ Have the contents of a floating box appear or disappear when an event occurs. (This uses the Multimedia ➪ Show/Hide Action.)

✦ Have the contents of a floating box appear or disappear gradually while fading in or out, or by some other special effect when an event occurs. (This uses the Multimedia ➪ Wipe Transition Action.)

✦ Use an Action to fill the content of a floating box. You can use several Actions to enable you to place graphics, such as the RandomImage Action, for example. To fill the floating box with text you can use the Document Write Action.

✦ Tie the text or graphic in your floating box into a Link Action. (This uses any of the Link Actions.)

The following third-party Actions use floating boxes, too:

✦ **ScrollIt** by Walter Blady lets you easily scroll the contents of a floating box up and down, and left to right. Learn more about it or order it from `www.wblady.com/actions4.html`.

✦ **Mouse Trail** by Oliver Zahorka of OUT Media Design GmbH is an action that makes the contents of a floating box follow your mouse as you move around the page. You can order this Action from `http://out.to/actions`.

✦   ✦   ✦

Adding Audio and Video

One of the most inviting things about the World Wide Web is its capability to deliver audio and video, enabling you to produce a true multimedia experience. It's the most exciting element of the Web, but it's also the most precarious. It's a little bit like the early days of color TV. Color TV was actually invented around the same time as black and white. However, had programs been produced for that color TV format, they could not have been seen on a black-and-white TV receiver; viewers would have needed two separate televisions. Because there was industry regulation, this non-compatible model never became part of our lives. Instead, the industry was mandated to produce a color transmission that could coexist. As a Web designer, you're sort of in the position of putting out a video for the black-and-white or the color viewers — or producing two versions to reach both.

You can place audio or video in your page and you can take steps to extend the chances that users will see or hear your files in a certain program (or using a certain plug-in), but ultimately, you have no control over whether your visitors have a player to play your video format, or which player your guests will use to play it if they have alternatives. (Sort of like being in radio in the early '70s and not knowing if listeners had stereo or mono.)

Because you have so many ways to create and deliver audio and video, the topic is too wide-ranging to discuss in this book. I'll have to leave you on your own to discover the world of Web audio and video. However, showing you *how* to put those media files on your page is exactly what this book is about. Although the creation of each type of audio or audio-visual delivery varies, their access from your page, or placement on your page, is very similar.

Bear in mind that GoLive lets you embed various media types on your page and link to them. But GoLive is not a media creation tool. You'll need to create your media files before you can place them on your page. You'll also need to determine whether they'll download from your own Web server or be streamed from a dedicated streaming server in order to prepare the files. Before using a multimedia file on the Web, it should be compressed using a tool such as Cleaner 5 or QuickTime Pro. This provides maximum quality with a minimum download time.

Tip   If you're planning on using anything other than original sound files or shareware you own, read "The Use of Music on a Multimedia Web Site," an article by Ivan Hoffman. You'll find it by following the "For Recording Artists and Song Writers" link at www.ivanhoffman.com.

Adding Sound and Video on the Web

It may help you to understand that the native HTML browser does not directly understand audio and video media types. Instead, an audio or video file is actually played within a Web browser (or designated player) thanks to the use of a plug-in.

The standard installation of both Netscape and Internet Explorer include a plug-in, called Default, that provides the capability to understand and handle most standard audio files and some video file types. Additionally, Netscape includes a plug-in called LiveAudio, which adds more multimedia functionality within Netscape.

Apple, RealNetworks, and Microsoft provide a standalone player and a plug-in as part of the standard installation. The plug-in provides most of the functionality of the standalone player, with the additional capability to play the files from within the actual page being viewed.

The way a browser knows which plug-in to call upon is by the *MIME (Multipurpose Internet Mail Extension) type* associated with the audio or video file. The user's browser has a list of every Mime type and the plug-in it should call upon when it sees that Mime type. GoLive knows most of the common Mime types and automatically writes them into your page's HTML when you place an audio or video file on your page. In any case where GoLive doesn't recognize an associated Mime type, you choose one when you embed the file.

Here's an overview of the installed user-base for these key plug-ins:

✦ QuickTime is always installed on the Mac, and chances are QuickTime has been already been installed on your Windows machine. QuickTime has been available for Windows since Windows 3.1. This means that you can deploy QuickTime-supported media on machines all the way back to Intel 80386 and Motorola 68030 with color ROMS. Most early computers that shipped with CD-ROM players came with examples that installed QuickTime with their Applications. QuickTime is the most-installed application on Windows after Microsoft Paint (which comes with Windows). In current versions of QuickTime (Versions 4.*x* and higher), the browser plug-in is installed to the correct locations automatically along with the player application. Some Windows users may have to download QuickTime independently, but it enables the mixing of over 25 media types in a single page. This means your browser page is more stable. QuickTime is the W3C and MPEG4 standard, so it's worth the download if you can encourage users to do it.

✦ RealNetworks' RealPlayer is a popular player for audio and video media. Used by many radio stations, RealNetworks has been adding additional features over the years. They have several server choices and a free and fee-based player. They specialize in streaming files. Your audience needs the RealPlayer to experience your content, such as music or video, but you cannot force users to download and install the player, leaving your message unheard by perhaps many visitors. However, this is a popular player, and it now comes bundled with Internet Explorer and Netscape, so this is less of an obstacle than it has been in the past.

✦ Another plug-in that provides multimedia functionality is Macromedia's Shockwave Flash plug-in, which has become somewhat of a standard, so these days it's also installed during most browser installations.

 New Feature

In previous versions of GoLive there was one generic plug-in icon you placed on the page, and then configured. GoLive 5 gives you a head start now, by providing these three key plug-ins preconfigured for you.

Methods of adding sound or video to your page

You have several ways to add sound and video to your page, as follows:

✦ If your goal is to have a user download a sound for playing later, you can do that by compressing it in a well-known Internet format, such as with WinZip or StuffIt, and linking to the compressed file. (This is covered in Chapter 11.)

✦ You can record a simple sound or some music, save it as a common audio file, and then embed it in the page, setting it to autostart so it plays automatically when the page loads. Likewise with a video — you can create a movie and then deliver it as QuickTime, Windows Media, or RealMedia, having it download to the user's computer as a *progressive download*. A progressive download is actually a regular download that you can watch as it is being copied to your machine. You place the file on your regular Web (HTTP) server. Then, when the user calls for it, the file is sent to the user's computer. When it arrives, it plays, or awaits the user's command to play it, depending on whether you set it for autostart or enabled user controls. This file then resides on the user's machine so when it's finished playing the user can play it again — if you provided controls.

✦ You can create a movie, and then deliver it as QuickTime, Windows Media, or RealG2 media by streaming it. Streaming is a unique serving process, done from a special server, called a streaming server (RTP/RTSP, for Real Time Streaming Protocol). Each format provides its own server software, dedicated to streaming that format. QuickTime is streamed from the QuickTime Streaming Server, an OSX server. RealAudio and RealVideo are served from the RealServer. Windows Media is served from NetShow Server. The reason for the dedicated server for each is the unique job it does. A regular (HTTP) server sends a file to the user but dismisses it once it is sent. A (QuickTime or Real) streaming server uses two-way communication, tracking the rate at which the user successfully receives the file and adjusting the serving rate accordingly. With streaming, the image or sound is there for the moment, but not cached or saved to the hard drive. When a guest at your site replays the sound or movie, it is streamed all over again. This method is the only way to go for live broadcasts. It's also the best way to protect from theft of material.

Note   To further add to the mix, you can either have your movie (whether downloaded or streamed) play on your page, or it can open within its own player window, independently of the page.

✦ You can create your A/V presentation within LiveMotion or Flash, and then embed that presentation on your Web page. This is the most reliable way to create click sounds at this stage in Web history. (You can also create your entire page in LiveMotion or Flash, and then link to the entire page, rather than to a page that contains the LiveMotion or Flash file. Because that's a different story, turn to Chapter 11 to learn about linking to that kind of page.)

You can create an SVG graphic embedded with controls such as zooming and embedded links, and then place that graphic on your page. But SVG (Scalable Vector Graphics) is so new that it requires an *SVG Viewer* in order to work in any browser, as of Internet Explorer 5 and Netscape 4.*x*. And, it has browser-imposed limitations.

Understanding embedding and linking

You actually have two ways to present video or audio on your page (as shown in Figure 20-1). One is to embed it — to have it actually play in a designated area of your page. The other is to have the play button in the page, but have the audio or video file play, not in the page, but in a separate player application. Embedding makes the experience more a part of your page. Linking provides flexibility such as the capability to display larger images without taking over your entire page, or playing longer movies or songs without using up the browser's RAM. Either way, an audio or video file relies on a Mime type, and the setup is similar.

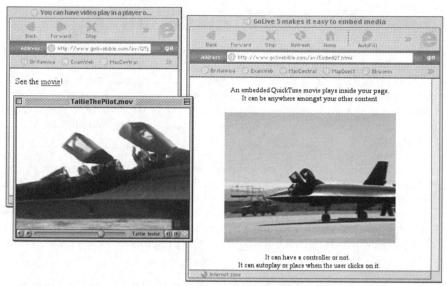

Figure 20-1: A QuickTime movie as seen in Internet Explorer 5 on the Mac. To the left, a plain link to a movie file and the resulting player window. At the right is the same movie, embedded with a plug-in and playing in place on its page.

If you're embedding the file, keep the following in mind:

✦ If placing a video, place it exactly where you want the player to appear.

✦ If placing a sound and its player will show, place it exactly where you want the player to appear.

✦ If the sound will be invisible and play as the page loads, place it as the very first thing on your page to have it begin as quickly as possible. Place it later in your page to delay playback. But remember that it takes time for the sound to download and kick into action.

✦ If the sound will be invisible and triggered by a user action (as opposed to autoplay), placement doesn't matter much. However, the closer to the top of the page, the faster it begins loading. This is important to know if the page has other large or time-consuming media, such as animated GIFs or high-resolution image downloads. You will have to strike a balance.

To embed a file, you use the GoLive Plug-in, which writes the <embed> tag into the page's HTML. To link a file, you create a link just like any other link. When you embed a file, you designate the file you're embedding by using a Point and Shoot button in the Inspector. That same file is the one you link to when creating a plain vanilla link.

Adding Shockwave/Flash to Your Page

Shockwave/Flash (SWF) files can be created in Adobe's LiveMotion or in Macromedia's Flash (from which the plug-in type derives part of its name). These animations are popular because they can contain user-event-triggered sounds, such as an effect when the mouse rolls over an area, and also contain links. (In fact, GoLive even enables you to change the destination of those links. See Chapter 11 to learn more about that.) As the SWF plug-in has become somewhat of a standard recently, SWF files are a fairly safe bet to use.

You can incorporate SWF files into your site in two ways. You can create an entire page that is SWF (see Chapter 11) or you can use the SWF plug-in to place the animation within a page as just a part of the page instead. The latter enables visitors using older browsers to see your page's contents, just missing the one animated part. Adding an SWF file to your page is very simple and straightforward, thanks to the SWF plug-in, which even guides users to the plug-in's download and update site as needed.

On the CD-ROM Doug LaMaster (age 12) has generously created the SWF file shown in the following steps for you to learn and experiment with. You can find it in the Exercises folder, under this chapter number.

You *could* place an SWF graphic into your page by simply dragging the graphic file from your Files tab into the page. However, this doesn't do the same thorough job that GoLive's preset plug-in placeholder does, so my strong recommendation is to place the plug-in first, as follows.

To place an SWF presentation into your page, follow these steps:

1. If it's not already there, place the .swf file in the Files tab of the Site Window so GoLive can manage it. (Remember that if that file isn't in your Files tab, it will appear as an Orphan file and will not upload with your site unless you correct that later.)

2. Drag the Flash plug-in icon from the Basic tab of the Objects palette into place on your page. Because your SWF animation is a visual element that becomes an essential part of your page, put the placeholder exactly where you want the graphic to appear.

   If you check out the Basic and More tabs of the Inspector (see Figure 20-2), you'll notice that this plug-in comes preconfigured with the correct Mime type, the coding for the object and embed tags, and even the code needed so your visitors can go directly to the Macromedia site to download the Flash plug-in if they don't already have it. This makes it easier for users to see your site; there's less risk that they'll go away and never get around to coming back.

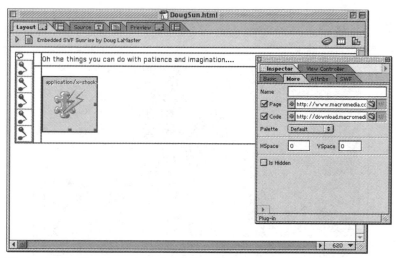

Figure 20-2: The More tab of the Plug-in Inspector with its default settings immediately after the SWF plug-in is placed

3. In the Basic tab of the Inspector, use your preferred linking method to link from the URL area to the .swf file, as shown in Figure 20-3. The graphic expands to its full size, taking its rightful position as a part of your page. You can move it if you'd like, just like you move any graphic. (See Figure 20-4.)

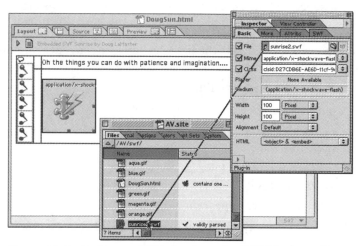

Figure 20-3: Linking an SWF plug-in to the SWF file that will become part of the page

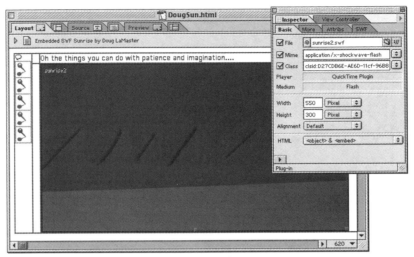

Figure 20-4: The SWF file is in place on the page.

4. *(Optional)* If you need to change the size or alignment of the graphic, you can do so within the Basic and More tabs of the Inspector.

5. In the Name field of the Inspector, enter a name for your graphic so you can reference it later, if needed.

6. *(Optional)* Customize your SWF image's settings for playback within the SWF tab of the Inspector shown in Figure 20-5. All of these settings are optional. *Autoplay* tells the animation to play as soon as the page downloads and enough information has loaded. *Loop* tells the movie to play over again when it reaches the end. *Quality* sets the balance between playback and download speeds, as follows:

   • *Default* uses the player settings.

   • *High* puts appearance quality over speed.

   • *Autohigh* is a smarter version of high, also compensating for below-specified frame rate speed.

   • *Autolow* accommodates lower speeds, giving energy to appearance when speeds are acceptable.

   • *Low* puts speed over appearance.

   Scale only comes into play when you override the plug-in's automatic sizing. Here are the options:

   • *Default* maintains the original proportions of the clip, adding borders to the manually sized plug-in area as needed.

Figure 20-5: The SWF tab of the Plug-in Inspector; it appears only when the Mime type is for SWF

- *No Border* also maintains the original proportions of the clip, but without adding a border. Instead, it crops the image as necessary.

- *Exact Fit* doesn't maintain the clip's original proportions; it forces the movie into the size you determine within the Basic tab.

What do you do if you want to use SWF but also want to accommodate those who don't have the plug-in installed? You don't want to lose them. . . . Enter the swfRedirect.action by Paul Vachier, which is available at: `www.adobe.com/products/golive/actions/main.html`. Create a page that doesn't have the SWF and put the swfRedirect.action in the Head of that page. Make that page the one people are sent to by default; send users to the SWF version of the page if the plug-in is detected. There's an alert message area where you can enter a message to the visitors that don't have the plug-in so they'll know they're missing something and can consider getting it for the future.

Adding a QuickTime Movie (or Sound)

QuickTime movies can either download from your own Web server or they can be sent from a QuickTime Streaming Server. When you create your QuickTime movie, you can create just one movie to be played, or you can create multiple versions and a reference movie (called a Master movie in Cleaner 5). If using the reference file method, you'll link to that ref file instead of linking directly linking to any one version. The reference file, in turn, points to the various versions and serves the appropriate version based on the user's QuickTime control panel.

QuickTime movie creation, in a professional program such as Cleaner 5, generates multiple movies, each optimized for a specific download speed. The actual movie version sent to the user is determined by the settings in a user's QuickTime control panel. This is the reason you may have several .mov content files.

When preparing your movie, be sure to generate versions for all speeds you'd like to accommodate, or at least for the slowest speed. If you don't create a file for 28.8/33.6 and a user arrives to your site at that speed (or with that speed mistakenly set in the QuickTime Control Panel), the user will not see your movie. Instead, the user will see the default movie—for example, a poster announcing that QuickTime 4 must be installed. Cleaner provides a premade default or enables you to choose your own default, and the Apple software (XLMtoRefMovie and MakeRefMovie) enables you to choose a default movie.

Determining which QuickTime files to upload and link to

The file you place on the page is determined by the serving method. QuickTime content files end with a .mov extension. You have one content file for each speed you optimize for. The pointer file ends with MSTR.mov if you're using Cleaner 5. If serving the content file progressively, place all of the files (content and reference) in your Files tab, and then link to the reference file. If you simply have one content movie and want to serve it from your site, link to that .mov file.

If the file(s) will stream, place the content files on the QuickTime Streaming Server, and then place the reference file in the Files tab and link to the reference movie file.

Files that will stream and therefore need to be send to the Streaming Server don't need to be copied into your files tab. They'll just waste space there. Instead, you can use the FTP Browser (Files ⇨ FTP Browser) to upload those files. See Chapter 27 to learn how to use the FTP Browser. The path to the streaming files is hard-coded into the reference file, so you'll need to prearrange this with your streaming host and movie creator. (If you're doing your own movie generation, you need to know where the files will be served from in order to complete the file creation process.)

 Note QuickTime movie creation in a professional program such as Cleaner 5, QuickTime Player Pro, or the GoLive QuickTime Editor (see Chapter 21) can generate multiple movies, each optimized for a specific download speed. The actual movie version sent to the user is determined by the settings in a user's QuickTime control panel.

After you know how you'll server your QuickTime audio or video, you can add the files to your Site Window and place the appropriate file on your page.

Linking to a QuickTime movie

At times you'll want users to view or hear your message independently of the browser (for example, when you're broadcasting live or they're listening/watching a long clip). By having the movie play within its own window via the QuickTime Movie Player, you enable your visitors to close your Web page or visit other pages in your Web site and still experience your content. One way to accomplish this is to place a Movie Poster on your page and have that poster call up the Movie Player.

Using a Movie Poster

Instead of having an entire movie download into your page, you can place a Poster — a still image from your movie — and have that poster call up the movie when clicked. To do this, you actually take a frame from the movie and then place that frame into the page by using the QuickTime plug-in icon and linking to it. Then set up the movie poster with a link to the actual movie. The movie's target can be a new browser window, the QuickTime Movie player, or the poster on the page.

If the target is that of the poster on the page, be sure to add 16 pixels of height to the poster to accommodate the movie's controller. Use a background color for the poster image. (The Color palette's color picker can help you pull a color from the movie poster to help blend the background.)

To make the movie poster, open your movie in the QuickTime Movie Player, move to the desired frame, and choose Edit ⇨ Copy. Then open a new Movie Player (File ⇨ New Player) and choose Edit ⇨ Paste. Save that new movie as a self-contained movie using File ⇨ Save and choosing Make Self Contained. Be sure to give the new movie the usual .mov extension. If there's a sound track (or other tracks), consider opening it the movie in the QuickTime Editor (see Chapter 21) and removing the sound, as it may sound odd. This also reduces the image size. Place this poster in the Files tab along with the movie. If you're using Cleaner 5, you can create a movie poster by checking the option for it and selecting the desired frame.

To deliver your file by linking, enter your text or place your button image as normal (see Chapter 10) and then link to the appropriate file in your Site Window. The file you link to is the same file you would link the plug-in to in order to embed the movie. To experience your movie, the user clicks a link.

Embedding a QuickTime movie in your page

Once you've determined which files to put in your Site Window and placed them there, you can add the file to your page. (If streaming, don't forget to upload those streamed files.)

Caution

If the QuickTime you're adding is a QuickTime VR (QTVR), and you happen to be placing it in a table cell, be aware of an odd bug that causes the movie to flash when the user's cursor inhabits the cell in the space alongside the movie. To avoid this flashing, put the QTVR movie in its own cell and set the cell to *exactly* the same size as the movie, with no spacing or padding around it. You can place your text in any adjoining cell.

You can place a QuickTime movie into your page by simply dragging it from your Files tab into the page or by placing the plug-in placeholder and then linking to it.

The results (as I write this) are the same except for the cache setting, which you can check or uncheck in the last tab of the Inspector.

To add a QuickTime movie (sound or video) to your page, follow these steps:

1. Place the movie into the desired position on your page in one of these ways:

   • Drag the QuickTime plug-in icon from the Basic tab of the Objects palette into place on your page.

   • Drag your movie from the Files tab directly into place on your page, and then use your linking method of choice (Point and Shoot or browse) to link from the File field of the Inspector to the movie within your Site Window.

   The file expands to its full size as GoLive reads the file type and sets the correct Mime information and the file's Medium, in the Inspector. If you have a plug-in installed that can play QuickTime (the QuickTime plug-in, for example), GoLive reports the Player. QuickTime uses the `<embed>` tag only; it doesn't need `<object>` controls, so the Class information area is grayed out.

Tip

If a player is reported in the Inspector, you can now make sure your file plays properly and that you have the correct file. You have four ways to check. In the bottom-left corner of the Plug-in Inspector, throughout all tabs, is a Play button that plays your movie in place while you're in Layout mode. The other way to check is to double-click the movie within the page. You can also switch to Preview or preview your page in the browser using the Preview button on the browser toolbar. Lastly, the Open Movie button opens your movie in the stand-alone QuickTime Movie Viewer. (You can use this to edit your movie, too. See Chapter 21 to learn about editing your QuickTime movies.)

2. *(Optional)* If you need to change the size or positioning of the movie, you can do so within the Basic and More tabs of the Inspector. (You can also size by dragging the handles of the plug-in icon in your page layout.) If no alignment is selected, the file is positioned at the top left by default. GoLive also enables you to specify a palette, which is a Windows setting from days gone by. The palette only effects very old computers, so it is highly unlikely your audience will be effected by it — default is recommended.

   To get an idea of how the width and height sizing works, set a background color and then experiment with the sizes. (Use a bright pink background or such so you can really tell what's happening.)

3. In the Name field of the Inspector, enter a name for your movie so you can reference it via JavaScript later, if needed. This adds the code `name="youname"` within the `<embed>` tag.

4. Provide a way for users to get the QuickTime plug-in. In case a user arrives at your page and doesn't have the QuickTime plug-in, the Page option tells the browser where to send the user to get it. The preconfigured SWF plug-in comes complete with this information, but for QuickTime you need to enter it by hand (or, if the URL is already in your External tab, Point and Shoot to it).

In the More tab, check Page, and then enter or link the URL of the QuickTime download page, as shown in Figure 20-6: **http://www.apple.com/quicktime/download/**.

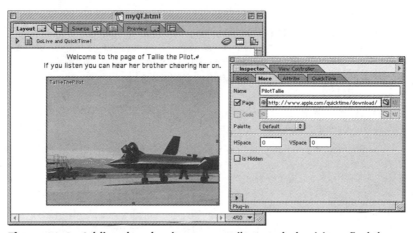

Figure 20-6: Adding the plug-ins page attribute to help visitors find the QuickTime plug-in if they don't have it

The code written into your `<embed>` tag is `pluginspage="http://www.apple.com/quicktime/download/"`.

With this attribute added, when the user arrives at the page, instead of being taken to the default plug-in directory, a new browser window opens directly to the Apple QuickTime download page.

Note

The next tab of the Plug-in Inspector is the Attributes (Attribs) tab. In this tab you could click New, enter the proper name for any attribute in the lower-left field, and then enter that attribute's value at the right. However, the next tab, labeled QuickTime, provides a visual interface for setting up some attributes. If you need to set up an attribute not accounted for in the visual interface, such as the field of view (fov) for a panorama, remember to enter it here. For a complete reference of attributes, check out `www.apple.com/quicktime`, and then follow the authoring link. The visual interface also removes unneeded attributes, but you can also select any attribute in the list and then click Delete to remove it.

5. *(Optional)* In the top part of the QuickTime tab, personalize the playback of your movies. Not all settings work for every movie, although in some cases the user's settings take precedent over what you enter. Here are the options:

- *Show Controller* places the standard QuickTime playback controls below the movie. When the controller is on, a dark strip appears at the bottom of the movie's area on your page while in Layout mode. The height of the movie area enlarges by 16 pixels to accommodate the controller (16 pixels is the standard size of the controller per the QuickTime specification).

- *Cache* enables the browser to cache as it downloads and plays. This makes replaying go faster.

- *Autoplay* tells the movie to play as soon as the page opens and the movie has enough information to do so. The exact amount of information that must be downloaded before the movie plays depends upon the way the movie was set up and is being served. (This setting overrides the user's QuickTime control panel.)

- *Loop* tells the movie to play over again when it reaches the end. (Helpful if your movie is a background sound.)

- *Palindrome* works in conjunction with the loop option. A normal loop gets to the end of the movie and begins again at the start. Palindrome causes the movie to play backwards once it reaches the end. Once back at the start, the cycle still begins again as with a regular loop.

- *Play Every Frame* forces the plug-in to play every single frame of the movie as it plays for the user. However, frame dropping is a way to compensate for erratic download speeds. Additionally, this attribute mutes your audio. Forcing each frame is not a good idea.

- *BGColor* provides a cohesive look to your movie in cases where you make the movie area larger than the actual video in order to add something extra to the movie controller or to have another video target the same space (keep reading). To add a background color, double-click the color swatch. This opens the Color palette. Then locate the desired color and click it. The newly selected color should appear in the color swatch.

- *Volume* enables you to preset a volume for the audio of your movie as a percentage of your user's volume. No sound is 0, and the loudest is 300 percent of the user's volume setting. (Although you can go up to 300 percent, chances are you'll cause distortion over 100 percent, not to mention dislike.) To set a volume, enter any number between 0 and 300. If you leave this blank, the volume is set at 100 percent. The user can then override this volume using the QuickTime controller (if you have it enabled) or the computer's volume control.

- *Scale* sets the scale of the movie within the given movie window size, a bit like zooming in. By default, the scale is 1, so the movie appears as normal. Entering 2 in the scale field causes the movie to appear twice as large, requiring a frame twice as large. Normally in QuickTime this automatically resizes the QuickTime movie window to accommodate the total movie image. However, GoLive does not do this, so you need to adjust the height and width manually. If you use a larger scale and don't resize the movie window, the controller does not show, as it is outside of the window's area.

6. *(Optional)* Use the Link and Target feature in the bottom part of the QuickTime tab to set the movie up to link elsewhere when the movie area (not the controller) is clicked. You can use this to achieve the following results:

   - Have your movie load and play in another browser window. (This is helpful when you don't want the movie taking up your entire page originally, but want a large area for it when it plays. For fastest initial page loading, use a Poster Movie in the original page. See the sidebar, Using a Movie Poster.)

   - Have the movie play within the QuickTime Movie Player. You can set the size of the movie within your page so the movie doesn't consume the page. When the user clicks the movie, the player opens to normal size, playing the movie in its original size. Even better, use a movie poster for the initial in-page image so only that small file needs to load into the page. Then have the movie poster call up the full-sized movie. This is a great way to prevent the user's RAM from being consumed within the browser. (See the sidebar, "Using a Movie Poster.")

   - Link to any Web page, to a JavaScript, or even to another movie. Check Link, and then enter the destination URL using your preferred linking method. (The code written when you check the URL is `href="./"`, where the "`./`" is replaced by the URL you enter in the URL field.)

7. Next, enter the target, as follows:

   - To have the movie appear in the QuickTime Movie Player, type in **quicktimeplayer**. This is the scenario depicted in Figure 20-7.

   - To have the movie appear in a new browser window (calling the user's default browser), choose Target ➪ New from the Target menu.

   - To have the URL appear in place of the movie on the page, type in **myself**. (You may have to tweak the size of the original movie space on the page to accommodate the new movie. Adding a background may help.)

   - If using a frameset, use the Target parameter in the normal manner, choosing a target frame.

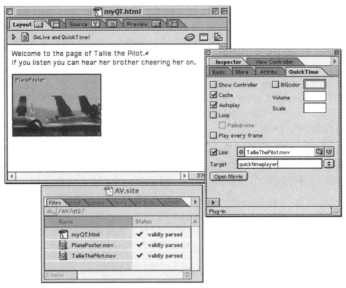

Figure 20-7: Setting up a Poster movie called PlanePoster that links to the full movie and opens it in the QuickTime Player

The Open Movie button opens your movie in the stand-alone QuickTime Movie Viewer, from which you can edit your movie. However, if you're working with multiple copies of the movie that have already been prepared for the Web, you'd have to prepare your edited movie all over again. To learn more about the QuickTime Movie Viewer, see Chapter 21.

Obtaining more information

To see QuickTime in action, you can view the live examples at `www.golivebible.com`. For more information about putting QuickTime on the Web, check the following sources:

✦ Visit `http://developer.apple.com/quicktime/index.html`.

✦ Read *QuickTime for the Web: A Hands-On Guide for Webmasters, Site Designers, and HTML Authors* by Steven W. Gulie, part of the QuickTime Developer Series by Apple Computer, Inc. (`http://developer.apple.com/techpubs/quicktime/qtdevdocs/QT4WebPage/qtdevseries.htm`).

✦ Read the Cleaner 5 manual.

Using RealMedia in Your Site

RealMedia (www.real.com/) is a system of delivering audio or video from a regular http Web server or a Real Streaming Server to a user's computer. You can serve RealMedia files on your site in two ways. One is to provide the entire file on a regular (HTTP) Web server; the other is to use a RealStreaming Server and stream your content. (A free version of this server exists for up to 25 streams. You can purchase RealServer software to run more concurrent streams.) The streaming options for RealMedia give you control over whether your users can record or download your steamed files. You set these options up in your content creation program when you prepare the file for the Web. To prepare your files to stream, you tell the file creation software where the streamed file will reside, and that path is written into the ram file — the file you'll link to from your Web page. Upon creation of the RealMedia file, you end up with at least two files. One is the actual content file, which will reside on the server. It will end with .rm (for RealMedia) or .ra (for RealAudio). You'll have one for each modem speed you're accommodating. You can use the FTP Browser (File ⇨ FTP Browser, see Chapter 27) to upload that file directly to the streaming server. The other file, ending with .ram (if steaming) or .rpm (if progressively downloading), is a pointer file (just text) that contains only the path to the actual content files. This is the file you'll place in your Files tab and link to from your page. To deliver a RealMedia file to your users, you can create a basic link that the user clicks, or you can embed the file into your page and use the preconfigured Real plug-in. Both methods are covered in this section.

When you create your RealMedia file using Cleaner 5 or RealProducer, you determine whether the file will download progressively or be streamed. You also determine which modem speeds you'll deliver. You can accommodate up to six audio and video speeds. (You'll need RealProducer Plus or Cleaner 5 to create all six speeds. With RealProducer Basic, which is free, you can choose two speeds.) The accommodations for these speeds are encoded into one content file.

Linking to call up a RealMedia file

At times you'll want users to view or hear your message independently of the browser — for example, when you're broadcasting live or they're listening/watching a long clip. By linking to your file and having it play within the RealPlayer window, you enable your visitors to close your Web page or visit other pages in your Web site and still experience your content. You can use the link technique whether you're serving the file from your regular Web server or streaming it from a RealServer.

Three scenarios exist for which you can provide a link, as follows:

✦ To have the user download the file, you link to the actual content (.rm) file. If you have two files (optimized for two different speeds), you will have two links. Your content files (.rm) go into the Files tab and upload to your regular Web server along with the rest of your site.

✦ To have the file play progressively (play but not actually download), you create a .ram file that points to the content files (.rm) on your Web server. You place both your content files and your .ram file in the Files tab and upload them all to your Web server, along with the rest of your site. In this case the ram file is `http://yourdomain/folderifany/movieorfilename.rpm`. The name doesn't matter as long as the link is valid and the ram file calls for the correct movie.

✦ To have the file stream, you create a .ram file that points to the content files (.rm). You place the .ram file into the Site Window, and then you place the content files on the RealServer. (Because these files don't need to reside on your regular Web server, they don't need to be in the Site Window. Instead, use the FTP browser, covered in Chapter 27, to upload to the RealServer.). Then you link to the ram file. The one-line content of the ram file in this case is `rtsp://yoursrealserverraddress/folderifany/movieorfilename.ram`. The name doesn't matter as long as the link is valid and the ram file calls for the correct movie.

Follow these steps to deliver your file via a link:

1. Enter your text or place your button image as normal (see Chapter 10).

2. Link to the appropriate file in the Files tab, depending on which method of delivery you're using. Here are the options:

   • To have the user download the file, link to the .rm file.

   • To serve the file progressively, link to the .ram file.

   • To stream the content file, link to the .ram file.

On the Mac, sometimes links don't launch RealPlayer, but instead download a RealMedia pointer file to the user's desktop or download folder. The RealNetworks Web site (`www.realnetworks.com`) discusses this in an article about configuring Web browsers.

Embedding RealMedia in a page

The advantage of using GoLive's Real plug-in to embed a file on your page is that it puts your video image directly on your page, as opposed to having it appear within the independent Player.

To place the RealMedia file in place within your page, you use the Real Plug-in icon. Dragging the file directly onto your page is not an option, as you'd be dragging a link on to the page, rather than a physical file. That's because you don't actually place the RealMedia on your page, but use a pointer to lead the way to the actual media file.

To display RealMedia in your page, follow these steps:

1. Place the .ram or .rpm file in the Files tab of the Site Window, depending on whether you're serving your files from the Real Streaming Server or serving progressively from your regular Web server, respectively.

2. Drag the Real plug-in icon from the Basic tab of the Objects palette into place on your page. If you're placing video or having the player show, place the placeholder exactly where you want the player to appear. If you're placing audio only and not providing any control, place the file close to the top of the page so it will begin to load as soon as possible. GoLive's Real icon automatically sets up the Mime type: audio/x-pn-realaudio-plugin.

3. With the Real plug-in placeholder selected on the page, link from the File field of the Plug-in Inspector to the .ram or .rpm file in the Files tab.

Tip

If a player is reported in the Inspector, you can now test the file. You have three ways to check. In the bottom-left corner of the Plug-in Inspector, throughout all tabs, is a Play button that plays your movie in place while you're in Layout mode. The other way to check is to double-click the movie within the page. You can also switch to Preview, or preview your page in the browser using the button on the toolbar.

4. *(Optional)* Change the alignment of the player within the Basic tab. The default is top left if none is selected. To add padding outside of your player area or bring the palette to the foreground instead of the default, background, use the More tab.

   Changing the height and width of the placeholder doesn't have an effect on the playback image; it just enlarges the console's buttons. When the image plays, the playback window grows to accommodate the image. (This makes it very hard to design around.)

5. Name this occurrence of your multimedia file using the Name field of the Inspector. This enables you to reference it via JavaScript later, if needed. This adds the code name="youname" within the <embed> tag.

6. Use the Page option to provide a way for users to get the Real plug-in if they don't have it. In the More tab, check Page, and then type in (or use an External link to) **http://www.real.com/**. This adds the HTML code pluginspage="http://www.real.com/" into the <embed> tag. When the user arrives at the page, instead of being taken to the default plug-in directory, a new browser window opens directly to the RealNetworks download page.

Note

You can skip the Attributes (Attribs) tab of the Plug-in Inspector, using the customized Real tab instead. Then, if the visual interface didn't provide something that you want, use the Attributes tab to add it by clicking New and hand-entering the parameter and value. You can also use this list to review attributes. To delete any attribute in the list, select it and then click Delete to remove it.

7. *(Optional)* In the Real tab, shown in Figure 20-8, personalize the playback of your movies, as follows:

   • *Autostart* tells the movie to play as soon as the page opens and the movie has enough information to do so. Playback won't be immediate, though, as some data needs to download before the movie (or sound) can play.

   • *No Labels* turns off display of information such as title, author, and copyright within the playback window.

Figure 20-8: The Real tab of the Plug-in Inspector enables you to set Real-specific controls.

8. *(Optional)* Choose your RealPlayer's playback control panel from the *Controls* menu in the Real tab of the Inspector. If you prefer not to provide the standard RealPlayer control panel — Play, Pause, Stop, Fast Forward, Rewind, and Volume — you can choose any one specific control. For example, if your movie is set to autoplay, you can provide just the Play button, which also enables users to pause. You can also build your own custom control panel. To learn how to do this, see the next section.

Building a custom control panel

When providing playback controls, you have the option to build your own custom controller by incorporating any of the possible controls available in the Real tab of the Real Inspector. For example, you can provide only the Play/Pause button and a volume control. To do this, embed your file as normal, making sure you name your file in the More tab of the Real Inspector. Then switch to the Real tab and proceed as follows:

1. If your file is visual, choose Image Window as the control. If it is audio-only, choose any attribute.

2. To add the next control panel element, place another Real icon into the desired position on your page, but don't link it to a source file because this icon will not provide media content.

3. In the More tab, enter the same name that you gave the previous Real icon to make it part of the same group.

4. In the Real tab, choose the desired control panel element from the Controls pop-up menu. These are the choices you have for custom controls:

- *Play Button* is a Play/Pause button.
- *Play Only Button* is a Play button.
- *Mute Control* is a Mute button.
- *Mute Volume* is a mute button and volume slider.
- *Position Slider* is a clip position slider.
- *Clip Information* shows information about the video or audio.
- *Home Control* is the Real logo.
- *Info Volume* shows presentation information and volume controls.
- *Info Panel* shows information about the presentation.
- *Status Bar* tells the viewer about the transmission.
- *Status Field* shows the viewer information normally displayed in the browser's status bar. (It still shows there whether this field shows or not.)
- *Position Field* shows the viewer where the presentation is in relation to the entire presentation.

Note   When you choose a control panel element, it should be automatically sized to its optimal viewing size. However, GoLive fails to do this properly, so your control button is rendered at the default size of 100×100 pixels (the size the Real icon is preset to). To remedy that, you need to open the Source Code window and manually edit the sizes. Real lists the recommended sizes at `www.realnetworks.com/devzone/documentation`.

5. Keep the Console setting at Default for all parts of your custom panel: the source file and the control elements. The other Console settings are for highly advanced control. They enable you to do things such as having two different videos play back within the same single window. This advanced customization is beyond the scope of this book, so check the RealNetworks Web site to learn what you need to do in order to build advanced custom controls like that.

Windows Media

GoLive doesn't provide a preprogrammed plug-in for Windows Media, so to place audio or video in Windows Media format, use the generic plug-in icon. In theory you can stream Windows Media from the Windows Streaming Server, called NetShow Server. But frankly, streaming Windows media provides little benefit. Even streamed, it only has one audio track, so no matter what the user's connection, everyone receives the same exact audio. While it does contain two video tracks, the track is selected upon the initial call to the file and not switched during download. The only difference between a file you prepare to stream and one you serve from your regular server is the second video track. (You *can* serve a dual video file, but the second track only adds to the file size.)

Setting up Windows Media is basically the same as setting up QuickTime or RealMedia; you either link to the .asf (content) or the .asx (pointer) file.

Embedding Other Media File Types in Your Page

GoLive can accommodate embedding any media type in your page via its Generic plug-in. In some cases GoLive will be great at helping you out, while in other cases you're on your own.

You have two ways to embed a file to your page. You can drag the file directly into place on your page or you can place the Generic plug-in icon first and then link it. Each has the same effect when dealing with file types other than SWF (which contains more information in the placeholder than can be read from an SWF file).

The placeholder method can be handy if you know you need a lot space on the page for a graphic or a sound player, but the sound or video is not available to you yet. In that case, use the placeholder and leave it unassociated with any file for now, and then return to this point after the file is available and in your Files tab. Meanwhile, bear in mind that this is the cause of the bug you'll see on this page.

To embed a sound or video file in your page, follow these steps:

1. If you have the multimedia file, place the file in the Files tab of the Site Window so GoLive can manage it. If not, skip this step and add the file later.

2. Do one of the following:

   • If you have your multimedia file, drag it into place on your page to have the file appear immediately on the page. If GoLive recognizes the file type, it sets the correct file information in the Inspector.

- Drag the Generic plug-in icon from the Objects palette's Basic tab into place on your page. Then use your preferred linking method to link from the URL area of what is now the Plug-in Inspector to the sound or video file. (After you link a file, the question-mark icon at the top right goes away.)

In layout mode the plug-in icon takes up visible space on your page, pushing your other elements aside, but if you are using a sound-only file and making it invisible, the plug-in really has no effect on page layout. Click the Preview tab of the Site Window to see the actual flow of objects on the page, or to preview it in your browser.

3. If GoLive doesn't recognize the file's Mime type automatically, check Mime, and then use the pop-up menu to select the appropriate Mime type for your audio file. (See Figure 20-9.) You can choose from about 11 audio file types and several video types, as well as other Mime types, too.

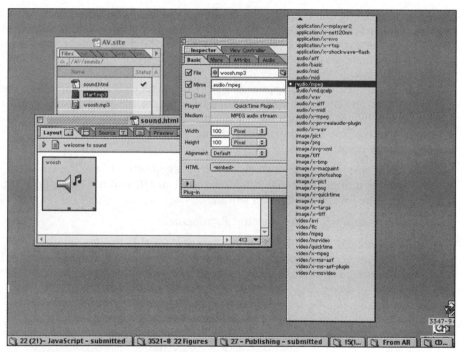

Figure 20-9: Choosing a Mime type

After you choose a Mime type, GoLive reports a Player and Medium, as follows:

- The Player is the name of whatever player, if any, that is installed on your hard drive and capable of playing that sound type for you. (It's mapped in Preferences under Plug-ins, so you can change it.) If no appropriate player is available on your computer, it will say, "none available."

If you don't have an appropriate player installed, you won't be able to test the sound file, but this doesn't effect the sound's usability for other users on the Web. Those user's browsers will be looking on their respective hard drives for a viable player.

- The Medium is the type of file that the browser will expect your sound to be.

If a player is identified, you can test that your file plays properly and that you have the correct file. You can click the Play button at the bottom of each tab of the Plug-in Inspector to play your file in Layout mode. You can double-click the file within the page, or you can switch to Preview. Or, preview your page in the browser using the button on the toolbar.

Note A full discussion of Mime types is beyond the scope of this book. To learn about them you can check out HotWired's WebMonkey Audio Mime Types. Go to `http://hotwired.lycos.com/webmonkey` and choose the multimedia link.

Note Wondering about the Class attribute? It goes along with the `<object>` tag to set up ActiveX. Should you choose to change the HTML settings to accommodate ActiveX, you'll need to know the Class of the object and enter it here (unless it sets automatically for you, as it may in Windows).

4. If the file does not appear at its proper size, or if for some reason you'd like to adjust the file's size, affecting its appearance on the page, enter the width and height to match that of the prepared image file or desired sound controller. (You can also size by dragging the handles of the plug-in icon in your page layout.)

   The size you set here changes the space allotted to the file when on your page; it doesn't change the file's actual size. If you're setting up a sound that will be invisible, skip this setting

5. *(Optional)* Choose a specific alignment.

6. *(Optional)* Set the HTML tag to be used for this file. By default a plug-in writes the `<embed>` tag into the page's source code, telling the browser to display the media in place on the page and to call up the plug-in.

   The addition of the `<object>` tag enables you to provide ActiveX controls for Windows users. If you know about the object settings for the file type you're adding and want to add an ActiveX controller, choose <object> & <embed>, and then set up the desired parameters.

7. Switch to the More tab of the Plug-in Inspector, and then enter a name for your media file in case you want to call it via JavaScript later on.

8. In case a user arrives at your page and doesn't have the necessary plug-in, you can use the Page option (called the `pluginspage` attribute) to tell the browser where to send the user to download it. Visit the plug-in's Web site

and locate a page that contains installation instructions. Then copy the URL and paste it into the Page field. (Or add the URL to the Externals tab and link to it.) The HTML this option writes is `pluginspage="url.com/thepage"`.

Note

If you're using one of the more common file types (see the sidebar, "How Does GoLive Know Mime Types?"), chances are your browser has a plug-in mapped for that file type and you won't need to worry about having users obtain a plug-in. The only time you need this is if you're using a newer or unique file type that isn't pre-configured (yet) by GoLive and needs a specific plug-in.

9. *(Optional per Step 7)* The Code option is only available when you use the <object> & <embed> tag. You'll need to consult the ActiveX protocols for an explanation about this parameter.

10. *(Optional)* The Palette setting pop-up dates back to the days of now ancient and out-of-use PCs, and it is highly unlikely your audience will be effected by it. The default is background and is all you need.

11. If your file will be visible to the user, you can add a padding space at the top and bottom and/or each side by entering the amount of space, in pixels. There's a horizontal and a vertical space control.

12. If it is sound you are adding, and the sound will play automatically and doesn't need controls, you can hide the sound. To do so, check Is Hidden.

13. If you are aware of specific attributes you need or want to set up, switch to the Attributes (Attribs) tab. For each attribute you wish to enter, click New, enter the proper name for any attribute in the lower-left field, and then enter that attribute's value at the right.

Attributes tend to be specific to each file type, so it is not possible to explain each attribute and its implications here in detail. However, the following sections provide a basic understanding of your options.

Adding audio attributes

If the file you're embedding into your page is an audio Mime type, the Plug-in Inspector provides another tab for you. After setting up the basic settings within the first two tabs of the Plug-in Inspector, turn to the Audio tab to set up audio-specific attributes. These settings enable you to choose the controls a user sees and can use.

As you choose settings in the Audio tab, they're reflected in the Attrib tab. While you can enter settings directly in the Attrib tab, it is easier to use the Audio tab. However, you might want to view this tab to see a summary of your settings.

How Does GoLive Know Mime Types?

GoLive comes preconfigured knowing each of the basic file types, their possible extensions, and the Mime types associated with them. Before you place any plug-ins in the GoLive folder's Plug-ins folder, if you pop any audio or video file on your page, you can see the choices of Mime types listed in the Mime menu within the Inspector. After you add your own plug-ins and restart GoLive, you can see the additions reflected in the Mime menu.

In addition to adding plug-ins to teach GoLive about a Mime type, you can enter new ones by hand. To do this, you need to know the file type information and then you enter it in GoLive's main Preferences window. See "Choosing Plug-in Preferences" and "Mapping a new extension or Mime type" later in this chapter.

Setting visibility

You can set your sound to be visible — that is, have a visible player — or to be invisible. All files are visible by default. To make your player invisible, switch back to the More tab of the Plug-in Inspector and check Is Hidden.

If you're using a sound that plays automatically on your page, consider keeping the sound visible and choosing just the stop button for its control so users can turn off the sound in case it's inconvenient to them. Use the width and height settings to make the button fit your page nicely.

Setting controls

If your sound's controller is visible, you can choose to use the standard controller from the Controls pop-up menu, choose any one specific control such as pause, or you can, in theory, invent your own control panel using the Is Mastersound option. However, the Inspector interface for creating custom controls is buggy to say the least. If you really want to create a custom control panel, I recommend that you look into the HTML code required for this feature and then use the Inspector in combination with hand-coding to set it up.

Timing

The timing attributes set the playback time and duration of play. The options are as follows:

✦ **Autostart,** enabled by default, tells the sound to play automatically as soon as it loads. If you want the user to control the playback or you will be incorporating playback into a timeline, uncheck Autostart.

✦ **Loop** enables you to have the sound play more than once. If you prefer the sound to not go on indefinitely, enter the number of times you'd like the sound to play.

✦ **Starttime** causes the sound begin a specific period of time after the sound loads into the browser. Enter the start time in minutes and seconds, as depicted. For example, 01:03 for one minute and three seconds in.

✦ **Stoptime** tells the browser how long after loading the sound to stop playing it. Like with starttime, enter the time in the minutes:seconds format.

✦ **Volume** presets a volume for your audio. Zero (0) is no sound, while 100 is the full volume of the user's speaker. Enter any number between 0 and 100.

Remember that audio and video on the Web are an inexact science, so be sure to test your page in as many browsers and on as many platforms as possible.

Using a Scalable Vector Graphic

Scalable Vector Graphic (SVG) is a promising new file format that, among other things, enables graphics to scale (hence the name) when the user resizes a browser window. While you might think of something called a Scalable Vector Graphic as a graphic, an SVG file has more in common with a multimedia file than GIF, JPG, or PNG. To begin with, it requires a plug-in of sorts — an SVG player to be precise. For another, it's included on a page via the `<embed>` tag, not a regular link like a graphic file. And lastly, SVG files can include interactive elements such as JavaScriptable commands, and provide for animation and zooming, too.

Note If you're interested now and wondering how you can create an SVG, look no further than Adobe Illustrator 9.0. Illustrator is truly on the cutting edge with this technology.

Although promising, SVG has several downsides at this time. To begin with, as with any new format, it does not yet enjoy built-in support within any browser; users need to download and install a viewer into their browser plug-ins folders to see the graphic. (You need a special viewer to see and use it in GoLive, too. See the note that follows.) Next is the same old issue of Internet Explorer not enabling JavaScript access to any plug-in on the Mac. So Mac users with Internet Explorer cannot experience any of the cool SVG interactivity. (So much for a fair-sized part of your viewership, once again thanks to Internet Explorer's programming.) Mac Internet Explorer users can see the animation in the file, but that's a small part of the interactivity. Additionally, both Netscape and Internet Explorer need extra RAM to use SVG and don't handle it well if a sufficient amount isn't allocated on the Mac.

Note In order for GoLive to recognize an SVG file, it needs the SVG Viewer. Adobe wrote an SVG Viewer and installs it into GoLive's Plug-ins folder automatically when you install GoLive. It's the only plug-in GoLive installs.

SVGs are placed on the page much like any other graphic, but don't appear in the page layout the way other graphics do. In order to see the graphic itself, you have to preview it.

To use an SVG graphic on your page, follow these steps:

1. Drag an uncompressed SVG graphic file from the Files tab into place on your page. (Compressed SVG files still require an uncompressed version, which defeats the purpose of compression.)

   A generic SVG placeholder appears in this place on the page, but rather than being the usual default placeholder size, it is the size of your actual graphic, as shown in Figure 20-10.

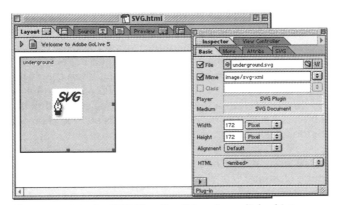

Figure 20-10: An SVG file after it has been linked into a page

2. To see what the graphic looks like for page-design purposes, click the Preview button (the forward arrow play symbol) at the lower-left corner of the Plug-in Inspector. (Normally, this preview enables you to play a QuickTime movie, but the first frame of the movie appears on the page. Only with SVG do you see nothing until this preview is on.)

3. *(Optional)* If you're using a compressed version of your SVG file on your page, turn to the SVG tab of the Plug-in Inspector and check the option for using a Compressed SVG. Believe it or not, this links the plug-in to the compressed file via the uncompressed file — and both files (uncompressed and compressed) have to reside together in your Files tab and on the server. That sort of defeats the purpose of compressing a file, doesn't it?

That's it. Everything else is set up for you. If you'd like to preview your full page in Preview mode, you can do so. The SVG file is fully visible there. However, to try the JavaScript interactivity, you need to preview the page in a browser. (This is always the case with JavaScript and GoLive.)

Note   To learn more about SVG, read Adobe's ReadMeSVGViewer.html file, installed into the Plug-ins folder of the GoLive folder during the default GoLive installation.

Because SVG is very new and not in common use, it's exciting to use it, but you should also accommodate users who don't have the reader yet. The SVG Redirect Action (by Paul Vachier) is just what you need. Create an alternate page that doesn't use an SVG and send users to that page as the normal link. In the Head of that page, add this action, which transports viewers to the SVG-charged page if the viewer is detected. You can also add a message to let viewers know about the SVG. You can find this plug-in at www.adobe.com/products/golive/actions/main.html.

Choosing Plug-in Preferences

You can use GoLive's Preferences to set up specific media types to work with the various plug-ins you have for GoLive.

The way a browser knows which plug-in to call upon is by the Mime type and class mappings you tell GoLive to write into your page's HTML. The user's browser has a list of every common Mime type and knows which plug-in it should call upon when it sees that Mime type. GoLive too has such a list, so it provides automatic detection of the Mime type and class when you place your media on a page. That list is visible to you, as well as editable by you. You can find it within GoLive's general preferences window.

Tip   Even if you're not interested in changing GoLive's Plug-in mappings or adding more by hand, I recommend taking a look at these preferences to get a good idea of what plug-ins and Mime are about.

You can do two things in the Plug-ins Preferences, as follows:

✦ You can change the player that a plug-in uses within GoLive. For example, if you have both Netscape's LiveAudio and QuickTime installed in GoLive's plug-ins and you want the LiveAudio player instead of QuickTime, you can change it here.

✦ You can tell GoLive to recognize a certain extension and associate it with a specific Mime type, even if you don't have that plug-in handy to install.

Changing a player

Follow these steps to change the player that a plug-in uses within GoLive:

1. Choose Edit ➪ Preferences and then select the Plug-ins icon.

2. Scroll through the list and click once on the Mime type/Plugin/Extension you want to reassociate.

3. From the Plugin pop-up menu, choose the new plug-in, as in Figure 20-11.

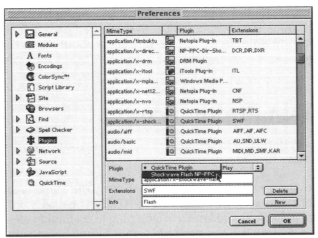

Figure 20-11: Changing the Shockwave Flash setting so the Flash plug-in handles SWF files in GoLive instead of QuickTime

4. *(Optional)* By default a plug-in is set to play when a file is previewed. If you prefer it not to play, choose Don't Play. (This appears to have an effect on the Mac but not Windows.)

If you know you want GoLive to use a specific player and you know that player is capable, but it's not listed in the pop-up menu, you probably don't have that plug-in installed. All eligible players that are installed appear in this menu for any given file type. Locate a copy of the desired plug-in and drop it into the Plug-in folder in GoLive's folder, and then restart GoLive and return to Preferences to make your selection.

Mapping a new extension or Mime type

The best and easiest way to tell GoLive about a new plug-in file type and to map that file type is by copying that file type's plug-in into the GoLive Plug-ins folder. When you do this, GoLive reads the new plug-in upon its next startup and knows all about the file type. Additionally, if the plug-in is a player, GoLive knows to use that player for your preview whenever you place a file of that type on your page. However, you may not always have access to a plug-in. There may be a time when you get word of a file type (extension) and just need to tell GoLive to choose the correct Mime when it sees that extension.

Note   Mime stands for Multipurpose Internet Mail Extension. It's a method by which files are identified on the Internet. Many Mime types exist, only some of which are for audio and video.

To set up a file extension to write a Mime type and associate a plug-in, follow these steps:

1. Choose Edit ➪ Preferences, and then select the Plug-ins icon.

2. Click New. The words type/subtype appear in the Mime type field as the format you need to follow.

3. In the Mime Type field, complete the information that will appear in the Mime type column. Type or paste the media file type (application, audio, or video), followed by a slash and the Mime type. Use the existing listings as a model.

   If a plug-in that can handle your newly entered Mime type is present in the plug-ins folder, GoLive automatically chooses it for you and it appears in the Plugin menu. You can change it if you'd like.

4. Enter the associated extension or extensions in the Extensions field so that GoLive will know to use your new Mime type when it encounters a file with this ending.

5. Enter any helpful information here. By looking at some of the prewritten file types, you can see that this is usually where details about the originator of the file type are recorded for your information. Perhaps you want to use this area to note your source, in case you question it or need to verify it later.

Remember, entering this information here makes it possible for you to select a Mime type in order to associate it with a file type. But that does not enable GoLive to play that file as a preview for you. For that you need the file type's actual player—which means you need to install its plug-in.

Using the Object Plug-in

The Object plug-in's full identity is W3CObject Control. It was originally developed specifically to enable ActiveX controls to work. However, along the way, the W3C officially adopted it and defined it as a generic element, giving it a lot of variations and parameters. The result seems to be general confusion as to how to use it and limited functionally compared to what they planned for it. Additionally, as it is Windows only and developed by Microsoft, it is not well supported in Netscape. So, as it stands now, for the most part it remains as a controller for providing ActiveX controls for Windows users using Internet Explorer. (Because it excludes all non-Windows users as well as Netscape-using Windows users, it's not a good idea to count on it for the Web; it can be useful within an intranet, however, if your intranet is limited to Windows and Internet Explorer.) Explaining the details of the Object's plug-in set-up is beyond the scope of this book. This section provides the basics only.

Note The instructions here are for GoLive for Windows only. Because the Mac does not use ActiveX, you cannot follow these steps; no Select button exists for you to choose your object, as in Step 2. However, if you take over a page that has the object in it, you can set or adjust the properties within the Inspector.

To add a W3CObject to your page, follow these steps:

1. Drag the Object placeholder into place on your page.

2. Select the Object's codebase by linking from the Base field.

3. Name the object.

4. Click Select to open the Insert Object window.

5. Choose from Create New, Create from File, or Create Control. Because you're most likely using GoLive to place your media files and using this to add a control, you will most likely choose Create Control.

6. In the Object Type list, select from the list of available controls, as in Figure 20-12, and then click OK.

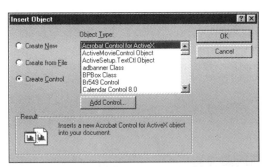

Figure 20-12: Choosing an ActiveX control

Note   You can choose objects such as a calendar that actually put a real, active calendar on your page for users to reference.

7. To resize the object with live feedback, press Control while you drag any corner handle. (You can also enter the dimensions in the Inspector, but you won't see the effect until the size settings are entered.)

8. *(Optional)* Use the other settings in the Inspector to set the horizontal and vertical space or set up a border. See Chapter 10 for more on these options.

9. In the Properties tab of the Inspector, set up the behavior of the control. — or just take a look at what's there in case you like the default configuration. Here are your options:

   • Choose a property from the list.

   • If the controller you chose has its own dialog boxes to help you select properties, use them.

   • In the value field for that property, now available at the bottom of the Inspector, enter the desired value and then press Enter to set it.

   • To add an entirely new value, click the New button. Then add both the Property name and the value in their respective fields at the bottom of the Inspector.

User-Triggered Sounds

Sound can provide background for you page, playing as soon as the page loads. However, it is more effective to use sound to add punch to your page, having it play within a timeframe or as the result of a user action.

One of the most frequently requested effects is to have a sound play as the result of a user's action. For example, you might want to have the sound of a camera shutter clicking when visitors click a camera image on your page. The possibilities are endless when you have this technology and an imagination. The problem is browser support.

Can it be done? Yes, via JavaScript that uses Java as well. Can all browsers (or just the big two) accommodate it? No. Unfortunately, Internet Explorer for the Mac cannot play sound on demand due to its programming.

The Netscape browsers have all supported JavaScript audio playback on all platforms since Version 3, when Netscape introduced its LiveAudio plug-in (installed by default as part of their browsers). But with Internet Explorer, support is not consistent. The Mac simply does not have a mechanism for JavaScript triggers. (No sound effect will work on any version 2.*x* browser on any platform.)

Because you cannot count on your user-triggered sound to be heard by everyone, it's a good idea to use such sounds as accents and not as an essential part of your site's message.

Using GoLive Actions to Trigger Sounds

GoLive includes two sound Actions: Play Sound and Stop Sound. These Actions, which are preprogrammed JavaScripts, work on sounds that you embed in your page. The safest sound file type to use for this is WAV. Unfortunately QuickTime (at least as of Version 4) does not have the Java hooks needed to take the play command.

To have a sound play upon a click or rollover, follow these steps:

1. Place the Generic plug-in at the top of your page so the sound will begin to load immediately as the page downloads.

2. Link the sound and set it up as explained under the section "Embedding Other Media File Types in Your Page" earlier in this chapter, and as follows:

   • Be certain to name the sound or it will not be available to call from the Action (or from any JavaScript).

   • Check Is Hidden so the sound's player will not be visible.

3. Add the text or graphic that will trigger the link.

4. Set up the link trigger as explained in Chapter 18 in the "Creating User-triggered Actions" section.

5. Choose Multimedia ➪ Play Sound from the Action menu, and then choose the sound by name from the pop-up menu in the lower part of the Actions palette.

OUTactions provides a free, fuller-functioning alternative to Play Sound, called SoundTools, that is on this book's CD-ROM in the GoLive Stuff folder. It is also available from www.out.to/actions.

Beatnik

Beatnik (www.beatnik.com) is the newest kid on the audio block. Although not at all part of the GoLive interface, it simply has to be mentioned in any discussion of user-triggered sounds. Beatnik is sort of a midi-style application in that it works with preinstalled small sound samples or, at most, by downloading a small set of sounds and sequences. So, instead of requiring actual entire music files, users have the result of hearing music immediately. There's no player to launch and no streaming and buffering. Instead, the sound samples are compiled and played on the fly in the browser, using JavaScript. It enables you to put sound behind your images so sound plays on rollover. (They call this Sonified Links and Navigation.) Beatnik also lets you provide music when the user clicks (called QuickClips) or background sound or music (called Ambient Sound). These sounds can play when the page loads or via a user-triggered action.

The catch? Visitors to your site have to download and install the Beatnik Player. (And, as I write this book, a player for Internet Explorer for the Mac is still a promise we await.) So again, bear in mind that some of your audience may not experience your effects, and don't rely heavily on them.

You can use Beatnik within minutes by using the predesigned sounds that come with it. Of course, you can create your own sound effects, too. The Beatnik Web site provides a clear series of tutorials and code you can copy and paste. But the best news is that free Beatnik Actions exist that have been created just for GoLive. John May of GoLiveHQ led the way with that. You can learn all about the actions and download them from GoLiveHQ (www.golivehq.com) by following the Software link. (With GoLive's new capability to enable users to create their own menus and Objects palette tabs, who knows what will be available to you by the time you read this? Check www.golivehq.com, www.beaknik.com, or www.golivebible.com for news on this front.)

✦   ✦   ✦

Creating QuickTime Movies in GoLive

In Chapter 20, I showed you how to add a QuickTime movie to your page. This chapter takes you deeper into the abilities of QuickTime and GoLive — showing you GoLive's Quick-Time Editor. With it, you can mix and match a wide variety of video and audio with text, clickable or automatic hyperlinks, and more to create event-filled QuickTime movies that can add to your site's presentation.

What, exactly can the QuickTime Editor handle and do? Pretty much everything QuickTime is capable of doing. On the video front, in addition to the various video formats, it handles still images, .swf files, MPEG files, streaming video, and more. On the audio front, it handles every common and popular format. It enables you to add text for things like subtitles, and even have that text trigger other media events upon rollover. (Multilingual subtitles, anyone?) Then there's the linking it can do so your movie can call up Web sites automatically, or if a user chooses to click. Truth is, there's more, but you'll have to read (or at least skim) this chapter to learn about it.

Although a part of GoLive, the QuickTime Editor pretty much stands on its own. You can create your QuickTime movie without opening a Site Window, and without gathering materials into a Site Window. Because all of what you do to your movie is saved within the QuickTime Editor, and not as a typical part of your GoLive site, you don't add the movie's elements-to-be into the Site Window. Instead, as you add tracks to your movie, the QuickTime Editor opens an Open dialog box you use to locate and import the file into the movie container itself.

Introducing QuickTime Movies

With GoLive, you can create a new QuickTime movie by creating a new QuickTime container and placing any existing video, audio, and so on into it, or you can edit an existing QuickTime movie to add any of the various items QuickTime supports. The GoLive QuickTime Editor is a full-featured QuickTime Editor, written fully to the QuickTime API (application programming interface) This means that nearly anything QuickTime supports can be done in this editor. Then, after you've finished creating your QuickTime masterpiece, you just pop it into your Web page the same way you add any other QuickTime movie.

Note   QuickTime must be installed on your computer to use the QuickTime Editor. If you don't already have it installed, use your GoLive CD-ROM to install it. The installation includes an easy-to-use Update application. You can run that Updater anytime to have Apple check for missing files over the Web. The Updater will also notify you if Apple has released a newer version of QuickTime than the one on your GoLive CD-ROM.

Whether you begin by opening an existing movie or creating a new blank one, your movie opens in the *Movie Viewer*. The QuickTime movie viewer is, in one tab, a QuickTime Player. In the other, it is a layout tool.

Tip   To help you see your movie clearly, you can magnify the window by choosing Movie ⇨ View Size, and then a size. This does not change the resolution of the movie — it just enlarges the window.

While you're working in the movie viewer, the Inspector acts as the QuickTime Inspector. From that window, you open the movie's TimeLine window — where you add the various tracks that comprise your movie. The blank tracks are, of course, added by dragging their icons from the Objects palette. There's an entire tab dedicated to QuickTime. As you work with a track, the Inspector provides a specific Track Inspector appropriate for that type of track. You can see some of these tools in use in Figure 21-1.

As you work in your movie's timeline, you can watch the resulting movie play in the movie viewer. When you step through your timeline frame by frame, each frame displays here.

The Movie Editor toolbar and Movie menu provide the rest of your tools. The menu provides things like window sizing, text options, and exporting. The toolbar is where you open the TimeLine Editor window; position, skew, or rotate a track of your movie; send a layer of it backward or forward; and more.

Figure 21-1: The QuickTime Editor tools, as seen in Windows

Note

Some types of tracks are only recognized starting with the QuickTime 3 plug-in (for example, MP3 and audio compressed using QDesign2, SWF, SML, or streams). However, a user's system has to be fairly outdated to be running a version older than that. QuickTime 4 is the current version as of this writing. The plug-in is available for free and is widely distributed as well as downloadable from Apple's Web site.

Getting Video In

The QuickTime Editor is a tool for editing movies, not a tool for capturing video from an external source. That calls for another type of dedicated software.

If you're on a Mac and have FireWire, you can use iMovie. If you're on a Mac without FireWire, you can use the Apple Video Player that's automatically installed on each Mac or a commercial software product such as Adobe Premiere.

On Windows, you can use Edit DV Unplugged, from DigitalOrigin (www.digitalorigin. com). The process varies, so check the manuals/help for the product you're using.

Getting Started

A QuickTime movie is a container. When you begin a new movie from scratch, you open a new empty container. When you open an existing movie, you open that movie in its container. Whether starting a new movie or editing an existing one, you can resize the container, set its background color, and make several adjustments to it. When you begin with a new movie container, you begin by adding content. That content may be an existing QuickTime movie, but it can just as well be nothing but text, or text and sound, or stills and a movie and text and sound. I could go on, but that would take the fun out of your discoveries.

Starting a new movie

You don't have to have a Site Window open in order to create a QuickTime movie. However, if you create your movie outside of a Site Window, remember that you'll need to add it to the Site Window later, in order to use it in your site.

To create a new QuickTime movie, follow these steps:

1. Choose File ➪ New Special ➪ New QuickTime Movie. This opens a New QuickTime Movie dialog box, as shown in Figure 21-2.

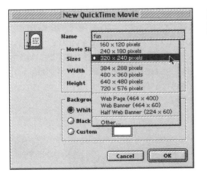

Figure 21-2: The New QuickTime Movie dialog box, where you set up your movie container

2. Select the name "Untitled" and replace it with a short descriptive name ending in .mov, such as "MyVacation.mov."

3. Set the size. Use the pop-up menu to choose from a variety of popular sizes (including banner sizes) or enter your own width and height.

4. Choose a background color. To choose from any color besides black or white, click the color swatch and then choose a color.

   When creating a QuickTime movie, your color choices come from your computer, not the GoLive Color palette. Still, if you're using your new movie on the Web, bear in mind the limitations of color on the Web. (See Chapter 2.) On the Mac, I suggest you use the HTML Picker to select your color.

If your movie is a video or other image that fills the entire dimension of your QuickTime window, the background color will never be seen. But if your image is a compilation that includes space between visuals, background plays a big role. (For example, if you're using subtitles that appear below the video instead of over it, the text should be easily readable on the background. You'll be able to choose a text color too, by the way.)

5. Click OK. Your new, blank movie container opens in the movie viewer, to its Preview tab, the .mov ending after the name you gave it. (See Figure 21-3.) Only the background color appears at this point. From here, you're ready to add tracks and create your movie.

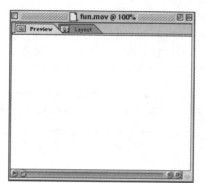

Figure 21-3: A new blank container in the movie viewer

Although you have a named document, your Movie window, this is not a saved file yet. If you close it at this point without saving, it will cease to exist. Once you add content to your movie, you'll be asked to save it if you try to close without saving, but it's important to know that your work within the QuickTime Editor is not automatically saved.

Opening an existing movie

You can open and edit any QuickTime or QuickTime-compatible movie file. (If you're not sure whether a file can be edited in GoLive, simply try. You can't harm a file by trying.) QuickTime supports every common, widely used video format in use within the video industry, including AVI, AVR, DV, M-PEG, MPEG-1, and OpenDML.

Before you edit a movie, as usual I recommend that you copy the movie to the Files tab of your Site Window. As with any other file, this leaves the original movie intact and provides a copy for you to work on and use in your site. You have two basic ways to open a movie:

✦ To open a QuickTime (or compatible) movie file from within the Site Window, simply double-click the movie.

✦ To open a movie that is not yet in your Site Window, choose File ➪ Open, navigate to the movie file you want to open, and then double-click the file to open it or click the Open button.

Both methods have the same result. The movie opens in the Movie Viewer window and the Inspector becomes the QuickTime Inspector. You can now add new tracks, swap one existing track for another, or edit a track.

If you do choose to edit the file before adding it to the Site Window, remember that you'll need to add it to the Site Window later in order to use it in your site.

Saving your movie

Changes you make to a movie are not automatically saved, so be sure to save your changes as you work. (Remember: save as soon as you do something you don't want to have to do all over again.) Also keep in mind the following points:

✦ If you open an existing QuickTime movie to edit it, just save normally as you work; the document already existed, so you won't see a Save dialog box.

✦ If you begin with a blank new container, when you go to save it you'll go through the regular process. I recommend saving as soon as you've set a custom background color or laid your first track.

To save a new movie, follow these steps:

1. Choose File ➪ Save to bring up your system's Save dialog box, as shown in Figure 21-4. Because you named the movie in the initial setup, it is already named here and you can leave the name as is.

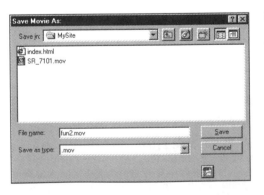

Figure 21-4: The Save dialog box (Windows) for a movie that began life in GoLive as an empty container

2. Choose the location in which you want to save your movie, as follows:

- If you have a Site Window open, you can save it directly to the Files tab. To do so, click the GoLive pop-up button and choose the root folder of your site.

- If you don't have a Site Window open, choose your desired location.

3. Click Save. A Progress bar shows you that a self-contained movie is being saved. Now you can move on in the production process. But don't forget to save!

Introducing the TimeLine Window and Inspector

Open your movie in the TimeLine window to see what it's made of. This movie was shot with a DV camera, and then compressed for the Web in Cleaner 5 (formerly called Media Cleaner Pro). Then we drag it into the Site Window and double-click to open it in GoLive. Now we can add value to it — add links, or add text to aid in telling the story or to enable accessibility.

Just like a film you see in a movie theater, a QuickTime movie is composed of audio and video tracks synchronized to play together. Each element you add to your QuickTime movie is added by adding a track within the TimeLine Editor, shown in Figure 21-5.

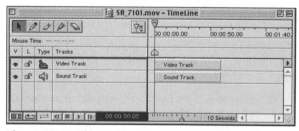

Figure 21-5: The GoLive TimeLine window with a movie in progress

To open the TimeLine window for a movie, click the Show TimeLine Window button on the toolbar. (First you have to open the movie, as described in the previous section.) After doing so, keep in mind the following factors:

✦ If the movie you're viewing the timeline for is new, the window will be empty when you first open it.

✦ When you first import a regular video into QuickTime, you have a *video track* that contains the images shot and a *sound track* that contains any sounds recorded when you recorded the video.

✦ If you're opening an existing movie, you will see whatever existing tracks have been created. (If that movie was created within another application, you won't see multiple tracks. Instead, you'll see one single track that contains all of the movies contents.)

The Track list

The left side of the TimeLine window is the Track list, a listing of each track within the movie. This is where you place the icons from the QuickTime tab of the Objects palette to place a track. The Track list has the following features:

✦ Beside the track's icon is the name of the track. By default, this name will be Video Track 1, Video Track 2, Sound Track 1, Sound Track 2, and so on. You can give it a new descriptive name by double-clicking its name and entering a new one (or you can change the name in the Inspector when the track is selected.

✦ Below the track's name you also see a triangle, if it's a text, filter, sprite, HREF, or chapter track. Clicking the triangle so it points downward reveals the details of that track, some within the Track list and other details in the section at the right. It's handy to see, but if you have several tracks and wish to save screen space, keep the details hidden.

✦ Beside the Tracks name column, the Type column shows you what type of track you have. The icons that appear here, under the Type column, match the ones in the Objects palette to help you easily identify the type of track.

✦ The Lock column—L—displays a Lock icon and enables you to lock a track against accidental editing. Click to lock, again to unlock. The word "locked" also appears when locked.

✦ In the left-most column—V, for view—is an Eye icon, which turns the track's contents on or off. When the eye is black, the visual content of that track is visible or the sound for that track is audible. Clicking the eye turns the track's contents off or back on. When off, the eye is gray. (This is consistent with viewing and hiding different layers in other Adobe software such as Photoshop.) If a track is off when the movie is saved for use on the Web, that content is not seen or heard in the final movie. However, it's still there to be turned on again in a later edit. When you hide your video, the Movie window displays only the playback controls.

If you prefer not to see the View, Lock, and Type columns, you can hide them by clicking the Show/Hide Track Info button, located beneath the View column. You may appreciate this when you've got a long timeline.

One of the powers of the Track list is the ability to drag the tracks within it up or down in the list. A track at the top of the list literally sits on top of a file beneath it. This enables you to stack and restack graphics as with a graphics program. The toolbar also has Bring to Front and Send to Back buttons that move a selected track up or down the list. You can see the track move in the Track list as you click the buttons. In addition, menu commands exist to do the same.

The content area and TimeLine

The right side of the TimeLine window displays the location and duration of each track, depicted as a bar. Above the Track bars, at the top of the area, is a timeline that represents the time span of your movie. This time span is relative; you can set it to represent any length of time by adjusting the scale with the *Time slider*. When the slider is furthest left, the timeline's scale is 1 frame, as reported to the right of the slider. That means each tick on the timeline represents one frame. At this point the timeline is the most spread out, providing a more detailed view of the timeline. This enables you to better view a specific piece of the movie. Each time you move the slider one notch to the right, the timeline's scale compresses, going from 1 to 2 to 4 to 6 to 12. From there, as you move the slider further right, the scale moves from frames to seconds, going to 1 second to 2, then 4 to 10 to 30 seconds, and then to one minute. As you compress the timeline, more of the video's timeline appears at once on your screen, but with less detail. (Back in Figure 21-5, the scale is set for 10 seconds per tick. The movie is one minute, so the bar covers six ticks on the timeline.)

At the top of the timeline numbers is the *Time cursor*—a blue triangle attached to a line that traverses all of the tracks' bars. As you use the playback controls (explained in the next section) to preview your movie in relation to the elements in the various tracks, the Time cursor moves across the timeline. You can also click a number in the timeline to move the Time cursor to that point, or drag the Time cursor to any part of the timeline. Playback then begins wherever the Time cursor is. In fact, playback happens *as* you drag the Time cursor. Watch the Movie window (whether its in Preview or Layout mode) and you'll see the movie play as you drag.

You also move the Time cursor to *markers* you place along the timeline. Markers are like bookmarks; they work along with the Marker button just to the left of the timeline to enable you to jump to any self-determined points within your movie. First you set and name your marker(s). Then you click the Marker button and drag down it's list of markers to select the one to which you want to jump.

To place a marker using a visual cue from your movie, drag the Time cursor to the point where you want the marker, watching the movie in the Preview tab to guide yourself. Then release the mouse and move the cursor just below the numbers so the grabber hand turns into a downward-pointing blue arrow and click to place the marker. The marker, named New Status by default, leaves the name selected so you can enter a short descriptive name (see Figure 21-6) that will help you choose it from the Marker menu later (see Figure 21-7).

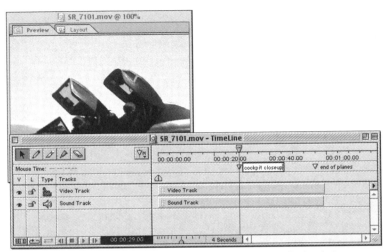

Figure 21-6: Setting a second marker to jump to a desired close-up. Another is set to just before a video track ends. (The blue arrow is the cursor.)

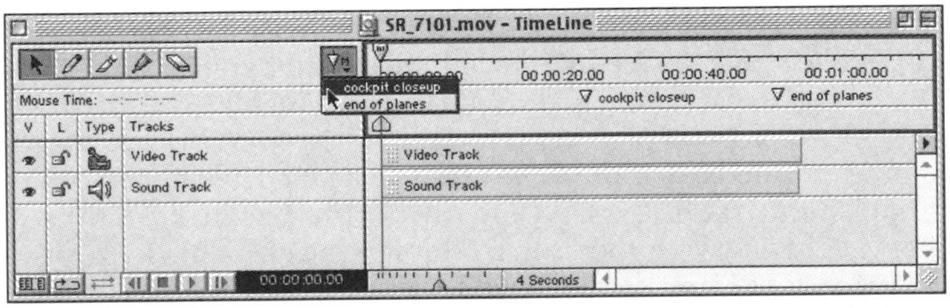

Figure 21-7: Using the Marker pop-up menu to move to a point in the movie

If you know where you want the marker, based on the start or endpoint of a particular track, and don't need the cue from the movie playback, just place the marker without using the Time cursor first.

The playback controls and clock

At the bottom-left corner of the TimeLine window are the standard video playback buttons. Beside them, a clock helps you see the real-life timing of your movie.

The playback controls, from left to right, do the following:

✦ **Loop** repeatedly plays the movie indefinitely until you click this button again to stop it.

✦ **Palindrome** works along with the Loop button. Instead of playing the movie from start to finish over and over, Palindrome causes the movie to play forward, then backward, and then forward again, and so on.

✦ **Step Backward** moves back through the movie from where you are, one step at a time.

✦ **Stop** stops the movie. Double-clicking Stop resets the movie to the beginning.

✦ **Play** begins playback of the movie. Clicking Play again pauses the movie. Then clicking again resumes playback.

✦ **Step Forward** moves forward through the movie, from wherever you are, one step at a time. The duration of a step varies depending on the type of movie you're working on. In a video clip, this is commonly a frame, with a frame being defined as the time interval recorded in the movie as the frame rate. To the right of the playback buttons is a clock that enables you to watch the timing of your movie as it plays. It's a regular clock timer, showing hours, minutes, seconds, and fractions of seconds. For example, at 29 seconds into a movie, it'll read, 00:00:29:00. You can see the numbers run as you watch the bar run across the tracks in the section above. By noting these numbers as your movie plays, you will know the points at which to place your chapters, text, and so on. (When you set the playback to Palindrome, you can see the numbers run backwards.)

The Inspector

The QuickTime Editor is no different from the rest of GoLive when it comes to interface. The Inspector plays its role here, too. For each window you select, and each track or sample you select, there's an Inspector to help you. Files you import and the elements you add within GoLive have Track Inspectors. The text or data you personally created in a GoLive track will have Sample Inspectors. Each provides the various options defined in the QuickTime API, enabling you to do everything QuickTime permits, within the familiar and easy-to-use GoLive Inspector. A couple of Inspectors are consistent, though, such as the Movie Inspector and the Track Inspector.

The Movie Inspector

When the movie viewer is on the Preview tab and is the selected window, the Inspector provides feedback about your movie, as shown in Figure 21-8. You can check back here from time to time to see how your movie is doing size-wise.

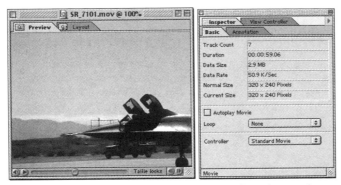

Figure 21-8: The Movie Inspector, active when the Movie window Preview is active

For the most part, this Inspector is not for setting options, but for the reporting of settings based on other changes made to the QuickTime movie. The following are its settings:

✦ **Track count.** The number of tracks that comprise the movie.

✦ **Duration.** The length, in minutes, of the total movie.

✦ **Data Size.** This reports the physical size of the QuickTime movie (the larger the file, the longer the download time before it appears in the users browser, or the longer it will take visitors to download the movie).

✦ **Data Rate.** The amount of QuickTime movie data, in kilobytes, that will play in one second.

✦ **Normal Size.** The width and height, in pixels, that the movie was set up to be.

✦ **Current Size.** The width and height in pixels that the movie is currently being viewed at. (You can view a movie larger or smaller by choosing a size from the Movie ➪ View Size menu.)

The Annotation tab enables you to add credits to your movie so users can learn about it when they play it within their QuickTime Players. (This info appears when the user chooses Movie ➪ Get Info while in the QuickTime Player.) You can use the Annotation tab to enter identification information anytime your Movie window is active and on the Preview tab. Simply enter the desired information in the appropriate fields, as shown in Figure 21-9.

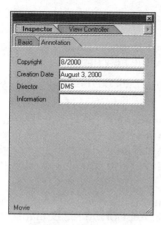

Figure 21-9: Adding annotations to a QuickTime movie

The Track Inspector

The Track Inspector (see Figure 21-10) has the same common elements for all visual items you place in your movie — that is, for everything in the QuickTime Objects palette but the two Audio icons or the organizational folder. It lets you position and size a track, as well as set its graphics mode. To activate the Track Inspector for a track, click the name of that track or click its bar under the timeline.

Figure 21-10: The Video Track Inspector

Note

For items such as text and sprites that are added directly into the movie, the sample track holds the unique data. It's the sample track that varies greatly with each type of track you place in your movie.

Here's what you can do in the main section of (almost) each Track Inspector:

✦ Name the track. (You can also name each track by double-clicking its name in the Tracks list to select the text, and then typing the new name.)

✦ Set the time, relative to the timeline, at which the track begins playing, as well as how long it remains a part of the movie.

✦ Set the position of the visual within the movie viewing area. The first field sets the distance of the left edge of the image from the left side of the video window. The next field does the same for the top edge and top of the movie, pushing the visual down within the movie window. (You can also do this by dragging the item in the Layout tab.)

✦ Check the Constrain Proportion box to maintain the relative size of the movie. This way, if you adjust the width of your movie later, GoLive recalculates the height automatically so the movie does not become distorted. This also prevents the "stretching" effect later, when a visitor to your site resizes the browser window.

✦ Choose a graphics mode that enables the visual element to become part of your page without competing with or covering up your other visuals, as happens when you add a visual over another. You have the following options:

 • *Dither Copy* has no translucency or transparency. It simply dithers colors as needed with lower screen depths (fewer number of colors on a user's monitor).

 • *Copy* has no translucency or transparency. It is best for line art or solid blocks of color that are not demanding of many colors.

 • *Blend* makes the entire image partly translucent or transparent. You control how much so by choosing a *control color*. The darker the color, the more transparent; the lighter the color, the more opaque.

 Blend adds a tint of the selected color to the image. QuickTime enables you to set translucency without having the tint by setting the hue angle and saturation to zero. However, those settings are not in the Track Inspector.

 • *Transparent* enables you to select one color that becomes transparent, so other visuals below can be seen. Only the exact color becomes transparent, though, so this is best with solid areas, such as with the background of a nonaliased text block. It works well on GIFs, but QuickTime already respects the transparency of a GIF, if it already has any. Used on a JPG, this can create an interesting effect.

 • *Straight Alpha* is for an image that has an alpha channel. In Photoshop, or your image creation software, you mask areas you want to turn transparent, and then make an alpha channel and set the details of pixel-level transparency. Then, in the QuickTime Editor, QuickTime respects that channel. In the Inspector, you don't choose a transparency color — a sign that it uses the images transparency.

- *Straight Alpha Blend* is also for an image that has an alpha channel. It's a mix of straight alpha, respecting the image's transparency, and a blend, which enables you to add another level of transparency or translucency. In GoLive, you do this by choosing a tint color in the Inspector.

- *Premul(tiplied) White* is specifically for an image that has a white background and a premultiplied white alpha channel.

- *Premul(tiplied) Black* is specifically for an image that has a black background and a premultiplied black alpha channel.

- *Composition (Dither Copy)* is the same as Dither Copy except that it is specifically for use when adding animated GIF files to your movie.

In each of the cases where a color is to be selected, an active color swatch is available, as in the rest of GoLive. To choose a color, click the color swatch and then choose from your computer's color options, or from the GoLive palettes, as the case may be. (Some color swatches here use GoLive's Color palette while others do not.) In the system palette, the color selected when you click OK is the color that's applied. In GoLive, the color you click while the swatch is selected is the one that gets set.

The Basics of QuickTime Editing

The essence of editing with the QuickTime Editor boils down to just two ways of adding and defining your movie's contents: importing files and adding GoLive-generated elements. To add your content — whether by importing a file or by and adding GoLive-generated elements — you drag the element's icon from the Objects palette and then use the Inspector and the TimeLine window to set it up.

Each of the icons on the QuickTime tab of the Objects palette shown in Figure 21-11 (except for the organizational Folder icon) enables you to add something different to your movie.

QuickTime tab

Figure 21-11: The QuickTime tab of the Objects palette

Importing files

Nine of the 16 icons in the Objects palette enable you to add an independently existing file into the QuickTime movie container. In each case, when you drag the icon from the Objects palette into the Tracks list of the TimeLine window, the icon doesn't actually make it to the page. Unlike when you're building an HTML page, and will need to upload the items you place on that page, with QuickTime you are importing the file into the QuickTime container. Therefore, in each case, you don't need to begin by placing the file in the Site Window. In fact, the file that would be copied in would be unnecessary and unused. Instead, these nine icons cause an Open, or Import, window to open on your screen. In that Open dialog box, you browse to the desired file and then click OK to import it.

As you work with the file you've imported, you don't affect the original file in any way. One key to understanding this is that you never actually edit the imported file. You just tell the QuickTime container which parts of the file it should play, where on the screen, when in the timeline, and in what order. If you later save the container as a self-contained movie, the parts of the file you use are copied into the movie. Six icons import a file immediately upon track placement, as follows:

✦ The **Video Track** icon is for adding moving video clips (and animated GIFs). You can add many formats. Using this to import a movie results in only the first video track of that movie being imported. You have a more flexible way to import from existing movies than using this icon. Instead, you can cut and paste (more on this later).

✦ The **MPEG Track** icon places an MPEG file into your movie. It appears as a single track regardless of whether the file contains video, audio, or both. You cannot edit the MPEG file, but you can add the usual QuickTime feature over it within your movie.

✦ The **SWF Track** icon enables you to incorporate a Flash or LiveMotion file directly into your movie. An SWF file can contain all sorts of audio and video, links . . . but when it is saved as SWF and comes into this editor, it counts as one file — a one-track SWF, not a breakdown of its workings.

✦ The **3D Track** icon is for adding a 3DMF file. That's a QuickDraw 3D metafile.

✦ The **Sound Track** icon enables you to add any digital audio such as sound effects, spoken voice, music (other than MIDI), and more.

✦ The **MIDI (music) Track** icon enables you to add general MIDI files to your movie. The advantage of using MIDI for your sound is file size. It's definitely a preferable way to go on the Web.

With each of these, you drag the icon into the Tracks list and then immediately locate and select the file to be imported. When you click Open in the Open dialog box, the file imports and appears as a single track in the Tracks list. The Inspector for each of these is identical. You can use the Inspector to set the start and end times of the video/sound — if you prefer that to dragging along the timeline. For each of the visual formats, you can use the Inspector to set the size and location of the file — in case you prefer numeric entries to dragging the images in Layout mode. And finally, you can set the image mode to one of nine modes including Dither Copy, Copy, Blend, Transparent, Alpha, Premultiplied Alpha, and Composition Dither Copy.

Two more of the QuickTime Editor's icons don't import a file immediately, providing an import interface in their Inspectors instead, as follows:

✦ The **Picture Track** icon is for adding still images. Still images come in for a very short duration, but because they're still, you can lengthen the duration without affecting the quality of the image or the size of the movie file.

✦ The **Sprite Track** icon is for adding still images and then animating them in all sorts of ways. It is necessary to know what sprites are capable of and have an idea of how to do it, or be willing to experiment a bunch to get to know what they can do. The Inspector looks simple, but it's powerful.

The picture and sprite tracks work a bit differently from the others as they don't do an immediate import. Instead, you do get to place them directly into the Tracks list, as shown in Figure 21-12. Then, you choose the Import command from the Inspector. If you choose to import a Photoshop graphic, GoLive presents an image conversion dialog box, and then converts that image and places it. Sprites are interesting creatures; single images that can move around in your movie, appear in many places at once, cause all sorts of actions to happen, and much more.

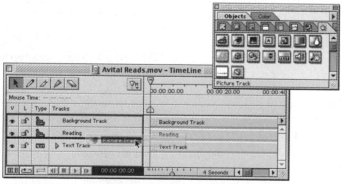

Figure 21-12: Dragging a picture track into place in the Tracks List. The dark line shows you where it is due to land.

One of the QuickTime icons in the Objects palette does not import a file at all. Instead, it links to the desired file. Specifically, the Streaming Track icon is also for adding audio or video (or audio *and* video) to a movie. But the essence of a streaming track is that the media streams down to the viewer, but the movie file remains in place on the streaming server. When you incorporate streaming media into your movie, you can include a pointer to the source of the stream but you can never import the actual audio or video data into your movie file. Each time the movie is played, the viewer's computer connects to the streaming server to get the streaming parts of the movie.

The difference with the streaming track is that its content is streamed, so it resides on a streaming server. To use this content, you link to it by entering its URL in the Inspector. But because in the end the video streamed is a visual part of the movie, you'll find the same exact settings in the Inspector's first tab.

Note   One reason to use a streaming track is so that viewers cannot copy/save your content. By placing a streaming track into your movie, the main movie can download, but the elements you stream are protected. Or, sometimes you want a movie to stream entirely, but you need to include an SWF or sprites, which cannot stream. In that case, you create one movie that contains those elements and include the streaming movie by using the streaming track.

Adding GoLive-generated elements

The rest of the icons in the QuickTime tab of the Objects palette are actually each a specially designed interface for incorporating a brand new element, such as text, into a QuickTime movie. In some cases, without GoLive, you'd import a text file. In others, you would type code. Because this is GoLive, you drag an icon and set up in the Inspector. The Inspector makes this an easy task, as always.

The icons that enable you to add things directly into the QuickTime container to stand alone or jazz up your imported files are as follows:

✦ The **Generic Filter Track** icon adds a special effect to one particular visual track in your movie. For example, it can show clouds behind an image or flames coming up around it.

✦ The **One-Source Filter Track** icon also adds a special effect to one particular track.

✦ The **Two-Source Filter Track** icon is used to create smooth (or interesting) transitions between two video tracks.

✦ The **HREF Track** icon provides for the addition of clickable links. Or, the user can be transported to the link's destination automatically, based on the movie's timeline. You can use this to automatically load Web pages in another frame at predetermined points in the movie. You can have only one HREF track in a movie, but you can place as many URLs as you want, each containing a link to another location.

✦ The **Chapter Track** icon enables you to divide your movie into multiple chapters. The movie still plays smoothly from start to finish. But alternately, the user can choose a specific chapter and start playing the movie from there. You place just one chapter track in a movie, adding all chapters into the submenu sample tracks for this track.

✦ The **Text Track** icon lets you add captions to your movie. For example, you might identify those who are speaking as on the TV news, or create a text version of what is said to aid the hearing impaired. It also enables you to create scrolling credits and such. You can choose any font, color, size, and so on — all under the Movie ⇨ Text heading, within four submenus.

With each of these tracks, the title track and a content subtrack exist. The subtrack contains the actual data, such as the chapter, the text, or the URLs. The master track and sample track each has its own Inspector, so experiment with each selectable item to discover your options and the editor's abilities.

To use a GoLive generated track, follow these steps:

1. Drag the icon into the Tracks list section of the TimeLine window to lay down the track.

   The name of the track appears in the Track list with a blue arrow to its left.

2. Click the blue arrow beside the track's name so you'll be able to add it and adjust your chapters.

3. Double-click the track's name in the Tracks list and name your track, just so you know what's on that track as you work. (Not all tracks can be named. If the name is gray in the Inspector, you know the name cannot be changed.)

4. Click the Create Sample button at the upper-left corner of the TimeLine window.

5. In the sample track for your track, move to the point where you want the object to begin and then drag to define its length (duration), as shown in Figure 21-13.

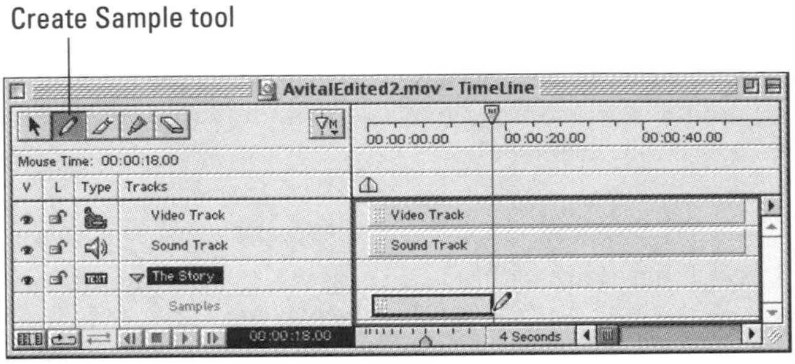

Create Sample tool

Figure 21-13: Using the Create Sample tool to draw out the timeframe for a track, in this case to display text

If you'll be placing multiple objects within a track, first lay the block you want to have go first. You can always add more after the first one, but you can't add anything in front of it. Dragging the first Sample bar takes the Master Track bar with it.

That's the basic set up. Like with the visual file imports, the first tab of the Inspector is for size and positioning, with the opportunity to see a color mode. Then, each track has its own unique tab or tabs in the Inspector, where options for that item make setting it up easy and understandable. For example, the Inspector for the Text Sample tab is shown in Figure 21-14.

Figure 21-14: Setting up a sample in the Sample Track tab's Inspector. Each tab of each sample track provides exactly what you need; in this example, it's a text editing interface.

Laying out your movie

The Layout tab of the Movie Viewer is very much like a page layout program. You begin a new Movie window by choosing a size for your movie and selecting a background color. As images and text are imported into your TimeLine window, they appear in the Movie Viewer window. Instead of selecting an object directly in the layout, you select a track in the Track list or select its bar to make that track's visible object become active. Selected visuals have the standard handles, can be dragged into place (as in Figure 21-15), and can be skewed and/or rotated. Any track can be sent to the front of the layers piled on it; layers can also move backward. On top of that, you can use any of nine filters to drop out colors within the image, creating some interesting effects.

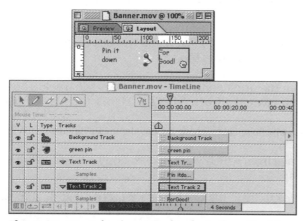

Figure 21-15: Selecting a track selects the object for editing. This image shows a movie container that has a background color set, an image placed within it, and two text blocks. The text is selected to be positioned.

To aid you in your layout, three commands appear under the Movie menu and in the toolbar: Hide Ruler, Show Grid, and Snap to Grid. The toolbar also provides options such as Bring to Front or Send to Back, which become active whenever a visual track is selected, and Skew, Rotate, and Scale, which become active whenever applicable.

Your movies can have text, such as credits that even roll, or captioning. To add text to your page, you begin by adding a text track. The Text Track Inspector is very much like the Inspectors for the other visuals. The text can move up or down through the layers, be transparent, scale, skew, and rotate. Use the Layout view to adjust it. Actually, you enter the text within the Inspector — but first there's a step to define the text space. Text can either be over your visuals or off to any side, depending on the dimensions you set for your window.

Tip   As you work in the Layout window, you can easily switch tracks by Control-clicking (Mac) or right-clicking (Windows) and moving between your layers within the contextual menu.

Copying Existing Tracks from Other QuickTime Movies

Now that I've outlined the various ways all tracks are added to the timeline, would you believe that I'm now going to show you an entirely different way? That's because if you want to import more than just the first video track of a movie — say you wanted to copy the audio — you're out of luck with the Import feature. Copying is the most flexible way to get things from one movie to another. You can copy any track from within another QuickTime movie. In fact, you can also copy any track from any other QuickTime-compatible movie, too.

To copy a movie, first you open the originating movie and copy the track. Then you open the destination movie and paste the track. That's it. Here's the play by play.

Follow these steps to import a specific track from an existing QuickTime movie:

1. Open the QuickTime movie from which you'd like to copy a track, using either of the following methods:

   - If this movie happens to be in the GoLive Site Window, just double-click it to open it.

   - More likely, this movie is not in the Site Window because it is not intended to be part of your site. In this case, use File ➪ Open to open the movie.

2. When the movie opens in a GoLive Movie Viewer window, click the Layout tab.

3. Click the Show TimeLine Window button in the toolbar.

4. In the Tracks list, click once on the name of the track you wish to import. (This selects the track.)

5. Choose Edit ➪ Copy to copy that track. (If it's not available, you're not in the Layout tab.) You can also drag the track directly from one TimeLine window to another. You are now finished with that movie and can close it. However, you might want to wait until you've successfully pasted the track and tested your new video.

   The beauty of this method is that you can copy any track you see within a movie. If you have multiple tracks to choose, Shift-click the tracks you want, to take more than one with you at once.

6. Open the target movie or create your new QuickTime movie. (If one is in the Site Window, double-click it.)

7. Click the Layout tab of the Movie Viewer window.

8. Click the Show TimeLine Window button in the toolbar.

9. Click once in the Tracks list to select the area, and then choose Edit ➪ Paste. (If it doesn't paste, you're not in the Layout tab.) The copied track appears, complete with its proper track icon.

From here you can adjust its position in the timeline, name it, and otherwise set it up just like you set up any track.

Adding Visual Tracks

If you're beginning your QuickTime creation with a pre-existing movie, it most likely already has a video track. Whether that's the case and you are adding another video track, or whether you've just begun a new blank movie and are adding your very first video track, the process is the same.

Note   You don't actually use GoLive to create a video track or to edit it. You must create your visual files elsewhere. The GoLive QuickTime Editor enables you to import these visuals in order to enhance them within the QuickTime container.

Each time you import a new visual element (or any element, really), it appears in its own track and is placed at the beginning of the timeline. You can position it within the timeline after you import it.

Note   If you want to import an entire movie containing an audio track as well as video, and perhaps multiple video tracks, this is not the technique to use. This only imports the first video track of any movie. To get hold of other tracks within a movie, you can copy and paste.

These directions assume you're already working in a movie and have the TimeLine window open.

To import a visual element, follow these steps:

1. Drag the appropriate track icon from the QuickTime tab of the Objects palette and drop it anywhere over the Tracks list. For visual elements, your choices are: Video, MPEG, SWF, or 3D. Unlike other icons you drag from the Objects palette, you don't actually place this one. Instead, when you drop the icon, the Open dialog box opens.

2. Navigate to the file you wish to add, and then double-click the file or select it and click Open or Convert. (If choosing a graphic that's not already a QuickTime video, the button says Convert instead of Open.) The visual element appears in the Movie Viewer window and as a track in the TimeLine window.

Note   You can import videos from the various (many) formats that QuickTime supports. When you select a video that is not QuickTime already, the button says Convert. After you click Convert, the movie is converted by QuickTime and appears in your TimeLine without further ado.

3. Double-click the name of the new video track to select it, and then enter a short descriptive name for the video track so you can identify it as you work.

4. If you don't want this item to begin at the starting point of your movie, move your mouse over the dots at the left of the bar until your pointer becomes a hand, and then click and drag it along the timeline, releasing it at the desired point.

Tip   As you drag the bar, the Time cursor moves along with it. If another visual track already exists in your movie, you can watch the movie play in the movie viewer as you drag, and use that as a clue for placement.

5. Edit the size and/or graphics mode of the video within the Track Inspector or by switching to the Layout tab of the Movie window and working visually.

Note   It's important to realize that if you use this method to import an entire QuickTime movie, only the first video track will be imported. Any secondary video tracks, any audio, and any other tracks will not import this way.

After you add a track, you can copy and paste that track within the same movie. Simply select the track you wish to copy, copy it using Edit ⇨ Copy, and then choose Edit ⇨ Paste. The new track is automatically created. The graphic mode of the track is copied. However, the layer information is not.

To delete a track, click the track to select it and then press Backspace/Delete. To delete the contents of a track that has samples, click the sample and then press Backspace/Delete.

Adding Sound and Music Tracks

Although called "videos," we tend to rely on audio to add to our visual experience. Normally, adding audio on the Web can be tricky, but when it's part of a movie, it becomes QuickTime no matter what format it would be if played directly from the Web page. That's one less plug-in or MIME type for you to worry about.

GoLive's QuickTime Editor has two different types of audio tracks: sound and MIDI (which is music). The MIDI track adds any general MIDI files to your movie, while the sound track handles all other audio. (MIDI, by the way, is for Musical Instrument Digital Interface.) Aside from the lack of need for video settings, the import of audio is just like importing visuals (discussed in the preceding section).

Note GoLive and QuickTime aren't audio editing tools. You'll need to set up your sound or music files fully in your sound editing software before you import them.

As with all elements you add to your movie from other file sources, you are actually importing the file into the QuickTime container. Therefore, you don't have to add the audio file to the Files tab or the Site Window.

Each time you add a new sound or music track, it is imported into its own track. This makes it easy for you to move each audio bit around on the timeline or delete the audio. The only thing you can't do in the QuickTime Editor is create audio transitions such as fade in or fade out. That must be done within the file you're adding, edited within the audio editing software.

Tip If your sound is a .mov file, you can open the sound movie in the Movie window using File ➪ Open, and then select the track (while in the Layout tab) and copy it. Then you can paste it into the TimeLine window.

To import an audio (sound or MIDI) file, follow these steps:

1. Drag the Sound or MIDI icon from the QuickTime tab of the Objects palette and drop it anywhere in the Tracks list of the TimeLine window. Drag the MIDI icon to add MIDI, or even karaoke (.kar). Use the Sound icon for everything else. Because you're importing the sound into the QuickTime movie container, not putting it on your Web page, the icon doesn't actually make it onto your page. Instead, when you drop the icon, the Open dialog box opens.

2. Navigate to the audio file you are adding. (If you're using Windows, don't forget to choose the type of file or all files so you'll find what you're looking for.) If you'd like to listen to the sound before importing it, click once to select the desired file, and then click the Play Sound button or icon that appears in the Preview area within the Open dialog box.

   To import the audio file, double-click the file or select it, as shown in Figure 21-16, and click Open. The new track appears in the Tracks list and the TimeLine bar is inserted at the starting frame of your movie.

3. Click the drag handle at the left of the sound's bar and drag it to the point in the timeline where you want it to play. The action in the movie can be an excellent guideline. Alternately, you can set the start time of the sound in the Inspector.

   If the sound's duration is too short to see it in the timeline, use the Inspector to set it up, as shown in Figure 21-17. Locate your desired start time by moving the Time cursor, and then note the time in the clock timer at the bottom of the TimeLine window. Then enter that time into the Start Time field of the Inspector.

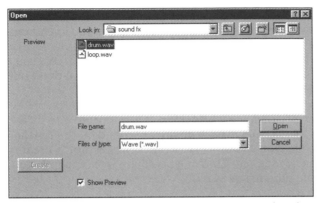

Figure 21-16: Selecting and/or previewing sound and music files

Figure 21-17: Placing a file by the numbers in the Sound Inspector when a file is too small to drag. After the number is entered here, Woa! will be 39.2 seconds in. (There happened to be a marker set prior to the import to denote the sound's entry point.)

4. *(Optional)* Drag the right edge of the sound's bar to alter the duration of the sound, or use the Inspector to do this. But, bear in mind that this doesn't cut the sound short; it compresses it instead, and can create an unwanted sound effect.

MIDI

MIDI has gotten a bad rap by some folks, and the reason is understandable. Fortunately, MIDI in QuickTime is not the animal that got that bad rap. Some MIDI players rely on a computer's sound card to synthesize MIDI — and the quality of sound cards can vary, which means MIDI can sound pretty bad. QuickTime, however, has a built-in MIDI synthesizer! This ensures that the sounds generated are the same across the board. (The quality of speakers and sound card still affect the sound, but not to the extent that a bad synthesizer does.)

Another thing affecting the quality of sound created with MIDI is the source of the MIDI sound files. QuickTime licenses (and uses) Roland's GS instrument set — high-quality stuff.

5. Double-click the sounds name in the Tracks list and give it a short descriptive name. (You can do this in the Inspector too, whenever the sound is selected.)

To test your sound, switch to the Preview tab of the Movie window, and then use the play controls there or in the TimeLine window.

If, at any time, you choose to delete a sound track, simply click the sound track to select it, and then press your Delete key or choose Edit ⇨ Cut on Mac or Windows (or Edit ⇨ Clear (Mac), or Edit ⇨ Delete (Windows). (If the Delete commands aren't available under your Edit menu, click any other track, and then reselect the track you wish to delete.

Adding Video Effects and Transitions

Filters and video transitions can go a long way to adding a polished real-movie touch to your movie. The QuickTime Editor divides the various effects into three icons in the QuickTime Objects palette tab.

Filters appear on their own track in the timeline, so you can add, edit, reorganize, or delete them without permanently changing the contents of the video track. This approach is very similar to the idea of layers in Adobe Photoshop, where you might add text or a drop shadow to a graphic by first placing each element on its own layer. That way, if you change your mind about the color of the text or the direction of the drop shadow, you can simply delete or edit that one layer. The other elements on the other layers are not affected.

You can apply three types of filters to a movie, as follows:

✦ **Generic Filter Track.** These three *generic* filters apply clouds, fire, or ripples. These do not act in conjunction with any of your existing visual tracks; each, if used, is a track unto itself, taking its own place as a visual element in your movie. Consider it like importing or pasting another image—except that they are meant to add effect to your own visuals.

✦ **One-Source Filter Track.** These 14 filters apply an effect to a single track (or one source) to somehow alter its appearance. Commonly used filters include Blur, Sepia-tone, Film Noise, and Lens Flare.

✦ **Two-Source Filter Track.** In video terms, this is known as a transition. This filter acts in conjunction with two movie sources, acting on the end of one and the beginning of the other, to create an effect that somehow makes the change from one video to another softer, smoother, or more interesting. Well done, a transition enhances the continuity of the story being told. The QuickTime editor has 13 transitions.

Adding a generic filter track

A generic filter is entirely the work of QuickTime. QuickTime generates the image, fully independent of your movies or images. Each of these effects exists on its own track and literally covers all other visuals that are beneath it. However, by controlling the transparency of the track's background, you can have your effect and visuals too. The filters are explained under Step 5 of the following instructions.

To add a filter track into a QuickTime movie, follow these steps:

1. Drag the Generic Filter Track icon from the Objects palette QuickTime tab into the TimeLine window.

   Consider where you want to place it. You might feel like you're working with the Mad Hatter as you experiment with this filter, but it's a case of up is down and down is up. If you add a filter *below a visual track* in the Tracks list, you are placing it *on top of that image* in the Movie window. Thus if you have, say, an image of leaves, and you want them to appear as if on fire, you put the generic filter track beneath the leaves track and select the Fire filter. That superimposes the fire over the leaves in the actual video.

   Fortunately, you can always drag the filter up or down within the Tracks list to change its stacking order after you see the effect.

2. Click the triangle by the generic filter track to expose the sample track.

3. Click the Create Sample button and, in the sample track, drag to define the start point and endpoint of the effect. You can always drag it around on the timeline to adjust it after you see its overall affect within your movie.

4. In the Generic Filter Sample Inspector, click Select.

5. When the Select Effect window appears, choose the desired effect (filter) from the list on the left.

Note If you do not have QuickTime installed on your computer (or if you have only the minimum QuickTime install) the preview may not work and a dialog box may tell you that you're missing some files. If this happens, connect to the Internet and authorize QuickTime or GoLive to download what it needs from the QuickTime Web site. Click OK when the download is complete, and resume.

GoLive gives you three generic filters to choose from:

- *Cloud* enables you to choose the cloud color and background color. If you wish to, click the respective color swatch, and then choose from your computer's color options. (This is QuickTime, so it does not use GoLive's Color palette.) The color selected when you click OK is the color that's applied. Drag the Rotation slider until the cloud suits you, and then click OK to apply the filter.

- *Fire* places flames at the bottom of your Movie window. Use the Spread, Sputter (the lower the sputter, the higher the flame), Water, and Restart sliders to adjust the flame's color, height, and intensity. Then click OK to apply the filter.

- *Ripple* causes everything under the ripple effect to waver as if it is under water. You don't have to set up anything here, but if you want to choose your own mask, click the Mask field to locate the masking graphic, and then select it and click OK to apply the filter.

As you choose one of the preceding options, it displays in the lower-left corner. Then, as you tweak it, you can see your results live in that preview.

6. Select the filter's Parent bar, in either the list or the timeline, in order to set the graphics mode for the filter track. Otherwise, the filter covers up your graphics or video and renders your movie fairly useless.

7. Choose your graphics mode from the Mode pop-up menu.

   For example, because the background of the fire is black, choose Transparent. Then pick black as the color to be made transparent.

8. Now that your effect is all set up, double-click the filter's name in the Tracks list and give it a descriptive name, such as "flames" if you're using the flame effect.

Click the Play button in the TimeLine window to view the filter's effect within the Movie Viewer window. (Move the Time cursor to the desired starting point first if you want to see only a portion of the movie.) You can also click the Play button in the movie viewer to see the movie.

If you decide you'd rather not use that filter, either click the Eye icon to hide it while you think it over, or select the filter's name or bar, and then use your Backspace/Delete key.

Applying a one-source filter track

A single-source filter changes the appearance of one track that you select for the time span that you select. A few of the common effects are blurring an image, tinting, embossing, and adding "noise" to the "film."

To apply a one-source filter track to a track, drag the One-Source Filter Track icon into place below the video track to which you want to apply the effect. Use the Create Sample tool to define the filter's start point and endpoint in the sample track of the timeline. Then do the following:

1. With the sample track selected, in the Inspector, click Select.

2. Choose one of the 13 effects (filters) from the list on the left.

3. Tweak the look of the effect using the options that appear for your selected effect. The preview area shows the results of your efforts.

4. After you select the desired effect and adjust it to your liking, click OK to apply it.

Click the Play button in the TimeLine window to view the filter's effect in the Movie Viewer window.

Applying a two-source filter track

You use a transition filter to supply a transition between two different tracks (sources). For this, you use both the filter track and the sample track. To apply a two-source filter track to a track, drag the Two-Source Filter Track icon into place between the two video tracks it will transition. Use the Create Sample tool to define the filter's start point and end point in the sample track of the timeline.

Then set up the transition filter by doing the following:

1. In the TimeLine window, select the two-source filter track.

2. Use the Source A pop-up menu in the Two-Source Filter Inspector to choose the outgoing movie clip. All eligible image tracks in your movie appear here. This is an excellent example of why naming a track is helpful.

3. Choose the incoming movie clip that from the Source B pop-up menu, as shown in Figure 21-18. If you want, you can enter a name for the effect or transition in the Title field. (You can also name your transition by double-clicking its name in the Tracks list.)

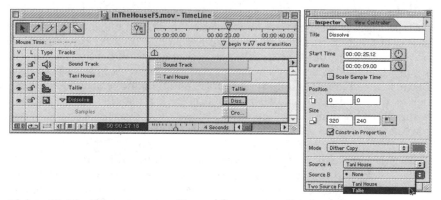

Figure 21-18: The two-source filter track set up to dissolve between two tracks, and the effect in mid-dissolve shown in the preview

4. In the TimeLine window, select the sample track (the partner to the two-source filter track you just set up).

5. Verify that the option to switch from video A to video B is selected. You can choose to go from B to A, but most people find that confusing to remember and plan in their heads.

6. Click the Select button.

7. From the list to the left, select a transition effect. Click a transition's name, and then watch the demonstration of that effect in the Preview field below the list. (If it is not animated, something is missing from your QuickTime installation in your computer.) Note the roles of A and B.

8. Use the controls to the right of the Effects list to customize any effect.

Click the Play button in the TimeLine window to view the transition in the Movie Viewer window.

Adding Sprite Tracks

Sprites are to animation what PostScript is to bitmapped imaging. They're the energy efficient recycling team of the animation world. Using sprites, you can place one image in your movie and call upon that image many, many times to give it the look of animation.

If you've used an animation program, you may be familiar with this — it's a fairly standard process. The QuickTime movie is considered a stage and your images are the cast of characters. You import your entire cast into the first keyframe of the sprite track, and then rather than copying each character and pasting it many times, you simply direct the character's behavior and the character follows your direction. Because the characters only appear once, and then move around as much as you desire, the file size stays small and your movie is most efficient for use on the Web. A sprite can be animated independently from other parts of a movie. A movie can have several sprites, each doing its own thing.

To begin, you create your still images of characters and other graphics for your sprite tracks within your graphic program of choice. You can use practically any graphics program, because QuickTime can handle just about anything: BMP, GIF, JPEG/JFIF, MacPaint, Photoshop, PICT, PNG, QuickDraw GX (Mac), QuickTime Image Format, SGI, Targa, and TIFF. Then, you import them into the QuickTime movie and proceed to set up their behaviors and actions.

To add an animation to your movie, you first add the sprite's track and set the "stage" for your animation. Then you add the sample tracks — individual paths within the sprite and set keyframes, which are individual points in time. Finally, you select the individual keyframes and bring in one of your characters at that point in time. By adding a character to multiple keyframes (you can duplicate a keyframe) and moving it around or changing its properties, you create animation.

Tip   If you have a sprite track that you like in another movie, you can open that movie, select and copy that track, and then paste it into your current move.

The Inspector does a lot of work for sprites; it changes when you select the sprite track, any subtrack, the individual sprite's keyframe in the timeline. . . .

Creating sprite and sprite sample tracks

The first step is to add the sprite track to your QuickTime container. Once its there, you import your characters and lay down the sample tracks on which the animation will happen.

To insert a sprite track into a QuickTime movie, follow these steps:

1. Drag the Sprite Track icon from the Objects palette's QuickTime tab into the place within the TimeLine window's Track list. (The sprite track contains a subsection called an action track — more on that soon.)

2. With the sprite track selected, open the Inspector (to the Basic tab) and replace the title "Sprite Track" with your own short descriptive name for your new sprite track. The Sprite Track Inspector sets the look and behavior of the entire sprite area, rather than that of any individual sprite.

3. Switch to the Sprites tab to build the stage for your animation. Make the following choices:

   - *Visible* enables you to have your sprite track appear when the movie begins, or be invisible upon playback. By default, this is checked and the sprite track is visible. (Apparently, the Eye icon in the TimeLine window has an adverse effect on sprites, boundary-wise.)

   - *Scale Sprites When Track Is Resized* enables images to scale the way they're designed to.

   - *Background Color* enables you to set a color other than the default black. The color swatch here works like the usual GoLive feature, so click to bring up the Color palette, and then click the color to set it. Your color will not appear in the Movie window yet.

4. Switch to the Images tab of the Inspector, uncheck Import Photoshop layers, if your images aren't layers, and click the Import button in the lower section.

5. In the Open dialog box, locate the images and click Add or Add All. Click Done to complete the import.

6. GoLive converts your images, asking you to choose JPG compression settings (even if you're importing a JPG). Make your choices, and then click OK. You only have to choose once—this choice applies to all images imported at a time. The images now appear, by name, in a scrolling list in the center of the Inspector. (When you click one, you can see its details.)

7. *(Optional)* To rename a sprite image, select the image and then rename it in the Name field below the Image list. This has no effect on your movie, but may make it easier to choose your characters later.

8. To add your first sprites to your timeline, switch to the Images tab of the Inspector and enter the number of sprite samples you want to add. Bear in mind that you can always add more later by returning to this Inspector.

Note

A sprite sample is an individual action track within your sprite. You can have three characters and three samples, so each character can walk its own road across your sprite. Or, you can have three characters but just one or two action tracks. Your third character may just be a guest star in another path. Two characters cannot appear at the same time in the same space (sample), but one can stand in for another.

9. *(Optional)* To move the entire sprite, background and all, either drag it within the Movie Window Layout tab or select the sprite track and use the settings in the Sprite Track Inspector's Basic tab (and watch the result in the movie viewer).

Note You can move the sprite around within the Movie window, just like any other visual object — but bear in mind, you're affecting the entire sprite, not any individual sample when you do this. It's for setting the sprite stage within the greater context of your entire movie, not for moving your characters across their sprite stage.

You can add more samples later by selecting the sprite track in the Tracks list, switching to the Sprites tab of the Inspector and entering the number of additional samples in the Add New Sprites field. Should you find you don't need one of your samples later on, you can easily delete it by selecting it in the Tracks list and pressing your Backspace/Delete key.

Positioning and animating individual actors

Now that your cast of characters is in the wings, ready to act, you can begin directing them. It's time to tell each one where to go, when to make itself visible or scarce, and how to play with fellow sprite samples. To do this, you select the individual sprite sample and set it up in the corresponding Sprite Sample Inspector.

Each sample track starts you off with one *keyframe*. A keyframe represents a moment in time in relation to your timeline. You set a keyframe at any point at which you want something significant to happen. Then, you select each keyframe, one by one, and use its Inspector to set its position, look, and (optionally) activity trigger.

Note If you've used GoLive to animate a floating box already, you may have enjoyed the Recorder as a quick and easy way to add motion to your page. Unfortunately, that feature isn't available here. To create motion for your sprite characters, you must do it the old-fashioned way, by placing a *keyframe* and numerically entering the desired position at that point in time.

To add a character into the sprite's scene, select a keyframe (diamond) within the timeline. You'll create the illusion of movement by setting up several keyframes that follow one another in the timeline. Once a keyframe is selected, use its Inspector (the Sprite Sample Inspector) to set up the details for that point in sprite time and sprite space, as shown in Figure 21-19.

Begin by choosing which image this keyframe controls, by selecting a character from the Image menu. Then choose among the following options to set up the look of the character:

✦ Define the image's graphic mode by choosing from the Mode menu. (See the "Introducing the TimeLine Window and Inspector" section earlier.)

✦ Click Visible if you want the selected character to be seen.

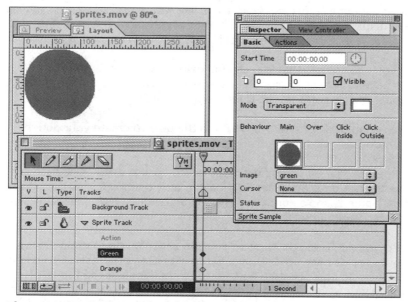

Figure 21-19: Setting up the initial appearance of a character

✦ Use the two position text fields to enter the position you want the character in at this point of the timeline. The left field is for pixels from the left side of the stage. The right is for distance from the top of the stage.

You can have sprite characters act as Event triggers similar to the way graphics can trigger actions on your Web page. This is where the Behavior options come in. Normally, a character's behavior is simply Main—like the Main state of a Mouseover button. But here in behaviors, you can turn your characters into clickable objects that behave like buttons.

The sprite behaviors you can choose from are as follows:

✦ **Main,** which is the main, default state of a character; the way it appears when nothing special is happening.

✦ **Over,** which is onMouseOver (on Enter).

✦ **Inside** is for when the mouse is pressed.

✦ **Outside** is for when the user drags the mouse outside of the sprite.

As with rollover button images in the Smart tab, one keyframe can have multiple images attached to it. With the rollover button, the button can have three images. With a keyframe, there can be four. To create an alter state, keep that keyframe selected, click the icon for the state you want to create, and then choose a character and cursor, and enter a status message. Then, like with your Web pages, you can set the message displayed at the bottom-left corner of the user's browser during a specific state, or behavior. To do this here, enter a message in the Status field.

Something you can do here that you can't do within GoLive's Actions or rollover button is to have the user's cursor change when it's over the sprite. You do this here by choosing a cursor from the Cursor pop-up menu.

After you've set up one keyframe, move on to the next to create your action sequence. To do this, you'll have to add more keyframes, of course.

Note To help guide yourself, so you can recall which track is which, give each of your sample tracks a descriptive name To rename one, double-click its current name, Sprite 1, Sprite 2, and so on in the timeline and enter a new one, being sure to press Enter/Return to set the name.

Add more keyframes to the timeline so you can set them up to create movement along time, as well as have other things happen as time progresses. To add a keyframe, select the Make Sample button (the Pencil icon at the top-left corner of the TimeLine window) and click at the desired point in time within the desired sample track. Each keyframe you create within a sample track automatically carries forward the settings from the last one on that track. This makes it very easy to create a continuing sequence.

What if you've set up an intricate set of behaviors for a keyframe and want them to carry on — or want something similar for another point in time? As you might expect in GoLive, you can press Option (Mac) or Alt (Windows) as you drag the keyframe you want to copy.

Note Don't forget to switch back to the Pointer icon after you finish adding keyframes. Otherwise, you won't be able to select a keyframe to set it up!

You can view your results in the Movie Viewer window. If you set up actions based on cursor movement, move your cursor around in the window to see the results. After viewing the animation, you may want to adjust the timing.

To move any keyframe ahead or backward, just drag it. If the Time cursor is in the way, move it over first. To delete a keyframe, select it and press Backspace/Delete.

Wiring sprites

In addition to having a character move around or change color (swap characters, really), you can attach an Action or Actions to it, just like you can do with text or objects on an HTML Web page that you create back in your Files tab. Instead of creating a link on your page and attaching an Action to the link, you choose a keyframe here. Once the keyframe is selected, you switch to the Actions tab of the Sprite Sample Inspector. This Inspector is very much like GoLive's Actions Inspector — only the actions are different.

Cross-Reference

Refer to Chapter 18 to become familiar with the Actions Inspector in order to best use this feature.

Sprite Actions are controls for what the sprite does when clicked. For example, you can make the movie loop or set the volume. Sets also exist for QuickTime VR and SWF.

Adding Text Tracks

A text track can be used to add captioning to your movie, such as for subtitles for a foreign movie, or to provide narration (accessibility) for your deaf viewers. You can have many text phrases appear in turn as the movie plays.

Setting up text sections is much like setting up chapters. You add one text track to your movie, and then add all of your text segments within the text track, using the Text Track Inspector to do so.

Note

In this example, the original move is 320×240 pixels. To provide room for a text track below the video, a new container was made, at 320×320 pixels. For a background, I picked a color that fit in with the video.

To create a text track, drag the Text Track icon into the TimeLine window, expand the arrow to see the sample track, and use the Create Sample tool to draw out the location time-wise where you want your first text to appear. Now you're ready to add the text. With the sample track still selected, move to the Inspector, which stands ready for your first text. Then follow these steps:

1. In the Text Sample Inspector, type your text into the large white field and then click Apply, as shown in Figure 21-20.

2. Click back on the sample track in the timeline to see how your text looks. The text appears, but it has a white background that covers up all of your visuals! It's also at the top of the movie, which may not be where you want it.

3. Click the text track's name or TimeLine bar to change Inspectors to the general Track Inspector, and then use the Mode pop-up menu to make the white background transparent. Choose Transparent, and then select white as the transparency color.

   When you can see your text and video together, you can move on to format your text, resize or reposition the text area, or make your text interactive — in any order. The next sections show you how to do each of these things.

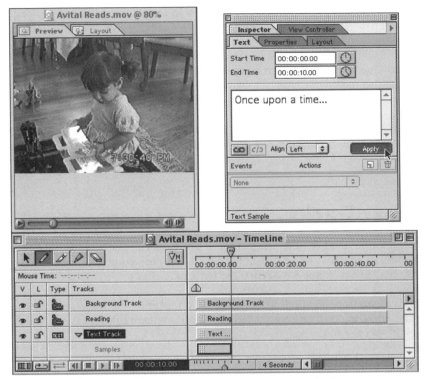

Figure 21-20: Setting the Inspector so you can see your text

Formatting your text

To work on the text, you select the text sample and then work with the Inspector and Movie menu. You can return to format your text any time.

If you begin by creating several samples in sequence, and then return to the first one to enter the text and format it, as you select each following sample, that sample inherits the formatting.

You can do any of the following to format your text:

✦ Select the text and use the options under the Text submenus of the Movie menu. You can choose a font, size, style, and/or color. You can select just a word to format. Each time you return here and make a change, click Apply to record that change.

✦ While anywhere in the Text field, use the Align menu under the text.

✦ Switch to the Properties tab to set scaling and scrolling.

Note For each sample block, you may have to return to the Properties tab and select Don't Auto Scale to avoid having your text scrunch.

✦ Switch to the Layout tab to set up margins and give the text a drop shadow, make its background transparent, or anti-alias it. (Anti-aliasing creates trouble for the transparency, though.)

Resizing and positioning your text area

Click the Layout tab of the movie viewer to position your text. Select the text sample in the timeline to select the text block. Then use the handles to resize. Remember, you can turn the grid on or off in the Movie menu. And notice that the Skew button is available in the toolbar, too.

If your text distorts as you resize the text area, select the text sample and then the Properties tab of the Inspector, and check Don't Auto Scale.

Note You can preview your work at any time, but you have to remember to switch to the Preview tab in order to do so

Making text interactive

Just like you can apply GoLive Actions to text links on your Web page, you can do the same here in the QuickTime Editor. It's really just an extension of editing your movie's text. The Actions you can apply here are not the same as the ones on your Web page, though. These are playback oriented for the most part.

To turn text in a QuickTime movie track into a link, follow these steps:

1. Select the text sample, and then go to the Text tab of the Text Sample Inspector.

2. In the text entry field, select the work you want to turn into a link and click the Make Link button.

3. Click the New Action button, and then choose your Action from the pop-up menu.

4. Set up the Action per its options. In Figure 21-21, the Action takes the reader to a URL so the setup is the link to the URL.

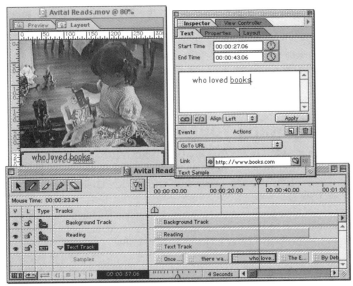

Figure 21-21: Turning text into a link that triggers an action. This one opens a URL when clicked.

Adding HREF Tracks

An HREF in HTML code is a link to any destination on the Web. An HREF track, therefore, adds a URL into a unique text track to your movie. When the movie plays and comes to the start time of the HREF track, if set to Autoload, the user is automatically transported to this link's destination. (The page opens in the user's browser, of course.) Otherwise, the link simply appears where you place it in your movie, available for the user to click, and then goes away when its duration is over. If no target for the URL is specified, the browser will stop playing the movie and jump to the location specified by the HREF segment.

Note   HREF tracks work well when used in a frames-based Web page. You can run the QuickTime movie or animation in its own small frame and direct the browser to display any HREF track links in another, larger viewing frame. This permits the browser to continue to play the movie while the link(s) are loading up at the same time, so people looking at your movies or animations don't have to choose between the movie and the link.

Follow these steps to add an HREF track to your movie:

1. Drag the HREF icon from the Objects palette into the Tracks list in the TimeLine window to place the track. It's not a visual track, so its placement doesn't matter. It's named automatically, and that name can't be changed.

2. *(Optional)* The HREF track is invisible by default, so the URL is hidden within your movie. If you want the URL to be seen, turn on visibility by clicking the Eye icon. You can then use the graphics mode to set up a transparency and use the text block's handles to resize and position the text.

3. Open the track to reveal the sample track, and then choose the Create Sample button (Pencil icon) to define the part of the timeline where you want the URL to be active.

4. With the sample track still selected, use the Inspector to define the URL using your preferred linking method. Figure 21-22 shows Point and Shoot. If using a relative URL, make sure the URL is relative to the movie, not relative to the HTML page that contains the movie (if the HTML page and the movie are in the same folder, this is automatic). If using frames, or if you want the target page to open in a new window, choose a target as usual.

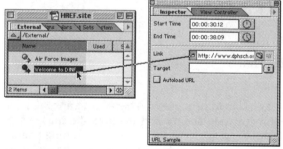

Figure 21-22: The first URL being added to an HREF track via the URL Sample Inspector

QuickTime movies support two special targets that are helpful even when not using frames — "quicktimeplayer" and "myself." If the URL specifies a QuickTime movie, and the target is "quicktimeplayer," the movie loads in the QuickTime Player application instead of in the browser. If the target is "myself," the new movie replaces the current movie, without otherwise changing the current Web page. When the link is defined, its URL appears in the Sample bar as feedback.

Adding Chapter Tracks

When my QuickTime-guru friend Keith demonstrates QuickTime for Apple Computer, people are always wowed by chapters. Yet, looking at QuickTime movies over the years, I rarely see them used. Chapters are a nice touch — and apparently one that'll impress a few people. At any rate, they can definitely make it easier for people to use your movie.

What is a chapter? Take a look at Figure 21-23. That pop-up menu at the lower right of the QuickTime window enables viewers to select from one of those predefined chapters. Upon doing so, the user is instantly transported to that part of the movie. Imagine how helpful that is in a product presentation or instructional video!

Figure 21-23: A completed QuickTime movie containing chapters

Note   I've placed chapter tracks last in this chapter, not because I think them least important but because I think everyone should add them as the finishing polish to a
movie. Although it's simple enough to move a chapter's starting point, having all
the pieces together may make it easier for you to determine just where a new
chapter should begin.

You add only one chapter track to a movie. Within that single track, you create each of your chapters. As you add chapters (samples), the chapter track grows, so begin by defining your first chapter — the one closest to the start of your movie.

To create a chapter track, follow these steps:

1. Drag the Chapter Track icon from the QuickTime tab of the Objects palette into the TimeLine window. By default, a chapter track is not visible when you add it. This is because a chapter is not a visual entity within a movie.

2. Click the blue arrow beside the track's name so you'll be able to add and adjust your chapters.

3. Double-click the track's name in the Tracks list and name your chapter. This name is only a guide for yourself as you work.

4. In the Inspector, in the "Act as Chapter Track for" pop-up menu, choose one of your tracks as the guideline for the chapters. Your chapters won't appear in the Movie window until you do this.

5. Click the Create Sample button at the upper-left corner of the TimeLine window.

6. In the sample track for your chapter track, move to the point where you want the first chapter to begin, and then drag to define the chapter marker. The sample has to be at least 275 pixels in order for it to appear in the Chapter list. (Unfortunately, you get no feedback about how many pixels in size your sample is, but I find that, at a time scale of four seconds, if all three rows of dots on the bars appear, it's long enough.)

   If you're using markers as a guide, use the dotted line in the timeline to notice where your sample will begin.

7. In the Inspector, enter a name for your chapter. This is the name viewers will see. It should be short and give the viewers an idea of what's at that point in the video.

Note   You can also use the Inspector to enter the starting point and duration of the Chapter bar if you prefer not to do it by dragging in the timeline. To change the hour, click the hours, and then type a new one. To change the minutes, select minutes and then adjust the timing. For seconds, click the seconds and do the same. However, you do have to begin the chapter's bar by dragging no matter what.

8. The Sample button remains selected until you choose another button, so go on to define your next chapter by dragging within the same sample line. Then name it, too. As you define each subsequent chapter, the endpoint of the Chapter bar extends toward the end of your movie. You don't have to have a chapter at the very end; the movie's over at that point anyway.

Note   You can also change the start time of the new chapter by changing the numbers in the Start section. If you move the start time backwards, the ending point of the previous chapter moves accordingly.

To edit your chapters later, return to this track and drag the entire bar to a new position or adjust the endpoint by dragging. Or, you can use the Inspector to enter new times. If, while using the Inspector, you cause an overlap, an Alert informs you and prevents it. To delete the chapter, select its bar and press Backspace/Delete. To totally remove all chapters, select the chapter track and then use your Backspace/Delete key, or choose Edit ➪ Cut.

Keep the Chapter bars visible so you can see the Time cursor move as you watch the movie. The bars can be seen anytime the blue arrow below the chapter track is pointing downward. (Click the arrow to turn it down, and then click again to turn it up and conceal the chapter markers.)

To test your chapters, watch the movie in the movie viewer, as follows:

✦ Click the Play button, and then choose a track from the pop-up list to the right of the Play bar.

✦ As you click each chapter's bar in the timeline, the Time cursor jumps to the beginning of that chapter. Then use the Step Backward button to move backward one frame at a time and see the exact point at which the chapter begins.

Saving and Exporting Your Movie

When you first begin working on a new movie and save it, it is flattened, which means all of its resources are in the one file and it can work on any computer platform. As you import items into your movie container, QuickTime tracks all the items you import, but those items are not necessarily really in the movie yet, with some elements actually residing in other source files and merely referenced in the one you're working on. Before you post your movie to your Web site, it's a good idea to flatten it. To do this, choose Movie ➪ Flatten Movie or File ➪ Save As. This flattening is actually making the movie *self-contained*—resolving the references so the movie can stand alone.

After you've done your final save, you can insert it into your Web page (see Chapter 21 to learn how). Then, as with all Web page content, you can, and should, view the Web page in as many browsers as possible on both the Macintosh and a PC, if you can.

Another option is to export the movie. Exporting provides the option to save the movie in one of many formats, as listed in the pop-up menu of the Export dialog box.

To export your movie, follow these steps:

1. Click the Export Movie button on the toolbar or choose Movie ➪ Export Movie to open the Export dialog box (see Figure 21-24). This looks like a Save dialog box, but it has two pop-up menus and options for compression.

2. In the Save dialog box, choose a file type for the export.

   Choose to make your file an AVI file, a BMP file, or DV stream, FLC, Hinted Movie, Image Sequence, Picture, QuickTime, or Text.

Figure 21-24: The Export Movie dialog box

3. In the Use field, choose compression methods and rates.

   If you've done an export before and want to use those same settings, keep Most Recent Settings selected. Otherwise, make your selection.

4. Click Options to bring up the Movie Settings dialog box, shown in Figure 21-25. In this dialog box you can choose from all of the compression methods that are built into QuickTime.

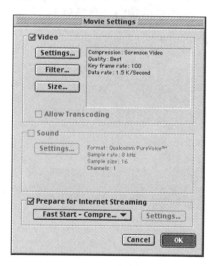

Figure 21-25: The main part of the Movie Settings dialog box. Each section contains powerful compression and rate transfer settings.

5. Click OK to close the Options, and then click Save to complete your save.

To turn your movie into a streaming movie, click the Export As Streaming Movie button in the toolbar or choose Movie ⇨ Export As Streaming Movie and choose your settings as the pop-up menus present themselves. You can learn more about streaming in Chapter 20.

Sometimes you may want to send someone one track of your movie. To do this, select the track you wish to export by clicking its name in the Tracks list, and then click the Export Track button on the toolbar or choose Movie ⇨ Export Track. Use the Export pop-up menu to choose the format you'd like for your track, and then edit the name of the movie, leaving the extension intact. The Options button in the Save dialog box provides some advanced settings. However, those settings are beyond the scope of this book so you'll need to refer to the QuickTime API for details on how to use them.

Using Your Movie in Your Site

When using any image on a Web page, it's important that the page know the image's dimensions so it can display it properly. The QuickTime Editor automatically includes the dimensions of your visual elements so GoLive can write them into the HTML of your page. This helps browsers display your pages more quickly, helping to guarantee that visual elements on your page will appear at the correct size.

✦   ✦   ✦

Creating Your Own JavaScripts

GoLive provides prewritten JavaScripts (Actions and the Rollover and URL Pop-up Smart Objects) that do everything, or just about everything, you'll commonly want to do with JavaScript. However, there may come a time when you'll want to do something not yet accounted for or foreseen by GoLive. Fortunately GoLive, like the Web, is about evolution and flexibility, so you're not limited to using its prewritten JavaScripts.

This chapter introduces you to GoLive's JavaScript Editor, a mini-application designed to make JavaScript creation easier for you. In this chapter, I show you how to place a script into your page, and then how to use the JavaScript Editor. I've also included a short tutorial you can follow to write your first script. You'll find that tutorial in the "Using the JavaScript Editor" section later in this chapter.

Of course, in order to write JavaScripts, you'll need to understand how JavaScript works. That's the topic of many a book in itself, so covering it fully is beyond the scope of this book. (You do want to be able to lift this book, I assume.) In order to get you started, though, take a look at Appendix B.

Using JavaScript

JavaScript can make Web pages friendlier in many ways. It can disable the Submit button until the user fills in all required form fields. It can make suggestions for a user hovering hesitantly over a button. It can generate an HTML page from scratch, as is done in the www.visibone.com/colorlab color scheme lab for the picked colors. JavaScript can also tailor a page to a user's environment, such as screen size, color depth, and/or browser version.

In more advanced applications, JavaScript can contribute to a very smooth chat interface. Or parts of a page can be opened and closed dynamically, like a tree of folders or message threads. JavaScript provides advanced interaction locally (on the client side), without waiting for slow dial-up connections.

You can add your own JavaScript in several ways, as follows:

✦ You can copy a JavaScript from elsewhere, and then paste it into GoLive's source mode.

✦ You can store the JavaScript in the Files tab of the Site Window as its own document, and then link to it.

✦ You can write your own JavaScript, hand-entering it in the JavaScript Editor.

✦ You can use the JavaScript Editor in conjunction with the JavaScript Inspector to build your own JavaScript with drag-and-drop ease.

Placing JavaScript into Your Page

Whether you're given a JavaScript that's prewritten and ready to use, or you are writing the script yourself, you begin by placing the JavaScript icon on the page.

A JavaScript can be placed in the header of your page or directly on the page. The location of the script determines when it will be executed. As your page builds in the user's browser, the browser reads the script and performs whatever function the script describes (tells it to do).

To have a script await a specific action, such as the user clicking an object on your page, place the script in the heading. That script is read and begins working while the page is loading, but isn't necessarily called into action until the event it awaits takes place. Typically this is used for scripts that contain functions triggered by the Onload handler of the page — an event that tells the script handling the event that the page and all of its elements have fully loaded — or any kind of function that is triggered from user interaction like image rollovers.

Scripts in the body begin working when the browser gets to their code. For example, a script can display the user's browser version in case, say, that matters to the quality of the presentation of your page and you want to let the user know.

Inserting JavaScript

Scripts can go in either the head or body elements of your page. To place a JavaScript into the header of your page, you use the icon from the Head tab of the Objects palette. To place a JavaScript in the body of your page you use the icon from the Basic tab of the Objects palette. (Both icons are Java beans with script scroll.) The head and body icons are not interchangeable; the body icon is refused within the head, whereas the head icon appears as text, not an icon in the body. The Inspector for each JavaScript icon is named to reflect the script's position, but the contents and functionality of both are the same. A script in the body of the page executes as the browser reads that part of the page.

A script placed in the header can run while the header of the page is being read, giving it a head start on the rest of the page. Putting a script in the header also enables the script to load and then await a specific user action that may take place on the page later on. Actually, you can also place a script in the body and have it contain functions that are triggered by a user action. However, the body is meant to contain content, so scripts that do not need to execute *while* the browser reads the page should be placed into the head to follow the correct programming method.

Placing a JavaScript in a page's header

To insert a JavaScript icon in the header of your page, follow these steps:

1. Open the Head section of the page by clicking the Toggle Head Section button (the triangle next to the Page icon).

2. Drag a JavaScript icon from the Head tab of the Objects palette into the Head section of your page, as in Figure 22-1. (Alternatively, you can double-click the icon in the Objects palette to automatically put it at the end of all the other elements within the Head section.)

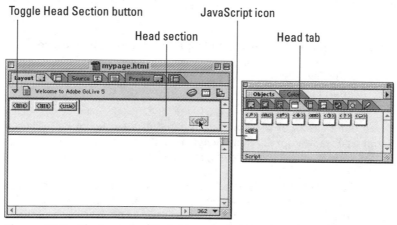

Figure 22-1: Placing a JavaScript icon in the Head section of the page

Tip   If the Head section isn't open (per Step 1) as you begin to drag the JavaScript icon into place, rest your mouse over the Toggle Head Section button (the triangle next to the Page icon) until the Head section springs open, and then continue dragging.

Placing JavaScript in a page's body

To insert a JavaScript in the body of your page, drag a JavaScript icon from the Basic tab of the Objects palette into place in the body of your page. Or you can double-click the icon in the Objects palette to have it automatically land at the end of all the other elements.

Note that when a JavaScript is placed in your page, its icon is visible in Layout mode but not in Preview, nor in your browser. The icon is shown in GoLive's Layout mode as a convenience for you to work with. If you check the page in Source mode, you'll find that GoLive puts JavaScripts between HTML comments. This common practice enables modern browsers that understand the `<script>` tag to interpret the script, but older browsers will merely encounter the comment tag and ignore it. If these comment tags weren't present, the script would appear in the browser as though it were part of the page's content.

Setting up for the JavaScript

After you place the JavaScript icon on your page, the Inspector becomes either the Head Script Inspector or the Body Script Inspector. These two Inspectors are identical in both appearance and function. (As you're working on your JavaScript later, the Inspectors for both become the JavaScript Inspector and offer the actual scripting snippets.)

To provide the information the Script Inspector needs, follow these steps:

1. Name your new script by typing a short descriptive name into the Name field, as shown in Figure 22-2. The name has no effect on the script but makes it easier for you to call it later.

Note   If you don't give your script a custom name, the JavaScript Editor lists it as Head Script 1, Head Script 2, Body Script 1, and so on. None of the three related Inspectors will reflect this default name, though.

2. From the pop-up menu labeled Language, select the browser version your script will support. This will place the corresponding JavaScript language version in the text box below it. In HTML 4, the Language parameter is required within the script tag (specifically, a `TYPE="text/javascript"` attribute, which GoLive does not write and all browsers question).

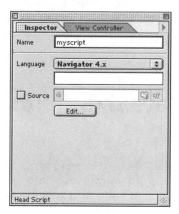

Figure 22-2: The Script Inspector

The inclusion of the Language parameter enables old JavaScript-capable browsers to ignore the script if it's written in a JavaScript version too new for them to understand. Only use the Language parameter if you're certain that parts of your script will be understood only by browser versions 3, 4, and above. When a Language parameter is selected, it appears in the text field below the Language menu, and your script, when viewed in the page's Source mode tab, will state the language within the script tag (`<script language="JavaScript1.2">`). One school of thought is that to enable the broadest user base to use your script, you should leave the Language pop-up menu alone and the text field below it empty. (Actually, `language` is deprecated.) Another is that you should use `JavaScript` as the language because it keeps IE from guessing the script could be VBScript. To do this, you choose Navigator 2.*x* (which writes `JavaScript`). This is all very transitional and unsettled.

3. Determine the source of the JavaScript file, as follows:

   • To paste in script code you've been given or to write your own script, click the Edit button. This opens the JavaScript Editor (and changes the Inspector to the JavaScript Inspector). In the JavaScript Editor, you can paste code you already have or write your own. (Later in this chapter I show you how to use the editor.)

   • To use an external JavaScript file, click the Source checkbox and then Point and Shoot to, browse to, or type in the location of the .js file. As with all files you use in GoLive, it's best to place your external JavaScript document into the Files tab of the Site Window before you use it in a page. Also, make sure the file's name ends with the .js extension. (To learn how to create the external script, read on.)

Whether you are creating a new JavaScript or want to edit an external script you've been given, you use the JavaScript Editor. This editor is explained after the next section.

Incorporating a Provided JavaScript into Your Page

When you ask for help on an e-mail list or visit a Web site that provides JavaScript code, you may be given the text to use, but it's up to you to put it into use in your page. You can turn this script into an external script and link it to your page, or you can place the JavaScript directly into your page.

Placing JavaScript code into an external JavaScript file

When someone provides you with JavaScript code that you want to use in multiple places, you might want to turn it into an external JavaScript document.

Follow these steps to create an external JavaScript document:

1. Drag a new blank page into the Files tab of the Site Window and give it a short descriptive name, ending with the .js extension. Or begin a new page by choosing File ➪ New Special ➪ JavaScript Document, but remember that you'll have to save this new document into your Files tab (root) when you save it.

2. Double-click this page to open it (unless it's already open). Because the page ends with the .js extension, it opens in the JavaScript Editor.

3. Paste the code you've been given into this page. You can use the error-checking buttons on the JavaScript Editor's toolbar to check the script.

4. Save the page.

You can now link to this document as an external JavaScript. You might bear in mind that external JavaScript libraries do not work in all browsers. For example, Netscape Navigator 3 Gold had major problems with it. However, you probably won't be counting on JavaScript to work in an older browser like that anyway.

Placing JavaScript code directly into your page

When you're provided with a JavaScript that you want to incorporate into your page, you don't actually have to use GoLive's visual interface, first placing a JavaScript icon on a page. If you prefer, you can easily paste the JavaScript directly into your page's code using the Source mode. (You cannot paste the script into the page in Layout mode because GoLive would interpret that code as page content. Outline mode enables you to browse to an external file but not to paste in a script's code.)

Each JavaScript begins with a `<script>` tag and ends with a `</script>` tag. You copy these tags and everything in between them, and then paste this script into your page. Or, a script meant for sharing may be marked by comment tags to guide you. For example, when you set up an account with TheCounter.com, the script they provide you for placement into your page clearly begins with a start comment (`<!-- Start of TheCounter.com Code -->`) and ends with an end comment, (`<!-- End of TheCounter.com Code -->`).

To paste a script into Source mode, switch to the Source tab, place your cursor at the point where the script should begin, click to insert the I-beam cursor, and then paste. After you paste the script and switch back to Layout mode, you'll see the JavaScript icon in the header or body.

After you're incorporated a JavaScript into your page, you may want to customize it for your site or expand upon it. You can use the JavaScript Editor to do this, so keep reading or come back to the next section when you're ready.

Introducing the JavaScript Editor

GoLive contains its own JavaScript Editor, complete with specialized features such as syntax highlighting and checking. If you're comfortable with the JavaScript language and you want to type in your own code, you can. If you'd rather have a helping hand writing your script, GoLive provides that, too. When you open the JavaScript Editor, the Inspector becomes the JavaScript Inspector, which works in conjunction with the JavaScript Editor, providing drag-and-drop building blocks for creating or editing JavaScript.

Testing a Hand-Coded JavaScript

To test your hand-coded JavaScript, preview the page in a browser. (This is necessary for GoLive-coded JavaScripts as well.) In Netscape, you can type **javascript:** in the URL field in order to open a console that displays any error messages (the debugger window). In Internet Explorer, errors in JavaScript trigger a dialog box that describes the type of error and the line number of the code.

You have three ways to open GoLive's JavaScript Editor, as follows:

✦ Double-click the JavaScript icon in the page (head or body). This is the fastest method, and it ensures that you open and edit the correct script.

✦ Select the JavaScript icon in the page, and then click the Edit button in the JavaScript Inspector. This method also ensures that you open and edit the correct script.

✦ Click the JavaScript Editor icon (the Java Bean) on the upper-right corner of the page window, and then choose the script you want to view and/or edit from the pop-up menu at the upper right.

When you're editing a JavaScript, you have two main tools: the toolbar and the JavaScript Inspector.

The JavaScript Editor toolbar

As you build or edit a JavaScript, the JavaScript Editor's toolbar (see Figure 22-3) can assist you by making it easier to view your script, and by providing error checking and feedback. Its use is very straightforward.

From left to right, the buttons on the JavaScript Editor toolbar are as follows:

✦ **Toggle Error Display.** When open, this area shows the details of the errors reported in the toolbar.

✦ **Check Syntax.** Clicking this button causes the JavaScript Editor to read the code you have created and look for syntax errors. Errors and warnings are then displayed. (When you click this button, the Error Display area closes automatically.)

✦ **Display Errors.** This button toggles between showing and hiding a list of errors in the top pane of the JavaScript Editor. (The button is gray when active.) The number of errors shows to the right of this button. Each error appears in the Error Display area, beside a Stop sign icon. When you click an error in the error display, the code in question becomes highlighted in the page. If you add code to your page while the errors are displayed, click the Check Syntax button again to check the new code.

✦ **Display Warnings.** This button toggles between showing and hiding a list of warnings in the top pane of the JavaScript Editor. (The button is gray when active.) Warnings notify you of code segments that use proper syntax but appear to create an untenable situation, such as a nested function definition. The number of warnings is shown to the right of the Display Warnings button. Each warning appears in the Error Display area, beside a Yield sign icon. When you click a warning in the error display, the code in question becomes highlighted in the page. If you add code to your page while the warnings are displayed, click the Check Syntax button again to check the new code.

Toggle Error Display

Check Syntax

Display Errors   New Script Item

Display Warnings   Delete Script Item

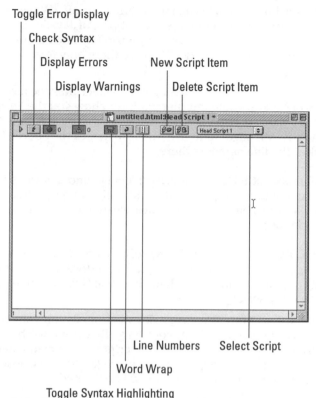

Line Numbers   Select Script

Word Wrap

Toggle Syntax Highlighting

Figure 22-3: The JavaScript Editor

Caution

Under certain circumstances, the displayed error message or warning complains about something that seems to be correct. This happens when all parts of the code are syntactically correct by themselves, but the script as a whole makes no sense. Thus, the Syntax Checker made a wrong assumption about which part of the code is supposed to be correct. For example, a "{ } mismatch" error can be caused by a missing semicolon (;).

✦ **Syntax Highlighting On/Off.** With syntax highlighting on, specific portions of your JavaScript code appear in different colors, enabling you to easily see exactly what's what. (See the "Setting the JavaScript Editor's Preferences" section later in this chapter to find out how to change the colors.) When gray, this button is on.

✦ **Word Wrap.** This button toggles word wrap on or off. (When on, the button is dark gray.) Many JavaScript lines run longer than will fit comfortably within the editor's window without scrolling, so Word Wrap helps you view the script more easily. This is a soft wrap, which doesn't actually place a carriage return or line feed into the line of code. (Physically breaking a line breaks the script.) It's for appearance's sake within the JavaScript Editor, and does not affect the script's source code at all.

✦ **Line Numbers.** This button toggles line numbers on or off. (When on, the button is dark gray.) Although line numbers are not part of JavaScript programming, they help you to easily see where things are. The line numbers do not show up in the actual JavaScript code. They are there only for reference within the JavaScript Editor.

Line numbers are a great help when debugging JavaScripts, because the debug windows of Netscape and Internet Explorer show you the line numbers where the errors occurred. However, these line numbers are counted from the start of the whole HTML page, so to use them, switch to the Source Code Editor and look at the line numbers there.

Note   Like the internal JavaScript Editor, the browser's debug functions can only make assumptions about the code it expects and the type of error arising from such an error. Sometimes it just comes close to the area where the error happens but is wrong on its conclusions.

✦ **New Script Item.** This button places a new script icon within the header of your page and opens a new, blank script window. (It does not create a script within the body of your document, perhaps because GoLive cannot know where to place a body script.)

✦ **Delete Script Item.** This button removes all code from within your script window and removes the script icon from your page. Be careful to check the name of the script that appears in the Select Script pop-up menu, because regardless of the script icon you selected in the page, the one whose name appears in the pop-up menu is the one that will be deleted.

✦ **Select Script.** This pop-up menu presents the names of all scripts in your document, whether they contain content or not. Selecting a script from this list displays it in the current editor window so you can view it or work with it. When you open the JavaScript Editor by clicking the JavaScript Editor button in the top-right of the Web page window, be sure to select your desired script from the editor so you work on the right script.

Whenever you launch the JavaScript Editor, the Script Inspector changes into the JavaScript Inspector. It now has three separate tabs: Script, Events, and Objects.

The Script tab

The first tab is labeled "Script," and it's identical to the basic Script Inspector (previously shown in Figure 22-2) except for the addition of a Functions listing. The Functions listing is empty at first, but you will fill it as you add functions to your JavaScript. Once functions are listed, you can navigate directly to any function in the JavaScript Editor by clicking it in the listing. This can save you lots of time that you would otherwise have to spend tracking it down within the code.

Note   In order to find a certain piece of code, you can always use the Find & Replace function.

The Events tab

The Events tab (see Figure 22-4) provides a full list of all events that you can add to your JavaScript. These events can be dragged into place within the JavaScript Editor to help you build your script.

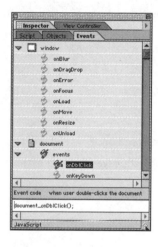

Figure 22-4: The Events tab

The available events listed are dependent upon your page. When you're working on a blank Web page, the only events that can take place (and, therefore, the only ones listed in the Events tab) are window and document events. As you add other elements to the page, those that can have events are automatically added to the listing under the appropriate category (window or document). For example, when you add a form to your page, form-relevant events appear under the document events listing. Or, when you add an image to your page, a set of image events appears under the document options.

To see the available events, after you select the Events tab, click the arrow (Mac) or plus sign (Windows) next to the category When you select any event within the JavaScript Inspector, a short description appears at the bottom of the Inspector beside the words "Event Code" to guide you in your choice. After you place this code onto the page, its code string appears in the white area below the code's description. Table 22-1 shows some common JavaScript events.

Table 22-1
Common JavaScript Events

Event	Meaning
onBlur	An element loses focus; it is no longer the selected or active element. For example, a window is moved backward as another becomes active.
onDblClick	The mouse button is pressed and released twice in rapid succession.
onDragDrop	A drag-and-drop operation is completed.
onError	An error occurs.
onFocus	An element receives focus.
onKeyDown	A key is pressed.
onKeyPress	A key is pressed and released.
onKeyUp	A pressed key is released.
onClick	The mouse button is pressed and released once.
onMouseOut	The mouse pointer moves off the object (leaves the area of the object).
onMouseDown	The mouse button is pressed.
onMouseUp	The mouse button is released.
onMouseMove	The mouse pointer moves.
onMove	A window is moved.
OnLoad	The page and all list elements are fully loaded into the browser.
OnUnload	The browser moves on to another page.
OnResize	A window is resized.

To add the code for an event to your script, drag the event name from the Events tab into the JavaScript Editor. The JavaScript Editor automatically names the function when you drop the object into it. The name is comprised of the name of the object, an underline, and then the name of the event. For example: `document_onMouseDown()`.

The Objects tab

The Objects tab (see Figure 22-5) contains objects and their available properties and methods that can become part of your script. As with the Events tab, you drag objects into your script. Actually, you don't have to drag an Object's icon to the page. Instead, you can select and drag an object's specific property or method to the page, and the editor writes the full code to include the object automatically.

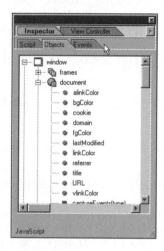

Figure 22-5: The Objects tab

To see the available object properties and methods, after you select the Objects tab, click the arrow (Mac) or plus (+) sign (Windows) next to the category (Window, Document, or Other) to view the listing of available object properties and methods.

Far too many properties and methods exist to explain here, but you can select any object within the JavaScript Inspector and learn a bit about it from a short description that appears at the bottom of the Inspector.

Note   A property is something that describes an object. (Properties have red squares.) A method is something an object can do, like get, open, close, clear, write, or capture. (Methods have green dots.)

When you drag an object property or method into the JavaScript Editor, the appropriate JavaScript referencing is automatically written as soon as you release the object. For example, to write `history.forward()`, open the window folder/list, and then open options under the *history* heading. In that list you see an object method called *forward()*. Simply drag *forward()* to the page, and the editor writes the entire string: `history.forward()`.

Using the JavaScript Editor

Now that you're familiar with the JavaScript Editor's interface, you pretty much know how to use it to compose a JavaScript. In this section you use this interface to create your first JavaScripts.

Basically, you begin every script by placing the highest-level object first. To select a Window Object, open the Window folder. To select a Document Object, open the Document folder. If you need to start with the window, select a Window Object. Next add either a method or a property. If you want to add a method, add it, followed by its parentheses ( ), and finally add the argument or arguments within the parentheses. If you want to add a property, simply add it. Properties have no arguments and thus have no parentheses.

To guide you in your search for code within the JavaScript Inspector, icons mark code segments in the Object tab as follows:

   ✦ The red square designates an object method (such as get, open, close, clear, write, or capture).

   ✦ The green dot designates an object property (which is an object description).

You may notice that sometimes items come into the code as lowercase while others have some uppercase characters mixed in. The standard of using an uppercase mixture helps you see second and third words within a multiword event, object, method, or property. However, names of properties and methods always start with lowercase. By convention, if a name starts with uppercase it references the class or type of an object (such as Array, Location, Math, Number, or String). Note that exceptions exist.

If the JavaScript you're working on is within your page, whatever you type into the JavaScript Editor instantly becomes a part of the code in that page. You cannot see it unless you have the Source Code window open, but it's there. This means you don't have to save the contents of the JavaScript Editor. But you do have to remember to save your page after you close the JavaScript Editor and return to the Web page you're working on. Of course, it is always best to save often.

Tip   If you find yourself using the same bit of code repeatedly, you can create a Text Macro that inserts that code with just the typing of a key combination. This can save you time and help you avoid typing errors. To learn how to create a Text Macro, see Chapter 14.

A script tutorial

To get a feel for using the JavaScript Editor along with the JavaScript Inspector, try creating this simple script, which writes monitor information into the user's browser. This JavaScript is written directly into the page, so no event handler exists.

To create your first JavaScript in the GoLive JavaScript Editor:

1. Drag a JavaScript icon from the Basic tab of the Objects palette into the body, as shown in Figure 22-6. Drop it exactly where you want the words that this script will write to appear.

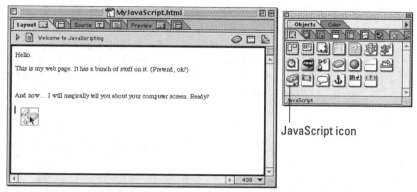

JavaScript icon

Figure 22-6: Placing the JavaScript icon into place on the page

2. Double-click the icon to open the JavaScript Editor. If it doesn't open to the Script tab, click that tab now.

3. Name the script **DocWriteJS** for this tutorial, as shown in Figure 22-7. (You can actually choose your own name, though, if you want.)

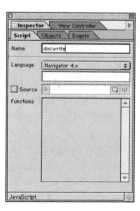

Figure 22-7: The Script tab of the JavaScript Inspector, as it should now appear

4. For this tutorial, either leave the language field blank or choose Navigator 2.x (which writes JavaScript). When this text field is empty, you are not including any Language parameter, and the code that is written is just ⟨script⟩.

   If you choose a language and then change your mind, just delete the language name from the text field. Or, after you've completed the script, you can delete the language in Source mode. (The final code at the end of this tutorial can be your guide.)

5. In this document write example, the highest level is the *Document Object,* so switch to the Objects tab and open the Document listing. Locate the method "write(text)" and drag it into the editor, as shown in Figure 22-8. (Remember, you're looking for an item by a red square. That visual clue can help you save time and make choices later on.)

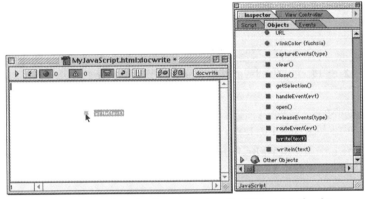

Figure 22-8: Dragging the Document write Object Method to the editor

The editor now displays `document.write(text)`. If you have Syntax Coloring on, the method appears as purple unless you've changed the default colors. Now you need to tell the browser what to write into the document. This information goes into the parentheses that follow the method.

6. Double-click to select the word "text" between the parentheses; it's there as a guide. Then type: **Your screen resolution is**. The script will display exactly what you type between the quotation marks. You can call this "hard-coding" text. You begin with a quotation mark and then enter the desired text and close with an end quotation mark. Don't forget to include a space to go between words. The editor now displays the following (as shown in Figure 22-9):

```
document.write("Your screen resolution is ")
```

If you have Syntax Coloring on, the text appears as brown unless you've changed the default colors.

Figure 22-9: The JavaScript Editor as it appears after you enter the first text of your message

7. To join the literal text with the property you seek, type a plus sign (+). (You are still working within the parentheses.)

You can type a space before and/or after the plus sign if you prefer. The spaces won't have any effect on the script and may make it easier for you to see what you're doing. (But "real programmers" don't use spaces.) With Syntax Coloring, the plus sign appears as black by default. The editor now displays:

```
document.write("Your screen resolution is "+).
```

> **Note**
>
> After you type an opening quote mark, the text you're typing appears in red — until you type the closing quote mark. That's the error-checking feature in action.

8. To tell the script to get and display information about the screen resolution, open Window in the Object tab, and then open Screen, and finally drag the property "width" into place immediately after the plus sign and before the closing parenthesis, as shown in Figure 22-10.

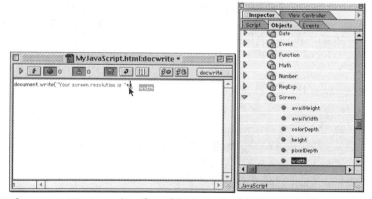

Figure 22-10: Dragging the Object Method (which gets the user's screen resolution) into place within the text that the script will generate

The editor now displays the following:

```
document.write("Your screen resolution is "+screen.width)
```

If you have Syntax Coloring on, the property appears as purple, like the method, unless you've changed the default colors.

Tip

How do you figure out what to drag and where to drop the dragged object? Because you need to get the property of an object, you begin your search under the Object tab. In this case the property you seek is the screen resolution, as stated by the hard-coded text, so logically you search for something that says "screen." Because green dots denote properties, you just have to check items that have green dots.

9. To join this property with more literal text, type another plus sign (+) immediately after "screen.width" and before the closing parenthesis. The editor now displays the following:

```
document.write("Your screen resolution is "+screen.width+)
```

10. To add more literal text — an *x* or the word *by*, as is common when stating dimensions — type another quotation mark, a space, and then your text, followed by another space and the end quotation mark. The editor now displays:

```
document.write("Your screen resolution is "+screen.width+"
by ")
```

11. To join this literal text with another property — in this case, the screen height — type another plus sign (+) immediately after the last quotation mark and before the closing parenthesis. The editor now displays:

```
document.write("Your screen resolution is "+screen.width+"
by "+)
```

12. To tell the script to get and display more information about the screen resolution, again in the Object tab, open Other Objects, and then open Screen, and finally drag the property "height" into place immediately after the last plus sign and before the closing parenthesis. (This follows the same logic as in Step 8.)

The editor now displays:

```
document.write("Your screen resolution is "+screen.width+" by
"+screen.height)
```

13. To tell the editor you're finished, type a semicolon (;) after the closing parenthesis. The editor now displays the following:

```
document.write("Your screen resolution is "+screen.width+" by
"+screen.height);
```

If you've performed each step in this tutorial as instructed and have errors and warnings turned on, there should be a 0 (zero) next to each button on the tool-bar. (If a number appears by either button, click the button to display the error notice.)

Caution

Do not count on GoLive to pick up on the errors in Object Property and Method capitalization. If *any* objects within the Other Objects section of the Objects tab write themselves with a capital letter in the first word, you will have to change the case yourself manually for the script to work.

14. Close the JavaScript Editor and switch to the Source tab of the page's window to view the full script (see Figure 22-11). The comment-like tags in front of your code (`<!--`) and at the end (`// -->`) are normal for demarcating a JavaScript. They're necessary to prevent errors in browsers that don't understand JavaScript.

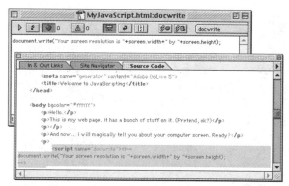

Figure 22-11: The final script, along with the code it generates in the page's source code

Note

In order to familiarize you with the JavaScript Editor, this tutorial covered adding a simple script to a page. Building a more intricate script, such as one that triggers upon a specific event, requires an understanding of JavaScript's Event flow hierarchy and is too much to go into within this book. If you're familiar with JavaScript, you'll be able to take it from here.

Note

To test your hand-coded JavaScript, preview the page in a browser. (This is necessary for GoLive-coded JavaScripts as well.) In Netscape, you can type **javascript:** in the URL field to open a console that displays any error messages (the debugger window). In Internet Explorer, errors in JavaScript trigger a dialog box that describes the type of error and the line number of the code.

JavaScript T'n'T

by Oliver Zahorka of OUT Media Design GmbH, Switzerland

Here are some tips to avoid booby traps and pitfalls when using JavaScript on your pages:

✦ Only use characters and numbers in variable names. Do not use punctuation marks (`.`,`;`:), quotation marks (`"` or `'`), or spaces—these have a special meaning in JavaScript.

✦ Do not start variable names with numbers.

✦ End all your statements with a semicolon (`;`). Most JavaScript parsers are very forgiving regarding the syntax structure of your scripts, but this is implementation dependent, and in case of ambiguity the script fails.

✦ Always use `var` to declare local variables that should be kept inside the scope of the current function or script. Otherwise you might unwillingly overwrite the content of a (global) variable still in use by another function of the script.

✦ Double-check whether you really compare two values for equality (`thisValue==thatValue`) or instead do an assignment (`thisValue=thatValue`).

✦ When naming objects in the various Inspectors, try to use unique JavaScript names (which also applies when using Actions for these objects). Otherwise, it may not be clear what object a JavaScript call refers to. For example, an image and a form that are both named "myNamedObject" cannot be accessed consistently under certain conditions. (See the next tip.)

✦ When accessing objects, use the more complicated but unambiguous notation referencing the proper object arrays. For example, use `document.forms["myNamedObject"]` instead of the shorter `document.myNamedObject`.

✦ When naming any kind of HTML object, try to avoid known JavaScript-reserved names. A good example of a bad name is "top" for a frame. Because "top" is a JavaScript keyword used for the topmost window in the event hierarchy, the script will behave unexpectedly if you try to access a frame named "top" via JavaScript.

✦ One source of confusion is the fact that JavaScript is case-sensitive. Therefore the name "myObject" and "MyObject" are not equivalent, but can be used to identify different objects.

✦ In Windows, some JavaScript functions that access URLs seem to fail. This is due to the fact that browsers are programmed to fetch a file via HTTP and not to access it on the local drive. If you think your JavaScript should work (and display an image, for example), try to copy your files to a regular Web server for testing.

Setting the JavaScript Editor's Preferences

You can set the JavaScript Editor's look and behavior for your own comfort. To set the JavaScript Editor preferences, choose Edit ⇨ Preferences. Select the JavaScript icon in the list at the left of the Preferences dialog box to see the main preferences. Then, in the list at the left of the Preferences dialog box, click the arrow (Mac) or plus sign (Windows) next to the JavaScript icon to reveal the other JavaScript preference categories (see Figure 22-12).

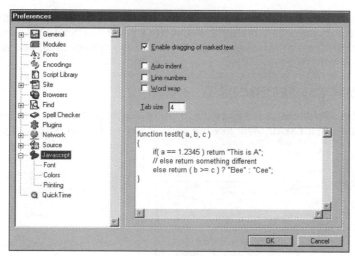

Figure 22-12: The JavaScript Preferences dialog box

The main JavaScript preferences are as follows:

✦ **Enable dragging of marked text.** By default you can drag and drop text. If for some reason you prefer to disable this feature, remove the checkmark by this option.

✦ **Auto indent.** The Auto indent checkbox is deselected by default. Select it if you want the JavaScript Editor to automatically subordinate lines of code by a preset amount.

✦ **Line numbers.** Line numbers don't have any effect on your script, and they appear only in the JavaScript Editor, but they can make troubleshooting much easier. To have line numbers appear in the JavaScript Editor, check this option. This option also appears in the toolbar. Your toolbar choice overrides the Preference setting.

✦ **Word wrap.** By default, your lines of code continue in a straight line, which can become very long. It's easier to read your code if you enable wrapping within the JavaScript Editor. (Like line numbers, this setting only affects the display in the editor and doesn't affect your script.) This option also appears in the toolbar. Your toolbar choice overrides the Preference setting.

✦ **Tab size.** The tab size determines the number of spaces each tab moves your JavaScript code, and actually does affect the JavaScript code. The Tab size text box is set to 4 by default. To change the tab size, select the default number and type the desired number over it.

To view the rest of the JavaScript preferences, click the arrow (Mac) or plus sign (Windows) next to the JavaScript icon in the list at the left of the Preferences dialog box. Then click Font, Colors, or Printing to see and set those options, respectively.

JavaScript font preferences

The JavaScript font preferences (see Figure 22-13) only affect the font used in the JavaScript Editor and are for your own viewing and editing — they don't affect your page or scripts.

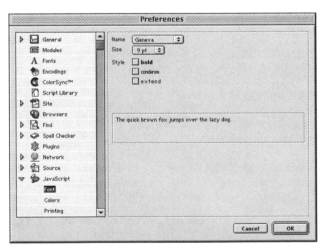

Figure 22-13: The Font Preferences dialog box (Mac). In Windows, make your choices from scrolling lists instead of pop-ups.

As you choose from the following options, you can see the results in the sample area:

✦ **Name.** Select a font face from the menu. You can use any font installed in your system.

✦ **Size.** Select a font size from the menu.

✦ **Style.** If you prefer your text to appear bolded, condensed, or extended, check the appropriate box.

JavaScript color preferences

The following are the available JavaScript color preferences:

✦ **Enable Syntax Highlighting.** This setting is deselected by default. In order to have the JavaScript Editor check your code's syntax and report it to you clearly, check this box. You can also turn on syntax highlighting from the JavaScript Editor toolbar. The toolbar setting overrides this application-wide preference.

✦ **Colors.** You may select a color for each syntax. To do so, click the color you want to change, and then choose a new color using your computer's color picker.

JavaScript printing preferences

The JavaScript printing preferences are as follows:

✦ **Printer Specific Settings.** If you plan to print your scripts and would like visual clues about your code's syntax so you can read it more clearly, turn on Printer Specific Settings and then check each desired setting. Here are the options:

- *Syntax Highlighting.* This enables the same colors you see in the JavaScript Editor to be printed. It is most beneficial if you have a color printer.

- *Bold Typeface Tags.* This prints all tags in bold so they stand out from the surrounding code.

- *Line Numbers.* This provides line numbering in your printout.

✦ **Use special font for printing.** This set of font preferences provides control of the font for printing your script. The options are as follows:

- *Name.* Select a font face from the menu. As with the onscreen font preference, you can use any font you have installed.

- *Size.* This sets the font size.

- *Style.* If you prefer your text to appear bolded, condensed, or extended, check the appropriate box.

✦   ✦   ✦

Adding Java Applets to Your Page

If you're even remotely interested in doing a Web page, or have perused the computer aisles of your local book store, you've certainly heard of Java. But what is it and what can it do for your site?

Java is a programming language developed by Sun Micro-systems in 1996. But it's *not just another programming language*. Java is platform agnostic, and therefore inherently cross-platform—and that's where all the excitement lies. This is big news on the Web because a programmer can write the application (actually, a mini-app, called an *applet*) once and it can run on any computer. The programmer just has to write the unique applet code, which then runs in conjunction with something called the Java Virtual Machine (JVM). The JVM is a player of sorts, created to play the individual Java applets each programmer creates. There's a virtual machine written for each computer platform. It's been around and been part of OS installs and/or browsers since 1996, so your common everyday Web surfer should have it installed and ready to run.

Introducing the Advantages of Java

Because the applet code is small, not needing the added weight of a full platform-specific application, Java is a good language for sending applications over the Web. The only code that has to be downloaded from the Web server to the user's machine is the applet-specific code. That code lives on your site's Web server as a separate document or series of documents. Inside the Web page, the `<applet>` links to them and tells the Web server to carry those files to the user's browser along with the rest of the page. When the browser sees the `<applet>` tag, it tells your computer to launch its JVM. From there, the JVM takes over, playing (executing) the downloaded applet files.

> **Note** Whenever you see a message in your browser's Status bar that says "Applet Loading," that's the JVM being called for, launching, and then beginning to read the applet's files. As soon as the files are read, the applet appears on the Web page.

So what can a Java applet do? Java applets can add a lot of functionality to your page, or you can use them just for fun. For example, an applet can provide links to other pages, provide a searchable database, provide a searchable guestbook, or show graphs and charts. If you're selling anything at your site, a currency converter can facilitate sales. Or an applet can provide a scrolling news area or banner. Or you can use Java to add a game to your site. A Java applet can also add a special effect in conjunction with another element on your page.

Java is a full programming language, so teaching you to create your own Java applet is well beyond the scope of this book. This chapter focuses on how to place a Java applet into your page. Zillions of prewritten applets are available on the Web, some free and others very reasonably priced, so you won't be hurting for good applets.

> **Note** Don't lose track of the differences between Java and JavaScript. Although alike in name, they are nothing alike in nature. JavaScript is a language that functions within the user's browser. Java is a standalone mini-application that runs within a separate application called the Java Virtual Machine.

Each Java applet has one master file that contains the base code for the applet. This is the file the Java plug-in links to. This base file then calls up any other class files, as needed. Parameters define, or help define, the way an applet functions. An applet usually comes with instructions stating parameter settings, or parameters may already be set. In some cases, a text file is provided and you customize that file. In some other cases, an applet may include graphic or other media files and perhaps you may substitute your own. In any case, a well written applet includes explicit directions. Once you understand the basics I show you here, you should be able to use any well-written applet with ease and confidence.

> **Caution** Do not change the name of any of the applet's files. All files need to be named exactly as the programmer named them. Java is case-sensitive so even capitalizing a word causes an error.

Adding a Java Applet to Your Page

Rather than actually place a Java applet into your page, as you can with JavaScript, you call a Java applet from a tag within your page. The actual applet files cohabit with the rest of your site files, first in the Site Window, and then later on the Web server. As with graphics and other media files, an applet is called from your page by a specific tag, and information unique to the one instance of its use is placed within that tag. In other words, you drag the applet files into your Site Window, and then use the Java icon to place the applet and the Inspector to set up the applet's attributes — much the same way you add any graphic file to your page.

To put a Java applet on your page, follow these steps:

1. Drag the Java applet's .class or .jar file into the Files tab of the Site Window so GoLive can manage it.

   If the applet has multiple files, place them within a folder of their own within the File tab to keep them organized.

Check the applet's documentation to learn which files are needed in the Site Window. There may just be one .class file or many. There may be .jar files, or sound, image, or media files. Other files may include plain text (.txt) files.

2. Drag the Java applet icon from the Basic tab of the Objects palette and place it on your page, as shown in Figure 23-1.

Java applet icon

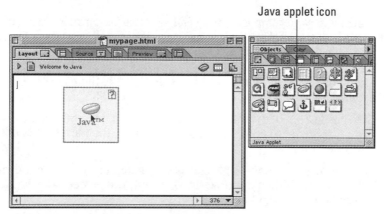

Figure 23-1: Placing the Java placeholder on the page

3. Set the applet's master .class file by linking from the Base field of the Inspector (now the Java Applet Inspector) to the designated .class file within the Files tab of the Site Window, as shown in Figure 23-2. (The Base file can also be a .jar file or a collection of files called a .zip file. You link to those same way.)

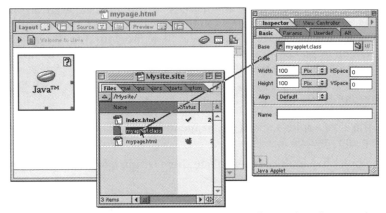

Figure 23-2: Linking to the file that contains the applet's base code

Use your preferred linking method (Point and Shoot, browse, or hand-entering). Or, as usual, you can Point and Shoot directly from the placeholder icon by pressing Command (Mac) or Alt (Windows) as you drag from the placeholder.

Note   A Java applet may be comprised of several separate files. If so, read the directions that come with the applet. These instructions should tell you which file contains the base code that you should link to.

After you link the placeholder to the JavaScript file, the base code is reported in the following two places, as reflected in Figure 23-3:

- The Code area of the Inspector reports the name of the base code file you just linked to. If the file is in a subfolder, the path to it is not included there.

- On the page, the name of the applet appears in the top-left corner of the placeholder. (When not linked to a script, the placeholder has a question mark in the top-right corner.)

Figure 23-3: The Java Applet Inspector after the main class file is linked

On the Mac you can preview the effect of the applet in your page now (if the applet runs from a link to a .class file and you have MRJ — Mac Runtime for Java — installed). Click the play button — the arrow — at the bottom-left corner of the Java Applet Inspector. If the applet doesn't require specific parameters, it plays. Otherwise, it will say "loading." Click the Preview arrow again to stop the preview. You need to stop it in order to continue working in the Inspector. (Windows preview is not possible because Windows does not have a virtual Java engine.)

4. Resize the Applet the same way you resize a graphic, as follows:

   • Drag one of the handles.

   • Enter the desired width and height in the Width and Height text boxes, after selecting the measurement unit — pixels or percentage — from the pop-up selection. (The unit of measure for both dimensions should match.)

   In this example, the height is 95 percent so it fills the browser page, while the width is 100 pixels. This applet lets you control the size of the text used, in pixels, so that size affects the width you set here. You can always return to the Inspector and change either dimension.

5. *(Optional)* In the HSpace and VSpace text boxes, set the amount of space, in pixels, that you'd like to have between the Java applet and any surrounding page elements. You may prefer to do this later, after seeing how the applet looks on the page.

   HSpace controls horizontal space — the space at the left and right of the applet. VSpace controls vertical space, which is the top and bottom space. You have no way to specify just left or right, nor just top or bottom.

6. *(Optional)* Select an alignment from the Align pop-up menu. Alignments for Java applets work the same way as for images (see Chapter 10).

7. Enter a unique-to-the-page name in the Name text field so it can be identified as a unique object on the page.

8. Turn to the Params tab and enter any required (and desired optional) parameters. A good applet comes with a list of all available parameters, noting which are necessary to enter and define. For each new parameter you want to create, do the following:

- Click the New button. This adds the words "param" and "value" to the list in the main section of the Inspector. The data entry fields for this new parameter are at the bottom of the Inspector, as shown in Figure 23-4.

- In the left field, the word "param" guides you to enter the name of the parameter. If it is not already selected, select "param," and then type your actual parameter. A parameter can be whatever the programmer sets it up to be. For example, it may be regcode, author, name, image, bgcolor, align, or target, just to name a few. Then press the Tab key to select the value field.

- In the right field, type the actual value that goes along with the parameter.

  As you enter each parameter and value, the HTML is written into the page within the applet tags, as shown in Figure 23-5, where a set of parameters has been entered.

  You can edit a parameter at any time. To do so, click the parameter in the list, and then edit the text within the two fields at the bottom of the editor.

Figure 23-4: The Params tab after the first new parameter is started

9. To facilitate accessibility, in the Alt tab enter alternative text that describes the applet into the Alt Text field.

10. To accommodate those who don't have Java capability turned on, do the following:

a. In the Alt tab check Show Alternative HTML, changing the Java placeholder icon to a green-framed area.

b. Click inside the white area within in green frame and type some text, or drag any regular page elements into the white area.

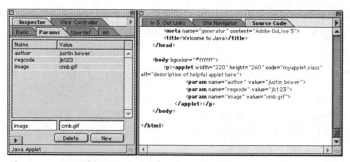

Figure 23-5: The Params tab after some parameters are added, and the resulting applet tag's code

For example, you can place an Image icon from the Objects palette, and then link it to an image. This way, the image will appear in lieu of the applet. Or, if you enter text here and format it, the text will be constrained by the green box, and will reflect any style formatting you apply to the text.

If you'd rather not use the Inspector to enter each parameter, you can give yourself a head start. Visit the Web page where you downloaded the applet, or open the applet's HTML help page within a browser or GoLive. Select and copy all of the text from the first `<param>` tag to the end of the last one. Return to your page in progress, place the cursor in front of the closing `</applet>` tag, and then paste. When you turn to the Inspector's Param tab, all of the copied parameters will be there.

Checking your results

After you've completed the entries in the Inspector, check your results. You have four ways to do so:

✦ *(Mac only)* While in Layout mode, click the button in the bottom-left corner of the Inspector to preview the applet from within the Layout mode of your page. The script may take a while to load so be patient. The button darkens during preview so you know it's running. It's possible that an applet will work here but not in a browser, so it's best to use this feature as more of a preview.

✦ Switch to the Preview tab.

✦ Use the Preview in Browser button to display the page in your browser. This enables you to watch the Status bar messages. Test in both Netscape and Internet Explorer.

✦ To test the applet across platforms and browsers, upload the pages to the Web server, and then have many users test it for you.

If the base file does not end with the .class extension, it will function fully in a browser, but you won't be able to preview it within GoLive.

Editing and deleting parameters

If you wish to change any parameters, click the parameter once in the Params tab of the Inspector, and then edit the value in the Value field at the bottom of the Java Applet Inspector. (The Java icon must be selected before you can see the Java Applet Inspector.)

To delete a parameter, click it in the Parameters list of the Params tab, and then click the Delete button.

Adding a Java Applet Using Cut and Paste

You can copy all of the sample applet code, and then skip the step of placing the Java placeholder onto the page. Copying the applet code doesn't place the applet's files into your site, so you still begin the same way. Here's what to do:

1. Drag the Java applet's .class, .jar, and/or other files into the Files tab of the Site Window so GoLive can manage it.

   If the applet has multiple files, place them within a folder of their own within the File tab to keep them organized.

Check the applet's documentation to learn which files are needed in the Site Window. There may just be one .class file or many. There may be .jar files, or sound, image, or media files. Other files may include plain text (.txt) files.

2. Copy the applet's sample code — from `<applet>` tag to `</applet>` tag from the documentation and paste it into the Source Code window of your own page, somewhere between the body tags.

3. Return to your own page, switch to the Source tab or open the Source Code window, the paste the applet code where desired within the body area.

You don't have to worry too much about where you paste the code because, after you paste it, you can return to Layout mode and move it into the desired position, align it, and so on. In some cases, such as when working on a grid, inserting the Java icon may push other items around on your page. While pasting the code, try to place it some place empty to avoid that from happening.

When you switch to Layout mode, you'll see the Java icon in your page. In addition, in the Java Applet Inspector, you'll see all of the defined parameters.

If you wish to change any parameters, click the parameter once in the Params tab of the Inspector, and then edit the value in the Value field at the bottom of the Java Applet Inspector. (The Java icon must be selected before you can see the Java Applet Inspector.)

Testing and Troubleshooting an Applet

To test your applet, use the Preview in Browser button on the toolbar. What should you expect when you do? You may first see the words "loading . . ." in the page where you placed the Java icon, and then the applet should appear. Then you should see the program run, so you'll see your image, the message scroller, the calculator, game, or whatever the applet creates. Meanwhile the browser's Status bar, at the bottom-left corner, shows you what is happening. It should say, "Applet loading," and then "Applet started."

The browser's Status bar also lets you see and understand what is happening in case of an error. Potential errors should be explained in the applet's documentation.

The most common error, which should not happen to you with GoLive's file management, is "Applet can't start: class _____ not found." This error happens under the following circumstances:

✦ One of the .class file names is changed. Even changing the case of a single character breaks the applet. Check back in the folder you downloaded and verify the names.

✦ The path from the Base field in the Java Applet Inspector to the base class file is not correct. If the file is in your Site Window and you used Point and Shoot to link to the file, this will not happen. If you browsed to the file, perhaps you didn't browse to the site's folder, but to the original download's folder by mistake.

If you see any other error message, note the message, and then check the applet's documentation. Potential errors should be explained there.

Adding a Login Applet to Your Page

Now let's look at Login Pass Applet, by Jacky Leung. This is freeware, available at `http://members.xoom.com/jackyhk`. This simple password login applet lets you pre-enter user login names and passwords. When a user comes to the login page, which contains this applet, and enters a login name and password, the entry is checked against the text file in which you pre-entered the info. It lets you have up to ten usernames.

Before you follow these directions, create the page to which the user will be taken when the correct username and password are entered. Also collect the list of logins and passwords if your users will choose their own.

This applet consists of two files: pass1.class (the base code) and in.txt (the file the applet checks against). The rest are for demonstration purposes and for your information only.

To set up this applet for use in your page, follow these steps:

1. Place the three files into the Files tab of the Site Window.

2. Open your page and drag the Java icon into place.

3. Link the Base Code field to the .class file.

4. Set the size of the applet area. The demo uses 367 as the width and 187 as the height.

5. Open the testpass.html file in GoLive and view the Source Code window. Copy the two required parameters — author and title — from the download page, and then paste them into the source code within the applet tag, or enter these two parameters within the Inspector. You must get them exactly correct, or the applet won't work.

6. Open the in.text file and, in the first line, remove the name of the default target page and enter the name of the page that a successful password will take your users to.

7. Enter the user login names and passwords for each user, as follows:

   • Remove the text in the second line and enter the login name for the first user.

   • Remove the text in the third line and enter the password for the first user.

   Continue entering logins and passwords for all additional users, placing the login on one line and the password on the next. Be sure to put each entry on a new line, two lines per user.

Note   If you are using a frameset, create another parameter called "targetframe" and enter the name of the target frame as you would in the Frame Editor.

Preview the applet-containing page in a browser. Enter a login name and password. If the entries are correct, you should arrive at your destination page. If incorrect, you should receive notice within the login page.

Getting More Java Applet Help

Thousands of prewritten Java applets are waiting online to be found and adopted. They range from decorative and fun to helpful and informative. Some are free. Others are available for small shareware fees, and yet others may be available for professional-level site license fees. Table 23-1 lists a few good sites where you might find the Java Applets of your dreams.

Table 23-1 Java Applet Sites	
Site	**Location**
Java Applet Rating Service	www.jars.com
Script Search	www.scriptsearch.com
Better Homepage	www.better-homepage.com/java/java-applets.html
Free Java Applets	www.free-applets.com
Gamelan	www.gamelan.com
Intel Web Applets	www.intel.com/cpc/webapplets
Java Boutique	http://javaboutique.internet.com or http://javaboutique.webdeveloper.com
Java Centre	www.java.co.uk
Sun Microsystems	http://java.sun.com/applets/index.html

You can learn more about Java applets by visiting the sites listed in Table 23-2.

Table 23-2
Java Applet Help Sites

Site	Location
Java Boutique	http://javaboutique.internet.com
Java Applet Rating Service	www.jars.com
Sun Microsystems	http://java.sun.com/applets/index.html
Gamelan	www.gamelan.com
Java for MacOS	www.apple.com/java

✦   ✦   ✦

Using Dynamic Link

When you visit an automated teller machine (ATM), you first enter your user identification and private password. Magically, the machine recognizes you and your account numbers. Then, when you ask for cash, or make a deposit, the machine debits or credits your account and gives you an up-to-date accounting. This occurs because you are actually filling *form* fields and pressing the Process button. Your actions enable the machine to update your account *dynamically*, because the machine is accessing a database stored elsewhere in the bank's system. This database holds the records to your account, although, aside from the bank employees, you are the only person who can access these records through the automated system.

Although this scenario is much more complicated in real life, the same sequence of events can happen in a Web page when you fill in form fields and click the Submit button to perform a search operation to find existing information. If you've ever posted a message to a bulletin board, your message may have been added as a new record in an online database. When you make online purchases, the site's shopping cart system could be based on an online database system. One method of enabling this Action to happen is the Active Server Pages technology. Active Server Pages (ASP) scripting is often used in e-commerce situations such as shopping carts. However, it is also a useful tool for managing, accessing, and disseminating important information in real time across a large company WAN (wide area network) as well as providing search capabilities to a Web site.

ASP provides dynamically linked information via VBScript, JavaScript, and linked databases. The technology was developed by Microsoft in 1996 to provide server-side scripting that is platform independent to the client (visitor). You can identify an ASP page by the .asp extension.

ASP pages are text files that contain embedded code that is created with VBScript (based on Visual Basic) or JavaScript and HTML tags. The server reads the scripting and strips the code from the source, leaving only the HTML code to display the document for the viewer. A benefit of using ASP is that your scripting is completely invisible to anyone viewing the source code through a browser, unlike most CGI scripts in which programming is visible in the source.

Introducing Dynamic Link

You may have noticed the .asp extension when you've performed a search request, or while filling a cyber-shopping cart online. That site is using a server capable of reading the VBScript embedded in the Web page to look up records in a database, or add items to your private database in the case of the shopping cart scenario. But, if you stop to look at the source view offered by all browsers, you don't see any scripting language. This is due to the magic of ASP. By the time you see a page, the server has read all of the embedded scripting, stripped the scripting code out and delivered you a page that contains only the HTML coding.

Dynamic Link is an Adobe GoLive module for providing dynamic database capabilities in the form of Active Server Pages (ASP) to the Web. Dynamic Link is not middleware software. It edits the HTML and ASP tags in your document so that you can create dynamic pages in the same manner you create static pages in GoLive.

When using Dynamic Link, you begin by creating a mock page, just like you create any other HTML page using GoLive. Because you don't actually have the data that will later be supplied by the database, you use placeholders to designate the elements that will later be filled with data when the final page is processed on the Web server. Your mock page looks very much like any HTML page you design in Adobe GoLive, giving you total control over the look of the page. A database designer then references your mock page as a model for designing the necessary tables. After the database is installed on the ASP server, you use the same mock-up page to link your design elements to the database fields.

One of the strengths of Dynamic Link is that you can design the look of the Web pages at the same time the database is being programmed. You don't need the completed database to create your design because you are already aware of what information, search functions, or presentation is needed. By placing mock content in the regular HTML page you build within GoLive, you can visually build the look of page, demonstrating how it will be viewed on the Web. To add your mock content, simply type the mock text or add mock graphics, just like you add any text or graphics to your pages. On the other hand, you can create your dynamic content and then lay out your ASP pages. Dynamic Link is very accommodating to individual work styles.

Dynamic Link has two components:

✦ The Dynamic Link module creates the Dynamic Link palette used to create the dynamic elements on your page.

✦ Server-side files, which are installed on the Web server (see the next section, "Hardware and Software Setup," for details). These files include utility files that contain a library of common ASP functions that are used by your ASP pages as well as ASP configuration files.

You then upload the generated ASP pages along with your site files to your server, where the encoded script is decoded by the server as the pages are called by your visitors. Your audience will not see the decoding taking place in the background.

Right now, Dynamic Link is for ASP technology only. Adobe plans to present Dynamic Link for other scripting languages, such as Jscript, PHP, and ColdFusion, in the future.

The Hardware and Software Setup

To create your initial mock pages, you don't need anything more than your regular copy of GoLive and a list of the information that the database will later provide and insert into your placeholders. After that, in order to match, or bind, your placeholders with the actual database fields, the database must actually be live on an ASP server, and you need access to that server. You must be connected to the database at all times during this part of the process.

Server Needs

The following Web servers are capable of running ASP:

✦ Microsoft Internet Information Services (IIS) software Version 4 or later.

✦ Chilisoft for ASP on a Unix server.

✦ Microsoft Commerce Server if you plan on creating e-commerce applications.

✦ Microsoft Personal Web Server. Although not viable for real-life Web serving, for the purpose of binding your mock page to the database and creating your ASP pages, Personal Web Sharing (PWS) will do well.

Note

Personal Web Server is available as part of the Windows 98 installation. You'll need the Windows 98 CD-ROM to install the Microsoft Data Access Components (MDAC), or you can download MDAC from microsoft.com.

✦ Peer Web Server for Windows NT Workstation — available as part of the Windows NT 4 Option Pack from `www.microsoft.com/ntworkstation/downloads/Recommended/ServicePacks/NT4OptPk/Default.asp`.

Personal Web Sharing is an excellent tool for testing your ASP pages. Instead of installing your databases on a live connection, install them into a Personal Web Sharing directory to find errors and troubleshoot before uploading to the server. If you are using Personal Web Sharing, you need to install the Config folder into the Wwwroot folder of your PWS.

Using the Dynamic Link interface on the Mac

You can use the Dynamic Link Module on a Mac as long as your databases are installed on the IIS server; it's just a matter of knowing the IP address and location of the database files in the directory. While your database may be live online, your pages are still being created and stored in your site file, so you can continue designing pages and uploading them as usual. You will, however, need to have someone else prepare your database if the database application is Access — or install Virtual PC and use Access in Windows.

If you are fortunate to also own a PC, you can network the two computers together and use Personal Web Sharing to serve your database. This is a completely offline operation, in that your final public server is never involved. This is also an excellent way to experiment with Dynamic Link.

Given you do not have an ASP-capable server at present, here are the steps necessary to access Personal Web Sharing via networked computers:

✦ Your computers must be networked via an Ethernet hub.

✦ Verify PWS is installed. If installed, you'll find it in the Start Menu ⇨ Accessories ⇨ Internet Tools.

✦ If PWS is not installed, you can install it by opening your Control Panel, and then Windows Setup. Locate Internet Tools and click Details. Here, you can check the box next to Personal Web Sharing to install it.

✦ Use Find and search for mdac 2.1. If installed, you are ready to continue. If no files are found, download the file from `www.microsoft.com/data` and install.

Now that you have PWS ready, you'll need to install the Dynamic Link files onto the root level of the server:

1. Locate the program folder for Adobe GoLive. Inside this folder is a folder named Dynamic Link.

2. Inside this folder is another folder named Examples. Open the nested folders and locate the folder called demo.

3. You will need to copy this folder to the PC. Timbuktu is an application you can use to transfer files between the two computers.

4. Now navigate back to the root level of your hard drive. You will see a folder named Inetpub.

5. Open this folder and the folder named Wwwroot. Here is where you'll paste the Demo folder you copied.

6. When the folder appears, right click the closed folder and choose Properties. Click the Web Sharing tab and choose Share this Folder. An alias will be assigned as \demo. Click Apply and close this window.

7. Now open the Demo folder and then the Config folder. Inside you will see a folder named Include.

8. Open this folder and locate the document named Friends. Open this file using Notepad. This file enables you to connect to the PWS from your Mac.

9. You are now going to give your Mac permission to access the PWS files. Scroll down to the bottom of the document. You will see the IP number 127.0.0.0. Place your cursor behind the last 0 and hit the Enter key. Now type in your Mac's IP address.

10. Save the document and close the file.

Now you are ready to connect from your Mac. When you tell Dynamic Link to make your page dynamic, you'll enter this address into the Config folder URL line: PC's IP address/demo/config. Dynamic Link will inform you if you are not successful, and will default to offline status. Once you are successful, you will be able to connect to any database that has been installed in the Demo\Config\Database folder.

If you do not know your PC's IP number, you can find it by typing **winipcfg** into the Run window.

Note   When creating dynamic pages on the Mac, change your Web settings (in the Edit Menu) for line-break characters to Windows (CR/LF). This will ensure your pages are compatible when installing them into your Personal Web Server directory.

That's it! You are now ready to design dynamic pages on your Mac!

Determining your database needs

Dynamic Link for ASP uses a database as its source for the dynamic content that will fill the pages you design within GoLive. You database must support OLE DB or ODBC interfaces to communicate between the Web server and the database. This is so the ASP code can query the database to find out things like the names of tables and fields in the database.

The most common databases ASP can be used with are as follows:

✦ Databases that are ADO (ActiveX Data Objects) compliant, such as Microsoft Access (Access 97 for best stability), Oracle, and Microsoft SQL Server.

✦ Any databases that can be accessed through ODBC (open database connectivity) such as FileMaker Pro, using the OLE DB driver so as not to lose primary-key information in your database tables.

✦ Microsoft Commerce Server (ASP).

Note If you plan to use Microsoft Access 2000, install the latest version of Microsoft Data Access Components (2.1 or 2.5.) You'll find this software at `www.microsoft.com/data`.

Setting up the Web server

In order for you to use Dynamic Link to create your ASP pages, you need to do a bit of easy configuration on the Web server that is serving the database. You need to install the Dynamic Link Config folder into your root folder (your own directory) on the server. You can use the FTP browser under your File menu to do this upload because this folder never has to reside in your Files tab (in the Site Window) and is only uploaded once.

To upload this folder, follow these steps:

1. In the FTP browser under your File menu, set up a path directly to your main server folder. For example, if you own a domain called `KevinTHEiDude.com`, you enter `KevinTHEiDude.com` as the server, and then, because this folder needs to reside within that root folder, leave the Directory field blank.

2. Locate this folder and then drag it directly into the main the FTP Browser window. You'll find this folder within the Adobe GoLive 5.0 folder:

   `Adobe GoLive 5.0\Dynamic Link\Server Pages\asp\config`

   The Config folder, now on your Web server contains four subfolders:

   • *Actions* and *Info* provide Dynamic Link programming instructions. After their initial upload to the server, you don't have to give their presence a second thought because you won't be accessing them directly.

   • *Database* is where you place the database that your ASP pages will interact with. What you place here depends on the application your database is programmed in.

   • *Include* comes preinstalled with Dynamic Link's ASP programming code.

Should you need help troubleshooting Dynamic Link, Adobe provides an online troubleshooting page to aid you in isolating and solving problems once you have installed the server files. This page is located in the Dynamic Link folder, in Examples ➪ asp ➪ config ➪ info. Locate the `troubleshooting.asp` file in the Info folder and upload it into the Info folder in your Config directory. To access the troubleshooting report, open the file using your browser. A typical URL would be `http://localhost/config/info/troubleshooting.asp`.

Caution When the Dynamic Link Config folder is uploaded to the public server, there could be a serious security risk because the Dynamic Link files provide powerful access to the server. You must ensure that permissions on the server are set so that the Config folder cannot be accessed by anonymous users over the Web. You can set a password for the Web folder by setting Basic Authentication on the server side, or use the IP authorization in the `friends.asp` file. This file is located in the nested folder named Include. Make sure you disable HTTP read permissions for the folder named Databases to ensure no one can download your databases.

Installing your database on the server

Put yourself back at the ATM machine. You have just entered your user ID and password. Records are being searched to verify your identity via the password you supplied. The next step might be to request an account balance update. To do that, a new set of records is searched to present the requested information on the screen in front of you. When you ask for your most recent deposits or last few posted checks, the screen magically displays the requested information in the form of a table. You might take a moment to marvel at how quickly your requests are answered!

ASP performs similar functions for the viewers of your Web pages. You can quickly supply information requested by keywords, or sort information by customer preference. Requests are made through forms, which are linked to database fields. You can use this same technology for e-commerce applications.

In order for Dynamic Link to communicate with your database and integrate with your GoLive HTML page, you must set your database up on the Web server. If you are planning to use MS Access, you can simply upload your database to the online directory. If you are using an Oracle SQL Server, any ODBC database, or FileMaker, you need to take a few extra steps.

Installing an Access database

To install an Access database, upload the database file to the Databases folder in the Config folder you previously installed on your Web server. The default location for installing your databases is the Config\Databases folder, but you can put them in a different folder on your PC if you prefer. You will need to edit the `GetDatabasePath()` function in `utils.runtime5.asp` to point to the location of your database files. Instructions on how to modify the function are included in the comments preceding the function definition.

Installing an ODBC, Oracle, or SQL Server database

If you have already been using Dynamic Link to access databases on the server, clear the cache so you'll be able to see any new or changed database files. The cache contents are only kept in memory, so you can clear the cache by quitting GoLive. Whether you've been running Dynamic Link already or not, it is, of course, a good idea to quit all running applications before an installation.

To install an ODBC, Oracle, or SQL Server database, follow these steps:

1. Locate the Databases folder in the Dynamic Link Config folder installed on your Web server.

2. Right-click to bring up the contextual menu. Select New Microsoft Data Link.

3. Locate the New Microsoft Data Link.udl created in the last step, right-click to select Rename, and give this file a name.

4. .Right-click the file again to select Properties.

5. Select the Provider tab and select the provider for your database.

6. Click Next and complete the necessary information in the Connection tab.

7. Click Test Connection, and then OK to save your settings.

8. When you open GoLive, you'll be able to select your database as a content source using Dynamic Link.

Note   If you use an ODBC driver with Oracle, you should use the Microsoft ODBC driver, which is named "Microsoft ODBC for Oracle," rather than the Oracle ODBC driver, named "Oracle ODBC Driver".

Adding a FileMaker Pro database

To install a FileMaker Pro database, follow these steps:

1. Open the ODBC control panel on your Web server.

2. Click the System DSN tab and then click Add.

3. Choose the FileMaker Pro driver in the Create New Data Source window and click Finish.

    You won't see the FileMaker Pro driver if it isn't already installed on your Web server. Ensure that Remote Data Access Companion is enabled (under File ➪ Sharing).

5. Enter **FMP** as the Data Source Name and Description.

6. Choose the Use Remote Connection option and set the server address to the IP address of the computer running the FileMaker Pro database.

    Your database will not work with the Web server if this option is not selected! If you are using the same machine as your Web server, choose Use Remote Connection and use the IP address 127.0.0.1

7. Create a .udl file as instructed in Steps 3 through 8 in "Installing an ODBC, Oracle, or SQL Server database."

8. Open FileMaker Pro and your database. Your database will now show as tables in the Dynamic Link New Content Source window.

ODBC versus OLE DB

Users should use OLE DB drivers whenever possible, as it supports the automatic detection of primary keys. Without a primary key specified, you may see incorrect results or behaviors when displaying multiple records in a table, or when updating or deleting records using a form. You can manually specify the primary key field by editing the `WrapRecordSet()` function call in the ASP file's `<head>` section. For example, change

```
set Article = WrapRecordSet(ArticleRecordSet)
```

to:

```
set Article = WrapRecordSet(ArticleRecordSet, "ID")
```

or, if more than one field comprises the primary key, enter each separated by commas:

```
set Product = WrapRecordSet(ProductRecordSet, "ID,SKU")
```

If you are using the OLE DB driver for your database (which is recommended), you do not have to edit this function call. The Dynamic Link module will automatically add the correct primary key field(s).

Unlike most databases, FileMaker Pro does not use the term "table" for a collection of data. The concept of a table is analogous to an individual FileMaker Pro database file. The collection of FileMaker Pro database files related to each other can be considered the "database." When you see the term "table" below, think "database file."

If you run into problems creating the .udl file or configuring the ODBC control panel, your database administrator and Web server system administrator can help.

Turning on Dynamic Link

When you first install GoLive, the Dynamic Link module is not enabled by default. To enable the module, open you're the GoLive Preferences (Edit ➪ Preferences) and then open the Modules section and check the box next to Dynamic Link. As noted in the Modules dialog box, you must restart GoLive in order for Dynamic Link to become active.

Note When creating mock or dynamic pages on the Mac, change the Web settings for line-break characters to Windows (CR/LF) for compatibility with the server software.

Creating Mock Pages

You may find it helpful to work from a guide when designing your ASP page. Dynamic Link can convert a static HTML page to an ASP file, so it is easy to create pages that flow with the general style of your site. It is not necessary, however, to create mock pages; you can make a new blank page dynamic and add links to your page elements as your build the page. In this case, you will not have a .html file and matching .asp file in your Site Window.

To design a mock page, begin a new blank page as normal and begin designing your page as normal by adding tables, placing objects, creating links to other site pages, and so on. You can also move it around within your Files tab as normal.

The text, graphics, tables, grids, and such that you design into your page will remain intact — a true part of your final page presented from the Web server. To aid you in visualizing how the finished page will look, add *mock content* to your page wherever data (text or graphics) from the database will eventually be merged in. If data will fall into a line of text, place mock text in with your text — for example, **Dear John Doe:**, with John Doe holding the place for the name-to-be. If a specific table cell will hold dynamic text objects (merged text), add some mock text that is similar to the format of the dynamic text. If you will be dynamically placing a graphic object onto the page, or into a table cell, link the object to a sample graphic. In other words, create your entire page as normal, just using dummy text and graphics where live items (called *objects* in Dynamic Link terms) will appear later, as demonstrated in Figure 24-1. You'll get to tell Dynamic Link which things are placeholders, so don't worry about them ending up being served to visitors.

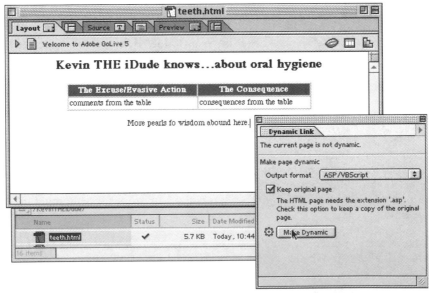

Figure 24-1: A mock page, ready to be made dynamic. The file name remains `teeth.html`, indicating that this is not a dynamic page. The table is formatted as it will appear in your dynamic page, but the table content is not available yet.

Note You don't *have* to add mock content into a table cell, because the cell itself can be designated as the placeholder during the binding process. However, for inline text, lack of dummy text causes Dynamic Link to choose one of your page's real words (which you will then lose when the page is served live) so you *do* need dummy text.

You are not limited to creating individual pages. You can create framesets in the same manner as if all your pages were going to be static pages.

Later, when you make the page dynamic, you use the mock content to denote where the database data will be inserted.

Making Your Page Dynamic

The Dynamic Link palette is your command center for setting up your dynamic content and connecting to your databases without manually entering coding and scripts. After you have completed a mock page, which will then be used as the model for generating the new .asp page, you activate this palette to get down to the business of going dynamic. Remember, to create the mock page, you follow normal workflow procedures.

When you're ready to create your .asp page, call up the Dynamic Link palette by choosing Window ➪ Dynamic Link. When the palette is first visible, you'll be politely informed that your page is not dynamic.

 Note If Dynamic Link is not listed in the menu, the module is not active. See the "Turning on Dynamic Link" section earlier in this chapter.

When you first open the Dynamic Link palette, it's inactive, as shown in Figure 24-2, waiting for you to instruct GoLive to make your page dynamic.

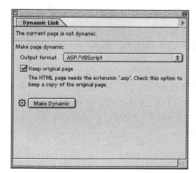

Figure 24-2: The Dynamic Link palette before it is activated. "Keep original page" is checked by default and the status informs you that the page is not dynamic.

A status message at the top of the palette reminds you that your present page is not dynamic. The main section of the palette contains the following controls to make your page dynamic:

✦ A pop-up menu provides two choices for output format: ASP/VBScript and Other Choices. The default, ASP/VBScript, is the one you use to create ASP pages. Other choices is presently reserved for the next versions of Dynamic Link, such as Dynamic Link for JSP, Mercantec, and others.

✦ An option to save the original page as HTML is on by default. This enables you to revert to your original page design, should you need to make changes or start again. If you are not going to first create a static HTML page, you can uncheck this box. No harm is done if you leave the box selected, but your HTML file will be blank.

Caution   Once you have made your HTML page dynamic, any changes made or new elements added to the .asp page will not be reflected in your .html (mock) document. If you drag an .asp document into the Site Window, a new HTML document is automatically generated. However, this document will be blank.

✦ The Make Dynamic button, next to a yellow Gear icon is your key to starting the dynamic process. When you're ready to start linking dynamic content, click Make Dynamic to create a new dynamic page. GoLive then converts your mock page to an ASP page, and it is appended with the .asp extension. This is your new ASP page — the page that will live on the server and be served to your visitors, replete with data drawn from the database. (Or, perhaps your page will carry data to the database instead.) If you leave the box marked "Keep original page" checked when you click the Make Dynamic button, a copy of your existing HTML page will be saved as well. You may want to check this button in case you want to return to the original page if you make a mistake.

✦ The bottom-left area of the palette, perhaps blank as you first view it, provides status messages as you work on your dynamic pages.

After you make your page dynamic, the next step is to link your new ASP page to the database it will work in conjunction with. The palette changes to provide the interface for setting up this connectivity, as shown in Figure 24-3.

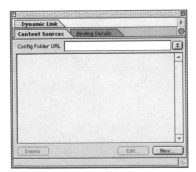

Figure 24-3: The Dynamic Link palette after it is activated. You are now ready to connect to an online database to begin binding content to your placeholders.

Tucked away in the upper-right corner is a tiny yellow gear called the Show All Dynamic Bindings button. When depressed, all bindings on the page become visible. A binding is the Dynamic Link term for a connection to a database object. By default, valid bindings are green and invalid bindings are red. (You can return to Preferences to change these colors, as you prefer.) You can use this feature to easily see which parts of your page will display content from the database and which parts are normal HTML.

Note Dynamic Link cannot verify valid links when in Offline mode. All of your bindings will appear as valid.

The two tabs within this palette—Content Sources and Binding Details—work in tandem. They're where all the action happens—where you link your placeholders to the actual tables of the database and to the specific form elements within. The Content Sources tab is where you choose the database that will provide your page's content. Specifically, it's your interface for choosing first the database, and then the table within that database, and finally the field you'll bind into your Web page. Enter the path to your Web server and to the Config folder within. In keeping with the example used previously, say your Config folder is within the domain KevinTHEiDude.com. In this case, you'd enter www.KevinTHEiDude.com/config.

If you are using Personal Web Sharing on a local machine and designing your page on a Mac, the URL will be the IP address of the local machine followed by /config. (When doing Personal Web Sharing, the Config folder resides in the Wwwroot folder of the Inetpub folder. If you are using Personal Web Sharing on a local machine and designing your page in Windows, the URL will be http://localhost/config.

The Binding Details tab is where you get down to the details of what happens between your database's fields. This can be a simple task such as replacing text or graphics or a more complicated task of filling a table, processing data in a form, or providing navigation from one dynamic page to another. The Binding Details tab changes much like the Inspector as different tasks are defined.

Choosing Content Sources and Binding Fields

After you've made your mock page dynamic and set up the path to your database within the Config folder, you are connected to the server and can begin to define your specific content sources.

Creating a content source

To create a new content source, follow these steps:

   1. Click the New button in the lower-right corner of the Content Source tab.

You are presented with a new window called New Content Source, as shown in Figure 24-4. This is where you will choose your database and tables, and create filters for the fields within those tables.

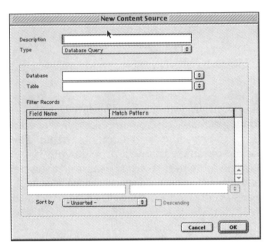

Figure 24-4: The New Content Source window defines the dsatabase and table that is associated with the page content.

2. In the Description field, type a concise name that precisely describes the intended use of this content source, as shown in Figure 24-5. This description cannot contain spaces or special characters.

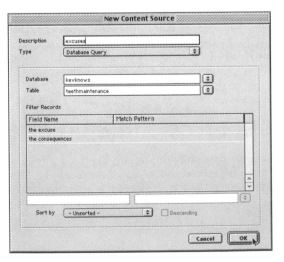

Figure 24-5: Configuring the New Content Source window. A descriptive name has been assigned to the chosen database and table. The table fields are displayed in the Filter Records area.

3. Use the pop-up menu to the right of the Type field to select either Database Query (selected by default) or Microsoft E-commerce Shopping Cart.

Note Selecting Microsoft E-commerce Shopping Cart indicates you are designing an ASP page that is used with Microsoft's Site Server Commerce Edition. This server adds a number of specific field names for building shopping cart applications on top of the fields of your database and expects these field names in your database also. The additional fields make it easy for computing and displaying shopping cart contents, total price, sales tax, shipping charges, and so on. You cannot use pages generated with this option enabled if you are not running Site Server Commerce Edition.

4. Use the pop-up menu to the right of the Database field to choose your database by name. All databases installed in the Config folder of your server are listed here as available data sources.

5. Use the pop-up menu to the right of the Table field to choose the table you want to use as the content source, or choose Custom SQL to enter your own SQL statements:

   • If you choose a table, the fields within that table are listed in the Filter Records list below.

   • When you choose Custom SQL, a blank text area is presented, ready for your input so you can type or paste your SQL statement.

Tip Spaces in table names will result in malformed SQL statements. An example is: `select from * The Big Table` (the table name is The Big Table.) You can add underscores between the words instead: The_Big_Table.

6. (*Optional*) Use the choices within the Sort By pop-up menu to sort the fields within the Field list.

When you're finished choosing all your options, click OK. This closes the New Content Source window and returns you to the Content Sources tab. If you will be calling fields from other tables in your database on one page, you must create content sources for each table. You accomplish this by clicking the New button again until all of the tables you will be using have been assigned description names.

You can return to this window at any time by highlighting the description title in the Content Sources tab and clicking the Edit button.

Binding a content source to a placeholder

Back at the Content Sources window, all of the fields within your content source (a.k.a. *table*) should be listed in Outline mode beneath the description (a.k.a. *name*) you gave your content source. You can now proceed to bind the placeholders on your pages to this content source via the Content Sources tab by following these steps:

1. On your page, select a placeholder object (your mock text or graphic) you wish to bind data to.

2. In the Content Sources window, locate the content field that will replace the mock content and check that field name.

Note The simplest tasks in Dynamic Link are the binding of text or graphics. For this reason, I use text in the example here.

3. Open the Binding Details tab (see Figure 24-6).

Figure 24-6: The Binding Details tab shows the assigned content source by the descriptive name you chose in the New Content Source window and the field that is bound to your placeholder.

The Bindings Detail tab changes to reflect the appropriate options for the type of mock content you have selected.

Bind To is checked by default. Your current content source is automatically displayed, as is the field you selected within the Content Source window, and the placeholder text is now surrounded by a green border, indicating a valid binding, as shown in Figure 24-7.

Figure 24-7: Binding borders surrounding text placeholders. If you like, you can turn off the borders with the yellow gear in the upper-right corner of the Dynamic Link palette.

4. (*Optional*) Use the filter options in the pop-up menu to the right of the Filter field to choose a formatting option for your data.

Note   If you apply an inappropriate filter to the dynamic content, an error message will be generated when previewed or displayed in a browser.

When applying filters, keep in mind that they are applied to the display of your dynamic content but do not alter the appearance of the placeholder in any way.

5. (*Optional*) To see a preview of how your final page will look to a visitor to your site, click the Preview tab of the page window, as in Figure 24-8.

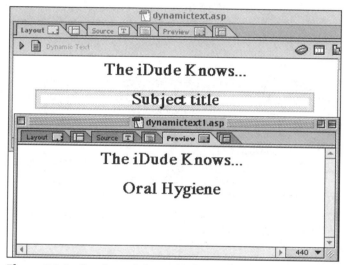

Figure 24-8: Preview of dynamic text replacing a placeholder

This live preview functions as long as you're connected to the database, which means as long as you're connected to the Web server.

 Note   To bind graphics to a graphic placeholder, the database must contain the URL of each individual graphic. Binding procedures are the same as binding dynamic text.

Creating dynamic tables

In addition to displaying information inline as text, you can display your data within a table. With Dynamic Link, you can format tables that automatically grow to contain the displayed cell content. The process for binding data to a table is very much the same as binding text.

When you are designing your Web page, add a table normally, formatting table cells as you wish them to be displayed along with text formatting within the cells. This text will be the placeholder for the dynamic content.

When your placeholder content is ready, bind the table to your dynamic content by selecting the contents of the first column or by simply placing your cursor in the cell you want replaced. In the Content Source tab, choose the field that will supply the content. Continue this step until you have completed binding the mock content in each of your table columns to the appropriate table field.

Now that you have specified the content for the individual columns, you need to tell Dynamic Link to replace each row in the table with the data from the content source, as shown in Figure 24-9.

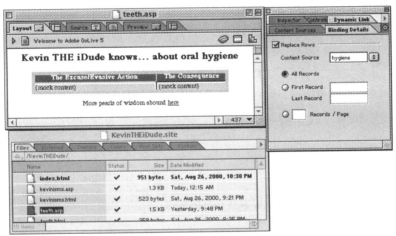

Figure 24-9: Replacing rows in the dynamic table

Select either the entire table or just a cell in the table. The Binding Details tab should still be in front. Choose the Replace Rows option. Several options exist for the displayed records:

- ✦ **All Records** displays all the records in your database field.

- ✦ **First/Last Record** specifies a range of records displayed from your database.

- ✦ **Records/Page** limits the number of records displayed.

Note   You are specifying the behavior for the entire table. You cannot have different behaviors for different columns. Replace Rows always applies to the entire table.

You can preview the table in Adobe GoLive or in your browser, and any additional rows needed will be created dynamically, as shown in Figure 24-10.

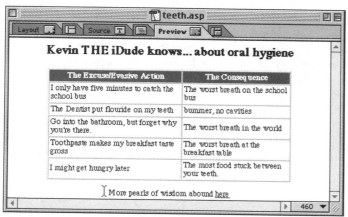

Figure 24-10: Previewing the dynamic table shows your table filled with data from your database table and the HTML table rows extended to accommodate the new items.

Creating Navigation Links

As your Web site grows, you will want to link your dynamic pages either to more dynamic Web pages or to and from normal HTML pages. You can create navigation links using the Dynamic Links palette.

Imagine you are back at the ATM machine exploring the details of your bank account. The first screen might only display your current bank balance. If you choose the option of viewing the last five checks posted to your account, a new table appears listing the check number and dollar amount of five checks. You just followed a link from one dynamic page to another.

Note Although link creation doesn't have to be your last step, logically and in practice, it is likely to be. Before you do this, you at least have to have your content sources defined.

To link to a regular HTML document, simply apply the link as normal, using the Text Inspector.

To create links from one dynamic page to another, create the mock pages for both the linking page and the destination page, and then turn both pages dynamic.

Preparing to link to a new dynamic page

As with regular HTML Web pages, a link can be triggered by text or a graphic image. In fact, you begin your link as normal, even though the actual destination of the link will be dynamically generated in this case.

Note   Up until now, you could preview dynamic pages in Preview mode or in a browser. The linking process, however, cannot be verified until the pages are installed on the server. You can install the site files on the Personal Web Server to accomplish this. This method keeps your work private until you are ready to publish your pages.

Normally, when you create a link in a static HTML page, you are requesting a new file in your site; however, when your pages are dynamic, you can either link to a different page or link to the current ASP page — updated with new dynamic content.

To create a link to a dynamic page, follow these steps:

1. In the .asp page that will contain the link, begin your link as normal:

   • Select the text or graphic that will initiate the link.

   • Click the New Link button in the Link tab of the Inspector.

   • Using your linking method of choice (for example, Point and Shoot), link to the .asp page that will be the target of the link. (This page should be within the Files tab of your Site Window and may be the same page that is currently open.)

2. In the Dynamic Link palette, choose the Binding Details tab, as shown in Figure 24-11.

Figure 24-11: Creating a link Action

Note   When creating a link, you do not begin by selecting a content source within the Contents Sources tab.

3. Check the Link Action option.

4. From the Link Action pop-up menu, choose the destination of the link. You can choose any of the following options:

- Show Details of Current Record
- Show Previous Record
- Show Next Record
- Show First Record
- Show Last Record
- Show Empty Records

5. Use the pop-up menu to the right of the Content Source field to select your content source.

6. Use the pop-up menu to the right of the Content Source field to choose the field name.

Passing values between two dynamic pages

Web pages are inherently *stateless*. This means that a dynamic Web page does not maintain a constant connection to the database while it is being viewed by a Web browser — the Web server sends the page to the browser and that's it.

In order for the Web server to know what information to send to you when you request the next page, you need to pass some information from the current page back to the server.

To pass this data between your dynamic pages, you can use either form fields or URL arguments. Form fields enable the user to enter data that can be used (for example) as the criteria for a database search. URL arguments are appended to the URL and take the form `www.mydomain.com/dynamicpage.asp?argument=value`. For example, if a user enters a first name in a form, and then clicks a submission button, the next page can greet the user by name. That next page simply writes the name value that was passed by the form.

Expert Tip If you want users to be able to bookmark your dynamic pages, make sure you add the important parameters needed to generate your page (such as primary keys) to the URL — pages that are generated purely by form submissions cannot be successfully bookmarked. — *Rob Keniger, big bang solutions,* `www.bigbang.net.au`

You can customize the control over the values passed to the new dynamic page by choosing Add Arguments to URL in the Link Action pop-up menu. To take advantage of this customization, before you create the link within the originating page, set up the destination page. To enable arguments, you must first prepare the target page, as follows:

1. Open the destination .asp page.

2. In the Dynamic Link window, click the Content Source tab.

3. Click the desired content source once within the list, and then click Edit.

This opens up the Edit Content Source window, shown in Figure 24-12, and, in the Filter Records list, displays all the fields available within that content source.

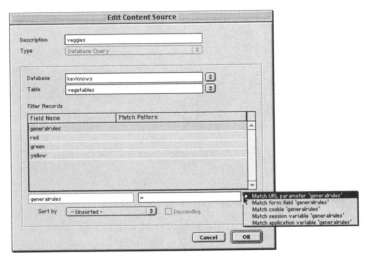

Figure 24-12: Applying Match Pattern filters

4. Click the desired field name once to select it.

This is the field you want to assign as a matching filter to parameters submitted via links from other pages.

The field name appears within the filter record text field directly below the Filter Records list.

5. From the pop-up menu to the right of the pattern field, choose the desired Match Pattern filter, as shown in Figure 24-12. The choices are as follows:

- Match URL ID parameter "field name"

- Match form field "field name"

- Match cookie "field name"

- Match session variable "field name"

- Match application variable "field name"

Note

Explaining all of the choices here is beyond the scope of this book. The database programmer should know what is needed here for your particular database.

If you want to use the values passed from the previous page via the URL, choose the Match URL ID parameter and set the name filter to match the URL argument from the linking page.

Your selection is also displayed under the Match Pattern column in the Filter Records list.

If you prefer a parameter that does not appear within the pop-up menu, type it directly into the Match Pattern text area. (The parameter you enter must be a valid parameter.)

The arguments you can enter include the following:

- *Text string.* Use the arguments of = "hello"
- *Number string.* 123
- *Script function.* For scripts you have written based on function

6. Click OK.

Linking the dynamic pages using dynamic URL arguments

After you have completed adding your arguments to the targeted link page, you then return to the page containing the originating text or graphic link.

To complete the process of creating a link to a new dynamic link, follow these steps:

1. Select the text or graphic link.
2. Click the Binding Details tab.
3. Choose the Link Action option, and then use the pop-up menu to select Add Arguments to URL.

   The Dynamic URL Arguments box now displays all the dynamic parameters that are available on the target page. You need to specify the value that is passed to the matching parameter on the target page.

Remember that you cannot verify dynamic links if the pages are not installed on the server. You will have to install the pages to check the validity of your links. Once you have installed these pages, however, you can preview the pages with dynamic links at the same time you are editing them by keeping a browser window open that points to the page you are editing. To preview the links, click the Refresh button in the open browser.

Dynamic Link Preferences

In order to make working in Dynamic Link more comfortable, you can set the look of your Dynamic Link interface. To do so, choose Edit ➪ Preferences, and then choose from the various settings offered, as shown in Figure 24-13.

Here are the settings to choose from:

✦ **Web Server HTTP timeout** is the amount of time Dynamic Link will wait before reporting an error in connecting to the content sources (your database files) for the page you are currently working with. The default is set at 15 seconds. If you make it any longer, you'll go crazy waiting for the server response status messages!

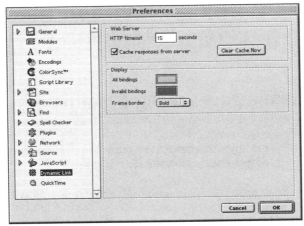

Figure 24-13: The Dynamic Link Preferences window for the Mac

✦ **Cache responses from server**, on by default, improves performance by caching Web server requests within GoLive. The cache is used by GoLive for retrieving table and field information for your content sources. When you make changes to an online database while you are also editing your ASP pages in GoLive, it's a good idea to turn off the cache so that GoLive stays in sync with your database. You can also clear the cache by using the Clear Cache Now button. Each time you restart GoLive, the cache is reinitialized because its contents are only kept in memory.

✦ **Display options** control the color of the frame borders that envelope your dynamic content:

All bindings will highlight your placeholder content that has been bound to your content source.

Invalid bindings indicate errors. The default colors are lime green for valid bindings and red for invalid bindings. You change the colors by clicking the color box and choosing a new color from the system's color picker.

You can also choose the thickness of the **frame borders**, which highlight your dynamic placeholders via the pop-up menu.

✦　　✦　　✦

Going Live – The Final Touches

◆   ◆   ◆   ◆

◆   ◆   ◆   ◆

After your pages are complete, come to this part to learn how to add some professional touches that'll help browsers find your site — and help visitors find what they seek at your site. Then learn about optimizing your site for delivery on the Web. This part shows you how to polish your site in a variety of ways. It's also where you'll learn how to get your site onto a server — to *go live* with it.

Optimizing and Problem-Solving

So you've built this great Web site, and you're getting close to putting it out there for the world to see. In this chapter and the next I discuss the finishing touches to ensure that your site is "leak-proof." I start with tips to help with last minute changes, and then discuss how to use GoLive's powerful error-finding and fixing tools, and finish with some tips on how to optimize your site and get feedback on how it looks on different platforms.

Finding and Replacing Body Text or Code

The only real constant in Web design is change. Inevitably at some point in the process you will make changes — either directed by a client, or due to factors outside the designer's control — such as a change in a URL or an e-mail address. GoLive's powerful Find and Replace features make this process a snap. You can search through the text on a page; the HTML code "behind" the page; search the site for page names, objects, URLs, e-mail addresses and colors. If you use a Mac, you can also create a site index that makes finding and replacing even faster. One caution — with all this power, you need to be sure of what you're asking to find and replace before you click the Replace button.

For basic finding and replacing, the default preferences are fine as they are, but you may prefer the different behaviors you can easily set for yourself. If you're delving into the world of using regular expressions, you may want to check out those preferences and add to those search patterns. Find preferences are covered at the end of this section.

Finding and changing text

You can use Find & Replace in Layout mode to search for text on your page or in Source view (including the Source Code window) to seek out HTML code elements. Either way, you can replace the found characters with new ones. (You can find text within Outline and Preview mode too, but cannot do a replacement in those views. The Replace buttons are simply not active.)

Searching text

To perform a search, follow these steps:

1. To search for the contents of a page, open the document you wish to search in the Layout view. Or, to look for code, open it in the Source tab.

Tip   To see your search in both modes, keep the page open to Layout and open the Source Code window (Window ⇨ Source Code) too.

2. Choose Edit ⇨ Find and, if it's not already active, bring the Find & Replace tab forward by clicking it.

3. Enter the text you're searching for into the text area at the top of the window.

   Text wraps within the search field, and then scrolls to contain large blocks of text. However, if you seek a longer string of text than the window can hold, you can either make the window longer, or click the pencil icon to open a separate Edit window that displays your text string in a larger, resizable area. (See Figure 25-1.)

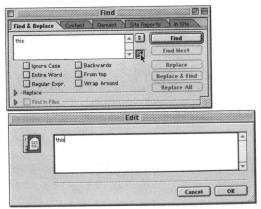

Figure 25-1: Setting up to perform a search for the word "this"

Tip

If you've previously done a search, you can easily repeat that search by clicking the double-headed pop-up menu to the right of the text-to-find area. The top part of this menu presents a list of text you've previously searched for. Instead of tying or pasting your search phrase again, simply choose it from this list.

4. *(Optional)* Select various search options:

   • *Ignore Case* disregards capital letters. In other words, "About Us" also finds "about us."

   • *Entire Word* lets you disregard words that are embedded in longer words. A search for the word "ant" does not produce the word "antidote."

   • *Regular Expr.* is for wildcard searches. This is an advanced feature, so ignore it while doing a typical search. The upcoming section, "Wildcard searches and regular expressions," discusses this feature.

   • *Backwards* changes the order of the search. Without Backwards selected, the search goes from the beginning of the document to the end. With Backwards selected, the search starts at the end and works its way to the top. (Notice this option actually changes the name of the next option from *From top* to *From bottom*.

   • *Wrap Around* starts the search again at the top of the document after it reaches the end.

To find text within your page without actually replacing it, use the Find or Find Next feature. To locate text one occurrence at a time, click Find. To find the next occurrence of the selected text, click the Find Next button. (By default, the open page becomes active at the first find so you need to bring the Find window forward again to click Find Next.) Once the last occurrence is found, or if no text is found matching the search, a beep sounds.

You can also locate text on your page without opening the Find dialog box. Just select the text you want to find, and then choose Edit ⇨ Find Selection. Or, to search for text you've previously entered into the Find dialog box, choose Edit ⇨ Find Next. These methods don't enable you to set detailed search criteria, though. Instead, they inherit the criteria last set when the dialog box was open.

Simply finding text within your page can be helpful, and may be all you need to do. But you can, of course, also have GoLive replace that found text with new text. The next section discusses replacing text.

Caution

Once you Replace text, you cannot undo the change in the traditional Undo manner. However, using some creative Finding & Replacing you can get the text back the way it was. (If you have any question about the replace process, duplicate the page before performing the replacement.)

Locating and replacing text

Follow these steps to locate and replace text:

1. You must find text before you can replace it, so enter your find criteria in the Find window. Without this criteria, all Find and Replace buttons are dimmed.

2. If it's not open already, click the arrow next to the word Replace to open the Replace section of the Find window.

3. Type or paste the text you want to replace in the window, as in Figure 25-2.

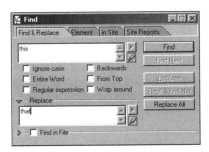

Figure 25-2: Setting up to locate the word "this" and replace it with "that"

Tip   You can easily repeat a past replacement. Click the double-headed pop-up menu to the right of the text-to-replace area and choose it from this list.

4. Click the appropriate button, as follows:

   • To replace only the currently found occurrence of the text that was located, click Replace.

   • To monitor the replacing as it goes along, select Replace & Find. This replaces only the currently found occurrence of what was found, and automatically finds the next occurrence.

   • If you're confident with all your criteria, you can select Replace All. This replaces all occurrences of the text that you seek.

Tip   You can replace found text with no text by not entering anything in the Replace window.

You can also repeat a currently set search and replace without opening the Find dialog box again. Just choose Edit ➪ Find Next, and then choose Edit ➪ Replace or Edit ➪ Replace & Find Next. Any search criteria last set within the Find dialog box is inherited and performed. This works in Layout mode and in Preview on the Mac only (on Windows it still works, but it changes the document window to Layout mode when it finds a matching occurrence). It also works within Source view and the Source Code window, but there, results can be disastrous if the text you change also occurs within your HTML code. If your goal is to change HTML elements in pages, you're safer using a better way, which I address later in this chapter in "Finding HTML code elements."

Find and replace in multiple files

To Find and Replace in multiple pages, close any open pages and begin from within the Files tab of the Site Window. Select Edit ⇨ Find to open the Find & Replace window. Input the text to be found into the Find text area. Go ahead and click the arrow next to the Find in Files box to expand the window. At this point you have several search method options. You can have GoLive search your entire site or narrow down the search to specific pages.

Searching the entire site

To search your entire site you don't have to open or use the Find in Files feature. Instead, you can follow these steps:

1. To begin, click Find.

   GoLive starts searching the first file in the Files tab. It opens the first document in which it finds an occurrence and selects the text the same way as when searching the document, as explained in the previous section.

2. If you want to replace the selected occurrence of the found text with your replacement text, click Replace & Find. If not, click Find Next.

   When a selection is found, the page that contains it becomes active so you have to click the Find dialog box once to make it active before you can choose Replace & Find or Find Next.

   Once it finds the last occurrence in a document it moves on to the next document, leaving the previous document open in its wake.

3. Close each window individually, saving those in which the changes suit you.

If you are certain you want all occurrences changed and don't wish to review each occurrence, simple click Replace All instead of Find, Replace & Find, or Replace. GoLive asks you if you're sure you want to do this — and for a good reason. Think about any possible replacements that may consequently happen. For example, if you replace "his" with "hers," will you end up turning "this" into "thers?" You easily could. That's a case where the Entire Word option prevents an error. Consider such events and choose your search wisely. After you proceed and the replacement is complete, an alert informs you of the number of changes made.

Caution   Make a backup of your site (or the pages you're about to work on) if you are going to make sweeping global changes in it. Remember that you cannot undo changes made with Find & Replace.

Searching specific pages

Rather than having every file in your site searched, it is safer and faster to designate the pages to be searched.

Here's how to select and search individual pages:

1. Click the blue arrow to the left of the Find in Files option—in the lower third section of the Find window.

2. Add the files to be searched by doing the following:

   • Drag HTML pages from the Files tab of the Site Window into the Files list area.

   • Click Add Files to open the Add Files dialog box in which you can specify which HTML pages to search.

   • Add all of your site's HTML pages, and then select and delete the ones you don't want to search. To add your entire site's files, click Add Site.

   The HTML file names you specify are listed in the scrolling box at the bottom of the Find window, as seen in Figure 25-3. The Find in Files checkbox is also checked automatically.

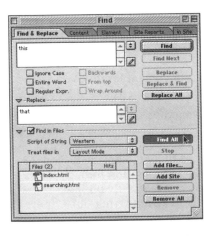

Figure 25-3: A setup to search for "this" and turn it into "that" within the Layout mode (body text) of two pages (Ignore Case has been turned on so "This" can be replaced as well as "this.")

3. *(Optional)* Remove any pages you don't want searched. To do so, select the file(s) and click Remove or press your Backspace/Delete key.

4. *(Optional)* If the text you seek is not written in the language reflected in the Script of String pop-up menu, choose the encoding that matches your desired language. (You must have that language ability installed in your system.)

5. Check that your search will take place in the desired part of your page. To search the content of your page, make sure the line above the files list says, "Treat files in Layout Mode." To search the HTML code of your page, choose Source Mode from this pop-up menu.

Caution   Making Find & Replace changes in Source mode can be tricky as many tags contain similar text.

6. Click Find All to have GoLive search all of your selected files.

Find All seeks out all occurrences, but does not make any replacements. When the search is complete, GoLive presents a hit count for each file in the scrolling list, as shown in Figure 25-4. As GoLive searches, an arrow points to the file currently being searched. The arrow remains on the last file searched. This completes the find part of the find and replace.

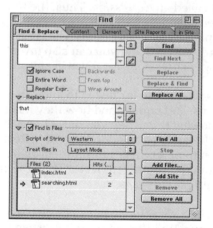

Figure 25-4: The results — hit count — of the search for "this" or "This." Each page shows two occurrences that may be changed.

If you prefer to simply make all replacements at this point, rather than reviewing the changes, skip the Find All button and click Replace All. However, it may be wise to at least wait and see how many hits are found first. The number of hits can be a great clue as to the wisdom of your criteria.

7. Make the change by doing this:

- If the number of hits look right to you and you are certain of your replacement, click Replace All.

- If you prefer to review your pages first, double-click the page to open it. The first occurrence of the found text is selected and awaiting your action. To replace the selected occurrence of the found text with your replacement text, click Replace & Find. To skip that occurrence and find the next one, click Find Next.

If, upon seeing the hit count or rethinking a page, you don't want to make changes to it, select that page within the Files list and click Remove.

8. Save and close the open page, and then double-click the next page to work on it.

Wildcard searches and regular expressions

Wildcard searches enable you to locate a wider range of text occurrences than normal, and even remember parts of what you've found. Wildcards are specially designated characters that act like the Joker (the wild card) in a game of cards. You enter the text you are seeking as normal within the Search area field but use these characters to enable GoLive to find, say any numeric digit instead of just a 1, 2, 3, and so on. Because wild characters work as part of a larger search string, the group of characters that comprise the search is called an *expression*. Thus, the term *regular expressions*. These expressions are often called global regular expression print (GREP) strings, or GREPs, from a Unix pattern-matching utility. GoLive comes preconfigured with many common wildcard searches and you can also invent your own. In fact, you can even save your own expressions for reuse in any site.

The secret to using regular expressions to stand in for text is to know each of the characters that comprise the expressions, and understand how they function and how to string them together. It's like knowing that when you put a 1 and then a + and then a 1 that you are intending for those 1s to be added together. Remember algebra, where you put some numbers into parentheses to set them apart and be counted as a whole by the numbers around those parentheses? Well, the same action happens here, but not always with parentheses.

So what are these special characters? They are actually the same characters you've been using since you learned to write, but with different meanings when used here. For example, the period (.) you use to end your sentences now becomes a placeholder for any character at all, and an asterisk (*) now acts as a placeholder for any number of characters. Sometimes a series of characters comprise a placeholder. Different groupings of characters have different functions. Table 25-1 presents each of the characters and show you what they do.

One problem with endowing your everyday characters with special wildcard powers is that if a question mark (?) is suddenly more than a question mark, what happens when you really want to find a plain old question mark in your text? The answer is to use a somewhat secret code that tells GoLive you really want that question mark to be interpreted as just a question mark. That (not so) secret code is a backslash (\)—the key under your Backspace/Delete key and above your Enter/Return key.

Caution If you do not have previous experience with regular expressions I recommend using them extremely cautiously. Multi-page replaces are *not* undoable. If you are not sure the expression does exactly and only what you want, use it on a copy of your site or file first. Regular expressions are the topic of entire books, and detailed explanations are beyond the scope of this book.

Performing a wildcard search

A wildcard search is done like any other search, typically with a Replace operation (or you wouldn't have much reason to bother). Follow these steps to perform a wildcard search:

1. Check the Regular Expr option below the search area field. This enables GoLive to recognize the wild characters and expressions.

2. Enter the text you are seeking within the Search area field, just like when doing a regular search, but use the wildcard rules to build your expression. (See Tables 25-1, 25-2, and 25-3 later in this chapter, as well as the guidelines that follow to learn the rules.) Here are the ways to choose an expression:

   • Choose a preconfigured or previously used regular expression from the pop-up menu to the right of the search area. This menu is shown in Figure 25-5.

   • Type in your own regular expressions from scratch.

   • Type your own using expressions from the pop-up menu within it to help build your own GREP faster.

   • If someone on an e-mail list has helped you out with the needed expression, copy it from the e-mail and paste it here.

Figure 25-5: Selecting a preconfigured expression on which to search

3. Enter the replacement text, if any.

4. Perform the find and/or replacement using the appropriate buttons, as described earlier in this chapter for a regular find and replace. If your expression is not properly laid out, an intelligent error message points out the error. It cannot troubleshoot your replacement errors—just the syntax of your expression.

Caution   Remember to check that you are set to work with your files in Layout or Source mode, as desired. The key is the *Treat files in* menu. Your page may be open and in Source mode, but if you're treating your files in Layout, the replacement takes place in Layout, not Source.

Instead of doing a replacement immediately, I strongly suggest you duplicate one page (Edit ➪ Duplicate) as the page to search, open it up, and then use Find to let GoLive point out what it finds with your expression. Click Find to see the first occurrence, and then Find Next to walk through the document. Be in Layout or Source mode, depending on what's appropriate for your search. If you're happy with what is found, you can go for the big replacement. Or, instead of using Find Next, try Replace & Find to step through the first replacements and check the result of the replacements as you go. Once you're confident your expression works for a page, you can use it on the rest of the pages in your site.

GoLive's Help provides a table of the common GREP expressions that you can use within your search strings. You can also find a more detailed chart with examples by Ken Martin at www.golivebible.com. Table 25-1 lists the wildcard characters you can use within your searches.

Table 25-1 Wildcard Characters		
Wildcard Character	**What It Does**	**Example**
. (period)	Stands in for any single character.	.at locates bat, cat, fat, hat, mat, pat, rat, sat, tat, vat (and any words you may have misspelled too)
[]	Stands in for a single character that you place between the brackets. If you place a statement for a range of characters, it finds whatever qualifies as a result of that statement.	[123] finds 1, 2, or 3; [1-3] also finds 1, 2, or 3; [a-p] finds any lowercase letter that is from a to p, including a and p. To have it find the same letters but in either case, add the other case: [a-pA-P]
-	Acts as a wildcard when used between two characters.	a-z finds any character from a up and through z.

Wildcard Character	What It Does	Example
-	When it precedes a *range of characters*, though, it no longer acts as a wildcard.	`[-QB]` matches either "-," or "Q," or "B." `[^-QB]` matches anything *except* either "-," or "Q," or "B." (In the last two cases, the "-" is simply a character, not a wildcard, because of its location.)
`[^]`	Is used with other characters placed between the caret (^) and the closing bracket to exclude those characters. Note that a caret standing alone, rather than in this grouping, has another role entirely. (See the list of Modifiers that appears in Table 25-3.)	`[^a-z]` finds any single character that is not a lowercase a, b, c . . . or z.
`\d` or `[0-9]`	Finds any digit.	`\d\d\d-\d\d\d\d` matches a seven digit phone number `[\(]?\d\d\d[-|\)]` finds area codes. (This works well in Layout. Not perfect in Source because it also finds the ISO number and perhaps other combinations that have three digits followed by a dash.)
`\D` or `[^0-9]`	Finds any character except for digits, including whitespace characters (tabs, line breaks, and so on).	In "3-D Movie" `\D` would match "-," then "D," then "(space)," then "M," then "o," then "v," then "i," and then "e."
`\w` or `[a-zA-Z]`	Finds any alphabetical character.	In "3-D Movie" `\w` matches "D," then "M," then "o," then "v," then "i," and then "e." (The space between the D and M is not an alpha character so it would not be found.)

Continued

Table 25-1 *(continued)*

Wildcard Character	What It Does	Example
[a-zA-Z]+	Finds any word (one or more consecutive alphabetical characters).	In "3-D Movie" \w+ matches "D" and then the word "Movie" as a whole word.
\W or [^a-zA-Z]	Finds any nonalphabetic character.	In "3-D Movie" \W matches "-," and then the "(space)" between the D and M
\s or [SPACE+\t]	Finds any white space character, including space, carriage return, and tab.	In "3-D Movie" \s matches only the "(space)" between the D and M. If you import text from another document and it contains carriage returns at the end of each line, this finds and removes them.
\S	Finds any character that creates space, like a tab, space, or return.	Searching "3-D Movie" matches "3," then "-," then "D," "M," "o," "v," "i," and "e" (skipping the space).
\r	Used only in HTML (Source code), this finds any line break.	\r\r finds any two consecutive returns
\t	Finds any tab character, such as indentations in HTML source code (unless the page has been indented by spaces).	\t\t finds any two consecutive tabs
\x00 - \xff	Finds any character, as identified by its hexadecimal ASCII value.	\x40 finds "@" \xDB matches "€" (Euro)

Table 25-2 lists the wildcard qualifier characters you can use within your searches. Remember that wildcard characters such as ^, ?, \, [, and] have special meaning in regular expressions. To tell GoLive that you want one of these characters to count as text (instead of as the special character) while using regular expressions, you need to precede the character with a backslash (\). Thus, a backslash followed by a question mark (\?) finds the question mark character—?—as normal text.

Now that you know the theory and rules behind GREP expressions, here are some helpful GREP examples that you can use, understand, and adapt. As you work, remember that using GREPs requires experimentation and patience unless you're a programmer. Have a backup of your site first, and then experiment.

	Table 25-2	
	Wildcard Qualifier Characters	
Qualifier	*What It Does*	*Example*
?	Used after a parenthesis, it sets the contents of the parenthesis, as an optional part of the search. Used after a character, the character is then an optional part of the search. (This is *Optional Part*, a predefined choice available in the pop-up menu.)	(Mr.)? Richard Gaskin **finds all occurrences of Richard Gaskin, both with and without the title. This is handy in order to say, make all instances of the name bold.**
+	A plus sign finds each occurrence of the character it follows plus any more immediate occurrences. If part of a string, if finds *one or more occurrences* of the search string it follows, when those occurrences are in a row.	In the sentence "I will go to the movies too on Tuesday with Tootie and Tony." a search for to+ (that ignores case) finds to, too, Too(tie) and To(ny). Be careful though, because it finds $100,000.00 as well at $10.00 in the wrong circumstance.
*	The star is equivalent to a ? and + *simultaneously*. The * matches *zero or more occurrences* of the preceding character (so the preceding character may not exist, may have a single match, or may have any consecutive number of matches). When it "finds" zero occurrences, it has nothing to select so GoLive displays a "not found" message.	In a Find for: Ke* within the string, "Ken is keen on kites and is a really keeeeen guy," the matches would be: "Ke," "Kee," "k," "keeeee"

Table 25-3 lists the wildcard modifier characters you can use within your searches.

Tip   You can use what you learn here to add to, or edit the preconfigured expressions by opening GoLive's Preferences (Edit ⇨ Preferences), selecting Find, revealing the subtopic, and choosing Regular Expressions. See "Setting Find Preferences" later in this chapter.

Table 25-3
Wildcard Modifier Characters

Modifier	What It Does	Example
|	Separates alternatives. (This bar is above the backslash on your keyboard.) (This is available as *One Word Of*, a predefined choice available in the pop-up menu.)	`this|that` finds "this" or "that."
( )	Encloses a search string so any words between them is interpreted as one, and then acted up accordingly within the encompassing sentence. (You may remember this from high school algebra.) Also, any search string in parentheses that was matched is *remembered* and can be replaced automatically in the Replace field by back-referencing. So the first matched parentheses would be accessed by \1,	`(Kenny|Anna|Jack) is a coconut.` Finds "Kenny is a coconut." and "Anna is a coconut." and "Jack is a coconut." The name in each of those sentences is *remembered* so using a back-reference in the replace field, such as `\1 is wonderful.` replaces the found sentences with "Kenny is wonderful." and "Anna is wonderful." and "Jack is wonderful." the second by \2, and so on.
^	In Layout mode this finds the start of a paragraph. In Source mode this finds the start of a line. Note that when in front of a range of characters, this caret becomes a wildcard instead.	`^NASA` matches "NASA" at the beginning of a line (or paragraph), but does not match "NASA" if it appears in the middle of a line (or paragraph).

Working with font tags

GoLive users frequently use a GREP to remove all the font tags that have found their way into a site and are no longer desirable when the power of style sheets is discovered. Because you're reading this book and are aware of how useful style sheets are, you may not find yourself knee-deep in font tags, but then again, you may be inheriting a site that presents a significant challenge. The challenge of removing font tags is a perfect example of how to use regular expressions in the real world. You have two ways you can remove your font tags. You can hard-code a search by entering the exact font tags you want to remove, but this requires a new search for every variation of font tags you have on your site. Or, you can do one search using a more flexible, all-encompassing expression. With the help of GREP fan Ken Martin, here is a demonstration of each method. (Thank you also to Henrik Madsen for posting the original example to the GoLive Talk list.)

In a case where the text from which you want to remove font tags has only a font tag, you can just do a regular Find & Replace by just typing it in exactly as it appears in the source of your file, and not even use regular expressions. In this example, the words on the page are "YourTextIsHere" and they have only one font attribute, which is a font size of 2. Here are the steps:

1. Enter the following in your Find field, substituting the actual tag you seek: **<font size="2">YourTextIsHere</font>**

2. In the Replace field enter the same text you already have on your page so when the string that includes your unwanted font tags are deleted, the text is put back in your page. Type: **YourTextIsHere**

3. Choose Treat files in Source mode so the code will be searched.

4. Perform your search as described earlier in this chapter.

To perform a more flexible and far-reaching search that removes any font tag attribute (not just font size 2), you would use a formula similar to the following one. Here are the steps:

1. Enter the following in your Find field: **<font[^>]*>YourTextIsHere</font>**. This search finds *<font*, then zero or more characters that are not >, then the >, then the words *YourTextIsHere*, and then *</font>*.

2. In the Replace field enter the same text you already have on your page so when the string that includes your unwanted font tags are deleted, the text is put back in your page. Type: **YourTextIsHere**.

3. Perform your search as described earlier in this chapter. Here are some of the attributes this search example finds and removes:

```
<font face="arial">YourTextIsHere</font>
<font face="comic sans">YourTextIsHere</font>
<font size="2">YourTextIsHere</font>
<font size="3">YourTextIsHere</font>
<font size="2" color="red">YourTextIsHere</font>
```

To further expand the flexibility of this search, you can add the ?, which means that the preceding character or pattern is optional. With this you can eliminate *every* font tag (both open and close), while leaving the content intact, and you don't need to hard-code your page's text into the Replace field. This search is shown in Figure 25-6. Here are the steps:

1. Enter the following in your Find field: **</?font[^>]*>**.

   This Find expression finds the opening tag (<), then optionally the closing tag (/), then it finds all possible font tags by finding font, then zero or more characters that are *not* >, and then it finds the closing bracket (>).

2. Nothing needs to be entered in the Replace field because the GREP leaves the text intact as perform your search.

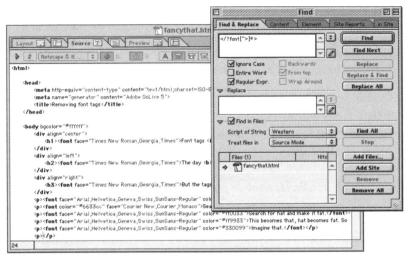

Figure 25-6: The setup for removing all font tags from a page called fancythat.html

Beware though, because this also means that *every* font tag will be removed, which may not be want you want. Regular expressions are very powerful and flexible, but need to be used carefully. On the other hand, `</?font[^>]*>` would be very useful if you wanted to remove all Font tags from your site so you can use Cascading Style Sheets (CSS).

If you knew that you wanted to replace all the font tags that contain `size="2"` with a CSS style called `bodycopy`, you can take advantage of regular expression's capability to remember matched patterns, called *back-references*. Here's how to do so:

1. Enter the following in your Find field: **<font(.*)? size="2"[^>]*>([^<]*)</font>**.

2. In the Replace field enter: **<span class="bodycopy">\2</span>**.

This GREP example looks for the beginning of a font tag (`<font`), and then finds and remembers zero or more characters that *may* precede the `size="2"` (in case color or face tags occur *before* the size tag). It continues, seeking zero or more characters that are *not* > (in case color or face tags occur *after* the size tag), then a closing bracket (>), and then zero or more characters that are *not* a bracket (<) (which will be the original text that was styled), and finally the closing font tag (`</font>`).

The contents in the parentheses are remembered and are accessible in the Replace field by \1, \2, \3 and so on. (back-references), in the order they were matched. The preceding replace string uses \2 because the first set of parentheses was used to find out if there were any characters before the size="2", so it was the second set that *remembered* the text you wanted to save.

Notice, too, that searching for `<font size="2"[^>]*>([^<]*)</font>` (which doesn't have that first set of parentheses) may not have done as well, because the size="2" may not have been the very first item in every font tag you wanted to match.

Tip   If you are not finding what you need, check to see if the Ignore Case checkbox is set the way you want.

Removing all occurrences of italic and bold

Another commonly requested replacement is to remove all italic and bold from a page. The trick, of course, is to do it but leave the text between the tags intact. The GREP for doing this is fairly simple:

Search for `</?(b|i)>`. This expression tells GoLive to find the opening bracket, optionally find the closing tag's /, and then find any occurrence of either a b which is part of the bold tag or an i which is the italic tag, and then find the closing bracket. Replace with nothing, which means, as with the font tag, leave the Replace field empty.

Note   Credit goes to Oliver Zahorka for posting the preceding GREP to the GoLive Talk list.

However, now that you're familiar with this helpful GREP, I should tell you that the Element tag contains a preconfigured task that does this just as well, or more easily. See the next section, "Finding HTML code elements," to learn about this feature.

Note   Want to check out a few more GREPs? Ken Martin has been kind enough to post some on his site at www.kpmartin.com.

Finding HTML code elements

Earlier in the chapter I mentioned a better way than Find & Replace to edit HTML code. Well, here it is. The Element tab lets you find and manipulate code elements using GoLive's HTML-savvy search engine, which recognizes HTML code and tags. You can add, delete, or modify attributes of existing tags. The best way to illustrate these functions is with an example, so first I give you the details of this search and replace feature, and then I provide an example.

The Element tab window is divided into three sections, as follows:

✦ **Search** (the top section) is where you select search criteria, including HTML elements and attributes.

✦ **Action** (the center section) is where you select actions you want carried out on any HTML elements and attributes found during a search.

✦ **Find In** (the bottom section)is where you can specify which files to search, just like in the Find & Replace window.

Name That Link!

By John Snippe, Designer, CyberNautica.com, design@cybernautica.com

Occasionally when developing, and particularly when dealing with middleware solutions, URLs are created that are not exactly memorable. (Okay, they're downright long and tedious) However, you sometimes need to be able to deal with these links within your Web pages in order to update their code. What is the easiest way to do this? Take advantage of the lesser-used Title attribute available in the Link Inspector and name that link!

After you name the link in Source mode, you can do a search on the title value you have entered (and presumably remember!) and can dig through source code to find the relevant line of code. This provides a 50 percent solution.

For the 100 percent solution, bring a GREP into the picture to *round-trip* an update. Here is a sample code string with a URL:

```
<a href="http://www.foobar.com/19278467/837r6jds/74jdjfbvch8348.
middleware title=your_title_here">foobar</a>
```

In this example, "foobar" is displayed on your page, the actual URL is `www.foobar.com/19278467/837r6jds/74jdjfbvch8348.middleware`, and "your_title_here" is the title entered in the Title field to make this URL memorable.

Now you can do a search or a search/ replace on "your_title_here" that enables you to replace or remove completely in one step. Here is a sample GREP to handle that on the preceding example (thanks, Ken Martin!):

```
<a href="[^\"]*" title="your_title_here">[^<]*</a>
```

Plug in the title you have chosen, and do what you wish in the Replace field of the Find dialog box window, which can also be manipulated with GREP.

Caution   Use this feature with caution and be sure you have a backup of your site before using this feature. You can easily do something you'll regret here.

If you're new to HTML or not fully comfortable with it, I recommend that you switch you page window to Source mode or open the Source Code window so you can see the tags that you're searching. This may help you choose your attributes and values.

To use the Element tab's search and replace, follow these steps:

1. In the top Search section, set up the search by doing this:

   • In the first pop-up menu keep Name is or choose Name matches.

   • In the pop-up menu to the right of the next blank field, choose one of the HTML tags from the list. (See Figure 25-7.) Or, enter your own criteria.

• Use the Attribute and Operator pop-up menus to complete your search criteria, if needed. Be sure to replace the generic word "value" with the actual value. These pieces appear in the larger search field.

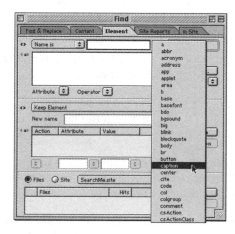

Figure 25-7: A partial list of the many elements from which to choose

Tip You can easily set up five predefined tasks. To do so, choose one from the Open Task pop-up menu. After you perform your own search and replace, you can save it as a task too. That way you can later choose it from the Open Task pop-up menu to do it again.

2. In the middle (Action) section, select and set up the actions you want to perform. You can do this one of two ways:

• Choose an action from the long pop-up menu at the top of this section. Their names are fairly descriptive of what they do. For example, to remove a set of tags, but keep the text between the tags, choose *Replace Element by its content*. When searching for a tag in order to change the tag's name, choose *Rename Element*, and then enter the new tag code into the New Name field, which automatically becomes available.

• Custom create an action by choosing an Action, Attribute, and Value. Click New Action to place generic text within each of the three columns, and then use the pop-up menu below each attribute's respective column to set up the action you wish to accomplish. Use the New Action button to add more actions and the Delete Action button to remove an action (after selecting it in the list first). Items within the pop-up menus change, depending on the criteria set in the top of the window.

3. Specify the files to be searched by using the Files or Site button:

• The Files button is selected by default. This option lets you add individual files. You can then use the Add Files button to open the Open file dialog box and add more files to the search.

- Click the Site button to add all HTML files in the open Site Window. You can then exclude any file from the search by selecting the file and clicking Remove.

Selected files appear in the Files list at the bottom of the field. Upon completing all criteria selection, the Start button becomes solid.

4. Click Start to begin the search.

An alert informs you of the number of files that will be affected and warns you that the action cannot be undone. Click OK to continue.

The Hits column lists the number of replacements within each page. You can view the results of any page by double-clicking the file name in the list. This opens the page in Layout view.

The best way to illustrate these functions is with an example. One function commonly requested on the GoLive Talk list is to change the background color in all the pages on your site. Here's how you can perform that task:

1. As the background color tag is a body element, you select body from the pop-up menu next to the Start button. The word "body" is placed by the "Name is" field.

2. From the Open Task pop-up menu, you select "Set background color." This automatically fills the Action/Attribute/Value window with the action words: set bgcolor white.

3. In the pop-up menu below the Value column, select and delete the default color's code. Open the Color palette, scroll to the desired color and drag that color into the Value field.

4. To change all HTML pages within your site, click the Site button. (If you have multiple Site Windows open, make sure the correct site is listed in the pop-up menu beside the Site button.

5. Click Start to begin the search; when the alert appears, click OK.

Because one background exists per page, they get one hit per page, so there should be a 1 in each line of the Files list, as shown in Figure 25-8. Each page now contains the desired background color.

Setting Find preferences

To view or change GoLive's Find preferences, open the Preferences window by selecting Edit ⇨ Preferences and clicking the Find icon at the left. Choose an option for what appears when a match is made. The pop-up menu offers three options:

✦ **Activate Document** opens the document and brings its window to the front.

✦ **Keep the Find Window in Front** keeps it in front of the document.

✦ **Close the Find Window** closes it.

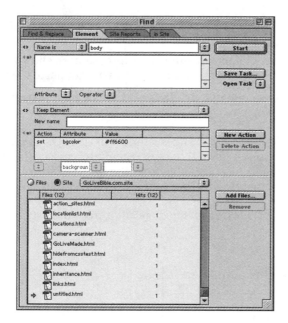

Figure 25-8: This search-and-replace operation found all 12 files in the site and set their background color to ff6600 (an orange).

As you use Replace and Find, you may want to return to this preference and set the Find window to remain in front, or at least, experiment with that option.

Choose one of the following to set the option that tells GoLive how to deal with text files when you search a site in the Source mode:

✦ **Use only HTML files** limits your search to Web pages.

✦ **Use HTML and text files** lets you search all text files in a site, including JavaScripts, external style sheets, and so on.

Using GoLive's help, you can search for patterns of text or code, rather than just for specific words. Several common patterns come preconfigured. As you get into using this feature, you may wish to add your own patterns — and this is where you add them.

Before you add a GREP (a.k.a. *regular expression*) to Preferences, try it to be sure it works. Then, return to the Find & Replace tab and choose that expression from the pop-up menu so you can copy it from the Search field to paste into Preferences.

To add a regular expression, follow these steps:

1. Click the arrow next to the Find icon to reveal the Regular Expressions topic and select the word Regular Expressions.

2. Click New.

3. Enter a descriptive name for your search, so you can choose it correctly from the pop-up menu when using Find.

4. Tab to the Regular Expression column and enter the expression, as shown in Figure 25-9. (If you copied it from the Find & Replace tab you can paste it now.)

5. Tab again and enter the replacement pattern. Leave it blank if no replacement exists (as in the example shown here).

As soon as you click anywhere within the Preferences window or click OK to close the window, your new expression is set. Click OK to close the Preferences window and save it. The newly entered GREP is now available from the bottom part of the Find & Replace pop-up menu and appears with your name so you can reuse it.

To remove an expression if it doesn't work as planned, select it from the list, and then click Delete.

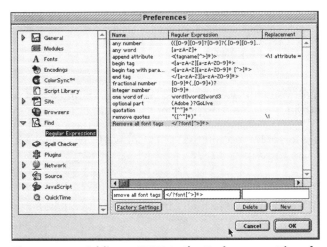

Figure 25-9: Adding a GREP to the Preference settings for GoLive's Find feature. As the name reflects, this one removes all font tags, both opening and closing.

Finding Files within Your Site

What happens when you *know* you created a URL for a certain site but just cannot see it listed among your many URLs when you need to link to it? As your site gets larger, it can become easy to lose track of a file, external URL, the name of a color, and so on. Fortunately, if you recall any part of the item's name, you can use GoLive's find feature to seek it out. The last tab of the Find window lets you find individual files or objects by name. This can be extremely helpful in large sites. You can find files by name or by any fragment of the name that you may recall. You can find colors, external links, and so on.

Locating items in your site

To seek out specific items within your site, follow these steps:

1. Within the Site Window, activate the tab in which you wish to search.

   If seeking a file within your site, go to the Files tab; if seeking an external URL, turn to the External tab, and so on.

2. Choose Edit ⇨ Find, and then click the in Site tab, or click the Find Files in Site button in the toolbar.

3. Select either Name or URL from the left pop-up menu:

   • Name enables you to search by the name you gave a file or address.

   • URL enables you to locate an External address by the actual URL, rather than the name you gave it, as is the case in Figure 25-10.

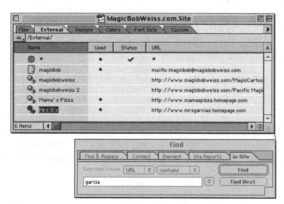

Figure 25-10: A search for "garcia" within the External tab reveals the URL for Mrs. Garcia's Restaurant, which the designer can't recall.

4. Set your search criteria by choosing from the options in the right pop-up menu. Your choices are *contains, is, begins with,* or *ends with*.

5. Type or paste in the file name or part of the file name that you know and want to find.

   Once you have performed a search for any text, that text is remembered and can be selected from the pop-up menu to the right of the text field so you don't have to re-enter it.

6. Click Find to begin the search.

   GoLive displays the first found result (in its embedded folder if applicable) by highlighting its icon.

7. Click Find Next to find the next file that matches the search.

Performing index searches (Mac only)

If you're on a Mac, you have one more way to save your sanity (or at least time), when you know you created a page but just cannot recall what you named that page. The Mac OS contains a feature called Apple Information Access Technology (AIAT) that enables users to index the contents of their hard drive, down to individual elements in files. To take advantage of this feature in GoLive, turn on the Find by Content module selected in the Module Preferences. It works whenever you have a Site Window open. (In the previous version of GoLive, this module, now called Find by Content, was called AIAT.)

Building an index

Before GoLive can search within your files, it must build an index of that site's files. You can do this during your first search, or beforehand. If you're building a large site, you may wish to build the index at the beginning and have it update automatically so it's ready and up-to-date whenever you need it.

Follow these steps to build the index at any time:

1. Choose Edit ⇨ Find and select the Content tab.
2. Click the Build Index button.
3. Check Auto Update, if it's not already checked.

The index appears as a file within your Site Window's files tab. It is named for your site with the word index at the end. You do not need to upload this file along with your site. It's just for internal use while working on your site within the Site Window.

Performing a search

To seek out any occurrence of text within your site, all you have to do is enter the words (or characters) you're looking for and press Enter/Return to do the search. The options explained as follows may make it appear more complicated than it really is.

Here are the steps to locate content within a file:

1. Choose Edit ⇨ Find and select the Content tab.
2. Enter the text you're searching for into the Search field at the top of the Find window.

   If you've previously performed the same search, you can choose it from the pop-up menu to the right of the Search field.

3. *(Optional)* If the language of the page(s) you are searching is other than the one who's encoding appears in the Encoding pop-up menu, use this menu to choose the encoding for the desired language. (GL-Western is the encoding for Roman alphabet languages.)

4. *(Optional)* If you have multiple sites open and wish to search a site other than the one named in the Site pop-up menu, choose the desired site from this menu.

5. By default, all occurrences of the finding are listed. To reduce the number of finds, select a relevance ranking from the pop-up menu at the bottom left corner of the window. For example, selecting 75 percent lists hits with a 75 percent ranking. You can always change the ranking later to lengthen or shorten the list.

6. Click Search. If you have not already indexed your site, GoLive asks you to do so now. Click yes to have GoLive index and search the site. Clicking No cancels the search. When the search is complete, a list of pages appears, along with a relevance ranking and the number of hits found on the page.

7. *(Optional)* Click the blue arrow to the left of a page to reveal the occurrences and read their context, as shown in Figure 25-11.

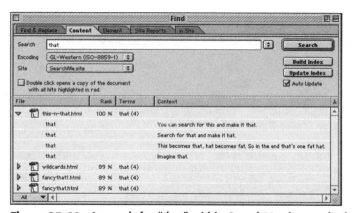

Figure 25-11: A search for "that" within SearchMe.site resulted in four pages with occurrences. The text of each occurrence can be seen in the Context column when the page results are revealed.

8. *(Optional)* By default, if you double-click any page listed within the find list, it opens a *copy* of the page or file and shows you every occurrence of the found text in red. If you prefer to have the *real page* open instead, uncheck the option.

9. *(Optional)* Double-click the page icon in the files list. The first occurrence found is highlighted, as in seen Figure 25-12.

   If you are finding a page to make a change, such as to add a comma, it is easier to open the original. That way you can find the text, edit it, save, and be done with it.

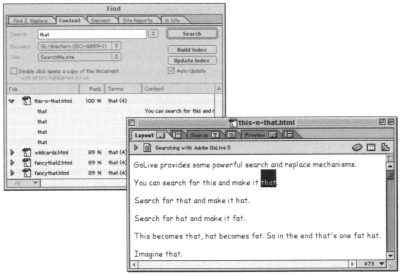

Figure 25-12: A searched page open to work within and save changes to, if needed

Note   If you have the option to open a copy of the document checked, the page that opens is a copy, as noted by its name, which begins with the words, "Matches in." Saving this page saves a new copy of the page.

If, before you do another search sometime in the future, you'd like to ensure that your index is current, you can click the Update Index button. Before you close the Find window, I suggest seeing that Auto Update is checked. That way, the index automatically updates as you build your site.

Identifying Bad Links

Links are unique aspects of the Web and a great part of the power of your pages comes from links. When you need to review the health of your page, to see that graphics are in place, that sounds are there to play, that files are there to download, where that page leads, and more . . . you're talking links. Needless to say, GoLive monitors your links at all times and provides plenty of feedback about their health. Chances are, you've seen green bugs as you've worked in GoLive. Those are link warnings. You may also have seen missing file icons, empty reference notations, and so on. That's what this section is about: Learning how to monitor and repair your links.

You have several ways to know that your link is complete—and when your link has an error. The Files tab of the Site Window, your main stomping ground for dealing with your pages and other files, is constantly monitoring the links within your pages—and letting you know when a problem exists. (You can't miss those odd green bugs.) As you work in Layout mode, GoLive can show you incomplete and invalid links by marking them in red. You can also see these errors in Outline mode. At any time as you work, you can also Preview your page and try the links. The In & Out Links palette is always available to lend a hand. The Errors tab of the Site Window can help too.

To repair a broken link, use any of the same methods you use to create the link in the first place.

Green bugs

You don't have to open every page to check for bad links. Green bugs in GoLive alert you to bad links. It appears in the Status column of the Files tab in the Site Window shown in Figure 25-13.

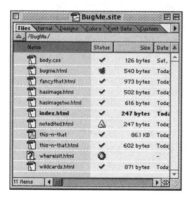

Figure 25-13: The Files tab reports the status of your pages at all times. The green bug tells you a link error occurs on a page.

Any time you see a green bug next to a page, it's a good idea to investigate. One way to learn the source of a bug is to open the page, turn Link Warnings on if it's not on already, and then locate and repair the red link warnings on the page. (See the following "Link Warnings" section.) Another way to look into a bug issue is within the In & Out Links palette. (See "Reviewing Links in the In & Out Links Palette" later in this chapter.)

When you successfully correct all bad links, the green bug goes away.

Note   The Files tab may also display a yellow caution icon. That's not a bug or bad link. It just means that the page has not yet been developed.

Link warnings

GoLive is constantly watching your site, checking that all your links are valid and that files are designated where they are requested. As soon as you create your link you can see whether it is valid or not. Just click the Link Warnings button (the Green Bug button) on the toolbar or choose Edit ⇨ Show Link Warnings. With Link Warnings turned on, a wide red border marks any bad links. In fact, the red points them out everywhere the link is, as shown in Figure 25-14. If a bad graphic exists, the bad link can either be to the graphic on the page or to the link that is its destination.

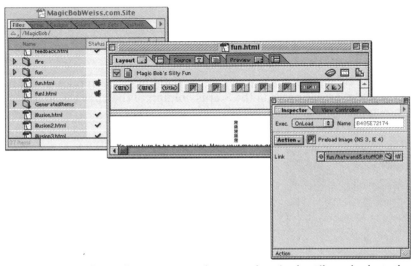

Figure 25-14: The path to an error. The green bug in the Files tab alerts the designer. In the open page, the red border points out the Head section. In the Head section the red points to the Action. In the Inspector, the red identifies a missing file.

The easiest way to learn exactly what the problem is and make the repair, is to select the red-bordered text or item and check out its Inspector. The Inspector also uses the red highlight to show you its problems. Of course, you can also repair the link via the Inspector just like you can create the link in the first place.

If the bad link is in the Head area, the arrow beside the Page icon at the top of your page is the item highlighted in red. Click the arrow so it points downward and reveals the icons in the Head section. The icon with the error is highlighted to point it out. Select it and use the Inspector to learn exactly what the problem it.

You can turn Link Warnings on and off at any time. If you have any content on your page already when turning on Link Warnings, GoLive checks all links and immediately shows you any errors. All new links you create are then checked as you create them.

You can easily change the color of the Link Warnings highlight. Go to Edit ➪ Preferences, open the General topic, and choose User Interface. There, you'll see the topic Marking and Link Warnings beneath it. (Actually, you'll see the bold red color swatch first, I bet.) Click in the color swatch to open your computer's color picker, and then choose a new color there. The color you choose takes effect in the preferences as soon as you click OK to close the Preferences window.

This color setting affects link warnings everywhere in your site. It's the color of a warning whether shown on the page, in the Inspector, or in the Header of your page.

In & Out Links palette

The In & Out Links palette doesn't mark or identify bad URLs, but it does alert you to links that lack a specified destination.

Within the Files tab of the Site Window, click the file you want to inspect. Open the In & Out Links palette if it's not already open. The selected file appears in the In & Out Links palette, with all links coming in to it shown to the left and all outgoing links at the right. The name and icon for the destination file appears next to each link. If a link has been started but no file is linked to it, the icon is blank and the words (Empty Reference!) appear, as shown in Figure 25-15. You can fix this by dragging the Point and Shoot button over to the desired file if you can recall which file is missing. The In & Out Links palette is covered fully later in this chapter.

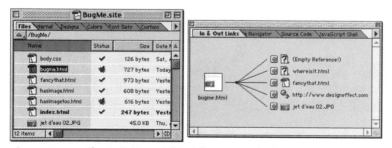

Figure 25-15 The In & Out Links palette reveals that, of the four links on the selected page, one, which reports "(Empty Reference!)," is incomplete. (Another bad link exists, due to a missing file.)

Note　When you place one of the palette's placeholder icons on the page and don't designate a file to fill it, or assign a link to it, that holder also reports an error.

Previewing links

Another way to discover broken links is to switch to Preview and try the links. You can't make any changes to the page in Preview mode so switch back to Layout mode to correct your link.

Some pages don't fully render in Preview so some links may not work. Another option is to click the Show in Browser button to preview your pages in a browser and try the links. After you're previewed the page in a browser, return to the page to fix the problem. You can choose Show in Browser again to have GoLive rebuild the page after you've made the corrections, and then test it again.

Using HTML Outline Editor mode

Another way to become aware of bad links is to switch to HTML Outline Editor mode while Link Warnings is on. In Outline Editor mode the reference to a bad URL is highlighted in red as in Layout mode. (See Figure 25-16.) But unlike in the Layout mode method, you don't have to check the Inspector to learn the link's destination. Instead it is clearly revealed in the outline. (See Chapter 3 to learn about Outline mode.)

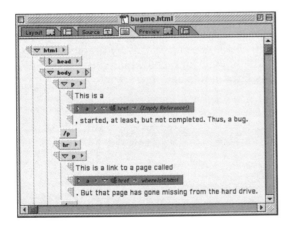

Figure 25-16: HTML Outline Editor mode clearly alerts you to link errors and displays the URL at the same time.

You can select the text of the bad link and correct it while in Outline mode. However, as with correcting a URL in the Inspector, this correction only fixes the one occurrence of the URL. If the URL is listed in the External tab of the Site Window, that listing won't be updated. It's far better to make the correction in the Site Window so all current and future occurrences of the URL are repaired and correct. If you correct it in Outline mode or in the Inspector, and then later click the Update button to do an update, the corrected URL is added to the Site Window. This leaves you with two URL files for the same location, and one is incorrect, which can be confusing. Then, if you later try to repair it in the Site Window, an error dialog box informs you that the URL you are attempting to use is already in use. You need to relink all uses of it the incorrect URL, and then delete it.

Using the Errors tab

The Errors tab also gives you a message when problems occur. Simply put, if a file is missing, it in a folder called Missing Files, and if a file is orphaned it appears in a folder called Orphan Files, as shown in Figure 25-17. You can inspect these files by selecting them and seeing what the File Inspector says, or by viewing their In & Out links. Details on this tab are provided in the dedicated section called, "Troubleshooting via the Errors Tab" later in this chapter.

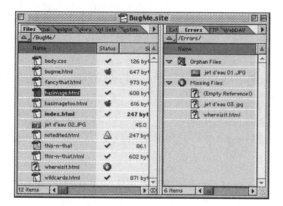

Figure 25-17: The Errors tab of the Site Window reveals missing or orphaned files that don't make it to your server without help.

Checking external links

One of GoLive's greatest powers is its capability to check your external links. It's incredibly easy to do and saves you an amazing amount of time. By running an external link check on your Site Window occasionally, you avoid getting those embarrassing broken link e-mails from your visitors. This feature not only checks links that you've used; it also checks links that may want to use.

Only two requirements are needed for checking external links. One is that the links must be noted in the External tab of the Site Window, as shown in Chapter 11. Just make the External tab active and choose Site ➪ Get References Used or click the Update button on the toolbar. The other requirement is that because checking requires GoLive to search the Web for the address's validity, you must be connected to the Internet.

Note   The only link GoLive cannot check is an e-mail address. The way to do that is to try sending an e-mail to the addressee.

To check your external links, follow these steps:

1. While connected to the Internet, bring forward the External tab of your Site Window.

2. Choose Site ⇨ Check External Links or bring up the contextual menu while pointing anywhere in the External tab and choose Check External Links from there.

Tip   If you want GoLive to check URLs before you actually use them on your site just have them in the External tab.

As GoLive verifies your links, a green connection icon appears in the Status column of the Site Window. When a link is verified, the usual black checkmark appears in the Status column. If an external link is not found, the Green Bug icon appears in the Status column. If a bad URL is inside a folder, a mini bug appears with an arrow pointing toward it. When you open that folder you see which file has the bug. Figure 25-18 demonstrates the various status icons.

New Feature   In Version 5, GoLive can even verify a link to an anchor within a page. Those links no longer appear as invalid when the link is fine.

If you have many external links (and especially if you have a slow Internet connection) this process can take a while. This is a good time to take a break, stretch, refocus your eyes, or remember to eat a snack.

To repair a URL, select its icon, and then correct it in the URL field of the Inspector. After you correct the URL, GoLive asks if it may update any pages that contain the link. Click OK to have all references to this link corrected. When the error is corrected, the bug disappears.

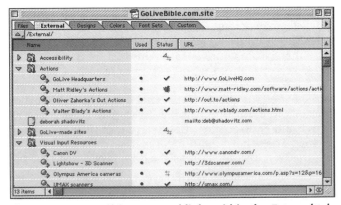

Figure 25-18: Verifying external links within the External tab of the Site Window. Files within two folders are still being checked, as is one other link. One link destination is invalid so it displays a bug.

Tip

You *can* edit the URL in the Inspector's URL field. However, that changes the URL only for that link rather than updates it in the Site Window. The better way to correct a faulty external URL is in the Site Window. If you make the correction in the Inspector, and then later click the Update button to do an update, the corrected URL is added to the Site Window. This gives you two URL files for the same location and one is incorrect, which can be confusing. If you later try to repair it in the Site Window, an error dialog box informs you that the URL you are attempting to use is already in use. You need to relink all uses of the incorrect URL, and then delete it.

Troubleshooting via the Errors Tab

The Errors tab is dedicated to showing you the files in your site that are causing, or will cause errors. That is, missing and orphaned files. Orphans are very easy to fix. Missing files may be more difficult as they are, well, missing.

You have three ways to open the Errors Tab, as follows:

✦ With the Site Window active, click the Green Bug (Link Warnings) button on the toolbar.

✦ Click the fly-out menu — the right-pointing arrow at the top right corner of the Site Window — and select Errors from the resulting pop-up menu.

✦ Click the double-headed arrow at the lower-right corner of the Site Window to open the right side of the Site Window. Then select the Errors tab.

When GoLive discovers an orphan or missing file, it creates a folder named Orphan Files or Missing Files in the Errors tab. (The folder disappears when no Orphans or Missing files exist, respectively.) Expanding the folders shows the problematic file(s).

Orphan files

An *orphan file* is a file called for by a page in your site, but not yet collected in the Site Window. Orphans don't show as missing or as errors in the Files tab or in the Link Inspector. However, as they are not yet part of your Site Window, it's very possible to upload your site to the server without them — which means your site will be incomplete when served live on the Web.

Orphaned files do not cause green bugs in a file's status column as they are available on the hard drive and the path to them is valid. However, orphans are not uploaded to your Web server unless you take the necessary steps. This is why they are pointed out in the Errors tab, as shown in Figure 25-19.

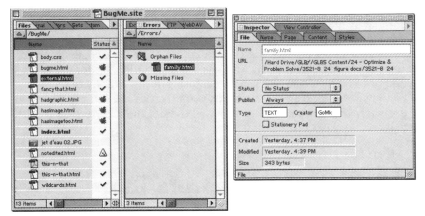

Figure 25-19: The Orphan Files folder reports family.html as an Orphan. Notice that the path reported in the Inspector is outside of the site's root folder and the page does not appear in the Files tab. The referring page (index.html), does not have a bug.

Orphan files can easily appear if you use the Browse button to add a file to your site. Using Browse doesn't physically add a new copy of a page to your site; it just creates a link to that file so the file is reflected within your site. Why are orphans really a problem if they are successfully reflected in your site and appear on your pages as valid links?

Assume that you've ended up in an orphan file situation by browsing to insert an image onto one of your pages. When you view that page on your own computer, that image is available on your hard drive so it appears on your page. You then upload your site to the Web server. All files that appear within your Files tab are sent to the server. But . . . that image is not in your Files tab so it is not uploaded. Now a visitor calls for your page. The page is sent to the user, but unless the computer you created the site on happens to be a Web server too, the path to that image cannot be completed so your image does not display. The same event happens when the orphan happens to be a page, a PDF, and so on. When that page or item is called for, it cannot be found so your site is incomplete.

What happens when the orphan happens to be a page that contains graphics, and the entire page and its graphics live outside of your site folder? Again, you have orphans. However, in this case, only the linked-to page appears as the orphan because GoLive only recognizes that page. GoLive is not yet managing the files that are on that page because the page is not yet managed via the Site Window.

Any time you use Browse to incorporate a file that is not already within your Site Window, you eventually have to get the file physically into your site folder, and consequently into your Site Window.

Note To clarify, if you use the Browse button to arrive at and choose a file from within your own site folder, the effect is the same as using Point and Shoot. This does not cause orphans. (You know you're at your own site's folder when the folder is named for your site and contains the three files: yoursite.site, yoursite.data and yoursite. This folder is the actual docs folder. The folder you browse to is yoursite. GoLive knows it as the root folder.)

Repairing orphans

Fortunately, it is very easy to repair an orphan file. To repair an orphan, simply drag the orphan file (its icon really) from the Errors tab in the Orphan file folder into your Site Window (or into a subfolder if desired.) GoLive presents the Copy Files window, reminding you that the page containing the inserted image needs to be updated. Click OK to have GoLive copy the image into your site folder and Site Window and update the page. When the orphan is corrected, it disappears from the Orphan file folder in the Errors tab and, if no more orphans exist, the entire folder disappears.

The other way to remedy an orphan is to use the Clean Up Site command. While cleaning up your site, just check the option for adding all referenced files. During the clean up, GoLive notices the file is referenced, but is not yet within the site's folder (Site Windows), so it copies the file into the folder for you.

Remember the example (shown previously in Figure 25-19) of the link to the page that lives outside your site folder? If you repair that orphan by dragging its Orphan file icon into your Site Window, it is successfully copied into the Files tab and GoLive can upload that page. However, the files that comprise the page still reside outside of the Files tab. Now that GoLive manages the page, it is aware of the files that are part of that page and those files are immediately noted as orphans that you need to drag over too. Another way to repair an orphaned page is to note the location of the page, and then go to that page in your computer (outside of using GoLive) and move the page and its contents into the Files tab the same way you learned to add files earlier in this book. You can bring the entire folder that contains the page and files, or you can just bring in the files. GoLive updates the links within the copy of the page it creates, so the page will find its contents without a hitch. (By the way, if you were to delete a page that causes orphan or missing files, those Orphans or Missing file icons go away.)

Locating orphans

To learn where an orphan file is, you can use any of these three methods:

✦ Select the Orphan file icon in the Orphans folder and look at its URL in the Inspector. That URL is the path to the file.

✦ Select the Orphan file icon in the Orphans folder, open the In & Out Links palette, and then move your mouse over the file's icon there. (See "Reviewing Links in the In & Out Links palette," later in this chapter.)

✦ Select the file icon (or link) on the page on which it is used, and then look at its URL in the Inspector.

Missing files

Two types of files are reported as missing: lost files and unknown files (which includes empty references). Both appear with a stop sign icon to alert you.

Lost files

A *lost file* is one that is called for by a page—to either inhabit that page or is a destination link from a page—but is nowhere to be found on your hard drive or on any other volume accessible to your site at the time. A lost file may have been in the Site Window at one time but was deleted, or it may never have been there at all.

Lost files often start out as orphans. It's all too easy for this situation to occur. Your lost file begins as part of a page that resides outside of your site and is not copied into the site when the page is copied over. Thus, it's an orphan. Later, the file is deleted (or the hard drive it was on becomes unavailable). After all, you have no way of knowing that this file is being used as part of a Web site so it is easy to delete it without realizing the repercussions. Thus, the page within GoLive that calls for this file can no longer locate the file—and it is noted as missing. As a missing file, it can no longer appear on the containing page so a placeholder appears in its place and it becomes listed in the Missing Files folder.

> **Note**   As you can see, it is all too easy for a file that is used in your site but is not copied into the Site Window to go missing and cause problems for you. The lesson to learn here is to always copy all files used on your pages into the Files tab. You can always delete a file later if you don't use it, but you cannot always locate a file after it's gone.

Another way files become lost is when you actually delete the file yourself. Say a file, such as a graphic, is used on a page. Later, you delete that graphic file. You're good and you delete via the trash button on the toolbar or by using the contextual menu. But that file is still called for by the page it was on so you have just created a Missing File. The page shows a green bug link error and the file is reported as missing.

Less often, files are lost when they are deleted from directly within the behind-the-scenes site folder on your hard drive, instead of from the Site Window interface. A file deleted this way is actually a different case though. In this case, the Site Window thinks the file is still there and doesn't report it as missing immediately. After you rescan the site though, GoLive notes the missing file. (See "Rescanning Your Site and Updating Links" later in this chapter to learn about the Rescan feature.)

> **Note**   Only physical files—files that can occupy the Files tab—can become missing files. After you've linked to an external URL or address, the link is written into the page and remains valid. even if the marker for that address is deleted. (You lose the benefit of having the one marker address many instances of it and make changing the address across the board easy, though.)

When a file appears as Missing, first check the Site Trash folder in the Extras tab to see if it's there. If it is, you can drag it back into place in the Files tab. If it's not there, the only way to repair a lost file is to locate that file (if you can) and copy it into the Site Window.

The Inspector may also inform you where your missing file was last seen by GoLive, although this is not guaranteed. Select the missing file's icon in the Missing Files folder, open the Inspector, and then check the URL field for the last known path. (If it's a long path, press Option (Mac) or Control (Windows) and click the Folder icon (now the Edit pencil icon on the Mac). This opens the Edit URL window, in which you can view the entire path to the file more easily. The last known location is also reported in the In & Out Links palette, as shown in Figure 25-20.

If you have another file in the Files tab or copy one in to replace the missing file, you can Point and Shoot from the missing file to the desired file to use it in lieu of the missing file. You can Point and Shoot from the Errors tab, the In & Out Links palette, or the File Inspector while that file is being inspected. Remember though, that this replacement is in effect for every occurrence of the missing file's usage in the entire site. You can also open the page that contains the error and link from there. In this case, only that occurrence of the used file is corrected.

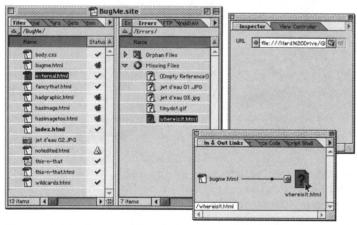

Figure 25-20: Reported in Missing Files, whereisit.html cannot be found. Its referring page, bugme.html reports an error. The last known address of this missing file was directly in the Files tab so it must have been deleted from there.

Caution

If you click a Missing file icon, and then use Point and Shoot or browse to repair the link, GoLive attempts to apply the correction to every broken link on your site, and provides a Change Reference window notifying you of the pages it wants to update. You can then select or deselect to repair the page(s) you need to. Note also that using the browse function to select a page already in your Site Window completes the link correctly. *(Thanks to Pete Zimowski for this information.)*

Missing files (empty references)

An unknown file, called an *empty reference*, is one whose link was started, but the destination of that link is unknown to GoLive. Thus, the only way you can figure out what the link was meant to do, is to open the page it is reported as being on, as seen in Figure 25-21. Perhaps that page will hold clues. For example, perhaps the link was descriptive text, or it was referred to from an image map or button whose destination is clear.

If the intended destination is already in your Site Window, you can link the Empty Reference icon to the destination file or marker. If the destination is a file, but not in the Site Window, you need to bring it in or create the marker for it before you can repair the link. Once the file is in place in the Site Window, you can link to it in several ways. You can Point and Shoot from the Empty Reference icon in the Errors tab, from the Empty Reference icon in the In & Out Links palette, or from the URL getter area of the Inspector while the file is selected and being inspected. Or you can open the page that contains the link and connect the link in the same way as when you normally create a link. In each case, you shoot to the file or address that is to be its destination.

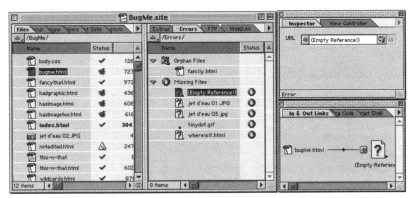

Figure 25-21: The Site Window and palettes provide no clues as to the destination intended for this link on the page called bugme.html. (The page however, may hold clues when opened.)

If the link was made in error, open the page that contains the link and unlink it. (See Chapter 11.)

Finding missing files within your site

GoLive may report a file as missing due to some confusion — or more likely because you've moved the file to the Site Trash. In this case GoLive can help you locate the missing file.

Control-click (Mac) or right-click (Windows) to bring up the contextual menu, and then choose Find. This brings up the Find in Site dialog box that automatically sets up the search. Just click Find and GoLive searches your site for the missing file. If the file is in your Files tab it is automatically selected for you. Of course you can also do this by simply searching through your list of files yourself. If the file is found within the Files tab, you can Point and Shoot to the found file to fix the reference.

Rescanning Your Site and Updating Links

As you add files in the GoLive Site Window, GoLive copies them into the behind-the-scenes site files (Root) folder on your hard drive. As you create new folders or delete old ones, move files around, add or delete files in your Files tab, GoLive does the same in the folders on your hard drive. These changes are tracked within the Site Document that you double-click to open the Site Window. The Site Document usually does an excellent job of keeping up, but at times it may not keep up or may lose track. Whenever you're not sure, you can rescan your site.

Another time to rescan your site is whenever GoLive shuts down without the proper File menu's Quit or Exit command (Ô-Q or Ctrl+Q). When this happens, you'll notice upon relaunching the site that not all the files you've added to your site appear, or that your recent folder organization isn't reflected in the Site Window. Files you *know* you added appear as missing and links you know are good appear with bug icons. In reality, your changes were made behind the scenes. The Site Window just doesn't show them. To rectify this, simply rescan the site. In other words, if you ever crash, freeze, or force-quit/escape, rescan the site next time you open it so you can see what is happening in your site.

One more time why you'll want to rescan is whenever you add files to your site at the desktop level by adding them to the behind-the-scenes site folder instead of to the Site Window. (Although I've recommended many times against adding files to this site folder, I know at some point you will do it anyway. For example, you may save the resulting file directly into the root folder when you're working within another program.) Anyway, when you return to the Site Window to place the file on your page, link to the added page, and so on, you'll notice that even though the image is physically in the Images folder, GoLive doesn't know it yet. Rescanning gives GoLive the opportunity to learn that a new item has been added to or deleted from the site.

Another benefit of rescanning your site is that GoLive double-checks and verifies your links.

You can rescan your entire site at once, just the Root level, any one folder of files in the Files tab, the entire data folder (the Extras tab), or any folder within the Extras tabs. This flexibility can save you time if your site has a lot of files.

To rescan a part of your site, click within that part of the site or open the folder you want scanned, and then do the following:

✦ Select the Rescan command from the Site menu. (If in your site's Files tab the command is Rescan Yoursitename, if in the Extras tab it is Rescan Yoursitename.data. If in a folder, it is Rescan NameOfFolder.)

✦ Select the Update checkmark button in the toolbar

✦ Open the Site Window to the section or folder you wish to rescan, and Control-click (Mac) or right-click (Windows) while anywhere in that area and choose Update from the contextual menu.

✦ You can also rescan your site via the Clean Up Site command. Use Clean Up Site, while the Rescan root folder option is selected.

Note   The Update button in the toolbar does not always perform a rescan. It actually always reflects the Rescan or Get command that is active in the Site menu. The Site menu's command (and therefore the Update command) change depending upon the tab that is active in the Site Window. Rescanning only occurs in the Files and Extras tabs, which are the tabs that contain physical files.

It's important to understand that the Rescan command synchronizes the site folders and the Site Document, but does *not* import files that are located externally. If you used the Browse button to connect your site to a page or file anywhere outside of your site's root folder, these commands do not copy that file into the site. Only the Clean Up Site command copies does this.

As soon as you make changes to a page, GoLive updates all references (links to and from the page). However, if you work with your pages in an HTML editor outside of GoLive, or edit your pages directly in Source code, there may be times when you want to make sure the links in all of your pages are fully up-to-date. You can do this whenever GoLive does a Rescan by checking the option ("Reparse files on harddisk rescan") to do so within Preferences, or you can reparse your links manually.

Follow these steps to have GoLive reparse your links each time you rescan the site:

1. Choose Edit ➪ Preferences, and then select the Site icon.

2. Check "Reparse files on harddisk rescan."

3. *(Optional)* If you don't want GoLive to go through all of your links, you can also check the option for "Reparse only changed files."

To manually reparse your links, follow these steps:

1. Close any open pages.

2. Make the Site Window active and bring the Files tab forward. (It doesn't matter whether any page is selected or no page is selected, but you must be in this tab for the command to be available.)

3. Press Option (Mac) or Ctrl (Windows) while you click the Site menu, and then choose Site ➪ Reparse All.

Note   This Reparse command only reparses links. It doesn't reparse the code against the Web settings or reformats code.

Reviewing Links in the In & Out Links Palette

The Web works amazingly through links and a great part of the power of your pages comes from them. When you need to see what is on your page and where that page leads, you're talking about links. GoLive enables you to view all the links in your page through the In & Out Links palette.

Just select any file in your Site Window, Navigation view, or Links view, and every link into — and out of — that page is yours to view and command. This palette shows you *all files* that comprise the page — the graphics (including a background image if one exists), QuickTime videos, sounds, external URLs, e-mail links, and so on. (Colors and font sets are not reported, as they are embedded code, not linked objects. However, you can inspect a color or font set to see on which pages it is used.) Any part of the page that's in the Files, Extras, or External tab is tracked and identified in the In & Out Links Inspector. When you click a graphic or other page element, the In & Out Links Inspector shows all the files in which that graphic is used.

Viewing a page's links with the In & Out Links palette

To open the In & Out Links palette, click the Open In & Out Links Palette button on the toolbar or choose Window ➪ In & Out Links. (If no file is selected, the palette is blank.) You can resize it or collapse it as with any other palette.

To view an item's links, select the item within the Site Window, Navigation view, or Links view. This selected item becomes the focus of attention. You can click any page, file, or marker shown in the palette to change the focus to that item.

All pages that link to the focus page appear on the left of the page. Any files that are used within the page are shown on the right. Also at the right are any internal pages, external URLs, and e-mail addresses that appear as links on the page. You can easily replace one page with another by dragging the Point and Shoot button to any other page within the Files tab of the Site Window.

When you view a graphic or other media item stored within the Files tab, pages that include the graphic appear on the left, as shown in Figure 25-22. When a graphic acts as a button, the page or object that button links to are not reflected in the In & Out Links palette. (Because colors and font sets are not a part of any graphic, they are not reported as links in or out of a file.)

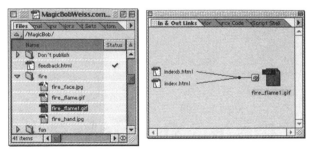

Figure 25-22: The pages using a graphic appear on its left

To replace one graphic with another, inspect the current graphic in the In & Out Links Inspector, and then drag the current graphic's Point and Shoot button over to the new graphic within the Files tab of the Site Window. Everywhere the graphic is used, the new graphic takes it place. The benefit of the In & Out Links palette is that you can see every page on which the graphic is used so you can avoid changing a graphic on a page where you don't want it changed. Or, you can note the page on which you don't want the graphic changed, and then open that page and change the graphic just on that page. A typical use for this feature is to replace one background image with another should you wish to give your site an entirely different look. (This is also discussed in Chapter 11.)

When you view an External URL or address stored within the External tab, the pages that use that address appear at the left, leading in to the address's icon. Figure 25-23 demonstrates the use of an e-mail address.

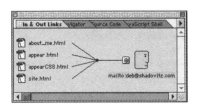

Figure 25-23: External addresses called for in a site are reflected in the In & Out Links palette

When you view a color stored in the Colors tab or a font set stored in the Font Sets tab, all pages that use this color or font set appear to its left leading into it. However, unlike pages, graphics, or other media, no Point and Shoot button exists to change the color or font set, as shown in Figure 25-24.

As stated earlier in this chapter, the In & Out Links palette can also tip you off to incomplete links. As you view a page, any links you've begun but have not specified a destination for, appear as a link but with the question mark document icon and the words (Empty Reference!). If you recall where this link is to lead, you can drag the Point and Shoot button to the missing file and complete the link. Otherwise, open the page, click the Show Link Errors (green bug) button to reveal the incomplete link, and then repair it from either the Inspector or the In & Out Links palette.

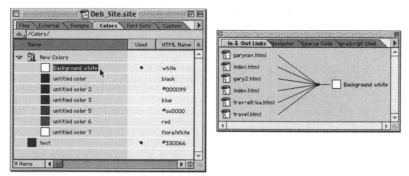

Figure 25-24: The In & Out Links palette reports use of colors (or font sets) but doesn't accommodate altering the color (or font set).

It's interesting to look at your files in the In & Out Links Inspector. Sometimes the feedback can be priceless. For example, say the Shockwave file in Figure 25-25 was provided by a Flash artist. By clicking the .swf file in the Files tab of the Site Window and viewing the file's links in the In & Out Links palette, you can see that some of the files this document has links to are not yet stored within the Site Window. Thanks to the In & Out Links palette, you know to request the missing files or to check your disks or hard disk for the missing files. After you locate the missing files, when you drag them into the Files tab of the Site Window the question mark disappears and an icon representing the file replaces it. Alternately, the designer can create the file and link, and then you can provide the page to which the link is designed to lead. The same is true for PDFs; you can inspect a PDF's embedded links and even change a link's destination.

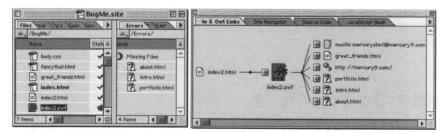

Figure 25-25: Selecting index2.swf reveals that three linked files are missing.

Changing the look of the In & Out Links palette

To change the look of the In & Out Links palette, click the arrow in the upper-right corner of the palette and select Palette Options. Select or deselect the features you want to best fit your needs. The options, shown in Figure 25-26, are discussed here.

In the In & Out Links palette, all items that link to, or are used by, a page always appear as icons representing their file types. However, a thumbnail represents the file of focus. The "Icon instead of thumbnail" option enables you to choose whether the document being inspected appears as a file type icon or a thumbnail.

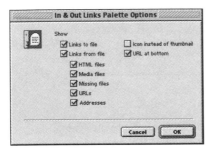

Figure 25-26: The In & Out Links Palette Options enable you to choose what you see in the palette.

You can turn any link type off in case it helps provide a clearer picture of what's on your page or in your site. For example, if you only want to see all URLs listed on your site you can turn everything off but the URL that links from the file. Likewise, you can view only e-mail addresses, only the HTML pages, or, only the media used. You can even see just missing files.

Finally, at the bottom left of the Link Inspector, the URL of the inspected item is reported by default. (If you're working on your hard drive, it's actually the current path to the file that is being reported.) You can turn it off by unchecking URL at bottom.

Printing an In & Out Links map

As you view the links in and out of any file in your site, you can print the view. To do so, click the arrow in the upper-right corner of the In & Out Links palette and select Print.

Cleaning Up Your Site

When your site is complete, you may wish to clean it up — that is, to remove all the extra files you've accumulated. (See, it's all right to put every possible graphic into your Site Window because you can remove all unused files before you save the site for posterity.) The truth is, those files can remain in the Site Window forever without ever being uploaded to the Web server, but in case you want to remove them, you can use the site Clean Up command. This command enables you to remove files, external links, colors, and font sets that are not used.

Note   Cleaning up your site also allows you to resolve orphan and missing files. Because of this ability, some people prefer to do a clean up even before their sites are complete. Although I've placed it here at the end of the process, you can use this feature to clear up your file situation any time while you're working in GoLive.

Setting Clean Up Site Preferences

The Clean Up Site Preferences are actually a list of the actual site clean-up actions. The options explained here show what Clean Up can do for you.

You can customize the Clean Up Site window for either the site you're working on or for all sites. You may want to set a generic preference you are comfortable with, and then tell GoLive to show you the various options each time you use the command so you can set the actions specifically for that cleaning event.

Site-specific preferences are stored within the Site Window and are passed along when you pass the GoLive site files to others. To customize the Clean Up Site window for the active (open) site, select Site ⇨ Settings or click the Site Settings button on the toolbar. Select Clean Up Site from the left menu and check the Site Specific Settings option at the top of the section. (The options are grayed out until you check this box.) The dialog box for these preferences looks just like the one shown in Figure 25-27, but when setting preferences for a specific site, the name of the site appears within the settings window's name. (These Preferences are the same as those shown here, except for the Site Specific Settings option at the top.)

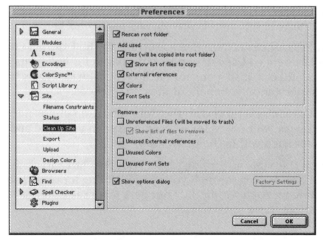

Figure 25-27: The Clean Up Site Options enable GoLive to collect files you've used that aren't yet in your Site Window and to remove those that you haven't used.

Application-wide preferences are attached to your GoLive Preferences file, rather than to the Site Window. The preferences you set for the program apply to all sites you create in GoLive, unless you apply other site-specific preferences to a site. To customize all GoLive sites, select Edit ➪ Preferences, expand the Site in the left menu pane, and click Clean Up Site, as shown in Figure 25-27.

Note   Regardless of the options you choose in either case, by selecting Show Options Dialog you have another opportunity to choose each option each time you clean up a site.

Rescan root folder

Rescan root folder tells GoLive to look at the files that are actually stored within your site folders on your disk and list them within the Site Window. (See "Rescanning Your Site and Updating Links" for a full understanding of this function.)

Add used

Add used tells GoLive to go to the pages in your site and collect the specifically designated items into the Site Window. This features includes the following preferences:

✦ **Add Used Files** tells GoLive to search your hard drive (and any other mounted disks) to locate and copy any orphaned or missing files it finds. This is important, as files that are not within your Files tab cannot be uploaded to the Web server and results in errors on your pages when people visit your site. This is, perhaps, the most important clean-up command. *Show list of files to copy* tells GoLive to show you which files it wants to copy. This command gives you the chance to see what files you've left out of your site, and provides you the opportunity to opt out of copying any particular file.

✦ **Add Used External References** is the same as turning to the External tab and choosing Site ➪ Get Referenced Used. It combs your pages for links outside of your site and creates URL or e-mail icons for each within the Externals tab. (See Chapter 11 to understand the benefit of these references.)

✦ **Add Used Colors** is the same as turning to the Colors tab and choosing Site ➪ Get Colors Used. It checks your pages for all colors used in your site and creates color swatches for each within the Colors tab.

✦ **Add Used Font Sets** is the same as turning to the Font Sets tab and choosing Site ➪ Get Font Sets Used. It goes through your pages noting font sets used and creates a set listing for each within the Font Sets tab. (See Chapter 8 to understand the benefit of these references.)

Remove

Remove, the next group of options, is for removing unused items. It's the add options in reverse. Remove tells GoLive to go through the pages in your site, note all files, external references, colors, or font sets used and keep them, deleting those that are in your Site Window but not used. Some people like these features because it keeps the Site Window efficient and makes it easier to locate what is needed.

(While Rescan and Add Used can be accomplished by other means, removal can only be accomplished using Clean Up Site.

Note I recommend always having "Show list of files to remove" buttons selected. This gives you one last chance to see the files or references about to be deleted because you cannot undo the deletion.

Show Options dialog box

The Show Options dialog box tells GoLive to show an options dialog window each time you choose the Clean Up Site command. With this selected, each time you choose Clean Up Site, the Clean Up options are once again presented to you for selection so you can select/deselect options for the clean-up you are currently doing. The resulting Clean Up Site Options dialog window offers exactly the same options and even looks almost identical.

I strongly recommend you keep this option selected. It not only provides you with the option to perform the various clean-up tasks, but also reminds you of what happens during the clean-up. It's not fun to accidentally remove URLs, e-mail addresses, colors, or font sets that you've worked hard to collect or set up. (It's not fun to delete files either, but they can be restored from the Site Trash or even your computer's trash—if you catch them in time, that is.)

Using Clean Up Site

To clean up your site, follow these steps:

1. Choose Site ⇨ Clean Up Site. Alternately, you can call up the contextual menu from either the Files tab or Extras tab and choose Clean Up Site.

Note You have another alternative to using the Clean Up Site command. You can switch to the Externals, Colors, or Font Sets tab of your Site Window, call up the contextual menu, and choose the Get or Remove command that appears with respect to that tab. That way you accomplish just what you need, without the hassle of selecting or deselecting other clean-up options. Consider these actions mini cleanups.

Remove? Not Me

I prefer not to use the remove options. Instead, I use my Site Window as a collecting point for all items that I hope to add to my sites. Having files in the Files tab does not cause them to be uploaded to the Web server. (The server is a place I *don't* want cluttered.) Having markers for External addresses, colors, or font sets does not take up any hard disk space or make a site file size larger. But having those markers in the Site Window does make it easier to use them later. The key to keeping these items in the Site Window is to label everything clearly and to organizing well.

2. Unless you've disabled the Show Options Dialog option, the Clean Up Site Options dialog window appears. Use this window to determine exactly what clean-up to perform. Click OK when you're done.

3. If you've opted to add used files, the Clear Site dialog box shown in Figure 25-28 appears, asking for permission to add orphan files to your Site Window. (If you don't have orphans, this step is skipped.) You can uncheck the Update checkmark to skip copying a file into your Site Window — although that is likely to be counterproductive. Click OK to let GoLive copy the used files into your site.

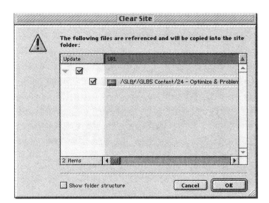

Figure 25-28: The Clear Site dialog box asks permission to add your orphan files to your Site Window.

Note Remember that GoLive is making a copy, not moving your original file. The original remains safely where it is.

4. If you've opted to add used files, the Copy Files dialog box asks permission to update the links from the files in your site to the file(s) being copied into your site. Click OK.

Note Because GoLive is making a copy of your originally linked-to file, the link within the linked-from (a.k.a. *referencing*) page must be updated to reflect the address of this new copy.

5. If you've opted to remove unused files, the Clear Site dialog box asks permission to remove all unused files from your Site Window. (If all files are used, this step is skipped.) You can uncheck the checkmark for any file to have that file remain in your Site Window for future use. Depending on your Preference setting for deletion, these files are either moved to the Site Trash within your Extras tab, or to your computer's Trash or Recycle bin. Click OK to have the listed and checked files deleted.

Tip If you use the removal option, I recommend designating removed items to be sent to the Site Trash, so you can get them back if you change your mind. To return a file to your site, simply drag it from the Site Trash folder in the Extras tab back into the Files tab.

If you've checked the option to add or delete external references, colors, or font sets, the respective tabs reflect the additions and deletions. As no physical files are involved, no dialog boxes confirm these actions.

That's it. Your Site Window should now be up to your specifications.

Flatten Script Library

If you've used any GoLive Action(s), a Component, or any of GoLive's Smart Objects from the Objects palette, you've used JavaScript in your site. Any time you use one of these items, GoLive looks at all the prewritten scripts resident in the Modules folder within the GoLive application folder — and it writes all the code for all of those JavaScripts (with all of their potential functionality). While this code enables you to do amazing tasks, not all the code generated to achieve this functionality is needed. All you really need is the code to perform the functions you've programmed your site to do. For the first time, in GoLive 5, you can remove the extra code, reducing the amount of JavaScript code the user downloads. You do this using the Flatten Script Library command in the contextual menu.

The secret to flattening your JavaScript library is to do it after you've completed development, right before you upload your site. This is because any time you work on an Action, Component, or Smart Object, GoLive refers to its Modules folder and writes the scripting for all of the items in that folder back into your external JavaScript document and you just have to flatten the library again.

When your site's development is done — for the time being — and you're ready to upload your site to the Web server, flatten the script library.

To flatten the script library for your site, simply point your mouse anywhere in the Files tab as you Control-click (Mac) or right-click (Windows). Choose Flatten Script Library from the resulting contextual menu. That's it.

Note   Any time you work on the site, flatten the script library again just before you synchronize the files with the server.

Creating Site Reports

GoLive's site reporting feature, new to Version 5, provides excellent feedback about the state of your site. (Although a part of the Find window interface, these reports are a whole 'nother ballgame, so I feel they merit a standalone section of this chapter on optimization.)

Using the Site Report's five subtabs, you can set a number of criteria for your search. After you make your selections and click the Search button, GoLive produces a separate window called a Site Report, which is viewable in the same way as a Site Window.

Note You can select criteria from one or all of the subtabs. When you select more than one set of criteria, GoLive uses "and" logic to look for results. In other words, if you select a search for files greater than 10K in size within the File Info tab, and then choose to seek files that contain external links within the Links tab, the generated site report contains only files that satisfy both the criteria.

Follow these steps to create a site report:

1. Select Site ⇨ Site Report or Edit ⇨ Find, and then click the Site Reports tab. Both selections take you to the same exact window. The Site Report tab has five subtabs. Pop-up menus and checkboxes make choosing within each tab easy.

2. Click a tab you want and choose any of the available selections. Your site report can comprise any combination of options from any tab; you are not limited to one tab at a time. The following are available options:

   • *File Info* enables you to find files by byte size, download time, and modification/creation date. The download time of an HTML file considers all elements that make up the page (images, sounds, and so forth.) when computing download time. In Figure 25-29, a site is being checked for all pages that take more than 30 seconds (user entered) at 33,600 bps (also user selected). If such pages exist, they are listed by name and can be remedied, if desired.

   • *Errors* report four types of common errors. Use it to learn about any pages that have title problems that can cause embarrassment and prevent your site from being found by the public. Choose Missing Attributes to help ensure accessibility and accurate image-rendering. Use the HTML error and warning flags to help your site's usability in various browsers. The error and warning browser sets that appear in the pop-up menus are defined in GoLive's application Preferences (Edit ⇨ Preferences ⇨ Source ⇨ Browser Sets.) You can change these sets in the GoLive Preferences.

   • *Site Objects* identifies where a particular Component or e-mail address is used, as well as lets you know whether you've used any particular font, font set, or color. To enable the report to seek a color, you can drag a color into the color swatch in the Use of color section.

   • *Links* reports pages with external links, pages with links to files with a particular extension (such as .jpg), and pages with links of various protocols.

   • *Misc* provides a report on one of the most important keys to site usability. It enables you to learn which of your pages, if any are a certain number of clicks away from any particular file, such as your home page. You can select the file using either the Point and Shoot or browse feature.

3. Click Search!

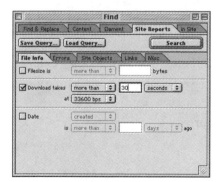

Figure 25-29: Checking a site to learn whether any pages will take more than 30 seconds at 33,6000 bps.

A progress bar appears while your site is scanned. The generated site report then appears in its own window, entitled "YourSiteName:Report Results." The top of the report tells you what you asked for, and how many files matched. Below the tabs is a list of the files found. The report looks very similar to your Site Window, and in fact it is. Selecting the Navigation or Structure tabs shows the same graphical depiction of the site provided by the regular Navigation view. (Design ⇨ Navigation view) You can use the View Controller to further filter your view.

The Structure tab provides a tree view of the file hierarchy of your site in which only files that conform to the query are shown. Also shown are folders containing the conforming files, folders containing those folders, and so on. The root of the tree is the site folder.

Saving and reusing a query

After you select your criteria, you can save it by clicking the Save Query button at the top of the Site Reports tab. Later, you can use the same criteria by clicking the Load Query button. A saved query can be used for any site you create or work on in GoLive. It can even be e-mailed to another GoLive-user. You can create and save a useful query, and then reload it to create a report for each site you create or work on in the future.

To save a query, follow these steps:

1. Click Save Query to open the Save dialog box.
2. Name the query, being sure to keep the .glsq extension in the file name.
3. Choose a folder in which to store the file.

To load and use a query, follow these steps:

1. Click Load Query to bring up the Open dialog box.

2. In the Open dialog box, locate, select, and open your saved query file.

   All query choices saved within that query take effect within the various tabs of the Site Reports dialog box.

3. Click Search to perform the search as normal.

Using document statistics

GoLive can look at your page and tell you the physical size of the page and the images on it, give you a character and word count, and inform you of approximate download times for a given modem speed. This feature gives you a good idea whether you are building a "bandwidth monster" that will take forever to download and completely frustrate your viewers. To use Document Statistics, open the page you want to inspect and select Special ⇨ Document Statistics. The Document Statistics window is shown in Figure 25-30.

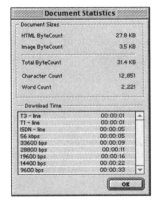

Figure 25-30: The Document Statistics for a page

Stripping Code

Some Web designers do their best to get a page down to as few kilobytes as possible, removing every possible extra character from the page. However, the trade-off is the excellence of GoLive's interface and the benefit is a moment so short your site's visitors will not notice it. If you feel you need to do this, you can export your site. See Chapter 27 to learn about export options.

Checking Browser Compatibility

GoLive's Preview mode gives you an idea of how your page will look in various browsers on Mac and Windows. However, to get the real picture, you may need to go a few steps further.

Test on your own computer

Without actually uploading your site onto a server, you can preview your site in all the browsers you have on your own computer, using GoLive's Show in Browser feature.

Try changing the resolution of your monitor to both bigger and smaller than the resolution with which you used to design. Consider those who run their monitors at a lower resolution to make bigger letters to serve "more mature" eyesight. Remember those who do not even know they can change resolution. Obviously, you can't design for everyone, but you may discover your masterpiece is less than masterful at a different resolution, perhaps requiring more scrolling than you really want.

Test from a server

To test further, you probably need to upload the site onto a server, which is covered in Chapter 27. You may want to upload the site into some sort of test folder, not the root folder of your domain on the server, so the public won't find your test site and see your site before it's ready for prime time. Simply create a folder on the server called *testsite* and upload the site into it. To view the site, the URL you type into your browser would look like `www.yourdomain.com/testsite`. Now you can look at it yourself or have your own group of "beta testers" look at the site.

Once you have the test site loaded, can discover more on your own. For example, if you have a fast connection at your home or office, you may have a rude awakening when viewing the site on a 56K or slower modem, which is still what the majority of the world will use to view your site. Although you're viewing the site on the same platform you built it on, it is still constructive to reconnect that old 56K modem and look at your test site through it. (If you have high speed access, use the back-up dial up access for this. Or get a free Internet account.)

If you use a Mac and have the processor speed, RAM, or disk space to use a Windows emulator (Virtual PC, for example), you can use a browser within the emulated operating system (OS) to view the site as "the other side" sees it.

Take every opportunity to view your site on as many browsers and platforms as possible. Does the person next door use another OS? What a great opportunity to meet your neighbors, make new friends, *and* view your site in another light. If your public library has Internet access, go there and look at your site (and tell them to get this book for their computer reference section).

Beta testing

Finally, you can always assemble your own crack team of beta testers, preferably people who have some experience with Web sites and browsers, which will help in the quality of the feedback you receive. One tester is probably not enough—five is a decent number to ask. Send them an e-mail asking them to test your site and include the URL. If you're part of any e-mail list, (especially a Web-related list) post the test request to the list.

Perhaps include a checklist of what to look out for: Link accuracy, plug-in performance (Flash, RealPlayer, QuickTime, for example), colors, text size, download times, and so on. You can also ask them to send you screen shots, especially of problem areas. Despite your best efforts, a misspelled word or some grievous grammatical error that you overlooked in your designing zeal may exist, and feedback from beta testers helps you improve your site.

✦　　✦　　✦

Polishing Your Web Pages

✦   ✦   ✦   ✦

In This Chapter

Helping visitors find
your Web site

Helping visitors find
what they need once
at your site

Ensuring that visitors
see your freshest data

✦   ✦   ✦   ✦

You're almost ready to go live with your site — to
upload or publish it for the world to see. However,
you need to consider just a few more matters so your site
has maximum efficiency and exposure. Call it your final site
tweaking. This chapter has two main goals. The first is helping visitors find your site. The second is helping visitors
find their way within your site.

Helping Visitors Find Your Site

You can do many things once your site goes public to let the
world know it's there. In fact, you can spend as much time
advertising your site as you do building it. But even before
you go live, you can set up your site to maximize your exposure potential by carefully considering the page title and
description the public sees, and the descriptive keywords
that only browsers and search engines see.

Finesse page titles

Although you have one Web site to be found, when it comes to
people finding you via search engines, you have not one site
to be found but many pages. Each page, providing different
content on your topic, provides another opportunity to tell
the world you have that content. Take advantage of this fact
by providing descriptive and accurate titles for your pages.
Not only will a well-thought-out title help visitors find your
pages, but once they do, a well-executed page title helps them
find the way back to your site. (Your pages don't *still* say
"Welcome to Adobe GoLive 5," do they?)

Presumably you named your page when you started it and presumably, if you're reading this chapter, you have the content of your page set. Now that you've lived with the page and title for a while, preview the page in a few browsers and see how the title appears in the browser window and how it bookmarks.

The title of each page plays a significant role in helping search engines find your page. Is it descriptive of the page? Does it contain the same words in your keywords so search engines see a match? Does it really help people know what they'll find if they take the time to click that link within the search engine?

The title is also the name used when the page is bookmarked or set as a favorite. Does it say the right thing to help visitors come back to it when they see it as a bookmark (or in the Internet Explorer history)? If it is clipped and appears as a mystical message, rethink it—again.

Adjust the title until it *really* works for you, like the one shown in Figure 26-1 works for Magic Bob. You can change it by selecting it at the top-left corner of your page.

Cross-Reference See Chapter 6 to learn about naming your pages.

Figure 26-1: A good page title appears in full, bookmarks in full, and tells readers what they need to know.

Adding keywords to your pages

Keywords provide information to search engines about the material on your site. A Keyword tag is actually a metatag, with the attribute, Keyword. If you check the HTML source code, you'll see that the Keywords icon simply puts a line something like the following into the code:

```
<meta name="keywords" content="professional magician, magic,
Magic Bob Weiss, LA magician for hire, Los Angeles magician for
hire">
```

What Words Should You Use?

The words on your page title should all appear as keywords too. Technically, it's the other way around, but I want you to really think out your page title. Search engines give your keywords more credibility when they appear in the title because the title is out there for everyone to see, unlike hidden keywords. This way, the engine developers figure you're not using the words to cheat and lure unsuspecting people to your site.

The words in your page *description* should be listed as keywords too. Again, the public may see your description, so if you're willing to put it out there for public inspection, the words are more likely to be accurate reflections of what viewers will really find at your site.

Common misspellings of your keywords, name, subject, and content should also be listed as keywords. The fact is, people misspell and even great spellers mistype. Or a person may be looking for you or someone listed on your site by name, but not know how to spell the name. You don't want to lose the chance to be found just because someone's brain or fingers are tired when they look for you, or because they don't know how to pronounce or spell your name.

Consider accommodating people whose first language is not the language of your site. If your site is in English, visitors from non-English-speaking countries may still be able to get a lot out of your site, or be willing to try. But they may not know the English spelling of the very topic of your site. By adding alternate language listings of the topic, you can help. While you can't list every possible language, or even every keyword in two languages, you can add good keywords for a few commonly spoken languages, so add the ones that most help your target audience.

Words within phrases count individually too, so don't repeat them. For example, if you enter "Corinne Fischer" as your keyword, it covers searches for Corinne or Fischer. However, to accommodate people seeking Cori Fischer, you need another Keyword entry: "Cori Fischer." A user search for Fischer, by the way, will also find other Fischers, but not if the person searching enters a phrase such as "Alex Fischer."

Note   Keywords that contain accent marks, umlauts, and other special characters are not a problem for GoLive. If your page contains such characters and you use the Add to Keywords feature, your keywords are added with the same marks. These entities are handled well by GoLive and are a part of the W3C specification. However, some search engine robots may not handle them well.

You have several ways to add keywords to your page. The fastest way to get started is to take a keyword from the text of your page. You can also add keywords that do not appear on your page. This way, you can add the common misspellings and other alternatives.

Adding keywords via the content of your page

It's easy to add keywords to your page after you use the words on your page. Using any of three GoLive commands (shown in the following procedure) automatically places the Keyword icon in the head section of your page for you.

To add a keyword or keywords (phrase) via your page's content, follow these steps:

1. Select the text that you would like to have act as your keyword. You are not limited to single words. You can select any consecutive words that create a phrase you'd like people to be able to search on.

2. Choose from one of the following commands to add your selected words to your keywords:

   • Special ➪ Add to Keywords

   • Press ⌘-K (Mac) or Ctrl+K (Windows)

   • Point to the selected text as you Control-click (Mac) or right-click (Windows) and choose Add to Keywords from the contextual menu

That's it. The first time you do this, GoLive automatically places the Keyword tag in the head section of your page, as you can see in Figure 26-2. After the first time, it simply adds more words to the tag. You can continue to add words that appear on your page this way, or you can enter more words directly within the Inspector or in the Source Code window (choose Window ➪ Source Code).

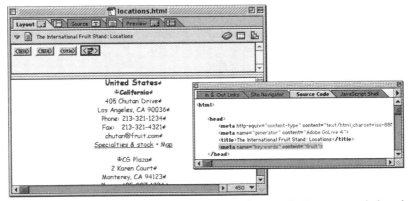

Figure 26-2: A word on a page, added as a keyword. The Keywords head item is created within the head section of the page and the metatag is written into the source code.

Tip

After you get your keywords listed, you can use the Inspector to move them up and down. The words listed first may be counted most heavily by a search engine. But trying to add them to your page in order of importance is difficult.

Adding the Keyword tag manually

If, for some reason, you want to take the extra steps of manually adding the Keyword tag to the head section of your page instead of starting by selecting a word from your page, you certainly can.

To manually place a keywords tag on your page, follow these steps:

1. Drag the Keywords icon from the Head tab of the Objects palette into the head section of your page. If the head section isn't open as you begin to drag, rest over the toggle (the arrow to the left of the Page icon) until it opens, and then continue to drag the icon into place.

2. Click in the field at the bottom of the Keywords Inspector, and then enter the desired keyword into it (as shown in Figure 26-3).

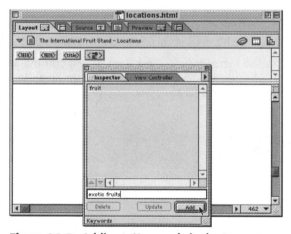

Figure 26-3: Adding a Keyword via the Inspector

3. Press Enter/Return or click the Add button. The keyword appears on its own line in the main text area.

Adding keywords not present on your page

There are bound to be words that are not on your page, or not on that particular page, that you still want to be referenced on the page because they relate to the site, or because they're the misspellings.

Follow these steps to add keywords that are not on your page via the Inspector:

1. Open the head section of your page and click the Keyword metatag once to select it. Doing so turns the Inspector into the Keywords Inspector.

2. Click in the field at the bottom of the Keywords Inspector, and then enter the desired keyword into it (as already shown in Figure 26-3).

3. Press Enter/Return or click the Add button. The keyword appears on its own line in the main text area.

Adding keywords into HTML directly

After you select and add the first couple of keywords, it's actually faster to add many of your keywords directly into HTML. The reason for adding two or three via the Layout mode interface first is to see the pattern needed to add words. In this case, each group is separated by a comma, followed by a space.

Here are the steps to add keywords directly into HTML:

1. Choose Window ⇨ Source Code to open the Source Code window. Position the window comfortably.

2. Locate the Keywords tag within the HTML code. The easiest way to do this is to click the Keyword icon in the head of your page because this selects the code.

3. Place your cursor after the last keyword, and then type a comma and a space and your next word or phrase, as has been done in Figure 26-4. Repeat this step for each additional word or phrase.

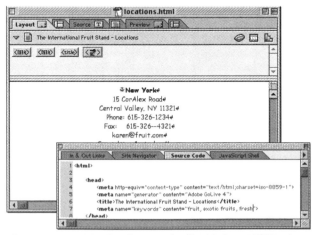

Figure 26-4: Entering keywords directly into HTML via the Source Code window

When you've added all the desired words (for the time being, until you think of more), click back on the page to continue working, or close the Source Code window.

Note You can also add keywords to source code using the Source tag. Just look for the Keyword tag at the top of the page within the `<head>` ... `</head>` tags.

Editing and deleting keywords

You can edit your keywords within the Inspector or directly in HTML. Within the Inspector, you edit a keyword by selecting it, make the changes in the text field at the bottom, and then click Update. To delete a keyword, select it in the list at the top, and then click Delete. To change the order of keywords in the list, click the keyword you want to move and use the arrows below the keyword list to move the selected keyword up or down, as shown in Figure 26-5.

Figure 26-5: Changing the order of a keyword within the Inspector. With the word "fresh" selected, the up arrow moves the word up one with each click.

Within the Source Code window, click the Keyword icon in the page's head again to select the code if you can't find it on your own. Then edit the words as within a word processor. (Changing the order can be much easier in the Inspector.) Again, you can also do this in the Source tab of the page window.

Adding a description

By providing a description for each of your pages, you give search engines something to consider as they rank your site, and also provide a good, solid blurb for the search engines to display when your site is listed.

GoLive doesn't come with a prewritten Description metatag so you get to try your hand at setting up your own to add your description. You may only get to do it once, however, because after that you can make it reusable.

Check Your Spelling — Again

If you've been progressing through this book to learn GoLive and build your site, you've known about the spell-checker ever since you've known how to put text on your page. Consequently, I hope your pages are displays of perfectly spelled words. But I want to do more than just remind you to perform that spell-check if you haven't done so yet. Now that you've added the description, I have an excuse to push you. After all, spelling errors *do* undermine your credibility.

By checking your spelling after everything else is present on your site, you ensure that even things such as the page description are correctly spelled. GoLive has powerful tools to correct spelling errors. You can check spelling on a single page, or check the spelling of every page in your site. Before your site goes live, run it through that spell-checker one more time. (To learn more about checking your spelling in GoLive, take a look at Chapter 8.) Just pay attention to the intentionally misspelled keywords so you don't correct them by mistake.

To add a description into your page's code, follow these steps:

1. Drag the Meta icon from the Head tab of the Objects palette into the head section of your page, as shown in Figure 26-6. If the head section isn't open as you begin to drag, rest over the toggle (the arrow to the left of the Page icon) until it opens, and then continue to drag the icon into place.

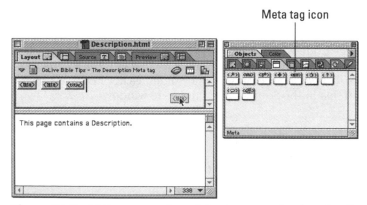

Figure 26-6: Adding a generic metatag to a page by dragging the object to the page's head

If you let go of the icon within the body part of the page, the code for the metatag appears on your page as text. Delete the text and try again.

2. With the Metatag icon selected in the head, choose HTTP-Equivalent from the pop-up menu in the metatag's Inspector, as shown in Figure 26-7.

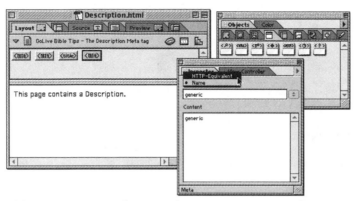

Figure 26-7: Setting the type of metatag to accommodate a description

3. The new tag is generic by default. Define it as a description tag by entering **description** in the small text field at the top of the Inspector.

4. Enter you page's description in the large Content field in the Meta Inspector.

The Inspector window is resizable so you can enlarge it to more easily read your description, if you'd like. It also scrolls as needed.

Tip

Instead of trying to compose your description in this small box, you can compose it elsewhere, and then paste it here.

You can also add a description directly into HTML, after getting a head start by dragging the Meta icon into the head of the page first. When the Tag icon is selected, so is the code in the Source Code window. Double-click the first occurrence of the word "generic," and then type **description**. Double-click the second occurrence of the word "generic" and type or paste your description. You'll also need to add the metatag type, which is a selectable item in the Inspector. You can either choose it in the Inspector (where your description appears if you click the page to set your code) or you can place your cursor after the word "meta," and then type **HTTP-Equivalent**. Figure 26-8 shows you what a description tag looks like in HTML as well as in the Inspector and in Layout.

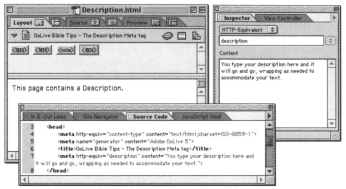

Figure 26-8: A completed Description tag's code, along with its appearance in the Inspector and the Meta icon within Layout mode

What's in a Name? It Can Break a Tie

By Mario and Sheri Salinas, Amazon-Networks

Most people have no idea of the good, or damage, they can do to their Internet efforts just by choosing the right, or wrong, domain name. The trick to thriving, in many ways, depends on choosing that good, pesky name.

Consider the criteria a search engine uses to measure how high up on its results list to place your site:

1. Whether or not the phrase being searched for appears in your domain name.

2. Whether or not the phrase being searched for appears in your page title.

3. The number of times the phrase being sought (in a search engine) shows up in the body of your page.

Now that you know that . . . you can understand the following: When all other things are equal, if two pages are weighted exactly the same for a search phrase, such as "Caribbean vacation," for example, and these two pages would normally turn up in the same place in a search results list, a search engine will usually give preference to the page that contains the search phrase in the domain name. Therefore, a page that contains "Caribbean vacation" 15 times in the body and title of the page and is housed at a domain name called www.caribbean-vacations.com will turn up much higher than an identical page housed at a domain called www.mels-exotic-travel.com. (Bear in mind, though, that these rules change constantly.)

This sidebar is excerpted from a fuller paper available at www.golivebible.com.

Redirecting your visitors to your new URL

If you've had a site up for a while, and now have your own domain name and want to start using it, will your previous visitors and all those people with your old business cards and brochures still come to the old site? This isn't much different from changing phone numbers. When people reach the old phone number, you arrange for a message at the old number that tells your callers the new one. As with a phone, you can put up a single page at the old site and use it to tell visitors about your new address. But on the Web you can even automatically transport visitors to the new address.

You don't actually have to tell visitors they're being taken to a new URL, but if you don't they won't know to bookmark, note, and give out your new address. It's better to let them know what's happening and why.

Choosing a Domain Name

By Mario and Sheri Salinas, Amazon-Networks

The most important reason search engine queries are so important is that a search engine delivers targeted results to prequalified interested parties. This is probably the most important value to being found in a search engine's results list. If someone finds your site in a search engine's results list, it's because they were actually looking for you. To be most precise, they were looking for your goods or services. There, that was it . . . your BIG CLUE. They were looking for your *goods* or *services*, not your company. (They don't even *know* your company yet.)

You can register your company's name as a domain (such as `www.allentowntravel.com`) for those customers that already know you exist, but for the rest, you need something that helps Web surfers find your site as easily as possible.

When you register a domain name, you need to register a two- to three-word combination of words that best describes what it is you sell. For example, if your company specializes in selling Caribbean vacations, your best domain names would be something like the following:

- ✦ `www.caribbeanvacations.com`
- ✦ `www.exoticvacations.com`
- ✦ `www.caribbeanhideaways.com`
- ✦ `www.exoticdestinations.com`
- ✦ `www.romanticvacations.com`
- ✦ `www.sexyvacations.com`
- ✦ `www.vacationhideaways.com`

This sidebar is excerpted from a fuller discussion available at `www.golivebible.com`.

Refreshing your page

The Refresh tag has two purposes. One is to redirect a browser from the page it's on to another page. This is commonly used when you move your site from one URL to another and you want your visitors to find your new location. You've probably seen pages that say "We've moved! Your browser will take you to the new site in five seconds, or click here to go to the new location." That's the Refresh tag in action.

The other purpose is to reload the current page. Although this may seem a superfluous thing to do, it can actually be very useful in one case. If you have time-sensitive data on your page, such as daily or even hourly stock price updates, then you need to make sure that your users can actually get to the current data. Because Web browsers cache pages and may use the cached version, not always checking for the latest version from your site instead, you can use the Refresh tag to force the browser to load from your site.

Follow these steps to use a Refresh tag:

1. Drag the Refresh icon from the Head tab of the Objects palette into the head section of the page. If the head is not open when you begin to drag the icon, pause over the toggle arrow to the left of the Page icon until the section opens, and then continue dragging the icon into place.

2. In the Inspector, enter the delay in seconds, as shown in Figure 26-9.

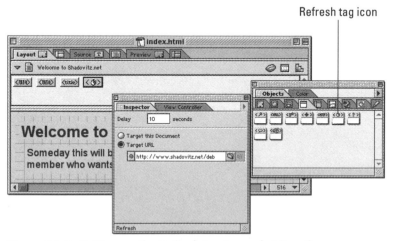

Figure 26-9: Setting up the Refresh tag to send visitors from one location to another after giving them time to read the page

Note Set the delay to at least a few seconds. Without a delay this feature interferes with the use of the Back button in a visitor's browser, because he or she will have difficulty backing up over the redirection page.

3. Set the target page:

- To refresh (reload) the current page, choose Target this Document.

- To have the browser redirect to another page, choose Target URL, and then select the target page as you would choose any destination (Point and Shoot, browse, or type/paste the URL).

Older browsers don't support browser redirection so, to cover all the bases, it's a common courtesy to provide a textual explanation of what is going on along with a regular link that leads to the new site. This also tells impatient people that they can click the link instead of waiting.

Note The Browser Switch Action is another mechanism for enabling the browser to perform a page change. Because it is an Action and it's most useful to detect browser versions and lead users of older browsers to a more usable alternative page, it is covered in Chapter 18, which covers Actions.

Helping Visitors Find Their Way Within Your Site

In this section I discuss ways to help viewers make maximum use of your site and how to facilitate maximum traffic on your site.

Adding a Table of Contents

If you've given a lot of thought to the design of your site, you will have a nicely laid-out site where people can find anything there with a few logical clicks. Now that your site is all set, you can add one last detail to help users find what they seek there. You can give your visitors a Table of Contents.

The Table of Contents is generated from within the Design module of GoLive. It's only available when the Navigation view (Design ⇨ Navigation View) is open on your screen. The site hierarchy you see within the main pane of your Navigation view is exactly what the Table of Contents will look like — except in list form. Your home page is always at the top. Below that, the first-level pages are listed, with the first page on the left as the first page listed in the Table of Contents. Beneath each of those second-level pages are any pages beneath each of those pages, also listed with left to right being top to bottom. In Figure 26-10, you can see a Table of Contents with three levels. You can simplify your Table of Contents by moving pages from the main pane of the Navigation view to the Scratch pane or by collapsing branches of the view, as shown in Figure 26-11.

Using Counters

It's nice to know something about the people who visit your site. Sometimes the information can help you provide better services, add new information, or redesign your pages to better serve your users. This kind of information is easy to obtain, doesn't breach your visitor's privacy, and can even be had for free.

TheCounter.com offers a free counter that provides statistics for your site. Register at www.thecounter.com, and then return there to view the statistics. When you register, you choose how the counter will look. It can be invisible, or display their logo either with or without the counter showing (low-traffic or new sites may not want visitors to see low numbers). Each week the company e-mails you a report telling you the number of visitors per day so you don't even have to hit your browser to get the basics. I'm sure other similar services exist, but this is one I can personally recommend. They don't know me. They just do a good job.

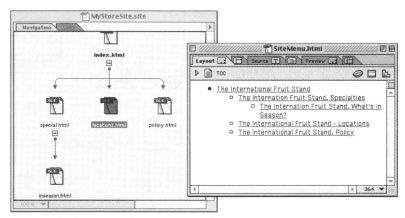

Figure 26-10: The Table of Contents is a reflection of your site's Navigation view. This Table of Contents was generated with all pages exposed.

Note   Up until now, the order of the pages within your site has not mattered because that order has no effect on the user's experience; it's how you present your site's organization that counts — and how you link your pages. But, when it comes to generating a Table of Contents, the presentation in the Navigation window does count.

The SiteMenu file automatically links to each page in your Site Window, but it doesn't have a link from any of your pages until you link it up. You can add it into your navigation bar or link it to any specific pages by using the usual linking methods.

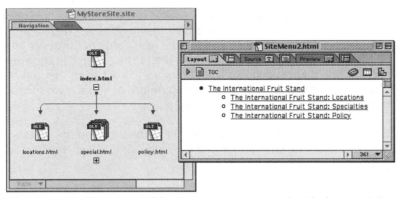

Figure 26-11: The same Table of Contents generated with the Specialties subpages hidden

Follow these steps to have GoLive generate a Table of Contents:

1. Choose Design ➪ Navigation View to open the Navigation view of your site.

2. *(Optional)* Arrange the icons in the Navigation view to reflect the organization you want in the Table of Contents. Remember the following points:

   • Only the pages visible in the Navigation view appear in the Table of Contents. Click the minus sign under any page to collapse the pages beneath it and exclude them.

   • Pages appear from top to bottom in the order they appear in the Navigation view from left to right. Drag any page to the left or right of another page on its same level to change the listing order.

Cross-Reference The Navigation view is covered in full in Chapter 29.

3. With the Navigation view as the active window, choose Design ➪ Create Table of Contents. (If this view is not active, the menu option is not available.) GoLive compiles the Table of Contents on a new page, named SiteMenu.html with a page title, and presents it to you.

4. Close the new page. It is saved automatically; you don't have to save.

5. Link your Table of Contents page into your site. It's a regular page so you can place it anywhere you place a page. You'll find it in a folder called NewFiles, which was automatically generated along with the Table of Contents.

6. *(Optional)* Edit the text as desired. The full page title is used to create the link that takes visitors to your page. Unfortunately, the same thing that makes a great page title also makes a tedious link and a redundant Table of Contents.

The Table of Contents is handy and it's easy to create, but unfortunately it's not dynamic. As you add to your site, or remove pages, you'll need to create a new one. The next one is entitled SiteMenu.html1. Linking the new Table of Contents into place in lieu of the old one is easy, of course. Just select the original in the Files tab and view it in the In & Out Links palette. Then Point and Shoot from that old one to the new one. Once the old one is unlinked, you can delete it. You'll have to edit the links on the new Table of Contents to shorten them.

Use an external style sheet to affect the look of your Table of Contents. This way you can link replacement Table of Contents to the same style sheet, easily maintaining the look you prefer.

Cross-
Reference   Chapter 17 discusses style sheets.

Consider an In-site Search Engine

If your site is large and information-packed, adding search capability to your site can be a great help to your visitors. A search engine enables people to find occurrences of a specific word rather than having to guess by document title, or section or link title. A search engine isn't a substitute for good navigation, but it takes the job of listing all of your content off your shoulders.

Programming a search engine is a major job and can be a major expense. Fortunately, you don't have to program one. When this topic comes up on the various e-mail lists, a few such search engines are recommended time and time again. As each one is bound to change the services it offers to meet customer demand (at Internet speed), I won't try to list their services. Instead, I encourage you to check each of them out and ask around.

One search engine stands out among the rest, due to its amazing integration with GoLive. As soon as the GoLive 5 SDK (see Appendix E) hit the streets, the folks at Atomz.com had a custom-made tool for adding its free search tool to your site — and all it takes on your part is choosing Special ➪ Insert Atomz.com Search. (You can drag the search form from the Atomz.com tab of the Objects palette if you prefer instead; it's just as easy and provides the same choice of basic or advanced search.) To learn about, sign up for, and download the custom GoLive Atomz.com site search tool, visit http://atomz.com/golive.

Although not integrated with GoLive, two other free search engines are Whatuseek (http://intra.whatuseek.com) and Free Find (www.freefind.com). Google (www.google.com) is also recommended by some.

Simplifying URLs within your site

The way folders appear in the Site Window is their path on your page. If a page called mykids.html is in a folder called Family, which is in a folder called Pages, the URL to that page becomes `www.mydomain.com/Pages/Family/mykids.html`. If you don't expect anyone to bookmark this mouthful, you may be fine. But if you do want people to recall the URL, consider making the path simpler. Perhaps you don't need to have a folder called Family, or maybe you don't need a folder called Pages. It's okay to move pages out of folders and up to the main level (or root directory) of your site.

To move a page out of a folder into the main level, follow these steps:

1. Click within the Files tab of the Site Window, and then return to the main folder, if you're not there already. To do so, click the blue arrow (Mac) or folder icon (Windows) at the top-left corner of the window, directly below the Files tab icon.

2. Expand the folder that contains the page to be moved, and drag that page up to the Name header. (This also works to move a file that is within a folder that's within another folder.) GoLive notices the page movement and requests permission to update all pages affected by the move.

3. Click OK to complete the update. Your new path to that page no longer includes the folder name.

Another reason to simplify the URLs on your site is that it speeds up the browser's page-building process. For one, long names such as `thefirstpageinthesitethat-peoplesee.html` rather than `index.html` contribute to file's (and site's) physical size every time that page is linked to. In addition, any time the user's browser or the Web server has to call upon a page or file, it has to match the request for the file to the actual file. The longer the name, the longer it takes to complete the match.

The names of the folders you use to organize your files also become part of the path to the file, so again, shorter is faster and code-efficient. The most important consideration in keeping name size small is your ability to keep track of your site. Theoretically, the smallest file size would come from naming your pages, folders, and images something like 1.html, 2.jpg, and so on, but you might have trouble keeping track of what's on your site.

The answer? Use the middle ground — abbreviate your file and folder names just enough so you can easily know what's in them. Take a look at your page names and change any that you can shorten. To change a page's name, close the page, and then select the name within the Files tab. This selects the actual name part of the file's name. Type your new and improved name. Press Enter/Return or click anywhere outside of the name's area to confirm the name change. GoLive tracks each page and file that refers to each page so it then asks you for permission to update all references to this page. Click OK. The new name is now fully functional.

To change a folder's name do the same, except when you select the folder's name the entire folder name becomes selected and can be edited. (There's no file name extension for GoLive to protect or for you to worry about.)

Dating your information

It's a good idea to let your visitors know how recent or up-to-date the information is on your site. GoLive's Modified Date Smart Object makes that easy to do. All you do is type a bit of intro text, and then drag the Modified Date Smart Object onto the page and choose from the Inspector how the time or date should appear. Once you put the Smart Object into place, GoLive adds the current date or time information to the page every time you save your page. If you'd like to have both date and time, you just add two Smart Objects. You can, of course, place this anyplace on your page, but commonly, it's placed at the bottom.

You might want to place date/time information on all of your pages, or on many of them. To speed up the placement of this information on the many pages within your site and other sites, set it up once, and then create a reusable object. To use the same exact introductory wording and look of the date and/or time within your current site, select it all and drag it to the Custom tab of the Site Window. To have that same introductory wording and look available to all sites you create in GoLive on your computer, drag it to the Custom tab of the Objects palette. In either case, all you have to do is drag the date-modified statement from the Custom tab in which you stored it into place on the page.

See Chapter 13 to learn about the Custom tab and other options for reusing items.

Putting this Smart Object in a component causes GoLive to track and record the date and time when the component was changed, not the specific page it is in. Therefore, the Smart Object does not actually state when the page was changed.

To put a date or time stamp on your page, follow these steps:

1. *(Optional)* If you'd like to have any text introducing the date and time, enter it and add a space. Leave the cursor flashing at the end of the text. For example, you can say: **This page was last modified on** . You can always add introductory or explanatory text later, instead, if desired.

2. Locate the Modified Date icon in the Smart tab of the Objects palette and do one of the following:

   • Double-click the Modified Date icon in the Smart tab of the Objects palette to have it land where your cursor is.

- Drag the Modified Date icon from the Smart tab of the Objects palette into place at the end of your intro text, or where you want the date or time information to appear.

3. In the Inspector, use the Format menu to select the language in which you wish to display the date or time. The language you choose changes the date and time formats to display in the selected language with the appropriate formatting options for that language. You can see this in Figure 26-12, where an English Modified Date is on the page and a French one is being set up.

Modified date icon

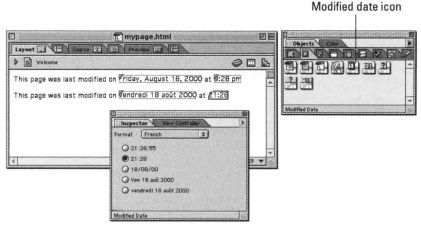

Figure 26-12: Setting a Modified Date Smart Object. You can choose from a variety of languages.

4. Click one of the radio buttons to determine whether your Modified Date object will show the date or the time, and in which format. Various options exist for each radio button. The effect is immediately visible on the page.

You can only select either a date format or a time format with one stamp icon. You cannot select both.

5. *(Optional)* Repeat the preceding steps to add another date or time Smart Object if you want both date and time on your page.

GoLive uses your own computer's system date and time to stamp pages so make sure your computer's date and/or time settings are correct.

The result of placing the Modified Date object is text on your page. This text takes on whatever formatting is set up within your page. If you use a style sheet that defines the overall look of your page's text (by using the Body tag as a style element), the date/time statement appears in that same text style. This holds true even if you create a reusable item that includes introductory text.

See Chapter 16 to learn about style sheets.

If you have not used a style sheet, but used the toolbar to apply font styling (adding the Font tag to your page), dragging the Smart Object within styled text causes the date/time to take on the same styling. But if you drag the Smart Object after styled text, it does not take on the styling. If you create a custom phrase, the phrase does not take on the styling in either case, as it contains its own paragraph tag.

See Chapter 7 for more about styling your fonts.

Remember that the Modified Date Smart Object is not going to report the current time to your visitors the way a clock does.

Keeping Your Data and Messages Fresh

Normally, when a browser calls for a page, it caches images in order to make it easier for a person to revisit that page. Without a cache, the browser must call for every item on your page again each time it returns. How much material is cached and how long it remains in a user's cache depends totally on the user's browser preferences. If any page within your site tends to present new information that changes frequently, you can tell browsers not to cache that page.

To tell a browser not to cache a page, you place the following HTML anywhere within the `<head>` and `</head>` tags of your source code:

```
<meta http-equiv="Pragma" content="no-cache">
```

Of course, you can also do this within the Layout mode, using the Inspector, as outlined in the following steps:

1. Drag the Meta icon from the Head tab of the Objects palette into the head section of the page you don't want cached. If, as you drag, you realize that the head section is not open, rest over the arrow to the left of the Page icon until the section opens, and then continue into the section.

2. Choose http-equiv from the pop-up menu at the top.

Where's the Checklist?

Many books on Web-site creation provide a final checklist. I'm proud to say I'm not offering you one. Not that it's not important for everything on your site to be in order. It is. It's just that I took a look at some checklists and, well, it turns out that GoLive already had everything on those lists covered. Between GoLive's constant link error-checking, and the details in this entire chapter and the previous one, everything on a checklist is covered. Everything — and more. That's GoLive for you.

3. In the next field, enter **Pragma**.

4. In the content field, enter **no-cache**, as shown in Figure 26-13.

Figure 26-13: Setting up the metatag that tells a browser not to cache a page

From now on, when this page is loaded into a browser, its contents will not be cached and all contents on the page will be pulled down from the server.

You don't have to type this code. Instead, open the ReusableItems.html page, which you can find on the CD-ROM that comes with this book. Drag its Metatag icon from the head section of the page over to the Custom tab of your Objects palette, as directed in the page.

✦   ✦   ✦

Publishing Your Web Site

After you've created your Web pages, tweaked them, and organized your folder structure, you're ready for your site to . . . go live. It's time to *upload* your site to a Web server. GoLive includes three tools and that enable you to get your site to the Web:

✦ **Site Window FTP** is an integral part of your site file management. It's the most convenient way to transfer files back and forth between your Web server and your Files tab. A good deal of GoLive's best power comes from using this feature.

✦ The **FTP Browser** is a generic FTP client you can use to access any FTP site regardless of which Site Window you're working in. It comes in handy when you want to reach an FTP site quickly. It's also most convenient when you want to see the overall structure of your Web server space and add new directories on the same level as the site you're currently working on.

✦ **Export Site** accommodates older browsers that require your site to be of a specific folder structure, or, for when you want to hand off a completed site ready for the Web, but without the site document.

Because the Site Window FTP is so powerful and makes GoLive so easy to use, I show you that upload feature first. After that, I cover the generic FTP tool and the Export command.

Before You Get Started

Are you considering whether your site is ready to go live? You like what you've got. The links that are there all work.

Everything renders nicely. But there's one effect you'd like to add, when you have the time. There's one or two more things you'd like to add to that certain information page, when you have the time.

What to do . . . go live with what you have, or wait until you've got the time to try those other things?

Go live! With the incremental update your Site Window provides, you can get your site up now, and then continue to work as time permits. Set your new, experimental pages to Publish Never in their Page Inspector and play to your heart's content. When they're ready to take their rightful place in your site, change their Publish status to Publish If Referenced, and then hit the Connect button and the Incremental Upload button. Any time you're in your Site Window, you're only four clicks away from the new and improved site of your dreams.

Setting Up Your Server Space

Once you purchase Web server space, it's up to you how you section that space off and post your site. In most cases, you'll simply send your site directly into the folder (a.k.a. *directory*) that you've purchased or been assigned. When you do, users enter the domain name and land directly at your site. But you can also subdivide your server space creatively.

Sharing a space among separate sites

You can divide your server space into several spaces, and then host a separate site in each folder. For example, I set up www.shadovitz.com to act as not only my own site, but to also be available for my family — and even friends. Within my space, my root folder, I created several other folders. I named one folder, "deb," and put my own site within that folder. The upload path for that is www.shadovitz.com as the server and /deb as the directory. Several other folders also exist within my root folder, each with a different folder name that becomes part of the URL to that site. Each folder contains an entirely separate site, created in its own GoLive Site Window. The site settings for each site are the same except for the folder name and the directory setting. Chances are, for a professional site, you won't do this type of thing, but as a just-for-fun family site, it worked well for me for years. After a while, I decided it would be nice to have a more professional URL, so I registered www.debshadovitz.com and my Web server administrator over at PGS Group pointed that URL directly to my deb folder. Thus, www.debshadovitz.com takes you to the same place as www.debshadovitz.com/deb.

While you might never use such a setup for your published sites, the same trick works brilliantly to create a secret test site that the public won't find.

Setting up a secret test site

Say you own www.mygreatsite.com. You need to test your new great site, but if you publish it by uploading it directly into the root folder of www.mygreatsite. com, the world may find it before you're ready for it to be found. You can publish it without keywords or a description, but you need to test the title. And if it's a good domain name, people will seek it out naturally, without the help of a search engine.

To keep your site from being seen prematurely, you can bury it inside of a folder and give that folder a name that won't pop into a person's mind with ease. Using either the Site Window FTP or the FTP Browser, create and name a single new folder inside your root folder. For example, name the folder something like **testmepleaseno1**. (To learn about adding a new directory, see those sections in this chapter where Site Window FTP and the FTP Browser are explained.) Then, enter the path to this folder as the destination to which you upload your site. While you're testing the site, give out this address. In this case, the test address would be www.mygreatsite.com/ estmepleaseno1.

When you're ready for the site to go public, you don't have to create a new Site Window. Just add a new server address setting that leads directly into the root level. Then upload the same now-finished files from your Files tab up to the root level of your site. You can use either of the two FTP features, or use the Export command to both test your site and publish it. (The Site Window FTP is, as always, easiest.)

After your site goes live to the world, you can still continue to use the subdirectory as a testing space.

Uploading your Site Via the Site Window

The FTP tab of the Site Window, dedicated to your site's file transfer, is one of the shining lights of GoLive. With this feature, uploading your site for the first time couldn't be easier . . . but the greatest power comes from the ease with which it enables you to change any page or pages and get them up to the server in minutes. With the ease of incremental uploads, it's easy to keep your site up-to-date. In the next chapter, I tell you all about updating your site. Here, I show you how to upload your site for the first time.

Note   You can upload your site using the FTP Browser window, but that doesn't let the Site Window track the upload. To use the Incremental Upload feature for all your future site updates, be sure to use the Site Window for your initial upload.

What, exactly can you do with the Site Window's FTP tab? You can upload your entire site, and then later upload only the files that have changed. You can use your Site Window to store files you're thinking about using but are not ready to use yet, and not have to worry about those files being uploaded. You can move a single file to the server. You can move a single file down from the server back to your Site Window, or even to your desktop.

The FTP settings you use to transfer your site this way become part of your site document's (a.k.a. *Site Window*) settings, so you can pass your site folder to a coworker or to a client and the recipient will still be able to do the uploads. Even if you have to trash your GoLive preferences, you won't lose these settings, which remain part of the site document.

One more thing to consider: You need to have space on a Web server arranged before you can go on. If you've got your server space set up or rented, you should have the domain name, path to your folder, username, and password at your fingertips, ready to add now.

Setting up access to the server

Before you can send your site's files to a Web server, you have to tell GoLive how to reach your server. To do this, you enter the path to that server—along with your username and password—into GoLive's FTP dialog box. The FTP address you enter here is recorded in the site document that you double-click to open the site. It becomes a part of the Site Window's preferences and travels along with the rest of the site information and tracking. This is great because when you pass the site to your client to maintain, or pass it to a coworker (or to yourself in another location), the FTP access information and file upload history go with it. At the same time, this Web server access is not available to everyone else who is using your computer (unless this Site Window is opened). If you want, you can add this server access to the general GoLive preferences later. Each time you enter FTP information, this option is available, and I list it as an optional step.

You'll need to be connected to the Internet in order to actually connect and upload your site, but you don't need the connection to enter the FTP settings for your site. You just need to have that Site Window open and active.

To set up the path to your Web site's location, follow these steps:

1. Click the Site Settings button on the toolbar. (Alternately, you can choose Site ⇨ Settings, or choose Settings from the contextual menu.)

   This opens a Preferences panel that contains preferences similar to application-wide preferences, but are (or can become) for this Site Window only. If not already at the FTP & WebDAV Server settings, click that section icon at the left.

2. Enter the address of the FTP server in the Server field. This is the main address, like www.yourdomain.com. It does not include the rest of the path to the site, if one exists.

3. If the site will not reside in the main level of the domain, but within a subfolder instead, enter the path from the main level to the site folder in the Directory field.

Depending on your server, when placing your site at the main level, you
will need to add a lone "/" to the Directory field. Finding the exact path that
your server wants may take some experimentation. In the example shown in
Figure 27-1, the site will reside at the main level, so the field is empty.

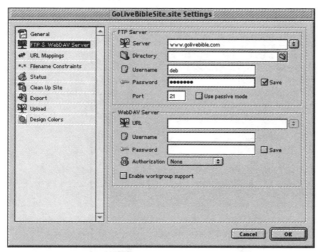

Figure 27-1: A completed set of FTP settings entered
within the Site Settings dialog box

4. Enter your username in the Username field. (You are asked to choose a username when you purchase your server space. If you're unsure of your username,
   ask your server administrator.)

5. Enter your password in the Password field. (Again, you should have provided
   the server administrator with your desired password at sign up.)

Username and password are usually case sensitive, as is the path to your site. If
your login isn't working, check that you have it entered exactly as your server
administrator set up for you.

6. To have the Site Window remember your password for future access, click
   Save. If you don't, you'll have to return to the site settings and enter your
   password each time you connect. (Not saving it can be a good security
   measure.)

If you don't save your password, and don't enter it before you try to log into your
server, you may receive an error message stating that login failed.

7. (*Optional*) Normally, the common port number used on all servers for FTP is
   21, so you can leave this preset. However, if your server uses a different port,
   your administrator will tell you to enter that specific number.

8. (*Optional*) Check the option to use passive mode if your server administrator recommends it.

9. (*Optional*) Move back to the pop-up arrow menu to the right of the Server field and choose Add Current Server, as shown in Figure 27-2—if you want these settings saved to the applications-wide preferences.

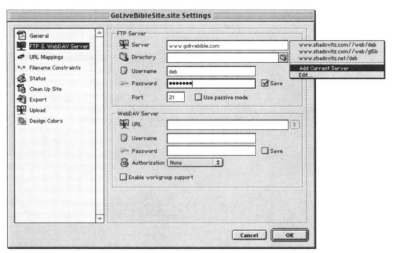

Figure 27-2: Adding a completed set of FTP settings to the general GoLive preferences

Tip   If you want to have easy access to this site's folder on the Web server, even when you don't have its Site Window open, save your site's FTP settings into the main GoLive preferences. When access information is in general application-wide preferences, you (and others who use your computer) can call up the site from within the FTP Browser window any time GoLive is running, without having to open the site's Site Window.

If you'll be dividing your site up among servers, or if you're using a separate directory as a test area, adding the server address to this list makes it a cinch to return again.

10. (*Optional*) If you want GoLive to strip certain code as it uploads your pages, set this option in the preferences. Click Upload from the Preferences list at the left, and then choose from the list of settings as shown in Figure 27-3. Check the option for "Site specific settings" so this will pertain to your current site only.

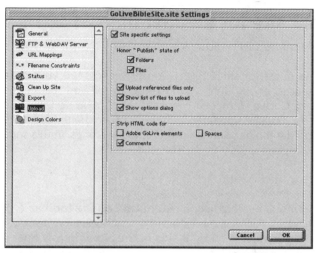

Figure 27-3: Setting GoLive up to strip comments from pages upon upload

Under "Strip HTML code for," choose any of the three options:

- You can remove all GoLive elements (which means the pages won't have this code if you need to import the site later).

- You can remove all spaces and have the code all run together (which technically makes the page smaller to download but harder to ever work with again).

- You can remove all comments from your pages (which doesn't alter GoLive's functions at all and may remove internal communications that you don't want broadcast to the world, or may remove your own guidelines).

11. (*Optional*) If you are accessing the Internet through a corporate network or have a firewall, you may need to set up proxy settings. These are located in the main preference area. To get to them, choose Edit from the pop-up arrow menu to the right of the Server field, and then choose the Network icon. (You can also get to them via Edit ➪ Preferences.) To learn about these settings, see "Setting FTP Preferences" later in this chapter.

12. Click OK.

Note   The lower half of this window is for WebDAV and is not an issue for uploading your site. (See Chapter 30 to learn about using WebDAV.)

Uploading your site for the first time

After you've set up your site's FTP settings, you're ready to upload your site.

 New Feature If, in the ultimate quest for small pages, you prefer to send your pages to the server without spaces, or you don't want viewers to see your comments, or you want to remove all GoLive elements—you can have GoLive do this upon upload. To do so, set this in your site's preferences before you do the upload. Click the Site Settings button on the toolbar, and then click Upload settings. In this settings area, check any desired option under "Strip HTML code for."

To upload your site (for the first time), follow these steps:

1. Click the FTP Server Connect/Disconnect button on the toolbar. (Alternately, you can choose Site ➪ FTP Server ➪ Connect, or choose FTP Server ➪ Connect from the contextual menu.) The right side of the Site Window opens automatically, bringing forward the FTP tab. The Files tab continues to display the files you've been working on, while the FTP tab becomes the window to your server.

   In the FTP tab, the status line at the lower left tells you it's "Connecting," then "Getting file list," and in a moment, "Connected." Because this is the first time you're connecting, the FTP tab is empty, as shown in Figure 27-4. (In subsequent uploads, your existing files will appear here. See Chapter 28 for more information.) If the server folder isn't empty, see the "What If I Already Have a Site on the Server?" sidebar at the end of this section.

   If, upon connecting, you notice you're in the wrong directory (folder), disconnect by pressing the same connection button (FTP Server Connect/Disconnect), click the Site Settings button on the toolbar, and then repair the entry. (If you try to select the address to repair it and cannot select it, you've forgotten to disconnect.)

Figure 27-4: Connected to an empty server space to upload a new site for the first time

2. Click the Incremental Upload button on the Site toolbar.. Unless you've already altered the FTP preferences, the Upload Options dialog box appears, as shown in Figure 27-5.

Figure 27-5: The Upload Options dialog box

3. In the Upload Options dialog box, check the options available and make any changes.

   • "Honor 'Publish' state of Folders and of Files" tells GoLive to upload the files (or not) depending on your choice for each file. (See "Setting the Publish Status" in Chapter 6 for an introduction to the Publish status feature. You can also learn more about how this feature works in the section entitled "Avoiding Accidental Publishing" in Chapter 28.)

   • "Upload referenced files only" instructs GoLive to upload only files that can be reached from your home page (index.html or default.html).

   • "Show list of files to upload" tells GoLive to present you with a list of all files it finds to upload. (The files it finds are based on your previous three settings.)

   • "Don't show again" stops this options dialog box from appearing each time you upload your site in the future. If you choose this, the current settings remain in effect. Without this dialog box appearing each time, if you want to change the settings, you can click Site Settings again and choose the Upload section in the Preferences window. In this section, you can also turn the option to show the Options dialog box back on.

   • Click "Set as default" to make these your default settings.

4. The Upload Site dialog box opens, as shown in Figure 27-6, presenting a list of the files GoLive has found to upload, based on your settings in the previous dialog box.

5. If you've made the proper choices in the File Inspector and the Upload Options dialog box, all of the files you've used in your site appear here. Keep them checked. If you realize a file selected for upload is not yet used and doesn't need to be uploaded, uncheck the Transfer box for that file.

6. After reviewing the files to be uploaded, click OK.

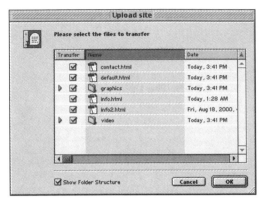

Figure 27-6: The Upload Site dialog box

The Uploading Files dialog box opens and shows you the transfer process. At the same time, the status area of the FTP tab tells you the files are uploading. Then the files appear in the FTP tab.

What If I Already Have a Site on the Server?

If you have a site already existing on this server in this location, you will have to decide what to do with the existing site. Do you want to delete it, or move it to another folder for safe keeping . . . just in case? (There shouldn't be any "in case" need as you've already tested your site fully, but I'm a just-in-case type of person.) Or, you can download the existing site to your hard drive for safekeeping.

To move the site to another folder for safekeeping, follow these steps:

1. Create a new folder within your server's directory.

2. Click within the FTP tab to make that the active tab, and then click the New Folder button on the toolbar. This puts a new folder (new directory) into your server space. Name it something like "oldsite."

3. Select all of the files within the FTP tab (which are all the files from your old site), but don't select the "oldsite" folder, and then all of the files into the oldsite folder.

    Should you, for some reason, need to revert to your old site again, you just have to open that folder (double-clicking does the trick), and then drag all of its files back out to the main level of the directory. Meanwhile, with all the old files safely tucked away, you can now upload your new site. The oldsite folder won't do any harm.

To download the existing site to your hard drive for safekeeping, use the Import from FTP Server feature under the Files menu. See Chapter 5 to learn how. This creates a new GoLive site that consists of the old site. You can then select all the files on the server and delete them by clicking the Delete Selected Item button on the toolbar (the trash can).

After you've uploaded your site, you can see one of the benefits of the Site Window FTP feature. Notice, as shown in Figure 27-7, that the files in your Files tab and on the server are visible side by side so you can easily notice which files are on the server. Additionally, you can expand each side of the Site Window and the columns within it to see the file information, such as the date a file was last modified.

Figure 27-7: A site newly uploaded via the FTP tab of the Site Window

Viewing your files in the FTP tab

You can easily see any file that's on the Web server by opening the folders within the FTP tab. To see what's within any folder within your site's main level, do the following:

✦ Click the arrow/plus sign to the left of the folder. This reveals the files within that folder in Outline view, with the files inside indented beneath the folder's listing. (You can see this in Figure 27-7.)

✦ Double-click the folder. This opens the folder so it becomes the main focus of the window, as shown in Figure 27-8. To return back to the main level, click the now upward-pointing arrow above the File list and to the left of the reported path you're viewing.

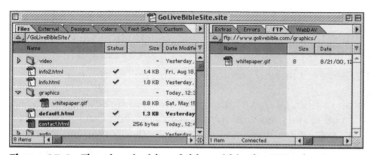

Figure 27-8: The view inside a folder within the FTP tab

Adding a new directory

Within your site, creating a subdirectory comes automatically, whether you realize you're doing it or not, because every folder within your Files tab becomes a new subdirectory within your site once you upload that folder to the Web server. But at times you may want to consciously create a subdirectory within your server space. To learn why you might do this, see "Setting Up Your Server Space" at the beginning of this chapter.

To add a new subdirectory to any server folder you have access to using the Site Window (FTP tab) FTP, follow these steps:

1. Set up the site settings to connect you to the main level of the server folder to which you have access.

2. Connect to the server.

3. Click in the FTP tab to select it.

4. Click the New Folder button on the toolbar.

   The new folder appears in the FTP tab, coming in with the name "untitled_folder" preselected.

5. Type a new name for the folder.

Once you've added the directory, if you want to upload a site's files to it, disconnect from the server. Then click Site Settings, go to the FTP settings, and add a slash and the name of your new folder in the Directory field. Next time you click to connect to the server, the FTP tab opens directly to the new folder.

Disconnecting from the FTP server

If you're using a dial-up connection to access your server, you'll want to disconnect as soon as you've completed the upload.

To disconnect from the server, do the following:

✦ Choose Site ➪ Disconnect.

✦ Point anywhere within the FTP Browser, and then Control-click (Mac) or right-click (Windows) and choose Disconnect from the contextual menu.

✦ Click the FTP Server Connect/Disconnect button on the toolbar.

The status area at the bottom left says "Disconnecting," and then the files disappear from the tab. If you're finished working on your site, you can just close your Site Window. The connection to the server is terminated automatically.

Using the FTP Browser

The FTP Browser is a generic FTP client, provided within GoLive for your extra convenience. Using this FTP client, it's easy to connect to any FTP server (provided you have access privileges) at any time while you're working in GoLive, regardless of the site you happen to be working on. Say, for example, you're working on one of your sites when another of your clients phones to ask you something. You want to check the server to discover the location of the file in question, or make sure its there. You could open that client's Site Window and connect using its FTP tab, but it's faster to simply open the FTP Browser and connect that way. I also find the FTP Browser the easiest way to add a subdirectory to my site. But I'll get to that in a moment.

Entering your FTP settings

Before GoLive can call upon your FTP server, you have to tell it where that server is. You also have to supply the username and secret password you set up with your server administrator. If you've looked at the site settings already, or used any FTP application before, these settings will be familiar. If you haven't, please refer to, "Setting Up Access to the Server," earlier in this chapter for details on this setup.

Meanwhile, here are the basics of FTP setup:

1. Choose File ➪ FTP Browser. (No button exists for this.)

2. Enter the address of the FTP server in the Server field. This is the main address — the domain.

3. To upload your site to a subfolder instead of the main level of a site, enter the path from the main level to the site folder in the Directory field.

4. Enter your username in the Username field.

5. Enter your password in the Password field.

6. (*Optional*) If you've been directed to access your server through a unique port number, or want to set Passive mode, click Advanced. Figure 27-9 demonstrates this.

7. Click OK.

You can optionally choose to save your settings at this point by clicking the arrow beside the Server field and choosing Add Current Server. However, it is often wiser to wait and save them after you've connected successfully and then disconnected. Waiting ensures that the settings are correct and prevents the confusion of inaccurate access settings appearing in the list. Additionally, after you connect GoLive automatically updates your directory path, so waiting enables you to save the actual path.

Note   To access your server through a firewall, or if you have other unique setup to do, see "Setting FTP Preferences" later in this chapter.

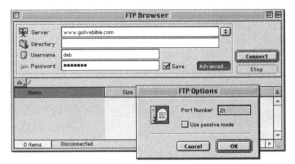

Figure 27-9: The FTP Browser access settings

Connecting to an FTP site via the FTP Browser

With settings entered, you can now connect to the FTP Browser, as follows:

1. Choose File ➪ FTP Browser. (No button exists for this.)

2. Choose the desired server from the arrow beside the Server field.

   This list contains all server settings you've entered here before and saved via the same menu, as well as any server settings you've entered directly under GoLive Preferences in the FTP Server section.

3. Click Connect or click the FTP server Connect/Disconnect button in the toolbar.

   The status area tells you the FTP Browser is getting the File list.

Upon successful connection, the files appear (unless the folder is empty) and the status area says "Connected." Now you can add files or folders, view or edit files, or delete files or folders, as detailed in the next section.

Working within the FTP Browser

While you're connected to your server, your files appear within the FTP Browser window. You can move files around within this window just like you move files in the Site Window; you can drag files between folders, move a file out of a folder up to the main level (by dragging it to the Name heading in the window), change names, and delete files. You can even edit the files on the accessed site.

Adding a new directory

You can add a new directory within your site's folder anytime you're connected to that server. You cannot add a directory outside of the folder to which you have access. For that, you need to contact the server's administrator.

To add a new directory within your site's folder, connect to your server and then do the following:

1. Create the folder in either of the following ways:

   • Click the New Folder button in the toolbar.

   • Control-click (Mac) or right-click (Windows) and choose New Folder from the contextual menu.

   The new folder appears within the FTP Browser window.

2. By default the new folder is called "untitled_folder." It's preselected, so name your folder by just typing or pasting a new name.

Once you have a new directory, you can add files to it by dragging files onto the Closed Folder icon, or you can open the folder and watch the results of adding files to it.

Uploading your site or pages

You can use the FTP Browser to upload any individual file, or even an entire site. To upload a file, just drag it into the FTP Browser window, as follows:

✦ You can drag files from the Files tab of your Site Window. (It doesn't make sense to do this, though, as the FTP tab is much more efficient for uploading.)

✦ You can drag a file from anywhere on your computer.

✦ You can use GoLive's Export feature to export the entire site, and then upload the exported files. To do so, open the folder that contains the exported files, select the entire contents, and drag them all into the browser window. (If you drag the entire exported folder into the browser, your site's address won't be `yourdomain.com`, but `yourdomain.com/thefoldername`.

To add your file into a specific folder, drag it onto the Folder icon. You can do this even if the folder is closed. When adding a file into the main level of the FTP directory, make sure no folder is highlighted when you release the mouse or the file will land inside the selected folder. (Of course, you can always open the folder and drag the file out later.)

Viewing your files

Within the FTP Browser window, shown in Figure 27-10, your site's files appear in a List view, as within the Site Window.

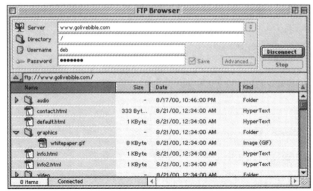

Figure 27-10: A site's files, as viewed within the FTP Browser window

To see what's within any folder within your site's main level, do the following:

✦ Click the arrow/plus sign to the left of the folder. This reveals the files within that folder in Outline view, with the files inside indented beneath the folder's listing.

✦ Double-click the folder.

This opens the folder so it becomes the main focus of the window. You can then return back to the main level by clicking the now upward-pointing arrow above the File list and to the left of the reported path you're viewing.

Cross-Reference

The FTP Browser is a fully functioning FTP client that can be used to rename and delete files as well. See Chapter 28 to learn more about using the FTP Browser.

Disconnecting from the FTP Browser

To disconnect from the server, do the following:

✦ Choose Site ➪ Disconnect.

✦ Point anywhere within the FTP Browser, and then Control-click (Mac) or right-click (Windows) and choose Disconnect from the contextual menu.

✦ Click the FTP server Connect/Disconnect button in the toolbar.

The status area at the bottom left says "Disconnected."

Tip

If you plan to access this FTP again (and are not concerned with other users having this access ability), this is a good time to save your FTP settings for easy access in the future. To save them, click the arrow beside the Server field and choose Add Current Server. This adds your server information to the FTP server preference in your application-wide GoLive preferences. (You can always delete the access info. See "Deleting a Server Setting" later in this chapter.)

Setting FTP Preferences

GoLive's FTP capabilities provide many services and options. GoLive usually provides the opportunity to set the various options as they become pertinent to what you are doing. But, of course, all options are also available at any time via the general Preferences window. This section covers all of the FTP preferences.

Updating FTP server settings

You actually have two places to enter FTP information: in the Site Settings dialog box and in the FTP Browser. These are the most logical places to add your FTP server settings because they provide the most direct interface for doing so. In each case, if you choose Add Current Server, you add your currently entered settings to GoLive's application-wide preference settings. You can also add your settings directly in the Preference Settings dialog box, as covered in this section.

Adding a new server setting

If you prefer, you can go directly to Preferences and add as many servers and settings for directories within servers as you wish. To do so, choose Edit ➪ Preferences, and then click the arrow by the Network icon at the left and click FTP Server. Then click New and enter your settings. (See Figure 27-11.) See the section on site settings to learn about each of the settings, if you need to.

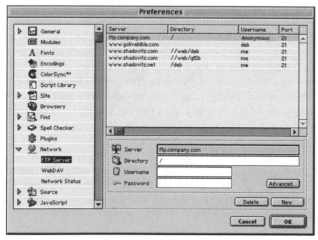

Figure 27-11: A new Web server access listing about to be entered; the result of the New button being clicked

You can also use this preferences area to delete a server. This can be handy if you saved settings that turned out to be wrong, or no longer want them available to everyone who uses GoLive on your computer.

Editing a server setting

To edit server access settings, click the line once that lists that server. When a server is selected, its FTP information appears in four fields below the list. Make your changes in those fields. To edit the port number or set the passive settings, click Advanced. This opens a window that contains those options for the currently listed server.

Deleting a server setting

To delete server access settings, click the line once that lists that server, and then click Delete. Deleting a server setting from the FTP Browser window or the general GoLive preferences (which is the same thing) also removes it from the list of saved servers within the site settings used by the Site Window FTP. If the server address you delete happens to be currently selected within the Site Settings dialog box, it is not lost. If it isn't, though, it's gone from GoLive altogether and will need to be re-entered if it is to be used again.

Uploading options

GoLive gives you several ways to determine which files will be selected for upload. These settings and options can greatly help you send only the necessary or desired files to the server. These options are set on a site-by-site basis. To set them, you can click the Site Settings button, or you can choose Edit ➪ Preferences and then open the Site section at the left.

Honor the Publish state of folders and of files

As you add a file to your site, or at any other time you're in the Files tab, you can select a file and set it to always be published, to never be published, or to be published only if it's accessible from the home page (which you're presumably using on your site). You can set folders as a whole to only be published if they're not empty, always, or never. Then, each time you perform an upload using the Site Window FTP server, the Upload Options dialog box gives you the option to tell GoLive to honor these settings.

But, in case you missed getting all Publish states in your files set in the File Inspector, you have another opportunity to have GoLive upload only the files that are reachable from your home page (`index.html` or `default.html`). Under Edit ➪ Preferences ➪ Site, just select the Upload Preferences section and then check "Upload referenced files only."

Then, to give yourself one final opportunity to determine not to upload a file, you can tell GoLive to show you which files it recommends updating. To do so, check Show list of files to upload here in the Upload Preferences.

And, just for good measure, in case you ever check the option not to show these options as you're actually doing the upload, you can reset it here by checking Show Options Dialog.

Stripping HTML code

GoLive can automatically strip the HTML code for spaces, GoLive-specific elements, and/or comments as it uploads your site. This is another site-by-site preference for the current site only — and for use upon upload only. The settings here don't have any effect on the settings for the Export command.

To set GoLive to strip code, chose Edit ➪ Preferences, and then open the sublistings for the Site icon in the menu to the left and choose Upload. Under the heading "Strip HTML code for," check any code you want removed from your pages on upload.

What happens when you remove GoLive code? Stripping the code makes all those HTML code checkers out there happy by removing any GoLive-specific code. However, that very code is what gives you GoLive's unique, easy-to-use capabilities. As long as you continue to work with your pages within the Files tab, it doesn't matter GoLive-wise what happens to the exported pages. They'll work on the Web, and that's what counts. But, if you don't have a safe backup and ever need to import your site from the server to start a new Site Window for your site, you'll be out of luck as far as using Smart Objects, Actions, and Components. Your grids will be gone, too. (For the inside scoop on what goes, you can choose Edit ➪ Web Settings, and then look at all items marked as Adobe GoLive Special. That's what goes.

General network options for FTP

The main tab of the Network Preferences window enables you to set up GoLive to use proxy servers, should you need one. It also enables you to set up other general preferences for your FTP access. Additionally, it includes support for Mac-specific Internet and password features.

To set up the general FTP preferences, choose Edit ➪ Preferences and then click the Network icon in the menu to the left, as shown in Figure 27-12. The following are the general network preferences for FTP:

   ✦ **Use FTP Proxy.** If your computer's FTP access is via proxy, check this option and then enter the host and port information in their respective fields.

   ✦ **Use HTTP Proxy.** If your HTTP access is via proxy, check this option and then enter the host and port information in their respective fields.

   ✦ **Keep connections alive** helps GoLive maintain your Internet connection if you use a dial-up connection. This can help prevent time-out errors as you're uploading files.

Mac-Specific Settings

The Internet Control Panel option (at the top of the Preference panel) enables GoLive to use the settings from your Internet Control Panel, if you've set them up and rely on them. To check, update, or enter your settings, click the Internet Control Panel to the right to open the Control Panel. To use these settings, check "Use always," and then click Import Now.

You can also have GoLive add the passwords for your access to our Keychain. Just check the main option, "Use system Keychain for passwords". Your passwords will automatically be added. If you prefer GoLive to prompt you each time, check "Ask before adding passwords."

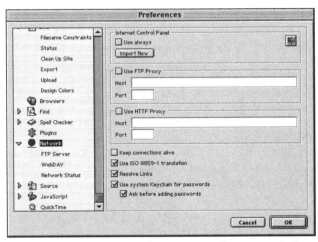

Figure 27-12: The Network Options Preferences window

✦ **Use ISO 8859-1 translation** is a file encoding specific to the Mac. It enables special characters to properly translate to the ISO standard, and is checked by default. This option is not necessary, and is not checked on Windows.

✦ **Resolve Links**, selected by default, commands GoLive to verify paths of any aliases that may reside on your server. If this process seems to slow you down, uncheck the option.

Tracking Server Access Errors

As you communicate with your Web server, GoLive tracks this communication. Actually, the server sends the messages and GoLive captures them for you to see. Most of the time, you will probably not even think of this log, but there may be times when it can come in handy. Should you have problems connecting, check it out. You can also print the messages so you can send them to your server administrator.

Note If the Network Status message window seems familiar, perhaps you've used WebDAV and seen it in action logging your file transfers to the WebDAV server.

Viewing server access messages

The access log continues to collect server messages, whether you have it open or not. This means you can keep it closed, and then refer to it only when you need to see what's going on.

Follow these steps to view the Server log:

1. To view the messages captured from your server, choose File ➪ Network Status.

2. To view the details of any message click its message header once in a list at the top of the window. The newest messages appear at the bottom. Icons let you know what type of message it is. (You can choose what types of messages appear here. See the "Setting Server Access Preferences section later in this chapter.)

   • Errors are depicted by the Stop Sign icon.

   • Warnings are depicted by the yellow Caution icon.

   • Status messages are depicted by the FTP icon. Each time you log on, a new session begins. It ends when you disconnect. Next time you connect, a new icon and message appear.

Note If you cannot connect at all, due to an incorrect address, path, username, or password, no message will be generated. Remember, the messages here are only those generated by the server.

3. Scroll through the message at the bottom of the window. The activities of a session are recorded from top to bottom, so the most current activity is at the bottom.

If you have a problem connecting, contact your server administrator for interpretation and a possible solution. You can easily save the error report as a text file any time, in order to pass it to your administrator.

When the connection is lost, GoLive may show "Unexpected Disconnect." Or, it may not know what the cause of disconnection was and instead may display an alert, stating the last message it received from the server. If you see odd or random messages that make little or no sense, it probably means the connection was lost and that's all GoLive knows. If you're certain your Web connection is solid, you might ask your server host what may be causing the problem. Or, try turning on Passive mode (see "Setting Up Access to the Server") to see if this helps. (It is also known to slow down server communication, though.)

What might you see in the log? Figure 27-13 provides a typical, successful logon and logoff message.

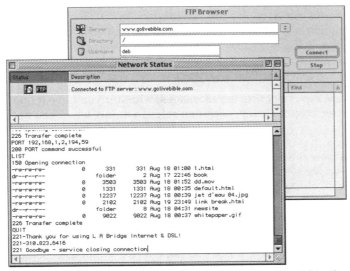

Figure 27-13: An example of a file transfer message within the Network Status window: a file uploaded, and then the Disconnect button used

Saving your server access log as a text file

You can save the server access log anytime while you have the Network Status window open you. Do the following:

1. Open your Network Status window by choosing File ➪ Network Status.

2. Point to the desired message within the top part of the window as you Control-click (Mac) or right-click (Windows) and choose Save As from the contextual menu.

3. In the Save dialog box, edit the file name as desired, but keep the .txt extension. (With this extension, anyone you send the document to will be able to open it.)

4. Choose a location for the file and click Save.

When you double-click the exported text file, you may see line numbers at the left side of the document window. This numbering appears if you have the Line Numbering option turned on in your preferences under the Source heading. These numbers do not appear when the file is opened in another application.

After saving a text document copy of any message, you can e-mail the file for troubleshooting purposes, or keep it for your own access records.

Caution   Upon printing an access message, you might be tempted to clear out that message. In fact, the contextual menu contains a Clear command. However, the Clear command clears your entire log, not just the message you are pointing to.

Setting server access preferences

By default, GoLive tracks any errors a Web server sends back when you try to access any Web server via GoLive. You cannot turn this default off.

In addition to errors, you can also have GoLive track all warnings sent by the server and/or all status messages. To do so, follow these steps:

1. Choose Edit ➪ Preferences, and then click the arrow by the Network icon at the left and click Network Status.

2. (*Optional*) Check the option to also track warnings.

3. (*Optional*) Check the option to also track status messages.

4. (*Optional*) Change the total number of items the Network Status log holds before discarding older information to make room for the new. By default, 50 messages are logged. You can retain as few as five, and as many as you'd like.

It's a good idea to keep the warnings and status messages logged because you can print the complete log in order to do troubleshooting — and when troubleshooting, too much information can be safer than not enough.

Exporting Your Site

These days, you typically want to use the Site Window's FTP feature to upload your site and let GoLive track the changes intelligently. But, GoLive also includes an excellent export feature — just in case you want to call upon it.

Unlike uploading, which moves your files to a server, exporting your site makes a copy of the site. You then upload the copy as desired. The copy of the site doesn't contain the site document or the GoLive data folder. It's just a plain, old-fashioned set of HTML pages. When you export, you give up the GoLive site management. More accurately, you maintain the site management in your Site Window, but the exported version is a standalone version of the site sans GoLive tools.

Some users prefer to export a site in order to turn it over to a client who won't be using GoLive and just wants to edit plain HTML. You can export, and then turn over the site's exported folder and let the client upload it and continue to work on it. (Or, you can hand your client an exported copy but do the actual upload using the FTP Browser window.)

GoLive Help also suggests that if you need to split your site among several servers, you might use export. But, you can color code your files (using the File Inspector) to designate various servers, and then use the pop-up menu in the site settings for FTP to connect to each server in turn and upload the correctly colored files. So, again, you can still use the Site Window.

New Feature With GoLive 4, if you wanted to strip out the GoLive code, the only way to do it was by using the Export command. But, now you can strip code on upload from the Site Window, too.

Setting export options

Before you export a site, you should look over the things that will happen upon export, and adjust them to your liking or the guidelines outlined here:

1. Open up the settings, as follows:

   - Click the Site Settings button on the toolbar (or choose Site ➪ Settings), and then choose the Export preference heading at the left.

   - Choose Edit > ➪ Preferences, and then, under the Site heading in the left pane, choose Export.

2. To set up the export for the site you're working on, but not other sites in the future, check Site Specific Settings at the top of the settings section.

3. Choose your export settings. (They are very similar to the upload settings.)

   - *Honor "Publish" state of Folders* tells GoLive to respect the setting you selected for each folder as it was selected in the Files tab. The setting is selected within that folder's File Inspector, from a menu called Publish.

   - *Honor "Publish" state of Files* does the same as the state for folders, but the Publish options are more specific. Files can be set to export (or upload) only If Referenced (reachable from the home page), Always, or Never. (If Referenced is safest and most respectful of your server space.)

   - If you have not set all of your files' Publish states to *If Referenced*, but like that feature, you can still benefit from it. Uncheck "Honor Publish state of files," which can cause information clash. This makes "Export referenced files only" an option.

   - *Export referenced files that are not part of this site* locates and exports copies of any orphan files you may have in your site. This enables those files, although not in your Site Window, to become part of your published site. The orphan files are sorted into a folder that's called Other, by default.

     This option works in conjunction with one of the folder name fields a bit lower down. You can choose your own folder names instead of keeping Other.

4. Choose your Hierarchy settings. This tells GoLive how to sort and reorganize your files:

   - *As in site* mirrors exactly the organization of your Files tab.

   - *Separate pages and media* separates your site's files and places all HTML Pages folders into a folder called Pages. At the same time, it puts all other files used in your site into a folder called Media. These two folders go into the enclosing folder, along with the home page, which remains outside of the Pages folder. The path to each of your pages is then `www.yourdomain.com/Pages/yourpage.html`. All media links are `www.yourdomain.com/Media/graphic.gif`.

This option works in conjunction with two of the folder name fields a bit lower down. You can choose your own folder names instead of keeping Pages and Media. Your server administrator might (but probably won't) tell you that specific names are needed, and then tell you those names.

- *Flat* puts all of your site's files into one folder. The path to every page and every graphic, sound, and so forth is then `www.yourdomain.com/yourpage.html`. (You might have a Web server administrator that insists on this structure.)

5. If you wish to have any of the following code removed from your pages during the export, you can check the option to strip that code. (See "Setting FTP Preferences" earlier in this chapter for details.)

- *Adobe GoLive Elements* are the GoLive tags and attributes that give you Actions, Smart Objects, Components, and so on. Stripping the code doesn't stop them from functioning on the Web. (In case you're considering this just to save download time, the truth is, the download time saved by cutting out this code is too little to even be counted.)

- *Comments* simply removes any comments hidden in the page.

- *Spaces* removes all spaces from your code, rendering it fairly unreadable as code but fully functional as a page. (If you're only reason to do this is to cut file size, bear in mind that no one will notice the difference in download time.)

6. Show Options Dialog enables you to see options as GoLive prepares the export, so you can recall what will happen and/or make any changes.

7. After your selections are complete, click OK.

Performing the export

To perform the export, follow these steps:

1. From the Site menu, choose Export site from its submenu:

- Site ⇨ Explorer ⇨ Export Site (Windows)

- Site ⇨ Finder ⇨ Export Site (Mac)

2. In the Export Site Options dialog box that appears, as shown in Figure 27-14 (unless you told it not to in Preferences), make any final export choices. Then click Export. Figure 27-15 shows the results of an export.

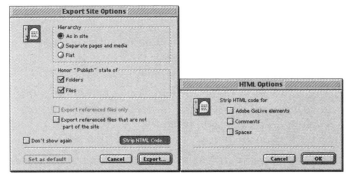

Figure 27-14: The Export Options dialog box

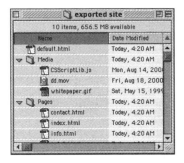

Figure 27-15: The result of an export where "Separate pages and media" is the hierarchy option selected

3. In the Save dialog box that appears, choose a location for your exported site, and then click Save. You don't have to create a folder in which to house your new export. GoLive creates one for you.

   There's a lapse of time as GoLive sorts and prepares the files, and then a progress bar to show it's working. When finished, a dialog box tells you the export was successful and reports the number of unreferenced files that were exported. (Files not referenced have no function on the Web, so take that as a warning that something may be unreachable when you're counting on it.)

4. Choose to see the details of the export by clicking Details or click OK to finish up.

   If you choose not to see the results, you're finished. If you click Details, an untitled GoLive page opens up, reporting what it found and did. Meanwhile, the site is already waiting on your hard drive. You can save the Details, or close and lose them. You are not asked if you'd like to save the Detail.html page when you close it.

If you'd like to upload the contents of the export folder to the Web and take the site live, use the FTP Browser. Just be sure to open the enclosing folder, and move everything but that folder up to the server.

✦   ✦   ✦

Using GoLive's Advanced Site-Planning Tools

P A R T

VII

◆   ◆   ◆   ◆

In This Part

Chapter 28
Updating Your Site

Chapter 29
Using the Site
Designer

Chapter 30
Authoring with
WebDAV

◆   ◆   ◆   ◆

A site is not very lively if you can't easily make changes to it after it's live. GoLive makes updating a cinch. I show you how to do it right here. After you get all the basics of site design down, and know the power of GoLive, you may want to become part of a design team — perhaps a team that presents design ideas to clients, or an international design team with codesigners all over the world. Powerful high-end professional design features are the subject of this part, too.

Updating Your Site

So . . . you've completed your site and uploaded it. Your site is now live. As you read this, people around the world can be visiting your site. All is good in your Web world. But time, information, and life don't stand still—and you don't want your site to either. One of the best powers of GoLive is the ease with which you can edit or add to your site. Editing can be as simple as double-clicking any of your pages, adding a few words, clicking the server connect button, and dragging the newly edited page over to the server. Or, you can add an entire section to your site, new navbar and all—but it's still point-and-shoot, drag-and-drop easy!

Fortunately, the editing process is no different from the initial page creation and GoLive easily accommodates tasks such as edits, added links, page or folder renaming, image changes, and so on. Thanks to Components, it's even easy to add new pages—and have them listed in the navigation bar. Then, life after edit is a simple upload, not any harder than the initial upload.

Editing Existing Pages

No matter how many times you read and reread your pages as you prepare them for the Web, as soon as you (or your client) live with them for a while, someone will surely want some changes. Whether it's a word here and there, an image change, or some other modification, the editing process is no different from the original page design process.

Uploading your site copied your pages to the Web server, leaving your local files intact within your Files tab—as they were, ready and willing to be worked on again any time. As you continue to work on your site, the uploaded copy remains intact, being viewed by the public. Within your Files tab, you can make all the changes your heart desires. Then, when you're happy with the changes, you can upload the new changes.

To edit an existing page, simply double-click the page in your Files tab and continue to design it just like you did before you uploaded the page.

Avoiding accidental publishing

If you are working on a page, or are editing several pages at once, there's a trick to help you avoid accidentally uploading pages as you're working on them. You can set the page's Publish status so GoLive won't even consider uploading the page.

In the Files tab, select the page about to be edited, and then choose Never from the Publish pop-up menu of the File Inspector, as shown in Figure 28-1. When the edit is complete, change the Publish state back to If referenced.

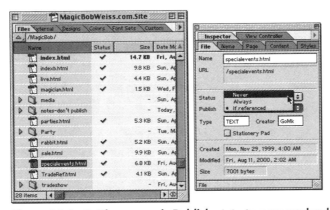

Figure 28-1: Setting a page's Publish state to never upload so it won't get caught up in an incremental or changed-pages upload

This Publish feature works in conjunction with the Upload Options dialog box that appears when you ask GoLive to do an Incremental Upload or to Upload Modified Items. When you let GoLive honor the Publish status of your files, the software doesn't even consider uploading your page(s) in progress. (It's a good idea to make this a habit anyway.)

Cross-Reference To learn more about the Publish feature, see Chapter 6, or see "Uploading Your Site for the First Time" in Chapter 27.

If you're just making a few quick changes to one or two pages and won't lose track of what you're changing and what you need to upload, this only adds extra steps that you needn't bother with.

Keeping a safe copy

Having a version of your site living on a Web server out in the real world is something of an edge — an extra backup. If, as you're editing your page, you do something that is somehow irreversible, such as an incorrect Search and Replace, you can always download the good version from the server back down to your Files tab, and then work from that good copy again. (But that doesn't mean you should stop backing up your work.)

However, before you begin any intricate changes on a page, you may want to take precautions by duplicating your page first.

To duplicate a page, do either of the following:

✦ Select the page in the Files tab, and then choose Edit ➪ Duplicate.

✦ Point to the file in the Files tab as you Control-click (Mac) or right-click (Windows) and chose Duplicate from the contextual menu.

The duplicate copy is automatically named with a 1 appended to the end of the name. Subsequent duplicates are appended with a 2, 3, and so on.

Keep the duplicate as the safe copy, and then make your changes to the original. Life is easy if your changes go well. But if they *don't*? If you mess up the original beyond use and want to revert back? The answer lies in the In & Out Links palette.

To revert to your original situation, links and all, select the original (now messed up) page and open the In & Out Links palette. Drag the Point and Shoot button from the original page over the duplicate page within the Files tab. The duplicate, although still named as a duplicate, has the exact functionality of the original page. You can then delete the ruined original, make a new duplicate, and try your changes again.

Note   Although *almost* identical, a duplicated page contains the same contents within the page, but a quick look at the In & Out Links palette reveals that no links connect to a duplicate. Because links into a page follow a page, not its name, changing a duplicate page's name to that of the original page doesn't connect the incoming links.

Don't forget that while you're editing the original page, you can set its Publish state to Never Publish, per the preceding tip section. Also set the duplicate to not publish. That way, if it ends up replacing the original, you won't publish it inadvertently either.

When your changes are complete, you upload the edited page once more. Because it has the same name as the page already on the server, it replaces the version on the server. See "Sending Your Changes to the Web" later in this chapter to learn about the ways you can upload your edited pages.

Renaming items within your published site

When you rename a page within your site, all files that interact with it are affected and need to be updated accordingly. GoLive closely tracks all links and asks permission to update all related files accordingly. This doesn't change after you upload your site; files and folders within the Files tab are still updated automatically when you change a file or folder name that involves them.

Now that these items are already on the server, that item and all related pages that are updated need to be uploaded to the Web server again. Not a problem. GoLive helps you take care of that with its Incremental Upload or Upload Modified pages command. Your changes hit the server running and can be on their way to someone's monitor in moments.

At the server, though, the newly renamed item isn't really renamed. The server doesn't know you changed the name of an existing item. It just sees a new item. (You and GoLive know it's the same file, with the same contents, links, and all. But the server doesn't know that.) The newly renamed file takes its rightful place within your site, performing as called up. Meanwhile, the original file sits there, keeping its old name and never being called for, because all references to the old name were updated. Because the server has no way of knowing that your site doesn't need the file, the file remains intact. You can leave it, or you can delete it; either way there's no harm. To learn how to delete a file, see "Deleting Items from Your Server" later in this chapter.

 Tip You can use the Incremental Upload to ensure that all necessary files are on the server — and that you didn't delete a file that's actually in use. If a file in use in your site is not found on the server, GoLive sees that it needs to be uploaded.

Renaming files that are already on the Web server is another story. See "Renaming Files or Folders on the Server" later in this chapter for details.

Editing a file directly on the Web server

You can actually edit a file as it's live on the server. This is possible within both GoLive File Transfer Protocol (FTP) clients: the FTP tab of the Site Window and the FTP Browser window.

What happens if you're editing a file when a visitor comes to your site? The file you've opened to work on remains intact on your site. As you work or view the file, it's still available to visitors.

You can use the following method to edit any page that GoLive can open: HTML files, external Cascading Style Sheets, external JavaScript files, and QuickTime movies. If you double-click a file of a type that GoLive cannot open, the Save dialog box appears. Here are the steps to edit a page:

1. Double-click the file.

The status message reports that GoLive is downloading the file. Along with the download of the page you double-clicked, any files on the page also download. If the file happens to be a page that contains six graphics, the status message says downloading seven times.

The page opens on your screen. As a reminder that you are working on a file that will be returned to the server as you save, the file name is appended with FTP//, as shown in Figure 28-2

Figure 28-2: A page on the server, opened from the FTP tab to be viewed or edited (the page is identical when opened via the FTP Browser)

2. Edit your page.

You can only alter text or work in source or outline views when editing an HTML file that's called on FTP.

In the case of the FTP Browser window, the drag-and-drop feature of the Site Window and Objects palette are not available, nor is Point and Shoot. With a page opened from within the FTP tab of the Site Window you can actually use features such as Point and Shoot but the references to the items you link to or add to your page are not written properly and won't function.

3. Save your changes.

Saving the page automatically opens the connection to the server, and puts the changed page up. As this happens two Save File to Server dialog boxes appear: first the Connecting progress bar, and then the Uploading file progress bar. That's it. Your changes are now live on the Web.

4. Close the file.

Note
You can also just close the file without doing the save. Per standard computer protocol, you're asked if you'd like to save the page. If you want to keep the changes and have them appear on the server, click OK. You also have the option to cancel the changes. If you are not ready for the new page to go live, cancel the save, and then choose Save As, saving the page to either the server (with a new name) or to your hard drive. You can then rename it and/or upload it later.

If you make a change on your site using either FTP window, GoLive recognizes the time of the change within the Site Window FTP. Thus, if you make changes to a file via the FTP Browser, the Site Window FTP tab accurately reports the latest dates. However, the Incremental Upload feature of the Site Window's FTP tab does not recognize that the file on the server is newer and will still want to upload the file that's on your hard drive in the Site Window's File tab.

 Note When you select a page in either browser window and view the Inspector, it provides FTP server access privilege settings. But when you have a page open via FTP, the Inspector provides the same interface as when you have the page open from within the Files tab.

Adding New Pages to Your Site

You add a new page after upload the same way as before. And, as before, where you add it depends on your site's file structure. You can add a page directly into the Files tab (which is the Root level of the site) or into a folder within the tab, or you can make a new folder and place new pages into the new folder.

Don't forget to link your new pages to your existing pages. Otherwise, your visitors won't be able to get to them. As you link the new page, pages, or section into your existing pages, GoLive asks you for permission to update all pages involved—just like before you uploaded your site. Keep the following two points in mind:

✦ If you have a small site you probably have links to every page listed within your navigation bar. If so, you may want to add links to the new pages into that navbar. If you're using a Component, this is easy to do.

✦ If you have a small site your main navigation may consist of links to each main area of the site. In this case, if you're adding a new main area, you need to add a link to the main page of that new area. Then, if you have a navbar that connects all of the pages within that area, you need to add a link to each new page within that area. Again, a Component makes that easy and makes adding or removing pages within the area later easy too.

If you plan on doing any type of upload to the Web server before these new pages are complete, set these pages to Publish—Never in the File Inspector as you add them to your Files tab. When it's time to upload them, select all of the new pages within the Files tab and change the Publish setting to Publish—If Referenced. That adds them to the collective uploading process.

When it comes time to upload the new pages, you may be taken aback by the number of pages GoLive recommends for upload. Remember, you don't only have to upload your new pages. You also have to re-upload all of the pages affected in any way by the addition of the new pages.

The new upload includes all pages that link to the new pages. If you're using a Component to provide your page links, every page that contains the Component is altered. Because it's so easy to change a link within a Component, it's easy to forget that the single Component affects many pages.

You also need to upload any new files used on the new pages. You may only be adding one new page to your site but that page may have five graphics and a file, sound effect, or movie that downloads when a link is clicked. In that case you have those five or more files to upload.

There will eventually be a time when, after creating a new page, you are so excited to get it up on the Web, and you drag the page to the server. You then open your browser and point it to your site to see how your new page looks live on the Web — and a puzzled look comes across your face as you wonder why all the images are broken. It'll take a moment before you realize that you forgot about dragging the page's images up to the server! After the palm of your hand comes down from your forehead, you'll laugh at yourself for forgetting what you *know so well*.

Deleting Items from Your Site

Before you ever upload your site, if you delete an item from the Files tab of your site, the item is no longer a part of the site. After you copy your site files to the server though, a copy of that item resides on the server regardless of what you do to its counterpart in the Files tab.

To delete a page, pages, or other files from your site, delete them as usual from within the Files tab. The repercussions of deleting a file from the Files tab after your site is live are no different than before.

Consider referring files

To check if a file is referred to by other links, select the file in the Files tab and view it in the In & Out Links palette to see where the file is used and whether it will be missed. If so, those links will break. Perhaps you're also deleting the pages that refer to it. If not, be sure to break the referring link. (To do so, select the complete text or the image, turn to the Links tab of the Inspector, and click the Remove Link button.)

Is the item to be deleted used on any page? (These would also include the incoming links.) If so, a generic placeholder appears in its place on that page. You need to remove the placeholder from the page.

The links to the right of the item to be deleted are not affected by the deletion. Some items may become unnecessary though, if they're not used elsewhere. You can discover whether the file in question is used elsewhere by clicking the file's icon within the In & Out Links palette. That file becomes the palette's focus and if it has no links coming in on the left, it is not used anywhere else. (It won't have links to the right because only pages can have items on them; you're viewing an item.)

After you delete the file, Rescan the site (Site ➪ Rescan *yoursitenamehere*) to check for missing files. Open the right side of the Site Window and select the Errors tab to see if any missing files are reported—and whether your newly deleted file is one of them. If it is, the file was still in use and, if missed, will cause errors. Again, the In & Out Links palette holds the secrets; select the Missing file icon and view it in the In & Out Links palette to learn where the file is missed. Then make the necessary corrections to your site to avoid errors.

Unnecessary strays

After you delete an item from your Files tab, that item is no longer used within your site and is no longer uploaded to your Web server. But . . . the server doesn't know that. The copy already on the server continues to reside there—and will remain there until you remove it.

The Customizable Upload Button

As you get used to doing uploads and discover the function you tend to use most, you can make that upload available on your toolbar. Or, more accurately, you can swap out the default upload button, Incremental Upload, for either of the other three upload commands—Upload Modified Items, Upload Selection, or Upload All. Click the Incremental Upload button, but hold your mouse button down until a small menu pops up, and then make your choice from that menu. The command that's checked when you release the mouse is the command that the button affects when quickly clicked, as you see here:

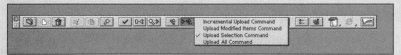

The Upload button currently set to upload selected files when clicked

If your favorite upload method is not Incremental Upload, you can set the button to Upload Modified Items, Upload Selection, or Upload All of the files in your Files tab. Whichever command you choose, the first upload step displays your upload options unless you've turned off that feature.

In this book I pretend that you have not discovered this feature or have not changed its command from Incremental Upload.

It's perfectly all right to leave the unused item on the server. It's simply not a part of the live site. You may wish to delete it though, so you can more clearly view your local files and live file side by side in the Site Window and notice the state of your site. (I'd delete it.) Deleting a file or folder from the Web server without removing the file from use on your site is another story. To learn how to delete a file or folder from your server, see "Deleting Items from Your Server" later in this chapter.

Sending Your Changes to the Web

Just as you have several ways to upload your site in the first place, you have several ways to update the files on your Web server. In fact, they're the same exact methods. So why have I separated the directions? Because you have more to consider when updating the files on your server and I want to make sure you're aware of them. For example, once you upload a changed page to the server, you replace the page that's currently being served — and you may not want to do that if that changed page is still a work in progress.

Updating your site via the Site Window

You can have GoLive automatically send your new or changed pages and files to your server in either of the following two ways:

✦ Incremental Upload

✦ Upload Modified items

Caution   If both the file in your Site Window and the file on the server have changed, GoLive has no way of knowing which file you really want to keep as live. Don't risk this confusion. If you know you've updated a file via the FTP Browser window, and then made even more changes in the Files tab, drag that page to the server by hand.

Incremental Upload

The Incremental Upload tells GoLive to look at each file within your site, note the date and time each file was last modified, and then compare those dates to the last modification date of each file in your Files tab. Then, determining which copy of each file is newer, it recommends a file be uploaded (if newer) or not uploaded if it's older.

Caution   GoLive is truly good at recognizing modification dates for alterations done directly on the server, or for files uploaded to the server in any other manner than via the Site Window. However, other factors affect the files it finds to upload. For one, the clock on the server can be different from your computer's clock so your local files or the ones on the server may not have accurate modification dates. Also, the various upload options take precedence over the dates.

To upload new and altered files, follow these steps:

1. Click the FTP Server Connect/Disconnect button on the toolbar. Alternately, you can choose Site ⇨ FTP Server ⇨ Connect, or choose FTP Server ⇨ Connect from the contextual menu.

   The right side of the Site Window opens to the FTP tab as it connects, gets the file list, and then displays the files that are on your Web server. The status area reports the number of items listed.

2. Click Incremental Upload.

   A progress dialog box reports that GoLive is searching for newer files. If none are found it reports that no newer local files exist.

3. If you kept the preference to show the Upload Options dialog box, it appears just like when you performed the original upload. Review the options available, make any changes, and then click OK.

4. In the Upload site dialog box that opens (unless you've told it not to in Preferences), review the list of the files GoLive recommends to upload, based on your Upload Options. Uncheck the Transfer checkmark for any file you're not ready to upload yet. Click OK.

To avoid the error of having an unfinished page replace a live page on your Web server when you are editing a file, select the file in the Files tab, set the Publish pop-up to Never, and then make sure that the Upload Options dialog box tells the Incremental Upload to respect the Publish options. Doing this can save you a lot of embarrassment.

The Uploading Files dialog box reports the file transfer as the FTP tab's status area reports that the files are uploading. Next, modification dates are synchronized. The new files then appear in the FTP tab.

Tip   If, for some reason, you experience a crash during an Incremental or Modified-items upload, modification dates may not be noted by GoLive. If this happens, some of your files may not have made it to the server and the dates may become confused. In this case, you can select the files that need uploading and drag them to the FTP tab yourself.

Upload Modified items

The Upload Modified items feature doesn't look at the dates of file changes on the FTP Browser window. This feature simply tracks which files are uploaded each time you upload. When you call it up, it notes whether you've saved any changes to the file via the Files tab of the Site Window since the last Site Window FTP and recommends a file for upload if it has been changed since then.

GoLive doesn't actually *always* publish every file you've modified. You may not want one or two to upload yet. If you've set your files up with Publish states and choose the Honor Publish states option, GoLive skips files set to not publish and publishes those set to always publish.

To upload files modified since your last upload, follow these steps:

1. Click the FTP Server Connect/Disconnect button on the toolbar. (Or choose Site ➪ FTP Server ➪ Connect from the main menu or contextual menu.)

   The right side of the Site Window opens to the FTP tab as it connects, gets the file list, and then displays the files that are on your Web server. The status area reports the number of items listed.

2. Do one of the following:

   • Choose Site ➪ FTP Server ➪ Upload Modified Items.

   • Point anywhere within the Files tab of the Site Window and choose FTP Server ➪ Upload Modified Items from the contextual menu.

3. The Upload Options dialog box appears just like when you did the original upload. Review the options available, make any changes, and then click OK. (Unless you turned off the preference for it, that is.)

4. In the Upload site dialog box that appears next, review the list of the files GoLive recommends uploading, based on your Upload Options. (Again, this appears unless you've told it not to in Preferences.) Uncheck the checkmark for any file you'd rather not upload. Click OK.

The Uploading Files dialog box reports the file transfer as the FTP tab's status area reports that the files are uploading, and then tells you it is synchronizing the modification dates. The new files then appear in the FTP tab.

Uploading all files

You can tell GoLive to upload all of your files, regardless of any dates modified. The Publish state you set up in each file's File Inspector is still honored if you tell GoLive to honor it during the upload. Follow these steps to upload all of your files:

1. While connected to the Web server, choose Site ➪ FTP Server ➪ Upload All from the main menu or contextual menu.

2. Depending on the options you've set, you see the Upload Options dialog box. If so, make your choices, and then click OK.

3. Again, you see the Upload site dialog box (unless you've turned this option off). This time it should list all of your files, except any that may be excluded due to Publish states set for each file or folder. Uncheck the checkmark for any file you're not ready to upload.

As the upload proceeds, a progress window lists each file as it is uploaded. GoLive then tells you it's synchronizing the file modification dates. The status message in the FTP tab keeps you informed too. Your newly uploaded files then appear in the FTP tab of the Site Window.

Uploading selected files

You have two ways to upload your own custom selection of files. You can select them and use the Upload Selection command, or you can drag the files to the server.

Whichever way you do this, don't forget about the files that comprise the page you're uploading. Those files need to be moved too. You also need to be sure you move them into the parallel position on the server, into the folder of the same name as where they are in the Files tab.

Uploading a selection via the FTP tab

Follow these steps to upload a selection using the FTP tab:

1. Connect to the Web server if you are not already connected.

   To connect, click the FTP Server Connect/Disconnect button on the toolbar. (Or choose Site ➪ FTP Server ➪ Connect from the main menu or contextual menu.)

2. In the Files tab, select the files you wish to upload.

3. Choose your upload activity in one of the following ways:

   • Choose Site ➪ FTP Server ➪ Upload Selection from the main menu.

   • Point to any selected file in the Files tab and choose Site ➪ FTP Server ➪ Upload Selection from the contextual menu.

4. Depending on the options you've set, you see the Upload Options dialog box. If so, make your choices, and then click OK.

5. If your option is set to show the list of files to upload, you see the Upload site dialog box. This time it lists only the files you selected in Step 1. Uncheck the checkmark for any file you're not ready to upload yet, and then click OK.

Note   If, in Upload Options, you told GoLive to honor the Publish state of files and any of the files you selected for upload are therefore disqualified from upload, those files will not upload. If this disqualifies all selected files, you may hear your computer working as GoLive processes, but nothing more happens as a result of this command.

The upload progress dialog box appears to show you what's happening (uploads and date synchronization), and then the FTP tab refreshes and the newly uploaded files and/or folders appear on the server.

Manually carrying files to the Web server

If you've changed one page and want to get it up to the server quickly you can hand carry that page all the way through cyberspace yourself. Just grab the page within the Files tab and drop it into the FTP tab, as in Figure 28-3. The uploading files dialog box flashes for a moment as your file finds its way, the synchronizing modification dates message, and then your changes await the world.

Figure 28-3: Dragging two pages and the file used on one page up to the server

Caution

While both methods here get your page to the server, they don't account for any files that are on the page. You have to remember to upload your graphics, sounds, and so on, too. You also have to remember to put them in the folder location parallel to their location in the Files tab so they can be found.

You can even carry a Web page to the server while it's open and being worked on! To do this, drag the Page icon at the upper-left corner of the page to the FTP tab of the Site Window. You have to be connected to the Web server, of course. The upload dialog box appears for a moment, the synchronizing modification dates message, and then your page appears on the server.

This option offers a unique advantage. If you do not save right before uploading the page, the uploaded version is the way the page looked when *last* saved. This means that if you begin working on the page and then realize you wanted to upload it before editing it, you do not have to lose your work by saving without changes and losing even the History file. Just drag the page's icon to the FTP tab and GoLive uploads the page exactly as it looked when you last saved it. You can then keep on working, saving when you like the way the page looks.

If you have *never* saved the page, you cannot drag the Page icon and you cannot upload page.

Updating files via the FTP browser

You can use the FTP Browser to send new or edited pages to the Web server. If you're already working within the Site Window, it doesn't make sense to open this FTP client and use it to upload new pages or files. If you've just completed a page or file edit, chances are good that you did the edit within the site's Site Window so you'd use the FTP tab to get that edit online.

The process for sending pages to your Web server after the initial site upload is no different than it is during the initial upload. Just drag the page into the FTP Browser window. Keep the following points in mind:

✦ You can drag files from the Files tab of your Site Window.

✦ You can drag a file from anywhere on your computer.

✦ You can upload files generated by GoLive's Export feature.

If you initially used Export to put the site up and have modified the site, it is safest to do a full export again and then upload the new export result. To do this, create a spare folder within the FTP browser window and move the existing files into that folder for safekeeping as you upload the new files. After you've tested the new upload, you can delete that folder.

To create a new folder into which you can move or place files, simply click the New Folder button on the toolbar. You can then drag files and folders around in the FTP Browser window just like you can in the Site Window. The interface is very similar.

Updating your server's files list

If you are making a lot of changes to the file structure within your site, it can be helpful to be sure you're looking at an accurate view of the site. To do this, use the Update command. When connected to an FTP server, the Update command sends a query back to the server, takes a look at what's there, and refreshes your FTP window. This works the same way in both the Site Window FTP and the independent FTP Browser.

While connected to the server, do one of the following to update the files list:

✦ Choose Site ➪ Update.

✦ Point anywhere within the FTP window, and then Control-click (Mac) or right-click (Windows) and choose Update from the contextual menu.

✦ Click the Update button (checkmark) in the toolbar.

The status area at the bottom left says Getting File List and the newly refreshed view of your FTP server appears.

Transferring Files to Any Site Anytime You're in GoLive

The FTP Browser can be very handy for the quick transfer of any files. For example, you may be busy working in one site when you need to act quickly within another site. Instead of opening that other site's Site Window, grab the FTP Browser window from the File menu. If the settings are entered, you can be at that site in moments.

Perhaps a coworker e-mails you a Portable Document Format (PDF) file that's meant to replace a PDF of the same name that's already in place. Or you have a link that downloads a compressed file, such as a software demo, and your client has updated the demo. Or someone else may be actively designing a site and just needs to toss a file up to the server for the coworker to download into the active Site Window and work with. Again, the new file has the same name so when you replace the existing file, all links to it still function.

Updating your Web site if you used export

If you use the Export command to prepare your site for the Web, you can use the FTP Browser window to upload the site. You can do this whether you used it on your initial upload or not.

The bottom line with Export is that if you're using it to generate your site, you should do a full new export each time you change the site and want to send the changes to the server. Trying to export sections of the site can lead to complications. It's best to be certain that all pages in the site are the newest versions. Do a new Export the same way you did the first, and then upload the new export in its entirety.

Renaming files or folders on the server

It's very easy to change the name of any file or folder already on the Web server, whether you're viewing the server's files within the FTP tab of the Site Window or the FTP Browser window. However, changing the name of a file or folder in use within the site affects all paths to that file or folder. You can rename files and folders within GoLive's File's tab because of GoLive's brilliant updating technique. But on the server, the new name won't be reflected within the other files so such a change will break the site. Keep Web server renaming to that of empty directories only.

To rename a file or folder that's on the server, do either of the following:

✦ Select its name, and then type or edit the name.

✦ Select the file, and then rename it in the Inspector.

The new name is reflected in the FTP window immediately. The status message reports the renaming, and then reverts to displaying Connected.

Deleting items from your server

Deleting a file from the server is the same within the FTP tab as in the FTP Browser. You can delete a file, files, folder, folders, or any combination of the two at the same time. Just be careful not to delete items that are called for within your site or you'll have broken links or missing images, sounds, downloads, and such. If you delete a file that is the destination of another link within your site, your visitors will see a dead link (404-file not found) error.

Note If you delete files that are called for within your site you *will* have broken links — but an Incremental Update will notice those files missing and recommend uploading them again. (The Update Modified items feature won't, unless you happen to have modified the local version of that missing item.)

To delete a file from the server, do one of the following:

✦ Select the items you wish to delete, and then click the Delete Selected Item (trash can) icon in the toolbar.

✦ Point to the file or folder you wish to delete, and then Control-click (Mac) or right-click (Windows) and choose Clear from the contextual menu. To remove several at once, select the items you wish to delete, and then call up the contextual menu and choose Clear.

✦ Drag the items you wish to delete out of the FTP Browser window and into your computer's Trash/Recycle bin.

An alert dialog box asks if you're sure you want to delete the files. Click OK. The status area at the bottom left informs you that the files are being deleted. The status message then changes to simply say Connected again and the files no longer appear in the Browser window.

Unlike deleting files from within the Files tab of the Site Window, files you delete from the server are really removed. No equivalent of a trash site exists on a server. You'd need access to the computer serving your site in order to possibly retrieve your deleted file.

Downloading Files from Your Server

There may be times when you want to grab a file that's on your server (and is part of your site) and bring it down to your hard drive to work with.

One such case may be if you, your client, or coworker modified a page directly on the server via the FTP Browser window. Or perhaps one of you had another file to add to the site and used another FTP client to place the file on the Web server so you can pick it up later and add it to the site. Or, maybe you've, well . . . messed up your local file on your hard drive and you want to bring the currently live page back to your Files tab so you can work from that copy.

In either case, it's easy to transfer files from the Web server to your Files tab or hard drive. It's actually the same process in reverse. You have the same options for downloading as for uploading. In case you're wondering, how you download a file is not at all tied to how you uploaded it in the first place.

Caution   Downloading a page to the folder that contains the same page name replaces the copy you already have in your Files tab.

Incremental downloads

If you've done a bit of editing via the FTP Browser window, or a coworker or client has made additions to the site, those changed or new pages are on the Web server, but you don't have them in your Files tab to work with. You can easily download those pages or files to your own Files tab by using the Incremental Download feature.

To download all new or changed pages from a site's Web server, follow these steps:

1. Click the FTP Server Connect/Disconnect button on the toolbar. Alternately, you can choose Site ⇨ FTP Server ⇨ Connect, or choose FTP Server ⇨ Connect from the contextual menu.

2. Click the Incremental Download button on the toolbar, or choose Site ⇨ FTP Server ⇨ Incremental Download.

3. Review the list of recommended files in the Download site dialog box (Figure 28-4). Uncheck any that you don't wish to copy down to your Files tab, and then click OK.

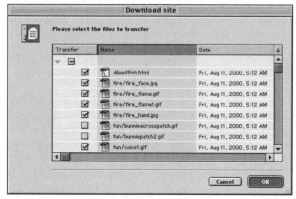

Figure 28-4: The Download site dialog box presents the list of files about to be downloaded. Two have been unchecked so they will not be transferred to the Files tab.

Progress dialog boxes keep you informed about what's happening, and then your files appear in the Files tab.

4. When the transfer is complete, depending on your Internet connectivity, you may want to disconnect from the server. To do so you can click the FTP Server Connect/Disconnect button on the toolbar, choose Site ⇨ Disconnect, or choose Disconnect from the contextual menu within the FTP tab.

Downloading selected pages using the Site Window FTP

If you're certain of the page or pages you want to download, you can grab and pull them down by dragging them over.

Caution   Bear in mind that when you download a file from the FTP tab to the Files tab, the downloaded file replaces the file on your hard drive.

Follow these steps to download a page or pages from your site:

1. Click the FTP Server Connect/Disconnect button on the toolbar. Alternately, you can choose Site ⇨ FTP Server ⇨ Connect, or choose FTP Server ⇨ Connect from the contextual menu.

2. Drag the desired file from the FTP tab to wherever you want it, as follows:

   • You can drag it to your Files tab. Doing so replaces the existing version of that file with the version that's on the server.

   • You can create a new folder in the Files tab, and then drag it into that folder. That places the version that's on the server into the new folder. This way you don't lose the version that's already in your Files tab.

   • You can drag the file to your desktop or to any folder on your hard drive. This copies the file to that location.

Another way to download selected items is to select the item in the FTP tab, and then choose Site ⇨ FTP Server ⇨ Download Selection. The selected files appear in your Files tab without further ado. The limitation of this command is that it only downloads your files to the main level of your site. Even if you have the Files tab open to a subfolder, the files land in the main folder (Root level).

Downloading pages using the FTP browser window

When you download a file, you're making a copy of the file so it's always safe to download any page. The original file remains intact on the server. Just be sure to mark or file the copy so you know what it is and why you have it.

To download a file via the FTP Browser window, simply drag the file to the desired destination on your hard drive.

Note   You don't necessarily need to download a file to edit it. See the previous "Editing a file directly on the Web server" section for more information.

✦   ✦   ✦

Using the Site Designer

C H A P T E R

29

Whether you've already got a site of any size or are just about to embark on a brand-new site, you'll find the site-design features in GoLive handy. You can use the Site Designer to plan the structure of your site, creating multiple plans and then accepting your favorite. You can sit down with clients or associates and move pages and entire branches around within any of your plans until the site suits everyone (or as many as possible). Then you can submit the design, which lets GoLive turn your plan into pages so you can get to work on the contents. And if someone rethinks the decision and prefers another plan (does that happen?), you can recall the first one and submit the new plan.

If you've already begun your site, you can still benefit from the Site Designer. In fact, Adobe created it with you in mind. Sites are bound to grow, and this makes it easy to see your existing site's structure, figure out where the new section best fits, and then plan the new section and incorporate it.

Before I get into how to use the Site Designer to plan a site from scratch, I'll show you how to use Navigation view to view your existing site. With understanding of site structure in mind, it should be easier to think in terms of a new site.

Viewing Your Site's Structure

One benefit of viewing your site in Navigation view is that you can get a good feel for your site's structure. Another is that you can add to your site in a logical, orderly manner. As your site grows, it gets harder and harder to visualize its structure — to recall exactly which pages link directly from the home page, which sections those pages represent, and how well the pages continue to represent the sections of your site. Do the pages that link to your sections really belong there? When you use Navigation view to review your site and add your new pages, you get a chance to see and to think about it.

The Design menu provides two windows that work together, each providing a different view of your site. The Navigation Hierarchy mode shows you how the pages in your site are intended to relate to one another. That is, it shows you which pages are accessed from other pages as substructures of those pages. It can also show you all links that are pending. Link Hierarchy mode is where you go to see how your pages physically link to one another.

Introducing Navigation view

In Navigation Hierarchy mode, you can add pages to your site, defining those pages' pending links to their related pages. Navigation view also enables you to drag your files around so you can visualize the structure. Pages are live here, so you can even double-click the necessary page(s) immediately and create the links while it's fresh in your mind. You can also delete pages in Navigation Hierarchy mode. Both of these views have a companion window called the Site Navigator (Window ➪ Site Navigator).

You can do a lot to customize the look of your files within these views, and even determine which files you see there. As always, it's the View Controller that provides this control. You can open it any time by choosing Window ➪ View Controller.

Note GoLive 4 contained a Site tab in the Site Window. In GoLive 5 the functionality of that Site tab has been made clearer and moved to its own free-floating window. It joins other design tools under a new Design menu. Navigational links and actual links each have a dedicated view now. Of course, you can drag the Navigation or Links tabs into the main Site Window if you prefer to keep all site views in the same window.

GoLive's Navigation view enables you to see your site's structure in a comfortable, familiar, organizational-chart layout. This view starts with the home page at the top because that's the first page your visitors see. From there, all pages that viewers can get to from the home page appear below it, and then any pages that link from those subpages appear beneath their respective pages.

To view your site's hierarchy, choose Design ➪ Navigation View. This opens the main pane of the Navigation view, as shown in Figure 29-1.

If you have just started a blank site, only your automatically generated home page (index.html) appears because no other pages exist in your site yet. If your site is already in progress, all of your pages should be there. You may see a plus sign to let you know more pages exist. If so, click the plus sign to reveal the pages.

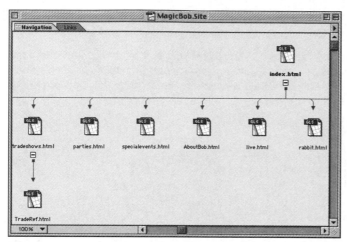

Figure 29-1: A site as seen in Navigation view. It contains several pages, noting the relationships between the pages.

Note

If you see only one icon with no plus sign, but you know your imported site is comprised of one or more pages linked from the home page, GoLive hasn't recognized your links. In that case, choose Design ⇨ Rebuild Hierarchy. This instructs GoLive to read all of your existing links, examine the file structure, and map them into a top-down conceptual view of your site. (Even if you don't have any pages linked to the home page, if you have other pages in your site and choose the option to Use Folder Hierarchy when you use Design ⇨ Rebuild Hierarchy, GoLive builds a conceptual Navigation view.) See the sidebar, "Rebuilding Your Site's Hierarchy."

Understanding Links view

The partner view in the Views window is the Links view. You can open directly to Links view by choosing Design ⇨ Links View, or you can click the Links tab anytime you're in Navigation view (and vice versa). Links view, as you might guess, presents a depiction of your site's actual links. In this view you can see all links leading out of a page as well as all links leading in. If that sounds similar to the In & Out Links palette, that's because it is. However, this Links view is far more reaching. This view displays the site's full hierarchy as it displays links. When you first look at this view and expand it, it can be overwhelming. However, you can easily determine what is shown there and how it looks.

Rebuilding Your Site's Hierarchy

GoLive can generate your site's Navigation view by looking at the organization of the files in your Files tab, the way they link to one another, and any pending links you have specified. When you call up the command, the Build Navigation Hierarchy dialog box you see here enables you to determine which of these links GoLive uses to do this.

The Rebuild Hierarchy dialog box and options

Links tells GoLive to read the actual links you already have and build the structure to show what you really have in place for users to follow and get to.

Folder Hierarchy tells GoLive to read all files in all of your folders and place them all in the main pane. For example, as a quick favor to a friend one day, I developed a few pages for him and put them in a folder of their own within my site to pop it on the Web quickly. This minisite had its own index.html page and a few offshoots, but did not link to my own index page in any way. However, with Folder Hierarchy on, the extra index page was displayed at the second level of my site, as it is linked from my index page. (I was trying to generate a table of contents, and it was very confusing.) By unchecking the Folder Hierarchy option, I enabled GoLive to generate my site structure by reading my links only, from my index page down, ignoring the stuff I have in folders.

Add Pending Links tells GoLive to show you all pages that are not linked to one another. This is not a view of what you want to have pending. It's a view of what you do not already have linked. Even if you have no desire to link two pages together, GoLive shows you the link is pending (which really simply means it does not exist). If you do not check this, no pending links are programmed. But as you drag pages from the Scratch panel into your site, those pending links are recorded.

The view you see in both of these tabs is really just another view of the pages that are in your files tab. When you click a page here, the Inspector becomes the File Inspector, just like when you select a page in the Files tab. When you double-click a page here it opens, too. Renaming a page here renames it just like in the Files tab as well.

In both views, you can hide or show branches of your site map to make viewing easier on large, complex sites, as follows:

✦ Click any plus sign to reveal the pages that link from any page, or the minus sign to collapse revealed pages. When pages are hidden, or collapsed, they appear as icons stacked behind the page to which they link.

✦ Select a page and then click the Unfold All button in the toolbar to expose everything from that page down. (A complementary Fold All button doesn't exist, so use the minus sign.)

You can choose from two orientations when viewing your site, as follows. You can switch orientations using the toolbar or by clicking a radio button in the View Controller.

✦ By default, Navigation view is Wide, that is, from the top down, with *parent* pages on top, *children* below, and *siblings* to each side. (At first wide may seem tall, but as a rule, as your site grows, it becomes wider and wider.) You can have it flow Tall — from left to right if you prefer, so *parents* are to the left of *children* and *siblings* are top and bottom. Just click the Orientation button on the toolbar. Click again to toggle back to top down view.

✦ By default, Links view runs sideways, showing links in on the left and links out on the right, like the In & Out Links palette. Clicking the Orientation button on the toolbar turns this view horizontal so links in come in from the top while links out are below.

Getting around in Site views

As your site gets larger you need an efficient way to navigate through the site's scheme. GoLive provides not one, but two tools for you to choose from: a free-floating palette and a retractable pane directly within the views. Both work the same way in Navigation and Links views. Here's how to use them:

✦ To open the Site Navigator palette, choose Window ⇨ Site Navigator. The Site Navigator opens as a small dockable palette just like the other GoLive palettes.

✦ To open the Panorama pane in the Navigation or Links view window, choose Panorama from the fly-out arrow menu at the top-right corner of the window. The Panorama pane opens to the top of the main pane when you view your pages top to bottom, or at the left of the main pane when you view left to right.

Within each of these miniature views, the red square is your navigation tool, and your cursor is a grabber hand. As you drag the square around, the pages it encompasses move within Navigation or Links views. Figure 29-2 shows the Site Navigator palette working in conjunction with Navigation view.

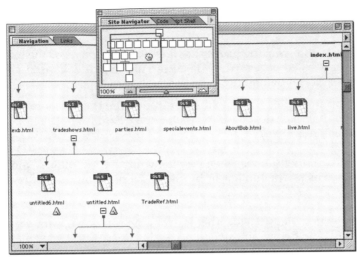

Figure 29-2: Drag the red box in the Site Navigator palette to move around within the Navigation or Links views.

Tip   You can also manipulate your site's items within the Panorama pane.

The one difference between these navigators is that the Site Navigator also enables you to zoom in or out on the Navigation and Links views. Use the buttons to each side of the slider, or slide the slider, to enlarge the page icons and see fewer pages, or reduce the icons and see more. (Coming in close on generic page icons isn't helpful or exciting, but you can turn those generic pages into mini page previews, making it a very handy feature.)

Customizing page icons and labels

GoLive provides a significant amount of customization so you can see your site's overview with a look and feel that works best for you. It can also go a long way toward providing you with a nice-looking presentation for clients or coworkers, if you're building a site for someone besides yourself.

Rather than viewing your pages as small generic icons, you can create a custom presentation that may go a long way to making your life easier. For example, you can set up custom icons that show your clients or team mates exactly what each page looks like and then use the page titles instead of abbreviated names. This makes it easier for people to follow.

The Navigation and Links views windows have extra panes that you can open via the fly-out menu at its upper-right corner. You can set up the view for each pane independently of the others. Just click inside a tab to select it, and then turn to this interface.

To customize Site view's icons and labels, you use the View Controller, which is the window twin to the Inspector. If the Inspector is open, simply click the View Controller tab to access it. Otherwise, choose Window ➪ View Controller. Then turn to the Display tab.

Note   If you throw away the GoLive preferences file to return to the program's default settings, you might still open your Navigation or Links windows and see your pages represented as something other than icons (the default view). This is because this preference is stored within the individual Site Document for each site, not in GoLive's application-wide preferences. Therefore, even if you trash GoLive's preferences, when you open an existing site, you'll see whatever was selected the last time someone worked on that site.

Viewing your structure as an outline

If, for some reason, you prefer not to view your site in a graphical display, as is the default, you can choose an outline list of your files. In Outline view (see Figure 29-3) you don't have the options for custom icons, but you do get to choose which information columns you view.

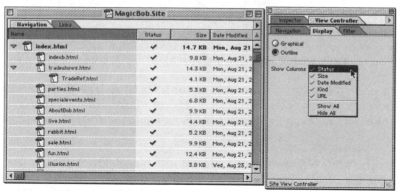

Figure 29-3: Outline view provides an OS-like view of your site's files.

Choosing a View icon

By default, you see your pages depicted with generic GoLive page icons. Instead, you can choose to view your pages as Thumbnails, Frames, or Ovals.

Thumbnails are reduced images of each page, as shown in Figure 29-4. GoLive renders these icons for you on demand, which means that when you change a page, GoLive updates the thumbnail associated with the page and redraws any views (for example, Navigation) that use the thumbnail. These icons don't necessarily capture your entire page, but they do a great job of displaying a miniature view of your page.

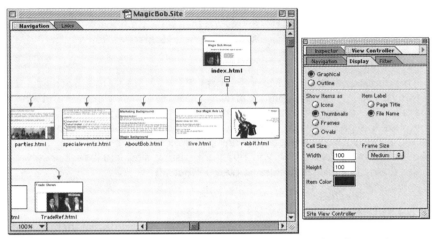

Figure 29-4: The same site shown in each prior figure in this chapter, but now in Thumbnail view

If choosing Thumbnails fails to display reduced images depicting your pages, tell GoLive to create the thumbnail images. Close all open pages and then choose Design ➪ Update Thumbnails. (The Navigation or Links window must be active for this command to be available.) This process can take quite a while, though, so don't do it while you're in any rush. (Take a stretch break while GoLive works for you.)

Frames are generic rectangles, as shown in Figure 29-5. By default they are white with black borders and black text. You can add color in place of the white by using the color option on the Display tab. You can also change their shape by using the size options.

Ovals are generic white circles. You can add color in place of the white by using the color option on the Display tab. You can also change their shape by using the size options. However, Adobe recommends that you do not use Ovals for display in the Navigation or Links view; save them for the Site Designer view, so you can more easily differentiate between task. The Site Design feature is covered under the section "Planning Your Site in the Site Designer" later in this chapter.

Setting labels

By default, the name of your file is the display label, but that name, being short and concise for speed and efficiency on the Internet, is not necessarily helpful to people trying to follow the flow of your site's pages. In addition, if your site is divided into sections and you have each section in a separate folder, and you then use a default home page within each section, your site may be peppered with pages just identified as index.html or default.html. That's not very helpful when it comes to identifying the pages in your site in order to do things like anchor design sections to them.

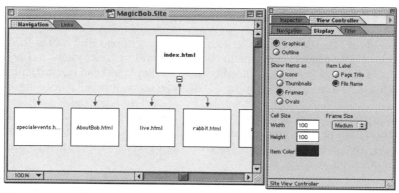

Figure 29-5: The same site using frame icons (set within the Display tab of the View Controller)

Instead, you can choose to display each page's title within the View Controller. The titles are far more descriptive — if you've used them well. (To learn about the importance of page titles, see Chapters 6 and 26.) That said, if many of your pages begin with the same phrase, displaying titles may count against you. Labels truncate to the size of the page's icon, so the name may be cut off before it can tell your viewers anything.

Tip

If the label is truncated, hover over the item. The full name appears in the status area of the window at the bottom-left side of the pane. In Windows, the full page title or file name is also displayed in a Tooltip.

Setting up cell and frame size

Cell size and *Frame size* work somewhat together. You can set the size of your pages when viewing Frames, Thumbnails, or Ovals. The easiest way to choose a size is to select Small, Medium, Large, or Wide from the Frame menu. That way, each shape maintains its default proportions. (If you're more daring, you can enter the desired width and height, in pixels. After you alter these numbers, the Frame menu uses your numbers to set small, medium, large, and wide icons.)

Setting your view's color

You can set the color of the items if they are set to Frames, Thumbnails, or Ovals. The color you select tints the entire icon. This can look nice with Frames or Ovals, but interrupts the true color of your thumbnail page icons. Choose a color the same way you do throughout GoLive; click the color swatch and then locate a color and click it. If that fails to set the color, drag the color onto the color swatch.

Filtering files viewed

The Filter tab of the Site View Controller enables you to choose which files (URLs, Addresses, and Media objects) you see in Navigation and/or Links view. In Navigation view the default settings work well. Filtering the files displayed can be particularly helpful in Links view where the hierarchy of links can go on forever if not simplified.

The choices are very straightforward, as you can see in Figure 29-6. Check a file type to display that file type, and uncheck any file types you don't care to see for the time being. The Toggle Media and Toggle Links buttons simply turn all media or link types off or on.

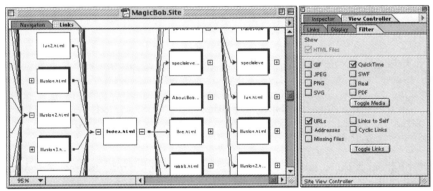

Figure 29-6: The Filter tab of the Site View Controller determines which files you see.

While you view your site in Links view, another filtering interface is available to help you determine what you see. This is the Links tab of the Site View Controller, shown in Figure 29-7. Again, you check and uncheck options to determine what you see.

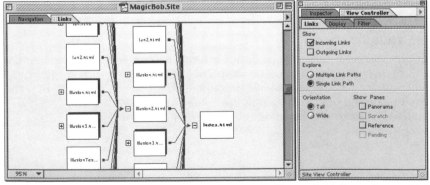

Figure 29-7: The Links tab of the Site View Controller further determines which files you do or don't see.

Using spotlights to focus in on page relationships

While you view your site in Navigation view, GoLive provides a great amount of feedback about the relationships between your pages and files. While you may be inclined to choose one favorite way of looking at your site, you're likely to want to view various relationships. For that reason, the spotlight feature (and various viewing Panes) can be selected not just from the Site View Controller, but from the fly-out menu of the Navigation or Links views window as well.

The spotlight feature enables you to focus your attention on specific sections of your site, based on the relationships between files.

To use a spotlight, follow these steps:

1. Select the file you want to learn about.

2. Choose the desired spotlight from the fly-out menu. (Alternatively, keep the View Controller open and click the desired option's radio button.) You have the following choices:

   • *Family* shows you all files that link into or out of the selected page. (In other words, the page's parents and children.) This "spotlight" is actually a highlight that encompasses the related files, as shown in Figure 29-8. To spotlight another family, just click the page whose family you'd like to see.

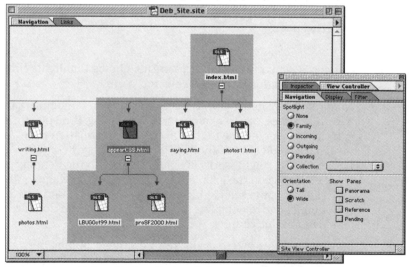

Figure 29-8: Using the Family Spotlight to see all pages that relate to a selected page

- *Incoming* shows you only those files that link directly into the selected page. The page being checked up on appears with a regular darkened selection, and the pages that are part of its family appear with a circular highlight. For example, in Figure 29-9, only one page (appearCSS.html) links into the selected page (LBUGOct99.html). (If you select a page expecting only a page or two to link into it but find a ton of pages highlighted, the pages are probably connected by a navbar.)

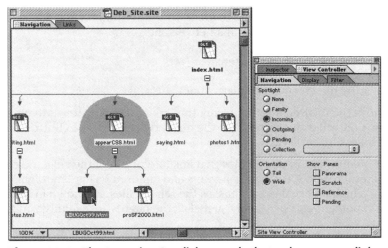

Figure 29-9: The Incoming Spotlight reveals that only one page links into the selected page.

- *Outgoing* is similar to incoming, but this choice highlights those pages that are destinations from the selected page.

- *Pending* shows you the links GoLive expects you to complete that you have not yet created. To demonstrate the linking, it displays arrows pointing from the source page to the anticipated destination page. Another window pane is dedicated to showing you which pages contain pending links. The Pending spotlight works in conjunction with the Pending pane. When you select a page in the main pane, the Pending pane shows all pages that need a link from the selected source page. You can Point and Shoot into the Pending pane to complete links. See "Seeking and Connecting Pending Links" later in this chapter.

- *Collection* enables you to easily see a unique grouping of pages that you specify. First you create the collection. Then later you can use that collective grouping as a spotlight again and again.

  To create a collection: Select one or more files and a spotlight, and then choose Design ➪ Remember Selection. To name the collection so you can recall what it is later on, choose Design ➪ Edit Collections, and then select the collection in the resulting dialog box (see Figure 29-10), enter a name, and click OK.

Figure 29-10: After you create a Collection, name it descriptively so you can recall what it is when you want to use it again.

To use a collection as a spotlight, you must use the Navigation view's View Controller because the specific collection cannot be chosen from the fly-out menu. Choose your desired collection from the Collection pop-up menu and the collection spotlight button automatically becomes selected, saving you a step.

To turn off a Spotlight, return to the fly-out menu (or View Controller) and choose Spotlight None.

Displaying pages and files within filtering panes

Show Panes opens any of the four additional information display panes within the Navigation or Links windows. Each pane enables you to view different files within your site. Panes can also be opened and closed by choosing them from the fly-out menu of the Navigation or Links view windows. (The fly-out menu is more convenient to use, as it requires fewer steps to access.)

Each of the file's panes has its own zoom pop-up menu at its bottom-left corner, so you can adjust the size of the files in each pane independently of the other panes. This way you can choose from quantity or quality, seeing what you need when you need it.

As any file is selected in any of these panes, you can view it in the In & Out Links palette to get the full story on its situation. You can also select a file and delete it by clicking the Trash can icon in the toolbar, as normal. External links cannot be trashed this way, though.

The Scratch pane

The Scratch pane is home to all files in your site that are yet unused. It enables you to see these files while working in Navigation view so you can remember to incorporate them into your site, or see how they may or may not fit. Because Links view is only about actual links, this pane is not available while you are in Links view.

If GoLive has built your Navigation view based on the links in your site, all pages reachable from the home page via links appear in the main pane, while pages that are not accessible from the home page appear in the Scratch pane. So in that case and as a rule, pages not linked appear as scratch. You can view these files by scrolling around within the Scratch pane. Other pages can reside in the Scratch pane too. In fact, using the contextual menu command, Move to Scratch, you can move pages out of the main view and into scratch view, even if they're linked. Scratch is sort of a holding tank for pages until you figure out where they fit in the visual scheme of your site.

Note   The key to understanding the Scratch pane is knowing that the links you create between pages do not define your site's hierarchy. You can have five levels of children and then have a child at level 4 link back to one at level 2. Navigation view shows you a conceptual view of your site's hierarchy, not its actual physical structure. This is why a page can be linked into your site but still be moved to scratch, or be visible in your Navigation view but not be linked in yet.

As you find a place in your site where an unconnected file fits in, you can drag it into place in relation to the existing page. This doesn't actually link that page; it simply marks your intent to link it into your site and helps you visualize where the page fits into the plan. See "Reviewing and Reorganizing Your Site's Structure" later in this chapter.

The Pending pane

As you work, you may want to see which page links are pending for any one particular page. To do so, choose Pending from the fly-out menu at the top-right corner of the Navigation view. This opens the Pending pane in the right side of the window. Then click once on the page that interests you. All pages awaiting links from that page appear in the Pending pane. (Note that the Pending pane shows links that are due to link *from* the selected page.) The pages in the Pending pane are live, so you can Point and Shoot to them, drag them, or double-click them to open them in Layout mode or any other page view. (For more on this pane, see "Seeking and Connecting Pending Links.")

The Reference pane

The Reference pane provides an area in which you can view all files that are referenced from the file you select in the main pane. This is your view to all of the embedded media objects on any selected page. Use the Site View Controller to choose an icon style and size. Supplement it with the pop-up arrow at the bottom-left corner of the pane to adjust the size of the icons you see in this pane.

Seeking and Connecting Pending Links

Recall that the page icons you see in Navigation view are "live" just like the page icons in the Files tab. All the same ways you can create links (by dragging pages from the Files tab onto open pages, or by Pointing and Shooting from one page to another) work here too. But here you have the added benefit of seeing which pages you have not yet linked and which ones GoLive expects you to link. So you can see which page needs a link, see the page it will link to, and actually create the link — a nice little package of functions.

The fastest way to see which pages need links (or which ones GoLive thinks needs links, at least) is to use the Spotlight feature. Just choose Spotlight Pending from the fly-out menu at the top-right corner of the Navigation view page, and GoLive presents you with red arrows that point out each expected link. Each arrow points from the page that is expected to contain the link toward the page expected to be the destination, as shown in Figure 29-11.

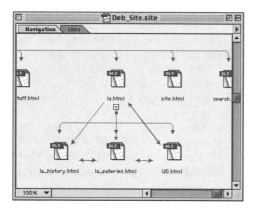

Figure 29-11: With the Pending Links Spotlight on, red arrows show links pending between a page and its children, as well as between the siblings.

The Pending pane provides you with a way to focus on any one page and the links that are pending for just that page. Choose Pending from the fly-out menu at the top-right corner of the Navigation view. This opens the Pending pane in the right side of the window. Then, in the main pane, click once on the page that interests you. All pages awaiting links from that page appear in the Pending pane, as shown in Figure 29-12. (Note that the Pending pane shows links that are due to link *from* the selected page.)

When you see a page that needs links, you can double-click that page from within the Navigation window to open it and create the links as needed. Because the pages that await the link from this page are already in full view within the Pending pane, you can Point and Shoot from the page's Inspector to that link destination right in the Pending pane. As you create physical links between pages, you can see the red pending arrows disappear.

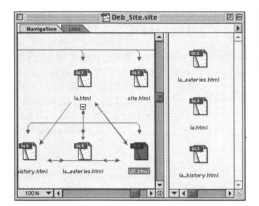

Figure 29-12: When a page is selected in the main pane, the Pending pane, if open, displays any pages that are pending links for that selected page (whether the spotlight is on or off).

Unfortunately, the pending links feature basically assumes links between every page and back. You may link from one page to another, but not want a link in the reverse direction (as is the case with a glossary-type window that uses the Open Window Action). However, GoLive assumes you want that link backward and lists it as pending. As I write this, you have no way to remove an unwanted pending link. (However, the programmers are very responsive, so there may be a way by the time you read this. Check for updates about things like this at www.golive bible.com.)

You have one more way to take note of any links pending for any particular page. That's the good old Inspector — or the Page Inspector, to be more precise. To see if links are pending on any page, or to learn about the links pending from a page, double-click the page to be examined. Click once on the Page icon at the top-left corner of the page (while in Layout view only) and turn your attention to the Inspector, which contains a Pending tab. This tab shows you all pending links from this page, whether still pending or not. Here are some other details:

✦ The Pending column points out that links are pending from the current page to the page listed. As you continue developing the page and you add a link to any of the pages that appear in this list, the page you've linked to remains listed, but the arrow under the Pending column is removed.

✦ The Nav (for Navigation) column contains an arrow that reports the relationship between the current page and the one listed. In other words, Nav reminds you of the direction users will travel on your site map when clicking the link to this listed page. The up arrow indicates a parent, the down arrow a child, the left arrow a previous sibling, and the right arrow a next sibling. These pages can be either resolved or unresolved links. If pages are not immediately related, no Nav arrow appears. For example, in Figure 29-13, the pending link between UG.html and la_history.html was created by the user and is not part of the normal hierarchy, so no arrow appears. The URL column further to the right is another reminder of where the link leads to.

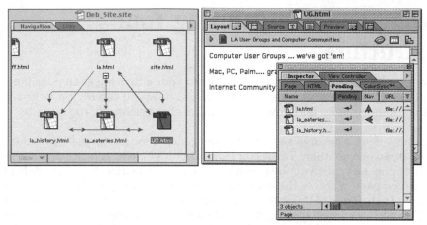

Figure 29-13: When a page is open and the Page Inspector is active, the Pending Tab reports all pending links and all link relationships.

Tip

You can resolve a pending link by creating the link while viewing the Pending tab. Drag the icon of the pending page from the Pending tab into any line of text in the (open) document you wish to link to. GoLive automatically creates a text link for you, with the text in the link being the name of the destination page. The default text is the name of the file. (This is the same idea being linking files in the Files tab by dragging them onto an open page.)

Because you access the Page Inspector from within the open page, you can call it up while you're working within the Files tab too, without first opening the Navigation view window.

You cannot actually create physical links within the Navigation view because GoLive has no way of knowing what element in that page you wish to link from, what the link should look like or say, or where on the page it should be placed. Only you can add that creative input. So there's no way around it; you have to open up a page in order to create the actual link. But GoLive can help make creating the links as easy as possible with the Navigation view (just like it does from any other view). You can use either of the following typical linking methods to create your link:

✦ Point and shoot from the open page or from the page's Inspector to any file anywhere within the Navigation view.

✦ Drag any page within the Navigation view onto another page to create a link.

Reviewing and Reorganizing Your Site's Structure

In Chapter 4, I showed you how to add pages to your site using each possible method, Navigation view included. Here I discuss how you can review your actual links and intended links, and how you can make changes or add to your site.

What exactly does it mean to say that the Navigation view shows you how your site's pages relate to one another? The relationship shows you which pages are accessed from other pages as substructures of those pages. For example, if five pages lead off of your home page, it shows the home page at the top, with it branching out to those five pages. Then, if one of those five pages has three below it, it shows those three under the one from which they connect. When you look at one of those three, you can follow the green arrows to see how users get back to the home page. If one of those three pages had a direct link back to the home page, though, that link would not appear in Navigation view because this view doesn't show you every actual link—just structure.

As you view your site's hierarchy, Navigation view enables you to clean up its organization. For example, upon seeing the pages laid out, you may realize that you have two similar branches that should be placed together as one substructure. In that case, you can move the top page from one of those branches over to the other and visualize the new flow.

Whenever you move pages around in the Navigation view, GoLive automatically updates or generates pending links to show you what you'd need to accomplish this flow in reality. To see this, turn on the pending links spotlight and then move some pages around in the hierarchy.

As you move pages around, you may want to add your own links that GoLive doesn't assume you'll want. You can easily do that by pressing ⌘ (Mac) or Ctrl+ Shift (Windows) as you Point and Shoot from the source page to the target page.

When you first create new pages in your Files tab or move pages into your Site Window, they are not physically linked into your site. Those files appear in the Scratch pane. Working in Navigation view gives you a good view of the pages not yet part of your site's navigation.

As you view your site's structure and view a page in the Scratch pane, you can get a clear idea of where the page fits into the structure and then drag the page from the Scratch pane directly into place by the page to which you would like it to link. Again, GoLive notes the pending links needed to fulfill this reality, and again, you can designate your own pending links.

If the pages in the Scratch pane happen to relate to one another, you can build their substructure within the Scratch pane and then move the entire substructure into place within the main pane by dragging its topmost page into place, as shown in Figure 29-14. (There has to be one top-most page in the substructure; you cannot place siblings at the first level in Scratch. To do that, move the pages into the main pane.)

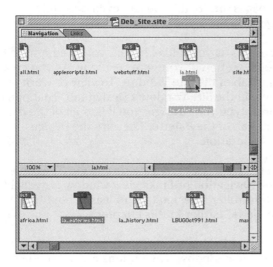

Figure 29-14: Drag a file from the Scratch pane into the main pane to define the intended relationship in the Navigation view.

You can also remove pages from the site's hierarchy by moving them into the Scratch pane. To do so, select the page or pages you wish to remove and then choose Design ⇨ Move to Scratch or choose the same command from the contextual menu as you point to any of the selected files.

The pages you view and arrange in Navigation view physically exist within your Files tab. When you work in this view, you're working with a reality. But there's another way to work in GoLive. Instead of creating real pages and manipulating their hierarchy, you can design a site in a purely conceptual manner, enabling you to create multiple "what-if" scenarios before deciding upon one to fly with. To do that you use the Site Designer.

Planning Your Site in the Site Designer

The GoLive Site Designer is a design canvas — a limitless pad of sketch paper where you can design your site or any section of a site, play with it until it looks and feels just right, and then try yet another design and another, or actually use any of the designs you create here. This is the tool to use if you're proposing a plan to a client, working on a large site as part of a team, or just to knock around a few ideas for your own site. It is intended for the development of individual sections to be anchored into existing site structures. (You can also use the Navigation view window to add pages and experiment, but to a different degree as you'll soon see.) An annotation feature enables you to post notes to yourself or to communicate thoughts to others right on the design canvas. (The notes also appear in an annotations list.) And because the pages are "real," you can even do some prototype designs in the Site Designer to show your clients or associates.

You can create as many separate designs as you'd like. In fact, you're supposed to. You should create one design for each section of your site, as a rule. As you create each design, it's listed in the Designs tab of the Site Window. To view or work on any design, just double-click its name in the Site Window's Design tab. That opens the Design Canvas on which you prototype your design. You'll find all of the design components you need under the Site tab of the Palette. They are the Design Section, Design Group, and Design Annotation.

As your design grows, you'll want an easy way to navigate through it. The same Panorama pane that you have in the Navigation or Links view window is available here. You choose it from the View Controller's Design tab. To learn about this feature, see "Getting around in Site views" earlier in this chapter.

You can also control the look of your Site Design. Again, it's the same controls and options as in the Navigation or Links view window. The options are in the View Controller's Display tab. To learn about this feature, see "Customizing page icons and labels" earlier in this chapter.

Rather than have many, many different pages all linking from the home page, large sites flow better when they have logical sections. That way, visitors enter the site at the home page, choose a section to visit, and explore within that section. For example, if seeking tech support, the tech support section would lead into the various tech support options. Following this model, you can create your site in Design Sections. Because you may want all pages within a section to share a common look or common subnavigation bar, you can base all pages in a section on one Stationery pad. To help your site's organization, you can place files within a section of their own folder in the Files tab. You create the folder within the Designs interface or use an existing folder. All pages in a section share a base file name.

The key to understanding what you do in the Site Designer is to understand what GoLive is doing behind the scenes as you work. When you create a design, GoLive stores it in a folder within the data folder of your site. As you add pages to your design, GoLive creates those pages as regular page files — but it doesn't place those pages in your Files tab, so they are not counted as part of your site. You can open those pages and add content to your heart's content. As long as you remember to save your page, GoLive stores it for you. As you move a page beside another page, seeing the black "relationship" line, GoLive notes that links are pending to accommodate that relationship. (Pending links are the green navigational links in the Site Designer; no red pending arrows appear here.)

You can open any page and create real links as you work. GoLive handles their URLs for you. When you submit a page or your entire design, GoLive moves the page(s) from the data folder to your site's root folder. You then see them in the Files tab as "real" pages. The links are updated behind the scenes for you, so all of your page design remains intact. You can continue to work on your pages as real pages. If you then find you need to recall the pages, GoLive simply moves them back to the data folder for you and updates the links again to accommodate their new paths. Again, you don't lose your work, and again, you can continue to design the pages. And, of course, you can resubmit the page(s) again later.

Preparing a site for a site design

The GoLive Site Designer works from within a Site Window so your designs can be stored in one convenient place and easily translated into a real-life site project. You can use it whether you're beginning a brand-new site or you've already begun work on a site.

To use the GoLive Site Designer from the very start to plan a new site, begin by creating the new Site Window. Go to the File menu and choose File ⇨ New Site ⇨ Blank. The designs you create at first will be *anchored* to the default index page that GoLive generates as the home page for any site.

To use the Site Designer to add a section onto your site, open your Site Window just like normal. As you create sections, you will choose an existing page within your site to anchor the new section to.

You use the Site Designer to design sections of your site — and sections need to fit into the grand plan of the entire existing site. So, in order to see your site (and because you'll need it anyway in a few minutes), open the site's Navigation view (Design ⇨ Navigation View).

If you are not already viewing your pages as Page Titles, you may be looking at several pages called index.html (If you've stored your previous site sections in their own folders and given each a lead page called index, this is the case). Open the Inspector to the Navigation view's View Controller and then choose to view your pages as Page Titles.

Now you're ready to begin your new design.

Give Your Pages a Head Start with Stationery

When you accept a design, GoLive creates the pages you've planned. But once these pages are generated, they exist physically in the Files tab — so if you want them to all contain a navigation Component or all have a specific background color or graphic, and so on, you'd have to open *each* page and place all these items. Instead, take advantage of stationery.

Create a basic Stationery page as the basis for the pages within a design group, as in the accompanying figure. Place the page's basic elements on this Stationery so they'll be there when the pages of your section are generated. If you need differing page layouts for different parts of your site, create different Stationery for each part. Here are some things you might do as part of a starter page:

✦ Create a dummy/starter style sheet and link it into this Stationery. If you anticipate using multiple external style sheets on some pages, add them too.

✦ Create a starter navigation bar Component; it doesn't even have to have text or a link — it just has to exist within your Components folder.

✦ Link in a graphic to stand in for the background graphic.

✦ Add a generic image placeholder, or use a dummy graphic to stand in for a logo and place it on the page where you expect to keep it.

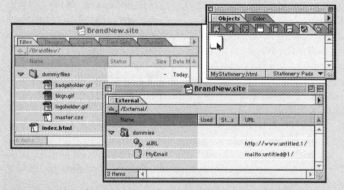

An example of a starter package. Each element is in place in the
Stationery that will be used to create the pages in this section.

Upon the page creation, you can develop the navigation bar. You can add to the external style sheet. You can use the In & Out Links palette to exchange any reference element in the Stationery for the real element by Pointing and Shooting just once instead of having to open perhaps hundreds of pages in order to add elements to them.

The elements I mention here are only the beginning. Follow the idea and include in your Stationery page(s) anything you can think of that you can later replace via the In & Out Links palette or by using search and replace.

The Stationery does not have to be complete. Even without much of the look, you'll save time.

Creating a new site design

You can begin your new site design no matter where you are in GoLive. However, because you need to see your design listed in the Designs tab in order to name it, it makes sense to be in the Design tab when you create the new design. Here are the steps:

1. From the Design tab of the Site Window, choose Design ⇨ New Site Design. The new design icon (called "Untitled Design") appears under the Designs tab of the Site Window.

2. Select the default name, "Untitled Design," and then give your new design a descriptive name so you can return to it easily as needed.

3. Double-click the new design name in the design list. This opens its design window, which is blank at this point, as shown in Figure 29-15.

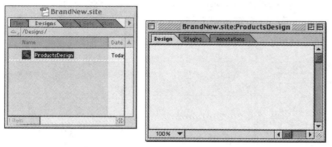

Figure 29-15: A new blank Design window for "ProductsDesign," shown in the Design's tab

The Design window has three tabs: Design, Staging, and Annotations. I'll explain each as they come into play, but here's a brief summary:

- You create the design in the Design tab.

- You see the list of pages-to-be in the Staging tab.

- Your annotations are listed in the Annotations tab, grounded to the design.

4. To create a proposed portion of your new site, drag the Design Section icon from the Objects palette's Site tab into the Design tab of the Design Window, as in Figure 29-16.

Although the item you're dragging is called a Section, you're really placing a single proposed page, not a group of pages. After you add the Section, you can add pages to it.

The design section appears in the Design Window, as shown in Figure 29-17. (It is displayed in whatever shape is currently selected in the Display tab of the View Controller.) It is named "index.html" by default. (Actually, it's more accurate to say its *lead page* is named index.html by default.)

Figure 29-16: Adding a new Design section to ProductsDesign

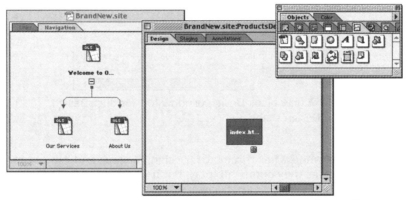

Figure 29-17: A new Design section as it first appears in the Design Canvas

Note

If you've changed your Preferences to use another name for the home page, that preferred name is used here too. For example, if you have your home page set to be default.html, then this page is called default.html too.

5. With the new section still selected, begin defining the new pages you're about to create by typing a name into the New Filename field of the Section tab of the Inspector (which as the Section Inspector now has two tabs: Object and Section). (Figure 29-18 shows this step and the next two steps completed.)

In this example, I am creating a section to display products, so I enter the Filename "products." The proposed pages will be "products1.html," "products2.html," and so on. This can save you a lot of time later because you won't have to go back and rename all of your pages. If you leave this blank, the pages will be either untitled.html, untitled1.html, and so on, or it will use the name of the Stationery if you use Stationery.

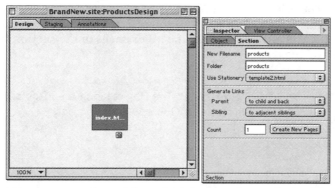

Figure 29-18: The Section tab of the Inspector as it should be filled out with the basic information for any section

Note

The Stationery option here enables you to begin all of a section's pages with a stationery pad. But what about the initially placed page? Unless there's an option for that in the Inspector by the time you read this, see the sidebar "Using Stationery for the First Page in a Section" later in this chapter and you'll be set. Or, if you're reading this prior to performing the steps, consider the solution suggested in the sidebar "Give Your Pages a Head Start with Stationery" earlier in this chapter.

6. In the Folder field of this section tab, enter a name or folder *and* subfolder name for your section's new folder. In this example, the folder name will be products. Keep the following points in mind:

   - If you have not yet created the folder to house your files, GoLive will create the folder for you.

   - If you want these files to go into a subfolder but don't yet have the enveloping folder created yet, enter a folder name, a slash, and then the subfolder name (**foldername/subfoldername**), and GoLive will create both folders.

   - If you already have a folder waiting for these files, enter that folder's name.

   - If you already have a folder waiting for these files but want these particular files to land in a subfolder that you don't have yet, enter the existing folder's name followed by a slash and the name of the folder-to-be.

   - If you don't specify a folder here, all files in this section are placed within a folder called NewPages.

7. To base all pages in this section on Stationery, choose that Stationery from the pop-up menu. (You have to create the Stationery before you can choose it.)

Tip

Be sure to read the sidebar entitled "Give Your Pages a Head Start with Stationery" to see how you can use Stationery before you go any further in your design.

8. With the Design Section still selected, activate the Object tab (shown in Figure 29-19) of the Section Inspector to give your new proposed page a title. (See Chapter 26 to learn about the significance of a page title.) Select the default title, "Welcome to Adobe GoLive 5," and enter your own. (This names just the one page object, not the other pages in the section that are the children of this page.)

Figure 29-19: The Object tab of the Inspector, which sets up the selected page only

Other information you can optionally enter here is as follows:

- Name this design section main page. This name doesn't play any role in the actual pages when they become part of your site. It's simply for display in the design section. If you go to the View Controller and choose Design Name as your Item Label, this name appears in the page icon instead of the file name that appears by default, or the other alternative of page title. However, as it stands now, this name must be entered on an object-by-object basis, by selecting each object and entering a name, because it is not inherited within a section. If you don't name each of your proposed pages (objects), when you choose the Name as the Item Label, those pages are named "No Name," which is pretty useless. Look for news at www.golivebible.com about this feature's functionality changing in future revisions of GoLive.

- Enter a target directory *only* if you want to create this particular page within a different folder from the rest of the section's files. This feature was really added to accommodate one-page sections, which are a rarity. You can easily skip this step, and then later move your main section page to the root level manually if you prefer it there. Or, you can enter this folder name later on before you submit or resubmit your design.

- Change the Filename *only* if you want this particular page to have a name other than the default name. If your new section will be housed in its own folder, using the name index.html (or whatever page name is your server's default home page) enables users to get to the page by typing just the domain and directory name without adding the page name to the path. The only time it is desirable to use a name other than your server's default is when the page will reside at the root level of your site where a page by the default name already exists.

9. With the Design Section still selected, switch to the View Controller and set up the look of your site design, as shown in Figure 29-20.

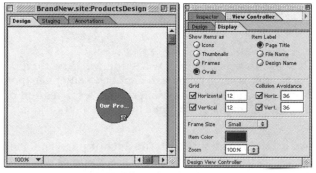

Figure 29-20: The Products Design site set up to work with comfortably. (The Display tab of the View Controller and the selected settings are shown here, too.)

Ovals are the recommended shape for pages. This is because the design is conceptual at this point and the other icons are more like real pages.

Choose the item label that works best for you. A page title that says welcome doesn't tell you anything about the page, because only "welcome" shows, so consider another title for the duration of your prototyping. The file name for your pages will tend to be something like products1.html at first, but you'll be changing names after you create the page objects. The design name label requires that you hand-name each page object after you add it.

Note The settings here are the same as those for the Navigation and Links view, so refer back to "Customizing page icons and labels" if you have any questions.

10. Look back at your site's Navigation view, opening it now if needed, and drag the anchor page anywhere into any white space in the Design Canvas, as in Figure 29-21. (You could drag in a page from the Files tab of the Site Window. It's just not in keeping with the visualization idea going on with the site-design process.)

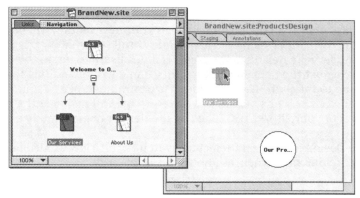

Figure 29-21: The first step in adding the anchor to the Products Design site

The *anchor* is the page to which your new section will directly relate and link when the section becomes reality. You can anchor to any page in your existing site. Your anchor page can become a parent to your new section or it can be a sibling. The anchor page appears in italics with an anchor icon at its lower-right corner.

11. Define your new section's relationship to the anchor page and anchor it by dragging the Design Section object into place alongside of the anchor page icon. Following the same method you use in Navigation view, drag the design object onto the anchor page and release the mouse when the dark line appears in the position where you want your new page to link.

In Figure 29-22, the Products section of the site will relate to the other (existing) sections as a sibling. Conceptually, it will come before the Services section of the site. Therefore, it is dropped at the left edge of the anchor page. The result, as shown in Figure 29-23, is that each page has a pending link to the other and the design you go on to create will have a known place in your site's universe when (if) it is submitted later on.

Note   After the first page of the Design Section is anchored, you can add children to it. Children pages are the only logical pages to add to a page in this position. A sibling page would lend itself to being another page anchored to Services or About Us instead.

12. Add the first children (pages below the first page of this section) by doing one of the following (no matter which method you use to do this, the new pages will use the information you set up in the Section tab):

   • With the section still selected in the design window, choose your link settings from the Section tab of the Inspector, and then enter the number of pages you want to create and click New Pages. Each page you add this way is at the same sublevel; all of these new pages are children of the main section page.

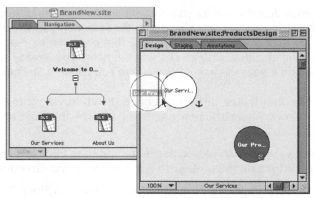

Figure 29-22: Anchoring the Products Design site to the anchor or page to which it will connect within the existing site

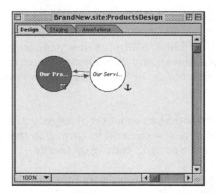

Figure 29-23: The would-be Products section of the site is successfully anchored into the existing site as a sibling to the Services section of the site. It is now ready to have children.

- With the section still selected, choose Design ➪ New Page. (Although this command only says the word Page, it is actually a special command for creating child pages.)

- Click the New Child Page button on the toolbar once to add one new page below the main section page. To add another page on the same level, reselect the main section page and click the New Child button again.

- Drag the Generic Page icon from the Objects palette's Site tab to the lower edge of the section icon and release the mouse when a dark line appears below the main section page. Repeat once for each page you want to add.

- Point to the page to which you'd like to add the new page and Control-click (Mac) or right-click (Windows), and then choose Page under New in the contextual menu. (Again this command is specially for creating child pages.)

Note You have no need to drag the icon for your Stationery over from the Objects palette to add a page, because all new pages already use the Stationery you selected in the Section tab. If you drag Stationery over this way, that page will be named "New from yourstationeryname.html" instead of using the name you already set up for the section. Only add a page this way if you need to add different Stationery.

13. Add more pages either below, beside, or above the children of the section's main page, as follows. Again, the new pages will use the information you set up in the Section tab.

   • Select the page you wish to add pages to, and then click any of the four New Page buttons on the toolbar to add a page in that direction.

   • Drag the Generic Page icon from the Objects palette's Site tab. As you move toward each edge of a page icon, a dark line shows you where the new page will land.

   • Select the page you wish to add pages to. Then choose Design ➪ New Page (to add a child page), New Next page, New Previous page, or New Parent page

   • Point to the page to which you'd like to add the new page and Control-click (Mac) or right-click (Windows), and then choose Page (to add a child page), Next page, Previous page, or Parent page from under New in the contextual menu.

Tip If, under any of the children, you want to add an entire set of pages, you may want to make that child's sublevel an entire new section on its own, with that child as the anchor. See "Adding subsections to a design," coming up shortly.

To change the default name of any page, complete or edit its title, or otherwise customize it, select it and turn to the Object tab of its Inspector. However, note that where it lists no Target Directory, the target directory is really the folder or folder/subfolder you entered in the Folder field of the Section tab earlier.

As soon as you add any page object to your site design, you can move it around, add more pending links to it or from it, or group it.

Adding subsections to a design

Most often, it is best not to add subsections to your design. The idea behind the Site Designer is that you create each new section of your site individually and anchor each section where it best fits into the site. However, there may be a time when you wish to add a subsection within any given section. For example, you might have one set of pages for which you wish to use a different Stationery.

In the example here, I might have one product line that differs from the others enough to merit another look, as I might for a home products line if the rest of the products are industrial. The new subsection might also be placed in a subfolder within the products folder, so the path to its folder might be products/home.

Using Stationery for the First Page in a Section

One feature missing as of this writing is the ability to use Stationery for the first page of any design section. However, you can do this yourself, thanks to a tip from the Site Designer's programmer himself. (Thanks, Lance.) You can do this any time after you place the Design Section in the design canvas, but before you add content to that page.

Return to your Site Window and reveal the left side of it. Select the Extras tab and open the Stationeries folder. Double-click the desired Stationery and choose New to open a new page. Switch to the Source tab of the page, select all the code, and then copy it. Then return to your design canvas and double-click the design section's page to open it. When it opens, switch to its Source tab, select and delete all of its code, and then paste the code you copied from the Stationery page. Switching back to the Layout mode, you should see the features of the Stationery. Save that page. Finally, return to the Stationery you copied the code from and close it without saving.

You have two ways to add new sections to your design. One is to repeat the motions for creating the first design section, making one of your design section pages its anchor. The other is to turn one of your first section's child pages into a section heading of its own.

To turn any section's child page into the parent of a section, select the page you wish to turn into a section, and then choose Design ➪ New Pages. Make your choices just like you did for the first section's creation. Check Make Parent a Section and then click Create.

To add a new Design Section, repeat the process of dragging a new Design Section from the Site tab of the Objects palette. Then set it up as you set up the first one on your page. Anchor your new section to one of the pages within your first design section.

Adding comments (annotations) to a design

You can easily share thoughts with others who are working with you on a design or add comments to your design presentation. You can place an annotation anywhere, including on a page icon. You can also move the note anywhere in the design window at any time later.

You can choose to have the subject or note content appear, and then choose where it appears in relation to the note icon. If the subject or note content appears, you can make the note any size by dragging a single handle that appears. Figure 29-24 shows several annotations in use within a client presentation.

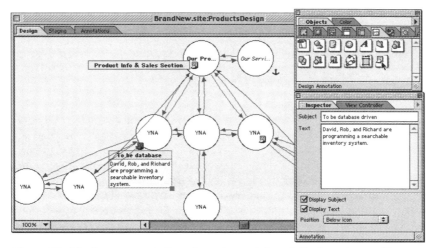

Figure 29-24: Some annotations in various states of display, along with the Inspector

Annotations also appear in the annotations tab of the Site Design window. There, you can read the subject and text in the annotation list, or by selecting an annotation and reading the text in the Annotation Inspector.

To add an annotation, follow these steps:

1. Drag a Design Annotation icon from the Objects palette's Site tab into place anywhere in the Design window, including on a page icon. A tiny note icon appears where you place the annotation.

2. Enter a subject into the Subject field of the Annotation Inspector.

3. Enter the note's content in the Text field of the Annotation Inspector.

4. By default only the tiny note icon appears where you place the annotation; however, you can change this behavior, as follows:

   • Check Display Subject to have the subject appear in a bold heading.

   • Check Display Text to have the note's content appear below the subject.

   • Use the pop-up menu to choose where the subject and/or text appears in relation to the note icon.

If you choose to have the subject and/or text show, you can resize the note by dragging the handle at the lower-right corner of the note.

Defining Links

As you add a page to your site design, you are telling GoLive how the page relates to the page it's beside. GoLive shows you the relationship by displaying green lines with an arrow from the originating page to the linked page. Those green links are also the ones that define your site as a "top-down hierarchy" like the one you see in Navigation view. In a top-down hierarchy, each page relates to the page it borders.

In the reality of your site, there will be times when you want a page to link not just to the page next to it as the green, top-down-hierarchy links expect, but to a page that is perhaps several jumps away. For example, each page at the end of a family unit path might need to link back to one of the family's top pages, because it contains the shopping interface or customer service form. Because GoLive doesn't know the content of your page to anticipate that, you can define that link intention yourself by creating an "ad hoc" link. The Site Designer calls these links Hyperlinks because they serve no structural purpose; only navigational. (Use of this term is a bit confusing because a hyperlink is, by definition, a link. Remember that the whole concept of a hyperlink is to enable people to jump from any point to *any* other. Thus, this feature enables you to define a *pending* hyperlink.)

To define your own ad hoc link that goes between any pages, just drag the Point and Shoot button on the page where you want the link, and then drag it to the destination page and release the mouse when the page icon becomes selected. (You know, Point and Shoot.) The result of Pointing and Shooting is a blue arrow, as shown in Figure 29-25.

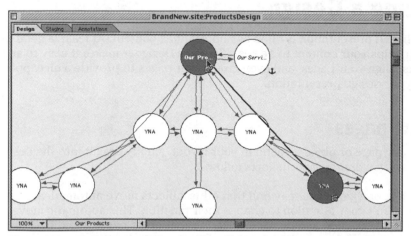

Figure 29-25: One user-defined ad hoc link at the left and another being defined via Point and Shoot

When you select a link, the Link Inspector provides a pop-up menu where you can choose the type of link you're working with. However, you have no real reason to do so. As you create and move your pages, dropping them into place, GoLive changes the links' hierarchy (green) accordingly. Those link choices in the menu are simply Parent, Child, Next [sibling], and Previous [sibling]. The blue links you create on your own are referred to there as a Hyperlink. When do you use the pop-up menu in the Link Inspector? If you Point and Shoot to create a Hyperlink, and then want to turn it into a Navigation, you can select the link and then choose the desired Navigation relationship link type. (But it is still easier to drag the page into place.)

One more type of link is listed. It's called Tour, and its purpose is to mark out a special path of pages for you so you can create a guided tour through your Web site for users. However, as I write this, with the release of GoLive 5, this link is only used within the Design Canvas. Therefore, once you submit your design for the real production work and check your link status in Navigation view, you don't have the ability to see this uniquely colored pending hyperlink. In the future, look for more about this cool idea.

Because links need to originate from content within a page, you cannot create a link simply by Pointing and Shooting from one page icon to another, but you can open any of the pages in your design and create the real links as you design the page. In Design view the green and blue links don't go away to show you that you've resolved a link. You just have to know it for the time-being. When you submit the site, you can view it in the Links view and see an accurate depiction of the state of your links.

Organizing a Design

Good polished presentation is often as important as content. At least, a good presentation helps your content to be seen. The Site Designer makes it easy to arrange your links, align your pages, and even group your pages to provide a nice, polished look for your design presentation.

Moving pages

To move any page or object around in your layout, simply drag it into the desired position. As you drag a page, its links follow.

As you move one page, you may find that other objects move automatically, although it isn't your intention to change their position. This automatic movement is the result of Collision Avoidance—a feature that helps pages avoid overlapping or obscuring other objects. By default, the Site Designer is set to maintain a minimum distance of 36 pixels between each page, so when you try to place a page closer than that to its neighbor(s), the neighbor(s) move the same distance as you are moving the initial page.

You can adjust the distance that is maintained, or even turn Collision Avoidance off, within the View Controller's Display tab. To set the distance you want maintained between pages to the left and right of the page(s) you're moving, enter the distance (in pixels) within the Horiz(ontal) field. To turn off horizontal avoidance and let next-door neighbors overlap, uncheck the Horiz(ontal) option. The Vert(ical) settings work the same, but control spacing for pages above and below the page you're moving.

Aligning pages

Pages are just like most other design elements you work with in GoLive — and therefore, the same Align palette that helps you on the Layout grid or in a floating box arranges your page icons nicely in the Design Canvas. In addition, the alignment commands are available in the contextual menu.

To align objects, simply select them and then click the desired button in the Align palette (Window ➪ Align), as demonstrated in Figure 29-26, or choose the appropriate command from the Contextual menu.

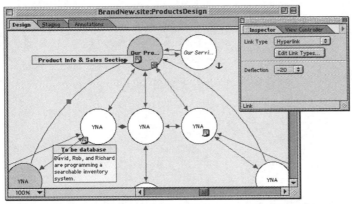

Figure 29-26: Distributing the space between three sibling pages using the Align palette

With one page selected, you can Align your page to its Parent (Align to Parent). With multiple pages selected, you can also align the pages with respect to one another (Align Objects) or average out the spacing between them with the Distribute Objects command

Tip   If, after distributing the space between pages, they become misaligned with regard to the parent and appear off center, group those pages and then align the group to the parent's center. You can ungroup them afterward.

To learn about the Align palette, see Chapter 7.

Arranging links

You can alter the look of the links (both green and blue) to help make things clearer to viewers. For example, you may want a line to circle around a page. To do so, simply select the link and drag its handle.

To select a line, click it. To select multiple lines more quickly, press the Shift key as you drag over any part of each line you wish to select. When you select a line, a single handle appears at the line's midpoint. You can drag that handle to change the arrow's arch.

You can also control the arch of each line. To do so, select the link, turn to the Inspector (called the Link Inspector), and choose a deflection angle from the pop-up menu. A negative number moves the handle to the left, while a positive number moves the handle to the right. In Figure 29-27, the blue (ad hoc) links have deflections of 20 degrees, each in the opposite direction. The link at the right curved outward from the center of the design prior to the deflection change from a positive to a negative number.

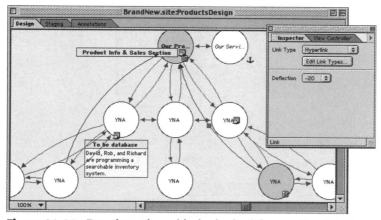

Figure 29-27: Experimenting with the look of the pending links in a design by choosing deflection angles

When you have a relationship that goes in both directions between a parent and child or between two siblings, you have two separate arrows by default. You can clean up the arrow clutter on your page by having any set of two lines appear as one double-headed line. To do this, drag one of those two lines onto the other. The fastest way to do this is to select all the lines you wish to set at once, and then turn to the Inspector, which becomes a Link Inspector, and use the Deflection pop-up menu to set all of the links' deflections to zero (straight lines), as shown in Figure 29-28. After you do this, if you move one of the pages, the line still appears as one. But, any time later, you can select the line and drag the handle to separate the lines.

Tip While you're making your presentation look nice, take a look at the Site Settings preferences. The Design Colors settings under Site Settings or Edit ➪ Preferences enable you to choose your own colors.

Grouping and ungrouping pages

You may already be used to the concept of grouping objects, either from the ability in the Layout grid or from other drawing programs. Like in those cases, you can group objects (pages in this case) in the Design window so you can treat them as one. You can group any page; the pages don't all have to be part of the same design section.

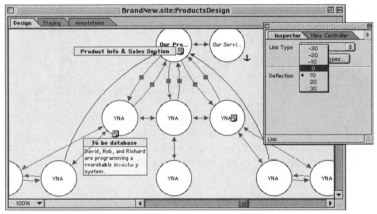

Figure 29-28: Setting up three separate sets of green links at the top of the design to merge into double-headed single arrows for clarity. All sets at the bottom are already merged.

Grouping files makes it easier to move them around. Just drag a group's title bar or border. Grouping files also enables you to collapse them from view in the layout. Just click the collapse group icon at the right side of its title bar.

 Expert Tip Use the Group feature to place all of the pages you anticipate linking within a navigation bar. You can pull the group to any location in the Design window, and the Navigation links will extend to continue to show you their intended relationships, even when you move a group. — *Steven Shmerler, Web designer, SASnet.com*

To group pages, do one of the following:

✦ Select the pages you wish to group together. Then point anywhere on any selected file and Control-click (Mac) or right-click(Windows) and choose Group. A group is created by encasing pages in a rectangle, as shown in Figure 29-29. If any pages exist within the range of the rectangular area that are not included in your selection, those pages are moved outside of this bounding area.

✦ Drag the Design Group icon from the Object palette's Site tab into place in the design view. Then drag the desired pages into the group boundary. By default, the boundary resizes automatically to accommodate your pages. (You can turn this option off by selecting the group and unchecking Auto Resize in the Group Inspector. In that case, you need to drag one of the group's four handles and expand it in order to add more pages to the group.) If any pages interfere with the range of the rectangular area, they are moved outside of the bounding area.

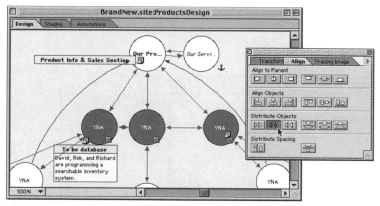

Figure 29-29: Three sibling pages grouped together — in this case to designate the contents of a navigation bar, per the title

After you group your pages, you can resize the group borders by dragging any handle.

Note   If you group a page and later add pages connecting to it, those new pages land inside the group. However, you can move them out by simply dragging them outside the group's boundary.

To help you identify the group later, select the group and turn your attention to the Group Inspector and do the following:

✦ Name your group. The name appears in the group's title bar.

✦ Color the group's bounding box by clicking the color swatch and choosing a color.

While in the Group Inspector, you also have the option to prevent the group region from resizing automatically when new pages are added to it. To ungroup pages, point to the group and Control-click (Mac) or right-click (Windows) anywhere on any selected file, and then choose Ungroup.

To delete a group, click its title bar or sides to select it and then press the Backspace/Delete key. Deleting a group does not ungroup it. Deletion deletes all of the pages in the group. If you do this in error, remember you can choose Edit ➪ Undo or undo it in the History palette.

Checking Your Design

Checking a design shows you whether your pages are connected by links to an anchor page or not. It also shows you whether the files will be placed in a folder or not. And if a problem occurs with a file's name, you're alerted.

You can tell GoLive to check your design any time a design is open while you're in any tab of the Design's window. However, to see the report on the check, you turn to the Staging tab. In the Staging tab, all of your proposed files appear in a folder called Design Pages, while all pages you've made live are in a folder called Live Pages. The anchor page(s) are also displayed, within a folder called Anchor Pages, of course.

To check a design, follow these steps:

1. Click the Check Design button on the toolbar, choose Design ➪ Design Staging ➪ Check Design, or choose Check Design from the contextual menu.

2. If you're not already there, select the Staging tab.

3. View the results in the Status and Check columns. The Status column is equivalent to the Status column in the Files tab. The status of your page's links appear here, link error bugs are here, and if a page has not been developed yet, it is reported as a generic page here. The Check column reports the stage of each page's check-in.

As in the Files tab of the Site Window, GoLive reports the status of each page in a column marked Status. You'll see the following icons and text:

✦ A yellow alert icon and the words "stage in scratch" tells you the page is not yet linked to any anchor page either directly or through its family's path.

✦ A stop sign and the words "file in use" tells you that the page is open. Close it before submitting the design (or in order to recall it).

✦ A stop sign and the words "target folder" tells you that the folder you requested in the Folder field of the Section Inspector's Section tab cannot be created upon submission of the design. (Or this message appears in the Target Dir field of the Object tab of the Page Inspector if the page is not within a section.) If you see this, return to the tab and enter a valid folder name.

Note   See "Turning Your Design into Real Pages," later in this chapter for details about submitting designs.

✦ A stop sign and the words "section name" tells you that the section page cannot use the name given because that file name already exists in that particular folder. Select the Section page and choose another name for the page, or choose another folder within its Inspector.

✦ A yellow alert icon and the words "file rename" tells you that the page's name will be renamed upon submission. For example, if you are submitting a page called untitled.html, but the target folder already contains a file by that exact name, the submitted page will automatically be renamed untitled1.html.

The URL column shows you where a file is located at the time. If a file is not part of the Files tab, its path begins with your design name. If it is in the Files tab, the path begins with the name of the folder it is in.

Presenting a Site Design

For the most exciting presentation, present your design live in GoLive by opening the Design tab of the Site Window and opening each design in turn. That way you can make changes on the spot. If a live presentation isn't an option, you can deliver it via the Web as (drumroll please) a Web site! Take screen shots of the design window, save them as GIFs, and then put them into Web pages using your Web design program of choice.

Another easier option is to save the design as a PDF (Adobe Acrobat portable document file) by printing to the PDF printer. That way you can e-mail or print the file, or print your site plans. The contents of the Design Window can be printed using the normal File ⇨ Print command.

Turning Your Design into Real Pages

After your associates, clients, or your own alter-egos agree on a site design, it's time to convert those proposed pages into real pages. This is called *submitting* your design.

To submit a design, make sure the design window is open and active, and then click the Submit Design button on the toolbar, choose Design ⇨ Design Staging ⇨ Submit Design, or call up the contextual menu from within the site design window and choose Submit Design.

Upon design submission, the following things happen:

✦ In the Design tab each page gains a mini document-in-folder icon to show the page really exists in a folder in the root level of your site.

✦ In the Staging tab the submitted pages (that's the entire design in the window) are moved to the Live Pages folder.

✦ In the real folders on your computer, the pages move into the root folder where all of your real pages, graphics, movies, and so on are stored. (Prior to this they are in the site data folder within a Design folder.)

✦ In Navigation view the pages appear. If they are anchored, they appear in the main pane in place within the site's hierarchy. (That means they look just like in the design view, but beneath their anchor.) If they are not anchored, they are scratch pages and appear in the Scratch pane.

Once a design is submitted, you work on its pages just like you work on any other Web page in GoLive.

You don't necessarily have to turn your entire design live at once. You can select specific pages and submit just those pages. In order to submit a page this way, though, the pages need to be connected to an anchor page. If you attempt to submit a page that isn't connected, an alert lets you know it cannot be done.

To submit selected pages, open the design window to the Design or Staging tab and select the pages you wish to submit. Then choose one of the following options:

✦ Design ➪ Design Staging ➪ Make Items Live in Site to add the page(s) to the site's actual hierarchy.

✦ Design ➪ Design Staging ➪ Make Items Live in Scratch to add the page(s) to the Files tab but not to the hierarchy displayed in the main part of the Navigation view. These files will be available in the Scratch pane of Navigation view so you can work with them and determine an intended place in the site's hierarchy.

Recalling a Design

Design submission is not final. In fact, the idea behind all this is that you can submit a design to see how it holds up in reality, and then recall it to tweak it. If you're considering more than one design, the recall feature enables you to submit each, in turn, look it over, and then recall it to try out the next one. When you recall a design, its pages are pulled from the Files tab and returned to the Designs folder. However, the folders the submission created remain in the Files tab.

Technically, you can work on a design in Design view even while it's submitted and live. However, this can become confusing. I recommend that you recall a design in order to work on it.

To recall a design, have the design window open and active, and then click the Recall Design button on the toolbar, choose Design ➪ Design Staging ➪ Recall Design, or call up the contextual menu from within the site design window and choose Recall Design.

Upon design, remember that the following things happen:

✦ In the Design tab the mini document-in-folder icons disappear.

✦ In the Staging tab the submitted pages move back to the New Pages folder.

✦ In the real folders on your computer, the pages move from the root folder back to the Design folder in the site data folder.

✦ In Navigation view the pages disappear.

To recall selected pages, open the design window to the Design or Staging tab and select the pages you wish to recall. Then choose Design ➪ Design Staging ➪ Send Items Back to Design.

✦   ✦   ✦

Authoring with WebDAV

As Web sites become larger and/or more intricate, chances are greater that you'll want to collaborate with others on a site's creation. To enable you to work collaboratively on your site, GoLive 5 adopts support of WebDAV. WebDAV, which is short for Web Distributed Authoring and Versioning, is an open programming standard that enables people to work together on the same site via the Internet protocol, HTTP. To take advantage of WebDAV, you need access to a Web server that can run it. The Web server itself needs to be running the WebDAV server extension or module to *be* a WebDAV server. This WebDAV server does not need to be the server that ultimately hosts the site. When the site is complete, you can do a regular FTP upload to your site host of choice from your computer or any of your coworkers' computers. Remember, the WebDAV server is only to help the developers share a site, not for end users to view the site.

Introducing WebDAV

Thanks to WebDAV, if you're part of a team, whether located within the same building or on opposite sides of the planet, you all can collaborate on your site. Just do an FTP-like site upload to a WebDAV server, give everyone a copy of the physical site folder and access to the WebDAV server, and you're set. The WebDAV server acts as the central repository for all pages and files. As you work on a page, you lock it so others can't change the page. When you're finished, you return access to the others again. Of course, while you're working on any page or file, your team members can still look at the page or file; they just can't change it.

Standard WebDAV enables you to lock or unlock and upload or download files. But GoLive goes farther by adding Workgroup Support, a one-step check-in and check-out process that automatically handles the file locking as it checks versions and downloads or uploads for you. Workgroup Support also gives you the ability to synchronize your files with the servers. In this chapter, I focus on Workgroup Support first, as it's the fullest featured. Afterward, I cover generic WebDAV workflow.

True to the spirit of the Internet, WebDAV makes the world yet again smaller and the people within it yet again closer. The only catch is that you need a WebDAV server. Not all servers can host WebDAV, but fortunately that's quickly changing. A complete list of supported servers is available at the WebDAV Web site, www. webdav.org. For a comprehensive tutorial on how to set up a WebDAV server, take a look at Jeep Hauser's write-up on GoLive Heaven, www.goliveheaven.com.

Beginning with WebDAV

At first, your design process is the same as always. Begin your site just like you begin any other site, creating it on your own computer, adding pages and files and content. You can take it as far as you'd like before putting it on the WebDAV server to share the files. Then, when you're ready to have others add input to the pages, and add pages or other files, connect to the WebDAV server for the first time and upload your site's files to the WebDAV server. Anytime after you send your files to the server, send your entire site folder — the one that contains your site document — to each of the people with whom you want to collaborate. Upon receipt of the site files, each collaborator opens the site the same way as normal, by double-clicking the site document or using File ➪ Open. Each then personalizes the site settings with a unique username and password, (set up by communication with the WebDAV server administrator) and then connects to the WebDAV server. Upon connection, each collaborator synchronizes the files that now reside on his or her computer with the files on the server. (The copies in the Files tab are known as the local files.)

You may be wondering exactly what files are being shared. Only the files that comprise the actual Web site are shared — that is, the actual files that are ultimately uploaded to the Web server. The site management files remain locally on each collaborator's computer. The idea behind this collaboration is not to have a lot of people access one site document (thus, Site Window) at the same time. It's to let each user contribute to different pieces of the site at the same time. Unfortunately, Components and Stationeries remain on their creator's computer; they are not part of the synchronization process. (But you have ways around this — more later.)

In order for collaboration to work smoothly, it is important that only one person works on a file at a time. As soon as a file is done being worked on, that file is then sent (uploaded) back to the server, replacing the copy that is already there. This way, each collaborator sees, and has access to, the newest version. Should two people edit the same file at the same time, there will be two different versions of the same page and a very real possibility that one person will upload a page only to have it replaced as soon as the next person uploads the other independent version. To avoid that problem, each user needs to lock any page or file on the server prior to working on it. Other users are then unable to work on that page or file, although they can still view it. And because the pages can be constantly changing, it's important for collaborators who are working on related pages to synchronize often, ensuring that they have the latest look, feel, and content.

Tasting the two WebDAV flavors

WebDAV in GoLive comes in two flavors. One is the generic WebDAV method of locking a file, and then downloading it, working on it, and then uploading the edited version to the server and unlocking it. In this case, each action is independent of the other and it's up to you to remember to do each of these steps.

The other method is GoLive's more sophisticated version, Workgroup Support, with which you check out a file and GoLive locks it, and then sends you the newer version of it if the one on the server is newer than your local copy. After you've completed work on the file, you check in the file and GoLive uploads your copy to the WebDAV server, and then unlocks it for you. With Workgroup Support, there's no risk of forgetting to lock a file before you edit it. The other advantage of Workgroup Support is that as soon as you turn it on, it locks all local files in the site on your computer. This prevents you from inadvertently changing a local file only to find someone else has it checked out and has made other changes to the same file.

There's something to be said for using each method, and the two are not mutually exclusive. You can switch between them by turning Workgroup Support on or off. While WebDAV, especially with Workgroup Support, enables you to easily pass pages or files between codesigners, Web pages are all about linked pages, so what you do on one page often affects another. A good site also needs a good file structure, so you're bound to want to move files around. In addition, you or your coworkers are bound to try various page designs, discarding some and changing others. You may also find yourselves changing file names. Some of these things can become confusing if you don't set up a good plan of communication between all collaborators. In this chapter, I try to point out the actions that can lead to confusion, so if you read through the workflow sections, you can anticipate potential problems and avoid or minimize them.

 Tip
Style sheets (covered in Chapter 17) prove extremely beneficial when using WebDAV. They easily enable you to change the look of your site without dealing with checking out every page whose look you want to change. Normally, if a page is checked out when you want to change its look, you're stuck. With a style sheet, you change the style sheet, upload it, and that's it. Users of checked-out pages will see the effect of your new styles as soon as they synchronize and download the revised style sheet. You can even use comments (a Workgroup Support feature) to inform coworkers of the style changes within the style sheet.

Division of Labor

As you become familiar with WebDAV and begin to use it, you may soon come to feel that the constant checking out and in or files can become tiresome, as can the dialog boxes that ask you to do so.

With good site planning and division of labor, you can avoid much of this. Find a way to divide your site into work sections so each coworker has one section to concentrate on and no one else will need to add to those pages or affect them. Then, each person can work without Workgroup Support, locking all of those files, and working in the Files tab without the constant communication to the server or the locked file messages of Workgroup Support. (This doesn't prevent the file's owner from periodically sending the pages to the server for others to view.) When the section is complete, those pages can be unlocked to enable access by others, or can remain locked for protection.

If you cannot figure out a way to give each worker a dedicated section, perhaps one or two can work this way. Or, alternate section assignments so each person can do the required part, and then switch to another section.

Setting Up for WebDAV

Before you can begin collaborating via WebDAV, you need to connect to the server, upload a copy of the site's files to the server, and give each collaborator a copy of the site. This section covers all the steps you need to get your team up and running.

Setting up preferences

WebDAV is a Web server feature so before you use it, you need to set up the preferences that provide your server access. If you don't enter these connection settings prior to connecting, when you attempt to connect, GoLive informs you they're needed and opens the Site Settings dialog box.

You can enter WebDAV server information in the following three places:

✦ **The WebDAV Network Preferences** are available to you whenever you're using your copy of GoLive. These settings are stored within the GoLive 5.0 Preference file. After you enter WebDAV access information here, you can call it up for use within any Site Window or any WebDAV browser window. When you pass your site files on to your coworkers or hand them off to a client, these settings are not carried over.

✦ **The WebDAV browser information** is also stored within the GoLive 5.0 Preference file and available to you whenever you're using your copy of GoLive. Actually, the settings you enter within the WebDAV browser can be added to the WebDAV Network Preferences area; just select "Add Current Server" after you make your initial connection to the WebDAV server. The WebDAV browser is a generic WebDAV client that enables you to access your site's files at any time your in your copy of GoLive. (For more about the WebDAV browser see, "Using the WebDAV Browser" later in this chapter.)

✦ **The site settings** are site-wide only. These are the settings you need to use WebDAV for your site. Site settings are attached to your site document, so anyone you send a copy of your site files to will have those settings. If you're planning to pass your site files on to your client when the site is complete, note that these site settings will be passed on to the user unless you delete them upon completion.

Note

If you're using firewall software, you may need to accommodate its setup requirements. This information is also entered in GoLive's Network Preferences, but within a different panel. Refer to the firewall documentation to learn what you need to enter. Then, click the Network icon under Preferences to enter the information. Entering it there enables the access info to be used for FTP transfer as well. See Chapter 27 to learn more.

GoLive-wide preferences

The application-wide preferences are the most useful, because you can call on them from either WebDAV client. You can enter as many as you'd like. To do so, follow these steps:

1. Choose Edit ➪ Preferences, and then click the arrow by the Network icon at the left and click WebDAV.

   The WebDAV setup appears at the right. (See Figure 30-1.)

2. Click New.

3. Enter the address of the WebDAV server in the Address field.

4. Enter your username in the Username field. (The server administrator must set you up with a username.)

5. Enter your password in the Password field. (The server administrator must set this up too.) A password is optional. You may not need one.

6. If a password is required, choose Basic as the Authorization option. If not, choose None.

7. *(Optional)* If you have move WebDAV servers to add at this time, click New again and complete the information for each.

8. Click OK.

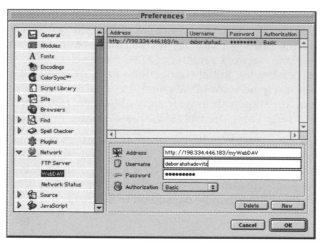

Figure 30-1: Setting GoLive's application-wide preferences for WebDAV access

At any time, you can return here and add more WebDAV servers. Simply click New again to add each new one.

If, as you're working in the WebDAV browser, you choose Edit to change any settings, GoLive presents this same WebDAV Preferences window for you to work within.

Note

You may notice that I introduced three places you can enter WebDAV settings, but only show two. That's because there's no need to enter settings in the WebDAV browser. Instead, you can be more efficient by entering the information in WebDAV preferences, just once, and then calling it up from the WebDAV browser.

Site-specific preferences

Site-specific preferences are attached to only the Site Window that's active when you set them. These preferences go with your site if you pass the site's file to another person.

You have two ways to enter site settings, as follows:

✦ After you've entered the WebDAV access information into the Preferences window, you can simply call them up from the Site Settings window, thereby entering them there too. If you pass the site to someone else, the recipient has this access information within the site settings. But when you (or anyone else) open another site on your computer, you'll be able to call those settings again from the Preferences window.

✦ You can enter the access settings directly into the Site Settings window, without ever entering them into the Preferences window. This way, the settings are stored only within the site document, and are not available to anyone else using GoLive on your computer.

To set up site-specific WebDAV preferences, follow these steps:

1. Click the Site Settings button in the toolbar, or choose Site ⇨ Settings. The Site Settings button is not available unless you have a Site Window open and active.

2. Click the FTP & WebDAV server icon.

   The lower half of the window is for WebDAV settings, as shown in Figure 30-2.

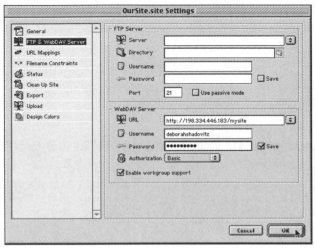

Figure 30-2: Setting up Site Window preferences for WebDAV access

Tip   If you've entered and saved WebDAV server settings under the General Preferences section (per the preceding section), you can simply click the pop-up list arrow to the right of the URL file and choose your server from there. When you do, the URL, username, and even password (if previously saved) is automatically filled in for you. In that case, skip to Step 8 that follows.

3. Enter the address of the WebDAV server in the URL field.

4. Enter your username in the Username field. (The server administrator must set you up with a username.)

Note   The WebDAV server administrator may not require authorization. However, even if it is not required, you'll need a unique username in order for GoLive to lock files for you. If your username is not unique, someone can guess it and then gain access easily as there would be no password match to complete the access.

5. If a password is required by the WebDAV server administrator, enter your password in the Password field. (The server administrator must set up the password for you first.)

6. *(Optional)* Check the Save option if you want GoLive to remember your password. Otherwise, you'll need to enter your password each time you access the server.

7. If a password is required, choose Basic as the Authorization option. If not, choose None.

8. *(Optional)* Check Enable Workgroup Support.

Tip

Workgroup Support, GoLive's own addition to the standard WebDAV functionality, saves you steps and eliminates user error. I highly recommend using this feature. See "Workflow Using Workgroup Support" to learn more.

9. Click OK.

At any time later, you can turn Workgroup Support on or off by returning to the site settings here and checking or unchecking the option.

Uploading your site to begin collaborative work

After you've set your upload preferences, you can upload your site to the WebDAV server. Initially, only one person on a team uploads the site. Once it's uploaded, the rest of the team open their local copies, connect to the copy on the WebDAV Server, and synchronize their local (hard drive) copies to the one on the server in order to join the collaboration.

You don't have to have general WebDAV preferences entered in order to upload your site or use WebDAV in any way. You only need site-specific WebDAV preferences to proceed.

Follow these steps to upload the site:

1. With the Site Window active, click the WebDAV server Connect/Disconnect button in the toolbar (or choose Site ➪ WebDAV Server ➪ Connect/Disconnect).

   The button will not be active if don't have a Site Window open and active. Click the Site Window to bring it forward.

Note

The WebDAV server Connect/Disconnect button in the toolbar is a toggle, as implied by its name. If you're not connected, this button connects you. After you're connected, the same button disconnects you from the WebDAV server.

If you have not yet set the site-specific WebDAV settings, a dialog box alerts you. Click OK to have the site-specific Settings dialog box open, and then enter the settings. Or, click Cancel until you can learn these settings.

As GoLive connects you, or attempts connection, a WebDAV Transaction dialog box appears. Then the right side of the Site Window opens to the WebDAV tab and the URL of the server appears at the top of the right side of the Site Window, below the tabs.

Three new buttons activate to the right of the WebDAV server Connect/ Disconnect button in the toolbar: WebDAV Synchronize All, WebDAV Upload Modified Items, and WebDAV Download Modified Items.

2. Click the WebDAV Synchronize All button in the toolbar (or choose Site ➪ WebDAV Server ➪ Synchronize).

GoLive checks the situation on the server and then reports all files of your site within the Synchronize dialog box, as shown in Figure 30-3. At this point, because you have never uploaded files to the server, all of your site's files should be listed as needing uploading to the server. Whenever a file in your Files tab does not exist on the WebDAV server, the file appears as gray on the server side of the Synchronize window.

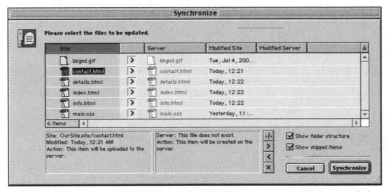

Figure 30-3: The Synchronize dialog box. Arrows pointing toward the server show the files needing to be uploaded to the server.

Note

Another way to get files to the server is to use the Upload Modified Items button or menu item. Physically, this serves the same initial purpose of getting your site's file up to the server. However, before you can use GoLive's Workgroup Support feature, you need to synchronize — literally. Because Workgroup Support looks for this synchronization in order to function, its easier to begin with the Synchronization command and save yourself a step later.

3. Click Synchronize to have all files upload. (Files travel in the direction the arrow points.)

Although you don't need to do this the first time, you can click the name of any file to learn about both the version on your hard drive (in the Files tab) and the one on the server.

The files upload and appear within the WebDAV tab of your Site Window, as in Figure 30-4. (The Synchronize dialog box closes automatically.)

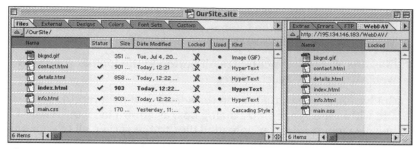

Figure 30-4: The Site Window, with local files at the left and the files on the WebDAV server appearing in the WebDAV tab

4. *(Optional)* If you won't be using the WebDAV server for a while, you can disconnect for now. You can click the WebDAV server Connect/Disconnect button in the toolbar to disconnect.

The files on your hard drive are now located on the server as well. You are ready to begin collaborative development — that is, as soon as your fellow developers have the same files and access. Otherwise, you don't have anyone to collaborate with.

Giving access to fellow developers

After you get your site-in-progress up to the WebDAV server, the next step is to give your fellow developers access to the site so they can join the collaboration.

In order for each member of your development team to be a full-fledged developer on the site, each needs a full copy of the site document. WebDAV does not provide a method for dispersing the physical site files. To do that, send your entire site folder (the main folder that contains the site folder, the .data folder, and the .site document) to everyone, either via FTP, e-mail, or disk.

After each person has a local copy of the site files, each can double-click the site document to open the Site Window, enter site-level WebDAV preferences (see "Setting up preferences" earlier in this chapter), connect, and then work as desired.

Users have two ways they can work using WebDAV. One way is the plain vanilla WebDAV method of manually locking and downloading files to work, and manually unlocking and uploading files to put them back into place for others to see and use. You can switch between methods any time, as long as you disconnect first. The other way is GoLive's enhanced method, which is a more automated or sophisticated method of check-in and check-out, called Workgroup Support. The method each user chooses is independent of the other users. You can use one while someone else uses another. Because Workgroup Support is simpler and more functional, I introduce it first.

Setting up if you're a codeveloper

With WebDAV, no concept of "owner" and "guest" exists. All site designers are equal. However, only one person starts the site and uploads it to the WebDAV server. The rest of the developers obtain a copy of the original site files, sign on to the WebDAV server and synchronize, and then begin working. Anyone can lock and download, or check in a file to work on it. And anyone can simply lock a file so others cannot change it.

Caution   If you are coming into the collaboration while it is somewhat in progress, and don't have the latest copy of the site files, ask your project leader for a current copy. Starting with a copy of the Site Window that closely matches the files on the WebDAV server can save you a lot of time getting up to synch.

Here's what you need to do to begin working:

1. Receive a copy of the site folder, complete with the site document, the .data folder, and the files folder.

2. Double-click the site document as normal.

3. Set up your site settings. (See "Setting up preferences".)

4. Connect to the WebDAV server by clicking the WebDAV server Connect/Disconnect button.

   Upon connection, the right side of the Site Window opens to the WebDAV tab and all files currently on the WebDAV server appear to you.

   If the site has not been synchronized, you should see the message: "Site files need to be synchronized. Do you want to do it now?" If so, click Yes.

Note   When you say yes to the Automatic Synchronization dialog box, only the files that you have in your local site will be synchronized with the content on the server. Other files that are part of the site will not appear to you. This is handy if you are only concerned with working on your part of the site.

5. *(Only if you do not see the Automatic Synchronization dialog box.)* Click the WebDAV Synchronize All button in the toolbar. (Alternately, you can choose Site ➪ WebDAV Server ➪ Synchronize or choose WebDAV Server ➪ Synchronize from the contextual menu called from within the Files or WebDAV tab.)

6. Perform the synchronization. If you are signing on at the very start of the job, there may be no file to synch, or there may be just one or two. But if you're coming in later, there can be many files in question.

For example, WebDAV may want to upload one of your files to the server. If this is so, chances are the file it is questioning actually still exists on the server but has been moved or renamed there. In this case, look for another file on the server that either has the same name but is in a different place or has a similar name or function. You can then look at the details of these files by clicking the file in the left side of the Synchronize window and reading about it in the field below. If you feel you have enough information to make a decision, you can take action (the actions you can take are described in the next section, "Synchronizing Files"). If not, choose to skip the file in question, and then ask your project leader.

You may also see a Warning icon, which signifies a conflict because both files have been changed and WebDAV doesn't know which you'll want. Select the file you want and look at the modification dates for each file to determine which way the file should go — up or down? Or, skip it until you can ask someone.

7. Begin working. (See "Workflow Using Workgroup Support," "Working with Basic WebDAV," or "Using the WebDAV Browser" later in this chapter for more information).

Note You may see some green bug errors when all of the new files arrive at your site. If so, you'll need to do some investigative work and repair some links.

Synchronizing Files

Whenever multiple copies of any document exist in different places at the same time, things can get confusing. File synchronization ensures that the site files you're working with are the same as the ones on the WebDAV server. It works the same whether you're using Workgroup Support or not.

It's the responsibility of each designer on your team to synchronize his or her local copy with the server copy. The more often everyone synchronizes, the more accurate the site will be. Or, perhaps you'll set up a synchronization schedule. For example, if you're all in different time zones and you're working all day, you synchronize before winding down for the evening. That way, the next shift (located in the next daytime time zone) has up-to-date copies to work from. In turn, those in that time zone, synchronize in order to let the next designers work. If work time overlaps, but you know a person will turn to a job at a certain time, synchronize before he or she comes on. All this said, you're not going to run into problems if you don't actually synchronize, because any files you'll be changing are locked against other's changes.

What, exactly, does synchronization do? It looks at the modification date of each file and compares the date of one on your hard drive with that on the server. Then it points from the newer file to the older one, recommending you replace the older ones on each drive with the newer versions from each. Thus, your new files are moved to the server and your older ones are replaced. If a file has been modified on your hard drive as well as on the server, GoLive doesn't make a decision as to which file to keep. Instead, it tells you there's a conflict and leaves it up to you to decide which to keep.

Caution GoLive does not have a mechanism to merge two different files into one. If you have two edited versions, you'll need to determine which to keep and manually incorporate the changes that were made within the file you're not keeping. For this reason, it's not a good idea to override the check-out or lock feature.

To synchronize your entire sites automatically, follow these steps:

1. If not already connected, click the WebDAV Server button in the toolbar. (The Site Window must be open for this button to be available.)

2. Click the WebDAV Synchronize All button in the toolbar. (Alternately, you can choose Site ➪ WebDAV Server ➪ Synchronize. You can also call up the contextual menu while Control/right-clicking within the Files tab or WebDAV tab, and then choose Synchronize.

Note You can also select specific files to synchronize instead of synching your entire site each time. To do so, select the files or folders you want to synchronize in the Files tab of the Site Window. Then choose Site ➪ WebDAV Server ➪ Synchronize Selection, or choose WebDAV Server ➪ Synchronize Selection from the contextual menu.

In the Synchronize dialog box, GoLive displays all of your Site Window's files and suggests a synchronization action, as follows:

- An arrow points in the direction the file will travel: from your Site Window to the server, or from the server toward your Files tab.

- If both files have been changed since the last synchronization, GoLive cannot know which file you wish to keep so it displays a yellow Caution icon. You must then make a decision, and choose Upload or Download. Or, you can choose to skip the file.

- If a file is missing, its icon is grayed out under the column it's missing from, and an arrow points from where the file exists (your local site folder or the server) to where it has been deleted.

When a file or folder is grayed out on the server side of the Synch window, the item has been deleted. Click the item and you'll see that WebDAV intends to upload your copy of it back to the server—thus, putting back the very item someone else deleted. If you see a gray item, unless you have good reason to copy it back to the site-in-progress, tell WebDAV not to upload your copy. To do so, select the item in the Synch list and click the X button at the bottom of the window. Then, when you synch and are asked if you really want to delete the item, say yes. After you synch, your copy of the file or folder will be gone too.

Note Folders appear without an Action status. (They move across if files exist within it that are moving.) To move an empty folder, create an Action by clicking the buttons at the bottom of the window. This Action doesn't appear in the top part. To learn the Action, you must deselect, and then reselect, the item's line and read the file report at the bottom.

3. *(Optional)* To learn the details of a file, select its icon in the leftmost column. The details about both versions appear below. The local file's information is in the Site (local file's) column, while the server file's details are in the Server column.

   This column tells you the file's location, its last date modified, and the planned action. Or, if the file doesn't exist, it says so.

4. *(Optional)* Click the Synchronization icon by any file to change its synchronization option. Each click cycles it to the next action. Keep clicking until you reach the desired option. (Or, with that file's name selected in the File row, click the desired Action button below.) You have the following options:

   • *Skip* tells GoLive not to synchronize the file. However, it does not dismiss the date conflict. The next time you synchronize, the same conflict will be there — that is, until one of the files is changed again. Whenever the file is changed in both locations, the conflict remains until one file is replaced, either way (even if you know they are both identical).

   • *Upload* tells GoLive to upload the file to the WebDAV server.

   • *Download* tells GoLive to download the file from the server to your hard drive.

   • *Delete* tells GoLive to remove the file from the server *and* from your hard drive.

5. Click Synchronize.

Synchronization can take a while, depending on the number of files and the transfer speeds. A dialog box keeps you informed.

Workflow Using Workgroup Support

After each of your teammates has a copy of the original site files and has the site-specific settings completed, work can begin.

GoLive's Workgroup Support makes collaborative development much more foolproof than generic WebDAV. As soon as you turn on Workgroup Support, GoLive locks all of your local files so you cannot edit them without checking them out first. With Workgroup Support on, whenever you want to work on a page, you check it out from the server. After you're finished working on it, you check the file back in so the site-in-progress reflects your additions or changes.

Once a file is checked in, your codesigners can also check it out themselves if they have something to add or change. Checking it out automatically performs a modification date comparison and, if the file on the server is newer than your copy, downloads the file from the server. At the same time, it locks that file on the server so others cannot change it while you're working on it. You then work on the file from your Files tab, developing the page as you normally design pages in GoLive.

Checking the file back in uploads the copy you just worked on back to the server and automatically unlocks the file for others to use. If you forget you're using Workgroup Support and double-click a file in the Files tab without checking it out, GoLive asks if you'd like to check it out or tells you the file is already checked out. This goes a long way to prevent multiple users from editing the same page at the same time, and negating one another's work. Of course, when you're not connected to the server, you can still open a page to look at it. Just tell GoLive you don't want to check it out. Don't make changes to that page, though, because you won't be able to save them.

Note
> The standard WebDAV procedure (that is, without GoLive's Workgroup Support) has a lot of potential for errors and can be a recipe for disaster. Instead of check-in and check-out, you manually lock a file, upload it, download it, and then unlock it. In addition, because it doesn't automatically lock your local files, it's far too easy to modify a page while someone else is also working on it in earnest, and then replace that page and lose all of your teammate's work. You may find standard WebDAV much easier and faster, or want to avoid it totally — depending on the division of labor your team works out.

Checking files out

In order to work with a file, you check it out from the WebDAV server. (Of course, you must be connected to the WebDAV server to check a file out, so the Check Out option doesn't appear when you're not connected.)

You can check out one file or multiple files at the same — even if you're not going to work within a file right away. Why check out a file if you're not about to work with it? Perhaps you want to ensure that no one else will work with it before you make important changes. Or perhaps you're about to change one page that affects another and you want to ensure that the affected page (or pages) is available to be updated.

Checking out a file is really simple. Just choose a check-out method from the contextual menu for that file. Here's the full story.

To check out a file or files, follow these steps:

1. *(Optional)* Refresh the lock status of the file(s) you are about to check out. That way, you know you have the ability to check out the page.

   While pointing anywhere in the Files tab, Control-click (Mac) or right-click (Windows) and then choose Refresh Lock Status from the contextual menu (or do the same from the WebDAV tab, but choose Refresh). On the Mac, you can press ⌘-R instead.

   If checking out multiple files, select those files and then point to any of the selected files to call up the contextual menu.

2. Check out the file using one of the following two methods:

- Point to the desired file, either in the WebDAV tab or Files tab, and then Control-click (Mac) or right-click (Windows) and choose Check Out from the resulting contextual menu. This method checks the file out, but doesn't open it.

- Double-click the desired file in the Files tab, and then click Yes when asked if you want to check it out. This method checks the file in and immediately opens it for you to view or work with. (Double-clicking doesn't work in the WebDAV tab with Workgroup Support turned on.)

Either way, to check out multiple files, use your preferred selection technique to select all desired pages/files and then point to any of the selected files to call up the contextual menu. However, double-clicking is not particularly speedy or efficient, because you're asked if you want to check out one file, and then must wait for it to check out and open before you're asked about the next one.

If a file has been checked out by someone else (but you didn't know because you didn't update the lock status), you'll receive a server error saying that it is already checked out.

If the Check Out command doesn't appear in the contextual menu, you don't have Workgroup Support turned on. Open the site settings (using the toolbar button or Site ⇨ Settings) and check Workgroup Support. Then try again. One other time the Check Out command doesn't appear is when a file is already checked out. When the Padlock icon appears in the Lock column, you won't be able to check out the file; the Check Out command is simply not an option.

Caution   If you attempt to check out a file and receive a network status warning that the file cannot be checked out because it is already locked, the next dialog box invites you to override the locked status. However, after making your changes, upon upload you'll reach a dead end. The bottom line is that as soon as you learn a file is locked, you should refrain from changing it and contact its owner and ask him or her to release the file.

The most recent version of the file is now on your hard drive, awaiting your design.

While a file is checked out, you see the following icons, as shown in Figure 30-5:

- ✦ You see a Pencil icon in the Locked column of your Files tab.

- ✦ You see a Pencil icon in the Locked column of your WebDAV tab, along with the name of the owner (you) in parentheses.

- ✦ All other users working on the site see a Padlock icon in the WebDAV tab, along with the name of the owner in parentheses.

- ✦ All other users see a Pencil icon with a line through it in the Files tab.

When a Coworker Disappears

What if one of your coworkers disappears for a while or his or her computer goes down, leaving the files checked out or locked and therefore inaccessible? While you can override a lock to change a file locally, that doesn't help you get the file to the server. WebDAV's lock mechanisms really do protect from that. So what can you do? The solution is to sign onto the WebDAV server using that user's username and password. Perhaps your WebDAV server administrator would be the person to do this, or the team leader if you have one. Actually, anyone who has the user's information can sign on using that teammate's username and password, and then unlock the files. Of course, it helps to know what stage that user is at so no incorrect files land in your site.

When GoLive 5.0 performs a file check-out, it requests an infinite timeout from the WebDAV server, thus you have no option to simply wait out the server timeout period in order to regain access to your site's files. Therefore, if you do not know the user's name and password, having the server administrator intercede is your only option.

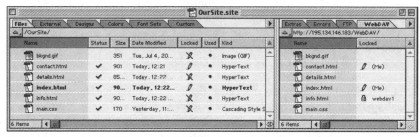

Figure 30-5: A Site Window, with two files checked out by this user and one checked out by a user named "webdav1"

Note

If you begin to work and find you're getting error messages or odd behavior, you most likely have turned Workgroup Support off and then back on. Every time you turn Workgroup Support off and then turn it on again, you *must* synchronize in order for it to work. Most of the time, you'll receive a notice requesting that you synchronize, but if you don't receive this notice, do it yourself. (see "Synchronizing Files").

Working with a checked-out file

After you check a file out, you've got the most up-to-date version of it sitting in your Files tab. Double-click that file to work on it. You can work on checked-out files just like you work with it normally — for the most part.

The only difference in page editing or development comes when you change a file that is called from another page or in some way affects another page. (For example, you change a destination or file name in a Component, or change the name of a page that another page links to, or when you move a file.) As always, GoLive tracks all changes and asks permission to update all pages affected by any change. However, in this case, GoLive doesn't necessarily have access to all affected pages. Any pages you happen to have checked out are available to update, but what about the others?

Here's what happens after you make a change to a page or file and it affects other pages:

1. You make a change to your checked out page and save it. (In the figures here, a link to the index page was added to the Component Navigation bar that's on all the pages.) GoLive tells you that a number of files must be checked out and asks if you'd like to check them out, as shown in Figure 30-6.

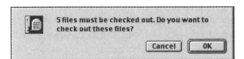

Figure 30-6: The dialog box states that five files are affected by the name change (four site pages and one Stationery).

 Note   GoLive is not actually counting the number of files that must be checked out at this point. It is actually counting the number of files that must be updated. For instance, in the example shown here, five pages are affected by the Component's edit (four pages plus a Stationery page), so you need to check out five pages. However, two of those pages are already checked out.

2. Click OK to let the check-out proceed. GoLive communicates with the server and calls for each page. The Network Status dialog box may open to let you know that some pages cannot be checked out (if you have it enabled in the Preferences window). That's normal communication; there's not anything bad or wrong happening. The Network Status dialog box just hangs out in the background. When the communication is complete, if any files are already checked out, or locked (by someone who has Workgroup Support off), an Alert message tells you, as shown in Figure 30-7.

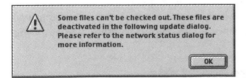

Figure 30-7: A warning that not all files can be updated

3. Click OK to dismiss the alert. (That's your only choice.)

An Update dialog box appears, as shown in Figure 30-8, showing you exactly which files need to be updated. Files that can be updated are solid and checked. Files that are not available, are grayed out and don't have a checkmark.

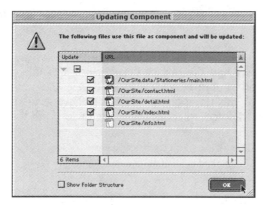

Figure 30-8: The Update dialog box, called Updating Component, shows that one file cannot be checked out. That file, info.html, is checked out (locked) by another user.

4. Upon seeing how many files need to be updated but are not available, decide whether to proceed with the update or not. To proceed, click OK. To avoid the update, uncheck the update boxes for all listed files and then click OK.

When the update is complete, the unlocked, updated files in the Files tab all reflect the change, as shown in Figure 30-9. If all files to be updated are available to check out, your update takes place and all is well and done. In this case, the locked page, info.html, was already checked out so it could not be updated, and the screen shows a bug to let you know.

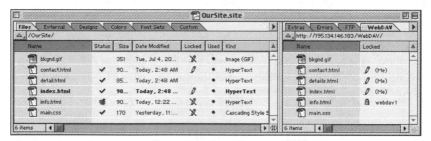

Figure 30-9: The Site Window, after the edit. One locked file reports an error.

GoLive should be able to update all files that were active and checked in the Update dialog box. You will have to update the other files yourself later on. If your update involved moving or renaming files themselves, then, in the Files tab, any file that could not be updated is designated by a green bug error. If your update was changing the content of a Component, pages that were not updated will still have the old Component content, and will not have any warning that the content is now outdated (see the "Sharing Components" section later for more info). This can help you later, in case you forget the update that was missed. As usual in GoLive, you can open a page and click the Show Errors button on the toolbar to highlight the error on the page. Then, you can repair the error. If only one or two pages need updating, manually locating the bug and performing the update can be effective.

But you may have many, many pages to update. Thankfully, a few tricks can help you automate the update.

Tip   If while updating a Component not all files are available, here's a way to easily update the rest of the page. When the rest of the files are available, open the Component in your Extras tab as normal, type a space at the end, and then undo the change. Close and save the Component. GoLive will want to update all affected files so it will again volunteer to check them out for you, and then do the update.

Adding files

You can add new files to your site the same way you normally add files. Newly added files are not locked, as they have not yet been in communication with the WebDAV server. There's no need to lock them yet because no one else has a copy of them, so there's no chance of two people altering the same file. Newly added files show as unlocked in the Locked column of the Files tab and don't appear at all under the WebDAV tab.

Newly added files can link to other files as normal, too. Whenever an affected file is on the server and not checked out by you, you'll be given the opportunity to check it out. If the affected file is already checked out, you'll be told it cannot be updated, and you'll need to address that page later.

When you're ready to share your files with the team, upload them by selecting them and choosing WebDAV Server ➪ Upload Modified Items (or, you can upload them when you synchronize).

Each time you synchronize, GoLive will see these files are not on the server and plan to upload them. When you're ready to share them, permit the upload. Until then, choose to skip those files.

Components and Stationery

WebDAV, (both with or without Workgroup Support) only works with the files in your Files tab. But under GoLive's normal organizational structure, Components and Stationery are not in the Files tab.

Using this organization, the person who created the Component sees all files as bug-free and is able to edit the Component. Meanwhile, because the Component is not shared between all designers, to everyone else all pages that contain the missing Component appear with errors — and these coworkers cannot edit the Component. Likewise, only the person who created the Stationery has the benefit of using it to easily create new, consistent pages. Fortunately, there's a solution to this.

Sharing Components

The secret to Components is not where they reside in the GoLive Site Window, but a bit of internal code. Therefore, after you create a Component, you can move it. You should do this before the initial upload of your site to the WebDAV server.

To share a Component via WebDAV, follow these steps:

1. Open the right side of your Site Window if it's not already open. (You can be doing this while connected to the WebDAV server or not.) Then select the Extras tab.

2. Click the arrow next to the Components folder to reveal your Components.

3. *(Optional)* Create a new folder in the Files tab. Give the folder a descriptive name to remind everyone it contains your Components. The normal folder is called "Components" so it may be helpful to avoid that exact name.) The name doesn't really matter. The folder just helps keep the site organized.

4. With the folder selected in the Files tab, open the Inspector to the File tab and set its Publish status to Never. That way, it won't land on your Web server when you publish the site.

5. Drag your existing Component(s) from the Components folder to the new folder in your Files tab.

6. To make sure that your Component still has its Component functionality, double-click it to open It, and then click the Page icon to turn the Inspector into the Page Inspector. Make the HTML tab active, and then click the Component button. Close the page, saving if asked. (If you have multiple Components, do this for each one.)

7. If the Component is already in use in your site, when GoLive wants to update the files that uses the Component, let it. In turn, you'll need to upload those modified files to the WebDAV server.

The Component, now living in the Files tab, will be treated like any other file by the WebDAV server. Allow it (and its folder) to be uploaded to the server and have everyone download it. As it is changed in the future, it'll be updated just like the other files. And because everyone has it, no one will have to contend with or ignore the error bugs.

Caution

As of GoLive 5.0, if you update the contents of a Component, it will prompt you to also update all pages that use that Component. However, if some of those files are not available (for example, if they are checked out by other users) and you still go ahead with the update/upload, the files that did not get updated will not receive any warning that the Component has changed, and will have the old Component content. It is much better to wait until you have access to all the files a Component is used in before you finalize an update.

The only difference usage-wise is that the Component is no longer draggable from the Objects palette because it no longer appears there. Instead, to place the Component, place the Component icon on your page and then link from the Component Inspector to the Component in the Files tab. Once you start using Components with WebDAV, all new Components should be created in the Files tab and not in the Extras tab.

Sharing Stationery

Stationery functions as Stationery, not because of where it lives in the GoLive Site Window but because its file type is turned into a Stationery template when it is saved as Stationery. After is it created, it can be moved and still retain its functionality. Its usage changes a bit, but that's easy enough to deal with.

To share Stationery via WebDAV, follow these steps:

1. Open the right side of your Site Window if it's not already open. (You can be doing this while connected to the WebDAV server or not.) Then select the Extras tab.

2. Click the arrow next to the Stationeries folder to reveal your Stationery.

3. *(Optional)* In the Files tab, create a new folder and give it a name that will remind everyone that it contains your Stationery. "Stationery" comes to mind as a suggestion, but it's up to you. (The normal folder is called "Stationeries," not Stationery. The slight difference can avoid confusion.) The name doesn't matter as this is just for organizational purposes, but I wouldn't give it the exact same name as "Stationeries."

4. With the folder selected in the Files tab, open the Inspector to the File tab and set its status to Never Publish. That way, it won't land on your Web server when you publish the site.

5. Drag your existing Stationery from the Stationeries folder to the new folder in your Files tab.

That's all there is to enable it to be shared. Share this folder and its contents along with all other files. Next time you synchronize or upload files, send this folder along. Anyone who downloads it can use it following the directions that come next.

Using Stationery from this new location is just a bit different. Because it is not in its assigned folder, it is no longer available from the Objects palette. Instead, follow these easy directions.

Follow these steps to use Stationery that resides in the Files tab:

1. Double-click the Stationery page. This automatically opens a new page created from the Stationery. Normally, when you double-click a Stationery page (when it resides in its proper folder), you are asked whether you'd like to modify it or create a new page from it. In this new location no dialog box exists. You just get a new page.

2. Begin to work on your new page, and then save it. As you save it, be sure it will land in your Files tab. You can easily do this by choosing Root from the GoLive pop-up menu in the Save dialog box.

Once you've saved the new page to the Files tab, it's just one of the gang, ready to be uploaded with the next batch of pages.

Deleting files

Deleting files can be tricky business with WebDAV, whether you're using standard WebDAV or Workgroup Support. (Deleting a new file that has never been synchronized or uploaded to the server is not an issue; new files are deleted as normal without complications.)

When you delete a file or folder within your Files tab, next time you synchronize GoLive attempts to download the same file or folder from the WebDAV server to your local hard drive copy. And when you delete from the WebDAV tab, the next time you synchronize GoLive wants to upload the same file or folder from the your computer to the server. So, what if you delete from your Files tab *and* from the server? Ah, you're all set then. But . . . next time one of your workmates synchronizes, GoLive will see the file on that computer and want to download that copy to the server. (Does this sound like fun yet?)

The key to successful collaboration is good communication and attention to detail. If you're keeping a log of your actions and sharing it with the other designers, you can let them know you're deleting an object. (GoLive and WebDAV don't have a log feature—that's up to you to create on your own.) And when you're synchronizing files, be sure to notice what's happening rather than automatically accepting the program's suggestions.

Deleting is the easy part. To delete a file or folder, point to it in the WebDAV tab, Control-click (Mac) or right-click (Windows) and choose Clear from the contextual menu. Then do the same in the Files tab (or select the object and click the Trash icon in the toolbar).

The hard part is keeping the file from coming back. It's up to your coworkers to pay attention when they synchronize. And it's up to you to do the same when they delete a file and you synchronize.

So, how do they delete the file? When they synchronize, just notice the file that shows as normal on their computers and gray on the server. Click it and note that it was deleted. (And you may know from your e-mail or other communications.) Then click the Synchronize Action button until the "X" appears to denote pending deletion. Each coworker only has to delete it once. That is, unless someone else sends it back to the server. . . .

Renaming files

Renaming files is even more tricky than deleting a file because two files are involved, not just one. The synchronization mechanism sees the newly named page as a newly created page, and the lack of the formerly named page as a missing page. I strongly recommend you don't rename pages unless you have a very serious reason to. (Remember, the page name is not its title. It will appear in a bookmark's URL, but not in the bookmark text or in the message conveyed to your visitors.) You have two ways to rename a file: on the server or in your files tab. Each has benefit and drawback.

Renaming a local file in the Files tab

While working with Workgroup Support on, you must have a file checked out in order to rename a file in the Files tab. Otherwise, you'll receive an Error dialog box stating that you cannot name it because the file is locked. Without Workgroup Support, you can rename without a warning. It doesn't matter if the file is locked on the server, because this renamed file will not be recognized as the same file that is locked.

To rename a file in the Files tab, follow these steps:

1. Rename your file as normal (without WebDAV). You must have a file checked out in order to rename it. (See Figure 30-10.)

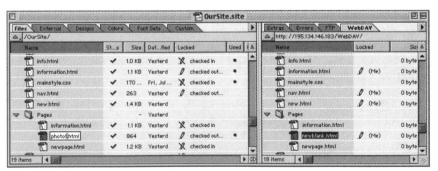

Figure 30-10: Renaming a file, once called `newblank.html`, in the Files tab. The file on the server does not change to correspond.

2. As you'd expect within the Files tab, any related files are updated by GoLive's usual update process. If any other files are affected, GoLive performs the usual update, as follows:

   • If all affected files are checked out, the update goes smoothly and all updating is done.

   • If any files are not checked out, GoLive asks to check them out. If all are available, they are all checked out and the update goes smoothly and all updating is done.

- If any files are not checked out, but some are not available, the unavailable files are marked with error bugs. You need to check them out later and relink to the newly named file.

3. Synchronize the renamed and any updated pages, as shown in Figure 30-11, so the newer versions are viewable by all coworkers. Because you have renamed the file, it appears as a new page to the server, so an upload is suggested — and is appropriate. The old-named file is still on the server and seen as a separate file. Click the Synch Action button until the "X" appears to delete that file.

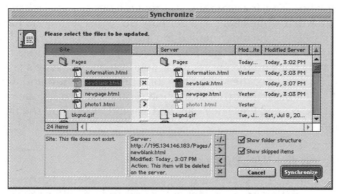

Figure 30-11: Synchronizing to add the "new" page to the server and delete the "old" page from the Files tab

4. Check in the file whose name you changed. Checking it in enables you to add a Comment, letting your teammates know that this file is the newly named file to add to their sites, and that the older named file is to be deleted from their sites. If you're finished with all of the files, check them all back in while you're at it. You can check the file out again immediately if you still want to work with it.

Note   In case you're wondering about using Upload Modified Items here, this option leads to the same Synchronize dialog box but will only show those files modified in the Files tab. It won't give you the opportunity to delete the old-named file from the server. Check-in is also not an option as you cannot check in from the Files tab and, even if you could, WebDAV sees two separate files now, not just one to be checked in and updated on the server.

Expert Tip   Adding a comment adds your name to the file history, so if you make a group habit of always noting the check-in time, the group has a shared history of who worked on the file and when (at least, when they finished working on it). Check out the "check in comment" shown in Figure 30-12 as an example. — *Cathy Scrivnor, Web site designer*

Figure 30-12: Synchronizing to add the "new" page to the server and delete the "old" page from the Files tab

Here's the complication: Say, for example, you rename `details.html` to `detail.html` (which isn't a worthwhile change to actually do, considering the hassle). Each of your coworkers still has the older-named file locally. Upon synch, each will see that the old file wants to upload as that file, according to WebDAV, does not exist there. If that file lands back on the server, it can end up on everyone's site again, so everyone has two copies of the same file — one being used and updated, while who knows what happens to the other. Somehow, you need to tell your coworkers not to upload that old-named file. They can, and should, download the newly named file, though.

Renaming a file on the WebDAV server

When you rename a file on the server, any pages that are affected are not updated by GoLive's normal updating process. Instead, you'll end up with pages of bugs that need repair.

To rename a file directly on the WebDAV server, follow these steps:

1. While connected to the server, in the WebDAV tab, point to the file you wish to rename and Control-click (Mac) or right-click (Windows), and then choose Rename from the contextual menu. This selects the file name, without selecting the extension.

   You do not have to have a file checked out in order to rename it. However, you cannot rename a file while someone else has it checked out or locked.

2. Make the name change, and then press Return/Enter or click anywhere off of the file name, as shown in Figure 30-13. The file name extension is not preselected, so it should remain intact.

Tip

On the Mac, you can also select the file name in the WebDAV tab and rename it. The Rename command is not necessary.

GoLive connects to the server. As it begins to communicate, you'll see the Renaming File dialog box, and then see your old name reappear in the WebDAV tab. Let the communication happen and it'll change back. The name updates on the server and in your WebDAV tab.

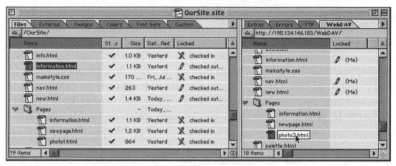

Figure 30-13: Renaming a file on the server by entering the new name in the WebDAV server tab

3. Changing a name changes it on the server but not in your local files, so you need to synchronize or download the modified pages. To save time, you can synchronize only that page, by pointing directly to that page to call the contextual menu when you choose Synchronize.

4. In the Synchronize window, let the newly named page download to you. You *don't* want the older-named page to download to the server, though, so be sure to set that file to Delete. See Figure 30-14.

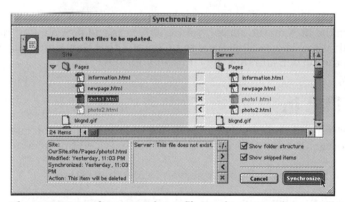

Figure 30-14: After renaming a file on the server, the new file needs to download, but the old file *must* be deleted to avoid confusion.

If the renaming affects any other pages, those pages are identified by a green error bug. You need to repair those bugs.

Moving files

Moving files creates the same complications as renaming a file. That is, WebDAV synchronization doesn't compensate for the fact that you're simply moving an existing file. Instead, upon synchronization, it wants to upload the newly moved page and download the page that is in the older location. To compensate for this, you can add comments to all moved files so your coworkers know what's happening, and know to delete the copies from the old location and upload the copies from the new location.

Note The confusion and complications that can arise from moving files around demonstrate the benefit of using the site design features to set up the structure of your site before sharing the site on the WebDAV server and beginning the actual content fulfillment.

Files can be moved directly on the server. While connected to the server, simply drag the files around within the WebDAV tab as you would with normal, local files. (It just takes a bit longer while the sever connects and communicates.) While you're at it, you can also move the parallel file in your Files tab. That way, when you synch, your file structure will match and you'll be less likely to mistakenly send files between your hard drive and the server, which creates duplicate files. When you synchronize your files, the moved files may be marked by a conflict alert stating that both files have been changed. Because you know they're the same file, you can skip the file.

When you move the files on the server, your coworkers will face a minor dilemma upon synchronization. They will all have to be careful that they don't put their local copies back on the server, and that they upload your new version.

Checking files in

When your work on a file is complete, at least for the time being, you can check it back into the server. Checking it back in gives other users editing access to the file.

To check a file or files into the WebDAV server, follow these steps:

1. Point to the desired file, either in the WebDAV tab or Files tab, and then Control-click (Mac) or right-click (Windows), and choose Check In from the contextual menu. (To check in several files at once, select those files, and then point to any one and call the contextual menu. To check in all of your checked-out files at once, call up the contextual menu while pointing to a blank area instead of a file.)

   If Check In doesn't appear in the contextual menu, it means that you are not connected to the Workgroup Support, or you don't have Workgroup Support turned on.

A progress window appears, showing you that the file is being uploaded to the WebDAV server, and then unlocked. When complete, your Locked icon disappears within your Site Window.

2. *(Optional)* You can use the Comment dialog box to communicate with your coworkers. Simply enter any comment or message when the dialog box presents itself. If multiple files are selected, and then checked in at once, one single Comment dialog box appears. Anything you enter in this Comment field is attached to each of the files. This makes it worthwhile to add comments about Component contents and their edits.

Caution

Each time you check in a changed file, the dialog box offers the option to turn off the Comment dialog box by way of a checkbox that says "Don't show again." However, no preference choice exists to re-enable this option, so it is *not* a good idea to turn it off—especially if you're using Windows. On the Mac, you can turn Comments back on by calling up the contextual menu, moving down the menu to highlight Check In, pressing and holding down Option, and then clicking Check In. In Windows, I have found no way to turn it back on as of GoLive 5.0.

If, for some reason, you prefer not to be given the option of adding a comment, you can turn it off by checking the "Don't show again" option anytime you see this dialog box. After you've turned it off, in order to add a comment, call up the contextual menu, move down the menu to highlight Check In, and then press Option (Mac) or the Windows key (Windows) as you click Check In.

Note

When Workgroup Support is active you cannot upload or download a file by dragging it from one tab to the other.

If you'd like your fellow designers to see how your page or file is progressing, but aren't ready to check it back in yet, synchronize to put your versions on the server without checking it in.

Editing a file someone else has locked

What happens when someone else has a file checked out, but you *need* to edit it? You only have read-only permission, so what do you do? To avoid confusion, the best thing to do is to contact your coworker and ask that the file be checked back in. However, if that's not possible, you can override the lock and go ahead with the change. WebDAV is so good, though, that as long as a file is locked on the server, you cannot override that page on the server. You won't be able to check your version in as normal, because you did not officially check it out. You cannot use the Upload Modified Files or Synchronize commands, because both result in an error.

Caution

Overriding the lock and changing your page is easy, but dealing with two versions of the same page—each of which may have significant changes—may not be. Consider this an emergency-only solution.

Why can't you upload your edited page? Consider what happens when the person who checked out the file officially checks it back in — as must be done. That file replaces your edited file — and your work is lost. You and your coworker may have made important changes, and there's no way to automatically merge these changes.

Follow these steps to override a Check Out lock:

1. In your Files tab, double-click the file. This opens a dialog box that asks if you'd like to check out the file.

2. Click Yes. An Alert message tells you the file is already checked out and asks if you want to override it.

3. Click Yes. The Lock column's icon changes to a broken pencil and the file opens. (It is not checked out on the server, but the local lock is removed.)

4. Edit the page as normal, and then save and close it.

5. Work out and follow a plan to ensure that no one's changes are lost.

If you break the lock and go ahead with edits, communication about your change is imperative. You'll need to work out a plan to determine whether your coworker has edited the page, learn which version has most extensive changes, and then decide which of you will incorporate the changes.

Here are a couple of ideas:

✦ The person who made the fewest changes, or easiest to reproduce changes, can e-mail the local file the other designer. (To locate the page, point to the page and call up the contextual menu, and then choose Reveal in Finder.) The recipient can incorporate those changes and upload the new file. Meanwhile, the other person deletes the local copy. When the fully incorporated page gets to the server, it will replace the void made by the deleted local copy.

✦ Taking advantage of the fact that a WebDAV is, indeed, an HTTP server (just running extra extensions), you or your coworker can view the page that's currently on the WebDAV server by viewing the page via the Web browser. (You do this by entering the address of the site and the path to the page in question into a browser and visiting the page.) Perhaps your coworker can then copy your work off of the page within the browser, and then paste it into the checked-out copy. When the checked-out copy uploads, it replaces your edited page and all is well.

Note   GoLive's Help tells you to override the lock by using your system's lock. The double-click method accomplishes the same thing, though, and is easier. What is the GoLive way? On the Mac, Control-click, and then choose Reveal in Finder. Press Command-I, deselect Locked with the Get Info window, and then close the window. For Windows, right-click the file and choose Reveal in Explorer. Then, choose File ➪ Properties, and then, in the General tab, deselect the Read-only checkbox and click OK.

Keeping your view of the site up-to-date by refreshing

If any of your coworkers are actively working on the site at the same time you are, files can change at any time. Page names may change. Page content may change. New pages may be added. Pages may be deleted. Graphics may change. Pages and graphics may be moved around. You know all this by now. . . .

The truth is, you're pretty safe from errors even if you don't refresh, because dialog boxes and errors point out the need to check out a file, or their already-locked status when you try to work with the files. Refreshing just saves you from thinking you can work with a file when you cannot.

Refreshing your WebDAV Files list and all information

Each time you connect to the WebDAV server, the current content of the server is shown to you in the WebDAV tab. But as you're hard at work on any particular page for a while, the site may be changing. There will be plenty of times you'll want to manually refresh the tab — well, not quite manually. GoLive does the work for you. You just manually tell it to.

Anytime you're working in the WebDAV tab, whether Workgroup Support is on or not, you can update the file listing as well as the Lock icons and the information that appears in the Inspector. Just control-click (Mac) or right-click (Windows) while you're anywhere within the WebDAV browser and choose Refresh from the contextual window.

Refresh lock status

It's also a good idea to keep your lock status icons up-to-date, too. Simply Control-click (Mac) or right-click (Windows) while you're anywhere within the Files tab of your Site Window and choose Refresh Lock Status. This ensures that the lock status you see in your Files tab matches the status on the server. It's particularly helpful after you've opened pages while offline, and have broken locks appearing as a result.

Disconnecting and reconnecting

While you're working with Workgroup Support, you can synchronize to be sure you have all current files, check out all pages or files you need to work on, and then disconnect and remain disconnected while you work. Then, anytime you need to synchronize again, grab another page, or check one of your pages back in, you can connect to do so.

Disconnecting

To disconnect from the server, click the WebDAV server Connect/Disconnect button in the toolbar (or choose WebDAV ⇨ Disconnect from the contextual menu). This doesn't do anything special with regard to your files. It just cuts your connection to the server. You know you're not connected when the WebDAV tab is empty.

If you're finished working on your site for any length of time, and are closing your Site Window, you don't have to bother to disconnect. Closing the Site Window will do the trick. There's no sort of special closing down procedure.

Reconnecting

After turning WebDAV on and doing the initial setup, each time you work on your site, you must reconnect to the server in order to check out the files you need, and then check them back in. If you already have all necessary files checked out, you can work on them without connecting to the server. However, if your work relates to other pages, you may want to connect in order to see what the latest versions of those pages look like.

Are you wondering why you have to reconnect to the WebDAV server in order to work on a file? It's because Workgroup Support locks your local files. If a file is not checked out when you disconnect after a work session, that file remains locked on your computer. When you open your Site Window again later and attempt to open the file, GoLive asks if you'd like to unlock the file. Remember that this is a warning to you not to alter that file.

Each time you open your Site Window to work, you need to take three steps to begin working anew, as follows:

1. Connect to the WebDAV server.

   With the Site Window active, click the WebDAV server Connect/Disconnect button in the toolbar (or choose Site ➪ WebDAV Server ➪ Connect/Disconnect, or Control-click (Mac) or right-click (Windows) while anywhere in the Files tab and choose WebDAV ➪ Connect). Upon connection, the files appear in the WebDAV tab.

2. Synchronize your local files to the WebDAV server.

   To do so, click the WebDAV Synchronize All button in the toolbar (or choose Site ➪ WebDAV Server ➪ Synchronize, or choose WebDAV Server ➪ Synchronize from the contextual menu). Then review the synchronization plan, make changes as desired, and click Synchronize.

3. Update the lock/check-out status of the files in the site. Control-click (Mac) or right-click (Windows) while anywhere in the Files tab and choose WebDAV ➪ Refresh Lock Status.

This ensures that you're working with the most up-to-date site design and makes it easier for you decide which files to work on.

Working when not connected

Granted, we live in a fairly wired world, but thankfully we're not yet connected everywhere all the time. You don't always have to be connected to your site's WebDAV server every moment you're designing the site. You can still look at a site's pages and even edit them while not connected.

Viewing files

When Workgroup Support is first turned on, all of the site's files are locked on your computer. When you're connected to the server, with Workgroup Support on, and double-click a file to look at or work with it, you receive a dialog box asking if you'd like to check out the file. But when you are not connected and double-click the file, the dialog box asks if you'd like to unlock the file. While you are not connected, it is perfectly OK to look at a file, but problems arise when you edit it.

To look at a page while not connected, follow these steps:

1. Double-click the page to open it. A dialog box appears, asking if you want to unlock the file.

2. Click No. The page opens so you can view it.

3. When finished viewing the page, close it without saving.

The lock status remains unharmed and all will be well when you reconnect later.

Editing files

In order to edit files when you're not connected to the server, check out the files before you disconnect. Checking out a file unlocks that file on your hard drive, giving you edit access and also preventing others from working on it while you're gone. While you're disconnected from the server, you can double-click any checked-out page and work on it to your heart's content.

The WebDAV Workgroup Acid Test

What happens if users cheat and edit files while offline, breaking locks and so on? Having put GoLive's Workgroup Support and WebDAV through the test, here is some of what I found.

Situation: A file is not properly checked out when you disconnect. While offline, you edit the file. Back online later, you choose the parallel file within the WebDAV tab and choose Check Out.

What happens? GoLive knows that the file on your hard drive is newer so it doesn't upload the older one from the server. It keeps your file intact and gives you Check Out status — but only after giving you an error message.

Situation: Two people try to check out a file at the same time.

What happens? Only one "wins," but because the timing is so tight, the other will not yet see the Padlock icon. Instead, the Network Status window opens automatically and displays an error that tells you the page is locked. The next time the status icons are updated, the lock displays.

When you are not connected to the server and do not have the file checked out, changing the page leads to grief. Because it's problematic and because you should avoid doing so, Workgroup Support does everything it can to prevent you. If, while not connected, you double-click a page you do not have checked out, and respond to the Unlock File dialog box by clicking Yes, you'll be able to edit the file but not save it. All you'll get when you try to save is an error. For situations like this, it's a good idea to document changes using the check-in comments. This dialog box appears whenever you check in a file, and can be very useful for noting the changes you've made in case others may have modified the same file.

Learning About a Site's Files

Much the same way that you can learn about a file in the Files tab of the Site Window while you're working on your site locally, you can learn about it from the WebDAV tab of the Site Window. As with local files, you simple select the file and then turn to the Inspector to learn about that file. What can you learn about a file that lives on a WebDAV server? You can learn its name, its location, the date and time it was created and last modified, and its size. You can also learn a few other things, including whether it is locked and who locked it. Perhaps most importantly, in the History tab you can view comments left by your coworkers — if you're taking advantage of Workgroup Support.

You can view file information whether you're using Workgroup Support or not; it always works the same way. To view any remote file's properties, you must connect to the WebDAV server and have the Inspector open.

To learn about a file, follow these steps:

1. Select the file in the WebDAV tab of the Site Window. If you're accessing your site within the WebDAV browser instead, select the files in that window. The feature works the same.

2. Use the four tabs in the Inspector to learn about your file. (If the Inspector isn't open, open it now.) The four tabs are as follows:

   • *File* shows you the file's name, the path to the file, the date it was created and modified, and its size.

   • *Special* shows you the file's content language, resource type, display name, and content type.

   The first three items of information are not automatically read by GoLive from the file. Instead, they appear if the server administrator entered the information on the WebDAV server side.

   • *Lock* shows you the file's lock status. It shows you the Lock icon, names the owner, states the type of access you have, and, in the Scope column, tells you whether the lock is exclusive or shared and when it will timeout.

- *History* shows you each date the file was edited, and by whom. It also displays comments if the past editors entered any. To learn about entering comments, see "Checking files in" under "Workflow Using Workgroup Support."

 If you don't see all the columns, and wish to, drag the bottom-right corner to widen the Inspector.

Monitoring Network Status

As you work, the Network Status window keeps you alerted to the state of the files you're working with, or trying to work with. By default, it opens automatically whenever it has a message for you. You can also open it yourself by choosing File ➪ Network Status.

The top of the Network Status window displays a status icon and short name, and a short description. The newest error message appears at the bottom of this list. The bottom of the window displays the details of any selected error description. To view any error details, click once on the error in the list at the top. Error details are written as HTML pages. The title of the message appears between a <h1> tag, and the details are immediately below. Read between the tags to get the message.

Here are the steps to set the behavior of the Network Status window:

1. Choose Edit ➪ Preferences.
2. Click the arrow to the left of the Network icon.
3. Click once on Network Status.
4. *(Optional)* Under "Track also," Warnings is on by default. If you prefer not to have warnings displayed, uncheck the option.
5. *(Optional)* Under "Track also," Status Messages is off by default. If you want status messages displayed, check the option.

   These are messages that give you the details about all server communication.
6. *(Optional)* By default, five warnings or messages are displayed in the Network Status window shown in Figure 30-15. You can choose to have 5, 10, 25, 50, 100, or an unlimited number of messages saved and displayed here.

 If, as you work, you receive network errors such as PROPFIND or one about the MOVE command, refer to the WebDAV Server tutorial by Jeep Hauser at www.goliveheaven.com.

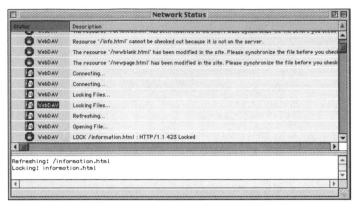

Figure 30-15: The Network Status window, displaying several error and status messages

Turning Workflow Support On or Off

Workflow Support is a GoLive enhancement to WebDAV. If, for some reason, you want to turn it off, you can. You can easily turn Workflow Support on or off, enabling you to switch between modes. All you have to do is check or uncheck the option in the site settings.

Note

Technically, you can Workflow Support on or off while you're connected to the WebDAV server. However, I advise that you disconnect first. It appears that file locks become confused when WebDAV server is turned on and off on the fly.

To turn Workflow Support on or off, follow these steps:

1. Click the Site Settings button on the toolbar or choose Site ➪ Settings to open the site Preferences window.

2. Click the FTP and WebDAV server icon on the left.

3. Check or uncheck "Enable workgroup support," depending on whether you're turning it on or off. When Workgroup Support is on, the Lock Status column should say checked in or checked out. When Workgroup Support is off, the Lock Status column should say locked or unlocked.

4. If the lock status in the Files tab doesn't change to reflect your current state, you need to refresh. Point anywhere within the WebDAV tab, Control-click (Mac) or right-click (Windows) and choose Refresh from the contextual menu. This updates the lock status so the files know how to behave. (If you have just turned Workgroup Support on, you can call up the contextual menu in the Files tab and choose Refresh Lock Status.)

Caution If you fail to refresh your site status after turning off Workgroup Support, double-clicking a file still asks you to check it in or out. This can be very confusing—to both you and GoLive. Likewise, if you turn Workgroup Support on and are not asked to check out a file, you will also have confusion.

Working with Basic WebDAV

GoLive's Workgroup Support enhances the standard WebDAV file in ways that avoid file-saving conflicts. However, because it also locks all files on your local drive, it may grow tiresome after a while. If you have a definite section of the site that is yours and only yours to work on for any block of time, you might prefer to turn Workgroup Support off and work in the generic locking system.

Workgroup Support is only available while you're working in a Site Window, so if you're working within the WebDAV browser, you'll need to work manually, as prescribed here.

While working without Workgroup Support, the act of synchronizing and downloading a file to work on it is separate from locking it. Thus, you have two steps: locking the file, and then downloading it if the server's file is newer. Likewise, when you've completed your work on a file, you must first upload it to the server and then unlock it. In addition, you'll need to synchronize your files manually. The other issue of concern about plain vanilla WebDAV is that you local copy of the files is not locked and the entire Files tab is dumb. This means that several people can work on the same version of a file, which means only one person's work will survive.

Tip Divide work up into clear, unrelated sections, and then lock all files within your section before working. Before changing a component that affects other pages outside of your section, ask for control of all of those related pages.

Manually locking files

With Workflow Support off, you *must* remember to lock any file on the server manually so that others can't work with it. Otherwise, you and another coworker *can* both be editing your respective local copies. Whether in the Site Window or the WebDAV browser, lock any file before you edit that file to avoid conflicting changes, redundancy, and confusion. All locking and unlocking is done directly on the server — from the WebDAV tab. (Lock commands are not available within the Files tab.)

Technically, and in the contextual menu, two levels of locking exist: exclusive and shared. An exclusive lock is the normal lock. It locks out all codesigners so only the owner can save changes to the locked file. Then there's a shared lock, but it doesn't really lock anyone out. Instead, it just alerts people that they are sharing access to the same file.

Tip   Before you begin locking files, you may want to update your view of the lock status so you can see which files are available to you. To do this, click anywhere in the WebDAV tab (not on a file) and call up Refresh from the contextual menu.

Locking a file exclusively

When you want to work on a file, and be absolutely certain that no one else replaces the file as you work on it, you can put an exclusive lock on the page. Be aware, though, that without Workgroup Support, other users can edit their own local copies. They cannot replace yours while it is locked, but they can replace it after you release the lock.

To lock a file within the WebDAV tab of the Site Window or the WebDAV browser, point to the file you wish to lock and Control-click (Mac) or right-click (Windows) on that file. You can also do any one of the following:

✦ To lock a file or the selected files, choose Lock from the contextual menu.

✦ To lock an entire folder at once, choose Lock All from the contextual menu. (If you're running on a Microsoft IIS 5 server, you cannot lock folders. Instead, open the folder and lock the files within it.)

Tip   To lock several files at once, select them all using your preferred selection technique. Then point to any of the selected files, call up the contextual menu, and choose the Lock command.

When a file is locked, keep the following points in mind:

✦ You see a pencil with "Me" in parentheses in the WebDAV tab

✦ Others see a padlock, along with the user's name in the WebDAV tab.

✦ Others have no feedback in the Files tab.

When you lock a file in plain WebDAV, you are locking the server copy of that file. This prevents anyone else from editing that page while you're working with it. It also prevents others from replacing the existing server version with any other version they may create on their own hard drives.

Unlike Workgroup Support, though, plain WebDAV doesn't lock all users' local files, so your coworkers can still make changes to their local pages — even after you lock a file on the server. However, because the file is locked on the server, local copies cannot be uploaded to server.

Should a coworker want to view the latest version of a locked page, it can be opened by double-clicking the file in the WebDAV tab (or WebDAV browser). The page is safely protected by the lock; viewers can look but cannot save changes to the page. Later, when you're finished and you upload and unlock the completed file, other users will see the padlock go away — when they log in anew, or refresh their WebDAV tab.

You can lock a file while Workgroup Support is off, and then check it back in while Workgroup Support is on, and vice versa (check one out, and then unlock it). I recommend disconnecting from the server between connections, though, because lock status may become confused.

Applying a shared lock

A shared lock lets several people have access to a file or files while locking others out. Those who are not given the shared lock status can read the document, but not save changes to it. However, those who share the access all have equal edit privileges to the file. Those users should maintain high communication to ensure no edits overlap.

 A folder cannot be assigned a shared lock so you'll have to select the folder's files and then apply the lock.

Although a Shared Lock command exists under the WebDAV tab's contextual menu, you, as a user, are not able to set up others to share the file status. This can only be done by the WebDAV server administrator. Check with your administrator if you'd like to pursue this feature.

When you have access to a file that has a shared lock, you see a Group icon (two faces like Apple's File Sharing group icon) atop a pencil, with your name beside it. If others are also sharing the file, instead of your name you will see "N users", where N is the number of users who currently have the file checked out. When a file has a group lock, but you're not part of the group, you see the Group icon without a pencil.

Making sure you work with current files

Without Workgroup Support, it's totally up to you to make sure you're working with the most recent version of a file. And, as you work on other parts of the site, it can certainly help to know you've got the most current version of the entire site. You have several ways to ensure you have the most recent version of the site's files. You can update a single page, download selected pages, download an entire file, synchronize all of your pages, or manually drag a page to or from the server.

One way to ensure you are working with the newest files is to let GoLive determine which files are newest — your copy or the copy on the server. You can easily do this using the Download Modified Items command.

To download all files that have been modified since you last updated the site, do one of the following:

✦ Click WebDAV Download Modified Items in the toolbar.

✦ Choose Site ➪ WebDAV Server ➪ Download Modified Items.

If, instead, you're certain of which file you want to work with, you can manually determine which files you carry down to your Files tab.

To download specifically selected files, select the files to be downloaded and then do the following:

✦ Choose Site ➪ WebDAV Server ➪ Download Selection.

✦ Drag the selected files from the WebDAV tab to the Files tab of the Site Window.

If you've been working with files within your Files tab and have one or more files that are ready to be delivered to the server, you can do a synchronization. Synchronization enables you to send your newest files to the server while also bringing other newer files down to your Files tab. To learn about synchronization, see "Synchronizing Files," earlier in this chapter

Caution If a file is not locked, it is entirely possible for two or more people to open and edit that file. If you save your changes and place them back on the server, the next person's save and upload will delete your file. Be sure to lock all files you're about to work with.

Managing files

You can work with files in the WebDAV tab or in the Files tab. The latter is easier. When you work directly in a file in the WebDAV tab, you are editing the file directly on the server and therefore the GoLive Site Window interface is not in effect. For example, you cannot Point and Shoot to link from a page on the WebDAV tab to another page in the WebDAV tab. (If you Point and Shoot to a file in the Files tab, you'll have an invalid link.)

After you've made sure you had the newest version of the file and locked the copy on the server, you can work with the file within the Files tab of your Site Window pretty much like you work when you're not using WebDAV at all. However, a big difference comes up when you make a change that affects other pages. Without Workgroup Support, you're on your own as far as making sure that all affected pages are updated and sent back to the server.

When you change the page or file in the Files tab, GoLive changes all related pages, as always, when it does its automatic update. But because no pages in the Files tab are locked, it may be updating pages that are currently locked on the server. This means it is updating pages that you cannot put back on the server. Changes are that the lock owner will send a revised version of that page to the server, and that you won't want to replace that new version with your own. So, the update you did is lost and you'll need to redo the change that is lost with it. Therefore, before you change the page or component that affects another page, make sure you have the latest version of all affected pages and lock all of these pages on the server.

Tip When a site-wide change is to be made, call for all files and lock them all before making the change.

As with Workgroup Support, WebDAV file name changes cause duplicate file issues. When you rename a file, like with Workgroup Support on, WebDAV will want to download the new-named file to the server and upload the old-named file to you. To learn more, see the "Renaming files" section earlier in this chapter.

Uploading files after an edit

After you've made changes to any file or files, you need to upload the changed files to the WebDAV server in order for other team members to see your work and know where the site stands. As with downloading, a few options are available.

Note Remember, you have to be connected to the WebDAV server in order to transfer files. If you're not connected, click the WebDAV Server button in the toolbar to open the right side of the Site Window and connect to the server. (The Site Window must be open for this button to be active.)

Uploading modified files

If you've worked on more than one page, or your work includes multiple files such as an external style sheet, graphics, and so on, the easiest and safest way to transfer your changes is to let GoLive compare the files and upload them for you.

To upload all files you've modified, do one of the following:

✦ Click the WebDAV Upload Modified Items button in the toolbar.

✦ Choose Site ➪ WebDAV Server ➪ Upload Modified Items.

Uploading specific (selected) files

If you know exactly which page or pages you've changed, and are certain of the pages you wish to update on the WebDAV server, you can select those pages and manually move them to the server. If you've only changed one page, this can be the most efficient. However, if your page or pages contain graphics or other media, don't forget that you may need to upload that media.

Tip If you'd like to add comments to your files as you place them back on the server, turn Workgroup Support on and do a check-in instead of just uploading and unlocking. Only Workgroup Support has the Comment dialog box. You have no way to add a comment without it being on.

To upload specifically selected files, follow these steps:

1. Select the files you want to upload. (These are the files on your own hard drive, in the Files tab of your Site Window.) Use the standard selection techniques: marquee or Shift-click.

2. Do one of the following:

- Choose Site ⇨ WebDAV Server ⇨ Upload Selection.
- Drag the selected files from the Files tab to the WebDAV tab in the right side of the Site Window.

Caution   If you inadvertently edit a file in your files tab — not aware for some reason that it has been locked — when you attempt to upload the file, you'll be unable to, receiving an error that tells you the server cannot find a lock token.

Finally, you can synchronize your site, sending all of your changed pages to the server and bringing newer pages to your Files tab. To learn about synchronization, see the "Synchronizing Files" section earlier in this chapter.

Using the WebDAV Browser

What about when you're not on your main computer and therefore don't have your Site Window handy? GoLive also enables you to view your WebDAV server files by way of the WebDAV browser, a more generic window to your files.

You can connect to your WebDAV server by choosing File ⇨ WebDAV Browser. Rather than presenting your files in the Site Window, this option gives you access within a more generic window. When you work in this window, you work more closely with the server. When you double-click a file, it opens the file from the server. When you save a change, it calls to the server and saves that change directly to the server.

Using this window, you can gain access to anyone's copy of GoLive, without having to affect any site-specific settings you've entered for your sites. However, while this window does give you access to the site files so you can edit them, it doesn't give you the benefit of the Site Window. For example, it isn't possible to link via Point and Shoot or even by browsing. Consider this access for emergency only.

Follow these steps to use the WebDAV browser:

1. Choose File ⇨ WebDAV Browser to open the WebDAV browser application.
2. Click the arrow button to the right of the Address field and choose the WebDAV server to which you want to connect. This automatically fills in the username and password for you.
3. *(Optional)* Check the Save option if you want GoLive to remember your password. Otherwise, you'll need to enter your password each time you access the server.
4. If a password is required, choose Basic as the Authorization option. If not, choose None.
5. Click Connect. Your site's files appear in the lower section of the WebDAV browser window.

6. Work on the site, remembering the following:

- *To look at a page or file*, double-click the file. A Progress bar shows you that the file is being downloaded from the server, and then the page opens up for you to view.

- *To edit a page or file*, lock the page by pointing to it, and then Control-click (Mac) or right-click (Windows) and choose Lock from the contextual menu. Then, double-click the page to open and edit it. Save as normal when done. When you save, another Progress bar shows you the file is being uploaded to the server. Don't forget to unlock the file when you're finished. Call up Unlock from the contextual menu to do so.

Because you're not using the Site Window when you use the WebDAV browser, you cannot take advantage of Workgroup Support features. Instead, you have to remember to lock your files prior to working with them, and then unlock them later on. For the most part, using the WebDAV browser is like working without Workgroup Support turned on. See the "Working with Basic WebDAV" section (earlier in this chapter) to learn about locking and file transfer.

Hosting After Development

What happens after your project is complete and it's time for your site to go live? That depends on your site hosting plans and where the WebDAV server came from.

A WebDAV server is actually also a regular Web server that just happens to have WebDAV extensions (or modules) installed. If this server is also to be your regular HTTP server, you can keep your site right where it is and just start giving out the address. If the site remains on the WebDAV server, all development team members can continue to work on the site, keeping it up-to-date and interesting from their corners of the world.

Caution Although it is possible to serve a live site from a WebDAV server, it is never wise to serve a site from a production server or computer. It's far better, and safer, to have one computer for production and another for live sites.

If the WebDAV server is meant as a staging area during production only, and another home awaits your site, you can go on to upload the site to its new home via GoLive's usual FTP methods. (That's the stuff covered in Chapter 27.) Of course, having the site served from a standard FTP server doesn't preclude you from keeping the site up-to-date. As shown in Chapter 28, GoLive's interface makes it very easy to update your site. The only difference is that, in order to avoid each designer having different versions, the update may be best left to one designated person.

✦　　✦　　✦

What's on the CD-ROM

The CD-ROM that accompanies this book contains a great deal of useful software and other goodies that will help you take full advantage of what you learn in this book.

Exploring the CD-ROM

On the CD-ROM you'll find the following:

+ Software (demos, freeware, and shareware) that can help you in your quest to produce great Web sites. All of the software on this disk works with the versions of Mac or Windows (as the case may be) that are required to run Adobe GoLive 5.

+ Exercises discussed within this book and the real-life versions of the templates shown in this book.

+ Graphics that you can *use* on your very own Web site.

+ Other GoLive tools to make your life easier.

You'll find a lot here so I've organized it to make it as easy as possible for you to use.

Freeware, shareware, and commercial demos

The software on this CD-ROM varies from freeware to commercial demos. Each piece of software includes its own licensing agreement or a similar document that you should read to completely understand how it's being distributed and what you need to do (if anything) to continue to use the software. Table A-1 lists the software found on the CD-ROM.

Table A-1	
Software on the *Adobe GoLive 5 Bible* CD-ROM	
Software Title	*Maker/Description*
Dragon Web Surveys (Mac and Windows)	Waves in Motion (www.wmotion.com). There's no easier way to create fabulous surveys for use on the Web and elsewhere.
DropStuff (Mac and Windows)	Aladdin Systems (www.aladdinsys.com/dropstuff). Aladdin DropStuff provides up to 20 percent better compression than Zip with simple drag-and-drop ease. The Windows version offers compress-and-mail, Zip compression, and Aladdin Expander.
DropZip (Mac and Windows)	Aladdin Systems (www.aladdinsys.com/dropzip). Aladdin DropZip is the easiest Zip compression utility available. The Windows version includes StuffIt compression, Zip-and-mail in one easy step, and Aladdin Expander for access to all popular file formats.
Gamma Toggle FKEY	Roland Gustafsson (www.acts.org/roland/thanks). With this applet a Mac user can see what a page looks like with a PC's gamma setting, which is a darker setting. Just press a key combination to toggle between the Mac and Windows gammas.
GoClick 3.0.1 (Mac)	Terry Morse Software, Inc. (http://terrymorse.com). Convert any document into a Web page with one click (after you set it up). Even the most complex document layouts are maintained.
Poll-it (Mac and Windows)	Waves in Motion (www.wmotion.com). When you don't need the full features of the Dragon, Poll-it is the choice for great polls on the Internet.
PopChar Pro	UNI Software Plus GmbH (www.unisoft.co.at). Better than KeyCaps, PopChar Pro means never having to search for a special character again. It even highlights recently selected characters so you can get right back to them.
Snapz Pro	Ambrosia Software (www.ambrosiasw.com/utilities). This screen-capture solution for the Mac captures desktops, windows, menus, or your own selection, saving images as GIF, JPG, and QuickTime movies directly into the application format of your choice.

Software Title	Maker/Description
Spell Catcher (Mac)	Casady & Greene (www.casadyg.com). One dictionary covers you in every program, checking spelling (specialized dictionaries too), auto-repairing common words and words you teach it. Includes definitons and thesaurus, word count, and text cleanup.
Spell Catcher (Windows)	Cassady & Greene (www.casadyg.com). One dictionary for just about everything you type. Includes medical, legal, engineering/scientific, and HTML dictionaries.
ZipIt! (Mac)	Thomas A. Brown (www.maczipit.com). ZipIt is a Mac program that zips and unzips archives in a format fully compatible with PKZip for Windows. Shareware.

Software solutions for e-commerce

When you make the jump into e-commerce at any level, you'll have plenty to do without reinventing the wheel. These are my favorite software solutions — made in GoLive with GoLive users in mind, of course.

✦ The **GoLive 5 CatalogBuilder** kit is an intuitive e-commerce front end for Adobe GoLive 5.0 and the CatalogBuilder shopping cart. It comes with an Extend Script that you place in the Extend Scripts folder within your GoLive 5 application folder and Model Site. The Extend Script adds a BuyObjects Tab to your GoLive Objects palette. You can use the Model Site alone or installed in the GoLive 5 Templates folder so that you can create e-commerce sites by selecting File ➪ New Site ➪ Copy from Template. Used together, the Extend Script and the Model Site enable a Web designer to create powerful e-commerce sites by simply dragging and dropping.

CatalogBuilder is a centerpiece of the modular, integratable e-commerce solutions created in collaboration between artist/Web designer Doug Fairchild and photographer/programmer Doug Alberts. Their goal for both programmer and nonprogrammer Web designers is to give them powerful and user-friendly e-commerce tools that combine the successful sales and marketing methods developed in the mail-order catalog field along with the power of electronic media.

✦ **Document Express Pro** is best described as a Customer Relationship Management (CRM) system — an e-mail response-management system that *doesn't* require a Web-hosted database. Instead, your database resides comfortably on your desktop computer so you can work with it easily without risking harm. It's a marketing center, enabling you to create Web forms to collect customer feedback, automate e-mail responses to your customers, and create customized marketing campaigns without losing personalization with your core customers. It can also be a sales center with the same flexibility and ease.

Document Express Pro was born out of Mark Teixeira's desire for people to have a low-cost, easy-to-use information gathering and response solution on virtually any Web site. All you need to communicate with your customers is Document Express Pro and a single dedicated POP e-mail account.

Exercises

Web site creation is a hands-on experience. It can be pretty hard to learn something if you don't have the materials you need to try it. I certainly don't want to see you spinning your wheels, spending valuable time trying to come up with files you can experiment with, so I asked some terrific GoLive users to pitch in. Table A-2 shows you which files to use.

	Table A-2 *Adobe GoLive 5 Bible* Exercises		
Chapter	**File Name**	**Author**	**Description**
10	Photoshop Mock File	Steven Shmerler	As discussed in Chapter 10, you can create a site mockup in Photoshop and bring it into GoLive. This standard 640×480 TIFF file is yours to practice using GoLive's Tracing Image feature.
11	Max.swf	Doug LaMaster	An SWF file with a link, so you can practice editing links via Point and Shoot. Because you need to embed this file, it is located in the Chapter 20 folder.
14	CustomPaletteItems. html	Deborah Shadovitz	A few items such as preformatted tables that might be handy as you create your pages. Maybe they'll give you some ideas for how you can use the Custom items feature yourself.

Chapter	File Name	Author	Description
15	FramePractice	Deborah Shadovitz	Curious about frames? Here's a frameset to open, inspect, and experiment with.
15	framesetExOUT.sit	Oliver Zahorka	This frameset focuses on the function of targets.
16	Form Variables Example	Rob Keniger	To demonstrate Variable and Cookie Actions, Rob Keniger put together a three-page site that uses them and explains what's taking place on each page. Check out the Head sections with the Inspector open to get the full story. This example requires a fully functioning Variable Action and therefore requires Robert McDaniel's Replacement Variable Action as noted in Chapter 16.
16	Replacement Variable Action	Robert McDaniels	This Action, discussed in Chapter 16, works in lieu of the Variables Action that you'll find installed with GoLive. This is an unofficial fix, done by a caring GoLive user. It works beautifully and enables you to try the Form Variables example created by Rob Keniger.
19	MyMovers DHTML folder	Cathy Scrivnor and Deborah Shadovitz	This site demonstrates how floating boxes can be animated. Open the TimeLine for each floating box and look carefully at the paths, keyframes, and scenes to see how each scene was done. Select a link and open the Actions palette to see how the scenes are attached. (We had some fun with this and hope you do too.)

Continued

Chapter	File Name	Author	Description
20	SWF files	Doug LaMaster	Curious about putting an SWF file on your page? Here are two to learn with. Max includes an external link so you can also practice changing link destinations in the In & Out Links palette.
22	jslimitselect.html	David Shadovitz	This is a simple JavaScript that you can add to your form when you want users to check or choose two (or three or four) items in a list, but no more than what you limit them to.
Appendix E (SDK)	Reversomatic	Rob Keniger	Ready to try customizing GoLive? Even if you're not a code person, you can try Rob's Reversomatic. He shows you how in Appendix E. Then open this to compare your results.

GoLive stuff

The CD-ROM has some great tools especially made for Adobe GoLive 5. Check out the following:

OUTactions

OUT Media Design GmbH is a maker of high-quality Actions that you can download from the Web and add to your GoLive Action collection to provide even more functionality to your site — with ease. On the CD-ROM, you'll find the entire OUTactions site (as of this writing). Open index.html in your browser and you've got a list of all OUTactions along with the description and a demo of each Action (as of this printing). Some of these great Actions are yours free of charge. You can access and use the free Actions by clicking the link within the description. OUT Media Design GmbH is located at Querstrasse 8, CH-8105 Regensdorf, Switzerland.

Among the free Actions are the following:

✦ **Browser test** is a switch that enables you to test for anything special you want to do on a certain browser.

✦ **Delay Action** enables you to delay the activation of an Action without relying on the timeline.

✦ **Execute JavaScript** enables you to, well, execute JavaScript code.

✦ **Redirect URL** works as a page loads. It's a great way to make a slide show using your HTML Web pages.

✦ **Sound Tools** improves upon the GoLive start and stop sound Actions, providing Internet Explorer compatibility.

As a special bonus, OUTactions also provides a set of form utility Actions not available anywhere else. The OUTactions bonus Actions are the following:

✦ **Field Count** provides welcome feedback to a user by counting and reporting the number of characters he or she types in a given Text or Text Area field. You set the maximum number of characters you want entered, and determine whether to count down or up from that number. The user sees the count in either the browser's status area or in another text field. When the user reaches the limit, a customized alert appears, and then the user can edit the text field or move on.

✦ **Limit Selection** enables you to prevent users from choosing more multiple choice responses than you request on a form. To use it you select the List Box on your form, and then attach the Action to it. You can choose the maximum number of responses and customize the message. (This Action is based on the LimitSelect JavaScript by David Shadovitz that is also on this CD-ROM but takes it further and makes it easier to apply.)

✦ **Check Box Group** and **Check Box Limit** work together to enable you to limit the number of checkboxes a user checks for a particular option. You can choose to have a customized alert appear when the limit is reached, or to have the first box automatically uncheck.

Actions by Matt Ridley

Matt Ridley has created some great tools for you to use in exchange for doing someone else a good turn later on. A variety of his "charityware" Actions are on this CD-ROM for your convenience; you can also find more at www.mattridley.com. Here's what you'll find on the CD-ROM:

✦ **Basic Dialog Action** (Netscape 4 and perhaps later) displays a floating, draggable, custom dialog box within the browser window. You can specify its background and title bar color, title and message text and color, and the button's label.

✦ **Emailer Action** enables you to set up a send e-mail link, completing the recipient's address, a subject, and a message.

✦ **FindOnPage Action** locates selected text within the current page. The search can be case-sensitive or not and can search forward or backward.

✦ **GetInfo Action** displays a dialog box providing the following information about the user who accesses the page: browser name and version number, exact date and time of page access (optional), the OS (optional), and the page that user came from that linked into the page this Action is on (optional).

✦ **ImageDialog Action** (Netscape 4 only) displays a dialog box similar to the Basic Dialog Action, adding the capability to place an image within the dialog box. (Matt recommends you read the directions for this carefully.)

✦ **OpenWindow 1-1 Action** lets the fresh air in. Actually, it enables you to create a custom browser window to provide supplemental information to your viewers.

✦ **ThirdVoiceHide Action,** by Jeremy Bowers, only runs if the page it's on is viewed with IE 4.*x* on Windows, because that's the only platform on which Third Voice (TV) is available (at time of writing). This Action doesn't stop TV notes from being added, but stops or makes it difficult for TV users to view existing notes.

✦ **ThirdVoiceRedirect Action** redirects users who have Third Voice to an alternate page/URL. This Action doesn't affect Mac or Unix users, or Netscape browsers on Windows.

Graphics

Looking to spice up your page? The following is a list of cool graphics you'll find on the CD-ROM:

✦ **Web Spice Clip Art Collection.** DeMorgan Industries Corporation's Web Spice (www.webspice.com) is an excellent clip art collection specifically designed for the Web, including nice backgrounds.

✦ **PhotoSpin.** PhotoSpin Inc. (www.photospin.com) sells excellent royalty-free photographs and artwork such as textures and photo objects. Backgrounds can easily be lightened and objects contain alpha channels for quickly pasting into backgrounds and otherwise altering for use on the Web. You'll find 35 JPGs to use here. (Thanks to Duane Pearson for providing these backgrounds.)

✦ **Photos by Gary Miller.** Gary Miller lives on a hill overlooking the water in Anchorage, Alaska. Each evening at the same time and from the same place, he took a photo (using his Olympus D340L) of the local sunset. His October

Sunsets collection is yours to use as you please. Other photos exist as well—some other great Anchorage area shots and more. The photos are fresh out of his camera, not manipulated in any way.

✦ **Photos by Paul Bradforth.** Paul Bradforth (www.pbi.dircon.co.uk) designs and produces all types of graphics and photo-composites to order, for Web or print, at reasonable rates. He's readied a few of my personal favorites for you to use. (See if you can tell which are done without any camera or film or lighting—completely digital. At least one is a 3D model done in Bryce.) Higher-resolution versions are available. [Paul retains the copyright to all of his work.]

✦ **Photos by Bob Ludlow.** Bob Ludlow, of Digital Photo Themes (www.photothemes.com), specializes in high-quality prints. To help you get started on your way to an interesting Web site, he has prepared some of his favorite shots as JPGs, ready for you to use on the Web. If you'd like a higher-quality version, or would like a high-quality print for your own daily enjoyment, contact Bob at his site or at ludlow@earthlink.net. [Bob retains the copyright to all of his work.]

✦ **Photos by Jonathan Nourok.** Jonathan Nourok (www.nourokphoto.com) is an assignment and stock photographer based in Long Beach, California. His images have been used all over the world by corporations and publishers. To get you started on the road to a great Web site, he shares two shots helpful for general use. [Jonathan retains the copyright to all of his work.]

✦ **Mark's Backgrounds.** Original backgrounds created just for you by Mark Jaress, digerati extraordinaire, because "GoLive Rocks!" They're optimized and ready to go, but you can alter them, or course.

✦ **The Famous Invisible GIF.** You've probably heard about the trick of using an invisible GIF as a space holder a zillion times. But where do you *get* one? And how do you pass it around if it's invisible? Well for one thing, when you create it, you don't give it a custom icon. (Sorry, I couldn't resist.) Steven Shmerler, the creative genius behind all the cool graphics in Chapter 10—and much of the wisdom you'll find there—makes life yet a bit more easy for you by sharing this GIF with you (1pixeltransparent.gif). Just remember that it's not his finest artwork. You'll find some of that at www.sasnet.com.

✦ **Deb's Backgrounds.** Yep, that's me. You're welcome to the few backgrounds I've created for my own use.

Note If you use any of these graphic elements in your site, I hope you will provide a credit or thank you to the contributor somewhere on the site. Thanks.

Music

Frédéric Berti is a musician now also in the Web design business — using GoLive, of course. He provides some of his original music to you for use on your site, or to play as musical inspiration while you work. (I wrote this book to this music.) You can learn more about him and his music at www.essania.net.

Color selection tools

In Chapter 2 I tell you about VisiBone's excellent Online Color Scheme Lab. Bob Stein has created an offline version. You know great color when you see it. This may help you see it. If you're working with clients, bring this CD-ROM along and the *offline* Online Color Scheme Lab may save you both a lot of time and energy.

Bob also provides the color wheel tables he originally made for Dave Raggett of w3.org (the guy who *invented* HTML tables), which to his great honor Dave cloned for his online reference. One has hexadecimal HTML codes, the other decimal RGB codes.

Firstuse.com

Firstuse.com (www.firstuse.com) is the first worldwide Internet-based registry that provides 24-hour, confidential digital fingerprinting and timestamped registration of intellectual property and important records in the event that someone ever challenges your ideas or the integrity of your files. Firstuse.com also provides education and resources to help manage, build, and protect records and intellectual property. Our packet of information includes a visual, step-by-step process for registration and verification, strategies for Web designers, and a description of Firstuse Direct, an Adobe plug-in that enables users to digitally timestamp, fingerprint, and register their files with Firstuse.com directly from the Adobe software program.

Client questionnaire

Back in the wild first days of the public Web, a few Los Angeles Web designers got together and, realizing that many people had no idea what this Web-thing really was, created a set of standards — Ethical Standards and Practices Initiative — for designers to follow. One of the outcomes was a set of questions to present to potential clients in order to guide communication and production. The Beachparty Web site (www.beachparty.org) encourages you to adapt this ClientQuestions.pdf for your own use. Be sure to visit the Beachparty site. The lessons it shares are worth the time spent reading.

✦　　✦　　✦

Index

Continued

Continued

Continued

Continued

IDG Books Worldwide, Inc. End-User License Agreement

READ THIS. You should carefully read these terms and conditions before opening the software packet(s) included with this book ("Book"). This is a license agreement ("Agreement") between you and IDG Books Worldwide, Inc. ("IDGB"). By opening the accompanying software packet(s), you acknowledge that you have read and accept the following terms and conditions. If you do not agree and do not want to be bound by such terms and conditions, promptly return the Book and the unopened software packet(s) to the place you obtained them for a full refund.

1. **License Grant.** IDGB grants to you (either an individual or entity) a nonexclusive license to use one copy of the enclosed software program(s) (collectively, the "Software") solely for your own personal or business purposes on a single computer (whether a standard computer or a workstation component of a multiuser network). The Software is in use on a computer when it is loaded into temporary memory (RAM) or installed into permanent memory (hard disk, CD-ROM, or other storage device). IDGB reserves all rights not expressly granted herein.

2. **Ownership.** IDGB is the owner of all right, title, and interest, including copyright, in and to the compilation of the Software recorded on the disk(s) or CD-ROM ("Software Media"). Copyright to the individual programs recorded on the Software Media is owned by the author or other authorized copyright owner of each program. Ownership of the Software and all proprietary rights relating thereto remain with IDGB and its licensers.

3. **Restrictions On Use and Transfer.**

    (a) You may only (i) make one copy of the Software for backup or archival purposes, or (ii) transfer the Software to a single hard disk, provided that you keep the original for backup or archival purposes. You may not (i) rent or lease the Software, (ii) copy or reproduce the Software through a LAN or other network system or through any computer subscriber system or bulletin-board system, or (iii) modify, adapt, or create derivative works based on the Software.

    (b) You may not reverse engineer, decompile, or disassemble the Software. You may transfer the Software and user documentation on a permanent basis, provided that the transferee agrees to accept the terms and conditions of this Agreement and you retain no copies. If the Software is an update or has been updated, any transfer must include the most recent update and all prior versions.

4. Restrictions on Use of Individual Programs. You must follow the individual requirements and restrictions detailed for each individual program in Appendix A of this Book. These limitations are also contained in the individual license agreements recorded on the Software Media. These limitations may include a requirement that after using the program for a specified period of time, the user must pay a registration fee or discontinue use. By opening the Software packet(s), you will be agreeing to abide by the licenses and restrictions for these individual programs that are detailed in Appendix A and on the Software Media. None of the material on this Software Media or listed in this Book may ever be redistributed, in original or modified form, for commercial purposes.

5. Limited Warranty.

(a) IDGB warrants that the Software and Software Media are free from defects in materials and workmanship under normal use for a period of sixty (60) days from the date of purchase of this Book. If IDGB receives notification within the warranty period of defects in materials or workmanship, IDGB will replace the defective Software Media.

(b) **IDGB AND THE AUTHOR OF THE BOOK DISCLAIM ALL OTHER WARRANTIES, EXPRESS OR IMPLIED, INCLUDING WITHOUT LIMITATION IMPLIED WARRANTIES OF MERCHANTABILITY AND FITNESS FOR A PARTICULAR PURPOSE, WITH RESPECT TO THE SOFTWARE, THE PROGRAMS, THE SOURCE CODE CONTAINED THEREIN, AND/OR THE TECHNIQUES DESCRIBED IN THIS BOOK. IDGB DOES NOT WARRANT THAT THE FUNCTIONS CONTAINED IN THE SOFTWARE WILL MEET YOUR REQUIREMENTS OR THAT THE OPERATION OF THE SOFTWARE WILL BE ERROR FREE.**

(c) This limited warranty gives you specific legal rights, and you may have other rights that vary from jurisdiction to jurisdiction.

6. Remedies.

(a) IDGB's entire liability and your exclusive remedy for defects in materials and workmanship shall be limited to replacement of the Software Media, which may be returned to IDGB with a copy of your receipt at the following address: Software Media Fulfillment Department, Attn.: *Adobe GoLive 5 Bible*, IDG Books Worldwide, Inc., 10475 Crosspoint Blvd., Indianapolis, IN 46256, or call 1-800-762-2974. Please allow three to four weeks for delivery. This Limited Warranty is void if failure of the Software Media has resulted from accident, abuse, or misapplication. Any replacement Software Media will be warranted for the remainder of the original warranty period or thirty (30) days, whichever is longer.

(b) In no event shall IDGB or the author be liable for any damages whatsoever (including without limitation damages for loss of business profits, business interruption, loss of business information, or any other pecuniary loss) arising from the use of or inability to use the Book or the Software, even if IDGB has been advised of the possibility of such damages.

(c) Because some jurisdictions do not allow the exclusion or limitation of liability for consequential or incidental damages, the above limitation or exclusion may not apply to you.

7. **U.S. Government Restricted Rights.** Use, duplication, or disclosure of the Software by the U.S. Government is subject to restrictions stated in paragraph (c)(1)(ii) of the Rights in Technical Data and Computer Software clause of DFARS 252.227-7013, and in subparagraphs (a) through (d) of the Commercial Computer — Restricted Rights clause at FAR 52.227-19, and in similar clauses in the NASA FAR supplement, when applicable.

8. **General.** This Agreement constitutes the entire understanding of the parties and revokes and supersedes all prior agreements, oral or written, between them and may not be modified or amended except in a writing signed by both parties hereto that specifically refers to this Agreement. This Agreement shall take precedence over any other documents that may be in conflict herewith. If any one or more provisions contained in this Agreement are held by any court or tribunal to be invalid, illegal, or otherwise unenforceable, each and every other provision shall remain in full force and effect.

my2cents.idgbooks.com

Register This Book — And Win!

Visit **http://my2cents.idgbooks.com** to register this book and we'll automatically enter you in our fantastic monthly prize giveaway. It's also your opportunity to give us feedback: let us know what you thought of this book and how you would like to see other topics covered.

Discover IDG Books Online!

The IDG Books Online Web site is your online resource for tackling technology — at home and at the office. Frequently updated, the IDG Books Online Web site features exclusive software, insider information, online books, and live events!

10 Productive & Career-Enhancing Things You Can Do at www.idgbooks.com

- Nab source code for your own programming projects.

- Download software.

- Read Web exclusives: special articles and book excerpts by IDG Books Worldwide authors.

- Take advantage of resources to help you advance your career as a Novell or Microsoft professional.

- Buy IDG Books Worldwide titles or find a convenient bookstore that carries them.

- Register your book and win a prize.

- Chat live online with authors.

- Sign up for regular e-mail updates about our latest books.

- Suggest a book you'd like to read or write.

- Give us your 2¢ about our books and about our Web site.

You say you're not on the Web yet? It's easy to get started with IDG Books' *Discover the Internet,* available at local retailers everywhere.

CD-ROM Installation Instructions

The software that's included with the *Adobe GoLive 5 Bible* CD-ROM is simple to install. Before you install anything, though, you must decide which programs you want (see the program lists in Appendix A) and then find them on the CD-ROM. To browse the contents of the CD-ROM, follow these steps:

1. Insert the *Adobe GoLive 5 Bible* CD-ROM into your CD-ROM drive.

2. On the Windows desktop, double-click the My Computer icon. When the My Computer window opens, find the icon for the CD-ROM drive (usually D:).

   If you are using a Macintosh computer, simply look for CD-ROM icon on your desktop and click it.

The CD-ROM contains folders that correspond to programs, GoLive Actions, GoLive 5 Bible exercises, graphics, music, and other media. Many of the files on the CD-ROM are resources that don't require installation. For those programs that do, each folder holds all of the files that are required to install that software. Once you decide which program you want to install, do the following:

1. Open the folder icon for the program you want to install.

2. What you see next varies depending on the software. If you see any files called "License" or "Readme," open them first. Double-clicking those files opens them using Notepad, a simple Windows applet for viewing and editing text documents.

3. When you finish viewing the Readme and License files (if present) you are ready to install the software. Browse through the contents of the program's folder until you find the installation file listed in Table A-1. It should be an executable file (ending in .exe).

4. Open the icon for the executable installation file. An easy-to-use installation wizard launches to guide you through the setup process. Each one is different, so just follow the onscreen instructions to complete the process.

For complete information about the contents of the *Adobe GoLive 5 Bible* CD-ROM, please see Appendix A.